Cracking the GRE

The Ultimate Guide to the Graduate Record Examination

Prof. Jagdeep I. Vaishnav

In association with Nishant B. Patel, MBA

Published by

An Imprint of dreamtech PRESS

Edition : 2005

Printed at : Himal Impressions, 168, Raja Garden, New Delhi-110015

Dedication and Acknowledgements

I dedicate this presentation to:

- My late parents: My mother Mrs. Sulochana Vaishnav who taught at the reputed Sophia School in Mount Abu and my father Mr. Indrajit C Vaishnav who was trained in criminal investigation at the world renowned Old Scotland Yard in England and retired as Inspector General of Police, Gujarat State.
- My sister Bhargavi R Nanavaty and my brother Mayur Indrajit Vaishnav
- My wife Bhavana, son Harsh and daughter Pooja
- Reverend Brother Jerald Anthony Keane (S.J.), and the Late Br. J B Judge (S.J.), who taught me at the St. Mary's High School at Mount Abu in Rajasthan, India.
- Mr. H R Patankar, IAS (Retired) who was initially the Principal Secretary of the Industries mines and Energy Department (IMED) and then Chief Secretary of the Government of Gujarat during the time I was with the Government of Gujarat in the IMED. He has been a source of great inspiration to me.

Jagdeep. I. Vaishnav
Author

I dedicate this presentation to:

- My parents Mrs. Sudha Patel who is with the Bharat Sanchar Nigam and Mr. Bipin Patel who is with the General Administration Department at the Secretariat in Gujarat. His literary leanings have been a source of inspiration to me.
- Mrs. Hetal Patel, my better half, who has lit my way through some rather lean patches with the beaming radiance of her personality.
- My little daughter Anya who has soft-landed on Mother Earth on November 8, 2003.

Nishant. B. Patel
Co-Author

Contents

Chapter 1 : Why should you read this book? ... 1
Chapter 2 : How should you read this book? ... 18
Chapter 3 : Understanding the System ... 19
Chapter 4 : Analytical Writing Assessment— Presenting your perspective on an issue ... 40
Chapter 5 : Analytical Writing Assessment—Analysing an Argument ... 45
Chapter 6 : Antonyms ... 49
Chapter 7 : Word Analogies ... 88
Chapter 8 : Sentence Completion ... 177
Chapter 9 : Reading Comprehension ... 224
Chapter 10 : Ages ... 263
Chapter 11 : Area and Volume ... 268
Chapter 12 : Arithmetic Progressions ... 275
Chapter 13 : Averages ... 282
Chapter 14 : The Circle ... 293
Chapter 15 : Exponents and Exponential Functions ... 299
Chapter 16 : Geometric Progressions ... 302
Chapter 17 : Highest Common Factors ... 310
Chapter 18 : Inequalities ... 312
Chapter 19 : Least Common Multiple ... 315
Chapter 20 : Least and Most ... 322
Chapter 21 : Line Graphs (and, of course, some other types of graphs) ... 332
Chapter 22 : Linear and Simultaneous Equations ... 340
Chapter 23 : Logarithms ... 346
Chapter 24 : Elementary Aspects of Statistics ... 354
Chapter 25 : The Number Line ... 362
Chapter 26 : Mathematical Operators ... 364
Chapter 27 : Mixtures ... 367
Chapter 28 : Divisibility Rules ... 373
Chapter 29 : Permutations, Combinations and Probability ... 381

Chapter 30 : Prime Numbers 391
Chapter 31 : Profit and Loss 397
Chapter 32 : The Pythagoras Theorem 403
Chapter 33 : Quadratic Equations 413
Chapter 34 : Ratio and Proportion 420
Chapter 35 : The Clock 425
Chapter 36 : Setting up Equations to solve Word Problems 429
Chapter 37 : Speed and Distance 435
Chapter 38 : Squares and Cubes 445
Chapter 39 : The Triangle 452
Chapter 40 : Work and Time 461
Chapter 41 : Getting into Shape 466
Chapter 42 : The Axioms 476
Chapter 43 : What is Data Interpretation? 480
Chapter 44 : Reading Bar Charts 485
Chapter 45 : Reading Pie Charts 495
Chapter 46 : Reading Tabulated Data 503
Chapter 47 : Quantitative Comparison (Practise Test-1) 516
Chapter 48 : Quantitative Comparison (Practise Test-2) 530
Chapter 49 : Quantitative Comparison (Practise Test-3) 542
Chapter 50 : Problem Solving (Practise Test-1) 553
Chapter 51 : Problem Solving (Practise Test-2) 565
Chapter 52 : Problem Solving (Practise Test-3) 576
Chapter 53 : Question Paper 1 586
Chapter 54 : Question Paper 2 628

Chapter 1

Why should you read this book?

Several questions may pop up in the prospective reader's mind when he picks up this book from a shelf in a bookstore.. Some of the questions are as follows:

- Why should I read this book when it doesn't even contain word lists?
- Why do I not see an array of mathematical formulae in this book?
- Most books mention Mathematics and Quantitative Ability as the subjects that one needs to study to crack the GRE. Will this book explain clearly as to what is the difference between mathematics and quantitative ability?
- Why do I not see any instructions on how to take computer adaptive tests? Why are guidelines on how to use the mouse missing? Why are guidelines on how to darken, the correct oval missing? Will I miss out on anything because of the absence of such instructions and guidelines?
- Why do I not see tips in this book on how to make guesses – whether smart or intelligent?
- None of the books that I have seen so far carry the actual past papers of the GRE. How will I ever know what is the EXACT (A) range and (B) level of skills that the GRE aims to test? Will this book be able to provide me with a scientific assessment of the EXACT range and level of skills? How will it make such an assessment? On what basis? What will be its methodology?
- Why is no CD attached to this book? Will this book be of help to me even then?
- Why do I not see Test Papers (or what some books refer to as **Diagnostic Tests**) at the very outset of this book?
- Why should I read this particular book when the market abounds in books professing to prepare me for the Graduate Record Examination?

We shall answer these questions one by one. Please be with us.

Why do you not see word lists in this book?

Word List is the title given to a **randomly selected** list of **words** the meanings of which **you**, dear reader, ought to know in the opinion of someone who does not tell you **why** he deems it necessary to know the very words that he has compiled and not others when the English language has now over 117,000 words. Why does this compiler of the so-called *Word List* not ask you to mug up the entire dictionary? That will make the breadth of your personal lexicon so vast as to put a don of the English language to shame?

How does one know how much is enough? How does one develop the skill of analysing a word and tell what it could mean with a fair degree of accuracy?

The Educational Testing Service gives you a comprehensive idea on the Test Taking Tips in its POWERPREP CD, and a range of topics with which they expect the test taker to be familiar with. Then they also give you a whole range of past papers administered at the GRE. This gives you a sample of the quality of questions that you will get at the examination. The implied warranty is that the quality of questions at the examination shall, at the very least, conform to the standard that has been set in these previous questions. The supplier of the ultimate goods is an eminent and premier institution. If you do not heed the sample and draw your lessons on what to prepare and how to prepare for the GRE on the basis of the sample, what will you reasonably use as a base for making preparations for the GRE? If someone ignores the primary source, what more reliable source can anyone look to?

We shall derive an estimate of the level of the word power that you shall need at the GRE on the basis of questions flowing from the primary source.

See the following words from an actual paper administered at the GRE. You are given five options and are to select one among these five options that has a word most nearly opposite in meaning to the given word.

	Which among the five options is most nearly opposite in meaning to the under noted capitalised word?	Option 1	Option 2	Option 3	Option 4	Option 5
1	SEMINAL	Oblique	Provincial	Incomplete	Fluctuating	Derivative
2	LACONIC	Operative	Acerbic	Voluble	Pompous	Erect
3	SYBARITE	Political aspirant	Habitual malcontent	Humanitarian	Veteran	Ascetic

Let us go from word to word.

1. SEMINAL

Do you know that the word **nasal** has the suffix –AL? Do you know that the suffix –AL means having the quality of? Therefore if someone who seems to speak as if he speaks from the nose is said to have a *nasal* voice or a voice with *the quality of the nose*?

Do you know the meaning of the word semen? It is what the male sexual organ secretes in order to fertilize the female ovum and this fertilisation leads to conception and ultimately childbirth. Semen is therefore the original source of life. Seminal is a word that means having the quality of the seed or origin and therefore **seminal** means **original**. Once you are clear with this, you know that oblique (that means tangential or indirect) need not have anything to do with the word seminal. It is possible for someone to be both tangential and seminal (or original) at the same time. You can be the origin of an oblique reference to someone's affair with another woman. Once you are able to derive that *seminal* means *original*, you can judge from someone's *provincial* dialect (meaning *someone having the quality of province*) as to which province he has been brought up. In this day and age a fellow may have origins in Germany but he may have studied in USA and you can only tell whether he has stayed in Texas or North Carolina for example. You can tell nothing about his origin (which is Germany). You then know that provincial does not have anything necessarily to do with origin as such. As far as the word *incomplete* is concerned, nothing incomplete can ever be original. Something can be deemed to be *fluctuating* if it is undecided or varying irregularly like the voltage that would damage the refrigerator if it fluctuates wildly. Nothing indecisive can be original, or seminal. If there is no relationship at all between seminal on one side and oblique, provincial, incomplete and fluctuating on the other, there cannot be antonymous relationship as well among these words.

If petrol is a derivative of crude oil and cheese is a derivative of milk, then something derivative is certainly not original. Here at least there is a relationship even if of opposites. Clearly, something derivative is the opposite of seminal.

Are you ever likely to forget the meaning of the word *seminal* from the detailed explanation that you see in the above paragraphs? **The detailed explanation is** not an isolated instance. It is **a representative sample.** It represents a genre called situational context. It differs vastly from mere contextual usage. As you go along you will see how significantly situational context differs from contextual usage.

2. LACONIC

From what will you learn the meaning of the word *laconic* in a manner that will engrave its meaning on your mind? From the Word List that says that *laconic* is terse or concise? Or would it not be easy for you to remember its meaning from the following situational usage?

Imagine that you have been trying to talk to the fellow in the next seat on a bus journey of some ten hours' duration and all that he has said during these ten hours is *really* and *is that so*. He does not say **yes** or no when **hmm** will do. He is *laconic* (or someone who speaks very less).

It is for this reason that the opposite of laconic is someone who speaks almost non-stop and is therefore voluble.

3. SYBARITE

See the following contextual usage of the word Sybarite:

Being a sybarite, he slept till late in the mornings.

What meaning could you derive of the word sybarite? Could the fellow be lazy? Could he be accustomed to reading till late at night? Is he an *ore* like *iron pyrite*? You can say nothing at all from the contextual usage.

From what will you learn the meaning of the word Sybarite once and for all? See the following explanation: The word *sybarite* comes from the ancient Italian city named *Sybaris* that was known for the self-indulgent and luxurious life style of its inhabitants. The opposite of someone self-indulgent is someone who is self-denying.

An *ascetic* is someone who practices severe abstinence or austerity especially for spiritual or religious reasons. An ascetic is therefore the precise opposite of someone who is a sybarite.

Can you ever learn meanings of words from drab *Word Lists* in which the eraser will rub ahead of the pencil, where you will start forgetting the meanings of a word as soon as you read the next word? There has to be a methodology that will make a permanent impression on your mind of the meanings of different words and this book presents that precise methodology of situational usage.

To give you an appetiser of the methodology that we are talking about, do you know why the word *content* means such greatly different things like: (A) *what is held* (in a vessel, book and so on) and (B) *satisfied*, *tranquil* and so on?

The word *content* has the prefix CON- that means *together* and the Latin root TENT- that means *hold*. Something that a vessel holds completely is its *content*. Whatever it does not hold completely, overflows. Whatever a book *holds completely is* its *content* or *subject matter*.

The prefix CON- also means *thoroughly*. This is why the word *content* also means *hold thoroughly* or *satisfied*.

Imagine that a lion has just killed a deer and has eaten twenty odd kilograms of meat that a lion normally does at a sitting. It can be said that he *holds* deer meat *thoroughly* in his stomach. Now imagine that another deer is passing by this resting lion. Imagine that this deer has been jilted by his lover doe and is contemplating suicide. The deer has begun to hope that the lion would eat him up and thus he would bid adieu to this big bad world. The lion makes no move. Let us suppose that the passing deer then asks the lion if he can do with deer meat without the slightest bit of running (some sort of home delivery as it were). The lion then burps loudly and says *no, thanks* because he is *content* (or, in other words, his stomach *thoroughly holds*). This means that when the lion is *content*, he is *satisfied*.

With the above methodology can you ever forget the different shades of the meaning of the word *content*? You cannot even if you want to. This is the methodology that you will see in this book all through. The meanings of hundreds of words are explained in such a lucid manner that learning will be a matter of joy.

Why do you not see an array of mathematical formulae in this book?

There is a huge difference between Mathematics and Quantitative Ability. Mathematics is all about method. Quantitative Ability is all about reckoning and estimation. None of the mathematics tests that you took at school and college had any options. None of the mathematics tests that you took at school or college forbade you from carrying rulers and compasses. Most of us got marks for the steps that we wrote in the course of solving problems even though the ultimate answers may have been wrong. There was reward for effort. The words Quantitative Ability or Quantitative Section are not ours. You will find these very words mentioned in the Test Taking Tips in the POWERPREP CD. If the intention was to take a test of mathematics there is no reason why this new bird called Quantitative Ability should have been mentioned at all. If you will see (A) the hundreds of questions in this book that aim to test EXACTLY the same range and level of skills that the GRE aims to test and (B) the lucid answers to each of these questions, you will find that there is not a single mathematical formula other than the most rudimentary that has been employed in solving these questions. The test is of logic.

Then what is the difference between Mathematics and Quantitative Ability?

We shall have to take recourse to illustrations in order to drive home the difference between Mathematics and Quantitative Ability. The illustrations that we present hereunder are live examples of questions from past papers of premier competitive examinations for management entrance and so on.

Illustration 1

Which among the following is a perfect cube? The options are as follows:

1: 2395346442 2: 2395346372 3: 2395346462 4: 2395346472

See the number of digits in the four options. There are ten digits in all four cases. How fast can you finish factorising four ten-digit numbers? Try the mathematics method and see for yourself if you want to. Is the examiner trying to find out the factorising skills of someone who sometimes shaves twice a day? What is the examiner trying to find out? He is trying to find out whether you can judge that:

- All four options are even numbers
- An even number is definitely divisible by 2.
- You cannot have a perfect cube unless you have three of each of the factors; this is why the cube of 6 is 216 which can be factorised as $2 \times 2 \times 2 \times 3 \times 3 \times 3$ and the cube of 15 is 3375 which can be factorised as $3 \times 3 \times 3 \times 5 \times 5 \times 5$.
- Since all four options are even numbers, the perfect cube among these four is bound to be divisible by $2 \times 2 \times 2$ or 8.
- All thousands and higher powers of 10 are divisible by 8. Therefore if you want to know whether the number 12256810320 is divisible by 8, all that you have to do is see the number made by the digits in the hundreds, tens and units places. In the case of 12256810320 the last three digits give the number 320 which is divisible by 8 and hence there is no need to do anything other than observe this simple fact in order to conclude that 12256810320 is definitely divisible by 8. There is no need to put pen to paper.
- Out of the four options, only in case of Option 4, the last three digits to the right give a number divisible by 8 and therefore if any number in the four options is a perfect cube, it is the number in Option 4. We trust you have started feeling the difference between Mathematics and Quantitative Ability.

Illustration 2

What is the remainder when 6 divides 4^{63}?

Ask yourself this: How long would it take you to multiply 4 by itself 63 times? A week? A month? Does this question pertain to mathematics at all? If not, what does this pertain to? Dear reader, it pertains to nothing other than simple common sense. It calls for being able to recognise a pattern being formed.

This is how we shall see the pattern being formed.

Divide 4^1 by 6 and we get 4 as the remainder.

Divide 4^2 (which is 16) by 6 and we get 4 as the remainder.

Divide 4^3 (which is 64) by 6 and we get 4 as the remainder.

Divide 4^4 (which is 256) by 6 and we get 4 as the remainder.

There is no need to go further than 4^3. The pattern is that whatever be the power to which you raise 4, if you divide 4^N by 6 where N is as large a natural number that you can think of, the remainder will invariably be 4. The question after all is about the remainder alone.

We trust you are slowly beginning to see the *succinct* difference between Mathematics and Quantitative Ability. We shall however see some more illustrations.

Illustration 3

A store has a parking lot that contains 70 parking spaces. Each row in the parking lot contains the same number of parking spaces. The store has bought additional property in order to build an addition to the store. When the addition is built, two parking spaces will be lost from each row; however, four more rows will be added to the parking lot. After the addition is built, the parking lot will still have 70 parking spaces, and each row will contain the same number of parking spaces as every other row. How many rows were in the parking lot before the addition was built?

(1) 5 (2) 6 (3) 7 (4) 10 (5) 14

Let us understand that if there were 5 rows in the parking lot before the addition was built then since 4 more rows were added to the parking lot, there are 9 rows now. If you want to park 70 cars in 9 rows that are laid out in such a manner that each row has the same number of parking spaces, you have to divide 70 cars in 9 equal lots. This is impossible since 70 is not divisible by 9. Option 1 is to be chucked out of the window for this reason alone.

If there were 6 rows in the parking lot before the addition was built, there was no way in which you could have parked 70 cars in 6 rows in such a way that each row in the parking lot contains the same number of parking spaces (and therefore the same number of cars parked in the parking spaces). This is because 70 is not divisible by 6 in the first place. Option 2 is to be kicked out for this reason.

There were 7 rows in the parking lot before the addition was built then since 4 more rows were added to the parking lot, there are 11 rows now. If you want to park 70 cars in 11 rows that are laid out in such a manner that each row has the same number of parking spaces, you have to divide 70 cars in 11 equal lots. This is impossible since 70 is not divisible by 11. Therefore Option 3 is to be crumpled and thrown into the wastepaper basket.

If there were 10 rows in the parking lot before the addition was built, then since 4 more rows were added to the parking lot, there are 14 rows now. If you want to park 70 cars in 14 rows that are laid out in such a manner that each row has the same number of parking spaces in every row, you have to divide 70 cars in 14 equal lots. This is possible since 70 divided by 14 gives 5. When the addition is built, two parking spaces are lost from each row. The fact that there are 5 parking spaces in each row now means that there were 7 parking spaces in each row earlier. Since 4 more rows were added to the parking lot and there are 14 rows now it means that there were 10 rows earlier. If you had wanted to park 70 cars in 10 rows such that there were 7 cars in each row, you jolly well could have. The short point here is that both the new number of rows and the old number of rows should divide 70. If they do not, the option should be thrown out by its ear. **Option 4** is correct for this reason.

In the case of Option 5 while the earlier number of rows (which is 14) can divide 70, the new number of rows (which would be 18) will not divide 70 and hence Option 5 is not workable.

Illustration 4

In a triangle ABC, AB = 6, BC = 8 and AC = 10. A perpendicular dropped from B, meets the side AC at D. A circle of radius BD (with centre B) is drawn. If the circle cuts AB and BC at P and Q respectively, then AP: QC is equal to

1. 1:1 2. 3:2 3. 4:1 4. 3:8

This is a matter of logic alone. A triangle with sides 6,8 and 10 units of measure is a right- angled triangle (since the sides are in the ratio of 3:4:5). Remember Pythagoras Theorem?

See the following triangle:

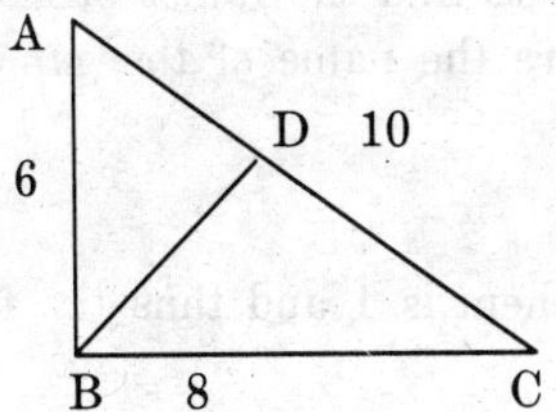

If you draw a circle of radius BD (with centre B), this circle will cut AB and BC at the same distance from B. This means that if the circle cuts AB at P and BC at Q, the length of PB and QB will be equal. This means that AP is what is left of AB after the circle cuts it at P and CQ is what is left of BC after the circle cuts it at Q. Now imagine that there are two brothers (one elder, the other younger) and their tiny sister.

Imagine that the elder brother has 6 chocolates and the younger brother has 8 chocolates. If the little sister, wants the same number of chocolates from each of her two brothers – let us say 3 chocolates from each of the two brothers - the elder brother will have fewer chocolates left than the younger brother. On this analogy, AP will invariably be **less than** QC. This is only at Option 4.

Also look at this from another refreshingly different angle.

Angles ACB and DCB are equal in the two right-angled triangles ABC and DBC (in right angled triangle DBC, angle ACB shows itself as angle DCB). Since the two triangles ACB and DCB are right angled each of the triangle had one angle of 90^0. Both the triangles have a common angle ACB. This means the third angle of the two triangles also has the same measure and therefore ACB and DCB are equiangular right angled triangles.

The ratios (I) and (II) where ratio (I) is the ratio between the side opposite to angle ACB in triangle ABC and ratio (II) is between the side opposite to angle DCB in triangle DBC will be the same since the two angles are equal. Ratio (I) can be clearly seen as 6/10 or 0.6. So will it be in the case of triangle DBC where the hypotenuse is 8. In other words, BD/ BC = 0.6 and hence BD = 0.6 times BC. We know that BC is 8 units in measure. Therefore BD = 4.8. Therefore AP = 6 – 4.8 = 1.2 and QC = 8-4.8 = 3.2. Thus AP: QC is 1.2:3.2 or 12:32 or 3:8. So Option 4.

The problem in this illustration comes from one of the toughest management entrance tests in the world. Ask yourself this: Have we used any formula? Have we used anything other than some simple logic for arriving at the correct answer?

The difference between Quantitative Ability and mathematics having been explained, there is no need for remembering any other than four or five of the most basic mathematical formulae such as that of the area of a circle, the area of a triangle, the circumference of a circle, the Pythagoras theorem and so on. This is precisely why you will not see any mathematical formulae in this book.

Illustration 5

If K = (P + Q)/(PQ) where K, P and Q are positive integers, how many values of K are possible?

(1) None (2) One (3) Two (4) Seven

When we settle down to solving a question with the kind of options you see above, we must realise that the four options are such that the moment you get three possible values for K, all that one has to do is to mark Option 4 as correct. This is essentially what sets quantitative ability apart from mathematics. If the question pertained to mathematics, it would have been necessary to reckon each of the seven possible values for K and the corresponding values of P and Q.

Secondly it must be remembered that we have three unknown quantities K, P and Q and we have not the faintest idea of what is the relationship between them. All that we are told is all three are positive integers. From the standpoint of mathematics this is not saying much at all. There are an endless number of positive integers.

When we see the expression (P + Q)/(PQ), we must be able to realise that:

- K is dependent upon the values of P and Q and therefore the whole idea is to find the values of P and Q that will give a corresponding positive integer value for K and therefore the name of the game is finding suitable values for P and Q
- (1/Q) + (1/P), which is what (P + Q)/PQ is really, is a positive integer
- Since Q and P are positive integers, the first possible value of either of them is 1 and thus the first possible value for K is 2
- Since we have already assumed 1 as the value for both Q and P, the next higher value for either is 2. This would mean that if both Q and P are equal to 2, K = 1 and this is the second possible value for K
- It is not possible for any one of P and Q to be 1 and the other to be 2 because this would mean adding 1 and 1/2 and thus would not give an integer.

- (1/Q) + (1/P) cannot ever add up to an integer if either Q or P or both of them were higher than 2. If there are two positive fractions one of which is ½ in value and the other is less than ½, their sum shall always be less than 1. This means any value for Q and P beyond 2 is out of the question and therefore there can be only two sets of values for P and Q: that would give integral values for K. When both P and Q are equal to 1, K = 2. When both P and Q are equal to 2, K = 1.

Illustration 6

(This illustration is drawn from an actual past paper of an examination rated as one of the toughest management entrance tests in the whole wide world)

DIRECTIONS *for questions 1 and 2:* A company imports component A from Germany and component B from USA. It then assembles them along with other components to produce a machine used in a chemical process. Component A contributes 30% to the production cost and component B contributes 50% to the production cost. The current practice is to sell the machine at a price that is 20% over the production cost. Due to foreign exchange fluctuations the German Mark has become costlier by 30% and the US Dollar by 22%. But the company is unable to increase the selling price by more than 10%.

Question 1

What is the current margin of profit?

1. 10% 2. 15% 3. 12% 4. 8%

Question 2

Suppose the US Dollar becomes cheaper by 12% of its original value, and the German Mark becomes costlier by 20% of its original value. To achieve a profit margin of 10%, the selling price must exceed the production cost by

1. 10% 2. 20% 3. 12% 4. 15%

Answer 1

We are given that Component A (imported from Germany) contributes 30% to the production cost and component B (imported from USA) contributes 50% to the production cost. This makes up only 80% of the production cost. This means that the rest 20% of the components come from the domestic market. This logical reasoning that 20% comes from the country itself is the first of the differences between Mathematics and Quantitative Ability.

Let us imagine that the total cost of production of a machine was 100 units of currency. This means that if the earlier cost of production was 100 units of currency, the selling price prior to exchange fluctuation was 120 units since the practice then was to sell at 20% over the cost of production. This means that the German component cost 30 units and the US component cost 50 units and therefore the indigenous component cost 20 units of currency. When the German Mark and the US Dollar became costlier respectively by 30% and 22%, the price of these currencies rose to 130% and 122% respectively of its earlier prices. This means that the company needed 39 currency units worth of German components (since 130% of 30 currency units is 39 currency units) and 61 currency units worth of US components (since 122% of 50 currency units is 61 currency units). These two add up to 100 currency units. Add the indigenous component of 20 units of currency and you come to the revised production cost of 120 currency units. If the company sells at the selling price of 120 units it is doing social service. It is not earning profit. If the company cannot increase the selling price beyond 10% of the selling price, it can go to 110% of the earlier selling price of 120 currency units and this makes 132 currency units the new selling price. This means that when the production cost is 120 currency units and the selling price is 132 currency units, the profit margin is (132-120)/120 = 12/120 = 1/10 or 10% and hence Option 1.

Answer 2

This is where Mathematics should take a well-deserved rest and let Quantitative Ability do all the work. If you wish to achieve a profit margin of 10%, it means that if the cost of production is, for example, 100 Zambian Shillings or

100 Saudi Riyal or whatever other currency, the corresponding selling price must be 110 Zambian Shillings or 110 Saudi Riyal or whatever other currency that you can think of. This is fundamental. It is for this reason that to achieve a profit margin of 10%, the selling price must exceed the production cost by 10% regardless of the currency and the cost of production. So **Option 1.**

This is one more illustration to show as to what sets Quantitative Ability apart from Mathematics. When the issue is Quantitative Ability, studying Mathematics is irrelevant whether the Mathematics is from the Vedas or it is from the annals of the Egyptian civilisation or from the Central Congo.

Why do you not see instructions on how to take computer adaptive tests when you rifle through this book? Why are guidelines on how to use the mouse missing? Why are guidelines on how to darken the correct oval missing?

In present times teaching an under graduate or a graduate how to use the mouse in a computer adaptive test or how to darken the oval for marking ones choice for the correct answer is like teaching fish how to swim. It is like teaching a bird how to fly. The idea in writing this book is to make a scientific estimate of the level of the skills associated with the Graduate Record Examination. The basis of scientific estimate of the skill level required for any examination is ideally the actual past papers. Luckily the POWERPREP CD that the ETS issues has sample questions, practise tests and Test Papers. Nothing could be more reliable than this which we shall refer to as the **Official Source**.

The focus of this book is clear. We see no need for wasting scores of pages on teaching young readers on how to pounce on the mouse, or on how to darken ovals. For those rare few that may want to practise clicking the mouse and so on, the POWERPREP CD has it all. We shall not carry coals to Newcastle. We shall not carry sandbags to the Sahara. Time is precious and so is paper. The idea is to achieve the desired objective with economy of effort. We shall devote our energies to systematically analysing:

(A) The range and level of skills that the GRE calls for

(B) The range and level of skills, you, dear reader, already possess

(C) What range and level of skills that you, dear reader, will require to develop which is really a matter only of subtracting (B) from (A).

Why do you not see in this book any tips on how to make guesses – whether smart or intelligent?

If someone unknown asks you as to what is her age and you make an estimate based on the person's outwardly appearance, the drooping shoulders, the abundant grey in the tousled hair and so on. You tell him that you will eat your hat if he is a day younger than 53. He then tells you that you may start with your hat and then if you still have any appetite left for hats he will give you his as well but he is in fact not a day over 43. We have assumed a male in this illustration. If instead we make such an error in guessing a female's age, Lord knows what can happen.

When you guess, you estimate. You speculate. You are asking for it.

We shall show you an illustration from some literature that aims to prepare young people for the GRE and the GMAT where there is a reference to an intelligent guess. The question and its explanation are as follows:
The question with its five options is as follows: What is the product of 21.84×32.78?

(A) 615.9152

(B) 715.8152

(C) 715.902

(D) 715.9152

(E) 725.9152

The explanation in the preparatory literature that we are talking about goes more or less as follows: **Since the product asked for will be greater than 21×32, which is 672, you can straightaway eliminate choice (A). Also each term has two decimal places, so the answer must have four decimal places.**

Thus you can eliminate choice (C). If you can't do the detailed calculation, then guess (B), (D), or (E). The correct answer, however, is (D).

Do you know why it is not necessary to guess even if you cannot do the calculations? Do we even need to tell you what will happen if your so-called intelligent or smart guess backfires in a system of negative marking? Do you know that insofar as the GRE is concerned, a wrong answer for something as simple as this may pull you into the abyss of a much lower strata of (easier) questions from which getting a sizable score might remain a pipe dream? Shall we tell you why there is no need to do any calculations **at all** in this very example? Follow us and you will be convinced that if there is any book that can help you prepare for the GRE, it is this which you are reading now.

Let us understand that:

The product of 21.84 × 32.78 is certainly bigger than 21 × 32

Multiplying 21 × 32 is the same thing as multiplying (20 + 1) × (30 + 2) which is as such (20 × 30) +(20 × 2) +(1 × 30) + (1 × 2) = 600 + 40 + 30 + 2 = 672. It is for this reason that Option A is to be kicked out of the window because choice A is less than 672. [The method shown here of multiplying 21 and 32 for example is the fastest way to multiply orally. At the most what you can do is to write down 600 + 40 + 30 + 2 when you multiply orally and add the four figures. **Remember: adding is always easier than multiplying**]

When you multiply 21.84 × 32.78 you **may** get a number that has 4 places of decimals. There cannot be a certainty about four places of decimals. Which is why we wish to show you under what circumstances you will **certainly** get a number with four decimal places and under what circumstances you will **not**. The reader of this book (or for that matter any of our books) should be so clear in his concepts that he will laugh at the suggestion of so-called *intelligent* guesses). 21.84 as we know is really 2184 / 100. The quantity 2184 is divisible by 4 for the reason that the last two digits (tens and units places) give a number divisible by 4 whereas all hundreds are divisible by 4 and therefore in order to determine whether a number is divisible by 4, it would suffice if we merely found whether the last two digits to the right are divisible by 4. As we know, if a number divisible by 4 were to be multiplied by 5, there would certainly be a zero as the last digit. It is for this reason that if we were to multiply 21.84 by 32.75 for instance (instead of 32.78 as given in the illustration) the answer would be 715.2600 but since the zeroes at the end are meaningless, what you are looking at is a number with two places of decimals. Check this stuff about two places of decimals with your calculator. The product of 21.84 and 32.75 has two places of decimals because (A) 21.84 which as such is 2184 / 100 has 4 as one of the factors and (B) 32.75 which as such is 3275 / 100 has 25 as one of the factors (as is the case with all numbers that end with any of the following last two digits: 25, 50, 75 and 00). Then again when we multiply 21.84 with 32.85 (instead of 32.78 as given in the illustration) we would get 717.444 (which has three places of decimals and not four). You may again check this out with your calculator. Why we are asking you to check with the calculator is because we want you to assimilate concepts and checking out with a calculator is only a methodology of **reinforcing** the concepts and **not learning** them. We will tell you why the product of 21.84 and 32.85 is a number that has only three places of decimals although you are multiplying two numbers each with two places of decimals. The reason is simple: the product of 21.84 and 32.85 has three places of decimals because (A) 21.84 which as such is 2184 / 100 has 4 as one of the factors and (B) 32.85 which as such is 3285 / 100 has 5 as one of the factors (as is the case with all numbers that end with any of the following last two digits: 15, 35, 45, 55, 65, 85, and 95). The product of 21.84 and 32.78 has four places of decimals because neither of the two numbers (although both are even) is divisible by 5.

From what we have seen so far, since 21.84 and 32.78 multiply giving a four-digit number in excess of 672, we are to concentrate on choices B, D and E that are respectively 715.8152, 715.9152 and 725.9152.

Now comes the beauty.

You will be convinced that it is only conceptual clarity that will help you decide as to which option is correct and guessing will be considered stupid. Add the digits of some of the following numbers that are divisible by 3: 12, 21, 36, 48. You will see that the digits add up to a number that is itself divisible by 3. (For example the digits in 21 add up to 3 and in 48 the digits add up to 12). 12, 21, 36, 48 and so on are all essentially multiples of 3. This is why when you multiply 32.78 with 21.84 you will get a number whose digits should add up to either 3 or a number divisible by 3. Add the digits in 715.8152 and you will get 7 + 1 + 5 + 8 + 1 + 5 + 2 = 29. This is not divisible by 3 and hence 715.8152 is not a valid choice. Having found that the digits in 715.8152 add up to 29, we need to see only 715.9152 whose total of the digits is bound to be 1 more than in the case of 715.8152 and should therefore add up to 30. This means that 715.9152 is bound to be divisible by 3 and hence this is the product of 21.84 and 32.78. This is the reason why choice D is to be marked as correct. **This is the reason why so-called intelligent guessing is mere speculation**. If you will see choice E, the digits will add up to one more than 30 and hence choice E will not be divisible by 3.

As far as this specific illustration is concerned, we trust you have now understood why it is not at all necessary that the multiplication of two numbers each with two places of decimals will give a product that will have four places of decimals.

This book will give you the entire range of concepts and comprehensive practice material that will eliminate the very need for guessing, the need for playing blind, the need for sailing by guess and by Godfrey (meaning, *without landmarks* so that you may land on the shores of China whereas your destination may have been Chile)!

A Scientific Assessment of the Skill Level associated with the GRE: How it is made.

It becomes extremely important to rely on the POWERPRED CD (the official Source) for making a reliable and accurate assessment of the range of skills required for the GRE. This is because all other sources may or may not contain any questions from the past papers at the GRE. Based on the pattern of questions in an examination, one can meaningfully prepare for that examination. Otherwise one plays blind.

One relies on the actual past papers of an examination in order to arrive at a scientific assessment of the skill level associated with that examination for the following reasons:

1. If, for example, the actual question papers of the past ten years have an average of 5 questions (out of 50) based on the Pythagoras Theorem, one must understand that studying this theorem is crucial to the preparation. However seldom, if ever, there have been direct questions at the GRE on the Pythagoras Theorem. Each question on this theorem would be so carefully worded so as to call for sharp comprehension to realise that the question pertains to this theorem. Some of the questions may be such that Old Pythagoras himself would have to scratch his head for a while before he would begin to realise that this question is based on this theorem. For example, it takes presence of mind to realise that the following question relates to this theorem: If u, v, w, and m are natural numbers such that $u^m + v^m = w^m$, then which one of the following is true?

   Option 1. $m \geq \min (u,v,w)$ Option 2. $m \geq \max (u,v,w)$

   Option 3. $m < \min (u,v,w)$ Option 4. None of these

   In order to solve such a question one must realise that in the case of natural numbers (which is what positive integers are), only the squares of two natural numbers can add up to the square of a third natural number. One has not seen any instance where the cubes of two natural numbers add up to the cube of a third natural number. The smallest possible values of two natrual numbers whose squares add up to that of a third natural number is in the case of $3^2 + 4^2 = 5^2$. Even in this case, if you were to see $3^2 + 4^2 = 5^2$ in the form of $u^m + v^m = w^m$, you will see that m is the least among m, u, v and w and hence Option 3. If you have heard of the phrase "Old wine in new bottles", then this question can be figuratively described as "the Pythagoras Theorem in fancy dress".

2. If, for example, the actual question papers of the past ten years have an average of 7 questions out of 50 based on the topic of Ratio and Proportion, one must realise that one must be ready to face any sizzling question based on this topic. However no examiner will be so naive to give you any direct question on Ratio and Proportion. He will not ask you what will be the price of a pound of nuts in which there are nuts of Type A costing $ 35, nuts of Type B costing $38 and nuts of Type C costing $43 per pound mixed in the ratio of Type A: Type B: Type C:: 3: 7: 9. Such questions appear in books that profess to prepare you for the GRE without knowing that such questions have never ever appeared at the real event and are not likely to appear at the real event for very obvious reasons. The typical question on the subject of Ratio and Proportion at the real event will be bunged to the student like this: A train approaches a tunnel AB. Inside the tunnel is a cat located at a point that is 3/8 of the distance AB measured from the entrance A. When the train whistles, the cat runs. If the cat moves to the entrance of the tunnel, A, the train catches the cat exactly at the entrance. If the cat

moves to the exit, B, the train catches at exactly the exit. The speed of the train is greater than the speed of the cat by what order?

Option 1: 3:1. Option 2: 4:1. Option 3: 5:1. Option 4: None of these.

While apparently the question may seem to pertain to Speed and Distance, what one must realise is that (A) the options have ratios alone (B) The speed of neither the train nor the cat is given (C) The length of the tunnel is not given either and what is given is the ratio between the distance from the entrance that the cat stands and the length of the tunnel. As soon as one realises that for determining Speed the least parameters that one needs is Distance and Time, since none of these parameters is given it would be naive to persist with examining this question from the standpoint of Speed and Distance. If, however, we proceed on the lines of **logic** alone then there is no need to put even pen to paper. If we assume that the tunnel is 8 meters long and go by the options for which we have no choice since we do not know either distance or speeds; we do not even know their ratios. This means that according to Option 1, the cat is 3 meters from the entrance. If the ratio of the speed of the engine and the cat were to be 3:1 as per the first option, this would mean that the train is 9 meters from the entrance since by the time the cat runs 3 meters, the engine runs 9 meters. If on the other hand, the cat runs towards the exit, then the cat runs 5 meters and the engine runs 9 + 8 = 17 meters whereas if 3:1 were their ratio of speeds, then the engine should have run only 15 meters. Option 1 is not workable. Turning to Option 2, if the ratio of the speed of the engine and the cat were to be 4:1 as per the first option, this would mean that the train is 12 meters from the entrance since by the time the cat runs 3 meters, the engine runs 12 meters. If on the other hand, the cat runs towards the exit, then the cat runs 5 meters and the engine runs 12 + 8 = 20 meters. Therefore the engine has run 20 meters by the time the cat has run 5 meters. This means that the ratio of the speeds of the train and the cat is indeed 20:5 or 4:1 and thus Option 2 is correct.

3. During the course of writing the several books that aimed at preparing students for management entrance tests (one of them rated as the toughest in the world) we have had occasion to solve thousands of questions from the actual past papers of so many management entrance tests. The list of these books is on the back cover of this book. What we have seen as the most important commonality between all of these tests is the fact that the **name of the game is logic** (whether the questions pertain to the Verbal Section or to the Quantitative Section or what-have-you.) We therefore place great emphasis on development of one's analytical reasoning. It is for this reason that we recommend this presentation to you so that your preparation is on the right track.

The risk of there being no question from the past actual GRE papers in other books is extremely high and only the utterly impudent would base their assessment of what is the event at the GRE on material other than that provided by the Official Source.

The question then is: **how does one reproduce the essence of what the GRE intends to test in each question from its actual past papers without reproducing the very text of the actual past GRE papers?**

We shall tell you with the help of the following illustrations that we present to you in tabular form how we have taken meticulous care to see that the essence of what the GRE intends to test is preserved without an iota of dilution or variation.

If the question in the actual past paper of the GRE were worded as follows:	We would have rewritten it as under:	So that both the original question and the rewritten question test the same range and level of skills that are as follows:
What is the unit digit of $(33)^3 \times (47)^4 \times (19)^{5}$?	What is the unit digit of $(23)^3 \times (27)^4 \times (29)^{5}$?	Whether one understands the fundamental aspect that when we multiply–say a two-digit number – what we are multiplying is (A) with (B) where (A) = a multiple of 10 + a positive integer less than 10 and (B) = another multiple of 10+ another positive integer less than 10

		Whether one understands that you shall have to add the following four things in order to reach the product AB: (I) the product of a multiple of 10 with another multiple of 10 that shall have zero in the unit digit with (II) The product of a multiple of 10 with another positive integer less than 10 that also shall have zero in the unit digit with (III) The product of a positive integer less than 10 with another multiple of 10 that shall have zero in the unit digit finally with (IV) The product of a positive integer less than 10 with another positive integer less than 10 that is the only quantity among the four quantities to have a unit digit which shall be the same unit digit that you will find in the product of (C) a positive integer less than 10 in A with (D) a positive integer less than 10 in B. This is why the product of 27 and 33, for example, is $(20 + 7) \times (30 + 3) = (20 \times 30) + (7 \times 30) + (20 \times 3) + (7 \times 3) = 600 + 210 + 60 + 21 = 891$ and this is also why the unit digit in the product of 27 and 33 is the same as the unit digit in the product of 7 and 3.

In view of the clarification that we have furnished to you in the above table, we may state that the questions that we present to you do certainly give us a very scientific assessment of the range and level of skills that one shall have to be ready with in order to emerge with flying colours at the GRE. The thousands of questions that you shall see in this book, wherein we have taken utmost care to preserve the essence of each question (with the methodology indicated in the above table), provide a scientific assessment of the level of the examination and the range of skills associated with the GRE. The result is that we have an accurate estimate of what concept notes to build in and of what level.

Why is no CD attached to this book?

CDs typically have test papers. In some cases the level of difficulty varies. There may be a CD in which when you are able to state which of the following five two digit numbers is a perfect square, a loud cheer emanates. You are thrilled. Your confidence rises. While as such there is nothing wrong with rising confidence, it is also important that the rise in confidence is backed to the hilt by complete assimilation of the fundamental aspects of different topics that the ETS – the agency that administers the GRE - expect you to be familiar with. In the absence of this conceptual clarity, the cheer from the CD may bring intoxication (figuratively, of course) and not confidence. It may, at best, bring **Dutch courage** (which as such is *temporary boldness induced by drinking alcohol*).

This of course is the least of the consequences of practising with test papers in CDs without first knowing (A) what the event is in the first place and then knowing (B) what is the level of skills that you will require in order to do well. An online assessment of either A or B is, in the very least, Utopia.

Let us elaborate on this a little further by drawing parallels from the experiences of a schoolboy leaping into a limpid pool of deep water in the middle of a forest where a school class have gone on a picnic. Nothing could be more enjoyable to our mind. But that is provided he knows that leaping in from a few inches and a few meters are two different ball games altogether. The small leap will take him certainly in the pool where after he may splash around and throw up huge sprays of water at his friends standing nearby. The atmosphere will be thick with good cheer. If however he leaps from ten meters with confidence based on the lessons that he has learnt, if any of course, on the little splash from two feet, he does not know what he is in for.

A leap from that kind of height should never be attempted till one is trained in (A) keeping one's hands and feet together not only while falling but also while entering the water (B) leaping in such a way that one certainly clears the jagged rocks on the cliff from one is jumping in. The consequences of not being trained in both (A) and (B) can be any or all of the following: deep lacerations, a skull fracture, spinal fracture, fracture in other limbs, haemorrhage, drowning. The atmosphere could get thick with broken bones and sprays of blood instead of with good cheer. We do not want any of our readers to go through any of these (figuratively) horrendous experiences and hence we have consciously left out the CD in this book. This is not the only reason why we have deliberately omitted a CD. The other reasons are as follows:

The CD could tell you which answer is correct but, typically, in a sketchy manner, why the particular answer is correct. You may have marked a different answer from the one that is shown as correct based on the conviction that your answer is right. You have no means of finding why you are wrong. You have virtually no means of finding why you are right as well.

We have based our estimate of the skill level associated with the GRE on the basis of the question bank in the Official Source. There could be no source as reliable as this to form the basis of such an estimate. In case of a great majority of the questions we have given a clear idea of the skills that the particular question tests. The solutions are lucid and it is our assurance to you that you will be able to understand the explanations whether the matter pertains to Quantitative Ability or to Verbal Reasoning or to Interpretation of Data. This is because logic is the prime ingredient of the great majority of solutions. **You will find that the solutions are, in a great majority of cases, miniature concept chapters in their own way. This is the reason why you may find repetitive requests in this book for reading each and every solution to the problems regardless of whether you are right or you are** wrong in your attempts to solve the problems on your own. The concept notes are drawn against the scientific assessment of the range and level of skills associated with the GRE. The concept notes and the accompanying exercises are sure to take the reader in stages to the level where he would have the confidence to excel at the GRE.

Most of the CDs attached to preparatory literature for competitive tests state that the question papers that they contain would give the user of the CD an idea of his potential score. What if a person who has no idea of the event at all leaps in head first into writing the test paper in the CD and finds that his score remains static at a level where he would find that getting into any worthwhile institution is a pipe dream? Has he bought the book and the CD with a view to learn that he is useless? The competitive examination is akin to a war game with an unseen enemy. No game (except solitaire which is reserved as such for the old and infirm) can be won without a clear strategy. There must be a plan for winning. If one fails to plan, one plans to fail. We do not want you to leap from ten meters into limpid pools in forests while on a school picnic without being trained in such leaps. We shall give you the necessary inputs. Thereafter you shall let out a little yippee when you take off with supreme confidence from ten meters into the cool waters below.

We would like to say this even at the cost of repetition that this book will give you:

(I) A precise idea of the event in which you have decided to take part

(II) A scientific estimate of the level and range of skills that are needed to do well at the GRE

(III) A reasonably good estimate of the level and range of skills that you already possess

(IV) A clear idea of what skills that you will have to develop in order to put up a brilliant performance at the GRE [which as such is (II) – (III)]

(V) Detailed concept notes and practice material that will ensure that you not only assimilate the concepts but also thoroughly enjoy doing this.

Please be sure that the test that you are to take is not a leap into a pool of water from a few inches or a foot high nearby rock face. It may really be a leap from ten meters and yet not seem like a leap from ten meters to some who have conceptual clarity. On the other hand, a leap from just one meter may seem like a leap from ten meters to someone who is not trained and (therefore) not confident. Hundreds of thousands of young people take the GRE all over the world for a limited number of admissions to premier colleges. It is a competitive examination and therefore no cakewalk. However if you are armed with the necessary concepts and have a clear-cut plan for emerging with flying colours, nothing can stop you from attaining your objective. This is one of the main reasons why you should read this book.

Why do you not see Test Papers (or what some books refer to as Diagnostic Tests) at the very outset of this book?

The doctor diagnoses patients who come to him with an illness. Neither are we doctors nor are you patients. There is one other place where they perform diagnostic tests if one can loosely refer to these interviews as diagnostic tests: when tiny tots have to start going to kindergarten, the toddler and his/her parents are interviewed by the kindergarten teachers where the child is asked as to what is the colour of this particular flower and so on. We (you and us) have a common objective: you should excel at the GRE. In attaining this objective, we will give you a precise idea of the skills that you shall require for faring admirably at the GRE and then we shall see what skills do you already possess and thereafter we shall decide what skills you shall need to develop or bring to gleam by brushing up. We shall talk of tests only thereafter. That is why the Test Papers (all followed by lucid explanations) are after the chapters containing concept notes and exercises. No one should really test anyone before facilitating his preparation. The idea is to impart confidence. Confidence can come only from clarity about what is the event in which one is set to take part and clarity about concepts and then clarity about the strategies associated with the event. We shall therefore draw a plan and work to it. Logically, tests that want to test what you have learnt should be at the end of sessions of learning..

Why should you read this particular book when the market place abounds in books professing to prepare you for the Graduate Record Examination?

The GRE is a competitive examination. It cannot be surmounted without an effective strategy. In order to develop a strategy, you must know precisely what the game is. It is for this precise knowledge and for formulating the strategy for winning that you should read this book. Let us give you a fair idea of what the GRE is all about and what is the name of the game at the GRE and then about what strategies to adopt as you go along.

Few competitive examinations are as transparent as the GRE. The ETS gives a CD to those who register for the GRE that has questions from their past test papers. If anybody wishes to derive a precise estimate of the examination there could be nothing that can be considered more reliable than these questions from the official source.

There is nothing new at all about educational institutions giving a Sample Test Paper in their bulletins and prospectuses. You can see any number of instances of this. Typically, there is an Answer Key to the Sample Test Paper. There are no solutions in such bulletins and prospectuses. The POWERPREP CD has solutions to the past test papers of the GRE. This is hugely commendable. The first inference that is to be drawn from the solutions is that everything is worked out. You will see no occasion when a question is posed to you is logically incorrect. You will see no occasion when the solution is incorrect, no matter how sketchy it may be. When you see that not a single question is logically incorrect, you are assured that the examiner's concepts are certainly in place. This cannot be said of so many other institutions – some of them greatly reputed – who provide Sample Test Papers (with the relative Answer Key) in their bulletins and prospectuses from which it can be seen quite frequently that questions are based on faulty logic.

The solutions that the POWERPREP CD provides are sketchy at the best. The solutions do not state for example what the examiner wants to test. The solutions do not tell you whether the correct inference will emerge verbatim or whether this will require your views. The solutions for example do not tell you how many correct answers to the questions on average out of the total number of questions asked in relation to the passages in the Verbal Section can be seen to emerge verbatim or how many will emerge nearly verbatim or how many will require your views on some issue that the author has raised.

If the solutions were to tell you for example that 85% of the correct answers emerge either verbatim or very nearly verbatim, the only skill that one must develop is to be able to scan the passage for verbatim answers. Then the secret will be out. If the solutions were to tell you that the matter pertains to your views about something that the author has contended, the skill to develop is to be able to cull out from the very tone of the question that what you are required to do is to present your opinion or perspective. The strategy then is to see what is the author's contention and then apply your thought to it. Do not look in the passage for an answer to such type of questions. This is because if the correct answer involves your opinion, the passage is wholly unlikely to have your opinion.

The solutions do not tell you that this thing is about logic alone. If they did, you would realise what is the event. **The idea in presenting such sketchy solutions is that you should find out the event.** You cannot expect the test administering body to make porridge out of the event and present it to you as your breakfast cereal. You **have to cull out what is the event. You have to decide what skills will this need. You have to decide what strategy will you need to win.** This is why the sketchy solutions in the Official Source will not be of help to you. This is why you will need to know how to reach the correct answer and what it takes to reach the correct answer and how to avoid the pitfalls and traps presented by some of the options that look perilously close. This is why the solutions in this book are so vital to your being able to meaningfully prepare for the GRE. That is why it is so important to read each and every solution that we have provided in this book.

Let us tell you a few things about the solutions in the Official Source. Let us start with the Verbal Section.

While the solutions tell you why a particular choice is correct, the solutions in the Verbal Section for example do not tell you why the others are wrong. It is possible that you may have got the correct answer through chance. On the other hand, it is likely that you may have given deep thought to the question and after what seems a powerful reason for your choice you may have elected a particular option and yet the CD tells you that your chosen option is wrong. **You do not know why you are right or why you are wrong.**

This is where we come in. We shall show you in what type of questions you can expect only a verbatim correct inference and therefore what precise skills are required for answering such questions. We will show you in what type of questions you will **necessarily** have to apply yourself to the question and why. We will show you not only why the particular choice is correct but also why the others are incorrect although some of them may seem perilously close to the correct answer. The idea is not to fill pages. If this was the objective, we could have served it eminently by writing reams of pages on how to click the mouse and how to darken the ovals and how to make so-called *intelligent* guesses and so on. **The idea is to help you develop that absolutely essential sense of reasoning that is the master key to any competitive examination be it the GRE or be it any other.**

The fact that the solutions in the Verbal Section or for that matter in the Quantitative Ability Section do not show you what is the precise skill level that the examiner is trying to test is quite understandable. The GRE is an examination that students from a wide range of disciplines take. Some may hail from engineering background whereas others may hail from pharmacy and some may, for example, hail from commerce streams.

The guiding consideration behind drafting the format of the GRE cannot be to test mathematical skills or else the examining body would exempt those who are from say Veterinary Sciences from writing the so-called mathematics section and instead put in questions relating to arthritis among Saharan camels or asthma among Australian sheep. The guiding consideration is to test the reasonableness of the candidate and little else. See the very words in the Test Taking Tips in the POWERPREP CD and you will find the word **basic** being employed several times while referring to skills in arithmetic, algebra and geometry. That is why the conventions are laid threadbare. That is why they tell you beforehand that if any square root is mentioned, the basic presumption is that you are to deal with only positive square roots. If the test was of mathematics, don't they know that a positive number can have both negative and positive square roots? Isn't a mathematics buff expected to know this very fundamental thing? That is why they give you a list of mathematical skills that they expect you to be acquainted with. If it was mathematics that they wanted to test why should they tell someone what sign stands for *greater than or equal to*? Anybody appearing for a mathematics test is expected to know such most elementary things.

The guiding consideration behind drafting the GRE cannot be to test whether the person writing the examination is a don of the English language. William Shakespeare, the great English poet and playwright, was reputed to have one of the widest personal lexicons (a *lexicon* is someone's *word stock*). People reading his works have spent sleepless nights in trying to find out for example whether he meant **humankind ness** or **human kindness** when he referred to somebody as **full of the milk of humankindness**. Even then if the words that he employed in the course of his glorious innings on Mother Earth were to be listed somewhere, this would not take more than a tenth of the total lexicon in any standard encyclopaedia. Therefore if you start off with mugging up "Word Lists" without knowing what the event is in the first place, what are you really trying to do? Are you trying to replace this great man; or outpace him? In order to help you reach a judgement about what the event really is, the ETS gives you the POWERPREP CD that has their numerous past papers. You have to decide what the event is. You have to decide what you shall have to do in order to emerge with flying colours. You will have to decide what range of skills you will need. You will have to see whether the matter is of logic skills to a great extent or it is of English language skills. You will have to ascertain what is the ratio in which (A) logic and (B) command over the English language are mixed in the GRE. Only then can you prepare meaningfully. But this analysis cannot be done meaningfully in an online test. Secondly, this analysis will necessarily have to be based on the actual past papers of the GRE that the ETS gives you. Nothing could be more reliable for doing this analysis. Nothing could tell you in a voice that could split a sensitive ear what the event really is. Using any other papers as the basis of your analysis of what the examination is all about really and thereafter preparation for the examination means that you are preparing for an unspecified event. It is for this analysis that we invite you to the presentation in this book in general and in this chapter in specific.

The fact that the Official Source does not present either this analysis or the detailed concepts you would need to fare admirably at the GRE is quite understandable. No one who administers a competitive examination would tell you what is the strategy for success. Have you ever heard of someone who organises a sports event between 13 and 19 October for example issuing a letter to those who are taking part in the 100 meters dash at what velocity and in which direction the wind blows in October at the venue? Have you ever heard of someone who is to take part in a 100-meter dash being told by the organisers that the Ethiopian participant can be overcome if you stay in lead till 85 meters because if he is not able to take a lead over the others till the 85-meter mark, he virtually gives up? Have you ever heard of someone taking part in a sprint event and told by the organisers that he should develop his arms as well as his legs because strong arms are vital for imparting momentum for the sprint? Do they write to the prospective competitors as to what they should eat and what to avoid and how much to run each day in preparation and so on? All this has to be derived by the people who take part in the 100 meters. But the people who are planning to compete at this event are a lot more fortunate than anyone planning to take on a competitive examination. At least they know what is the event. Those who prepare for competitive examination without ascertaining the event beforehand from the very literature that the test administering body issues to them beforehand may have been toiling for a boxing bout whereas the event may be chess.

We may mention that the Official Source has so-called *strategies* in relation to different topics. Why we refer to these as *so-called strategies*, we shall clarify. See the strategy in the Official Source for the questions on antonyms that goes more or less as follows:

Remember:

- Antonyms are generally nouns, verbs, and adjectives.
- Look for the word most nearly opposite in meaning to the given word.
- Try to define words precisely.
- Use the given word in a sentence to help establish its meaning.
- Look for possible other meanings before finally choosing an answer.
- Use your knowledge of prefixes and suffixes to help define words you do not know.

If they tell you to look for a word that is most nearly opposite in meaning to the given word, this is only a **reiteration** of the meaning of the word *antonym*. Where is the strategy in this reiteration? If you are told that the idea is to hit your opponent so hard with your gloved fist that he falls to the mat and cannot get up till the referee counts ten, you are only being told the **objective** of the boxing match and **not the strategy**. Strategy would be to avoid his lunges and play around till Round Seven by when he tires out completely even if he scores many points till then. He can stuff his points in his pipe and smoke them at leisure after you knock him out in Round Eight. Seem to him that you are a gone case. Let him feel overconfident. Let him become carefree. Let him drop his guard. Then give him one haymaker on his front teeth. Let him spit out a few of the thirty-two teeth that God has blessed him with. Let him spit out blood. Blood shatters his confidence. Batter him then. This is strategy. Asking you to ensure that your boxing shorts are properly laced or not to curse the referee no matter what the provocation are only directions, not strategy.

Asking you to try to define words is another tall order. Can anyone define death for example? Does it need to be defined? Who are we to define words? Are we lexicographers? Within a minute that you have at the most, can you be reasonably expected to first define a word and then use the given word in a sentence?

As regards the knowledge of prefixes and suffixes to help define words, prefixes can change the very nature of a word. When you are asked to **eject** something it means you are to **throw out** something whereas if you are asked to **inject** a fluid you are to forcefully **throw in** the fluid into the sick child's veins because she will not accept an injection willingly. The two words EJECT and INJECT have different prefixes. EJECT has E- as the prefix whereas INJECT has IN- as the prefix. The prefixes materially change the nature of the word that they are used for forming. The word INJECTION has a suffix –ION that makes a noun out of the verb INJECT without in any way changing the nature of the word to which it is attached since an **injection** also **involves throwing in something forcefully**. However mere prefixes and suffixes cannot help you define words. The reason why the words EJECT, INJECT and INJECTION all involve throwing something is because the Latin root JECT- means *throw.*

A strategy to proceed with defining words from the prefixes and suffixes is like telling someone that the strategy is to drive pell-mell without telling where one is to go eventually whether pell-mell or at a snail's pace. It is not even a direction leave alone a strategy. This is where we come in. We present in this book a wide range of roots of words with situational usage so that the meanings of so many words at the very core of the English language will be permanently ingrained in your memory. We shall not dwell any further on this. Please see the Official Source yourself and see if you can find any strategy. If you cannot – and this is eminently likely - please be sure that they are not expected to give you any. If you seek strategy in their CD and yet do not find it, you are being unreasonable in trying to find it when it cannot be reasonably expected to be there. Let your quest for strategy rest here. You will find strategy in this book.

Chapter 2

How should you read this book?

We shall now deal the question: How should you read this book?

First read the chapter *Understanding the System*. This should acquaint you with the objectives that have guided the design of the GRE and the topics that one is expected to have familiarity with as also the skills that one would need to excel at the GRE.

Then read the concept notes one by one. At the end of the concept notes there are exercises (with, of course, lucid solutions) that are designed to ensure complete assimilation of the relevant concepts. It is suggested that you may take up for study a chapter under the Verbal Section. You would do well to start with the Chapter titled *Antonyms*. You may then take a few chapters under the Quantitative Section. You should ideally start with the Chapter titled *Ages* and then move on till you reach the chapter titled *The Circle*. You may then return to the Verbal Section to the chapter titled *Word Analogies*.

In between you may turn to the Section on Analytical Writing Assessment. You may like to access the following website where you will see the list of topics that the ETS has set out for the GRE in regard to presentation of one's perspectives: www.gre.org/issuetop.html and the following website for the pool of Arguments: www.gre.org/argutop.html. The Issues and Arguments drawn from their official pool would provide the necessary and relevant topics on which one must have one's viewpoints clear. This should greatly facilitate preparation for the Analytical Writing Assessment.

Thereafter you may read a few chapters under the Quantitative Section. This variation will ensure that you have variety fare when you read.

You may then turn to the Practice Tests and take one by one the Practice Tests, alternating between the Verbal Section and Quantitative Section for reasons of variety.

Finally you may take the Question Papers 1 and 2 at the very end. These practice tests would provide you with top of the line (and yet relevant) practice material since it aims to test EXACTLY the same range and level of skills as do the questions that you will see in the POWERPREP CD that the ETS issues to those who register for taking the GRE. We have provided lucid solutions to each and every question whether in the exercises at the end of each chapter, or in the practice tests or in the question papers.

Please feel free to write to us at jivaishnav@yahoo.com if you find any difficulty in solving any question from any other official pool of questions. Please send the question by way of an attachment to your e-mail. Whenever you write to us, please do write to us (at your option of course) where and what you study (or where and what have you studied). Your educational background would help us in deciding how should we present the solution to you. Please write to us the source of the question(s). We shall deeply appreciate your responses in regard to the quality or quantity of the presentation in this book.

Authors.

Chapter 3

Understanding the System

The Graduate Record Examination (GRE) conducted by the Educational Testing Service of the USA (ETS hereafter) is designed to assess the skills of graduate students aspiring to pursue studies in graduate schools and fellowship programmes in the USA in particular as also in some educational institutions located outside the USA. Students from numerous countries aspire for admissions to institutions that consider scores at the GRE for granting admissions. The idea is to have a test that measures skills acquired in (A) Verbal Reasoning, (B) Quantitative Ability and (C) Data Interpretation over a period of time. This means that inputs that one needs for the GRE are those that one has acquired at school and not further.

There are some really laudable aspects of the GRE that makes it such a transparent process.

The ETS has spelt out what they want to test really in the GRE and what topics they expect the test takers to be familiar with when they take the GRE. We shall see both of these from section to section as under:

THE VERBAL SECTION

The verbal section measures your ability to analyse and evaluate written material and synthesize information obtained from it, to analyse relationships among component parts of sentences, to recognize relationships between words and concepts, and to reason with words in solving problems.

The verbal section contains the following question types:

- Antonyms
- Analogies
- Sentence Completion
- Reading Comprehension

THE ARITHMETIC SECTION

- Arithmetic Questions may involve: arithmetic operations, powers, operations on radical expressions, estimation, percents, absolute value, properties of integers (e.g., divisibility, factoring, prime numbers, odd and even integers), the number line
- Algebra Questions may involve: rules of exponents, factoring and simplifying algebraic expressions, understanding concepts of relations and functions, equations and inequalities, solving linear and quadratic equations and inequalities, solving simultaneous equations, setting up equations to solve word problems, coordinate geometry, including slope, intercepts, and graphs of equations and inequalities, applying basic algebra skills to solve problems
- Geometry Questions may involve: parallel lines, circles and their inscribed central angles, triangles (including special triangles), rectangles, other polygons, area, perimeter, volume, the Pythagorean theorem, angle measure in degrees

Math Symbols and Other Information

The following information applies to all questions in the quantitative section:

These common math symbols may be used:

$x < y$ (x is less than y)

$x \neq y$ (x is not equal to y)

$\sqrt{X}$, (the non-negative square root of X, where $X > 0$)

$|x|$ (modulus of X or, in other words, the absolute value of X, where X is a real number)

n! (n factorial: the product of the first n positive integers)

m || n (line m is parallel to line n)

$m \perp n$ (line m is perpendicular to line n)

(Angle ABC is a right angle)

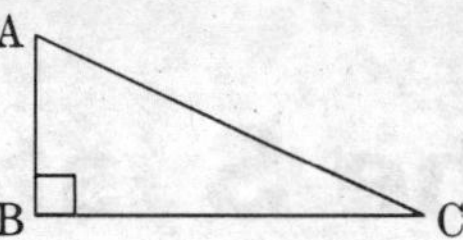

Numbers: all numbers used are real numbers.

Figures: the positions of points, angles, regions, etc., can be assumed to be in the order shown; angle measures are positive

A line shown as straight can be assumed to be straight-figures lie in a plane unless otherwise indicated

Do not assume that figures are drawn to scale unless it is stated

THE DATA INTERPRETATION SECTION

Data Analysis Questions emphasize understanding basic principles and reasoning within the context of given information. Questions may involve: (I) elementary probability (II) basic descriptive statistics (III) mean (IV) median (V) mode (VI) range (VII) standard deviation (VIII) percentiles (IX) interpretation of data in graphs and (X) tables (XI) line graphs (XII) bar graphs (XIII) circle graphs (XIV) frequency distributions

This is the broad syllabus of the Graduate Record Examination (the GRE) insofar as the Data Interpretation Section is concerned in the very words of the Educational Testing Service that conducts the GRE. The test administering body itself tells you what is the range of topics the students must be familiar with. That makes things fairly transparent. It is also important to note that there are clear conventions laid down. For example, if you are asked to reckon with $\sqrt{X}$, then you are to consider only the positive square root of X if X is not equal to zero. This shows clarity on the part of the examiner.

We shall tell you why the laying down of convention is so significant. See what utter confusion the absence of convention can lead to.

See this question from the past paper of a Management Entrance Test reported to be one of the toughest in the whole wide world: Let $K = \sqrt{N} - \sqrt{(N - 1)}$ where N is a natural number. Then K:

(I) Increases with N

(II) Decreases with N

(III) First increases with N and then decreases with N

(IV) First decreases with N and then increases with N

Natural numbers, dear young reader, are those that you can count on your fingers. This means all natural numbers are positive integers. This also means that the very first value for N is 1. If we take N = 1 then $K = \sqrt{N} - \sqrt{(N - 1)} = \sqrt{1} - \sqrt{(1 - 1)} = \sqrt{1}$. In the absence of clearly laid down convention, $\sqrt{1}$ can be either + 1 or – 1. It cannot have both positive and negative values. This is because you have to compare the next possible value of K when N = 2 with the value of K when N = 1.

When N = 2, $K = \sqrt{N} - \sqrt{N - 1} = \sqrt{2} - \sqrt{2 - 1} = \sqrt{2} - \sqrt{1}$. We know that $\sqrt{2}$ is approximately either + 1.4 or –1.4 therefore when N = 2, K can have the following four possible values: (1) $K = \sqrt{2} - \sqrt{1} = 1.4 - 1 = 0.4$. (2) $K = \sqrt{2} - \sqrt{1} = 1.4 - (-1) = 1.4 + 1 = 2.4$ (3) $K = \sqrt{2} - \sqrt{1} = -1.4 - 1 = -2.4$ (4) $K = \sqrt{2} - \sqrt{1} = -1.4 - (-1) = -1.4 + 1 = -0.4$

Therefore when N = 2, K can be any one of this four things 2.4, 0.4, –2.4 or –0.4. When N = 1, K can be any one of these two things 1 or –1. What will you compare? When you want to compare two quantities both quantities must be certain. If you are to decide who is taller Jim or Tim, one important thing is to know the heights of the two boys. It must be certain that you are talking about Tim Smith and Jim Lake and not Tim Donnelly and Jim Eastwood. Without this clarity, comparison becomes impossible.

Confusion in the mind of the examiner becomes clearly manifest in posing a question where none of the options are workable in the absence of a clear-cut convention. As far as GRE is concerned the conventions are clear-cut and so is the range of topic that student must know. This is the beauty of the examination.

What separates the GRE from a school –level test is however *breadth of perception.*

We can almost hear some of you asking the meaning of breadth of perception. We shall have to necessarily use illustrations to drive home this point.

Illustration 1

Imagine that you are told that Liquid D is an admixture of Liquids A, B and C in the ratio of 3:4:11 and the ratio of the prices of Liquids A, B and C is 13: 11: 7. You are then asked as to how much would 2 litres of Liquid D cost as a percentage of the price of 5 litres of Liquid D.

Now see what is meant by breadth of perception. The fellow learning mathematics at school will leap and get hold of pen and paper and then add 3, 4 and 11 and arrive at the fact that Liquid A, B and C respectively constitute 1/6th, 2/9th and 11/18th of Liquid D. He then gazes blankly at the figures that he has before him. He does not know how to proceed. The graduate student knows that whatever be the price of a litre of Liquid D, the price of 2 litres of Liquid D will fundamentally be 2/5th of the price of 5 litres of Liquid D and therefore the crux of the question is expressing 2/5th in percentage terms; 2/5th is 40%. The answer to the question is that 2 litres of Liquid D will cost 40% of the price of 5 litres of Liquid D. The ratios of the three liquids have nothing to do whatsoever with this question. Nor have the ratios of the pieces got to do anything with the question **this realisation is what determines breadth of perception.**

Illustration 2

Imagine that you are asked as to what will be the remainder when 8 divides 9^{63}. The person skilled at mathematics may be able to answer this question in a few days time since multiplying 9 with itself 63 times is a Herculean task and then dividing the result with 8 will be another huge task. The person with breadth of perception realises that 9^{63} is essentially $(8 + 1)^{63}$. In the expansion of 9^{63} there will be 8^{63} and 8^{62} and 8^{61} and so on till 8^1 with integral co-efficients (all of which are essentially multiples of 8 and therefore eminently divisible by 8) whereas there will be one and only one term at the end that will have nothing to do with 8. This last term will be 1. Thus when one divides 9^{63} with 8, the remainder is 1. This is what the graduate student who has seen a lot more of the world after finishing school will say in a minute. He has been putting shine on the skills that he has acquired at school. This shine is what is being tested at the GRE.

The Important Aspects of the GRE

The following are the most important aspects of the GRE:

- In the computer-based General Test, the verbal and quantitative sections are adaptive. The Analytical Writing Assessment Section is not computer adaptive.
- At the start of each section, you will be presented with a test question of medium difficulty. What is medium and what is difficult is never defined by the ETS. It is not written alongside the question whether it is of medium difficulty or easy or tough. When the ETS have not defined what they call medium difficulty and what is not, we are not to depend on anyone else's judgement about the level of difficulty of a particular question. Ignore anyone who professes to present to you questions for example with Difficulty Level 1 as the easiest and Difficulty Level 10 as the toughest. These so-called difficulty levels are all homemade. They have no basis. It would be logical to make an assessment whether a question is easy or medium or tough from the actual questions in the Official Source. This is why we have focussed on

questions from the Official Source for developing our concept notes and exercises. The idea is to enable the reader to find himself capable of answering **any** question popped up at him. He would not need to make a so-called *intelligent* or *smart* guess. If he decides to guess (or speculate), it is because he has not assimilated our concept notes.

- The ETS has a marvellous system whereby the student community judges whether a question is easy, or moderately easy or moderately tough or tough. **Even the paper setter at the GRE does not determine whether a question is tough or easy. Students the world over who have written the GRE in the last three years decide which question is easy and which is tough.** If you will see in the official publications of the ETS, they clearly lay down the scoring methodology. The ETS has carried out a survey of what percentage of students was able to answer each particular question in the past three years. The findings of this survey are available for the world to see in their official publications. If the ETS finds that, for example, less than 20 percentage of all the students who wrote the GRE the world over have answered Question A correctly, that question would be classified as tough whereas a question where over 80% of the students have answered it correctly is classified as easy and so on. When this finding is in the official publications of the ETS, relying on any CD other than the POWERPREP CD is fraught with the risk of being led astray. **Who except the ETS can tell you how many percent of the students who wrote the GRE the world over found Question A easy and how many found Question B tough?**
- If you answer the first question correctly in each section, the next question typically will be one of greater difficulty. This is why it is of paramount importance to be solid on concepts.
- If you answer the first question incorrectly, the next question typically will be one of lesser difficulty. This is why if you guess and fall flat, you may find it difficult to register a decent score at the GRE.
- As you answer each question, the computer scores that question and uses that information, as well as your responses to any preceding questions and information about the test design, to determine which question will be presented next.
- The computer does not always select a tougher question when you answer a question correctly or an easier question when you answer incorrectly. This is because the test design includes several factors in addition to the difficulty level of the questions. Therefore to say that the level of difficulty rises with each question correctly answered is not correct. The examination takes an overall picture of the examinee.
- The computer-adaptive GRE General Test is designed such that the questions you see are influenced by three factors: (A) Difficulty level of the questions already answered (correctly and incorrectly) (B) Required variety of question types and (C) Coverage of specific content.
- The next question posed to you will be the one that best reflects both your previous performance and the requirements of the test design. This means that different test takers will be given different questions.
- Because each question that the computer selects for you is determined by your answers to previous questions, you cannot move on to the next question before you answer the question that appears on your screen. This is why one must be solid on concepts.
- Once you answer a question and confirm your response, you cannot return to that question and change your answer. The computer has already scored that answer and used it as a factor in selecting succeeding questions.
- Your score in each section will be based on the number of questions you answer as well as on the difficulty levels of the questions you answer correctly and incorrectly. Typically, a correct answer to a difficult question has a greater positive effect on your score than does a correct answer to a relatively easy question. **It is also possible to earn a very high score even if you answer several questions incorrectly.**

As to questions such as the following, we request you to look up the POWERPREP CD. We see no need for reinventing the wheel.

(I) At what periodicity is the GRE held?

(II) How much time do you have for writing the GRE?

(III) How many questions are generally asked in each of the three sections (Verbal, Quantitative Ability and Analytical Writing Sections)?

We feel that the focus of our effort should be to give a clear picture of the event and what skills are called for and therefore we shall quickly get on with the task. All that we can say that is for the year 2005 (when this goes to press), the GRE has, in all, three sections including (1) the Analytical Writing Section that has writing assignments on two topics one is of 45 minutes' duration and the other is of 30 minutes' duration, (2) the Verbal Section of 30 minutes duration that has 30 questions involving Sentence Completion, Reading Comprehension, Antonyms and Analogies and (3) the Quantitative Section of 45 minutes duration that has in all 28 questions involving Quantitative Comparison and Problem Solving.

An Assessment of the Skill Level associated with the GRE

We shall first see from some questions from the Official Source of the GRE what skills are required in the Verbal Section and then in the Quantitative Ability Section. Nothing can help us understand the system better.

The Skill Level associated with the Verbal Section

The Verbal Section presents questions under these following topics:

- Antonyms
- Analogies
- Sentence Completion
- Reading Comprehension

We shall take an overview of the skills that they want to test at the GRE under each of these sub-topics. We shall base our assessment of the required skills on the questions in the official source.

Antonyms

The questions on Antonyms measure your (A) vocabulary and (b) skills to reason from a given concept to its opposite.

Here is a sample question.

Find the word most nearly opposite in meaning to the word DIFFUSE from out of the following options:

(I) Contend (II) Imply (III) Concentrate (IV) Intend (V) Rebel

The *official solution* (which is what we shall hereafter refer to each of the solutions provided to questions in the official source) goes more or less as follows: To diffuse means to spread out and concentrate is most nearly opposite in meaning to diffuse. Hence Choice (III) is the best choice.

We shall now see what skills would come handy to us for solving this question in particular and based on that assessment what skills shall we need for the GRE as a whole. **See the following solution that we present:**

The word DIFFUSE has the prefix DIF- (that means *away from* or *apart* or *in different directions* or *the reversal or undoing of an action*) and the Latin root FUS- (that means to *melt*; *pour*). DIFFUSE therefore literally means to *pour away from something* and hence to *spread out*, *scatter*. If something diffuses, what is happening is the *reverse of concentration*. We shall therefore infer that **the knowledge of the structure of the English language that comprises of roots, prefixes and suffixes would help us with this question in particular and with other questions of which this is only a sample.**

We shall also use this opportunity to understand what the words *contend*, *imply*, *concentrate*, *intend* and *rebel* mean and, if possible, how these words have found their place at the core of the English language.

The words CONTEND and INTEND are derived from the Latin TENDERE- that means to *stretch* or *strive*. The prefix CON- means *together* (in the context of *content* which means something that a vessel *holds together*) or *thoroughly* (in the context of content which means *thoroughly* pleased or satisfied). If somebody *contends* that Marilyn Monroe was the most beautiful woman on earth, it means that he *thoroughly holds* the opinion that if any woman on this earth is to be judged as the most beautiful, it was Marilyn Monroe.

The prefix IN- means so many things depending upon the context. Something that is **inflexible** is not flexible. Someone who is brilliant or **ingenious** has genius in him.

If someone were to **intend** to help a classmate with studies, what he is **striving for in this objective** is to see that the classmate gets better scores at the end of the term examination.

The word IMPLY consists of the prefix IM- (that means the same thing as IN- in English) and the Latin root PLY- (that means to *fold* or *twist*). **When someone twists the meaning of what he wants to say rather than saying it directly in so many words, he does this to imply a meaning** to what he says. When some student gets a poor score at mathematics and his father tells him that it must have taken great effort to get such a score, what he **implies** is that the score is poor because he has not been putting in efforts.

If being a judge **implies** that one must mix in only the most limited circles, it means that one of the aspects **folded into the position of a judge** is limited socialisation.

The word **concentrate** that comprises of the prefix CON- (that we have seen earlier means together) and the word CENTRE (which we all know means the centre or the focus) literally means *to get together towards the centre* or in other words to *intensify*, *collect at a common centre* and so on. The Latin suffix –ATE in the word concentrate is used to form verbs such as agitate, migrate, rotate and so on.

The word **rebel** consist of the prefix RE- that means a whole lot of things depending upon the context as under:

1. Motion backwards or away, as in the words *recede*, *remove*, *revert*
2. Reversal or withdrawal, as in the words *recant*, *redeem*, *resign*, *revoke*; secrecy, as *revert*
3. Opposition, as in the words *rebel*, *reluctant*, *resist*;
4. Negation, as in the words *reprobate*, *reprove*
5. Frequent or intensive force, as in the words *redouble*, *redound*, *regard*, *research*

In the word *rebel*, the prefix RE- means *again* as in its context 5 above and the Latin word BELLUM means *war*. A rebel literally is someone who declares war again and again or someone who is a **revolutionary** or an **insurgent**. Once one knows that BELLUM is Latin for war, it would be easy to recall the meanings of the words **bellicose** (that means *inclined to fighting*) and **belligerent** (that means *aggressive* or *argumentative* and so on).

We may mention that what you see above is not a sample of the question alone but A REPRESENTATIVE SAMPLE of the solutions that we have provided in this book all along. The one thing that will be very clear is that the solutions that we have provided are not only detailed but far superior to what one sees anywhere (including from the official source).

We may jot down the following lessons from the above sample question and the solution that we have provided:

1. The English language has a deep-seated structure derived primarily from Latin
2. This structure can be learnt with ease if explained in a manner that makes learning a matter of joy
3. There were five options for the word most nearly opposite in meaning to the given word DIFFUSE
4. The given word DIFFUSE and the five options all had a word that lay at the core of the vocabulary in the English language
5. In view of (4) above, the skills tested are those relating to words at the core of the English language
6. We have permanently engraved the meaning of the given word DIFFUSE and its shades from its origin and the meanings of the words in the options also with the methodology of roots, prefixes and suffixes
7. Mugging up the meanings of words will get us nowhere

This is our assessment of the skills required for doing well at the Antonyms Sub-Section in the GRE. We have also arrived at a conclusion regarding the methodology that we shall have to adopt in order to develop/sharpen the skills that are required/we already possess but need to be sharpened. What you shall see in this book is this very methodology of roots, prefixes and suffixes not only in course of explaining the meaning of the given word and the correct choice for the antonym but for all other words in the options. This is done with the intention of increasing the reader's personal lexicon till it has the necessary expanse with which he can meet any competitive examination, no matter how tough, head on.

Analogies

The questions on Analogies measure your ability to recognize (A) relationships among words and the concepts they represent and (B) parallel relationships.

Here is a sample question.

Find the word pair that has the nearest relationship to that in COLOUR: SPECTRUM from out of the following options:

(I) Sound: Waves (II) Cell: Organism (III) Dimension: Space (IV) Tone: Scale (V) Verse: Poem

The *official solution* goes more or less as follows: The relationship between Colour and Spectrum is not only that of part to whole. If this were true, Verse: Poem or Cell: Organism could also be correct. A spectrum consists of progressive series of colours just as a scale consists of a progressive sequence of tones. This is why the correct choice is (IV) Tone: Scale.

Now see why the Official Solution will not be of help and why the solution that we present to you would be extremely helpful to understand what is really being tested.

If you see the Official Solution, they do not tell you why the relationship between Colour and Spectrum is not only that of Part to Whole. The spectrum that you and I know has VIBGYOR with Violet first and Red last. Talking about **progressive sequence**, I know for example that I used to score marks that put me at the bottom of the class while Harvey Almeida always stood first in class because he had the highest marks. The progressive sequence would then begin with me and end with Harvey. How a progressive sequence would have Violet at its least term and Red at its highest term beats me. It is mind-boggling. Does violet weigh less than red? Is Red the tallest of the seven colours? Can Red spit farther than Indigo? The severe limitations of the official explanation need not be even discussed. If you wish to develop the skills that will enable you to do well at the GRE, you will have to lean on preparatory material with the kind of explanations that will make understanding things both easy and enjoyable. This is where this book comes in.

We do not know whether you have noticed this: **all the words** that we see in (A) the given word pair and (B) in the options are words that we have used day in and day out during school and college days.

All of us have seen the spectrum in science class in middle school. When white light diffracts through a prism, it breaks up into its component colours such as Violet, Indigo, Blue, Green, Yellow, Orange, and Red (remember the acronym VIBGYOR?). Thus each of these colours is a part of which the spectrum is the whole. Yet, for a moment let us consider that prima facie the relationship between Colour and Spectrum seems to be that between Part and Whole. However the relationships between Cell and Organism and Verse and Poem are also that of Part and the Whole. A cell is the smallest part of an organism as we have learnt early on in our school days in science class. From even earlier days in school we learnt that a verse is a part of a poem when we recited, for example, the verses of *Mary had a Little Lamb* (when we were tiny tots) and of the poem *Charge of the Light Brigade* (possibly during the eighth or ninth form in school). The first inference is that we have to look for another relationship between Colour and Spectrum. The other inference is that we are not to look at Options (II) and (V) now that we know that both these options present the same relationship of Part: Whole and that our energies are to be focussed on Options (I), (III) and (IV) for deriving the unique relationship between Colour and Spectrum that can be found in only one of the options. This means that we are now to look at the following word pairs only: (I) Sound: Waves (III) Dimension: Space (IV) Tone: Scale.

Sound propagates (or travels from place to place) through waves. We have learnt this in our middle school days. Colour does not propagate through spectrum. As a matter of fact the spectrum **splits** a ray of light into its component colours. This is why Option (I) will not be of help.

As regards Dimension and Space, if your bedroom has a good deal of space, it must be that it has large dimensions as compared to a cramped bedroom of small dimensions. Dimensions determine the quantity of space. For example, the product of (A) the length of the floor, (B) its breadth and (C) its height determines the space in a factory. The colour does not determine the quantity of the spectrum. This is principally because the spectrum does not have quantity at all save for the number of colours at all. This is why Option (III) will not do.

This means that we are to look for a common relationship between Tone and Scale and Colour and Spectrum. Logically, the relationship between Part and Whole can cover two types of relationships:

(1) Where there is no difference between the component part and the whole. For example if two chocolates taken out of a box of chocolates is a part and a box of chocolates is the whole, then the part and the whole are both chocolates and therefore the same thing. In this variant of the relationship Part: Whole there is monotony. A few verses make a poem and a million cells make an organism. There is monotony in the relationship in both cases.

(2) When there is difference between the component part and the resultant whole. For example, in a car there are tyres and tubes and an engine and a chassis and so many parts that make the whole that the automobile is. There is however a variety of components that goes into making the whole.

A spectrum cannot have only Red colour. Then there would be no spectrum at all. All you would have is a ray of red light. Variety is therefore the essential ingredient of a spectrum. As such we know that the only option left is Tone: Scale. The question is: how would this work?

The word **tone** has so many shades of meaning as follows:

- If someone could tell which instrument was being played from its *tone*, he could distinguish the *individual characteristics* of a wide variety of musical instruments.
- If someone asks you to *tone* down the volume of the record player, he is asking you to reduce or *soften* the volume.
- If you can tell from a pencil portrait whether the model sat facing the sun or against it, this is because the artist was able to achieve a light and shade effect by producing *corresponding gradations* or *tones* in the single colour that he used for making the drawing. In effect he has made a *scale* of colours from a single colour by employing different tones of the colour.

The word **scale** has so many shades of meaning that we shall see as follows:

- If the cake that you have bought is on the *scale*, it is put on a *device to weigh things*.
- If you are planning to *scale* the mountain, you want to *climb* the mountain.
- If the masterpiece by the great painter that you saw in the museum has a *scale of shades of red*, it means that it has a *series of tones of red colour* produced by mixing red colour with different proportions of white or black

As we have seen in the above explanation, a scale of colour of shades of red consists of a variety of tones of red colour. Therefore the correct choice is **Option (IV)**.

Please note that the above solution is substantially different from the *official solution* not only in terms of detail but also in terms of depth of analysis. All along in this book you shall see explanations that will enable you to build the skill of reasoning that is most important in order to do very well at the GRE. You might also like to notice that although most of us knew beforehand the meanings of the different words in the given word pair and in the options, the level of reasoning skills that are called for is very high. That is what we have learned while trying to understand the system. This is the skill that is to be developed. This is the skill that this book will help you both develop and sharpen as you go along.

Sentence Completion

Questions on Sentence Completion measure your ability to recognize words or phrases that both logically and stylistically complete the meaning of a sentence.

Here is a sample question.

Complete the following sentence by choosing the words in the blanks from the five choices furnished below the question.

Early ________ of hearing loss is ________ by the fact that the other senses are able to compensate for moderate amount of loss, so that people frequently do not know that their hearing is impaired.

(I) discovery.. indicated (II) development.. prevented (III) detection complicated

(IV) treatment .. facilitated (V) incidence .. corrected

The *official solution* goes more or less as follows: The statement that the other senses compensate for partial loss of hearing indicates that the **hearing loss is not prevented or corrected**; therefore, choices (II) and (V) can be eliminated. Furthermore, the ability to compensate for hearing loss certainly does not facilitate the early treatment (IV) or the early discovery (I) of hearing loss. It is reasonable, however, that early detection of hearing loss is complicated by the ability to compensate for it. The best choice for the correct answer is (III).

The thrust of the argument in the official solution is that since the other senses compensate for partial loss of hearing, hearing loss is not prevented or corrected and that the ability to compensate for hearing loss certainly does not facilitate the early treatment or the early discovery of hearing loss.

Prima facie, the statement that other senses compensate for partial loss of hearing seems bizarre. There are five senses (and five corresponding sense organs in brackets) as follows: sight (eyes), smell (nose), hearing (ears), touch (skin) and taste (tongue). To imagine that for example that the tongue could compensate for moderate hearing loss in any way is quite confusing (leave alone the tongue compensating for moderate hearing loss to an extent that the person does not realise that he has a hearing impairment). It would be real odd if the nose could see someone making faces at you while you are fast asleep. However the idea is to apply **our logic** to the problem on hand without going into the depth of the logic in the official solution.

If you see the wordings in the official solution, it is stated that **loss cannot be prevented if there has been partial loss**. This sounds real odd. **If there is a partial loss, partial loss cannot be prevented**. Yet however it is possible that in spite of partial loss, loss can be both prevented and corrected.

See the following illustration.

Imagine that a maidservant is cleaning up things and accidentally the handle of the broom in her hand bangs against a jar full of honey. The jar develops a crack. A quarter of all the honey that there was in the jar at the outset leaks out. There is partial loss of honey. In order to stop the outflow of honey, the maidservant applies a sealant to the crack. The loss is prevented. The problem is corrected. The maidservant tops up the honey in the jar with honey from another jar in order to obviate the prospects of the lady of the house shouting at her. The partial loss is compensated.

We have seen an instance where there was **partial loss, compensation, prevention of loss and correction** all happening simultaneously. We have seen an instance where the ability to compensate for partial loss has nothing to do whatsoever with either early treatment or early discovery of partial loss.

Now look at it this way. From the sentence, with its blanks and all, it is quite clear that since other senses compensate for moderate hearing loss, people frequently do not know that their hearing is impaired. Even if one cannot understand the logic behind other senses compensating for moderate hearing loss, it is easy to understand the other part of the sentence that people frequently are not aware that they have a problem with their hearing.

Therefore when someone with a hearing impairment is sitting next to you in the train and asks you how many hours to go till (say) Brighton and you say **three** in a soft tone, he does not hear you and asks you to speak a bit louder saying that there is too much noise all around. You speak loud enough for him to hear. He has got the information that he wants. He is still unaware that he has a hearing impairment. When his family have had enough of shouting in his ears all the while, they take him to the doctor.

He has meanwhile bought a small hearing aid concealed behind his earlobe and when the doctor asks him in a loud voice as to how long has this been going on, he tells the doctor to please desist from shouting.

The doctor is taken aback. He looks askance at the family who have briefed him that the fellow is more or less stone deaf. The doctor and the patient converse in such a soft tone that the man's family find it difficult to catch what they are saying to each other. It is their turn to seem hard of hearing. At the end of it all, the doctor tells the man's family that he seems not to have any hearing impairment worth the name. The person's family looks stupid in front of the doctor because the man has carried an invisible device on him that compensates for moderate hearing loss.

Now ask yourself this: what among the five options for the second blank has the compensatory mechanism (the concealed hearing aid) done here?

(I) Has it indicated early discovery of hearing loss?

(II) Has it prevented early development of hearing loss?

(III) Has it complicated the early detection of hearing loss?

(IV) Has it facilitated early treatment of hearing loss?

(V) Has it corrected early incidence of hearing loss?

You will find that the only thing that has happened is that it has complicated the early detection of hearing loss. This is how the problem has to be dealt with. Some of you may say that the solution that we have presented is too detailed. However, the idea in presenting a detailed solution is to help develop the **reasoning** that the official solution cannot be even expected to help develop. Reasoning seems to be the sole skill that the GRE seems to call for whether in relation to the Verbal Section or the Quantitative Section.

Look at the strategies that the Official Source presents as follows (more or less):

(I) You should read the incomplete sentence carefully and look for key words or phrases.

(II) Complete the blank(s) with your own words; see if any options are like yours.

(III) Pay attention to grammatical cues.

(IV) If there are two blanks, make sure that both parts of your answer choice fit logically and stylistically into the sentence.

(V) After selecting an answer, you should read the sentence completely again to see if it makes sense.

You will find that none of the strategies from the Official Source could have worked in their own sample question. One would never have the time for finding one's own words for filling in the blanks. When this goes to press the English language has some 117000 words. Which words should I choose to fit in? What will I do with their options in the meantime? Make a pickle out of them? Use them for my sandwich filling? Where does grammar come in here at all? About two blanks, one cannot hope to fit one word from one choice and another blank with a word from another choice. You have to choose only one option. What use is the strategy in (IV) above?

Please remember that it is not our idea at all to criticise or belittle the official source in any way. The GRE has a transparent process. It has several unique features such as a statement of the purpose of the examination, the broad structure, the conventions, what it wants to test and so on are all in black and white. This is really admirable. This is something that every institution conducting competitive examinations ought to do.

The official source has given more than enough in giving out a sample test. The solutions are a bonanza because you can be sure that they have everything perfectly worked out and there is nothing slipshod about the official source unlike so many competitive examinations where mistakes abound. The idea is to drive home the point that the official source cannot be expected to give you either a clear cut statement that the name of the game is reasoning and logic or what strategies you should adopt for scoring well. They are not there to spoon feed the test taker. They are there to test him and evaluate him. He will have to derive his own lessons about the pattern of the examination and the strategies that he will need in order to shine out. Therefore even expecting inputs such as detailed and lucid solutions to questions in the sample test that the official source supplies and strategies for success is itself grossly unrealistic.

Reading Comprehension

What the Section on Reading comprehension purports to measure is your ability to (A) read with understanding, insight, and discrimination and (B) analyse a written passage from several viewpoints.

Look at the lessons that one should derive from the official statement of purpose for the Reading Comprehension Section:

- When the official source itself says that they want to test whether you can read with discrimination (or in other words, *judgement*), reading everything before deciding what is worth reading is wholly unreasonable.
- When the official source says that they want to test whether you can analyse a passage from several perspectives, one must realise that one's analysis is not going to be in the passage and therefore if one sets off looking for an answer in the passage to questions involving one's analysis, one would be about as reasonable as Don Quixote charging at the windmills.

Passages, as the official version goes, are taken from the humanities, social sciences, and natural sciences. This means that the passages that you would be up against could relate to virtually anything under the sun.

In regard to what one is to do after reading the passage, one is to choose the best answer to each question. One is required to answer all questions following the passage on the basis of what is **stated** or **implied** in the passage.

Here is a sample passage and a sample question.

Every lover of words knows that these little symbolic units of meaning can be as contradictory as sub-atomic particles sometimes are. This may well be nature's quixotic way of laughing at our desperate need to explain everything. It gives us a full stop, but watches helplessly, as we expand it into three dots and continue to search.

Although the measurement of the velocity of sub-atomic particles precludes the measurement of their position and vice versa, it hasn't stopped nuclear physicists from trying to search from attempting to pin down, to explain. And it is important.

In a book on quantum physics called **In Search of Schrodinger's Cat**, *John Gribbin says something very fascinating. If a mythical god with a magical pair of infinitesimally small pliers started the task of removing one atom from a molecule of hydrogen (if I remember correctly) every second from the time of the Big Bang... today, it would take another million years for him or her to complete the task. Phew!*

But it is still important to try. Why? If everything is so small and the now proved quantum world is essentially indefinable, why do we go on trying to define? Because we must. It is as important to be rigorous and empirical as to accept the indefinable. Lest we forget, it is through absorption in the act of definition that we first encountered the indefinable. And it is still found there more easily than anywhere else.

But for the effort to define, how would we find the indefinable? But for the setting of limits, would the notion of the limitless have ever arisen? Didn't William Blake once remind us that we never know what is enough; unless we have known what is more than enough?"

The question along with the choices is as follows:

From the passage it can be inferred that:

(I) To understand a system, we should investigate within its boundaries.

(II) To understand a system, we should investigate beyond its boundaries.

(III) To understand a system, we should be rigorous.

(IV) To understand a system, we should be empirical.

(V) To understand a system, we should investigate both within and beyond its boundaries.

Now see the solution that we present.

Having driven home the point that it would be grossly unreasonable to expect that the official solutions whether they pertain to Sentence Completion or Analogies and so on would be either detailed or lucid (or both), we have decided to skip the part about analysing the official solution insofar as it pertains to Reading Comprehension. We would like you to straightaway look at this solution that we have provided.

See the words of the question. The mandate in the question is **to infer from the passage**. This means that you are not to apply **your** viewpoint or judgement about any issue raised in the passage.

The words to note are at paragraph 4 in the passage. "It is still important to try. Why? If everything is so small and the now proved quantum world is essentially indefinable, why do we go on trying to define? Because we must. It is as important to be rigorous and empirical as to accept the indefinable. Lest we forget, it is through absorption in the act of definition that we first encountered the indefinable. And it is still found there more easily than anywhere else."

At this stage we find it necessary to understand the meanings of a few words that occur in the passage. This is with a view to learning the meanings of words used in situational contexts.

Rigorous can mean *harsh*, *severe*, ***meticulous***, *exacting*, ***uncompromising*** and the word **empirical** means *experimental* (that means *guided by observation and not only by theory*).

Paragraph 4 in the passage says that *it is as important to be rigorous and empirical as to accept the indefinable*. This means that we are to be **both** (A) rigorous and (B) empirical; we cannot be either (A) or (B). This means that Option (III) and (IV) are to be ruled out because these options talk respectively about only (A) and only (B). We must then notice that all the other options talk about a **boundary**.

See the words "*The emphasis is both on defining and to accept the indefinable.*" Something can be defined if it lies within the sphere of human knowledge or understanding. If it lies outside that sphere, it is indefinable. But when can you conclude that something is indefinable? You can arrive at this conclusion only after you have tried to find out whether it is definable or indefinable, meaning whether it is within the sphere of human knowledge or outside that sphere. And, dear reader, this act of trying to find out is what is known as **investigation**.

There are some questions that one ought to ask himself when up against such a passage and the question that has followed.

What is a boundary? What would the boundary wall of your house do? It would define the extent of the land that you own. The boundary walls tells the world that the land that lies outside your boundary walls is not your land.

Now suppose there was a bicycle lying parked outside the boundary wall of your house. It has been lying for a couple of days. There is no claimant. You wish to find out as to who could possibly have left it there. What will you need to do in order to find this out? You will have to investigate. What is the starting point of this investigation? Going outside the boundary wall. You would want to see whether it is a child's bicycle or an adult's? Whether it is new or looks used? Whether you have seen such a bicycle before? Whether any of your friends have been riding such a bicycle? Whether there is some stolen stuff under the seat?

Can you possibly investigate meaningfully by remaining within the boundary wall? Whom will you ask, pray? Your mother? Your pet?

What is true of the investigation about the bicycle is also true of a system. If one wants to understand a system, then: (A) One must know what it already has and then (B) what it will need. For doing (A) one has to find out from within and for doing (B) One has to find out from outside the system.

So, a **boundary** is that which **defines** the limits. The emphasis is therefore on **remaining within** (as seen from the meaning of the word rigorous (*uncompromising*) and **investigating** (meaning *trying to find out by experiment*) **beyond the boundaries of a system**. Hence **Option (V)**.

With this we come to the end of our solution to the question. We shall now see the official version of the strategies that are suggested in regard to Reading Comprehension in general. The official version goes more or less as follows:

(I) Read the passage closely and proceed to the questions thereafter or skim the passage, then reread the passage closely as you answer the questions.

(II) You may like to try it both ways with sample questions to see what works best for you.

(III) Answer the questions on the basis of the contents of the passage.

(IV) Separate main ideas from supporting ideas.

(V) Separate the author's own ideas from information being presented.

(VI) Ask yourself as follows: What is this about? What are the key points? How does the main idea relate to other ideas in the passage? What words define relationships among ideas?

As regards strategy (I), the word or is out of place in a strategy. A strategy is essentially a game plan for success. If I am a hockey coach for a team I have to tell the team to either (A) attack from the word go or (B) be on the defensive from the word go. I cannot tell them to either attack or defend. The team will be thoroughly confused about what to do. They may end up losing.

As regards strategies to separate main ideas from supporting ideas and to separate the author's own ideas from information being presented, while they could be workable if you had a few hours for each passage, these strategies cannot work within time limits. You have a minute for each question. As regards asking yourself what is this about, if you were to see the sample passage, it might initially seem like something about words, thereafter about velocity of particles, then about quantum physics and then about mythology and so on. A strategy as proposed in (V) above will lead to utter confusion and a whopping headache as a result of the chaos. It would be infinitely safer to rely on the methodologies that we have presented in this book.

The Quantitative Ability Section

The reader will recall having read in the inaugural chapter in this book where we have set out how Quantitative Ability differs from Mathematics. The Quantitative Ability Section at the GRE has the following broad components:

The quantitative section of the GRE General Test measures the following:

(A) Basic mathematical skills

(B) Understanding of elementary concepts relating to mathematics

(C) Ability to reason quantitatively and solve problems in a quantitative setting

The reader will please note that the **ability to reason gets tested all along whether questions pertain to the Verbal Section or to the Quantitative Ability Section.** The focus on developing reasoning or logic skills should therefore become sharper and sharper if one is to excel at the GRE. This assessment is not a matter of inference. We can read the emphasis on logic skills from the literature that the official source provides for enabling preparation for the GRE.

The Quantitative Ability Section has broad content areas as follows:

(A) Quantitative Comparison

(B) Problem Solving — Discrete Quantitative

(C) Problem Solving — Data Interpretation

Let us see what skills are required in respect of each of these broad areas under the Quantitative Ability Section. We shall go from area to area, starting with Quantitative Comparison.

Quantitative Comparison

Quantitative comparison questions are designed with the objective of measuring the ability to (A) reason quickly and accurately about the relative sizes of two quantities and (B) perceive that not enough information is provided to make such a decision

Here are two sample questions and the directions in regard to the sample questions:

Mark 1 if the quantity in Column A is greater

Mark 2 if the quantity in Column B is greater

Mark 3 if the two quantities are equal

Mark 4 if the relation cannot be determined from the information given

Sample Question Number	Column A	Column B
1	9.8	$\sqrt{100}$
2	$(-6)^4$	$(-6)^5$

The solutions that the official source has provided go more or less like this:

Solution to Sample Question 1

$\sqrt{100}$ denotes 10, the positive square root of 100. (The GRE follows convention used in most standard text books; For any positive number x, $\sqrt{x}$ denotes the non-negative number whose square is x.) Since 10 is greater than 9.8, the best answer is (2). It is important not to confuse this question with a comparison of 9.8 and x where $x^2 = 100$. The latter comparison would yield (4) as the correct answer because $x^2 = 100$ implies that either $x = 10$ or $x = -10$, and there would be no way to determine which value x would actually have.

Solution to Sample Question 2

Since $(-6)^4$ is the product of four negative factors, and the product of an even numbers of negative number is positive, $(-6)^4$ is positive. Since the product of an odd number of negative numbers is negative, $(-6)^5$ is negative. Therefore, $(-6)^4$ is greater than $(-6)^5$ since any positive number is greater than any negative number. The best answer is (1). It is not necessary to calculate that $(-6)^4 = 1296$ and that $(-6)^5 = -7,776$ in order to make the comparison.

Now see the solutions we shall present to you.

If you will see the Solution to Sample Question 1, while the question itself is so simple that there is virtually no need to provide anything other than the mere reiteration of the convention at the GRE that you are to consider only the positive square roots of given numbers. The word *non-negative* is out of place. The word *positive* would be certainly more apt. The reason is: a number can be either negative, zero or positive. If you are to consider only non-negative square roots, you are to consider only positive square roots. The square root of only zero can be zero. As we know zero is neither positive nor negative. **Thus it would be far simpler to say that the positive square roots need only be considered.**

Secondly when the question clearly involves comparison between (A) 9.8 and (B) $\sqrt{100}$ (which is 10 as per the convention at the GRE), where does any confusion with x come in? What is x? In algebra one uses alphabets such as x and y to denote unknown or uncertain quantities. Since both 9.8 and 10 are known quantities, x has no role to play here. If you wish to steer clear of confusion, you will do well to refer to the concept notes and practice material in this book alone.

If you will see the Official Solution to Sample Question 2, it would be apt to conclude saying that the quantity (A) will invariably be a positive number since any number whether positive or negative when raised to the power of an even number will yield a positive number and the quantity (B) will invariably be a negative number since it involves raising a negative number to the power of an odd number and since fundamentally since a positive number is invariably greater than a negative number, the quantity in Column A is always greater than the quantity in Column B. The hint about not calculating the actual values of $(-6)^4$ (which they have worked out to 1296) and that $(-6)^5$(which they have worked out to -7776) in order to make the comparison is unnecessary. The actual calculations are at all feasible since you are dealing with small powers of (–6). What if the question were to require you to compare between $(-6)^{64}$ and $(-6)^{65}$? Should anyone even dream of working out the actual values of $(-6)^{64}$ and $(-6)^{65}$?

We may also like to mention that most questions that you will see in the official source are not lollipops that you see in the Sample Questions that the official source has provided. This is why one should broad base one's assessment regarding the skills required at the GRE and see the hundreds of questions and their breathtakingly simple and logical solutions in this book. Only this can build and sharpen conceptual clarity.

As regards the strategies emanating from the official source, these are more or less as follows:

(I) Avoid lengthy calculations if possible.

(II) Try to arrive at a quick estimate of the correct answer.

(III) Do consider all kinds of numbers before finalising your decision.

(IV) Geometric figures may or may not be drawn to scale. Comparison should be based on the information that is given coupled with your knowledge of mathematics rather than on mere appearances.

You will see that at least the two Sample Questions that you saw above there was no need to calculate anything at all, leave alone lengthy calculations. Regarding estimating the answer, we have designed the presentation in this book with a view to providing the reader with such a vast array of concept notes and practice material that we would be disappointed if the reader even **dreams** of estimating anything. We would like the reader to be so solid about concepts. When you are specifically asked to compare between **two given numbers**, it would be imprudent to consider any other kinds of numbers before finalising your decision. If however the quantitative comparison should involve unknown quantities, then only will the question assuming values: positive, negative, zero, fractions and so on will arise.

The moral of the story is that a strategy has to be specific to a situation. When one is up against a jackal in a forest one may decide to use the strategy of hitting the animal with a stone. When a more ferocious animal is even suspected to be in the vicinity, it would be prudent to put as much distance between him and you as possible. This is what we mean by specificity in regard to strategy formulation. You will find that specificity in this book in abundant measure. You will be ready for all sorts of situations.

While the two Sample Questions that we have seen above involve nothing other than mere reasoning, it must be made clear to the reader that one need not assume that these two questions represent the level of difficulty (or should we say *ease*?) that you are likely to encounter at the GRE. Like we have said before, the basic presumption is that the first question is of medium difficulty. There cannot be any presumptions about any questions thereafter. This is not a conjecture. This is what the official source says. The official source has not laid down any parameters that would help you or for that matter anyone determine whether a question is easy or medium or tough. The official source has laid down parameters regarding only one aspect: Analytical Writing Assessment. They have clearly laid down what are the ingredients for an essay to get a score of 6, what would earn a score of 5 and so on. The ETS is so specific about this single aspect. Therefore if you see any preparatory literature for the GRE that gives you a series of questions that is Level 1 and another that is Level 10, you are looking at so-called levels of difficulty that is a matter of perception of the compilers of that material. It has no official seal. It is all home made.

All that you must realise is that from the first question at your GRE test, one must be ready for **anything**. Read on and you will be.

Problem Solving - Discrete Quantitative

Discrete quantitative questions are designed with the objective of measuring (A) basic mathematical knowledge and (B) the ability to read, understand, and solve a problem that involves either an actual or an abstract situation.

The reader would do well to mark the words *basic mathematical knowledge*. This is only to be expected when the GRE is meant for students from myriad disciplines. The qualified engineer may be sitting next to someone from pharmacy when writing the GRE. Both draw from the same pool of questions.

Each question in this section has all the information needed to answer it, except for basic mathematical knowledge, which is assumed to be common to the backgrounds of all those appearing at the GRE. This too is quite simple to understand. No question will tell you how to formulate an equation or whether what you need to do is addition or subtraction.

Here is a sample question.

Sample Question

When working, a certain person takes 16 complete steps in 10 seconds. At this rate, how many complete steps does the person take in 72 seconds?

(1) 45 (2) 78 (3) 86 (4) 90 (5) 115

Solution to Sample Question

The official version of the solution to the sample question runs something like this: 72 seconds would mean 7 ten-second intervals plus 2/10th of such interval. The person who takes 16 steps in 10 seconds will take (7.2)(16) steps in 72 seconds.

(7.2) (16) = (7) (16) + (0.2) (16) = 112 + 3.2 = 115.2

Since the question asks for the number of complete steps, the best answer choice is (E).

That brings us to the end of the official solution. If you have noticed, there is detailed calculation and then a precise answer is reached. The answer is one that cannot be altered by Isaac Newton himself or for that matter any other great mathematician.

Thereafter saying that (E) is the **best choice** seems bizarre because one would then be inclined to believe that other choices could have worked and what one is doing in the process of marking (E) as the best choice is what is known as *intelligent guessing* or, what the official source says with fair frequency, *estimation*. To this we have only question that we are certain will meet with the silence characteristic of only graveyards: what is the next best choice?

Look at how we present the solution to this sample question.

The fact that there are sixty seconds in a minute is not a closely guarded atomic secret. If a person takes 16 steps in 10 seconds, he would take 6 times 16 steps in a minute. That makes 96 steps in 60 seconds. We all know that 72 seconds is more than 60 seconds. We can therefore see why the person will certainly take more than 96 steps in 72 seconds. There are five options. Only one has more than 96 steps. This is Option (E) and for this reason Option (E) is to be marked as correct. We are not multiplying 96 with 72 and dividing the result with 60 for the sole reason that we are not schoolboys. We are not sitting in class waiting eagerly for the teacher's beaming smile when he finds that we have answered his question correctly. We do not want to hear him saying *Here Timothy, you are right, by Jove. Take this toffee.* We would have taken the trouble to put pencil to paper and would have done any calculations at all if there was another option that had a number greater than 96.

Let us yell this message sky high: *We are not fond of toiling. We are reasonable people. If you wish to test our reasoning, so be it. We shall use only reasoning.*

As regards the suggested strategies in the Official Source, the official version of the strategies recommended goes something like this:

(I) Determine what is given and what is being asked.

(II) Scan all answer choices before answering a question.

(III) Scan answer choices to decide the level of approximation required.

(IV) Avoid long computations.

(V) Use reasoning instead, when possible.

Since the official solution indicates that not a single strategy out of the recommended strategies has been followed either in letter or in spirit, we are not going to offer any comments as regards strategies from the official version. You be the judge.

Problem Solving — Data interpretation

The underlying objective behind Data interpretation questions is to measure your ability to

(A) Synthesize information and select suitable data for answering questions and

(B) Determine whether the information provided to you is sufficient for answering a question

Question regarding Data interpretation usually appear in sets of more than one question and are based on data presented in charts, tables or graphs.

Here is a sample question.

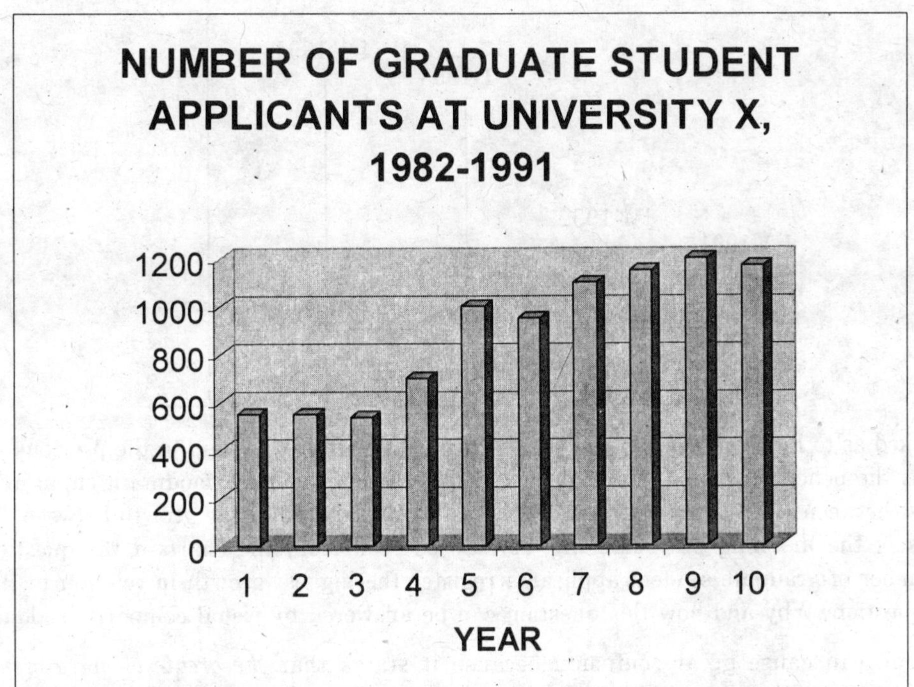

NOTE: In the chart above year 1 corresponds to 1982, year 2 corresponds to 1983 and so on till year 10 corresponds to 1991.

Question: In which of the following years did the number of graduate student applicants register the highest growth in relation to the previous year?

(A) 1985 (B) 1986 (C) 1988 (D) 1990 (E) 1991

The Official Solution goes very nearly like this: You can answer this question directly by visually comparing the heights of the bars in the graph. The greatest increase in height between two adjacent bars occurs for the years 1985 and 1986. The best choice for the answer is (B).

The Strategies as suggested in the Official Source are as follows:

(I) Scan the data to see what it is about.

(II) Try to make visual comparisons and estimate products and quotients rather than perform computations.

(III) Answer questions only on the basis of data given.

As regards the Official Solution, there is a hint about visually comparing the bars. There is a solution all right. But it is of not much use to someone who has not spent his best days on this earth in pouring over graphs and charts. The hint is useless for someone like you and I who do not eat, sleep and think Statistics. We are novices to charts and graphs. There is no mention of **what** should you see in particular. As such the entire bar chart is visible. The question is: what should you focus on? The solution that we shall provide will be such that you will understand exactly:

(I) Why and how this question can be answered by visual comparison alone?

(II) When would visual comparison not be sufficient?

(III) What would you have to do when visual comparison is not sufficient?

Now see our solution. The question is about in which year there was the highest growth in relation to the previous year. Imagine that a father has marked his son's height with a pencil on a wall on the 1st January every year as follows:

If you were then asked as to in which year do you see the highest growth in relation to the previous year, all that one has to imagine that the pencil marks of the height are coffee parlours along a mountain climb and see where the climb is the steepest between each coffee parlour. This is visible in the case of the growth between 1st Jan 1992 and 1st Jan 1993. **This is the meaning of visualising**. It may be seen from the chart in the question that in 1986 we see that the number of graduate student applicants register the highest growth in relation to the previous year. This answers the question: Why and how this question can be answered by visual comparison alone?

The Official Solution can cause great confusion because it states that *the greatest increase in height between two adjacent bars occurs for the years 1985 and 1986* whereas it should be **between** the years 1985 and 1986 (and not **for**).

Now as regards the second question: When would visual comparison not be sufficient? Imagine that the markings that the father has made of his younger son's height on the wall are as follows:

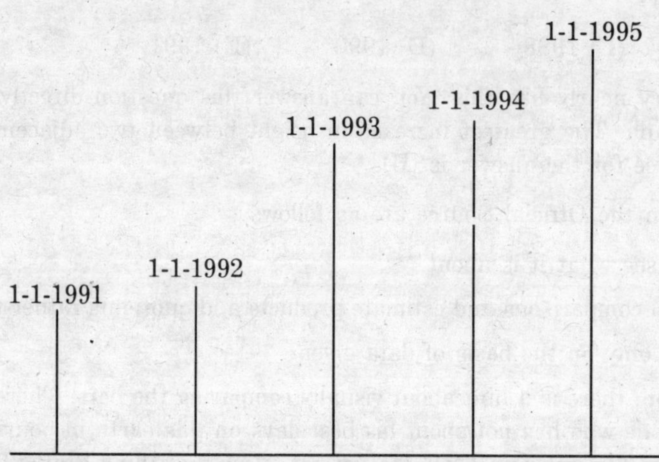

If we were to see the markings of height each year of the younger lad, our visual finding is that the toddler seems to growing virtually by the same rate each year. We would then be in a dilemma.

To find out in which year was the growth highest in relation to the previous year, put a pencil with its lower edge resting on the tops of 1-1-1991 and 1-1-1995. Imagine that the dotted line in the diagram below is the lower edge of the pencil and you will see that the top of 1992 is below the edge of the pencil. This will be possible to see in computer adaptive tests as well. The inference to be drawn is that while there has been virtually steady growth throughout, the top of 1-1-1992 is below the edge of the pencil and hence from 1-1-1992 to 1-1-1993 there is a slightly steeper climb than for the rest of the years.

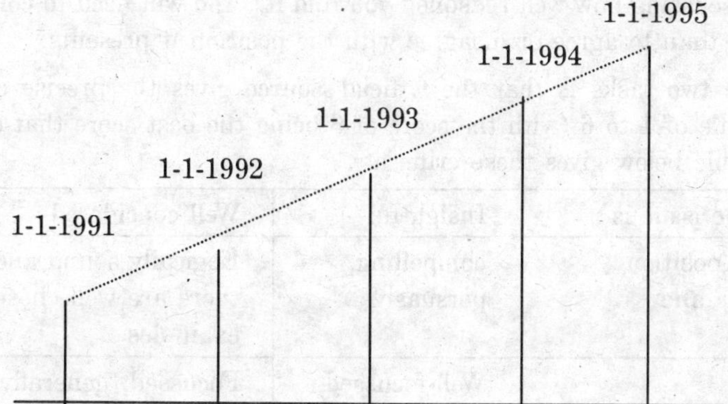

If there are two or more instances where the top lies below the edge of the pencil, then it would become necessary to actually divide the height in the year given in the option by the height in the previous year one by one and see in which option do you get the largest fraction. Mind you we are not asking you to divide the increase in height by the height in the previous year. We are asking you to divide the actual height in any year by the height in the previous year. The reason for this is simple:

For purposes of understanding the underlying rationale behind dividing the actual height in any year by the height in the previous year (and not the increases in height over the previous year height) let us restrict ourselves to the two heights as on 1-1-1992 and 1-1-1993 to see which height shows the greatest growth rate in relation to previous year. If you see the heights on (A) 1-1-1992 and (B) 1-1-1993, they are essentially (A) (Height on 1-1-1991 + increase in height between 1-1-1991 and 1-1-1992) and (B) (Height on 1-1-1992 + increase in height between 1-1-1992 and 1-1-1993). Therefore when we compare the actual heights (A) and (B) in relation to the previous year what we are doing is effectively comparing as follows:

To the Right Side we have (Height on 1-1-1991 + increase in height between 1-1-1991 and 1-1-1992)/ (Height on 1-1-1991). To the Left Side we have (Height on 1-1-1992 + increase in height between 1-1-1992 and 1-1-1993)/ (Height on 1-1-1992). This means that:

To the Right Side we have 1 + [(increase in height between 1-1-1991 and 1-1-1992) / (Height on 1-1-1991)]. To the Left Side we have 1 + [(increase in height between 1-1-1992 and 1-1-1993)/ (Height on 1-1-1992)].

In this comparison we can safely cut the 1 on both sides because they add the same value and **hence in directly comparing the actual height in any year by the height in the previous year** (instead of the increases in height over the previous year height) **what you are effectively doing is comparing** (A) Increase in height between 1-1-1991 and 1-1-1992)/ Height on 1-1-1991 with (B) (Increase in height between 1-1-1992 and 1-1-1993)/ (Height on 1-1-1992). This is what you are asked to do in any case. You are bypassing a whole lot of calculations in the bargain. This answers the third question: What would you have to do when visual comparison is not sufficient?

This brings us to the last section that we are going to deal with (although you might find this section at the beginning of the GRE Test): the section on Analytical Writing Assessment.

The Analytical Writing Assessment Section

The Analytical Writing Assessment Section is the first section in the GRE Test. This section has two components as under:

1. A 45-minute session in which you are required to present your perspective on an issue. You will have a choice between two issue topics. Each topic will state an opinion on an issue of broad interest. You will be asked to discuss the issue from perspective(s) of your choice. It is expected that you provide relevant reasons and examples to explain and support your views

2. A 30-minute session in which you are required to analyse an argument. The computer will present to you an argument to analyse. Unlike in the case of the task involving perspectives on an issue where you will have two choices of issues, you will not have choice of arguments that you will be required to analyse. This task would present a different challenge from that of the Issue task. You will be required to make a critical assessment of

a given argument by discussing how well **reasoned** you find it. You will need to consider the **logical soundness** of the argument rather than to agree or disagree with the position it presents.

The first landmark of these two tasks is that the Official Source gives the precise criteria for determining the scores of these tasks on a scale of 1 to 6 (with the score of 6 being the best score that one can get). Nothing could be more transparent. The table below gives these criteria.

If your presentation on the issue is	Insightful	Well considered	Clear
If you have developed the position that you take with reasons and examples that are	compelling, persuasive	Logically sound and/or there are well chosen examples	Relevant and/or there are examples
If your analysis is	Well-focussed, well-organized and connects ideas logically	Focussed, generally well organized, and connects ideas appropriately	Adequately focussed and organized
If (A) the quality of your expression and (B) your vocabulary is	(A) Fluent, precise (B) Effective	(A) Clear, good (B) Appropriate	Reasonably clear
If your presentation shows the following position in regard in your degree of ease with the conventions (i.e. grammar, usage and mechanics) of standard written English although	Comfortable Minor errors	Comfortable Minor errors	In Control Some errors
You get a score of	6	5	4

The second landmark of this task, while it is apparent from highlighting of the words **reasons and logical soundness** and so on in the above paragraphs, is the fact that like the other sections of the GRE, this section too is designed to test reasoning and logical skills more than anything else.

The third landmark of this task is that **what you write has got to be entirely original**. You are asked to present your perspective and therefore this insistence on originality is very easily understandable. The emphasis on originality is seen in the relative guidelines set out hereunder in regard to **Essay Similarity** that you may also see in the POWERPREP CD:

Your essay responses on the analytical writing section will be reviewed by ETS essay-similarity-detection software and by experienced essay readers during the scoring process. Based on widely accepted criteria of plagiarism within United States graduate schools and universities, ETS may cancel test scores of any test taker when there is substantial evidence that an essay response includes, but is not limited to, any of the following:

- *Text that is substantially similar to that found in one or more GRE essay responses;*
- *Quoting or paraphrasing, without attribution, language or ideas that appear in published or unpublished sources;*
- *Unacknowledged use of work that has been produced through collaboration with others without citation of the contribution of others;*
- *Essays submitted as work of the examinee when the ideas or words have, in fact, been borrowed from elsewhere or prepared by another person.*

When one or more of the above circumstances occurs, your essay text, in ETS's professional judgment, does not reflect the independent, analytical writing skills that this test seeks to measure. Therefore, ETS must cancel the essay score as invalid and cannot report the GRE General Test scores of which the essay score is an indispensable part.

Our objective in designing the contents of this book is to prepare the reader for the best scores. We shall not prepare him on how to win by slender margins. We shall not prepare him to give the opponent a black eye before sinking on the canvas and allowing the referee to count till ten. We are not going to train our reader for avoiding a straight-sets loss at tennis. Our objective is to train him to win and only win. The strategies that we shall present are designed with that clear objective in view all the while.

This is why we shall give sample perspectives and analysis of arguments designed with the objective of enabling the reader to earn the tallest score that is possible. This is the reason why we have desisted from giving the criteria that would fetch scores below 4 in the table above. The idea in giving criterion for scores from 4 to 6 is only to drive home the point that the process at the GRE for evaluation is rather transparent. We would like our readers to target at and then prepare for nothing less than the best scores.

This chapter is an introductory to the event at the GRE, the system at the GRE and its transparency. This chapter is designed to also drive home the following principal aspects:

- Why the assessment of the event at the GRE should be made on basis of only the material and test papers from the Official Source and nothing else
- Why the assessment of the event at the GRE will help reach a decision regarding what should be the range of skills in one's armoury
- Why the Official Source cannot even be expected to give anything other than very sketchy solutions to the practice tests and no solutions at all to the questions in the Test Papers that they provide
- Why the Official Source cannot even be expected to give strategies for the GRE and therefore what strategies we shall have to evolve as we go along

To our mind, the above purposes have been served. This is why we bring the curtain down on this chapter. Before we take leave, we shall request you to please see the relative chapter in this book where we have provided some sample questions regarding presentation of one's perspectives on an issue and analysing an argument. In that chapter you shall also see the relative model answers designed with the objective of getting only the best possible score and see what aspects of the answers conform to the criteria for getting the best scores.

Chapter 4

Analytical Writing Assessment— Presenting your perspective on an issue

We take it that you have seen the detailed guidelines in regard to the Analytical Writing Assessment Section in the chapter titled Understanding the System. The presentation regarding Perspectives on the Issue has necessarily got to be original. We however give hereunder some Model Issues, Model Presentations and Comments on the Model Presentation. We trust these would enable you to formulate your strategies for this section.

Present your perspective on the issue below, using relevant reasons and/or examples to support your views.

ISSUE NO.1

"In our time, specialists of all kinds are highly overrated. We need more generalists — people who can provide broad perspectives."

MODEL PRESENTATION

The rapid social and technological change that we see today have led to increasing life complexity and psychological displacement, both positive and negative effects among persons in Western society call for a balance in which there are both specialists and generalists.

We need specialists to allow society as a whole to meaningfully assimilate the masses of new information and knowledge that have come out of research and have been widely disseminated through mass global media. As the head of Pharmacology at my university once said (and I paraphrase):"I can only research what I do because there are so many who have come before me to whom I can turn for basic knowledge. It is only because of each of the narrowly focussed individuals at each step that a full and true understanding of the complexities of life can be had. Each person can only hold enough knowledge to add one small rung to the ladder, but together we can climb to the moon." This illustrates the point that our society's level of knowledge and technology is at a stage in which there simply must be specialists in order for our society to take advantage of the information available to us.

Simply put, without specialists, our society would find itself bogged down in the quagmire of information overload. While it was fine for early physicists to learn and understand the few laws and ideas that existed during their times, now, no one individual can possibly digest and assimilate all of the knowledge in any given area.

On the other hand, over specialization means narrow focii in which people can lose the larger picture. No one can hope to understand the human body by only inspecting one's own toe-nails. What we learn from a narrow focus may be internally logically coherent but may be irrelevant or fallacious within the framework of a broader perspective. Further, if we inspect only our toe-nails, we may conclude that the whole body is hard and white. Useful conclusions and thus perhaps useful inventions must come by sharing among specialists. Simply throwing out various discoveries means we have a pile of useless discoveries, it is only when one can make with them a mosaic that we can see that they may form a picture.

Not only may over-specialization be dangerous in terms of the truth, purity and cohesion of knowledge, but it can also serve to drown moral or universal issues. Generalists and only generalists can see a broad enough picture to realize and introduce to the world the problems of the environment. With specialization, each person focuses on their research and their goals. Thus, industrialization, expansion, and new technologies are driven ahead. Meanwhile no individual can see the holistic view of our global existence in which true advancement may mean stifling individual specialists for the greater good of all.

Finally, over-specialization in people's daily lives and jobs has meant personal and psychological compartmentalization. People are forced into pigeon holes early in life (at least by university) and must consciously attempt to consume external forms of stimuli and information in order not to be lost in their small and isolated universe. Not only does this make for narrowly focussed and generally poorly-educated individuals, but it guarantees a sense of loss of community, often followed by a feeling of psychological displacement and personal dissatisfaction.

Without generalists, society becomes inward-looking and eventually inefficient. Without a society that recognizes the importance of broad-mindedness and for sharing generalities, individuals become isolated. Thus, while our form of society necessitates specialists, generalists are equally important. Specialists drive us forward in a series of thrusts while generalists make sure we are still on the jousting field and know what the stakes are.

COMMENTS ON THE MODEL PRESENTATION

This is an outstanding analysis of the issue — insightful, well reasoned, and highly effective in its use of language. The introductory paragraph announces the writer's position on the issue and provides the context within which the writer will develop that position: "In this era of rapid social and technological change leading to increasing life complexity and psychological displacement . . . ."

The argument can be divided into two parts. The first part presents a strong case for specialization, mainly in the field of medicine. The second part presents an equally strong, well-organized case against overspecialisation based on the following three main reasons:

(1) Logical (where it is argued that narrowly trained specialists often fail to understand the whole)
(2) Moral (where the argument is that generalists usually understand what is needed for "the greater good")
(3) Personal (where the thrust of the argument is that specializing/pigeonholing too early can be psychologically damaging)

The careful line of reasoning in the argument is further strengthened by the skilful use of testimony from an expert (quotation from a prominent medical researcher) and vivid metaphor (such as *to inspect only one's toenails is to ignore the whole body*).

It is not the reasoning alone that distinguishes this response. The language is precise and often figurative (*"bogged down in a quagmire of information overload," "a pile of useless discoveries,"* and *"specialists drive us forward in a series of thrusts, while generalists make sure we are still on the jousting field"*). The reader is constantly guided through the argument by transitional phrases and ideas that help organize the ideas and move the argument forward. This is an exceptionally fine response to the topic.

ISSUE NO.2

"It is unfortunate that today's educators place so much emphasis on finding out what students want to include in the curriculum and then giving it to them. It is the educators' duty to determine the curriculum and the students' duty to study what is presented to them."

MODEL PRESENTATION

The statement above conceals interesting connotations far above curriculum development. Issues of classroom control and development of scholarly talents are at stake, not simply a debate over which books are acceptable or over revisionist histories.

The statement itself is a bit misleading in that in my experience, student control over curriculum hardly existed. Each year, there were certain course offerings made available, and students were to choose from those offerings, of course bearing in mind requirements for graduation set forth by the administration. On a classroom level, the immediate, initial material may have been somewhat directed by the students, but this was a part of the process allowed by the teacher/professor in order to gain the interest and attention of the students. However, too much of any one thing becomes problematic; letting students set the curriculum, as with letting students choose and design their own major in college, serves ultimately to dilute the quality of the educational experience unless a single advisor can devote significant amounts of time to the individual student. This amount of time, or even the expense to the student of this individual attention, seem to indicate that resources would be better allocated elsewhere.

Of course, any school in which the students decide "what goes" is bound to have problems controlling students. Once the educators, be they administrators or teachers, are under the control of students, even a democratic situation would be like holding royalty accountable to the mob. Presently, students hear for hours that they should not forget to use a condom in the heat of the moment, and educators think the message gets through, while half the kids can't even remember to bring a pencil to class. Students go to school not to simply learn the Pythagorean theorem, but to learn direction and receive guidance. This cannot occur when students are in charge, and standards, already hard to find in America's contemporary public schools, will become unenforceable. If students dictate and administrators do, students will never learn academic responsibility, and if they can't be held accountable for homework, what other responsibilities will they avoid when they get older?

But in another sense, teachers and students do exist in a partnership of sorts. Teachers are there to satisfy the needs of the student, and the student, while perhaps not being the most experienced/ knowledgeable person on what his/her needs actually are (versus wants), at least should be afforded some say. In addition, we must remember what the purpose of education is, and that there are different levels of education.

In high school, the focus is not so much on learning actual material. The focus is on developing study habits, and on social interaction. The best secondary schools promote an environment in which individual creativity and pacing can be developed, where students are taught to think on their own, and learn to debate and argue in a scholarly way, through writing and other formal methods of discourse. Group collaboration and interpersonal skills are developed and honed. The actual details of what is studied and tested is of less importance. Whether a student reads Maya Angelou, or Yeats, or Euripides essentially is beside the point as long as a student's mind is cultivated, not just their ability to record and recite. What is important is that secondary students develop and grow in the hands of the professionals.

The secondary educational experience is designed to prepare a student for college. It is in college where the individual learns to examine the world and how it works, and the individual's place in it.

As for duty, it is the educators' duty not simply to determine the curriculum, but to present it effectively. They cannot half-heartedly paint it on the blackboard, they must enliven it and actually teach. Hard work must be lauded, while freeloaders are punished. These are the duties of teachers, and the duty of the students is not just to learn or study, but to grow. An independent mind is what students need, and that mind has to be in a position to want and be able to question beyond the material presented, not simply to question its legitimacy. That distinction, though subtle, is the difference between letting the students follow a self-destructive course of premature self-determination on the one hand, and permitting on the other hand the fostering of great talents through a cooperative, mentoring relationship.

COMMENTS ON THE MODEL PRESENTATION

This is an insightful, well-articulated discussion of curricular responsibility and the larger issue of academic responsibility. After a brief introduction examining assumptions implied by the topic, the writer skilfully develops the position that letting students dictate the curriculum could dilute the educational experience. Allowing students to determine the curriculum, the writer claims, will deny them the guidance and direction they need to learn academic responsibility.

The argument is strengthened by the discussion of how teachers and students can work in partnership to satisfy the needs of students. The argument is further advanced with concrete examples from high school courses showing how teachers provide guidance for students through group collaboration, development of interpersonal skills, and preparation for college. The examples are varied (from condom use to reading Angelou, Yeats, or Euripedes) and used effectively to further support the writer's position.

In the conclusion, the writer thoughtfully discusses how educators should not only determine the curriculum but also present it in an enlivened and appropriate manner. The final sentence, contrasting a "self-destructive course of premature self-determination" and "a cooperative, mentoring relationship," ties the ideas together.

The response is clearly organized, although the writer does not rely on conventional phrases (such as "first," "second," etc.) to signal the organizational structure. Instead, the organization and focus progress through the line of reasoning that moves fluently and coherently from one paragraph to the next.

Language use is generally precise and effective (e.g., "holding royalty accountable to the mob"), and sentence structure is well controlled (e.g., "hard work must be lauded, while freeloaders are punished"). The few errors are minor, the kind that can easily be made — and forgiven — under testing conditions.

This outstanding response received a score of 6.

ISSUE NO.3

"The best ideas arise from a passionate interest in commonplace things."

MODEL PRESENTATION

Even the most brilliant thinkers, from Socrates to Satre, live lives in time. A childhood, an adolescence, an adulthood; these are common to me and you as well as the greatest writers. Furthermore, many of the great thinkers we esteem in our Western culture lived somewhat uneventful lives. What distinguished their life from say a common labourer was their work. Therefore, what provided the grist for their work? One might say that they were brilliant and this alone was sufficient to distinguish their lives from the masses. Intellect alone cannot devise situations or thoughts from nowhere; there must be a basis and that basis is most common, if not always, observation of the common, of the quotidian. Critics of this idea may argue that these thinkers were products of fine education and were well schooled in the classics. This, they may point to, is the real basis for their knowledge. I would argue that although it may be a benefit to study classics and be well schooled in diverse disciplines, these pursuits merely refine and hone an ability each and every person has, the ability to study human nature. Where best to study human nature than in the day-to-day routine each one of us can witness in him or herself or those around us.

I propose that the two best disciplines to understand this power of the commonplace and its ability to cause a groundswell of thought are philosophy and literature. Every school of philosophy, from the Greeks to our day, share a common mission or intent and that is to understand and explain human existence, with all of its concomitant features. Generally speaking, the Greek philosophers, epitomized in Aristotle, attempted to set down rules for human behaviour founded on logic. These rules applied not only to the rare forms of human behaviour but largely focused on the more mundane motions of daily life. Many of Aristotle's rules were based on his observations of others as well as himself. Contrast this venture with the existentialists of our century who attempted to look behind the real motivations of human behaviour as well understand man's relation to the Universe. To do this, what did these philosophers do? They studied those around them; they submerged themselves in the commonplace, in cities with hordes of anonymous people. While the existentialists, as well those philosophers before exploited their uncommon education and intellect, the basis for their movement was ordinary human behaviour and existence.

Finally, literature is similar to philosophy in that it seeks to explain and understand human behaviour and therefore rooted in the commonplace. Nevertheless, its relative strength over philosophy is literature's ability to emotionally and spiritually move the reader through the use of contrived situations and fictional characters. It can do this when even the central theme of a piece maybe love between a man and a woman (e.g. commonplace). Literature also distinguishes itself from philosophy in that the breadth of the fiction may be huge. The plot and the detail can be quite ordinary or fantastic. However, this does not mean that the central themes of all literature, whether ordinary or fantastic, deal with human beings and the problems they find in the world, something that we all share.

In conclusion, I hope it has been shown that a passionate desire to understand and explain human behaviour, the significance of our existence and deal constructively with the challenges of life are the centrepieces of at least in two of the most influential areas in human thought. What is more commonplace than the existence of man.

COMMENTS ON THE MODEL PRESENTATION

This is a well-focused and insightful analysis of the issue. Beginning with the observation that the greatest thinkers "live lives in time," the writer reasons that the great thinkers develop their ideas through observation of common occurrences and everyday reality. One of the strengths of this response is the way in which it thoughtfully considers the opposing claim: that great thinkers are primarily the product of fine education, and that, being "well schooled in the classics," they are far removed from everyday life. The writer notes that, while it "may be a benefit to study classics," it is nevertheless true that being "well schooled in diverse disciplines" will simply "refine and hone an ability to study human nature" in its everyday manifestations. This observation is indicative of the writer's sophisticated grasp of the complexities of the issue.

The writer goes on to demonstrate the intellectual "power of the commonplace" by skilfully developing two compelling examples from academic life: philosophy and literature. Aristotle is cited as a philosopher who studied the "more mundane motions of daily life." Similarly, the writer explains, twentieth-century existentialists, in attempting to understand man's relation to the universe, found inspiration in the commonplace.

Another strength in this essay is the way it introduces an idea and then builds on that idea as the argument unfolds. For instance, in a discussion of the existentialists in the second paragraph, the writer expands on an earlier point about "thinkers" in general: the existentialists may have "exploited their uncommon education and intellect," but the "basis for their movement was ordinary human behaviour and existence." It is logical connections such as these that make for a coherent and well-focused discussion.

The writer uses language fluently and controls sophisticated syntax throughout the essay: "I would argue that although it may be a benefit to study classics and be well schooled in diverse disciplines, these pursuits merely refine and hone an ability each and every person has, the ability to study human nature."

This is not a flawless paper: word choice, for example, is not always precise. But the essay's cogent analysis, effective organization, and sophisticated sentence structure merit a solid score of 6.

Chapter 5

Analytical Writing Assessment—Analysing an Argument

We trust you have seen the detailed guidelines in regard to this in the chapter titled Understanding the System. While the presentation whether in regard to Perspectives on the Issue or Critique on the Argument has necessarily got to be original, we give hereunder some Model Arguments, Model Critiques and Comments on the Model Critique. We trust these would enable you to formulate your strategies for this section.

Discuss how well reasoned you find the following arguments.

ARGUMENT NO.1

Hospital statistics regarding people who go to the emergency room after roller-skating accidents indicate the need for more protective equipment. Within this group of people, 75 percent of those who had accidents in streets or parking lots were not wearing any protective clothing (helmets, knee pads, etc.) or any light-reflecting material (clip-on lights, glow-in-the-dark wrist pads, etc.). Clearly, these statistics indicate that by investing in high-quality protective gear and reflective equipment, roller skaters will greatly reduce their risk of being severely injured in an accident.

MODEL CRITIQUE

The notion that protective gear reduces the injuries suffered in accidents seems at first glance to be an obvious conclusion. After all, it is the intent of these products to either prevent accidents from occurring in the first place or to reduce the injuries suffered by the wearer should an accident occur. However, the conclusion that investing in high quality protective gear greatly reduces the risk of being severely injured in an accident may mask other (and potentially more significant) causes of injuries and may inspire people to over invest financially and psychologically in protective gear.

First of all, as mentioned in the argument, there are two distinct kinds of gear - preventative gear (such as light reflecting material) and protective gear (such as helmets). Preventative gear is intended to warn others, presumably for the most part motorists, of the presence of the roller skater. It works only if the "other" is a responsible and caring individual who will afford the skater the necessary space and attention. Protective gear is intended to reduce the effect of any accident, whether it is caused by an other, the skater or some force of nature. Protective gear does little, if anything, to prevent accidents but is presumed to reduce the injuries that occur in an accident. The statistics on injuries suffered by skaters would be more interesting if the skaters were grouped into those wearing no gear at all, those wearing protective gear only, those wearing preventative gear only and those wearing both. These statistics could provide skaters with a clearer understanding of which kinds of gear are more beneficial.

The argument above is weakened by the fact that it does not take into account the inherent differences between skaters who wear gear and those who do not. If is at least likely that those who wear gear may be generally more responsible and/or safety conscious individuals. The skaters who wear gear may be less likely to cause accidents through careless or dangerous behaviour. It may, in fact, be their natural caution and responsibility that keeps them out of the emergency room rather than the gear itself. Also, the statistics above is based entirely on those who are skating in streets and parking lots which are relatively dangerous places to skate in the first place. People who are generally more safety conscious (and therefore more likely to wear gear) may choose to skate in safer areas such as parks or back yards.

The statistics also does not differentiate between severity of injuries. The conclusion that safety gear prevents severe injuries suggests that it is presumed that people come to the emergency room only with severe injuries. This is certainly not the case. Also, given that skating is a recreational activity that may be primarily engaged in during evenings and weekends (when doctors' offices are closed), skater with less severe injuries may be especially likely to come to the emergency room for treatment.

Finally, there is absolutely no evidence provided that high quality (and presumably more expensive) gear is any more beneficial than other kinds of gear. For example, a simple white t-shirt may provide the same preventative benefit as a higher quality, more expensive, shirt designed only for skating. Before skaters are encouraged to invest heavily in gear, a more complete understanding of the benefit provided by individual pieces of gear would be helpful.

The argument for safety gear based on emergency room statistics could provide important information and potentially saves lives. Before conclusions about the amount and kinds of investments that should be made in gear are reached, a more complete understanding of the benefits are needed. After all, a false confidence in ineffective gear could be just as dangerous as no gear at all.

COMMENTS ON THE MODEL CRITIQUE

This outstanding response demonstrates the writer's insightful analytical skills. The introduction, which notes that adopting the topic's fallacious reasoning could ". . . inspire people to over invest financially and psychologically in protective gear," is followed by a comprehensive examination of each of the argument's root flaws. Specifically, the writer exposes several points that undermine the argument:

- that preventive and protective gear are not the same
- that skaters who wear gear may be less prone to accidents because they are, by nature, more responsible and cautious
- that the statistics do not differentiate by the severity of the injuries
- that gear may not need to be high-quality to be beneficial

The discussion is smoothly and logically organized, and each point is thoroughly and cogently developed. In addition, the writing is succinct, economical, and generally error-free. Sentences are varied and complex, and diction is expressive and precise.

In sum, this response exemplifies the very top of the 6 range described in the scoring guide. If the writer had been less eloquent or provided fewer reasons to refute the argument, the paper could still have received a 6.

ARGUMENT NO.2

The University of Claria is generally considered one of the best universities in the world because of its instructors' reputation, which is based primarily on the extensive research and publishing record of certain faculty members. In addition, several faculty members are internationally renowned as leaders in their fields. For example, many of the faculty from the English department are regularly invited to teach at universities in other countries. Furthermore, two recent graduates of the physics department have gone on to become candidates for the Nobel Prize in Physics. And 75 percent of the students are able to find employment after graduating. Therefore, because of the reputation of its faculty, the University of Claria should be the obvious choice for anyone seeking a quality education.

MODEL CRITIQUE

While the University of Claria appears to have an excellent reputation based on the accomplishments and reputations of its faculty, one would also wish to consider other issues before deciding upon this particular institution for undergraduate or graduate training. The Physics and English departments are internationally known, but these are only two of the areas in which one might study. Other departments are not listed; is this because no others are worth mentioning, or because no other departments bothered to turn in their accomplishments and kudos to the publicity office?

The assumption is that because English and Physics have excellent brains in the faculty offices, their teaching skills and their abilities to pass on knowledge and the love of learning to their students are equally laudable. Unfortunately, this is often not the case. A prospective student would certainly be advised to investigate thoroughly the teaching talents and attitudes of the professors, the library and research facilities, the physical plant of the departments in which he or she was planning to study, as well as the living arrangements on or off campus, and the facilities available for leisure activities and entertainment.

This evaluation of the University of Claria is too brief, and too general. Nothing is mentioned about the quality of overall education; it only praises the accomplishments of a few recent graduates and professors. More important than invitations to teach elsewhere, which might have been engineered by their own departmental heads in an attempt to remove them from the campus for a semester or two, is the relationship between teacher and student. Are the teaching faculty approachable? Are they helpful? Have they an interest in passing on their knowledge? Are they working for the future benefit of the student or to get another year closer to retirement? How enthusiastic are the students about the courses being taught and the faculty members who teach those classes? Are there sufficient classes available for the number of students? Are the campus buildings accessible; how is the University handling all those cars? Is the University a pleasant, encouraging, interesting, challenging place to attend school? What are its attitudes about education, students, student ideas and innovations, faculty suggestions for improvement?

What about that 75% employment record? Were those students employed in the field of their choice, or are they flipping burgers and emptying wastebaskets while they search for something they are trained to do. A more specific statement about the employability of students from this University is needed in order to make the argument forceful.

The paragraph given merely scratches the surface of what must be said about this University in order to entice students and to convince them that this is the best place to obtain a quality education. Much more work is needed by the public relations department before this can be made into a four-colour brochure and handed out to prospective students.

COMMENTS ON THE MODEL CRITIQUE

The writer of this outstanding response acknowledges that the University of Claria may "appear" to have a sterling reputation, but cogently argues that such a reputation is perhaps unwarranted in light of the thin and misleading information provided. The paper's insightful critique targets several instances of unsound reasoning in the argument:

- that the argument identifies academic achievements in only two departments;
- that publications and research prove little about the quality of teaching at Claria; and
- that the student employment statistics lacks specificity and may be entirely bogus.

The writer probes each questionable assumption and offers alternative explanations, pointing out, for instance, that invitations for faculty to teach elsewhere may have been purposely arranged in order to temporarily remove them from campus and that the employed students may be "flipping burgers and emptying wastebaskets."

In addition, the response perceptively analyzes many features — omitted by the argument — that could more convincingly make the case that Claria is "the obvious choice." The writer suggests that the search for a quality education would, at least, need to investigate the teaching strengths of the faculty; ideally one would also ask about research facilities, the university's physical plant, availability of classes, even parking arrangements!

Although the fourth paragraph ("What about that 75% employment record?") interrupts this discussion, the response is, on the whole, logically and effectively organized. Each paragraph develops the central premise: that the argument is uncompelling because it fails to use more valid indices of educational quality.

The writing is succinct, graceful, and virtually error-free, distinguished by impressive diction ("kudos," "laudable," "engineered," "entice"), as well as syntactic sophistication. For all of these reasons, the response earns a 6.

ARGUMENT NO.3

"According to a recent report from our marketing department, fewer people attended movies produced by Silver Screen during the past year than in any other year. And yet the percentage of generally favourable comments by movie reviewers about specific Silver Screen movies actually increased during this period. Clearly, the contents of these reviews are not reaching enough of our prospective viewers; so the problem lies not with the quality of our movies but with the public's lack of awareness that movies of good quality are available. Silver Screen should therefore spend more of its budget next year on reaching the public through advertising and less on producing new movies."

MODEL CRITIQUE

The advertising director first needs to determine the relative proportion of movie goers that choose to see Silver Screen films. That will help him to understand his market share. If the population in general is attending less, then he may still be out-profiting his competitors, despite his individual sales decrease. In fact, his relative sales could be increasing. Determining where he stands in his market will help him to create and implement an action plan.

Another important thing to consider is the relative cost of attending movies to the current standard of living. If the standard of living is decreasing, it may contribute to an overall decrease in attendance. In that case, advertising could be very helpful, in that a clever campaign could emphasize the low cost of movies as compared to many other leisure activities. This could offset financial anxieties of potential customers.

Finally, it is important to remember that people rarely trust movie reviewers. For that reason, it is important that the films appeal to the populace, and not critics alone. The best advertisement in many cases is word of mouth. No matter what critics say, people tend to take the opinions of friends more seriously. This supports continual funding to produce quality movies that will appeal to the average person.

There is no reason that silver screen should not spend more on advertisement, however, there is reason to continue to invest in diverse, quality films. Furthermore, the company must consider carefully what it chooses to emphasize in its advertisement.

COMMENTS ON THE MODEL CRITIQUE

Although the response begins by stating that the argument "is relatively sound," it immediately goes on to develop a critique. The response identifies three major flaws in the argument and provides a careful and thorough analysis. The main points discussed are that

- the fall-off in attendance might be industry wide
- the general state of the economy might have affected movie attendance
- movie goers "rarely trust movie reviewers"

Each of these points is developed; together they are presented within the context of a larger idea: that while spending more money on advertising may be helpful, the company should "continue to invest in diverse, quality films."

This is a smoothly written, well-developed analysis in which syntactic variety and the excellent use of transitions make for a virtually seamless response. This paper clearly merits a score of 6.

The argument presented above is relatively sound, however, the author fails to recognize all the elements necessary to evaluate his situation. The idea that more money be invested in advertising may be a helpful one, but perhaps not because people are unaware of the current reviews. To clarify, it may be necessary to advertise more in order to increase sales, however that could be due to many circumstances such as a decrease in the public's overall attendance, an increase in the cost of movies, or a lack of trust in the opinions of the reviewers.

Chapter 6

Antonyms

The English language has a deep-seated structure. The core words of the English language form its framework. On this framework rests a huge and constantly growing collection of words. This is because the language has grown by taking on words from a wide range of languages as far and wide as Hindi (the words *bungalow, veranda, jungle, pundit* and so on are derived from Hindi) and French (while thousands of French words find place in English language, some illustrations are the words *connoisseur, adieu, parlance, parsimonious*, and so on).

The fountainhead of most European languages is Latin. It has provided structure to the English language. It becomes important to learn the basics of the structure of the English language. The best way to do this is to learn how words have been evolved as we come across core words that are a part of the framework of the English language. This would make sure that we learn not only how a particular word is formed but also how it can be used to mean different things in different contexts. This learning process has to be gradual and enjoyable. Care has been taken to make it both.

You would surely have come across the words mediation (which means being instrumental in trying to resolve the dispute *between* two parties), intermediary (which means someone who brings two parties together for business or other dealings), median (which means a line joining midpoints or a middle term or number), medieval (which means pertaining to the Middle Ages) and Mediterranean (which means the sea which is in the middle of terrain or land masses of Europe and Africa). If one were to know what MED means, one may not even need to refer to a dictionary if it is not handy. One may be able to sense the meaning of the word and if it is in contextual usage, one may even be able to feel the meaning of the word. So powerful is the methodology of learning about the evolution of words.

The English language has over a hundred thousand words. Learning them all is well nigh impossible. And yet if one is to be ready for a test of one's understanding of the English language, one should be ready with a large personal lexicon. What is large is a subjective matter. What is large for the ant may be chickenfeed for the elephant. It is in the context of the great size of the task of learning the meanings of thousands of words that the learning methodology assumes great significance. Learning can result in assimilation if learning were to be an enjoyable experience. It is our endeavour to make it just that.

Trying to learn a couple of thousand words through such lacklustre and impersonal methodologies as Word Lists (as so many books are wont to describe a list of words that the student is expected to consign to memory) may prove enormously futile. On the other hand someone who is aware of this deep-seated structure of the English language has a clear edge over someone who has been mugging Word Lists. The difference between one and the other will be as clear as between one who knows why and another who merely knows how. The one who knows why can at any time refresh his memory about how.

In the table below, you will see a word in the first column to the left of the table. Pick the antonym (the word opposite in meaning) of this word from the five choices given in the remaining columns. The answers follow. It is recommended that you invariably read the detailed answers regardless of whether you are right or wrong.

Here then is the first of our practice sessions with antonyms.

The Word	Option1	Option2	Option3	Option4	Option5
Morose	Overawed	Agitated	Cherubic	Decisive	Cheerful
Persevere	Put into	Send out	Bring forward	Give up	Take away
Pungency	Boredom	Redundancy	Unresponsiveness	Blandness	Insignificance
Offhand	Appropriate	Accurate	Universal	Disputatious	Premeditated
Dispatch	Aversion	Irregularity	Heedlessness	Leisureliness	Serenity
Sedulous	Presumptuous	Ponderous	Treacherous	Careless	Useless
Expire	Evolve	Stabilize	Come to life	Grow to fruition	Bring to light
Warrior	Commentator	Liaison	Lobbyist	Emissary	Pacifist
Indelibility	Availability	Comprehensibility	Decidability	Erasability	Retractability
Gossamer	Sincere	Taciturn	Intense	Awkward	Ponderous
Craven	Indifferent	Presumptuous	Valorous	Scrupulous	Petulant
Insularity	Overzeal- ousness	Cosmopolitanism	Susceptibility	Willing hospitability	Knowledgeable consideration
Tortuous	Enduring	Informal	Cautious	Simplistic	Straightforward
Divestiture	Monopolization	Consultation	Subsidization	Promotion	Acquisition
Metamor- phose	Examine in haste	Prepare in advance	Descend slowly	Remain unaltered	Move ahead

The correct answers are in the table below. If you will see the detailed explanations, you will see which option is correct and which is not. Besides, you will see why one option is correct and why the others are not. You will observe that it would be ever so important to have a fair idea of the deep seated structure of the English language rather than of merely trying to memorise thousands of words without being aware of their meanings that would be so easy to understand to learn and appreciate from contextual usage. What you will also see is the frequent doses of etymology (a study of how words are evolved or formed). These have been put in to ensure that not only you do not understand the particular words but also what words with similar origins could mean. You may be able to judge the meanings of words with fair accuracy.

Etymology by itself is too heavy a dish to digest. It has to be taken in small doses in order to sustain interest. But when you are taken through the etymology of words as and when you see them being used in a context, there is likelihood of being able to sustain interest. It is with the objective of making learning an enjoyable experience that etymology is being presented to you.

We are certain that the methodology that is presented hereunder will ensure complete assimilation of the meanings of words and their shades – wherever necessary. We have consciously avoided long winding lists of even more long winding words in this book in order to prevent the eraser rubbing ahead of the pencil. With such lists of words, there is every possibility of one forgetting a word (leave alone its meaning) before reading the next word. Such lists have at best soporific value. They would be ideal as lullabies. It is for this reason that we would like to request the reader to read each and every explanatory answer regardless of whether you are right or wrong. There is every possibility that you may learn so many new words and what is more, the exact meanings of these words may remain ingrained on your memory. Such is the power of the methodology that is presented to you here.

The Given Word	Detailed Explanation as to why not any of the other words would fit as the antonym of the given word and what the other words mean (with contextual usage)
Morose	Have you heard of the words mortal, moribund, moron, morgue, morbid, mordacious, morbidity, and mordant that all have something to do with death or ding? The word mortal comes from the Latin word MORS, meaning someone or something destined to die. This is why human beings are referred to as *mortals*. So when you and your friends are about to sit for lunch and notice that there is someone who generally does not mix with your group has not brought his lunchbox but seems hungry and ask this person whether he would like to break bread with lesser mortals, you are as such asking him whether he would like to share the food that other human beings whom he considers as below his status have pooled. Those who die but are yet not forgotten are often referred to as *immortals*, meaning those who (figuratively, of course) do not die. Those of you know where Crimea is, read on. Those who do not, it is in Russia. In the Crimean War sometime in the mid 19th century, a whole brigade of British cavalry was killed. This episode has been *immortalised* by Lord Alfred Tennyson in his famous poem *Charge of the Light Brigade*. This poem will ensure that the brigade will remain alive in the memory of people forever. It would therefore be evident that someone who is lively would be the opposite of someone who is *morose*. Someone *overawed* is someone who is greatly impressed. The word awe means wonder, amazement or admiration. It is possible for someone to be overawed without seeming lively. Someone who can render a song or two in a tolerable tune may overawe someone who is mercifully unaware of tune and rhythm. Therefore merely being overawed need not mean that one is lively. An *agitated* person could be perturbed. Someone who is perturbed may not be lively as well. Someone given to anger or frequent mental turmoil is quite likely to be not lively. A lively person is cheerful and is generally able to face life with composure and is therefore not likely to be angry or disturbed at a slight provocation. Someone *cherubic* is someone who is sweet and innocent. Even here liveliness may not be present. Someone innocent may be either free from blame or may be free from cunning. Someone may ask a cherubic girl if she would like to accompany him to the cinema. She may say that she would rather sit and pray through the evening. Someone *decisive* may be able to make up his mind. He may not be hesitant. A decisive match may be the one that will decide who will win the series or the trophy. But someone decisive may not necessarily be lively. He may decide to kill himself and may implement that decision. A lively person loves life. When you cheer your favourite team, you shout hurrah. You are animated. Someone who is cheerful is lively. Thus *cheerful* is the precise opposite of morose. Incidentally the word animated comes form the Latin word ANIM (meaning life, spirit, mind or soul). Thus when you see **an animated film**, what you are seeing is **sketches being brought to life**. An animated discussion is a lively discussion. An animal is something that possesses the characteristics of life. This is why animosity is the ferocious quality of animals and when someone harbours animosity, he is hateful. That is why someone who is *equanimous* maintains mental balance during periods of adverse circumstances (the word equanimous has the prefix EQUI – meaning *equal* – and ANIM – meaning *mind*)
Persevere	Have you heard of the words perfect, pervading, and perforate? The word perfect reminds you of someone who is thorough in his work. If the fragrance of the cake that your mother has put in the oven is pervading the house, it means that it has spread everywhere. If a paper is perforated, there are holes everywhere. All these words speak of a job done thoroughly. Someone who gives up

.	cannot be said to have persevered. Thus to *give up* is the antonym of persevere. If you *persevere* with your plans, it means that you are thoroughly committed to translating your plan to reality. You will not give up even if there are odds. That is why mountain climbers persevere even if there are great hazards. Climbing snow-capped peaks is no picnic. *Severe* means harsh, rigorous or unsparing. The prefix PER along with SEVERE adds up to mean *to do something thoroughly and with rigour*. When you put something into another, you might implant, inject or infuse something. You might inspire (meaning either take a breath or put liveliness into a party or make someone confident). The prefix IM or IN (both mean the same thing as IN in English) are indicative of something being put in. This is worth remembering. To send out would mean *to emit*. The word emit incidentally consists of the prefix E (meaning *out*) and the root MIT (meaning *send*). It is for this reason that when you *emit* six whistles, you could be sending out a signal to your girl friend to meet you in the park at six. The root MISS also means to *send*. Thus emission is *sending out*; emissions from a factory may be fumes or contaminated water. It is for this reason that an *emissary* is someone who has been sent out by his country to represent his nation in a foreign land. When you remove something from another, what might you be doing? Would you be extracting? Would you be excavating? The important thing to see here is that the prefix EX generally means *out* although sometimes it may also mean *thoroughly* as in the case of an expert. It is for this reason that *extremes* are the out ends. When you bring forward, you might advance something. If you bring forward the date of your return to your country from your vacation trip to Mauritius from June 1 to May 23, you have *preponed* your return. When you have *propagated* a theory you have tried to bring it forward for the attention of so many people. The prefixes AD, PRE and PRO are generally used to form words that tend to mean *doing* or *bringing forward*. In the word *persevere* the prefix is different. Quite frequently, it helps to know what the prefix has to say about the word to which it is prefixed.
Pungency	Have you tasted mustard sauce? Does it not cause a tingling sensation on the tongue? Have you had a bite of radish? Does it not cause irritation on the tongue? Things that cause irritation to the sensory organs are pungent. That is why some spices are pungent. They are pungent because they possess the quality of *pungency*. Something that is bland is tasteless or insipid. A cup of tea brings cheer. It invigorates you. A cup of *bland* tea might put you to sleep. Thus blandness is the antonym of pungency. Something bland may cause boredom. But boredom may be the effect of blandness that may be the cause. Since cause is not the same thing as effect, blandness is not the same thing as boredom. When something is available in a quantity that is far more than what is required, it may become *redundant*. When something is no longer needed, it becomes redundant. Redundancy may cause boredom in some instances. Someone may be lecturing and may use the same sentence over and over again, although the language may change. He may keep saying: "You know" or "You see" every now and then. The audience may have gone to sleep. He may have become redundant. But one may also see someone who is vigorously rubbing wax polish on a wooden floor that is already shining. While the act of rubbing polish may have become redundant in your viewpoint, the person who is rubbing away may be deeply enjoying that activity; if he were not he would have gone to sleep using the polishing cloth as his makeshift pillow. Something pungent may evoke response; you may sneeze when accidentally smelling pungent chilly powder. But this response is the effect of which pungency is the cause. Someone unresponsiveness to the pungent smell of chilly powder may be unresponsive to the fragrance of roses as well for the simple reason that acute sinusitis may have virtually taken away his sense of smell altogether. But just as responsiveness to something pungent is an *effect* of which pungency is the cause, so is unresponsiveness.

	Notice the word *sign*. What do you do when you sign a contract regarding the terms of your employment with a company? You give an indication or a signal that you have understood the terms and agree to abide by it. How do you ask the fellow at the head of the queue for movie tickets to purchase your ticket? You make a sign. You may have said nothing. Yet you have imparted meaning to your gesture.
	You are at the stock exchange watching the proceedings. At your mere nod, your share broker buys a huge amount of shares. Your nod is a sign that has meaning. It carries weight. It is *significant*. Notice that significance or insignificance (that means the lack of significance) has nothing to do with pungency at all. For an antonym there has to be a relationship in the first place even if it is an inverse relationship.
Offhand	Imagine that your friend has just returned from your school's Annual Sports Day where he has been sitting and cheering the participants and shovelling oodles and oodles of popcorn into his interiors. Now imagine that someone asks him as to what event did he win. He tells offhand that it was the 100 meters. On being asked his timing he replies offhand that it was some 9 seconds or so. On being congratulated – in very wry tones, of course – for having left the world record for the event in shade, he realises that even if it had to be a fib, it should have been thought of earlier. When you do something without premeditation (thinking beforehand) you do it offhand. Therefore premeditated is the antonym for offhand.
	The word *accurate* comes from the Latin CURA that means *care*. When you do something with accuracy, you do it with care. Just because you have done something with premeditation, it does not mean that it is accurate. For example in the previous illustration it is possible to know who holds the world record for the 100 meters and what is his timing. Suppose that the chap who has lied earlier now knows that the world record is 9.8 seconds and thus after careful thinking he says that he ran the 100 meters in 12 seconds, even then he will not be accurate. He is still fibbing.
	A movie meant for universal exhibition means that all including children can see it without restriction. A universal phenomenon is something which is seen whether in Mongolia or in Indonesia or in any other part of the world. For example the day being of 24 hours duration is a universal phenomenon. But the sun shining at midnight is a phenomenon only in – say - Norway. It is not a *universal* phenomenon. However, the word *universal* has nothing to do with the word *offhand*.
	The word *appropriate* has several shades of meanings. If some feel that capital punishment is not appropriate till all efforts to reform the criminal are exhausted, they feel that execution would not be a correct or fitting punishment. If someone is used to appropriating the most comfortable chair, he takes for himself this chair. If the bank decides to sell the mortgaged property and appropriate the sale proceeds towards the loan in default, they intend to apply the money realised from sale towards the loan. Offhand is doing something without thinking. Just because something is done with prior thought, does not mean it is the opposite of offhand. For example one may write a letter. It requires thinking. Yet writing a letter is not the opposite of doing something offhand.
	The word dispute means a quarrel. Someone disputatious is fond of quarrelling. Quarrels may even be without prior thought. They may erupt in a flash. But just as writing a letter is not the opposite of doing something offhand; a quarrel is not a synonym for something offhand.
Dispatch	When you carry out a task with dispatch, you have accomplished it promptly. The antonym of dispatch should therefore mean doing something without promptness.
	Serenity is peace of mind. When someone is serene, so many things are possible: one may do things promptly, one may not do things promptly or one may not do anything at all. A person who does things promptly may not be serene. For example, someone who irons clothes before rushing to office may even be using swear words while ironing. The serene person has a smile on his face while ironing. Both can be prompt. The difference will only be of the mental state while doing work. Someone meditating may have a serene mind. He may be doing nothing.

	Someone who does things leisurely is doing things without haste. He displays the quality of **leisureliness** that is therefore the antonym for dispatch. Someone who does not pay heed (or *attention*, in other words) displays the quality of heedlessness. There is nothing to prevent him from doing things promptly. He may promptly switch on an electric iron for ironing his clothes without paying heed to his wife who has been shouting that the iron has a problem of leakage of current. In being heedless he may get a horrible electric shock. Someone doing things without paying heed is quite likely to be guided by haste alone and not caution. Someone doing things in an irregular fashion may or may not do things promptly. Someone who exercises with the skipping rope may promptly finish a thousand skips and yet may be irregular. He may do it once in a month. Mere irregularity does not imply lack of promptness. The word *aversion* has the prefix A (that means – among many things - *away*) and is derived from VERTERE (which in French means to *turn*). The tendency to turn away from something is known as aversion. Therefore aversion means dislike, distaste, unwillingness or shunning. When you do things with dispatch, you may like what you are doing or even dislike what you are doing. An executioner may have to hang a convict at 4 a.m. He may hate what he is doing although he may be prompt. Mere aversion does not mean that one does things without dispatch or promptness. Someone with an aversion to studies, may not study at all.
Sedulous	If you are to succeed at the competitive examination, you will have to receive sedulous or persistent or painstaking coaching. When one does something persistently, it has to be with zeal. Therefore something done in a sedulous manner is something done with zeal or persistence. The antonym of sedulous would be something done without zeal or persistence. The word *presume* comes from the prefix PRE that means *before* and SUME that means *take*. Therefore someone who does things without proper authority or sanction may be described as *presumptuous* because he takes this authority for granted. This does not mean that someone who does things in a presumptuous manner does things without zeal. As a matter of fact more than ordinary zeal may even be the motivating factor for doing things in a presumptuous manner. Therefore presumptuousness would not be the antonym for sedulous. The word ponderous comes from PONDUS that means weight. Something of great weight or something clumsy may be ponderous. Someone may be seen eating with the slow ponderous concentration of a jersey cow. When you ponder over a matter, you weigh it in your mind and therefore if you are pondering on what to do next, you are carefully thinking about your next step. Ponderous may therefore be clearly ineligible for being an antonym for sedulous. It may, at times, come perilously close to being a synonym. Zeal is always taken in its positive connotation. The unholy haste displayed by a mass murderer to relive the strain on the earth's resources to whatever extent that he can by killing as many of its population that he could, would not be considered as zeal. Treachery is violation of faith. Someone treacherous cannot be considered as zealous. He also cannot be considered as someone who does things carelessly. Before someone violates the trust that another reposes in him, he has to carefully develop a relationship so that people trust him. Therefore treacherous cannot be an antonym for sedulous. The antonym of sedulous would be something done without zeal or persistence. Something done in a careless manner cannot ever qualify to being done in a persistent manner. You cannot be careless and persistent at the same time just as you cannot have boiling ice cream. Therefore careless is the antonym for sedulous. Someone who does things in a careless fashion at least does things. A carelessly made meal may come in handy if you are really hungry. Someone useless may not be capable of doing anything at all.

Expire	The word expire comes from the prefix EX (that means *out*) and SPIRARE (that - in Latin - means to breathe). When dying, someone breathes out for the last time. To *expire* may mean – in addition to mere *breathing out* (as opposed to *inspire* that means *breathe in*) – to *die*. If a drug is marked with an expiry date, it means that it will have to be used before that date only where after its utility may have *expired* (or died). Therefore the antonym of expire should mean to breathe in or come alive. But something that comes to life is necessarily animate. The word *evolve* comes from the prefix E (that means *out*) and the French verb VOLVERE (that means *to roll*). Something that rolls out – meaning it gradually comes into view or being – is said to have evolved. It is not necessary that something that has evolved is animate. One may evolve a plan to win the next elections. This plan is not animate. Therefore *evolve* would not be an antonym for expire. Something that seems to have stabilized may not be necessarily animate. Someone's blood pressure may stabilize as a result of drugs. While the person is animate, his blood pressure is not animate. It is only a measure of the state of bodily function. If something comes to life, it is necessarily animate. A party comes to life with the rock group making its entry. This is because the people attending the party come alive; the people get up and dance. The tablecloths and glasses and crockery do not get up and swing to the tunes of the band. Therefore the phrase 'come to life' would be the antonym for the word *expire*. Fruit is what the soil produces. It calls for a great deal of effort by the farmer. The fruit of one's labours may mean a successful outcome. To grow to fruition means to bear fruit or become fruitful or real. If someone's persistent efforts come to fruition, it does not mean that whatever is produced is animate. When you bring some object to a light source, the idea is to reveal it. The object itself may be inanimate. One can bring to light even a plot or a conspiracy, none of which are living things.
Warrior	A warrior is one who goes to war. A warrior is thus a fighting man. Someone who does not want to fight would therefore be the antonym for warrior. A commentator may have little to do with war or an alternative to war. A commentator has no place on the battlefield where bullets are flying. He may make a commentary on non-war events such as sports events. Liaison means communication or contact. A company's liaison officer would be engaged in maintaining contact between the company and the organisations that the company deals with. A liaison between a man and a woman may mean an illicit affair. Quite clearly liaison has nothing to do with either war or alternative to war. A lobbyist is one who takes up the cause of some interest group. Some persons may be interested in an infrastructure project whereas others are against the project because of large-scale loss of fauna and flora. The environmental group lobbies *against* the project. The lobbyist has little to do with a war or otherwise. An emissary as we have seen earlier is someone who has been sent to represent (his people or his country as the case may be). He may be deputed to bring peace between two warring factions or he may have been sent to ensure that satisfactory arrangements have been made in regard to a cricket match between two national teams. He may or may not have anything to do with wars. The pacifist comes from the Latin PACIFUS that means peace. The Pacific Ocean is named thus because it is a calm ocean whereas the Atlantic is not. A pacifist brings peace through reconciliation, which is the opposite of war. A pacifist is of a peaceful temperament. Thus a pacifist is the antonym for a warrior.
Indelibility	You would surely have seen the words *impossible* (that means *not possible*) and *inadequate* (that means *not adequate*). The prefixes IM and IN are variations for *not* in English. It is for this reason that something *indelible* is something that cannot be deleted and its antonym is something that can be deleted. To *delete* means to *erase*.

	Availability has nothing to do with deletion. You delete something that you do not require. Something may be available either by a natural process or it may be produced on the basis of a perceived need. A printed receipt for the money that you have paid at a store may be available and yet may be indelible. The word comprehensibility is made of the prefix COM (that means completely or jointly) and PREHENDRE (that means *to seize*). A *comprehensive* article in a newspaper is that whose crux you can seize completely or in other words understand its meaning completely. It can also mean someone or something that is seized of all relevant facts and thus can be said to be *complete* and *thorough*. A comprehensive price quotation for a computer – for example – includes basic price, taxes, transportation costs, installation expenses and so on. It is a complete and thorough, *all-inclusive* quotation. Decidability comes from the word *decide* (which means to make up one's mind about something). One may decide to make a memorial for someone. If it has anything to do with deletion, then a decision to make a memorial would mean making the memorial for erasing the chap's memory. This would be illogical. No memorial can succeed in erasing memory even if it states that it has been made for that purpose. It will remind of the person each time one passes by and reads what is inscribed. **Erasability** is the quality of being erased or deleted. It is therefore the antonym for indelibility. Have you noticed that the words *extract* (meaning to pull or draw something out from another thing – which is why you have an *extract* of the proceedings of a board meeting), *distract* (meaning to pull or *draw away* one's attention), *protract* (meaning to pull or draw forward and therefore extend), *contract* (meaning to pull or *draw in*) all have TRACT in them? Have you seen that while the invariable presence of TRACT imparts the meaning of *pull* or *draw* to each word, the meaning of the word changes completely with the prefix? This is because the prefix can materially or completely change the meaning of a word. When you make a commitment to take the family to the movies and then you find that you have to be at the airport to meet your boss, you may have to *retract* (or *draw back*) your commitment. Retractability is the quality of something that makes it *retractable* (or *possible to pull back*).
Gossamer	The word *gossamer* is really a mix of the words *goose* and *summer*. During summer (when goose is eaten) one finds spiders webs floating in the air. This light floating film is known as gossamer but figuratively gossamer is something light and delicate. The antonym of something light and delicate is something that is weighty or heavy. A person is sincere if he does his duty in an earnest manner. However, a person need not be heavy or weighty – either actually or even figuratively - in order to be sincere. A child can be sincere about the study without being either heavy or weighty. The words *tacit* and *taciturn* come from the Latin TACERE that means *be silent*. A tacit agreement is an agreement that is neither written nor spoken. It is signified by silence. Someone taciturn is characterised by very little speech. He is uncommunicative. If he can say *hmm*, he will not take the trouble to say even *yes*. A taciturn person also need not be weighty. As luck would have it, only human beings speak. Therefore if anyone can be silent (in its contextual meaning of *not speaking*), it can be only human beings. It is not as if taciturn persons speak only when they have some weighty thing to say. They say very little or nothing at all – weighty or light-hearted. It is for this reason that the antonym of gossamer cannot be taciturn either. Something may burn intensely. Passion can be intense. Yet passion is not a human being and therefore intense cannot be taciturn. Suppose that a person has been taught that a paunch is a certain indication of overeating and one generally overeats when stressed. He gets a job. His employer has a massive paunch. He then

	asks the employer as to why he has been overeating. The question would not only be awkward but might cost him his job. Someone who ponders over what he is to ask another person would weigh the question in his mind before bunging it to the other person. He would not be generally found posing awkward questions. The word ponderous would be the precise antonym of gossamer for the reason that *ponderous* means *weighty* as seen from an earlier explanation about the origin of this word in this chapter.
Craven	Someone *craven* is one who is *cowardly*. Many other words can be used to describe a coward such as *lily-livered*, *chicken-hearted*, *timid*, *fearful* and so on. The antonym of craven would therefore be someone who does not show unworthy fear in the face of danger. In short, *brave* would be the exact opposite of *craven*. An *indifferent* person is one who does not care or is uninterested. A coward may or may not be uninterested. He may be interested in running off to a far away place before the fight starts. He may be uninterested in martial art. A *presumptuous* person is one who takes things for granted. He does not wait for authority to do something. But for instance if my office assistant allows the boys to take a day off while I am out of station without my permission, he may have seemed presumptuous but this does not mean that he is brave. There is no bravery associated with giving people a day off in anticipation of sanction from the higher ups. Valour is bravery. Valour is courage. **Valorous** would then be the antonym of craven. It is a different matter, however, that discretion is the better part of valour sometimes. When the children yell that there is a poisonous snake in the garden, there would be little point in rushing forth to hold the cobra by his neck when one has no prior experience in snake catching. But then if one is fearful of a poisonous snake, such fear may not seem **unworthy** fear. One is not likely to be teased if he admits that he is scared of snakes. The whole town is horrified of them. Scruples are one's moral principles. One chap may have no hesitation whatsoever in wringing a partridge's neck and chucking the bird into the fire to barbecue. Another may not be able to sleep if he has even **seen** such an act. Scruples are therefore not absolutes. Generally speaking they are matters about which an individual may have doubts in his mind about their morality. Someone who is scrupulous may not be valorous. Because scruples are relative things. What is sauce for the goose may be poison for the gander. Valour and courage are, on the other hand, absolutes. The other day I was at the railway ticket booth waiting for my turn in the queue. The fellow ahead of me leant on my shoulder of the chap ahead of him in order to be able to keep standing and tie his shoelaces. After having tied up, he continued to lean on the other's shoulder till the other could bear it no longer. With a good deal of **petulance** in his voice he asked the other if he thought he was a ruddy orthopaedic. However in the instant case there was, to my mind, some justification for bad temper. Someone petulant is one given to being ill tempered as a rule. Too frequent anger is indicative of inability to cope with Life's problems. To that extent someone petulant may be even cowardly.
Insularity	It would be interesting to know what the word *insular* means. INSULA in Latin means *island*. We have seen the word peninsula being used to describe the Indian sub-continent (or Italy or Greece for that matter). The word *peninsula* consists of the prefix PENE that means *almost* or *nearly* and INSULA that means island. Some landmass that has water all round is an island whereas a landmass that has waters almost all around is a peninsula. An inhabitant of an island is *insular*. Someone insular, figuratively of course, is isolated or detached. He is ignorant of other cultures. The antonym of insular therefore would be someone who adopts other cultures. Since the matter is about cultural awareness, zeal – whether in abundance or in short supply has nothing to do with insularity. Overzealousness therefore cannot

	be an antonym for insular. One can be overzealous about the culture of one's own tribe, for example, and, for this reason, be insular. The prefix COSMO in the word *cosmopolitanism* means the *world* or *universe*. *Polity* is an organised society. An organised society in which there would be people from so many cultures from all over the world would be where you would find *cosmopolitanism*, which in turn is the antonym for *insularity*. Someone susceptible to colds, for example, is someone who catches colds at the drop of a hat. Susceptibility is that quality that makes people susceptible. This has nothing to do with cultures, however. Someone *insular* is *ignorant* about other cultures. A person possessing willing hospitability may be hospitable to persons of his cultural background alone. He may be a great host to his cousins but not to the visiting student delegation from another nation. There is nothing to presume that someone hospitable is aware of other cultures as well. Imagine that someone wants to buy a house. He does not know what the market price is or what the quality of construction nor about clarity of title of the land. He seeks help from someone who has been in the line of real estate for long. After *knowledgeable consideration* – meaning viewing the proposal to buy the house with the knowledge that the gentleman has acquired over the years – he says that the quality of construction is doubtful, the prospective buyer is saved from a bad bargain. This is what knowledgeable consideration means. But this too has nothing to do with cultural insularity or integration.
Tortuous	The word *tortuous* is used to describe something that twists and turns. If you are on a pilgrimage to a mountain shrine and the gradient is sharp and the road has many twists and turns, the route can be described as steep and *tortuous*. Even discussions can be tortuous if events take many turns during the course of discussions. This is a figurative use of the word tortuous. The antonym of tortuous is something that is not turning and is therefore straight. Something that is *enduring* is what lasts for long. In my ancestral home one can see a wooden staircase with many twists and turns but it has lasted for over a century. Something that is merely enduring does not mean that it has no turns. The word *form* means a pattern or type. If the custom at a training establishment is to dress for dinner in dark suits with light ties then such a dress is formal and anything other than that is informal. This is because the prefix IN or IM (both of which mean the same thing) means NOT in English. Informal is therefore what does not conform to a pattern. Since tortuous is about twists and turns, *informal* has nothing to do with it. The word *caution* means *care* or *warning*. The word *cautious* is an adjective used to describe someone who exercises caution. Since tortuous is about twists and turns, *cautious* has nothing to do with it. Someone can be described as a *simple* person if he is not proud or is unspoiled; in short a simple person has no complications. The word *simplistic* means simple to an extreme. Let us see an illustrative usage of the word *simplistic*. If someone buys shares of a company with the *simplistic* assumption that when the market improves, the stock he has bought will look up is a little simplistic if he has not studied the company in which he has invested. It is likely that this company is terminally sick. In the absence of the word straightforward, this would have been close. However since the exact antonym follows soon after, *simplistic* may not do. **Straightforward** is the precise antonym for tortuous.
Divestiture	The word *divestiture* has the prefix DI that means *away from*. This is why *divert* means to turn (attention) away from, *disable* means away from ability and so on. The word VEST means garment. An investiture ceremony is one where the king-to-be is clothed in the powers of king. He is invested as King. It is not necessary that only rulers be invested. Someone may be invested as

	Office Superintendent in an office with three clerks and a single messenger. He assumes office the day he is invested. You may invest money in a business organisation. You acquire assets in that organisation. Divestiture is the precise opposite of investiture. Divestment is the opposite of investment. Therefore the antonym of *divestiture* is *investiture* or *acquisition*. The word *promotion* has the prefix PRO that means forward. *Motion* means movement. Someone who moves ahead in the hierarchy has been given a *promotion*. Someone who has moved a project idea forward by setting up a venture to realise the potential in that idea is the *promoter* of the venture. Somebody who *acquires* a project (which has been set up by someone else) takes control of its management. He however does not become the promoter in the strict sense of the word because the promoter is as such the originator. The word subsidize has the prefix SUB that means *under*. Therefore a *subject* is the person who is ruled by the King and a *subordinate* is someone below someone else who is in the ordinate (meaning ordered) hierarchy of an organisation. A subsidy is an assistance that the government generally provides to its citizens. The subsidy is a means to place artificial buying power in the hands of people who may need something but may not be able to afford it at the market price. Thus, for example, the government may subsidise power in a cold country where people need heating in their homes regardless of whether they can afford it or otherwise. *Subsidization* is a modality of providing subsidy. It has nothing to do, however, with divestiture. You have a persisting backache. You have been seeing your physician regularly about this ailment, He has been giving you medicine. The pain persists. He asks you to consult a specialist who has had special training in treating back pain. You consult people when you want a way out of a problem. You consult people who have requisite knowledge to guide you. *Consultation* is therefore a modality of seeking advice. Consultation too has nothing to do with divestiture. The prefix MONO means *single*. Therefore monogamy is a system where only one spouse – at a time – is allowed and monologue is one-way communication. The word monopoly comes from the word MONO and the French word POLIEN that means *to sell*. Monopoly is therefore a situation where only one party produces or sells something. Monopoly may be either legal (such as a government organisation being the only one allowed to run train services) or it may be because no other business organisation has either the financial capacity or technical competence (or maybe both) to produce the commodity. *Monopolization* is the making of a monopoly. One can monopolize a conversation by not allowing the others to speak. *Monopolization* too has nothing to do with divestiture.
Metamorphose	The word metamorphose has the prefix META that means something occurring separately and therefore is used to denote *change*. The word MORPHE means form. A *change in form* is therefore *metamorphosis*. Something that has undergone metamorphosis can be said to have *metamorphosed*. Therefore the antonym of metamorphose is to be in a state of no change. When you move ahead, you progress. Progress is change by its very nature. *Move ahead* would therefore not be the antonym for the word *metamorphose*. When there is change, a thing alters in state either partly or wholly. **To remain unaltered** is antonymous to *metamorphose*. When you descend slowly into a mineshaft, for example, you change the depth at which you are located from time to time although the change may be gradual. Anything involving change is therefore not appropriate for being an antonym for *metamorphose*. To *examine in haste* has nothing to do with change or the lack of it. Nor for that matter does *prepare in advance* has anything to do with change. Before we come to the end of this exercise let us ask ourselves this question: why is it that the

	words *eject* means to throw out, *reject* means to throw back, *inject* means to throw in something forcefully, *deject* means to throw down (one's head in disappointment), *project* means to throw forward an image or a scheme that has some cost today but benefits tomorrow (meaning some time after). Why is that a *projectile* is something that has been thrown forward, an *object* means an aim, to *object* means to throw something into a discussion or debate to denote your reservations about an argument or a point being made. This is because the root JECT means *to throw*. The prefix E means *out*, RE means *back*, IN means "in" as in English, DE means *down*, PRO means *forward* and OB means *against*.

This is why:

- The pilot throws himself out of the aircraft with engine failure when he *ejects*.
- When you *reject* something what you effectively do is to throw it back (meaning not to accept).
- When you *inject* a vaccine, the child cries because the forceful throwing of vaccine in his body is a matter that he does not appreciate.
- When climbing the *projecting* rock you had to climb something jutting out.
- The *projected* profits of the company seemed too ambitious when seen with the profits actually earned.
- The *projector* is used to *throw* an image on a screen.
- So many in the crowd hung their heads in *dejection* when their favourite team lost by a narrow margin.

So when you see -JECT in any word, remember that it has got to do with a throw.

We shall now move on to the Second Practice Session with Antonyms. Please see the given word and mark the option that you feel is antonymous to the given word.

The Word	Option1	Option2	Option3	Option4	Option5
Fluent	Insensitive	Inappropriate	Derogatory	Halting	Hypocritical
Ally	Mediation	Felon	Adversary	Inventor	Conspirator
Flustered	Mute	Calm	Heavy	Ingrained	Courageous
Waterproof	Soggy	Natural	Unglazed	Viscous	Permeable
Accelerate	Swerve	Arouse	Dispel	Reject	Retard
Emit	Absorb	Demand	Mistake	Prevent	Require
Metamorphosis	Relief from strain	Continuation without change	Cyclical motion	Dogmatic persistence	Varied activity
Dissonance	Concord	Confederacy	Collusion	Consent	Contract
Broach	Keep track of	Lay claim to	Close off	Soothe	Simplify
Ferment	Solidity	Purity	Lucidity	Transparency	Tranquillity
Hapless	Excited	Elated	Fortunate	Completely self reliant	Assured of success
Plethora	Vacuousness	Narrowness	Choice	Dearth	Confusion
Posture	Walk clumsily	Behave naturally	Impose arbitrarily	Publicize widely	Explain carefully
Noisome	Attractively fragrant	Subtly Flattering	Consistently patient	Softly glowing	Gradually diminishing
Abrogate	Uphold	Defer	Discuss secretly	Admit willingly	Read thoroughly

Hereunder are the answers to the above Practice Session. Please read the detailed explanations regardless of whether you are right or wrong.

The Given word	Detailed Explanation as to why not any of the other words would it as the antonym of the given word and what the other words mean (with contextual usage)
Fluent	The word *fluent* comes from the Latin word FLUERE that means *flow*. It is for this reason that the word *influence* can mean either (1) something flowing into another or (2) the effect of someone's directions/ideologies/thought processes flowing into another person's behavioural pattern. Someone who speaks in a manner that reminds one of a flowing stream is said to be *fluent* in speech. Someone can be said to be fluent in a foreign language if he has command over that language. He can speak without interruption. He would not need to say: "how do you say it?" and "what's it called?" every now and then. The antonym of *fluent* would be *that which does not flow smoothly*. Someone responsive to another's feelings or pain can be said to be *sensitive*. *Insensitive* is the very opposite of the word sensitive. A person who is insensitive to another's pain can also speak in a fluent manner. He may let loose a barrage of words, a volley of the choicest abuses, all in a manner that would seem to resemble the gushing flow of a stream. Therefore there is nothing to presume that someone *insensitive* would not be fluent in speech. If the police are *interrogating* some people in connection with a recent murder, they are asking him questions. If the authorities of one country require some information or evidence from a person or authority in a foreign country, it is the practice to ask for such information through what is known as a *Letter Rogatory* sent to a court in the foreign land. ROGARE in Latin means *to ask*. The prefix DE means *down* or *down from*. It is for this reason that the word *derogatory* means *asking down* or remarks and questions or disrespectful behaviour that may pull down someone's reputation or behaviour that will lower a person's esteem. However there is nothing to presume that someone making derogatory remarks may be any less fluent than the most fluent orator. As a matter of fact speaking well of someone is difficult. Speaking ill of someone is rather easy and therefore someone derogatory may very well be fluent. **Halting** is the antonym for fluent. One takes a halt when one has been going on for long. Halting speech is that in which there are breaks. The speech is in fits and starts. A stream does not flow for a while and take a recess. The word *hypocritical* comes from a Greek word HYPOCRISIS that means *acting a theatrical part*. A theatre actor has to pretend for his bread and butter. He always has to be someone else. The word *hypocritical* means pretending to be more virtuous than what one really is. Someone hypocritical would tend to put on airs of being virtuous and it is because of this pretension that he is deceitful, dishonest or lying. The antonym for hypocritical would thus be truthful or unpretentious. Someone fluent is not necessarily unpretentious or truthful. As a matter of fact in order for him to get away with the impression of being virtuous, he will necessarily have to be glib and fluent. A halting speech would on the contrary give him away.
Ally	An *ally* is a partner, associate or helper. You would have noticed the word *alliance* that means a partnership or association and *allied* that means related or connected. Someone who is the opposite of a friend or helper and thus is an *enemy* would be the antonym of an ally. An enemy is hated. We have seen the words with the letters MED in them that mean *middle*, and therefore *mediator* means someone who goes in between (brings about a compromise or settlement or a business transaction and so on). A mediator is therefore who helps settle some dispute and is therefore not an antonym for ally. A *felony* is a grave crime or sin. A *felon* is someone who commits felony. He does not qualify as an antonym for ally. He is not an enemy in the strict sense that he does not nurse hatred against someone whom he commits felony. In order to nurse hatred the enemy must know the person whom

	he hates. In the case of a person who knocks some passer-by on the head with a blunt stick and relieves him of his purse and cash, there is no need for the felon to know his victim or to say: "How are the wife and children, my dear Mr. Simon? Kindly convey my regards to them" before knocking him on the head and robbing him. The word *adversary* has the prefix AD that means *to* and is derived from VERSUS that means against. Someone who is against another is an *adversary* or *enemy*. **Adversary** is therefore the antonym for ally. The prefix AD finds application in so many commonly used words. An adventurer is someone who is inclined to ventures or daring feats. An advocate is someone who speaks or pleads for someone else. The word invent has the prefix IN and comes from the French verb VENIRE that means *come*. An *inventor* is someone who comes into or discovers or is the creator. An inventor has nothing to do with hatred. The words *inspiration* (breathing in), *respiration* (breathing in and out and thus breathing again), *perspiration* (meaning *breathing through* the skin that becomes moist when the activity level goes up substantially) and so on, come from SPIRARE that means *breathe*. The word *conspirator* has the prefix CON that means *together* and thús a conspirator is someone who is breathing against or plotting against someone else. He is one among others who are plotting against someone. He is thus an ally for those with whom he is working.
Flustered	The word *fluster* means *hurry*, *confusion* or *panic*. Someone who has a peg or two more than what he can stomach can also be flustered; alcohol confuses, you know! The opposite of *flustered* is someone who is in command of his senses: someone who is unhurried. Someone who cannot speak is *mute*. Someone who does not speak is also mute just as someone could be a *mute* spectator to another person being robbed whereas he could as well have come to the other's help. A mute person need not be in command of his senses. Either he does not have the faculty of speech or he is so terrified of a person harming another that he is not able to speak. Someone who is **calm** is in charge of his senses. His calmness is deliberate. Thus calm is the antonym of flustered. The word *heavy* means *serious* or something or someone with great *weight*. This has nothing to do with command of senses. A person can be heavy and flustered as well; a drunken fatso is an example to hand. The word *grain* has some interesting shades of meaning. Wheat is a grain and so is corn. This is the usual meaning of the grain that we all know. The other meaning is *constitution* or *texture*. For example, veneers are thin sheets of richly *grained* (or richly *textured*) wood that are glued to furniture to create a superb finish. If a lady finds it difficult to withstand sycophancy because it goes against her *grain*, it means sycophancy is against her *constitution*. The word *ingrained* means *built into the texture or constitution*. If someone wants to please others out of an ingrained habit, it is because the habit to please other is part of his constitution. He is made that way. However, ingrained has little to do with fluster or calm. Either fluster or calm can be ingrained in one's temperament. The word *courageous* is commonly used. It means brave or daring or a quality displayed by someone who faces danger in spite of fear or lack of confidence. Therefore someone *courageous* is not necessarily calm. If he wants to stop someone robbing another, he will have to *rush* to the victim's help. He may have to *bash* the robber. He may have to throw a handy stone at the robber's head.
Waterproof	The word *proof* has several shades of meaning. Some evidence that establishes the validity of an argument is its *proof*. In the printing business, a trial text that has to be checked so as to eliminate errors is the *proof* of that text. As a verb, *to proof* something is to make it impervious

	against another. When you *waterproof* something, it means that it will not allow water to get in. Something that will *allow* water to get through is thus the opposite of waterproof. A soggy soil is one in which it has water in plenty. A soggy shirt is one that is saturated with sweat or water, as the case may be. The soil is soggy because it has not allowed water to *go through*. Its sogginess is because of *retention* of water. Something that is not manmade is *natural*. It can be a lisp. It can be a stutter. It can be a bird. There is nothing to suggest that merely because something is natural it will allow water to pass through. You do not see water entering a camel's mouth and going out through the ears, although the camel is natural. A thin coating of glaze is applied on pottery so as to make it impervious to water. Glaze can be seen on tiles as well. A glaze on a cake, is an icing that is a thin coating of sugar. Something that is unglazed will not necessarily allow water to pass through. Neither will glazed cake or unglazed cake allow water to *pass through*. It will *retain* water and become *soggy*. Try pouring a tumbler of water on a piece of pastry and see for yourself. A fluid – or better still semi-fluid – that seems thick and sticky can be described as a *viscous* fluid. Glycerine is one such fluid. Molasses is a dark-brown viscous liquid obtained as a by-product in the processing of sugar, particularly cane sugar. Something viscous may retain water. Glycerine and molasses will mix with water, for example. Filters of crushed sand or charcoal are used in filtration of water. These filters are *permeable* to water. They allow the water to pass through but the impurities are not allowed to go through. This separates the impurities from the drinking water. **Permeable** is thus the antonym of waterproof.
Accelerate	To *accelerate* when driving is to increase the speed of the vehicle. To accelerate the cure of a disease is to hasten the pace of its cure. The opposite of *accelerate* is *slow down*. When you *swerve* your motorcycle, you change direction or turn rapidly. This may be done at speed as the word *rapidly* suggests. If you slow down and turn, then you *turn* and not *swerve*. When you arouse someone from sleep, you wake up the person who has been in a state of no activity (that sleep essentially is) to a higher state of activity. There is no slowing down; whatever arousal is, it is hastening the pace of activity. The word dispel has the prefix DIS that means *away* and comes from the French PELLERE that means *to drive*. When you *dispel* someone's misconceptions you *drive* them *away*. When a drug *dispels* inflammation, it *drives* the inflammation *away*. One cannot imagine driving something away without hastening the pace. The word *reject,* as we have seen earlier means "*to throw back*" and therefore "*not to accept*". If you do not accept something it is not necessary that you slow down. As a matter of fact, if you are driving and the other persons in the car request you to drive slow, you may *reject* this request and drive on at maybe even a faster pace. The word *retard* comes from the Latin TARDUS that means slow. The prefix RE means *back*. You can go back only to an earlier state. If the earlier state was slow, the present state is fast. So going back from fast to slow would involve reducing the pace. Therefore **retard** is the antonym of *accelerate*.
Emit	The word *emit* has the prefix E (that means *out*) and comes from the Latin root MIT or MISS (that means *send* or *let go*). When you find that someone enjoys *emitting* an air of harshness, it means that the person enjoys *sending out* an impression of harshness. The opposite of *sending out* is *taking in*. The word *absorb* has the prefix AB (that means away from) and is derived from the French verb

	SORBERE that means to suck in. When a handkerchief *absorbs* perspiration, it *sucks in* the perspiration away from the skin. **Absorb** is therefore the antonym of emit. To *demand* means to ask. There is no sucking in. If a child demands attention by crying, is it sucking anything in? A *mistake* is an error and has nothing to do with sucking in or sending out. To *prevent* means to stop from happening. If a bomb disposal expert prevents a bomb from exploding, would he be sucking in either the bomb or its contents? When you require a break from work, you need it. It has nothing to do with sucking in anything.
Metamorphosis	A metamorphosis is a complete change in appearance or condition or character. Someone who has all along been bad-tempered comes back and is cheerful all day ever after attending a programme on self-improvement can be said to have undergone a metamorphosis. The opposite of metamorphosis is no change in form or character or appearance. If a sales representative has been struggling for months and his boss asks him to go on a paid holiday so that he may have some relief from strain, the whole idea is that he should have a change of activity. He should relax. Relaxation will change his form; he may return looking livelier. There is implied change in relief from strain even if the change is short-lived. **Continuation without change** is the opposite of metamorphosis. Cyclical motion by its very nature means change from - say - State A to another state and then another and finally back to State A. Change is, therefore, implicit in cyclical motion. A *dogma* is a *set belief* either authoritatively laid down by a religious authority **or** it may be *an arrogant declaration of opinion*. Dogmatic persistence may involve a change in appearance. For example, if the religious head wants that all men should grow beards, this may in itself means change in appearance. Someone who was clean-shaven only the other day may sport a flowing beard today. Variety is the spice of life. It means change. Varied activity thus cannot be the opposite of metamorphosis.
Dissonance	The word dissonance has the prefix DIS that means *away* and the French SONARE that means *sound*. Something away from sound - that which is not in harmony - is *dissonant* and its quality is *dissonance*. Several other words such as *consonance*, *resonant* and so on can now be understood in all their shades once one is aware of the meanings of the different prefixes and the word SONARE from which these words are derived. The opposite of dissonance is harmony. It would be interesting to see the range of words with the Latin root CORD: some of these words are *accord*, *record*, *discord*, *concord* and so on. The word *concord* has the prefix CON that means *together* and the Latin root CORD that means *heart*. When the hearts are together – meaning there is harmony or agreement – there is **concord**. This then is the antonym of dissonance. *Confederacy* is an alliance. It may be even for an unlawful purpose although not necessarily so. For example the Maratha *Confederacy* in India that comprised of several ruling families, dominated the Indian subcontinent. The purpose of confederacy may however even be unlawful. Two criminals may enter into a confederacy to kill the new entrant into the underworld. Hence the word *harmony* cannot be employed to describe confederacy since the word *harmony* has necessarily positive connotations whereas confederacy has both positive and negative connotations. One comes across collusions where people make false or inflated claims under accident insurance policies and milk the insurance companies. Such frauds are possible because the insurance surveyors and the staff at the insurance companies are in *collusion*. The word *collusion* has necessarily negative implications and therefore although the people in collusion may be working together, the word *harmony* cannot be used to describe their relationships. The word consent means agreement or acquiescence in a proposition. It is possible that a boy may agree to marry someone for whom he has no liking merely because the dowry is attractive. Here there is consent but not harmony.

	The word *contract* has interesting shades of meaning. The prefix CON means together and TRACT means *pull* or *draw*. Thus something that becomes smaller when subjected to cold, *contracts* because its elements *pull together*. When some persons interested to do business with one another sit down together and draw the terms on which they shall be guided in their business dealings, what they *draw together* is the *contract*. However business dealings are meetings of profit motives and not meetings of hearts. There is no place for the word *harmony* in such transactions.
Broach	When a young man plans to settle down in life, he decides to meet her girlfriend's father and *broach* the issue of marriage. What he would do is to *introduce* the topic of marriage in their conversation. When a barrel of wine was *broached* at the festival, it was *broken open* or *pierced*. The opposite of broach is *not to introduce or not to open*. When you keep track of the prices of the shares that you have invested in, you effectively *approach* or *broach* the subject of their prices regularly. If you were to ask your share broker as to "What's with me darlings?" instead of asking for the prices of the particular shares, he will bang the phone down. You have got to be specific. You have to ask about the prices of shares by mentioning the names of the stocks. The stock broker does not know who your darlings are. When you lay claim to being the only person to have eaten a dozen hamburgers at one go, you cannot help *broaching* the issue of the hamburgers. When the Taliban decided to *close off* the Hindu temples in Afghanistan, what they did was to stop any approach to these temples. Thus to **close off** is the opposite of broach. When you *soothe* someone who has just lost a family member, you have to broach the topic of death. There is no way you can comfort or *soothe* someone without raising this issue. When you want to *simplify* the method of working of an arithmetic problem you cannot avoid mentioning the problem.
Ferment	The word *ferment* has some interesting shades of meaning. When you want that the cake batter should *ferment*, you add yeast to it. Yeast, however, is as animate as a human being if not more. But if someone is unable to sleep since his thoughts are in *ferment*, it means that his mind is in a state of *agitation* or *tumult*. The opposite of *ferment* would therefore be *at rest* or *peace* or *calm*. But both *calm* and *peace* are in the context of **mental state** that is the prerogative of animals. A lion can be calm if his interiors are bursting with the meat of a deer that he has just devoured. However his calmness is at his option. He may decide to forget calmness as soon as he is hungry. If you were to try cracking a coconut on the head of a priest in a temple, he could yell with pain. A temple however cannot help being calm even if thousands of coconuts are broken on its floors every day. The temple has no choice. It is inanimate. When you are struck by the *solidity* and magnificence of an ancient fort, you are impressed by its *material strength* or *compactness*. The *solidity* of someone's arguments is the soundness or strength of its reasoning. There can be peace and calm in the fort. However since *calm* or *peace* as opposite to *ferment* is with respect to mental state, *solidity* will not serve as antonym for *ferment*. Purity is a virtue that makes things pure. Therefore, for example, gold can possess purity. But pure gold cannot possess calm or peace with respect to mental state. Something that is easy to understand is *lucid*. If you were to dive into a lagoon and see the plants at its bottom, the waters may be described as *lucid*. *Lucidity* is what makes things lucid but it has nothing to do with *calm* and *peace* in the context of mental state. A lucid explanation is inanimate. It cannot be calm. Glass allows light to pass through and therefore one can see what is at the other end through the glass itself. This property of glass is known as *transparency*. Thus figuratively, if the procedures at a government office are such that there is nothing that you cannot see or nothing that is

	hidden, such procedures are transparent. However neither glass nor procedures are animate and cannot possess either peace or calm with reference to mental state. The mental state in which a person is at peace or is undisturbed is known as *tranquillity*. Since the mind is the prerogative of animals alone, tranquillity is the antonym of *ferment*.
Hapless	Have you noticed that the word *perhaps* means *if by chance something happens*? Have you noticed that the word *mishap* means something that happens by *chance*? Have you noticed that the word *happening* means something that occurs by *chance*? Have you also noticed that the three words that we have just seen have the letters HAP in them? Would it now surprise you to know that if someone is *hapless* it means he is not *lucky*? A hapless person is someone who has no chance. The opposite of *hapless* would then be *lucky* or *fortunate* and so on. When someone is *excited*, his activity level increases. Someone can be excited at the thought of meeting his girlfriend in the park after dark. He can be excited if when he is sitting with his girlfriend, some goons come up to him and mark lecherous remarks about his lady. He in his excited state throws his fists at the goons. The goons bash him to a pulp. Is our friend lucky just because he is *excited*? Suppose someone has long been preparing for a competitive examination. He has been studying hard. He has all his mathematical formulae at his fingertips. He is elated when he enters the examination hall because he is self-assured. Then the first question that turns up in the computer adaptive test is one in which he is asked to say how long was the race in which the gold medallist finished so many meters ahead of the silver medallist and when the silver medallist finished, the bronze medallist was so many meters behind him. He is only told that the three ran at their respective constant speeds. He knows that speed equals distance divided by time. He is not given time, or distance or speed. He has not the foggiest idea of how to proceed. Is he lucky merely because he was *elated* before he entered the examination hall? Fortunate, quite clearly, is the antonym of hapless. While being completely self-reliant is admirable it is not necessary that someone completely self-reliant is that condition at his option. Suppose someone is an orphan. He has no one to pay for his school fees. He then does menial jobs and sleeps in the porch to work his way through. While his industry is admirable, his fortune is certainly not. Suppose the person in the above illustration whom we have seen studying hard were told by the coaching class that now that he knows his mathematical formulae, he can treat success as his. Is he not assured of success? Is he still fortunate?
Plethora	*Plethora* means over-abundance or excess. If you are not able to select a book for self-improvement because there is *plethora* of such books at the bookstore, it means that there are too may of such books or, in other words, there is an excess of such books. The opposite of plethora should therefore be a situation in which there is not enough of something. The word *vacuousness* comes from vacuum. So if someone has a vacuous expression, it means that he seems blank, or deadpan. If, on the other hand, someone is vacuous in your viewpoint, then he is stupid or inane. Someone vacuous has nothing. The absence of something does not qualify for short supply. For obvious reasons, therefore, vacuousness is not the opposite of plethora. Narrowness is the state in which you see something small of breadth or maybe lacking range or width. But just because a garment store sells narrow trousers it does not mean that the store does not have enough of such trousers. *Choice* is something that can be exercised when there is enough to choose from. If you go to a restaurant and the choice is cheese sandwich or bread and

	cheese, it would not require genius to learn that the choice is limited and that the menu at the establishment does not have enough things on offer. If on the other hand the young man who wants a life partner has so many beauties running after him, he – lucky fellow – has *choice*. The word *choice* would therefore remind one of abundance rather than shortage. **Dearth** means scarcity or short supply and thus is the opposite of plethora. The word *confusion* has the prefix CON that means together and the Latin root FUS that means to *pour* or *melt*. When things pour or melt together- like so many choices coming up at the same time - there is confusion. Before you have completed speaking to a lady customer on one phone, the other one rings and before you are through with the second lady customer, the third rings and so on. Unfortunately, you refer to the third caller – a muscular gentleman with a walrus moustache – as *madam*. There is confusion. Confusion also reminds one of abundance.
Posture	To drive home the point that this whole issue of antonyms is more about logic than anything else, it must be noticed that all options are in verb context. It is for this reason that the word *posture* should also be seen in its verb connotation and not noun context. Logic by itself however cannot be of much help unless one is ready with nuances of words in order to cope with questions like this. The word *posture* as a noun means the manner in which one carries oneself (someone may have a hunched posture and another may be ramrod straight) and it may also mean attitude (someone may take up an aggressive posture at the slightest incitation). As a verb *posture* means to *put on airs* or *artificial behaviour* with a view to impress another person. The opposite of the word posture in its verb context would be *not to behave artificially*. One may walk clumsily if he is imitating a clumsy person. Another would walk clumsily because such is his natural manner of walking. What is clumsy is a matter of opinion and circumstance. Someone who walks smartly without a rucksack on his back may walk clumsily if the backpack is too heavy. There is no implied unnaturalness about a clumsy walk. **To behave naturally** is the opposite of posture as a verb. Something that is done on the basis of mere opinion or a whim or fancy is *arbitrary*. If the regime in a nation decides to impose prison sentences without a legal trial on immigrants against whom a native has lodged a police complaint, such sentences would be then be *imposed arbitrarily*. This has nothing to do with natural behaviour. This has to do with behaving *against* the laws of natural *justice* and not about behaving natural *tendencies*. If a political party decides to publicise widely all its achievements, then it uses such media of publicity as are necessary or feasible. The choice could be natural media such as walking from place to place, attracting crowds with whistles and then yelling their achievements to gatherings if the budget does not permit anything beyond. On the other hand there could be radio and television broadcasts and large-scale banquets if the party has enough to spend. However this has nothing to do with natural behaviour simply because natural behaviour is something an individual (and not an organisation) is capable of. Imagine that it is in your nature to provide only broad guidelines and leave details to those whom you nurture. You then send out an office assistant to buy saffron. He comes back with a couple of tons of saffron that costs you the sky. You are on the verge of bankruptcy. Thereafter whenever you send out someone to buy things, you explain carefully as to what he should buy, how much, from where, what quality, what price and so on. Merely because you explain carefully it does not mean that you are behaving naturally.
Noisome	This is a word that is rather easily misunderstood. *Noisy* is what is characterised by excessive noise. Something *noisome* is what stinks to the high heavens. The opposite of noisome is something that is fragrant. The word *subtle* has both positive and negative overtones and means *expertly* or *cleverly* on the one

hand and *artful* or *cunning* on the other. A table tennis player may surprise his opponent with a *subtle* variation in service. Here this subtle variation is possible because of expertise. Some politicians may say one thing while their *subtle* meaning (or cunningly concealed meaning) is something else. Someone who flatters another does it because he has an objective to attain. He cannot afford to make flattery subtle in such a manner that the other person cannot understand it otherwise his efforts may go in vain. Flattering statements – subtle or otherwise - can only be *pleasing* but *not fragrant*.

Someone rushing pell-mell to make use of the water closet may find that someone else has occupied it. He has to wait or in the alternative walk to another one that is a mile away. So he waits patiently. Merely because he is consistently patient, it does not mean that he is fragrant. Sit next to someone in a similar predicament and find out. If a person's skin is softly glowing it means that it has a slight shine about it. Now imagine that this person is the one waiting with consistent patience to make use of the water closet and you will see why something that is softly glowing need not be fragrant as well.

The word gradual is derived from the Latin root GRAD or GRESS that means *step*. AL is a suffix that means *pertaining to*. *Gradual* thus means *step by step*. Something that is gradually diminishing is reducing in intensity in steps and not suddenly.

Imagine that the patience of the fellow waiting for making use of the water closet is now gradually diminishing. Is he necessarily fragrant then?

Attractively **fragrant** is the opposite of noisome.

Abrogate

The word *abrogate* has the prefix AB that means *off* or *away from* and is derived from the Latin ROGARE that means either of (1) *ask* or (2) *propose a law*. This is why *interrogate* means ask someone asking another (the prefix INTER means *between* and ROGARE means *ask*). *Abrogate* therefore means *away from proposing a law* and therefore *cancel* or *repeal* a *law*. The opposite of *abrogate* should be *making a law* or *continuing to recognise the authority granted*.

When a lower court has passed sentence of life imprisonment on an accused and the appellate court decides to *uphold* this judgement, it effectively decides that the sentence be continued without modifications. The higher court does the precise opposite of cancelling the lower court's sentence. Uphold would therefore be the opposite of the word *abrogate*.

The word *defer* has some interesting shades. When you want to delay things you *defer* doing them and thus allot low priority to them. When you meet someone you respect you *defer* to him by bowing your head. Surprisingly one word can mean allotting *low priority* and showing *great respect* in a single breath. This is the beauty of the English language. However to explain these shades of the word defer, DE is the prefix that means *down* and the Latin root FER that means to *carry* or *bring*. When you carry down something in the order in which things are to be done, you *defer* the item. When you *bring down* your head as a mark of respect to someone for whom you have regard, you *defer* to that person. Clearly the word *defer* has nothing to do with granting or cancelling any authority or making/cancelling a law. When you *discuss secretly* you want that none other than you and the chosen few persons should hear what you are saying. If a law or lawfully granted authority has to be cancelled, the fact of its cancellation has to be shouted from the rooftops – if not literally then at least figuratively. Any act passed by the government of a civilised nation has to be published for the knowledge of its citizens in what is known as a gazette. This is because the citizens should know at all times as to what is legal in their country and what is not. There is a basic presumption in law that all citizens are aware of the law of their land and the maxim is *ignorantia juris non excusata* (meaning ignorance of law is not an excuse). No citizen can say after murdering another that he was not aware that murder is a crime in this country or else he would have stopped at slapping the hapless victim. The word *admit* has several shades of meaning that we shall see in this chapter. To admit means to *own* (or accept responsibility for doing

	something) and to *allow in*. When you *admit willingly*, either you willingly own that the windowpane that has been broken is because you clobbered the ball when you were playing cricket in the street or you greet someone who wants to come into your house. This too has nothing to do with granting or cancelling a law or authority. When you read thoroughly, you read every word. This does not mean that reading thoroughly has anything to do with making or cancelling laws. It is common to see old folk sitting on park benches and reading the newspapers so thoroughly that they have got even the advertisements by heart. Are they cancelling any law by reading (newspapers) thoroughly?

Incidentally we have seen the word *dispel* in this exercise. To *dispel* means to drive away. Other words based on the French PELLERE (to drive) are compel, impel, propel and expel. See how the prefixes change the meanings of the words completely. The word *compel* has the prefix COM that means with or together or completely. Thus if you *compel* someone to do something that he does not like, you *force* (or *completely drive*) him to do it. When the schoolmaster expelled a youngster from the class, he *drove* him *out*, as the prefix EX (that means *out*) suggests. When the pump in a machine works as the *impeller*, it *drives* the fluid *in* the machines. Thus to impel someone is to urge someone or incite him whereby you are putting a drive *in* him, as the prefix IM (that means in, suggests).

We have also seen the word *emit* that has the prefix E (that means *out*) and comes from the Latin root MIT or MISS (that means *send* or *let go*). When you find that the streetlights *emit* a vague hum, it means that there is an odd humming sound that the streetlights are *sending out*. There are several commonly used words based on this root MIT or MISS. The core words of this root are: *admit, commit, dismiss, emit, missile, permit,* and *transmit.*

Admit literally means "to let go"; it is used to mean "to let in; to allow to join; to grant something as true."

The words based on admit are	That mean
Admissible	Allowable
Inadmissible	Not allowable
Admission	The act of admitting; permission to get in; a confession
Admittance	The right to enter a place; entrance

The word commit literally means "to send together" but is now "to do; to entrust to the care of someone or something; to devote oneself to some issue; to place someone in custody, for example in a mental asylum or jail." Words based on **commit** are:

Commission that means *entrusting to someone*; *an authority granted to act as specified*; *performing*; *a fee* given to an agent for services rendered

Committee that means a group of persons asked to report on some matter

The word *dismiss* means "to send away; to discharge from service; to order someone to go or be removed; to reject. A word based on *dismiss* is *dismissal*, meaning " the act of dismissing or the state of being dismissed."

A *missile* is "something that can be sent; any object intended to be thrown; a guided rocket."

Omit means "not to include; leave out." A word based on *omit* is *omission*, meaning "the act of omitting; something that has not been included."

Permit is "to send or let someone or something to go through; to allow."

Words based on *permit* are	That mean
Permissible	Something that can be allowed
Permission	The act of allowing; a formal consent
Permissive	Granting permission; lenient

To *transmit* means "to send across; to send something from one place to another; to pass on a message, disease etc." Words based on *transmit* are:

Transmitter – a device by which news are sent across; it is also a person who passes on news, disease, information etc.

Transmission – the act of transmitting; that which is transmitted; the system in an automobile that sends motive power from the engine to its wheels.

Please see the following sentences that have these core words from the Latin root MIT or MISS in context that makes it so easy to understand and appreciate their different shades of meanings:

1. The club may not **admit** you if you are not in a formal dress.
2. He will get **admission** to the school only on the basis of his performance at a written test.
3. You will have to **admit** that you were wrong in your diagnosis in this case.
4. I would not **commit** such a mistake again.
5. The charges against him being proved, the judge **committed** him to prison.
6. He was **commissioned** into the Philippines Army as an officer in 1985.
7. The bank charges **commission** for issuing drafts.
8. A **commission** was appointed to investigate the Stock Market scandal.
9. The opposition leader heads the Public Enterprises **Committee** of the Parliament.
10. All purchases exceeding $2000 per instance can be made only after obtaining the written approval of the Purchases **Committee**.
11. The clerk who was involved in the bank fraud has been **dismissed** from service.
12. He would **dismiss** any suggestion to reduce his jurisdiction.
13. Any public servant convicted of a crime, faces **dismissal**.
14. That car does not **emit** much smoke.
15. When the bullet hit him, he **emitted** a cry of pain and sank to the ground.
16. If the car's **emission** exceeds the norm, the Transport Commissioner will not register it.
17. The boy sent out a paper **missile** with a rubber band that he quickly hid.
18. "Apollo 12" was the first manned **missile** to land on the moon.
19. I would suggest that you **omit** sugar from your diet; it may help control weight.
20. His **omission** from the team comes as a surprise.
21. The college would **permit** entry only to those who have a visitor's pass.
22. I would **permit** you to raise questions, but only after the lecture is complete.
23. A foreigner's working in this country is **permissible** only if he has a valid visa.
24. He asked for **permission** to state his case before the court.
25. The telex machine can **transmit** messages rapidly.
26. This is a facsimile **transmission**; the original document will arrive in post.
27. There is nothing wrong with the car's engine but the **transmission** has a problem.
28. You can **remit** money now through the Internet.
29. Radio **transmission** of the President's nationwide address is scheduled for 8 p.m. tonight.
30. He has been able to achieve so much as a result of **unremitting** effort.

We could now look up the dictionary to see the meanings of the following words: Emissary, Intermission, Intermittent, Missionary, Missive, Remiss, Remission and Remit.

We have also seen the word *concord* in the above exercise and the detailed explanations. The word comes from the Latin root CORD that means heart. Several other words flow from this root. The three core vocabulary words from CORD are *cordial*, *accord*, and *record*.

Cordial is CORD + the Latin suffix IAL (meaning *pertaining to*); *cordial* thus means *pertaining to the heart; warm and hearty; friendly and sincere*; the noun *cordial* means *a stimulating drink; a medicine given as a stimulant for the heart or circulation.* A word based on *cordial* is *cordiality* that means *warmth of feeling.*

Accord comes from the Latin prefix AC (meaning *to; at*) and CORD; *accord* thus literally means *at heart* or as a verb it means to *be of one heart or mind*; as a noun it means *harmony; agreement.* The words based on accord are:

Words based on *accord* are	That Mean
Accordance	Agreement; harmony; conformity
According	On the authority of; as stated by
Accordingly	Consequently; correspondingly

Record is the Latin prefix RE (meaning *back; again*) + the root CORD (meaning *heart*); *to record* thus means *to put something in the heart or mind again, as by writing it down.* Thus *record* means *to write down, for preserving an account of something; register in permanent form.* As a noun, *record* means *a written or permanent account,* as a grooved disc *that reproduces sound.*

1. They gave us a **cordial** welcome.
2. I find lemon **cordial** most refreshing, particularly during summers.
3. Her tastes **accord** with mine.
4. I shall act in **accordance** with your instructions.
5. **According** to me, we should not go out in this weather.
6. There will be dignitaries at tonight's function, so please dress **accordingly**.
7. Our teacher wanted us to **record** our impressions of the trip to the science fair.
8. You will be considered for promotions only if your **record** is satisfactory.
9. My sister presented me with a **record** of instrumental music played by a renowned orchestra.
10. The Imperialists sowed the seeds of **discord** between the two communities.

You will recall seeing the word *gradual* in this exercise and an explanation of why it means step by step. The word *gradual* is derived from the Latin root GRAD or GRESS that means *step*. The core words in the vocabulary that flow from this root are: *aggression, gradual, graduate, progress.*

Aggression is the Latin prefix AG (meaning *to; toward*) + the Latin root GRESS (meaning *to step or go*) + the suffix ION (meaning *the act or state of*); *aggression* means *to take a step toward someone:* the stance or attitude of *an attack.*

Words based on *aggression* are	That Mean
Aggressive	Characterized by vigorous activity; disposed to forceful approach or attack
Aggressor	A person who attacks

Gradual is the Latin root GRAD (meaning *to step or go*) + the suffix AL (meaning *pertaining to*); *gradual* means *moving or changing slowly, step by step* (and therefore *slowly*).

Graduate is the Latin root GRAD (meaning *to step or go*) + the suffix ATE (meaning *to take or make*); graduate means *to take a step* (out of the college after successful completion of the study programme); *to receive a diploma or degree for completing a course of study at a school or college.* A word based on *graduate* is *graduation*, meaning *the act of graduating; a ceremony at which degrees or diplomas are awarded;* it also means *calibration of an instrument such as scale, thermometer etc. wherein if the temperature rises, there are steps on the thermometer that indicate the temperature.*

Progress is PRO, the Latin prefix meaning *forward* + GRESS the Latin root GRESS, meaning *to step or go*; *progress* is *step forward; advancement; improvement.*

Words based on *progress* are	That Mean
Progression	An act of progressing; an advancing sequence
Progressive	Moving forward; aiming at progress

Take a look at the following sentences wherein the different words flowing from the root GRAD or GRESS are used in context. This contextual use should be able to convey the various shades of meaning of these words.

1. **Aggression** is round the corner, with the enemy moving troops close to the border.
2. What your company needs is an **aggressive** sales effort.
3. Our brave army has defeated the **aggressors**.
4. There seems to be a **gradual** change in him for the better.
5. He **graduated** this year in science.
6. My son **graduated** at the top of his class in engineering.
7. The thermometer was **graduated** in centigrade.
8. The tax slabs are **graduated**; higher the income, higher the tax incidence.
9. What is the **progress** in your project so far?
10. We must step up the pace of **progress** to start commercial production by the month end.
11. The series 7,14,21, 28 is a mathematical **progression**.
12. There has been **progressive** increase in the level of noise pollution here.

Now that we know that the root GRAD, GRESS means *to step or go*, you could analyse the words in the table given below and write down their possible meanings. You could then look up the dictionary and see their meanings and see how effective is this method of learning. This will teach us to refer to the dictionary. The pencil and the jotter will never let you down. The need for reference to the dictionary will diminish once we write things down after we have learnt them.

To kick off, the word *digress* should mean *step away from* and therefore *stray from* the topic or chosen route. Check this in a dictionary and verify whether it is correct. It should be fun deriving the meanings of words from their roots.

The Word	The meaning of the word according to your analysis of the word after knowing the meaning of the root GRAD or GRESS
Digress	
Digression	
Digressive	
Regress	
Regression	
Regressive	
Transgress	
Transgression	
Transgressor	

The Latin root FER means *to carry; bring.* The core words are: *confer, differ, offer,* and *transfer*.

Confer is the Latin prefix CON (meaning *together with*) + the Latin root FER (meaning *to carry; bring*): *confer* literally means *to carry or bring together* or *to give or bestow* or *to consult together.* A word based on *confer* is *conference* which means *a formal meeting to discuss some important issue.*

Differ is the Latin prefix DIF (meaning *apart*) + the root FER (meaning *to carry; bring*); *differ* means *to carry oneself apart from others; to disagree; not to be like others.* Another word based on *differ* is *difference* which means *the state of being unlike others; a distinguishing trait.*

Offer is the Latin prefix OF (meaning *before*) + the root FER (meaning *to carry; bring*); *offer* means – literally- *to bring something before someone* or *to propose*; as a noun it means *a proposal.* A word based on *offer* is *offering* meaning *that which is offered; a gift offered to a place of religious worship;* it may also mean flowers offered in a temple.

Transfer is the Latin prefix TRANS (meaning *across*) + the root FER (meaning *to carry; bring*); *transfer* means *to carry across; to cause the title of goods, property to pass from one person to another; to move from one place to another.*

Words based on *transfer* are	That Mean
Transferable	That which can be transferred
Non-transferrable	That which cannot be transferred
Transference	The act of transferring

Take a look at the following sentences wherein the different words flowing from the root FER are used in context. This contextual use should be able to convey the various shades of meaning of these words.

1. He decided to **confer** his property to the orphanage.
2. The President of India **conferred** the Padma Bhushan on Pandit Ravi Shankar, the great musician.
3. The Police Commissioner held an emergency **conference** with his deputies to decide plans to cope with the sudden outbreak of riots.
4. The look-alike twins **differ** in eating habits.
5. His judgement on the case **differs** from the other two judges on the Bench.
6. His **offer** at the auction of the mansion was the highest.
7. Since he was unwell, I **offered** to take him to the hospital.
8. My uncle **offered** me a ride on his new motorcycle.
9. It is normal for devotees to make an **offering** of their hair at the Tirupati temple in India.
10. The citizens protested against the Municipal Commissioner's **transfer**.
11. The company **transferred** him to Hong Kong.
12. A promissory note is **transferable** by endorsement and delivery.

You may like to see some more words that are based on the root FER on the next page. See if you can derive their meanings from your understanding of the root FER and the prefixes and suffixes. You may then check what you have derived with a dictionary and see how effective is the method of learning the meanings of words from their roots.

The Word	The meaning of the word according to your analysis of the word after knowing the meaning of the root FER
Deferential	
Prefer	
Preference	
Preferential	
Refer	
Reference	
Referendum	
Sufferance	Here the prefix SUF is a variant of the prefix SUB that means *under*.

We now move on to the Third of our practice sessions with antonyms. Given below are words for which the antonyms have to be located from among the five options against the words in the tables.

The Word	Option1	Option2	Option3	Option4	Option5
Boisterous	Grateful	Angry	Clever	Frightened	Quiet
Jabber	Tickle	Argue	Stroke	Speak slowly	Joke inaptly
Amalgamate	Separate	Fixate	Terminate	Calibrate	Correlate
Endorse	Provoke criticism	Receive payment	Submit unwillingly	Oppose publicly	Perform quickly
Gist	Artificial manner	Trivial point	Informal procedure	Eccentric method	Singular event
Anarchy	Courtesy	Hope	Order	Neutrality	Importance
Breach	Garner	Solder	Keep silent	Move forward	Give approval
Extant	Extensive	Extraneous	Extricable	Extinct	Extra
Spiritual	Eclectic	Figurative	Ephemeral	Immoral	Corporeal
Incursion	Loss of respect	Lack of resolve	Reparation	Relapse	Retreat
Tractability	Infertility	Implausibility	Incorrigibility	Impenetrability	Indefatigability
Savant	Flatterer individual	Bore	Unlearned person	Unprincipled	Misunderstood advisor
Aver	Collect	Augment	Placate	Deny	Encourage
Facetious	Lugubrious	Contentious	Ingenious	Prodigious	Audacious

Herein below are the answers and the detailed explanations as to why a particular word or phrase is the apt choice for the antonym for the given word and why the others are not. The idea in giving the complete picture and not just the correct option is to be able to develop the analytical ability that would make it possible to eliminate the wrong choices by sheer reasoning instead of guessing. No matter how intelligent the guess, it remains a guess, which is a matter of speculation no matter how intelligently done. In the converse nothing can be above reasoning. If your reasoning skills were sharply honed, there would be no need to guess and be at the mercy of chance. This is the reason why it is strongly recommended that you go through the explanatory answers regardless of whether you are right or wrong.

There would be another thing that you will notice as you go along. Knowledge of the origin of some core words in the English language can help you tell as to what should be its meaning and the shades of the meaning even if you come across a word that you have not heard before. This knowledge would be an invaluable help in any examination where the extent of one's awareness of a language is tested. Mugging long lists of words without contextual usage is an exercise in futility. The earlier one understands this, the better it is. If your mental axe is sharp, there is no need to worry whether your axe can cut an elm after you have been able to bring an ash tree to the ground with a resounding crash. **The sharp axe will cut anything**, whether it is a matchstick or a redwood tree.

We have put together the various roots of the English language with their core words and their contextual usage in sentences to drive home not only the meaning of a particular word but also its nuances.

The Given Word	Detailed Explanation as to why not any of the other words would fit as the antonym of the given word and what the other words mean (with contextual usage)
Boisterous	The word *boisterous* has both positive and negative overtones. Someone who is excessively cheerful and lively can be described as *boisterous*. A party where there is loud laughter and great cheer can be described as a *boisterous* party. Someone who speaks in a rough and loud tone can be described as *boisterous*. The opposite of this would be someone or something that is *not* loud. When someone obliges you or helps you, you thank him. This is because you are grateful for the help. Anyone incapable of gratitude is not capable of any noble human sentiment. Yet it is not necessary that gratitude be expressed in soft tones alone. Suppose a helicopter flies overhead and drops food packets to people marooned in rising floodwaters of the river on whose banks they reside, if there is any way of ensuring that the expression of gratitude (from the people who have picked up the food packets) reaches the pilot's ears, it is shouting till the heavens tremble. Anger raises voices. Someone angry is most likely to be loud. It is not necessary that clever people are always soft-spoken. If you were to see the annual function at a medical college, the young medicos in the making may bring the ceiling down with shouts of *encore* (or *once more!*) after a particularly entertaining performance. The Parliament in session, now televised in most countries, is another illustration of this. Are the parliamentarians not clever? Merely because someone is frightened it does not mean that there will be no shouting. In fact people are known to have screamed loud enough to pierce onlookers' eardrums when frightened. Someone who is not noisy is quiet. This is the opposite of boisterous.
Jabber	When someone speaks rapidly and in a manner that you cannot understand what he is saying, you ask him to quit *jabbering*. The opposite of this is speaking in a manner such that you can understand exactly what he is saying. Senseless talk can also be jabber even if it is fluent. There are various ways in which people can be tickled. One is to run fingers softly along someone's soles. The sensation resulting from this is tickling and may cause laughter. The other is intellectual tickling such as asking brainteasers and so on. When someone tickles another it is not necessary that he should say anything at all, leave alone *slowly*. There are two principal ingredients to an argument: logic and volume. People take recourse to shouting after the logic in their arguments is over. Thus volume is always at the expense of logic. So long as there is logic, one may speak in a cohesive and lucid manner. Once this is exhausted, people may, in all probability, jabber when they argue. When someone *strokes* the fur of one's pet cat and talks to the pet, it is not necessary that he should speak at all. But even if he speaks, whatever he speaks will seem Double Dutch to the pet, which can understand no human language. Only human beings can speak. When a human being speaks slowly and in a language that the person to whom he is speaking can understand, what he speaks will not be jabber. Thus when you **speak slowly**, you do not jabber. **You make sense**. Imagine that there is a funeral procession. The pallbearers are carrying the coffin. The relatives are wiping their eyes. Someone decides to relate a quip about the corpse having woken up when

<table>
<tr><td></td><td>the coffin banged against a low tree. He will be lucky if people do not slap him for his inapt (or inappropriate) joke. To joke inaptly is the same thing as to jabber.</td></tr>
<tr><td>Amalgamate</td><td>The prefix A has several shades of meaning. It can mean intensify such as in amass (which is an intensification of mass when one can amass wealth) or both intensify and be off from as in abandon (which means intense joy and also to go away from). The word amalgam is derived from the French AMALGAMARE that means to mix thoroughly. Somebody can be said to be an amalgam of wit and elegance if the two qualities are intensely mixed in his character. Mercury, the only liquid metal, has the property of amalgamating with several metals except iron and platinum. This is why mercury is used for extracting gold from its ore; the amalgam is distilled after amalgamation to extract gold.
The opposite of mix thoroughly is to separate.

When you pour kerosene into water, it does not mix. Something is separate if it is not mixed and thus to separate is the opposite of amalgamate.

The suffix ATE is used to form verbs such as donate, orate, create and so on. It is known as verb suffix. To make stable or fixed is to fixate. When a baby's attention is fixated on a toy elephant he does not amalgamate with the toy or else the baby would probably need to be distilled to bring him back to human form.
When some rail line comes to an end at a junction, it terminates there. When a business contract is terminated, there is no more business agreement thereafter. To terminate is to bring to end. Have we not seen the star sign Libra? It means the scales. How does one know how many pounds does a thing weigh when it is put on the scales? One learns from the markings on the scales. These markings are known as calibrations. To calibrate is to make marks telling us measures. When you calibrate the scale, the markings do not mix with the scale because if they did there would be no way to know what is what.

When you see some known face on a train you try to correlate the person with the face. Then it strikes you that this is the fellow who used to flick the sandwiches from your lunchbox at school. Does the fellow mix with the face (or with the sandwiches for that matter) because you have been able to correlate him?</td></tr>
<tr><td>Endorse</td><td>The word endorse comes from the word DORSDUM that means back. When you sign on the back of a cheque, you endorse the cheque thereby authorising someone else of your choice to receive the value in that cheque. It has your approval. You have backed it. When you endorse someone's views, you back or support his views. The opposite of endorse would thus be to oppose.

You can oppose something if the action is incomplete or there is room for retraction or modification. Suppose someone publishes something inflammatory about some religious practices. It can provoke criticism. It cannot be opposed because the act of publishing is complete. A movie is released. It has obscene material. It can be criticised but not opposed. It is released.
When you receive payment for a cheque, for instance, there can be no opposition to this. The matter is over.

When someone pays some unreasonable tax after raising objections, he can be said to have submitted unwillingly. But even the act of paying tax is complete. On the other hand, if people rise against this tax and decide that none shall pay it and the matter shall be taken to the streets, there is opposition to the tax because it is not paid.
To oppose publicly is not to approve. This is the opposite of an endorsement.

Imagine some freshman being ragged by the seniors and is asked to shave his head. Imagine that he shaves his head quickly. He has performed quickly something that he has been asked to do</td></tr>
</table>

	whether willingly or otherwise. But the act of shaving the head is complete. There is only compliance, no opposition.
Gist	Imagine that the *gist* (or *central idea*) of someone's lecture is: how to speak effectively in public. You reach late and find that the speaker is summarising his lecture as follows: (A) one must prepare talking points beforehand (B) one must use simple language (C) one must not repetitively keep saying "you know" and "you see" (D) one must be able to judge from the faces in the audience whether they are enjoying or bored. You get the *gist* (or *main part*) of what he is saying. Something that is *not the main part* is the opposite of *gist*. Oxygen is not visible. It is a part of the air. Yet it is needed for giving artificial respiration to patients. It has to be extracted from the air in an *artificial manner*. The artificial manner is the only way to get oxygen into a bottle for giving artificial respiration. Here the artificial manner *itself* is the gist of bottling oxygen. Not only it is the main way of doing so, it is the *only* manner. Nothing can be more central than *only*. Imagine that there is a drama being enacted. Some greatly talented actor is playing the part of an army lieutenant colonel. He has the crowd in tears. On the way out from the auditorium, somebody says that the play was just about average since they had not taken care to see to details as seen from the fact that the insignia on the actor's uniform was that of a full colonel and not a lieutenant colonel. The point that this person is making is trivial or unimportant in the context of the superb and convincing role-play. A trivial point is thus the opposite of the gist. Imagine that you are an ace at computer software design. A company in this line needs your services. You meet the company's top management who have invited you to dinner and cocktails. The procedure of interview is informal because *you are being sought*. Here the informal procedure is the *only* way in which this exercise can be conducted. If on the other hand you were to be a fresh graduate with no practical experience responding to an advertisement for a job, it is unlikely that your interview would be informal. Something *odd* or *whimsical* is *eccentric*. Imagine that an old lady's sons have taken her to a psychologist for consultation. They think she is an odd person and needs therapy. The psychologist asks her what she has been doing so that they think she is odd. They tell him that she has been making omelettes. He then asks them what do they have against her making omelettes because he likes making omelettes himself. The old lady then tells the psychologist that he must visit her place. She has trunks and trunks full of omelettes. Now the psychologist realises that the *gist* of the whole thing is that the old lady has gone nuts. She is an eccentric. However she can be considered eccentric or whimsical if eccentricity or whimsicalness is her principal aspect. Something *singular* is that which is *unique* or *extraordinary*. Imagine that a uniformed officer has been scratching his shins everyday till they bleed after he takes off the socks that he has to wear as a part of his uniform. Now imagine that a witch doctor rubs some ointment on his feet and then chants some mantra. Oodles of little worms emerge from his shins. It may be the ointment alone that may have done the trick. The mantras may have had little role to play in the episode. Yet, he is cured. This is an *abnormal*, *extraordinary* or *singular event*. Yet it is not *trivial* by any stretch of imagination.
Anarchy	The word *arch* means principal or main. So many commonly used words flow from the Latin root ARCH that means *the one who rules* and ARCHY that means *a system of rule*. Some of these are *monarch*, *patriarch*, *matriarch*, *monarchy*, *oligarchy* and so on. If you see the words *anhydrous* (that means *without* water) and *anaerobic* (that means *without* oxygen), *anaesthesia* (that means *without* sensation), it is not too difficult to understand that the prefix AN means *without*. Therefore *anarchy* is a situation where there is no rule or order. The opposite of anarchy is a situation in which there is rule or order.

	The word *courtesy* means politeness. Some companies show their politeness and goodwill to those who offer business to them by offering gifts. Thus if a government official goes on a foreign jaunt *courtesy* a company that has substantial dealings with the government, it means that the foreign trip is funded by the company.
	If at the end of an enthralling recital there is a huge applause for the singer, then the singer may *courtesy* to the crowd by bowing to them. It is essentially a voluntary act. The word *courtesy* therefore does not mean rule or order.
	Someone may *hope* for winning a lottery. He buys a lottery ticket. But there is no rule that whoever buys a lottery ticket must win it. Thus *hope* cannot be the opposite of *anarchy.*
	Since *anarchy* means the absence of order, the word order is the opposite of anarchy. When order prevails, so does the rule of law.
	Two men are fighting like madmen over some land. A third takes no sides and thus maintains *neutrality* to the fight because he thinks it is not his business at all. Yet the fight is indicative of lack of order.
	Imagine that there is a famine. Food is scarce. There is strict rationing. Yet someone is able to get more than his share because he is in a position of importance. The rule is that only fixed quantities would be given irrespective of a person's social standing. Yet *importance* is what is helping the fellow bend the rules. The rule might prevail by and large but not for him.
Breach	Imagine that there is a canal flowing through farmland. If you wish to draw water from the canal, you have to pay for the water. Some farmer wishes to draw the water but not pay for it. He then breaks the canal wall adjacent to his field. He thus *breaches* the canal. The opposite of *break* is to *join*.
	Imagine that there is prohibition in a state. Yet somebody brews liquor. He has committed a *breach* of the law by breaking it.
	The word *garner* comes from the *granary*, which is a storehouse for grain. If squirrels *garner* nuts for the long winter, they *collect* food for the days when none will be available. They are not *joining* the nuts.
	Solder is a metal alloy usually of tin and lead used for *uniting* or *joining* less fusible metals under heat conditions. On an exceptionally cold day, when you see a young lady passing by with her frozen fingers soldered to her fruit basket, the fingers are (figuratively of course) are so firmly fixed to the basket that they seem joined to the basket. Solder is the opposite of breach.
	You may *unite* with a cause by demonstrating with those who are protesting against some action. But if you keep silent, it may not necessarily mean that you are united with the protestors. Your silence may be because of fear of reprisal. Your silence may be due to your being in favour of the action against which there is protest but you do not want to be singled out as one in favour of something that lots of people are protesting.
	One who may be promoted in an organisation would *move forward* in the hierarchy. This does not mean he is being united with the company staff. He may already be united and it is because of his commitment to the company that he is moving forward.
	When you *give approval*, you signify that you are in favour of the proposed course of action. It may so happen that there may be an isolated instance of someone approving the proposal whereas there may be a public outcry against it.
Extant	If the country's *extant* laws require that immigrants have to seek a work permit before they can take up a job, it means that a work permit is a must for immigrants (who wish to take up employment) under the *prevailing* laws. Something *in existence* or something *current* is *extant.* The opposite of this is something that is not prevailing.

	A garden is *extensive* if it occupies a large space. Some lecture that has been going on for very long is *extensive*. If some scientists have done *extensive* research on the medicinal properties of turmeric, they have done *comprehensive* research. These contextual usages convey the shades of meaning of the word *extensive*. Something that is extensive may or may not be prevailing. If two nations were engaged in an extensive battle before they signed a peace agreement, the battle is over now. It is not prevalent. Imagine that Mr. A is seeking admission to an educational institution. He has done extremely well at the entrance test as well as at the interview. Someone with a lower score than Mr. A's is admitted because his father is a top bureaucrat and Mr. A is sidelined. This means that the chap who has been admitted has been granted admission on *extraneous* considerations. This is because the score at the entrance test and the performance at the interview is the main criteria whereas the parentage of the person admitted is not the main criteria. If water is filtered, this is because mud is considered *foreign* or *extraneous* to water. Something can be extraneous provided it is in existence. Something that is not prevalent cannot be extraneous simply because it is not there. If someone has been sinking in a waterlogged patch of land, then he can be *extricated* from the quagmire by throwing a rope to him. Something that can be *extricated* is *extricable*. However the fellow in our story sinking in the sand must be alive or must be prevalent (meaning visible above the surface) so that he can be extracted because only then can he make use of the rope thrown to him. After he is not prevalent, he can only be fished out. Amen! You are on a visit to Mongolia and the guide tells you that some tribe in Lower Mongolia is now *extinct*. It means that you cannot meet any member of this tribe because they are all lounging in Heaven. Extinct is the precise opposite of extant. Imagine that you are eating at a fast food joint. The pizza that you have ordered has *extra* cheese in the topping. But something extra has got to be prevalent at the very least. In fact it is more than what should be normally prevalent.
Spiritual	Man has two kinds of needs: *material* (such as food, shelter, clothing, wealth and so on) and *spiritual* (such as peace of mind, love from the family, respect in society, religion and so on). The *material* needs are all tangible (meaning things that can be touched by the hand) whereas the *spiritual* needs are intangible (meaning things that can be felt only by the mind or soul but not by the hand). Clearly the opposite of spiritual is material or something that has form or shape and can be touched by the hand. The origin of the word *eclectic* comes from a Greek word that means to *select* and is used to describe philosophers who selected such doctrines that pleased them from different schools of thought. The word eclectic has now come to mean *wide-ranging*, *broad-based* or *liberal*. A *doctrine* as you know is a general principle or belief that a religion lays down for its followers to follow. But you cannot see or touch a *doctrine*. When you see an elephant at the zoo and hail "Hey, elephant! Want a banana?" you are being literal. There is no comparison of the elephant with anything else. But suppose you are talking to some friends about someone whose name you have forgotten but who weighs thrice as much as she should and refer to her as *the elephant*, you are being figurative. You are using figures or are being symbolic in your speech. But just because something is figurative it does not prevent it from being tangible. As a matter of fact if someone were to meet the bulky lady whom he has been figuratively referring to as *the elephant* and ask her if she has broken loose from the zoo, he might get to see that she is certainly very tangible; her slap will leave a cherry-red impression on his cheek. Some moths have very short lives. They are described as *ephemeral*. Thus something that is short-lived or transitory is known as *ephemeral*. Imagine that you are walking along a dried riverbed. There is a heavy cloudbank. Imagine that there is a sudden cloudburst and a tremendous

	amount of rain. Suddenly there is a gush of water. The river comes alive. Imagine the situation a few days later when there is sunshine but no river. The river is *ephemeral*. The river, even if ephemeral, is eminently tangible. If you do not get out of the way of the rushing waters, you might find yourself swimming for dear life in its swirling waters. Someone or something that does not adhere to morals (or accepted principles of virtuous and upright behaviour) is *immoral*. However virtue is not tangible and so also is its lack. The word *corporeal* comes from the French CORPUS that means *body*. Thus something that has body and form is called *corporeal*. It is eminently tangible. The fat lady whom our friend in a previous paragraph has just asked whether she would like him to escort her back to her rightful place in the zoo is *corporeal*. She is tangible. See the mark her fingers have left on our friend's cheek. Thus **corporeal** is the opposite of spiritual.
Incursion	The word incursion comes from the Latin root CUR that means *to run* or *go*. Thus incur means *to go* or *run into*. When you hit the ball for a six while playing cricket in the street and shatter someone's windowpane, he would like you to know that you have *incurred* (meaning *run into*) his displeasure by chasing you with his heftiest walking stick in his hand eager to establish contact with your back. When you want to *assault* someone else, you have to run into him. No one generally walks up to be bashed. An *incursion* is a *raid*, *invasion*, *assault* or *attack*. The opposite of an incursion is *to go* or *run away from*. When someone who is respected for his integrity and uprightness is caught in a trap laid by the Anti-Corruption Bureau, it means *loss of respect* for him. However loss of respect is not the same thing as running away from something. Respect is not something actual. It cannot run away from someone. It has neither any feet nor any transportation mode. When someone cannot make up his mind as to what to do, he is said to have *lack of resolve*. Now imagine that a young lad goes to the railway station and is considering whether to take the first train or the second. Before he can resolve the issue, the first train goes away. Time and tides wait for no one. Nor do trains. He takes more time to make up. The second train has also run away. The next train is due next morning. When the fellow has lack of resolve, *he* does not run away from anything but other things such as opportunities run away from him. At the end of the First World War, Germany the defeated country signed the Armistice (peace agreement, in other words). They accepted to make reparations, thereby agreeing to make monetary compensation for things that they had destroyed: houses, trains, ships, and so on. *Reparation* comes from the word *repair* that means *to mend*. It therefore means *compensation* or *redress*. When you make reparation, you are *running towards* something that you ought to do, not *running away* from something. When a fellow has malaria, he takes medicine. He is then asked to take *prophylactics* (medicines that will ensure that the disease does not occur or recur). He does not take these prophylactics. The disease recurs. He has a *relapse* of malaria. When there is a relapse, the disease *runs towards* the person once again. Imagine that an army is fighting the enemy army. There is heavy casualty on the side of Army A. It feels that it has had enough of punishment from Army B. Army A then decides to *retreat* (or *run away*) from Army B. **Retreat** is the opposite of incursion.
Tractability	We have in this exercise seen the words *contract*, *tractor*, *detract* and so on that flow from TRACT that means to *pull* or *draw*. Something that is easily pulled is *tractable*. Its quality is *tractability*. Something that is manageable or obedient has tractability. An obedient person can be easily *drawn in*. His wife tells him in the middle of a card game that it is time for dinner and he is drawn in because he is tractable. Something that is not obedient or cannot be managed trait which is opposite to the quality of tractability. It is not possible to *draw* it *in* easily. The opposite of *tractable* is *obstinate* or *recalcitrant* or *disobedient*.

	Imagine that a farmer has been sowing seeds on a patch of land. He waits for days and weeks but nothing grows. He then concludes that the soil has *infertility* or is incapable of producing. The soil is not disobedient. It breaks when he puts in the plough. It absorbs the water that he puts in. It merely produces nothing. He can *draw* nothing from it: in or out. Someone tells you that he has just returned from an overseas trip. You ask him how long it took for him to get a passport. He says that he did not need a passport since he was invited by the government of that country to lecture to the university professors there about quantum mechanics. You start smiling at how he has been fibbing. You then ask him as to what is the meaning of the words *quantum mechanics*. He tells you that they are automobile mechanics of great physical size. You start roaring with laughter. His tale is *implausible* or *unbelievable*. His yarn has the quality of *implausibility*. He is *easily getting drawn into* questions and then ridicule when he displays implausibility. We are looking for the opposite of someone who can be easily drawn in. The word *incorrigibility* comes from *corrigible*. It has both positive and negative implications. Someone with whom you cannot find a fault is incorrigible. If a physician has great command over forensic medicine (the branch of medicine dealing with its application in detection of crime where – for example – an expert can match the hair that the victim had clutched during the scuffle, with the hair on the head of the murder suspect and confirm or otherwise that the accused is indeed the murderer) his statement in court during the trial can be *incorrigible*, meaning his analysis is so good that you cannot find fault with it. If someone has taken to drinking and his wife has been pleading with him to give up this bad habit. He does stay off for a few days. He then starts drinking with renewed vigour. He is *incorrigible* or his habit cannot be corrected. He does not obey. His **incorrigibility** is the opposite of tractability. His wife cannot aspire to *draw him in* and share with her the joys of sipping – say - lemonade instead. The drunk *cannot be drawn in* while he is hitting the bottle with his friends. He is *obstinate*. If the forest in an area is so thick that it is not possible to go deep inside, it is *impenetrable*. If a mystery is so great that it cannot be understood then it is *impenetrable*. Impenetrability is the quality that makes things impenetrable just as stupidity makes people stupid. The opposite of tractability is some quality that makes things easy to draw away. If a mystery is impenetrable, what can you expect to *draw* from it, let alone *in* and *easily*? The word *indefatigability* comes from FATIGUE that means tiredness. Something that cannot be easily tired is *indefatigable*. Someone who wants to get into a prestigious medical school studies hard for the entrance test. He fails the first time. He then studies even harder for the second attempt. He fails again. He studies like a man possessed for the third trial. His parents try to persuade him to switch to fine arts. They try to *draw* him *in*. He says no. He will have nothing other than medical education even if he has a white beard when he gets through the entrance test. He is *indefatigable*. He cannot get tired of trying. But suppose his parents ask him to drink a glass of milk (that he hates) before going to bed and he complies without a whimper. He is still *tractable*.
Savant	The French language has given so many words to the English language. Unlike the English language that has only one verb – *to know* for knowing something or someone, the French language has two separate verbs: SAVOIR (used in context of knowing *things*) and CONNAITRE (used in the context of knowing *human beings*). The word *savant* is used to describe a learned person. The opposite of a savant is someone who is not learned. Imagine that a university vice-chancellor is due to retire from service. He is to be replaced. The state education minister shall decide finally as to who will be the next man in. Now imagine that a professor sidles up to the minister at a function and tells him that the state has been doing so well in the education field after the minister has taken office and that he hopes that in the forthcoming elections he wins and continues being the minister in charge of education. Is it not possible that a learned person is a flatterer?

	Suppose that you have accidentally entered the club where an astronomer is a member. He greets you and offers you the chair next to his. He then tells you as to how far is Pluto from Neptune in kilometres and then tells you how the hydrogen rings around some other planet can obstruct light. By the time he begins to tell you a funny thing about the atmospheric conditions in Mercury last winter, you want to be excused to attend to an urgent call of nature. You resolve never to sit next to him even if it comes to standing at the club functions. Is it not possible for a learned person to be a bore? An **unlearned person** is one who is not learned. He is the opposite of a savant. Imagine that you are seeing a learned physician. He prescribes medicines for your ailment. At the year-end, the pharmacist in the office complex where the physician has his clinic, hands him a part of what he has earned by selling medicines according to the physician's prescriptions. The learned physician accepts the kickback. Is this learned person not an *unprincipled individual*? Whom will you take advice from? Will you take from someone who is not learned or from someone who is learned? Suppose that you go to a lawyer in regard to some property matter. He tells you that you have not a hope of winning the case. You think that he does not know his stuff well. You think that he is a stuffed shirt. You go to another lawyer who sees no reason why you should not win hands down. You persist with the litigation and the case is not even admitted for hearing for want of merit in your case, let alone being resolved. Is not the first lawyer *learned*? Is he also not a *misunderstood advisor*?
Aver	If you read two authors on the same subject and find that what one of them says is true about some matter, and the other fellow states that it is false then you are confused; the reason for the confusion is that what one *avers*, the other denies. To state or to declare something as true is to *aver*. The opposite of this is to state something to be false. The word *collect* comes from the Latin root LECT that means *to read* or *choose*. The prefix CO means *together* or *with others*. To *collect* means to *choose together*, to *assemble*, to *bring together for a hobby* or to *accumulate*. However this has nothing to do with stating something to be false. When someone does jobs after his regular working hours to *augment* his income, he does these to *increase* his income. To *augment* therefore means to *increase*. This again has nothing to do with stating something to be false. When a man has had a tiff with his wife about the extra amount of salt in the omelette that she cooked for breakfast, he brings home a bottle of perfume on his way back from the office, to *placate* her. What he is doing is trying to *appease* her. He is trying to *make peace*. Thus to *placate* means to *appease* or *pacify*. The word *placate* too has nothing to do with stating things to be false. After she accepts the gift, he may tell her that she would do well to put less salt as a matter of course since his doctor has advised him to go easy on the salt. He has not said that the complaint about excess salt was false. Therefore even this has no connection whatsoever with stating things to be false. The word *deny* has some interesting shades of meaning. It means *saying no*. So when someone denies that he has any knowledge of a fraud that has been committed in his office, he is saying no. He therefore states that if there is any belief that he has any knowledge about the fraud being perpetrated, it is a false belief. If he denies a statement made in the charge sheet to the effect that he is involved, he is saying that such a statement is false. If a person on a fast denies himself food, he is saying no to food. To deny is the opposite of to aver. A father may *encourage* his son to speak the truth always. To encourage means to *give courage*. The word encourage can be used only in positive contexts. To state or to declare something as true is to *aver*. One cannot encourage anyone to say something that he knows is untrue.

<table>
<tr><td>Facetious</td><td>Something said in a jocular or non-serious fashion is facetious. For example when someone says that war is a method of controlling population, he is being facetious. This is because war kills innocent people: men, women and children who have nothing to do with the dispute between nations. A war is a really serious matter. If you wish to control population, then people have to be educated in methods of limiting family size. War can never be the answer for population problems. The opposite of facetious is serious.

The word lugubrious means mournful or dismal. It is the opposite of facetious.

If a tract of land is a contentious issue between two nations, it means that there is a dispute about which of the two should really own that tract. On the other hand if someone is contentious, it means that he easily takes to dispute or quarrels and is argumentative. If some issue is contentious and the two nations are frequently close to war on that issue, it means that the issue is serious.

But then a bone may be a contentious issue between two dogs. Or if some person fights with others on such issues as which football team should win the forthcoming Premier Football League; which is more pungent: red chilly or pepper; which is a better drink: tea or cocoa, the issues are not serious even though contentious. Thus just because something is contentious it does not necessarily mean that it is serious.

The word ingenuous comes from the Latin root GEN that means to beget or to produce. The prefix IN has several shades of meaning. The prefix IN can mean in, internal as in words like inborn, inland; IN can mean against such as in the word inconsistent (against consistency). Something that is in the state in which it was born (innocent as all babies are) is ingenuous. Babies are not capable of committing trickery and therefore someone ingenuous can be also be naïve or simple. Someone ingenuous cannot be serious.

If a child can work sums involving calculus before it is put to school, it is prodigious, meaning it is amazing or abnormal. If your barber charges you a huge sum for the haircut, he would be charging you a prodigious sum, which is a mammoth sum (what is mammoth and what is a pygmy is a matter of time and circumstance; someone in Class VIII may look extraordinarily tall and muscular in comparison to his toddler cousins but a decade later he may still be five foot four whereas the cousins are all six-footers). Someone prodigious may not be serious at all. It is not impossible to visualise a seven-foot tall fellow playing marbles with little children in the street.

Audacity is courage, rudeness or impudence. In an age when women posing for portraits were dressed to their teeth and any exposure of body parts was gross indecency, a model that broke free from the prevalent beliefs and posed for a nude portrait may have been termed as audacious; here the word audacious means brazen or shameless. An army general, who surrounded by the enemy on all sides, leads a do or die effort and defeats the enemy is an audacious or daredevil general. The army general would be both serious and audacious. Someone audacious posing for nude photographs cannot be called serious.</td></tr>
</table>

We have seen the word anarchy and its meaning in the above exercise. There are several words that flow from the Latin root ARCH. There are some similar roots and these are: ARCHEO-, ARCHI-, -ARCH and –ARCHY.

The Greek root ARCHE- or ARCHEO- means *ancient*. *Archeology* (now spelt *Archaeology*) is ARCHEO- (meaning *ancient*) plus the Latin suffix –LOGY (*meaning science* or *study of*); archaeology (now spelt *archaeology*) means *science* or *study of ancient human cultures*.

ARCH- or ARCHIi are Greek roots meaning *chief; principal*. (There is no *e* in this root.) Note the four core words formed from this root – *architect, archenemy, archangel and archbishop*. The word *architect* is the Greek root ARCHi- plus the Greek root -TEKT (meaning *worker*); *architect* (means *principal worker*); the word now means a person who designs and draws up plans for buildings and supervises their construction. But if someone has been described as the *architect* of some company's downfall, it means that he is the chief worker of that downfall (meaning, *someone chiefly responsible for the company's debacle*).

ARCH- and ARCHY- are two roots having similarity.

The Greek root ARCH- means *a ruler; a person who rules*" and ARCHY- means *a particular kind of rule.*

Monarch is the Greek root MON- (meaning *one; single*) plus ARCH-; a *monarch* is a person who rules alone; a king or sovereign.

Monarchy is, therefore, (1) a system of rule wherein a person rules alone or (2) a land ruled by a monarch. For example, Great Britain is a constitutional monarchy.

Matriarch is the Greek root MATRI- meaning *mother* plus –ARCH meaning *a ruler*; a *matriarch* is a woman who rules or leads a large family or tribe by hereditary rights. Similarly, *matriarchy* means *a society ruled by a woman.* For example, *matriarchs* ruled in Central Africa during the early twentieth century.

The Latin root PATRI- means *father*; what could the word *patriarchy* mean?

If you remember, we have seen the word *incursion* in this exercise. It comes from the Latin root CUR-, CURS- and COURS- that means *to run; go.* The core words based on this root are: *concur, current, occur and recur.*

Concur is CON- (the Latin prefix meaning *together*) + CUR- (the Latin root meaning *to run; go*); *concur* literally means *to run together*; it means (a) to agree or approve (b) to happen at the same time.

Words based on *concur* are	That Mean
Concurrent	Happening at the same time
Concourse	A coming together, as of streets, or a place where people, traffic etc. come together.

Current is the Latin root CUR- (meaning *to run; go*) + the Latin suffix -ENT (meaning the same thing as -ING in English); *current* means *going, running, moving.* Thus it means *any continuous movement of something such as water in a river or stream; continuous movement of electricity in an electric wire. Current* as an adjective means *something that is happening in the immediate present; moving with the time.* A word based on *current* is *currency*, which means (a) money that is in circulation as a medium of exchange (b) general acceptance or circulation (such as in *the belief that deep breathing exercises can cure hypertension has gained currency*).

Occur is the Latin prefix OC- (meaning *toward; against*) + CUR- (meaning *to run; go*). *To occur* literally means *to rush towards something or someone*; thus *occur* means *to happen; come about; come to mind.* A word based on *occur* is *occurrence*, meaning (a) an event or instance (b) the act or the fact of occurring.

Recur is the Latin prefix RE- (meaning *back; again*) + the Latin root CUR- (meaning *to run; go*); *recur* means *to go* or *happen again or happen repeatedly.*

Words based on *recur* are	That Mean
Recurrence	Happening again
Recurrent	Happening again and again

We shall now see contextual use of these core words in sentences that should drive home the precise meanings of these words flowing from the root CUR and also their nuances.

1. All members of our housing complex concurred about the need for hiring better security guards.
2. The judge passed two concurrently running sentences for two different counts (which means that if one sentence is for five years and the second is for seven years, the convict does only seven years in prison and not twelve).

3. The **current** of the river in spate is frighteningly swift.
4. His clothes are of **current** fashion.
5. The Euro **currency** is accepted all over Europe barring some few countries.
6. The fashion trends that the cinema idol set have gained wide **currency**.
7. **Occurrences** of theft have increased since our old watchman retired.
8. The pain in my ear does **recur** every monsoon.
9. Ever since I have been taking precaution, there has been no **recurrence** of malaria.
10. Unless you sleep under a mosquito net, malaria is likely to be your **recurrent** malady.

Now that you know the roots CUR, CURS and COURS, you can analyse the words in the table given below and write down their possible meanings. You can then look up the dictionary and see their meanings and see how effective is this method of learning.

The Word	The meaning of the word according to your analysis of the word after knowing the meaning of the root CUR, CURS and COURS
Discourse	
Excursive	
Precursor	
Discursive	
Incur	
Precursory	
Excursion	
Incursion	
Recourse	

If you remember we have seen the word *collect* in this exercise that is based on the root LECT. There are two other similar roots to LECT and these are LEG- and LIG-.

The Latin root LEG-, LIG- or LECT- means *to choose or to read.* The core words are: *collect, elect, eligible, legible, select.*

Collect is COL-, the Latin prefix meaning *together* + LECT-, the Latin root meaning *to choose*; *collect* originally meant *to choose together*; now it means *to assemble; to bring together for a study or hobby; to accumulate (such as dust or dirt).* A person's *collection* of paintings is something he has assembled after carefully choosing them.

Words based on *collect* are	That Mean
Collection	The act of gathering; that which is gathered or assembled
Collective	Common; something done together with others
Collector	Someone who carefully and painstakingly collects art pieces, coins and so on

Elect is E-, the Latin prefix (also spelt as EX-) meaning *out* + LECT-, the Latin root meaning *to choose*; *elect* means *to pick out especially for an official position by voting; select.* The noun *elect* means *those who are chosen or favoured.*

Words based on *elect* are	That Mean
Election	The act of choosing
Elector	The one who chooses
Electorate	The body of people who vote

Eligible is *E-*, the Latin prefix (also spelt as EX-) meaning *out* + *leg-*, the Latin root meaning *to choose* + the suffix *–IBLE*, meaning *able to be*; *eligible* means *able to be chosen* or *that can be chosen or picked out for something; suitable; qualified and desirable, as for an official position or marriage.* A word based on *eligible* is *eligibility,* which means *suitableness*.

Lecture is a word that comes from the root LECT- (meaning *to read*) + -URE, the suffix meaning *the act of*; *lecture* means *the act of reading; a discourse on a specific subject delivered before an audience.* To *lecture* is to *deliver a lecture.*

Legible is the root *LEG-*, meaning *to read* + *-IBLE*, the Latin suffix that means *able to be; able*; *legible* means *able to be read or that can be read.* A word based on *legible* is *illegible* that means *not able to be read.*

Select is the Latin prefix *SE-*, meaning *apart* + *LECT-*, the root meaning *to choose; select* means *to choose something apart from the rest;* as an adjective it means *choice* or *exclusive.* Words based on select are:

Words based on *select* are	That Mean
Selection	The act of choosing; a collection made with care
Selective	Careful in choosing

1. Students may **collect** their mark sheets from the college by the evening of 25th March.
2. He **collects** antique furniture.
3. Mrs. Edwin has a magnificent **collection** of stamps.
4. The business tycoon is a **collector** of vintage cars.
5. You may take pizza; I **elect** a plate of ginger fried rice.
6. Mandela is among the **elect** in statesmanship.
7. I stood for **election** to the post of General Secretary in our college students' union.
8. Nobody other than **electors** listed at this centre is allowed to enter these premises.
9. False promises will not fool the **electorate** any more; if you want votes you will have to fulfil the promises in your election manifesto.
10. You will be **eligible** for a driving license only after you turn eighteen.
11. He is regarded as the most **eligible** bachelor in town.
12. I am scheduled to **lecture** at the business school next Monday.
13. I found his **lecture** most interesting and useful.
14. You will do well to improve your handwriting; it is barely **legible**.
15. You call this **illegible** scrawl a love letter?
16. I want you to carefully **select** the further course of study.
17. The new confectionery has a wide **selection** of pastries.
18. He will not take anything other than the best, **select** mangoes.
19. The club is **selective** is about its membership; admission is granted only after an interview.

Now that we know that the root LEG-, LIG- and LECT- means *to choose or to read*, we could derive the meanings of the following words, as we understand them from the viewpoint of their roots. We could write the meanings of the words in the spaces against each of them and look up the dictionary and see if we have arrived at the correct meanings of the following words:

The Word	The meaning of the word according to your analysis of the word after knowing the meaning of the root LEG-, LIG- and LECT-
Elective	
Intelligent	
Lectern	
Lecturer	
Legend	
Selectivity	

We have seen the word *ingenuous* in this exercise. It comes from the Latin root GEN-, GENIT- that means *to produce; give birth*. The core words are *genesis, genius, genial, genuine, genital, progenitor*.

Genesis is a word that comes from the Latin root GEN- (meaning *to produce; give birth*) and means *creation; beginning; the birth or origin of; the origin or something.*

Genius also comes directly from the Latin root GEN- (meaning *to produce; give birth*) and means *the inborn spirit of a person* or *a person with extraordinary inborn intelligence.*

Genial also comes from the Latin root GEN- (meaning *to produce; give birth*) and means *of inborn or natural kindness; giving comfort or warmth of life.* A word based on *genial* is *congenial* meaning *sympathetic or agreeable.*

Genuine comes from a Latin word based on GEN- (meaning *to produce; give birth*); *genuine* means *natural; inborn; original; authentic; real.*

Genital is the root GENIT- (meaning *to produce; give birth*) + the Latin sufix –AL (meaning *pertaining to*); *genital* means *pertaining to the birth-giving organs or process*; *genitals* are *external sexual organs.*

Progenitor is the Latin prefix PRO- (meaning *before*) + the root GENIT- (meaning *to produce; give birth*) + the Latin suffix –OR (meaning *the person or thing that performs an action* just an actor is someone who performs an act; *progenitor* means *an ancestor; forebear.*

Let us see some sentences in which these core words are used. The contextual usage will drive home the precise meanings of these words and so also their shades of meanings.

1. The **genesis** of your problems lies in your lethargy.
2. Our mathematics teacher was a **genius**.
3. His attitude to me has been **genial**, although we have had our differencсs of opinion.
4. The atmosphere in our office is **congenial**.
5. The Aborigine is the only **genuine** Australian; the rest of them are immigrant.
6. The painting has been copied well; it is difficult to tell the **genuine** from the imitation.
7. Charles Darwin advanced the theory that the ape is the **progenitor** of modern man.

Now that we know that the root GEN-, GENIT- means *to produce; give birth*, we could derive the meanings of the following words, as we understand them from the viewpoint of their roots. We could write the meanings of the words in the spaces against each of them and look up the dictionary and see if we have arrived at the correct meanings of the following words:

The Word	The meaning of the word according to your analysis of the word after knowing the meaning of the root GEN- and GENIT-
Genitive	
Congenital	
Indigenous	

Chapter 7

Word Analogies

The word *analogy* means so many things, some of which are as follows: similarity, parallel, correspondence, likeness, resemblance, correlation, relation, equivalence, and similitude. But the crux is correspondence. The word correspondence comes from the word RESPONSE and has the prefix CO- that means together and therefore the word *correspondence* means *responding together* or *agreement* or *harmony* or *matching*.

I remember the days when I was a bachelor and my younger brother and I used to stay together and cook our own meals. Our grandmother was a thorough vegetarian whereas we cooked either fish or meat everyday. We used to visit her frequently. Sometimes I would go alone and at other times my brother would go alone to look her up. Quite frequently we met her the same evening but at different times. When she would ask as to what we had for dinner one of us would say that we had vegetable curry and rice for dinner and the other would say it was lentil soup, vegetable stew and chapattis. She used to be exasperated. How is it, she would say, that the two of you have different things, for dinner when you cook together? We then decided that our answers should correspond. We would then decide beforehand what our fib would be. Our answer was the same.

Quite frequently, major competitive tests have a few questions on analogy. The idea is to give a pair of words that have a relationship and then one is required to find out from among the given options as to which relationship either bears the nearest relationship to the given pair, or sometimes, which pair has the least correspondence to the given word pair. The skill in arriving at the correct answer often takes a fair understanding of the English language; sometimes the issue may even be that of general awareness and quite frequently, the matter pertains to logic. But logic in isolation may or may not work. It therefore becomes imperative to build the requisite skills and hone them to a state where no matter how difficult the question, the answer would emerge from the deadly combination of general awareness, one's understanding of the meanings and the nuances of different words and then reasoning which would lend the cutting edge to one's skills for being able to spot analogies in a flash.

In this chapter we shall see the very best illustrations of word analogies. A given related pair of words or phrases will be followed by options in which there shall be pairs of words/phrases. We shall then see (A) which of the options has the relationship that matches the one expressed in the original pair and (B) why. We shall not stop at this. We shall also learn as to why the other options will not do. This would put matters beyond debate or hesitation. Besides, this would help immensely as we face similar questions in the examinations to come.

Please see these illustrations and the detailed explanations as to which ones will click and which will not. You will also notice that there is a profusion of etymology. However mere etymology may act as a lullaby to some of you and therefore there is ample contextual usage so as to drive home the meanings of words and then you shall be able to retain the meanings of words and their nuances in your mental armour till Kingdom Come. It has been our endeavour (when I use the word our, I mean Nishant - the co-author and I) to make the business of learning the etymology of words as enjoyable as possible because we firmly believe that if learning gives you joy, the assimilation will be jolly nearly complete.

Illustrations 1 to 5

DIRECTIONS *for questions 1 to 5:* **In each of the following questions, a related pair of words or phrases is followed by five lettered pairs of words or phrases. Select the lettered pair that best expresses a relationship similar to that expressed in the original pair.**

1. GARBLED: COMPREHEND

(A) convoluted: tangle (B) obscured: recognize
(C) emancipated: free (D) expunged: excite
(E) determined: placate

Answer 1

Something garbled is something mutilated or distorted or tampered. Imagine you want to send a telegram to your friend that she has passed the Degree Examination with a first division. Your message that you have delivered to the Post Office is as follows: "Congrats; you are through degree examination with first class". What may happen, unfortunately, is that the message that the person may actually receive may be " Concrete; you are not through degree examination with first class". The whole thing seems to convey a wrong message ultimately. The message you have sent has got distorted in the process of transmission. This is what a garbled message would be, something corrupted or obscured. Confusion will be confounded. Something garbled is not comprehensible, whereas to comprehend is to understand. So the relationship between Garbled and Comprehend is that between Distorted (or Corrupted or Obscured) and Understand (or recognise).

Hence the correct choice of the pair analogous to the given word pair is at **option (B) obscured: recognize.** As regards the others, let us see why they will not work.

Option (A) convoluted: tangle; convoluted is the prefix *con-* (meaning *together*) and *volute* (meaning *rolled longitudinally upon itself*) and thus convoluted would mean mixed or distorted and thus also garbled. Whereas a *tangle* means knot or something *entwined* and therefore *confused*. It may so happen that you are going for a walk and your shirt may get *tangled* in the bushes and it may take you some time to take it from the thorns and things. So convoluted and tangle are synonymous, whereas the given word pair are antonymous.

Option (C) emancipated: free; emancipated and free are synonymous. The word emancipates comes from the prefix *e-* (meaning *out*) and *mancipium* (meaning slave) and thus to *emancipate* means to *free* just as in "Abraham Lincoln proposed a bill for *emancipation* of slaves in America."

Option (D) expunged: excite; expunged is the prefix *ex-* (meaning *out*) and the root *pungere-* (meaning to *prick*). Expunged therefore means to prick out or remove or take out. If you have taken your shirt from the pricks (the thorn in which it got entangled in the explanation regards Option A above) then it becomes free.

Let us see a contextual usage of the word *expunged*. Imagine that an honest government officer is not carrying out the will of his superior officer who is corrupt. When the honest officer's annual confidential reports are to be written, the superior officer wishes to take revenge. He writes an adverse confidential report. The officer is not considered for promotion. He goes in appeal and he is informed that he is not being promoted because of adverse remarks in his confidential rolls. He then appeals against these adverse remarks. The superior officer is unable to justify adverse remarks and these are then *expunged* (or deleted in such a fashion as if they did not exist at all) from his annual confidential rolls.

To excite means to animate, move, thrill, discompose, or inflame. In excitement, one may even become distorted. One newspaper correspondent was sent to cover the great work being done by Lawrence of Arabia. In his tremendous excitement at meeting such a great person, the journalist introduced himself to Lawrence as "I am Lawrence of Arabia". He got hugely confused in his excitement (here the word excitement is used in the context of thrill). As such there is no relationship between *expunged* and *excite*.

Option (E) determined: placate; something determined is something that has been made clear. The word *determined* comes from the word *terminal* that means the end and the prefix DE- means *down*. Thus something of which the *end* is *drawn down* or *fixed* is *determined*.

If you are at a railway station and are not able to make up your mind as to which train to travel and then you find that all the trains have gone off the matter has got determined for you. At least till the next day. You can go home today and rest in its comfort. On the contrary if you take train A to get to your destination, it is determined that you do not have to think of the other trains now. The word *determined* is as such antonymous to garbled.

To *placate* means to appease or make peace with. Imagine that two fellows have been throwing fists at each other over a girl and you go in and separate them. You tell them to cool off. They stop fighting for the time being. You tell them to see whether she has soft corner for anyone of them and then if need be settle matters amicably. This may not necessarily mean that they comprehend or understand. All you may do is to buy peace. They may be at each other's throats once again. Thus the relationship between determined and placate is not the same as between Garbled and Comprehend.

Thus only Option B will work.

2. HEAT: CALORIMETER

(A) Distance: odometer (B) Gasoline: tachometer

(C) Wind: velocity (D) Rain: humidity

(E) Ocean: tide

Answer 2

Option (A) Distance: Odometer; Distance can be measured in several units of measure such as inches, meters, miles and so on depending on whether you are measuring the size of your biceps or the distance between your residence and the airport. Heat can be measured in units called calories, which are frequently used to find out the energy value of foods. A calorimeter is the apparatus for measuring heat. The relationship between Heat and Calorimeter is that of something and the device for measuring that thing.

An odometer is an instrument for measuring the distance travelled by a wheeled vehicle. When in a car, the odometer is known as the milometer. It is also an instrument for measuring distances in surveying. The relationship between distance: odometer is that between something and the apparatus for measuring it.

As regards Option (B) gasoline: tachometer; gasoline is a fuel that drives cars and scooters and motorcycles and a tachometer is the apparatus that measures the number of revolutions per unit of time. A tachometer in your motorcycle measures the revolutions per minute (which is known as RPM in brief) made by the engine's drive shaft. A tachometer may also be used for measuring the velocity of a moving fluid but then it measures the velocity and not the fluid. (So a tachometer is not the device for measuring gasoline.) So the relationship between gasoline: tachometer is not that of something and the device for measuring that thing.

Option (C): wind: velocity; Wind velocity is the rate at which the wind blows. It is not a device. An instrument or device for measuring the speed or velocity of engines, vessels, projectiles, etc. is known as a velocimeter.

Option (D): rain: humidity; This is a cause and effect relationship. Rain causes humidity. Humidity does not measure the amount of rain. A device known as Rain Gauge measures the amount of rainfall (usually in number of inches).

Option (E): ocean: tide; The tide is an indication of the direction of flow of water in the ocean. At high tide, the water flows towards the shore and at low tide, away from it. There is no relationship of something and the device for measuring that thing. Nothing can measure the ocean as such.

So only Option (A) will work.

3. ALLY: WAR

(A) Patriot: brawl (B) Crew: ship

(C) Spouse: marriage (D) Peer: class

(E) Team-mate: game

Answer 3

An ally is a person who joins forces or unites with some other person or country. An ally is therefore some sort of partner. Two nations may go to war. A third nation becomes an ally of one of them. There may be a business ally as well. He helps someone in business.

A war is essentially between nations but it can be a conflict between smaller units as well. Two tribes may go to war. The essence of war is that it is a matter where one takes on the other with the objective of winning and thus there is always a strategy in a war, no matter what its size may be.

Option (A) **patriot: brawl;** A patriot is one who is fervently loyal to his nation. But this means that there are only two parties in this: the nation and the patriot. He is not an ally since an ally is essentially a third party. Since a patriot is not an ally, Option A does not match.

Option (B) **crew: ship;** A crew is the number of human beings that are required to operate a ship. The ship as you know is inanimate and it will require someone to put in the fuel and another to direct it and a third to clean the decks and serve dinner to the passengers and so on. Thus the relationship between crew and ship is that of operator and the device that is operated. But the crew is neither a partner of the ship nor an ally.

Option (C) **spouse: marriage;** A marriage is between two parties. A spouse is a partner but not an ally. One can have several allies just as the Allies in the Third World War meant an alliance between UK, USA, France, and so on. Two partners make a marriage (at least in the civilised world). Besides, marriage is not an institution that is meant either for war or for business. (At least that is not the intention behind marriages). Thus the relationship is not the same as between ally: war.

Option (D) **peer: class;** A peer is someone who is your equal in status or rank or class. If you are designated as a Manager in a company, the other Managers are your peers. The relationship between peer and class is that of what constitutes the genre and the genre itself.

Genre, incidentally, means *type* or format or *style*. For example realistic paintings are part of a *genre* in which the style is to paint real things, as they seem to the human eye. Abstractionist paintings are a part of the genre in which the painter paints things as they appear in the mind's eye. His theme in the painting may be emotion, which is not visible to the human eye but it may be visible to the artist through his mind's eye. The two *genres* - realistic and abstractionist -are therefore *formats* of painting.

Option (E) **teammate: game;** A teammate is an ally. You can have several allies. A game is played with the objective of winning and further it is a matter of strategy. On all counts therefore, teammate: game qualifies for the pair being analogous to ally: war and hence **Option E.**

4. EAVESDROP: CONVERSATION

(A) Shoplift: customer
(B) Trespass: property
(C) Gossip: discussion
(D) Arrest: suspect
(E) Subpoena: witness

Answer 4

To *eavesdrop* means to overhear a conversation that you are not supposed to. If the schoolteachers are in their staff room and discussing the performance of some students in the subjects that they have taught, this conversation is essentially private till the mark sheets are in the hands of the students. No one other than those who are *authorised* to hear this conversation should be present when they talk. Imagine that some student is waiting by the window of the staff room and overhears this conversation. He has been *eavesdropping* on this conversation.

Incidentally, the projecting edges of the roof of a house from which raindrops fall to the ground are known as its *eaves*. An eavesdropper would need to stand near them to be able to overhear conversations that he is not supposed to. This is how the word *eavesdropping* has evolved.

The relation between eavesdrop: conversation is that of something that you are not authorised to do and the area where you are entering (figuratively, of course since the private conversation is an area that an eavesdropper would tread on without authority). Incidentally when the police tap the telephone lines to overhear what criminals are plotting to do so as create law and order disturbances, this is not a case of *eavesdropping* since such overhearing is with *due authority* given to them by law.

Option (A) **shoplift: customer;** If a person were to steal goods from a shop, he would be doing something that is a patently unauthorised thing to do. This is because stealing involves taking away goods without the permission of the owner. But it will remain unauthorised all through. No law can provide authority for stealing. However a shoplift can (unauthorizedly, of course) carry away goods from a shop. He does not carry away customers. Thus the relationship between shoplift: customer **will not qualify** for being analogous to eavesdrop: conversation.

Option (B) trespass: property; A trespass is what a person would commit if he was not authorised to enter some premises (or property) and yet has. He has done something that he is not authorised to do. But a trespass is against private property. So if you find someone who has entered your house without your permission, and you find that he has a wonderful remedy for the ailment that your grandfather has been suffering from, it may so happen that you may actually buy the remedy, give him money and then give him a cup of tea. You may also request him to keep coming over whenever he would pass by next. So what has started out as a clearly unauthorised action, you can yourself not only ratify it but also convert it to an invitation for future visits. **But it is dependent upon your will whether to ratify the trespass or not.** A trespass when it started out was **clearly unauthorised**. The trespasser too is an unauthorised entrant upon the conversation that he was not authorised to hear.

As such therefore the relationship between trespass: property would be analogous to eavesdrop: conversation.

Option (C) gossip: discussion; A gossip is idle talk or someone who indulges in idle chatting. A discussion is something that has the element of seriousness in it. But neither require authorisation whereas the crux of eavesdropping is that it is unauthorised. The relationship between gossip: discussion is that between something light-hearted and something serious and would not be analogous to eavesdrop: conversation.

Option (D) arrest: suspect; The police would arrest a suspect (suspected for a crime, of course which eavesdropping is not). The relationship between **arrest: suspect** is a **legal action** taken against someone who is believed to have done something illegal (which is different from something unauthorised like eavesdropping). As such therefore the relationship between arrest: suspect would not be analogous to eavesdrop: conversation. The arrest is authorised per se.

Option (E) subpoena: witness; A subpoena is a Court order, which makes it necessary for a certain person to remain present in the Court at a fixed time and if the person against whom the subpoena is issued does not comply, then there is provision of punishment. A subpoena is generally issued to a witness but not necessarily so. A subpoena may even be issued, for example, to someone who may be able to give documentary evidence although he may not be a witness to the crime. However the relationship between subpoena and witness is that of a Court order and one to whom it is issued. But a subpoena is something patently authorised by law. As such therefore the relationship between subpoena: witness would not be analogous to eavesdrop: conversation because eavesdropping is clearly unauthorised from its very outset.

Therefore, only **Option (B) trespass: property** would fit the bill.

5. **PALPABLE: TOUCH**

(A) Malleable: gild
(B) Palatable: ingest
(C) Pliable: mould
(D) Edible: cook
(E) Appreciable: please

Answer 5

Something *palpable* is that which can be touched. The sense of touch determines whether a thing is palpable just as the sense of vision determines whether a thing is visible. A banana is palpable because you can touch it with your hand. The mercy of god, however strongly one may believe it exists, cannot be felt by the hand. This is because it is abstract. So the relationship between palpable and touch is that between the characteristic and what determines whether something has the characteristic. What is to be borne in mind is that something palpable has necessarily got to be physical unless one uses the word palpable in the figurative sense such as in "the tension in the house was *palpable*". But **palpable** cannot be abstract.

Option (A) malleable: gild; Something malleable is that which can be hammered or pressed to a shape such that it does not fracture or *break* and also that it does not return to its original shape. Aluminium is one metal that is malleable. That is why you see aluminium sheets. The word-*malleable* is generally used in the case of metals. Incidentally metals that can be drawn into wires are known as *ductile* metals; aluminium is both ductile and malleable. Copper is another ductile metal; the copper wires through which electric supply reaches our houses are testimony to the ductility of copper.

If you see a sword that seems to be made of gold, it is likely to be a *gild* sword, meaning an iron sword on which there is a coating of gold. To *gild* is to cover with gold. There is no relationship between malleable and gild. Gold has to be electroplated on to another metal surface so as to gild the latter. Besides it is not the gild that makes the other metal malleable unlike in the case of touch that decides whether something is palpable.

Option (B) palatable: ingest; Something palatable is that which brings pleasure when eaten. Therefore bitter medicines may be edible but not palatable. To ingest means to take in but does not mean doing it with pleasure. A child may refuse to ingest a plate of cereals for hours and may all the while hold it in her hands. If someone merely ingests something it does not mean that the thing ingested is palatable as well. The relationship between palatable and ingest is not the same as in the case of palpable and touch.

Option (C) pliable: mould; A mould is a die. It is a hollow form into which a fluid is poured (and even iron and steel can flow when heated to the required temperature) or plastic material is pressed to harden into a required shape. Something pliable is that which can be made to take a different shape. So a mould would determine whether a thing is pliable. Something that takes the shape of the mould is patently pliable. So the mould decides whether a thing is pliable. Therefore the relationship between pliable: mould is the same as between palpable: touch.

Option (D) edible: cook; In my bachelor days I had engaged the services of a cook to relieve myself of the daily grind of cooking, although it is a different matter that I could not stomach him for long. The last thing that can be said about the things that he cooked is that they were edible. One can cook inedible things as well. People who have stayed in hostels should know.

Option (E) appreciable: please; This is a close one. If something that can please, it can be said to be appreciable. But the sole reason why this relationship will not do is the fact that what can be touched is strictly physical whereas what is appreciable may not necessarily be physical. It can be abstract as well. On a hot summer afternoon, a tall glass of cool lemonade may please one no end. One may even dip one's finger in the lemonade and smack one's lips after tasting the traces of lemonade that have clung on to one's fingers after one has touched it. One can be tickled pink with the jokes that the comedian has been cracking but the jokes cannot be touched.

Thus **Option (C) pliable: mould;** So far we have been seeing word analogies where we are to determine which among the given pairs of words in the options very nearly corresponds to the relationship between the word pair given at the outset. Now let us look at the other variety - the word in the options that is very nearly the opposite in relationship to the word given at the outset. We have so far been seeing harmonious relationships. We shall now to see disharmonious relationships. We shall determine mismatches.

Illustrations 6 to 15

DIRECTIONS *for questions 6 to 15: Each question below consists of a word printed in capital letters, followed by five words or phrases. Choose the word or phrase that is most nearly opposite in meaning to the word in capital letters.*

Since some of the questions require you to distinguish fine shades of meaning, be sure to consider all the choices before deciding which one is *best*. However this is an exercise devised for learning. A wrong answer should not be a matter of concern at this stage. The idea behind this exercise is to see the detailed explanations and hone one's reasoning skills from these explanations. The strop on which you will hone your reasoning skills is built into the detailed explanations. Not reading them merely because you are right will not be the proper thing to do since you will deprive yourself of the chance to hone your mental axe.

6. REDUCE:

(A) Exploit (B) Amplify (C) Omit

(D) Displace (E) Diversify

The word *reduce* comes from the Latin root DUC- (meaning to *lead*). The prefix RE- means *back. Reduce* therefore means to *lead back* or *bring* to a *lower state* of size, numbers, value etc., briefly meaning to become less in any manner. To reduce is to diminish in size or quantity or volume. The word opposite in meaning to *reduce* is that which should mean **to increase in size or quantity** and so on.

Option (A) exploit; The word exploit is made up of the prefix *ex-* (meaning out) and the Latin root PLIC- (meaning *fill up, finish, fulfill*). Thus to *exploit* is to *fill* out meaning *take out some resources from where they are and fill them somewhere else.* (such as one would *exploit* natural resources for one's own advantage and someone would *exploit* his staff for maximizing profits or a bowler may *exploit* the pitch conditions and so on). It is for this reason that an extraordinary achievement is also known as an *exploit* (but this is only in the noun sense where one's chest would swell - or fill out - with pride as a result of having attained such an achievement). (If one's chest swells, it is because one takes some air out from the atmosphere and fills it into one's lungs.) If one were to exploit a mine, one would only reduce the amount of ore in it. To exploit is a cause of which reduction may generally be the effect.

Option (B) amplify; The word *amplify* comes from the word *ample* that means *enough*, *abundant*, *more than enough.* When you have ample clothing, it means that you have more dresses than what you need. If your wardrobe is reduced to three shirts, it means that you do not have enough clothes. To *amplify* would mean *to increase in size or volume* and is the precise opposite of *reduce.*

Option (C) omit; The word omit comes from the Latin root MIT- and the Latin prefix O-. *Omit* originally meant to *send something toward another person*; now it means *not to include*; *leave out*. A word based on *omit is omission*, meaning *the act of omitting*; *something that has not been included.* When you *omit* something it is not necessary that something or someone becomes the opposite of *reduced.* If an athlete is *omitted* from his country's Olympic team, it does not necessarily mean that he will grow in size. He may sulk and deny food. He may become as thin as a rail.

Option (D) displace; To *displace* is to put out of place. The word *displace* may mean to *expel*, *relocate*, *dismiss* and so on. This is because the prefix DIS- means *away from.* Just because you *displace* something, it does not mean that it will become the opposite of *reduced.* If a senior employee displaced by junior officer, it would mean that the junior person takes the senior's place. The senior may be allotted some other work or he may even be dismissed. On the other hand he may get a better job, with a higher pay and responsibilities. There is no implicit increase in his position or remuneration. Whatever increase is implicit is in that of the junior man but the person displaced is the senior officer, not the junior officer.

Option (E) diversify; The word diversify comes from the Latin root VERT- or VERS- that means to turn. The prefix DI- means *apart, in different directions.* To *diversify* means *to turn to a different direction* or *take up different activity or activities* or *to have variety.* When you *diversify* an investment, you invest the amount in such a way that you put it in a variety of investment avenues. If I were to have a hundred thousand dollars to invest, I may invest this sum in five different banks. I have only diversified the investment, not increased or expanded it. This would not qualify for the opposite of reduction.

Thus only **Option (B): amplify** is the opposite of reduce.

7. LETHAL:

(A) Protected (B) Painless (C) Pleasant

(D) Stimulating (E) Harmless

Answer 7

Something *lethal* is that which kills or is extremely dangerous. The bite of a cobra can be *lethal.* This is why most people run for their dear lives when they see one. The opposite of *lethal* is that which causes no harm and hence the choice of the word opposite to *lethal* is *harmless.* We shall now see in which of the options do we see a word similar to harmless (or maybe harmless itself.)

Option (A): Protected; Why do sentries mount a guard to protect the armoury? Why should they protect the guns if the guns are harmless? Aren't electric wires protected with the help of a protective coating? Does it mean that the current flowing through it at 220 Volts is harmless? Something that is protected need not be harmless.

Option B: Painless; Have you heard of death sentences carried out with an injection that kills the convicts without causing them pain? Isn't the injection both lethal and yet a painless way of killing someone instead of the early days when executions were carried out by hanging or decapitating the person with a sword? Is such a painless injection harmless? This option does not qualify to be the opposite of *lethal.*

Options (C) & (D): Pleasant & Stimulating; Isn't whiskey pleasant and stimulating (and so are cigarettes)? Would anyone smoke or drink if it did not bring him pleasure? Have you heard of people lounging in bars and sipping quinine at leisure even though quinine (some horribly bitter medicine) can cure and prevent malaria?

Are cigarettes harmless? Then why do we see the statutory warning on cigarette packs that cigarette smoking is injurious to health? Options (C) & (D) do not qualify to be the opposites of lethal.

Thus Option (E), which incidentally is the exact opposite of lethal. If a snake is seen in your backyard and the wild life specialist tells you that it is a harmless rat snake and twirls it around the necks of his own little children, would you not ask to have the thing around your neck as well?

8. **RATIFY:**

(A) Veto (B) Negotiate (C) Postpone
(D) Debate alternatives (E) Draft proposals

Answer 8

To *ratify* means to *confirm* or *validate* (an act, agreement, etc., esp. one made in one's name by someone else) by signing or *giving formal consent or sanction.*

Imagine that a company's Board of Directors have resolved that business deals in excess of a hundred thousand dollars shall be referred to the Board (at its meeting, of course) before it is finalized. A director of that company has gone abroad and finds some business proposal really worth entering into and signs the relative contract in the name of the company. He does not have sanction for entering into this deal and yet has proceeded to enter into the deal in anticipation of sanction because he knows that there is clear merit in the deal and that the Board is sure to approve it after he explains the pros and cons of the transaction. The company at its next meeting of the directors may ratify this and thus the action taken in anticipation of sanction may be deemed to have the due sanction. This kind of post-facto sanction is very normal if the proposition is attractive and there is not enough time to hold a board meeting. The opposite of *ratify* would *be not to confirm.*

Option (A): Veto; To veto is to reject or turn down. Now imagine that the Board of Directors of the company in the above transaction meets and the Director who has proceeded in anticipation discusses this deal in the Board. Imagine that the Board feels that while the price of the bicycles that the Director has negotiated is attractive, the country to which the bicycles are to be exported is in a grave foreign exchange reserves position and thus the chances of getting the money at all are dim. It may so happen that the company that has bought the bicycles in the foreign country may have the local currency to pay for the bicycles that they have imported but looking to the foreign exchange position of the country to which the bicycles have been exported, the reserve bank of that country may not allow the foreign currency to be sent out. The result would be that if the local currency of that country is – let us give it a bizarre name – Equayquakes, they are worth nothing outside the country in which Equayquakes is the currency. The Board may then veto the proposal to export bicycles (or say no to confirming the transaction). Thus to *veto* is the precise opposite of to *ratify.*

Option (B): Negotiate; To negotiate may mean so many things: if one were to negotiate, say with a workers union one may discuss certain norms of productivity, or finalise a wage increase and so on. The process of finalising an agreement is on. If someone is driving a car and there is a sharp turn, then when he has completed driving on the turn he has *negotiated* (or *dealt with*) this sharp turn. If he does not successfully negotiate this sharp turn, the car may go into a spin and turn turtle or maybe it will crash into the valley below.

As we have seen in the above illustration of the company director finalising a deal and the board refusing to ratify it, when the board either ratifies or vetoes the deal, it does what is *correct* according to its mind. Before you ratify something, you also have the option of not ratifying it. Insofar as the turn in the road is concerned, you have no time to sit and consider whether it is right or wrong. Negotiation is the only thing to do. The other option is to plunge into the valley. To *negotiate* is not the opposite of *ratify*.

Option (C): Postpone; To *postpone* would be to put off. Some deal that is ratified is final and binding on the person or company that ratifies it. Postponing does not necessarily mean that the thing is rejected. Suppose the deal that we are talking about is put up to the Board of Directors who want to wait for a letter of credit from, say, a London-based first class bank that will pay the bill for the bicycles in US Dollars (and not Equayquakes) to the exporting company, then the Board may postpone the decision on the deal till such a letter of credit is received. Such a letter of credit will ensure that the amount of the bill for the bicycles exported will definitely reach the company. When it is received, the Board may confirm the deal. Thus when you merely *postpone* a decision, it does not mean that you *veto* or *ratify* the decision. Postponing means to defer the decision on something; the ultimate decision may be *for* or *against* something.

Option (D): Debate alternatives; Whether you want to ratify something or veto it, there must be a clear decision. When you debate alternatives it means that the process of taking a decision on some matter is on. The pros and cons are being weighed. There is no decision at all so far.

Option (E): Draft proposals; If someone is busy with a draft proposal it means that things are at a preliminary stage (as indicated by the word *draft*) The proposal is on the drawing board or *on the anvil* as it is figuratively said. For some proposal to be rejected or approved, there must be a clear-cut proposal in the first place. A draft proposal is not a proposal. If you want to break the Berlin Wall, then there must be a Berlin Wall. You cannot break its drawings with hammers.

9. **RESOLUTION:**

(A) Vacillation (B) Organisation (C) Condemnation
(D) Hybridisation (E) Altercation

Answer 9

It is normal for people to take a *resolution* on New Years. Some resolve not to drink alcohol thereafter. Others resolve never to drink water thereafter. A resolution means a *decision*. It has finality as its prime ingredient. The opposite of resolution is that which should have the lack of finality as its prime ingredient. So if you have not *finally* made up your mind about something, you have not made a resolution.

Option (A): Vacillation; When a young man is seeing several lovely young ladies and cannot make up his mind whether lady A or lady B or Lady C will be the lady in his life (his wife, in other words), he is in a state of *vacillation* or *indecision*. Vacillation is the action or habit of wavering between opinions, options; it also means hesitation. He finally makes up his mind to marry lady A because her father is a millionaire; he has made a *resolution* (whether correct or otherwise is not the moot point). He has made up his mind. Thus vacillation is the precise opposite of *resolution*.

Option (B): Organisation; Imagine that you are put in charge of the organisation of a quiz contest. You will have to decide the contents of the quiz. You will have to decide where to hold the contest, who will participate, when will be the preliminaries and when the finals, what will be the prizes, who will foot the bill and so on. You will have to arrange things with finality. You cannot put off the decision on the venue till the date of the contest because on the fateful day all the halls in town may be full and you might have to sit under the deep blue sky. Organisation is characterised by order and arrangement. There is finality in it. There is *decision* in it. *Organisation* cannot be the opposite of *resolution*.

Option (C): Condemnation; Condemnation is pronouncing adverse judgement. A convict could be condemned to life imprisonment if found guilty of murder. There is finality in condemnation as well. The judge has made up his mind.

Option (D): Hybridisation; Through a process called cross-fertilisation, a new variety of grain or plant or even an animal is produced. An example is hybrid corn. Another example is the **tigon** that is a result of mating between a tiger and a lioness. The tigon is not what nature gave you. It is a hybrid. It has been developed through crossbreeding. Hybridisation is crossbreeding. It is out of context with resolution. Whatever is hybridised, however, is final since the process of hybridisation increases genetic variety. Therefore *hybridisation* is not the opposite of *resolution*.

Option (E): Altercation; An altercation is a fight, a showdown and it may be physical.

Imagine that two men have been driving cars. One of them takes a turn without indicating that he is turning. The other's car ploughs into the chap's who is turning. There is damage to the car that is turning. Both men get down. "You careless moron", says the one who has turned without signalling, "Cough up a thousand dollars for the repairs or I'll bash you to a pulp this minute". The other chap says, "It is your fault, you should be the one paying, you dithering idiot." "You want your teeth to be on the floor without the intervention of a dentist?" asks the first. "Hold your horses, blighter, or you will get it in the neck" says the other. They are considering a fight. Even before they get down to blows, each has decided that he is right. Once they get down to blows - or in other words, have an *altercation* – the decision to fight it out is taken. Thus *altercation* cannot be the opposite of *resolution*.

Vacillation is therefore the right choice.

10. **HERMETIC:**

(A) Abundant (B) Derisive (C) Permeable
(D) Steadfast (E) Corpulent

Answer 10

A major problem in food preservation is spoilage due to micro-organisms. However, enzyme activity virtually ceases in the absence of water. In order to ensure that dried and canned foods are stored even at high temperatures, the cans in which these are preserved, are sealed in such a way that there is no contact with the external environment that has moisture. Such sealing is known as *hermetic* sealing. *Hermetic* is airtight. Something *hermetically sealed* is that *which is not influenced by outside elements.* Its opposite is that *which is influenced by outside elements.*

Option (A): Abundant; The word **abundant** means **plenty**. It is possible to see plenty of cans of processed foods at a large department store. Just because such cans are abundant, it does not mean that they have contact with the outside elements.

Option (B): Derisive; Imagine that the two men that we have just seen fighting when one's car ploughed into the other's have begun exchanging blows. The chap who has turned without signalling (who, in fact, is at fault) delivers a haymaker to the other chap (who, in fact, is not at fault). The latter can take it no more and falls to the ground. The chap who is in the wrong then says, "You weakling, don't fight if you do not have the brawn". He then bellows with a *derisive* laughter (meaning *loud* and *mocking* laughter). *Derisive* is that *which derides* someone. Something derisive is that *which mocks someone.* In our little story, the well-directed punch thrown by the chap with the derisive laughter has come into contact with the other chap's chin.

Option (C): Permeable; Something *permeable* is that *which allows contact with the outside elements.* A permeable membrane may allow water to seep in. A permeable soil may allow water to flow through it to the lower layers of soil. It comes into contact with the moisture from external sources. **Permeable is the precise opposite of hermetic.**

Option (D): Steadfast; For those of you have seen the epic Titanic where the sinking of the then largest and most luxurious passenger ship on its maiden voyage has been depicted so well, you might remember that the captain of the ship stood *steadfast* to the wheel and sank with it. Some four men who were playing violins on the deck when passengers were running for dear life, stood *steadfast* to their task and sank with the ship. Would the captain not have been tempted to get onto a lifeboat and save himself? He too would have a wife and children and so would have the violin-playing quartet. Something steadfast is that which does not yield or is of unshaken loyalty and thus would not allow any outside elements to influence it. This cannot do as an opposite for *hermetic*.

Option (E): Corpulent; The word corpulent comes from the word CORPUS that means body. Someone corpulent is one who can be referred to as a fatso. He is fat because of the influence of his internal elements such as (A) insatiable appetite or (B) hormonal imbalance (C) utter lethargy, and so on. Corpulent, therefore, cannot be the opposite of hermetic.

11. BURNISH:

(A) Lighten (B) Hide (C) Dull

(D) Heat slowly (E) Close tightly

Answer 11

Burnished is the past tense of *burnish* just as furnished is the past tense of *furnish*. See the contextual usage of the word *burnished* in this sentence: The *autumn green of the trees* was *gilded* and *burnished with the low sunlight*.

Gilded - as we have seen earlier - means something with a coating of gold. Gold is a shining metal, as we all know. When the autumn green has been *gilded* and *burnished*, it means that something burnished shares some characteristic with something that has been gilded. You can have ice cream that is frozen and hard. This is because something frozen is also hard. You cannot have milk that is watery and thick. This is because these two adjectives are self-contradictory. *Burnished means made glossy or polished*. The opposite of this is *something that is not glossy* or not polished.

Option (A): Lighten; Imagine that you are walking up the steps leading to a mountain shrine. You ask someone walking down as to how many more steps does one have to climb. You are told that there are only six thousand more steps. You stagger. The knapsack on your back is cutting into your shoulder blades. Even the camera seems to weigh a ton. Your brother offers to take the knapsack to *lighten* your burden for a while. You gladly hand it over.

To *lighten* is to reduce, something you would do if you were to *lighten* the workload on someone else. Just because your burden has been lightened, does it mean that the lightened thing – meaning you – lacks polish or gloss? Quite clearly, this option has nothing to do with the word burnish.

Option (B): Hide; The *hide* is the *skin* of an animal. This is what it means as a noun. So if someone says that he has rhino *hides* for sale, he is dealing in rhino *skins*. (This means that the rhino that was under the skin is now back to the Almighty).

If the children are playing *hide* and seek, some of them *conceal* themselves at places where finding them would pose momentary difficulties to those who are looking for them. If a man who has stolen a polished gold bracelet decides to hide it under the seat of his bicycle, the gloss in the bracelet would not reduce as a result of it being hidden. To *hide* is to conceal. This has nothing to do with polish or gloss.

Option (C): Dull; What is dull and what is not, is a matter of people's opinion most of the time. This is because it is Man who has built up the vocabulary. Most things are relative, therefore. In this manmade vocabulary, the word dull has several shades of meanings, which we shall see in the following contextual usages:

An afternoon on which the habitual drunk has found no money to buy whiskey is a *dull* afternoon to him although the birds may be tweeting till their throats are aching.

A day on which there is a cloud cover and there is *no sunshine* is a *dull* day according to the weather bulletin although you learn that you have topped your class at the end-semester examinations and therefore that day is one of the brightest days in your life

You tell a classmate a joke that split your sides with laughter when you heard it the first time, but he does not even sport a smile. He merely asks you as to when are the next terminal examinations to begin. The sweetness in your joke is lost on the desert air. He is a *dull* person (at least in your assessment).

You are out buying the blue skirts that you need for your sister's school uniform and there are two that you have short-listed. One of them has a glossy finish. It shines. The other is not glossy. It is dull. You are in a dilemma as to which one to buy.

Dull is that *which lacks polish* and dull **is therefore the precise opposite of burnish.**

Option (D): Heat slowly; To *heat slowly* is neither here nor there. Does water develop a glow when heated slowly? Does not the gas mantle glow when heated slowly? *Heating slowly* has nothing to do with polish or gloss.

Option (E): Close tightly; To *close tightly* is also neither here nor there. Do the chocolates in the jar shine because you have closed the jar tightly? Do their wrappers lose their gloss because you have shut the jar tightly?

12. **MITIGATE:**

(A) Adore (B) Saturate (C) Proclaim
(D) Exonerate (E) Intensify

Answer 12

To *mitigate* means to *make milder* in manner or attitude, make *less hostile*; *mollify*. We shall see some sentences with contextual usage of the word *mitigate* so as to understand its meaning and the nuances of the word:

- People who have pain in the joints are advised to do specific exercises that would *mitigate* their pain. (Here the pain would be *reduced in intensity*; this is the meaning of the word *mitigate* in this particular context.)
- Protective films on windowpanes *mitigate* harsh sunlight.
- I am usually tense before examinations but my scores at the preliminaries had been so good that my anxiety was substantially *mitigated* this time. (Here the word *mitigate* means *alleviated*)

The opposite of *mitigate* is to *make worse.*

Option (A): Adore; Students often adore their teacher. The teacher is their ideal and they have deep respect for the teacher. A lover may *adore* his girl. He holds her very dear. To adore means to *have deep respect for something*. This is not the same thing as making it worse. This option would thus not work. We shall move on to the next.

Option (B): Saturate; The word *saturate* comes from the Latin word SATURAT that means *full* or *satiated*. Let us see some sentences in which the word is used contextually so as to understand its various shades of meaning:

- Ten units that together have more operating capacity than the aggregate demand in the country are now manufacturing soda ash. The market for soda ash is *saturated*. (Here the word *saturated* indicates *glut* or *oversupply*.] This does not make things worse for those buying soda ash. They may be able to buy at lower prices. Consumers may benefit eventually. Their hardships on account of inadequate supply of soda ash may get *mitigated*.
- The mountain climbers' clothes were *saturated* (or drenched) with rainwater. This by itself may not make things worse. Worse may be if they catch a severe cold. In the other event, they may simply change and move on.

To *saturate* thus would not qualify as being opposite to *mitigate*.

Option (C): Proclaim; The word *proclaim* comes from the Latin root CLAM- or CLAIM- that means to *cry out* or *shout*. The Latin prefix PRO- means forward. Thus to *proclaim* is to announce publicly. If the government were to *proclaim* tax concessions, this would make matters better. Normally people announce the good news. When you shout to people it is with the intention of making yourself heard. No loser proclaims that he has been beaten but the winner would proclaim victory. When a government has been able to increase the rate of employment or increase the rate of growth of gross domestic product, it *proclaims* this achievement. This option would therefore not work as an opposite to mitigate.

Option (D): Exonerate; The word *exonerate* that has the prefix EX (that means *out*) comes from the word ONUS (that means *burden* or *blame*). When an army officer has been (falsely) charged with dereliction of duty and the court of inquiry finds that in fact whatever that he has done is in keeping with his responsibilities, the court *exonerates* him (or frees him from blame).

To *exonerate* is to pronounce someone *free from blame.* This too makes matters better for the chap who has been blamed. Since the opposite of *mitigate* is to *make worse,* this option will not work either.

Option (E):Intensify; When the battle *intensifies,* the shelling gets heavier. When the pain gets *intensified,* it becomes aggravated. Things become worse. To intensify means *to make intense or aggravate.* Thus to *intensify* is the precise opposite of *to mitigate.*

13. **PELLUCID:**

(A) Similar (B) Opaque (C) Extravagant
(D) Insane (E) Cowardly

Answer 13

Imagine that you are on a summer holiday. You have been staying at a beach resort. You have been frolicking in the lagoon. The water gets agitated. Even then you find that you can see the bottom of the lagoon. Such seawaters are pellucid. The waters are transparent. They allow the light to go through. You are reading a book while on holiday. Each word is clearly understandable. So well is the book written! The language of the book is, figuratively of course, *pellucid* (or very clear). Something *pellucid* is crystal clear. So something that is confusing and therefore not clear is the opposite of *pellucid.*

Option (A): Similar; Imagine that two of your friends, Sam and Tim, are identical twins. They look amazingly similar. You frequently end up calling Tim as Sam and vice versa. But this is because they are *identical* twins. Even their mom gets mixed up sometimes. Now imagine that you know another pair of brothers, Ted and Bob, who look similar but there is no confusion as to who is who. You never refer to Ted as Bob or vice versa. There is no confusion at all. *Similar* is neither here nor there and would not do as an opposite to *pellucid.*

Option (B): Opaque; Something *opaque* is that *which does not allow light to go through it.* You cannot see what is on the other side of it. The question of seeing what is behind an opaque object therefore does not arise. There are people sitting behind a frosted glass wall that is made of *opaque* glass. They are discussing a plan to sabotage the festivities that you have been planning meticulously. You cannot see who they are. You are confused. The wall does not allow you to see through because it is opaque.

Had they been sitting behind a transparent glass wall, you would have been able to clearly see who are the ones planning to sabotage your programme. Thus **opaque is the opposite of pellucid.**

Option (C): Extravagant; Have you heard of the word **vagrant**? Those who wander from place to place and do not have a fixed address are called *vagrants.* The word extravagant comes from *vagrant* and means someone who lives beyond the bounds of reason and shows no moderation. Someone astonishingly excessive or exceedingly elaborate is called *extravagant.* He speaks forty five words where five would have sufficed. His extravagance is clearly discernable. A reasonable man lives within his means. Someone extravagant is one who lives beyond his means and overspends. He buys an after-shave lotion worth a hundred dollars without flinching. Unfortunately, however, when he buys this lotion, he has to show his money to the shopkeeper. Without this show, the lotion is put back on to the shelf. Extravagance shows clearly in his behaviour just as the bottom of the blue lagoon was visible when you were out on your summer holiday. *Extravagant* therefore cannot be the opposite of *pellucid.*

Option D: Insane; You meet this fellow in the street who holds his palms one on top of the other and asks you the colour of the elephant in his palms. He can hide neither the elephants nor his insanity. His insanity is as clearly visible as the bottom of the blue lagoon. An *insane* person is *one who is off his rocker.* He is nuts. Insanity is not a characteristic that one can reasonably hope to conceal. *Insane* therefore cannot be the opposite of *pellucid.*

Option E: Cowardly; Imagine that your ladylove has been seeing some other young man these days. They are both out shopping when a ruffian makes a pass at her. The chap escorting her tells her in a shrill voice that they should be moving out to a place where there are gentlemen. The ruffian then turns to him and asks as to what would he prefer - a chop on the neck or a punch in the solar plexus. The escort now starts shivering. You then turn up on the scene and bash the ruffian black and blue. Your ladylove realises that you are the man in her life and walks off with you. Is the fellow's *cowardice* not as clearly visible as the bottom of the blue lagoon? Not only can he not hide it, his shivers proclaim his cowardice. Someone *cowardly* is one in whom the *lack of courage* is apparent. Like insanity, cowardice too is difficult to keep under wraps. *Cowardly* therefore cannot be the opposite of *pellucid*.

14. DUCTILITY:

(A) Air of command (B) Tendency to inhibit (C) Harshness

(D) Consciousness (E) Brittleness

Answer 14

A *ductile* metal is that *which can be drawn into wire form* (without fear of returning to its original shape). If a bar of copper is put into a wire-making machine and drawn into a wire, the wire does not again become a bar on its own. It stays as wire. This is what makes copper a *ductile* metal. This is why a rod of aluminium can be twisted to make a loop. It *obeys* the force that bends it. As against this your schoolteacher can ask you to bend over and touch your knees if you have not done your homework and you will too because you obey. But he cannot bend the stick of chalk and make a loop out of it. The chalk will break but not bend. However, figuratively, someone *ductile* is *compliant* or *malleable*. A ductile person can be manipulated. He obeys his wife when she asks him to be at home at seven sharp for dinner because her mother is to be with them for dinner. The opposite of something ductile is that which does not obey or change shape.

Option (A): Air of command; The air is in the atmosphere. Someone with *an air of command* has an *atmosphere* around him that makes others do what he tells them to do. Someone with an air of command is one who generally *issues commands*. But an air is an impression as well. A bureaucrat with an air of command knows that when he issues orders, those at the receiving end of orders have to obey them because if they do not, he can take departmental action against them for insubordination. Someone with an air of command may however fall to the feet of someone to whom he dare not issue orders. He may himself become ductile. If the political boss wants that the Civil Supplies Officer (CSO) who has been frequently raiding the petrol pumps - a majority of which are owned by the political boss's cousin - be transferred to an innocuous position, then the bureaucrat in charge of the Civil Supplies Department might have to obey the political boss. If he does not transfer the CSO, he may be transferred to an innocuous position himself. This option will thus not do as the opposite of ductile.

Option (B): Tendency to inhibit; To *inhibit* means to *forbid*. The word comes from the prefix IN- (that means *in*) and the root HABERE (meaning *hold*). Thus, to *inhibit* means to *hold in*. If a person is too dependent on his parents, this may inhibit his progress because it may so happen that he gets admission to a premier college but since it is in another town and would mean leaving the parental home, he may refuse admission and prefer to stay on and study in a second-rung institution in the town where his parents reside.

Another person's shy temperament may *inhibit* him from *mixing* with his classmates. In the converse, to *exhibit* means to *hold out* or *show to others*.

If a chap has the *tendency to inhibit*, he *restrains*. But a chap who tends to inhibit may not be able to do so for long. The word *tendency* means inclination. But this does not mean forever unchanging. The shy person may find that a glass of sherry loosens his tongue a bit. He does not clam up when he meets his classmates at the reunion. He may end up cracking the choicest jokes that he has read when in self-imposed seclusion and have the town rolling with laughter. When the effect of the sherry wears off, he may return to being an introvert. He is back to his original form whereas something that is ductile does not return to original form. This option will also not do as the opposite to *ductile*.

Option (C): Harshness; The word *harsh* has several shades of meaning that we shall see as we go along. If the punishment for theft in a particular country is chopping off the hands, it is terribly *harsh*.

Imagine that there is a function to commemorate the foundation day of your residential complex. The chap in flat no. C-101 has not the faintest idea of melody. Yet when urged to sing, he takes to the microphone and renders a song for an hour. His *harsh* (or *discordant*) notes are jarring to the ears.

You are in Siberia during December and find the winter severely cold and then feel that the Siberian climate is terribly *harsh.* The word harsh here means *severe.*

You are standing at the bus stop in a town that is new to you. You ask the gentleman next to you in the queue as to which bus would take you to Bliss Avenue. He looks at you coldly and asks you whether you can read and says that if you *can* read, the bus routes are all in the timetable on the bus stand. This is a *harsh* or *curt* reply.

Now why harsh cannot be an antonym for ductile:

The chap in C-101 can learn to play the accordion instead of singing and his notes may thrill everyone and the whole party dances to his tunes.

Have you heard of Siberian summers when the flowers bloom and the flamingos fly about and the birds chirp? The Siberian climate does not stay harsh forever. It keeps changing. Something ductile remains bent when bent. Something harsh can be ductile as well.

Option (D): Consciousness; Imagine that a boxer is in a championship fight with another. One of the boxers - Mr. A -delivers a full-bodied punch into the solar plexus of the other- Mr. B. The referee starts counting. Mr. B is blissfully unaware of what is going on. He has fainted. He then regains consciousness. He asks why the stars are visible in broad daylight. His people are happy that he has at least regained consciousness. He has woken up. *Consciousness* in its one shade of meaning is *waking up*.

Now imagine that a chap weighs thirty kilograms more than what he should. He feels intense pain in the chest one day. The doctors tell him that if he loves dear life he should take up regular exercise and control his diet so that he should knock off thirty kilograms at the very least. The fellow realises that unless he does what the doctors tell him, it is curtains. He exercises regularly. He eats sparingly. He is conscious of the fact that if he wishes to live, he should live a life of regularity and moderation. But that does not mean that he is not ductile. He is doing exactly what the doctors have told him. He is bending to the doctor's orders.

Option (E): Brittleness; We have seen two shades of meaning of the word ductile; one of them is that which can be drawn in wire form and the other is manageable or pliable or obedient.

A *brittle* young lady is one *who is extremely nervous*. She is likely to break apart (not literally but figuratively, meaning to completely lose self-control) at the slightest annoyance. A *brittle* substance is that *which breaks easily* and is therefore *fragile*. *Brittleness* is thus the tendency to break but not to yield or bend. Something that breaks when you try to bend it has the characteristic of brittleness. ***Brittleness is thus the precise opposite of ductility***.

15. COMITY:

(A) Paranoia (B) Inertia (C) Discord
(D) Inequity (E) Frustration

Answer 15

Comity is *courtesy, civility, kind and considerate behaviour towards others*. *Comity* therefore means a situation where there is meeting of the hearts. If someone were to tell you that Germany came back into the comity of nations after the Second World War, it would means that Germany is back into the association of nations for mutual benefit. The opposite of comity is that in which there is a lack of civility.

Option (A): Paranoia; Imagine that a young fellow joins a large organization. He hails from a minority ethnic group. He works well. A promotion is due. Someone who performs better is promoted and our man is overlooked. He feels that he is being ill treated because he is from a minority section. Then there are instances when someone is on leave and the absentee's work has to be allocated to those present. Our man feels that he has been allotted more than ordinary amount of work because the bosses have decided to harass him. His behaviour reflects his thought processes. He becomes rude and irritable. Another promotion opportunity is denied to him as a result of his attitudinal change. He *feels* all the more *persecuted* - or, in other words, he *feels singled out* for *ill treatment*. He has become *paranoid*.

Now imagine that a father feels that his daughter spends too much time at her college. He suspects that she has been having affairs with her classmates. He lifts the extension in the other room when someone telephones her. He follows her to the college. When her class goes on a picnic, he hides himself at a spot from where he can see what the class is doing to his lass. He has become *deeply suspicious*. He has become *paranoid*.

The tendency to suspect others or to believe that one is being unfairly used is *paranoia*. Someone paranoid becomes paranoid when in company of others. Mark the word *suspicion*. It means that the chap is not sure. If a person is sure that he is being unfairly used in an organization, he should resign his job. The world is full of opportunities for those capable of delivering the goods (including couriers and delivery boys). The fact that the person from the minority continues to be within the organization or that the suspicious father cannot tell his daughter to leave the house if he is so sure that she is footloose means that he lacks the courage to go out of the civil society of which he is part. *Paranoia* is therefore not the opposite of comity.

Option (B): Inertia; Inertia is the *lack of drive* or the *lack of will to change*. Someone who watches the television all day long while lying on the couch may have *inertia*. He does not have the will to change his horizontal position. He is simply too lazy.

There is another variant to the meaning of the word *inertia*. Imagine that a coastal village has been hit by a tidal wave. So many have lost their lives, so many are homeless, so many have nothing to eat. The district administration should rush to the village and ensure that the people have food and shelter and are rehabilitated. If the administration does not take any action even in such dire situations, then it can be said that the administration is suffering from inertia or, in other words, it is not sensitive to the sufferings of its people.

The opposite of *comity* is lack of civility. But lack of civility means *hostility* just as lack of manners is rudeness. In order to be hostile one has to have negative emotions. Civil people say good morning to one other when they meet in the morning. Someone who lacks civility may ask the person who wishes him good morning whether he has nothing better to do than going around saying good morning to all and sundry. But the inert person does not respond at all. Someone who has *inertia* has no emotions at all. Thus *inertia* would not do as the opposite of *comity*.

Option (C): Discord; The word discord consists of the prefix DIS- (meaning away from) and the root CORD- (meaning *heart*). Thus literally *discord* means *away from heart* - meaning that the hearts do not meet. A situation where you see lack of harmony is that of *discord*. Harmony is a precondition for civility and the lack of harmony would bring about the very opposite of comity. If a community lives in harmony, it cannot hope to do so except when there is *comity* or *civility* among its members. If there is *discord*, the comity is gone. Mind you, an occasional quarrel does not automatically mean that there is discord among the community. But when quarrelling becomes a regular feature, then *discord* has set in. Thus *discord is the precise opposite of comity*.

Option (D): Inequity; The words *equity, equitable, inequity, inequitable, equinox* and so on come from the Latin root EQUI- that means equal. Just as laxity is the state of laxness, equity is the state of equality. This means that equity is a state in which there is justice because everyone is equal in the eyes of the law.

Imagine that Mr. A, a police inspector is due for a promotion to the rank of a police superintendent. His performance has been excellent. A police superintendent has retired. Mr. A is posted in his place so that he starts officiating in a higher position than his substantive position. This is unique. There is no precedent of someone holding higher position even temporarily. This means that Mr. A is certain to be promoted. A kind of promise is held out to him in his being posted in a higher position. Now when the promotions are announced, Mr. A is overlooked. He feels aggrieved. He appeals for promotion on grounds of *equity* and fair play. The meaning of the word *equity* here is *justice*.

A company issues *equity* shares. People subscribe to the issue. Some get shares and become equity shareholders. The meaning of the word equity is that if the company gives dividend to anyone, it shall either give to all *equity* shareholders or to none. It also means that each share has one and only one voting right - not more nor less! This is because all *equity* shareholders are equal in the eyes of the company. The meaning of the word *equity* here is *equality*.

Inequity is the *lack of fair play and justice*. When you do not get from society what you think is your right then you feel that you have been treated with *inequity*. The judge's decision anywhere in the whole wide world will seem *inequitable* to the person against whom it has gone. That does not mean that the judge has to pronounce the defence and the prosecution as being both guilty or both not guilty. Thus *inequity* is not the opposite of comity simply because there is no connection between them. To cut a long story short, what is inequity and what is equity is a matter of individual perspective but *discord* is not. When you see two people in *discord* tugging at each other's hair and raining blows and abuses, no one will judge this as just another way of expressing mutual love and admiration.

Option E: Frustration; *Frustration* may mean a *state within oneself where one may feel dissatisfied* with the outcome of one's efforts. But *frustration* implies only one person whereas there must be at least two persons if there is to be civility or comity. A man may doff his hat to a lady whom he meets while on a walk. This is a gesture of civility. But if he doffs his hat to a non-existent lady, he is bonkers. There must be at least two for civility.

Exercise 1

DIRECTIONS *for questions 1 to 10: Each question has a pair of CAPITALIZED words followed by four pairs of words. Choose the pair of words which best expresses the relationship similar to that expressed in the capitalized pair.*

1. ATMOSPHERE: STRATOSPHERE

(1) Nimbus: Cloud (2) Instrument: Calibration
(3) Aircraft: Jet (4) Climate: Rain

Atmosphere: Stratosphere; The *stratosphere* is the *upper layer of the atmosphere.* The relationship is that between the whole and its upper layer just as between milk and the cream floating on its surface or a boiling liquid and the froth on top. We have to look for this relationship from among the options.

Option (1): Nimbus: Cloud; A *nimbus* is a *rain cloud.* It may be worthwhile recalling the four major types of clouds that there are: cirrus or high altitude clouds, **altocumulus** or middle clouds, **stratocumulus** or lower clouds, and **nimbus** which may be low or may not be low since they have vertical development and may go as low as 1 km or as high as 13 km from ground. But nimbus is a cloud, all the same. Since nimbus is not necessarily a low-cloud, the relationship is strictly not as between the species itself and its higher level.

Option (2): Instrument; Calibration. An instrument is calibrated; for example a thermometer is calibrated into degrees and each higher degree indicates higher fever. Whenever one comes across a word with LIBR or LIBRA in it, one should remember the zodiac sign of the scale and remind oneself that the word is designed to denote a scale such as the word calibre indicates *one's standing on a scale where skills are measured.* A person of higher calibre would be ranked high on the scale than those lower than him in calibre.

Of what use a scale that we use in geometry if the inches in centimetres and so on are not marked on it? At best we can use it for drawing straight lines but you can measure nothing accurately with it. An instrument can thus be utilised effectively provided it is calibrated or else one has to go by approximation. But calibration is an integral part of the instrument. The calibration is not at a higher or lower level than the instrument itself.

Option (3): Aircraft: Jet; Here the relationship is that of a species like the aircraft and a highflying variety of the species that the jet is. The relationship fits exactly with the relationship expressed in the original word pair. Hence **Option 3.**

Option (4): Climate; rain. Here there is no such relationship as between Atmosphere: Stratosphere; rain is not at a higher altitude than the climate. If there is rain then it is rainy climate; if it does not rain - as in deserts - then it is a dry climate. Those who have been going to mountain resorts would have noticed that it is possible to see rain falling at a lower level than the hill station whereas the climate in the hill station may be bright and sunny.

2. FOOD: GOURMET

(1) Book: Critic (2) Art: Connoisseur
(3) Sports: Fan (4) Craft: Skill

Food: Gourmet; A *gourmet* is *a connoisseur in the matters of food and drink*. For those who may find it difficult to remember the meaning of the word connoisseur, I may attempt to make a permanent record of its meaning in your mind.

Connoisseur comes from the French verb CONNAITRE means to *know*. The French language has two different verbs for to *know*. For knowing human beings, the verb is CONNAITRE pronounced as KO-NAY-TRUH whereas for knowing non-humans the verb is SAVOIR pronounced as SAA-VAH. It is for this reason that someone learned is known as a savant in English because savant comes from the French verb SAVOIR; a savant is one who is well read and reading involves books that are not human. The use of the verb CONNAITRE here is for the *one who distinguishes*.

A person who has expertise in the line of art is an art *connoisseur*; a person *who knows drink and food* is a *gourmet*. The relationship between a gourmet and food is that of someone who has excellent tastes and the things about which he has excellent taste.

Option (1): Book: Critic; A critic may be knowledgeable since his services are used for the purpose of an objective evaluation; but the critic criticises as well. He may or may not be an expert in the field, depending on in which context the word critic is used.

At this stage, I am reminded about a story of someone who did not play bridge and yet sat with a foursome at his club. He *criticised* every move made by the fellow next to whom he sat. Tired of his constant criticism, the four players decided to play a trick on him when he got up to attend to a call of nature. When he came back the cards were dealt. The first person tore up his cards and said two FARFLES (A word that you will see in no dictionary since it was invented on the spot by the four players). Another said three TARTLES. The man next to whom the critic sat called three and a half FARFLES. At this the critic exclaimed: How can you call three and a half FARFLES with such lousy cards? He was criticising a game which he could not have had the foggiest idea simply because it was not a game at all. It was a mere ploy to confuse him. The moral of the story is that it is not necessary that a critic would know the subject well. He may criticise for the sake of criticising.

Option (2): Art: Connoisseur; Just as food is something about which a gourmet *knows well*, so is art a subject about which a connoisseur knows well. Hence **Option 2**, fits the bill admirably.

Option (3): Sports: fan; A fan is one *who is inordinately fond of a sport* or sports. It is not necessary that he know the sport(s) well or at all. A grandma once developed a great liking for cricket. In her days there was no television. You read what happened next day in the newspapers. She would, therefore, be found immersed in the cricket column. She found to her utter surprise that one day the total score of the team was written without the word "total" against it. Only the figure was highlighted. She then asked her grandson as to why this chap Mr. Total did not play this test match although he seemed to score the highest number of runs every time. The grandson suitably briefed her. The moral of the story is that just because someone is a fan of some sport or game, it does not mean that this person knows the game well; like the grandma, the fan may not know the game at all.

Option (4) Craft: skill; The word *craft* has several shades of meaning. If one reads that the river *craft* capsized mid-stream and there were only a few survivors, it means that the *riverboat* capsized. If someone has been asked to *craft* the royal crown, he has been asked to *make* the crown. If the goldsmith's son does not show interest in his father's craft but wishes to study medicine instead, it means that he is not interested in his father's profession that calls for *manual skills*. If some renowned lawyer is treading on the toes of the others in his town, his competitors may tell his potential clients of how he failed in this case and how in the other case he showed near innocence of legal procedures. There may thus be craft afoot to bring a bad name to him. Here the word craft means *cunning*. *Craft* and *skill* is the same thing in the normally understood meaning of the word craft. The gourmet is a human being. Craft is not. Thus this option will not do.

3. **NORTH: SOUTH**

(1) Black: White (2) Yellow: Orange

(3) Red: Maroon (4) Blue: Indigo

North and South are the opposite among the four cardinal directions: North, East, West and South of which the word news, incidentally, is an acronym. The relationship between North and South is that of opposites.

Option (1): Black and White; This is the correct choice because of the precise oppositeness of the two colours. These two colours are not shades of each other. Thus Option 1.

Option (2): Yellow: Orange; Yellow is mixed with red to form orange. Orange is therefore a shade of yellow (and so also of red).

Option (3): Red: Maroon; Red with a tinge of blue makes maroon. Maroon is therefore a shade of red and so also of Blue.

Option (4): Blue: Indigo; Indigo is a darker shade of blue. Indigo is deep violet blue.

4. **BRAND: PRODUCT**

(1) Pepsi: Cola (2) Aircraft: Flying Machine
(3) Tim: Boys (4) Sports car: Automobile

The relationship between a brand and the product is that the former is a specific name for the latter which is a common name for a class of things.

Option (1): Pepsi: Cola; These are two distinct brand names of the product - called *aerated drinks*. Pepsi is the brand name under which one company markets its aerated drinks and Cola is the brand name of that another company uses for marketing its aerated drinks.

Option (2): Aircraft: Flying machine; An aircraft is an *airplane*. It is not a brand name. Neither is flying machine a brand name for airplanes. Both are airplanes without any particular brand names.

Option (3): Tim: Boys; Tim is a name and boys is the general term for male offspring produced by parents. So while all fellows called Tim are boys, all boys are not called Tim. The relationship is that of Brand: Product. Hence Option 3.

Option (4): Sports car: Automobile; A sports car is an automobile specially designed for racing. But sports car is not a brand name. The relationship between a sports car and an automobile is the relationship as between a specially designed product and the product itself.

5. **DROUGHT: FAMINE**

(1) Poverty: Plenty (2) Drip: Fluid
(3) Camera: Film (4) Training: Skill

The term drought refers to a period in which there is an *unusual scarcity of rain*. Water-supply reservoirs become empty and wells dry up. There is no water for irrigation to crops. Crops dry up as well. As a result there is shortage of food and this food shortage is called famine. Thus drought causes famine. The relationship is thus as between Cause and Effect. Let us see the relationships in the different options and see where we find a cause and effect relationship.

Option (1): Poverty; Plenty. Poverty is a situation caused by not having enough. If there are not enough jobs and agricultural produce finds no buyers at a price equal to the cost that the farmer has incurred in producing it, then even if the farmer has produced great quantities of agricultural produce he will have to face poverty. Poverty and plenty can co-exist.

In several developing countries it is possible to see palatial houses where people live in the very lap of luxury side by side with hutments in which you see poor people living in utter squalor. But poverty does not cause plenty. Both are opposite situations caused by inequitable distribution of wealth in the society. Thus poverty and plenty are opposites or antonyms but not cause and effect.

Option (2): Drip: Fluid; You might have seen drips being administered to patients in hospitals and ambulances. The drip is the flow of nutrients (quite frequently mixed with medicines that flow into the patients body specially when he cannot be administered these medicines orally or does not retain them if given orally). The fluid is what causes the drip. The relationship is inverse to drought and famine because drip is the effect and fluid is the cause. What will the drip do in the absence of fluid? Tell jokes to the patient? This option will not do either.

Option (3): Camera: Film; The word film has some shades of meaning. If you are going to the department store to buy film for your camera before pushing off on your skiing vacation, it means that you are out to buy a roll of cinematographic light-sensitive tape on which the snaps that you will shoot will emerge when developed. When you see a film, you see a drama or event captured on cinematic film. But the film can be of use only if there is a camera. Both are complementary products just like a tennis racket and a ball, both of which are necessary to play tennis. But suppose you have given the film for developing to the photo laboratory after your return from the skiing holiday and have not bought another roll, does it mean that your camera is not a camera? A camera may or may not contain film. The camera does not make the film. The film is not because of the camera. The effect is not of cause and effect.

Option (4): Training: Skill; Suppose a carpenter who possesses great carpentry skill has been blessed with a baby boy. All that the baby knows is how to gurgle and wail loudly when he wants to be fed. Imagine that the boy is growing up and comes to a stage when he can handle a saw. Will it naturally occur to him that synthetic resin is to be used for bonding the plywood and the veneer? Certainly not! His father will have to teach him carpentry skills starting from the very beginning and then gradually groom the boy till the boy can make marvellous furniture without any training inputs from his father. But what is necessary for the boy to reach that ultimate stage? Training. Here the relationship is precisely that of Cause and Effect. Training is the cause of which skill is the effect. Hence **Option 4**.

6. **SALT : SALTY**

(1) Sweet : Sugar	(2) Cow : Bovine
(3) Bitter : Sour	(4) Taste : Flavour

If you put sugar in your tea, it becomes sweet. If you put salt on finger chips they become salty. In the relationship Salt: Salty, *salt is the cause of which salty is the effect*. Let us see the different options and find such a relationship.

Option (1): Sweet: Sugar; Something becomes sweet because you put sugar in it. The relationship between sweet and sugar is that of Effect and Cause. It is because of sugar that a thing becomes sweet. This is not the relationship that we are looking for. It is the precise inverse, as a matter of fact.

Option (2): Cow: Bovine; This calls for some knowledge of the various families of animals.

The cats are called *felines*. The tiger, lion, jaguar, and leopard are called *big cats*. The feline family also includes the cheetah, jaguar, lynx, and puma (also known as the *cougar* or *mountain lion*).

The horse is a part of the *asinine* family. Some of the other members of this family are zebras, the mule and the ass.

The kangaroo is a part of the *marsupial* family of animals. The term marsupial refers to a group of mammals that are distinguished by their ability to carry their young in an abdominal pouch for a period of time following birth. The marsupial family includes such animals as the kangaroo, opossum and the koala, all three found mainly in Australia.

The cow is a representative of the *bovine* family. So are the yak and the ox and the buffalo, deer and so on. The *bovine* family of animals *ruminates* on the food that they eat. The relationship between cow and bovine seems to be that of Sub-species: Species. Here prima facie the relationship does not seem to be that of cause and effect (although a cow does give birth to a calf which too is a bovine animal and thus a cow could be the cause of another bovine animal) and therefore we shall have to see the other options.

Option (3): Bitter: Sour; There is a tree called cinchona that grows in South America. If one were to bite a piece of its bark, the two eyeballs would turn 360 degrees in their sockets (figuratively of course) because the bark is horribly bitter. Once in a while an almond can also turn out to be bitter. This is because the guy who sells you almonds does not taste each and every almond before he delivers them to you. The lemon is sour to taste. Bitter and sour are thus two distinctly different tastes. However, it is not because of bitter that something becomes sour. The relationship is not that of cause and effect.

But the words bitter and sour can be used in a figurative context as well. A child is told not to touch a flame. He disobeys. A shriek follows. The child learns from *bitter* (or painful, agonising or harrowing) experience that flames are not to be touched.

Imagine that a man worked for a textile company. The company has downed shutters. The man has not been paid his provident fund and gratuity and so on (that we shall collectively refer to as terminal dues). He writes several letters to the management. There is no reply. The directors have migrated to a snow-capped hill station. He makes representations to the Labour Commissioner. He waits. There is no reply. He has no money to eat. He has no energy to follow up. He complains all the while. He is sullen. He is *bitter*. He is *sour*. In a figurative sense, both tastes can be used to describe the same thing. However the relationship between bitter and sour in the figurative context is that between synonyms but not as between cause and effect.

Option (4): Taste: Flavour; What does a curry which has no salt *taste* like? Imagine that you have bought cheese in which the manufacturer has inadvertently forgotten to put salt. Will it not *taste* bland? It is the salt that enhances the *flavour* of the cheese. However whether the cheese has taste or not can be only be determined after you taste it. Here the relationship is that of *effect and cause* since it is because of flavour that taste emerges. In determining a cause and effect it is important to understand that the cause comes first and the effect follows. You and your girl are out for a walk and someone makes a pass at her you bash him. He falls. His falling is the effect of your bashing. The cause invariably precedes the effect.

Now one is in a bit of a fix. The cow gives birth to a calf. The calf in turn is a bovine animal. Here the Cause: Effect relationship is established. Thus **Option 2, Cow: Bovine.**

7. **DIVIDE: UNITE**

(1) Split: Apart (2) Marriage: Divorce

(3) Fission: Fusion (4) Chasm: Gap

Let us see the relationship between **Divide and Unite**. Imagine that the employees of a company have formed a trade union. They have great unity. They fight back united when the management tries to exploit them. Now imagine that a leader of the union wants to form a separate union. Some men join him. Others stay on in the other union. The former union is divided into two unions. *Divide* and *unite* are thus opposites. It is this relationship that we have to look for in the options.

Option (1): Split: Apart; Imagine that you are sharing a chocolate bar with a friend. You split the bar by breaking it. The two parts become apart. This is a cause and effect relationship, it is because of the split that things go apart. *Split* and *apart* are synonymous in nature. This will not do since we are looking for opposites.

Option (2): Marriage: Divorce; As such *marriage* and *divorce* seem to be opposites. But they are really not opposite. A marriage is a legal union. Therefore an illegal union should really be the opposite of marriage. A divorce only annuls a marriage. Further, a marriage does not divide but it unites two people, nor does divorce unite anyone. This option is therefore not in sync with the main analogy of divide: unite where division comes first and unity later.

Option (3): Fission: Fusion; As children one must surely have seen flatworms. If you cut a flatworm into two, one piece of the worm goes off in one direction and the other in the other. This is something that seems so difficult to understand. But there is a reason for this. Many flatworms are also able to reproduce asexually both by binary *fission* - that is, by pinching themselves apart to become two-and by regeneration, producing an entire new worm from a piece that has been cut off. Quite clearly, fission *divides*.

Everyone remembers Elvis Presley the great singer for his *fusion* (or *bringing together*) of the country sound with black rhythm-and-blues influences and the new rock-and-roll style. Here fusion *unites*. Thus the relationship between *divide* and *unite* is the same as in *fission* and *fusion*. **Option 3** is apt.

Option (4): Chasm: Gap; The Grand Canyon in Arizona, USA is one of the wonders of the world. It is an almost one mile deep chasm (or gap in the surrounding mountains) created by the Colorado River. It may be seen that *chasm* and *gap* are synonyms; a *chasm* is a break and so is a *gap* (the other synonyms of chasm and gap are *hiatus, recess, break, pause, rift* and so on). Both *divide*. This is why this option is not workable.

8. **CRIME: PUNISHMENT**

(1) Lawyer: Judge (2) Court: Room

(3) Accused: Defendant (4) Homicide: Penalty

Crime: Punishment; This is again a cause and effect relationship. A chap commits a crime and this is why he is punished. Crime is the cause of which punishment is the effect. Let us see the various options where this cause and effect relationship emerges.

Option (1): Lawyer: Judge; The *lawyer* only represents the chap who commits a crime. Someone else commits the crime. The *judge* only decrees the punishment. The lawyer does not cause the judge. Both are part of the judicial system. There is no cause and effect relationship.

Option (2): Court: Room; The *court* does not create the *room* whereas the reverse is necessary for a court unless it is the intention of the judicial system to enjoy the open air while working. Here too there is no cause and effect relationship.

Option (3): Accused: Defendant. These are synonyms; the one who is accused of a crime is the defendant. Here too there is no cause and effect relationship.

Option (4): Homicide: Penalty; The word *homicide* has several shades of meaning. Homicide, in criminal law, is the killing of a human being by the act, procurement, or negligence of another. Homicide covers not only the crimes of murder and manslaughter but also the taking of a human life under circumstances justifying or excusing its commission. Thus, the killing of an enemy on the battlefield as an act of war is considered justifiable homicide, and killing, without malice, to save one's own life or the lives of one's dependants is termed excusable homicide. But when someone murders another he committs homicide. He is to be punished. Thus homicide is the cause of which *penalty* is the effect. So the relationship is that of cause and effect and hence **Option 4.**

9. **NUTS: BOLTS**

(1) Nitty: Gritty (2) Bare: Feet
(3) Naked: Clothed (4) Hard: Soft

Those of you who have seen nuts and bolts, the nut is a small usually square or hexagonal flat piece of metal, wood, etc., with a hole through it for screwing on to a *bolt* to secure or adjust it. The nut is useless without the bolt and the bolt is useless without the nut. Therefore *Nuts* and *Bolts* are components complementary to one another (unless, of course, one is talking about almonds or peanuts which are nuts too but then you do not bolt almonds or peanuts). Speaking figuratively, when you are learning a language and have understood the grammar and the pronunciation and are able to express yourself in that language, you have got the **nuts and bolts** of the language. Nuts and bolts together as a phrase make *the essence* or *the heart of the matter*. But we have to look for a complementary relationship. Let us see the various options.

Option (1): Nitty: Gritty; Imagine that you are keen to buy a new house. You see a nice, new bungalow. The owner has agreed to sell it to you. The basic decision for buying the property is taken. The following are some of the important things that may have to be worked out before you hand over the money to him:

In whose name does the property stand?

Where is the permission for building the bungalow?

Is there an existing mortgage on the property?

What about the water source?

Has the property tax been paid up to date?

What you are doing, infact, is working out the *nitty-gritty*, or in other words, the basic facts of the matter.

Nitty-gritty is the essence or the heart of the matter and figuratively it is the same thing as nuts and bolts. The two terms *nitty-gritty* and *nuts and bolts* are used as complements to denote the heart of the matter.

Option (2): Bare: Feet; There is nothing complementary about this relationship. Imagine that on a moonless night, someone has carefully folded and kept all his clothes on a rock by the side of a lake and jumped in. He swims to his heart's content and comes out to reach for his clothes. He discovers that some other chap in need for a good pair of clothes has run away with his clothes. Now he is bare (or naked). How does he reach home? He has his feet with which to run. The feet will not refuse to run because he is bare. They will run faster, as a matter of fact.

Option (3): Naked: Clothed; This does not throw up a complementary relationship at all. This is because any complementary relationship cannot have opposites. The tennis ball cannot be the opposite of a tennis racket. As a matter of fact, unless someone throws off his clothes, he cannot hope to be naked.

Option (4): Hard: Soft; These are opposites too and do not have a figurative usage when read in conjunction. As a matter of fact, no figurative use can have two contradictory words in conjunctions because that will make the figurative use illogical. So **Option 1.**

10. **JUST: ARBITRARY**

(1) Order: Chaos	(2) Fair: Whimsical
(3) Hope: Surprise	(4) Proper: Improper

The word *just* that means *fair* or *impartial* comes from justice that means *fairness* or *fair play*. Therefore an umpire has to be *just*.

According to criminal procedure codes of civilised countries, if the police have to arrest someone in connection with a crime, then they must produce the arrested person within 24 hours before a judicial magistrate and give satisfactory reasons to the magistrate for the arrest of the person. This is with a view to ensuring that the arrest is not *arbitrary* (or, in other words, according to the will, whim or pleasure of the arresting official). If there were no such code, then the police official could, for example, arrest and put in jail, someone who has come to the help of a young woman whom the police official's son has been trying to molest. There would be no fairness left. The country could become a police state.

Arbitrary is therefore the exact opposite of *just*. The relationship between just and arbitrary is that between fair and unfair and is therefore of antonyms. Let us see the various options and find out which pair matches this relationship.

Option (1): Order: Chaos; The word *order* has several shades of meaning. *Order* can mean neatness if you have put your clothes in neat *order* in your wardrobe. If your motorcycle is in good working order, it is in good condition. If the boys are to stand in queue in ascending order of their height, it means that they have to stand in an *arrangement* where the shortest boy is first in the line and the tallest boy is last. If the judge finds that the people in the courtroom have started shouting when the accused makes a certain statement and asks for order to be restored, he is seeking *orderliness*. If there is no *order*, there is *chaos*. The clothes in your wardrobe are thrown carelessly, the boys are standing according to their will and the shorter boys cannot see the magic show that the school has organised, the motorcycle sputters and spills oil all over the place, the court room reminds one of a fish market. The absence of order is chaos. The relationship between order and chaos is antonymous. But in just and arbitrary, both just and arbitrary are adjectives whereas in order and chaos, both are nouns and we shall have to look further.

Option (2): Fair: Whimsical. Imagine that a kingdom has an old monarch. One day he goes hunting and sees a beautiful spot by the lake. He decides to set up a new capital there. He sets a time limit for construction of the new palace and roads and courthouse and so on. The new capital is now functional. A few months later, he finds the new place boring. He now wants the capital to go back to where it was. Again there is a flurry of activity. A huge lot of money is wasted in transfer back and forth. There is not enough reason for shifting out. There isn't enough reason for shifting back. Things work according to his fancy. He likes a woman so he marries her regardless of whether she is already married. He does whatever suits his *whim* (or *fancy* in other words). He does not entertain debate and discussion. He is *whimsical*. He is *arbitrary*. As we have seen, *just* is *fair* and *arbitrary* is *whimsical* and all the four words in italics are adjectives. The relationship matches exactly and thus **Option 2** matches.

Option (3): Hope: Surprise; Imagine that someone has not been studying and has done badly at the examination and even then nurses the *hope* that he will pass with distinction. His *hope* is not backed by effort. Imagine that you have done extremely well at the written test and interview for commission into the army. You *hope* you will make it. When you *hope* to be commissioned into the army and then your name does not figure on the army's website where they have posted the results, it comes to you as a surprise. In the converse your friend has not done well and yet gets in. For him too this is a *surprise*. In the two cases, surprise has negative and positive connotations. However, *hope* and *surprise* are nouns whereas *just* and *arbitrary* are adjectives.

Option (4): Proper: Improper; The word *proper* has several shades of meaning. If you are out to play cricket, the proper (or *suitable, appropriate, right*) dress is white shirt and trousers and white shoes. If you meet an elderly person in the street and refer to him as old boy, you do not know the *proper* (or *correct*) manner of addressing elders (although it may be proper for the elderly person's peers to address him in this manner). If the librarian asks you to put the book back in its *proper* place, he is asking you to put it in its specific place. If someone makes a proper mess of things, he is making a complete or utter mess of things. The word *improper* is the opposite of *proper*. The relationship although antonymous does not match because *proper* may not be *just*. There is nothing *fair* or *impartial* about having to wear a helmet when riding a motorcycle although it may be proper (or a right thing to do).

All four relationships given in the options are that of opposites. The closest, however, is Fair: Whimsical since *fair* is *just* and *whimsical* is arbitrary. Hence **Option 2.**

DIRECTIONS ***for questions 1 and 2: Each question has a pair of CAPITALISED words followed by four pairs of words. Choose the pair of words which best expresses the relationship similar to that expressed in the capitalised pair.***

1. **MIND: MATTER**

(1) Physical: Spiritual (2) Abstract: Concrete
(3) Action: Reflection (4) Theory: System

The word *mind* has several shades of meaning. When you *mind* the class, you are seeing that no one misbehaves which means you have charge of the class. When somebody tells something that offends you and you mind his words, you are offended by his words. When some elderly person is getting down the stairs in the night and you ask him to *mind* the step, it means that you ask him to be *careful* of the step that he might not be able to see. If you have been giving unsolicited advice to someone and he asks you to *mind* your own business, he is asking you to *concentrate* on your business. If the teacher asks you to *mind* her words, she is asking you to *pay attention* to what she is saying. If someone is of unsound mind, he is nuts.

Something that *matters* has *significance.* If there is some floating matter in the swimming pool, it is some *waste* that should be removed. If you have hit the window while trying to get up and have hurt yourself and noticed that your cousins are laughing, you tell them that it is no laughing *matter* (or *occasion* or *event*).

In the present context, mind and matter are two opposites. The brain is a part of your body. There are some who can touch the brain. The butcher, for example, can touch the brain of the animals that he kills. The neurosurgeon too touches the patient's brain when he operates on it. But the mind is abstract. It cannot be touched.

Matter is that which *can be touched.* The table is made of solid matter. The hamburger is an edible matter. What we have to look for is the option that gives something *abstract* on the left and something *tangible* (or, in other words, something that can be touched) on the right.

Option (1): Physical: Spiritual; Something *physical* is that which *can be touched.* This is because it has a body. When somebody seeks material bliss, he is looking for things like brand-new cars, a huge mansion with a swimming pool and so on - things that can be touched. When someone seeks spiritual Bliss he seeks peace, mental poise - things that *cannot be touched.* The relationship between *Physical* and *Spiritual* is exactly reverse of the relationship in the capitalised pair.

Option (2): Abstract: Concrete; When a thing matters, it weighs, it is firm and solid. *Abstract: Concrete* best matches the relationship expressed here. *Concrete* is also solid, such as when one is asked to bring up a concrete plan for increasing company's profits. Hence **Option 2.**

Option (3): Action: Reflection; When you perform something, you take *action.* When you run, your legs perform action. This is a physical action. When you take legal action, you file a case. You have to take physical action such as typing your case, meeting a lawyer, paying him fees that he can touch with his hands and so on. All these *actions* are also *physical.* After you have made some remark that your mother has not liked, you decide upon *reflection* (meaning thinking it over in your mind) that you shall now onwards be polite. Reflection is something that you can do only in your mind. The relationship between *Action* and *Reflection* is exactly reverse of the relationship in the capitalised pair.

Option (4): Theory: System; A *theory* flows from the mind. But a system may or may not be physical. A locking system at the bank has got to be physical because if it is not then looters will walk away with the cash in the bank and no one will stop them. If an office has a system where the staff meditates every evening, this system is about the mind. You cannot see what the people are doing in their minds when meditating. If the universe is a system, you cannot touch it. Can you *touch* the *system* of Christianity? Thus a system may or may not be physical. Thus the relationship between *Theory* and *System* is not necessarily as that between *Mind* and *Matter*.

2. **FAÇADE : BUILDING**

(1) Fence : Garden (2) Dial : Watch
(3) Neck : Bottle (4) Page : Book

The word *façade* comes from the word *face*. The face is what you see. It is the exterior or an outward *appearance*. A man may have a long moustache, piercing eyes and an imposing jaw. Yet he may leap onto the dining table when he sees a cockroach or lizard although none are capable of bringing the slightest harm to him. A man may be a coward from within but his façade may be that of a dauntless person. A building may have an impressive façade and yet the place may stink to high heavens when you enter it. The building is thus what is behind the *façade*. The relationship between a façade and a building is that between the external appearance of something and what is behind the façade. You cannot see the façade when you enter the building and conversely, you cannot see the building when you are looking at the façade.

Essentially a façade while it consists of the two dimensions of an object that one sees - meaning its external appearance - but is part of the third dimension behind it. Now let us see where we shall see this relationship among the options.

Option (1): Fence: Garden; You can see a fence when you are inside the garden. Therefore this relationship is not like that between *Façade* and *Building*.

Option (2): Dial: Watch; You cannot see the *dial* if you are in the *watch* (meaning you have opened up the watch) and if you see only the dial you cannot see the watch (meaning the third dimension that has the operating system of the watch). Therefore this relationship is similar to that between *Façade* and *Building* and therefore **Option 2.**

Option (3): Neck: Bottle; A neck of the bottle is that part of the bottle from where you pour in or pour out the contents of the bottle. You can see both the neck and the bottle simultaneously. Imagine that a bottle is large enough to accommodate a full-grown man. He can see the neck when inside the bottle and he can see the bottle when looking down the neck. A dial is the only part of the watch that is externally visible. It is those two dimensions of a watch that one sees (merely because a dial is circular is does not mean that it is one-dimensional; a circle is essentially a regular polygon of countless number of sides). A neck is a part of the bottle; one can see both the bottle and the neck together.

Option (4): Page: Book; You can, see the *page* of a *book* only after you have crossed its *façade*, which is the cover of the book. Therefore this relationship, if anything, is the reverse of the relationship between façade and building.

DIRECTIONS ***for questions 3 to 5: Each question has a pair of CAPITALISED words followed by four pair of words. Choose the pair of words that best expresses the relationship similar to that expressed in the capitalised pair.***

3. **UNITY: DIVERSITY**

(1) Single: Multiple (2) One: Many
(3) Homogeneous: Heterogeneous (4) Singular: Plural

The word *unity* comes from the word *unit* that means one. *Unity* is the quality of *oneness*. When there is *unit* in a housing complex, it means that the people living in the complex live like one family. When a resolution t issue bonus shares to the shareholders of the company is adopted unanimously in the general body meeting, means that the shareholders are of *one mind* on the issue of the bonus shares

Diversity is a condition of *variety*. When a fishbowl has only goldfish, although there may be a hundred goldfish in it, there is only one variety of fish. When the fishbowl has two goldfish and two Malawi cichlids (blue fish from Malawi that are highly prized by those who love keeping aquariums in their homes), then there is diversity in the fish in the fishbowl. The goldfish do not yawn out of the boredom of seeing only fish of their own kind. (Yawning is okay when you are outside water but one does not know whether fish can safely yawn when in water). When there are at least two of a kind, there is *diversity*.

The word diversity comes from the Latin prefix DI- that means *away from* or *apart* and the Latin root VERT- that means *turn*. To *divert* means to turn (one's attention) from something and therefore towards a *different* thing. Diversity is therefore the quality that makes things different and hence when there is diversity there cannot be unity. Thus the relationship between *Unity* and *Diversity* is that of opposites.

If you were to see the **options 1, 2 and 4, Single: Multiple, One: Many, Singular: Plural** all may denote the relationship between one of a kind: several of a kind (such as one man: several men). There can be a single Alsatian (a large furry dog that puts the fear of God in people who have the misfortune of being chased by them) and multiple Alsatians; there can be one elephant and many elephants. There is no presumed diversity.

Option (3): Homogeneous: Heterogeneous indicates precisely the relationship between one of a type: many of different types (which is the meaning of diversity). *Homogeneous* is that which is uniform in character throughout, whereas *heterogeneous* is characterized by diversity and is the precise opposite of homogeneous. Hence Option 3.

4. **DOUBT: FAITH**

(1) Atheist: Religious (2) Skeptic: Pious

(3) Cerebral: Dull (4) Impolite: Courteous

If you have a lingering doubt, that the fellow who sold you the second-hand motorcycle has forged the signature of the true owner on the forms, that you shall have to file with the Vehicle Registration Authority for transferring the motorcycle in your name, then you have no faith in him. Therefore either you can have doubt or you can have faith. The words, doubt and faith, are thus opposites. We shall have to find such a relationship from among the given options.

Option (1): Atheist: Religious; An atheist is one who does not believe in God and does not even doubt his existence. He is convinced that God does not exist. While someone religious may have a deep faith in God, the word atheist to this option will not work for the reason that the atheist is sure that there is no god.

Option (2): Skeptic: Pious; There are different shades of meaning of the word *skeptic*. If a magician is performing and someone shouts from the audience that the pigeon that flew off from his hat was in the hat itself, the magician may call the heckler and show him the hat and when the *skeptic* certifies that there is no pigeon in it, the magician may proceed to pull out another pigeon from this "certified" hat. Here the word *skeptic* means someone who doubts. If the minister of a church says that there is no place in heaven for *skeptics*, he means that those who are non- Christians (or disbelievers of the Christian faith) will have to stay outside heaven. A pious person is one who is deeply devoted to religion. One cannot be deeply devoted to football, for example, unless one is sure that football is not the same thing as twenty-two idiots chasing a single ball and thousands of people wasting their precious time in watching these twenty-two idiots. The pious person is deeply devoted to his faith and has therefore no doubts whatsoever of the existence of God. The relationship between *Skeptic* and *Pious* matches the relationship between *Doubt* and *Faith*. Hence Option 2.

Option (3): Cerebral: Dull; Let us see the shades of meaning of the word *cerebral* from the following contextual usages:

- If a chap has had *cerebral* injuries in an accident, it means that there are injuries to his *brain*. Cerebral is *what pertains to the brain* and is not relevant because something cerebral has nothing to do with doubt.
- If someone has described the physical relationship between two lovers in his book in a more delicate and *cerebral* way than other authors do, then he has described such a relationship in a *more intellectually appealing manner* than the others who have described such relationships.

The word *dull* is used to describe something *lacking enthusiasm* or *shine* or lacking *intellectual capacity* or *something that does not stimulate intellectually*. Thus a boy who prefers to watch television serials while lying on the couch instead of playing anything may seem *dull* to his classmates who are playing squash on Sundays and baseball on weekdays. A silver teapot that has not been polished for some time may seem *dull*. A fellow who has slept all through a late-night movie even though his girlfriend was with him may have found the movie *dull* (and then his girlfriend in turn may have found him dull). But *cerebral* has nothing to do with *doubt* nor has *dull* anything to do with *faith* although cerebral: dull is an antonymous relationship.

Option (4): Impolite: Courteous; Someone who is *impolite* behaves in a *rude* or *offensive* manner. An impolite man may speak with his mouth full. He may use swear words. He may shove people when walking through a crowd. He, however, is sure that there is nothing wrong in what he is doing. Anyone who has the slightest doubt that the snake in his bedroom may be poisonous will leave it well alone and call the fire brigade or a professional snake catcher. Anyone who has no doubt whatsoever that the snake is a harmless grass snake (although people around him tell him not to touch it because it may be venomous) will hold it by its tail and try to throw it out the window (and in the process get bitten by the snake which turns out to be a King Cobra). So it is with *impolite* people. They too have *no doubt* that what they are doing is only proper. It is for this reason that the relationship between *Impolite* and *Courteous* will not match the relationship between *Doubt* and *Faith* although the relationship is antonymous.

5. DEMAND: SUPPLY

(1) Labour: Capital (2) Require: Offer

(3) Give: Take (4) Accept: Reject

Imagine that some men are out to have a good time and they have hired a rowboat on a moonlit night for a spin around the lake. Imagine that the lake is situated in a state where the manufacture, sale and drinking of liquor (whether at home or in a public place) is prohibited. The men yearn for a drop or two to enliven the proceedings. They ask the boatman if he can manage to get them some bootlegged stuff. This is their *demand*. It can be satisfied with the *supply* of whatever is demanded. The boatman knows where to get a bottle on the sly. He knows he can make some extra money in the deal. He will not suggest that buttermilk if consumed in the right frame of mind can bring great cheer as well. The demand is for liquor and nothing else will work. If he procures the bottle, the demand is satisfied. If the demand is for tweed, then jute cloth will not do. Thus *Supply* is the effect of which *Demand* is the cause. We shall have to see the options to get this Cause and Effect relationship.

Option (1): Labour: Capital; The word *labour* has several shades of meaning. If you labour for attaining some objective, you are *working hard* to get something that you badly want. The people *who do manual work* are *collectively called labour*. If you emphasise a point over and over, you are said to *labour* on that point. The word *labour* in the context of *capital* would mean *workforce*.

Capital means the money needed for running an industry or business. Capital is put to risk in the business. With capital, you can buy machines, raw material, spares and so on. You may need capital for day-to-day expenses as well. The other meanings of capital are apparent in the following sentences:

- London is the capital of UK
- The young artist's sitar recital was a *capital* (or *excellent*, *splendid*) performance
- *Capital* punishment is now banned in Lower Mongolia; they have now changed laws to provide for life imprisonment instead of hanging
- Napoleon's attack of Russia during the harsh Russian winter was his *capital* (or *greatest*) mistake; 90000 troops perished and he had to retreat.

As such both labour and capital are the key inputs for the industry. No industry, not even financial services industry, can run only on capital. You would need some people to clean up the offices, some men to serve tea in silver teapots to gullible investors and so on. Labour and capital would thus go hand in hand and are therefore complementary. But labour is not the cause of which capital is the effect. Therefore Option 1 will not do.

Option (2): Require: Offer; The fellows in the boat (in a couple of paragraphs above) required alcohol. They demanded (or asked for) a bottle. The boatman agreed to get them a bottle on the sly. He got one. The demand was met by supply. If the men in a town have no razors and are going about with their beards touching their knees, some young entrepreneur may get some razors and sell them to the fellows who have been busy picking lice from their beards. Offer (to supply razors at the marked price) is a result of demand (raised by men stumbling over their own beards because they do not know how to shave their beards) and hence the relationship in **Option 2** matches with the relationship between the words in the capitalised pair.

Option (3): Give: Take; There is no implication of demand in the word *give*. Suppose someone has been enchanted with a bottle of perfume in a departmental store but does not have the money. He then proceeds to conceal the bottle in the inner recesses of his coat, blissfully unaware that the close-circuit camera has conveyed the images of his act to the security guard who can lift a full-grown man with his little finger. The guard comes over and tells our friend that he is going to give it to him. No man can be so daft as to assume that what he is to be given is the bottle. The guard is going to give him a bone-rattling uppercut on his chin. And that too without the fellow's demanding it! This supply, unlike the chap selling razors with a fat price tag, will come free of cost. The relationship between give and take does not necessarily mean a commercial transaction. What the guard may want to give, the thief may not want to take. A give and take could even be gifts changing hands. So this option would not do either.

Option (4): Accept: Refuse; When you seek something that you need and are ready to pay for, you create a demand for the thing you need. You **accept** after supply but not before. To accept is at a stage later than demand. It is thus not synonymous with demand and hence for this reason alone this option will not match with the capitalised pair. The word *refuse*, incidentally, has an interesting meaning. When the garbage collector comes by, you hand over your *refuse* (meaning things that you do not need, for being *poured back* or recycled to the extent that is possible).

DIRECTIONS ***for questions 1 to 3: Each question has a pair of CAPITALISED words followed by four pairs of words. Choose the pair which best expresses the relationship similar to that expressed in the capitalised pair.***

1. **BARGE: VESSEL**

(1) Cargo: Hold (2) Link: Chain

(3) Shovel: Implement (4) Squadron: Plane

The word *barge* has several meanings that we shall see emerge in the following contextual usages:

- If you *barge* in when some friends of yours are partying, then you enter uninvited.
- If you are in the bazaar and you *bump* into someone, you *barge* into him.
- If the port in which the ship is to unload cargo is not deep enough, then the cargo is loaded into a flat-*bottomed boat* that reaches the cargo to the dock. Such a boat is known as a *barge*.
- When the river has to be crossed and there is no bridge, your car can be put into a barge, which is again a flat-bottomed boat and *ferried* to the other side.

A *vessel* can be a *cooking utensil*; it can be a ship or any craft that can be used for navigating on waters. A vessel can also be a *tube in the body carrying blood*.

In the relationship between a *barge* and *a vessel*, the *barge* is a special variety of vessel; a barge is one of the species of *vessel*.

Option (1): Cargo: Hold; The merchandise that a ship carries is known as its *cargo*. A ship when its carries cargo, has to put it in a place where it is not affected by the ever-present moisture in the sea air. Such a place is known as the ship's *hold* (or, in other words, *the place that holds the cargo*). The relationship between cargo and a hold is that of the thing contained and a container. This relationship will not work for the simple reason that whereas the cargo may be meat, the hold may be a steel container. A cargo is not a type of hold unlike a barge which is a type of vessel.

Option (2): Link: Chain; A chain has several links. A link is one of those that make the chain just as a barge is one of the things that make the genre of the vessel. This relationship is identical to that between barge and vessel and hence **Option 2** is correct. Incidentally the word *genre* means *genus* or *species*. Portrait painting was the primary *genre* of paintings till artists started painting abstract paintings, leading to the evolution (or *birth*) of the abstract paintings genre. The word *genre* comes from the Latin root GEN- that means to *beget* (or *give birth to*). From this root several core words have found their way into the English language. These core words are genital, congenital, genuine, genial, genius, genesis and so on. These core words have been contextually used in sentences (elsewhere in this book) that should drive home the exact meanings of these words and also their shades of meaning.

Option (3): Shovel: Implement; A *shovel* is a *spade-like implement* or a tool used to dig into the soil or to put coal into the boiler of a steam engine. To *shovel* food into one's mouth is to eat greedily. The shovel is an implement and to that extent the relationship between a shovel and implement matches that of barge and a vessel. The difference between these relationships becomes clear when you see the reverse. An implement can be a nail-cutter that does not shovel anything nor has any similarity to a shovel either in terms of size or function. In the case of a barge and a vessel there may not be a similarity in size, but there is a complete similarity in the essential function of the two. This similar function is carrying people and cargo from place to place. It is for this reason that Option 3 will not work.

Option (4): Squadron: Plane; A squadron is the collective name for some twelve fighter aircraft used by the air force of a country. The number of aircrafts in a squadron differs from country to country but twelve is the average. The relationship between a squadron and a plane is that of a collective name and a single constituent. This relationship will not match with the relationship between a barge and a vessel because the squadron is not the species of which the plane is the genus.

2. **DOGGEREL: POET**

(1) Soliloquy: Playwright (2) Symphony: Composer

(3) Pulp-fiction: Novelist (4) Caption: Cartoonist

A *poem or verse of a poor or undignified type* is called *doggerel*. Those of the undignified kind abound but they cannot be written here for very obvious reasons. No poet would like to write poetry that he himself would like to refer to as doggerel. Whether a poem is of a poor quality or doggerel is what the reader decides. Thus it is the poet who writes poems that are judged as doggerel. The relationship between doggerel and poet are that of a creation and creator.

Option (1): Soliloquy: Playwright; A *soliloquy* (pronounced SOH LILO QUEE) is something that someone in a drama speaks to himself. SOLO means *single* and LOQUERE is a French verb that means to *speak*. The relationship between a soliloquy and a playwright (meaning the chap who writes plays) is that of a creation and the creator. There is however this essential difference between a soliloquy and a doggerel. A Doggerel is essentially of a poor quality. A soliloquy can be deeply philosophical. Those who have read Mac Beth by William Shakespeare would remember Mac Beth's moving soliloquy about sleep. For those who have not had the pleasure of reading this epic, Shakespeare described sleep thus in Mac Beth's soliloquy after he murders the King of Scotland (while the King was fast asleep) to fulfill his wife's ambition to make himself the King: *Sleep that knits up the raveled sleeve of Care; Sore labour's bath, balm of hurt minds; Great Nature's second course, Chief Nourisher in Life's Feast*. This is one instance of a deeply philosophical soliloquy. This is why this option will not do.

Option (2): Symphony: Composer; A *symphony* means a marvelous *musical composition* played by an orchestra. The word *symphony* comes from the prefix SYM- that means together and the Latin root PHONO- that means *sound* or *voice*. A symphony is that in which there is musical harmony either instrumental or of singers in a choir. Sound as we know gives rise to either noise or music depending on whether the people are in the same note (or *harmony*) or in different notes (for example when quarrelling that would make *cacophony*). A symphony and the composer bear the relationship between a creation and its creator. A symphony may be of exceptional quality and maybe timeless. Mozart, Bach, Beethoven, Schubert and other famous composers have left a legacy of soul-stirring symphonies that are evergreen. These symphonies shall be remembered for ages to come. This is why this option will not do since *doggerel* is essentially poetry of a low or undignified type.

Option (3): Pulp-fiction: Novelist; Here too the relationship is that of a creation and its creator. The *novelist* writes *fiction*. Just as *doggerel* is poor or undignified poetry, a *novel of poor quality* is known as *pulp-fiction*. We have seen several novels that have been dramatized or been made into movies. Movies have been made from epics too. The memorable movie, My Fair Lady, was an adaptation from the play Pygmallion (by G B Shaw, the great English playwright). But then there are movies that are adaptations from martial arts fiction. While such movies can be of great interest to many, few would enjoy reading martial arts fiction because there would be little reading material that can be of interest. What can you read? Such fiction is an instance of pulp-fiction. A few pages of reading such text and one could be in deep sleep. This is why Option 3 will do.

Option (4): Caption: Cartoonist; The word *caption* as such means a *heading*. In the context of cartoons, since a cartoon usually consists of sketches, how does one tell the reader what the person in the cartoon is saying? How does the cartoonist show a particular political leader making a blunder while inaugurating the orphanage? It is for this reason that the cartoonist puts headings or words in little rings in the cartoon. These words are called legends or captions.

In Caption and Cartoonist, we again see the relationship between a creation and its creator. But cartoons are usually extremely sharp and witty. A cartoon of poor quality will not carry in the newspapers. This is because the newspaper industry lives on sensational issues and things. The printed material has to be such that arouses great interest. This is why Option 4 will not do either.

3. **PARADIGM: PATTERN**

(1) Skeleton: Flesh (3) Container: Content

(3) Maxim: Theory (4) Structure: Framework

A *paradigm* is an *example* or *pattern* followed. A particular post office which is essentially a branch of the Post Department may be lucky to have an exceptionally customer service oriented Postmaster. The chaps going there to buy stamps and to send letters by registered post may be heard whistling a merry tune when they emerge from the post office as they have been treated very well. This may be an isolated instance of excellent customer service. The Postmaster is transferred and another gentleman assumes office. He is sullen. No one now likes to even pass by the post office. People go in only if it is very necessary.

When a bank (as a whole) lays claim to be in *paradigm* banking, they are claiming that they shall follow a *pattern* of customer service where customers will be treated with utmost courtesy and care regardless of:

(A) Where their branches are located, and

(B) Who runs the branches

Thus *paradigm* and *pattern* are the same things and therefore here one is comparing synonyms. Let us see in which option we get this relationship.

Option (1): Skeleton: Flesh; The *skeleton* is only the *framework* on which the *flesh* adheres. Skeleton is not flesh. The relationship is not synonymous and will not do.

Option (2): Container: Content; *Container* and *content* are different. The *container* may be made of steel, which one cannot hope to eat whereas the *content* of the container may be Swiss chocolates that would be a delight to eat. Things that are different cannot be synonymous.

Option (3): Maxim: Theory; We shall see the essential difference between a *maxim* (which is a *rule* or a *proverb*) and a *theory* from the following context.

- In the law there is a *maxim* that states that the burden (or, in other words, the responsibility) of proof is on the prosecution. This means that the rule is that the prosecution (meaning the side which is saying that the accused has done this wrong or committed the crime) should prove the crime. If the prosecution cannot prove the guilt of the accused, the accused is deemed to be not guilty. This means that it is not for the defendant (meaning the accused) to prove that he is not guilty. If this *maxim* were not in the law, then the police would at their whims and fancies, charge anyone and everyone including the gentlest people of crimes. It is for this reason that the said *maxim* (or, in other words, *rule*) is implemented in most civilized countries.

- For those who want to succeed in the competitive examinations, the *maxim* is that the early bird catches the worm. Here the word *maxim* means a proverb.
- When you study law, you might see a *theory* that advocates reform in place of punishment. The main point of this theory is that a criminal takes to crime because of social influences and it is the responsibility of society to reform him rather than to punish him so that he becomes a good and noble citizen like anyone else. This theory further states that each successive punishment might make him a harder criminal. Notwithstanding this theory, however, proven murderers are being executed. This theory remains a theory only. It is not applied.
- When Archimedes was in his bath, he discovered the reason why things float. He advanced the *theory* of buoyancy. This theory was found to be of practical application. In fact the entire shipping industry works because this theory is correct. How else can one expect steel vessels of great weight to float on water? Thus *theory* is a system of ideas or hypothesis confirmed by observation.

We have seen what a *maxim* is and we have seen what a *theory* is. From the illustration above, it can be seen that a *maxim* is not the same thing as a theory. Since the relationship is not that of synonyms, this option will not do.

Option (4): Structure: Framework; Those who have seen high-rise buildings being constructed, would have seen that there is a *structure* of steel (or maybe steel-reinforced columns) and beams. This is the *framework* of the building. Once this structure is complete they make walls of brick and then put flooring, sanitary fittings, plaster and so on. The walls, the plaster and the sanitary and electrical fittings are things that are later made to fit into the structure. Thus *structure* and *framework* are synonymous and hence this option bears the same relationship as that between *paradigm* and *pattern.* Hence **Option 4**.

DIRECTIONS ***for questions 1 to 10: In each of the following questions a pair of words with a certain relation between them is given followed by lettered pairs. Select the lettered pair wherein the words have the closest relationship to that of the original pair.***

1. **SAPLING: GREYHOUND::**

1. Creeper: Plant	2. Tree: Bush
3. School: Boys	4. Freshman: Graduate

The word *sapling* has several shades of meaning. *Sap*, as you know, is vital juice that makes a tree grow. The suffix -LING is used to denote *small things* such as in the words fledgling, hireling, stripling (a youth not yet fully grown), trifling (insignificant or small), nestling (a bird not old enough to fly and therefore completed to be in the nest) and so on. A *sapling* is therefore a *small plant*. Sap, however, flows through animals and thus figuratively a *sapling* means an inexperienced person or even a baby greyhound. The greyhound is a dog characterized by considerable ferocity. The relationship between a sapling and a greyhound is that of a young one of an animal and the animal itself and therefore of the diminutive and the large thing.

Option (1): Creeper: Plant; A *creeper* is a kind of *plant* that climbs trees. A *creeper* may be small or it may be enormous. The trumpet *creeper* grows up to forty feet, which by no means is small. A *plant* may or may not be diminutive. If it is diminutive, it cannot be the main. Therefore the relationship between a *creeper* and a *plant* is not necessarily of diminutive and large.

Option (2): Tree: Bush; A *tree* is a grown plant. A *bush* is a plant that grows to small heights. A tree when compared to a bush is like a full-grown man standing next to a dwarf. Thus, the relationship, if at all between a *tree* and a *bush* is inverse to that in the capitalized pair. This option will also not do.

Option (3): School: Boys; *School* is a large collection of boys (and maybe girls if it is co-educational). Boys are men in the making; they are diminutives of men. School, however, is not the diminutive of boys and we shall have to move on.

Option (4): Freshman: Graduate; A *freshman* is one who has *just entered college* whereas a *graduate* is one who has *finished college* (and successfully or else he would be referred to as a college drop-out). A *freshman* is therefore a *graduate* in the making and hence the relationship in **Option 4** matches with that in the capitalized pair.

2. **HERD: ELEPHANTS::**

(1) Wave: Whales (2) Fleece: Sheep

(3) School: Gamblers (4) File: Soldier

A *herd* is a collection of animals. There are some collective nouns for animals that are worth knowing and these are as follows:

A *school of fish* is a large number of fish swimming together (swimming because they can do nothing else).

A *pride of lions* is one in which there are lions in numbers.

A bevy of dogs is one in which dogs are travelling in company of fellow dogs. (The word bevy is used for describing a gathering of beautiful girls as well).

A litter of piglets is one in which there are many young pigs talking about the exploits of their fathers.

A pack of hounds is one in which hounds are in the company of other hounds.

A drove of livestock is one in which cattles are out seeking greener pastures. Incidentally, when people attend a political speech in droves, it means that there are a number of people.

A flock of sheep is one in which sheep are out in their numbers.

A kennel of dogs is a gathering of dogs.

The *elephant* is an animal that usually moves in *herds* unless of course a single elephant is being used for a joy ride by human beings that have the uncanny knack of keeping the wildest animals in control. The relationship between *Herd* and *Elephants* is the collection of animals and the animals themselves.

Option (1): Wave: Whales; *Whales* in their collection are known as a school of whales. *Wave* is therefore not the collective noun for whales and this option will not do.

Option (2): Fleece: Sheep; The *fleece* of a *sheep* is the wool on its body. *Fleece* is therefore not the collective noun for *sheep* and this option will not do either. Incidentally the word *fleece* can be used as a verb as well. If you have bought a shirt for a certain sum and your friend has bought a shirt of the same brand, quality and size for half that sum, the shopkeeper from whom you have bought the shirt seems to fleece (or rob or cheat) people.

Option (3): School: Gamblers; The English language has some oddities. A pineapple has neither pine nor apple. A sweetmeat has no meat in it because a sweetmeat is a cake or a pie that the confectioner makes. Rum is an alcoholic drink and something rum is something strange or odd.

Oddly, therefore, a collection of *gamblers* is known as a *school* of gamblers. Hence **Option 3** is correct.

Option (4): File: Soldier; The word *file* has several shades of meanings. A *file* is one in which you keep documents and papers. A file can be used to manicure your nails. A *file* can be used to smoothen wooden surfaces. If the drillmaster asks your class to stand in single *file*, it means that the classmates have to stand one behind the other. One boy, however, cannot stand in file. It is for this reason that a file cannot be the collective noun for a soldier in the singular although a *file* can be a collection of soldiers in their plural. Just as it takes two to tango, it takes at least two soldiers to make a *file*. Thus Option 4 will not do.

3. **KOWTOW: BOW::**

(1) Abjure: Renounce (2) Gauche: Spruce

(3) Garble: Represent (4) Boisterous: Bubbly

To *kowtow* to someone is to *surrender* to his wishes or to *bow before* him figuratively. So kowtow and bow are synonyms. A poor nation may have to *kowtow* to a rich nation if it wants to receive aid from the rich nation. Thus the relationship between *Kowtow* and *Bow* is that of *synonym*.

Option (1): Abjure: Renounce; The word *abjure* is made up of the prefix AB- (that means *away from*) and the root JURARE- (meaning *swear*). If a chap takes an oath that he will stay away from cigarettes, he would have to *abjure* or *renounce* smoking. When a country's head of government is appointed to office he takes an oath of allegiance or loyalty to the country and its constitution. He is not going away but into the oath. When this head of government feels that he has had his fill of political office, he may decide to renounce office. *Abjure* is to *renounce* and these are synonyms as well. Both are verbs. The relationship matches with the capitalised pair and thus Option 1 is correct.

Option (2): Gauche: Spruce; The word *gauche* means left in French. Left-handed people were believed to be *awkward*. Gauche (pronounced GAUSH) is *unsophisticated* and *spruce* is *trim* or *smart* and is the precise opposite of *gauche*. Both are adjectives. The relationship is antonymous and will not do.

Option (3): Garble: Represent; When one *garbles* a message, he distorts it. A spy wanting to convey that he has just sent the secret defence plans of the enemy country to his country's defence headquarters may send a cable saying that Mrs. Dalhousie is safe and sound in hospital with blood pressure in control now. The reason for garbling such a message is quite obvious. If the cable mentions that the atomic bomb drawings have been copied and sent to the Mongolian defence headquarters, the chaps will be arrested and then hanged without delay. To *garble* is to *distort* some matter or story whereas to *represent* is to *tell it like it is*. These too are opposites and will not match the relationship in the capitalised pair.

Option (4); Boisterous: Bubbly; A *boisterous* party is one in which the noise level is substantially high. *Boisterous* is *noisy* and *bubbly is full of enthusiasm*; one can be quite enthusiastic being noisy - for example, someone enthusiastic about keeping the whole place clean may be able to sweep and scrub the whole house without uttering a single word.

A person, who may be deaf and dumb from birth, may be bubbly when he learns that he has stood first in the Master of Arts examination held by the university this year. Bubbles are not known to make noise, you know! As such, therefore, there is no established relationship between boisterous and bubbly.

4. **BOVINE: OX::**

(1) Lupine: lion (2) Vulpine: Vicious

(3) Pavonine: Pigeons (4) Asinine: Ass

Bovine family of animals consists of cows, bulls, buffaloes, yak and so on and an *ox* is a member of the bovine family. The relationship is that of class: member.

Option (1): Lupine: Lion; A *lupine* is a leguminous plant. A *lion* belongs to the feline family and has nothing to do with lupine.

Option (2): Vulpine: Vicious; *Vulpine* is an adjective that means something which resembles a fox and the characteristic of the fox is slyness. The fox, however, belongs to the canine family that also has dogs and wolves and such other similar animals.

Option (3): Pavonine: Pigeon; The word *pavonine* means something that has to do with a peacock. So the correct choice is Pigeon.

Option (4): Asinine: Ass; Asinine: ass where the *ass* is a member of the *asinine* family that also covers horses, zebras and so on. Option 4 therefore.

5. **SCULPTOR: STUDIO::**

(1) Baker: Shop (2) Painter: Shack

(3) Musician: Conservatory (4) Acrobat: Trapeze

The relationship between *sculptor* and *studio* is that between a professional and the place of his profession. We have to examine the options for locating such a relationship.

Option (1): Baker: Shop; The baker bakes in the bakery. Whatever he bakes, he has to sell it in order to bring home the bacon (or in other words, to earn for feeding the family). This is why whatever he bakes, either he sells directly to retail customers or sells it to other shopkeepers so that his products get a wide coverage and buyers. When he sells to other shopkeepers, he need have only delivery vans. When he sells himself, he has a *shop*. But once in the shop, he becomes a shopkeeper and therefore wears two hats: one of the baker when he bakes and the other of the shopkeeper when he sells what he bakes. Essentially however the baker's profession is carried out in the bakery and hence the relationship between the *baker* and the *shop* does not match that in the capitalized pair.

Option (2): Painter: Shack; A *painter* works in his studio. A *shack* is a *small house* usually a temporary structure. There are various other names for such homes one of them being a *shanty*. Every man has the dream of being wealthy and the painter is no exception to this ambition. If he resigns to the fact that he shall live in a shack, there is little point in painting. There are painters who make more money than industrialists. Some paintings sell for more than what an average individual could earn in a lifetime. Therefore to presume that a painter works in a *shack* is illogical.

Option (3): Musician: Conservatory; The word conservatory comes from the French verb SERVARE that means *to keep*. The prefix CON- means *together*. A *music or drama school* is known as a *conservatory*. A musician in order to excel at his profession has to be with others of his ilk. Imagine that a chap is learning to play the flute. He must have an idea of rhythm in order to play in a concert. If he does not, he will create chaos. The relationship between a musician and the conservatory matches that between the sculptor and the studio. Hence Option 3 is correct.

Option (4): Acrobat: Trapeze; An acrobat is one who does breath taking gymnastic exercises. There are acrobats who ride bicycles on a high wire. There are others who walk on high wires. There are some who ride motorcycles on the walls of a well. There are some who leap through rings that have a fire burning around them. There are some who swing out from somewhere near the top of the circus dome and catch another swing that is propelled towards them. The last variety of acrobats are called trapeze artists because the arrangement of swings from where they launch out and catch other acrobats in mid-air is called the trapeze. There are some who leap into a well from high minarets. There are a variety of activities that the acrobats perform. Trapeze is a prop for only one of them. This is why the relationship between an acrobat and a trapeze is not the same as that between the sculptor and the studio because the trapeze is not the only place where you see acrobats in action.

6. **HIDE: RHINOCEROS::**

(1) Skin: Sheep (2) Calyx: Petal

(3) Metal: Box (4) Armature: Dynamo

The word *hide* has interesting shades of meaning. As a verb, it means to *conceal* just as when you do want to spring a surprise on someone, you *hide* in the wardrobe and then, when the person is in vicinity, you leap out and say 'boo' to frighten the person. If you are buying a sheepskin jacket, the jacket is made of the *hide* (or *skin*) of a sheep. The word *hide* meaning animal skin is however used for the skin of large animals since only such skins can be tanned for making leather. If you did not like the driver of your school bus because he was very rude, you did not like his *hide* or *rudeness*.

Option (1): Skin: Sheep; A rhinoceros is a large animal and therefore its skin is eminently eligible to be referred to as hide. The general relationship between Hide and Rhinoceros is that between Surface and the Whole. The specific relationship between Hide and Rhinoceros in the context of an animal - which is what both the rhinoceros and the sheep are - is thus that of the skin and the animal. **Option 1** matches the relationship in the capitalized pair because the *skin* of a *sheep* is its exterior cover and the *sheep* is an animal.

Option (2): Calyx: Petal; The *calyx* is the number of leaves forming the *outer casing of a flower*; the latter, also has many *petals*. But since the *flower* is not an animal and also because the Skin: Sheep relationship in Option1 has tallied exactly, this option will not do.

Option (3): Metal: Box; A *box* is usually made of paperboard or wood or metal, but the selection of the material from which a box is made depends on its use. However, a *box* is not always made of *metal* and therefore this relationship will not do either.

Option (4): Armature: Dynamo; An *armature* is seen in a *dynamo*, which is a device that converts mechanical energy to electrical energy with a rotor cutting a magnetic field in it and generating electrical impulses that are used to provide sparks for igniting the mixture of fuel and air sprayed in the cylinders in internal combustion engines. It houses the rotor generating electromagnetic impulses and has copper wires wound around it to carry the current to the battery. As such, an *armature* is the surface of the dynamo. But since the *dynamo* is not an animal, this relationship will not do either. There is one more reason why this option will not do. An *armature* is what makes and breaks the current and therefore is a moving part of induction coils. One might also see the *armature* in an electric bell that moves to and fro when someone presses the switch. An armature is therefore not necessarily the outer part of an electrical device.

7. MURMUR: THUNDER::

(1) Wave: Shake (3) Cry: Roar

(3) Sniff: Inhale (4) Quiver: Fear

Imagine that a dictator rules a country. He is all-powerful. No one dares to defy his orders. The dictator starts having people killed even if guilty of small crimes. The dictator then starts having people framed. Slowly the people start gathering courage to voice dislike for his actions. Yet they speak softly lest someone tells him. Their dislike of the dictator is expressed in *murmurs*. Then the voice of protest grows till it becomes extremely loud like the *thunder* in the dark cloud-laden skies. One can murmur to someone who is very near. One cannot hope to communicate something by murmuring to someone who is a mile away. People watching this might take one for a nut.

Murmur is to speak softly and gently. *Thunder* is to shout in a state of intense agitation.

Option (1): Wave: Shake; When the President is passing through your town in a motorcade and you are watching, you wave your hands at him in a gesture of greeting. When you and your sister are out shopping and a ruffian nudges her insolently, you shake your umbrella at him before you hit him on the head with it. When you shake your umbrella it moves from side to side; when you *wave* your hand it also moves from side to side. The question is only of the intensity of moving from side to side. *Wave* is a gentle action of moving things from side to side whereas *shake* is an intense one. The relationship in *Wave: Shake* matches with that in the capitalized pair and therefore Option 1.

Option (2): Cry: Roar; The word *cry* has several shades of meaning. A baby cries when she wants milk; she to wails. When someone dies in the neighbour's family and they *cry*, they weep because of the grief caused by a loved one's death. When a thief accidentally overturns the lamp in a house from which he is about to escape with the life's savings of the people in it and the grandma lets out a *cry*, she shouts.

A lion *roars* just as the horse neighs or the cat mews or the bird chirps. But the word *roar* can be used figuratively to describe someone *shouting* or *laughing loudly*.

Imagine that two men stake claim over a property. One of them is staying on it and the other has entered the premises with accomplices with a view to have the occupant thrown out. The man (with the accomplices) cries to the one inside: Come out you vermin or I'll have you cut to pieces. The man inside *roars*: You idiot, get off or I will bash you and your friends to a pulp. Then he emerges from the house. The accomplices recognise the chap as the one who recently won the gold at the National Karate Championship. They flee. A *cry* and a *roar* are both sounds of high intensity, however, and this option will not do.

Option (3): Sniff: Inhale; When you *sniff*, you are audible. When you inhale, you are not likely to be audible; *inhaling* is a quiet process. The relationship is reverse of murmur: thunder.

Option (4): Quiver: Fear; The word *quiver* has several shades of meaning. Imagine you were to meet someone out hunting with a bow and arrow. This person would have to carry more than one arrow in order to be certain to kill something for the family's next meal. But holding several arrows in one hand and then using the arrow with the other hand may not work. Deer may run close to him to tease him and when he misses they may all roar with laughter. So that he can carry enough stock of arrows easily on his back, he puts them all in a case, called *quiver*.

Imagine that you have just finished school and your entire class is to go on an excursion to a mountain resort. You are to leave tomorrow. You are greatly excited at the prospect of the outing, of seeing snow-capped mountains, at the train ride, at the prospect of bathing in mountain springs. You are in a *quiver* or in a *state of great excitement*.

Imagine that there are women working in a tea estate. One of them sees a King Cobra with its raised hood. She runs for dear life and so do the others. When they are at a safe distance from the reptile, the woman who saw the serpent stops and shakes violently out of fear. She is in a *quiver*. Thus *quiver* is the effect of which fear is the cause. This relationship will not do since we are looking for a relationship indicating a difference in the intensity of two actions and not a relationship of cause and effect.

8. **PAPER: PAPYRUS::**

(1) Epigraphy: Stone (2) Epitaph: Grave

(3) Notes: Books (4) Parchment: Hide

The early Egyptians made *paper* from a plant called *papyrus*. *Paper* is essentially the parchment (or, in other words, thin layer) made from cellulose which is derived from the papyrus plant.

Incidentally, the word *paper* can be used as a verb as well. When the walls of a house are covered with decorative paper, one is said to have *papered* the walls. When two brothers have had a difference of opinion on the division of their ancestral property and their sister has *papered* over these differences, it means that she has brought about a situation such that the brothers do not now quarrel in the open (and therefore their differences are not visible).

Back to *Paper* and *Papyrus*, the relationship between these two is that between Finished Product and Raw Material. Let us see where we find this relationship among the options.

Option (1): Epigraphy: Stone; The word *epigraphy* comes from the Latin root GRAPH- that means *to write* or *draw* something in a specified manner. GRAPHY is the art of such writing or drawing. From this root several words emerge, some of them being photography (PHOTO means light), telegraph (TELE means over long distances and a telegraph is something written over a long distance), geography (GEO means the earth and geography is what is written about the earth). The prefix EPI is used in the context of something *near* as in epicentre of the earthquake, something on as in the case of an epigraph where something is written on a stone (by carving with a chisel of course) and something over as in the case of the epidermis, which is the outermost layer of the skin. Epigraphy means either (A) the art of *writing on a stone* or (B) collective writings on stone as seen in some archaeological sites. However the relationship between *Epigraphy* and *Stone* is not that of finished product to raw material. *Epigraphy* is an art and art only starts the process of artful things being made whereas a finished product denotes the end of a process.

Option (2): Epitaph: Grave; As we have seen above, the prefix EPI- means on, and GRAPH means something *drawn* or *written*. It is for this reason that an *epitaph* is an *inscription on a grave* where a brief write-up is written about the fellow whose mortal remains are inside the *grave*. While an epitaph is a finished product, the grave is not its raw material. If anything, the stone (on which the *epitaph* is inscribed) can be deemed as a raw material, but certainly not the *grave*. It is for this reason that this option will not do either.

Incidentally, the word *grave* also means something *serious* as in a *grave* mistake. The word *grave* comes from GRAV- the Latin root that means *heavy*. Something that makes a thing weighty or serious is *grave*.

Option (3): Notes: Books; Before an author decides to send a *book* for publication, he makes *notes* and from these *notes* about what he wants to write and what interesting observations have inspired him and so on, he writes the *book*. Thus the *book* is the finished product of which the *notes* maybe deemed as the raw material. However the relationship in this option is inverse to the one in the capitalised pair.

Option (4): Parchment: Hide; A *parchment* is the *skin of an animal* prepared for bookbinding; this is the skin you see in leather bound books. The *parchment* is the finished product after it has been subjected to the process of tanning. It is made from *hide* (which means *skin*) that is the raw material. Hence, *Parchment: Hide* gives a relationship similar to the one in the capitalised pair. Thus **Option 4** is correct.

9. **MODESTY: PURITY::**

(1) Plurality: Unity (2) Loquacity: Taciturnity

(3) Plenty: Scarcity (4) Honesty: Probity

The word *modesty* has several shades of meaning, which we shall see from the following contextual usage, which though on the face of it, may seem lengthy but it is designed with a view to drive home, the nuances of a single word and hence this slight elaboration:

- Imagine that you are in the clinic of a renowned medical practitioner. He takes a look at the sores on the skin of a patient and says that the problem is not within his capacity to handle. He then recommends another doctor. If he were a vain person - meaning someone with an exaggerated sense of self-importance - he would not have admitted that he does not know how to treat the person. He would probably have tried out some remedy or the other instead of saying that he does not know how to go about this one. The fact that he has admitted that he does not know how to treat this patient means that he has *modesty* or *humbleness*.

- Imagine that you and your classmate has finished college. You have a good job while his salary is small, which you can judge from the *modesty* or *inexpensiveness* of his clothes.
- Imagine that a factory owner has been hearing that the trade union leaders want higher salary for their members. He asks them to come to his office to discuss the matter. He is expecting them to ask for a huge hike. Instead they ask for a small and reasonable pay increase. He is surprised by the *modesty* or *smallness* or fairness of their demands.

We now know that *modesty* means humility (and therefore self-control), reasonableness and no extravagance and so on. *Purity* is the quality that makes things pure. If someone drinks with *modesty* he drinks in a reasonable manner and thus it never shows on him. He does not stagger. He is never boisterous. The difference between the modest person and someone who is pure is that a pure person will not drink at all. It is the highest stage of modesty. If the gold bracelet that you have bought has a *modest* amount of silver mixed in it, the amount of silver is reasonably *small*. But if the bracelet is *pure* gold, then it has nothing other than gold. Let us look for this relationship among the options.

Option (1): Plurality: Unity; Imagine that your class is to go on a picnic. One group prefers a mountain resort. Another feels that the beach would be ideal. A third feels that the wildlife reserve would be the best. There is plurality of opinions on where to go. If on the other hand, the teacher asks those students who would like to go the nearby ski resort, to raise the right hand and it so happens that all students are in favour of the ski resort, then there is unity (meaning oneness) regarding where to go. Plurality and unity are therefore opposites because if there is plurality then there cannot be unity and vice versa. Thus this option will not do.

Option (2): Loquacity: Taciturnity; *Loquacity* is the quality that makes people loquacious. A person who is loquacious is given to *speaking profusely* whereas a *taciturn* person is one who is *reserved in speech* and thus these are opposites. Thus this option will not do either.

Option (3): Plenty: Scarcity; Imagine that you are out for a drive in the countryside and are hungry. You decide to stop at a restaurant and when you come to a town en route, you find that there are many places to eat. You have plenty of choice. But imagine that you are out of gasoline and walk to the nearest town with a jerry can and at every petrol station you are told that they have run out of gas, there is a *scarcity* of gasoline. *Plenty* and *Scarcity* are opposites and hence this option will not do either.

Option (4): Honesty: Probity; The word *honest* has several shades of meanings. An honest police officer is one who does not take bribes. He has *probity* or *integrity*. An engineer who designed the building that collapsed recently was honest enough to admit that he had purchased inferior quality cement from a supplier because the supplier was his classmate. He is honest only to the extent that he is frank, candid or truthful. He does not have *probity* since he has purchased inferior cement knowingly. Therefore someone can have *honesty* but not necessarily probity but someone who has probity necessarily has *honesty*. Thus the highest form of *honesty* is *probity* and hence this relationship matches with the relationship in the capitalized pair. Hence **Option 4.**

10. PREDICTION: ASTROLOGY

(1) Forecast: Meteorology (2) Omen: Evil

(3) Premonition: Tragedy (4) Probability: Statistics

The word *prediction* comes from the Latin root DICT- that means to *say* or *speak*. The prefix PRE- means *before* and therefore if one says that something will happen before it actually does, then it is a prediction or in other words foretelling. One can foretell on the basis of observation of past trends or on the basis of mathematical calculation. If someone, however, sees that the sky is red and then says that there will be a death of some great person today, either he is relying on the fact that every day a whole lot of people return to the Almighty and that there is a great probability that one of them might be great or he is making a statement on the basis of his sixth sense or gut feeling but essentially without an adequate basis. This is the difference between a *prediction* and premonition; the former is based on study whereas the latter is based on intuition but without an adequate basis.

Incidentally, the word premonition comes from the Latin root MONIT- that means to warn. This is why the chap who minds the class when the teacher is away to see the principal on some urgent matter is called the monitor (the one who warns) of the classroom. The device in the intensive care unit of a hospital that warns if a patient's pulse falls or blood pressure rises and so on is known as a monitor. You shall see all core words based on this root, in this book.

As we have seen, a prediction is something that is foretold on the basis of observation. *Astrology* is the supposed art of being able to foretell the impact of the position of the stars on the course of human lives. Astrologers would probably study an array of patterns of star positions and then base their predictions on the basis of such patterns. The relationship between *Prediction* and *Astrology* is something foretold and the Basis Thereof.

Option (1): Forecast: Meteorology; The scientific study of weather conditions and climatic phenomena is known as *meteorology*. When a weatherman makes a *forecast* about the weather, he does so on the basis of this science. The *forecast* has scientific basis. He does not see a black sparrow flying from right to left and then, based only on the path that the sparrow takes, says that it would rain the next day. The relationship between *forecast* and *meteorology* is the same as between prediction and astrology hence **Option 1.**

Option (2): Omen: Evil; An *omen* is an *indication* of things to come. The young marketing executive has been making inroads into the market shares of the competition. His regional manager has just handed in his resignation. The managing director rings up the marketing executive and asks him whether he would like a holiday abroad before assuming higher responsibilities. This is a good omen for the young lad because while the boss has told him nothing specific, this might mean a big leap.

Now imagine that a marriage ceremony is on and suddenly the groom's younger sister's hair is caught in the table fan. There is chaos. She has to be rushed to a hospital. The groom's mother, with no basis for such a feeling, starts feeling that the marriage may be a disaster because the accident was a bad omen. An *omen* may be good or bad but whether an *omen* is good or bad is judged on the basis of gut feeling and not an adequate basis. It may so happen that the young marketing executive may get only much larger sales targets. It may so happen that the bride and groom may be lovebirds all their lives and seldom be seen out of each other's arms notwithstanding the groom's mother having felt that the marriage would be a disaster. Since there is a scientific basis or a database for an *omen*, this option will not do.

Option (3): Premonition: Tragedy; *Premonition* as we have seen is only on the basis of gut feeling and there is not an adequate basis for a *premonition* or forewarning. Neither for that matter is *tragedy* a basis on which the *premonition* is based. Hence this option will not do.

Option (4): Probability: Statistics; *Probability* is the mathematical measure of the likelihood of some event happening based on the study of the favourable cases and the total number of cases. When a dice is thrown up, the probability of getting one is one in six because there is one case when it will be favourable (when the face that turns up has one spot) and six total cases (since there are six faces out of which when you throw the dice exactly one face will be seen on top). Probability itself, is a part of the science of statistics and it foretells nothing. What is more *statistics* is definitely a science whereas astrology is only a supposed art. This option will therefore not do.

DIRECTIONS ***for questions 11-15: Each question below has two CAPITALISED words which have a certain relationship between them. The relationship could be synonymous, antonymous, part-whole etc. Following the pair, are four other pairs, each designated by a number 1, 2, 3 or 4. Select the numbered pair wherein the words have a relationship closest to that of the original pair.***

11. CLERGY: LAITY::

(1) Single: Pair (2) Employer: Industry

(3) Host: Show (4) Wholesale: Market

We have quite frequently heard the word layman being used to describe someone who is untrained or inexperienced, haven't we? When people of the Christian faith join seminaries to become priests, they start off as lay priests. They are priests in the making. Those who are *learning to be priests* or nuns are collectively known as *laity* just as the collective noun for human beings is humanity. The *clergy* (meaning those who are *priests* already) trains the laity. The *clergy* leads the *laity* to priesthood. Let us see where this relationship is seen among the options.

Option (1): **Single: Pair;** The relationship between *single* and *pair* is that of One: Two. The clergy leads laity whereas one does not necessarily lead two. Someone with 1 mark out of 50 at Mathematics would not lead but be behind the fellow with 2 marks out of 50 in the same subject if ranked according to marks at this subject. Thus this option will not do.

Option (2): **Employer: Industry;** An *employer* sets up an opportunity for employment. It does not mean that every *employer* leads an *industry*. An employer may employ someone for massaging his feet. Is massaging someone's feet an industry? This option will not do.

Option (3): **Host: Show;** There are some very well known television programmes that are *hosted* by renowned people. The Oprah Winfrey Show for example is hosted (or led) by Oprah Winfrey; the theme of this show is to openly discuss controversial subjects. The *host* leads the show facilitating the participants. This relationship matches with that in the capitalized pair and hence **Option (3)** is correct.

Option (4) **Wholesale: Market;** Imagine a farmer growing cabbages in his farm. Daily he reaps a thousand bulbs of cabbage. He would like to sell them so that he can give his family things other than cabbages. You cannot wear cabbages, can you? So he looks for buyers. He has the choice of selling the cabbages by himself in which case he will have to put them in a truck and drive around in towns and cities shouting "Cabbages, anyone?" till he is blue in the face. If he manages to sell any cabbages, the transaction will be a retail sale. As another alternative in which he can sell them all to a chap who deals in vegetables in bulk- a gentleman called the wholesaler. The transaction will then be *wholesale*. However, the farmer grows cabbages for meeting the demand for cabbages. A system in which one set of people demand some goods and another supply these goods is known as the *market*.

There are two principal components of any *market*: *wholesale* and retail. *Wholesale market* does not lead or conduct the *market*; it only forms a part of the market. Furthermore, both clergy and laity comprise of human beings whereas wholesale and retail market do not comprise of human beings; they are systems set up by human beings.

12. TUXEDO: SUIT::

(1) Taffeta: Silk (2) Buckram: Lining

(3) Tweed: Cloth (4) Cashmere: Wool

A *tuxedo* is a short dinner jacket worn over trousers. If you wear trousers but not a tuxedo, you are clothed but not *suited*. If you wear a tuxedo (and a pair of trousers of course), you are in a *suit*. A *tuxedo* is thus a part of a *suit* of clothes. The relationship between tuxedo and suit is that between part and whole. Let us now examine the options.

Option (1): **Taffeta: Silk;** *Taffeta* is a soft and lustrous variety of *silk*. The word *taffeta* can be used figuratively as well. Imagine that you ask someone to recite Twinkle, Twinkle Little Star and the blighter recites this well known nursery rhyme in the following form: Scintillate, Scintillate Diminutive Asteroid. The fellow's language is taffeta (or, in other words, bombastic). The relationship between taffeta and silk being that of a variety of some material: the material itself, it does not match the relationship of part: whole in the capitalized pair. *Taffeta* does not make silk. We shall have to move on.

Option (2): **Buckram: Lining;** The inside layer of something is its *lining*. Woolen coats have a lining of which the innermost is soft linen. Over this inner layer of linen, there is sometimes a smooth silk lining. The idea of making the lining is to provide additional protection against cold. The silk in the lining makes the garment more comfortable to wear. *Buckram* is a kind of cotton fabric used for making linings. Thus the relationship between buckram and lining is that the former is a part going into making the whole (and this whole is *lining*) which is the latter. Hence **Option 2.**

Option (3): **Tweed: Cloth;** It is not unusual to see so many things bearing the names of the places of their manufacture or origin. The Astrakhan hat is a fur cap named after the port of Astrakhan on the Caspian Sea. The Panama hat, the Bermuda shorts, Cashmere wool (named after Kashmir, an Indian province) and so on are examples of things bearing the name of the places of their origin. Tweed is the name of a river in Scotland, a country famous for its whiskeys, woolen garments and the bagpipe. In the vicinity of this river, a coarse woolen fabric is manufactured. This fabric, known as tweed, has a rough surface. Tweed is thus a variety of cloth. Tweed however, does not make cloth in the same sense as a tuxedo makes a suit and hence this option does not fit.

Option (4): Cashmere: Wool; As we have seen earlier, the *cashmere* variety of *wool* does not make *wool* and hence this option will not do either.

13. MACULA: SKIN

(1) Stain: Carpet (2) Vein: Eye

(3) Sheath: Nerves (4) Cloud: Space

A *macula* is a permanent *spot* or stain on the skin, usually congenital. The relation between macula and skin is that of spot or stain on a surface and the surface itself. We shall now see the options.

Option (1): Stain: Carpet; When children play on a *carpet* and spill ink, they cause a stain on the carpet. Stain and Carpet bear the same relationship as in the capitalized pair and hence **Option 1**.

Option (2): Vein: Eye; Blood is the vital fluid that every part of the human body needs. A *vein* is the capillary that carries blood to the *eye*. The difference between a macula on the skin and a vein in the eye is that the macula is not necessary whereas the vein is absolutely vital. Without *veins*, blood supply will cease and the consequences are not difficult to imagine. Secondly a vein is not a spot. A spot has a small usually circular area. It is therefore two dimensional. A *vein* is essentially three-dimensional.

Option (3): Sheath: Nerves; The *sheath* of a sword is what people in the old days would use as a cover for the sword when the sword was not in use. When in use, they used to put the sword into other people's bodies. In the modern days and age the sword has only ornamental value. The *sheath* is therefore a *covering*. It has nothing to do with stains. Since the sheath is not a stain for this reason alone, this option will not do.

Option (4): Cloud: Space; A cloud is not a stain on *space*. A *stain* is uppermost and therefore on the surface of something. The surface of *space* is indeterminate. One does not know where space ends. If somebody is under a cloud, then he is suspected of an involvement in some crime. Here too the *cloud* is not a stain. The stain is the suspected involvement in a crime and not the *cloud* under which the fellow figuratively is. Furthermore the stain is on his reputation. The reputation is abstract where as in the given word pair, skin is physical.

14. MAESTRO: ORCHESTRA

(1) Conductor: Bus (2) Bell: School

(3) Singers: Dancers (4) Ringmaster: Circus

A *maestro* in the generally used context is someone who is *adept at music*. A maestro could therefore be a singer or composer, conductor or instrumentalist with great command over music. However the term *maestro* is used to describe a *great performer in any art*, profession, etc. In the specific context of an orchestra, a maestro is the one who conducts it. The relationship between a maestro and an orchestra is that between a conductor and the thing he conducts.

Option (1): Conductor: Bus; fits like a shot.

Option (2): Bell: School; A bell does not conduct (or direct) a school in the same sense as a maestro conducts the orchestra. It only announces the starting time and closing time, breaks and resumptions. Its role is thus sporadic or on and off. A maestro has a constant role to play in the orchestra for as long as it plays.

Option (3): Singers: Dancers; Singers do not conduct the dancers. They are people from two different professions. Secondly because a person sings, it does not mean that he is a maestro. I sing too but none except the very strong hearted will be able to withstand me.

Option (4): Ringmaster: Circus; The ringmaster in a circus conducts some of the animals such as horses and chimps and so on. There is however a huge difference between an orchestra and a circus. The orchestra necessarily has human talent at play. The circus has animals performing. The relationship at option (1) is closer by far because when the conductor conducts the bus, he is conducting the human beings in the bus; he has no role to play in the conducting of the bus as a vehicle. This is the driver's bother. The conductor is in the bus because human beings get in and want to go somewhere. He has to tell them the fare; he has to tell them where to get off; he has to sell them tickets for if he does not then the bus owner goes bankrupt before you can say Mary had a little lamb; he has to give them change; he has to tell some of them that the bus does not go where they want to go and so on. The interface is between the *conductor* and human beings as in the case of a *conductor* and the *orchestra*.

15. MORDACIOUS: SARCASTIC

(1) Herbaceous: Green (2) Vivacious: Alert

(3) Curvaceous: Sleek (4) Audacious: Honest

Have you not heard the words morgue (a cold storage where dead bodies are kept in hospitals), and morbid (that means dreadful or gloomy as is a tragedy where many have died)? Something mordacious is characterised by biting sarcasm or invective. It is figuratively akin (or similar) to biting with the fangs of words. There is a similarity between a *sarcastic* remark and a *mordacious* remark. Let us see the similarity and yet the subtle difference in the meanings of the two words from the following contexts:

Imagine that a family is sitting to dinner and the curry is saltier than usual. The father asks the mother who has cooked the meal whether the table salt has become rather inexpensive considering that it has been used liberally. This is a sarcastic remark, criticising and teasing, making mockery of the fact that a more than normal quantity of salt has been added to the curry.

Now imagine that the father instead of merely criticising says that the curry has been made with a design to kill him since the lady of the house knows that extra salt will cause his blood pressure to shoot up. This is not teasing or taunting. It is downright *mordacious*. It is biting *criticism*. There is a mention of death with the intention of causing great pain and anguish to his wife over so small a matter.

Therefore *mordacious* is characterised by *acute sarcasm*. *Mordacious* is thus the acute form of something sarcastic. Let us see the options and see where we see such a relationship.

Option (1): Herbaceous: Green; An *herbaceous* plant is a *soft plant* that does not form woody stems. It is leafy and looks like grass. Something herbaceous is therefore green and thus herbaceous and green are synonymous. *Herbaceous* is not an acute form of green. It only bears green colour. This option will not do.

Option (2): Vivacious: Alert; The word *vivacious* comes from the French verb VIVERE that means to live. Thus the phrase 'Vive La Difference' means long live the difference. Someone out on a holiday at a sea resort swimming in the clear blue waters and having a great time may exclaim 'C'est La Vie' that means this is the Life! A *vivacious* person enlivens others. A *vivacious* girl may bring a dull party to life. An *alert* person hosting a party may be *alert* and may quickly fill the glasses of the guests as and when they are empty. Mere drinks, however, do not make parties come alive.

An *alert* watchman may keep constant vigil but his wife may take to snoring each time they are alone together because he makes no conversation other than about his muzzleloader. An *alert* person is alive. He is quick in attention. But the guard's wife may be *vivacious* and her jokes may make others roar with laughter. *Vivacious* is the acute form of alert. This relationship matches with that in the capitalized pair and hence **Option 2** is correct.

The word *acute* means *sharp*. It is not as if only pains can be acute. Someone's sense of hearing could be acute or keen. While on this word, have we not come across the words acuity as in the Professor's acuity or sharpness at mathematics or someone having an acrimonious debate (or sharp exchange of words)? These words are derived from the Latin root ACU- and ACR- that means sharp.

Option (3): Curvaceous: Sleek; Something that has *curves* is *curvaceous* just as something that has a good price (or good value) is precious. The word *curvaceous* is normally used in describing a shapely woman in view of her conspicuous curves. Something *sleek* is that which is *smooth* and *polished* just as a brand new expensive car may be. A person may have a smooth way of speaking and therefore may be described as one having *sleek* speech. Someone *curvaceous* may or may not be *sleek*. A shapely woman may burp in full view of others at a party. *Curvaceous*, since it may or may not be sleek, is not necessarily an acute form of *sleek*.

Option (4): **Audacious: Honest**; An *audacious* person is one who takes a challenge, is *bold* or *defiant*. A man commits theft. The police try to figure out who committed the crime. They fail to locate the thief. The thief may become *audacious* and may steal an even more expensive gold broach. Thus there is no relationship as such between *Audacious* and *Honest*. Hence this option will not do.

We have seen the word 'reduce' in this exercise, that means to bring to a lower state of size (when somebody exercises regularly and then finds that his waist measures 34 inches which earlier measured 40 inches, he has reduced in size), numbers, value etc.; to become less in any manner of size, numbers, value etc.

Words based on REDUCE are	That mean
Irreducible	That which cannot be reduced
Reduction	The act or reducing

The other core words flowing from this root DUC-, DUCT- are: *conduct, introduce, produce.*

Conduct is the Latin prefix CON- (meaning *with*; *together*) + the Latin root DUCT- (*to lead*); *conduct* means *to go with someone* or a group in order to *lead* him/them; *escort*, *guide* or *direct*. It also means to *direct*, *guide* or behave oneself or behaviour. A word based on *conduct* is *conducive*, meaning *helping, guiding, leading to a result*.

The word **introduce** consists of the Latin prefix INTRO- (meaning *within*) and the Latin root DUC- (to *lead*); *introduce* means *lead someone within something* or *into something*; *make a person an acquaintance of some other person*; *to present*; *to insert*; *to start* or *bring into use.*

Words based on the word INTRODUCE are	That Mean
Introduction	The act of introducing; a person's first knowledge of that which leads up to what follows
Introductory	Serving as an introduction

The word **produce** has the Latin prefix PRO- (meaning *forward*) and the Latin root DUC- (meaning to *lead*); produce literally means to *lead forward*; it means to *bring forth*; *something that is brought forth*; *to bring about*, *create*; *a yield* (such as fruits or vegetables).

Words based on PRODUCE are	That mean
Product	Something that is produced or brought forth
Production	The act of production
Productive	That which tends to produce goods or profits; causing or resulting in production
Productivity	The state of being productive; rate of producing

We shall now see some sentences that should drive home the exact meanings of the words based on the Latin root DUC, DUCT- since there is no substitute for contextual usage in order to understand their full import and their various shades of meanings.

You will notice, for example, that in some cases the word:

- **Conduct** means to *guide* or *direct* whereas in others it means behaviour.
- **Introduction** means a prologue whereas in other contexts it is a preliminary that is used for acquainting people with one another.

- **Produce** means crops and in other contexts it means to *bring forth*.
- **Reduce** means to lower in rank whereas in other contexts it means **reduction in weight.**

Here are the sentences with the contextual usage of the words as aforesaid:

1. The guide *conducted* us around the museum.
2. Zubin Mehta *conducts* the New York Philharmonic orchestra.
3. His *conduct* has been upright.
4. They will *introduce* you to the club members.
5. If the class gets restless, the professor *introduces* some humour to provide relief.
6. This program is only an *introduction* to higher-level mathematics.
7. The *introductory* chapter was so gripping that I could not help reading the book in one sitting.
8. The city of Vienna *produced* great intellectuals and artists.
9. That factory *produced* alcohol from molasses, till a ban on molasses came into force.
10. We have decided to *produce* a variety entertainment show on our school's annual day.
11. Agricultural *produce* is sold in bulk at this market yard.
12. The rumour was a *product* of his pervert mind. (Here what is produced is abstract)
13. During recession, it becomes difficult to find buyers for industrial *products*.
14. With unsold goods piling up, the company stopped *production* at the factory.
15. Unless the *productivity* rises, we will have to retrench some staff.
16. By way of punishment for disobedience, he was *reduced* in rank from major to captain.
17. I want to *reduce* my daily intake of cigarettes.
18. The accident *reduced* him to a physical wreck.
19. To control blood pressure, you will have to *reduce* body weight by at least ten kgs.
20. Our office expenses have come down to an *irreducible* minimum.
21. The consultants suggested staff *reduction* in order to bring about higher profits.
22. The union will not agitate against *reduction* in pay.

The Latin root VERT- or VERS- means to *turn*. The core words based on this root are: *avert*, *convert*, *divert*, *reverse*, *subversive*.

Avert comes from the Latin prefix A- (another spelling of AB-) meaning *away* + VERT- meaning to turn. *Avert* means to *turn one's eyes or head away from something*; *to ward off a danger*.

A Word based on AVERT is	That means
Aversion	Extreme dislike; that which makes one turn away.

Convert comes from the Latin prefix CON- meaning *thoroughly*; *completely* + VERT- meaning *to turn*. *Convert* means *to turn completely from one thing to another; change to another form*, *character*, *religion*, etc.; to *transform*. It also means a person *who changes his belief*, especially his religious beliefs. Words based on *convert* are:

Words based on CONVERT are	That Mean
Conversant	Familiar with
Conversation	Friendly talk or an exchange of ideas.
Conversational	Having to do with or resembling conversation, especially informal conversation.
Conversationalist	A person who likes to talk or who is good at making a conversation.
Converse	To talk informally together; exchange ideas; the opposite or "turned around" side of something; the contrary or reverse.
Conversion	The act of changing something into another form; the act of changing to a new religion or way of thinking.
Converter	A person or thing that converts.
Convertible	Capable of being converted or changed in character; a convertible thing, especially an automobile with a folding top that can be lowered or raised.

Divert comes from the Latin prefix DI- (another spelling of DIS-) meaning *apart*; *in different directions* + VERT- meaning *to turn*. So Divert means *to turn in a different direction*; *turn aside* from a set course; to *distract*; *to entertain*. Words based on divert are:

Words based on DIVERT are	That mean
Diverse	Marked by differences; not alike; varied in kind or form.
Diversion	A turning aside; an entertainment, amusement, or pleasant past time.
Diversity	Complete difference; variety; multiplicity.

Reverse comes from the Latin prefix RE- meaning *back* + VERS- meaning *to turn*. *reverse* means *turned* backward; having an *opposite direction*, *character*, etc; to *turn upside down*, *inside out*, or *in an opposite direction; set aside*, *overturn*, or *turn backward* or to the rear ; *that which is directly opposite; a setback*.

Words based on REVERSE are	That mean
Reversal	The act of reversing; something that is reversed; a setback.
Reversible	Capable of being reversed.
Reversion	A return to a former condition, state belief, practice, etc,
Revert	To go back to a former place, state, condition, etc.

Subversive comes from the Latin prefix SUB- meaning *from beneath; up from under* + VERS- meaning to turn + the Latin suffix -IVE meaning *tending to. Subversive* means *tending to overturn* or *overthrow something, especially a government*, *from its very foundations*.

Words based on SUBVERSIVE are	That mean
Subversion	The act of overthrowing something or the state of being overthrown.
Subvert	To overthrow from the very foundation.

We have seen the word **proclaim** in this exercise. The word **proclaim** means to *cry out in front of people* or *make an announcement*. Remember to cry does not necessarily mean to weep. If a warrior makes a war cry, it means that he shouts a word in challenge. He does not weep. If he did, he would not be able to fight anyone.

The Latin root CLAM- or CLAIM- means to cry out; shout. The core words are

The Word	The meaning of the word based on the root CLAM- and CLAIM-
Declaim	The Latin prefix DE- means completely and CLAIM- means to *cry out*; *shout*; *declaim* thus means to *speak loudly* and fully or *to give a formal speech* (as opposed to speaking softly or informally)
Exclaim	The Latin prefix EX- means out + CLAIM- (meaning *cry out*; *shout*); *exclaim* thus means to cry out suddenly; exclamation means a *sudden cry* or shout or a phrase that *expresses surprise or fear etc.*; *exclamatory* means *pertaining to expressing surprise*
Proclaim	PRO- (the Latin prefix that means *before*) + CLAIM- (meaning *to cry out*; *shout*); *proclaim* means to *cry something out before the people*; to *announce*; *make clear*); *proclamation* means a *public announcement*

1. The Principal *declaimed* our marks to the entire school in the assembly.
2. "What huge muscles that sailor has!" he *exclaimed*.
3. The Prime Minister *proclaimed* a statewide holiday on Thanksgiving.
4. His dress *proclaimed* his economic condition.
5. In a *proclamation* that was televised, the President declared a state of emergency.

You have seen core words flowing from the Latin root CLAM- and CLAIM-. You have seen prefixes such as A-, DIS-, AC-, and RE-. WE would suggest you analyse the following other words also flowing from the root CLAM- and CLAIM- and write the meaning of these words in the column against these words. You may then check the meanings with a dictionary.

The Word	The meaning of the word according to your analysis of the word after knowing the meaning of the root CLAM and CLAIM
Acclaim	
Disclaim	
Acclamation	
Clamour	
Disclaimer	
Reclamation	

We have seen the word **unanimous** in this exercise. This word is prefixed by UN- that means one and is derived from the Latin root ANIM- that means *life, soul, mind* or *spirit*. There are six core words with the root ANIM-: *animal, animate, animosity, equanimity, magnanimity, unanimous*.

The word *animal* has the Latin root ANIM- which means *life* plus the Latin suffix –AL which means *pertaining to; characterised by*; *animal* therefore means *that which is characterised by life; a living being.* It is, however, generally used to describe living beings other than human beings such as tiger, lion, snake, bird, fish or insect.

Animate means ANIM meaning *life* plus the Latin suffix –ATE which means *having* or *being*. *Animate* can mean *having life; full of life; living* or *to give life to; to make alive* depending on the context in which it used.

1. I enjoy watching the **animated** cartoon feature of Popeye on television.
2. When the environmentalists speak about the possible large-scale damage to the environment on account of the mammoth irrigation project that the government is planning, they speak with **animation**.
3. This table is an **inanimate** object.

Animosity; this word has the Latin root ANIM plus the Latin suffix -ITY meaning *condition; quality. Animosity* means *the quality of animals* or *hatred in specific*. Let us see the word *animosity* in a context that would make it easy to understand its exact meaning. We shall be able to visualise the husband and wife actually behaving like ferocious animals once we see the contextual usage.

There was a great deal of *animosity* between the husband and wife after his extra-marital affair was discovered.

Equanimity – the Latin prefix EQU- meaning *equal* or *even* plus the root ANIM- meaning *mind* plus the Latin suffix –ITY meaning *the state, condition, or quality of*, add up to *equanimity* which means *of even mind; calmness; composure, steadiness under difficult or adverse circumstances*. Let us see the word *equanimity* in a context that would make it so easy to understand its exact meaning.

1. The politician maintained *equanimity* even while insults were flung at him.
2. Although he was sentenced to death, the *equanimity* of the accused when the judgement was pronounced was remarkable.

Equanimous means *even tempered*. Thus when you say that meditation has slowly changed someone from a hot tempered to an *equanimous* person, the exact meaning of the word goes home.

Unanimous is the Latin prefix UN- which means *one*, plus the root ANIM- meaning *mind* plus the Latin suffix –OUS meaning *being; having. Unanimous* means *of one mind; everyone sharing the same view; showing the approval of all concerned*. Let us see this word used in context: The members of the housing society **unanimously** re-elected the entire panel of office bearers.

A word based on *unanimous* is *unanimity* meaning *state of being unanimous; complete agreement*. Let us see this word used in context: The jury reached *unanimity* on finding the prisoner guilty of the charge of murder.

We have seen the word *refuse* in this exercise in the content of *garbage* as one of its meanings. The word refuse comes from the prefix RE- that means back and the Latin root FUS that means *pour back*. Garbage is something that one may not like to retain and therefore when the garbage collector comes over, one hands it to him for being recycled or *poured back*.

The Latin roots FUS-, FUND-, FOUND- mean to melt; pour. The core words are: *confuse, foundry, fusion, refund*.

The word *confuse* has the Latin prefix CON- (meaning together) and the root FUS- (meaning to *melt; pour*); confuse literally means *to melt together*, or *to mix up mentally*. Two words based on *confuse* are :

Confound meaning, *to confuse; mix up; bewilder*

Confusion meaning, the *state of being confused*

Foundry is a word based on the root *FOUND-* (meaning to melt; pour); *foundry* is a place where metal is molten and poured into casts.

Fusion is a word based on the Latin root FUS- (meaning *to melt; pour*) + the suffix -ION (meaning *the state or process of*); *fusion* is the *process whereby things are melted or blended together*, or the *result of melting or blending together*. Two words based on fusion are:

Infuse meaning, *pour in, inspire something*

Fuse meaning, a device in an electrical circuit which melts and breaks an overloaded *circuit* before there is further damage due to an overload such as fire etc.

Refund has the Latin prefix RE- (meaning *back*) + the root FUND- (meaning *to melt*; *pour*); *refund* means "to *pour back; give or pay back* "

Let us now see core words flowing from the Latin root FUS-, FOUND-, FUND- in contextual usage:

1. The twins look so alike that their teacher sometimes **confuses** one with the other.
2. In the new school, there was **confusion** among the teachers about the syllabus.
3. In that newly married couple, one sees a complete **fusion** of two souls.
4. After the **fusion** of political party A with another party B, the new party retained the name of party B.
5. The jailer tried to **infuse** a sense of morality into the inmates.
6. They won the war because their General **infused** tremendous courage into the troops.
7. Zinc **fuses** with copper to form brass.
8. Had it not been for the **fuse** melting, the overload would have burnt the entire wiring,

Since we know that the Latin root FUS-, FUND-, FOUND- means to melt; pour, we can look up the dictionary and see the meanings of the following words:

Diffuse	Effusion	Profusion	Suffuse
Diffusion	Effusive	Profusive	Suffusion
Effuse	Profuse	Refuse	Transfuse

We have seen the word *content* in this exercise. The word has interesting shades of meaning. When you know that the *contents* of a box are Swiss chocolates, you know *what is in it*. When you have gorged all the chocolates someone asks you whether you would like some chocolate, you say you are full i.e. You are *content* or *satiated*. We shall now see, how such diverse meanings of a single word can emerge.

The Latin root *TEN-, TENT-, TIN-*, or *TAIN-* means *to hold*. The core words formed from this root are: *contain, continent, detain, lieutenant, pertain, pertinacious, retain, tenacious.*

Contain comes from the Latin prefix *CON-* meaning *together* + *TAIN-* meaning *to hold. Contain* means *to hold something together* in a holder; *to hold* or *be able to hold*; to *include*; to *keep within bounds or restrain*. The core words based on this root are:

Container: a *box, carton*, can, jar, etc., *that holds or encloses* something.

Containment: the *act or fact of containing or restricting*

Content: The word *content* has the prefix CON- that means *together* and the root TENT- that means *hold*. Something that a vessel holds completely is its *content*. Whatever it does not hold completely overflows. Whatever a book holds completely is its content or subject matter. The prefix CON- also means *thoroughly*. This is why the word *content* also means *satisfied*.

Imagine that a lion *holds* deer meat *thoroughly* in his stomach. Now imagine that another deer is passing by this resting lion. Imagine that the deer has been given a raw deal by Life and is contemplating suicide. The deer has begun to hope that the lion would eat him up and thus he would bid adieu to this big bad world. The lion makes no move. Let us suppose that the passing deer then asks the lion if he can do with deer meat without the slightest bit of running (some sort of home delivery as it were). The lion then says *no, thanks* because he is *content* (or, in other words, his stomach *thoroughly holds*). This means that when the lion is *content*, he is *satisfied*.

Continent: It comes from the Latin prefix *CON-* meaning *together* + *TIN-* meaning *to hold* + the Latin suffix *–ENT,* which is the same as our English suffix *–ING*,. A *continent* means *a mass of land* that is holding together; one of the *large land masses of the earth.* Someone who holds himself back thoroughly or completely when a whiskey bottle is opened at a party (or even otherwise) and refuses to have a single drop or someone who holds himself back in the face of temptations such as sexual entincements can be described as *continent*. A *continent* person is thus *self-restrained*. A word based on *continent* is:

Continental: *of, on, or resembling a continent*

Detain: It comes from the Latin prefix *DE-* meaning *away* + *TAIN-* meaning *to hold. Detain* mean *to hold away from someone that which belonged to him*; *to withhold freedom* from someone; *to stop* or *delay*; *to confine* in jail. A word based on *detain* is: -detention

Detention: the *act of detaining or confining* someone; the state of being confined or delayed.

Lieutenant: It comes from the French word LIEU meaning *place* + the Latin root *TEN-* meaning *to hold* + the Latin suffix – *ANT,* which is the same as the English suffix, *-ING. Lieutenant* means *holding the place of another* or *acting in lieu of another*; a person having the power to act for or represent his superior (and therefore *deputy*); a *commissioned officer ranking below a captain* in the army.

Pertain comes from the Latin prefix *PER-* meaning *through*; *throughout* + *TAIN-* meaning *to hold. Pertain* means to *have a hold throughout something*; *to have to do with or have reference to something.* Words based on *pertain* are:

- **Pertinent:** *related to the matter at hand*; *relevant.*
- **Impertinent:** disrespectful; unmannerly; impudent; not pertinent; irrelevant.
- **Pertinacious:** It comes from the Latin suffix *PER-* meaning *thoroughly*; *completely* + the word *tenacious. Pertinacious* means *sticking stubbornly or with determination to a purpose or opinion.*

Retain: Retain comes from the Latin prefix *RE-* meaning *back* + *TAIN-* meaning *to hold. Retain* means *to hold back something for oneself*; *to keep or continue to keep something in one's possession*; *to keep something in use*, practice, etc.; *to keep in mind or remember*; *to reserve the services* of a lawyer or other representative by paying him a fee." Words based on *retain* are:

Retainer: a *servant*; a *fee paid to engage or keep a representative* such as a lawyer.

Retention: the *act of retaining* or *state of being retained* or kept; the *ability to remember*; *memory.*

Retentive: *able to keep things*, especially in memory.

Tenacious comes from the *TEN-* meaning *to hold* + the Latin suffix – *ACIOUS* meaning tending to; inclined to. *Tenacious* means *tending to hold something* strongly, such as an opinion, belief, etc.; *stubborn.*" A word based on *tenacious* is:

Tenacity: the state or quality of holding firm; stubbornness; determination.

We have seen the word *grave* in this exercise that generally denotes a *place of burial*. However a *grave* mistake means a serious mistake. The Latin root GRAV- means *heavy.*

The word *grave* means something *of great importance*; *solemn*; *dignified*; *sombre. Aggravate* and *gravity* are the two other core words based on the root GRAV-.

The word **aggravate** has AG- the Latin prefix meaning *to* + the Latin root GRAV- (meaning *heavy*) + the suffix –ATE (which is used to form verbs); *aggravate* means *to make heavy*; *to worsen*; *to make more unpleasant* or *more burdensome.*

The word *Gravity* has the Latin root GRAV- (meaning heavy) + the suffix –ITY (meaning the *state or quality of*;gravity is *heaviness*; *the force that the earth exerts on an object that makes it fall towards the centre of the earth*; in another sense, gravity means *seriousness.*

Some words based on *gravity* are :

Gravitate: to **move as if attracted** by the force of gravity

Gravitation: the act or *state of gravitating*

Gravitational: pertaining to the force of gravity or to gravitation.

Let us see the core words flowing from the root GRAV- in context:

1. Do not give any more antacid to the patient; it will *aggravate* his indigestion.
2. The dispute between the two men became *aggravated* when one of them slapped the other.
3. The company is passing through a *grave* financial crisis.

4. Isaac Newton enunciated the three laws of *gravity*.
5. We came to know of the *gravity* of his malady only after receiving the medical report.
6. He has the habit of *gravitating* towards the topic of chronic constipation.
7. The earth's *gravitational* pull keeps the moon circling around it.

If you remember, we have seen the word *prediction* in this exercise. *Prediction* means being able to say that something is to occur before it actually happens. The word *prediction* comes from the Latin root DICT- that means *to say* or *speak*.

The Latin root DICT- means to say or speak. The core words are: contradict, dictate, diction, predict.

The word contradict has the Latin prefix CONTRA- (meaning "against") + the Latin root DICT- (meaning "speak; to say"); *contradict* means "to say against; to hold that the opposite of what is being said is true; to deny the truth of a statement." Two words based on *contradict* are:

Contradiction: a *denial*; a statement that denies another

Contradictory: that *which contradicts*

The word *dictate* has the Latin root DICT- (meaning *to say*; *speak* + the Latin suffix –ATE (which is a word-ending used to form verbs); *dictate* means *to say something, so that it can be recorded*; to *issue commands* or *make laws with authority*. The words based on *dictate* are:

Dictation: act of dictating letters, notes etc.; that which is dictated

Dictator : one who dictates (the laws), especially one who rules with an iron hand

Dictatorial: like a dictator; tyrant-like

The word *diction* is the Latin root DICT- (meaning "to say; speak" + the suffix – ION (meaning "the state or quality of being"); diction means the *quality of one's speech* and *use of words*. A word based on *diction* is **dictionary**, meaning *a reference book in which words of a language and their meanings are listed*.

The word predict has the Latin prefix –PRE (meaning before) and the Latin root DICT- (meaning *to say* or *speak about an event before it*); *predict* means *to say before the event actually happens*; *to foretell*; to say what may happen in the future." Two words based on *predict* are:

Predictable: that *which can be predicted*

Prediction: *a forecast*

Let us see the words emanating from the Latin root DICT- in contextual usage that will drive home the precise meanings of these words and their various shades of meaning:

1. Kindly do not *contradict* me at this stage; please let me complete what I have to say.
2. The Minister issued a statement today that *contradicted* what he said a few days ago.
3. The accused made *contradictory* statements during cross-examination by the prosecution.
4. I want you to quickly type the office memorandum that I have *dictated*.
5. The political party, that won the recent elections, was new to governance and thus bureaucrats *dictated* policy.
6. Hitler was a *dictator*.
7. While your vocabulary is adequate, please try to improve your *diction*.
8. Nostradamus could *predict* disasters.
9. The *prediction* for tomorrow's weather is that it would be a sunny weather in most parts of the country.

We have seen the word **premonition** in this exercise. *Premonition* means a *warning of something* that is likely to happen. It is based on intuition and not on the basis of some scientific study. The Latin roots *MON-*, *MONIT-* mean *to warn*; *advise*. The core words are: *admonish, monument, monitor* and *premonition*.

Admonish has the Latin prefix *AD-*, meaning to + *MON-* the root meaning *to warn*; *advise* + the suffix *-ISH*, that is used to form verbs; *admonish* means "*to warn*; or *advise* someone who makes a mistake. A word based on *admonish* is *admonition* meaning *the act of admonishing*; *a mild warning.*

Monument is a word that comes from *MON-*, the root meaning *to warn*; *advise* + the suffix *-MENT*, meaning *the act or means of*; *monument* is the *means of advising someone* about something; a thing such as a statue built as a reminder of a person or an event; tombstone; *a work of art*, *literature* that is considered to *have lasting value.* A word based on *monument* is *monumental*, meaning *of great value*; *larger than life*; *massive.*

Monitor is *MONIT-*, the Latin root meaning *to warn*; *advise* + *-OR*, the Latin suffix meaning *a person or a thing that does something*; *monitor* means a person or a thing *that advises* or warns ; a student who is appointed for maintaining order in a classroom; a device which is used to keep a check on information such as pulse rate; blood pressure; a person who listens to radio or television broadcasts to check on matters of quality, accuracy, compliance with law etc." A word based on *monitor* is *monitory*, meaning *warning.*

Premonition has *PRE-*, the Latin prefix meaning before + *MONIT-*, the Latin root meaning *to warn*; *advise* + *-ION* , the Latin suffix meaning the *act or the state of*; *premonition* means the *state of being warned before the happening of an event*; a natural instinct whereby one gets a warning of events that are going to happen in the future; *intuition.*

A word based on *premonition* is *premonitory*, meaning that *which gives a warning beforehand.*

Let us see some core words flowing from the Latin root MON-, MONIT- used in context in the following sentences:

1. The company felt it proper to only *admonish* him for the mistake and close the issue.
2. The students paid no heed to the teacher's *admonition* and continued to make a deafening din.
3. The Taj Mahal is a *monument* that a Mogul King built out of love for his wife.
4. Dr. Vikram Sarabhai did *monumental* work in the field of space research.
5. The *monitor* was asked to list students who had not completed their homework.
6. The professor's *monitory* look was enough to bring the class to order.
7. The whole day I had heartburn and this was to me a *premonition* of the accident in my chemical factory.
8. His sudden loss of weight and a constant headache was a *premonitory* symptom of cancer. (*Please note that there is no investigation done to diagnose cancer; loss of weight may be due to fasting and a constant headache may be due possibly to chronic constipation or sinusitis*)

We have seen the words *acute* and *acuity* in this exercise. The Latin root ACU- or ACR- means sharp. Here are five core words in which the root acu- or acr- appears: *acrid, acrimony, acuity, acumen, acute*

Acrid comes from ACR- meaning *sharp* and the Latin suffix –ID meaning *having a particular quality*. Thus *acrid* means *having a sharp quality in taste or smell*; bitter or burning to the senses.

Acridity means *the state or quality of being acrid*

Acrimony; the suffix –MONY means *quality of being*. Acrimony means *sharpness of speech or temper*

Acuity; -ITY means state, condition or quality of being

Acumen comes directly from the Latin meaning sharpness of mind or senses

Acute comes from a Latin word to sharpen. Acute means *sharp* or coming to a sharp point

Let us see core words flowing from the Latin root AC-, ACR- in the following contextual usages:

1. The *acrid* smoke hurts my eyes.
2. The *acridity* of the smoke, from the burning tyres, made his eyes water.
3. The political debate was full of *acrimony* with the ruling party coming under fire for not having fulfilled its election promises.

4. The parliamentary discussion, on the Women's Representation Act, turned into an *acrimonious* debate.
5. The teacher has great mental *acuity*.
6. He is an industrialist with great business *acumen*.
7. An *acute* angle is an angle less than ninety degrees in measure.
8. He is suffering from an *acute* pain in his knee joints.
9. Several third-world countries have been able to overcome an *acute* food crisis, due to large-scale application of inorganic fertilisers.
10. The mathematics teacher has a quick, *acute* mind.
11. His rotting tooth was causing *acute* pain and the painkiller was taking long to ease the agony.

We have seen what it takes, to be able to correctly answer questions in this section. We shall now move on to some practice tests that should help us not only to completely assimilate the necessary concepts and refine them, but also able us to decide the question-specific strategy that we shall need in order to be able to succeed at this sub-section in the Verbal Section at the GRE.

There are lucid solutions at the end of the tests. The solutions are written with the objective of giving you the very best. This is because you, dear reader, deserve the very best. You will see in a great majority of the solutions that the solutions are miniature concept notes. It is for this reason we strongly urge that you read each solution, whether you are right or you are wrong.

Practise Test 1

DIRECTIONS *for questions 1 to 12: In each of the following questions, a related pair of words or phrases is followed by five pairs of words or phrases. Select the word pair that best expresses a relationship similar to that expressed in the original pair.*

	The Word	Option 1	Option 2	Option 3	Option 4	Option 5
(1)	Adult: Child	Horse: Mare	Cat: Kitten	Swine: Sow	Human: Animal	Cow: Herd
(2)	Mansion: Residence	Limousine: Automobile	Chandelier: Candle	Tuxedo: Wardrobe	Diamond: Rhinestone	Yacht: Harbour
(3)	Envelop: Letter	Scarf: hat	Box: Bag	Crate: Produce	Neck: head	Blood: Heart
(4)	Choreography: Dance	Ceremony: Sermon	Agenda: Advertisement	Poetry: Recitation	Instrumentation: Conductor	Plot: Story
(5)	Overdose: Prescription	Deprivation: Materialism	Indiscretion: Convention	Affliction: Sympathy	Adventure: Expedition	Drug: Medicine Medicine
(6)	Evaporate: Vapor	Petrify: Stone	Centrifuge: Liquid	Saturate: Fluid	Corrode: Acid	Incinerate: Fire
(7)	Shard: Pottery	Flint: Stone	Flange: Wheel	Cinder: Coal	Fragment: Bone	Tare: Grain
(8)	Mercenary: Money	Vindictive: Revenge	Scholarly: Library	Immaculate: Cleanliness	Thirsty: Water	Belligerent: Invasion
(9)	Hammer:Anvil	Knocker: Door	Stick: Gong	Hand: Drum	Pestle: Mortar	Gavel: Lectern
(10)	Numb: Insensitive	Reflect: Luminous	Burnish: Lustrous	Heckle: Raucous	Repulse: Odious	Braid: Sinuous
(11)	Exorbitant: Moderation	Dispassionate: Equanimity	Macabre: Interest	Perfidious: Loyalty	Brilliant: Gullibility	Lavish: Extravagance
(12)	Troubled: Distraught	Annoyed: Disillusioned	Disturbed: Interrupted	Covetous: Rapacious	Outmoded: Ostentatious	Tranquil: Placid

Answer 1.

ADULT: CHILD; An *adult* is what the child becomes when it reaches full growth. Thus the relationship between *Adult* and a *Child* is that between a grown-up and growing. Let us see where we see such a relationship among the five options. An *adult* is not an *adult* merely because he/she can see movies that are not for universal exhibition or not merely because they can vote at the elections. An adult is one capable of sexual reproduction.

Option (1): Horse: Mare; A *horse* is the male of the species where the *mare* is the female. Both are necessarily fully-grown. This option will thus not do.

Option (2): Cat: Kitten; The *infant of the cat* is a *kitten* and a *cat* is a fully-grown adult male or female cat although male adult cats are often called tomcats. Here the relationship matches with that in the capitalised pair and hence **Option 2**.

Option (3): Swine: Sow; The swine is an adult pig and the sow is a female adult pig. Both are necessarily fully-grown. This option will, thus, not do either.

Option (4): Human: Animal; A *human* being is a member of the animal kingdom. The only difference is that *human* beings have the faculty of thinking. Yet Human is the sub-species of the Animal species. This option too will, thus, not do either.

Option (5): Cow: Herd; A *cow* in the singular is one *cow* grazing away, detached from her kith and kin. A *herd* of *cows* would have a number of *cows*. The *cow* is one among the *herd* that is the collective noun for cows. This option too will, thus, not do.

Answer 2.

MANSION: RESIDENCE; A *mansion* is a large and stately *residence*. The Divisional Commissioner in our city lives in a *mansion*. The *mansion* is his *residence*. My little cottage in the same lane as his is a simple *residence*. The relationship between Mansion and Residence is that of Large and Stately: Simple. Let us see where this relationship is seen among the options.

Option (1): Limousine: Automobile; When someone says that the President's *limousine* has bulletproof windows, he means that the large and stately car (or *automobile*) is designed to protect him from snipers. When I say that the *automobile* that I bought a year ago is running along smoothly, it means that my ordinary car is in good condition. The relationship between *Limousine* and *Automobile* matches that in the capitalised pair and hence **Option 1** is correct.

Option (2): Chandelier: Candle; When we sold our ancestral home, the *chandeliers* fetched a considerable sum of money. *Chandeliers* are branched supports for lights that you see hanging from the ceiling. Chandeliers in the modern day hold electric lights but in the early days, they held *candles* since there were no electric lights. Thus a *chandelier* is what holds a number of *candles*. However, a chandelier is not a stately form of a candle. It is at best something that holds *candles*. Thus this option is not workable.

Option (3): Tuxedo: Wardrobe; A *tuxedo* is a short dinner jacket. A *wardrobe* is what holds a person's clothes. The other meaning of *wardrobe* is the collection of the clothes one has. A tuxedo is in the singular. It therefore cannot be the stately form of a wardrobe. A *mansion* if sold would fetch a huge price to the owner as compared to an ordinary residence. A second-hand *tuxedo* may be had for a small sum. If used for long, one may even give it away to the servants. Thus this option is not workable either.

Option (4): Diamond: Rhinestone; A *diamond* is a precious stone. A *rhinestone* is normally an artificial gem cut to resemble a *diamond*. A diamond is not necessarily large. It may be as small as a grain or rice. A rhinestone may have a size resembles a large diamond. There is no relationship between **Diamond** and **Rhinestone** that would match **Mansion: Residence**.

Option (5): Yacht: Harbour; An industrialist may own a *yacht*, which then may be a small luxury boat that the industrialist may use for cruising. A boat-race freak may own a *yacht* that may be a small race boat. Either way, a *yacht* is small and hence fails to relate to a mansion, which is necessarily a large and stately house. This option is not workable either.

Answer 3

ENVELOP: LETTER; An *envelope* (or *envelop* as it is spelt in American English) is the outer cover in which a letter is put for sending it. The relationship between an *envelop* and a *letter* is that of an Outer Cover to its Content. Let us see the options and find out where such a relationship emerges.

Option (1): Scarf: hat; A scarf is usually a long narrow piece of silk worn as a muffler around the neck or as a neckerchief or cravat also won around the neck but under a shirt collar, or as a bandanna on the head. It has nothing to do whatsoever, with a *hat*. A scarf is not necessarily an outer cover whereas the envelope is necessarily one and therefore this option will not do.

Option (2): Box: Bag; A *box* is an outer cover in which you put things and so is a *bag*. They are both outer covers and hence this option will not do either.

Option (3): Crate: Produce; A *crate* is something in which one normally packs agricultural *produce* such as apples, oranges, mangoes and so on. The relationship between *Crate* and *Produce* matches with that in the capitalised pair. Option 3 is right.

Option (4): Neck: Head; A neck is not at all a cover. It is what the *head* rests on. This option will also not do.

Option (5): Blood: Heart; The *blood* has to flow within. If it flows out it means curtains for the one bleeding. It is, in fact, the heart that contains blood in it and hence if at all there relationship between the two, it is in a way inverse to that in the capitalised pair.

Answer 4

CHOREOGRAPHY: DANCE; People can dance in the street without a formal structure to their dance. There is no harmony in a street dance. One dancer raises his hand and the other dancer inadvertently brings his nose in the way of the raised hand and the result is a bleeding nose and then chaos. People can dance on a stage as well.

The difference between street dances and staged performances of dance is that the latter is designed to present the effect of harmonious movements of the dancers. It is for this reason that a staged dance has an arrangement that is decided beforehand by a *choreographer* (meaning someone proficient in the art of *choreography* or the art of dancing). Thus the relationship between Choreography and Dance is arrangement (of an event): The event itself. Now let us see the options.

Option (1): Ceremony: Sermon; Let us see when *ceremonies* usually take place and then decide whether *ceremonies* themselves need be by arrangement. There may be a marriage ceremony, a child's christening ceremony (when the child is given a name to which he may answer when called), a burial ceremony or a ceremony commemorating the valiant soldiers of a nation who have laid down their lives while defending the country. Clearly, ceremonies are necessarily arranged. But as we have seen, while a ceremony may be an arrangement that is decided beforehand, it may not have anything to do with *sermons*. A *sermon*, incidentally, is normally understood as being a religious lecture. But there can be other forma of sermons as well. If a teenager has been regularly going to parties and returning drunk in the dead of the night (meaning the middle of the night) and his father gives a *sermon* to him about his behaviour, then the *sermon* is as such a dressing-down or a reprimand. There need not be any ceremony in such a sermon. The father may use profane language and also his hand to drive home the point that he is striving to make, while the priest does not slap the congregation when he delivers a sermon. This option will not do.

Option (2): Agenda: Advertisement; If the Board of Directors of a company were to meet on a particular day to discuss how much dividend should be paid to the shareholders, then the *agenda* of the meeting is to decide how much dividend should be recommended for payment. Here the event is: how much dividend? *Agenda* is thus the arrangement of *things to be discussed*.

If I were to tell my children on a Sunday that we are going out for a stroll and then three hours later, one of them asks me in an irritated tone about what the agenda is, it means that the child now wants to know where we are going and how far. The child wants to know whether anything is decided beforehand, or the whole thing is unscheduled. Here too, the word agenda stands for an arrangement. Here the question is: Where are we going and how far is it now?

An *advertisement* is issued for the information of the public at large, usually with a view to promoting a product (such as a shampoo of a particular brand, of course, since no company will advertise that people should use shampoo without telling them the brand name that the company have given to their shampoo) or a cause (as in the case of a government advertisement telling citizens to get their children inoculated against polio). An advertisement is not an event. It is a means to inform or bring about the event: in one case the event may be huge sales of a company's branded shampoo and in the other it may be to ensure that every child below, say, five years of age is inoculated against polio. It is for this reason that this option will not do.

Option (3): Poetry: Recitation; *Poetry* is the art of writing poems. Poetry is also the collective noun for poems. Poetry is thus the art or work of a poet. Poetry is itself an arrangement of words that rhyme and poem. *Recitation* is not what poetry seeks to arrange. Poetry may be read quietly. One may take a poetry book, lie down in bed and read without a single word being spoken and therefore the chance of a poetry being heard by the others, if any, in the room is nil. When someone recites, one reads aloud. Someone doing recitation need not recite poetry alone. He may recite a passage from a novel as well. Poetry therefore does not arrange the event of recitation. Thus this option will not do either.

Option (4): Instrumentation: Conductor; *Instrumentation* can mean so many things. If an engineer were looking after the instrumentation of his fertiliser plant, he would be designing the various instruments to control the reactions and measure the amount of, say, sulphur being poured into the reaction chambers. If the national anthem is to be set to *instrumentation*, then musicians – some with violins, others with oboes, some with drums and so on – will practice how to play it to perfection. *Instrumentation* is thus an arrangement of events such as control of temperature or playing of the national anthem on musical instruments. But the *conductor* cannot be an event. He, in fact, would ensure that those playing the national anthem adhere to the arrangement. This option will then not be of much use. Since it could at best be the reverse of the relationship in the original pair.

Option (5): Plot: Story; Have you heard a story without a *plot*? When we were children, a cousin, who used to tell us *stories* about the exploits of someone called Jack, would go on and on, inventing the plot as he went along. We would plead with him to shut up. To this day we never miss a chance of ribbing (or *teasing*) him for this although he is now a renowned surgeon. A plot is the arrangement of a story and the story is the event that is arranged. This relationship matches the one in the capitalised pair and hence **Option 5** is correct.

Answer 5

OVERDOSE: PRESCRIPTION; An overdose is more than what one should take. The word prescription comes from the word SCRIBE that means *write* and the prefix PRE- that means (i) *before* if you were to *prepone* your journey or go before the scheduled departure or (ii) the plot *earlier in importance* if some belief were to be *prevail*, or (iii) *exceedingly* as in the case of someone being *predominant* in his sphere of specialisation.

When a doctor *prescribes* a particular medicine, he writes the important medicine that one should take. The doctor also writes how much medicine one should take in a single dose and the periodicity of the dosage. You cannot down the whole strip of antibiotics in one gulp. The doctor's prescription is a part of the convention of medicine and its dosage. The word convention means CON- the prefix that means *thoroughly* or *together* and the French verb VENIRE that means *to go*. Convention means *thoroughly going together* and therefore some *accepted usage* in which there must be harmony. A *convent* is a place in which people *thoroughly go* and therefore they stay there and are given thorough religious instruction. This is why a *convent* is where nuns stay.

The relationship between *Overdose* and *Prescription* is between *excess* and *reasonable Quantity*. Now let us see the various options.

Option (1): Deprivation: Materialism; When you pass by a hutment and see the people living there with poor water supply, lack of adequate sanitation and so on, you say that they are living in a state of *deprivation* that means *hardship* or *poverty* or a situation of disadvantage. The word *deprivation* cannot gel with overdose because overdose means excess and deprivation means a shortage. This option will thus not do for this reason alone.

Incidentally, materialism means a tendency to prefer material comforts of life such as cars and air-conditioners and so on instead of spiritual values such as mental peace and knowledge.

Option (2): Indiscretion: Convention; The word *discretion* comes from discern that means to *understand*. When you understand that beyond three cups of tea per day is not good for your health, then you drink tea with *discretion* or moderation. You do not allow yourself an overdose of tea. Indiscretion is the precise opposite. If the doctor tells you that you should take only two tablets of calcium in a day and you down the whole jar, it means that you are acting with indiscretion. You are not reasonable. As we have seen earlier, the doctor prescribes medicines and their dosage in accordance with a *convention* and therefore the relationship between *Indiscretion* and *Convention* matches with that in the capitalised pair. Hence **Option 2**.

Option (3): Affliction: Sympathy; Let us see what *affliction* means from its contextual usage. Diarrhoea in which there is watery bowel movement is a temporary *affliction* (or *disorder*) caused by poisonous or indigestible substance lodged in the intestines. An affliction may be the *effect* of an overdose. *Sympathy* is feeling sorry for others or being affected by the grief of another. It is for this reason that this option will not do.

Option (4): Adventure: Expedition; Overdose means something more than what is reasonable. What is an overdose is not a matter of debate once there is a prescription. Such is not the case with *adventure*. What is adventure and what is more than adventure are both difficult to define simply because there cannot be a limit up to which something can be considered adventure. For a sissy, adventure can stop at walking a mile away from home without one's parents accompanying him. For another person, climbing the world's highest peak is *adventure*. There cannot be an upper limit to adventure whereas for an overdose there has to be an upper limit and hence this option will not do either.

Option (5): Drug: Medicine; The normal meaning of a *drug* is something that can cure an affliction or malady. Medicine is that which a doctor prescribes from accepted usage and hence *medicine* denotes a convention. A drug, however, does not necessarily mean *medicine*. Even hashish is a *drug* and so is marijuana. No doctor will prescribe marijuana. Mere *drug* does not mean overdose at all just as liquor does not mean drinking beyond reasonable quantity. If *drug* itself is not indicative of overdose, this option cannot work.

Answer 6

EVAPORATE: VAPOR; When water *evaporates*, it forms water vapour (spelt VAPOR in American English). When petrol *evaporates*, it forms petrol vapour. The relationship between Evaporate and Vapor is thus between Cause and Effect. Let us now see the options.

Option (1): Petrify: Stone; Have you heard of the word *petroleum*? The word petroleum comes from the Latin PETRA that means rock and OLEUM that means oil. Literally *petroleum* means oil from the rock. When someone becomes so terrified that he cannot move, then he is *petrified* (or in other words *still as a rock*). A stone as we know is a rock; what is a stone and what is a rock is only a matter of dimension. The small rock is a stone. When the molten lava petrifies it becomes stone. Here is the Cause and Effect relationship that we are looking for. Thus **Option 1** is correct.

Option (2) Centrifuge: Liquid. The word *centrifuge* comes from CENTRI that means centre and FUGUS that means *flying* or *fleeing* (have we not heard that a *fugitive* is the one who commits a crime and then *runs* or *flees* from the law?). A centrifuge is a mechanical device that spins furiously generating forces that may go up to thousands of times the force of gravity and is used to separate heavier liquids from the lighter ones such as cream from milk. A centrifigue may separate one heavy liquid from another such as milk from cream. But the centrifigue is not the cause of which the liquid is an effect. The *centrifigue* is not a cow, is it? Hence this option will not do.

Option (3): Saturate: Fluid; To *saturate* means to satisfy or overfill. You *saturate* the bed of roses in the garden with water. The relationship between *Saturate* and *Fluid* is that between *something that is done* and *what it is done with*. This relationship is thus that of effect and cause and hence inverse of what is in the capitalised pair. This option will not do either.

Option (4): Corrode: Acid; When doubts and cynicism *eat away* the self-confidence of a person, they *corrode* that person's self-esteem. When rust *corrodes* the water pipes in buildings, the pipes are *eaten away* or *eroded*. Acid can *corrode* several metals since acids have the ability to chemically react with a lot of substances and form new substances that may not have the same physical strength or properties of the substance before the reaction with acid. Thus the relationship between *Corrode* and *Acid* is thus that of effect and cause and hence inverse of what is in the capitalised pair. Hence this option will not do either.

Option (5): Incinerate: Fire; The *cinerary* urn is the container that holds the ashes of someone who has been consigned to flames (after death, of course). The key word here is CINIS that means *ashes*. It is normal to see the father of the house separating papers that he needs to preserve and papers that he no longer needs. He then puts a match to papers that he no longer needs and *incinerates* them. When you want to *incinerate* something, you must have *fire*. The relationship between Incinerate and Fire is that of effect and cause and hence inverse of what is in the capitalised pair. Hence this option will not do either.

Answer 7

SHARD: POTTERY; The word *shard* means so many things as follows. All essentially mean a part: fragment, piece, particle, scrap, bit, chip, sliver, splinter, paring, shaving, remnant

A *shard* is thus a broken piece of pottery. The relationship between *Shard* and Pottery is that of broken part: whole. It may be noted that Shard and Pottery are not necessarily complementary. If the handle on a teacup has broken off, the broken handle becomes a *shard*. And yet there is nothing to stop you from drinking tea out of such a cup. Only you do not have a handle. The cup can hold tea and you can hold the cup all the same.

Option (1): Flint: Stone; The word flint has several shades of meaning that we shall see in their following situational usages:

- *Flint* to other emotions, the man broke down when his daughter was leaving his home after the marriage ceremony was over. (Here the word *flint* means *hard* or *unyielding*)
- The early man used two pieces of *flint* stone that he rubbed violently against each other and the resultant sparks lit fires.

Clearly, *flint* is a variety of hard stone. Both flint and stone are wholes. There is no Part: Whole, relationship between Flint and Stone and thus this option will not do.

Option (2): Flange: Wheel; The word *flange* means a projecting flat rim, collar, or rib, serving especially for strengthening, attachment, or (on a wheel) maintaining position on a rail. Thus the wheels of trains have *flanges* on them that keep them moving on the rail track; the *flange* is an integral part of the *wheel* and without it the *wheel* will stray from the rail track and the train would then be derailed. The wheel will be of little use without the flange. Thus a *flange* and a *wheel* are complementary where one is useless in the absence of the other. The relationship between Flange and Wheel is not akin to that between Shard and Pottery because a shard is a broken piece of pottery whereas a *flange* is not a broken part of the wheel.

Option (3): Cinder: Coal; The word *cinder* can mean two things. A *cinder* track is made of *burnt* brick. Motorcycle races are normally held on *cinder* tracks on which the motorcyclist does not slip. If people pick up the *cinder* from wood or *coal* fires, they do so to get residual pieces of partly burnt wood or coal that still have some capacity to burn.

The relationship between *Cinder* and *Coal* is that between partly burnt substance and the substance itself. This relationship is also not in keeping with broken part: whole as seen in Shard: Pottery.

Option (4): Fragment: Bone; The word *fragment* comes from the Latin roots FRANG-, FRING-, FRACT-FRAG- that mean *break*. That is why a *fracture* is a broken bone. That is why something *fragile* is that which can be easily broken. It may be noticed that if one were to know the basic structure of the English language that comes substantially from Latin – the mother of all European languages – it could be immensely helpful. If a man fell from the first storey and a *fragment* of the bone in his right thumb was picked up before he was rushed to the hospital, it means that a *piece* of his bone was found lying near where he fell. The relationship between Fragment and Bone is akin to broken part and whole and hence **Option 4** is correct.

Option (5): Tare: Grain; A *tare* is the seed of a plant grown as fodder. If in the process of cleaning wheat after it is harvested the *tares* are separated from the wheat, it means that the small fodder seeds that grow alongside wheat are separated from the main grain. The reason for separating tare is that it is about as useful as are stones and stalk that are separated too when wheat is chaffed after harvesting and drying. The relationship between Tare and Grain is akin to unwanted things: wanted things. Thus this option will not do.

Answer 8

MERCENARY: MONEY; A mercenary is a soldier who fights for a country other than that of his birth; the motive for fighting is therefore not patriotism or military service (no country can ask a person other than its national to join its army) but only money. Thus mercenary forces may be hired when one's own forces are felt to be inadequate. The word *mercenary* does not apply merely to warriors. A lady who married an old wealthy man for his money was tired of his peevish temperament and decided to divorce him when she felt that she should find some way other than a *mercenary* marriage to come into money. Thus the relationship between *Mercenary* and *Money* is that between means and end. Now let us see the options.

Option (1): Vindictive: Revenge; The word *vindictive* comes from the Latin word VINDICTA that means *revenge*. A *vindictive* person does something for the sake of revenge just as a mercenary fights for the sake of money. Let us see what the word vindictive means from the following contextual usage.

Imagine that someone is working in an organisation and has a boss who cannot hear *no* for an answer. Imagine that our friend has asked the boss for a day's leave because his wife has to be taken to the doctor's. The boss declines leave, saying that there is this draft budget to be made and leave can be granted only after the work of drafting the budget is over. Imagine that our friend then tells the boss that because there is a medical emergency, he has come only to inform that he will not be in the next day and not to ask for leave. The boss keeps this refusal, to attend office, in mind. Now imagine that our friend has done an excellent job and is considered for a foreign posting. When asked for his recommendation, the boss reports adversely on our friend. He gets nothing out of this action except mere revenge. The boss is terribly *vindictive*. Thus **Option 1** is correct.

Option (2): Scholarly: Library; Someone academically brilliant could be described as *scholarly*. While the books in the library may be the means by which the person reading them may become scholarly, this relationship may at best be seen as end and means. Of course, it is not as if scholars read only in libraries. They may read at home. They may read books that they have purchased. Yet the fact remains that this option will not do.

Option (3): Immaculate: Cleanliness; If a chap's dressing is *immaculate*, he is so well dressed that you cannot find any fault with it. If a man is convinced of his wife's *immaculate* purity, it means that he is sure that there is not a spot, stain or blemish on her loyalty to him. Cleanliness may keep things clean. It is not necessary that a clean person is also of *immaculate* morality. He may bathe thoroughly before setting out to seduce women. But even if something *immaculate* is the result of moral cleanliness, then at the very best the relationship between Immaculate and Cleanliness is that between end and means and hence inverse to that in the capitalised pair. This option too will not do.

Option (4): Thirsty: Water; When a person is *thirsty*, he may want to drink water. Thus thirst is the effect of having been *without* water. However a person may be *thirsty* for success in which case water will be of not much help. In any case, the relationship between Thirsty: Water is not as between means: end and hence this option is not workable.

Option (5): Belligerent: Invasion; A *belligerent* person may mean someone *inclined to war* or *quarrelsome* or *argumentative* person. Someone who goes to a bar and starts drinking may be full of humour when the first peg is resting in his stomach. When the third goes in, he may become *belligerent* (and start *quarrelling* with the bartender who may have advised him that any more liquor may not be good for him). The question of his going to war does not arise when he is barely able to stand on his feet.

The word *invasion* comes from the French verb VADERE that means to go and this with the prefix IN- that means *in* (as in *income*) or *upon* or *against* (as in the word *intrude*) makes INVADE that means to *go upon* or *enter forcefully*. An *invasion* may thus have several diverse connotations that we shall see in the following contextual – situational (more than contextual as a matter of fact) – usage:

- When the enemy country launched an *invasion* against our country, we were drafted into the army and had to go to war. (Here the word invasion means *war*)
- I was reading my girlfriend's letter when I saw that my younger brother was peeking into the letter. He was thus making an *invasion* (or *intrusion*, *infringement*) into my privacy.
- In my country, home is protected from *invasion* by a police officer who will need to have a search warrant issued by a judicial magistrate before he can come in and search the home. But, surprisingly, the Income Tax Department officers seem to have greater powers than the police because they can *invade* the privacy of a man's home without a search warrant. (Here the word *invasion* means *raid*).

The relationship between *belligerent* and *invasion* is like between *someone who tends to do something* and *what he does*. This does not match the relationship between mercenary and money because a mercenary fights for money and thus gets money because of his being a mercenary whereas a belligerent person does not fight for invasion. He may get a broken nose if he is belligerent but not strong enough. Thus this option is not workable either.

Answer 9

HAMMER: ANVIL; Those of you who have seen a shoemaker at work will recall that he puts a shoe on an *anvil* and *hammers* the nail in while the shoe is on the *anvil*. An ironsmith too has an *anvil* on which he puts red-hot iron and uses the hammer to give it the desired shape. The *hammer* and the *anvil* are thus complementary devices just as a tennis racket and a ball. If the ironsmith has only an *anvil* and no *hammer*, with what will he give the desired shape to the iron lemp? Let us see where we find this relationship among the options.

Option (1): Knocker: Door; When someone comes to your house, he rings an electric bell. Imagine that there is a power cut. What use is the electric bell? If he wants to convey that he is at the door, he has to knock. In order that he can do so with ease, a *knocker* is provided on the *door*. However, the *knocker* and the *door* are not complementary because you can make use of the door even without the *knocker*.

Option (2) Stick: Gong; If you have seen the gong that was used to strike the bell announcing that school was over for the day and when you ran for the school bus, the sum and substance of the gong was a stick at the end of which there was some hard thing with which you could ring the bell. But the gong and stick are not complementary. The stick is a part of the gong just as the strings are a part of the tennis racket. One can sound the gong even without the stick.

Option (3): Hand: Drum; You could play the *drum* with your *hand*. Yet the *hand* and the *drum* are not complementary. The *drum* will not shy away from you when you try playing it with drumsticks. This option will not do.

Option (4): Pestle: Mortar; The *pestle* is a hammer with which one crushes things placed in a vessel of marble, brass, or other hard material, with a cup-shaped cavity in which ingredients for pharmacy, cookery, etc., are pounded with a *pestle*. This *vessel* is known as a *mortar*. The *pestle* and *mortar* are complementary because if you have put some medicinal herbs into the mortar and wish to crush them, with what can you crush them other than with a *pestle*? One cannot use one's rifle to crush the herbs in a mortar. Thus Option 4 is correct.

Option (5): Gavel: Lectern; One may see the *gavel* in a courtroom when there is too much noise and the judge bangs the *gavel* (or a *small hammer*) on his desk to bring the courtroom back to order. One may see the gavel at an auction when the bidding stops and the highest bidder waits for the chap conducting the auction to bang the gavel on his desk to indicate that the thing that he is auctioning has been sold.

A *lectern* is the stand on which a lecturer puts his notes during the course of his lecture so that he can refer to them. Clearly, a gavel has nothing to do whatsoever, with a lectern.

Answer 10

NUMB: INSENSITIVE; When a surgeon operates on a patient's kidney stone, he engages an anaesthetist who in turn injects some drug into the patient's spine so that patient's body *becomes numb* from the waist down, or in other words, the body becomes *insensitive* to pain from waist down. Thus Numb: Insensitive are synonymous. When you see both of them as adjectives. However, the word *numb* can be used as a verb as well. If the cold will numb your fingers, it will freeze them or make them insensitive. Thus *Numb: Insensitive* can bear the relationship of Cause: Effect. Let us now see the options.

Option (1): Reflect: Luminous; While travelling at night on the highway, we see a continuous string of shining objects that tell us where the middle of the road is. This is because when it is dark we cannot see the road - which is black too - and thus are not able to see which is the right side and which is the left side of the road. It is important to know, however, which side is right and which left since in a country where you are required to drive to the left, driving to the right may mean a head-on collision with an approaching vehicle and then curtains. Such devices, called cat's eyes, reflect the light from the headlights of your car and become *luminous* (or shine). However, when you are sitting all by yourself and reflect upon your recent performance at the examinations (meaning, you *think deeply* about where you went wrong and how you would do better hereafter and so on), you do not develop a *luminous* glow. Thus there is no necessary relationship between Reflect and Luminous.

Option (2): Burnish: Lustrous; When you *burnish* the silver tea set with an oxidant, you *polish* the silver. The silver that was dull now becomes *lustrous*. When someone compliments you for the fine burnish on the tea set, he is complementing you for the excellent *polish* on the silver. The word *burnish* can thus be used as a noun and also as a verb just as the word *run* can be a noun when you have scored a hundred *runs* and as a verb when you *run* to catch the bus home. You burnish something to make it lustrous, just as the cold that will numb the fingers, will make them insensitive. Thus **Option 2** is correct.

Option (3): Heckle: Raucous; Imagine that a drama with a misleading title is being enacted at a theatre and some members of the audience, who have come with the hope of hearing jokes, are not thrilled with the deeply philosophical soliloquy that the star of the show has launched. These simple folks then start *heckling* the actor (*sit down and give yourself rest*, they shout). One would heckle with the intention of making the actors nervous or jeer at them in a *raucous* or *jarring, ear-piercing* voice. Thus a chap would *heckle* in a raucous voice if he has any hope of being heard by the actors. There are two parties to the transaction of Numb and Insensitive. The first party is the one who makes numb and the second party is the other who becomes insensitive. In the case of *Heckle* and *Raucous* there is only one party – the heckler. He *heckles* and his voice becomes raucous. The actor may have acted in hundreds of plays and may have seen both the dark and the bright side of acting. It is not necessary that the actor may become raucous because of the heckler. He may be entirely unaffected by the *heckling*. He may even smile in the direction of the heckler.

Option (4): Repulse: Odious; If you have heard or felt someone's *pulse*, it indicates the heartbeats. The word *repulse* has the prefix RE- that means *back* and therefore means *beat back*. So when the young lieutenant *repulsed* the enemy attack, he *beat* the enemy *back*. They had to retreat. On the other hand, when you were out on your usual morning walk and the sight of the rotting dead animal *repulsed* you, it beat you back or *disgusted* you.

A child that throws tantrums all the while may be an *odious* or *hateful* child. If a country makes it compulsory for all adults below the age of, say, forty five to join the army in the current battle against another nation, it would seem *odious* (or hateful) to most of its citizens. Something hateful, like the rotting corpse on a morning walk, may *repulse*. The relationship between *Repulse* and *Odious* is that between effect and cause. Thus this option will not work.

Option (5): Braid: Sinuous; If a fellow were to be slapped while trying to put a carnation in the *braid* of the new girl in his class, he is trying to put a flower in her *plait* (interwoven locks of hair). If the road to the hill station is *sinuous*, it goes up *winding*. If the girl in whose braid the fellow was trying to put a flower now seems to like him because of his *sinuous* body, it means that he has a *lithe, supple* body (in which there is the likelihood of many curves). If *sinuous* oil merchants dominated the Chamber of Commerce in your town, then it means that the few oil merchants dominating the Chamber of Commerce are *crooked*. The words *braid* and *sinuous* have no relation as such and therefore this option will not do.

Answer 11

EXORBITANT: MODERATION; If you remember that the earth moves around the sun in an orbit, it means that the earth is moving in its **normal track** around the sun. The prefix EX- means *out of*. Something out of its normal track – such as something costing much more than what it should cost - is *exorbitant* or *unreasonable*. When you eat butter in *moderation* (meaning in *reasonable quantity*), you do not have to worry about putting on weight. An exorbitant person is one who spends beyond reason and therefore lacks *moderation*. This is the relationship in the capitalised pair of words. Now let us see the options.

Option (1): Dispassionate: Equanimity; The word *passion* can mean so many things that we shall see in the following contexts:

- If a man is desperately in love with a girl, he is burning with *passion* for her. [Here *passion* may indicate things so diverse as adoration, sexual desire or lust]
- If your neighbour's son has a *passion* for motorcycles, he is crazy for them.
- If a man while quarrelling about a place to sit in a bus throws a punch at another in a fit of *passion*, he is in a state of mad rage or in a burst of anger.

A *dispassionate* person is one who is away from *passion* (as indicated by the prefix DIS- that means *away from*). He is cool and collected. Sorrow does not overlay disturb him and good news does not make him overjoyed. He has a balanced mind. This is why judges decide legal matters in a *dispassionate* manner; they are fair and do not consider extraneous issues such as the gender or caste and creed of the accused in deciding the case.

Equanimity means a *state of equal mind* when there is complete mental balance (this is because the prefix EQUI- means *equal* and the Latin root ANIM- means *life*, *soul*, *mind*, or *spirit* and the suffix –ITY is a suffix used for making nouns such as in *nicety*, *cordiality*, *vivacity* and so on).

It should now be easy to see that someone can be *dispassionate* if he has *equanimity*. The relationship between *Dispassionate* and *Equanimity* is that of effect and cause (It is important to remember that someone can become dispassionate due to **presence** of equanimity). If a person has *equanimity*, the effect is that he becomes *dispassionate*. The relationship between the capitalised pair is effect and cause due to **absence** of moderation. This option has a distinctly reverse relationship than in the capitalised pair.

Option (2): Macabre: Interest; The word *macabre* means something *gruesome*, dreadful, horrifying or shocking. Let us see the precise meaning emerge in the following context:

A young man was hell bent on becoming a pianist. His father was extremely wealthy and wanted him to run the family business. He ran away from his parental home to pursue his passion. He took piano lessons and did odd jobs such as sweeping floors or cleaning lavatories to keep body and soul together. His father found out where he was and offered the young man a large allowance so that he could pay for piano lessons and yet live in luxury but with the condition that he must return home and stand a test by a renowned pianist who must certify that the fellow has the potential. If the pianist certified to the contrary, then he would join the family business. The young man agreed. He played in presence of the maestro who said that the young lad did not have even an outside chance. The young man then started attending to the father's business. However, the lad learnt that the maestro was paid to give an adverse opinion and one day there was a loud report of a gun going off and it was found that the young man had shot himself through the head. This was a *macabre* end to the life of a fine young man. Quite clearly *macabre* and *interest* have nothing to do with each other. A macabre story may evoke great interest. Thus this option will not do.

Option (3): Perfidious: Loyalty; A *perfidious* person is one who is *disloyal* or *treacherous* or double-dealing. If a thief is caught because his ally has told the police where he was in in lieu of a pardon for his involvement in the theft, then the *perfidy* (or *treachery*) of his ally has given him away. A person becomes *perfidious* when he **lacks** loyalty. Thus the relationship between *Perfidious* and *Loyalty* matches that in the capitalised pair. Hence **Option 3** is correct.

Option (4): Brilliant: Gullibility; The word *brilliant* can means so many things.

- A star in the sky can be *brilliant* because it is shining intensely.
- The fellow who topped the Secondary School Board examination was *brilliant* (or he was academically very bright or extremely intelligent).
- If the sitar recital was *brilliant*, it was because it was magnificent.

Gullibility is the quality that makes a person trust others rather easily. He is easily cheated. Let us see this word in the following situational context:

A young man stood near the Eiffel Tower and wiped his eyes from time to time. Another young man soothed him. Some foreign tourists saw this and asked why the man was crying. The other fellow told them that the Eiffel was his by family heirloom but since he was in dire financial straits he was forced to consider selling it. The tourists – majority of them being some very brilliant college professors on a vacation in France - made a contribution and gave him a large sum of money to help him tide over his temporary problems. He was never seen or heard again. He took advantage of the tourists' *gullibility*.

Clearly, there is no relationship between Brilliant and Gullibility. This option will not do.

Option (5): Lavish: Extravagance; Have we not heard of *vagrants* who roam around without a permanent home? The word *extravagance* comes from the prefix EXTRA- that means *situated outside, more than* and the French verb VAGARE that means *wander*. Someone *extravagant* roams far away from the norms of spending (and therefore far outside his means since what is a legitimate expense and what is not is generally decided by the extent of income) and hence he is *lavish*. The relationship between Lavish and Extravagance is that between effect and cause due to the **presence** of *Extravagance*. This is why this option does not match with the relationship in the capitalised pair.

Answer 12

TROUBLED: DISTRAUGHT; Let us see what the words *troubled* and *distraught* mean from the following contexts:

- The batsman has been *troubled* by the bowler's good-length deliveries.
- The elderly lady was *troubled* by chronic constipation.
- The economy was *troubled* by war and poverty.
- *Distraught* by his wife's death during childbirth, he vowed never to look at the child's face.
- A man who claimed to be *distraught* over assassination of the president, killed the President's assassin in the courtroom by shooting him point blank.

As it would seem quite clear, *distraught* is necessarily the much higher form of troubled. Secondly, only an individual can be *distraught* whereas even groups of individuals – sometimes as large as a nation – can be troubled. If a person is troubled the trouble can be physical or mental. If the person is distraught, the mind alone is in a state of deep disturbance. Now let us see the options.

Option (1): Annoyed: Disillusioned; Let us see what these two words mean from their following situational usage:

When the cobra is *annoyed*, he spreads his hood.

Annoyed at having been cheated at the card game, the newcomer to the club slapped the dealer.

When he migrated to this country, he was under the impression that there were plenty of employment opportunities but when he found out that he would not get a decent job because he was black, he was *disillusioned*. (Here, if you notice, the fellow's illusions or wrong notions or false dreams were shattered. The man may not get annoyed at all. All that will happen is that he will loose interest in continuing. He may realise that getting *annoyed* would get him nowhere and he may then simply board the next homebound ship)

Clearly, there is no relationship between *Annoyed* and *Disillusioned*. If there is no relationship between two things, one can never be the higher form of the other.

Option (2) Disturbed: Interrupted; Let us see the shades of meaning of these two words from their following contexts:

Financial difficulty *disturbed* his plans to buy a new flat.

Disturbed by the neighbour's loud music, he could not sleep till the wee hours of the morning.

He was fast asleep on a train when the guard *interrupted* his sleep to inform him that his wife had given birth to a healthy baby boy and both mother and child were in good health. He was overjoyed.

When the steward *interrupted* the meeting to ask him if he would like soup to be served now, the director told him that he would tell him when to serve soup and the board would not like to be *disturbed* now.

As we have seen, in the case of the young father being interrupted in his sleep, he is not *disturbed*. On the contrary, he is thrilled. In the other case of the board meeting, disturbed means the same as interrupted.

Disturbed is not necessarily the higher form of Interrupted. Hence this option will not do.

Option (3): Covetous: Rapacious; A person who is yearning for something, or is *greedy* for some possession is *covetous* about it. A *covetous* person has an ardent desire for something. However, merely because someone has ardent desire, it does not mean that he will do anything to get what he wants. Full many a man have looked at the girl next door when she is at her window and have burned with love for her and yet have been satisfied with merely glancing at her for years on end. The word *rapacious* comes from *rape* that is a violent method of getting something that someone has yearned for. Therefore if *covetous* is a kind of greedy, *rapacious* has greater degree or greadiness. **Option 3** is correct.

Option (4): Outmoded: Ostentatious; The word mode means fashion or some way in which things are done. If a chap has been wearing knickerbockers when the mode (or fashion in which clothes are worn) is denims, his dress is *outmoded* or out of fashion. If the neighbours had organised lunch with thirty varieties of sweets during their son's marriage, then the event was *ostentatious* (or *showy*). As such there is no relationship between outmoded and ostentatious. Hence this option will not do.

Option (5): Tranquil: Placid; Let us see the words *placid* and *tranquil* in their contextual usage:

The sea was *placid* barring a few ripples due to the wind.

Yoga makes its practitioner mentally balanced and *tranquil*.

A *placid* person is one who is not easily disturbed. This is the same thing as *tranquil*. Both placid and *tranquil* are *peaceful*. One is not the higher form of the other and hence this option will not do.

We have seen the word *rapacious* in this exercise that comes from the word *rape*, which denotes violent lust or yearning for someone. Rapacity is that quality that makes someone rapacious.

We present to you this little quiz that we have chosen to title **Urban Nouns**.

The reason for selecting this title is that the quiz has some eight-letter words that end with the letters CITY. Given below are hints as to what the noun means. All other letters have been erased except for the suffix "–city". The blanks indicate the number of letters erased. To get things going, if the clue is cruelness or brutality, then the word is ATROCITY. The idea behind this quiz is to make learning a matter of joy and we trust you will enjoy this little quiz.

Try and fill the blanks in the words at from 1 to 15.

		HINT
1	- - - - city	defiance
2	- - - -city	old age, senility
3	- - - -city	space
4	- - - - city	happiness
5	- - - - city	savagery
6	- - - - city	usage of threats
7	- - - - city	wisdom
8	- - - - city	obscenity
9	- - - - city	shortage
10	- - - - city	firmness
11	- - - - city	quality of venom
12	- - - - city	speed
13	- - - - city	truth
14	- - - - city	liveliness
15	- - - - city	hunger

The answers to the above quiz are as under:

1. Audacity	5. Minacity	9. Scarcity	13. Veracity
2. Caducity	6. Rapacity	10. Tenacity	14. Vivacity
3. Capacity.	7. Sagacity	11. Toxicity	15. Voracity
4. Felicity	8. Salacity	12. Velocity	

You will remember that somewhere in this exercise we have been able to relate fragment to bone as broken piece to whole because we were able to derive from the Latin root FRAG- that a *fragment* is a broken piece.

Let us once again see the origin of this word and other core words emanating from the Latin root FRANG-, FRING-, FRACT-, FRAG that means "to break". Some words based on this root are *fraction, fragile, fragment, infringe.*

Fraction has the Latin root FRACT- (meaning to break) + the suffix -ION that is used to form nouns; a fraction is *a part broken off from a whole thing*; a small portion. Fractional, a word based on fraction, means " partial, being a fraction."

Fragile has the root FRAG- (meaning to break) + the suffix –ILE (meaning *able to be*); fragile is *something that can break easily*. Fragility is that quality of an object which makes it easily breakable.

Fragment is FRAG- (to break) + the suffix -MENT (meaning the *condition of being*; fragment is *something broken off*; a small part of the whole. Two words based on fragment are :

Fragmentary: *made up of unrelated bits* and pieces; *broken*

Fragmentation: the act of *breaking* into fragments

Infringe has the prefix IN- (meaning *in* as in English) + the root FRING- (meaning to break); infringe means *to break into another person's time* or privacy or rights etc. *Infringement* means, *breach of rules.*

Let us now see core words flowing from the Latin root FRANG-, FRINH-, FRACT- and FRAG- in contextual usages as follows.

1. The *fraction* one half, in percentage terms, is fifty percent.
2. I want my entire salary in one go; do not make *fractional* payment.
3. Be careful when you carry that parcel; the contents are *fragile.*
4. The old lady looked gaunt and *fragile* after her long fast.
5. We found that the cook would often *infringe* on our privacy.
6. The motorist was fined for *infringing* traffic rules.
7. France exploded a nuclear device in *infringement* of the pact between nuclear powers.

Since one knows that the root FRACT- means *to break*, may be we could look up the meanings of the following words in the dictionary:

Fracture	Frangible	Infraction	Refract	Refraction	Refractory

Practise Test 2

DIRECTIONS *for questions 1 to 12: In each of the following questions, a related pair of words or phrases is followed by five pairs of words or phrases. Select the word pair that best expresses a relationship similar to that expressed in the original pair.*

	The Word	Option 1	Option 2	Option 3	Option 4	Option 5
1	SCALPEL: SURGEON	Laser: Agronomist	Magnet: Ecologist	Syringe: Geologist	Telescope: Astronomer	Microscope: Geometrician
2	DOOR: ROOM	Rudder: Anchor	Boat: Ship	Patio: Terrace	Hatch: Hold	Basement: Attic
3	CORRAL: HORSES	Den: Lion	Meadow: Sheep	Herd: Cattle	Nest: Birds	Coop: Chickens
4	CANVAS: PAINTER	Leather: Shoe	Brush: Palette	Chisel: Wood	Marble: Sculptor	Hammer Carpenter
5	PANEGYRIC: EULOGIZE	Balled: Stigmatise	Ode: Criticize	Lampoon: Satirise	Tirade: Entertain	Treatise: Dispute
6	GLOSSARY: TEXT	Bibliography: Source	Abstract: Dissertation	Legend:	Index: Catalogue	Abbreviation: Footnote
7	LULLABY: SONG	Narrative: Volume	Lecture: Tutor	Paragraph:	Diatribe: Discourse	Invective: Compliment
8	FERVOUR: ZEALOT	Antipathy: Philanthropist	Improvidence: Spendthrift	Concision: Politician	Determination: Ecologist	Nonchalance: Acrobat
9	ASSUAGE: SORROW	Retaliate: Antipathy	Dampen: Ardour	Entrust: Reliability	Counsel: Reluctance	Withhold: Appreciation
10	DIE: SHAPING	Glue: Attaching Attaching	Anchor: Sailing	Drill: Boring	Pedal: Propelling	Ink: Printing
11	PERFUNCTORILY: INSPIRATION	Insolently: Veneration	Ardently: Passion	Phlegmatically: Composure	Surreptitiously: Obsession	Haltingly: Reluctance
12	FAWN: IMPERIOUSNESS	Equivocate: Directness	Elaborate: Originality	Boggle: Imagination	Manipulation: Repression	Coddle: Permissiveness

Detailed Solutions:

Answer 1

SCALPEL: SURGEON; A scalpel is a small light knife that the surgeon uses to make cuts during the course of surgery on a patient. The relationship between Scalpel and Surgeon is that of an Instrument and its professional user.

Option (1): Laser: Agronomist; The word *laser* is an acronym for Light Amplification by the Stimulated Emission of Radiation. Powerful laser beams can be focused on a small spot with enormous power density. Consequently, the focused beams can readily heat, melt, or vaporize material in a precise manner. Laser finds application in communication systems because laser light can travel long distances in space with very little reduction in strength of the signals it carries. Laser has application in surgery as well. Laser light can cut and cauterise small tissues in seconds without damaging the surrounding tissues.

An agronomist is a person who is an expert in the science of soil management and crop production. He has little use for lasers. The tools of his trade are soil samples and water samples and laboratories where these are analysed. Therefore this option will not do.

Option (2): Magnet: Ecologist; A magnet is a piece of iron that has the property of attracting other pieces of iron. An ecologist is one who specialises in that branch of biology that deals with the relationships of organisms inter-se and with their physical environments. An ecologist may, for example, be seen wading into a pond to study how frogs behave when they are transferred from brackish water to sweet water and so on. Another shade of meaning to the word ecologist is someone who is involved in the politics of protecting living organisms from damage due to pollution and large irrigation projects and so on. You might see an ecologist launching a fast-unto-death programme in protest against the possible submergence of trees in a project involving the construction of a large dam across a river. Quite clearly, an ecologist has nothing to do with a magnet as such in the course of his profession whereas a surgeon uses a scalpel in the course of his profession. Thus this option will not do either.

Option (3): Syringe: Geologist; A *syringe* is a device that a doctor uses to inject medicines into a patient's body. A *geologist* is someone who is engaged in the science of geology – or the study of the earth, covering aspects such as its structure and how it has evolved since its formation. If a *geologist* ever uses a *syringe*, he would do so if he decides to change his profession to being a quack and then one must scamper from him. A geologist has no use for a syringe and thus this option will not do either.

Option (4): Telescope: Astronomer: An *astronomer* specialises in the science dealing with all the celestial bodies in the universe, including the planets and their satellites, comets and meteors, the stars and interstellar matter, the star systems known as galaxies, clusters of galaxies, and quasars (that are stars located millions of miles away). In order that he can study such bodies at all, he must be able to see them in the first place. Secondly, if an *astronomer* wants to study a distant planet in the sky, he should be able to see its surface and if he uses only his eyes to do so, all that he can see at the end of his study is that the planet twinkles. He will be reduced to chanting the famous nursery rhyme: *Twinkle, twinkle, little star* and so on. He can see distant objects with far greater clarity than his eye affords him, with the aid of a device known as a *telescope*. Thus, a *telescope* is an instrument that an astronomer employs in the course of his profession and hence **Option 4** is correct.

Option (5): Microscope: Geometrician; A microscope is an optical device that helps one see micro-organisms. Like the telescope, the *microscope* also magnifies things many times over. A *geometrician* is someone who specialises at geometry, which we all know is the branch of mathematics dealing with the areas, volumes and so on of different figures such as triangles, squares and etc. He too, has not much use for a *microscope* during the course of his profession and hence this option will not do.

Answer 2

DOOR: ROOM; A *door* is an access to a room. But this is if one wants to be choosy. It is not as if a room cannot do without a door. The relationship between *Door: Room* is access: space.

Option (1): Rudder: Anchor; A *rudder* is that part of a *boat* that can change its direction. *Rudders* can come in very handy when, for example the boat is running head-on into a large wave. It is located at the rear of the boat. I remember the days when my little brother (now only 47 when this is being written) and I visited an uncle. Both of us were expert oarsmen yet when our cousin would take us out boating, he would insist on rowing all by himself. We would then turn the rudder a bit when he would try to steer the boat through a narrow passage. The boat would invariably rub against the rocks on the side much to his annoyance. We knew where the *rudder* was and what it did. He did not.

An *anchor* is something that is dropped from a boat which due to its sheer weight sinks into the sand below and does not allow the boat to drift. As such, a *rudder* and an *anchor* do not match the relationship between an access and the space to which it provides access. Hence this option will not do either.

Option (2): **Boat: Ship**; A *boat* is a small version of a *ship*. This relationship will not do either.

Option (3): **Patio: Terrace**; A *patio* is an inner space open to sky. It is some sort of veranda or a *terrace*. These two are synonymous in the sense that both are open to sky. Both can be said to provide access to the *wild blue yonder* (meaning the blue sky). This option will not do either.

Option (4): **Hatch: Hold**; A hatch is the little door that opens into the hold of a ship (the *hold* of a ship is the space where one might put cargo). The relationship between *Hatch* and *Hold* matches with that in the capitalised pair and hence **Option (4)** is correct.

Option (5): **Basement: Attic**; A *basement* is that part of the house which is below the living area on the ground floor. The attic is usually a small room at the top of the house. For those who wish to remember the meaning of the word attic once and for all, remember that lunatic is a word used to describe chaps who have moonlight in their *attics* (meaning those who are light in their heads or *attics*). A basement can be accessed only through the door of the house (provided of course the house has a door) and so can an *attic* be. This option will thus not do.

Answer 3

CORRAL: HORSES; *Horses* are essentially wild animals. With man's capacity to make lions leap through burning rings, few animals as such remain eligible for being referred to as wild. However, all animals make their own residential arrangements except when they are domesticated by Man. Thus animals live in man-made dwelling as well. A *corral* is one dwelling space where man keeps horses. The relationship between *Corral* and *Horses* is man-made living space for animals: animals that stay in them.

Option (1): **Den: Lion**; A *lion* though he roams free in nature needs a place where he can chat with his kith and kin. He thus makes a living space called a den. The relationship between Den: Lion is that of living space made by animals: animals that stay in them and will not tally with the relationship in the capitalised pair.

Option (2): **Meadow: Sheep**; A *meadow* is a large tract of *land* usually *covered with grass*. *Sheep* only graze on the meadow not live in it. Thus this option will not do.

Option (3): **Herd: Cattle**; A cow when loafing around alone is a cow in the singular. Animals that provide large-scale employment to Man are collectively referred to as *cattle*. Livestock would thus provide employment to some as milkmen, to some as makers of woollen garments and to others as butchers and so on. Man keeps livestock in spaces he calls *stockades*. A large number of livestock is known as a *herd*. Since a *herd* is not a living space for *cattle*, this option will not do.

Option (4): **Nest: Birds**; A *nest* is a living space that *birds* make for themselves. Thus this relationship does not match with that in the capitalised pair.

Option (5): **Coop: Chickens**; *Chickens* are the favourite food of many human beings. When people want to eat *chickens*, they would like ready access to them. Going after them with guns and slingshots and so on would be entertaining to some but terribly cumbersome to most others. This is why people keep chickens in manmade spaces; called *coops*. Hence **Option 5** is correct.

Answer 4

CANVAS: PAINTER; A *painter* needs two principal complementary tools of his trade. *Paint* is the first one and what to paint on is the second. He paints on paper, walls, glass, canvas and so on. When he paints, he expresses himself either by depicting what his eye sees (when he would be doing realistic painting) or what his mind perceives (when he does abstract painting). Thus the relationship *Canvas*: *Painter* is that of one of the surfaces (on which the artist works): artist.

Option (1): **Leather: Shoe**; A *shoe* is generally made of *leather*. The relationship *Leather*: *Shoe* is that of raw material: finished product and will not do.

Option (2): **Brush: Palette**; Painters who find that painting with their fingers is inconvenient often take recourse to a paintbrush. They often find that a flat vessel, which is called a palette, is necessary for mixing various colours. The relationship *Brush: Palette* will not do.

Option (3): Chisel: Wood. When a carpenter wants to cut a large piece of wood, he uses a saw. When he is fitting wood to some small area and finds the saw too large a device for cutting small pieces of wood, he uses a small sharp device for lopping off small pieces of wood. Such a device is known as a *chisel*. Some *chisels* are used for chipping stone as well and are used by sculptors. Since a chisel is not a surface to work on, and for that matter *wood* is not an artist, this relationship will not do either.

Option (4): Marble: Sculptor; A *sculptor* is an artist who carves a variety of surfaces such as stone, wood, marble and so on. Thus **Option 4** is correct since marble is a surface on which the *sculptor* works.

Option (5): Hammer: Carpenter; A *hammer* is a device for inserting nails into wooden surfaces on which the carpenter works. Even if we were to grant the status of an artist to a carpenter (as such a carpenter is an artisan), the surface on which he works is wood and not hammer. Hence, this option will not do.

Answer 5

PANEGYRIC: EULOGIZE; The prefix PAN- is used to describe a large range. It is for this reason that *Pan American* Highway runs across the Americas (both North and South America) and a *panorama* is an unbroken view of the whole area surrounding the observer. The word GYRATE means *to revolve* or *move around*. When someone *moves in a large area*, he does so either physically or his achievements are made known to a large number of people by way of public praise, glorification or eulogy. Thus *panegyric* means a eulogy or public praise. The relationship between *Panegyric* and *Eulogize* is that between cause and effect. Now let us see the options.

Option (1): Ballad: Stigmatise: A ballad is a song in praise of someone. Lord Alfred Tennyson, the famous English poet, wrote a ballad in praise of the valour of some six hundred English warriors who laid down their lives while fighting valiantly in the Crimean War. His ballad is titled *The Charge of the Light Brigade*. The ballad starts like this: *'Half a league, half a league onwards, All unto the Valley of Death, Rode the six hundred'*. Quite a few of us have read this ballad while at school.

A *stigma* is a blemish. It is a stain on someone's character. A ballad can bring glory, it cannot stigmatise. Thus this is not a case of cause and effect and will not do.

Option (2): Ode: Criticize; An *ode* is a dignified poem sung in order to glorify someone or something. An *ode* to a tree would then be expected to sing praises of the shelter it provides and how it enriches the atmosphere and so on.

When you *criticize* someone, you find faults with that person and therefore the word *criticize* necessarily has negative overtones. An *ode* glorifies someone and when you criticize someone you try to lower his image in the eyes of others. Therefore, this too is not a case of cause and effect.

Option (3): Lampoon: Satirise; The defence minister of a certain country once saw the Chief of Army Staff of that country walking down the corridor of the Defence Headquarters with many of his staff officers. While returning to his chamber, the minister saw the same contingent walking in another corridor. Known for his *lampooning* of the army, the minister inquired the Army Chief whether he would just keep parading all day or do some administrative work too. A *lampoon* is thus a *virulent* satire or *mockery*. The word *virulent* comes from the word *virus* and thus means *poisonous* or *harmful*. Lampoon is thus the cause that can satirise. Lampoon: Satirise is a cause: effect relationship and hence **Option 3** is correct.

Option (4): Tirade: Entertain; A *tirade* is a *long-drawn speech* denouncing something or someone but it is least likely to *entertain*. In an election speech, the speakers from the party in opposition may let loose a tirade against the policies of the government in office. Quite naturally, they would do nothing other than denounce the party in power if they ever want to sit on the treasury benches. If anything, a *tirade* may put a reasonable person to sleep. But a tirade cannot entertain. Hence this option will not do.

Option (5): Treatise: Dispute; A *treatise* is a written *work dealing methodically with a subject*. It has nothing to do with a *dispute*. They are totally different things. Hence this option will not do either.

Answer 6

GLOSSARY: TEXT; A *glossary* is a list of terms (with explanations, of course) that people would not generally understand. For example, if cricket were being introduced to a country that has not the foggiest idea of the game, then the phrase *'bowled a maiden over'* would generally be perceived as someone *having charmed a girl to fall in love with him*. The glossary of terms would then have to specify that *'bowled a maiden over'* means to have *bowled six balls (after which the bowler has to hand the ball to someone else) without yielding a single run*. The relationship between *Glossary* and *Text* is that of explanations of difficult and technical terms generally not understood in the *text*: whole text and thus glossary is a part of the *text*.

Option (1): Bibliography: Source; Quite frequently, when we read books – specially, books relating to professional courses – there is a list of references to other books that the author has consulted. Thus a *bibliography* is a list of *sources* to which the author has referred. The relationship between *Bibliography* and *Source* is that of list of sources: source. A *bibliography* is certainly not a list of terms not generally understood and hence this option will not do.

Option (2): Abstract: Dissertation; The Latin root TRACT- means to *draw* or *pull*. The prefix ABS- means *away from*. An *abstract* drawn from some text means the *synopsis* or *précis* of that text. A *dissertation* is an *extended scholarly essay* submitted for some academic qualification such as Doctor of Philosophy. An abstract, if it is a précis or a synopsis, must be understood. Therefore an abstract is not a list of terms that are not generally understood and thus this option will not do.

Option (3): Legend: Map; The idea in drawing a *map* is to present areas covering, say, thousands of square miles on a piece of paper. The central point in drawing a map is therefore reducing something to a rather small size. Thus at some places the letters HW-S may appear and at others NMON may appear. The letters HW-S to some may mean *Homework for Saturday* while NMON may mean nothing whatsoever. However, HW-S may denote **State Highway** and NMON may denote **National Monument**. Since space is a constraint, HW-S would do admirably instead of writing State Highway so that they can be presented on a map. A list of such words and what they mean if given along the map would then serve as a legend or glossary for the map. Thus Option 3 is correct.

Option (4): Index: Catalogue; If you were to enter a library and want a book about grasshoppers, you will have to ask for a catalogue of books on the subject of grasshoppers. If you were to select a particular book out of this *catalogue* and decide to look up this book you will have to look for the *index* find on which page will you see the chapter on what grasshoppers do in their free time, so an index is essentially a list depicting what is where. An *index* is not a list of terms people do not generally understand. There is no relationship as such between *Index* and *Catalogue* and hence this option will not do.

Option (5): Abbreviation: Footnote; The word *abbreviation* comes from the word *brevity*, which is the quality that makes things *brief*.

If someone were to tell you a joke that takes an hour to narrate, laughter is the least likely outcome. In all probability, you might go off to sleep after being tired of pleading with the fellow to come to the point. This is why it is said that *brevity is the soul* (or *essence*) *of wit*.

An *abbreviation* is a *contraction of a long name* or term. This is why UK is the abbreviation for the United Kingdom and VIP for Very Important Person. However, abbreviations are generally understood and do not have to explained. A footnote is what you see at the end of a page where you might see a reference to another book or the detailed explanation of some term. *Footnotes* are incidental to the text and they are not the main text. This is why this option will not do either.

Answer 7

LULLABY: SONG. A *lullaby* is a cradlesong. It puts a child to sleep. Not all songs have similar effects. There are songs that motivate people to dance. Some others bring tears to people's eyes. Then there are others that whip up patriotism and by the time the song is over, people hearing it may be seen leaping onto their horses with their swords flashing and the riders would be seen galloping towards the enemy. A lullaby is, however, one among the many types of song.

Option (1): Narrative: Volume; In the days prior to television, when you wanted to know what was happening in the cricket test match between two nations, you switched on the radio. You could get a *narrative* of who scored how much and who got out for how many runs and so on. A *narrative* is thus an account of a series of events. Now, as you can see what is happening, on a television screen, the narrative media is replaced with picture media. A *narrative* person is one who is talkative. Narrations can be at high or low volume. As a matter of fact, in the case of a radio, you can control the *volume. Narrative* therefore, has little to do with volume and this option will not do.

Option (2): Lecture: Tutor; A *tutor* when he teaches a number of persons may find a need for giving a *lecture*. Ordinarily, however, a tutor is one who gives tuition to either an individual or a small group of persons. In such cases he can do without a lecture. A lecture is not a variety of *tutor* and hence this option will not do either.

Option (3): Paragraph: Page; A *paragraph* is not one variety of *page*; it is only a part of a *page* most of the times and hence this option will not do either.

Option (4): Diatribe: Discourse: Imagine that a country is passing through an economic phase in which there are too many people who have little to eat and only a few who live in the lap of luxury. Imagine that a politician wants to change the system for which he must be in a position of power. He gathers labourers and lets loose a *diatribe* against the rich people, cursing them for exploiting the poor by extracting too much work from them and giving too little wages. He breathes fire in his speech.

Now imagine that a priest is talking to his congregation. He is giving a speech on the merits of abstention and purity of the soul. What he is giving, is a *discourse*. He too, may become emphatic. A diatribe is a variety of discourse. Thus **Option 4** is correct.

Option (5): Invective: Compliment; Imagine that a person goes to a bar. He asks for a double scotch and downs it before you can say *Mary had a little lamb*. He then asks for a refill and downs that as well. The alcohol goes to his head. He asks the bartender for a third round. The bartender then tells him that he has had enough. The drunk breaks the glass. He catches the bartender by his hair. The security guard is then summoned. He catches the drunk by his collar and throws him out. While going out, the drunk uses a whole lot of four-letter words; shameful language that cannot find place in print. The drunk is uttering *invectives*. A *compliment* is quite the reverse of an invective. Thus this option will not do.

Answer 8

FERVOUR: ZEALOT. Imagine that you are on vacation in a remote corner of Africa. The sun has set. A troop of local dancers has come to your hotel. The music starts, slowly at first. The tempo then picks up. A few of the guests join the dance. Many more join up gradually as the tempo rises sharply. There is handclapping that adds to the fervour that the music is generating. All the guests are now dancing in frenzy. *Fervour* therefore means *intense zeal*.

Now imagine that a certain country that is being ruled by foreigners is seeking independence. The independence struggle would mean that thousands of people would have to rise in revolt. So many people would lose their lives when the foreign power tries to curb the revolt by use of force. Clearly, unless the people who participate in revolts are *zealots*, the struggle would not succeed. People would have to be so zealous for the cause of independence that even bullets would not deter them.

A *zealot* is one who is carried away by excess zeal. He is a fanatical enthusiast. Thus the relationship between Fervour and Zealot is that of cause and effect. Let us now see the options.

Option (1): Antipathy: Philanthropist; Imagine that a religion prescribes idol worship. Now imagine that a small group of people practicing this religion have started feeling that idols should not be worshipped because nothing can represent the Almighty. They break away from the religion. There are no wars between the two groups. There is no mutual hatred either. There is *antipathy* between the two groups or contrariness of opinion just as there would be *antipathy* in the agriculturist populace when the government decides to tax agriculture incomes. The farmer may dislike the government. The converse is not true.

A *philanthropist* is one who has love for mankind. The prefix PHIL- means *loving, having an affinity* for and the word ANTHROPOS means human beings. A *philanthropist,* for example would give money for an orphanage, build and donate a hospital for the poor, pay for education of children of poor parents and so on. The opposite of *philanthropist* is a *misanthrope* (the prefix MIS- meaning *hating* as in the case of *misogamist* who hates marriage). Therefore there is no relationship, not even an antonymous relationship, between Antipathy and Philanthropist. This option will not do.

Option (2): Improvidence: Spendthrift; Have you not heard of a *provident* fund? It is a fund into which people deposit money all the while that they earn. They can fall back upon this provident fund in days when they are unable to earn their livelihood. The word *provident* means *that which provides*. One can save money only when one spends less than what one earns. Thus *providence* means *economy* or *careful budgeting. Improvidence* means the very opposite. A person given to improvidence spends without a care in the world. He is a *spendthrift*. Thus *improvidence* is the cause of which *spendthrift* is the effect. Thus **Option 2** is correct.

Option (3): Concision: Politician; The word *concision* comes from the word *concise* that means brief but easily understandable. Speeches are the tools of the trade of a politician. While politicians may or may not be concise, it is politics that makes a politician, not concision. *Politics* incidentally is the struggle for power. Thus there is no relationship between Concision and Politician, leave alone a cause: effect relationship.

Option (4): Determination: Ecologist; An ecologist as we have seen earlier is either (A) someone who specialises in the branch of biology that studies the inter-se relationships of living organisms and their relationship with their physical environment or (B) someone keenly involved in the activities of protecting living organisms from damage due to pollution and so on. He has to have determination if he is variety (B). But determination would make someone determined; determination would not make someone an ecologist. Somebody with the determination to drink a whole bottle of liquor will become drunk but he will not become an ecologist. Hence this option would not do.

Option (5): Nonchalance: Acrobat; The other day, the gentleman next door took ill and we had to rush him to hospital. We rang his son. He came hours later. Some medicines were urgently needed. He went out to buy them. An hour later one of us went to see where he was. The young fellow was leisurely smoking a cigarette at the hospital entrance. His *nonchalance* surprised me. *Nonchalance* means lack of enthusiasm or unconcern.

An *acrobat* is one who performs breathtaking gymnastic feats such as tightrope walking or he could be a trapeze artist in a circus. An acrobat swinging from one trapeze to the other must display great concern for his life first of all. If not, then as is the case with all who lack enthusiasm he too would be yawning with fair frequency and may miss the swing that is coming his way when stifling a king-size yawn. If the trampoline has gone to the laundry, it can be mighty dangerous. *Nonchalance* can make bores or dispassionate people but certainly not *acrobats*. Thus this option will not do either.

Answer 9

ASSUAGE: SORROW. I had severe pain in the joint of my right shoulder. Massage with turpentine *assuaged* (or, in other words, *soothed, alleviated, eased*) the pain considerably. I could even play a game of squash that evening.

One summer afternoon, two urchins rang the bell. My wife opened the door. The boys asked for drinking water. It took two large mugs of water to *assuage* (or *slake, quench*) their thirst.

In the above two situations, we have seen the shades of meaning of the word *assuage. Sorrow* is *grief*. **Sorrow diminishes if assuaged**. This is the relationship between Assuage and Sorrow. Now let us see the options.

Option (1): Retaliate: Antipathy; Imagine that there is hostility between two countries. The armed forces of one country open fire on an assembly of people in a village across the border. The other army *retaliates* by shelling a school building across the border. To *retaliate* means to pay back in the same manner. As we have seen earlier in this exercise, *antipathy* means *opposition in viewpoints* or opinions. If there were antipathy between two groups, retaliation would only widen the divide between them or worsen the condition instead of assuaging the problem. Thus this option will not do.

Option (2): Dampen: Ardour; My brother's son is a great fan of Mark Waugh, the famous Australian batsman. His *ardour* for the cricket star is apparent from the dozens of posters in his room; he sends e-mails to Mark Waugh every other day. On a recent visit to Singapore, the young fellow took a flash trip to Australia to meet Mark Waugh. Clearly, the word *ardour* means intensity of feeling. When you *dampen* your school uniform, you make it wet. When your hostel warden *dampens* the mood at the party by announcing that all are to break up at eleven, he *lessens* the fun that people are having. Thus ardour *diminishes* if dampened, just as sorrow *diminishes* if assuaged. Thus **Option (2)** is correct.

Option (3): Entrust: Reliability; You can find out whether your new private secretary is reliable by entrusting to him the bookings for your forthcoming business visit to a neighbouring town. If you find that he has made proper travel arrangements and bookings at a decent hotel, you can find out whether he is more reliable by entrusting him with the arrangements for your visit abroad. Thus to increase *reliability*, one has to *entrust*. The relationship between *Entrust* and *Reliability* is thus opposite to that in the capitalised pair and hence this option will not do.

Option (4): Counsel: Reluctance; Imagine that a boy is *reluctant* to study. He fails the end-semester examinations. His parents counsel him to pay more attention to study. He decides to focus on studies and passes the retest with decent marks. Now imagine that a married young man has a passionate affair with the married lady next door. Their meetings have been clandestine. Both think no one knows about their affair yet they are *reluctant* to let their affair affect their respective family lives. The young man's parents counsel him against such a relationship. The young man and his paramour elope leaving their respective families. Here *counsel* has had no effect on the problem. *Counsel* may indeed have been the cause for aggravation. Thus there is no necessary relationship between *Counsel* and *Reluctance* and this option will not do.

Option (5): Withhold: Appreciation; Imagine that a factory owner has just finalised the accounts for the last financial year and found that profitability has gone up sharply. He buys himself a new limousine. He finds that profits have gone up sharply since the new manager has joined. He wants to convey appreciation of the new manager's efficient working and give him a big bonus of say a hundred thousand pounds. He conveys this wholehearted appreciation to the new manager. On second thoughts he decides to give only ten thousand pounds for the present and *withhold* the rest for some other day. Is he likely to increase or diminish appreciation by withholding? The *appreciation* remains undiminished. It cannot be equated with money. Only the *amount of bonus* will diminish by withholding. So this option will not do.

Answer 10.

DIE: SHAPING. You might have seen a die at the workshop of a blacksmith or at the mints where currency coins are made. A die is a device for shaping bulk material. In the process of minting currency coins, metal is forced to flow into two matching dies, each of which bears a reverse engraved design of the relief pattern to be formed on the finished coin or part. A die, therefore, does the shaping. Now let us see the options.

Option (1): Glue: Attaching; If you want to affix postage stamps on an envelope, you would put *glue* on the reverse of the stamp and then affix the stamp on the envelope. Once it is affixed, it can only be torn but not detached. If you want to *attach* a photocopy of your mark-sheet with your application, for admission to a university, you attach the photocopy with a stapler. If the university people want to keep the photocopy separate from the application letter, they can detach it from the letter by taking off the staple pin. *Attaching* is similar to linking. The photocopy will remain whole if detached, unlike the stamp, which will be torn. **Glue** does the **affixing** but **not attaching**. Hence this option will not do.

Option (2): Anchor: Sailing; An *anchor* keeps the boat moored at the place where you want to keep it in the waters. But it is not the *anchor* that does the sailing. The sails do the *sailing*. A boat can do without an anchor. At best, you may tie it with a rope to a post on the shore. But if you want to go sailing, this can be done only if you have sails. This option will not do either.

Option (3): Drill: Boring; If you want to bore a hole into the wall for hanging the photograph of you being awarded your degree in convocation, you will need a drill to do that. Thus drill does the boring. **Option (3)** is correct.

Option (4): Pedal: Propelling; The word *propel* comes from the Latin root PELL- that means *drive* or *push*. The prefix PRO- stands for *forward* or *in favour of*. Thus, *propelling* means *driving* or *pushing forward*. A *pedal* can propel a bicycle but not an automobile. If you were to use *pedals* to propel cars, there would be no use for petrol although it would take hours to cover small distances. Besides, this would be terribly tiring.

Thus a *pedal* does not necessarily do propelling and hence this option will not work.

Option (5): Ink: Printing; If ink alone could do *printing*, we would see large blots of *ink* but no letters. It has to flow on paper through a device such as a pen that regulates where it should flow and how much. Thus, it is the *printer* that does the printing. Thus this option will not do either.

Answer 11

PERFUNCTORILY: INSPIRATION; The prefix PER- means *through*. The word *function* means *work*. Perfunctory therefore literally means *through work*. When one reads the history lesson for the sake of reading alone but not with interest, he is said to have read perfunctorily. Ask him when British dominion ended in Hong Kong and he is blank although he may have read it only the previous day. When you ask your teacher as to when the class would go on a picnic and she says: *We'll see*, her reply is perfunctory.

The word *inspiration* comes from the French verb SPIRARE that means *breathe*. When you breathe in, you *inspire*. You may breathe in air into your lungs or you may breathe in enthusiasm into someone for the task that he is entrusted to do. He is not happy about the work that has been given to him. He is sullen. *I know how difficult the task is but if anyone can do it, only you can do it*, you say, and the fellow starts the work and whistles all along till he finishes. You have provided *inspiration* to him. There are other words that flow from the verb SPIRARE. Some of these words are **aspire** (the prefix A- may means *away* or *on* or *up* or out and when you *breathe up* you take a deep breath and when you make up your mind to join, say, the army you *aspire* for a commission in the army), *conspire* (when some people speak together in soft voices that seem to be the sound of breathing when they hatch a plot or plan a *conspiracy*), and so on.

Quite clearly, anything done *perfunctorily* lacks *inspiration*. Now let us see the options.

Option (1): Insolently: Veneration; Imagine that a factory owner has employed a young man. He has been meeting production targets. Yet the owner does not pay him the promised bonus. There is a trade union in the factory. He goes to the union and asks them what he should do to get his due. The union leader escorts the young worker to the owner. They request for the bonus. The owner says nothing doing. They then bang his desk *insolently* and shout at him. They threaten to go on strike if the fellow is not paid. When something is done *insolently*, it is done in a disrespectful manner.

Now imagine a totally different scenario where this young man has been paid bonus in time. The owner also helped him with money when the young man's mother was hospitalised. The trade union want to go on strike on some other issue. The young worker refuses to take part saying that he holds the owner in *veneration* (or *deep respect*) and will do nothing that will disrupt production. Anything done insolently is done **without** veneration and hence **Option (1)** is correct.

Option (2): Ardently: Passion; My nephew admired Mark Waugh *ardently*. He was passionate about the great Australian cricketer. Anything done *ardently* is **with** *passion* and hence this option will not do.

Option (3): Phlegmatically: Composure; We would do well to see how the various shades of meaning of the word *phlegmatic* have come about. *Phlegm* – which quite clearly is the source of the word *phlegmatic* – is the thick viscous fluid secreted by the mucous membranes of the respiratory passage. As you know, the throat sits at the head of the respiratory passage and people clear their throats to clear the phlegm. At the same time, people who like to think coolly about a course of action or what to reply, clear their throats. Hotheaded people start off without a pause; their replies are off-the-cuff; their actions are not well considered. This is why the word *phlegmatic* in one of its shades means *cool*, *composed*, *tranquil* and so on.

As we also know, when there is too much of phlegm, we may have fever and recurring headaches that affect our capacity or inclination to get up and go. This is why *phlegmatic* means *sluggish* or *uninterested* in its other shade of meaning.

However, anything done *phlegmatically* is done **with** *composure*. Thus this relationship is opposite to that in the capitalised pair and thus this option will not do.

Option (4): Surreptitiously: Obsession; Let us see the meaning of the word *surreptitiously* from a situational context. You will notice that it has been our endeavour to give situational contexts as frequently as possible in order to drive home the meanings of words and their various shades in the contexts of situations in place of one liners. This is because the one liner context is a poor teacher; the situational usage on the other hand engraves the meanings of words on one's memory.

Imagine that a fellow is out on a conducted trip of Europe. The travel agency has put him up in a swank hotel in Rome. Our man, however, is obsessed with stealing things. The travel agency has arranged with the reception desk to wake up all the passengers at six the next morning. The phone rings at six. Our man quietly cuts the cord linking the telephone instrument with the plug and *surreptitiously* slips the telephone instrument in his bag.

Another young man is madly in love with the sweet damsel next door. Her father does not approve of the match since the boy comes from an economically lower stratum of society. The two however meet *surreptitiously* in bye lanes, taking care to see that no one known to them sees them or else the father may throw a fit. Quite clearly, *surreptitiously* means *secretly* or in a clandestine manner. Also quite clearly, had the fellow, who tucked the telephone instrument into his bag or the young couple who met *surreptitiously*, not been obsessed respectively with stolen things or love, neither would have the need to do things in clandestine fashion. Had the thief asked the reception desk if he could take away the instrument, there would have been either a reprisal or peals of laughter at the stupidity of the request. Had the girl's father permitted her to meet her young lover, there would be no need for playing hide and seek.

The word *obsession* comes from the Latin root SESS- that means to *sit*, or *settle*. The prefix OB- means *against* or *towards*, or *in a way* it depends on the context. The suffix –ION denotes a *state of*. A *state of sitting in front of* – with the determination not to get up till the desired thing is got – is *obsession*.

Anything done *surreptitiously* is done with *obsession* and hence this option will not do.

Option (5): Haltingly: Reluctance; I remember the time when my sister's son came to my place for the summer vacation. He was not too keen on the outdoors. I asked him if he would like to come on a short hike with me. He asked me how many miles that would be. I said fifteen, at the outermost. He said something haltingly about the pain in his sole and the doctor having advised him not to overstrain. I took him along notwithstanding his reluctance. We saw a pond brimming with alligators. We saw a panther drinking from a stream in the forest. He was thrilled. He is reluctant no more. Now whenever we meet, he asks me when we would go on our next hike. Quite clearly, when something is done or said *haltingly*, it is with *reluctance* and this option will not do.

Answer 12

FAWN: IMPERIOUSNESS; The word *fawn* can be used as a noun, adjective or as verb. In each case it has various shades of meaning. What is the commonality behind these shades is something that we shall see as we go along.

A *fawn* is the young one of a deer. So if the deer in the zoo is due to fawn, it means that the deer is due to deliver soon. Of course, only deer can fawn, not lionesses.

A *fawn* is normally of a beige colour or yellowish-brown colour. Thus a *fawn* jacket could be yellowish-brown. This is *fawn* as an adjective.

When you hold out a sugar cube to a *fawn*, the little darling wags her tail in order to show her eagerness to get munching on it. This the lion cub will seldom do. A two–year old lion cub might attempt to eat not only what one is trying to give but also the person as well. People who yearn passionately for a thing *fawn*, or wag their tails figuratively, and thus behave in a servile or sycophantic manner. They do not have the courage to snatch it away from the person from whom they are likely to get it.

The word *imperiousness* comes from the word *imperial* that is *related to the King*. The King does not *fawn*. Others *fawn* when they want something from him. This is why when someone fawns he cannot possibly have *imperiousness*. Now let us see the options.

Option (1): Equivocate: Directness; *Equivocate* comes from the prefix EQUI- that means equal and VOCATE that means *speak*. When one speaks something with *two equal meanings*, he is said to *equivocate*.

A Scottish army general was on his way back from the battlefield where he had inflicted a humiliating defeat upon the enemy. Three witches met him on his return. One prophesised that he would be the King of Scotland.

Another told him that *'none of woman born'* would harm him. Eventually he became King. With one prophesy having come true (primarily because the general killed the King and usurped the throne), he was sure that no human being could harm him. He became reckless and utterly arrogant. He was not aware that there were two meanings to what the witch had prophesised. There was a rebellion. The King's men deserted him. He was up against a young man who had been delivered by Caesarean section (meaning he was **not born in the normal course**). The young man chopped off the King's head. If the witch had used *directness* in her prophesy, she would have said that none except someone born of caesarean section would harm the fellow. He would have been on his guard then. But then there would not have been a story to narrate. The moral of the story, as far as we are concerned, is that if someone would equivocate, there would be no directness in his speech. Thus **Option (1)** is correct.

Option (2): Elaborate: Originality; The word *elaborate* comes from the word *labour* that means *toil*. The prefix E- means *out*. When a speaker toils or takes extensive pains to bring out what he is trying to say to an audience, he is said to be *elaborate*. When someone works out an *elaborate* plan to hike his company's market share, the plan is worked out with great care and toil and it is thus *very detailed*. If I wish to *elaborate* on a theme for a drama, I must know the theme in and out although I may not be the playwright. The chances that one who is elaborating has originated the content are very high. If Isaac Newton had to elaborate on the Laws of Motion at a scientific conference in the old days, it was because no one knew about these laws. It is not necessary that one would elaborate on a topic and yet not have originality. Thus this option will not do.

Option (3): Boggle: Imagination; The word *boggle* has so many shades of meaning that we shall see in the following usages:

- When I took my motorcycle to the garage, I asked the mechanic to see that it was restored to top working condition. When I went to pick it up a week later, he gave me a whopping bill. I *boggled* (or *wavered*) at the thought of paying so much.
- When I saw a serpent creep behind the sofa in my farmhouse, I boggled at the very sight. (Here when I say I was *boggled*, it means I was *very scared*)
- When I saw the Grand Canyon, its great depth *boggled* (or *amazed*) me.

Whichever way you look at it, there must be some imagination at work, in order to get boggled. When the repair bill boggled me, I imagined that it would take me at least two hundred days of working overtime in order to be able to pay it. When I saw the serpent I imagined what could happen if it bit me. When the depth of the canyon boggled me it was because I was trying to imagine how many pieces would I break into if I were to slip and fall in it.

Clearly, if something would *boggles* anyone, it is because of his imagination. This is why this option will not do either.

Option (4): Manipulation: Repression; The word *manipulation* has several shades of meaning that we shall see in the following situational usages:

- Imagine that a real estate developer wants a bank loan to finish constructing his latest multi-storey residential complex of flats that have not been selling. The bank asks him to give a proof showing that a majority of the flats have been booked. He issues allotment letters to some friends and relatives whom he persuades to put small initial booking amounts with him with an understanding that no further amount than this small amount need be paid and when the flats are sold to some genuine buyer, such booking amounts would be refunded to them. The list of bookings that the real estate developer then submits to the bank seems to give the impression that the majority of flats have been booked. The developer has carried out *manipulation* of the record of bookings (meaning *he has managed by unfair means* to present a situation wherein it would seem that the majority of flats are booked).
- Imagine that you have engaged a chef to turn out a lavish spread on your parents' silver wedding anniversary. The chef has put the cake in the oven, which he inspects periodically. He has put the soup on the boil in one vessel and is stirring it every now and then. He has put the stew to simmer in a large utensil. He is stirring the meat curry. He is carrying out *manipulation* (or *skilful physical dealing*) of four cooking vessels at a time.

The word *repression* comes from the word *press* and the prefix RE- that means *back*. When someone **presses back** some fact so that it does not come into public view or knowledge, he has indulged in *repression* of that fact. The word *repression* has several shades of meaning that we shall see with the help of the following:

- Imagine that a school class is on a picnic. Imagine that the bully of the class is asking everyone to line up for a demonstration of his skills at swimming. Imagine that he is walking up to the water but slips on the moss below and falls with a loud thud. Imagine that he has tears in his eyes. The whole class want to laugh their hearts out but have no choice but to *repress* their laughter lest the fellow would get even for this. Here *repress* means *hold back* and hence *repression* means *holding back* or *restraint*.
- If a country was trying to break free from foreign rule and the rulers had let loose a reign of terror and *repression*, this means that the rulers were crushing any attempt at starting a liberation movement or they were *quelling* the independence movement.
- If you will recall the instance of the real estate developer, he *repressed* (or *deliberately held back*) the fact that the bookings were bogus although he knew that the bookings were bogus. For him in specific and even generally, *manipulation* in its context of doing things by unfair means is not possible without *repression* of the truth. Thus this option will not do.

Option (5); Coddle: Permissiveness; The word *coddle* is used to describe what parents to do to their children when they *featherbed* them or *spoil* them. Quite frequently children do not know what is good for them. It is for the parents to teach them what is good and what is not. For example, children frequently have tooth decay caused by eating too much of sugary stuff. Yet parents permit them to hog sweets.

Permissiveness is a state in which there is too much liberty. Thus if parents *coddle* their children, this is only because parents have *permissiveness* or *leniency*. Hence this option will not do either.

As would be apparent from the various explanations of how words have evolved, the English language has a deep-seated structure. We shall strive to see all major roots of words in the language. As a part of this ongoing exercise, let us recall the word *propel* in this exercise and see the core words emanating from the Latin root from which the word *propel* has been derived.

You use a pedal to propel your bicycle. You use petrol to propel your car. The word propel comes from the Latin root *PEL-, PELL-, PULS-* that means to drive; push. The core words emanating from this root are: *compel, impel, repel.*

Compel is *COM-*, the prefix meaning together + *PEL-*, the root meaning to drive; push; *compel* means *to push together*; *to urge forcefully*; *to force* or *require by law*; circumstance etc." Words based on *compel* are:

Compelling: forceful; overpowering

Compulsion: the act of compelling or state of being compelled; force

Compulsive: forceful

Compulsory: required; without an option

Impel is *IM-*, the Latin prefix meaning on + *PEL-*, the root meaning *to drive*; *push*; *impel* means *to drive on*; *force or drive someone or something to an action*; *urge on*. Words based on *impel* are:

Impulse: a sudden urge to take some action

Impulsion: the act impelling or state of being impelled

Impulsive: given to acting on sudden inclination without prior thought; brought on by impulse

Repel is *RE-*, the Latin prefix meaning back + *PEL-*, the root meaning *to drive*; *push*; *repel* means *to drive or force someone or something back*. Words based on *repel* are :

Repellent: that which tends to repel; offensive or disgusting

Repulsion: a feeling of extreme dislike, disgust or horror

Repulsive: disgusting

Now let us see some contextual usages of the core words emanating from this root and understand not only their precise meanings but also their various shades of meaning:

1. Some Islamic countries *compel* even foreign women to wear the veil.
2. I have a *compelling* need for rest now.
3. He lied before the inquiry officer under *compulsion* from his superior.
4. He is a *compulsive* smoker.
5. Uniform will be *compulsory* for all military staff attending the parade.
6. Only a monetary crisis would *impel* him to economic activity.
7. She is reckless with money; she purchased an expensive fur coat on *impulse*.
8. The manager tends to be guided more by *impulsion* than finality; he takes only short-term views.
9. Do not be *impulsive* in choosing your career; the matter requires deep thought.
10. Cockroaches *repel* my sister.
11. Our valiant army *repelled* the enemy.
12. You will have to take a water-*repellent* jacket on the expedition.
13. I was overcome with *repulsion* when I saw the squalor in which he lived.
14. It is his mannerism more than body odour that makes him *repulsive*.

We may also recall having come across the word *obsession* in this exercise, a word that comes from the Latin root SESS- (one among the three similar roots *SED-*, *SID-*, or *SESS-* that all mean *to sit; settle*).

The core words are *preside, reside, sediment, session.*

Preside comes from the Latin prefix PRE- meaning before + *SID-* meaning to sit. Preside means *to sit before others* in the *place of a leader*; *sit in authority*; *act as chairman*. Some other words based on *preside* are:

President: the person chosen to preside over any organization, group, nation etc., the chief executive.

Presidency: the office of a president or the time that a president is in office.

Presidential: of, for, or pertaining to a president, the presidency, or the election of a president.

Reside comes from the Latin prefix *RE-* meaning *back* + *SID-* meaning *to sit*; *settle*. Reside means *to settle back or stay at a place*; to *make one's home at a particular place*; *to exist as a quality in something*; to *be vested in as a right*. Words based on *reside* are:

Residence: the place or house where a person lives.

Residential: a person who lives in a place; having a residence; staying in or being affiliated with a place in connection with one's official work.

Residential: of, pertaining to, or suitable for residences or homes.

You might like to see this rather interesting usage of the word *reside*: The powers to grant mining lease *reside* in the Commissioner of Industries.

Sediment comes from the Latin root *SED-* meaning *to sit*; *settle* + suffix *–MENT* meaning *the act or result of*. *sediment* means *the result of something settling*; *matter that settles or is settling to the bottom* of a *body of liquid*."

Session comes from *SESS-* meaning *to sit*; *settle* + *–ION* meaning *the act or state of*. *Session* means *the sitting together of a legislative body*, a court etc., for the purpose of doing business; a *single meeting of an organized group*; a school; term.

Practise Test 3

DIRECTIONS *for questions 1 to 12: In each of the following questions, a related pair of words or phrases is followed by five lettered pairs of words or phrases. Select the lettered pair that best expresses a relationship similar to that expressed in the original pair.*

	The Word	Option 1	Option 2	Option 3	Option 4	Option 5
1	CLOT: DISSOLVED	Enthusiast: Influence	Cartoon: Distorted	Crowd: Dispersed	Chain: Disengaged	Disciple: Inspired
2	STUDY: LEARN	Pervade: Encompass	Search: Find	Gather: Win	Agree: Keep	Accumulate: Raise
3	APPLE: FRUIT	Egg: Chicken	Rung: Chair	Wool: Fabric	Fuse: Dynamite	Wick: Candle
4	TABLECLOTH: TABLE	Tent: Ground	Shirt: Hanger	Window: Sill	Sheet: Mattress	Cloud: Earth
5	FERTILIZE: GROW	Immunize: Resist	Nourish: Enrich	Heat: Burn	Graft: Multiply	Prune: Dwarf
6	AUTHORITA-TIVENESS: PUNDITS	Dedication: Signatories	Sobriety: Executors	Sensitivity: Literati	Recklessness: Warriors	Allegiance: Partisan
7	FRESCO: WALL	Fountain: Courtyard	Parquetry: Floor	Thatch: Roof	Statuary: Passage	Gargoyle: Gutter
8	STRUT: WING	Lever: Handle	Axle: Wheel	Buttress: Wall	Beam: Rivet	Well: Pipe
9	ATTENTIVE: OFFICIOUS	Doubtful: Ambiguous	Absorbed: Engrossed	Refined: Snobbish	Magisterial: Authoritative	Impromptu: Spontaneous
10	AUDACIOUS: TREPIDATION	Refractory: Intransigence	Laconic: Volubility	Sordid: Aspiration	Cursory: Accumulation	Derisive: Subordination
11	BLANDISH MENT: COAX	Medal: Honour	Budget: Save	Diary: Reminisce	Concert: Play	Plea: Threaten
12	RELEVANT: CRUCIAL	Marginal: Unique	Perceptible: Obvious	Apparent: Real	Peripheral: Central	Possible: Desirable

Answer 1

CLOT: DISSOLVED. A *clot* is a lump (usually semi-solid) in some fluid that obstructs the flow of the fluid. Thus a nick, while shaving, may cause a drop or two of blood to ooze out; a clot soon develops and stops the flow. If the clot is dissolved, the fluid starts moving again. A *Clot* and *Dissolved* thus cannot co-exist. Now let us see the options.

Option (1): Enthusiast: Influence; Someone very keen on football is a football *enthusiast*. Someone who seldom misses a chance to go to a classical musical concert is a classical music enthusiast. A person may be very keen about physical exercise. He may be a fitness freak or an aerobics enthusiast. On the other hand, his wife may hold the view that turning the pages of a newspaper is enough exercise for a day. The poor husband may desperately try to get her to exercise but there may be no influence of his exhortations. It may so happen that a smart young man may take up the flat next door and the wife may realise the need for slimming and the poor husband's efforts may now start bearing influence on his wife. Thus *Enthusiast* and *Influence* may or may not co-exist. Hence this option will not do.

Option (2): Cartoon: Distorted; Comical or satirical situations may be represented in so many ways: photographs, portraits, caricatures or cartoons and so on, of which the photograph may seem to be the quickest of all the methodologies and portrait the slowest. A photograph would be feasible only if the situation was real and not when it is imaginary. A portrait might take weeks or months by which time the humour in a situation may have either diminished considerably or evaporated entirely. If time is of essence, the cartoon must reflect ready wit and the cartoonist for example would have to blow a long nose out of proportion with the dimensions of the rest of the face if the reader is to be able to tell who the subject of the caricature is. If he is to draw the nose in proportion with the rest of the face, he must paint a portrait and thus must have the subject of his caricature, posing for hours. No one in his right mind would pose for caricatures. When you blow things out of proportion, you distort them. Thus *Cartoon* and *Distorted* are normally feasible only when they co-exist and hence this option will not do.

Option (3): Crowd: Dispersed; Imagine that a guru is teaching his numerous disciples crowding around him about how to get rid of fear. Imagine that while this lecture is on, the sun sets and a lion roars in the vicinity – although it is only later found that the lion was in a cage in the zoo nearby. The guru runs for dear life and so does everyone in the crowd, after having realised that the guru himself does not seem too sure about the subject matter of the discourse. The crowd disperses. It may be noticed that *Crowd* and *Dispersed* cannot co-exist. This is why **Option (3)** is correct.

Option (4): Chain: Disengaged; If you were to *chain* a person to some place, you would tie him there with a *chain* so that he is not free to move. If the prisoner becomes *disengaged* he is free to move. It may so happen that the prisoner may cut the *chain* around his wrists and run leaving the entire chain where it fell. It may also happen that the prisoner may gather strength, enough to pull the peg on which the chain is tied, right out of the ground and run with the chain still adorning his wrists. In either event, the man has become disengaged, the only difference being that in the first instance he is free of the chain as well and in the other, he is still attached to the chain. Thus *Chain* and *Disengaged* may or may not go together and hence this option will not do either.

Option (5): Disciple: Inspired; We have seen the origin of the word *inspiration* in a prior exercise and have learnt that it means to *breathe* in (either air into the lungs or life or enthusiasm in the person whom one inspires). A disciple is an ardent follower of the person of whom he is a disciple. A person would not even faintly consider being someone's disciple unless he was deeply inspired by the master. Thus *Disciple* and *Inspired* necessarily co-exist and hence this option will not do either.

Answer 2

STUDY: LEARN; A person who wants to become a doctor, must study medicine. The relationship between *Study* and *Learn* is that of What you do: What you get as a result.

Now let us see the options.

Option (1): Pervade: Encompass; If you enter a room and find that a sweet fragrance *pervades* the room, the fragrance is everywhere *within* the room.

On the other hand, if your study of the design of buildings is to *encompass* the entire range of buildings such as temples, old residential buildings, low-rise flats and high-rise towers, then the scope of your study would cover diverse types of buildings and anything can be covered only *externally*. The relationship between *Pervade*: *Encompass* is that of *what happens within*: *What happens without* (the word *without* here means *outside*). Hence this option will not do either.

Option (2): Search: Find; You are about to go out so you look for your wallet. But you find that it is not in its usual place, you *search* for it for some ten minutes at the end of which, to your great relief, you find it in the trousers that you dumped in the laundry bag. Therefore *Search* is what you do and *Find* is what you get as result of *search*. Hence Option (2) is correct.

Option (3): Gather: Win; The word gather may or may not have anything to do with win. If you are at the casino and *win* a jackpot, you may find that the money is pouring out from the machine and may need a small bucket to gather what`you win. But then you gather the money only *after* you *win*. You do not *win* because you *gather*. Shepherds *gather* firewood when they are out grazing their cattle. Do they *win* anything in the process? Thus this option will not do either.

Option (4): Agree: Keep; *Agree* may not have anything to do with *keep*. When we were children, my brother, sister and I frequently played teacher turn by turn. We *agreed* that my brother would be teacher first and I next and my sister last. We were to keep doing what the teacher ordered. When my brother played teacher, he would punish us both, making us do sit-ups and to stand on the make-believe benches. When it was my turn to play teacher, my brother would back out of what we had *agreed* to *keep* (keep doing what the teacher ordered, that is). He would say that he was not playing anymore since he had a lot of homework to finish. Clearly, we would keep to what we had agreed while he would not. Hence this option will not do either.

Option (5): Accumulate: Raise; Imagine that an uncle of yours is visiting you. He has kept a whole lot of money in his trouser pocket that, unfortunately for him, has developed a sizeable hole. Coins drop on to the carpet when he walks to the door while rushing out to catch the train home. When you *accumulate* the coins that are lying on the ground, you are gathering them. You might even *raise* the money for the new tyre that you badly need for your bicycle.

Now imagine that this uncle of yours is *accumulating* shares of a certain pharmaceutical company that he is sure will appreciate greatly and when he sells them he will be able to *raise* the amount, that he needs for a new flat. When he is *accumulating* shares, he is buying them (because shares do not drop out of leaking trouser pockets). Now then, when he has bought a large number of shares, some children die when they are administered the pharmaceutical company's injections and the company's plant is sealed. The shares plummet. There are no buyers. Then the shares are delisted. Your uncle is not able to sell them. The shares are not worth a dime. Has he been able to *raise anything* by accumulating? Thus this option too will not do.

Answer 3

APPLE: FRUIT; An *apple* is a variety of fruit. An apple can be called a *fruit* without hesitation.

Option (1): Egg: Chicken; Imagine that you are doing a vacation job as a waiter in a restaurant and a man orders chicken sandwich but you serve him an *egg* sandwich instead, asserting that the *chicken* essentially is only an advanced form of *egg*, you will get the boot from the restaurant management. An *egg* is certainly not a variety of *chicken*. It is for this reason that this option will not do.

Option (2) Rung: Chair; A ladder normally has two parallel bars and *rungs* in between on which you step and climb the ladder. This is why when somebody is promoted, he is said to have climbed one more *rung* in his organisation's hierarchy. Chairs as such do not have rungs except in the case of high chairs on which people sit at bars (to get high or maybe higher?). Rungs may be of help to short customers who may need to be (first *seen* and then) attended to by the bartender. However, since the rung is not a variety of chair, this option will not work.

Option (3) Wool: Fabric; *Wool* as we all know is a variety of *fabric* and hence Option 3 is correct.

The word wool can be used figuratively in a variety of ways. If somebody is trying to cheat another, he is trying to *pull the wool* over the other's eyes.

If some person has, for example, learnt yogic healing from a guru and is now sure that yoga is the only way to get well, he is said to be *dyed in the wool* of '*yogic*' healing.

Option (4): Fuse: Dynamite; A *fuse* is a device that ignites a dynamite. It is not a variety of *dynamite*. The *fuse* and *dynamite* are complementary to each other. A complementary thing cannot be a variety of the other. Is the tennis ball a variety of tennis racket? This is why this option will not do either.

Option (5): Wick: Candle; A candle has a thick thread of cotton running all through. This thread is known as the *wick* of the candle. On one end the wick pops out and when you want to light the candle, you light this *wick* at one end. On the other end, you have to scrape the wax a bit to see the other end of the *wick*. If you want to light the candle at both ends, you will face no resistance whatsoever from the *wick*. However, someone who rapidly spends whatever he has—is said to be *burning his candle at both ends*. Thus, since a wick is *a part* of the candle (and not a variety of a candle), this option will not do.

Answer 4

TABLECLOTH: TABLE; Every *table* has a top, either of wood or stone such as marble. In order to cover the top, people put a *tablecloth* on table tops. A *tablecloth* is a cover and the *table* top is what it covers although a *tablecloth* is not strictly necessary to make the *table* of any greater use. The *table* can be as functional in the absence of the *table cloth* as in its presence. Also, a table cloth can be of use with or without a *table*. You can use it as a blanket if there is nothing else handy.

Option (1): Tent: Ground; A *tent* is a cover just as a tablecloth is. But the tent cannot be pitched without the *ground* underneath. You cannot pitch a *tent* in midair can you? Thus this option will not do.

Option (2) Shirt: Hanger; A *shirt* can serve a purpose only when not on a *hanger* –you can wear it only then. A *hanger* can serve a purpose when there is no *shirt*. You can hang a skirt or even a pair of trousers. You can use a couple of wooden *hangers* to light a campfire if you please. Thus this option will not do either.

Option (3): Window: Sill; The small projection of wall or wood just below the *window* is the *window sill*. *Window* covers nothing. Since a window is not a cover at all, this option fails on the first count and will not do.

Option (4): Sheet: Mattress; A *sheet* covers a mattress. The *mattress* can function merrily in the absence of the *sheet*. Do the *mattresses*, on which wrestlers wrestle, have *sheets* on them? If they did, one of the wrestlers could strangle the other with the *sheet*, (something not too difficult to imagine when boxers have bitten the ears of their opponents). A sheet can be of great help even in the absence of *mattresses*, for example when you are waiting for a bus in the wee hours of a cold morning and have only a *sheet* to keep you warm. Thus Option (4) will do admirably.

Option (5): Cloud: Earth; A *cloud* would seem to cover the *earth* if one were to see things from a space shuttle. However there is a great difference between the manner in which a tablecloth covers the table and the way in which a *cloud* covers the earth. You can lift the table cloth, fold it and put it into the cupboard. The *cloud* cannot be lifted and folded. Hence this option will not do.

Answer 5

FERTILIZE: GROW; A seed has to *fertilize* in order to *grow* into a plant. Pregnancy starts when the male sperm *fertilizes* the female's ovum (or *egg*). Only then does the child start to grow in the mother's womb. Thus you need to *fertilize* something for it to grow. Now let us see the options.

Option (1): Immunize: Resist; When somebody is to go to a country where malaria is rampant, he takes a dose of anti-malarial medicine to *immunize* (or *become resistant to*) himself against an attack of malaria. The polio vaccine is given at Family Health Centres to *immunize* a child against polio. It enables the child to *resist* an attack of polio. Thus to immunize is necessary for something to *resist* disease. Hence **Option (1)** is correct.

Option (2): Nourish: Enrich; When you *nourish* a child, you give him proper food that is essential for growing. When you enrich a child's vocabulary, you instil in him the zeal for learning new words all the while. If someone thinks that a cabaret is the only source of entertainment, you take him to philharmonic concerts to *enrich* his taste. When the government consciously promotes private enterprise, it is trying to create entrepreneurs who will eventually create more jobs and then better goods and eventually this would *enrich* the nation or make the nation wealthier. When you enrich the cake with icing, you do so in order to *decorate* the cake or improve the quality of its appearance and/or its taste. When you *enrich* someone or something, you increase its wealth or quality. In the case of the chap, who was taken to the philharmonic orchestra so as to enrich his taste, there may not be any need to *nourish* (or feed) him. Therefore there is no necessary *nexus* (or *connection*) between *Nourish* and *Enrich* and hence this option will not do.

Option (3): **Heat: Burn**; It is not necessary that there should be *heat* before a chap suffers a *burn*. He may suffer a *burn* due to steam. He may develop sunburn even while sunbathing in temperatures in which one would need to be neck deep in woollens indoors. A chap may suffer a *burn* even while neck deep in woollens, due to the reflection of the sun's rays from snow, when on a mountain climbing expedition. Thus this option will not do either.

Option (4): **Graft: Multiply**; The word *graft* has several shades of meaning that we shall see from its following situational usages:

- When a shoot of a plant is inserted into a slit made in another plant or stock, from which the shoot receives sap (the word *sap* means *vital fluid*) and on which it grows, then a *graft* has been made. Branches or buds of trees known to produce good fruit are *grafted* to stronger trees that produce fruit of indifferent quality.
- If the employees in a factory find that their salary is too poor for a whole day's *graft*, then they think that they are being underpaid for a whole day's *hard work*.
- If the general manager decided to fire the purchases manager because the latter was taking *graft* from the suppliers, it means the purchases manager was taking *bribe* from the suppliers.

In none of the above cases there was any multiplication. In the case of the graft of the plant for a better fruit yield, there was a better plant but not multiplication. In the case of workers putting in a whole day's graft, there was exploitation. In the case of the purchase manager, he lost his job. Since there is no relationship as such between *Graft* and *Multiply*, this option will not fit.

Option (5): **Prune: Dwarf**; We shall see the nuances of the word *prune* from the following:

If a company decides to *prune* its workforce by offering an attractive voluntary retirement scheme, the idea is to *diminish* the workforce *by removing unwanted* or *superfluous* workers.

If the farmer has decided to *prune* the orange trees, the idea is to *cut dead or overgrown branches* so that the yield of the tree increases.

If the editor felt that some of the sentences in the manuscript needed to be *pruned*, the idea was to *shorten* the sentences and *make* them *precise*.

A *dwarf* tree is a tree that is *noticeably small* in relation to other trees of the same kind just as the *dwarf* in the circus is noticeably small. When you *prune*, you may actually increase yields, you may *cut unnecessary parts*. A *dwarf* tree has small branches and trunk and yet all of them are necessary. A **dwarf** in the circus has small legs, hands and arms but all of them are necessary. Therefore pruning is not necessary for something to be a dwarf and hence this option will not do either.

Answer 6

AUTHORITATIVENESS: PUNDITS; The word *pundit* is contributed to the English language by Hindi and means *someone very well versed in his specialised field of knowledge*. A person who is a pundit in his subject has authority over his subject. People refer to a pundit in constitutional matters when there is an issue that requires expert advice from someone who can be relied on for advice in matters of constitutional law. Their advice is treated with respect just as the advice from someone in place of authority is treated with respect. This is why the pundit has authority over his subject. *Authoritativeness* is one of the prime qualities of pundits. Now let us see the options.

Option (1) **Dedication: Signatories**; To be a *signatory* to a cheque, the very first requirement (after a fountain pen of course) is a cheque book and then adequate balance at the bank to cover the cheque. If the balance is not enough to cover the cheque, then one must be prepared to become a "guest of the government". *Dedication* is the least of the requirements for being a *signatory* not only in the present case but also if one were to sign the warning that a traffic magistrate would give one for ignoring the red light. There being no necessary relationship between *dedication* and *signatories*, this option will not do.

Option (2): **Sobriety: Executors**; A sober person is someone who is in command over his mental faculties and therefore a rational person. Thus someone who has had a peg or two more than what he can drink without swaying from side to side, is not likely to be sober. The quality that makes a person sober is *sobriety*. The word *executors* means persons who are authorised to execute the will of someone who has died leaving written instructions about what should be given to whom out of the material things that the person has left behind on mother earth before launching on a journey in the general direction of Heaven. It is necessary that a person who is making a will should make it while he is cold sober (or else he may end up bequeathing all his earthly possessions to the bartender). Imagine that a fellow has made a will and appointed his brother's three sons, as the executors (meaning the fellows who will actually take custody of the material possessions of the dead man and tell the dead man's daughter's husband that *here, you take this rosary and this book of wise sayings that the old man has willed to you* and tell the daughter to take the three million dollars in the bank accounts) Even if the *executors* are swaying under the influence of alcohol while reading the will, nobody other than the executors of the will can execute the will. The prime quality of *executors* is authority and not sobriety. There may be any number of sober people in the hall, where everyone has gathered, to hear the will being read. Yet none other than the authorised *executors*, can give effect to the will. Thus this option will not do.

Option (3): Sensitivity: Literati; *Sensitivity* is a word that has several shades of meaning.

If my skin has *sensitivity* to soap, it means that when I use soap, I get irritation and itching all over.

If a person has *sensitivity* to even slight irritations, it means that his cauldron of temper is always boiling; he gets annoyed at slightest provocation.

If the artist's paintings have appealed to the *sensitivity* of many people who saw the exhibition of his paintings, it means that his style of painting has touched the finer senses of the people.

Imagine a person has no *sensitivity* in the matters of the fine arts and you take him to a temple, in your city, that people come to see from the world over, for its carvings. He takes a look at the carvings and yawns so loudly that you turn red with embarrassment.

Men of letters or learned class are known as the *literati*. The word *literati* is thus a collective noun. It is not necessary that *literati* have *sensitivity* to irritation. You might try to tease an author till you are blue in the face and yet he will not lose his cool. An author, as such, is able to perceive and express the feelings of an another person. This he cannot hope to do if he is not *sensitive* to the pains and joys of others. If a judge has *sensitivity* to a woman 's weeping, he will not pass death sentence on a convict whose wife is present in the courtroom. He will himself weep with the fellow's wife and may drown the sound of the wife's sobs with his loud wails. He cannot continue as a person of the learned class if he has *sensitivity* of the connotation employed here. *Literati* may or may not have *sensitivity* whereas pundits have got to have authoritativeness. **Option (3)** will not do for that reason.

Option (4). Recklessness: Warriors; People can show recklessness in many ways as follows:

- By spending far beyond income
- By driving vehicles at breakneck speeds
- By hitting out at a cricket ball without estimating where it would pitch and then lobbing a lollipop to the wicketkeeper

If you were to see the commonality in all the above illustrations of *recklessness*, one thing will stand a mile out: *recklessness* smacks of little or no strategy. A *warrior* without strategy is a sure case for defeat. This is because a war is a game involving strategies that each of the two sides work out from time to time after seeing what the other is doing and then only is victory, the basic aim of a war, possible. Thus *recklessness* is the least of the likely qualities of a warrior.

Option (5): Allegiance: Partisan; *Allegiance* means *loyalty*. If I were to owe an allegiance to the conservative party in my country, my loyalty would lie with that party. If a policeman owes allegiance to his duty and not to his religion, he would not hestitate to open fire on people of his own faith if they were to indulge in arson and rioting. Consider another case, if the national football club team is to be selected by the head of the football federation and the head were partisan towards members of his community, he would pick people not according to their merit alone but by their birth. Thus if a chap is partisan, he must owe so much allegiance to some person or cause that it makes him act in a manner in which he is guided by extraneous matters rather than by merits of the case. Thus **Option (5)** is correct.

Answer 7

FRESCO: WALL; *Fresco* is a method of painting on *walls* wherein water colour is applied to fresh plaster so that when the plaster dries, the water colour dries with it and becomes embedded in it. Many Italian church ceilings have frescoes of angels. The famous artist is a space within a building which is open to sky, Michelangelo, specialised in this art form. The relation between *fresco* and *wall* is that of an art form and the surface on which it is *embedded*.

Option (1): Fountain: Courtyard; A courtyard is a space within a building which is open to sky. Often there are fountains put up in *courtyards*. However, a *fountain* is not an art form and hence this option will not do.

Option (2): Parquetry: Floor; Blocks of different types of woods are arranged in a geometric pattern on *floors*. This art form is known as *parquetry*. Thus the relationship between Parquetry and Floor is: an art form the surface on which it is embedded—hence **Option (2)** is correct.

Option (3): Thatch: Roof; A *thatch* is a *roof* made of straw, reeds or palm leaves. One sees thatch roofs in tropical climates since a *thatch* provides insulation against heat. Since *thatch* itself is a form of *roof* this option will not do.

Option (4): Statuary: Passage; The word *statuary* comes from the word *statue* and has several meanings. *Statuary* is the art of making statues. If the municipality of your town wants to place a bust of some eminent person of the town a pedestal in the centre of the town square, they will have his bust made at the *statuary*, which is a place where statues are made. If you walk through a passage in which there are several statues arranged in rows by the side of the passage, then its a statuary you are walking *through*. However the statues are not embedded on the *passage* whereas a fresco is embedded on the wall. Moreover, statues are art forms and not statuary. Thus this option will not do either.

Option (5): Gargoyle: Gutter; The word *gargoyle* comes from the word *gargle*. You gargle with salt water when your throat is sore. The mouth is open when one gargles. A *gargoyle* is a *statue depicting an open mouth* – sometimes a human mouth and at other times an animal's – at the opening of a *gutter* from which rainwater drains out. The *gargoyle* is however a statue and since the *statue* is an art form and not the *gargoyle*, this option will not do either. What is more, it is not that the gargoyles can be seen only on gutters whereas frescoes are seen only on walls. Gargoyles can be seen carved on the bases of candlesticks and on table legs as well. Thus even if one were to assume for a moment that a *gargoyle* is an art form, it is not restricted to *gutters*, whereas frescoes are restricted to walls.

Answer 8

STRUT: WING; The word *strut* has several shades of meanings. To *strut* means to stand out or project.

When a person with an inflated sense of self-importance walks about, he walks with his chest (if not the chest, then his ego) projecting. He then walks with a swagger, in other words, he *struts*.

Several birds strut when in courtship mode. When a male peacock wants a mate, he *struts* about spreading his feathers.

A *wing* of the house is its extension. If a footballer plays on the right wing, he is playing on the right side. If the artillery is that *wing* of the army that provides firepower, it is an operational unit of the army specialising in providing firepower. A bird *flies* with *wings*. If a wealthy person takes a needy person under his *wing*, he takes the person under his care and *shelter*. Such are the different shades of meaning of the word *wing*.

In houses made of wood, diagonal timbers support the principal rafter or beam, which supports the ceiling. These *diagonal timbers* are known as *struts* and they resist the pressure exerted by the very weight of the principal rafter. In an extension (also known as *wing*) of such wooden houses, the principal rafter extends up to the wing and the struts support the structure.

In aircraft wings, there is a beam that extends from the fuselage (meaning the body of the aircraft) to the wingtips. There are *struts* in this beam that divide the stress on the beam in the wing and thus provide support to the beam in the wing.

In helicopters the rotors are mounted on *struts* and move around them. In helicopters, the rotors themselves are the wings of this type of aircraft.

Briefly, a *strut* is the support to a *wing*. Now let us see the options.

Option (1): Lever: Handle; A lever is a mechanical device to transmit force to a point other than to where it is applied. When you take an ordinary crowbar and try to lift a heavy iron pipe with it, you force on that end of the crowbar which is in your hand whereas its the other end of the crowbar that lifts the pipe. Thus lifting takes place in a crowbar through transmitting of force. Hence a crowbar is an example of a *lever*. A pair of scissors too is essentially a lever with the fulcrum in the centre of the lever. The *handles operate* the scissors but do not support it. Therefore this option will not do.

Option (2): Axle: Wheel; In cars, an *axle* is the central rotor of a wheel around which the *wheel* moves. Both the axle and the *wheel* move. The *axle* is the fulcrum of a lever consisting of the crank and *wheel*. The crank transmits the rotation caused by the engines to the axle. The axles in turn move the wheel. In the case of strut and wing – even if we were to talk about the strut and wing of a helicopter - the strut supports the wing. In the case of an *axle*, the *wheel* is either pegged to the chassis or held by nuts and bolts that you have to remove when you want to change a flat tyre. Thus, the *axle* does not support the *wheel*. This is why this option will not do either.

Option (3): Buttress: Wall; Imagine that a family is discussing whether the youngster should go to the engineering college in another town or study in the one in his town. His mother argues against moving to another town. The father feels that the quality of education in the college in the other town is better and thus the fellow should go there even if it means expense on staying in the hostel.

The youngster's uncle lends more support to the father's argument, saying that the other college has a better placement record. The uncle is said to *buttress* the father's argument or *strengthen* it by providing additional support. A *buttress* in the context of a wall is the structure of wood or stone to provide extra support or strengthen the wall. This relationship is akin to that between a strut and a wing. Therefore, **Option (3)** is correct.

Option (4): Beam: Rivet; If you have seen high-rise buildings under construction, you must have seen vertical pillars made of either steel or reinforced cement called concrete and horizontal structural supports to the frame of the building. The vertical pillars are known as columns and the horizontal structural supports are known as *beams*. A *rivet* is usually a short nail or bolt to fasten metal plates together. *Rivets* are rather visible in railway bridges. The *beam* supports the structure; it does not support the *rivet*. Thus this option will not do.

Option (5): Well: Pipe; A *well* does not support the *pipe* that goes into it for pumping out water nor is it the other way round. The *well* is supported by support walls made usually of stone that prevent the sides of the *well* from collapsing. Thus this relationship will not do either.

Answer 9.

ATTENTIVE: OFFICIOUS; There are several shades of meaning of the word *attentive* that comes from *attention* and means *paying attention*. If the class is *attentive* while the teacher is teaching how to solve quadratic equations, the class is *paying attention* or *concentrating* on what is being taught. Let us see the capitalised pair of words are used in the following illustrations:

1. You are at a party. If the hosts personally receive guests at the door and ensure that each guest has a pleasant time, then they are *attentive* or *gracious* hosts.
2. The other day I rang a chap who was a colleague of mine during my tenure with the government. A female voice came on the line and I could hear the fellow telling her to ask the caller to hold the line for a while as the Honourable *Joint Secretary* was talking on the other line. When the fellow came on the line, I asked him if he had a receptionist at home as well. No why, he said, that was his daughter. I thought the fellow was rather *officious* (or, in other words, *self-important*). He could as well have asked her to say that *her father* would soon be on the line. The chap was attentive to see that his importance must be emphasised to those with whom he interacted.
3. The other day I was compere at the passing out ceremony of athletes from a major sports training institu-

tion, when an official came over and without so much as a by-your-leave, jolly nearly snatched the microphone from my hand and announced that athletes who had not produced no-dues certificates from their respective hostels shall not get their diplomas. I thought that this was a bit too *officious* (or *nosy* or *domineering*). A moment later the head of the institution summoned him and gave him a dressing down first for snatching the microphone and then for announcing something, that he was not authorised to announce.

As may be seen from illustrations 2 and 3, both persons were too *attentive* to convey self-importance. They were *attentive* to peripheral issues and not the main issue whereas the attentive hosts at illustration 1 were *attentive* to **the main issue** of making people comfortable.

Option (1): Doubtful: Ambiguous; As we have seen earlier, the word *ambiguous* means *something which has two meanings* so that the one, who hears an ambiguous statement, is doubtful about what it really means. When a chap says that *flying planes can be dangerous*, one may either interpret this as (A) flying an aircrafts can be a dangerous profession or that (B) flying aircraft can be dangerous if they plunge to the ground amidst human settlements. Even a sign may be *ambiguous*. If you are in a bilingual country where C stands for cold in English and for hot in the other language, one may get singed with a hot shower although one may have turned on what appeared to be the cold shower.

However, something *doubtful* need not be *ambiguous* as well. If your favourite football club is scheduled to play their league encounter next Sunday and their participation is doubtful, since many players were injured in a bus accident on their way home from the practice session, there is only *doubt* but no *ambiguity*. Hence this option will not do.

Option (2): Absorbed: Engrossed; If a tablecloth *absorbed* the water that was accidentally spilt on the dining table, it means that the cloth *took in* the water. The tabelcloth cannot be *engrossed* in the water although it can *absorb* it. On the other hand someone *engrossed* in a piano recital is hearing with *rapt attention*. He is thoroughly *absorbed* in the music. Thus *absorbed* and *engrossed* are synonyms but *engrossed* is not necessarily higher form of *absorbed*. Hence, this option will not do.

Option (3): Refined: Snobbish; The word *refined* has several shades of meaning that we shall see as we shall go along.

If the castor oil that one had to take was *refined*, it was *purified* by various processes such as filtration done over and over again through different filters. (The oil was free from impurities)

If the audience behaved in a *refined* manner throughout the play, it appreciated softly when applause was due and did not boo even though there were boring scenes. (The audience was free from rudeness or vulgarity)

If the speech that the Principal was to deliver at the school's Foundation Day was *refined* by the Vice-Principal, it was made free from imperfections or defects.

Now let us see the meaning of the word *snobbish*.

- Imagine that you have bought a used car in a reasonably good condition and are out on a drive when you meet a friend at the traffic lights. You tell him that you got this used car at a bargain price. He says that he never buys anything other than new cars. He is being *snobbish* or *arrogant*.
- Imagine that you treat your friends to a lunch an inexpensive place. After the lunch you ask one of them if he liked the food. He says that only once in a while he eats plain fare so long as the company is good. Is he being *snobbish* or *condescending*.

A snob is arrogant, proud and has an exaggerated sense of self-importance and considers very many people as not up to his status. Unfortunately, however, for snobs, people who seem to think that there are very many people below him in status, there aren't many. Arrogance is the prime characteristic of those who are snobbish and so is rudeness. Just as an officious person thinks that he is rather attentive, so does a *snobbish* person think that he is too *refined*. This is why **Option (3)** is correct.

Option (4): Magisterial: Authoritative; A magistrate is authorised to administer the law (or, in other words, to see that it is implemented). A magistrate has got to be *authoritative*, meaning that he has got to exercise authority or powers vested in him. If you were to see the capitalised pair – ATTENTIVE: OFFICIOUS

– the magistrate is not officious (this mean that the magistrate is not meddling in other people's business or has a sense of exaggerated self-importance). He is official. If two group of persons have been fighting and the police brings them to the magistrate, they cannot ask the magistrate to keep out of their private fights. A free-for-all between two groups is a law and order problem. The magistrate has to enforce the law. He has powers to punish those indulging in so-called "private fights". This is the difference between officious and official; the first may or may not have authority; the second **necessarily** has authority. This is why this option will not do.

Option (5): Impromptu: Spontaneous; If you were to play a part in a drama in your college's annual function and were to forget some lines, some chap, not visible to the audience, sits backstage with the text and prompts you (meaning he tells you what to say next). The fellow prompting you, is in a *state of readiness* with the text. The prefix IM- is a variant of the prefix IN- meaning *not*. If you have some guests who have come in unannounced and you make a quick meal and then all of you sit to lunch, you are having an *impromptu* lunch (meaning an event for which you were not ready and thus it was a *makeshift* or *spontaneous* lunch). Thus *impromptu* and *spontaneous* are synonyms and *spontaneous* is not a higher degree of *impromptu*. Thus this option will not do either.

Answer 10

AUDACIOUS: TREPIDATION; There are several shades of meaning of the word *audacious* and *trepidation* that we shall see from the following contexts:

- If a writer presents unconventional views *without a fear of public protest*, his work is *audacious* or *bold* and *intrepid*.
- If a dancer takes off his/her clothes on stage, it is an *audacious* (meaning *shameless*) act of flouting decorum.
- The speaker at the symposium is shaking with fear of public speaking. His speech is marked with *trepidation*.
- If a chap is not well prepared for an examination and writes it with *trepidation*, he is in a state of mental confusion.

Thus an audacious person does not have fear, or trepidation. Now let us see the options.

Option (1): Refractory: Intransigence; Let us see what *refractory* means. The word *refractory* comes from the Latin root FRACT- that means *break*. The prefix RE- means *back* or something in *opposition*. If someone has a severe skin eruption and has tried an antibiotic and yet the problem persists, the skin problem is *refractory* to the antibiotic or *does not break* or *yield to the medicine*. The skin problem *breaks out again or comes back* or recurs.

If a father is trying to wean away his son from excessive television viewing and finds that the son just does not obey, the son is *refractory* to his father's efforts to mend his ways (meaning the son is *disobedient* or *recalcitrant*). *Intransigence* comes from IN- that means *against* and TRANS- that means *across*. Thus *intransigence* is the characteristic of a person that turns him against going across to the other person's view or opinion. A person who is *intransigent* is *uncompromising*, not ready to make any concessions.

Someone who is *refractory*, necessarily has *intransigence*. Thus this option throws up an opposite relationship to that in the capitalised pair and will not do.

Option (2): Laconic: Volubility; I remember the time I was on a long bus journey and trying to chat with the man in the next seat. I must have spoken a few hundred sentences and he said not so much as *hmm*. I then came to the conclusion that Fate had put me – a *voluble* person - in the company of a *laconic* person. I must keep shut and conserve energy. A *laconic* person (meaning *someone given to speaking very little*) does not have *volubility* (the characteristic of *speaking too much*) and hence **Option (2)** will fit like a shot.

Option (3): Sordid: Aspiration. The word sordid has several shades of meanings:

- If two lovers end their lives by jumping before a running train because their parents would not allow them to marry, it is a *sordid* (or *horrible*) end to their love story.

- You pass by a colony of people living in squalor and filth, the colony is a *sordid* (or *dirty, squalid*) slum.
- The word *toilet* is a pleasant term whereas *lavatory* would be a *sordid* (or *base*) way of referring to the same thing.

Aspiration means *breathing in*. When you *yearn* to see the beautiful girl whom you admired deeply while at college, you take a deep breath in nostalgia. When you want to make a serious attempt at the country's toughest management entrance test, you take in a deep breath as you do when you set a goal for yourself. Aspiration therefore means yearning, desire, ambition, objective and so on. As such there is no relationship between the two words *sordid* and *aspiration* and thus this option will not do.

Option (4): Cursory: Accumulation; When you take a *passing* or *quick* look at the book that someone has recommended to you and decide that you would be better off not reading it, you have given it a *cursory* look. You take a *cursory* look at another book about philosophy and find it interesting and buy it. It is one more book added to your accumulation of books. Thus something *cursory* may or may not translate into accumulation. Hence this option will not do either.

Option (5): Derisive: Subordination; *Derisive* means *mocking, ridiculing* and *satirical*. If a chap has been telling his friends that he is sure to top the class and ends up just scraping through the examination with bare minimum pass marks, he may invite *derisive* (or *mocking*) laughter from his classmates.

The word *subordinate* comes from *ordinate* that means to *appoint* a person to official duty. The prefix SUB- means *lower in rank* or *secondary*. *Subordination* means *submission* or *to make lower in rank or importance to someone else*. If the people in a country that has a monarch at the head of the government, want that there should be a democratic system of government, then they are seeking *subordination* of the monarch to the collective will of the people, which means that the monarch should be lower in rank (or importance) to the people's will.

As such derisive and subordination have little to do with each other and hence this option will not do.

Answer 11

BLANDISHMENT: COAX; The word *blandishment* has several shades of meaning that we shall see as we go along:

Imagine that a crow is sitting on the branch of a tree. The crow has a large piece of meat in its beak. A hungry fox stands below, with its mouth watering at the sight of the meat. The fox then tells the crow that it has been long since he has seen someone as beautiful as a crow. The crow does not respond. The fox then persists in his *blandishments* and says that he would give his eye-teeth to hear the crow sing in his amazingly beautiful voice. The blandishments take effect. The crow opens his mouth to sing. The meat falls out. The fox grabs it and scampers away. *Blandishment* here means *cajolery* or *deceitful alluring*.

Now imagine that a married man is alone, his wife having gone to her parents. There is a single girl next door, who the fellow eyes for a fling. She is aware of her plainness. He hears her sing and when she comes to the balcony, he praises her voice. He also tells her that she looks very elegant in the new dress. She thanks him for his kind words. He asks her whether they could go out to dinner that evening. The *blandishments* fall flat. She says *no*. *Blandishment* here means *gentle flattery*.

If you were to see the above two illustrations, it would be easy to notice that in both cases the purpose of giving *blandishment* is to coax someone into doing what the person desires. Thus the relationship between BLANDISHMENT: COAX is that of means: end.

Option (1): Medal: Honour; One gives a *medal* to *honour* someone. The *medal* is a means by which one seeks to *honour* someone meritorious. Thus **Option (1)** is correct.

Option (2): Budget: Save; A *budget* is a mechanism of matching income to expense. One decides what one wants to do and then estimates how much it would cost and thereafter one finds out how the expense is to be funded. Imagine that a new industrial unit for manufacture of glass is being put up. The *budget* for the plant is a hundred thousand dollars. It is estimated that it would take three years from the date of placing order for the equipment to their supply. It is then quite plain that for three years there will be only expense and no revenue. Revenue can be generated only if production starts and products start selling in the market. You can *save* money only if income is in excess of expenditure, not otherwise. As we have seen above, *budget* may mean not only no savings but no revenue either, just expense. Thus this option will not do.

Option (3): Diary: Reminisce; A *diary* as we all know is a record of the highlights of what one has been doing. One cannot write every little thing one does, in a diary, because then one can do little else. If one has clocked thirteen seconds at the school athletics competition and stood first, one writes this in the diary so that many years later when one's obese, television-watching couch potato children brag their having done 100 meters in twenty nine seconds flat, one can open the diary and show them one's timings. A diary can help *reminisce* (or *remember*). But one can very fondly remember things that one dare not put down in one's diary. My brother and I used to get slightly tipsy after taking a few swigs from our uncle's rum bottle and then replacing what we had imbibed with plain water. Had we written this in our diary and had the old man read it, he would have caned us mercilessly. Thus this option will not do either. One can reminisce very well without looking up the diary.

Option (4): Concert: Play; When the chaps proficient at the piano and the violins and the drums and the saxophones and so on are playing together a composition with the directions of a conductor, they are playing in *concert* or *harmony*.

It is not as if one has to give a concert to play something. One can play a game of squash without a single tune being sung. One would be barely capable of singing while playing squash. The steering wheel of the car can have *play* (meaning the amount of turning that one has to impart to it before the wheels start turning in response to the steering) without even a hint of a concert. A sly person can *play* two adversaries against each other to derive some benefit for himself. Thus this option will not do either.

Option (5): Plea: Threaten; A *plea* is an *appeal* or *prayer* or even a *mere statement* if it is used in noun context as follows:

- The judge dismissed the defendant's *plea* (or *an argument advanced in justification*) that the accused had a grave and sudden provocation to commit the crime.
- The King heard the *plea* (or *prayer*) of the murderer's mother and stopped his execution scheduled for May 2, ordering that the convict's sentence be reduced to life imprisonment instead.
- The accused entered a plea of not guilty (meaning that when presented the charge sheet, he made a *statement* that he was not guilty).

When one makes a request, prayer or statement in a court, one does not *threaten*. *Threatening* is antithetical to making *pleas*. This is why this option will not do either.

Answer 12

RELEVANT: CRUCIAL; Before the technician at the blood bank taps a donor's blood, he would like to know *relevant* facts such as whether the donor has tested positive for AIDS, or he has diabetes, high blood pressure, low haemoglobin and so on. Here *relevant* means *important* or *material*.

The other day when the carpenter came in to repair the dressing table, he came prepared with all *relevant* things such as nails, chisel, little pieces of wood, cloth on which to rub his hands when they were stained, emery paper and so on. Here *relevant* means *pertaining* to the task at hand but not necessarily important. Are little pieces of wood or used emery as important as a history of diabetes or the AIDS virus?

The word *crucial* comes from the word *crux* that means the *most essential aspect*. If the final game in the World Cup Table Tennis Tournament is at a *crucial* stage it means that one wrong move by the chap, who has advantage, may result in his losing the match. If the two enemy nations are holding a *crucial* round of talks, it means that if the talks succeed, there could be lasting peace between them but if they fail, war could be the unavoidable result. Thus, the word *crucial* means *of great importance*.

As we have already seen, something can be *relevant* without being important let alone being of great importance. Thus something *relevant* is at a lower stage and something *crucial* is at a much higher stage. Now let us see the options.

Option (1): Marginal: Unique; The word *marginal* comes from the word *margin*. If a candidate wins a race by a narrow *margin*, then the margin is the *difference* between the time taken by the winner and the runner-up to finish the race. If the difference is small, then the difference is *marginal* (meaning *small*). If the difference between the votes cast in favour of Candidate A and Candidate B in an election is marginal, then it could be anything between a couple of votes to a few thousand votes. If the difference is *unique*, then it can either be *only one* vote or *such a large number of votes that such a thumping defeat has never been recorded before*. Thus *marginal* and *unique* need not necessarily mean that unique is the higher stage of marginal. Hence this option will not do.

Option (2): Perceptible: Obvious; The word *perceptible* comes from the Latin root CEPT-that means *seize*. The prefix PER- means *through*. The suffix –IBLE means *that which can be*. *Perceptible* is that which can be seized. So if someone has perception, he can catch or seize the meaning of a statement through the words in which the statement is clothed. If something is *perceptible*, then its meaning *can be seized or caught through*. If there is a perceptible change in one's attitude, then it means that there is a visible change in one's behaviour If a person has all along been hot headed, then one can see him changed to a level headed person.

If you notice that a person's hairline has receded perceptibly, it is he is balding. If a person is *obviously* bald, he has no hairline at all. No effort is required to arrive at the inference that he is balding. Thus *Obvious* is the higher stage of *Perceptible* and hence **Option (2)** is correct.

Option (3): Apparent: Real; Something *apparent* is that what appears. If two persons have been quarrelling and one has been threatening the other to break his neck, it may be *apparent* that the man issuing the threat may actually deliver a deadly blow. If things boil down to a fight, it may happen that the fellow who has been issuing threats collapses under a single blow that the threatened person delivers expertly. What was *apparent*, is then not real.

Suppose the police is investigating the death of a woman in suspicious circumstances and feel that the apparent reason for the death is suicide because of persistent financial difficulties that she was experiencing. Suppose this turns out to be the real reason. Here what was *apparent* was also *real*. Thus this option will not do since *real* is not necessarily the higher stage of *apparent*.

Option (4): Peripheral: Central; If a company that has built a name for itself through manufacturing of high-tech machinery has also been making shoes and finds that the *peripheral* businesses must be sold so that the company can focus its energies and resources on the areas of its core (or *central*) competence, then in this context, *peripheral* means that which is of less importance. Therefore *Peripheral* and *Central* are antonyms and hence this option will not do since in order for one thing to be a higher form of another, there has got to be a synonymous relationship between the two.

Option (5): Possible: Desirable; Something *possible* may or may not be *desirable*. If a person is sick and the doctor says that it is *desirable* that he stops smoking for a fortnight, it may be *possible*. He would have to have the necessary resolve. Conversely, it may be *possible* for him to smoke a pack of cigarettes in an hour notwithstanding the doctor's advice. All one would need is a pack of cigarettes and a lighter; this, however, is not desirable since there is no necessary relationship between the two, this option will not do.

Chapter 8

Sentence Completion

Filling blanks in sentences, from a range of options, is a certain feature at the Graduate Record Examination (GRE). The idea is to fill in the choice that best fits the meaning of the sentence as a whole.

The skills may involve any of the following: (A) A fair understanding of the English language or (B) Mere logic or both (A) & (B).

However logic may not stand to much good in the absence of fundamentals and it is with the intention of imparting these fundamentals that this chapter has been devised. The methodology involves some illustrations followed by detailed reasoning of why a particular word will fit and why would the others not. This is quite different from what one sees in most books professing to prepare young aspirants to face major competitive examinations.

What you will witness here is a very different scenario. The pattern of the examination is laid threadbare. There are chapters that give the concepts that are very necessary for meeting the challenge of the competitive examination. The concepts are carried in illustrations that will hit the nail on the head. Then there are exercises that will ensure complete assimilation. Care has been taken to put in lucid solutions to each and every question in the exercises to ensure that not an iota of doubt lingers.

We shall see the illustrations first and then the exercises with explanatory answers.

Illustration 1

DIRECTIONS *for questions 1 to 5: Each sentence below has one or two blanks, each blank indicating that something has been omitted. Beneath the sentence are five lettered words or sets of words. Choose the word or set of words for each blank that best fits the meaning of the sentence as a whole.*

Question 1

When an oppressed group revolts against a society, one must look for the____ forces that led to the group's ____ that society.

(1) disparate .... acknowledgement of

(2) specific .... dependence on

(3) altered .... redistribution within

(4) focused .... interference with

(5) underlying .... alienation from

Answer 1

An oppressed group is that which has been overpowered or enslaved. Why did the Indian Independence Movement pick up great momentum after General Dyer ordered firing, that killed hundreds of innocent people in Amritsar? Because it meant that one could not express one's views even peacefully. It meant that the people who were massacred, were not considered a part of the society and were alienated. There is no need to look further than Option (5). The answer lies in a couple of logical questions that one should ask oneself.

But we shall not move on to the next question straightaway. We shall see why the other options will not work. This will only reinforce the choice of the correct answer from the standpoint of logic.

Option (1): *Disparate* means unequal or diverse. If an oppressed group revolts, there must be a strong common agenda. There must be unity of purpose. No group can hope to rise in revolt if its forces are disparate. If, however, the group *acknowledges* the society, they will not need to revolt. When, for example, would someone acknowledge another person as his master? When he accepts the other. Thus this option will not work.

Option (2): While there is nothing wrong with the usage of the word *specific* in the first blank, the problem lies with *dependence* in the second blank. When would you depend on someone else? When you trust him or need him. Would anyone revolt against someone he trusts? Thus this option will not work either.

Option (3): The question is what are *altered* forces? *Altered* means changed. If a group were to rise in revolt, they cannot change the common agenda as they go along. Nothing will bind them. Secondly, once some group is redistributed within a society, the group melts and becomes one with the society. Then there is no cause for a revolt against the society. Thus this option will not work.

Option (4): While there can be no *revolt* unless the forces are focussed, the problem lies with the word *interference*. Who can interfere? What is *'inter'* other than *'from within'*? If you are *within*, you are a part of society. Then the need to revolt does not arise. If the group interferes with the society, they cannot be an oppressed group at all. On the contrary, if Group A can interfere with the functioning of the society, Group A is in a dominant position. There is no need for Group A to revolt. Thus this option will not work.

What is the lesson that we have learnt here? We have come to know that the matter, at least insofar as it relates to this particular question, is that of logic and not command over the English language.

Question 2

Every novel invites us to enter a world that is initially strange; our gradual and selective orientation to its manners .... infants' .... to their environment.

(1) imitates .... welcome

(2) completes .... introduction

(3) resembles .... adjustment

(4) alter .... blindness

(5) reinforce .... resistance

Answer 2

If the world is strange to an infant, what is he required to do? If an infant sees a strange face it may either start crying or smile at the strange person. Over a period of time the infant learns to cope with the strangeness, meaning to *adjust* to the strange environment.

Option (1): Mark the words 'our selective orientation'. The word 'our' refers to those who are not infants. Who would *imitate* whom? Would the infant *imitate* the adult or will the adult *imitate* the infant? If the adult were to gradually *imitate* an infant, his family will send him to a nearby mental asylum. Option (1) will not work for this reason.

Option (2): If one novel – let us say novel A – were to complete the infants' *introduction* to their environment, they would not have been infants at all, in the first place. An infant is a child in a very early stage after birth. The matter is so simple. Have you seen any infant reading a novel? I would wake up in cold sweat if I were to even dream of an infant reading a novel. Option (2) will not work.

Option (3): To *resemble* means to look like. This is a far cry better than *imitate* in Option (A). The action of adults can *resemble* the adjustment of an infant to the new environment but it cannot *imitate* the child. We know that infants finally *adjust* to their strange environment. [They have no choice, of course, once they are out in this world]. Secondly, their adjustment will necessarily have to be gradual. It is not expected of an infant (meaning, someone not even an year old) to get up and make his own dinner if his mother has gone out shopping and he feels hungry in her absence. **Option (3) is correct** since the word *adjustment* is most appropriate.

Option (4): First of all, infants are not blind to their environment, except those most unfortunate few who are blind at birth. But even in the latter cases, gradual and selective orientation will not *alter* this condition of *blindness*. It may also be mentioned that it is not possible for an infant to be blind in a figurative way as an adult can be; for example an adult can be figuratively blind if he is reckless or is deficient in moral or intellectual perception. An infant is a child in the *earliest* period of life after his birth when he can scarcely be expected to display intellectual or moral perception or recklessness for that matter. All that can be expected of an infant is that he should sleep long, wake up, drink milk, smile a while and again go back to sleep. Option (4) will not work either.

Option (5): With a pencil, write the words in this option in the blanks and see what will be the meaning of the sentence. If a novel were to *reinforce* an infant's *resistance* to his environment, that infant would have to read the novel to begin with. This would be absurd. The next thing that the infant, who can read a novel, might do is get up and shave.

What is the lesson that we have learnt here? We have come to know that the matter, insofar as it relates to this particular question also, is that of logic and not command over the English language.

Question 3

Superficial differences between the special problems and techniques of the physical and those of the biological sciences are sometimes cited as evidence for the _____ of biology and for the claim that the methods of physics are therefore not adequate to biological enquiry.

(1) autonomy

(2) vitalism

(3) purposiveness

(4) obsolescence

(5) irrelevance

Answer 3

First let us understand the precise meanings of the five words from (1) to (5) and then see which will fit in.

Option (1): *Autonomy* comes from the prefix *AUTO-* (meaning *self*) and *NOMOS-* (meaning *laws*) meaning someone who can make one's own rules and regulations or someone who can decide for oneself: *autonomous* thus means *independent*.

Option (2): *Vitalism* is the doctrine or theory that the origin and phenomena of life are due to or produced by a vital principle, distinct from a chemical or physical forces. Vitalism therefore feels that it is above sciences. If a chap is not prepared to believe, for example, that the stem supplies nutrients to the plant, then he is not likely to believe in either biology or physics. For him since biology and physics are not there at all, there is no question of any difference between them.

Option (3): *Purposiveness* means *having a purpose*. **Option (4)**: *Obsolescence* is *disuse*. Something is obsolete if it not used any more. *Irrelevance* is lack of significance; something would be irrelevant if it was beside the point.

Now let us see which word would fit in. The statement being made is (A) there are superficial differences (or insignificant) differences between techniques of physics and biology and (B) claims that the methods of physics are not adequate to biological enquiry (or in other words methods of physics are not sufficient to derive answers to biological problems). These two statements mean that although there is not much difference in the **special problems** and techniques of biological and physical sciences, biological science is not dependent upon physics for answering questions posed to it. It is an independent science and thus autonomous.

So **Option (1)**: **autonomy** is correct. **Option (2)** will not do because *vitalism* does not even recognise biology. Since biology is a science with so much research taking place in its field, the words, irrelevance and obsolescence will not do either. If you were to imagine that there is superficial (meaning insignificant) difference between trousers and shirts, then there is need for only one of them. The other has not much purpose. Superficial difference between special problems of physical and biological sciences will be an evidence of the *lack* of purposiveness of one of them. This is why option 5 will not do.

Question 4

As the creation of new knowledge through science has become ____ , resistance to innovation has become less ____ , taking the form of inertia rather than direct attack.

(1) controversial .... sporadic

(2) institutionalised .... aggressive

(3) essential .... effective

(4) public .... circumspect

(5) suspect .... lively

Answer 4

Let us understand some words. *Innovation* means creation of something new. Inertia is a state in which a body has no motion. *Sporadic* is now and then, not continuous.

Aggressive comes from the prefix *AG-* (meaning towards) and the root *GRESS-* (meaning *step*) and the suffix -*ION* (meaning the *state of* or the *condition of being*); if you wish to attack someone who has been harassing your girl friend, you have no choice but to take a step towards him (he cannot be reasonably expected to come to you for receiving his quota of bashing). Thus *aggression* means *direct attack.*

Essential means necessary.

Circumspect comes from the prefix *CIRCUM-* (meaning *round*) and the root *SPECT-* (meaning *to see*); the word means one who looks around before doing something and is thus *cautious* or *careful.*

When a body is not moving, it means that it is doing nothing. It is in a state of *inertia.* Something taking the form of X *rather than* Y means that the earlier form was Y and now is X. So the present form of resistance to innovation is inertia. The earlier form of resistance to innovation was direct attack. This means that we shall now have to locate such a word for the second blank that indicates *direct attack.* We have no choice other than Option (2).

We may note that this is the *fourth consecutive problem* which requires more logic than mastery over the English language. This should get one to start realising that eventually this may turn out to be a test of logic alone.

Question 5

Lizzie was a brave woman who could dare to incur a great danger for an adequate ____ .

(1) risk

(2) combat

(3) object

(4) event

(5) encounter

Answer 5

What is the meaning of *adequate*? Enough. What is the meaning of the words *incur a great danger*? Take a great risk! Who but a complete moron would take a *great* risk for an *adequate* risk in Option (1)? Option (2): A *combat* is a fight. What does one fight for, other than to achieve a specific objective?

Option (3): What is an *object*? An object can mean a thing, or something thrown or a desired result.

Why does one take a risk at all? To attain something, to realise one's purpose or attain some object. None other than Option (3) can work.

Illustration 2

DIRECTIONS *for questions 6 to 15: Each of the sentences below has one or more blank spaces indicating that something has been left out. Following each sentence, five words or sets of words are given. Choose the word or set of words that makes the sentence most meaningful.*

Question 6

The doctor_____aside his doubts _______ as he was busy and had no time to spare.

(1) dismissed, subversively

(2) brushed, perfunctorily

(3) discussed, intermittently

(4) aired, recklessly

(5) voiced, truculently

Answer 6

Let us understand a few words. **Option (1)**: To *dismiss* means to sack. The word dismiss comes from the prefix *DIS-* (meaning away apart), and the root *MIT-* or *MISS-* (meaning *send*). So if you *dismiss* someone, you send him home permanently (meaning *fire* him) or if you *dismiss* someone's theory then you send the theory away (or you ask him to try his theory on someone else but not you).

The word *subvert* comes from the prefix *SUB-* (meaning *down* or *under*) and the root *VERT-* (meaning *turn*). *Subvert* therefore means, to *upset* or *overturn*. A *subversive* element is one who causes damage from within or one who undermines one's own party or group.

Option (2): The word *perfunctorily* has the prefix PER- (meaning *through*) and comes from the word *function* and thus *perfunctorily* means *through function* and thus *carelessly* or *quickly* or *offhand*.

Option (3): *Intermittent* is the prefix *INTER-* (meaning *between*) and the root *MIT-* (meaning to *send* or *let go*); *intermittently* means occurring at intervals, not continuous.

Option (4): *Reckless* means without care. When you *air* your opinion, you express it. When a programme is *aired*, it is *broadcast*. When you *voice* your opinion, you *speak* it out.

Option (5): *Truculent* is *aggressive, bad-tempered* or *belligerent*.

Whose doubts would a doctor deal with? The patient's, of course! Who can *air* or *voice* doubts? The patient, of course! The doctor can only hear them, not give voice to them. Options *4* and *5* get eliminated for this reason alone. If the doctor does not have time, he may not hear them. The doctor can *discuss* the patient's doubts only when he has time, because *discussion* implies *seriousness*. Option (3) will not work for this reason. As regards Option (1), one can put aside something. One cannot dismiss aside anything. This is why Option (1) will not work. He may thus *brush* them aside. With the above explanations, the doctor can only *brush* aside the patient's doubts. Hence **Option (2)**.

Question 7

The_____printed greeting cards for every occasion and each person have driven the traditional Chinese cards with______ out of the market.

(1) ubiquitous, calligraphy

(2) unctuous, cartography

(3) ultra vires, callisthenics

(4) normal, engravings

(5) blasé, fortitude

Answer 7

Cartography is drawing of charts or maps. Charts and maps have no place on greeting cards. The words *Calligraphy* and *Callisthenics* are derived from the Greek word *Kallos* that means beautiful. *Calligraphy* is beautiful handwriting. The word *Callisthenics* means physical exercises done with a view to make the body beautiful. You cannot put physical exercise on greeting cards.

The word *engraving means carving*. You can have carving on stones not on greeting cards.

Fortitude is courage or strength (a meaning that is not too difficult to derive if you know that a fort is built for giving strength to a place's defences). You cannot have greeting cards with courage either, simply because courage is abstract.

Ubiquitous means something that is *present everywhere*. What has been driven out of the market? Traditional Chinese cards. What has replaced them? Printed cards. What can be *ubiquitous*? Something available in plenty. Which is likely to be *ubiquitous* – printed cards or cards with beautiful handwriting? The answer is clear: Option (1).

Unctuous means *oily* or *greasy* and also *sycophantic*.

Blasé means bored of pleasure. While the word normal needs no explanation, since the cards are printed for every person and for every occasion, the word *ubiquitous* would fit most aptly in any case.

Question 8

________decisions had to be made by leaders during our________ struggle for freedom.

(1) Catastrophic, gargantuan

(2) Astronomical, grandiose

(3) Momentous, titanic

(4) Herculean, monumental

(5) Stentorian, omniscient

Answer 8

A *catastrophe* is a disaster. *Gargantuan* is of extremely large size.

Astronomical is sky-high because that is where the objects of astronomic study lie. A thing is said to be astronomically priced if its price is extremely high. *Grandiose* means *pompous* or *pretentious*. A grandiose building would mean an imposing or majestic building.

The word *momentous* means *decisive*, *vital*, or *of great historical significance*. *Titanic* means great. A *stentorian* voice is that which is roaring, or ear-splitting.

An *Omniscient* person is one who knows everything.

Now the question is, which pair of words would fit in. For the first blank *Catastrophic*, *Astronomical*, and *Stentorian* are out of question. You cannot make astronomical decisions either. The stars do not ask human beings to decide which path they should take and where they should be generally found. Human beings can only watch the stars.

As regards *Herculean*, the word comes from mythology Hercules, who completed extraordinarily difficult tasks had exceptionally large muscles and great strength. Thus while the decisions must surely have been difficult to make, what the decisions themselves were doing was making history. If you succeed in the struggle, you become an independent nation, if you fail you continue being slaves. Hence only the word *momentous* would fit into the first blank. Thus Option (3).

Question 9

_______ is often the reason for _______ of ideas in treatises of great length.

(1) Verb, obduracy

(2) Verbiage, obfuscation

(3) Verbose, obsolescent

(4) Veracity, obscurant

(5) Prolix, velleity

Answer 9

There can be clarity in ideas or confusion or shortage or redundancy or irrelevance. Whatever it be the word in the second blank has got to be a noun. So it is in the first blank, where there has got to be a subject and hence it has to be a noun.

With this let us see the meanings of the different words here.

The word *verb* needs no explanation. But it is not a noun. Secondly, unless there are verbs there can be no clear flow of language. So a *verb* can make a flow of words clear, and only a lack of a verb can make confusion or haze. *Obfuscation* is a noun that means the action of making something confusing or dim. Option (2) seems to the best bet so far.

Verbiage is a noun that means superfluous abundance of words. This can make reading a tedious affair. It can lead to haze. *Obduracy* is a noun that means stubbornness. Someone obdurate is someone who is inflexible. An idea cannot be obdurate. Only one who is not ready to accept new ideas can be obdurate.

Something *obsolescent* is something *outdated*. The word *obsolescent* is therefore an adjective. *Veracity* is a noun that means truth. *Obscurant* as a noun would mean someone who makes something obscure (or confused) and *obscurant* as an adjective means something that makes obscure.

Prolix is an adjective that means long-winded (comes from the word *prolific* that means of great abundance). *Velleity* is a noun that means a mere wish without the action to realise this wish.

Now about what will fit in the blanks.

If there is no *verb*, ideas cannot flow in a sensible language. *Verb* cannot be a reason for *stubbornness. Verbiage* – meaning superfluous abundance of words which can lead of *obfuscation* or make ideas confusing. The words *verbose* and *obsolescent* are adjectives and therefore do not qualify. *Veracity* or truth will on the contrary, make things clear. Thus Option (4) will not work either. As regards Option (5), *Prolix* is an adjective and will not work as a candidate for the first blank.

Hence Option (2) is the correct choice.

Question 10

_______ can be defined as unnecessary _______ or the employment of more words than are necessary.

(1) Simile, ambiguity

(2) Cliché, raillery

(3) Epigram, verbosity

(4) Redundancy, repetition

(5) Euphemism, analogy

Answer 10

A *simile* is a figure of speech involving the comparison of one thing with another of a different kind. So when you say that the ride was smooth as silk, you are using a *simile*. But in order to compare, you need to employ two words in place of one. Only then a simile becomes possible. There is no unnecessary word in a simile. Option (1) will not work for this reason.

Ambiguity means lack of clarity.

A *cliché* is a stereotyped expression something that is repeated frequently. *Raillery* means a good-humoured ridicule. Cliché cannot be good-humoured. Cliché can be boring.

An *epigram* is a short and witty poem or a concise and pointed expression. There can be nothing unnecessary in an epigram, which by its very definition is short. *Verbosity* is the tendency to speak too many words for describing too little. It would be out of place with epigram.

Something redundant is that which is superfluous. *Redundancy* means being redundant. *Repetition* is patently unnecessary if you are speaking to someone who can catch what you have said the very first time. Repetition is also unnecessary if the fellow to whom you are speaking is hard of hearing. It would be better to tell him just once in a loud voice. Thus Option (4) is correct.

Euphemism is an understatement that puts a point across politely. Politeness cannot be unnecessary. Thus 'he passed away' is a euphemism for 'he died'.

Question 11

Sometimes text books alone are not enough;______sources like libraries and guides supply students with more information.

(1) suppliant

(2) complementary

(3) adventitious

(4) adscititious

(5) adventurous

Answer 11

The point that is being made here is that textbooks are not enough and you will need other sources such as libraries and guides to give more information. The word that we are searching will describe the other sources.

Let us see the meanings of some words.

Suppliant means a beggar or pleader; in short someone who seeks. Libraries cannot be beggars nor can guides be beggars.

Complementary means that which does what the other cannot do. [*Supplementary* means something in addition to the main; this is the vital difference between these two commonly misunderstood words]. What is stated here is that textbooks are not enough. But the word complementary cannot be used here because both are required. Tea and coffee are supplementary products; either you have one or you have the other. But a tennis racquet and a tennis ball are complementary. You would need both to play tennis.

Adventitious comes from the word *advent* (meaning *coming*). So *adventitious* means accidental or foreign. Libraries are neither accidental nor foreign.

The word *adscititious* means *supplemental*. Hence Option (4).

Question 12

The shortage of____________was a serious______________faced by fleeing refugees

(1) carpet, problem

(2) blankets, treat

(3) vitals, poser

(4) victuals, threat

(5) viands, condition

Answer 12

This is a question of mere logic.

Refugees are those who are running from somewhere or have come running from somewhere. Carpets are luxuries. When you have run away leaving behind all your possessions, the first in the list of priorities is food, then clothing and then shelter.

Vitals are life-sustaining forces – the air, water and so on. These can never be unnecessary unless the intention is to end life.

A *poser*, however, is a brainteaser. Fleeing refugees are people who are running away from their home. They have to worry about where to go, where to stay, what to eat and so on. If someone asks a fleeing refugee a brainteaser, there is every possibility that the running refugee may request him to shut up.

Victuals are life-sustaining foods. Their shortage can be a serious threat. Thus **Option (4)**.

Viands are victuals but then the shortage of viands can be a serious threat, not a serious condition.

Question 13

The ________ public were kept away from the starlet who was sitting behind an ________ glass wall of the lobby, where she was being interviewed by the press.

(1) efficient, obdurate

(2) efficacious, effete

(3) efflorescent, oracular

(4) officious, opaque

(5) official, obtuse

Answer 13

Obdurate is stubborn; the honour of being *stubborn* belongs to animals, not glass. Secondly, if the public were *efficient*, they would manage to see the starlet no matter what the hindrance. This is the meaning of efficiency. The word *efficacious* is used for those who have the capacity to attain the desired result. The glass wall would have been no hindrance if the public were *efficacious* and their objective was to meet the starlet. Secondly *effete* means effeminate or degenerate. A glass wall has no gender and cannot be effeminate.

The word *efflorescent* that comes from the word flower means *bursting into flower*. If the public could be efflorescent, then there would be flower buds coming to see the starlet. Only buds can become flowers. **Oracular** can mean *prophetic* or *ambiguous*. A glass wall can scarcely be expected to be either.

If the public had been *officious* (meaning *self-important* or *prying*), they would not have been able to pry only if the glass wall were not to allow prying. Thus *opaque* (that which does not allow light to pass through) in the second blank fits in very well. Thus **Option (4)** is the correct one.

Obtuse means either dim-witted or of an inclination more than 90 degrees and less than 180 degrees. A wall cannot be dim-witted. If it is obtuse in angle, it will not be able to stand at all.

Question 14

_______ or wavering may have its weak points but it has given us some of Shakespeare's most ________ lines in "Hamlet".

(1) Vaccination, mellifluous

(2) Procrastination, meretricious

(3) Vacillation, memorable

(4) Vicissitude, metrical

(5) Verisimilitude, mediocre

Answer 14

This is a question of mere logic. When we see the word 'but' after the words 'weak points', we must bear in mind that:

(A) Something may have weak points but what it has given is something strong or worth remembering.

(B) The word in the first blank must have the same meaning as wavering.

Vaccination can give you protection from a disease but vaccination cannot give you any lines from any poem.

Procrastination means the tendency to put off work. Even this is not likely to give any lines from any poem. *Meretricious* is something having the characteristics of a prostitute. Shakespeare's lines can scarcely be referred to as this.

Vacillation means *wavering*. Something can be *memorable* if it is worth remembering. Option (3) fits like a shot.

Vicissitude means *difficulty* and since the word in the first blank must mean *wavering*, this word will not do nor will Option (4).

If something has given most *mediocre* (or, *ordinary*) lines then it cannot give us anything worth remembering.

Question 15

The_______dos and don'ts that appeared in the income-tax forms made his head reel.

(1) warren

(2) welter

(3) maze

(4) windfall

(5) wrangle

Answer 15

If a fellow's head reels then he is confused. Therefore there are things in the income-tax forms that lead to confusion.

A densely populated *cluster of houses* is known as a *warren*. A *welter* is a contrasting mixture of immaterial things. A *maze* is a tangle or confusion or complex of networks. A *windfall* is an unexpected profit. A *wrangle* is a fight. The dos and don'ts in an income-tax form cannot be anything other than a *welter* because welter leads to confusion; welter cannot be confusion itself. Maze will not do because maze itself is confusion whereas we are looking for something that would lead to confusion.

With this we come to the end of this chapter, in which we have explained, in a vein as light as possible, why the skills required for filling blanks are more of logic than anything else.

Exercise 1

DIRECTIONS *for questions 1 and 2: In each of the following sentences, a part of the sentence is left unfinished. Beneath each sentence, four different ways of completing the sentence are indicated. Choose the best 'alternative' among the four:*

1. ____________, the more they remain the same.

(1) The more the merrier (2) The less the dynamism

(3) The more things change (4) The more pronounced the transformation

2. The stockmarket is probably ______. And the way the market has been plunging says a lot about investor's confidence.

(1) the best barometer to assess the sentiment of the public

(2) an ideal indication of the health of public sentiment

(3) the least imperfect mechanism for judging the quantity of the sentiment of the public

(4) the best indicator of public sentiment

Answer 1

The reference to 'they' in the second half of the sentence is to something in plural.

'Dynamism' and 'transformation' in statements (2) and (4) are singular. When you talk about a fellow's dynamism you say that his dynamism is remarkable. When you are surprised to see a fellow, normally a very bad tempered person, changed into an equanimous man, you say that the transformation in the fellow is a matter of great surprise.

The more in statement 1 indicates a singular noun as evident from 'the' preceding 'merrier'. Statement (3) is then the obvious choice since it is the only option where the subject – **things** - is in the plural. Hence Option (3).

Answer 2

While all options are similar, statement 4 is most apt being brief. Instead of 'sentiment of the public' and 'health of public sentiment', it comes directly to the point that the other three statements mean to convey. Hence Option (4).

Exercise 2

DIRECTIONS *for questions 1 to 3: In each of the following sentences, a part of the sentence is left unfinished. Beneath each sentence, four different ways of completing the sentence are indicated. Choose the best alternative among the four.*

1. ________ that in this apparent mess, two things need not be interfered with

   (1) It is important (2) It is of cardinal important

   (3) It should be urgently understood (4) It cannot be emphasised

2. The highest reward for a man's toil is not what he gets for it but what ________.

   (1) he makes out of it. (2) he gets for others.

   (3) he has overcome through it. (4) he becomes by it.

3. Wines that yielded a good commercial profit ______ in the same limited areas of France as now.

   (1) seem to have been produced

   (2) appear to have a remarkable semblance

   (3) bear a significant similarity in terms of production to those grown

   (4) appear to have been similarly produced

Answer 1

There is an apparently messy situation but two things need not be interfered with. This is the important message that must be delivered. The choice is Option (1) because it is brief and emphasizes importance without being long drawn such as the sentence in option 4. Cardinal in Option (2) is an adjective that goes with *importance* and not *important*. Since importance is a noun whereas important is an adjective. A thing can be cardinally important but not *cardinal important*.

About statement 4, the central idea is to emphasize the importance of not interfering with two things whereas statement 4 says precisely the reverse.

Option 1 must be preferred to option 3 since the former states that there is something important. If a thing is important, it is implied that it should be dealt with soon. The word *important* covers both *urgency* and the *need to understand*. So **Option 1**.

Answer 2

The highest reward for a man's toil (meaning hard work) would be something other than what he gets for it (meaning, something other than wages) as might be seen from the sentence that is required to be completed. This is because wages is the ordinary reward for someone's hard work.

Option 1 says "he makes out of it" which is the same thing as wages or earnings but only put differently.

Option 2 may not gel well since there is every likelihood of the man toiling for himself. Quite unfortunately, although many people would like to work for others, the ground reality is that those who are in a position to do so are those who have provided enough for themselves. It is only after their pockets are full, that they can think of working for others. Furthermore, since they are already well off, they need not actually toil – whether for themselves or for others. Those who are toiling, are very likely to toil only for themselves.

As regards Option 3, whatever be the reward for toiling, a reward has a meaning only if it is retained. What one has overcome, is gone as soon as it is overcome. If I overcome financial difficulties, they are gone the moment I overcome them. If someone manages to overcome a serious illness, that illness is gone the moment it is overcome.

The obvious choice is, what **he becomes** *by it.* In toiling for myself, I may have become capable of putting hard and sustained effort. I may have become rich. I may have become sturdy. I may have become famous. Thus Option 4.

Answer 3

Mark the words wines that yielded a good commercial profit... The topic of discussion is something that happened in the past.

If someone says that he kicked his classmate, the kick has been delivered already. This means the past tense is to be employed in the sentence.

Among the four options, only Option 1 is in the past tense. Thus Option 1 alone can work.

Exercise 3

DIRECTIONS *for questions 1 to 5: In each of the following sentences, part/parts of the sentence is/are left blank. Beneath each sentence, four different ways of completing the sentence are indicated. Choose the best alternative from among the four.*

1. In pursuance of their decision to resist what they saw as anti-labour policies, the company employees' union launched agitation to__________.

   (1) show their virility

   (2) reaffirm their commitment to the company

   (3) bring down the government

   (4) demonstrate their strength

2. The safest general characterisation of the European philosophical tradition as it has developed up to now, with all its diverse proponents, is that it consists of a ________ Plato.

   (1) series of footnotes to

   (2) set of prologues to

   (3) collection of chapters on

   (4) string of commentaries to

3. The interest generated by the soccer World Cup is _______ compared to the way cricket ________ the nation.

   (1) milder, fascinates

   (2) lukewarm, electrifies

(3) tepid, inspires

(4) unusual, grips

4. No doubt, it was our own government but it was being run on borrowed ideas, using ________ solutions.

(1) worn out

(2) second hand

(3) impractical

(4) appropriate

5. The telephone symbolises that awkward ________ in all communication technologies; while it ________ to bring us together, it keeps us apart.

(1) paradox, needs

(2) irony, intends

(3) paradox, tries

(4) irony, wishes

Answer 1

It is important to note the meanings of a few words here. ***Virility*** is male sexual potency or manliness. A trade union is the least likely of the forums where one can display *virility*. Option 1 therefore would be absurd. As regards Option 2 ('commitment to the company') an agitation would involve go-slow, strike and so on, all of which would have adverse impact on the company's productivity. An agitation is the least likely of the ways in which a trade union shows commitment to the company because such commitment would mean higher productivity. As regards Option 3, an agitation by the trade union of a company may mean loss of production and thus lesser excise and – if the profit for the relevant year is adversely affected – lesser income tax. As we know, excise and income-tax are sources of revenue for the government. Such an agitation does not affect a government as substantially as to bring it down. The rationale is that if there is a loss of production of a particular commodity of Company A and yet there is a demand for it, then the unsatisfied demand will be satisfied by Company B that will produce this commodity. The government will realise the shortfall in internal revenues from a source other than Company A. Thus **Option 4,** since a trade union is a forum to display collective strength and collective bargaining capacity.

Answer 2

Look at the words *'diverse proponents'*. *Diverse* means *various* and a *proponent* is someone who brings forward a proposal or theory. (Remember *pro* is forward or favouring). Thus there have been *various* or *several* persons who have influenced European philosophy. It is not as if Plato was the only one who influenced this philosophy.

A *prologue* is a preamble and the words 'prologue', 'collection of chapters' and 'string of commentaries' to Plato would lead to the impression that Plato was the sole influence on European philosophical tradition whereas Plato was not. Options 2, 3 and 4 would thus get eliminated. Hence **Option 1: a series of footnotes**, since a footnote is *additional* or *incidental* information.

Answer 3

The word in the first blank cannot be a comparative word since the words immediately succeeding the blank is 'compared to..' Hence Option 1 is out since the word 'milder' is a misfit as it is a comparative term. *Lukewarm* and *tepid* mean the same thing; they are synonyms. But cricket cannot *inspire* a nation; the word *'inspire'* means to animate or motivate with a noble cause. Thus *grips* and *electrifies* are eligible to be in the second blank. But the word 'unusual' is neither here nor there. What is more, unusual itself is a comparative term. Thus the first blank is 'lukewarm' and the other is 'electrifies'. Hence, **Option 2**.

Answer 4

The word *'borrowed'* essentially means *second hand*, because one borrows a thing from another person. Secondly, one borrows something from someone when one needs it. There is a perceptible need for the second-hand item. So a worn-out thing is unlikely to be borrowed and so is an impractical thing.

The words 'no doubt' at the start of the sentence would be out of place if the ideas were indeed appropriate in the sense they were correct. The word *appropriate* means either *correct* or *seize*. If the ideas were correct, then the words no doubt, would also be out of place. Hence, **Option 2**.

Answer 5

Although the words *paradox* and *irony* are perilously close in meaning, *paradox* is a self-contradiction and an *irony* is a satire. However, it is the second blank that would decide the issue.

A telephone is a mechanical device and cannot be said to have a need just as a cow needs fodder. The words *intend* and *wish* are indicative of a human mind [or, in a broader sense, the mind of animates], which a telephone does not have. Hence **Option 3**: ***paradox*** and ***tries***.

Exercise 4

DIRECTIONS ***for questions 1 to 5: In each of the following sentences, parts of the sentence are left blank. Beneath each sentence, four different ways of completing the sentence are indicated. Choose the best alternative from among the four.***

(1) Though one eye is kept firmly on the ________ the Company now also promotes ________ contemporary art.

1. present, experimental
2. future, popular
3. present, popular
4. market, popular

(2) The law prohibits a person from felling a sandalwood tree even if it grows on one's own land, without prior permission from the government. As poor people cannot deal with the government, this legal provision leads to a rip-roaring business for ______ who care neither for the ________ nor for the trees.

1. middlemen, rich
2. the government, poor
3. touts, rich
4. touts, poor

(3) It will take some time for many South Koreans to ________ the conflicting images of North Korea, let alone to ________ what to make of their northern cousins.

1. reconcile, decide
2. understand, clarify
3. make out, decide
4. reconcile, understand

(4) In these bleak and depressing times of ________ prices, non-performing governments and ________ crime rates, the matinee idol has given us, a lot to cheer about.

1. escalating, increasing
2. spiralling, booming
3. spiralling, soaring
4. ascending, debilitating

(5) The manners and ________ of the nouveau riche is a recurrent ________ in the literature.

1. style, motif
2. morals, story
3. wealth, theme
4. morals, theme

Answer 1

Contemporary is that which is prevalent and therefore something that is ongoing or present. Since contemporary is 'present', the word that fits in the first blank, is "future". The clue lies in the usage of the word though; which means "nevertheless; yet; indeed and **the word in the first blank should mean something other than contemporary. This is only in Option 2.**

Answer 2

Since poor people cannot deal with the government, there will be **touts** who will manage to obtain permission from the government for felling sandalwood trees; thus this will be a big business opportunity for touts who, since they deal on behalf of the poor with the government, care neither for the poor nor for the government. So **Option 4**. The word *tout* although refers to an intermediary, is used essentially in a derogatory sense; people who procure tickets of the races, railways, cinema etc. and sell them in the black market are examples of touts; so are those who procure customers for prostitutes. The primary concern of the tout is his money and morality is farthest from his mind when he does business.

Answer 3

Imagine that you are faced with this problem of what to make with eggs. (A) poached eggs or (B) an omelette. What you have to do is to **decide** between (A) and (B). Thus the word in the second blank is *decide*. This means we have to choose between Option 1 and 3 only.

Conflict means anything from a heated argument to a full-scaled war. If there is a conflict, you do not need to *make out* that there is a conflict. The sharp words or blows or artillery fire and so on will speak for themselves. As regards some people engaged in conflict, there are only three options (A) let them fight (B) reconcile or resolve their differences or (C) you join in. As far as we are concerned only **Option 1** is workable since it mentions the word *reconcile*.

Answer 4

When the government is non-performing, prices and crime tend to increase rather steeply. There is neither law and order in the society nor any control on the market. Option 1 mentions *increasing* crime-rate; an increase from 100 crimes to 101 crimes is an increase and so is an increase from 100 crimes to 200 crimes but the latter is a soaring crime rate. Secondly 'booming' is used to describe sudden spurts in economic activity or profits and is therefore invariably used in the a positive context, not in case of crime. *Debilitating* is weakening in the context of fatigue or illness and is not used to describe a crime rate if it was rising rapidly. Thus Option 3.

Answer 5

A motif is essentially (A) an ornamental design in the context of dresses or (B) a theme in the context of folklore or literature. Thus both *motif* and *theme* (a theme is a "central idea") could fit into blank no.2.

Recurrent fever means occurrence of fever every now and then. Recurrent story means same story every now and then. One story cannot make literature.

The choice for the word for the first blank is between " morals" and "wealth". If you wish to describe someone's wealth you have to use figures: 5 cars, 6 mansions with swimming pools, 90 kilograms of gold and so on. This description cannot be regarded as literature. *Style* is virtually the same thing as *'manners'* since style is also excellence of manners. The obvious choice for the first blank is *'morals'* since *'morals'* means "habits of life with regard to right and wrong conduct, specially sexual conduct. With morals as the word in the first blank, the word in the other blank has to be either **theme** itself or a word that means theme. Thus **Option 4.**

Exercise 5

DIRECTIONS ***for questions 1 to 5. In each of the following sentences, parts of the sentence are left blank. Beneath each sentence, four different ways of completing the sentence are indicated. Choose the best alternative from among the four.***

(1) But________________are now regularly written not just for tools, but well-established practices, organisations and institutions, not all of which seem to be________________ away.

1. reports, withering 2. stories, trading 3. books, dying 4. obituaries, fading

(2) The Darwin who ________________ is most remarkable for the way in which he __________ the attributes of the world class thinker and head of the household.

1. comes, figures 2. arises, adds 3. emerges, combines 4. appeared, combines

(3) Since her face was free of ____________________, there was no way to __________ if she appreciated what had happened.

1. make-up, realise 2. expression, ascertain 3. emotion, diagnose 4. scars, understand

(4) In this context, the ______________ of the British labour movement is particularly__________.

1. affair, weird 2. activity, moving 3. experience, significant 4. atmosphere, gloomy

(5) Our intellectuals may boast, if they are so inclined, of being ____________ to the most elitist among the intellectual__________ of the world.

1. subordinate, traditions 2. heirs, cliques 3. ancestors, societies 4.heir, traditions

Answer 1

Suppose you wish to let others know about the well-established practices in specific being followed in your organisation or about your organisation as a whole, how would you do so? You could write a report in a magazine. You could write a story. You could write a book. All three are therefore tools with which you attain the purpose of informing others about something that you deem worth informing. Thus stories, books and reports can be written *about* something but not *for* something.

Now let us see what are tools? Tools are devices. A story, a book and a report are all devices by which you can inform others about something of interest. ***You cannot write a tool for a tool.***

Only an obituary can be written *about* somebody or thing. Thus **Option 4** where an obituary may be written for tools (that have ceased to be deployed or for practices that have ceased to be prevalent and so on).

Answer 2

Darwin's remarkable feature is the manner in which he deals with the attributes of (A) the world-class thinker and (B) head of the household. The obvious choice for the second word is combines since Darwin is both (A) and (B) and has to combine these attributes in order to be admired for his having balanced these two remarkably different roles. The word *appeared* is out of context with the present tense of the sentence and hence the only choice for the first word is *emerges* and thus Option3.

Answer 3

Something happened to her but the moot point is whether she herself appreciated what happened. What one would need to do is to *ascertain* whether she has herself appreciated what happened and the lack of expression leaves no way to ascertain this.

Thus, the choice for the first word rests on *expression* since a face free of expression would make it difficult to ascertain whether she has appreciated what had happened. Thus **Option 2**.

Now look at this from a logical point of view. If a person has undergone trauma, how can you tell that there has been a traumatic experience? Will it elongate his nose?. If a person has undergone emotional turmoil, and yet you cannot find out whether the person has had such an experience, it means that the person's face does not reveal his emotional trauma. Expressions can tell whether there has been an emotional trauma and lack of facial expression makes it difficult to say this. Once this is clear, ask yourself whether:

(A) Make-up can hide emotions?

(B) Emotions can hide emotions?

(C) Scars can hide emotions?

Only expressions can show emotions and lack of expressions can hide emotions. Thus only **Option 2** will work.

Answer 4

A labour movement can be said to have "affairs" (meaning matters to deal with) but not "affair" since the movement itself is a collective activity. An affair is a matter of romance. A trade union can have an affair only if it consists of either only one man or only one woman. But then it cannot be a union where plurality is a prime requirement. You cannot have one-man unions, can you? So Option 1 will not work.

About the word *moving*, it can mean *proceeding from one place to another* or *emotionally touching*. No labour movement can move from one place to another. If anyone, its *members* can move from one place to another. As regards *emotionally touching* – the other possible meaning of the word *moving*, the activity of a labour movement can seldom be expected to bring emotions and tears. So Option 2 will not work either.

A gloomy atmosphere is not a likely characteristic of a labour movement. There can be a gloomy atmosphere in the office premises of the labour movement. Some leader may have died. But there cannot be a gloomy atmosphere in the labour movement itself. So Option 4 will not do either.

Since the statement is written in a context – as apparent from the very words in this context.... – the *experience* of the labour movement would be particularly *significant*. Thus **Option 3**.

Answer 5

If our intellectuals were to boast, they could scarcely be expected to boast about being **subordinates** to elitists. Thus Option 1 will not work.

In Option 2, while the boasting may be about exclusivity, the word *clique* is used to describe **petty exclusivity**. *Elitist* means *the best*. The word *petty* means worthless or of insignificant value. **Nothing petty can be elitist.** So Option 2 will not work.

Look at this from a logical standpoint. Are you aware that an ancestor is someone who is dead long ago? Suppose you have been to your girlfriend's place and her father says that you may leave. What is implied is that you must go now. When I say it may rain tomorrow, what is implied is the likelihood of rain in the future. Clearly the word "may" indicates future tense. An ancestor is already gone. So Option 3 will not do either.

That leaves us with **Option 4**. Intellectuals may boast about elitist *traditions*. What are traditions? Traditions are things that have been a custom for many generations. If my grandfather has made some tradition, I can only be an heir to it.

Exercise 6

DIRECTIONS *for questions 1 to 10: Each of the sentences below has one or more blank spaces indicating where a word (or words) has (have) been left out. Following each sentence, four words or sets of words are marked 1 to 4. You have to select the appropriate word or set of words to make the sentence most meaningful.*

1. I have begun devoting all my time to writing and this has....... with my...... of any further knowledge.

   (1) hindered, gaining (2) interfered, acquisition
   (3) prevented, getting (4) contradicted, desire

2. Human memory being...........oral..........of large bodies of old literature is not possible and this accounts for corruption or variation in the existing texts of ancient literature ancient literature.

   (1) weak, recitation (2) fallible, transmission
   (3) mechanical, communication (4) neglected, quoting

3. Science is neither.............nor.............It is only amoral.

   (1) good, useful (2) bad, useless
   (3) moral, immoral (4) ethical, spiritual

4. Concern for..........pollution is still..........to a few specialists, and it has not yet permeated the social structure.

(1) intense, delegated (2) environmental, confined

(3) contaminated, given (4) water, experimental

5. In..........countries and new democracies, there is no immediate danger of the kind of..........which advanced capitalist countries face.

(1) developing, crisis (2) affluent, dilemma

(3) progressive, self-sufficiency (4) welfare, problems

6. ....is rather out of place at a..........meeting; trifling gaiety must give place to seriousness.

(1) Truancy, marital (2) Fluency, managerial

(3) Pantisocracy, poetic (4) flippancy, funeral

7. All the citizens must..........the use of nuclear and chemical weapons if we want our children to..........a better world.

(1) integrate, disinherit (2) indict, inter

(3) interdict, inherit (4) intrude, inveigh

8. The prospect of finding gold in the abandoned..........proved to be a..........as the gold digger soon found out.

(1) pits, judas tree (2) quarry, jeremiad

(3) site, jejune (4) canyon, mirage

9. The..........teachings of the alchemists have proved to be the..........of modern chemistry.

(1) herculian, anchor (2) hermetic, foundation

(3) heretic, justification (4) hazardous, attic

10. After visiting the beautiful mountains and lakes of Switzerland, Shelly was..........with a desire to write some of his most famous poems describing the..........power of nature.

1. imbued; illimitable 2. infiltrated, incendiary

3. imbibed, implacable 4. immune, illusive

Answer 1

For the first blank, *hindered*, *prevented* and *contradicted* are out of the reckoning since these words do not require the word 'with' to follow them. Interference is something that is done with someone else. Hence the only workable option is Option 2.

Answer 2

As regards Option 1 even if human memory were weak, oral recitation is absolutely possible. One can read from a text. If memory is fallible, it could fail. Consider Option 2, transmission means sending something from one place to another or from one person to another. Hence Option 2 would do very well. Option 3 will not do because if human memory were mechanical, there would be no corruption during transmission. It would be as simple as recording something on a cassette and transmitting it.

Answer 3

Amoral is unconcerned with morality. Something amoral is therefore neither moral nor immoral. So Option 3.

Answer 4

Only *environmental* and *water* are the two words eligible to go into the first blank. Something cannot be experimental to a specialist. A specialist is one who is thoroughly knowledgeable in his field of specialisation. If a field is a matter of experiment to somebody, he is not yet a specialist in that field. Hence Option 2.

Answer 5

A new democracy is not necessarily a developed country. India became a democracy in 1947 when it was very poor. The word *developing* may fill the first blank. The second blank is about a danger and self-sufficiency is certainly nowhere near being a danger. *Self-sufficiency* would, on the contrary, put someone out of the danger of being at the mercy of someone else. *Dilemma* and *problems* are too mild to go with danger. *Crisis* fits the bill well. Hence **Option 1**.

Answer 6

The end of the sentence suggests that the tone at the meeting must be serious and anything other than serious would be out of place at that meeting. This means that out of the options, only a funeral meeting would qualify for this condition. Hence **Option 4**. *Flippant* means disrespectful or shallow. At a *marital* meeting (to celebrate a marriage), while there has to be seriousness, it is not necessarily so; marriages are social gatherings where merrymaking is presumed. At a meeting of managers, *fluency* (of thought process and strategy formulation) is an essential requirement and cannot be considered out of place. But *flippancy* is certainly out of place at a funeral where whatever jokes one has in his repertoire must be saved for an occasion other than a funeral.

Answer 7

Blank 2 must take a word which should mean passing on of something, in this case a better would to our children. Hence the word inherit. Hence **Option 3**. To *inter* means to bury. Burial is essentially after death. We want our children tô live. Thus *inter* would not work in the second blank. To *inveigh* means to speak vehemently. This would presuppose bitterness which has no place in a better world.

Answer 8

A *quarry* is an open mine. Gold is found in quarries. A *jeremiad* is a lamentation. Hence, **Option 2**. Incidentally the word *quarry* also means prey just as the deer is the usual quarry of the Asiatic lion. The word *jejune* comes from juvenile meaning relating to the young and therefore naïve or childish. While the abandoned *canyon* can also do, a canyon may or may not contain gold. It is not necessary that just because there was gold in a canyon in the famous thriller *McKenna's Gold*, there would be gold in every canyon. A canyon is a deep cleft created by a river flowing in a highland. A prospector looking for gold would be better off prospecting in a quarry in which, since it is a mine, the possibility of gold being found would be more unless other prospectors who came to the quarry before him, have walked away with all the gold.

Answer 9

Let us see the candidates for the first blank. The word *Herculean* means *huge* and has to do with size whether of a person or of an effort and would not do; hazardous is out of place since hazardous teaching would not create any science, in which order is presumed; heretic is a non-believer and someone who does not believe in a subject can hardly be expected to teach it. Hermetic comes from hermit and a hermit is one who is devoted to his religion. An alchemist devoted to chemistry is a hermit insofar as his devotion to chemistry is concerned. Hence **Option 2**.

Answer 10

In the context of the beautiful mountains and lakes of Switzerland, the word in the second blank must mean something that would describe the power of nature as without limit. Hence **Option 1: imbued, illimitable.**

Something *incendiary* is that which can burn. When nature burns things, like it does in dry bushes and grasslands (a phenomenon known as bushfires) the tendency of anyone – poet or no poet – would be to run for safety instead of sitting there composing poems. If the poet persists with writing poems while a bushfire is raging, neither the poet nor his poems will survive to relate to us how beautiful nature was when things were burning.

Implacable means that which cannot be appeased or something that is harsh or cruel. When a chap sees the cruel power of nature – such as an earthquake bringing down a high rise building - he will be inclined to run and save his life rather than write. To *imbibe* means to take in. Shelly may have imbibed something such as tea, sandwiches, liquor, philosophy and so on. But Shelly could not have been imbibed by anyone else.

The power of nature is not illusive at all. If one sees a beautiful lake and leaps in overlooking the fact that he can't swim, the poet himself must vanish till the body comes floating to the surface. If he has to make an effort to swim, it means the water is tangible and not elusive. If the water were elusive, there would be no lake at all. If a chap thinks that the hardness of a rock is illusive, all he should do is bang his head on the rock and find out for himself that it is absolutely real.

Exercise 7

DIRECTIONS *for questions 1–9: Each of the sentences below has one or more blank spaces indicating that a word has been left out. Following each sentence four words or sets of words are given, marked 1 to 4. Choose the word or set of words that makes the sentence most meaningful.*

1. The children .... their parents to be allowed to go out for the circus that in the end the parents ....

   (1) malingered, dissented (2) importuned, relented

   (3) requested, condoned (4) communicated, regretted

2. .... of our responsibility will lead to ....

   (1) Dereliction, opprobrium (2) Direction, obloquy

   (3) Fulfillment, odium (4) Neglect, encomium

3. The contractor's .... made him resort to adulterating building materials.

   (1) serenity (2) avid (3) asperity (4) cupidity

4. The .... went on and on the most of the audience did not understand his................

   (1) politician, encomium (2) braggadocio, gibberish

   (3) banker, diatribe (4) play, jeremiad

5. Many substances shine and dazzle, but the pride of place must go to diamonds which......... especially under fluorescent lights.

   (1) coagulate (2) corrugate (3) coruscate (4) contemplate

6. He had an .... to .... and would rather lose a case than resort to trickery.

   (1) Aversion, adoration (2) telepathy, administration

   (3) antipathy, chicanery (4) sympathy, fraud

7. Frequent .... repasts made him a mass of obese flesh and his .... cheeks looked like overblown balloons about to burst.

   (1) gluttonous, flaccid (2) garrulous, bold

   (3) omnivorous, ecstatic (4) calorific, withered

8. The .... performance of Uriah Heep and the impression it leaves on our minds in an .... mark of Dicken's genius.

   (1) serrated, indelible (2) imperious, indefeasible

   (3) unctuous, irrefutable (4) servile, ingratiating

9. The decision comes at the end of .... consultation between the government and various political parties in the troubled border state rocked by prolonged terrorist ....

   (1) hectic, mayhem (2) empty, rampaged

   (3) countless, troupes (4) feverish, explosives

Answer 1

The crux of this sentence lies in determining what is at the end. The parents took a stance different from the one that they had been taking all along. If they had dissented at the end, the presumption is that they had agreed at the beginning and if this were true there would have been no need for the children to persuade their parents to allow them to go to the circus. The only word that fits at the end is ***relented***; this means agreed after all. Hence **Option** 2.

Answer 2

Dereliction means *abandoning* (or, in other words, *running away from duty or responsibility*) and *opprobrium* means *shame*. Hence **Option 1**. As regards Option 2, it is possible to direct someone's action. One cannot direct someone's responsibility and hence this will not work. *Obloquy* means *shame* or *disgrace whereas*. If one fulfils his responsibility it should bring satisfaction or honour. *Odium* means hatred. This option will not work. *Encomium* means high-flown praise. Neglect is not likely to bring about any praise. Hence option 4 will not do.

Answer 3

The contractor has been responsible for adulterating building materials. This means he has been driven by greed. If he had been *serene* (meaning *quiet and in control of one's faculties*) then he would not have been resorting to such unethical practices. A serene person is at peace with himself. A greedy person wants more and more and is not likely to be serene. Avid is an adjective that means *keen* and the blank does not belong to an adjective but to a noun. This is because we are looking for something possessed by the contractor, as is evident from the word 'contractor's'. *Asperity* is *harshness* or *severity* and someone severe is uncompromising whereas the idea behind using substandard material is to make more money from the contract than what was due. This means the contractor intended to appropriate someone else's money for himself. Cupidity is the tendency to appropriate another's wealth and hence **cupidity** is the appropriate word for the blank. Hence Option 4.

Answer 4

To *brag* means *to boast* and *gibberish* is *nonsense*. The fact that the crowd did not understand what the fellow was saying means that what he was saying did not make sense. So the second blank belongs to a word that means *nonsense*. An *encomium* is high praise (in high flown language); a *diatribe* is a stream of abuse and a banker is not expected to make such diatribe. **Braggadocio** (from the word bragging) is the first blank and **gibberish** the second.

Answer 5

Coagulate means *to come together*, *thicken* or *become crystalline*. When you put curd in milk, the milk coagulates. *Corrugate* means to *form a wavy pattern* like you see on asbestos sheets or packing boxes. *Contemplate* means *to think* and diamonds cannot be reasonably expected to contemplate since they do not have a mind. **Coagulate** here may be apt since the dazzling lights might seem to bring the diamonds together in a mass. *Coruscate* means to glitter or sparkle. Since coruscating itself means sparkling and diamonds sparkle even in the dark.

Answer 6

Chicanery is trickery or fraudulence in legal matters and hence **Option 3**: *antipathy*, *chicanery*. The first blank appears after the article 'an'. This means that the word in the first blank must start with a vowel (because if the word were to start with a consonant, then the preceding article would have been 'a' and not 'an'). This means we are to look at options 1 and 3 only. *Aversion* is hatred. *Adoration* is admiration. One cannot have aversion and adoration for something at the same time.

Answer 7

A repast is a meal. If the fellow's cheeks were overblown, it means that he was eating far more than what he should. *Thus gluttonous* (a word used to describe somebody who eats in a manner as if there is no tomorrow) in the first blank and **flaccid** (toneless flesh, hanging) in the second blank. An *omnivorous* person is one who eats both (A) Vegetarian and (B) Non-Vegetarian food. But a repast (or meal) cannot be omnivorous. It has to be either (A) or (B) or both (A) & (B). An ecstatic person is someone jumping with joy. A meal cannot be expected to jump with joy. The word *withered* means *dried up*. If a fellow's cheeks are withered, he cannot be obese. If your new neighbour is *garrulous*, it means he chats or chatters too much. No meal or repast can talk.

Answer 8

If some performance leaves an impression on our minds, we remember it for long. It can be either a happy event or an unfortunate event. If someone's genius leaves an impression on our minds, such an impression is the result of an admirable performance.

A *serrated* animal is one which has small sharp teeth. It can leave impression on our skin or on our flesh but not on our minds.

An *unctuous* person is one who is either *servile* or *glib* (or *smooth*, *urbane*, *polished*). A polished performance would certainly leave a positive impression. Something *irrefutable* is something that cannot be denied. The two words complete the meaning of the sentence hence Option 3 is the right answer. An *imperious* person is someone who is overbearing, highhanded or domineering. A performance cannot be imperious. Something *indefeasible* is that which cannot be made void or it cannot be annulled. Therefore a contract can be indefeasible but not a mental impression.

A *servile* person is one who behaves like an overly obedient servant. He is a sycophant. A servile person is not likely to leave a positive impression on anyone's mind. An *ingratiating* person is one who seeks the favour of another. He is a sycophant. Only a human being can become ingratiating. A mark cannot become a sycophant. Thus Option 4 will not do.

Answer 9

There is a state rocked by terrorists. If a mother rocks the child's cradle, the cradle moves to and fro. The child goes to sleep. If terrorists rock a state the state will not go to sleep. Terrorists create chaos and terror.

Option 1 would do well since consultation is likely to be *hectic* (or, in other words, very busy) and *mayhem* means chaos or terror which the terrorists would create.

Option 2 is very unlikely because an *empty* consultation would mean that there is nothing worthwhile discussed or decided. A state rocked by terrorists would need to have serious consultations and bold decisions about how to deal with terrorists.

Option 3 is not workable for two reasons: (1) with the word *countless*, the word *consultation* in the singular would not do. (2) only drama artists and dancers come in *troupes*. Terrorists do not come dressed for disco dancing.

Option 4 is not workable since *feverish* means having *fever*, *red-faced*, *nervous*, *excited* and so on. The word *feverish* would describe an animate thing but not consultation.

Exercise 8

DIRECTIONS ***for questions 1 to 5: Each of the sentences below has two blank spaces which are meant to be filled with one of the four choices numbered 1 to 4. Select the appropriate pair of words that make the sentence most meaningful.***

1. Murder is.........killing of another during the commission of a crime and manslaughter, a lesser crime, is the unintentional or........... killing of another.

   (1) deliberate; benevolent (2) accidental; mercy

   (3) intentional; accidental (4) purposeless; casual

2. German measles can result in foetal anomalies if contracted during the first trimester of pregnancy, and so all women who are likely to..........exposure and who are not.........should be vaccinated.

(1) face; brave
(2) risk; immune
(3) contact; protected
(4) confront; defenceless

3. In "there isn't an atom of truth in that story", "atom" is not used ....but only ....transferred sense of "something infinitesimally small".

(1) properly; metaphorically
(2) originally; secondarily
(3) correctly; indirectly
(4) literally; figuratively

4. While a prefix is a meaningful element attached to the beginning of a word to change the meaning, like "ante" meaning "............................", as in "antebellum", a suffix is an element added to the end of a word to change its meaning or ....as "able" in countable.

(1) against; form
(2) before; shape
(3) before; function
(4) against; function

5. "Ethnic cleaning may seem to be a/an...................term to denote the voluntary evacuation of the minorities to expedite the conversion of a territory into one inhabited by one ethnic, a racial group, but, it is only a/ an......................for the merciless massacre of the minorities.

(1) harmless; metaphor
(2) clear, simile
(3) political; euphemism
(4) innocent; euphemism

Answer 1

The killing of a human being by another human being is known as *homicide* (a word that comes from the Latin HOMO that means *human being* and –the suffix CIDE that means *killing*). There are various forms that homicide takes, depending upon whether the homicide is intentional or accidental or through negligence and so on. If homicide has been committed with criminal intention, then it is known as murder. If homicide has been committed in defence of the country (such as by soldiers in the course of war) then it is a justifiable homicide. If homicide is committed without malice and in self-defence, then it is known as excusable homicide. Where homicide is a result of someone's negligence, then it is known as *culpable* (meaning, *deserving punishment*) *homicide not amounting to murder*.

Murder means **premeditated** killing of one or more human being(s) by another human being(s). So murder is essentially **intended**. Unintentional killing is itself **accidental**. Hence **Option 3**.

As regards Option 1, no crime can be benevolent. This is why option 1 will not do. As explained above, murder is not an *accidental* killing at all and hence Option 2 will not work. As regards Option 4, *purposeless* people are excused if they loaf around and do nothing worthwhile all day long. But murder cannot be *purposeless*. Something intentional has got to have purpose. Whatever intentional action one takes is always towards realisation of a purpose.

Answer 2

The word *foetal* comes from *foetus*, which is an unborn baby. The word *trimester* means *three months*. If someone has had *exposure* to radiation, he has *come into contact* with radiation. If someone has had *exposure* to financial management of a large company, he has *experience* of managing finances of large companies. If someone is guilty of indecent *exposure*, he/she has shown such of his/her body parts in public that civilised people do not do.

For the first blank, *face*, *contact*, and *confront* will not do. If someone strips in public, this does not amount to *exposure* till someone faces the stripper. *It is the stripper who is faced*. As regards someone who has *exposure* to – say – flying combat aircraft, he has *experience* of flying such aircrafts. Such an experience could not have come about by his merely confronting or making a contact the aircraft. Experience comes out of learning something and hence experience or exposure is an internal process in this particular context. Thus Option 2 seems the best bet. In order to crosscheck, let us ask ourselves this simple question: who would need vaccination? Someone who is not immune. So the second blank belongs to the word *immune* and the first blank belongs to those who are likely to *risk* exposure. Hence **Option 2**.

Answer 3

A *metaphor* is a figure of speech that makes an analogy between totally dissimilar things. If you have just returned from a town in which you have seen that the people are busy, you may metaphorically describe the town as a beehive of activity. As we know, an atom is an infinitesimally small part of an element. Therefore using the word atom to describe something infinitesimally small is comparing two like things and therefore there is no metaphor employed. Option 1 will not do for this reason. If the idea is to say that there is not even the smallest truth in the story, then one uses the word atom in its *figurative* sense and not *literal* sense. One cannot use the word atom in the literal sense since a story is not an element like carbon or copper or uranium and so on. Since the word atom has been used, there is a direct reference and hence Option 3 will not do. Figurative use of words is made when you wish to compare something with another. An immature adult can be *figuratively* described as childish. He does not become a child by such usage. Someone very stubborn can be described as *stubborn as a mule*. He does not become a mule in the process. Hence **Option 4**.

Answer 4

The prefix ANTI- means *against* and ANTE- means *before*. (*Antecedents* means things that a fellow has done before. When one checks a prospective son-in-law's antecedents, the intention is to make sure that one is not giving one's daughter in marriage to a chap who is a Dr. Jekyll during the daytime and a Mr. Hyde after dark). So, we must look at Options 2 and 3 only.

Words, as we know, do not have any shape at all. They have functions. If, for example, you say that you are thirsty, you use the word "thirsty" to convey that you want water. That is the function of the word "thirsty". A suffix changes the function of a word. Thus **Option 3**.

Answer 5

No killing can be harmless, not even killing time (which is harmful too). Merciless killing of the minorities cannot be *innocent* either. Options 1 and 4 will not do for this reason. If you refer to someone cool as a cucumber, fat as a pig, and so on you are using similes. Cleaning is a process that brings cleanliness. Mass killing of human beings cannot bring cleanliness. You can compare mass killing with manslaughter but not with things that bring cleanliness.

Ethnic cleaning here, is a term used for merciless killing of minorities, as seen from the concluding line. A *euphemism* is an understatement. Politics is about the struggle to get power over people and unless the reason for someone killing another is personal enmity, the killing of minorities (who may have become immensely wealthy and are therefore hated in a country where there is utter poverty) is nothing other than a political matter. Hence **Option 3**.

Exercise 9

DIRECTIONS *for Questions 1 to 5: There are two gaps in each of the following sentences. From the pairs of words given, choose the one that fills the gaps most appropriately. The first word in the pair should fill the first gap.*

Question 1

The British retailer, M&S, today formally __________ defeat in its attempt to __________ King's, its US subsidiary, since no potential purchasers were ready to cough up the necessary cash.

(1) admitted, acquire
(2) conceded, offload
(2) announced, dispose
(4) ratified, auction

Question 2

Early ________ of maladjustment to college culture is ____________ by the tendency to develop friendship networks outside college which mask signals of maladjustment.

(1) treatment, compounded
(2) detection, facilitated
(3) identification, complicated
(4) prevention, helped

Question 3

The ______ regions of Spain all have unique cultures, but the ______ views within each region make the issue of an acceptable common language of instruction an even more contentious one.

(1) different, discrete
(2) distinct, disparate
(3) divergent, distinct
(4) different, competing

Question 4

A growing number of these expert professionals ________ having to train foreigners as the students end up ________ the teachers who have to then unhappily contend with no jobs at all or new jobs with drastically reduced pay packets.

(1) resent, replacing
(2) resist, challenging
(3) welcome, assisting
(4) are, supplanting

Question 5

Companies that try to improve employees' performance by ________ rewards encourage negative kinds of behaviour instead of ________ a genuine interest in doing the work well.

(1) giving, seeking
(2) bestowing, discouraging
(3) conferring, discrediting
(4) withholding, fostering

Solution

Answer 1

M&S were not able to find potential purchasers. This means that they were trying to sell something. This means Option 1 will not work since M&S would be trying to buy something if they were *acquiring* whereas here the intention is to sell. Secondly, when a chap is defeated, he does not *announce* defeat; if any announcement is made, it is that of a victory by the winner. The loser admits, accepts or *concedes* defeat. A defeat, by its very nature, is something that the defeated person does not shout about from rooftops. While Option 1 has the word *admitted*, Option 1 is not workable for the reason outlined above. So only Option 2 will work.

About *ratifying* defeat, one can ratify (or, in other words, *treat as something that is correctly done*) something that someone else has done on his behalf without his prior knowledge or approval. If, for example, my brother were to negotiate and finalise the sale of our ancestral property (which we wanted to dispose of but were not finding ready buyers) at a very attractive price while I was away on a tour so that such an attractive offer does not go past, I would ratify (take as correct) what he has done because it is in my interest as well. But if one loses, one has to lose by oneself. You cannot assign the job, say, of losing a boxing match to someone else. You have to take the punches on your own jaw and when you feel that you have had your fill, you tell the referee (tacitly, of course, by lying down on the mat and not opening your eyes till the count of ten is over) to declare the other man as the winner.

Answer 2

This is a question of mere logic. Look at the statement, which says that friendship networks outside college *mask* maladjustment. Who wears a mask? Someone who does not want to be identified wears a mask. Why? He wears a mask to complicate (make it either impossible or very difficult his identification. So Option 3.

Answer 3

There are some regions of Spain that have unique cultures. There are views that are making an issue of the common language of instruction, which is causing contention or a quarrel. If there is a quarrel about the common language, there has got to be more than one region. So, both *different* and *distinct* would seem to qualify for the first blank.

Now as regards the second blank, which should clinch the issue, the word *discrete* is an aggregate of the suffix *DIS-* (that means *away from*) and the Latin root *CRET-* (that means *to grow together*) and thus *discrete* means *separated* or *detached from one another*. Regions that are detached from one another would not even aspire for think of a common language. The word *disparate* means *essentially different* or *incommensurable*. Regions that would not commensurate with the others would not aspire for a common language either.

Whether in India or in Spain, or for that matter anywhere in the whole wide world, the common language has to be decided out of several different languages and hence there is a competition among the different regions for what should be the language acceptable to all; every region would like its language to be accepted as a common language. It is for this reason that the word in the second blank should be *competing*. Thus **Option 4**.

Answer 4

If the teachers have to unhappily contend for no jobs or jobs at drastically reduced pay packets, then it means that those trained foreigners would replace them. This means that expert professionals would resent (resentment comes out of unhappiness) having to train foreigners. Hence logically only **Option 1** will work.

As regards Option 2, if the chap who is presently working as a teacher does not have a job, what is left for the trained person to challenge him for? Will he challenge him at Indian arm wrestling?

As for Option 3, what assistance will a teacher, who has no job, need? Will the trained person help the unemployed teacher with counting the number of flies that the latter has killed in a day?

As regards *supplant* in Option 4, it means replacing someone by essentially underhand means. An individual teacher can be replaced by underhand means, but to expect the foreigners to replace the native teachers by underhand means, is expecting too much.

Answer 5

This is a matter of sheer logic. If there is a *negative* behaviour, it can only be on account of not giving rewards. Thus the word in the first blank should be *withholding*. The words *bestowing* and *conferring* both mean giving with a flourish or in style. If the Arjuna Award is to be given to an outstanding sportsperson, it is not merely *given* (one does not say, "here, you who play hockey fairly well, take this little packet and show your Mom and Dad what is in it when you reach home"); it is *bestowed on* the player or *conferred* upon him in a ceremony with pomp and pageantry. Thus **Option 4**.

We have seen what it takes to be able to correctly answer questions in this section. We shall now move on to some practice tests that should help us not only to completely assimilate the necessary concepts and refine these concepts, but these tests should also help us to be able to decide the question-specific strategy that we shall need in order to be able to succeed at this sub-section in the Verbal Section at the GRE.

Needless to say, there are lucid solutions at the end of the tests. Most of the solutions are miniature concept notes. It is for this reason that we strongly recommend that you read each solution regardless of whether you are right or you are wrong.

Sentence Completion Practice Set 1

This question includes sentences that have one or two blanks, each blank indicating that a word has been omitted. Beneath each sentence are five words or sets of words. Choose the word or set of words for each blank that *best* fits the meaning of the sentence as a whole.

Question 1

Natural selection tends to eliminate genes that cause inherited diseases, acting most strongly against the most severe diseases; consequently, hereditary diseases that are______ would be expected to be very _______, but, surprisingly, they are not.

(1) lethal...rare (2) untreated...dangerous (3) unusual...refractory

(4) new...perplexing (5) widespread...dangerous

Question 2

Although ancient tools were _______ preserved, enough have survived to allow us to demonstrate an occasionally interrupted but generally ______ progress through prehistory.

(1) partially...noticeable (2) superficially...necessary (3) unwittingly...documented

(4) rarely...continual (5) needlessly...incessant

Question 3

For centuries animals have been used as _______ for people in experiments to assess the effects of therapeutic and other agents that might later be used in humans.

(1) benefactors (2) companions (3) examples (4) precedents (5) surrogates

Question 4

The pressure of population on available resources is the key to understanding history; consequently, any historical writing that takes no cognisance of _________ facts is ______ flawed.

(1) demographic...intrinsically (2) ecological...marginally

(3) cultural...substantively (4) psychological...philosophically

(5) political...demonstratively

Question 5

During the opera's most famous aria the tempo chosen by the orchestra's conductor seemed_______, without necessary relation to what had gone before.

(1) tedious (2) melodious (3) capricious

(4) compelling (5) cautious

Question 6

The state is a network of exchanged benefits and beliefs, _______ between rulers and citizens based on those laws and procedures that are _______ to the maintenance of community.

(1) a compromise...inimical (2) an interdependence...subsidiary (3) a counterpoint...incidental

(4) an equivalence...prerequisite (5) a reciprocity...conducive

Question 7

An investigation that is ___ can occasionally yield new facts, even notable ones, but typically the appearance of such facts is the result of a search in a definite direction.

(1) timely (2) unguided (3) consistent

(4) uncomplicated (5) subjective

Question 8

Like many eighteenth-century scholars who lived by cultivating those in power, Winckelmann neglected to neutralize, by some ____ gesture of comradeship, the resentment his peers were bound to feel because of his ______ the high and mighty.

(1) quixotic.. intrigue with (2) enigmatic...familiarity with (3) propitiatory...involvement with

(4) salutary...questioning of (5) unfeigned...sympathy for

Question 9

The characterization of historical analysis as a form of fiction is not likely to be received ________ by either historians or literary critics, who agree that history and fiction deal with ______ orders of experience.

(1) quietly...significant (2) enthusiastically...shifting (3) passively...unusual

(4) sympathetically...distinct (5) contentiously...realistic

Question 10

Documenting science's _______ philosophy would be ______, since it is almost axiomatic that many philosophers use scientific concepts as the foundations for their speculations.

(1) distrust of...elementary (2) influence on...superfluous (3) reliance on...inappropriate

(4) dependence on...difficult (5) difference from...impossible

Answer 1

This is a matter of logic more than anything else.

Inherited diseases and hereditary diseases are the same thing. Before the first blank, there is a mention of some *consequence* of something that acts most strongly against the most severe diseases. It is not as if all hereditary diseases are most severe but the type that is being discussed here is the most severe type. Therefore whatever word that fits into the first blank, it should be a substitute for the words *most severe*. As such, both *lethal* and *widespread* would prima facie seem to fit the bill (although it is not necessary that a widespread disease is dangerous; conjunctivitis may be widespread and yet not dangerous) whereas lethal is necessarily dangerous. **Lethal** should fit the bill for the first blank but we must also see whether **rare** fits the second blank to confirm our finding.

When some toothpaste claims to remove the most stubborn plaque, the expected *consequence* of its use should be that either there should be no plaque left or if there is any, it should be only in traces. If someone were surprised after using such a toothpaste, it would be to see that the plaque persists noticeably. Similarly, when something acts most strongly against the most severe diseases, one would expect that the diseases should be eliminated altogether or if not, they would be expected to occur very rarely. Therefore the word in the second blank should be **rare**.

Option 1 should be marked as correct.

Answer 2

Imagine that you have been cleaning the attic at your grandfather's place where you find the following things:

- Some gorgeous silk gowns that have been wrapped in a shawl with mothballs placed in the gowns to keep parasites away

- A collection of classics in which parasites have made gaping holes with the result that over half of the books are worthless

Of these two things, which one was preserved? The answer is clear: the collection of gowns. Which one of the following sentences would you rate as correct?

1. The collection of gowns has survived although it was preserved.
2. The collection of classics has survived although it was not preserved.

Quite clearly Sentence 2 is correct because *although* means *in spite of*. Something has survived *although* care was not taken to preserve it. If you see the options, all but Option 4 say that the ancient tools were preserved; some say that they were preserved *partially*, others say they were preserved *superficially*, *unwittingly* and some other option says they were preserved *needlessly*. But in all these four options one fact emerges: the tools have been preserved with varying degree of care. Option 4 is the only one where there is a hint about no care being taken to preserve anything. Then the fact that enough have survived is not **although** (meaning in spite of) they are preserved but **because** they are preserved.

Then as regards the second blank, it is meant for the opposite of occasionally interrupted. Two possible phrases could be the opposites of 'occasionally interrupted':

(1) Always interrupted (this is not among the options but even if it was, there would be no progress and hence this can never be true)

(2) Generally uninterrupted. (this is among the options and very possible because if something is occasionally interrupted, progress is still possible just as it is when we stop for a cup of tea at a motel while going on a long drive)

Thus, since the opposite of *interrupted* is *continuous*, only Option 4 will work. This is why **Option 4** is to be marked correct.

Answer 3

A *benefactor* is someone who does good deeds for someone else. He is aware that he is doing something good. He is doing it out of his own will, voluntarily. An animal does not possess either this awareness or will. Therefore an animal cannot be a benefactor.

If someone is your companion, he walks with you and goes to the cinema with you. Therefore if animals were companions to human beings in experiments, both humans and animals would be employed in experiments. Then the question of using therapeutic (meaning, medicinal) agents **later on** in human beings would not arise.

Imagine that you are telling your new neighbour that you love fast food. He says that he has no idea of what fast food means. You then tell him, for example, that pizza is a fast food and that burgers are another example of fast food. You cannot give the example of a radish as fast food. All examples of fast food should be fast foods in the first place. This is why animals cannot be used as examples for people. At the most, people can be used as *examples* for people.

A *precedent* could mean any of the following things:

1. Imagine that someone in the army has been requesting for an accommodation. There is a house vacant in the navy colony but not in the army colony. If someone from the army has been allotted a house in the navy colony in the past, such allotment is a *precedent* or a *standard* or *an example* that such a thing can be done without fear of the earth shaking
2. If a company has put in an advertisement for recruiting engineers and the condition *precedent* is that the applicant should have a university degree in engineering, it means that this condition has to be met *before* recruitment.

Considering the above usages, animals cannot be expected to serve as a standard or an example for people nor can they be expected to meet any conditions, mainly because if you want someone to meet your condition, he should be able to understand what you are saying; animals cannot be expected to understand this. You can tell your prospective tenant that you will lease the house provided he vacates it at the end of two years. You cannot make your pet dog understand such a condition even if he has been with you for donkey's years (meaning, a very long time).

Therefore **Option 5** is the most natural choice. This fits in admirably because if you are, carrying out some experiments on animals now to be used later on humans what you are doing is using animals in place of human beings and therefore animals are a substitute for human beings. The word **surrogate** means *substitute.*

Answer 4

This is entirely about logic.

The central idea is the pressure of population on available resources. That is why the word *key* (that means vital or most important and so on) has been used to describe population pressure. The word in the first blank should relate to population. Therefore the word **demographic** would fit in admirably in the first blank. As to why the other words will not fit is quite clear. For example, ecology is the environment and does not mean population.

Answer 5

This is about logic up to a great extent. A famous orchestra cannot be expected to be *tedious* (or *boring*). If the tempo chosen now has been melodious then it means that it could earlier have been unmelodious. No orchestra can hope to be unmelodious and famous at the same time. The word *capricious* means something that is unpredictable. This could fit in admirably. If something does not bear any relation to what has gone before, only then could it be called unpredictable.

If the tempo had been *compelling*, then it could mean that earlier it was not compelling. No conductor will ever decide to conduct an orchestra if any member of that orchestra will not play his instrument according to his wishes. There could be cacophony if the conductor signals someone to stop playing and yet he carries on.

If the word in the blank were to be *cautious*, it would mean, since there was no necessary relation to what had gone before, the earlier tempo was without caution. A conductor has to be cautious all the while. He has to be attentive to who is playing what and how. If he is not cautious, there will be cacophony. He has to be careful that his baton does not fly off into the audience because if it does, someone may end up with a broken nose.

Option 3 is to be marked as correct.

Answer 6

The second blank will help in short-listing the options that we will look at. The question is: can laws be subsidiary or incidental to maintenance of community? What is more important: maintenance of community or law? Imagine that someone has committed a murder in cold blood and the law finds him guilty. If the law decides to execute him, the community will lose a member. Can anything be maintained if it keeps losing its ingredients? And yet can any community, in which the murderer goes unpunished, ever hope to stay together as a community? The murderer will go on a murdering spree. What is law after all? It is a code of things that should not done and it specifies what punishment would be meted out if that code were violated. The intention behind this code is that community, or life, must be maintained. Law can thus never be incidental or subsidiary to the maintenance of the community. The word *inimical* comes from the word *enemy* and means *harmful*. How can law ever be *inimical* to the maintenance of the community? The very intention behind law is that it should be *conducive* to community living. Thus **Option 5** emerges as the clear choice.

About law being a prerequisite – meaning something that is required beforehand - to the community, the need for law came after man started living in community. When man roamed the earth dressed only in a leaf and spoke no language, he needed none of the institutions of the community such as law, education, marriage, judiciary, trade unions and so on. So law cannot be a prerequisite to the community; it was in fact the reverse that was true.

We shall doubly ensure that we are on the right track when we choose Option 5. What is the meaning of 'exchanged benefits and beliefs'? Can beliefs be exchanged? Suppose A is a Christian and B is a Muslim. Can you imagine that they exchange beliefs and thereafter B becomes a Christian and A a Muslim? Can you exchange your belief that you are a hunk with someone who is not? Exchange of beliefs is not possible. All one can do is that one can believe, that is, if you pay taxes, the state will give you protection and water supply and electric power and so on. The state gives these benefits with the belief that the citizens will pay for them. There has to be reciprocation between the state and the citizens.

Answer 7

The word **typically** has to be noted. It means *normally* or *characteristically*. Imagine that you are attending your first day at college. You have worn jeans to college. You are told that since you are not aware of the unwritten code, your seniors will not take you to task for this, but from tomorrow onwards you must remember that *typically* the freshman has to be in formals only. This means that whatever you have done now, is *but* typical or *not* typical.

There are two essential points being made in the sentence: (A) An investigation can occasionally yield new facts (B) but typically new facts emerge out of a search in a definite direction. This means that (B) is typical whereas (A) is not and therefore (A) is not a result of a search in a definite direction. All we have to do now is to ascertain which among the options qualifies for being *without a definite direction*:

Option 1: *timely.* What is the meaning of timely? Something that is done in time is timely. This means that someone tells someone else to do something by such and such time and the other fellow completes the work timely. There is a chap who issues directions about when should the work be done. He guides. This cannot qualify as being without a definite direction.

Option 2: *unguided*. What does a guide do? He gives a definite direction. Therefore unguided means without direction. The clear choice is **unguided** that is **Option 2**.

Option 3: *consistent*. If what you have done is consistent with someone's wishes, then there is a person who issues directions with which your actions have to be consistent.

Option 4: *uncomplicated*. Imagine that you are to meet your friend at a spot that you have not seen before. He gives you directions. You act accordingly. You reach the spot without any difficulty or complications. If something is uncomplicated it means that there are directions on how to do it and you have followed these directions thereby finding the task uncomplicated.

Option 5: *subjective. Subjective* means *biased* or *individualized*. Imagine that you are out to buy a house. You see a nice cottage with a 'For Sale' sign and meet the owner. He quotes price A whereas you quote price B, which is much lower. Whether the offer of either party is reasonable can be said only after knowing the fair market price from parties not interested in the transaction but knowledgeable in the line. This is because you want to pay the least possible and he wants the most possible and therefore the price quotated by each will be *guided* by this self-interest. Clearly, something subjective cannot be unguided.

Answer 8

Let us go from option to option.

Option 1: If this were true then the word in the first blank would be *quixotic*. The word *quixotic* comes from the famous fictitious character Don Quixote who was eccentric. The question is, can any eccentric gesture neutralize any resentment at all? If you make faces at someone, the chances are that if he has any resentment towards you, then the resentment will only *increase*. This is why this option will not do.

Option 2: If this were true then the word in the first blank would be *enigmatic*. The word *enigmatic* comes from the word *enigma* that means a *mystery*. If someone were to make an enigmatic gesture, it would be very difficult to understand what the gesture means and therefore it is highly likely that an enigmatic gesture would only **increase** misunderstanding and resentment. For that reason this option will not do.

Option 3: If this were true then the word in the first blank would be *propitiatory*. The word *propitiatory* has the prefix PRO- (that means *favouring*) and means *appeasing*. An appeasing gesture can certainly neutralize resentment. This option can do well. What is more, if someone, from any strata of society, were *involved* (meaning *associated* or *connected with*) with those in power and wealth, it is likely to cause resentment among one's peer groups (or, people of similar status). We shall, however look at the others and see whether any other option is close.

Option 4: If this were true then the word in the first blank would be *salutary*. The word *salutary* comes from the word *salute*, which is a gesture of greeting and thus means *beneficial* or *valuable* or *timely*. A gesture of comradeship could well be salutary. We would then, do well to look at the word in the second blank. Winckelmann was one among 18th century scholars who lived by cultivating those in power. Here the meaning of the word *lived* is *earned a living*. The meaning of *cultivate* here is to seek *friendship* or to *curry favour*. The meaning of the word *question* here, is to *challenge* or *raise doubts about*. If a fellow is currying favour with the high and mighty in order to bring home the bacon for self, wife and children, how can he dare to question those mighty people? He would have to starve if he did that. This option will not work.

Option 5: If this were true then the word in the first blank would be *unfeigned*. The word *unfeigned* comes from the verb *feign* that means to *pretend*. If a schoolboy does not want to go to school, he can *feign* a stomachache. He can double up writhing in fake pain. His mother will then ask him to lie down for a while. If a gesture were feigned, scholars – whether from the 18th century or the 21st century- will be able to make out that the fellow making the gesture is pretending. Thus the gesture is very likely to be *unfeigned* if made by a scholar to his fellow-scholars. The question then is: can the words *sympathy for* do in the second blank? Who is likely to have sympathy for whom? Is the servant who is cleaning a mountain of dirty dishes after a seven-course dinner likely to have sympathy for his employer? Or is the reverse more likely where the employer gives his raincoat to the servant who has been drenched because he has no rainwear? If at all, it is the high and mighty that are likelier to have sympathy for the scholar who makes a living by currying favour with them. Quite clearly, *sympathy for* will not do in the second blank and therefore this option is not workable.

Option 3 will thus be the correct choice.

Answer 9

The correct answer can emerge only from logic.

Historians are those who write history and literary critics are those who evaluate the quality of literature. Let us understand what is the difference between history and literature. Old facts are history. Fiction constitutes literature. But at the same time one must remember that all fiction is not literature. If a man has been having an extra-marital affair on the sly and tells his wife some fictitious story about how much work there is at the office, his story is fiction but not literature.

Let us understand what the words *'characterization of historical analysis as a form of fiction'* mean. If one were to suggest a particular tablet as a remedy to cough and then, on being told that the patient is a child who would not be able to swallow a tablet, he suggests a cough syrup saying that the syrup is a form of the remedy, what he means is that the syrup is only a form in which the remedy appears. These words would then seem to mean that someone is trying to pass off a proposition that historical analysis is only a form of fiction. When something is not likely to be received, then it may not be received:

(a) quietly (there may be protest), or

(b) enthusiastically (the welcome may be cold) or

(c) passively (there may be violent reaction) and so on.

Except for the word *contentiously* (that means *with a dispute*), the first word in all other options is eligible for the first blank.

The matter then, will have to be seen from the viewpoint of the second blank. The eligible words in the second blank, from option 1 to 5 (in that order) are *significant*, *shifting*, *unusual*, *distinct*, and *realistic*. It must be remembered that whichever of these five words is correct must relate to both history and fiction. Straightaway, therefore, *realistic* should be struck off. *Realistic* is something that *appears real*. Fiction may be realistic; a man may want his wife to pay for his liquor from her income and may invent some story about his wanting to pay for the treatment of a poor colleague's son in pain. The wife may indeed give the money seeing that her husband is in tears while relating the harrowing tale of the *suffering* boy which he has made sound very realistic (or, *seemingly real*). History however, is real not realistic. Shifting means that which changes places. When some people shift house, they go to another house. Fiction cannot change places with history (or, in other words, facts). *Shifting* will not do for the second blank. The word *significant* will not do either, because it is not necessary that all fiction is *significant*. For example, a poor excuse may be fiction not significant. Then about the word *unusual*, it means *that which is away from a set pattern* or *order*. Something that is unusual cannot conform to an order of experience. Therefore *unusual* will not do either. The only choice is the word *distinct*, which should do very well because, history, as we have seen, is about facts and fiction is not about facts and the two are about two *different* or **distinct** things. Thus **Option 4** is to be marked as correct.

Answer 10

It has been our endeavour to give you, dear reader, the very best. This is because you deserve the very best. The question is: why is this the best? This is the best because we have been giving you the meanings of words and their nuances in not just one-liner contexts; but in *situational contexts* so that you understand their full import and your retention of their meanings is permanent.

Let us understand what the word *axiom* means. An axiom is a generally an accepted principle or rule that requires no proof. Let us see some illustrations of axioms so that the meaning of the word goes home once and for all:

Axiom (I) The product of two positive numbers is invariably positive

Axiom (II) No sentence can be true and false at the same time

Axiom (III) The whole is greater than any of its parts

If it is axiomatic that many philosophers use scientific concepts as the foundations for their speculations (meaning theories), it means that many philosophers rely on science. It also means that science has some say in matters of philosophy and thus science has influence on philosophy. If someone relies on other, there cannot be distrust between the two. Therefore Option 1 will get eliminated on that account alone.

When you are documenting something, what are you trying to do? You are keeping records. Why? To be used later on. What for? To prove or disprove something. We are told that it is axiomatic that many philosophers rely on science. What would you call an attempt to prove something that requires no proof? Such an attempt would be *unnecessary* or *superfluous*. Such an attempt cannot be *inappropriate* (or *unsuitable*). If it is horribly hot, a sweater is not necessary. Then in the sweltering heat whether a red sweater will be suitable with the beige trousers is not to be debated at all. When proving something is not necessary at all, then trying to prove it cannot be *elementary*, or *difficult* or *impossible*.

People have accepted axioms as truth. Any attempt to prove them will be superfluous. Hence **Option 2** will do very well.

Sentence Completion Practice Set 2

This question includes sentences that have one or two blanks, each blank indicating that a word has been omitted. Beneath each sentence are five words or sets of words. Choose the word or set of words for each blank that best fits the meaning of the sentence as a whole.

Question 1

Her _____ should not be confused with miserliness: as long as I have known her, she has always been willing to assist those who are in need.

(1) intemperance (2) intolerance (3) apprehension (4) diffidence (5) frugality

Question 2

Physicists rejected the innovative experimental technique because, although it ______ some problems, it also produced new ______.

(1) clarified.. data (2) eased.. interpretations (3) resolved.. complications
(4) caused .. hypothesis (5) revealed .. inconsistencies

Question 3

The spellings of many Old English words have been _____ in the living language, although their pronunciations have changed.

(1) preserved (2) shortened (3) pre-empted (4) revised (5) improved

Question 4

Social tensions among adult factions can be _____ by politics, but adolescents and children have no such _____ for resolving their conflicts with the exclusive world of adults.

(1) intensified .. attitude (2) complicated .. relief (3) frustrated .. justification

(4) adjusted .. mechanism (5) revealed .. opportunity

Question 5

Kalama maintains that an infant's reactions to its first stressful experiences are part of a natural process of development, not harbingers of childhood unhappiness or _____ signs of adolescent anxiety.

(1) prophetic (2) normal (3) monotonous (4) virtual (5) typical

Question 6

During the 1960's, assessment of the family shifted remarkably, from general endorsement of it as a worthwhile, stable institution to widespread ___ it as an oppressive and bankrupt one whose _____ was both imminent and welcome.

(1) flight from .. restitution (2) fascination with .. corruption (3) rejection of .. vogue

(4) censure of .. dissolution (5) relinquishment of .. ascent

Question 7

It comes as no surprise that societies have codes of behaviour; the character of the codes, on the other hand, can often be _______

(1) predictable (2) unexpected (3) admirable (4) explicit (5) confusing

Question 8

Far from viewing Jefferson as a sceptical but enlightened intellectual, historians of the 1960's portrayed him as ______ thinker, eager to fill the young with his political orthodoxy while censuring ideas he did not like.

(1) an adventurous (2) a doctrinaire (3) an eclectic (4) a judicious
(5) a cynical

Question 9

In a _____ society that worships efficiency, it is difficult for a sensitive and idealistic person to make the kinds of _____ decisions that alone spell success as it is defined by such a society.

(1) bureaucratic .. edifying (2) pragmatic .. hardheaded (3) rational .. well-intentioned

(4) competitive .. even headed (5) modern .. dysfunctional

Answer 1

This is a question of logic to a significant extent. The sentence says that something should not be confused with someone's miserliness. When can one get confused between two things or people? When they are strikingly similar. If they are dissimilar, there can be no confusion. One can get confused between two identical twin brothers but not between twin brother and sister. The word in the blank should therefore be a synonym for miserliness.

Miserliness can reasonably be found in a miser. A miser is one who uses things sparingly. *Intemperance* is *lack of control* or moderation, particularly in the context of consuming alcohol. Intemperance is therefore about using too much without restraint and would not qualify as being synonymous with miserliness. *Intolerance* is not being able to tolerate behaviour or remarks. It has nothing to do with using things – whether sparingly or otherwise - and hence would not do as a synonym for miserliness.

The word *apprehension* has diverse meanings. From the following situational usages, it will become clear that *apprehension* has nothing to do with use of anything and therefore it will not do:

- If someone about to sit for an examination has *apprehensions* about whether he would be able to clear it, he is *afraid* or *nervous* or *diffident*.
- If the police have succeeded in the *apprehension* of the suspects who have long been evading arrest, they have succeeded in *arresting* them.
- If a problem lies outside my *apprehension*, it is not within my *capability to understand* it.

As we have seen above, one of the meanings of apprehension is *diffidence* therefore since apprehension is ineligible to be in the first blank, so is diffidence. This means Options 3 and 4 are not to be considered at all.

This means that Option 5 is to be marked as correct, not because it is the only one left but because *frugality* is the tendency to make sparing use of resources.

Answer 2

This is almost entirely about logic too.

When does one reject something? One rejects something when it is not acceptable. The word in the second blank should be what the innovative techniques produced and yet was not acceptable. Can new data be unacceptable to physicists? Unless there is a problem with the data, there is no point in rejecting data. Data is something that you gather during the course of observation. Physics is a science based on observation. It cannot be averse to data, more particularly to new data. Physicists would on the contrary welcome new interpretations, and new hypothesis, since both would throw new light on existing theories or rules. This means that we must to look only at Options 3 and 5.

If it were Option 3, physicists would welcome techniques that resolved problems but if new problems or complications arose, they would have adequate reason to reject such techniques.

If it were Option 5 then techniques that *revealed* problems rather than provided solutions, would be rejected right away; then the word *although* would become unnecessary. Then physicists would reject new techniques *because* they revealed problems. If something has been rejected *although* it has done something to problems, then whatever it has done to problems is in the direction of solving or reducing them. Then the word in the first blank should definitely be *resolved* and not *revealed*.

Thus Option 3 is to be marked as correct.

Answer 3

The word *although* means *notwithstanding the fact that* or *despite the fact that*. The word *although* is used in the context of a development or proposition that is opposite to something that was earlier such as in the following illustrations:

- These mangoes have gone bad *although* one cannot see any significant change in their texture.
- *Although* the doctors tried very hard, they could not save the patient.

The word in the blank is, therefore, something that is opposite to *changed*. Nothing other than *preserved* will work for an opposite to *changed*. Hence Option 1.

Answer 4

This is a matter of logic as well once we are able to spot the fact that the word ir the first blank is something that adolescents and children do for resolving their conflicts with adults. Let us see which of the options will work. Let us go from option to option.

Option 1: If this were right then the sentence would read as follows: **Social tensions among adult factions can be *intensified* by politics, but adolescents and children have no such *attitude* for resolving their conflicts with the exclusive world of adults.** Do we not know the meaning of the word *intensified* that means *increased* or *aggravated*? Imagine that two brothers have been fighting about sharing the family assets. Imagine that one of the brothers gets into a fit of rage and slaps the other. The other chap retaliates by slapping even harder. The conflict between them gets intensified. Can a conflict ever get resolved if it is intensified? This option will not work.

Option 2: If this were right then the sentence would read as follows: **Social tensions among adult factions can be *complicated* by politics, but adolescents and children have no such *relief* for resolving their conflicts with the exclusive world of adults.** Can any conflict get resolved if it gets *complicated*? This option will not do either.

Option 3: If this were right then the sentence would read as follows: **Social tensions among adult factions can be *frustrated* by politics, but adolescents and children have no such *justification* for resolving their conflicts with the exclusive world of adults.** This would mean that frustration is a justifiable means of resolving conflicts.

Before finding our whether frustration can ever be a justifiable means of resolving conflicts, let us understand the different shades of meaning of the word *frustrate*.

- When you *frustrate* someone who is trying to improve his marks at the school examinations, you dishearten him.
- When you *frustrate* someone who is trying to jump the queue for tickets at the cinema, you obstruct him.

Can disheartening someone or obstructing something, ever be a means of resolving conflicts? Conflicts have to be resolved through negotiations, not through obstructions and disheartenments; on the contrary, these may intensify conflicts. This option will not do either.

Option 4: If this were right then the sentence would read as follows: **Social tensions among adult factions can be *adjusted* by politics, but adolescents and children have no such *mechanism* for resolving their conflicts with the exclusive world of adults.** Let us understand the different shades of the meaning of the wor *adjust* from the following situational usages:

- When you *adjust* the schedule of the vacation that you have been planning, keeping in mind that your brother is due to be back shortly from UK to spend a few days with you, you plan it in such a way that there is no conflict between the schedule of your outing and your brother's arrival.
- When your bank writes to you to *adjust* your loan account, it means that they want you to pay the amount overdue so that there is no conflict between the terms of the loan and your account position.

Clearly, conflicts can be resolved if one makes adjustments. The next question is: whether adjustment can be a mechanism for resolving conflicts? The answer is: if at all a conflict is to be resolved, meaning an acceptable settlement is to be reached, then any of the following can happen:

(a) One party to the conflict withdraws his contention saying that he does not now want what he has been agitating about; this even both parties in the conflict may possibly do and part as friends

(b) One party to the conflict decides to accept a position that is less than what it has been contending for.

(c) The other party also decides to accept a position that is less than what it has been contending for.

In all the above three situations, adjustment serves as a mechanism for resolving conflicts. Therefore Option 4 will do very well.

By now, it must have become clear that the correct choice of word for the first blank can only be a manner of resolving conflicts. Nothing else. If social tensions are *revealed* they only come to light. Merely revealation of social conflicts does not mean they are resolved. This is why Option 5 will not do.

Answer 5

Kalama, whoever he or she may be, maintains (meaning *says*) something about an infant's reactions while the infant is still an infant. This is clear from the usage of the present tense in the words '... first stressful experiences are part of...'. Secondly when Kalama says that the first stressful experiences are '...not harbingers of childhood unhappiness or ____ signs of adolescent anxiety' Kalama wants you to pick a word that is the synonym of harbingers. This is because when the teacher says that if he finds John playing practical jokes or doing any ___ while the class is in progress, he will punish him, what the teacher means to put in the blank is the word *mischief*, which in turn is a synonym for practical jokes.

With the above clarification, let us go from option to option:

Option 1: *prophetic*. If this option were correct, then the sentence would run as follows:

Kalama maintains that an infant's reactions to its first stressful experiences are part of a natural process of development, not harbingers of childhood unhappiness or *prophetic* signs of adolescent anxiety.

The word *harbinger* means a forerunner. If dark clouds are harbingers of rain, it means that the dark clouds announce approaching rain. If pimples on the face are harbingers of adolescence, it means that the body sends pimples as an advance party to announce that adulthood is coming. What a harbinger does is inform about the occurrence of something before it actually occurs. This is precisely what the word *prophetic* means. It tells about something that is likely to occur in the future. **Option 1** would seem to fit like a glove for two reasons: (1) the word in the blank is synonymous to the word harbingers and (2) the child remains a child.

Option 2 to 5: If these options were correct, that is if you were to put any of the words *normal*, *monotonous*, *virtual* or *typical* in the blank, it would mean – for example – that the first stressful signs of childhood unhappiness are *normal* signs of adolescent anxiety, this would mean that what the *child* is feeling are the *normal* signs of *adolescent* anxiety. This would be stupid. The word *virtual* in the blank would mean *more or less*. This again would be a self-contradiction because if a child can feel *any* normal signs then the only normal signs that he can feel are those related to childhood phenomena. The child cannot feel normal signs associated with adolescence. One can reasonably expect a child to sing in a girlish voice. One cannot expect the child to sing in a baritone voice that will crack the windowpanes. This, one can reasonably expect only when the child has grown up. All four options from 2 to 5 will not work for reasons of logic.

Answer 6

Let us understand some words here, so that we kill two birds with a stone whereby we:

- understand the meanings of words from not just contextual usage but situational usage as well that would ensure that we retain the meanings of words in our personal lexicon forever
- reach the right answer through reasoning and crosscheck our choice in the bargain

The word *restitution* has the prefix *RE-* that means *back* and comes from the French verb *STATUTERE* that means *to establish*. *Restitution* would then mean *establishing back*. Thus if the government were to take possession of a farmer's land for making a railway line through it and the court – on hearing the farmer – orders *restitution* of the land to the farmer, it means that the land has to be *established back* or *returned* to the farmer.

The word *vogue* means fashion or popular acceptance. If denims were in vogue in the 1970s, it means denims were considered very fashionable in the 1970s.

Dissolution means many things depending upon the context:

- If the process of making tea involves *dissolution* of sugar in water, then it involves melting of sugar in the water and mixing with it.
- If the partners of a firm have decided to announce *dissolution* of the firm it means that the firm will *break up*.
- If the *dissolution* of the newly rich is creating a general antipathy towards them, then the newly rich could be *engaged in debauchery or immoderation* and so on.

The word *ascent* means *climb*.

Having seen the meanings of some words that we may not have been familiar with, let us see how we shall tackle this question from the point of view of logic.

What does something do when it is *shifts*? It changes its initial position, place or preference and so on. The word *shift* implies change.

The word *endorsement* – with which the word shift is associated in this sentence – comes from the word DORSUM that means *the back of something.* Imagine that I owe you a sum of money and give you a cheque drawn in your name for that sum. Now imagine that you owe the same sum of money to your friend. You wish to pay the debt to your friend. You then *endorse* the cheque by writing the name of your friend on the back of the cheque. This *endorsement* is your instruction to the bank to pay the amount of the cheque to your friend. If a popular sportsman *endorses* a brand of sports shoes, he declares that he *approves* of the particular brand.

The word *change* can be used to describe a wide variety of changes such as:

- A change from a higher state to a lower state of the same thing; if a gambler has changed the frequency of his visits to the gambling den, he has come to a reduced level of involvement with gambling
- A change from a lower state to a higher state of the same thing; someone may change the usual level of his food intake from eating sparingly to walloping as if there is no tomorrow
- A change from one state to another altogether; an alcoholic may change to a teetotaller

In the present case, there is a change from a general endorsement to something widespread. There is no difference between *general* and *widespread.* If someone says that the law in this country is generally obeyed, then it can be reasonably inferred that what he means is that there is widespread compliance with law. One cannot say that the law is generally complied with if only he and his next-door neighbour comply with the law. Since the shift is from general endorsement to something widespread, the shift is not from one state of something to another state of the same thing. It is a complete change. Therefore the word in blank after the word *widespread* will have to be antonymous to *endorsement* (or *approval*). The word *censure* is the best choice and hence Option 4 is to be marked as correct.

Let us see why the other options will not do.

Option 1: flight from .. restitution. If one does not approve of some course of action, he may very well fly from it. If a dictator is ruling a country and people do not approve of his rule, then the choice is between staying and opposing his actions and being harassed or in fleeing from the country. As such, there is nothing to prevent the words *'flight from'* from taking the first blank. What seals the matter is that *restitution* – or in other words *return* - of something oppressive and bankrupt, can never be welcome. This is why restitution will not do in the second blank.

Option 2: *fascination with .. corruption.* In this case neither is fascination an opposite of endorsement nor can corruption of something bankrupt and oppressive, ever be welcome.

Option 3: *rejection of .. vogue.* In this case *rejection* may fit in the first blank but how can something oppressive and bankrupt be in *vogue* (or having *popular acceptance*)?

Option 4: *relinquishment of .. ascent.* The word *relinquishment* comes from the verb relinquish that means to *let go* and thus means *letting go.* The meaning of this word will emerge in the following situation:

- My colleague and I were being considered for promotion. While the process of appraisal was on, he developed heart problems. He decided on *relinquishment* of his right to be considered for promotion because he thought the added responsibility might mean enhanced stress.

The word *relinquishment* cannot be an antonym for *endorsement.* In the above illustration, we saw that my colleague's relinquishment was a matter of his own will. In the world endorsement, Approval implied. When you endorse, you approve. The opposite of this can only be rejection or some action showing disapproval. This is why Option 4 will not do either.

Answer 7

Suppose I were to tell you something as follows: "My brother is an exceptionally good singer; on the other hand I..." and then I would stop in mid-sentence to pick up the phone. With what words would anyone reasonably expect that I would have finished the sentence? I would have said that: "...on the other hand, I am a hopeless singer." This means that whatever would be said after the words *'on the other hand'* must be opposite to whatever was said before the words *'on the other hand'*.

Let us see what the sentence tries to say before he comes to the words *on the other hand*. It says that something comes as **no surprise**. The blank is after the words *on the other hand*. Therefore the word in the blank should be opposite in meaning to the words *no surprise*.

Let us see which option would fit. Suppose Option 1, that is, the word *predictable* were correct. If something is predictable, there can be no surprise. If a chap has been swaying after drinking too much, then it can be predicted that he will soon fall into the gutter. When he actually does fall into the gutter, it is no surprise. This is because it was only expected. Option 1 will not do.

Option 2, that is, the word unexpected is the precise opposite of expected. Thus **Option 2** will do very well. The word *admirable* cannot be antonymous to *'no surprise'* because one can reasonably admire people who do things that cause surprise and wonder. You admire a magician, for instance, when he pulls a rabbit out of his hat. Similarly anything *explicit* – or *clear in expression* - cannot be antonymous to expected. If a schoolmaster tells his class that those who will not be able to recite the table of nineteen on the next day must expect punishment, anyone who is not able to recite these tables should come prepared to receive punishment.

Anything *confusing*, cannot cause surprise. It is necessary to know, what is happening, before one is surprised. In a state of confusion one does not know what is happening.

Answer 8

There are some important things that have been mentioned about Jefferson in the sentence:

- Jefferson, whoever he may have been, was **not** perceived as an **enlightened** (or *civilised* or *cultivated*) person
- Jefferson, was **not** perceived as **sceptical** (or *suspicious* or *cynical*) person
- Jefferson was eager to fill the young people with his political orthodoxy (this can be reasonably be done only by teaching; filling anyone with one's ideas is not the same thing as filling mattresses with cotton)
- He censured things that he did not like

With this in mind, let us see which option will work:

Option 1, if correct, would mean that Jefferson was *adventurous*. If a young fellow does not like to get up from the couch on which he likes to sit and watch television and gets irritated when someone asks him to get up and play with the children next door, can he ever be adventurous? Being Adventure means a having a lust for new things. Adventure is possible only for those enthusiastically looking forward to newer challenges. Option 1 cannot do because Jefferson censured ideas he did not like, just as the young fellow did not like the idea of playing with other children, although it was a good idea.

Option 2, if true would mean that Jefferson was a doctrinaire. The word *doctrinaire* comes from the word *doctor*, which is a term used for referring to a person of exceptional learning. This is why a doctorate degree is awarded to those who have mastered the subject of their specialisation, even if the subject is Medieval History. This is why a doctrinaire person is likely to be a pedantic theorist. A doctrinaire person is also likely to be dogmatic about his work. It is likely that he considers himself as an authority on the subject and can brook (or *tolerate*) no discussion. We are told that Jefferson censured things that he did not like. This is not what enlightened persons do. One can hope to become enlightened only if one can at least listen to the other person's viewpoint. Thus two things become clear: Old Jeff was teaching (meaning he was a *doctrinaire*) and was not ready to listen to any contrary opinion (meaning that he was dogmatic and therefore *doctrinaire*, not enlightened). **Option 2** will do very well.

The word *eclectic* at Option 3 means a teacher with interest in a wide range of topics. Such a person cannot be *doctrinaire* (or *dogmatic*). If you have an interest in a wide range of topics, you cannot be reasonably expected to master a wide range of topics. *A doctrinaire person cannot look beyond his own subject or beliefs.* A *judicious* person is one who is fair, just and enlightened. We are told that Old Jeff was not enlightened. A *cynical* person is one who is sceptical. We are told that Old Jeff was not sceptical. This means that Options 3, 4 and 5 will not do at all.

Answer 9

The sentence in the question tells us these few things:

- The society in the sentence is of the type that worships efficiency
- The kinds of decisions that have to be taken are difficult for sensitive and idealistic persons

With these things in mind, let us see which option will work:

Option 1: *bureaucratic .. edifying*. The word *bureaucracy* means a government run by bureaucrats – or in other words, *high government officials* or *the civil servents*. That the word *bureaucracy* has also come to mean red tape, does not necessarily mean that the bureaucracy does not worship efficiency. However, there can be a bureaucratic organisation or system. But there cannot be a bureaucratic society. You cannot have a majority of people in the society who are high government officials, can you? This is why Option 1 will not do.

Option 2: *pragmatic .. hardheaded*. The word *pragmatic* means *practical*. Let us see the difference between a *pragmatic* person and a *sensitive* person through this illustration.

Imagine that a person is in his car waiting for the traffic lights to turn green. Imagine that a young urchin comes and asks him whether he would like to buy the brown bread that he has baked. The person takes one look at the bread and finds that it does not meet the criteria of either brown or bread. He then says, *no thank you*. The urchin persists and says that he has not had food for three days and was counting on him to buy the bread so that he could buy some food for himself. The *pragmatic* person in such a situation would first of all tell the fellow to try elsewhere but if the urchin persists for too long, he would advise the urchin to consider eating the bread that he already has. The *sensitive* (as different from *sensible*) person (who, for some strange reason, assigns the function of thinking to his heart rather than to the brain) would buy the bread and not flinch when the urchin does not care to return the change. The pragmatic person can take hardheaded decisions. Since he thinks with his head and not with his heart, he is very likely to be effective. Thus Option 2 will do very well.

Option 3: *rational .. well-intentioned*. A rational person is a *reasonable* or sensible person. He thinks with his brain. The word *reasonable* may work in the first blank. However, going back to above illustration of the sensitive person buying some so-called bread from the urchin, a well-intentioned person would not buy the bread either, because this would make the urchin try this trick on other gullible people and ultimately make him a trickster and fraudster. This is why *well-intentioned* will not do for the second blank.

As regards Option 4, **there is no such thing as even headed**. The word *even* can have the following meanings:

- If one has an *even* chance of getting admission to a prestigious school, he has an *equal* chance
- If a snake finds it difficult to glide on an *even* surface, he cannot move on a *smooth* surface
- If someone is *even*-tempered, he is *cool* and *composed*
- If someone has an *even* number of coins, then the number of coins he has is divisible by two

One can be level headed (or *practical*) or clear-headed (or *clear thinking*) or muddle-headed (meaning *idiotic*). This is why Option 4 will not do either. The word *dysfunctional* comprises of the prefix DYS- (that means *away from*) and *function* (that means *work*) and means *not working*. Can a decision that does not work ever spell success? Option 5 will not do for this reason.

Sentence Completion Practice Set 3

This question includes sentences that have one or two blanks, each blank indicating that a word has been omitted. Beneath each sentence are five words or sets of words. Choose the word or set of words for each blank that *best* fits the meaning of the sentence as a whole.

Question 1

The _______ of mass literacy coincided with the first industrial revolution; in turn, the new expansion in literacy, as well as cheaper printing, helped to nurture the _______ of popular literature.

(1) building .. mistrust (2) reappearance .. display (3) receipt .. source

(4) selection .. influence (5) emergence .. rise

Question 2

The sheer diversity of tropical plants represents a seemingly _______ source of raw materials, of which only a few have been utilised.

(1) exploited (2) quantifiable (3) controversial

(4) inexhaustible (5) remarkable

Question 3

During a period of protracted illness, Marian became infirm, _______ both the strength to work and many of the specific skills she once possessed.

(1) regaining (2) denying (3) pursuing

(4) insuring (5) losing

Question 4

Unfortunately, his damaging attacks on the ramifications of the economic policy have been _______ by his wholehearted acceptance of that policy's underlying assumptions.

(1) supplemented (2) undermined (3) wasted

(4) diverted (5) redeemed

Question 5

In parts of the Arctic, the land grades into the land-fast ice so _______ that you can walk off the coast and not know you are over the hidden sea.

(1) permanently (2) imperceptibly (3) irregularly

(4) precariously (5) slightly

Question 6

In the machine like world of classical physics, the human intellect appears _______, since the mechanical nature of classical physics does not _______ creative reasoning, the very ability that had made the formulation of classical principles possible.

(1) anomalous .. allow for (2) abstract .. speak to (3) anachronistic .. deny

(4) enduring .. value (5) contradictory .. exclude

Question 7

It is puzzling to observe that Jones's novel has recently been criticized for its _______ structure, since commentators have traditionally argued that its most obvious _______ is its relentlessly rigid, indeed schematic framework.

(1) attention to .. preoccupation (2) speculation about .. characteristic (3) parody of .. disparity

(4) violation of .. contradiction (5) lack of .. flaw

Question 8

To have true disciples, a thinker must not be too _________: any effective intellectual leader depends on the ability of other people to _________ thought process that did not originate with them.

(1) popular .. dismiss (2) methodical .. interpret (3) idiosyncratic .. re-enact

(4) self-confident .. revitalize (5) pragmatic .. discourage

Question 9

For some time now, _______ has been presumed not to exist: the cynical conviction that everybody has an angle is considered wisdom.

(1) rationality (2) flexibility (3) diffidence

(4) disinterestedness (5) insincerity

Answer 1

The question is: what happens when you nurture something? It **grows**. The seed that you nurture rises above the ground and becomes a plant and then grows taller day by day till it comes to its full height. When you nurture an ill feeling against someone who has been scoring better marks than you at examinations, then the ill feeling grows.

Literature can be either popular or unpopular. Only popular literature will sell just as anyone planning to make a living by selling sandwiches can hope to do so if his sandwiches are tasty (and therefore popular) among his customers. If the sandwiches are yuck (and therefore unpopular), the seller will starve. Popular literature is that which more and more people want to read.

Literature is the collective noun for material published with the intention that people should read it. This means that literature can be reasonably expected to be in printed form. If printing becomes cheaper, books will become cheaper. There may some people who want to read books but can not afford them. If the prices of books reduce, a whole lot of people may afford to read. Cheaper printing can only have beneficial effect on popular literature. With cheaper printing, popular literature can only rise. This is why only **Option 5** will do because the word *rise* alone can fit into the second blank.

As regards the other options, if something is *mistrusted* it cannot become popular; Option 1 will not do for this reason. The *display* of literature is possible by putting books in public view. This is possible even if popular literature is expensive; it is not necessary that only inexpensive books can be displayed. It is for this reason that Option 2 will not do. The source of literature is the author community, not cheap printing. If authors do not write, what can one print even if printing were to be free of cost? Thus Option 3 will not do either. The influence of popular literature is nurtured by the quality of the literature and not by cheap printing. This is why Option 4 will not work either.

Answer 2

Let us see which one of the options fits in:

Option 1: If this were true then the sentence would be as follows: **The sheer diversity of tropical plants represents a seemingly *exploited* source of raw materials, of which only a few have been utilised.** What is the meaning of the word *exploited*? If some storekeeper *exploits* his staff, he makes them work for long working hours without paying additional wages. He uses every bit of their capacity to work. They get exhausted. If the source of raw materials has been exploited, there cannot be few that are utilised; on the contrary, there are few that are **not** utilised. Thus Option 1 will not do for this reason.

Option 2: If this were true, then the sentence would be as follows: **The sheer diversity of tropical plants represents a seemingly *quantifiable* source of raw materials, of which only a few have been utilised.** If something is quantifiable, it can be expressed as a quantity. If the number of children in a school who have passed the year-end examinations with distinction is quantifiable, it is because you can count and tell exactly how many children have passed with distinction. This is because distinction is an absolute term: the school could set down what is distinction: for example 70% and above could be the norm for a distinction. However, if we were to quantify the number of brilliant children, this would be impossible merely because brilliant is a relative term. A teacher may think that many children in his class are brilliant whereas the headmaster may not go with that view. The word diversity means variety and is thus a relative term. It cannot be quantified. This is why Option 2 will not do.

Option 3: Raw materials are things that people need to make other things. If raw materials are *controversial* (in other words if there is a dispute about their applicability or quality or their effect on the quality of output), then people will **not use** such raw materials. However if anything can be controversial it can be the raw material itself, not its diversity. Something – say, fish – can have diversity if there is a wide variety of fish. If there are over ten thousand variety of fish, there can at best be a controversy on whether fish should be a source of food or otherwise, but there can be no controversy about the **diversity** of fish. This is why Option 3 will not work.

Option 4 will work because diversity can be *inexhaustible*. If something is inexhaustible, then whatever you utilise from this inexhaustible supply is will mean only a small quantity. What is small and what is large is again a matter of relativity. A sugar cube may seem an awesome structure to an ant while it may not even be visible to an elephant. Therefore when you say things like *small*, you are talking in relative terms and then the matter boils down to comparing, which is another way of saying that the matter pertains to ratios. In a ratio there is a numerator and a denominator. If what you have utilised is in the numerator, then the comparative value of how much you have utilised out of the total can be ascertained if the source is in the denominator. If something inexhaustible (or *endless*) is in the denominator, then the fraction will seem paltry. This is because the denominator is countless, whereas the numerator is small. This is why the words ***only a few*** can be used.

Suppose you meet someone at a party and find that he can recite the very best among poems without pausing for breath, you can say that his memory is *remarkable*. Now suppose that you meet another man at the party whose nose reminds you instantly of the story of Pinocchio, his nose is *remarkable*. Thus the word *remarkable* can have a positive connotation where it would mean *wonderful* and a negative connotation where it would mean *conspicuous* or *peculiar*. Either way, it is not something that *seems* one thing and *is* actually another. Someone can be *seemingly* bold but may scramble up the sofa if he sees a cockroach. The word *seemingly* therefore may mean something that is *deceptive*. If somebody has a small nose, then there is no way in which that nose can be *seemingly* outsize. This is why Option 5 will not work.

Answer 3

The word *protracted* means *long drawn*. Logically, when someone is ill for a long time, the likeliest after effect he would experience is loss of strength. Thus Options 1, 3 and 4 will get eliminated on the grounds that it defies logic to assume that someone will *regain* (or *get back*), *pursue* (or *run after*) or *insure* (or *protect*) strength in a protracted illness.

About Option 2, what can one deny? One can deny something that one does not want. A politician can deny having made some statement if he later on finds that there is a controversy about it. One can deny medicines if given forcibly. But one cannot deny skills or strength. This is simply because no one can give strength or skills forcibly.

This means that **losing** strength is what can happen logically as a result of a long-drawn illness and hence Option 5 is to be marked as correct.

Answer 4

Let us understand what the word *ramifications* means by observing its use in a situational context as under:

A great majority of senior citizens put their life's savings in government securities. Reducing the rate of interest on government securities would mean lower interest burden for the government, but one *ramification* of such a move on the income flows of senior citizens, would be that they would have to start looking for work in order to supplement their income.

The word *ramification* here means a *result* or *consequence*, generally one involving complications.

Somebody made some damaging remarks on the complications that would arise due to the economic policy and yet the same person wholeheartedly accepted the basis on which the policy was formed. This means his **earlier stand has become weak**. With this, let us see which option will work.

Option 1: *is supplemented.* The word *supplement* means different things as follows:

(A) A diet *supplement* is usually some food given in addition to the normal intake to add nutrients that are not there in the usual diet and to thus *end* a deficiency.

(B) If you are reading a *supplement* of a newspaper, you are reading – for example -a separate section attached to the newspaper in which the tourism infrastructure in a particular region may have been highlighted.

A supplement therefore adds to something so as to make it better. This means the 'damaging attacks' as mentioned in the statement, would gain strength. This is contrary to what has been given. Thus Option 1 will not do.

Option 2: *undermined.* What do you do when you mine something? You extract material out of it. When you undermine, you extract material from under something. So if one were to stand somewhere unaware that someone else is digging under the ground on which he is standing, what is likely to happen to the ground on which he is standing? It may become weak and may even cave in. *Undermine* means to *weaken*. This is exactly what has happened to the earlier stand of the person in the sentence. **Option 2** would do very well.

Option 3 would not do because the person's remarks would have been *wasted* only if no one had heard (or, for that matter, *read*) them. When someone makes remarks, he does this in any of the following ways:

A. He mutters them so that only he knows what he speaks

B. He writes remarks on a sheet of paper and reads them and then tears the paper to bits

C. He makes remarks while speaking to an audience

D. He writes remarks and these are read by other people; possibly these remarks are published

If the case was A or B above, then, since no one else had heard the remarks, the sentence in the question would not have arisen. The fact that there is an observation about his remarks means that the remarks were heard/read by other people. His remarks could go waste even if people did not take his remarks seriously about which there is no suggestion in the sentence. This means that the question of his remarks going waste would not arise. This is why Option 3 will not do.

As regards Option 4, it is logical to expect that only those persons or things that have the capacity to take a particular direction or path can be *diverted* (or *turned away* from something). A car can be diverted. So can a stream can be diverted. Remarks cannot turn right or left. This is why remarks cannot be diverted.

As regards Option 5, it is important to see the different shades of meaning of the word *redeemed* as seen from their following situational usages:

- If a person has pledged his insurance policy for taking a loan from a bank, he can *redeem* this policy (or *regain* it) once he repays the loan.
- A neighbour of mine very frequently quarrels with others. He is thus known for his bad temper. One day a child in our residential complex was hurt in an accident. The usually bad-tempered person rushed the child to the hospital and since his blood matched, he donated blood and saved the child's life. He *redeemed* himself or *compensated* for his bad temper.

The word *redeemed* in Option 5 would not do since we are told that the remarks were made weak and not made better or were compensated for.

Answer 5

There are some words that one would do well to know.

When the crew in an aircraft asks the passengers to *fasten* their seat belts,. the idea is to tie the seat belts so that the belt *holds* one securely. This is why *land-fast* ice means ice that *holds on* to land.

If there is ice on land and the sea is frozen, one can make out which is which only if there is a significant change in topography between the land and sea. If one walks in through a door when it is dark and falls flat, it is because one could not see the doorstep. But if one does not notice the doorstep when it is bright, one deserves to fall. The doorstep rises above the surface at the door as the entrance so that you *perceive* (or *notice*) where the outer surface ends and the inner floor starts.

If the land *grades* into the land-fast ice in such a manner that one can walk off the coast and not know you are over the hidden sea, it means that the *gradient* between the coast and the frozen sea is so gentle that you do not know where the coast has ended and where the sea has begun. This means that the change in gradient is so gradual as to be *imperceptible* (or *it cannot be easily noticed*). This is the reason why **Option 2** will do very well.

Land is land. Ice is frozen water. They cannot fuse *permanently*. The ice melts in summers. If there is a slight dip in the land and then there is a steep climb, such a gradient is an instance of an *irregular* gradient. If the gradient is *irregular* then it is all the more perceptible. A *precarious* gradient is one in which one wrong step sends one plummeting into the valley down below. One has to be blind to not to notice such a gradient. A *slight* pain when the doctor is injecting a drug is *still a perceptible pain*. Doctors tell children that there will be only *a slight* prick when the medicine is injected. Yet children wail. These are the reasons why Options, 1, 3, 4 and 5 will not do.

Answer 6

Let us understand a few words and their meanings, so that we can decide as to what should be the course of action that we should pursue in cracking this question:

- The volume of water expands when water is heated and contracts when it is cooled. However water expands instead of contracting when cooled or frozen from 0 to –4 degrees Celsius. This phenomenon is known as the *anomalous* expansion of water.
- Something that can be touched is physical; something that cannot be touched is *abstract*; for example, the mercy of God is abstract and so is intellectual brilliance.
- After World War II, television gained popularity. Many broadcasters predicted that the radio would fade away. To rely on sound, when visuals were available, seemed an *anachronism*. The prefix ANA- means *up*, *back*, *again* or *anew* and CHRONO in Latin means time. An *anachronism* is something or someone out of harmony with the times.
- If an athlete is capable of *enduring* a gruelling marathon, he has the *capacity to last* the entire duration of the race.

As may be seen from the above terms and their meanings that stand out from their contexts, all the first words in the Options 1, 3 and 4 seem to be candidates for the first blank. It is the second blank that will seal the matter.

If we consider Option 1, the question that arises is: Can something of a mechanical nature *allow for* (or *permit*) creative reasoning? What is *mechanical nature*? If you were to turn on the washing machine, is it ever possible that it will play your favourite melody on the accordion? Never. If you were to turn on the refrigerator will it ever make a hasty breakfast for you if you are getting late for office? A machine does what it is programmed to do: nothing more or nothing less. Reasoning is thinking. Quite clearly anything of mechanical nature will not allow for creative thinking. Thus **Option 1** is to be marked.

Options 2, 3 4, and 5 get eliminated on grounds of logic alone. Can Classical Physics stand on the dais and *speak* to an audience? Can this subject *deny*, for example, that it has overeaten? Can it *value* friendships or gold bracelets? Can it *exclude* singles from dance parties? It cannot do any of these.

Answer 7

See these two situations and ask yourself in which of the two would you criticise the dinner that your cook has made?

Situation A: The curry tastes great and so does the accompanying rice.

Situation B: The curry tastes yuck and the accompanying rice has singed (or *burnt slightly*).

Clearly, if there is any situation in which one would criticise, it is in Situation B where there is a defect. It is clear that the novel has been criticised and not Jones. There is no need to refer to Jones as *it*. It is then also clear that the novel cannot be criticised for something that it cannot do, or omit to do, or commit on its own. The defect has to be that of omission (by the author, of course) and not of commission (by the book), since the book can commit nothing. If, as in Option 1, Jones had paid attention to the structure of his novel, it would have been like the curry in Situation A. This is why Option 1 will not do. As regards speculation about structure, the word the *speculation* means *guessing* in the absence of certainty. Is it ever possible for a novel to *guess* what its structure is? Can a novel ever *speculate* on the stock market? The word *parody* means *lampooning* or *mimicry*. Can a novel ever *lampoon* a friend who has been slapped by a lady whom he had been teasing? Can a novel ever *violate* anything at all, let alone its own structure? Can one ever visualise a policeman stopping a novel for *violation* of traffic rules by riding a motorcycle without a helmet? This is why Options 2, 3, and 4 will not do.

As regards Option 5, the novel can surely be criticised for a *flaw* in its structure. This is because the *flaw* (or *defect*) is attributable to the author omitting something while designing its structure. Thus Option 5.

Answer 8

Let us understand a few things as follows:

- One can hope to become an effective intellectual leader only if what he says impresses people so deeply that they act according to his suggestions. This means that if I wish to become an intellectual leader, I must ensure that people do not dismiss my thought processes (although, as far as I am concerned, they can jolly well stuff the thought processes of others into their sandwiches and eat them).
- My thought processes originate in me and not with other people.
- Too much of anything is harmful and therefore, too much *popular*, too much *methodical*, too much *idiosyncratic* and so on, are very eligible for fitting in the first blank.

With this in mind, let us go from option to option and see which option will work for the second blank alone:

Option 1: If other people dismiss what one thinks, there is no way one can become either effective or a leader. He can only become the butt of their jokes. This is why Option 1 will not do.

Option 2: The question is: Who can *interpret*? Someone who *interprets* the presence of excess of a particular gas in the atmosphere as a sign of an impending earthquake, understands this phenomenon himself and tells it to others. If he does not understand, he talks through his hat. If someone wants to be an intellectual leader, he must interpret thought processes that originate either in him or in his own guru. His disciples must listen to him instead of each one going about interpreting thought processes that do not originate in him. Thus Option 2 will not do.

Option 3: The question is: What does the word *enact* mean? When you *enact* the Prohibition Act, for example, you pass a law that bans consumption of alcohol. When you *enact* a drama, you *represent* the scenes from that drama on the stage. When someone *enacts*, it is not necessary that he is doing something according to another's thought processes. The playwright could himself be the principal actor in the drama. When you *re-enact* a drama, you *reproduce* the drama that someone else wrote. Thus when you *re-enact* something, you *act according to the words of another person*. If someone wants to be an effective intellectual leader, others must act according to what he thinks (and not just hear him and go away stifling yawns all the way home). This is precisely what *re-enacting* someone else's thought processes means. Option 3 fits like a glove.

Option 4: What do you do when you *revitalize* something? When you *revitalize* the community science centre in your town, you *bring back life into it*. This means that it was either dead or dying and has come back to life because of your *initiative* (which is the quality of leaders). If your entry at a party *revitalizes* it, the party comes back to life with your arrival. People who had been discussing the heat and humidity for the past hour are now talking about classical music or abstractionist painting. If people can revitalize someone else's thoughts, the people become leaders themselves. They will no longer be disciples. Besides, can *people* ever be a leader (in the singular)? This is why Option 4 will not do. As regards Option 5, if people *discourage* someone from expressing his thought processes, that person cannot be an intellectual leader at all, let alone effective intellectual leader. For instance, he tells his disciples to observe a day's fast for cleansing the body and the disciples tell him to sit down and stop giving advice. Can such a person have any disciples at all? Option 5 will thus not do either.

Answer 9

Let us understand what the word *angle* means in this context.

If an elephant's corpse is found lying in the jungle but the ivory is untouched, someone who is in the business of ivory looks at the dead animal from his business *angle* and looks out for the first opportunity when he can cut the teeth of the animal and flee. The forest department views this from the *angle* of law, as an act of poaching and the attendant discredit that this could bring to them if the news spreads. The person in the luggage manufacturing business would see the corpse from the angle of a huge source of leather. The vultures look at the corpse from the *angle* of a feast that could last a fortnight. When everybody has an *angle* to something, it means that everyone has some or the other interest in that thing. This means that if everybody has an angle, what cannot exist is a state in which there is no interest; such a state is called **disinterestedness**. Thus Option 4 fits like a shot.

Chapter 9

Reading Comprehension

The competitive examination has no set syllabus. If the examiner decides to let you have a few passages and then some questions emanating from the passages, he is not bound to put in passages relating to any particular subject or subjects. The sky is the limit for him. And so it is for those of you who wish to take on such an examination. The ETS has set out in the Test Taking tips in the POWERPREP CD that the Reading comprehension Section measures your ability to read with understanding, insight, and discrimination and to analyse a written passage from several perspectives. They have also stated that passages are taken from the **humanities, social sciences, and natural sciences.** This is a fairly exhaustive syllabus to say the least. One should then be ready for anything.

The question then is: how much should you read before feeling confident about being able to meet the Reading Comprehension Section in the GRE head on? Ask yourself this: is it possible to say with any degree of confidence that what one has read will suffice insofar as the possible range of topics goes? Anyone saying that so much is enough is talking through his hat.

Then what is it that must be borne in mind for preparing for taking on the passages in the Reading Comprehension Section and the questions emanating there from?

While the range of topics is so diverse that none can predict that a particular topic will be covered, there is one fact that has to be seen here that is true of the GRE: most questions call for your opinion on the basis of the text of the passage. Quite frequently the questions tell you which line in the passage has the quoted text to which they are making reference. This is extremely helpful, to say the very least. This means that insofar as such questions go, reading the passage before reading the question would be futile even if you had the time, which you do not in any case.

What we shall see is a passage as under on the Humanities (which covers learning or literature concerned with the human culture) and see what kind of questions could we – you and I – supposing we were examiners can possibly ask the person to whom this passage and the questions emanating there from are to be administered.

The PASSAGE starts here: "I suppose that very few people know how Mrs Albert Forrester came to write *The Achilles Statue*; and since it has been acclaimed as one of the great novels of our time I cannot but think that a brief account of the circumstances that gave it birth must be of interest to all serious students of literature; and indeed, if, as the critics say, this is a book that will live, the following narrative, serving a better purpose than to divert an idle hour, may be regarded by the historians of the future as a curious footnote to the literary annals of our day.

Everyone of course remembers the success that attended the publication of *The Achilles Statue.* Month after month printers were kept busy printing, binders were kept busy binding, edition after edition; and the publisher, both in England and America, were hard put to it to fulfil the pressing orders of the booksellers. It was promptly translated into every European tongue and it has been recently announced that it will soon be possible to read it in Japanese and in Urdu. But it had previously appeared serially in magazines on both sides of the Atlantic and from the editors of these Mrs Albert Forrester's agent had wrung a sum that can only be described as thumping. A dramatization of the work was made, which ran for a season in New York, and there is little doubt that when the play is produced in London it will have an equal success. The film rights have been sold at a great price. Thought the amount that Mrs Albert Forrester is reputed (in literary circles) to have made is probably exaggerated, there can be no doubt that she will have earned enough money from this one book to save her for the rest of her life from any financial anxiety.

It is not often that a book meets with equal favour from the public and the critics, and the critics, and that she, of all persons, had (if I may so put it) squared the circle must have proved the more gratifying to Mrs Albert Forrester, since, though she had received the commendation of the critics in no grudging terms (and indeed had come to look upon it as her due), the public had always remained strangely insensible to her merit. Each work she published, a slender volume beautifully printed and bound in white buckram, was hailed as a masterpiece, always to the length of a column, and in the weekly reviews which you see only in the dusty library of a very long-established club even to the extent of a page; and all well-read persons read and praised it. But well-read persons apparently do not buy books, and she did not sell. It was indeed a scandal that so distinguished an author, with an imagination so delicate and a style so exquisite should remain neglected of the vulgar. In America she was almost completely unknown; and though Mr Carl van Vechten had written an article berating the public for its obtuseness, the public remained callous. Her agent, a warm admirer of her genius, had blackmailed an American publisher into taking two of her books by refusing, unless he did so, to let him have others (trashy novels doubtless) that he badly wanted, and they had been duly published. The reception they received from the press was flattering and showed that in America the best minds were sensitive to her talent; but when it came to the third book the American publisher (in the coarse way publishers have) told the agent that any money he had to spare he preferred to spend on synthetic gin." Here the passage ends, and here begins our desperation as to which question to ask the fellow who is taking the examination and why ask him such a question at all.

The possible objectives behind administering this passage in particular and a passage in general could be as follows:

- To find out whether our imaginary candidate belongs to the variety that would instead of cottoning on to the discussions about cotton, would order for a large peg of gin with lemon when the discussions at his office is about a gin that the management wishes to acquire so as to hedge against vagaries of supply and price of cotton
- To find out whether our imaginary candidate understands the meaning of phrases with contextual usage. For example, he is told that Percy was sitting in his drawers when the police barged in. Does our imaginary candidate visualise the man Percy sitting in the drawers of his office table or his dressing table or does he visualise Percy sitting in his underpants?
- To find out whether our imaginary candidate can discern from the passage whether Mrs. Albert Forrester was a successful author or the other thing?
- To find out whether our imaginary candidate can discern as to which one of the four given options was employed in the process of blackmailing of the American publisher that is being described in the passage
- To find out whether our imaginary candidate can figure out as to who is the author of *The Achilles Statue*?

  Now, let us see what kind of questions we would formulate and the options that we would devise so as to test the imaginary candidate.

Question 1

As seen in the passage, what would be the nearest meaning of the words "squared the circle"? Options: (1) Settled the outstanding differences (2) Did something impossible (3) Drew a square outside a circle (4) Made some remark out of context

Answer 1 and how it is derived

Can it be seen from the text in paragraph in the passage that Mrs. Albert Forrester – whoever she may have been, may God bless her – was an author whose books were really well written according to the critics but they did not sell. Does one have to be a genius to perceive that they were not selling? Especially when it is written in so many words?

Does one have to be a literary giant to perceive that the *book* referred to in the opening line of paragraph 3 in the passage is *The Achilles Statue* that has been authored by Mrs. Forrester? Does one have to be a master of the English language to know what is the meaning of the words: "from the editors of these Mrs Albert Forrester's agent had wrung a sum that can only be described as thumping"? The obvious meaning is that

Mrs. Forrester made a pile of money from the book. The word "thumping" has been used in the context of the money that the agent wrung out of the editors and not in the context of use of force that the agent employed in trying to extract money from the editors.

Now does one have to be a don of the English language to realise that (A) None of Mrs. Forrester's previous books were selling and (B) Her book *The Achilles Statue* was selling like hot cakes and raking in the moolah by the bushels and thus when she "squared the circle", what she did was something that was not happening so far and thus the only option that fits at all - leave aside for a moment options fitting like gloves - is Option 2: Did something impossible?

Question 2

Regarding the blackmailing of the American publisher by Mrs. Forrester's agent, it can be said that: (1) Her agent forced him to buy two volumes of her book *The Achilles Statue* (2) Her agent forced him to buy two of her trash books (3) Her agent forced him to publish two of her books when the American publisher wanted desperately two books of poor literary value but high degree of saleability (4) None of these

Answer 2 and how it is derived

What is the probable cost of two volumes of her book even if one were to assume that they were highly priced? Would it be so high as to necessitate blackmailing anyone for selling just two volumes of *The Achilles Statue*? Secondly, is it not clear that *The Achilles Statue* was doing roaring business as it is? When does one blackmail someone else? When one has something that the other person requires badly and is prepared to pay a price (even if figuratively) for it! Who needed trash books? The American publisher!

What is a trash book? Some book that has poor literature in it! Why would a publisher want it? He would want it so that he can publish it and then sell it to that overwhelmingly large section of the reading populace who read poor literature and make a neat pile for himself. So Mrs. Forrester's agent would use this as an opportunity to make the American publisher agree to publish (this is the implied meaning of the word "buy") Mrs. Forrester's two books that were not selling before he gets him two of the trash books that the American publisher wants badly. Thus Option 3.

Question 3

According to the passage, who is the author of *The Chilly Statue*? (1) Mr. Albert Forrester (2) Carl van Vechten (3) Mrs. Albert Forrester (4) Cannot be found from the passage

Answer 3 and how it is derived

If the book "*The Chilly Statue*" has been mentioned anywhere at all, it is certainly not in the passage that we have bunged to our imaginary candidate. If the passage makes mention of any book it is *The Achilles Statue*.

Young Achilles – whoever he may have been, God bless him – may have been feeling chilly or his manner may have become chilly (meaning unresponsive or aloof) but that does not convert *The Achilles Statue* into *The Chilly Statue*. So Option 4: Cannot be found from the passage.

The whole idea in slightly changing the name of the book and then bunging a question to the unsuspecting fellow is to see whether the fellow writing the examination is awake at all or has he succumbed to the lullaby of boredom.

Question 4

In regard to *The Achilles Statue* it has been stated in the passage that "this is a book that .., may be regarded by the historians of the future as a curious footnote to the literary annals of our day". Which one of the following reasons, if true, would, in your opinion, best support the above contention?

(1) *The Achilles Statue* was a great novel but its grain was significantly different from the undercurrent of the author's previous publications

(2) In regard to *The Achilles Statue*, the author's agent had to extract a huge order by blackmailing an American publisher

(3) *The Achilles Statue* was a trash book produced by the author who has been known for her faultless literary style

(4) The author's prior books were not selling and *The Achilles Statue* sold like hot cakes

Answer 4 and how it is derived

One must appreciate that what is required here is your opinion and if one expects one's opinion by way of a part of the text in the passage, one is carrying an unnecessarily huge opinion of oneself.

It would be appropriate to see which of the options is actually **refuted** by the text in the passage and for this we may see from option to option:

(1) *The Achilles Statue* was a great novel but its grain was significantly different from the undercurrent of the author's previous publications

About this there is mention at the outset that the said novel was one of the great novels of those days. Barring this, there is neither any statement in support nor any in opposition.

(2) In regard to *The Achilles Statue*, the author's agent had to extract a huge order by blackmailing an American publisher

The factual position as seen from the text was significantly different from the one stated above. *The Achilles Statue* was a hit and one does not need to go the lengths of blackmailing someone else in order to sell books that are recording huge sales on their own. The statement made above is, on the contrary, therefore, refuted in the passage.

(3) *The Achilles Statue* was a trash book produced by the author who has been known for her faultless literary style

One cannot be so naïve as to treat a book already referred to as "one of the great novels of our times" as a trash book.

(4) The author's prior books were not selling and *The Achilles Statue* sold like hot cakes

The annals of literature – meaning records regarding literature – luckily consider the quality of literature produced. The annals of literature are not books of accounts, wherein would be written the sales generated by different pieces of literature. Society would be extremely poor if the esteem accorded to a literary work or to the producer of that work were in direct proportion to the money it brought in. Pornographic magazines would then rule the roost.

Besides, there is nothing per se curious about one book selling and the others not.

Which all means that, if anything, one has to look at Option 1. A book that has literary style or content from an author's previous publications may seem curious. Besides there is mention – at the very outset - of the peculiar circumstances under which it was written.

Question 5

Please see the following words in the passage "It was indeed a scandal that so distinguished an author, with an imagination so delicate and a style so exquisite should remain neglected of the vulgar." Which of the following is the furthest in meaning to the intended meaning of the word "vulgar" as used in the passage. Options: (1) Pleasing (2) Delicate (3) Indecent (4) Well-read

Answer 5 and how it is derived

If one were to know by now that the whole passage is about a book, then it might take a moment that the word furthest in meaning from vulgar is well read. As such the most widely perceived meaning of the word vulgar is indecent or obscene but the contextual usage here of the word is to describe the public that had neglected the author.

The public, if it were to look for ways for neglecting an author, would have little choice of methodology save that of not reading (and therefore not buying) what the author writes. By now it would certainly dawn on our imaginary candidate – to whom we are administering this passage and the questions there under - that the person neglected was the author and those who neglected the author are the common people (in other words, the public).

The passage states that well read persons praised the author's works. Thus the class of people who do not qualify for being referred to as "vulgar" are the well-read people. Hence Option 4.

If one were to assess whether the objectives that we had set out at the very beginning of the passage have been served, one should think that they have been eminently served. It becomes necessary to move on to see what variety awaits us at the GRE and what skills are required to derive correct answers that have been raised in relation to passages. It is with this end in view that we present to you the following practice tests in order to familiarise the reader with the level of the passages that are found in the official source and what skills are needed to succeed at this particular section.

It will be our endeavour to give ample practice material in this book so that you can hone your skills. We will not say that the material has the same level of difficulty as in the GRE. We will give you material that tests EXACTLY the same level and range of skills that the ETS aims to test through the Practice Tests that you might see in the official source. We will give you the answers [not just the answer key, mind you] in a language that is lucid and the complete sequence of how these answers have been derived.

You deserve the best and we shall give it to you.

Practice Test 1

The questions 1 to 8 in this group are based on the content of Passage 1 whereas Questions 9 to 11 in this group are based on Passage 2 and Questions 12 to 14 are based on Passage 3. After reading the passage, choose the best answer to each question. Answer all questions following the passage on the basis of what is stated or implied in the passage.

Passage 1

The development of intelligence among early large mammals of the grasslands was due in great measure to the interaction between two ecologically synchronised groups of these animals, the hunting carnivores and the herbivores that they hunted. The interaction resulting from the differences between predator and prey led to a general improvement in brain functions; however, certain components of intelligence were improved far more than others.

The kind of brain function favoured by the interplay of increasingly smarter catchers and increasingly keener escapers is defined by attention - that aspect of mind carrying consciousness forward from one moment to the next. It ranges from a passive free-floating awareness to a highly focussed, active fixation. The range through these states is mediated by the arousal system, a network of tracts converging from sensory systems to integrity centres in the brain stem. From the more relaxed to the more vigorous levels, sensitivity to novelty is increased. The organism is more awake, more vigilant; this increased vigilance results in the apprehension of even more subtle signals as the organism becomes more sensitive to its surroundings. The process of arousal and concentration give attention its direction. Arousal is at first general, with a flurry of impulses in the brain stem; then gradually the activation is channelled. This begins concentration, the holding of consistent images. One meaning of intelligence is the way in which these images and other alertly searched information is used in the context of previous experience. Consciousness links past attention to the present and permits the integration of details with perceived ends and purposes.

The elements of intelligence and consciousness come together marvellously to produce different styles in predator and prey. Herbivores and carnivores develop different kinds of attention related to escaping or chasing. Although in both kinds of animal, arousal stimulates the production of adrenaline and norepinephrine by the adrenal glands, the effect in herbivores is primarily fear, whereas in carnivores the effect is primarily aggression. For both, arousal attunes the animal to what is ahead. Perhaps it does not experience forethought as we know it, but the animal does experience something like it. The predator is searchingly aggressive, inner-directed, tuned by the nervous system and the adrenal hormones, but aware in a sense closer to human consciousness than, say, a hungry lizard's instinctive snap at a passing beetle. Using past events as a framework, the large mammal predator is working out a relationship between movement and food, sensitive to possibilities in cold trails and distant sounds – and yesterday's unforgotten lessons. The herbivore prey is of a different mind. Its mood of wariness rather than searching and its attitude of general expectancy instead of anticipating are silk-thin veils of tranquillity over an explosive endocrine system.

Question 1

The author is primarily concerned with:

(1) disproving the view that herbivores are less intelligent than carnivores

(2) describing a relationship between animals' intelligence and their ecological roles

(3) establishing a direct link between early large mammals and their modern counterparts

(4) analysing the ecological basis for the dominance of some carnivores over other carnivores

(5) demonstrating the importance of hormones in mental activity

Answer 1

Let us see what is the author's primary concern. Let us go from option to option.

Option 1: disproving the view that herbivores are less intelligent than carnivores.

Please see the words in the first paragraph in the passage where it is stated that *using past events as a framework, the large mammal predator is working out a relationship between movement and food, sensitive to possibilities in cold trails and distant sounds – and yesterday's unforgotten lessons. The herbivore prey is of a different mind. Its mood of wariness rather than searching and its attitude of general expectancy instead of anticipating are silk-thin veils of tranquillity over an explosive endocrine system.* When the large predator does not forget yesterday's lessons he is sharp enough to remember them. The herbivore is wary or careful all the while and if one wants to fill the stomach, care cannot be a part of the menu because care is abstract whereas you need something material so as to be able to eat it. This means that it prefers to wait rather than search for food and hence what the author is trying to say is that the herbivore is less intelligent than the carnivore whereas Option 1 says the precise opposite and hence will not do.

Option 2: describing a relationship between animals' intelligence and their ecological roles.

We must try to find out what are the ecological roles of animals. See the first paragraph where you will see the words *two ecologically synchronised groups of animals: the hunting carnivores and the herbivores that they hunted.* The words synchronised has the prefix SYN- (that means *together*) and the Latin root CHRONO that means *time* and therefore *something that happens together in time* is *synchronised.* The ecological role that animals generally play is either that of predator or prey. What the passage says about these two varieties of animals and their intelligence is that although there is arousal in both kinds of animal, the effect of arousal in herbivores is primarily fear, whereas in carnivores the effect is primarily aggression. This is primarily because if a prey is not afraid, the predator will eat him without moving an inch from where he is standing. If the predator is not aggressive, he will starve. One cannot visualise lions or tigers going out shopping for meat and haggling with the butcher over the prices. Option 2 will do very well unless there is a better choice in the options to come.

Option 3: establishing a direct link between early large mammals and their modern counterparts.

All that the passage mentions is about early large mammals in paragraph 1. The modern counterpart of these mammals is not even mentioned anywhere in the passage leave alone establishing a direct link. This is why Option 3 will not do.

Option 4: analysing the ecological basis for the dominance of some carnivores over other carnivores.

The whole thing is between carnivores and herbivores and not between some carnivores and other carnivores. This is why Option 4 will not do either.

Option 5: demonstrating the importance of hormones in mental activity

If one wants to talk about the importance of petrol in an automobile, then one should talk about what petrol does in an automobile and what would happen if the petrol got over. If however one were to be found talking about what automobiles have done to the consumption of petrol worldwide, the logical deduction is that the fellow is talking about the importance of automobiles to petrol consumption and not the converse. There is mention of what the mental activity of arousal does to hormones and not what hormones do to mental activity. Option 5 cannot be inferred. Hence **Option 2** is to be marked as correct.

Question 2

The author refers to a hungry lizard (in the last paragraph in the passage) primarily in order to:

(1) demonstrate the similarity between the hunting methods of mammals and those of non-mammals

(2) broaden the application of his argument by including an insectivore as an example

(3) make a distinction between higher and lower levels of consciousness

(4) provide an additional illustration of the brutality characteristic of predators

(5) offer an objection to suggestions that all animals lack consciousness

Answer 2

Let us see where the words *hungry lizard* occurs in the passage and we shall find these words in the following words: "The predator is searchingly aggressive, inner-directed, tuned by the nervous system and the adrenal hormones, but aware in a sense closer to human consciousness than, say, a **hungry lizard**'s instinctive snap at a passing beetle." The words *inner-directed* mean that if an animal is hungry he will hunt for food and if he is not he will sit quietly and wish Merry Christmas to those animals that are passing by and whose cousins he has just eaten.

When a hungry lizard snaps at a passing beetle, it means that he is not searching for something to eat although he wants something to eat. If the hungry lizard were to search for food (rather than wait for a beetle to pass by) as predators and human beings do, then the lizard will be the one who will be passing by a bee when the bee is sitting and buzzing away in G Minor (and not vice versa). The author therefore tries to say that the consciousness of some predators is closer to human consciousness whereas the consciousness in other predators like the lizard is less similar to human consciousness. The author thus uses the hungry lizard to make a distinction between higher and lower levels of consciousness. Hence **Option 3** will fit like a shot.

Question 3

It can be inferred from the passage that in animals less intelligent than the mammals discussed in the passage:

(1) past experience is less helpful in ensuring survival

(2) attention is more highly focussed

(3) muscular co-ordination is less highly developed

(4) there is less need for competition amongst species

(5) environment is more important in establishing the proper ratio of prey to predator

Answer 3

Animals do not have IQ scores nor do they give out answers to mind boggling arithmetic problems in a flash. We shall therefore have to see what - in the author's views - is less intelligent in the context of animals.

If you were to see the concluding lines in the passage it would become clear that the large predators use past events as a framework to work out a relationship between movement and food whereas the herbivore is wary rather than searching and expects rather than anticipates. This means that the predator – say, a lion - may, for example, remember that the last time he stalked a deer with the wind blowing towards the deer, the deer was able to smell the lion a mile away with the result that the lion had to go to bed hungry that night. He would not repeat this and draw a lesson from this event; he would stalk the deer against the wind now onwards. The herbivore **expects** food rather than anticipates food. No one can be reasonably expected to go to a zebra with a stack of green grass. The zebra will have to organise his own meals. He cannot expect. But he does not understand this. He expects that he will be able to drink at the waterhole even when the waterhole is teeming with lions. He forgets that his mother and father both disappeared into the insides of these lions when the two of them were celebrating their marriage anniversary with a drink at the waterhole where lions were holding their annual general meeting. Who can save him?

Having realised that a less intelligent animal is one that does not derive lessons in survival from past events, it is easy to appreciate why Option 1 fits like a shot.

Question 4

The sensitivity described in the penultimate sentence in the passage is most clearly an example of

(1) "free-floating awareness"

(2) "flooding of impulses in the brain stem"

(3) "the holding of consistent images"

(4) "integration of details with perceived ends and purposes"

(5) "silk-thin veils of tranquillity"

Answer 4

We shall first see what words describe **sensitivity** in the penultimate sentence in the passage. These are as follows: *Using past events as a framework, the large mammal predator is working out a relationship between movement and food, sensitive to possibilities in cold trails and distant sounds – and yesterday's unforgotten lessons.*

For the predator what is movement? Have you heard of crocodiles wearing shorts and playing squash for the sake of exercise? A crocodile would get up and move only when he is hungry. He performs movement as a means to get to the passing herd of wildebeest on their annual migration from Place A to Place B via the Zambezi River in which the crocodile in our story has built a little cottage for self and family. This is because wildebeest do not come to him and ask him whether he would like them for dinner. Secondly since the movement is made with the objective of snapping up a wildebeest or two from the herd, the purpose of the movement is clear. He is aware that the summer is here and so will be the wildebeest on their migratory trail. He has worked out a relationship between movement and food. This is precisely what is meant by integration of details with perceived ends and purposes. Hence **Option 4**.

If you were to see the words *free-floating awareness* in the passage, these words are prefixed by the word *passive*. The crocodile in our story would have to go hungry if he were to remain passive while the wildebeest cross the Zambezi River. This is why Option 1 cannot do.

If you were to see the words *flooding of impulses in the brain stem*, the words are used to describe arousal at paragraph 2 in the passage where it is said that arousal is at first general where there is a flurry of impulses in the brain stem and then there is concentration or the holding of consistent images. So when the crocodile sees the wildebeest, he has a rush of impulses in the brain and then there is holding of consistent images. Sensitivity starts thereafter. He realises that it is summer and that the wildebeest are not here to make faces at him from a safe distance. They are here to cross the river like last year and the year before and so on and the time has come to grab a couple of them and make sandwiches for the children out of them. This means that the crocodile has forgotten yesterday's lessons. Options 2 and 3 will not work for this reason that these two options describe a situation before sensitivity sets in.

As regards Option 5, a silk thin veil of tranquillity over an explosive endocrine system in herbivores such as the zebras in our story means that while they seem to be tranquil and blissfully ignorant of the presence of the same lions who feasted on their parents, the moment they realise that the lion is not here to make a sketch of the zebras but is actually stalking them, they break into a frantic run. By then however it is too late. Had the zebra been sensitive, it would have realised that the lion is out to kill him long before the predator actually sets up a chase. This is why a silk thin veil of tranquillity is not sensitivity. Option 5 will not do for that reason.

Question 5

The author's attitude towards the mammals discussed in the passage is best described as

(1) superior and condescending

(2) light-hearted and jocular

(3) apologetic, conciliatory

(4) wistful and tender

(5) respectful and admiring

Answer 5

By now it must be clear that the author tells us why he considers the predators more intelligent and the herbivores less intelligent.

Let us see when someone's attitude could be *superior* and *condescending* (or *snobbish* in other words). Imagine that an experienced boxer is pitted against a rookie (as they call someone who is playing for the first time in a major tournament) at the National Boxing Championship. The bell rings and the fight begins. The old-timer tells the rookie to last at least the first round with him. This is snobbishness or condescending behaviour. There is no reason for an *author* to feel superior to animals. Thus Option 1 will not do.

I can be light-hearted or jocular towards someone else provided the other person understands what I am saying. Imagine telling the pet cat that old joke about two drunks where one cannot find the keys and so on. Can I reasonably expect the cat to laugh? Option 2 will not do for this reason.

One can be *apologetic* (*regretful* or *sorry*) or *conciliatory* (or *pacifying*) towards another if he has offended someone. Imagine that someone has been visiting a friend after long. The host's sister-in-law brings in the tea tray and lays it gracefully on the centre table. Imagine that the guest tells the host that he is lucky to have such a well-mannered housemaid and the host clarifies that she is a relative. The guest could be apologetic to the host and his sister-in-law for having put his foot in his mouth. How can one ever be apologetic to animals? Will they understand if you said sorry to them? Option 3 will not do either.

If someone from a village has recently relocated to a city where he is at college and is *wistful* for his beloved, he is *longing* for her or is *melancholic* or *sad*. If the owner of the store where a young man is employed is *tender* towards him, he is *kind* or *softhearted* towards him. If an author wants to be either tender or wistful for an animal, how does he expect that the animals will understand the depth of his emotions expressed in the passage? Will the animals borrow his reading glasses and read the passage? Option 4 will work.

One can be respectful and admiring towards another person or thing without the slightest necessity of the other person hearing or understanding him. You can admire a flamingo's feathers in any language you like without fear of the bird understanding a single word. This is why Option 5 will do very well.

Question 6

The author provides information that would answer which of the following questions?

(i) Why is an aroused herbivore usually fearful?

(ii) What are some of the degrees of attention in large mammals?

(iii) What occurs when the stimulus that causes arousal of a mammal is removed?

(1) (i) only (2) (iii) only (3) (i) &(ii) only (4) (ii) &(iii) only (5) (i) (ii)&(iii)

Answer 6

See the question. When you are asked something that the author provides, please be assured that your opinion is not sought. The answer is bound to be in the passage and that too either verbatim or very nearly that.

Please see the last paragraph in the passage where you will see the following words: Although in both kinds of animal, arousal stimulates the production of adrenaline .....by the adrenal glands, the effect in herbivores is primarily fear....... **Using past events as a framework, the large mammal predator is working out a relationship between movement and food, sensitive to possibilities in cold trails and distant sounds – and yesterday's unforgotten lessons.**

As regards question (i) the author tells us that the effect of arousal in herbivores is primarily fear. As regards question (ii) the author tells us that the large mammal is working out relationships between movement and food and is sensitive to distant sounds. About question (iii) the author tells us nothing; all he says is about stimulus comes in at arousal. There is no mention in the passage about what happens to a mammal when stimulus is removed. Thus Option 3.

Question 7

According to the passage, improvement in brain function among early large mammals resulted primarily from which of the following?

(1) Interplay of predator and prey

(2) Persistence of free-floating awareness in animals of the grasslands

(3) Gradual dominance of warm-blooded mammals over cold-blooded reptiles

(4) Interaction of early large mammals with less intelligent species

(5) Improvement of the capacity for memory among herbivores and carnivores

Answer 7

Please see these words in the first paragraph in the passage: The development of intelligence among early large mammals of the grasslands was due in great measure to the interaction between two ecologically synchronised groups of these animals, the hunting carnivores and the herbivores that they hunted. The interaction resulting from the differences between predator and prey led to a general improvement in brain functions.

Option 1 emerges verbatim if you know that a hunting carnivore is the predator and the herbivore that they hunt is prey and that interaction between predators and prey is the same thing as interplay.

Interaction can mean so many things such as: (A) discussion where one party opens a topic and the other party responds and then the process carries on for some time (B) reciprocal action where one does something to another and the other does something in response.

It is not reasonable to imagine that a panther will discuss the weather with the deer and the deer will suggest that they discuss the latest trends in cinema instead. Between predators and prey, there cannot be discussions on any topic at all no matter how interesting it may seem to human beings. Therefore interaction between predator and prey can only take the shape of the predator stalking the prey and the prey running for dear life and this interaction or interplay may result in either (A) the predator bagging the prey or (B) the prey escaping the predator and bragging to its children about how it gave a lion a run for its money the other day.

Question 8

According to the passage, as the process of arousal in an organism continues, all of the following may occur except

(1) the production of adrenaline

(2) the production of norepinephrine

(3) a heightening of sensitivity to stimuli

(4) an increase in selectivity with respect to stimuli

(5) an expansion of the range of states mediated by the brain stem

Answer 8

In the last paragraph in the passage you will see that as the process of arousal in mammals continue, there is production of adrenaline and norepinephrine. Option 1 and 2 are borne out from the passage.

If you were to see paragraph 2 you will see the following words: Arousal is at first general, with a flurry of impulses in the brain stem; then gradually the activation is channelled. This begins concentration, the holding of consistent images. This is what heightening of sensitivity to stimuli means. Option 3 can be inferred from the paragraph.

Option 4 can also be inferred from paragraph 3. Please, however, see these words in the last paragraph in the passage: Herbivores and carnivores develop different kinds of attention related to escaping or chasing. Although in both kinds of animal, arousal stimulates the production of adrenaline and norepinephrine by the adrenal glands, the effect in herbivores is primarily fear, whereas in carnivores the effect is primarily aggression.

Selectivity is a tendency in which one chooses one thing but not the other. If a child is selective while eating, it may mean – for example - that while she may eat egg sandwiches by the dozens, she may not touch the vegetable salad. The selectivity that the author is talking about is the fact that while stimulus makes the predator aggressive, it makes the herbivore fearful. Each selects what it should make of the stimulus. If the predators and prey did not have selectivity with respect to stimuli, then any of the following may happen:

(A) Both the panther and the deer will become aggressive towards each other and the deer may charge at the panther instead of running from him

(B) Both the panther and the deer will become fearful of each other and they will run in opposite directions when they meet and the panther will starve to death or opt for eating grass in order to avoid starvation

This means that **Option 5** cannot be inferred and has to be marked as correct.

Passage 2

Great comic art is never otherworldly, it does not seek to mystify us, and it does not deny ambiguity by branding as evil whatever differs from good. Great comic artists assume that truth may bare all lights and thus they seek to accentuate contradictions in social action, not gloss over or transcend them by appeals to extra-social symbols of divine ends, cosmic purpose, or laws of nature. The moment of transcendence in great comic art is a social moment, born out of the conviction that we are human, even though we try to be more. The comic community to which artists address themselves is a community of reasoning, loving, joyful, compassionate beings, who are willing to assume the human risks of acting rationally. Great comic art arouses courage in reasons, courage that grows out of trust in what human beings can do as humans.

Question 9

The passage suggests that great comic art can be characterised as optimistic about the ability of humans to

(1) rid themselves of pride

(2) transcend the human condition

(3) differentiate clearly between good and evil

(4) avoid social conflicts

(5) act rationally

Answer 9

What is optimism? It is a temperament that makes people hopeful. Imagine that a boat has capsized in the river and rescue work is in progress. Optimists will hope that most people will be saved whereas the pessimists will feel that no one can be saved. Optimism is thus necessarily a positive trait.

Now as regards the question, please see these words in the last lines of the passage: Great comic art arouses courage in reasons, courage that grows out of trust in what human beings can do as humans. If you trust the human beings who are engaged in rescue work and are confident that they shall do their best even at the risk of their lives, you as a bystander at the mishap will get courage from their efforts. You too will hope that most people will be saved. If comic art arouses courage in reasons, it means that comic art arouses the courage to act in a reasonable manner. Thus **Option 5** is inferred verbatim.

Courage is a positive trait. Foolishness is negative. Yet quite frequently there is a thin line dividing what is courageous and what is foolish. Imagine that two people have jumped into the river when the rescue team is trying to do its very best. One of them is a strong swimmer and the other knows not how to swim. On the face of it, both may seem equally courageous. However, a strong swimmer would qualify to be rated as courageous. A man who does not know how to swim is foolish. He may in fact add himself to the number of persons to be rescued.

Question 10

It can be inferred from the passage that the author admires great comic artists primarily for their

(1) ability to understand the frequently subtle differences between good and evil
(2) ability to reconcile the contradictions in human behaviour
(3) ability to distinguish between rational and irrational behaviour
(4) insistence on confronting the truth about the human condition
(5) insistence on condemning human faults and weaknesses

Answer 10

When you admire somebody, you speak well of him. If a girl were to admire a boy she would not say, for example, that he is of average height and speaks with a stutter. A girl who says that the fellow is never otherworldly would not seem to admire some boy whereas some girl who says that he is simply out of this world would be able to give the impression that she is admiring the boy. We shall therefore have to quickly look for a word or phrase that one would use in admiration.

See these words in the passage about comic artists: *Great comic artists assume that truth may bare all lights and … seek to accentuate contradictions in social action.* If it were said that great comic artists were truthful, it could be taken as admiration for the qualities of these artists. If you admire truth, you are admiring truth; you are not admiring great comic artists. To *accentuate* something is to *highlight* or *emphasise* it. If you are reading a novel and *accentuate* a phrase in it by drawing a line under it, you are only deciding what you will like to recall from the book. You admire the phrase. If great comic artists accentuate something, then it is a case of great comic artists admiring something and not the author admiring great comic artists.

Now see these words in the passage: *The moment of transcendence in great comic art is a social moment, born out of the conviction that we are human*. The word *transcendence* means *excellence* or *predominance*. If a chess grandmaster acknowledges the *transcendence* of another grandmaster it means that he accepts the other person's *excellence* at the game. The word *transcendence* is thus indicative of admiration. *Conviction* means the courage to stand up for what one believes is right or correct. Between two persons where one who is convinced about what he thinks is right and another who is not so sure, the only one who will insist about what he thinks is right is the fellow who is sure. The conviction that we are human means that great comic art is convinced that the truth is that we are human and insists on it. Thus Option 4.

Question 11

Which of the following is the most accurate description of the organisation of the passage?

(1) A sequence of observations leading to a prediction
(2) A list of inferences drawn from facts stated at the beginning of the passage
(3) A series of assertions related to one general subject
(4) A statement of the major idea, followed by specific examples
(5) A succession of ideas moving from specific to general

Answer 11

When you predict you forecast something which means that you say today something that may happen in the future. If you wish to predict rain, for example, then you will have to say that it will rain tomorrow and hence in every prediction there will have to be a future tense. If you see the paragraph, there is only present tense employed all through. Thus Option 1 will not work.

If you see the words at the beginning of the passage, you are told something that great comic arts *assume*. A fact does not have to be *assumed*. If you know that someone is ten years old, then the fact is that he is ten years old. Once you are aware of that fact, you need not assume the fellow's age. Thus since there are no facts stated at the beginning of the passage, Option 2 would not work.

An assertion does not mean that it is the truth. An assertion is merely an insistence or emphasis. If I make an assertion that I am most handsome, I am merely emphasising what is my view or opinion about me. It may be miles away from the truth. If you will see the passage it has opinions of the author. About a general subject, great comic art seems to fit very well since the whole passage is about great comic art. Option 3 should do very well unless we find another option that is close.

About Options 4 and 5, it would be noticed that there is no specific example at all and hence these two options will not do. This means **Option 3** is correct.

Passage 3

The dark regions in the starry night sky are not pockets in the universe that are devoid of stars as had long been thought. Rather, they are dark because of interstellar dust that hides the stars behind it. Although its visual effect is so pronounced, dust is only a minor constituent of the material, extremely low in density that lies between the stars. Dust accounts for about one percent of the total mass of interstellar matter. The rest is hydrogen and helium gas, with small amounts of other elements. The interstellar material, rather like terrestrial clouds, comes in all shapes and sizes. The average density of interstellar material in the vicinity of our sun is 1,000 to 10,000 times less than the best terrestrial laboratory vacuum. It is only because of the enormous interstellar distances that so little material per unit of volume becomes so significant. Optical astronomy is most directly affected, for although interstellar gas is perfectly transparent, the dust is not.

Question 12

According to the passage, which of the following is a direct perpetual consequence of interstellar dust?

(1) Some stars are rendered invisible to observers on Earth.

(2) Many visible stars are made to seem brighter than they really are.

(3) The presence of hydrogen and helium gas is revealed

(4) The night sky appears dusty at all times to observers on Earth.

(5) The dust is conspicuously visible against a background of bright stars.

Answer 12

If we are to find out what is the direct perpetual (meaning, something that is either *unchanging* or *does not stop*) consequence (meaning, *result*) of interstellar dust, then we are required to find out something that happens all the while because of interstellar dust. Secondly since interstellar dust is the cause we shall have to scan the passage and find out where we see the words *interstellar dust*.

Please see the following words: *Rather, they are dark because of interstellar dust that hides the stars behind it*. Clearly, interstellar dust hides the stars behind something. As regards whom does it hide the stars from, it is from human beings on Planet Earth. This is because the passage is meant for reading by human beings on Planet Earth. This is why Option 1 fits like a shot.

Question 13

It can be inferred from the passage that the density of interstellar material is

(1) higher where distances between the stars are shorter.

(2) equal to that of interstellar dust

(3) unusually low in the vicinity of our Sun

(4) independent of the incidence of gaseous components

(5) not homogeneous throughout interstellar Space.

Answer 13

As regards density of interstellar material please see the following words in the passage: *The average density of interstellar material in the vicinity of our sun is 1,000 to 10,000 times less than the best terrestrial laboratory vacuum*. The key word here is **average**.

If the average age of children in a class is 12, it does not mean that all children are exactly 12 years old. It means that some children are 11 and others are 13 whereas some others are 12.

If you are at a party hosted by a couple who are both schoolteachers and you find that all the guests are schoolteachers as well, the crowd is *homogenous* meaning *all* are of *the same* kind. This means that if interstellar material has *average* density, then some matter is heavier than the average and some is lighter than the average and the average density is thus the mean density. This also means that the density of interstellar matter is not all the same everywhere and hence **Option 5** emerges in a flash.

Question 14

It can be inferred from the passage that it is because space is so vast that

(1) little of the interstellar material in it seems substantial.

(2) normal units of volume seem futile for measurements of density

(3) stars can be far enough from Earth to be obscured even by very sparsely distributed matter

(4) interstellar gases can, for all practical purposes, be regarded as transparent

(5) optical astronomy would be of little use even if no interstellar dust existed.

Answer 14

The first thing to be noted is that we are to find out something that is a result of space being vast and hence the vastness of space is the cause and we are to find out the effect.

While the passage does not have the words *vast space*, there is a reference to enormous interstellar distances (that means vast space) in the following words: *It is only because of the enormous interstellar distances that so little material per unit of volume becomes so significant. Optical astronomy is most directly affected, for although interstellar gas is perfectly transparent, the dust is not.* The inference that flows from this is that even if the interstellar material is present in traces (because that is the meaning of little material per unit volume), the interstellar material has significance.

Now let us go from option to option and find out which one shall fit into the inference that we have derived.

Option 1: The passage says that the little material per unit volume is significant. This means that whatever interstellar material there is, has significance and therefore matters. Option 1 says that little of interstellar material is substantial which means that a major part of interstellar material is not substantial. This is in direct contrast to the above inference.

Option 2: Normal units of volume seem futile for measurements of density. One can measure the density of milk that we get at home. One can measure the density of honey that we have just bought from the apiary. But measuring the density of interstellar material requires a space journey of billions of miles. Since the passage does not mention any attempt to actually measure the density of interstellar matter, option 2 would not work.

Option 3: stars can be far enough from Earth to be obscured even by very sparsely distributed matter. If something is *obscure*, it cannot be seen or heard distinctly. If the population in a desert is *sparse*, it means that few people live in a vast area and therefore the population density is very low. If interstellar matter can be significant even if distributed sparsely, they must be able to do something significant or not allow something significant from happening. If sparsely distributed interstellar matter does not allow stars to be seen clearly, the matter is significant. Option 3 would fit like a shot provided no other option is close.

Option 4: interstellar gases can, for all practical purposes, be regarded as transparent. When the passage says that interstellar gases are perfectly transparent, then they are perfectly transparent whether the purpose is practical or impractical.

Imagine that you were to go to a goldsmith's shop to see how much you can get out of the bracelet that your grandmother gave you years back. The goldsmith takes one look and says that while there are impurities, the gold can be taken as pure for all practical purposes, what he means that the gold is very near to pure. But if the gold were to be perfectly pure, then the usage of the words *for all practical purposes* would be inappropriate. This is why Option 4 will not do.

Option 5: optical astronomy would be of little use even if no interstellar dust existed. If you see the last line in the passage it says: *Optical astronomy is most directly affected, for although interstellar gas is perfectly transparent, the dust is not*.

To *affect* means to *have effect on*. If one's personal computer is affected by a virus, the virus has had an effect on the computer. The computer is useless till it is repaired. We call the vendor and he sends someone over to repair the PC. He charges a hefty bill. If the PC were to be of little use even if no virus existed, then why would we have bought it at all? Do we buy useless things? Are we dealers in scrap? This is why Option 5 will not do.

Hence Option 3.

Practice Test 2

Passage 1

In his 1976 study of slavery in the United States, Herbert Gutman, Mike Fogel, Engerman, and Genovese, has rightly stressed the slaves' achievements. But unlike these historians, Gutman gives plantation owners little credit for these achievements. Rather, Gutman argues that one must look to the Black family and the slaves' extended kinship system to understand how crucial achievements, such as the maintenance of a cultural heritage and the development of a communal consciousness, were possible. His findings compel attention.

Gutman recreates the family and extended kinship structure mainly through an ingenious way of what any historian should draw upon quantifiable data, derived in this case mostly from plantation birth registers. He also uses accounts of ex-slaves to probe the human reality behind his statistics. These sources indicate that the two-parent household predominated in slave quarters just as it did among freed slaves after emancipation. Although Gutman admits that forced separation by sale was frequent, he shows that the slaves' preference, revealed most clearly on plantations where sale was infrequent, was very much for stable monogamy. In less conclusive fashion Fogel, Engerman, and Genovese had already indicated the predominance of two-parent households; however, only Gutman emphasises the preference for stable monogamy and points out what stable monogamy meant for the slaves' cultural heritage. Gutman argues convincingly that the stability of the Black family encouraged the transmission of – and so was crucial to – sustain the Black heritage of folklore, music, and religious expression from one generation to another, a heritage that slaves were continually fashioning out of their African and American experiences. Gutman's examination of other facets of kinship also produces important findings. Gutman discovers that cousins rarely married, an exogamous tendency that contrasted sharply with the endogamy practices by the plantation owners. This preference for exogamy, Gutman suggests, may have derived from West African rules governing marriage, which, though they differed from one tribal group to another, all involved some kind of prohibition against unions with close kin. This taboo against cousins' marrying is important, argues Gutman, because it is one of many indications of a strong awareness among slaves of an extended kinship network. The fact that distantly related kin would care for children separated from their families also suggests this awareness. When blood relationships were few, as in newly created plantations in the southwest 'fictive' kinship arrangements took their place until a new pattern of consanguinity developed. Gutman presents convincing evidence that this extended kinship structure – which he believes developed by the mid-to-late 18th century, provided the foundations for a strong communal consciousness that existed among slaves.

In sum, Gutman's study is significant because it offers a closely reasoned and original explanation of some of the slaves' achievements, one that correctly emphasises the resources that slaves themselves possessed.

Question 1

According to the passage, Fogel, Engerman, Genovese and Gutman have all done which of the following:

(i) discounted the influence of plantation owners on slaves' achievements

(ii) emphasised the achievements of slaves

(iii) pointed out the prevalence of the two-parent household among slaves

(iv) showed the connection between stable monogamy and slaves' cultural heritage

(1) (i) and (ii) only (2) (i) and (iv) only (3) (ii) and (iii) only (4) (i) (iii) and (iv) (5) (ii) (iii) and (iv)

Answer 1

If you are asked something about what Fogel, Engerman, Genovese and Gutman have all said or done, it means that **all four** – without exception - have said or done something common. With this let us see the statements (i) to (iv).

Statement (i): discounted the influence of plantation owners on slaves' achievements. This seems illogical per se since plantation owners were the ones who employed slaves and made them work from morning to night till they fell from exhaustion. The plantation owners would not have allowed the slaves to achieve anything other than toil. However if we see the passage, we shall see the following words in regard to the influence of plantation owners on slaves' achievements: *In his 1976 study of slavery in the United States, Herbert Gutman, Mike Fogel, Engerman, and Genovese, has rightly stressed the slaves' achievements. But unlike these historians, Gutman gives plantation owners little credit for these achievements.* Two things stand out from these words:

(1) Fogel, Engerman, Genovese and Gutman have all stressed or emphasised the slaves' achievements.

(2) Gutman has not given much credit to plantation owners for the slaves' achievements. This means that Gutman was the only one who discounted the influence of plantation owners on slaves' achievements. Statement (i) is wrong.

Since Statement (i) is wrong, we are not to bother about Options 1, 2 and 4. We should now scrutinise Options 3 and 5 only and see which one of these is right. Options 3 and 5 both have Statements (ii) and (iii) in common. We should therefore see whether Statement (iv) is correct.

Statement (iv): showed the connection between stable monogamy and slaves' cultural heritage. If we were to see these words it will become clear that Gutman was the only one who showed the connection between stable monogamy and the slaves' cultural heritage: *only Gutman emphasises the preference for stable monogamy and points out what stable monogamy meant for the slaves' cultural heritage.* This statement is wrong. This means Option 3 is to be marked as right.

See the importance of logic. We were able to arrive at the correct answer from seeing only two statements out of the four given to us.

Question 2

With which of the following statements regarding the resources that historians ought to use would the author of the passage be most likely to agree?

(1) Historians ought to make use of written rather than oral accounts

(2) Historians should rely primarily on birth registers

(3) Historians should rely exclusively on data that can be quantified

(4) Historians ought to make use of data that can be quantified

(5) Historians ought to draw on earlier historical research but they should do so in order to refute it

Answer 2

This is what the passage says about resources that the historians must use: *Gutman recreates the family and extended kinship structure* ***mainly through an ingenious way of what any historian should draw upon quantifiable data,*** *derived in this case mostly from plantation birth registers.*

The following three things can be inferred from the above words:

- If it is the author's view that any historian should draw upon quantifiable data, it means that it is what he feels all historians should do whether it is Historian A or Historian B and so on.
- In the present case if the data is to be drawn mostly from birth registers, it is the author's view that birth registers are not the only source from which data should be drawn.
- The birth register here is specific to the present case and not to a general source from which a historian should draw quantifiable data.

Now let us see the various options.

Option 1: Historians ought to make use of written rather than oral accounts. It is not necessary that written accounts carry quantifiable data. If you were to read an essay about how one spent the summer vacations reading and swimming and so on, nothing quantifiable may emerge at all although the essay is a written account of what one has done during the holidays.

Option 2: Historians should rely primarily on birth registers. This is contradicted from the last of the three inferences that we have drawn above.

Option 3: Historians should rely exclusively on data that can be quantified. If one is to rely exclusively on data that can be quantified (in other words *quantifiable data*), it means one is not to rely or make use of anything else. What we have inferred is that historians should make use of quantifiable data but not only of quantifiable data. What the author says is that historians should make use of quantifiable data. If you tell someone that he should wear a tie, it does not mean that he should wear only a tie and nothing else. Option 3 will not work for this reason.

Option 4: Historians ought to make use of data that can be quantified. This is what the author says. If you ought to reach office in time, it means you should reach office in time. Option 4 will do very well.

Option 5: Historians ought to draw on earlier historical research but they should do so in order to refute it. Whatever the author says about what historians should do is in the three inferences above. Earlier historical research finds no mention. Hence Option 5 will not work.

Question 3

Which of the following statements about the formation of the Black heritage of folklore, music, and religious expression is best supported by the information presented in the passage?

(1) The heritage was formed primarily out of the experiences of those slaves who attempted to preserve the stability of their families

(2) The heritage was not formed out of the experiences of those slaves who married their cousins

(3) The heritage was formed more out of the African than out of the American experiences of slaves

(4) The heritage was not formed out of the experiences of a single generation of slaves

(5) The heritage was formed out of the slaves' experiences of interdependence in newly created plantations in the southwest.

Answer 3

Please see these words in the passage where we find mention of the formation of the Black heritage of folklore, music, and religious expression: *Gutman argues convincingly that the stability of the Black family encouraged the transmission of – and so was crucial to – sustain the Black heritage of folklore, music, and religious expression from one generation to another, a heritage that slaves were continually fashioning out of their African and American experiences.*

The following things can be inferred from these words:

- The stability of the Black family encouraged the transmission of this heritage
- The heritage was not formed in one generation but over generations
- The slaves were continually fashioning (meaning, *building* or *constructing*) this culture out of their African and American experiences but not from either of the experiences alone

Option 1 is wrong because the slaves did not just *attempt* to preserve the stability of their families. They *succeeded*. They had stability. After Sir Edmund Hillary and Tensing successfully scaled Mount Everest, if someone were to say that they *attempted* Everest, he would need a psychiatrist.

Option 2 says about something altogether different from the two factors that contributed to the heritage: stability of the Black family and the slaves' African and American experiences. It does not say anything categorical. If your car is stalled on a highway and the first mechanic says that it is not because of the weak battery that it has stopped and the second says that it is because of the overheated radiator that it has stopped, the second mechanic is to be believed because the first is not sure.

Option 3 says that it was more out of the African experience than out of the American experience that contributed to the formation of the Black heritage of music and so on. This contradicts the third of the three inferences that we have drawn.

Option 4 confirms the second of the three inferences that we have drawn and hence **Option 4** is right.

Option 5 sings a different tune altogether from what the author says about the formation of Black heritage. It mentions nothing about stability of the Black family or about African and American experiences.

Question 4

It can be inferred from the passage that, of the following, the most probable reason why a historian of slavery might be interested in studying the type of plantations mentioned in lines 6-7 at paragraph 2 in the passage is that this type would:

(1) give the historian access to the most complete plantation birth registers

(2) permit the historian to observe the kinship patterns that had been most popular among West African tribes

(3) provide the historian with evidence concerning the preference of freed slaves for stable monogamy

(4) furnish the historian with the opportunity to discover the kind of marital commitment that slaves themselves chose to have

(5) allow the historians to examine the influence of slaves' preferences on the actions of the plantation owners

Answer 4

The question tells us very specifically where to locate the type of plantations: see lines 6 and 7 where it says: *Although Gutman admits that forced separation by sale was frequent, he shows that the slaves' preference, revealed most clearly on plantations where sale was infrequent, was very much for stable monogamy.* This means that slaves preferred stable monogamy.

When we see these lines we are able to locate just one type of plantation: where sale was infrequent. Since sale frequently led to separation, slaves preferred those plantations where sale was infrequent because this meant that they would not have to separate from their marriage partners.

Monogamy means marriage to one person at any given time. This can mean that someone would not be married to more than one person at a time. But it could also mean, for example, that a husband may divorce his first wife and marry another woman and then divorce her and marry someone else and yet he would not have more than one wife at any time.

Stable monogamy means marriage to one person and not to anyone else thereafter. It means marital commitment. Option 4 is to be marked as correct.

While the other options are far away from monogamy (leave alone stable monogamy) Option 3 might prima facie seem to be close but it really isn't for the reason that while the whole thing is about slaves, Option 3 talks about *freed* slaves. A freed slave, incidentally, is not a slave anymore just as molten ice cream isn't ice cream anymore.

Question 5

According to the passage, all of the following are true of West African rules governing marriage mentioned in lines 16-19 at paragraph 2 EXCEPT:

(1) The rules were derived from rules governing fictive kinship arrangements

(2) The rules forbade marriages between close kin

(3) The rules are mentioned in Herbert Gutman's studies

(4) The rules were not uniform in all respects from one West African tribe to another

(5) The rules have been considered to be a possible source of slaves' marriage preferences

Answer 5

Let us see these words where we are able to spot the West African rules regarding marriage in lines 16-19 of paragraph 2 in the passage: *Gutman discovers that cousins rarely married, an exogamous tendency that contrasted sharply with the endogamy practices by the plantation owners. This preference for exogamy, Gutman suggests, may have been derived from West African rules governing marriage, which, though they differed from one tribal group to another, all involved some kind of prohibition against unions with close kin.*

The following can be inferred from these words:

- The rules may have been the reason for the preference for exogamy (meaning *marriage with those outside one's community, clan* or *tribe*)
- The rules differed from one tribal group to another
- All the rules involved some kind of prohibition against unions with close kin

Now let us see which option will fit.

Option (1): The rules were derived from rules governing fictive kinship arrangements. This is not inferred since we are not told what is the source of these rules: West African rules governing marriage.

Option (2): The rules forbade marriages between close kin. This is indeed inferred as we have seen above.

Option (3): The rules are mentioned in Herbert Gutman's studies. The fact that Gutman has mentioned these rules means that these rules are mentioned in Herbert Gutman's studies. Gutman could not possibly have mumbled these rules in his sleep.

Option (4): The rules were not uniform in all respects from one West African tribe to another. This too is inferred as we have seen above.

Option (5): The rules have been considered to be a possible source of slaves' marriage preferences. When the rules are about slaves and their marriage preferences, this too is inferred. Surely the rules could not have been for plantation owners because the latter were known to marry their cousins, which is in contrast to what the slaves did.

Option 1 is to be marked as correct.

Question 6

Which of the following statements concerning the marriage practices of plantation owners during the period of Black slavery in the United States can most logically be inferred from the information in the passage?

(1) These practices began to alter sometime around the mid-18th century

(2) These practices vary markedly from one region of the country to another

(3) Plantation owners usually based their choice of marriage partners on economic considerations

(4) Plantation owners often married earlier than slaves

(5) Plantation owners often married their cousins

Answer 6

As may be seen from the question, the examiner wants you to apply logic in answering it. Therefore one has to make a reasonable choice of the correct option.

As we have seen in the previous answer, plantation owners often married their cousins as is evident from the fact that they were *endogamous* (or those who practice marriages within their community). Hence Option 5.

Question 7

Which of the following best describes the organisation of the passage?

(1) The author compares and contrasts the work of several historians and then discusses area for possible new research

(2) The author presents his thesis, draws on the work of several historians for evidence to support his thesis, and concludes by reiterating his thesis

(3) The author describes some features of a historical study and then uses those features to put forth his own argument

(4) The author summarises a historical study, examines two main arguments from the study and then shows how the arguments are potentially in conflict with one another

(5) The author presents the general argument of a historical study, describes the study in more detail and concludes with a brief judgement of a study's value

Answer 7

It is reasonable to expect that if there is a brief summary of the passage, it will be at the end. It will tell in a nutshell what the author has been trying to say all along in the passage. The possible rationale for the summary at the end of the passage is that those who have attempted to read it and have dozed off may wake up.

If you were to see these words at the end of the passage, they summarise what the author has been saying: *In sum, Gutman's study is significant because it offers a closely reasoned and original explanation of some of the slaves' achievements, one that correctly emphasises the resources that slaves themselves possessed.* The following can be inferred from these words:

- One thing stands a mile out: whatever the author of the passage says is about Gutman's study in the main.
- The author presents the findings of Gutman and not his own
- The other thing that stands out is the fact that the whole thing is about slaves in America. Now that slaves have been freed long back, the whole thing is history.
- Gutman is a historian

The first two of these inferences contradicts Options 1, 2, 3 and 4. Thus Option 5.

Question 8

Which of the following is the most appropriate title for the passage based on its content?

(1) The influence of Herbert Gutman on historians of slavery in the United States

(2) Gutman's explanation of how slaves could maintain a cultural heritage and develop a communal consciousness

(3) Slavery in the United States: New controversy about an old subject

(4) Black heritage of folklore, music, and religious expression: Its growing influence

(5) Black family and extended kinship structure: How they were important for the freed slaves

Answer 8

If there is a summary at the end of any passage, it comes in handy not only for putting an end to the snores of the public who started out reading it and then succumbed to the pressure of sleep soon after start. It could come in handy for deciding what is the title of the passage. This is because it is a nutshell account of what the author wants to say. The title has also to tell in a nutshell what the whole thing is about otherwise people may go off to sleep while reading long titles.

Let us see the summary once again: *In sum, Gutman's study is significant because it offers a closely reasoned and original explanation of some of the slaves' achievements, one that correctly emphasises the resources that slaves themselves possessed.*

These things can be inferred:

- Gutman explains some of the slaves' achievements.
- Gutman's explanation is original (meaning he hasn't copied it from some other source)
- The slaves have achieved something noteworthy.

If you wish to show the influence of Gutman on the historians of slavery in America, then you have to show what Gutman wrote and what the others wrote and then how they eventually had similar views to Gutman's views. This means that while the limelight may be on Gutman, some focus should be on the other historians as well whereas the summary itself talks about Gutman and none else. Option 1 is thus wrong.

Since what we get is Gutman's explanation, Option 2 would be a good choice if none other were close. Since there is no controversy, Option 3 is wrong as well. A controversy would mean that there would be a debate about something. If Gutman monopolises the passage, there is no debate. Whom will he debate with? Himself? The Black Heritage mentioned in the passage pertains to slaves. The slaves have long been freed. When there are no slaves left, how can the heritage exist in the first place, leave alone have a growing influence? Option 4 will not work for this reason. The term *Black family* pertains to slaves and not *freed* slaves. Option 5 will not do for this reason. Hence **Option 2**.

Passage 2

"I want to criticise the social system, and to show it at work, at its most intense" Virginia Woolf's provocative statement about her intentions in writing *Mrs. Dalloway* has regularly been ignored by the critics, since it highlights an aspect of her literary interests very different from the traditional picture of the 'poetic' novelist concerned with examining states of reverie and vision and with following the intricate pathways of individual consciousness. But Virginia Woolf was a realistic as well a poetic novelist, a satirist and social critic as well a visionary: literary critics' cavalier dismissal of Woolf's social vision will not withstand scrutiny.

In her novels, Woolf is deeply engaged by the questions of how individuals are shaped (or deformed) by their social environments, how historical forces impinge on people's lives, how class, wealth, and gender help to determine people's fates. Most of her novels are rooted in a realistically rendered social setting and in a precise historical time.

Woolf's focus on society has not been generally recognised because of her intense antipathy to propaganda in art. The pictures of reformers in her novels are usually satirical or sharply critical. Even when Woolf is fundamentally sympathetic to their causes, she portrays people anxious to reform their society and possessed of a message or program as arrogant or dishonest, unaware of how their political ideas serve their own psychological needs. (Her writer's diary notes: "The only honest people are the artists," whereas "these social reformers and philanthropists... harbour... discreditable desires under the disguise of loving their kind..."). Woolf detested what she called "preaching" in fiction, too, and criticised novelist D. H. Lawrence (among others) for working by this method.

Woolf's own social criticism is expressed in the language of the observation rather than in direct commentary, since for her, fiction is a contemplative, not an active art. She describes phenomena and provides materials for a judgement about society and social issues; it is the reader's work to put the observations together and understand the coherent point of view behind them. As a moralist, Woolf works by indirection, subtly undermining officially accepted mores, mocking, suggesting, calling into question, rather than asserting, advocating, bearing witness: hers is the satirist's art.

Woolf's literary models were acute social observers like Chekhov and Chaucer. As she put it in *The Common Reader*, "it is safe to say that not a single law has been framed or one stone set upon another because of anything Chaucer said or wrote; and yet, as we read him, we are absorbing morality at every pore." Like Chaucer, Woolf chose to understand as well as to judge, to know her society root and branch – a decision crucial in order to produce art rather than polemic.

Question 9

Which of the following would be the most appropriate title for the passage?

(1) Poetry and satire as influences on the novels of Virginia Woolf

(2) Virginia Woolf: Critic and Commentator on the 20th century Novel

(3) Trends in Contemporary Reform Movements as a key to understanding Virginia Woolf's Novels

(4) Society as Allegory for the Individual in the Novels of Virginia Woolf

(5) Virginia Woolf's Novels: Critical Reflections on the Individual and on Society

Answer 9

We shall have to go from option to option and see which one fits in.

Option 1: Poetry and satire as influences on the novels of Virginia Woolf. Let us see where we find mention about poetry and satire. If we were to see the concluding lines of paragraph 1 in the passage, we shall see these words: *But Virginia Woolf was a realistic as well a poetic novelist, a satirist and social critic as well a visionary..*

Look at this logically. If it is *because* of exercise that someone is hungry, then one says that the exercise made him hungry. Hunger is because of the influence of exercise. If on the other hand if you were to hear him saying but he is hungry, it means that he is hungry even though he did not do exercise. The word *but* in the above sentence means that Virginia Woolf was a satirist and social critic and not because poetry and satire influenced her novels. If she was influenced by poetry and satire, then the wording of the sentence would have been: *and therefore Virginia Woolf was a realistic as well a poetic novelist, a satirist and social critic*. Option 1 will not do for this reason.

Option 2: Virginia Woolf: Critic and Commentator on the 20th century Novel. First of all there is no mention of any date or year in the passage that would give the impression that Woolf did her act in the 20th century. For a moment even if we let that pass, then a casual glance at the paragraph will tell us that whatever criticism there is, it is about the works of Virginia Woolf. Woolf has criticised no one except for the mention of her having detested *preaching* in fiction (as may be seen at the conclusion of paragraph 3) by the novelist D H Lawrence in particular. Since D H Lawrence was not the only 20th century novel writer, saying that Woolf commented on the 20th century novel in detesting one novelist (and not *novel*) would be a sweeping generalisation. Option 2 will not work either.

Option 3: Trends in Contemporary Reform Movements as a key to understanding Virginia Woolf's Novels. If you want to use the contemporary trends as a key to understanding Virginia Woolf's novels, then these contemporary trends must be mentioned somewhere. *Contemporary* means that which is happening at the same time. If we will see the paragraph, no such trends are mentioned. This is why Option 3 will not do.

Option 4: Society as Allegory for the Individual in the Novels of Virginia Woolf. There are some shades of meaning for the word *allegory* that we would do well to know.

We would all know the *allegory* (or *a fable in which there is a moral*) of the race between a rabbit and the tortoise where the tortoise won because he was perseverant. The moral of this allegory was: the low and steady win the race. We would also recall George Orwell's allegorical book *Animal Farm* (1945), which was a condemnation of totalitarian society based on the Russian Revolution and its betrayal by Stalin. The animals who symbolised the common people of Russia, dissatisfied with their servitude to humans, take over their farm intending to run things fairly, but are betrayed by the pigs who symbolised the communists who adopt the commandment, "All animals are equal, but some animals are more equal than others".

Having appreciated that an allegory is symbolism, look at this logically. For example, an individual's behaviour and morals can create an allegory for the state of decay in society but how can you have society symbolising individuals? If you see the first paragraph, some *Mrs. Dalloway* - a character that we do not know is whether fictitious or real – is the allegory for the social system that Woolf wants to criticise. This is the exact opposite of Option 4.

Option 5: Virginia Woolf's Novels: Critical Reflections on the Individual and on Society. This is the only one left. However that is not the only reason why it is to be marked as correct. This title can partly be seen as apt from (A) the opening lines of the passage where Woolf in her own words wishes to criticise the social system and (B) the opening lines of paragraph 2. Hence **Option** 5.

Question 10

In the first paragraph of the passage, the author's attitude towards the literary critics mentioned can best be described as:

(1) disparaging

(2) ironic

(3) facetious

(4) sceptical but resigned

(5) disappointed but hopeful

Answer 10

Since the question is specific about which paragraph to refer, this must be taken as a godsend and we must rush to the first paragraph without a moment's delay. We shall see the following words there in regard to the author's attitude towards literary critics: *literary critics' cavalier dismissal of Woolf's social vision will not withstand scrutiny.*

It will be worthwhile understanding what *cavalier* means. The cavalier is a cavalryman, a horse mounted soldier. The cavalier sits on a horse and when he talks to others he looks down on the one he talks. Figuratively, the attitude of someone who behaves condescendingly with others or is standoffish to others – keeping aloof or reserved – is known as a *cavalier* stance. Cavalier dismissal means dismissing in a manner that would be belittling.

Scrutiny is examination or evaluation. When someone scrutinises the examination papers, the idea is not to see how much they weigh. The idea is to see how many answers are correct and how many wrong. If something will stand scrutiny it will be proved correct. If it cannot, it will be proved wrong or erroneous.

Since the author says that the critics' cavalier dismissal of Woolf's social vision will not withstand scrutiny, it means that if ever the critics views are judged by someone later on, they will be found to have been wrong in their criticism. There is no doublespeak. The author feels that the critics are wrong and he says this in so many words.

We shall have to see which of the options has a word or phrase that is synonymous to *cavalier*.

Option 1: disparaging. If a father is so fond of his child that he will not tolerate anything spoken *disparaging* about the child, this means that he cannot tolerate anything that will lower the child in the eyes of others. *Disparaging* could do as synonym for *cavalier* since when a cavalier speaks to others from a horse he would tend to treat others disparagingly.

Option 2: ironic. If it is *ironic* that a novelist died before he could receive the literary award that was announced, it is *paradoxical*. If a school student comes home with his scorecard and his father seeing that he has got only 10% marks at arithmetic tells him in an *ironic* manner that arithmetic seems to be his forte, the father is *ridiculing* or *scoffing* at the son. His tone is *sarcastic*. He says something other than what he means. Since the author has called the critics' views of Woolf's social vision as wrong, it means that the author says what he means whereas if he were ironic he would say something other than what he means.

Option 3: facetious. Imagine that an earthquake strikes a city and hundreds of people are dead. A husband and wife are watching the newscast on television and the husband says that these hundreds are free from the bother of paying income tax. The wife tells him that he is being *facetious*. What she means is that he is being *inappropriately humorous*.

Option 4: sceptical but resigned. In an argument between two people about who is right, one person feels that he is right but it is no use arguing now with the other because it will be an endless argument since the other person does not wish to listen to reason, then he tells the other person: *You win, okay*! He does not say what he means. This is why Option 4 will not do.

Option 5: disappointed but hopeful. The author says that the critics are wrong. If he were to say that he hopes that the critics will see the light and change their views, then the author could be said to be disappointed but hopeful. He says no such thing in the paragraph that we are to focus on in the terms of the question itself.

Hence Option 1.

Question 11

It can be inferred from the passage that Woolf chose Chaucer as a literary model because she believed that:

(1) Chaucer was the first English author to focus on society as a whole as well as on individual characters

(2) Chaucer was an honest and forthright author, whereas novelists like D. H. Lawrence did not sincerely wish to change society

(3) Chaucer was more concerned with understanding his society than with calling its accepted mores into question

(4) Chaucer's writing was greatly, if subtly, effective in influencing the moral attitudes of his readers

(5) Her own novels would be more widely read if, like Chaucer, she did not overtly and vehemently criticise contemporary society

Answer 11

Let us see from the passage why Woolf chose Chaucer as a literary model. Please see these words in the last paragraph: Woolf's literary models were acute social observers like Chekhov and Chaucer. As she put it in *The Common Reader*, "**it is safe to say that not a single law has been framed or one stone set upon another because of anything Chaucer said or wrote; and yet, as we read him, we are absorbing morality at every pore.**" The following can be inferred from these words:

- Since Woolf was a novelist and she chose Chaucer as a literary model, Chaucer too must have been a writer
- Chaucer could not have dictated or written laws since he was an author and not a dictator or statesman. The law that the above words refer to is Chaucer's code of morality
- Chaucer put this code so cleverly in his writings in such a manner that even though he did not write anything directly about morality, the reader was able to see his code of morality and absorb every lesson in morality that Chaucer gave
- Chaucer's writing had a powerful influence on his readers since they were absorbing his morality in every pore

The third of the above inferences is what subtlety means and hence Option 4 emerges straightaway.

Question 12

It can be inferred from the passage that the most probable reason Woolf realistically described the social setting in the majority of her novels was that she

(1) was aware that contemporary literary critics considered the novel to be the most realistic of literary genres

(2) was interested in the effect of a person's social milieu on his or her character and actions

(3) needed to be as attentive to detail as possible in her novels in order to support the argument she advanced in them

(4) wanted to show that the painstaking fidelity in the representation of reality did not in any way hamper the artist

(5) wished to prevent critics from charging that her novels were written in an ambiguous and inexact style

Answer 12

Please see these words at paragraph 2:

(A) In her novels, Woolf is deeply engaged by the questions of how individuals are shaped (or deformed) by their social environments, how historical forces impinge on people's lives, how class, wealth, and gender help to determine people's fates.

(B) Most of her novels are rooted in a realistically rendered social setting and in a precise historical time.

A is the cause of which B is the effect. Option 2 is to be marked as correct because it emerges verbatim. The social *milieu* means social *surrounding* or social *environment*.

Question 13

Which of the following phrases best expresses the sense of the word "contemplative " as it is used in line 2, paragraph 4 in the passage?

(1) Gradually elucidating the rational structures underlying accepted mores

(2) Reflecting on issues in society without prejudice or emotional commitment

(3) Avoiding the aggressive assertion of the author's perspective to the exclusion of the reader's judgement

(4) Conveying a broad view of society as a whole rather than focusing on an isolated individual consciousness

(5) Appreciating the world as the artist sees it rather than judging it in moral terms

Answer 13

Let us see the sentence where the word contemplative is used so that we shall be able to see its contextual usage. The sentence in Line 2, Paragraph 4 is as follows: Woolf's own social criticism is expressed in the language of the observation rather than in direct commentary, since for her, fiction is a contemplative, not an active art.

Quite clearly the meaning of *contemplative* in the present context is *something that does not involve acting* (or doing something). We should therefore look for a verb that means *not doing anything actively*. Among the five options, *avoiding* at Option 3 is the only verb that qualifies. Thus Option 3.

Question 14

The author implies that a major element of the satirist's art is the satirist's:

(1) consistent adherence to a position of lofty disdain when viewing the foibles of humanity

(2) insistence on the helplessness of individuals against the social forces that seek to determine an individual's fate

(3) cynical disbelief that visionaries can either enlighten or improve their societies

(4) fundamental assumption that some ambiguity must remain in a work of art in order for it to reflect society and social mores accurately

(5) refusal to indulge in polemic when presenting social mores to readers for their scrutiny

Answer 14

We should see the passage for what constitutes the major element of the satirist's art which we shall find in the following words in paragraph 4: *As a moralist, Woolf works by indirection, subtly undermining officially accepted mores, mocking, suggesting, calling into question, rather than asserting, advocating, bearing witness: hers is the satirist's art.*

These things can be inferred:

- Woolf was a moralist
- Whatever she had to say about officially accepted customs (which is the meaning of the word *mores*), she said indirectly
- Some of the ways in which she expressed herself indirectly were mocking, suggesting, questioning rather than saying anything assertively, and so on

Satire means mockery, ridicule. If you wish to ridicule someone who has three tyres of fat around his waist, calling him a fatso is a direct reference to his chubbiness. This may be rude and may offend. If however you ask him if he is on a crash diet, you are teasing him by saying other than what you mean. With this clarification, let us see the options and find out which one will fit.

Option 1: consistent adherence to a position of lofty disdain when viewing the foibles of humanity. The word *disdain* means *disregard* which is a feeling toward someone not worth noticing or below someone's dignity. The prime element of disregard is not expressing anything in order to show that the other person is not worth bothering about. Satire cannot be conveyed without expressing oneself. Option 1 will not do for this reason.

Option 2: insistence on the helplessness of individuals against the social forces that seek to determine an individual's fate. Imagine that your class teacher is showing you all the answer sheets for the mathematics test that she gave you last week. One of your answers is correct according to your view whereas the teacher has marked it wrong. When you insist that your answer is correct, you are entering into an argument. There can be no indirect way you can say that your answer is correct. Thus Option 2 will not work as well.

Option 3: cynical disbelief that visionaries can either enlighten or improve their societies. A *cynic* is someone who doubts all the while. He despises human sincerity and merit. If you tell a cynic that the person who got the highest mark at the common entrance test for medical colleges in the country is the son of a civil servant, he would probably say that the fellow must have got the question paper beforehand. You tell him that your country's contingent at the Olympics are likely to return with at least 5 gold medals and he says they will be lucky if they can make it to any of the heats, the morons. Cynicism is not satire. It can be expressed only directly. This is why Option 3 will not do either.

Option 4: fundamental assumption that some ambiguity must remain in a work of art in order for it to reflect society and social mores accurately. Satire means expressing indirectly but not indistinctly. If someone speaks with ambiguity, it will be difficult to judge what exactly he wants to say because ambiguity would lend two meanings or indistinctness to something said or written. Satire would give a single clear meaning to what one wants to convey. This is why Option 4 will not do.

Option 5: refusal to indulge in polemic when presenting. *Polemic* means a controversial argument or discussion. When one wants to present a point of view and chooses not to indulge in polemic, then since there can be only two ways of what one wants to say – direct and indirect - the only other way to present one's view point is indirectly. Say what you want but do not assert. This is precisely what we have inferred in the last of the three inferences that we have made at the outset. Hence **Option 5**.

Question 15

The passage supplies information for answering which of the following questions?

(1) Have literary critics ignored the social criticism inherent in the works of Chekhov and Chaucer?

(2) Does the author believe that Woolf is solely an introspective and visionary novelist?

(3) What are the social causes with which Woolf shows herself to be sympathetic in her writings?

(4) Was D. H. Lawrence as concerned as Woolf was with creating realistic settings for his novels?

(5) Does Woolf attribute more power to social environment or to historical forces as shapers of a person's life?

Answer 15

The passage shall supply information for answering just one of the five questions and therefore there is no need to be perturbed if one is not able to find the required information as one starts seeing the options one by one which we shall begin hereunder.

Option 1: Have literary critics ignored the social criticism inherent in the works of Chekhov and Chaucer? This is to be seen from the logical point of view. If one wants to see whether someone's classmates have commented on Sam's new hair cut, it is important to see if Sam has had a hair cut at all, old or new. Let us see whether there is social criticism inherent in the works of Chekhov and Chaucer. We shall have to scan the passage and locate references to these two gentlemen. The words are in the last paragraph and are as follows: Woolf's literary models were acute social observers like Chekhov and Chaucer. The word acute means sharp. A referee at the football match has to be a sharp observer and award free kicks and things when there are infringements. A sharp referee need not criticise the player who has inadvertently touched the ball with his hand. That is not his job. Similarly an acute observer need not necessarily criticise. He can observe and write down what he wants to say. All that the passage says is that Chekhov and Chaucer were **acute social observers**. Since one is not able to find out whether there is social criticism inherent in the works of Chekhov and Chaucer, our scrutiny of the passage to find information that would answer the question in Option 1 should stop here.

Option 2: Does the author believe that Woolf is solely an introspective and visionary novelist? Let us see what the author says about Virginia Woolf and we shall find his views in these words in paragraph 4: *Woolf's own social criticism is expressed in the language of the observation rather than in direct commentary, since for her, fiction is a contemplative, not an active art. But Virginia Woolf was a realistic as well as poetic novelist, a satirist and social critic as well a visionary.*

As far as *visionary* is concerned, the author has used this very word for Virginia Woolf in paragraph 1.

The word *introspective* has the prefix INTRO- (that means *within*) and the French verb SPECTERE (that means *look*) and therefore *introspective* means that which has the quality of *looking within* and hence *reflective*, *contemplative* or *meditative*. This too the author says in paragraph 4 while using the word **contemplative** to describe Virginia Woolf. **Option 2** is correct.

Option 3: What are the social causes with which Woolf shows herself to be sympathetic in her writings?

Let us see from the passage as to with whom is Woolf sympathetic and we shall find that **she is sympathetic with the causes of social reformers** but there is no mention of any specific social cause(s) as may be seen in the following words at paragraph 2 in the passage: *The pictures of reformers in her novels are usually satirical or sharply critical. Even when Woolf is fundamentally sympathetic to their causes, she portrays people anxious to reform their society and possessed of a message or program as arrogant or dishonest, unaware of how their political ideas serve their own psychological needs.* This is why Option 3 will not do.

Option 4: Was D. H. Lawrence as concerned as Woolf was with creating realistic settings for his novels? As regards D H Lawrence, Woolf detested (*despised* or *hated*) him for *preaching* (or *moralising*) in fiction. Had he been as realistic as Woolf, there would have no need to hate him. On the contrary Woolf would have admired him. Option 4 will not do for this reason.

Option 5: Does Woolf attribute more power to social environment or to historical forces as shapers of a person's life? The word *attribute* comes from the word tribute. If the shooter *attributes* his success to his parents' constant motivation, what he is saying is that this success is a tribute to his parents' motivation. He assigns his success to them. About Woolf attributing power to social environment or to historical forces as shapers of a person's life, let us see these words at paragraph 2 in the passage: *In her novels, Woolf is deeply engaged by the questions of how individuals are shaped (or deformed) by their social environments, how historical forces impinge on people's lives, how class, wealth, and gender help to determine people's fates.*

All that these words mean that Woolf is deeply concerned with (which is the meaning of *deeply engaged*) questions of how individuals are shaped by their social environments and how historical forces help to determine people's fate. There is no comparison between which plays a greater shape to a person's life: social environment or historical forces. This is why Option 5 will not do.

Practice Test 3

Passage 1

It is a popular misconception that nuclear fusion power is free of radioactivity; in fact, the deuterium-tritium reaction that nuclear scientists are currently exploring with such zeal produces both alpha particles and neutrons. (The neutrons are used to produce tritium from a lithium blanket surrounding the reactor.) Another common misconception is that nuclear fusion power is a virtually unlimited source of energy because of the enormous quantity of deuterium in the sea. Actually, its limits are set by the amount of available lithium, which is about as plentiful as uranium inn the earth's crust. Research should certainly continue on controlled nuclear fusion, but no energy program should be premised on its existence until it has proven practical. For the immediate future, we must continue to use hydroelectric power, nuclear fission, and fossil fuels to meet our energy needs. The energy sources already in major use are in major use for good reason.

Question 1

The primary purpose of the passage is to

(1) criticise scientists who believe that the deuterium-tritium fusion reaction can be made feasible as an energy source

(2) admonish scientists who have failed to correctly calculate the amount of lithium available for use in nuclear fusion reactors

(3) defend the continued short-term use of fossil fuels as a major energy source

(4) caution against uncritical embrace of nuclear fusion power as a major energy source

(5) correct the misconception that nuclear power is entirely free of radioactivity

Answer 1

Let us go from option to option and see which is the correct primary purpose of the passage.

Option (1): criticise scientists who believe that the deuterium-tritium fusion reaction can be made feasible as an energy source. Imagine that you have hosted a party. Every dish is very spicy. There is nothing for those who cannot stomach spice. Some people are not eating anything. If you wish to criticise the caterer to whom you entrusted the arrangements which of the following would you tell him: (A) or (B)?

(A) Here, do you see that most people drink a glass of water after every morsel because the food is terribly spicy? Do you see that the children are all going hungry? You call this food? Do you know that most of it will go waste?

(B) Do not be under the misconception that food is tasty merely because it is spicy. In future, keep spice to the minimum. Keep food that people are used to eating. They do not use so much spice for a good reason.

Criticism will take the form of (A) and caution will take the form of (B). This whole passage is talking about form (B). What is more, there is no specific mention that scientists are the ones who have been harbouring misconceptions. There are popular misconceptions. This means that many ordinary people have these misconceptions mainly because they do not know what is what. Scientists will not come under this category. Option 1 will not do for this reason.

Option (2): admonish scientists who have failed to correctly calculate the amount of lithium available for use in nuclear fusion reactors. Option 2 will not do because there is a note of caution and not admonishment (or *scolding*).

Option (3): defend the continued short-term use of fossil fuels as a major energy source. If the idea is to defend continued short-term use of fossil fuels as a major energy source, then there is no need for research in controlled fusion that the passage says must continue. There would be no need to say that one must continue to use fossil fuel for our immediate requirements of energy either. If you find that fossil fuel is better, then use it as long as you can. Why limit its use to the immediate term?

When would you defend something? When it is under attack, of course. There is no attack on the use of fossil fuels. On the contrary there is a recommendation on continuing its use till nuclear energy is found to be a practical energy source. Option 3 will not do for this reason.

Option (4): caution against uncritical embrace of nuclear fusion power as a major energy source. This is clearly discernable and hence **Option 4**.

Option (5): correct the misconception that nuclear power is entirely free of radioactivity. If someone has been under the misconception that he is terribly handsome and a girl tells him that he looks like someone straight out of a comic book, she has done her bit to dispel that misconception. If it is the primary idea of the passage to correct (or *dispel*) this misconception then it has been stated in the first sentence in the passage that nuclear power is not free of radioactivity. Nobody is saying that nuclear power is entirely free of radioactivity. Option 5 will not work for this reason.

Question 2

It can be inferred from the passage that the author believes which of the following about the current state of public awareness concerning nuclear fusion power:

(1) The public has been deliberately misinformed about the advantages and disadvantages of nuclear fusion power

(2) The public is unaware of the principal advantage of the nuclear fusion over nuclear fission as an energy source

(3) The public's awareness of the scientific facts concerning nuclear fusion power is somewhat distorted and incomplete

(4) The public is not interested in increasing its awareness of the advantages and disadvantages of nuclear fusion power

(5) The public is aware of the disadvantages of nuclear fusion power but not of its advantages

Answer 2

The word misconception comprises of the prefix MIS- (that means *wrong*), the other prefix CON- (that means *thoroughly*) and the Latin root CEPT- (that means *take, seize*). *Misconception* therefore means *thoroughly taking or seizing some wrong* (notion) and therefore *misconception* means *misapprehension*, *misunderstanding*, *mistake*, *error*, misinterpretation, the wrong idea, a false impression, or *delusion*. As may be seen from the way the word has originated, a misconception is because of **taking** (and not been given) a wrong interpretation and therefore cannot be a result of deliberate attempt to misinform. Option 1 will not work for that reason alone.

As regards Option 2, it will not do because it contradicts the contention towards the end of the passage that nuclear fission power is a more reliable source than nuclear fusion. About nuclear fusion, there is also a contention in the passage that it is yet to be established as a practical energy source whereas nuclear fission power is already established.

Regarding nuclear fusion there are two popular misconceptions one of which is about the scientific aspect of radioactivity. Anything to be popular must be known to the public. If a film star of Country A lands in Country B and does not find people leaping over one another for his autograph, it is because the public in Country B do not know him. **A popular misconception, therefore, is a wrong impression in the public mind.**

The other popular misconception is about nuclear fusion power being unlimited in supply, which is not a scientific matter. The public is unaware that nuclear fusion is not free of radioactivity. This is their incomplete and somewhat distorted awareness of the scientific facts concerning nuclear fusion power. Option 3 will do very well.

About Option 4 there is no mention in the passage about whether the public is interested or otherwise in increasing or decreasing its awareness and therefore there is no need to presume things. Option 4 will not work for this reason.

About Option 5, the public is aware of the advantages of nuclear fusion power but not of its disadvantages since there is a popular misconception that nuclear fusion power is free of radioactivity. Option 5 in fact contradicts the first popular misconception stated at the very beginning of the passage and will not do.

Question 3

The passage provides information that would answer which of the following questions?

(1) What is likely to be the principal source of deuterium for nuclear fusion power?

(2) How much incidental radiation is produced in the deuterium-tritium fusion reaction?

(3) Why are scientists exploring the deuterium-tritium fusion reaction with such zeal?

(4) Why must the tritium for nuclear fusion be synthesised from lithium?

(5) Why does the deuterium-tritium reaction yield both alpha particles and neutrons?

Answer 3

Let us go from option to option and see which question is answered by the information in the passage.

Option 1: What is likely to be the principal source of deuterium for nuclear fusion power? As may be seen in line 6 the sea is the principal source for deuterium. Option 1 is correct.

Option 2: How much incidental radiation is produced in the deuterium-tritium fusion reaction? The passage only tells us that the deuterium-tritium fusion reaction produces alpha particles and neutrons but not how much. This question cannot be answered from the information given in the passage.

Option 3: Why are scientists exploring the deuterium-tritium fusion reaction with such zeal? The passage only tells us that the scientists are exploring this reaction with zeal but not why with so much zeal.

Option 4: Why must the tritium for nuclear fusion be synthesised from lithium? About this too there is no information in the passage.

Option 5: Why does the deuterium-tritium reaction yield both alpha particles and neutrons? This too is not explained. We are only told that the reaction produces alpha particles and neutrons.

Question 4

Which of the following statements concerning nuclear scientists is most directly suggestive in the passage?

(1) Nuclear scientists have long been aware of the most important facts surrounding the deuterium-tritium fusion reaction.

(2) Nuclear scientists exploring the deuterium-tritium reaction have overlooked key facts in their eagerness to prove nuclear fusion practical

(3) Nuclear scientists may have overestimated the amount of lithium actually available in the earth's crust.

(4) Nuclear scientists have not been entirely dispassionate in their investigation of the deuterium-tritium reaction

(5) Nuclear scientists have insufficiently investigated the lithium-tritium reaction in nuclear fusion

Answer 4

Option 1 would be illogical if it were true. If the scientists have long been aware of the most important facts surrounding the deuterium-tritium fusion reaction why are they currently exploring the deuterium-tritium reaction? If you have known for long that two and two adds up to four, why strain oneself in finding out what do two and two add up to now? Don't we have better things to do?

Option 2 is also illogical given the contention in the passage that nuclear fusion power is yet to be established as practical.

Option 3 is illogical given that the passage states that there is a popular misconception (in the minds of the public and not in the minds of scientists) about the lithium actually available in the earth's crust.

Option 4 is correct since scientists have been exploring the deuterium-tritium reaction with such zeal. Zeal is passion. If the scientists were to be dispassionate (*not passionate* or *not zealous*) about the deuterium-tritium reaction, they would start yawning uncontrollably each time this reaction is even mentioned to them instead of exploring it with zeal.

About Option 5 there is no mention in the passage about any lithium-tritium reaction.

Passage 2

It has long been known that the rate of oxidative metabolism (the process that uses oxygen to convert food into energy) in any animal has a profound effect on its living patterns. The high metabolic rate of small animals, for example, gives them sustained power and activity per unit of weight, but at the cost of requiring constant consumption of food and water. Very large animals, with their relatively low metabolic rates, can survive well on a sporadic food supply, but can generate little metabolic energy per gram of body weight. If only oxidative metabolic rate is considered, therefore, one might assume that smaller, more active, animals would prey on larger ones, at least in groups. Perhaps they could if it were not for anaerobic glycolysis, the greater equalizer.

Anaerobic glycolysis is the process in which energy is produced without oxygen, through the breakdown of muscle glycogen into lactic acid and adenosine triphosphate (ATP), the energy provider. The amount of energy that can be produced anaerobically is a function of the amount of glycogens present – in all vertebrates about 0.5% of their muscles' wet weight. Thus the anaerobic energy reserves of a vertebrate are proportional to the size of the animal. If, for example, some predators had attacked a 100-ton dinosaur, normally torpid, the dinosaur would have been able to generate almost instantaneously, via anaerobic glycolysis, the energy of 3,000 humans at maximum oxidative metabolic energy production. This explains how many large species have managed to compete with their more active neighbours: the compensation for a low oxidative metabolic rate is glycolysis.

There are limitations, however, to this compensation. The glycogen reserves of any animal are good, at most, for only about two minutes at maximum effort, after which only the normal oxidative metabolic source of energy remains. With the conclusion of a burst of activity, the lactic acid level is high in the body fluids, leaving the large animal vulnerable to attack until the acid is reconverted, via oxidative metabolism, by the liver into glucose, which is then sent (in part) back to the muscles for glycogen resynthesis. During this process the enormous energy debt that the animal has run up through anaerobic glycolysis must be repaid, a debt that is proportionally much greater for the larger vertebrates than for the smaller ones. Whereas the tiny shrew can replace in minutes the glycogen used for maximum effort, for example, the gigantic dinosaurs would have required more than three weeks. It might seem that this interminably long recovery time in a large vertebrate would prove a grave disadvantage for survival. Fortunately, muscle glycogen is used only when needed and even then only in whatever quantity is necessary. Only in times of panic or during mortal combat would the entire reserves be consumed.

Question 5

The primary purpose of the passage is to:

(1) refute a misconception about anaerobic glycolysis

(2) introduce a new hypothesis about anaerobic glycolysis

(3) describe the limitations of anaerobic glycolysis

(4) analyse the chemistry of anaerobic glycolysis and its similarity to oxidative metabolism

(5) explain anaerobic glycolysis and its effects on animal survival

Answer 5

We shall go from option to option and see which gives us the primary purpose of the passage.

Option 1: refute a misconception about anaerobic glycolysis. If the idea were to *refute* (or *prove wrong*) a misconception (or *wrong impression*) about anaerobic glycolysis, then it would be necessary to state what is the misconception first of all. If there is any misconception mentioned anywhere it is about oxidative metabolic rate in these words in the first paragraph: *If only oxidative metabolic rate is considered, therefore, one might assume that smaller, more active, animals would prey on larger ones, at least in groups*. There is no misconception about anaerobic glycolysis and hence Option 1 will not do.

Option 2: introduce a new hypothesis about anaerobic glycolysis. If you wish to introduce a new hypothesis about anything one must state why the old one will not work. The passage on the contrary states at the end of the first paragraph that anaerobic glycolysis is a great equaliser. The passage further explains how anaerobic glycolysis compensates for low oxidative metabolic rate. There is no new hypothesis about anaerobic glycolysis and hence Option 2 will not do either.

Option 3: describe the limitations of anaerobic glycolysis. This option is illogical since anaerobic glycolysis has been described as *the great equaliser*. When you want to describe someone as a great mountaineer, you write the names of peaks that he has climbed. If instead you write the names of the peaks that he tried but failed to climb, it will be difficult to justify your calling him a great mountaineer.

Option 4: analyse the chemistry of anaerobic glycolysis and its similarity to oxidative metabolism. Since anaerobic glycolysis is the great equaliser to oxidative metabolism, the two have different functions to perform. If you were to imagine that oxidative metabolism to be an acid, then anaerobic glycolysis would be the alkali and vice-versa. If you were to imagine that oxidative metabolism were to be the privilege to some class of persons in securing admissions to medical colleges and anaerobic glycolysis to be an act of the democratic government that treats all at par, then the two have diversely different functions. Hence this option will not work.

Option 5: explain anaerobic glycolysis and its effects on animal survival. This the passage does very well in the following words at the end of paragraph 2: *This explains how many large species have managed to compete with their more active neighbours: the compensation for a low oxidative metabolic rate is glycolysis*. Hence Option 5.

Question 6

According to the author, glycogen is crucial to the process of anaerobic glycolysis because glycogen:

(1) increases the organism's need for ATP

(2) reduces the amount of ATP in the tissues

(3) is an inhibitor of the oxidative metabolic production of ATP

(4) ensures that the synthesis of ATP will occur speedily

(5) is the material from which ATP is derived

Answer 6

Let us see why glycogen is considered to be crucial to the process of anaerobic glycolysis. We shall see this in the following words in the last paragraph: Anaerobic glycolysis is the process in which energy is produced without oxygen, through the breakdown of muscle glycogen into lactic acid and adenosine triphosphate (ATP), the energy provider. The amount of energy that can be produced anaerobically is a function of the amount of glycogens present – in all vertebrates about 0.5% of their muscles' wet weight. Thus the anaerobic energy reserves of a vertebrate are proportional to the size of the animal.

These six things can be inferred from the above words:

- Energy is produced through anaerobic glycolysis

- Anaerobic glycolysis produces energy through the breakdown of muscle glycogen into lactic acid and adenosine triphosphate (ATP)
- ATP provides energy
- The amount of energy that can be produced anaerobically depends upon the amount of glycogens present
- The amount of glycogens present depend upon the net weight of an animal
- The bigger a vertebrate animal is, the bigger are its anaerobic energy reserves

We shall now go from option to option and see which one will fit in for the reason why glycogen is crucial to the process of anaerobic glycolysis.

Option 1: increases the organism's need for ATP. This even if true may explain why ATP is necessary for an organism but still does not explain why glycogen is important for the process of anaerobic glycolysis. This is similar to saying that exercise increases someone's thirst but not explaining why exercise is necessary for keeping fit. This option will not do.

Option 2: reduces the amount of ATP in the tissues. Tissues are not mentioned anywhere in the passage and hence this option will not do either.

Option 3: is an inhibitor of the oxidative metabolic production of ATP. ATP is produced by anaerobic glycolysis and not by oxidative metabolism. Hence this option will not work.

Option 4: ensures that the synthesis of ATP will occur speedily. ATP is produced by breakdown of muscle glycogen and breakdown is the opposite of synthesis. Synthesis takes place by the combining (or *union* or *fusion*) of two or more things to make something else, not by breaking down of things.

Option 5: is the material from which ATP is derived. This is the third of the six inferences that we have made above and hence Option 5 is correct.

Question 7

According to the author a major limitation of anaerobic glycolysis is that it can

(1) produce in large animals more lactic acid than the liver can safely reconvert

(2) necessitate a dangerously long recovery period in large animals

(3) produce energy more slowly than it can be used by large animals

(4) consume all of the available glycogen regardless of need

(5) reduce significantly the rate at which energy is produced by oxidative metabolism

Answer 7

Let us see where we see the limitations of anaerobic glycolysis are mentioned and then see which one of these is the major limitation. We shall see these limitations in the following words: ....*the compensation for a low oxidative metabolic rate is glycolysis. There are limitations, however, to this compensation. The glycogen reserves of any animal are good, at most, for only about two minutes at maximum effort, after which only the normal oxidative metabolic source of energy remains. With the conclusion of a burst of activity, the lactic acid level is high in the body fluids, leaving the large animal vulnerable to attack until the acid is reconverted, via oxidative metabolism, by the liver into glucose, which is then sent (in part) back to the muscles for glycogen resynthesis. During this process the enormous energy debt that the animal has run up through anaerobic glycolysis must be repaid, a debt that is proportionally much greater for the larger vertebrates than for the smaller ones. Whereas the tiny shrew can replace in minutes the glycogen used for maximum effort, for example, the gigantic dinosaurs would have required more than three weeks. It might seem that this interminably long recovery time in a large vertebrate would prove a grave disadvantage for survival.*

These things can be inferred from the above words:

- Anaerobic glycolysis compensates for oxidative metabolic rate
- There are limitations to anaerobic glycolysis

- When a large animal completes a short burst of energy, it runs up an enormous energy debt
- Since one can run up a debt only when one spends more than what one has, the large animal becomes weak after a short burst of activity
- Large animals become much weaker at the end of a short burst of activity than do small ones
- Tiny animals can replace this energy quickly
- Dinosaurs were large animals
- Large animals would require very long time for replacing this energy
- This long time for replacing energy would prove a grave disadvantage for the survival of large animals
- Anything that proves a grave disadvantage for survival has a major limitation
- Whatever major limitation that anaerobic glycolysis has with respect to animals, this limitation is with respect to large animals

Against the backdrop of these inferences, **Option 2** emerges as correct straightaway.

Question 8

The passage suggests that the total anaerobic energy reserves of a vertebrate are proportional to the vertebrate's size because

(1) larger vertebrates conserve more energy than smaller vertebrates

(2) larger vertebrates use less oxygen per unit weight than smaller vertebrates

(3) the ability of a vertebrate to consume food is the function of its size

(4) the amount of muscle tissue is directly related to its size

(5) the size of a vertebrate is proportional to the quantity of energy it can utilise

Answer 8

Let us see where the passage suggests why the total anaerobic energy reserves of a vertebrate are proportional to the vertebrate's size. We shall see the reason in the following words in the passage: *Anaerobic glycolysis is the process in which energy is produced without oxygen, through the breakdown of muscle glycogen into lactic acid and adenosine triphosphate (ATP), the energy provider. The amount of energy that can be produced anaerobically is a function of the amount of glycogens present – in all vertebrates about 0.5% of their muscles' wet weight. Thus the anaerobic energy reserves of a vertebrate are proportional to the size of the animal.*

The clear inference is that the total anaerobic energy reserves of a vertebrate are proportional to the net weight of the vertebrate's muscles. **Option 4** emerges as correct right away.

Question 9

The author suggests that, on the basis of energy production, a 100-ton dinosaur would have been markedly vulnerable to which of the following?

(I) repeated attacks by a single smaller, more active adversary

(II) sustained attacks by numerous smaller, more active adversaries

(III) an attack by an individual adversary of similar size

(1) (II) only

(2) (I) & (II) only

(3) (I) & (III) only

(4) (II) & (III) only

(5) (I) (II) and (III)

Answer 9

Let us see the words where the author talks about energy production and to what are large animals vulnerable. These words are in the first paragraph: *Very large animals, with their relatively low metabolic rates, can survive well on a sporadic food supply, but can generate little metabolic energy per gram of body weight. If only oxidative metabolic rate is considered, therefore, one might assume that smaller, more active, animals would prey on larger ones, at least in groups.*

These things can be inferred from the above words:

- Although the words 100-ton are not mentioned anywhere, a 100-ton dinosaur would surely not blush when classified as a very large animal
- Very large animals can produce little energy in relation to their body weight
- Smaller animals are active animals and can therefore produce substantial energy in relation to their body weight
- Smaller animals in groups would prey on large animals if one were to view things on the basis of energy production alone and therefore it would not be unusual to see a mice bringing down a lion and eating him up

  Statement (I) talks about a single animal attacking a very large animal. Statement (III) talks about a single large animal attacking a single large animal of the same size. Since the whole thing is about small animals in groups attacking a very large animal, only Statement (II) will work and hence Option 1.

Question 10

It can be inferred from the passage that the time required to replenish muscle glycogen following anaerobic glycolysis is determined by which of the following factors?

(I) rate of oxidative metabolism

(II) quality of lactic acid in the body fluids

(III) percentage of glucose that is returned to the muscles

(1) (I) only

(2) (III) only

(3) (I) & (II) only

(4) (I) & (III) only

(5) (I) (II) and (III)

Answer 10

Please see these words in the passage from which we shall be able to see the factors that determine the time required to replenish muscle glycogen following anaerobic glycolysis: *the compensation for a low oxidative metabolic rate is glycolysis. There are limitations, however, to this compensation. The glycogen reserves of any animal are good, at most, for only about two minutes at maximum effort, after which only the normal oxidative metabolic source of energy remains. With the conclusion of a burst of activity, the lactic acid level is high in the body fluids, leaving the large animal vulnerable to attack until the acid is reconverted, via oxidative metabolism, by the liver into glucose, which is then sent (in part) back to the muscles for glycogen resynthesis.*

The following things can be inferred from the above words:

- Anaerobic glycolysis compensates for a low oxidative metabolic rate and therefore the lower the oxidative metabolic rate, the faster the anaerobic glycolysis and vice versa
- The rate at which anaerobic glycolysis occurs is determined by the rate of oxidative metabolism
- Lactic acid level is high in the body fluids of large animals after a burst of activity
- The high level of lactic acid weakens the large animal

- The lactic acid is reconverted into glucose
- A part of the glucose is sent back to the muscles for synthesising glycogen again
- More the glucose sent back to the muscles, the more muscle glycogen will be synthesised

In addition to the above we have seen in an earlier answer that anaerobic glycolysis produces energy by breaking down muscle glycogens.

From what we have inferred, Statement (I) emerges from the first and second inference that we have made above. Statement (II) emerges from the third inference above. Statement (III) emerges from the last two of the above inferences.

Thus Option 5.

Question 11

The author is most probably addressing which of the following audiences:

(1) College students in an introductory course on animal physiology

(2) Historians of science investigating the discovery of anaerobic glycolysis

(3) Graduate students with specialised training in comparative anatomy

(4) Zoologists interested in prehistoric animals

(5) Biochemists doing research on oxidative metabolism

Answer 11

We must remember that the question requires you to exercise your judgement and reasoning. You will have to evolve the correct answer. You will not see the correct answer emerging verbatim from the passage principally because if anything it would be the author's reasoning that will emerge from the passage. **Your** assessment is most unlikely to emerge verbatim from the passage.

Now please see the opening lines of the passage: It has long been known that the rate of oxidative metabolism (the process that uses oxygen to convert food into energy) in any animal has a profound effect on its living patterns. The high metabolic rate of small animals, for example, gives them sustained power and activity per unit of weight, but at the cost of requiring constant consumption of food and water. Very large animals, with their relatively low metabolic rates, can survive well on a sporadic food supply, but can generate little metabolic energy per gram of body weight.

These things can be inferred from the passage:

- Whosoever is the audience needs to be reminded what oxidative metabolism is all about because there is a sentence in brackets telling what oxidative metabolism really is
- Whosoever is the audience needs to be reminded what gives sustained power to small animals
- Whosoever is the audience needs to be reminded why large animals can generate little energy in relation to their body weight

With this now let us see the options and see which one will fit in.

Option 1: College students in an introductory course on animal physiology. When you talk to college students who have been studying a subject for long, you know that there is no need to tell them what some terms pertaining to their subject mean. But when you talk to college students who are being introduced to a subject, you ought to tell them the meanings of terms pertaining to their subject if you do not want that the room should resonate with their yawns. Option 1 seems very logical.

Option 2: Historians of science investigating the discovery of anaerobic glycolysis. Even about anaerobic glycolysis, there is a small explanation as to what this means in the opening lines of paragraph 2. Anyone investigating the discovery of anaerobic glycolysis need not be told what it is. An investigator should have at least that much knowledge about the subject that he wishes to investigate. Option 2 will not do.

Option 3: Graduate students with specialised training in comparative anatomy. Graduate students with specialised training in comparative anatomy need not be told what the elementary terms used in their subject of specialisation mean. Option 3 will not work for this reason

Option 4: Zoologists interested in prehistoric animals. The entire passage is about anaerobic glycolysis. Since we know for sure that anaerobic glycolysis is not a prehistoric animal, we need not bother about this option.

Option 5: Biochemists doing research on oxidative metabolism. If a biochemist doing research on oxidative metabolism needs to be told what it is, then the next thing will be that biochemists should learn that A stands for Apple, and B for Ball and so on; biochemists should be studying in Kindergarten. Option 5 will not work for that reason.

Hence **Option 1**.

Question 12

Which of the following best states the central idea of the passage?

(1) The disadvantage of a low oxidative metabolism rate in large animals can be offset by their ability to convert substantial amounts of glycogen into energy

(2) The most significant problem facing animals that have used anaerobic glycolysis for energy is the resynthesis of its by-product, glucose, into glycogen

(3) The benefit to animals of anaerobic glycolysis are offset by the profound costs that must be paid

(4) The major factor ensuring that a large animal will triumph over a smaller animal is the large animal's ability to produce energy via anaerobic glycolysis

(5) The great differences that exist in metabolic rates between species of small animals and species of large animals can have important effects on the pattern of their activities

Answer 12

There are two principal scientific terms mentioned here with so much frequency that one would get the impression that the passage is about these two scientific terms in the main just as when your cousin talks about his girlfriend mentioning her name a dozen times in a row without allowing you to put in a word, you may safely deduce that the topic of his monologue is his girlfriend. These two scientific terms mentioned frequently are: Oxidative Metabolism and Anaerobic Glycolysis.

About Oxidative Metabolism we are told that it has a profound effect on any animal. Anything that has a profound effect on another may be safely considered as some topic of importance.

We are also told that if one were to consider Oxidative Metabolism alone, then one would see situations where groups of small animals would prey on large animals. This would therefore lead to a situation wherein some ants may drag an elephant by its tail, which we would find so difficult to imagine

We are told that anaerobic glycolysis compensates for Oxidative Metabolism and if A compensates for B that is something of great importance, then A could safely be considered as something of great importance as well.

Since anaerobic glycolysis compensates for Oxidative Metabolism, the latter must have some drawbacks just as someone's lovely voice compensating for his looks means that his looks are his drawback.

In view of the above, **Option 1** seems the best choice. About Option 2, by-product means something that is not an important product. A by-product cannot be the central idea of a passage just as crumbs cannot be the theme of the discussions that bakers may have during the annual general meeting of their industry association. About Option 3, Anaerobic Glycolysis enables animals to produce energy without oxygen.

Anaerobic glycolysis gives energy to animals. If this benefit were to be offset by the profound costs to be paid, it would mean that the animal is better off without energy. While the adverse aspects of having energy are not known, the outcome of **not** having energy for an animal is death. Option 3 would therefore be a most illogical choice. About Option 4, a large animal is only expected to prevail over a small animal. There would be need to worry if one were to see the reverse process where a panther is running for his life with a pack of squirrels baying for his blood. Option 4 would also be illogical for that reason. About Option 5, since Anaerobic Glycolysis compensates for Oxidative Metabolism, the latter has disadvantages that are offset by the advantages of the former. If at all, Anaerobic Glycolysis should be the theme of the passage and not Oxidative Metabolism. This is why Option 5 will not do either.

Passage 3

Tocqueville, apparently, was wrong. Jacksonian America was not a fluid, egalitarian society where individual wealth and poverty were ephemeral conditions. At least so argues E. Pessen in his iconoclastic study of the very rich in the United States between 1825 and 1850.

Pessen does present a quantity of examples, together with some refreshingly intelligible statistics, to establish the existence of an inordinately wealthy class. Though active in commerce or the professions, most of the wealthy were not self-made, but inherited family fortunes. In no sense mercurial, these great fortunes survived the financial panics that destroyed lesser ones. Indeed, in several cities the wealthiest one percent constantly increased its share until by 1850 it owned half of the community's wealth. Although these observations are true, Pessen overestimates their importance by concluding from them that the undoubted progress towards inequality in the late 18th century continued in the Jacksonian period and that the United States was a class-ridden, plutocratic society even before industrialisation.

Question 13

According to the passage, Pessen indicates that all of the following were true of the very wealthy in the United States between 1825 and 1850 EXCEPT:

(1) They formed a distinct upper class

(2) Many of them were able to increase their holdings

(3) Some of them worked as professionals or in business

(4) Most of them accumulated their own fortunes

(5) Many of them retained their wealth in spite of financial upheavals

Answer 13

Let us go from option to option and see which one fits about the very wealthy in the United States between 1825 and 1850.

Option 1: They formed a distinct upper class. If we were to see the following words at the beginning of paragraph 2, we will see that there was an inordinately wealthy (abnormally rich) class and therefore there was a distinct upper class: *Pessen does present a quantity of examples, together with some refreshingly intelligible statistics, to establish the existence of an inordinately wealthy class.* If two lads in Class V stand six feet tall whereas the others in his class are in the range of four feet, these two are inordinately tall and therefore form a distinct class of tall boys. Option 1 is inferred from the passage.

Option 2: Many of them were able to increase their holdings. Towards the middle of paragraph 2 we shall see the following words that will testify to the fact that Option 2 is inferred as well: *Indeed, in several cities the wealthiest one percent constantly increased its share.*

Option 3: Some of them worked as professionals or in business. Please see these words in paragraph 2 that will show that Option 3 is inferred from the passage but Option 4 is not: *Though active in commerce or the professions, most of the wealthy were not self-made.*

Option 4: Most of them accumulated their own fortunes. This is not inferred and thus **Option 4** is to be marked as correct.

Option 5: Many of them retained their wealth in spite of financial upheavals. Please see these words in paragraph 2 from where we can infer Option 5: *In no sense mercurial, these great fortunes survived the financial panics that destroyed lesser ones.*

Question 14

The author's attitude toward Pessen's presentation of statistics can be best described as

(1) disapproving

(2) shocked

(3) suspicious

(4) amused

(5) laudatory

Answer 14

Let us see the following words in the passage where one can see the author's attitude towards Pessen's presentation of statistics: *Tocqueville, apparently, was wrong. Jacksonian America was not a fluid, egalitarian society where individual wealth and poverty were ephemeral conditions. At least so argues E. Pessen in his* ***iconoclastic study*** *of the very rich in the United States between 1825 and 1850.*

Religious images or idols are known as *icons*. An *iconoclast* is someone who destroys icons or, figuratively, someone who destroys a general belief. General beliefs cannot be broken unless one presents exceptionally strong arguments. General beliefs are not pieces of pottery that we can break them with our fingers. It takes great courage to first of all even *present* a case against a general belief. Besides courage it takes a powerfully meritorious argument to destroy a general belief. Therefore one who presents an *iconoclastic study* (a study that breaks a widely accepted belief) is to be admired and hence Option 5 emerges straightaway.

Question 15

Which of the following best states the author's main point?

(1) Pessen's study has overturned the previously established view of the social and economic structure of early 19th century America

(2) Tocqueville's analysis of the United States in the Jacksonian era remain the definitive account of this period

(3) Pessen's study is valuable primarily because it shows the continuity of the social system in the United States throughout the 19th century

(4) The social patterns and political power of the extremely wealthy in the United States between 1825 and 1850 are well documented

(5) Pessen challenges a view of the social and economic system in the United States from 1825 to 1850, but he draws conclusions that are incorrect.

Answer 15

If you see the opening sentence of the passage, you will find that the fellow Tocqueville was wrong. This means that Option 2 is ruled out straightaway. A wrong analysis can remain a definitive account of something only till such time that it is proved wrong and not thereafter. Since the very first line says that Tocqueville was wrong, the question of his analysis having remained the definitive account of the United States in the Jacksonian era does not arise.

If you will see these words in the opening paragraph, you will find that Pessen was concerned only about the very wealthy in the USA in the early 18th century and thus he focussed his energies on just the very rich and not about the economic and social structure: *At least so argues E. Pessen in his iconoclastic study of the very rich in the United States between 1825 and 1850.* A study on economic structure would cover all the economic strata of people – the poor, the middle class, the higher income group and the aristocrat - that make the economic structure. Pessen does not mention anything about social structure at least in this passage. Option 1 would not work for this reason. Since Pessen deals with the periods 1825 to 1850 and not the entire 19th century, Option 3 would get eliminated on this account.

As regards Option 4, the political power of the extremely wealthy is not mentioned anywhere in the passage leave alone this being well documented. Since Pessen presented an iconoclastic study, Option 5 is correct.

Chapter 10

Ages

There are the following important aspects to be borne in mind all the while in regard to problems involving ages of people:

Ages are generally expressed in whole number of years. This is a basic presumption about ages of people:

Imagine that someone is X years of age today and another is Y years of age today. Imagine that X grows older by 5 years. Y will not stagnate in the meanwhile. He will also grow older by 5 years. Therefore if you are to add their ages after 5 years, the total will be X + Y + 10.

The ages of two persons (or even that of the whole town for that matter inter-se) can bear a certain ratio only once and never can they bear the same ratio ever again nor could have they had the same ratio in the past. This is simple to understand once you come to grips with the fact that the day a chap is born, he is zero years of age whereas his father may be say 27 years. The ratio of 27 to zero is infinity as will be the case when the denominator in any division is zero. A year later the father is 28 and the son is 1 year old. The ratio has changed from infinity (meaning unfathomably big) to a mere 28: 1. Three years later the father is 30 and the son is 3 years old. The ratio has changed – decreasing each time – from infinity to 28:1 and then to 10:1. The ratio will only keep decreasing non-stop and if the ratio between two numbers keeps **decreasing** non-stop, then the same ratio occurs only once and never before nor never after. For that matter, in the converse, the ages of the son: father will be a constantly increasing ratio and therefore it is easy to appreciate that it could have been a certain ratio only on one occasion: never before or never after.

If you are told that the ages of two persons add up to some definite figure, then effectively there is only one unknown. For example if you are told that a father's age and the age of his son adds up to 72, it means that if you were to assume that the father 's age is F years, and the son's age is S years, since F + S = 72, you know that F = 72 – S. So the ages of the father and the son are respectively (72 –S) and S. There is only one unknown and that is S. The moment you know what S is, you also know what F is. When you write the father's age in any equation, there is no need to write it as F; you can safely write it as (72 – S) and thereby keep the number of unknowns to only one.

If you are told that the ages of two persons bear a certain ratio, it gives no idea whatsoever of the individual ages. If you are told that John is twice Sam's age, John can be a 2-year old child and Sam would then be a little baby with a milk bottle stuck in his rosy lips. In the alternative John can white moustaches at 80 and Sam can be a 40-year old with a jet-black beard and riding a Harley Davidson.

If you are told that the ages of two persons add up to a definite figure and also, for example, that the first chap is thrice the other's age (meaning the ratio of the two persons' ages), you can find the exact ages in a flash. For example if you are told that a father's age and the age of his son adds up to 72 and that the father is thrice the son's age, you know that (1) F = 72 - S and (2) F = 3S and therefore (3) 3S = 72 – S and then to reach the conclusion that S = 18 and therefore F = 54 is a matter of a jiffy.

If you are told that the ages of two persons bear a definite ratio at a given point of time and that the ages after a certain number of years shall bear another but definite ratio, then again you can find the present ages of the two in a flash. Imagine that you are told that a father is thrice his son's age and that after 9 years the ratio will be 7:3, you need no further information to be able to find their present ages. This is because if you were to assume that the father's age is 3S (where S is the son's age) then (3S + 9): (S + 9) :: 7:3. This is better expressed as

(3S + 9) / (S + 9) = 7/3. What becomes immediately evident is that there is only one unknown that you are operating with and that unknown is S. If you can find S all you have to do to find F is to multiply S with 3. Now if (3S + 9) / (S + 9)= 7/3, then 3(3S +9) = 7(S + 9) and thus 9S + 27 = 7S + 63 and thus 2S = 36 and so S = 18. Since the pop is thrice the son's age, F = 54. Incidentally the above is also true if you are told the ratio of two persons' ages before a certain number of years (say before 15 years) and the ratio of their ages after a certain number of years or even before some more years (say 20 years).

The difference between two people's ages remains constant during their lifetime. The difference is an absolute figure. If a father is thrice his son's age and their ages add up to 72, then their ages are 54 and 18 respectively. The difference in their ages is 36 years. So when the son was born, the father was 36 years old. This difference between their ages is independent of the ratio of their ages; the ratio is a comparative figure and changes every year but the absolute does not change because that is the meaning of *absolute*.

Let us look at another fundamental about ages. For determining the ratio of present ages of two persons, one does not need to know their actual age difference if you are given as to what was the ratio of their ages when one of the two was the same age as the other is today. But from this you can only find the ratio of their present ages and not their actual ages. If a mother was thrice her son's age when she was the son's age, then she could have been her son's age only before a number of years equal to their age difference. If I am 50 years old today and my wife is 45, I was her age 5 years back (which is 50 – 45 = 5 years ago). If the mother is M years today and the son is S years today, then the mother could have been as old as the son's present age before exactly (M-S) years. Before (M – S) years, the mother's age was S years. Before (M – S) years, the son's age was [S – (M – S)] years = 2S – M years. [Relating this to the illustration of me – let my age be I years - and my wife (whose age we shall take as W years), if I am 50 today and she is 45 today, I could have been 45 only before 5 years and she would then have been 40 and if you put I = 50 and W = 45 in 2W – I, then only can you get 40 which is her age when I was her present age]. So back to the case on hand of a mother who was thrice her son's age when she was the son's age, S = 3(2S – M) and therefore S = 6S – 3M and hence 5S = 3M or M:S as 5:3. We have been able to arrive at the ratio of the present ages of the mother and the son without knowing the actual age difference between the two. If you assume the mother to be 55 years and the son 33, then the mother was 33 before 22 years and the son was then 11. If you assume the mother to be 45 years and the son 27, then the mother was 27 before 18 years and the son was then 9. In either event, the mother is thrice what her son's age was when she was her son's age and the present ratio of their ages is 5:3. This is irrespective of the actual difference in their ages.

Problem 1

The sum of the ages of a mother and daughter is 45. Five years ago, the product of their ages was 4 times the mother's age then. What are their present ages?

The detailed solution

Let the mother's present age be M and the daughter's present age be D. Then M + D = 45 or Equation (1) M = 45 – D.

5 years earlier their ages were (M – 5) and (D – 5) respectively and their product was 4 times the mother's age then. So (M – 5) × (D – 5) = 4 × (M – 5) and hence D – 5 = 4 so D = 9. Substituting the value of D as derived in Equation (1) above, one gets M = 45 – 9 = 36. So the mother is 36 and the daughter is 9 years old today.

Problem 2

A who is 15 years senior to B, says "You were 75% of your present age when I was your age". What are their present ages?

The detailed solution

75% is 75/100 or 3/4. Now let A's age be A and B's age be B. The first thing that emerges is A = B + 15. A was B's age 15 years back when B was (B – 15) and A's age then was B.

So B – 15 = ¾ × B and hence ¼ × B = 15 or B = 60 and thus B = 60 and A is 75. The present ages of A and B are respectively 75 and 60 years.

We shall now see problems 3 and 4 that stem from a common set of information given in problem 3.

Problem 3

Two women Shiny and Grace know that both their ages were integers. They are heard conversing as under:

Shiny: I am certainly not over 30

Grace: You are at least 5 years older than I, and I am 28.

Shiny: You are at least 29.

None of the above statements were true.

How old is Shiny? Options (1) 27 (2) 29 (3) 31 (4) data insufficient.

The detailed solution

If all three statements were untrue, then the following can be deduced:

(A) Shiny is over 30

(B) The age difference between Shiny and Grace is less than 5 years

(C) Grace is not 28

(D) Grace is less than 29 years old.

If Shiny is 31, then only her statement that she is certainly not over 30 can be false. So Shiny is 31.

Problem 4

How old is Grace?

Options: (1) 27 (2) 29 (3) 31 (4) data insufficient.

The detailed solution

If Shiny is 31, then Grace has to be lesser then 29 since if Grace was even 29, Shiny 's statement that Grace was at least 29 would be true. So Grace could be 27 and then the first half of her statement that she is 28 years old is also false and the other half of Gracc's statement that Shiny is at least 5 years older than her is also false because Shiny would be only 4 years her senior in age. So Grace is 27.

Now let us climb up a little to more complex problems that involve more than just arithmetic.

Problem 5

If the square of Tina's age is added to Mary's age, the sum is 62; but if you add the square of Mary's age to Tina's age, the total comes to 176. Can you say what are their respective ages?

The detailed solution

Two equations may be quickly jotted down. Tina's age may be denoted as T [and nothing other than T if one were to take it as x, then if one finds the value of x, one would have to see as to whom does x refer to and this would mean effort that one would do well to avoid.]

$T^2 + M = 62$

$M^2 + T = 176.$

Now T is below 8 because if it was even 8, then T^2 itself would be 64. Secondly $M^2 + T = 176$ and hence $M^2 < 176$ and since the nearest perfect square to 176 is 169 which is the square of 13, since $M^2 < 176$, M could have no higher value than 13. If M is to stop at 13, then since $T^2 + M = 62$, $T^2 = 49$ even if we were to assume the highest possible value (13) for M and hence $T = 7$. If T were to fall anywhere below 7, it could be 6 and then since $T^2 + M = 62$, $6^2 + M = 62$ and hence $M = 26$ and hence M^2 would be well over 400 since 20^2 itself is 400 and then the value of $M^2 + T$ will jump over the moon. Thus T is definitely 7 and therefore M is definitely 13. This is a matter of logical deduction and not mathematics. This is what separates quantitative skills from mathematics.

Now for some exercises that you may like to take up on your own. The answer key is furnished at the end of the exercise and so also are the detailed solutions.

EXERCISE

1. The ages of a family of four are in the proportion of 20:19:11:10 and six years hence their ages will be in the proportion of 22:21:13:12. What was the ratio of the ages of the second oldest among members and the second youngest among the members when the youngest of them was born?
2. My elder brother's age and my ages are such that:

   If 18 is added to the sum of our ages then the total is twice my elder brother's age and

   If 6 is deducted from the difference of our ages, then you get my age. What are our ages?
3. Tina, the elder of the two sisters, and Mina, the younger, were telling their music teacher that:

   3 years back Tina was 7 times Mina's age

   2 years back Tina was 4 times Mina's age

   Last year Tina was 3 times Mina's age and

   This year Tina is 2.5 times Mina's age.

   What are the present ages of the two sisters?
4. My gardener does not remember his precise age but when the census people came to survey, he said he was 2 years younger to one of his brothers, 4 years younger to another and his mother was 20 when he was born and that the average age of the four of them is 39. What is his present age?
5. The difference between the square of the present ages of my son and my daughter is equal to 2 times the sum of their present ages and 3 years hence the ratio of their ages will be 5:4. What are their present ages?

ANSWER KEY

1. 9:1
2. 30 and 12
3. 10 and 4
4. 32
5. 7 and 5

SOLUTIONS

1. Imagine the present ages of the four to be 20x, 19x, 11x and 10x. The ages of the second oldest and the second youngest among the four is thus 19x and 11x. 6 years hence the two will be 19x + 6 and 11x + 6 years respectively. And this will then be in the proportion of 21:13. So:

   $(19x + 6) / (11x + 6) = 21/13$ and hence $13 \times (19x + 6) = 21 \times (11x + 6)$ or $247x + 78 = 231x + 126$. Thus $16x = 48$ and thus $x = 3$. So the second oldest and the second youngest are respectively 19×3 and 11×3 or 57 and 33 years old today. The youngest among them is $10 \times 3 = 30$ years old. This means that when the youngest was born, the ages of the second oldest and the second youngest were respectively 27 and 3 and the ratio of their ages at that stage was 27:3 or 9:1.

The important point here is to calculate with reference to the ages of only the two – namely the second oldest and the second youngest – who have been referred to in the question and not to bother about the ages of all the members of the family.

2. My elder brother's age and my ages are such that:

   If 18 is added to the sum of our ages then the total is twice my elder brother's age and

   If 6 is deducted from the difference of our ages, then you get my age.

   If my brother is B years old and I am I years old, B + I + 18 = 2B or (1) B = I + 18 and (2) B – I – 6 = I. Substituting the value of B from equation (1) in equation (2), we get I + 18 – I – 6 = I or 12 = I. So I am 12 years old and my brother is (12 + 18) = 30 years old.

3. Let Mina's present age be M and Tina's present age be T.

   3 years back Tina was 7 times Mina's age. So T – 3 = 7× (M – 3) and hence T – 3 = 7M – 21 or T = 7M – 18.

   2 years back Tina was 4 times Mina's age. So T – 2 = 4× (M – 2) and hence T – 2 = 4M – 8 and thus T = 4M – 6.

   T = 7M – 18 and T = 4M-6 so, 7M – 18 = 4M-6 and hence 3M = 12 and M = 4. Thus T = 4M-6 or 4 × 4 – 6 = 16 – 6 = 10.

   What are the present ages of Tina and Mina? 10 and 4 respectively.

4. My gardener does not remember his precise age but let it be G at present age.

   When the census people came to survey, he said he was 2 years younger to one of his brothers who since he will always remain 2 years senior is today G + 2, since the gardener was 4 years younger to another the other brother is G + 4 and his mother was 20 when he was born so his mother is G+20.

   Since that the average age of the four of them is 39, their total age is G + (G + 2) + (G + 4) + (G + 20) = 156 so 4G + 26 = 156 and so 4G = 130 and thus the Gardener is 130/4 = 32 and ½ years old today.

   But since one expresses age not only in integers but also in the number of completed years, the gardener is 32 today.

5. The difference between square of the present ages of my son and my daughter is equal to 2 times the sum of their present ages and 3 years hence the ratio of their ages will be 5:4.

   If my son is S years old and my daughter is D years old today, then $(S^2 - D^2) = 2(S + D)$. The difference between the squares of two numbers is equal to their sum multiplied by their difference. Hence (S + D) × (S – D) = 2(S + D) and so S – D = 2. So S = D + 2.

   Three years hence, their ages will be S + 3 (or D + 2 + 3 = D + 5) and D + 3 and these will be in the ratio of 5:4. Thus (D + 5) / (D + 3) = 5/4. Hence 4 × (D + 5) = 5 × (D + 3) and thus 4D + 20 = 5D + 15 and D = 5. The son is D + 2 and is thus 7 years old and the daughter is 5 years old.

Chapter 11

Area and Volume

Area, in mathematics, is the size of an enclosed region, given in terms of the square of a designated unit of length such as square centimetres and square feet and so on. There are formulae for finding the areas and volumes of geometric figures.

The triangle is the first geometrical figure that comes to mind. The perimeter of a triangle is equal to the sum of measures of its three sides. The perimeter relates to a single dimension of the triangle because the perimeter is essentially how much would you have to walk if you were to walk once along the three sides of a triangle starting from any vertex and returning to the same vertex.

The area of a triangle is 1/2 the product of its base and height. See how this formula has been evolved. Imagine that you are trying to find out the area of the triangle ABC as given below:

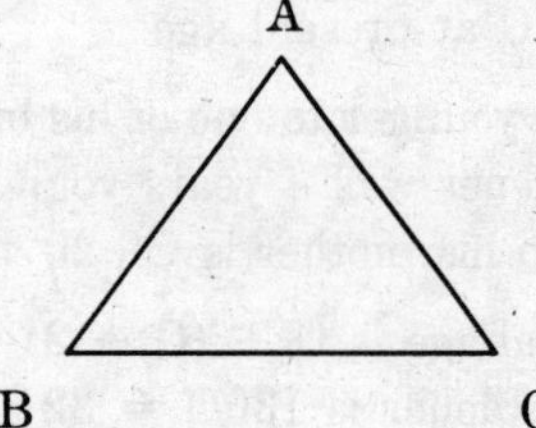

Draw:

(1) A line FG parallel to BC and passing through the vertex A

(2) A perpendicular from the vertex B to touch the line FG at D and

(3) A perpendicular from the vertex C to touch the line FG at E.

(4) A perpendicular from the vertex A to touch BC at H.

The figure that you will see shall be as under:

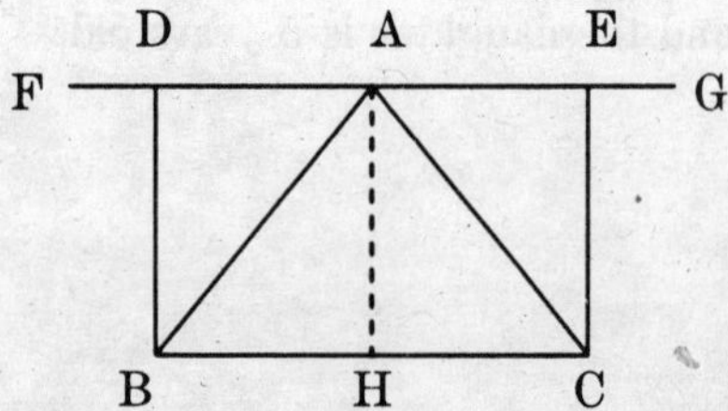

One will realise that the triangle ABC is essentially two parts out of the four equal parts that one can divide the rectangle DECB: these four equal parts are triangles ADB, ABH, AHC and ACE. The area of the rectangle BDEC is the product of its sides BC (which, incidentally is, the base of the triangle ABC as well) and BD (which is equal in measure to AH, the height of triangle ABC). The area of the triangle ABC would thus be half the area of the rectangle DECB and thus would be equal to 1/2 the product of its base and its height. As to why the area of a rectangle is the product of its length and breadth is simple to understand. Imagine that we are to find out the area of a rectangle of 3 units length and 2 units breadth. Divide the two long sides into three equal parts of 1 unit each and the two smaller sides into two equal parts of 1 unit each and put a mark at each of these divisions. Now join these marks as follows and you will find that you are staring at six squares each of which has sides measuring 1 unit.

3 units

2 units

Thus the area of the rectangle of 2 units length and 3 units breadth is 6 square units which is the product of the length and the breadth of the rectangle and this will hold good for all rectangles irrespective of their dimensions.

A square is a rectangle with this little difference that whereas in a rectangle the measures of the length and breadth differ, the length and the breadth are the same in a square. Hence the area of a square is then the square of the measure of its side.

A cube is a figure that has six faces each of which is a square of each side of the same length. The surface area of a cube is 6 times the square of the measure of its side.

The founding fathers of geometry discovered a remarkable constant relationship between the square of the measure of the radius of a circle and the area of the circle. They found that the area of a circle- found as accurately as possible by dividing a large circle into a vast number of circles of small side – is almost invariably equal to 22/7 times the square of the radius. They called this constant π and thus the area of a circle is π times the square of its radius or πr^2. By observation that could probably have involved making a large circle with a string and then straightening out the string to see whether there is a relationship between the length of the string (which is the circumference of the circle) and the radius of the circle, the perimeter of circumference of a circle was found to be 2π times the radius or $2 \pi r$.

While trying to find the general formula for ascertaining the volume of a cube, what may have happened is- of course, this is my conjecture - that a wooden cube of say 2 units may have been taken and each of its sides marked into 2 equal parts of 1 unit each. The markings on each face may have been joined so that each face looks like this:

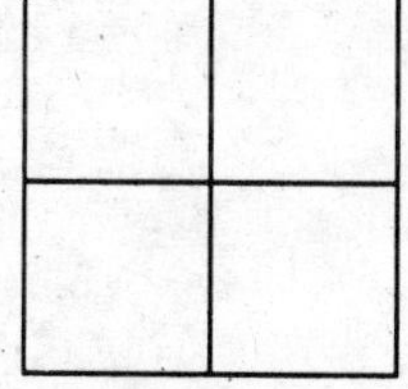

The cube may have been cut along the markings and it would have been found that one gets 8 smaller cubes of side 1 unit. If one were to call this small cube of side 1 unit as 1 cubic unit, then the volume of the cube is 8 cubic units, which incidentally is equal to side × side. While experimenting with a wooden block that has the top face a rectangle of length – say – 2 units and breadth – say- 3 units and a height (which is the third dimension of this figure and every figure that does not have a third dimension can have only surface area but not volume; you cannot sip tea in a flat circular piece of china, can you?) of 5 units, it was found that there were 30 blocks of 1 cubic unit and hence it was found that the volume of a geometric figure of three dimensions is equal to the product of the surface of the face of any figure and its height. This is why the volume of a cylinder that has a circle as a face is $\pi r^2 h$. An inverted cone ABE, if seen in cross section, is a third of a cylinder seen as a rectangle ABCD in cross section as per hereunder:

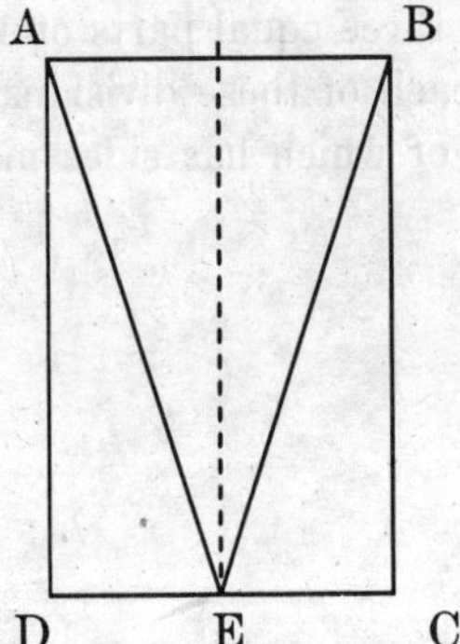

The base of the inverted cone with diameter AB is a circle of area πr^2 and the height of the cone is the perpendicular from E, the tip of the inverted cone to the diameter of the circular face at the top of the cone (this perpendicular is shown in a dotted line in the above figure). The height of the cone is also equal to the height of the cylinder itself.

The area of a cylinder is the product of the perimeter of its circular face and its height. The area of the cylinder that looks like a rectangle ABCD in the above figure is thus $2\pi\ r$ times the height of the cylinder where r (which is 1/2 AB) is the radius of the circular top face of the cylinder and either AD or BC is the height (we shall call this height h) of the cylinder. The area of the cone ABC being a third of the area of the cylinder for the same reason that the cone - which is a triangle in cross-section - is a third of the rectangle ABCD which really is the cylinder in cross-section, the area of a cone = 1/3 times $(2\pi \times r \times h)$ square units or $2/3 \times \pi \times r \times h$ square units.

A cylinder if open at both ends has an area of $(2\pi \times r \times h)$ square units where r is the radius of its circular base and h its height. If both ends of the cylinder are closed, its area increases to the extent of the area of the two circular faces and thus becomes $(2\pi \times r \times h) + (2\pi \times r^2)$. If one of the faces of this cylinder were open, its area would increase to the extent of only one of the circular faces and would thus be $(2\pi \times r \times h) + (\pi \times r^2)$.

A cylinder whether open at both ends or at one or at neither of its two ends would have the same volume throughout. Merely because you put a lid on a cylinder, you cannot add to what it can hold inside (and what it can hold inside is known as its volume). It is a different matter that a cylinder open at both ends can actually hold nothing. A cylinder being a circle when seen from the top has a base area of $(\pi \times R^2)$ square units and if the height of the cylinder were to be of H units, then its volume is equal to $(\pi \times R^2) \times H$ cubic units.

A parallelogram is a four-sided figure that has the two pairs of opposite sides equal in measure and parallel.

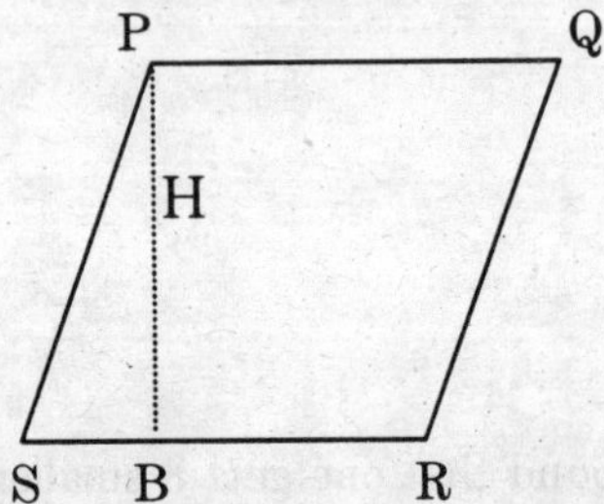

A parallelogram PQRS with base B (meaning the length of the side SR) and vertical height H (meaning the measure of the perpendicular distance from the vertex P at the top of the figure to its base SR) is drawn above.

In parallelogram PQRS,

(1) PQ is parallel to SR

(2) PQ = SR

(3) PS is parallel to QR

(4) PS = QR

A parallelogram of base B units and vertical height H units has an area of $B \times H$ square units.

A trapezium is a four-sided figure with one pair of its sides parallel but not equal. The other pair of sides is necessarily not parallel although they may be equal in measure. A trapezium PQRS is drawn below.

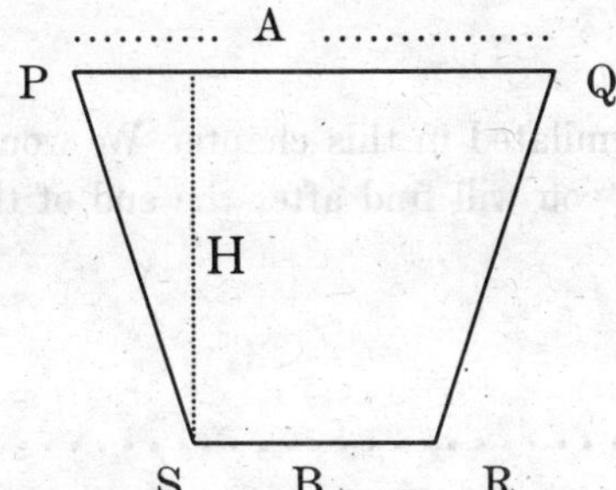

The area of this trapezium of the two unequal but parallel sides of A and B units and the vertical distance between the parallel sides of H units is $1/2 \times H \times (A + B)$ square units. If a third dimension were added to the trapezium PQRS, it would have height H as the third dimension. Both the upper and bottom surface of the resultant object would look like trapezium PQRS. The volume of the resultant object would be = Area of PQRS $\times H$.

A sphere is a solid object, on the surface of which every point is the same distance from a fixed point known as the centre. From every aspect it has the same appearance. A cricket ball is a common example of a sphere. The area of a sphere with radius R units is $4 \times \pi \times R^2$ square units and the volume of such a sphere = $4/3 \times \pi \times R^3$ cubic units.

Seldom would one come across direct questions at major competitive examinations on topics of Area and Volume. The ones that we recollect are as follows although there may not be any need to remember the formulae for the areas and volumes of any significant number of types of geometric figures beyond the most elementary type of such figures.

Illustration 1

Two full tanks, one shaped like a cylinder and the other like a cone, contain jet fuel. The cylindrical tank holds 500 litres more than the conical tank. After 200 litres of fuel has been pumped out from each tank the cylindrical tank contains twice the amount of fuel in the conical tank. How many litres of fuel did the cylindrical tank have when it was full? The Options are as follows:

(1) 700 (2) 1000 (3) 1100 (4) 1200

The Solution

Clearly, there is no test of knowledge about areas of cylinders or cones, if you were to see the solution to this, which is as follows:

The shapes of the tanks are of no consequence in the context of the fact that one is given neither their radius or, for that matter, any of the dimensions. But the fact is that the cylindrical tank has a volume of 500 litres more than the other tank and also that if 200 litres of fuel is pumped out from each tank, then the cylinder contains 2 times the fuel in the conical tank. Now let us go by the options.

- As per Option 1 – 700: the conical tank would have volume of 200 litres and if 200 litres were pumped out from both tanks, there would be no fuel left in the conical tank, and the question of comparison with the residual volume in the cylindrical tank does not arise, since there is no fuel left in the latter.
- Option 2: If the cylindrical tank were to hold 1000 litres, then the volume of the conical tank would be 500 litres. If 200 litres are taken from both tanks, the residual volume of fuel would be respectively 800 and 300 litres and this is not a case of the residual volume of fuel in the cylindrical tank being twice that in the conical tank.

- As regards Option 3, if the volume of the cylindrical tank were to be 1100 litres, then the volume of the conical tank would be 600 litres and taking away 200 litres from each would mean that the cylindrical tank has 900 litres left whereas the conical tank has 400 litres left and yet again this is not a case of the residual volume in the cylindrical tank being twice the residual volume of fluid in the conical tank.
- Option 4 therefore.

We shall now move on to a small exercise that shall reinforce all that we have assimilated in this chapter. We would strongly recommend that you check your answers with the detailed solutions that you will find after the end of the exercise.

EXERCISE

1. A rectangular pool 20 metres wide and 60 metres long is surrounded by a walkway of uniform width. If the total area of the walkway is 516 square metres, how wide, in metres, is the walkway?

   (1) 43 (2) 4.3 (3) 3 (4) 3.5

2. A cone C and a hemisphere H stand on the same circular base. If the solids have the same volume, what is the height of the cone compared to the diameter of its base?

   (1) 1/2 the diameter (2) diameter (3) 2/3rd the diameter

   (4) No meaningful relation exists

3. 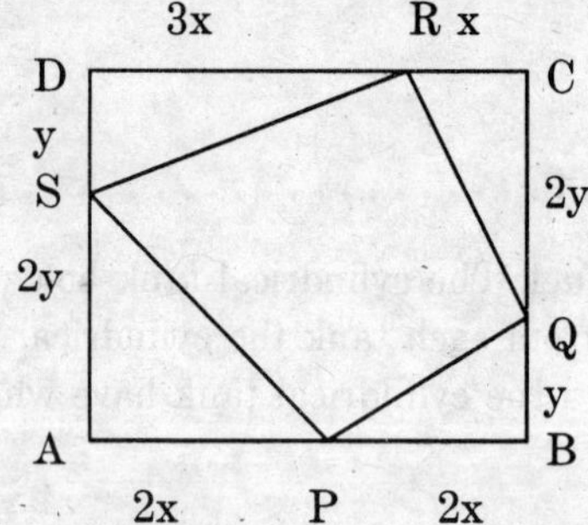

   ABCD is a rectangle P,Q,R,S are points on AB, BC, CD, DA respectively, such that AP = AB/2, BQ = BC/3, CR = CD/4 and DS = DA/3. If the area of PQRS is k times the area of ABCD, then k is equal to

   (1) 1/2 (2) 2/3 (3) 13/24 (4) 3/4

4. The sides of a rectangle are all produced in order, in such a way that the length of each side is increased by 'k' times itself. The area of the new quadrilateral formed becomes 2 ½ times the area of the original rectangle. Find 'k'.

   (1) 1/3 (2) 1/4 (3) 1/2 (4) 2/3

5.

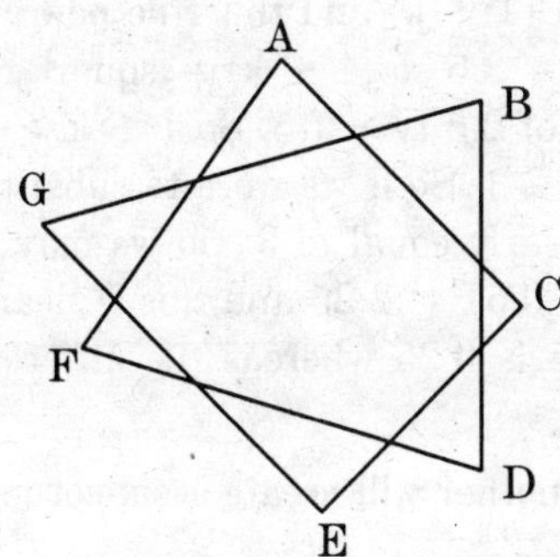

All line segments are straight. Find the sum of the angles at the seven corners A,B,C,...G marked in the diagram.

(1) 360^0 (2) 450^0 (3) 540^0 (4) 630^0

6. Which of the following will not enable you to construct the parallelogram ABCD?

(1) AB = 10, BC = 6 (2) AB = 10, angle A = 70^0, AC = 12

(3) AC = 12, BD = 8, AB = 10 (4) AC = BD = 12, AC perpendicular to BD.

7. The number V represents the volume of a sphere in cm^3, and the number S represents its surface area in cm^2. If V = S, what is S equal to?

(1) 9 (2) 27 (3) 27π (4) 36π

Solutions

1. If the pool is a rectangle its area = 20meters × 60 meters = 1200 square meters, and if the walkway is say x meters, the sides of the outer rectangle is (20 + 2x) × (60 + 2x).

Area of the walkway= $(20 + 2x) \times (60 + 2x)-1200 = 1200 + 4x^2 + 160x-1200 = 516$. Thus $4x^2 + 160x - 516 = 0$ or $x^2 + 40x - 129 = 0$. So $(x - 3) \times (x + 43) = 0$. Hence x = 3. The walkway is 3 meters wide. **Thus Option 3.** As a matter of fact, the fastest way of solving this is to replace the values of x among the four given options; only the integral number need be tried first and 3 is the only one qualifying among the options. Why we are not to touch 43 is that if 43 were correct, the dimensions of the pool would increase by 86 meters. The area of pool and walkway would then be (20 + 86) × (60 + 86) = 106 × 146 that would be somewhere near 1400. As against this the area of the pool is 1200 sq. meters. The area of the walkway would be in thousands of meters if 43 was to be the width of the walkway.

2. Let us assume the radius of the circular base to be R and the height of the cone to be H. So the radius of the cone and the hemisphere are both = R since the cone and the hemisphere rest on the same circular base. The volume of the cone = $1/3 \times \pi \times R^2 \times H$ = the volume of the hemisphere (which is half a sphere which has volume of $4/3 \times \pi \times R^3$) $= 1/2 \times 4/3 \times \pi \times R^3 = 2/3 \times \pi \times R^3$. Thus $1/3 \times \pi \times R^2 \times H = 2/3 \times \pi \times R^3$. So H = 2R and the height of the cone is twice the radius of its circular base and hence = **Diameter** of the circular base.

3. The rectangle has length of 4x and breadth of 3y and thus its area is 12xy. The area of PQRS is = area of rectangle – the sum of the areas of the triangles DSR, SAP, PQB and RCQ.

The area of any triangle is 1/2 × base × height. Since the four corners of the rectangle contain right angles, all four triangles DSR, SAP, PQB and RCQ are right angled and thus their height is the side opposite the hypotenuse. The areas of the triangles DSR, SAP, PQB and RCQ are 1/2 (3xy + 4xy + 2xy + 2xy) = ½ × (11xy). Thus the area of PQRS = 12xy – (11xy/2) = 13xy/2. The **area of PQRS as compared to the area of ABCD is = (13xy)/2 ÷ 12xy = 13/24.**

4. If I were to increase the side of a rectangle measuring 6 inches by 1/2 times itself, the new length would be 6 + [1 + (1/2)] = 9. If the original rectangle has length of L and breadth B, then its area is L × B. If the

new area is $2.5L \times B$, and that each of the length and breadth have been increased by k times their original measure, this means that the new length is $L(1 + k)$ and the new breadth is $B(1 + k)$ and thus the new area is $L \times B(1 + k)^2$. So $L \times B \times (1 + k)^2 = 2.5 L \times B$ and hence $(1 + k)^2 = 2.5$ so $(1 + k)$ = square root of 2.5. Now we know that the square of 1.5 = 2.25 and hence the square root of 2.5 is > 1.5. So $1 + k > 1.5$ and hence $k > 0.5$ and hence among the options the only value of $k > 0.5$ is 2/3. So if we were to substitute this value of k in $(1 + k)^2$, we would get $(5/3)^2 = 25/9 = 2.7777$ which is nearly equal to 3. So we may see the option 3 which is 1/2 and substitute this value in $(1 + k)^2$ and we get $(1 + 0.5)^2 = 2.25$ and this is nearest in value to 2.5 among 2.25 and 2.7777. The difference between 2.5 and 2.25 is 0.25 whereas the difference between 2.7777 and 2.5 is 0.2777. Hence **Option 3**.

5. The figure that you see is seven-cornered. A triangle when intersecting with another will create a six-cornered figure.

   A quadrilateral intersecting with another quadrilateral will create an eight-cornered figure. As such a figure with seven corners is possible when a quadrilateral intersects with a triangle so that the four corners of the quadrilateral add up with the three corners of a triangle to give seven corners. The four angles of a quadrilateral add up to 360 and the three corners of a triangle add up to 180^0. Together the seven corners add up to $360 + 180 = 540^0$. Thus **Option 3**.

6. A figure of three sides can be drawn only if one knows the:

   (A) Measures of the three sides or

   (B) Measures of two sides and angle that is contained in the side opposite to the sides whose measure is given

   (C) Measures of two angles and the measure of the side where both the given angles are held. In a parallelogram, opposite sides are equal and opposite angles are equal. So one should need to know two sides and an angle and only then can one construct a parallelogram. Not before. Hence **Option 1** will not enable construction of the parallelogram.

7. The volume V of a sphere = $4/3 \times \pi \times r^3$. The surface area S of a sphere = $4 \times \pi \times r^2$. If V = S, as given, then $4/3 \times \pi \times r^3 = 4 \times \pi \times r^2$. Thus r = 3 and hence $S = 4 \times \pi \times r^2 = 4 \times \pi \times 9 = 36\pi$.

Chapter 12

Arithmetic Progressions

As you would probably know, the word ***progression*** is a sum of the prefix ***pro*** (that means *forward*)+ the Latin root ***gress-*** (that means *step*) and the noun suffix ***–ion***. Something that goes forward step by step – as different from surging forward – is a progression.

Progressions are something that we learnt at school and it will not take much to refresh our memory.

- A series of numbers such as 1, 3, 5, 7, 9 and so on – let us call this Series A – is such that each term is exactly 2 more than the previous term. The common difference of this series is 2. Any term in this series minus the immediately previous term gives the common difference of the series.
- A series of numbers such as 3, 7, 11, 15 and so on – let us call this Series B – is such that each term in the series is exactly 4 more than the previous term. The common difference of this series is 4. Any term in this series minus the immediately previous term gives the common difference of the series.
- A series of numbers such as 15, 9, 3, –3, –9 and so on – let us call this Series C – is such that each term in the series is exactly 6 less than the previous term. The common difference of this series is -6. Any term in this series minus the immediately previous term gives the common difference of the series.
- A series of numbers such as 5, 10, 20, 40, 80 and so on – let us call this Series D – is such that each term in the series is exactly 2 times the previous term. Any term in this series divided by the immediately previous term gives the common ratio of the series. The common ratio of this series is 2.
- A series of numbers such as 7, 21, 63, 189, 567 and so on – let us call this Series E - is such that each term in the series is exactly 3 times the previous term. Any term in this series divided by the immediately previous term gives the common ratio of the series. The common ratio of this series is 3.

Series A, B and C are known as Arithmetic Progressions whereas Series D and E are known as Geometric Progressions.

In the Series A (meaning 1, 3, 5, 7, 9,...and so on till the nth term), it will be seen that:

When n = 1	The sum of n terms of series is	Average up to the nth term is
1	1 itself	1/1 = 1
2	1 + 3 = 4	4/2 = 2
3	1 + 3 + 5 = 9	9/3 = 3
4	1 + 2 + 5 + 7 = 16	16/4 = 4

The general formula for the sum up to the nth term in an A.P., even if you find it difficult to remember is the n × the average up to the nth term. This is because the average is total of n terms divided by the number of terms so in the converse the sum of n terms is average of n terms × n (which is the number of terms).

In this chapter we shall deal with Arithmetic Progressions.

An Arithmetic Progression is that in which there is a constant difference between any term in the sequence and its immediately preceding term. So if the term that starts the sequence is A and the constant difference of the arithmetic progression is D, then the second term in the series is A + D, the third term is A + D + D (or in other words, A + 2D) the fourth term is (A + 3D) and so on.

Thus the Nth term of an arithmetic progression is A + (N – 1) × D, where A is the first term in the progression and D is the constant difference in the arithmetic progression. As we have seen at the very outset, the common difference may be negative or positive. Of course, there is nothing stopping the common difference of an Arithmetic Progression being zero. The one interesting aspect of an Arithmetic Progression with a common difference of zero is that it will simultaneously fulfil the condition of being both an Arithmetic Progression and a Geometric Progression.

As we have seen the condition for an Arithmetic Progression is that any term in this series minus the immediately previous term gives exactly the same result throughout whereas the condition for a Geometric Progression is that any term in this series divided by the immediately previous term gives the same result throughout. So if we were to see an Arithmetic Progression starting off with the number 4, then the series will run like this: 4, 4, 4, 4, 4, 4, and so on. You will see it fulfilling the condition for a Geometric Progression as well since any term divided by its immediately preceding term gives exactly 1 all through.

If all terms in an arithmetic progression ("AP" hereafter) are added, a general formula may emerge. Let us look at the following:

If the AP were to have n terms, it would run as	Where n =	Then the total of its terms would be
A, (A + D), (A + 2D)	3	3A + 3D
A, (A + D), (A + 2D), (A + 3D)	4	4A + 6D
A, (A + D),..... (A + 4D)	5	5A + 10D
A, (A + D),..... (A + 5D)	6	6A + 15D

If we were to try to evolve a formula on our own in regard to the sum of an arithmetic progression up to the Nth term, we should be able to see from the above table that A occurs thrice when we are looking at the first three terms of the series and four times when we are looking at the first four terms of the series and so on and therefore it can be safely stated that if you were to add up the first N terms of the Arithmetic Progression, A would occur exactly N times and therefore one of the ingredients in this sum of the first N terms of an Arithmetic Progression is A × N. The other ingredient is 3D when we add the first three terms (D + 2D or in other words D(1 + 2)) and 6D (D + 2D + 3D or in other words D(1 + 2 + 3)) when we add the first four terms and 10D when we add the first four terms (D + 2D + 3D + 4D or in other words D(1 + 2 + 3 + 4)). So if there are N terms then D is multiplied by the sum of 1 till (N-1) in the sum of the Arithmetic Progression up to N terms. So the sum of the first 7 terms of an Arithmetic Progression starting with A with a common difference of D will be 7A + D(1 + 2 + 3 + 4 + 5 + 6) = 7A + 21D. And mind you, even calculating the sum of 1 till 6 or for that matter 1 till N is no great shakes. The sum of 1 to 6 is its average (given by the first term 1 + the last term 6/2 = 7/2 = 3.5) multiplied by 6, which is 3.5 times 6 = 21, which is the number of terms in the sub-series of 1 till 6. This is worth noting. One may forget a formula. But if one knows how a formula is evolved, one need never worry about forgetting formulae. You can devise them yourself anytime you like. This is because you know the underlying rationale. You are king!

It is important to remember that if the sum up to say the 6th term is given and so also the sum up to the 5th term, then as to how to find out what is the 6th term is rather simple. All you have to do is to subtract the sum up to the 5th term from the sum up to the 6th term.

If an AP runs like this: 4, 6, 8, 10, 12, 14 then the sum up to the nth term is as follows:

If N =	Then S_N =	And S_{N-1} =	$S_N - S_{N-1}$ =	T_N =
2	10	4	6	6
3	18	10	8	8
4	28	18	10	10
5	40	28	12	12

Putting this in algebraic language, $S_N - S_{N-1} = T_N$ where T_N is the nth term of the progression. And this is not true just of arithmetic progressions but also of geometric progressions. Of course, if we were to see this from the purely logical standpoint the utter simplicity of this will hit us like a wall. If six schoolboys have a certain number of marbles between them and if you count the marbles that any five of them have, you cannot help knowing exactly how many marbles does the sixth boy have.

One other interesting aspect of Arithmetic Progressions is that if there is an odd number of terms in such a progression, then the middle term is the arithmetic mean of the progression. Imagine an arithmetic progression of three terms as follows: a, (a + d) and (a + 2d) then (a + d) is the middle term and also the arithmetic mean of the three terms. So it will be in the case of a, (a + d), (a + 2d), (a + 3d) and (a + 4d) where (a + 2d) is the middle term and also the average of the five terms.

Then again there is a unique situation when the common difference of an arithmetic progression is zero when the arithmetic progression is also a geometric progression. The reason for this is simple and can be explained in two different ways:

(A) If an arithmetic progression is also a geometric progression then if we were to imagine that the first term of that geometric progression were A and the common multiple (meaning the number that you need to multiply the first term in order to arrive at the second term and the same number that you will need to multiply with the second term in order to arrive at the third term and so on) were R, then the first three terms of such a Geometric Progression would be A, AR and AR^2. If this progression is also an AP, then the difference between the third term and the second term is equal to the difference between the second and the first term. In such a case, $AR^2 - AR = AR - A$, or $R^2 - R = R - 1$ or $R^2 - 2R + 1 = 0$, or $(R - 1)^2 = 0$ or R = 1. When you multiply any number by 1, its value remains the same. This means that the first term of the AP is the same as the second and the third and so on. This means there is no difference between any of the terms and the common difference of the AP is zero.

(B) If an arithmetic progression is also a geometric progression then if we were to imagine that the first term of that AP to be A, the second term to be A+D and the third term to be A + 2D, then the third term divided by the second = second term divided by the first and this means that (A + 2D)/(A + D) = (A + D)/A and hence (A + 2D) (A) = (A + D) (A + D) and thus $A^2 + 2AD = A^2 + 2AD + D^2$; thus $D^2 = 0$ and hence D = 0.

Having grasped where the clutch is and where the accelerator and so on, we shall proceed with the driving lessons.

Problem 1

If the Jth term of an AP is K and the Kth term of that AP is J, what is the common difference of the progression?

The detailed solution

The logical approach to this problem is as follows:

As we know, J is the 10th letter of the alphabet and K is the 11th. Let us take J as 10 and K as 11. Then if the 11th term is 10 and the 10th term is 11, the 11th term minus 10th term should give you the common difference and this common difference is 10–11= –1.

To demonstrate that all other methodologies shall be subordinate to logic, we shall see the Mathematical Approach and see that this is always true. If the Jth term of an AP is K it means that A + D(J – 1) = K and if the Kth term of that AP is J it means that A + D(K – 1) = J. We have two equations:

Equation (A): A + D(J – 1) = K or A+ DJ –D = K

Equation (B): A + D(K – 1) = J or A + DK– D = J

If we were to subtract Equation (A) from Equation (B), we would get D(K – J) = (J – K) and thus D(K – J) = –1(K – J) and thus D = –1. The short point is that logic will always prevail.

Problem 2

What would be the 25th term in the AP 2,5,8,11...?

The detailed solution

The first term in the series is 2 and the common difference is 3 and hence the 25th term would be First Term + 24 times the Common Difference = 2+(24×3)= 2+72=74. Thus the 25th term in the AP 2,5,8,11,... is 74.

Problem 3

If the sum of N terms in an AP is $5N^2+3N$, which of the following series would qualify for being such a series:

Option 1: 8, 18, 28

Option 2: 5, 15, 25

Option 3: 8, 18, 34

Option 4: None of these

The detailed solution

Take N = 1 and then if the sum of N terms is $5N^2 + 3N$, then sum up to the first term – which is effectively the first term itself – is 8.

The sum up to the second term – where N is 2 – is (5 × 2 × 2) + (3 × 2) = 20 + 6 = 26 and hence the second term is 26 – 8 = 18.

The sum up to the third term – where N is 3 – is (5 × 3 × 3) + (3 × 3) = 45 + 9 = 54 and thus the third term is = (sum up to the third term) – (sum up to the second term) and is thus 54 – 26 = 28.

Option 1 fits the bill.

Problem 4

If the Nth term of an AP is 5N + 2, then what is the common difference of the series?

The detailed solution

The series can be constructed like this:

When N =	5N+2 =
1	7
2	12
3	17

The first three terms of the series are 7, 12 and 17. There is no need to go further. The common difference of the series is 5.

Problem 5

What term of the AP 11, 15, 19... is 99?

The detailed solution

The Nth term of an AP is equal to [First Term + (N-1) times the common difference]. If we were to assume that 99 is the Nth term, then 99 = 11 + 4(N – 1) and thus (N – 1) = 22 and so N = 23. This means that 99 is the 23rd term of the AP.

Problem 6

The Nth term of the AP 10, 8, 6 ... is (1) 12 + 2N (2) 12 – 2N (3) 2N – 2 (4) 2N + 8?

The detailed solution

Here if take N as 1, two options would fit: Option (2) 12 – 2n and Option (4) 2n + 8 since in both cases one would get 10 as the answer and 10 is indeed the first term. So one should try with N = 2 and see where it fits in. Options 1 and 3 would get eliminated straightaway since with N = 1, Option 1 would mean 14 as the starting term which it is not and Option 3 would mean Zero as the starting term which it is not.

We are given that the second term is 8 but by Option 4 we would get the second term as 2 × 2 + 8 = 12. With Option 2 one would get 12 –(2 × 2) = 12 – 4 = 8. Since we know that the second term is 8, Option 2 fits admirably.

Now it is time to move on to exercises and see whether we have understood the concepts outlined herein in their entirety.

EXERCISE

1. Is 76 a member of the series 4, 9, 14, 19...?

   Options: (1) Yes (2) No (3) Cannot say

2. What is the 20th term of the arithmetic progression 5, 11, 17...?

   Options: (1) 121 (2) 119 (3) 123 (4) 117

3. If the Rth term of an AP is S and the Sth term is R, then the (R+S) th term will be:

   Options: (1) R + S – 1 (2) R – S + 1 (3) R – S (4) None of these

4. If the Qth term of an AP is 2Q-1, then the sum up to the Qth terms is:

   Options: (1) $Q^2 - 1$ (2) $(2Q - 1)^2$ (3) $Q^2 + 2$ (4) Q^2

5. The first term of an AP is 5 and the fifth term is 7. The number of terms in the series so that the sum will be 63 will be:

   Options: (1) 9 (2) 7 (3) 8 (4) 10

ANSWER KEY

1. Option 3
2. Option 2
3. Option 2
4. Option 4
5. Option 1

SOLUTIONS

1. Is 76 a member of the series 4, 9, 14, 19...? On the face of it this seems to be an Arithmetic Progression starting with 4 and with a common difference of 5. Therefore all terms in the progression end with either 4 or 9 and thus any term ending with 6 has no place in this series if it were indeed an Arithmetic Progression. But while an Arithmetic Progression is a series, all series are not Arithmetic Progressions just as while all cows are animals, the converse is true. [If the converse were true, even human beings would be cows]. In the absence of a specific statement that the series is an **Arithmetic Progression**, it is difficult to say whether 76 is a member of what has been described merely as "the series". What can happen is that if "the series" is not an AP, the series may be so designed - for example that:

Up to the	What you have to add to any term to get the next term is
First four terms	5
Next four terms	4
Next four terms	3
Next four terms	2
All subsequent terms	1

So "the series" may run as: 4, 9, 14, 19, 23, 27, 31, 35, 38, 41, 44, 47, 49, 51, 53, 55, 56, 57, 58, 59, 60...and so on till 76.

Unless there is a clear assertion that the series 4, 9, 14, 19... is an AP, one cannot say whether the number 76 is or isn't a member thereof.

2. What is the 20th term of the AP 5, 11, 17...? The first term is 5 and the common difference is 6. The Nth term of any AP starting with A, and having common difference of D is = [First Term + ((N-1) times the Common Difference)] and the 20th term is therefore $5 + (19) \times 6 = 5 + 114 = 119$.

3. The Rth term of an AP is S and the Sth term is R. Let R = 3 and S = 4 and then the 4th term is 3 and the third term is 4 so the common difference of the AP is –1. If the 4th term is 3 and the series has common difference of –1, the 5th, 6th and 7th terms will respectively be equal to 2, 1 and 0. Since the 7th term is zero, let us see as to which among the options gives zero when R= 3 and S=4.

   (1) $R + S - 1 = 3 + 4 - 1 = 6$

   (2) $R - S + 1 = 3 - 4 + 1 = 0$

   There is no need to go further. **Option 2** is correct.

4. The Qth term of an AP is 2Q-1. The letter Q denotes a number. Q is faceless. We have to make it come alive by giving it some value. First let us assume that Q=1 and then Q=2 and so on and let us see what emerges in the table below:

When Q =	2Q – 1 =	Sum up to Qth term
1	1	1
2	3	1 + 3 = 4
3	5	1 + 3 + 5 = 9
4	7	1 + 3 + 5 + 7 = 16

The AP is thus 1, 3, 5, 7 and so on. As may be seen from the above, the sum up to the Qth term is equal to Q^2.

5. The first term of an AP is 5 and the fifth term is 7.

In an AP, the Nth term is = First Term + (N – 1) times the Common Difference.

The fifth term will be 5 + (4 times D) = 7, and hence 4D = 2 and D = 1/2.

The series is thus 5, 5.5, 6, 6.5, 7, 7.5, 8, 8.5, 9, 9.5 and so on.

If the first option were true then we should get 63 as the total of the first nine terms. We should check whether this is indeed the case. Up to the first nine terms, even if we are to ignore the .5 in 5.5 and .5 in 6.5 and so on, there are two each of 5, 6, 7 and 8. That should make 10 + 12 + 14 + 16 = 52. Then if were to add the halves in 5.5, 6.5, 7.5 and 8.5 that we have not included in the first count, these four 0.5's should get us 2 more taking the total to 54. Add to this 9 (which is the 9th term) and we get 54 + 9 that makes 63 and thus **Option 1** is correct. Having found that Option 1 is correct, there is no need to go further.

Chapter 13

Averages

Two little children are counting the number of toffees each one has. While young Tim has ten of them, Sally has only six. Sally wants more than what Tim has whereas Tim wants to keep clutching on to the ten of the best that he has. As a modality of breaking the deadlock, the children's father suggests that the two share the toffees equally. The two children count the toffees that they have in the aggregate and the count stops at sixteen. The father divides the toffees equally between the two children. Each child is satisfied that none has more than the other. Tim has eight toffees and so does Sally. This equal number of toffees is what is the average of what the two had earlier. Thus average of two numbers is their total divided by two. To my mind, this would be far easier to understand and assimilate than outlining a formula for the average. First of all there is the fear of misplacing the formula so that you cannot retrieve it quickly from your mental wardrobe when you want it the most. Second, the competitive examination, as such, is about your conceptual clarity and therefore it is of utmost importance to know the underlying principles rather than merely knowing the formulae themselves.

Another interesting aspect of the above sharing pattern is that since there are two persons where one has more than the other, sharing equally would mean that the child who has more, gives some of what he has to the child who has less. There is one giver and one receiver (which is very natural, considering that there are only two parties to the transaction). What the giver gives is what the receiver receives. What the giver gives is exactly equal to the difference between what he has and the average of the two. What the receiver receives is exactly equal to the difference between what he has and the average of the two.

Ted, Bill and Alice have respectively 15, 12 and 21 postage stamps of value to philatelists. They want to find out how many would each of the three have had, had they shared the stamps equally between them. They count the stamps and the total comes to 48. They divide 48 by 3 and get 16. Thus had they shared the stamps equally, they would have had 16 each. The average of these three numbers is thus (A) the total of the three numbers – meaning 48 - divided by (B) the number of numbers – meaning 3.

An interesting aspect of the above sharing pattern and of all averages of series of numbers having more than two terms is that since there are more than two persons, it is likely that:

- Some of the terms may have value higher than the average
- Some of the terms may have value equal to the average
- Other terms may have value lower than the average

Therefore, if five boys who have respectively 31, 37, 43, 49 and 55 marbles decide to share the marbles equally, they would have to find the average first. In the instant case, the average would come to 43. Boys who have 49 and 55 marbles are those who have a number of marbles higher than the average and will have to give respectively 6 and 12 marbles to those of the others who have a number of marbles that is less than the average. The boy with 43 marbles has the average of the numbers. He has to neither give nor receive. The boys with 31 and 37 marbles have to receive respectively 12 and 6 marbles from those who have 55 and 49 respectively– meaning from those who have higher than the average.

The average of a series of numbers is thus A/B where A is the total of the all the numbers and B is the number of terms in the series.

As we have seen, the average is what each one would have had, had they shared equally. It is not necessary that the average of a series be invariably among the terms in the series. It may be or it may not be. In the case of Tim and Sally, as also in the case of Ted, Bill and Alice, we have seen the average number is not a part of the series.

But there are instances when the average number is **certain** to be a member of the series. For example if you are looking at a series of consecutive natural numbers, then the average of this series will invariably a part of the series so long as the series has an odd number of terms. Look at the following such series and you will see that the average of the series is invariably a part of the series:

Series A: 1, 2, 3, 4, 5, 6, and 7. This series of natural numbers has seven consecutive positive integers. The total of the series is 28. Do it manually and satisfy yourself that this is indeed so. Secondly, by totalling things manually we learn not to lean on the pocket calculator for trivia. This would help immensely since the competitive examination, as a genre, does not permit use of the calculator. What would be of interest is to see that regardless of whether the number 1 starts the series or whether the number 1001 starts the series, you will see that the average of the series is invariably a member of the series. It is recommended that you take a couple of other starting numbers for the series of natural numbers with different number of terms – but with the condition that the number of terms is invariably odd each time - and see for yourself that the average of the series is invariably a part of the series.

Series B: 3, 5, 7, 9, and 11. This series of natural numbers has five positive integers such that the difference between any term and its immediately preceding term is exactly 2. The total of this series of five terms is 35. Its average is 7. You will see that the average term is invariably a part of the series of any numbers – whether natural numbers or negative numbers or fractions – so long as:

- There are odd number of terms in the series and
- The difference between any term and its immediately preceding term is exactly the same throughout

See the series –5, –2, 1, 4, 7 that has five terms such that the difference between any term and its immediately preceding term is exactly 3, or the series –4.5, –6.75, –9.00, –11.25, –13.50, –15.75 and –18.00 that has seven terms such that the difference between any term and its immediately preceding term is exactly –2.25. The average of the series -5, -2, 1, 4, 7 is 1 and the average of the series –4.5, –6.75, –9.00, –11.25, –13.50, –15.75 and –18.00 is –11.25. In both cases, the average of the series is invariably a member of the series. Incidentally a series of numbers such that the difference between any term and its immediately preceding term is exactly the same all through is known as an Arithmetic Progression.

You would do well to see an Arithmetic Progression with an even number of terms as follows and find its average: 1.35, 5.35, 9.35 and 13.35. The Arithmetic Progression has 4 terms (which makes it an even number of terms) such that the difference between any term and its immediately preceding term is exactly 4. You will see that the average of this series is 29.40/4 = 7.35 and is not a part of the series. The second lesson to be kept in mind is that in a series of numbers having an even number of terms such that the difference between any term and its immediately preceding term is exactly the same all through, the average of the series is never a part of the series.

The average of a series of consecutive numbers increases by exactly 1/2 when a number is added to the top of the list. In the converse, this average would reduce by 1/2 when the highest number in the series is deleted. Please see the following:

If the series were	Then its total would be	Then its average would be
1,2	3	1.5
1,2,3	6	2
1,2,3,4	10	2.5
1,2,3,4,5	15	3

The average of a series of consecutive numbers **invariably increases** when any number **except the mean number or any number higher than the mean number** is subtracted from between the series. Therefore if you were to subtract the number 2 from the series of numbers 1, 2, 3, 4 and 5, the average before subtracting is 3 and the average after subtracting is 3.25. This is because you have deleted a number less than the average. If you were to delete 3, the average would remain unaffected at 3, whereas if you were to delete the number 4 - which is a number higher than the average – then the average reduces to 2.75.

If the mean number were subtracted, there would be no difference in the average. If the highest number is subtracted, the average invariably decreases by exactly 1/2 and further, that the **average of a series of consecutive numbers cannot reduce by more than 1/2 regardless of the number deleted.**

Please see the following:

If the series were	Then its total would be	Then its average would be	Remarks
1,2	3	1.5	
1,2,3	6	2	
1,2,3,4	10	2.5	
1,2,3,4,5	15	3	
1,2,3,5	11	2.75	Decreases because 4 which is dropped is higher than the mean
1,2,4,5	12	3	Unchanged because the mean number 3 is dropped
1,3,4,5	13	3.25	Increases because 2 which is dropped from the series is lower than the mean

The average of a series of any numbers **remains unchanged** when **the mean number** is deleted from the series. If any number higher than the mean number is deleted, the average **invariably** decreases.

If the series were	Then its total would be	Then its average would be	Remarks
3,5,6,7,9	30	6	
3,5,7,9	24	6	Unchanged because the mean number 3 is dropped
3,6,7,9	25	6.25	A number lower than the mean is off and so average goes up (Since 5 is dropped)
3,5,6,7	21	5.25	A number higher than mean is off and so average goes down (Since 9 is dropped)

The average of a series of consecutive numbers is = (the first number + last number)/2. This is seen from the following:

If the series of consecutive numbers were to comprise of	The aggregate of the series would be (A)	The number of numbers in the series would be (B)	The average of the series = A÷B
1,2	3	2	1.5
1,2,3,4	10	4	2.5
4,5,6,7,8	30	5	6
a,(a+1), (a+2), (a+3)	4a + 6	4	a + 1.5

Irrespective of the starting number of a series of consecutive numbers, its average is = (the first number + last number) ÷2. This is also true of a series in Arithmetic Progression, the series of consecutive integers being nothing other than an Arithmetic Progression of numbers with a common difference of 1. The reason why this is so, is not difficult to understand for anyone regardless of his educational background.

Imagine an Arithmetic Progression starting with A as the first term and D as the common difference. The average of n terms = (the sum of n terms) / (n). The sum of n terms would be (A + A + D + A + 2D + A + 3D and so on till A + (N – 1)D). This would then add up to N(A) + D(the sum of integers starting with the first integer and goes as follows: 1, 2, 3 and so on till N-1). It is important to remember that:

The sum of the first three integers is equal to $^4C_2$, which is (4 × 3)/(2 × 1) = 6

The sum of the first four integers is equal to $^5C_2$, which is (5 × 4)/(2 × 1) = 10

The sum of the first N integers is equal to $^{(N+1)}C_2$, which is ((N + 1) × N)/(2 × 1)

Therefore in N(A) + D(the sum of 1, 2, 3 and so on till N-1), we can arrive at the sum of 1, 2, 3 and so on till N-1 which would be $^{(N-1+1)}C_2$ which is $^NC_2$ = ((N) × (N – 1))/(2 × 1). The sum of the Arithmetic Progression starting with A and having a common difference of D would then be N(A) + D(the sum of 1, 2, 3 and so on till N – 1) = [N(A) + D(N) × (N – 1)]/(2 × 1) and thus the average of this Arithmetic Progression would be N(A) + D((N) × (N – 1))/(2 × 1) / N = A + D × (N – 1))/2 = 2A + D(N – 1)/2. Now 2A + D(N – 1) = A + A + D(N – 1) = First Term (which is A) + Last Term (which is A + D(N – 1)) and thus the average of any Arithmetic Progression is (First Term +Last Term)/2.

It is important to remember this fundamental aspect of the average of a series of consecutive numbers because if you are asked to add all numbers from 1 to 100, all you have to do is add 1+100 and you get 101/2 = 50.5 and now multiply 50.5 by 100 which is the number of numbers in the series and the sum of all numbers from 1 to 100 is 50.5 × 100 = 5050.

If you add up all numbers from 11 to 20, then the total is (11 + 20) × 10/2 = 310/2 = 155.

Having seen the concepts underlying averages, we shall see some problems drawn from the very best competitive examinations and shall see how the concepts that we have outlined above shall be applied in solving the problems. In some of the problems – whether in this chapter or elsewhere - we shall see options whereas in others we shall not. This is simply because wherever the whole thing is about clarity of concept, the option is to be seen only after the concept becomes clear. We shall learn to lean on the options only in order to accelerate our quantitative skills.

Problem 1

In a class of Q number of boys, the average age is P years. Now three boys leave the class and yet the average age of the class remains unchanged. The ages of two among the three boys who have left are 12 and 14. What is the age of the third boy who left the class? The options are: (1) QP – 26 (2) 3QP – 16 (3) P + 26 (4) 3P – 26

The Detailed Solution

If you were to see the options, the one thing that emerges clearly is that you are expected to demonstrate nothing other than the utter clarity of your concepts regarding averages. Which is why the above concept notes become so tremendously pertinent. What is more, the problems that you shall see here onwards will enhance the level of your perception step by step to such a stage that no matter how difficult a question is flung at you, you shall face it with equanimity and shall be able to answer it correctly with ease of effort.

The total age of the class is ascertainable. Three boys have left. The ages of two of those who have left is known. The third chap's age is an unknown figure. Imagine that a class has five boys. On average each one has five sweets. That makes 25 sweets. Now imagine that three boys have left. The average of the sweets that each boy has now in class is 4. Two boys remain in the class. An average of 4 sweets per boy makes a total of 8 sweets. This means that 17 sweets have gone out. Two of those who have gone out have 4 and 6 sweets respectively. That makes 10 out of the 17 sweets that have gone out. So the third boy has 7 sweets.

Back to the problem on hand, one thing is certain: the age of the fellow whose age is unknown is equal to: The total age of the class before the three boys left – The total age of the class after the three boys left (because up to this stage you will know the total age of the three boys) – 12 – 14.

The class originally had Q number of boys. Their average age was P years. Therefore the aggregate age of the class was Q × P years. Three boys have left. The number of boys is now Q-3. Yet their average age is P so their total age is P × (Q – 3). The difference in the total age of the class before the boys left and after the three boys left is (Q × P) – [P× (Q – 3)] = QP – QP + 3P = 3P.

So the total age of the three boys who have left is 3P and of these three, the age of two adds up to 26 and hence the third boy's age is 3P-26. Therefore **Option 4.**

However, if one were to remember that if the mean number were subtracted, there would be no difference in the average, this problem can be surmounted in lesser time than it takes to say: "Mary had a little lamb." Three boys leave a class and yet the average age of the class remains unchanged at P. This only means that the average age of the 3 boys who left is also P. Their total age is thus 3P and two boys' ages add up to 26. So the third boy's age is 3P – 26.

Problem 2

There is Q number of boys in a class and the class teacher is retiring. The boys collect a total of $ P by raising an equal contribution from every boy in order to buy a present for their teacher but the teacher says the gift is too expensive and she goes to the shop from where the gift was bought and exchanges the gift with a lesser expensive gift that costs $ R. She gives the remaining amount to the prefect of the class who has to distribute the remainder back among all the boys. Four boys, however, do not want their share in the amount being refunded and the prefect has to then distribute to the remaining boys accordingly. How much does he have to give back to each boy?

The options are: (1) {[(P –R)/Q] + [4(P –R)/Q]} ÷ (Q – 4) (2) [P –R]/[Q – 4] (3) [P – Q]/[R – 4] (4) [Q – R]/[P – 4]

The Detailed Solution

This too is about the depth of one's understanding of averages.

$P has been collected. $R has been spent. The remaining amount is $(P-R) and this has to be distributed equally among (Q – 4) students since four of the students do not want their share in this remaining amount and the remaining amount of $(P – R) has to be returned to (Q – 4) boys and hence the prefect should return $(P – R)/(Q – 4) to each boy. The correct answer is **Option 2.**

Problem 3

A team has won 60% of the 60% of the matches it has played so far in the tournament. What percentage of the remaining matches it can afford to lose so that the average wins is exactly 75% of all matches it has to play in the tournament?

The Detailed Solution

Since one is working in percentage terms- and, mind you, per cent means "per hundred" - let us assume that the total number of matches to be played is 100. 60% of 100 is 60 and out of 60 it has won 60% meaning 60 × 60/ 100 = 36 matches. It has now to play 40 matches.

It has to win exactly 75 matches in the tournament. It has won 36 and has to win 75 – 36 = 39 out of the remaining 40 matches that it has to play. So it can afford to lose 40 – 39 = 1 match out of the remaining 40 matches that it has yet to play. 1 out of 40 is 100/40% or 5/2 or 2.5%. So the team can afford to lose 2.5% of the remaining matches in the tournament.

Problem 4

The average age of a class of 40 students is 12. Two students aged 16 and 14 leave the class, and a pair of twins joins the class. The average age of the class now goes up by 1.25%. What is the age of the twins?

The Detailed Solution

Two students exited and two entered the class of 40. The number of students thus remained unchanged after these changes. However the total of the ages of the students before two students left was = 40 × 12 = 480. Two students with total age of 30 left. The total age was reduced by 30 to 450. A pair of twins joined up. Their total age increased the prior average by 1.25%. As you know 1.25 is 1 integers and 1/4th. This means 1.25 is 5/4. 1.25% of 480 is = 5× 480/ 100 × 4 = 2400/400 = 6. The addition to the total age of the class is 6. So the new total of the class was 480+6=486. The total before the twins entered was 450 and this increased by 486 – 450 = 36. So the twins were each 36/2 = 18 years old.

Problem 5

A teacher once asked a student to write a series of consecutive numbers starting with 1 on the blackboard. She then asked another student to calculate the average of the series. Then she rubbed out one number from the series and found that the new average was 22 integers and 31 upon 43 (just as 1 and 1/2 is one integers and one upon two). Which number did she rub out?

The Detailed Solution

Look at the denominator in 22 integers and 31 upon 43. The denominator is 43. And this denominator is the number of terms remaining after one term has been deleted. This means that the number of terms before any term was deleted is definitely equal to: An integral multiple of 43 + 1. Since 1 is the first positive integer and 2 the next, the number of terms in the series before anything was deleted could have been 44 or 87 and so on. Now our analysis shall begin. We must remember that:

1. The average of any series of consecutive numbers = (First Term + Last Term) /2
2. The average of any series of consecutive numbers cannot decrease by more than 1/2 even if the highest term in the series is deleted.

If the first term were 1 and the last were 44, then the average would have been (44 + 1)/2 = 22.5. If the first term were 1 and the last were 87, then the average would have been (87 + 1)/2 = 88/2 = 44. Since the average has remained near 22, the first clear inference is that there were exactly 44 terms at the outset and out of these 44 one term was deleted. The total of the first 44 consecutive positive integers is 44 × (44 + 1)/2 = 990.

22 integers and 31 upon 43 means ((22 × 43) + 31)/43 = 946 + 31/43 = 977/43. If this is the average of 43 terms, then the total of the remaining terms is 977. Since the total was 990 and has reduced to 977, it is clear that the number 13 was erased.

Problem 6

If the average of 7 numbers is 7 and the average of another 9 numbers is 9, then what is the average of all numbers together? The options are: (1) 8 (2) 8.125 (3) 7.825 (4) 9.275

The Detailed Solution

The average of 7 numbers is 7 and thus their sum is $7 \times 7 = 49$. The average of the other 9 numbers is 9 and thus their sum is $9 \times 9 = 81$. So the total of all 16 numbers is $49 + 81 = 130$ and the average of these 16 numbers is $130/16 = 65/8$ which makes it just a wee bit more than 8 which is what **Option 2** really is.

Problem 7

I am throwing a large party and am out buying mushrooms. If the price per kilogram of mushrooms were reduced by £2, I am able to buy 2 more kilograms for £99. What was the earlier price of mushrooms?

The Detailed Solution

Reducing a problem to a smaller scale helps greatly in being able to arrive at the strategy to crack it. It is with this intention that we present to you this methodology of shrinking the problem.

Suppose I had £12 with which I set out to buy cakes and found that had I been able to bargain and buy cakes at £1 less per kilogram, I could have been able to buy 1 more kilogram than what I could have been able to buy earlier.

As we know £12 can be factorised in many ways such as: (A) £1 per kg × 12 kg (B) £2 per kg × 6 kg and (C) £3 per kg × 4 kg and (D) £4 per kg × 3 kg, and so on.

Had the price been £1 per kg. I would have been able to buy 12 kg earlier but if the price were to reduce by £1 per kg, the cakes would be given free of cost and not sold. The baker would probably starve if he were to persist with this for long. Had the price been £2 per kg. I would have been able to buy 6 kg earlier but if the price were to reduce by £1 per kg, the new price would be £1 per kg and hence I would have been able to buy 12 kg which takes up the number of kg that I could have bought by 6 kg instead of 1 kg as has been stated in the question. Quite obviously, the only option that fits in is £4 per kg as the earlier price of cakes. This is the only option in which the difference between the factors of 12 is exactly 1.

In the present question, what becomes clear is that if I could factorise 99 into two factors such that the difference between these factors is 2, I could spare myself a whole lot of headache. Factorising 99 in this manner is not difficult at all considering that it is even visibly divisible by both 9 and 11. This is the answer. If the earlier price was £11 per kg, then I could have bought 9 kg but if it drops by £2 to £9 per kg, I could buy 11 kg, which is 2 kg more than what I could have bought earlier.

Problem 8

I have bought a variety of shirts @ \$40, \$30, \$25 and \$10 per shirt and find that the average price of the shirts that I have bought is \$27 per shirt. What could be a possible value of the number of shirts that I have bought @ \$30 per shirt? The options are as follows:

(1) 3 (2) 2 (3) 1 (4) 4.5

The Detailed Solution

It is important to remember the difference between mathematics and quantitative skills. This problem is a clear instance of a problem calling for quantitative skills rather than any mathematics. You know that the average price is the total price of all the shirts divided by the number of shirts bought. In order to be able to arrive at this average one should know both (A) the total price of all the shirts as the numerator and (B) the number of shirts bought as the denominator. You are told neither (A) nor (B). Therefore this will essentially have to be a test of quantitative skills where logic will rule the roost.

Add the unit prices of the shirts other than that variety costing \$30 per shirt and you will find that it will be \$75. When you see 27, the first thing is that it is divisible by 9. The digits of the number 75 add up to 12 and since it is an odd number, 75 is divisible by 3 alone. Since the average price is divisible by 9, the first thing that is necessary is that the total price of all shirts must be an integral multiple of 9. This means that I must add a number whose digits add up to 6 or 15 or 24 and so on so that the digits in the total price of the shirts add up to 9 or an integral multiple of 9, which is an essential condition for the average price (\$27) to be an integral multiple of 9. Which means that if I were to multiply 30 with 2 (by buying two shirts @ \$30 per shirt), I would get 60 which if added to 75 would give 135 that is clearly divisible by 9. To crosscheck, if I were to divide 135 by 5 (the number of shirts bought) I would indeed get \$27 as the average price of the shirts. Hence **Option 2**.

It is of great importance to be able to discern which options are workable and which are not only from a glance at the options. Unfortunately however those options that are not workable do not have tuskers or walrus moustaches and it can be only conceptual clarity that alone can enable you to distinguish between those of the options that are to be ignored right away and those that might be workable. Which is why - dear reader - let us show you how you can eliminate the unworkable options so that you can focus your energies on those that are.

Option 4 is stupid in any case since no one buys shirts in fractions. If you were to try option 1 or 3, you would have an even number of shirts. This means that since the average is an integral number, the total price would necessarily have to be an even number. With 1 shirt, you get \$105 as the total price and since 105 is not an even number, Option 3 has to be scored off without a second look. Option 1 would mean 3 shirts of \$30 each and since with 1 shirt of each variety you get an odd number total of prices, with 3 of \$30 variety, you will continue to get an odd number as the total price of all shirts since 30 itself is an even number and any addition of an even number to an odd number is bound to result in an odd number. So Option 2 stares at you in the face as the correct option from the viewpoint of logic alone without having to put pen to paper.

Problem 9

The average amount of money with A, B and C in their purses is DM (Deutsche Mark) 450, the average of the money with B, C and D is DM 475. How much does D have in his purse if A has DM 500? Options: (1) DM 575 (2) DM 475 (3) DM 375 (4) DM 675

The Detailed Solution

The first thing to see is that B and C are common in the two trios. The first point of difference is that in the case of the first trio of ABC and the second trio of BCD, the second trio has a higher average. This means that D has a higher amount than A. The second point of difference in these two trios is that the average of the second trio is DM 25 more than that of the first trio and this means that the second trio has DM 75 more than the first trio. But since only A and D are not common to both trios, it means that D has DM 75 more than A. Since A has DM 500, D has DM 575. Hence **Option 1**.

EXERCISE.

1. An organisation conducts nature appreciation camps and in one instance it finds that the average fee it has recovered from the participants is equal to the number of the participants. What among the following could be a value for the total fee it has recovered for the camp?

   (1) 3561 (2) 3681 (3) 3721 (4) 2504

2. X number of men went on an excursion and their average contribution was \$X. However, they found that if Y men out of those who went on the excursion had contributed \$Y on average, the average contribution for the remaining would have increased to \$Z. This means that:

   Option (1) $X \times (Z - Y) = Z^2$ Option (2) $Z \times (X - Y) = X^2 + Y^2$

   Option (3) $X^2 - Y^2 = Z^2$ Option (4) $X = Z - Y$.

3. A series of consecutive odd integers has 17 members. If the average of this series is N, then N is definitely divisible by:

   Option (1) 17 Option (2) 9

   Option (3) 16 Option (4) None of these.

4. A man has three children A, B and C whose average age is 21. If the ratio of the ages of A the eldest and B his immediately younger sibling is 7:6, it then can be said for sure that:

   Option (1) C is 5 Option (2) C is 11

   Option (3) B could be 24 or 18 Option (4) A could be 35 or 28

5. A lady pilot flies her aircraft along the edges of a square of each side 200 kilometres. She does the first side @ 200 miles/hour, then turns immediately each time thereafter and does the next @ 400 miles/hour, the third @ 600 miles/hour and the fourth @ 800 miles/hour. What is her average flying speed in miles/hour?

ANSWER KEY

1. 3721
2. X = Z – Y
3. None of these
4. C is 11
5. 384 miles/hour

SOLUTIONS

1. If there are n participants, then the average fee per participant should also be n and this means that the total fee should be $n \times n = n^2$. Which means that whichever figure for the total fee recovered in the camp should be a perfect square. 3561, 3681 and 3721 are all in the region of 3600, which is the square of 60. 3561 is less than 3600 and since it ends with 1, it could be the square of 59 but if one finds the square of 59 – the simplest way of doing so is to consider 59 as (60 – 1) and find $(60 - 1)^2$ which is equal to 3600 – 120 + 1 = 3481. Since 3581 is not the square of 59, let us see which among 3681 and 3721 could be the square of 61 (since both end with 1 and could be the squares of 61) and we find that 3721 is the square of 61. Hence 3721 is the figure for the total fee recovered in the camp.

2. X men went on an excursion and their average contribution was \$X. Thus the total contribution would have been $X \times X = X^2$. However, they found that if Y men out of those who went on the excursion had contributed \$Y on average (meaning Y men had contributed \$$Y^2$ in all), the average contribution for the remaining would have increased to \$Z. Let us assume X to be 4 and Y to be 3. This means that 4 men would have had to collect \$16 in all. Of this 3 men collected \$3 each and thus their total contribution would have been \$9. This means that the remaining one person would have to contribute \$7 (which is \$16 minus \$9) instead of the initial contribution of \$4 that was envisaged. Thus the average contribution for the remaining one person increased to \$7. Hence Z = 7 when X = 4 and Y = 3. Let us see which among the given equations from among the given options is satisfied by the above referred values of X, Y and Z.

   a. $X \times (Z - Y) = Z^2$; Is $4 \times (7\text{-}3) = 3^2$? No.

   b. $Z \times (X - Y) = X^2 + Y^2$; Is $7(4 - 3) = 4^2 + 3^2$? No.

   c. $X^2 - Y^2 = Z^2$; Is $4^2\text{-}3^2 = 7^2$?No.

   d. $X = Z - Y$; Is $4 = 7 - 3$? Yes.

Hence Option 4.

3. A series of consecutive odd integers has 17 members. Let us first assume the series to start with 1 and end with 17. The average of this series is 9. But this is not the "be all and the end all" of our simple experiment. Let us then assume another series to start with 2 and end with 18. This series too has 17 members. The average of this series is 10.

   You get two values for N in the two little experiments; the first time N = 9 and the second time N = 10. But one thing emerges very clearly: N cannot be said to be **definitely** divisible by any of the first three options. Hence **Option 4.**

   The lesson to be learnt here is that one should experiment with at least two sets some elementary numbers in order to be able to reach a conclusion that something is definitely is or is definitely not. Had we stuck to the first experiment of 1 to 17, we would have seen that the average is 9 and this is divisible by 9 we would have rushed headlong into a hasty generalisation. In order to avoid committing the fallacy of hasty generalisation it is important to base your judgement on basis of wide observations.

4. A man has three children A, B and C whose average age is 21 and their total age is thus 63. If the ratio of the ages of A the eldest and B his immediately younger sibling is 7:6, then if we presume that they are respectively 7x and 6x years of age, then 7x + 6x + the age of the youngest child will add up to 63. Let us see under what circumstances this is feasible but it must be borne in mind that since 7x + 6x add up to 13x and that if x is 5 then the total of the ages of the two elder children itself crosses 65 whichever values of x that we may assume cannot be 5 or more and thus we shall have to work from 4 downwards:

If X =	7X =	6X =	7X + 6X =	Then the age of the youngest child is [63 –(7X + 6X)] =
4	28	24	52	11
3	21	18	39	24

With x = 3, the youngest child turns out to be older than the eldest and this is not workable. Hence only x = 4 is workable and the youngest child is definitely 11 years of age. Thus **Option 2.**

5. Average speed is = total distance covered divided by the total time taken. The time taken for each leg of journey is as under:

Distance (miles)	Speed (miles/hour)	Time taken=Distance/Speed (Hours)
200	200	1
200	400	½
200	600	1/3
200	800	¼
	Total time: (While adding fractions it is important to be able to express the different fractions with a common denominator so that one has then to add only the numerators with the denominator remaining constant)	= 1+ ½ + 1/3 + 1/4 = 12/12 + 6/12 + 4/12 + 3/12 = 25/12

So while she covers 800 kilometres in all she takes 25/12 hours. Her average speed is thus = total distance ÷ total time = 800 × 12/25 = 384 miles/hour. Average speed is (A) Total distance covered divided by (B) Total time taken and therefore it is not a simplistic average of the four speeds divided by 4. Speed tells you the relation between distance and time taken to cover that distance and without calculating the total time taken for four journeys undertaken at different speeds, the average speed is not possible to calculate.

Chapter 14

The Circle

If you were to see a square first and then a pentagon, hexagon, octagon in that sequence, you will realise that with the addition of the number of sides to a regular polygon, the polygon starts getting rounder and thus the resemblance to a circle keeps increasing. This is essentially because a **circle is a regular polygon of n sides.**

So if you were asked as to which is higher: the circumference of a circle drawn **outside** a regular polygon or the circumference of a circle drawn **inside** the **same** regular polygon, it should not take you a moment to answer correctly that it is the circumference of the outer circle which is definitely higher than the circumference of the inner circle.

So if you were asked as to which is higher: the perimeter of a regular polygon of 37 sides drawn **outside** a circle or the perimeter of a regular polygon of 93 sides drawn **inside** the same circle, it should not take you a moment to answer correctly that the perimeter of the outer polygon is definitely higher than the perimeter of the inner polygon regardless of the number of sides of these two regular polygons.

In a square, its two diagonals intersect at right angles and create four right angles at the centre of the square. With this the measure of the angles in a square is 360°. This is true of all regular polygons. If you were to link the vertices of the polygon to its centre, then the total measure of all angles subtended at the centre is 360°. This means that the perimeter of a regular polygon subtends an angle of 360° at the centre of the polygon. The circle is no exception to this since a circle is essentially a regular polygon of n sides. Thus the circumference of a circle subtends an angle of 360° at the centre of the circle.

There is a constant distance between the centre of a circle and any point on its edge – (better known as its circumference.) This constant distance is known as the radius of the circle. If a straight line joins any two points on the opposite sides of the centre of a circle and passes through the centre of the circle, then the measure of this line is two times its radius. Such a line is known as the diameter of the circle. Hence the diameter of a circle is 2 times its radius or, in the converse, the radius of a circle is half its diameter. A line joining any two points on the circumference of a circle without passing through the centre is known as the chord of the circle.

The diameter and a chord differ in this respect that while a diameter is also a chord of the circle, a chord is not a diameter if it does not pass through the centre of the circle.

If you were to draw radii (which is the plural of *radius*), from the centre of the circle and measure the angles between each of them, and add these up, be sure that the total would come to 360°. In the circle, this total of the angles between radii from the centre of the circle, which would come to 360°, is often referred to in π radians where one π radian is 180°. So the total of the angles subtended at the centre of a circle is 2π radians.

If one were to draw two diameters of a circle that intersect at right angles, then these diameters would divide the circle into four quadrants; each of these quadrants subtends an angle of 90° or $\pi/2$ radians at the centre of the circle.

There is a relationship between the circumference of the circle and its radius. The circumference or the length of the periphery of the circle is 2π times its radius where π is a constant. The area of the circle is π times the square of its radius. In mathematical terms, the area of a circle is $\pi \times r^2$. The constant π has an approximate value of 22/7.

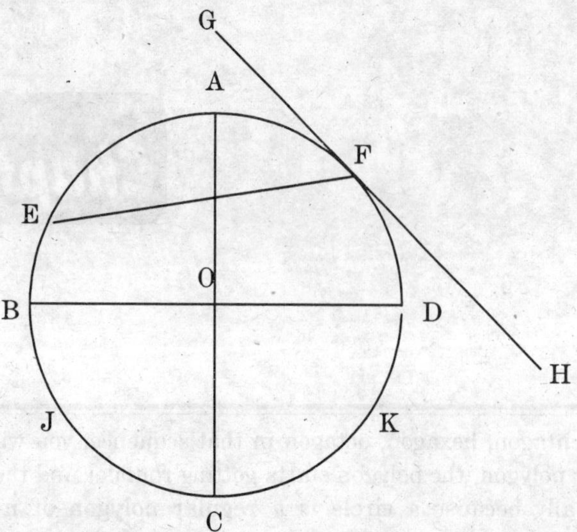

See the above circle. It has its centre at O. Each of AO, BO, CO, and DO are the radii of the circle. BD is the diameter of the circle (and so is AC). Both diameter pass through the centre of the circle. Quite apparently the diameter is the twice the radius. EF is a chord of the circle because it joins two points E and F on the circumference of the circle. But EF is not its diameter. This is because the qualification for a diameter is that it should not only join any two points on the circle but also pass through the centre of the circle.

Each of angles AOB, BOC, COD and DOA are equal to 90° or $\pi/2$ radians, since π radians means 180°.

If one were to walk on the periphery of the circle between any two points on the circumference – let us say from point J to the point C – then one would have walked along an arc of the circle.

The line GH touching the circle at point F is a tangent to the circle. It only touches the circle. If you were to join the points F and O and with a protractor measure the angle OFG, you would find that it is 90°. So also would be the angle OFH. This is a property of the tangent to a circle.

If you were to mark any point on the circumference of the circle and join this point (let us call it I) to the points B and D which are the two ends of the diameter, then you find that the angle BID would be 90°, no matter where the point I is located so long as it is on the circumference of the circle. This is a property of the circle. We would recommend that you actually mark a point I on the circle in the above figure and form triangle BID. Please also measure angle BID with a protractor. You will find it is 90^0.

If one were to mark two points J and K on the circle and join the four points E, F, J and K by straight lines, one would see a quadrilateral EJKF taking shape. If one were to measure the following four angles by means of a protractor and jot down their values, one would find that: (I) Angle JEF + JKF = 180° and (II) Angle EJK + EFK = 180°. This means that in a quadrilateral drawn in a circle with the four vertices of the quadrilateral lying on the circumference of the circle, the opposite angles are supplementary (meaning, they add up to 180^0). This is a property of the circle and the quadrilateral that we have visualised is known as a cyclic quadrilateral. Incidentally, Supplementary Angles are those that add up to 180° and Complementary Angles are those that add up to 90°.

If two tangents are drawn from a common point to a circle so as to touch it at two different points, then the length between the point of contact of the first tangent and the common point and the length between the point of contact of the second tangent and the common point has the same measure. Please see this for yourself by marking two tangents emanating from a common point – the point H, for example – tó touch the circle at two different points. Seeing is believing!

If two tangents are drawn from a common point to a circle so as to touch it at two different points, and then if a straight line is drawn so as to join the centre of the circle to the common point from which the two tangents are drawn, then the angles between (A) the two tangents and (B) the line joining the circle centre and the common point of the tangents have the same measure. This means that a line drawn from the centre of a circle to the point from where two tangents are drawn to touch the circle at two different points, then this line from the circle centre to the common point divides the angle between the two tangents into two equal parts. We would suggest that you draw a tangent from H to touch the circle at a point other than F and mark that point as L. Join OH. You will find that OH divides angle LHF into two equal parts.

If two or more circles are drawn from a common centre with radii of different measures, then these circles are known as concentric circles. Suppose two circles are drawn from a common centre with radii of different measures and the measure of the radius of the larger circle is R and that of the inner circle is r, then the area of the outer circle will be $\pi \times R^2$. The area of the inner circle will be $\pi \times r^2$. The difference between the areas of the two circles will be $(\pi \times R^2 - \pi \times r^2)$ or $\pi (R^2 - r^2)$.

Suppose two circles are drawn from a common centre with radii of different measures and the measure of the radius of the larger circle is R and that of the inner circle is r, then the circumference of the outer circle will be $2\pi \times R$. The circumference of the inner circle will be $2\pi \times r$. The difference between the circumference of the two circles will be $(2\pi \times R - 2\pi \times r)$ or $2\pi (R - r)$.

So if one is given the areas of two concentric circles and their circumference then it is possible to find the radius of both the circles because you know what $\pi (R^2 - r^2)$ is and what $2\pi (R - r)$ is. Since π is a constant term and has an arithmetic value, from $2\pi (R - r)$ you can find out what $(R - r)$ is and once you know what $(R - r)$ is you can find out the value of $(R + r)$ since $(R^2 - r^2)$ is nothing other than $(R + r) \times (R - r)$. Knowing the values of both $(R + r)$ and $(R - r)$, one can find the value of both R and r.

When a chord is drawn from two opposite points on the circumference of the outer circle of two concentric circles, this chord touches the inner circle at two points that lie on this chord of the outer circle. Thus such a chord would be common to both the circles. The distance between (A) Point of intersection of this common chord with the inner circle and (B) The point where the chord touches the circumference of the outer circle is the same on both sides of the common chord.

The above information about the circle is what is perceived to suffice for purposes of competitive examinations. This perception is based on the fact that a competitive test of the objective type is designed to ascertain the depth of one's thinking and it is not a test of one's mathematical skills alone. Such tests are meant for aspirants from diverse disciplines and one is not expected to be an expert at Geometry, for example.

With this, let us see some problems and their detailed solutions that will not only refresh the important aspects of what we learnt at school but also further strengthen what we have learnt.

Problem 1

There are two concentric circles with centre O. PQRS is a square, inscribed in the outer circle. PR is one of the diagonals of PQRS. QS is the other. PQRS also circumscribes the inner circle, touching it at points B, C, D and A. What is the ratio of the perimeter of the outer circle to that of polygon ABCD?

(1) $\pi/4$ (2) $3\pi/2$ (3) $\pi/2$ (4) π

The Detailed Solution

It would be worth drawing the figure roughly as under:

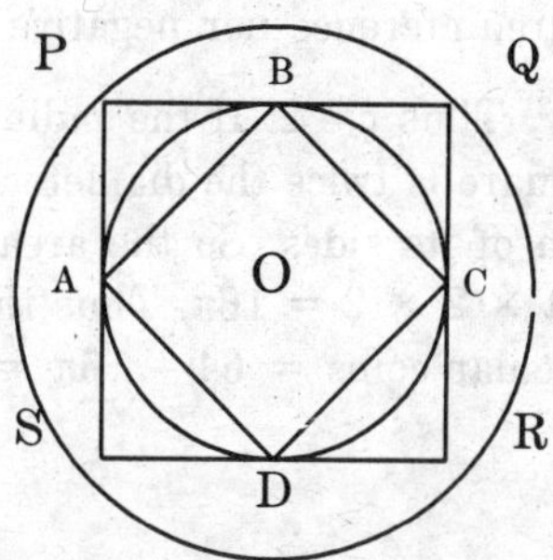

The circumference of the outer circle is $2\pi \times r$ (the radius). PR is the diagonal of the square PQRS and since PO is r (the radius of the circle), 2r is its diameter. PS the side of the square PQRS = $\sqrt{2}r$. Thus the measure of each side of a square = its diagonal divided by $\sqrt{2}$. PS = BD = $\sqrt{2}r$ and since BD is the diagonal of the polygon ABCD, each side of the polygon ABCD = r. Thus the perimeter of the polygon ABCD = 4r and the ratio of the perimeter of the outer circle to that of the polygon ABCD is $2\pi r/4r = \pi/2$. Thus Option 3.

Problem 2

Four identical circular coins are placed inside the square ABCD as in the following diagram:

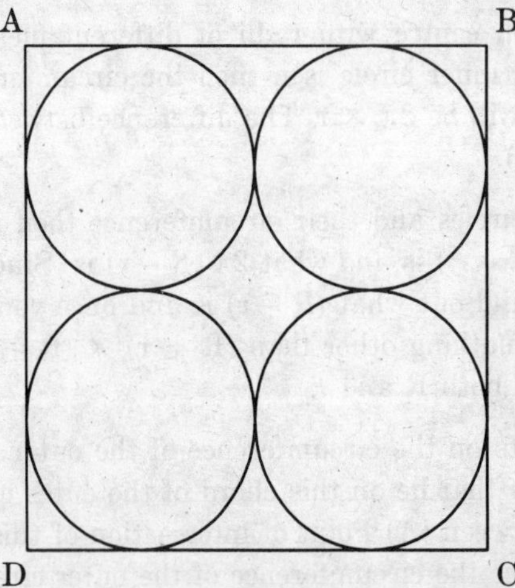

If for each coin, (area/circumference) = (circumference/area) then the area not occupied by the coins in ABCD is:

(1) $8(4 - \pi)$ (2) $16(8 - \pi)$ (3) $16(4 - \pi)$ (4) None of these

The Detailed Solution

In each coin, area/circumference= circumference/area. This means that the fraction represented by the area as a numerator and the circumference as the denominator has the same value as its inverse. Fundamentally, a fraction can be equal to its inverse in only two circumstances:

- ✓ The first is when the numerator is equal to the denominator, which means that the fraction has a value of exactly 1
- ✓ The second is when the numerator is opposite in sign to the denominator, which means that the fraction has a value of exactly -1

In no other circumstances can a fraction be equal to its inverse. The logical reason for this is as follows:

Imagine that a fraction with N as the numerator and D as the denominator is equal in value to its inverse. This means that N/D = D/N and therefore $N^2 = D^2$. This means that either N = D or N = – D. If N = D, it means that the value of the fraction is N/N or 1. If N= - D, it means that the value of the fraction is -D/D or –1. In the present case, however the reasonable inference is that the area equals circumference. This is because a circle can neither have negative circumference nor negative area.

If the circumference = area then $2\pi r = \pi r^2$. Thus r= 2. If the radius of each coin is 2, then the diameter of each coin is 4 and thus the breadth of the square is twice the diameter of the coins, which is 8. The breadth of a square is constant and equal to the length of its sides. So the area of the square is 8×8=64 whereas the area of the four coins is $4 \times \pi \times r^2 = 4 \times \pi \times 2 \times 2 = 16\pi$. Thus the area not occupied by the coins = area of the square minus the area of the four circular coins = $64 - 16\pi = 16(4 - \pi)$. So Option 3.

Problem 3

Three circles with centres P, Q and R, each with radius 20 cm, intersect one another as shown in the figure below. The length of AB = 12 cm, CD = 10 cm and EF = 5 cm. What is the perimeter of the triangle PQR?

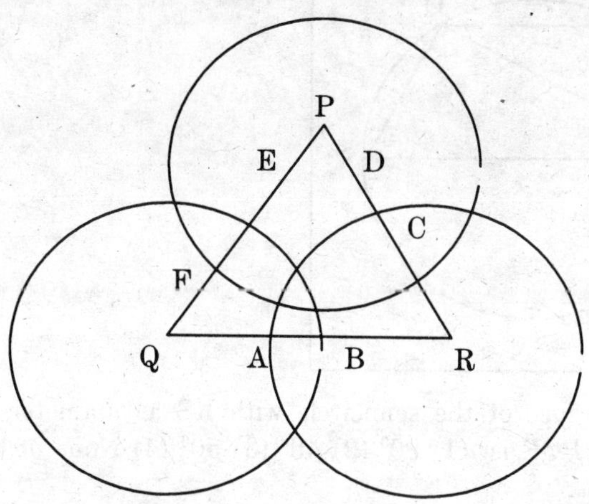

(1) 60 cms (2) 81 cms (3) 87 cms (4) 93 cms

The Detailed Solution

If there is any apparent visual aberration in the question, it is intentional. The perimeter of the triangle is PQ + QR + PR. All three circles with centres P, Q and R have identical radius of 20 cm each.

- QR = QA + AR. We know that AR is 20 cm since it is the radius of circle with centre R. QA + AB = 20 since QB is the radius of the circles with centre Q. Since AB is given as 12, QA + 12 = 20 and hence QA = 8; so QR = 8 + 20 = 28.
- QP = QF + FP. We know that FP is 20 cm since it is the radius of circle with centre P. QF + FE = 20 since QE is the radius of the circles with centre Q. Since FE is given as 5, QF + 5 = 20 and hence QF = 15; so QP = 15 + 20 = 35.
- PR = PD + DR. We know that DR is 20 cm since it is the radius of circle with centre R (the positions of the points D and C are misleading in the diagram). PD + DC = 20 since PC is the radius of the circles with centre P. Since DC is given as 10, PD + 10 = 20 and hence PD = 10; so PR = 10 + 20 = 30.

The perimeter of the triangle PQR = PQ+QR+PR = 35+28+30=93. So **Option 4.**

Problem 4

Four small discs, each of radius 5 cm, are cut from a circular disc of radius 20 cm. The ratio of the left out area to the cut out area of the disc is:

(1) 2:1 (2) 3:1 (3) 4:1 (4) 1:1

The Detailed Solution

Four discs each of radius 5 cm are cut. Their aggregate area is $4\times \pi\times r^2$ which is $4\pi \times 5^2 = 100\pi$. The area of the larger disc is $\pi \times R^2$, or $\pi \times 20^2 = 400\pi$. The left out area is $400\pi - 100\pi = 300\pi$. Therefore the area of the left out area to the cut out area is $300\pi : 100\pi$. This is 3:1. Thus **Option 2.**

Problem 5

Look at the figure below:

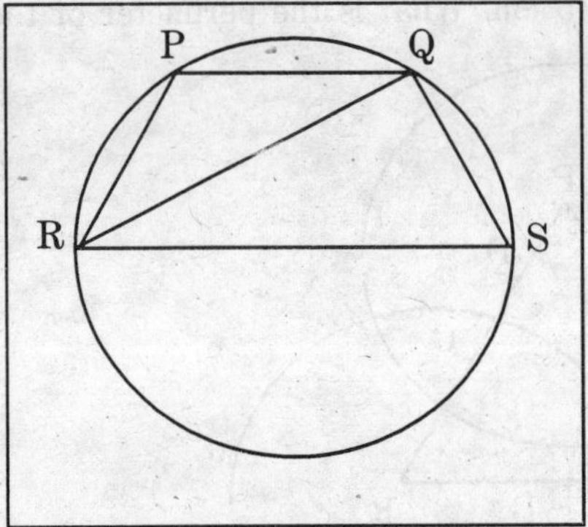

P and Q are points on the circumference of the semicircle with RS as diameter. Angle RSQ = 70^0 and angle PRQ = 30^0. Then, the value of angle PQR is: (1) 90^0 (2) 40^0 (3) 50^0 (4) None of these

The Detailed Solution

It is a fundamental of the circle that if a quadrilateral is inscribed in a circle, the opposite angles are supplementary, meaning that they add up to 180 °. It is called a cyclic quadrilateral. **(A) Supplementary angles add up to 180° and (B) complementary angles add up to 90°. It is another fundamental of the circle that if the ends of the diameter are joined by a line to any point on the circle then the angle at the point on the circle is 90°.** In the present case, RS is the diameter and point P on the circle is linked to the two ends of the diameter RS by straight lines. Therefore angle RQS is 90°. In the present case, angle RSQ is given as 70°. Therefore angle QRS is 20° (since in the triangle QRS, one angle RQS is 90 and another RSQ is 70 and thus the third angle SRQ is 180 – 90 – 70 = 20). Since QRS is 20°, the angle PRS (which is a sum of angles PRQ and QRS and is thus (30 + 20) meaning 50°. In the case of the cyclical quadrilateral, the opposite angles add up to 180 °. So angles PRS and PQS are opposite and supplementary and therefore angle PQS + angle PRS = 180 and so PQS is = 180 – 50 = 130 °. Now angle PQS is a sum of angles PQR and RQS. RSQ is 90° as may be seen from the above fundamental in relation to triangle with two vertices on the diameter and the third on the circle. So angle PQR + 90 = 130 and thus PQR = 40 °. Hence **Option 2.**

Chapter 15

Exponents and Exponential Functions

The Exponent is a term used in mathematics to indicate the number of times that a quantity is to be multiplied by itself. An exponent is usually written as a small number or letter at the upper right of the expression, as in A^2, which is read as squared and means $A \times A$; $(A + B)^3$, which is read (A + B) cubed and means $(A + B) \times (A + B) \times (A + B)$; and $\sin^4 A^0$, which is read sin A^0 to the fourth power and means that sin A^0 is to be multiplied by itself four times.

Exponents obey certain rules called the laws of exponents. These rules are set out and explained hereunder:

(1) $A^X \times A^Y = A^{(X+Y)}$

When you multiply any number A raised to a certain power X with the same number A raised to another power Y, the product is equal to A raised to the power of (X+Y).

This could be better understood by illustrations rather than by words. Let us imagine that A=2, X=3 and Y=5. Then $A^X \times A^Y = 2^3 \times 2^5 = (2 \times 2 \times 2) \times (2 \times 2 \times 2 \times 2 \times 2) = 2 \times 2 \times 2 \times 2 \times 2 \times 2 \times 2 \times 2 = 2^8$

(2) $A^X \div A^Y = A^{(X-Y)}$

This too could be better understood by illustrations rather than by words. Let us imagine that A = 3, X = 4 and Y = 2. Then $A^X \div A^Y = 3^4 \div 3^2 = (3 \times 3 \times 3 \times 3) \div (3 \times 3) = 3 \times 3 = 3^2 = 3^{(4-2)}$

(3) $(A^X)^Y = A^{XY}$

If we were to imagine that A = 3 and X = 2 and Y = 3, then $(A^X)^Y = (3^2)^3 = (9)^3 = 9 \times 9 \times 9 = 729$. If $(A^X)^Y = A^{XY}$, in the present case $(3^2)^3$ should be equal to 3^6. The question is then: Is $(3^2)^3$ equal to 3^6? If it is then $(3^2)^3$ should be equal to 3^6. We have already found that $(3^2)^3 = 729$. Let us see whether $3^6 = 729$. As we know, $3^6 = 3 \times 3 \times 3 \times 3 \times 3 \times 3 = 729$ and it is proved that $(A^X)^Y = A^{XY}$.

(4) $A^0 = 1$

Having understood that $A^X \div A^Y = A^{(X-Y)}$, it is easy to understand that $A^X \div A^X = A^{(X-X)} = A^0$. Now $A^{(X-X)}$ is really $A^X \div A^X$, which is really dividing a number A^X by the same number A^X and hence bound to result in 1. This is why regardless of the value of A, the value of $A^0 = 1$.

(5) $A^{-X} = 1/A^X$

Having understood that $A^X \div A^Y = A^{(X-Y)}$, it is easy to understand that $A^0 \div A^2 = A^{(0-2)} = A^{-2}$. Thus if we were to take A as 2 and X as 0 and Y as 3, $A^X \div A^Y = A^{(X-Y)} = 2^0 \div 2^3 = 2^{(0-3)} = 2^{-3} = 1 \div 2^3 = 1 \div 8 = 1/8$. Therefore it is easy to understand that A^{-X} is merely the inverse of A^X. Therefore, if $3^2 = 9$, then $3^{-2} = 1/9$.

(6) $A^{1/X} = \sqrt[X]{A}$

What this rule states in effect is that:

$8^{1/3} = \sqrt[3]{8} = (2 \times 2 \times 2)^{1/3} = (2^3)^{1/3}$. Having understood the rule that $(A^X)^Y = A^{XY}$, $(2^3)^{1/3} = 2^{3 \times 1/3} = 2^1 = 2$. Therefore whether you say $8^{1/3}$ (read as 8 raised to the power of one-third) or the cube root of 8, both mean the same thing and both mean 2.

These rules hold irrespective of whether A, X, and Y are positive integers, negative integers or fractions. While we have seen in the above illustrations that $A^X \times A^Y = A^{(X+Y)}$ where A = 2 and X and Y are 3 and 5 respectively (and therefore all three are positive integers), let us see some illustrations where some or all of A, X, and Y are negative integers or fractions. But before we start off, let us remember that – for example – if 2 × 2 × 2 × 2 × 2 × 2 = 64 then:

- Since $8 \times 8 = 8^2 = 64$, therefore 8 is the square root of 64 which means that if you were to raise 64 to the power of ½ (expressed as $64^{1/2}$ or $\sqrt{64}$), then you would get 8.
- Since $4 \times 4 \times 4 = 4^3 = 64$, therefore 4 is the cube root of 64 which means that if you were to raise 64 to the power of 1/3 (expressed as $64^{1/3}$ or $\sqrt[3]{64}$), then you would get 4.
- Since $2 \times 2 \times 2 \times 2 \times 2 \times 2 = 2^6 = 64$, therefore 2 is the sixth root of 64 which means that if you were to raise 64 to the power of 1/6 (expressed as $64^{1/6}$ or $\sqrt[6]{64}$), then you would get 2.

Now let us imagine that we are carrying out the multiplication as follows: $64^{1/2} \times 64^{1/3}$. We know that $64^{1/2} = 8$ and $64^{1/3} = 4$ and therefore $64^{1/2} \times 64^{1/3} = 8 \times 4 = 32$. Let us see whether $64^{1/2} \times 64^{1/3} = 64^{(1/2 + 1/3)} = 64^{5/6}$. Since we know that $64^{1/6} = 2$, therefore $64^{5/6} = (64^{1/6})^5 = 2^5$. We know that $2^5 = 2 \times 2 \times 2 \times 2 \times 2 = 32$ and therefore it is conclusively proved that $64^{1/2} \times 64^{1/3} = 64^{(1/2 + 1/3)} = 64^{5/6}$.

Let us now suppose that we are carrying out the following division: $64^{1/2} \div 64^{1/3}$. As we have seen earlier, $64^{1/2} = 8$ and $64^{1/3}=4$ and therefore it should be easy to understand that $64^{1/2} \div 64^{1/3} = 8 \div 4 = 2$. Let us now see whether having known that $A^X \div A^Y = A^{(X-Y)}$, $64^{1/2} \div 64^{1/3} = 64^{(1/2 - 1/3)} = 64^{(1/6)} = 2$. Since we know that $2^6 = 64$, $64^{(1/6)}$ is really $(2^6)^{1/6} = 2^{6 \times 1/6} = 2^1 = 2$. We have now clearly understood **why** $A^X \div A^Y = A^{(X-Y)}$.

So if we were to multiply as follows: $(1/64)^{1/2} \times (1/64)^{1/3}$, we know that this is equal to $(1/64)^{5/6}$ which in turn is $(1/2)^6)^{5/6} = (1/2)^5 = 1/32$. The short point is that the rules of exponents hold irrespective of whether you are dealing with positive integers, negative integers or fractions.

If the exponent in an expression involves an unknown or variable, such as a^x or 3^y, the resulting function is called an exponential function. Which is why if you are told that the distance between your house and the town library is 2^x km and that x is such that $2^x = \mathbf{x}^2$ but the distance is definitely less than 10 kilometres, it must strike one that there are only two possible values for x that will satisfy the condition that $2^x = \mathbf{x}^2$. These possible values of x are 2 and 4. When x = 2, $2^x = \mathbf{x}^2 = 4$ and when x = 4, $2^x = \mathbf{x}^2 = 16$. Since you are told that the distance is definitely less than 10 km, the only possible value of x that will work is x=2 and thus the distance that you are asked to find is 4 km.

We shall see another marvellous illustration regarding exponential functions that should ensure that we understand all its relative aspects and also sharpen one's reasoning skills.

Consider this: You are told that the surprise test a class teacher took the other day had N questions. For J= 1,2,3.... N, there are $2^{(N-J)}$ students who answered J or more questions wrongly. If the total number of wrong answers is 57, how many questions did the surprise test have? Your options are: (A) 5 (B) 4 (C) 3 (D) Cannot be determined

If there were five questions in the examination, then N = 5 and a fellow writing an examination cannot hope to write more wrong answers than the number of questions asked in the examination. Some of the students could have answered 1 question wrong. Some others may have answered 2 questions wrong whereas there may have been some students who may answered 3 questions wrong and so on. What can be seen is:

- The number of students giving 1 wrong answer (when J = 1) is = $2^{(5-1)} = 2^4 = 16$. Therefore the number of wrong answers on this account is 1 × 16 = 16.
- The number of students giving 2 wrong answers (when J = 2) is = $2^{(5-2)} = 2^3 = 8$. Therefore the number of wrong answers on this account is 2×8=16.
- The number of students giving 3 wrong answers (when J = 3) is = $2^{(5-3)} = 2^2 = 4$. Therefore the number of wrong answers on this account is 3×4=12.

- The number of students giving 4 wrong answers (when J = 4) is = $2^{(5-4)} = 2^1 = 2$. Therefore the number of wrong answers on this account is 4 × 2 = 8.
- The number of students giving 5 wrong answers (when J = 5) is = $2^{(5-5)} = 2^0 = 1$. Therefore the number of wrong answers on this account is 5 × 1 = 5.

In sum, the total number of wrong answers is 16 + 16 + 12 + 8 + 5 = 57. Therefore Option A is to be marked as correct. We may mention that if J = 0, the **number of students** giving wrong answers would be the highest. This is because the number of students giving wrong answers has been defined as $2^{(N-J)}$ where N is the number of questions at the examination and J is the number of wrong answers. $2^{(N-J)}$ can be higher when J is as at its least and insofar as wrong answers go, there cannot be anything less than zero. However the number of zero wrong answers = [No. of wrong answers(which is zero)/ student] × [No. of students giving zero wrong answers] = 0. That is why we have not taken J = Zero while calculating the total number of wrong answers.

It may be mentioned that the illustrations that we have given are drawn from the actual papers of management entrance tests that are believed to be among the toughest in the world. If you, dear reader, were to assimilate the methodology in these illustrations and the concept notes above, no problem on this topic - no matter how tough - will pose any difficulty to you.

Chapter 16

Geometric Progressions

As we have seen earlier, the word ***progression*** comprises of the suffix ***pro*** that means forward and the Latin root ***gress*** that means step. Thus a progression is essentially something that goes forward in steps as different from sudden movements such as leaps and bounds. Which means every number in an arithmetic progression (AP) or for that matter a GP, is a distinct step away from its predecessor in the progression. In an AP where the result of subtracting the immediately previous term from any term is the same throughout the progression, that step is the common difference. In the case of the GP where the result of dividing any term by its immediately previous term is the same throughout the progression, that step is the common ratio.

A Geometric Progression (GP hereafter for the sake of brevity) is a progression where there is a first term in the sequence and the second term is a multiple of the first term and in order to arrive at the third term in the progression, the second term has to be multiplied by the same multiplicand with which the first term was multiplied in order to arrive at the second term. So if the first term in the GP is A and the second term is AX, the third is AX^2, the fourth is AX^3 and so on such that the Nth term is $AX^{(N-1)}$.

To cite an example of a GP, see the following series:

GP 1: 1, 3, 9, 27, 81... Each number in the GP is 3 times its previous number. Therefore 3 is the common ratio of this GP

GP 2: 2, 9, 40.5, ... Each number in the GP is 4.5 times its previous number. Therefore 4.5 is the common ratio of this GP

GP 3: 8, 4, 2, 1, 1/2... Each number in the GP is 0.5 times its previous number. Therefore 0.5 is the common ratio of this GP

As we have seen earlier, the Nth term is $AX^{(N-1)}$. So if one is asked as to what term of the GP – 5, 10, 20.. is 320, all one has to do is to presume is 320 is the nth term and if it is so then $5 \times 2^{n-1} = 320$ and then dividing both sides by 5, we get $2^{n-1} = 64$. Now 2^6 is 64 and thus $2^{n-1} = 2^6$. Thus $n - 1 = 6$ so $n = 7$. So 320 is the 7th term in the GP 5, 10, 20..

If a GP has **A** as its first term and **R** is the common ratio of the GP, then the second term is $A \times R$ and the Nth term is $A \times R^{n-1}$. The sum S_N of such a series is given by the following formula that is not so difficult to remember: $S_N = A \times (R^N - 1)/(R - 1)$.

For those who find it difficult to remember formulae, if one knows how a formula evolves, not only will he not need to remember the formula, but if woken up in the middle of the night and asked to explain why is that the sum of N terms of an Geometric Progression is $A \times (R^N - 1)/(R - 1)$, he will stifle a yawn and then give a small sermon on the evolution of this formula in specific and other formulae in general. So complete will be his command over the subject.

A Geometric Progression where the first term is A and the common ratio is R, goes like this: A, AR, AR^2, AR^3 and so on such that the Nth term is $AR^{(N-1)}$. The sum of this progression is $[A+AR+AR^2+AR^3 +\ldots AR^{(N-1)}]$ or $A \times [1 + R + R^2 + R^3 +\ldots R^{(N-1)}]$. Let us assume progressively climbing values of N and understand why $[1 + R + R^2 + R^3 +\ldots R^{(N-1)}]$ will be equal to $(R^N - 1)/(R - 1)$.

If N = 2, then $[1 + R + R^2 + R^3 +\ldots R^{(N-1)}] = [1 + R]$ and $(R^N - 1)/(R - 1) = (R^2 - 1)/(R - 1) = [R + 1]$. We can thus see that so far $[1 + R + R^2 + R^3 +\ldots R^{(N-1)}] = (R^N - 1)/(R - 1)$.

If N = 3, then $[1 + R + R^2 + R^3 + \ldots R^{(N-1)}] = [1 + R + R^2]$ and $(R^N - 1)/(R - 1) = (R^3 - 1)/(R - 1) = [R^2 + R + 1]$. We can thus see that so far $[1 + R + R^2 + R^3 + \ldots R^{(N-1)}] = (R^N - 1)/(R - 1)$.

The fact that $(R^N - 1)/(R - 1) = (R^{(N-1)} + R^{(N-2)} + \ldots R^3 + R^2 + R + 1)$ explains why the sum S_N of a geometric Progression is given by the formula $S_N = A \times (R^N-1)/(R-1)$.

The reason why – for example – $(R^8 - 1)$ when divided by $(R - 1)$ will always give $(R^7 + R^6 + R^5 + R^4 + R^3 + R^2 + R - 1)$ is because $(R^8 - 1)$ is nothing but $[R^8 - R^7 + R^7 - R^6 + R^6 - R^5 + R^5 - R^4 + R^4 - R^3 + R^3 - R^2 + R^2 - R + R - 1]$ which is $[R^7 (R - 1) + R^6 (R - 1) + R^5 (R - 1) + R^4 (R - 1) + R^3 (R - 1) + R^2 (R - 1) + R (R - 1) + 1(R - 1)]$ or $(R - 1) \times [R^7 + R^6 + R^5 + R^4 + R^3 + R^2 + R + 1]$. It is for this reason that $(R^N - 1)/(R - 1)$ will always be $(R^{(N-1)} + R^{(N-2)} + \ldots R^3 + R^2 + R + 1)$.

Let us see this formula at work as follows.

Let the GP be of N terms where N = 4	Then A =	And R =	The value of A/ (R-1)	And $(R^N - 1)$ is	Then $A \times (R^N - 1)$ / (R - 1)	Sum of the series done manually is
1, 3, 9, 27	1	3	1/2	$(3^4 - 1) = 80$	40	40
7, 14, 28, 56	7	2	7/1	$(2^4 - 1) = 15$	105	105
5, 15, 45, 135	5	3	5/2	$(3^4 - 1) = 80$	200	200

It is important to remember that if the sum up to say the 6th term is given and so also the sum up to the 5th term, then as to how to find out what is the sixth term is rather simple. All you have to do is to subtract the sum up to the 5th term from the sum up to the 6th term.

If a GP runs like this: 4, 8, 16, 32, 64, 128 then the sum up to the Nth term is as follows:

If N=	Then S_N =	And S_{N-1} =	So $S_N - S_{N-1}$ =	Thus T_N =
2	12	4	8	8
3	28	12	16	16
4	60	28	32	32
5	124	60	64	64

Putting this in algebraic language, $S_N - S_{N-1} - T_N$ where T_N is the Nth term of the progression. And this is not true just of geometric progressions but also of Arithmetic Progressions.

Problem 1

If the three terms of a GP add up to 14 and the sum of their squares is 84, what are the three terms?

Options: (1) 1, 4, 9 (2) 2, 4, 8 (3) 1, 3, 9 (4) 2, 5, 7

The detailed solution

Among the options only Option (2) 2, 4, 8 and Option (3) 1, 3, 9 are GPs since in the other options, while the terms do add up to 14, there is no common ratio. It cannot be 1,3,9 since it does not add up to 14 in any case. The choice is automatic: Option 2.

While this illustration seems a trifle simplistic, there are important lessons to be derived from the above illustration and these are as under:

- It is important to see prima facie how many among the options do qualify for being a GP in the first place because those that do not are to be thrown into the dustbin right away
- It is important to see whether the total of the terms in those options that do qualify for a GP adds up to 14 because if it does not, this saves a whole lot of bother

- If I were to add three odd numbers, I would never get a total that is an even number that 14 is; therefore this is the first reason why Option 3 would get eliminated right away.
- The squares of odd numbers are also odd numbers and adding three odd numbers would give me another odd number and thus I would never be able to get 84, which is an even number; Option 3 has to be thrown out for this reason as well.

The idea is to build up a sense of analysis that would help in being able to discern options that are clearly not workable prima facie and this would save a whole lot of bother.

Problem 2

If the sum of three terms in a GP is 26 and their product is 216, what are three terms?

The detailed solution

There are two ways of looking at this. As to which way would you choose, would depend on your mental make-up. We shall give you both methodologies and you may decide for yourself as to which one would suit you.

Here if we assume that the first term is A, and the common ratio of the GP is R, then the three terms are A, AR and AR^2 whereas their product is A^3R^3. This means that if $A^3R^3 = 216$ and $6^3 = 216$. So AR = 6. If AR = 6, then 6 can be factorised as follows: 1 × 6 and 2 × 3. If A = 1, then R = 6. This would thus mean that A, AR and AR^2 would respectively be 1, 6 and 36 and their sum would be 43, which is not in the scheme of things. If A = 2, then since AR = 6, R = 3, then A, AR and AR^2 would respectively be 2, 6 and 18 and their sum would be 26, which is exactly as per the scheme of things. Besides, the product of 2, 6 and 18 would be 216 and there would be a common ratio of 3. This would work admirably. **The three terms are therefore 2, 6 and 18.**

Now look at this from another angle. If AR = 6, then the factors of 6 are 2 × 3 and 1 × 6. So A can be anyone of 1, 2, 3 and 6. You have to analyse and see which of 1, 2, 3 and 6 can be a value for A and which cannot.

The reason why A cannot be 1 is that if A is 1, then the other two numbers would have to add up to 25 (which is an odd number) and also multiply to get 216. This means then that the factors of 216 will have to be such that one of them is odd and the other even because only then will they add up to an odd number. The number 216 (which is an even number with its digits adding up to 9 which gives a clear signal that 216 is divisible by 9 and 3 and 2) can be factorised into two factors where one is odd and the other even in the following manner: 1 and 216, 3 and 72, 9 and 24; in none of these three cases will the sum of the factors be 25.

The reason why A cannot be 3 is because if A is 3 then the remaining two numbers must add up to 23 (and therefore one of the factors must be odd and the other even) and must multiply to get 72. The factors of 72 that meet this criterion are 1 and 72, 3 and 24, 9 and 8. None can meet this criterion.

The reason why A can be 2 is because if A is 2 then the remaining two numbers must add up to 24 and must multiply to get 108. The factors of 108 that meet this criterion are 6 and 18. What is more 2, 6 and 18 would make a Geometric Progression with a common ratio of 3. **Thus the GP is 2, 6 and 18.**

The reason why A cannot be 6 is because if A is 6 then the remaining two numbers must add up to 20 and must multiply to get 36. The factors of 36 that meet this criterion are 2 and 18. But 6, 2 and 18 or for that matter 6, 18 and 2 cannot form a Geometric Progression.

If you have noticed, we have solved this question on basis of analysis alone and no formulae or detailed calculations at all.

Problem 3

If A, B and C are the 3rd, 6th and 9th terms in a GP, then:

(1) $B^2 = AC$ (2) $A^2 = BC$ (3) $C^2 = AB$ (4) None of these

The detailed solution

This is more a matter of logic than mathematics. Let us show you why.

The powers of 2 are fairly easy to remember but even if one does not remember them, it will not cause any problems because you can leave the powers of 2 as they are meaning starting with 2^0 and then on to 2^1, 2^2 and so on till 2^8, the 3rd term will be 2^2, the 6th term will be 2^5, and the 9th term will be 2^8. The 3rd, 6th and 9th terms in this GP will be 2^2, 2^5, and 2^8. Quite clearly, the square of the 6th term will be the product of the 3rd and 9th terms because the 6th term is the middle term between 3 and 9. In this same series if you were to see the 1st, 2nd and 3rd terms, the 2nd term is midway between 1st and 3rd terms and since the 1st term is 2^0, the second term is 2^1, and the third term is 2^2, the square of the second term is equal to the product of the 1st and 3rd terms merely because it is midway between the two terms.

For those who still are in touch with mathematics, they may like to see things in the following fashion.

If the Nth term of a GP is XY^{N-1}, where X is the first term in a GP and Y is the common ratio of the GP, then the 3rd, 6th and 9th terms in that GP are respectively XY^2, XY^5, and XY^8 and thus:

$XY^2 = A$

$XY^5 = B$

$XY^8 = C$

Let us see which of the options is true. If option 1 is true then $B^2 = (XY^5)^2 = X^2Y^{10}$. And then $AC = XY^2 \times XY^8 = X^2Y^{10}$; so both B^2 and AC are equal to X^2Y^{10} and thus – either way – Option 1 is correct.

Problem 4

The sum of N terms of a GP where the nth term is $7 \times 5^{N-1}$ is given by:

(1) $7/4 \times (5^N + 1)$ (2) $7/4 \times (5^N - 1)$ (3) $7/4 \times (5^N)$ (4) None of these

The detailed solution

Listen, dear reader, when you are given letters like N in place of numbers, N will not whisper in your ear as to what is the correct answer. You will have to assume some value for N and then try and arrive at the correct answer.

Let us assume a certain value for N and thus let us take N = 2. So the two terms of the GP are as follows: $7 \times 5^{1-1}$ and $7 \times 5^{2-1}$. The terms are thus 7 and 35 and add up to 42. Let us see which of the options give us 42 as the answer.

Option 1: $7/4 \times (5^N + 1) = 7/4 \times (5^2 + 1) = 7/4 \times (25 + 1) = 7/4 \times 26 = 91/2$ which is a fraction.

Option 2: $7/4 \times (5^N - 1) = 7/4 \times (5^2\text{-}1) = 7/4 \times (25 - 1) = 7/4 \times 24 = 42$ which is what is given.

Hence Option 2.

Problem 5

If the sum of four numbers in GP is 40 and the arithmetic mean of the first and last is 14, the required numbers are:

(1) 1,3,9,27 (2) 27,9,3,1 (3) Both 1 and 2 (4) None of these

The detailed solution

If one were to add the terms in the series at both options 1 and 2, the total would be 40. Both are GPs.

In option 1, the common ratio is 3 whereas in option 2, the common ratio is 1/3.

Further, in both cases the arithmetic mean of the first and last numbers is 14. So both options 1 and 2 are correct.

Problem 6

If the (J+K)th term of a GP is M and the (J-K)th term of the GP is N, then the Jth term is:

(1) $(M / N)^{0.5}$ (2) $(M - N)^{0.5}$ (3) $(M \times N)^{0.5}$ (4) None of these

The detailed solution

There are two ways of looking at this. J, K, L and M and so on are all substitutes for numbers. Man has devised algebra. Man can both create and reveal its dark secrets. None can stop you from assuming some values for J, K, M and N. The ideal thing would be to assume some values in keeping with their order in the alphabet. J is first and N is last in this ascending order. Besides, we have to assume such value for J and K that will give a positive value for (J – K) since there is a $(J - K)^{th}$ term. So let J be 5, K be 4, M be 3 and N be 2. The reason why we are assuming that M is 3 and N is 2 is that if we were to assume that M = 2 and N = 1, then in Options 1 and 3, M / N would be the same as M × N.

Thus here since the (J + K)th term of a GP is M and the (J – K)th term of the GP is N, it means that 9th term of the GP is 3 and 1st term is 2. In a Geometric Progression, the 9th term is (First term × $(\text{Common Ratio})^8$) and therefore the 9th term divided by the first term would give $(\text{Common Ratio})^8$ and here $(\text{Common Ratio})^8$ would be equal to 3/2 and thus the Common Ratio is $(3/2)^{1/8}$. The Jth term is 5th term which would be (First term × $(\text{Common Ratio})^4$) which would be $(2 \times (3/2^{1/8})^4) = (2 \times (3/2)^{1/2}) = (4 \times (3/2))^{1/2} = (6)^{1/2}$. Let us see which of the options fit in.

Option 1: $(M / N)^{0.5} = (3/2)^{1/2}$; this is not what we have got above. We want $(6)^{1/2}$. Option 1 will not work.

Option 2: $(M - N)^{0.5} = 1^{1/2}$; this is not what we have got above. We want $(6)^{1/2}$. Option 2 will not work either.

Option 3: $(M \times N)^{0.5} = (3 \times 2)^{1/2}$; this is exactly what we have got above. **Option 3** will work admirably.

Now let us see the other method. Let us take the series as follows:

The first term is A and the common ratio is X. Then the Nth term is $A \times X^{(N-1)}$ and thus the (J + K)th term is $A \times X^{(J+K-1)}$ and the (J – K)th term is $A \times X^{(J-K-1)}$. Now we are told that the (J + K)th term of the GP is M and the (J – K)th term of the GP is N.

Thus:

$A \times X^{(J+K-1)} = M$

$A \times X^{(J-K-1)} = N$

M × N gives us $A \times X^{(J+K-1)} \times A \times X^{(J-K-1)} = A^2 \times X^{(J+K-1+J-K-1)} = A^2 \times X^{(2J-2)}$.

Now the Jth term of the GP is $A \times X^{(J-1)}$.

$A \times X^{(J-1)}$ is the square root of the expression $A^2 \times X^{(2J-2)}$ because if you were to arrive at the square of the expression $A \times X^{(J-1)}$ then you would get $A^2 \times X^{(2J-2)}$; thus the Jth term is $(M \times N)^{0.5}$. So Option 3.

Let us look at this fundamentally.

Take a series that starts with A as the first term and the common ratio of the GP is R. Let J=3 and K=2. So the series would be as follows:

T_1	T_2	T_3	T_4	T_5
A	AR	AR^2	AR^3	AR^4

Now since we have assumed that J = 3 and K = 2, then $T_{(J+K)} = T_{(3+2)} = T_5 = AR^4 = M$

and $T_{(J-K)} = T_{(3-2)} = T_1 = A = N$.

So $M \times N = AR^4 \times A = A^2 R^4$.

T_J is T_3 since J we have assumed as 3 and thus $T_J = AR^2$.

Now $M \times N = A^2 R^4$ and this is the square of T_J which is $= AR^2$.

So, $T_J = (M \times N)^{0.5}$.

EXERCISE

1. The sum of a series of N terms in GP whose Nth term is $9 \times (3^{N-1})$ is given by

   Options: (1) $9/2 \times (3^N + 1)$ (2) $9/2 \times (3^N - 1)$ (3) $9/2 \times (3^N)$ (4) None of these

2. How many terms of the GP 2/9, –1/3, 1/2... would add up to 55/72?

   Options: (1) 5 (2) 7 (3) 9 (4) 11

3. If –2K, 3K–2, 4K + 24 are consecutive terms of a G.P., then K is equal to

   Options: (1) 2, 2/17 (2) –2, –2/17 (3) –3/5, –4 (4) none of these

4. If in a GP in which all terms are positive integers, the difference of the fifth term and the third term is equal to the sum of the fourth term and the third term, then the common ratio of the GP is:

   Options: (1) = 1st term (2) = 2rd term (3) 2 (4) None of these

5. If the 7th term of a GP is 448, and the 3rd term is 28, then the common ratio of the GP is:

   Options: (1) 2 (2) –2 (3) T_7/T_6 (4) All of these

6. If in a series, the difference between the fifth term and the third term equals twice the fourth term, then the series is in:

   Options: (1) AP (2) GP (3) In both AP and GP (4) None of these

7. The sum of the series $4/7, -5/7^2, 4/7^3, -5/7^4$... to infinity is equal to:

   Options: (1) 23/48 (2) 48/23 (3) 49/48 (4) 5/49

ANSWER KEY

1. Option 2
2. Option 1
3. Option 2
4. Option 3
5. Option 3
6. Option 1
7. Option 1

SOLUTIONS

1. The Nth term of a Geometric Progression is $9 \times (3^{N-1})$. Which means that the first two terms of the GP are $9 \times (3^{1-1})$ and $9 \times (3^{2-1})$ or 9 and 27 respectively. Thus when N = 2, the sum of the series of the N terms is 36. Let us see which of the options in which if one were to substitute the value of N as 2 will give 36.

   Option 1: $9/2 \times (3^N + 1) = 9/2 \times (9 + 1) = 9/2 \times 10 = 45$. Option 1 is not workable

   Option 2: $9/2 \times (3^N - 1) = 9/2 \times (9 - 1) = 9/2 \times 8 = 36$. **Option 2 is correct.**

2. The sum of N terms of a geometric progression is given by the expression

   $A \times (R^N - 1)/(R - 1)$ where A is the first term in the series and R is the common ratio.

   Here the common ratio is $-1/3 \div 2/9 = (-1 \times 9)/(3 \times 2) = -3/2$. The sum of N terms is 55/72 when A= 2/9 and R is –3/2.

   $55/72 = [(2/9) \div (-3/2 - 1)] \times (-3/2)^N - 1 = (2/9 \div -5/2) \times (-3/2)^N - 1$

   So $(-3/2)^N = -243/32$. Since 243 is 3 raised to the power of 5 and 32 is 2 raised to the power of 5, N = 5.

3. If –2K, 3K–2 and 4K + 24 are consecutive terms of a geometric progression, then

   $(3K-2)/(-2K) = (4k + 24)/(3k-2)$.

   This is because a geometric progression is made by multiplying the starting term with the common ratio and hence if the first term is A, and the common ratio is R then the terms of the progression are A, AR, AR^2, AR^3, AR^4... and if one were to divide any term by its previous term, one would get the common ratio.

   If $(3K-2)/(-2K) = (4K+24)/(3K-2)$, then $(3K-2) \times (3K-2) = -2K \times (4K + 24)$

   This means that $9K^2 - 12K + 4 = -8K^2 - 48K$ or $17K^2 + 36K + 4 = 0$.

   If you see this in the standard form of the quadratic equation $[AX^2 + BX + C = 0]$, if $B^2 > 4AC$, the equation has two real roots. In this case $B^2 = 36^2 = 1296$ and $4AC = 4 \times 17 \times 4 = 272$. This means that there are two real roots.

   Further since the constant term is positive and the coefficient of X is also positive, both the roots are negative. This is only in the case of Options 2 and 3. If we were to employ option 2, the first root if it is –2, should give zero if substituted as a value of X in the equation $17K^2 + 36K + 4$. If X = –2, then $17K^2 + 36K + 4 = 17 \times 4 + (-72) + 4 = 68 - 72 + 4 = 0$. If you were to see Option 3, if one of the roots is –4 (which is easier to work with than the other root which is a fraction), this will not give zero when substituted for X in the equation $17K^2 + 36K + 4 = 0$. $[17 \times 16 + (-144) + 4 = 272 - 144 + 4 = 136]$. This is sufficient to infer that **Option 2 is** the **correct** answer.

4. In a GP in which all terms are positive integers, the fifth term is $A \times R^4$, $A \times R^3$ is the fourth term, the third term is $A \times R^2$ where A is the first term of the GP and R is the common ratio.

   The difference of the fifth term and the third term is = $AR^4 - AR^2$ and this is equal to the sum of the fourth term and the third term. So $AR^4 - AR^2 = AR^3 + AR^2$ and hence $(R^4 - R^2) = (R^3 + R^2)$ and dividing both sides by R^2 we get $R^2 - 1 = R + 1$ and hence $R^2 - R - 2 = 0$. Thus $(R - 2) \times (R + 1) = 0$ so R could be 2 or –1. Hence **Option 3**.

5. The 7th term of a GP is AR^6 and is 448, and the 3rd term is AR^2 and is 28. Dividing the 7th term with the third term, we get $(AR^6)/(AR^2) = R^4 = 448/28 = 16$. Thus R could be equal to either 2 or –2 but not both +2 and –2 simultaneously. If Option 1 is true then R = 2 and this means that –2 is not a value for the common ratio. If Option 2 is taken as true, then the value of R is –2 and then +2 is not a value for the common ratio. Fundamentally "All of these" could be a valid option provided all the options yield the same result. But +2 is not the same thing as –2. Since the common ratio could be either +2 or –2, the choice could be neither Option 1 nor Option 2. But fundamentally, T_7/T_6 will also give the common ratio of the GP no matter whether the common ratio is positive or negative and hence **Option 3**. This is because in a Geometric Progression, the Nth term denoted by T_N when divided by $T_{(N-1)}$ will always give a constant value no matter what the value of N. This is the hallmark of a Geometric Progression.

6. If the series is an AP then the fifth term, fourth term and the third terms are respectively (A + 4D), (A + 3D) and (A + 2D).

   If the difference between the fifth term and the third term equals twice the fourth term, then $(A + 4D) - (A + 2D) = 2 \times (A + 3D)$ and hence $2D = 2A + 6D$ and hence $4D = -2A$ or $D = -A/2$. This means that if we were to assume that the first term in a series is 4 and the common difference is –2, then the series will be 4, 2, 0, –2, –4 and so on. This is indeed an Arithmetic Progression.

If the series is a GP, then fifth term – third term = $AR^4 - AR^2$, where A is the first term and R is the common ratio of the GP and since this difference is equal to twice the fourth term, $AR^4 - AR^2 = 2 \times AR^3$ or dividing both sides by AR^2, we get $R^2 - 1 = R$ and hence $R^2-R-1=0$. This equation when seen in the general form of the quadratic equation $AX^2 + BX + C = 0$, we see that $B^2 < 4AC$ and that this equation cannot have real roots. Hence R is not real and there can therefore be no GP if the common ratio is not real. Hence the series is in AP only.

7. The sum of the series $4/7, -5/7^2, 4/7^3, -5/7^4$ would comprise of two separate Geometric Progressions as under:

Series 1: $4/7, 4/7^3$, and so on, and

Series 2: $-5/7^2, -5/7^4$, and so on

The sum to infinity of series 1 is given by $A \times (R^N - 1)/(R-1)$, where $A = 4/7$ and $R = 1/7^2$ or 1/49.

As N becomes larger, R^N will tend towards zero since R is a fraction. So with a large value of N, $A/(R - 1) = (4/7) \div (1/49 - 1) = (4/7) \times (-49/48) = -7/12$. And $(R^N - 1)$ will become –1 since R^N will tend towards zero. So $A \times (R^N - 1)/(R - 1) = -7/12 \times -1 = 7/12$.

About the sum to infinity of series 2 where $A = -5/7^2$ and $R = 1/7^2$ or 1/49, as N becomes larger, R^N will tend towards zero since R is a fraction. So with a large value of N,

$A/(R - 1) = -5/49 \div -48/49 = 5/48$

And $(R^N - 1)$ will become –1 since R^N will tend towards zero.

So $A \times (R^N-1)/(R - 1) = -5/48$.

In order to arrive at the sum to infinity of the given series, one will have to add 7/12 (which is nothing but 28/48) and –5 /48 and that would give you 23/48.

Chapter 17

Highest Common Factors

There may be common factors between two numbers or there may be no common factors at all. For example, if you were to see any three prime numbers - let us say 2, 5 and 19 – there are no common factors between these three numbers. For that matter there will be no common factors between any prime numbers. Therefore in so far as prime numbers go, since 1 is the only common factor between prime numbers, the least common positive integer factor is the same thing as the highest common positive integer factor in the case of prime numbers.

There is a distinct lower limit to the least common factors when you deal with positive integers. That least common factor is 1. In so far as fractions go, there is no lower limit to the least common factor.

See the two fractions 1/2 and 1/4. As we know, 1/2 is nothing other than 2/4 and thus when we try to find the highest common factor between ½ (which as we have seen is 2 × 1/4) and 1/4 (which really is 1 × 1/4), the highest common factor is 1/4. But if we were to try and find the **least** common factor between 1/2 and 1/4, this is a bottomless pit. The reason is simple: 1/2 and 1/4 can well be seen respectively (for example) as 6/12 (which really is 6 × 1/12) and 3/12 (which really is 3 × 1/12) and that is why I would, for example, state that the least common factor between 6/12 and 3/12 is 1/12. You would then say that 1/2 and 1/4 can be seen (for example) as 6000/12000 (which really is 6000 × 1/12000) and 3000/12000 (which really is 3000 × 1/12000) and that is why you would for example state that the least common factor between 6/12 and 3/12 is 1/12000. Therefore while there is no lower limit to the least common factor between fractions, there can be a distinct upper limit to the highest common factor in case of fractions as well as integers which we shall see as we go along. It is for this reason that when we shall hereafter talk of common factors between integral numbers, we shall reckon with only integral factors.

There will be common factors between two numbers in the following situations:

- One of the numbers is a multiple of the other: for example, between 18 (which as such is 2 × 3 × 3) and 36 (which as such is 2 × 2 × 3 × 3) the latter is 2 times the former and therefore while the lowest common factor between these two numbers is 2, the highest common factor (HCF) between these two numbers is 18 itself (since there are three common factors to 18 and 36 and these are 2, 3 and 3).
- In the case of fractions such as 1/3 and 1/6, since 1/3 is effectively 2/6 and therefore since 1/3 is a higher multiple of 1/6, the highest common factor between 1/3 and 1/6 is 1/6. This is analogous to the situation in the case of integers that we have seen in the above illustration of 18 and 36.
- Some of the numbers are multiples of another number that may not be mentioned in the series of numbers at all. For example in the case of 24, 36, 60 and 84, the four numbers when factorised would give the following factors:

  (I) 24 = 2 × 2 × 2 × 3

  (II) 36 = 2 × 2 × 3 × 3

  (III) 60 = 2 × 2 × 3 × 5

  (IV) 84 = 2 × 2 × 3 × 7.

The common factors are between 24, 36, 60 and 84 are 2 × 2 × 3 (as highlighted) and hence the highest common factor of these four numbers is 12. Which is not mentioned among the series of numbers 24, 36, 60 and 84.

We shall now see a few problems that will call for our understanding the nuances of HCFs. Problem 1 is taken from the past paper of one of the toughest management entrance tests in the whole wide world. Once we see it being cracked, you will become confident that you can crack any question on HCFs, no matter how tough.

We have deliberately avoided giving notes on how to find the HCF of 125 and 425 for example because no competitive examination would present such lollipops. Only a middle school student would be pardoned if we were to expect such initiation to the concepts of HCFs. The graduate student would be at best be considered naïve if he were to expect such methodologies. What is tested in his case is the breadth of his perception and his logical skills. Anyone introducing the graduate student to such elementary aspects of HCFs such as how to find the HCF of 125 and 425 for example would be even dafter.

The illustrations that we present here are designed to drive home those concepts about HCFs that can be reasonably expected at competitive examinations such as the GRE. That is why the level of the illustrations, whether in this chapter or elsewhere in this book, is appropriate to a competitive examination like the GRE.

Problem 1

Three pieces of cakes of weight 9/2 lbs, 27/4 lbs, and 36/5 lbs respectively are to be divided into parts of equal weights. Further, each part must be as heavy as possible. If one such part is served to each guest, then what is the maximum number of guests that could be entertained?

The Answer

This is a matter of logic. The three pieces of cake can be expressed as 9/2, 27/4, and 36/5 lbs. If one wishes to express these three fractions with a common denominator (so that a comparison becomes meaningful), the LCM of 2, 4 and 5 is 20 and thus they can be expressed as 90/20, 135/20 and 144/20 or: $(9/20) \times 10$, $(9/20) \times 15$ and $(9/20) \times 16$ pounds.

As we have seen earlier, there is no lower limit to the lightest cut that you can serve to each guest. You can go down to milligrams and then micrograms and thereafter to molecules and then to atoms and so on. The heaviest cuts from these can only be 9/20 pounds. You could then entertain: $10 + 15 + 16 = 41$ guests.

Problem 2

At a garment factory, the remaining length of cloth after pieces of cloth are cut from different lengths of cloth are called rags. Therefore if three pieces of 2 meters each are cut from a 6.1 meter long piece of corduroy, then you have 0.1 meters of rags.

Three pieces of cloth of length 31.5 meters, 43.5 meters and 54 meters respectively are to be cut into smaller pieces of equal length. If it is decided to cut smaller pieces of the maximum possible length what is the length of each of the smaller pieces if there are no rags left after the process of cutting pieces of equal length is over?

The Answer

31.5 meters, 43.5 meters and 54 can be seen as 3150 cm, 4350 cm and 5400 cm respectively. Between these three numbers 3150, 4350 and 5400, one can see from a preliminary glance alone that the number 10 seems to be a common factor to all three. After dividing these three numbers by 10 (which involves nothing other than crossing out the zero at the end in 3150, 4350 and 5400), one realises that we are left with 315, 435 and 540. If a non-zero number ends in either 5 or 0, it is certainly divisible by 5. Dividing each of 315, 435 and 540 by 5 we are left with 63, 87 and 108.

If one were to add the digits in 63, 87 and 108 one would realise that all three numbers are divisible by 3 as well. If we were to divide each of 63, 87 and 108 by 3 we would be left with 21, 29 and 36. As we know 29 is a prime number and therefore even if 3 were to be a common factor between 21 and 36, since 3 is not a factor of 29, the highest common factor of 3150, 4350 and 5400 is $10 \times 5 \times 3$ (since we have been able to divide 3150, 4350 and 5400 (all three) by 10, 5 and 3). This means that all three of 3150, 4350 and 5400 are divisible by 150. Therefore one can cut pieces of length 150 cm (or 1.5 meters) from each of the three pieces of cloth of length 31.5 meters, 43.5 meters and 54 meters respectively without having any rags left over. One would then have respectively 21, 29 and 36 pieces each of 1.5 meters length.

Chapter 18

Inequalities

We would surely have seen linear equations such as X + 7 = 21 from which we are able to derive without too much strain that X = 14. When two sides of an equation are **not equal** in value, then this gives rise to an inequality. We shall see illustrations about inequalities and see how we shall deal with inequalities.

Let us see the following problem: A, B and C are non-zero real numbers. We are to find out the situation in which (A + B – C) is invariably greater than (A – B + C). Sounds tough? It isn't really. We shall see as we go along.

We are only told that all three unknown numbers are real numbers. This means that A, B and C could take positive values or negative values or even zero. In this case, the question specifically states that the three numbers are non-zero and hence we are to exclude zero as a possible value for all three.

As you will observe, A is common to both expressions. If A has a positive value, A will add the same value on both sides. If A has negative value, A will subtract the same value on both sides. Imagine that four boys are sitting on a seesaw. Two of these boys have the same weight. Let us call them Tim and John. We shall call the other two boys with unequal weight as Ricky and Jim. Tim and Ricky sit on one end of the seesaw. John and Jim are on the other side. If you wish to see which pair is heavier of the two pairs (I) Ricky and Tim or (II) John and Jim. There is no reason why Tim and John should not get off. They are of the same weight in any case. Ask them to get off and you will soon find that what you are essentially doing is comparing the weights of Ricky and Jim. Similarly in the two expressions (A + B – C) and (A – B + C), cancel A from both sides and you are then comparing (B – C) with (–B + C). While you are weighing Ricky against Tim, if you were to make them wear a coat of the same weight, it will not affect the result. If Tim is heavier than Ricky, then Tim will be heavier than Ricky even if they wear coats of the same weight. And vice-versa!

Therefore when you are to compare (B – C) with (–B + C), you can safely add C on both sides and also B on both sides. Thus you are really comparing 2B with 2C, which again boils down to comparing B with C. Thus effectively in comparing (A + B – C) with (A – B + C), what you are really comparing is B against C. Given that B and C could take either positive values or negative values, if both have positive values, you cannot say who has more value: B or C? This is because both B and C are unknowns and there is no upper limit to positive values. Similarly if both B and C have negative values, you cannot say who has more value: B or C? This is again because both B and C are unknowns and there is no lower limit to a negative value.

Therefore there is only one situation in which you can say that B is greater than C. This is when B is positive and C is negative. This is because fundamentally all positive numbers have greater value than all negative numbers.

The moral of the story is that (A + B – C) is invariably greater than (A – B + C) when B is a positive number and C is a negative number.

Now let us move on to another problem regarding inequalities.

If N is a natural number, what is the range of values for the unknown term X when you are given that [1 – (1/N)] < X ≤ [3 + (1/N)]?

This question calls for some analysis. There is no need to calculate anything. However there is more to logic to this than anything else and we shall see how and why logic alone will work.

First we shall see why logic alone will work. This is because there is an inequality and there are two unknowns – X and N. There would have been room for algebra if we were looking at equations. But since there is an inequality, we have no choice but to proceed logically.

Then as regards how logic will work, let us jot down – as under – some inferences that we shall reach:

- N is a natural number, the least of which is 1. Natural numbers are those you can count on your fingers and therefore all natural numbers are positive integers such as 1, 2, 3 and so on.
- To the left of the inequality $[1 - (1/N)] < X \leq [3 + (1/N)]$, we have $[1 - (1/N)] < X$. This means that X has certainly greater value than that of $[1 - (1/N)]$.
- In the expression $[1 - (1/N)]$, there is a constant figure and a variable figure. The constant figure is 1, which does not alter in value with increase or decrease in the value of N. The variable figure is 1/N, which as such is a positive fraction since N is always a positive integer. What is more, 1/N is a fraction with a fixed numerator and therefore the value of 1/N increases when N reduces and – in the converse - the value of 1/N decreases when N increases. It is also interesting to note that 1/N can have its highest value when the denominator N is at its lowest possible value. As we know 1 is the very smallest natural number and therefore the highest possible value of 1/N is when $N = 1$.
- The expression $[1 - (1/N)]$ essentially involves the subtraction of a variable term from a fixed term and therefore the value of $[1 - (1/N)]$ will be its lowest when 1/N is at its highest possible value. Thus the lowest possible value of $[1 - (1/N)]$ is when $N = 1$ and therefore the lowest possible value of $[1 - (1/N)]$ is $[1 - 1] = 0$. What is established is the fact that since X has certainly greater value than that of $[1 - (1/N)]$, X is certainly greater than zero.
- We may now move on to the other side of the inequality, which is $[3 + (1/N)]$. We are given that $X \leq [3 + (1/N)]$. This means that X can have a value equal to the highest value of $[3 + (1/N)]$. It also means that X can take values less than this highest value of $[3 + (1/N)]$. But what is certain is that X cannot take any value greater than the highest possible value of $[3 + (1/N)]$.
- As regards the expression $[3 + (1/N)]$, this too has a fixed term: 3. This too has a variable term: 1/N. The value of the expression $[3 + (1/N)]$ is highest when 1/N is at its highest. This means that the highest possible value of the expression $[3 + (1/N)]$ is $3 + 1 = 4$.

Interestingly, 1/N will go on diminishing in value as N increases from 1 to 2 and 3 and so on. Therefore we have now reached two major conclusions:

(I) X is invariably greater than zero and

(II) X can take a value as high as 4 but X can certainly not be more than 4 and therefore X can be either equal to 4 or less than 4.

With this analysis, we reach the hidebound conclusion that the range of values for X is as follows: $0 < X \leq 4$.

We may mention that both the illustrations that we have given above are questions from the past papers of one of the toughest competitive examinations in the whole wide world and if this is what it takes to crack such tough questions, the clear inference is that at least insofar as questions pertaining to inequalities go, logic alone is what is put to test.

Let us see a few more questions regarding inequalities in order to understand and assimilate the underlying concepts completely.

Problem 1

X and Y are real numbers satisfying the conditions $2 < X < 3$ and $-8 < Y < -7$. Which of the following expressions will have the least value?

1. X^2Y 2. XY^2 3. 5XY 4. None of these

The Solution

We must remember that although algebra is a branch of mathematics, algebra is Man's brainchild. We must also remember that merely because unknowns such as X and Y are mentioned, it does not automatically mean that the question pertains to algebra. Man has devised a system of substituting alphabets in place of numbers. If anyone can assume certain values for unknowns, Man can.

What must be derived from the question is that X is certainly positive and Y is certainly negative. We must also remember that irrespective of whether a number is positive or negative, its square is invariably positive. Thus XY^2 in Option 2 is a product of a positive number X with another positive term Y^2. This is why XY^2 will invariably be positive. This is also why both X^2Y in Option 1 and 5XY in Option 3 will invariably be negative since in both these cases a positive term (both X^2 and X are positive) is multiplied with a negative number Y.

Fundamentally all negative terms are less in value than positive terms and therefore Option 2 will have to be chucked out by its ear and what we shall do is to evaluate whether X^2Y is less than 5XY and then whether there can be a still lower negative term than X^2Y or 5XY. This will help us decide whether Option 4 is correct.

Between X^2Y and 5XY (both of which are negative) the common factors are X and Y. Since we are to find out which is less: X^2Y or 5XY, we shall have to decide which is higher in value: X^2 or 5X. We multiply – say – minus 2 first with 3 and then with 4, we get –6 and then –8 of which –8 is lower because a negative term –2 is multiplied by 4 which is a higher positive term. Thus all that we are to effectively determine is which is higher in value: X^2 or 5X. In this problem we are told that X is positive, this means that in comparing X^2 with 5X what you are effectively comparing is X with 5. Since X is less than 3, 5 is higher. Therefore 5X is higher than X^2. Thus 5XY is lower than X^2Y since Y is negative.

Now As regards Option 4, having found that 5XY is least among the three options, it would not take long to understand that – for example- 6XY would be even lower than 5XY and 7XY would be lower still. But we are to choose from the three given options and therefore stop at Option 3.

Problem 2

If $X > 5$ and $Y < -1$, then which of the following statements is true?

1. $(X + 4Y) > 1$ 2. $X > -4Y$ 3. $-4X < 5Y$ 4. None of these

The Solution

Let us derive these following inferences from the question and then apply logic to crack this question:

- X is invariably a positive number whereas Y is invariably a negative number.
- There is no upper limit to the value of X and for that matter there is no lower limit to the value of Y.
- In the case of Option 1, in the expression $(X + 4Y)$, X can take a small positive value (say, $X = 6$) whereas Y can take a huge negative value (say, $Y= -1000$). The expression $(X + 4Y)$ can therefore take a huge negative value since Y is a bottomless pit and hence Option 1 need not be true.
- As regards Option 2, X can again take a small value and Y can take a huge negative value. Therefore –4Y will take a huge positive value and hence Option 2 need not be true either.
- As regards Option 3, X can take a small positive value (say, 6) and therefore –4X can take a small negative value (say, –24) whereas Y can take a huge negative value (say, -1000) and hence 5Y can take a huge negative value (say, –5000). Option 3 need not be true either.

Thus **Option 4** is to be marked as correct.

With that we come to the end of this concept note on Inequalities. We may mention that the above problems too have been derived from the past papers of an examination that is reckoned as the mother of all competitive examinations and the skills needed for solving these problems are logical skills alone.

Chapter 19

Least Common Multiple

This is a subject that was probably taught to us at middle school. It might seem a trifle strange that it should crop up again in our curriculum. We shall begin by assuring the reader that it is not our intention to take you back to middle school. The competitive examination is essentially a test of your breadth of perception and not of your skills at solving mathematical problems. This is why they give you options. Show us one school examination where you get four options and have to merely to tick one of them. The competitive examination is not a retest of **what** you have learnt at school. It is a test of **how** you are able to apply the elementary aspects of what you learnt at school to cope with the complexities of everyday life.

The presentation that we shall make on the subject of the Least Common Multiple is aimed at broadening of the reader's breadth of perception. The reader who expects the rigmarole of numbers and practice sessions based thereon may meet with a little disappointment initially. But as he will read on, he will find so many new angles to what he has learnt. His concepts will take on a gleam as a result of reading this chapter in particular and the book as whole with a great deal of enjoyment.

During the course of our writing a whole range of books to help aspirants prepare meaningfully for competitive examinations (and you might find the names of all these books on the back of this book) we have seen umpteen problems in regard to Least Common Multiple (LCM) but seldom have we seen any problem involving something as simple as calculating the LCM of integers possibly because there is not too much challenge here nor does it call for conceptual clarity as much as the calculating of an LCM of fraction does. The questions that we have seen generally involve calculating the LCM of fractions. What is important is to grasp the methodology of finding the LCM of fractions. This methodology will weave into it the methodology of calculating the LCM of integral numbers.

We shall begin the process of refreshing what we have learnt at school by looking at some illustrations. Among the various illustrations is one in which we are to imagine a situation that would generally occur at an age when one has finished school. You will see this illustration in due course.

Illustration 1

Ted and Mark are back from school one day and find that there are two pies of identical size in the refrigerator. Ted eats a third of one pie and Mark eats 3/8th of the other. Who has eaten more?

Ted has eaten 1/3rd. Mark has eaten 3/8th. I do not know who has eaten more. All I know is that effectively, Ted has walloped 1 piece out of 3 pieces of the same size and Mark has eaten 3 pieces out of 8 pieces of the same size.

I would have been able to tell who ate more had each of the two pies been cut into the same number of pieces of equal size and the number of pieces should have been such that I should be able to:

(A) divide the number of equal-sized pieces into three equal parts in which each part would have a whole number of pieces; this means that the number of pieces that I should be able to divide the pie should be a multiple of 3 and also

(B) divide the number of equal-sized pieces into eight equal parts in which each part would have a whole number of pieces; this means that the number of pieces that I should divide the pie should be a multiple of 8.

A number can be divisible by both 3 and 8 only if both 3 and 8 are factors of that number. The first such number that is divisible by both 3 and 8 is 24 (which really is the product of 3 and 8 since 3 and 8 have no common factors).

If the pie were to be cut into 24 pieces, since Ted ate 1/3rd of the pie, it means that he ate 8 pieces out of 24 equal pieces into which the pie could have been cut and Mark (who ate 3/8th of the pie) ate $3 \times 3 = 9$ pieces out of 24 equal pieces into which the pie could have been cut. Mark has eaten more.

We have assumed that the pie could have been cut into a number of equal pieces that is a product of 3 and 8 that are in the denominators in the two fractions that represent what Ted and Mark respectively ate? We have done this in order to make meaningful comparison. And what after all is 3×8? It is the LCM of 3 and 8.

Illustration 2

Imagine that:

- every sixth minute starting from 0900 hours on a particular day, a man shouts his girlfriend's name from a spot below her balcony and then quickly ducks away from her sight (and also her father's sight) for fear of her father aiming his shotgun on the young suitor
- every seventeenth minute from 0900 hours on that particular day, she emerges momentarily on the balcony and waves in the direction from where she heard her name being called.

At what time will the lovers be able to see each other for the first time? Quite obviously, the **first time** that they can see each other should be after the least time that they have started the process where one shouts and the other appears in the balcony at the peculiar time intervals stated above. We shall see when and how they see each other with the help of the following table:

The boy shouts at the following times	The girl waves at the following times	The result is:
0906 hours	0917 hours	They do not see each other
0912 hours	0934 hours	They do not see each other
0918 hours	0951 hours	They do not see each other
0924 hours	1008 hours	They do not see each other
0930 hours	1025 hours	They do not see each other
0936 hours, 0942 hours and so on with 6 minutes time interval each time till 0948 hours, 0954 hours, 1000 hours, 1006 hours, 1012 hours, and so on till 1042 hours	1042 hours	They see each other and are all smiles and she asks him to throw a rope ladder (which he has got handy) on which she climbs down and elopes with him; then they live happily ever after

If you see the above table that has a fairy tale ending, the chap is shouting every 6th minute. The girl is making her appearance on the balcony every 17th minute. When he shouts for seventeen times, he sees her. When she emerges for the sixth time, she sees him. His seventeenth shout is after 102 minutes from 0900 hours (meaning 9:00 AM). Her sixth appearance is after 102 minutes from the first appearance. They can see each other only when the number of minutes elapsed from the start is such that this number can be divided by both his and her time intervals.

Now suppose at the stroke of 1042 hours, the two had met and she had asked for a rope ladder, which the fellow did not have handy with him. And while he had gone to fetch a rope ladder, her father had been on rounds with his shotgun fully loaded and this made eloping impossible. Now when could they have seen each other again? After another seventeen shouts from the boy and another six balcony appearances from the girl; something that would have happened after another 102 minutes or 204 minutes from 0900 hours which would be three hours and twenty four minutes after 0900 hour or at 12:24 PM.

Had they been thwarted again at 12:24 minutes they would have to keep shouting names or making balcony appearances respectively till every integral multiple of 102 minutes elapse from 0900 hours and this would have probably meant that the two would have fainted from exhaustion.

In this illustration we have seen that the first time that they saw each other was 102 minutes from start and they could have kept seeing each other at every integral multiple of 102 minutes. But the least time for their meeting would have been 102 minutes because this is the least common multiple of 6 and 17. The other common times are after 204 and 306 minutes (and so on) both of which are common multiples of 6 and 17 but they are merely common multiples and not the least common multiples of 6 and 17.

An interesting aspect of the Least Common Multiple (which we shall refer as LCM hereafter) of 6 and 17 is that this LCM can be arrived at only by multiplying the two since (A) 17 is a prime number and (B) 6 is not a multiple of 17. The LCM is the least common multiple; 6 and 17 have no common factors except 1 (if you see 6 as 6 × 1 and 17 as 17 × 1). In order to find their LCM, the two shall have to be multiplied without any choice in the matter.

If it were to so happen that every 17th minute starting from 0900 hours on that particular day, the man shouts his girlfriend's name and every 34th minute from 0900 hours on that particular day, she emerges momentarily on the balcony and waves at him, they would have met each other on the 34th minute after 0900 hours. This is because 34 is the LCM of 17 and 34 since both 34 and 17 have 17 as a factor but 17 does not have 2 as a factor and thus the LCM of these two numbers is equal to 17 (the Common Factor of the two numbers) multiplied by 2 (the Factor that is not common to either of the numbers 17 and 34).

Illustration 3

Here is a question from the past paper of one of the most widely held entrance tests in the world. The question (with the accompanying options) goes as follows:

The jewels in a crown consist of diamonds, rubies and emeralds. If the ratio of diamonds to rubies is 5/6 and the ratio of rubies to emeralds is 8/3, what is the least number of jewels that could be in the tiara?

(1) 16 (2) 22 (3) 40 (4) 53 (5) 67

Let us see how we can crack this.

When somebody tells you that the ratio of diamonds to rubies is 5/6, what he means is that there are 5 diamonds for every 6 rubies.

Similarly when you are told that the ratio of rubies to emeralds is 8/3, it means - in the converse – that the ratio of emeralds to rubics is 3/8, which, in turn, means that there are 3 emeralds for every 8 rubies.

In both the ratios, the comparison is with respect to rubies; in the first case the number of diamonds gets compared with the number of rubies and in the second case the number of emeralds gets compared with the number of rubies.

One must also remember that the number of gems can only be integral. Anyone saying that some crown has - say - 2.25 diamonds would look silly at the very least.

Thus:

If the number of rubies were	Then the number of diamonds would be 5/6th the number of rubies and this would make	Then the number of emeralds would be 3/8th the number of rubies and this would make
6	5 × 6/6 = 5 diamonds	3 × 6/8 = 18/8 = 9/4 emeralds which is not a whole number of emeralds

12, which is the next higher multiple of 6. One has no choice but to move on to the next higher multiple of 6. Only then can we maintain a whole number of diamonds and try to find a situation where the number of emeralds is also a whole number. If one moves on to a number that is not a multiple of 6, then even the number of diamonds would become fractional. Then the whole thing will seem like a kitten trying to catch its own tail, going round and round without getting anywhere.	5 × 12/6 = 10 diamonds	3 × 12/8 = 36/8 = 9/2 emeralds which is not a whole number of emeralds
18, which is the next higher multiple of 6	5 × 18/6 = 15 diamonds	3 × 18/8 = 54/8 = 27/4 emeralds which is not a whole number of emeralds
24, which is the next higher multiple of 6	5 × 24/6 = 20 diamonds	3 × 24/8 = 72/8 = 9 emeralds which certainly is a whole number of emeralds

From the above table, we find that the least possible number of rubies is 24, of diamonds is 5/6th of 24 or 20 and the least number of emeralds is 3/8th of 24 or 9 emeralds. The total number of jewels is thus at least 24 + 20 + 9 = 53. Hence Option 4.

Illustration 4

Let us move on to another question from the past paper of one of the most challenging management entrance tests in the world. The question (with the given options) goes as follows:

At a bookstore, **MODERN BOOK STORE** is flashed using neon lights. The words are individually flashed at intervals of 5/2, 17/4, and 41/8 seconds respectively, and each word is put off after a second. The least time after which the full name of the bookstore can be read again is:

1. 49.5 seconds   2. 73.5 seconds   3. 1744.5 seconds   4. 855 seconds

Let us see how we will solve this.

There can be two situations when the three words MODERN, BOOK and STORE can flash simultaneously and one has to be sure which of them will be least:

- The lights flash at every 5/2, 17/4 and 41/8 seconds and this would mean that one can see the word MODERN flashing every 5/2 seconds, the word BOOK flashing every 17/4 seconds and the word STORE flashing every 41/8 seconds
- They are on for one second each time that they flash and this would mean that on adding 1 to each of 5/2, 17/4 and 41/8 seconds, one can see the word MODERN every 7/2 seconds, the word BOOK every 21/4 seconds and the word STORE every 49/8 seconds

Talking about things happening at the same time, if you were to shout "Ho" every second minute and I were to shout "Ho" every third minute and starting at say 8 AM, I shall shout at 8.02, 8.04, 8.06, 8.08, 8.10 and 8.12 AM whereas you will shout at 8.03, 8.06, 8.09 and 8.12 AM. The first time that we shout together is at 8.06 AM and the next time that we shall shout together shall be at 8.12 AM.

Interestingly the first time that we shout together exactly 6 minutes from the time we started and the next time that we shout together will be 12 minutes after starting off. Have you noticed that both 6 and 12 are multiples of 2 and 3? Are we aware that if a particular number is a multiple of different other numbers, then it can be called a common multiple of those different other numbers just as a house that a husband and his wife own jointly is their common property? Taking this illustration further you will find that the third time that the two shouts synchronise will be at 18 minutes from start and the fourth time that this happens will be at 24 minutes from start and so on till the neighbours call the police. Have we noticed that 6, 12, 18 and 24 and so on are all (common) multiples of 2 and 3 and of these four (common) multiples of 2 and 3, 6 is the **least** common multiple?

In the question on hand:

- The first time when the three words MODERN, BOOK and STORE can flash simultaneously will be at a number of seconds that is the least common multiple of 5/2, 17/4 and 41/8 seconds; in order to understand this better let us convert the three fractions 5/2, 17/4 and 41/8 so that the three have a common denominator and since 8 is already a multiple of both 2 and 4, all we have to convert – for example – the fraction 5/2 to a denominator of 8 is to multiply both numerator and denominator by 4 when 5/2 can be seen as 20/8. The three fractions 5/2, 17/4 and 41/8 will thus be seen as 20/8, 34/8 and 41/8.
- The second time when the three words MODERN, BOOK and STORE can flash simultaneously will be at a number of seconds that is the least common multiple of 7/2, 21/4 and 49/8 seconds. The three fractions 7/2, 21/4 and 49/8 will thus be seen as 28/8, 42/8 and 49/8

The least common multiple of 20/8, 34/8, and 41/8 seconds will be a much greater number than the least common multiple of 28/8, 42/8, and 49/8 seconds since between 20 (which is 2 × 10) and 34 (which is 2 × 17) the number 2 is the only common factor. The number 41 is a prime number and can have no common factors with any number at all. The least common multiple of 20, 34 and 41 will be (A) 2 × 10 × 17 × 41.

In the second instance, the lights will be seen for the first time at the common multiple of 7/2, 21/4, and 49/8 seconds. These three fractions are as such 28/8, 42/8 and 49/8. If we were to find the LCM of 28, 42 and 49, we would find that 7 is common factor of all three numbers which when factorised would be expressed as (2×2×7), (2 × 3 × 7) and (7 × 7). The LCM of (2 × 2 × 7), (2 × 3 × 7) and (7 × 7) is (B) 2 × 2 × 3 × 7 × 7.

Therefore there will be two situations when the three words can be seen together:

(A) At a number of seconds equal to 2 × 10 × 17 × 41/8, and

(B) At a number of seconds equal to 2 × 2 × 3 × 7 × 7/8

The question is: which is bigger – (A) or (B)? While comparing the two, we need not worry about the denominator 8. It is common to both fractions. 2 is common to both numerators and need not be bothered about. The numerator in (A) would be 170 × 41 that would be over 6800 even if we round off 41 to 40 and ignore 2, whereas the numerator in (B) would be 6 × 49, which would be a little less than 300. Clearly (B) that is equal to 2 × 2 × 3 × 7 × 7/8 or 147/2 or 73.5 seconds will be the least number of seconds when the three words MODERN, BOOK, and STORE can be seen together. Hence **Option 2** is the correct answer.

However once you are convinced that the correct answer is a multiple of 7 for sure, it is recommended that you quickly dividė the options by 7 and even then you will find that the Option 2 is divisible by 7. This is a step faster than the previous one of actually calculating the LCM. This is what sets Quantitative Ability apart from Mathematics and thus logic plays a substantial role at competitive examinations.

Illustration 5

See another problem from a past paper of a major competitive examination. The question (with the relative options) goes as follows:

A red light flashes 3 times per minute and a green light flashes 5 times in two minutes at regular intervals. If both lights start flashing at the same time, how many times do they flash together in each hour?

1. 30 2. 24 3. 20 4. 60

Having grasped the concepts of LCM, it now seems only proper that we economise on the time and effort in calculating. We shall, therefore, quicken the pace. The red light flashes once in 20 seconds and the green light flashes once in 24 seconds. If both start flashing at the same time, they flash simultaneously for the first time after a number of seconds that is the LCM of 20 (which as such is 4 × 5) and 24 (which as such is 4 × 6). In trying to find the LCM of 20 and 24, we must remember that 4 is a common factor to both, 5 is a factor of 20 but not of 24 and similarly 6 is a factor of 24 but not of 20. The LCM of 20 and 24 will thus be 4 × 5 × 6 that is 120. If the lights flash simultaneously ever y 120 seconds, they flash together every 2 minutes. They therefore flash simultaneously for 60/2 = 30 times each hour. Thus **Option 1.**

Before we move on to another chapter, we shall jot down some important aspects of Least Common Multiples that follow:

- It is possible to find the LCM of both whole and fractional numbers
- The LCM of whole numbers is the product of the numbers if the only common multiple of these numbers is 1. This is why the LCM of – say – 5 and 7 is 35; there are no common factors between 5 and 7 except 1.
- If there are two fractions with the same denominator but different numerators such that one of the numerators is a multiple of the other, then the fraction in which the numerator is a multiple (of the numerator in the other fraction) is the LCM of the two fractions. This is why the LCM of, say, 1/4 and 3/4 is 3/4 and the LCM of – say – 2/7 and 4/7 is 4/7.
- If there are two numbers in which the factors of one number are two whole numbers – say A and B – and the factors of the other number are – say – B and C, then the LCM of the two numbers is A × B × C. One would be able to divide (A × B × C) with both (A × B) and (A × C). This is why the LCM of – say – 15 (which is 5 × 3) and 35 (which is 5 × 7) is 105 (which is 5 × 3 × 7).
- We can derive the LCM of two numbers by multiplying the factor(s) that is/are common to both numbers with the factor(s) that is/are not common to both. This is why the LCM of 12 (which is 2 × 2 × 3) and 42 (which is 2 × 3 × 7) can be derived by multiplying the common factors of 12 and 42 (and these are 2 and 3) with the factors are not common to both. There are two 2s in 12 whereas there is only a single 2 that is common to both numbers. The factor 7 in 42 is not common either. This means that factors not common to 12 and 42 are 7 and 2. The LCM of 12 and 42 is thus 2 × 3 × 2 × 7 = 84.
- If we wish to find the LCM of two fractions where there are different numerators and denominators, the first step is to find a common denominator, which in turn means finding the LCM of the denominators. Then the two fractions have to be expressed with reference to the same denominator. This may give you a new set of numerators. Then the LCM of the new numerators is to be found. The LCM of the new numerators divided by the LCM of the denominators gives the LCM of the fractions. If you are told that one light flashes every 5/6th of a minute and another flashes every 6/5th minute, and the two of them flash together for the first time at – say – 8.00 A.M. then one can find when they shall flash again for the first time as follows: First find the LCM of the denominators 5 and 6. This is 30. The fractions 5/6 and 6/5 when expressed with reference to 30 as the denominator become 25/30 and 36/30 respectively. The new numerators are then 25 and 36 in which there are no common factors and hence the LCM of the new numerators is 25 × 36 = 900. The LCM of 5/6 and 6/5 is thus 900/30 = 30. The two lights shall therefore flash simultaneously for the first time at 30 minutes from start at 8.30 A.M.
- When asked to find the LCM of a fraction and whole number, it makes sense to express the whole number with respect to the same denominator. This is why when asked to find the LCM of 3/5 and 2 it makes sense to look at 2 as 10/5. The LCM of 3/5 and 10/5 is = (the LCM of 3 and 10)/5 = 30/5 = 6.

Before the curtain falls on this chapter I would like to share with you some curious phenomena that I came across recently. These phenomena are as under:

(I) I was climbing a flight of stairs the other day. I climbed a fair number of steps taking two steps at a time from the very beginning. Yet there was one step remaining at the top of the stairs. I then climbed taking three steps at a time from the bottom of the stairs and to my utter surprise I found that even then there was one step remaining at the top of the stairs. I then decided to take four steps at a time to see if there would be any step left at the top of the stairs. Just then my brother came in and I mentioned this curious phenomenon to him. He said that even if I were to try running up the flight of stairs taking 4 steps at a time and then 5 steps at a time and finally 6 steps at a time, I would still see that each time I would have to climb exactly one last step before reaching the top of the stairs. Can you tell me what was the number of steps in the staircase if I were to tell you that the number was between 100 and 150?

(II) The other day I was arranging some toffees in heaps and found that if I had put 4 toffees in each heap, I would have had 3 left; if I had put 5 in each heap, I would had 4 left; if I had put 6 in each heap, I would have had 5 left but if I would have put 7 toffees in each heap, I would have had no remainder. What was the minimum possible number of toffees that I was trying to arrange?

Do write your answers to me at jivaishnav@yahoo.com.

Chapter 20

Least and Most

Questions involving finding the least possible value and the most possible value for expressions are a regular feature at most premier competitive examinations. What is least and what is most, however, is a matter of circumstance.

If a father were to bring ten bars of chocolate and ask the eldest of his three children to distribute these in such a way that the youngest gets the most out of these ten bars, this would mean that the youngest child could claim all ten bars because the least that the others can get is nothing. The most that the youngest child could get is in that situation when the others get the least that they could get. If all chocolate bars were, however, to be given to one person out of three, then there is no distribution. Thus the least that each child could get is one bar. This means that the most that the youngest child could get is eight bars since the other two children would get one bar each.

Imagine that the father in the above illustration brings the ten chocolate bars and asks the eldest child to distribute these in such a way that the following terms are met:

- The bars are not to be broken
- Each one must get a distinct number of bars
- The youngest shall get the most but yet he shall not get more than thrice anyone else
- The eldest shall receive the least.

Suppose the eldest child was to look dazed and ask for our help, how would we help him distribute the ten bars?

Since the eldest is to get the least, could he get one bar? If he gets one, then there are nine bars to be distributed between the other two. This means that the various combinations that the middle child and the youngest could get are respectively (A) 2 and 7 (B) 3 and 6 (C) 4 and 5. In all three cases, the youngest gets more than three bars and this means that he gets more than thrice what the eldest gets. Thus 1 as the possible number of bars for the eldest is not workable.

If the eldest gets 2 bars, there are eight bars to be distributed between the other two. This means that the only combination for the other two is 3 and 5 since each one is to get a distinct number of chocolate bars and therefore the possible combinations of 2 and 6 & 4 and 4 will not work. Thus 2, 3 and 5 bars for respectively the eldest, second child and the youngest is a workable combination.

Now for the sake of analysis let us see whether 3 would do as a possible number of bars for the eldest. If the eldest gets 3, the other two would have to share 7 bars and this is only possible if the second child takes 3 and the youngest takes 4. But this would mean the same number of bars for the eldest and the second child and this is not in the scheme of things. We have to stop analysing here and decide that the only workable combination is 2, 3 and 5 as we have seen earlier.

We shall now see some further illustrations in regard to Least and Most. Each illustration is at a higher level of difficulty than its immediate predecessor. The idea is to gradually upgrade one's skills and ensure assimilation as well as clarity of concepts. It is suggested that you may please attempt the problems in the illustrations and regardless of whether you are right or wrong, go through the solutions each time. A whole lot of fundamentals would get clear. The best part is that while referring to the solutions, the reader will be able to develop the technique of reducing problems to smaller levels and then deriving lessons from this reduced level that will help to crack the larger problem in a jiffy.

Problem 1

Imagine that A, B and C are positive integers meeting the condition that A < B < C and A + B + C = D. What is the smallest value of D that does not determine A, B, C uniquely?

Options: (1) 9 (2) 6 (3) 7 (4) 8

Solution

Since A, B and C are distinct positive integers, if we see the possible value of D as 9 at Option 1, the following values of A, B and C can emerge:

A =	B =	C=	A + B + C =
1	2	6	9
1	3	5	9
2	3	4	9

Thus there are more than one possible values for each of A, B and C and one cannot say that 9 as a value for D determines unique values for A, B and C.

As per Option 2, the following values of A, B and C can emerge:

A + B + C = 6, when A = 1, B = 2, C = 3

There can be unique values for each of A, B and C and one can therefore say that 6 as a value for D determines unique values for A, B and C.

The question is whether 6 is the smallest possible value for D that determines A, B and C uniquely? For this we may move on to the other options.

As per Option 3, the following distinct values of A, B and C can emerge:

A + B + C = 7, when A = 1, B = 2, C = 4

There can be unique values for each of A, B and C and one can say that 7 as a value for D determines unique values for A, B and C. The question is whether 7 is the smallest possible value for D? We may move on to the last option and see whether it does or does not determine unique values for A, B and C.

If we see the possible value of D as 8 at Option 4, the following values of A, B and C can emerge:

A=	B=	C=	A + B + C =
1	3	4	8
1	2	5	8

There will not be unique values for each of A, B and C and one can say that 8 as the least value for D does not determine unique values for A, B and C.

Problem 2

119 persons have enrolled for a table tennis tournament. All pairs are to be paired for the first round, but because there is one person who does not find a partner in the first round, he will get a bye and move to the second round. This pairing process continues till the next round, with a bye to any player who does not find a partner. What is the minimum number of matches that must be played till the winner of the tournament is decided?

Solution

One has to see this problem on a smaller scale and evolve a hypothesis.

If the number of contestants was	Then there would be	The total number of matches would be
1	No match: who will the single fellow play with? His shadow?	0
3	1 match between two players (when the third fellow gets bye). The winner would play the final with the fellow in bye.	2
5	2 matches where 4 will play (when the fifth fellow gets bye). From two winners of round one, the bye will be added to make 3 players; there will be one match in the second round and 1 player will be in bye. From the second round there will be one winner who will play the final play with the fellow in the bye.	2 + 1 + 1 = 4
7	3 matches where 6 will play and 1 player will be in bye. From three winners of round one, the bye will be added to make 4 players. There will be two matches in the second round. From the second round, there will be two winners who will play the final.	3 + 2 + 1 = 6

Quite clearly, there will be one match less than the number of players if one is in bye for the reason that there is an odd number of contestants and if you make pairs, the number of persons who can play at any time can only be even.

Taking off from this, if there are 119 players, there will be 118 matches before the winner emerges. Needless to say, there will be not enough time to see if the hypothesis that we have evolved stands the test of 119 players. If it does for three or four different values for an odd number of players, it will do for 119 as well.

Problem 3

The English football team this year has so far played 2/3rd of the matches it is scheduled to play this year and has a record of 17 wins and 3 losses. What is the greatest number of matches it can afford to lose out of the remaining games to be played this year so that the record of wins is at least 75% of total games that it will play this year?

Solution

The fact that the team has won 17 and lost 3 means that the team has so far played 20 matches. If 20 matches is 2/3rd of the matches it has to play this year, then the total number of matches to be played this year is 30.

If the team wants that the record of wins is at least 75% (or 3/4th) of total games that it will play this year, it must win at least 3/4th of 30 or 22.5 matches. One cannot win fractional number of matches. Hence exactly 23 matches must be won. Having won 17, 6 more must be won out of the remaining 10. Thus the team can afford to lose at the most 4 matches.

Problem 4

If L and S are respectively the largest number and the smallest number formed from the five digits 0, 1, 2, 3 and 4 using each digit exactly once, what is the value of (L-S)? Options: (A) 29763 (B) 41976 (C) 32976 (D) 29634

Solution

Fundamentally, the greatest number that can be formed from any five digits is that when the highest digit is in the ten thousands place, the next highest is in the thousands place, then the third highest in the hundreds place and then the second lowest digit in the tens place and the lowest digit in the units place.

In the converse, the smallest number that can be formed from any five digits is that when the smallest digit is in the ten thousands place, the second smallest is in the thousands place, then the third smallest in the hundreds place and then the second highest digit in the tens place and the highest digit in the units place. Provided, however, that if zero is one of the digits, then zero shall not be in the ten thousands place since zero at the beginning of a five-digit number makes the number effectively a four-digit number and it would then no longer qualify to be a five-digit number. If therefore zero is one of the digits, it will figure in the thousands place and the second lowest digit will appear in the ten thousands place.

The greatest number L derived from the five digits 0, 1, 2, 3 and 4 using each digit exactly once is thus 43210 and S the smallest number derived from the five digits 0, 1, 2, 3 and 4 using each digit exactly once is thus 10234 and the difference between L and S will be = 43210 − 10234 = 32976.

Problem 5

Imagine that you are in a vault where there are diamonds each worth USD 4 million and weighing 300 grams each and rubies each worth USD 5 million and weighing 400 grams each. Your bag, however, cannot carry more than 12 kg. What combination of diamonds and rubies would you carry so that the value of the precious stones that you carry away is maximised?

(1) 20 diamonds and 15 rubies

(2) 8 diamonds and 24 rubies

(3) No diamonds and 30 rubies

(4) 40 diamonds and no rubies

Solution

This is a case involving what is known as extreme analysis. One extreme is that one carries only diamonds and no rubies and the other extreme is that one carries only rubies and no diamonds.

If the bag can carry 12 kg and:

(I) Diamonds weigh 300 grams each. It means that the bag can carry at the most 40 diamonds if it carried only diamonds.

(II) Rubies weigh 400 grams each. It means that the bag can carry at the most 30 rubies if it carried only rubies.

What needs to be seen is - what will maximise value?

(A) Only diamonds valued at 40 × 4 = 160 (ignoring millions)?

(B) Only rubies valued at 30 × 5 = 150(ignoring millions)?

(C) A mixture of diamonds and rubies?

The ratio between the weights of Diamonds and Rubies is 3: 4. Thus if the capacity of the bag is fixed, the number of either only Diamonds or only Rubies that you can carry will bear an inverse ratio of 4:3. For example, if the bag could carry only 6 kilograms, then you could carry either only 20 diamonds or only 15 rubies, which too would be in the ratio of 4:3.

The ratio between the unit value of Diamonds and Rubies is 4:5. The ratio between the value of either only Diamonds or only Rubies that you could carry would then be (4 × 4): (5 × 3) or 16:15. This means that if you carried only Diamonds you would be able to carry maximum value and if you carried only rubies, you would be able to carry minimum value. Any combination of diamonds and rubies that would weigh the maximum that the bag can carry would then only have value that would be less than that of only Diamonds and more than that of only Rubies. If the idea is to maximise value, then there is no other choice than carrying only Diamonds. See this being demonstrated in the following table:

In case the bag in the above question can hold only 24 gm and that a diamond weighs 3 gm and costs USD 4 a piece and a ruby weighs 4 gm each and costs USD 5 a piece, then

	Diamonds	Rubies	Aggregate weight	Aggregate worth
If I were to carry	8	0	24 gm	32
If I were to carry	0	6	24 gm	30
If I were to carry	4	3	24 gm	16 + 15 = 31

In the above example of reducing the problem to a smaller scale, there is only one intermediate combination and even this proves that it is not worthwhile taking the trouble of calculating the worth of different combinations of Diamonds and Rubies. Any combination of Diamonds and Rubies will be worth more than that of only Rubies and less than that of only Diamonds. This is for certain. Thus Option 4 is to be marked as correct.

Reducing the problem to a lower level has this advantage that it saves a lot of bother. It is also a rather effective method of problem solving. This is primarily because if any problem looks huge, reducing the problem to a small size will take the fear of the problem away. Secondly, if one is given four different combinations as options, the extreme analysis may not be worthwhile. But if one of the options states "None of these" then the extreme analysis and reduction of the problem to a lower level becomes extremely imperative to see whether a pattern is emerging and if it is then what it is. When deciding on " None of these" as the correct option, one has to be dead certain that the other options are wrong.

Problem 6, 7 and 8

Let us see these three questions flowing from the same set of information.

The information is as follows:

Four boys - P, Q, R and S collected marbles. Among them they collected 100 marbles. No one had less than 10. All had an even number of marbles. None had the same number of marbles.

Problem 6

If one of the boys had the largest possible number of marbles, then how many marbles are in his collection?
(A) 64 (B) 54 (C) 60 (D) 58

Problem 7

After a few days it was found that the boy with the largest collection had 54 marbles, what is the difference between the maximum possible number of marbles and the second largest collection?

(A) 30 (B) 18 (C) 26 (D) 12

Problem 8

If P had 54 marbles and Q had two more than twice the number collected by R, then how many marbles did Q have: (A) 10 (B) 30 (C) 22 (D) 26

Solution

There are some fundamental things to be remembered:

- If the quantity to be allocated among different persons is fixed, then one person among the many can have the highest possible if the others have the least possible. If I decide to distribute ten chocolates between two children, then what is the highest possible that one can have? The total number minus the lowest possible what the other can have. If the elder child decides to make do with one, the younger can have nine. If it is intended that both should have an even number of chocolates, then the one with the least can have only two and the one with the highest can have eight.
- If a fixed quantity is to be allocated among different persons, then two persons among the many can have the highest possible if the others have their least possible. If I decide to distribute ten chocolates between four children, then what is the highest possible and the second highest possible that two of the children can have? The total number minus the lowest possible what the other two can have.

If it is intended that the minimum number of chocolates that any child can have is 1, then the following combinations are possible:

- 1 + 1 + 4 + 4; this however will not enable one to distinguish between the highest and the second highest
- 1 + 1 + 3 + 5; the highest has 5 chocolates and the second highest has 3 whereas the other two have an equal number of chocolates and not a distinct number of chocolates

If it is intended that the minimum number of chocolates that any child can have is 1, and that the children should have a distinct number of chocolates, then only the following combination is possible: 1+ 2 + 3 + 4

So in the present case, there are 100 marbles. The quantity is fixed. This has to be distributed among the four in such a way that none had less than 10; all had an even number of marbles and none had the same number of marbles, then the least anyone can have is 10, the second least is 12 (because the numbers have to be distinct), the third least is 14 and this makes 36 in all. So the fellow with the highest possible number has **64 marbles**.

After a few days it was found that the boy with the largest collection had 54 marbles, this means that the three remaining boys had between them 46 marbles. The second largest collection is possible if the least and the second least is 10 and 12 respectively (meaning at their respective minimum) and thus second highest is 100 – 54 – 12 – 10 = 24. So the difference between the maximum possible number of marbles and the second largest collection is 54 – 24 = 30.

If P had 54 marbles, then Q, R and S had 100 – 54 = 46 marbles among them. If Q had two more than twice the number collected by R, then if we see from the options, if:

(A) Q had 10 marbles, R had 4 marbles and this is not in the scheme of things since the least number of marbles is ten

(B) Q had 30 marbles, R had 14 marbles and then since Q + R = 44, S could have had only 2 marbles of the 46 remaining after deducting P's 54 marbles form the 100 in all; this is not in the scheme of things since the least number of marbles is ten

(C) Q had 22 marbles, R had 10 marbles and between Q and R this makes 32 marbles and so S has 46 – 32 = 14; this is as per the scheme of things since the least number of marbles is ten and all have a distinct number of marbles. This is the correct option.

(D) Q had 26 marbles, R had 12 marbles and thus S had 8 marbles (46 –26 –12) and this is not in the scheme of things since the least number of marbles is ten

Problem 9

Of 933 boxes of peaches, each box has at least 110 and at most 134 peaches. The number of boxes containing the same number of peaches is at least: Options: (1) 311 (2) 3 (3) 2 and (4) Cannot be determined.

Solution

All you are told is that the boxes have at least 110 peaches and at most 134 peaches. Let us imagine that there are only three varieties of boxes: Variety One that contains exactly 110 peaches, Variety Two that contains exactly 111 peaches and Variety Three that contains exactly 134 peaches. The least number of boxes of say Variety One is possible when Variety Two and Three have the most number of boxes between them. Thus the least number of boxes of say Variety One is one and the most number of boxes that Variety Two and Three can have between them is 933 –1 or 932. This 932 can be in the following illustrative combinations:

	Variety One with 110 peaches in each box	Variety Two with 111 peaches in each box	Variety Three with 134 peaches in each box
Combination No. 1	1	1	931
Combination No. 2	1	2	930
Combination No. 3	1	3	929
Combination No. 4	1	931	1

In Combination No. 1, you have the most number of boxes with the same number of peaches (namely 134 peaches). In Combination No. 2, you have the least number of boxes with the same number of peaches (namely 111 peaches). In Combination No. 3, you have the second least number of boxes with the same number of peaches (namely 111 peaches).

Fundamentally, when we use the words *same number*, we are trying to compare. For comparison purposes we need at least two of a kind. Thus the least number of boxes containing the same number of peaches can fundamentally be only two. Hence Option 3.

Problem 10

P, Q, R and S are positive real numbers such that P × Q × R × S = 16. What is the least possible value of (1 + P) × (2 + Q) × (1 + R) × (2 + S)?

Solution

Let us imagine that this problem was on a smaller scale as under:

(1) P × Q =16

(2) We have to find the least possible value of (1 + P) × (2 + Q)

If P × Q = 16, then the following situations are possible:

(A) P can be 1 when Q is 16 when the value of (1 + P) × (2 + Q) is 2 × 18 = 36

(B) P can be 2 when Q is 8 when the value of (1 + P) × (2 + Q) is 3 × 10 = 30

(C) P can be 4 when Q is 4 when the value of (1 + P) × (2 + Q) is 5 × 6 = 30

(D) P can be 8 when Q is 2 when the value of (1 + P) × (2 + Q) is 9 × 4 = 36

(E) P can be 16 when Q is 1 when the value of (1 + P) × (2 + Q) is 17 × 3 = 51

One thing emerges clearly from the above analysis: least possible value of (1 + P) × (2 + Q) is when P and Q are equal in (C) above. In (B) above the least value of 30 is a matter of chance. The moment you swap the values of P and Q, the value would become higher than the least. But in case of (C) above, even if you swap the values of P and Q there would be no difference at all principally because P and Q are equal.

In the question there are four multiplicands: (1 + P), (2 + Q), (1 + R), and (2 + S). Various combinations of P, Q, R and S are feasible but the lowest possible value of the expression (1 + P) × (2 + Q) × (1 + R) ×

$(2 + S)$ will emerge for sure only when the four $P = Q = R = S = 2$; with these values you will find that the value of the expression $(1 + P) \times (2 + Q) \times (1 + R) \times (2 + S)$ will be $3 \times 4 \times 3 \times 4 = 144$. Take any other combination of values for P, Q, R and S among the following illustrative combinations and find out for yourself that 144 is indeed the least possible value of the expression $(1 + P) \times (2 + Q) \times (1 + R) \times (2 + S)$:

(I) $P = 1, Q = 1, R = 1, S = 16$

(II) $P = 1, Q = 1, R = 2, S = 8$

(III) $P = 1, Q = 1, R = 4, S = 4$

(IV) $P = 2, Q = 8, R = 1, S = 1$

Problem 11

A school class was at the airport to see off John - one of their classmates - who was proceeding abroad to attend a student exchange programme. Jim, Bill, Bob, Ted and Dick found the weighing scale interesting. They stood on the scale in twos each time such that no pair was repeated. They then found the following readings of weights in kilograms: 70, 72, 73, 74, 75, 76, 77, 78, 80, and 81. If Ted was the heaviest of the five, what could be Ted's weight in kilograms if no two boys had the same weight?:

Options: (A) 39 (B) 44 (C) 42 (D) 40

Solution

There are five boys. Each weighs different. Let the lightest to heaviest be denoted by the following symbols:

L_1 (lightest), L_2, M (middle of the range), H_2 and H_1 (heaviest) in ascending order of weight; this would mean that $H_1 > H_2 > M > L_2 > L_1$

The boys are being weighed in pairs; if the weights of pairs are arranged in ascending order, the following order will emerge: $(L_1 + L_2) < (L_1 + M) < (L_2 + M) < (M + H_1) < (H_1 + H_2)$

Assume values of 1,2,3,4 and 5 for L_1, L_2, M, H_2 and H_1 respectively and see for yourself that the above order will hold.

Now among the options, if $H_1 = 39$, then since $H_2 + H_1 = 81$, $H_2 = 42$. This is not workable since H1 is the heaviest.

In the present case: $(H_2 + H_1) = 81$, $(M + H_1) = 80$, $(L_1 + M) = 72$ and $(L_1 + L_2) = 70$.

If $H_1 = 44$, $H_2 = 37$ (i.e. 81 – 44) and $M = 36$ (i.e. 80 – 44) and then since $L_1 + M = 72$, $L_1 = 36$. This is not workable since the weight of the boy in the middle of the range would then be the same as that of the boy with the least weight.

If H_1 is 42,then H_2=39 (i.e. 81 –42) and $M = 38$ (i.e. 80 – 42) and then $L_1 = 34$ (i.e. 72 – 38) and since $(L_1 + L_2) = 70$, $L_2 = 36$. We have thus got values for the five different weights that fulfil the criteria that $H_1 > H_2 > M > L_2 > L_1$.

So Ted whose weight we have assumed as H_1 weighs 42 kg.

Problem 12

If $|Q-5| = 3$ and $|3P - 5| = 13$, what is the minimum possible value of Q/P? (A) 4/3

(B) –2 (C) –1/3 (D) None of these.

Solution

There are four situations possible: (1) $Q - 5 = 3$ and thus $Q = 8$; (2) $Q - 5 = -3$ and thus $Q = 2$ and

(3) $3P - 5 = 13$ and thus $P = 6$ and (4) $3P - 5 = -13$ and thus $P = -8/3$.

Q/P can have the following four possible values: (1) 8/6 or 4/3 (2) 8 ÷ –8/3 = –3 (3) 2/6 = 1/3 and (4) 2 ÷ -8/3 = –3/4.

The least possible value of Q/P among the four above is –3. Since -3 does not figure among the options, *none of these*. The bottom line is that if *none of these* is among the options, then one's analysis must be complete so that one is not caught napping.

Problem 13

At a competitive examination, at most C candidates out of 2C+3 can be selected. If the number of different ways of selecting at least one candidate is exactly 63, what is the maximum number of candidates that can be selected?
(A) 5 (B) 4 (C) 2 (D) 3

Solution

At most C candidates can be selected out of 2C + 3. If the number of candidates selected were C (where C = 5,4,2 or 3) then these were selected out of a total number of 2C + 3 = 13, 11, 7 or 9 respectively) candidates. The number of ways of selecting 1 candidate out of 2C+3 (where 2C + 3 = 13, 11, 7 or 9 when C = 5, 4, 3 and 2 respectively) is $({}^{2C+3}C_1)$ i.e ${}^{13}C_1$, ${}^{11}C_1$, ${}^{7}C_1$ and ${}^{9}C_1$ (respectively equal to 13, 11, 7 and 9). At the stage of ${}^{2C+3}C_1$ we do not get 63 as an answer. This means that we shall have to add this to the number of ways in which one can select two candidates out of 2C + 3 since at least 1 means 1 or more and to a further number of ways for selecting three candidates and so on till we reach a total of 63 number of ways.

Of these ${}^{13}C_1$ and ${}^{11}C_1$, or ${}^{13}C_2$ and ${}^{11}C_2$ and so on will invariably be multiples of 13 and 11 respectively and thus either ${}^{13}C_1 + {}^{13}C_2$ and so on, or ${}^{11}C_1 + {}^{11}C_2$ and so on, will invariably give integral multiples of either 13 or 11. Let us see this alive.

Let us find the values of ${}^{13}C_3$ and ${}^{13}C_5$ for example. ${}^{13}C_3$= (13 × 12 × 11)/(3 × 2 × 1) = 286 which is 13 × 22. It must be borne in mind that ${}^{13}C_3$ has 13 in the numerator but can not have 13 in the denominator. Since the denominator does not have 13, no factors of 13 are possible in the denominator since 13 is a prime number. Similarly ${}^{13}C_5$, which is (13 × 12 × 11 × 10 × 9)/(5 × 4 × 3 × 2 × 1) = 13 × 11 × 9 or 13 × 99 has 13 in the numerator but not in the denominator and therefore is bound to be a multiple of 13. So it will be with 11 since 11 is also prime. Furthermore, the sum of two multiples of 13 will always be multiples of 13. This is because if you take one such multiple as 13A and the other as 13B, the sum of these two will be 13A + 13B = 13(A + B). So it will be with any other number. The sum of two multiples of – say 9 – will thus be always be a multiple of 9 and so on.

Back to the question at hand, since 63 is neither a multiple of 13 or 11, we may not reckon either 13 or 11 as a value for (2C + 3) and focus on 7 and 9 as values for (2C + 3) since 63 is a multiple of both 7 and 9.Let us see this in the following tabular form.

The number of ways of selecting	Out of 2C+3 candidates where	
	2C+3 = 7	2C+3 = 9
1 candidate	${}^{7}C_1$ =7	${}^{9}C_1$ = 9
2 candidates	${}^{7}C_2$ =21	${}^{9}C_2$ = 36
3 candidates	${}^{7}C_3$=35	${}^{9}C_3$ = 84
TOTAL	63	129

The number of ways of selecting 3 candidates out of 7 is ${}^{7}C_1$, ${}^{7}C_2$ and ${}^{7}C_3$ is 7+21+35=63. Thus the total number of candidates (2C+3) out of whom the selection was made is 7 and since 2C+3=7, the number of candidates (C) selected is 2.

Problem 14

A man decides to acquire a triangular plot of land that is right angled and has plot area of 50 square meters. He needs to build a boundary wall around it. He finds that the cost of building the wall is \$ 30 per running meter. If he wants to keep the cost of building the boundary wall to the minimum, what should be the minimum cost that he will have to incur on the boundary wall? (A) \$960 (B) \$1380 (C) \$1170 (D) \$1020

Solution

The crux lies in keeping the length of the boundary wall to the minimum because only then will the cost of the wall remain at the minimum, there being a direct relationship between the length of the boundary wall and the cost of building.

In a right-angled triangle, the square on the hypotenuse is equal to the sum of the squares on the other two sides.

If a right-angled triangle has an area of 50 square meters then ½ × base × height= 50 square meters and hence the product of the base and height should be equal to 100. It would be important to do an extreme analysis, keeping the base large and the height small and progressively decreasing the base and increasing the height.

It must be remembered that the square of the hypotenuse has a direct relationship with the measure of the hypotenuse itself. The bigger the hypotenuse the bigger will be its square.

If Base = B	Height = H	B×H =	$B^2 + H^2$ = Hypotenuse^2	B + H =
50	2	100	2500+4=2504	52
25	4	100	625+16=641	29
12.5	8	100	156.25+64=220.25	20.5
10	10	100	100+100=200	20

The wall has to be built along the perimeter of the triangle. The perimeter of the triangle = B + H + Hypotenuse. The least cost of the boundary wall is possible when the length of the boundary wall is at its minimum and therefore (B + H + Hypotenuse) is at the very least possible.

The square of the hypotenuse is the smallest when the hypotenuse itself is the smallest among the different possible values for the measure of the hypotenuse.

Quite clearly, the hypotenuse is the smallest when the two sides are equal in measure. Again, B + H is also the smallest when B = H. So the perimeter of the triangle will be the smallest when the two sides are 10 meters each and then the hypotenuse which is the square root of 200 will be about 14 meters and the aggregate of the three sides will be 10 + 10 + 14 = 34 meters. The cost of constructing the boundary wall at \$30 per running meter = 34 × 30 = \$1020.

Chapter 21

Line Graphs (and, of course, some other types of graphs)

When we talk about a line we invariably refer to a straight line. A straight-line joins at least two points. Each point that lies on a graph has a position with respect to the x and y-axis. This position is determined by x and y co-ordinates. Thus if you are to find where the point (3,2) lies, what you would have to do is to start from the origin (meaning, the point 0,0 where the two axes intersect) and move 3 units along the x-axis to the east and on having reached 3 units away from the origin swerve north and go up 2 units vertically along a line parallel to the y-axis and stop there and say: "Whew, I have reached point (3,2)."

The co-ordinates in a line graph obey an equation that sets out a linear relationship between x and y (and not x and/ or y in their higher powers such squares and cubes and so on). As to what is meant by linear relationship, we shall see as under.

Let us see two graphs where in one case there is a linear relationship between x and y and another where one of x or y is in a higher power. If the equation of a line graph is say $x - 2y = 3$, some of the co-ordinates on this line will be as follows and if the equation of another graph is $y = x^2 - 2$, the co-ordinates would be as under:

In the equation $x - 2y = 3$			
When x=	–1	0	1
Then y=	–2	–1.5	–1
Therefore x – 2y =	3	3	3
In the equation $y = x^2 - 2$			
When x=	–1	0	1
Then y=	–1	–2	–1

In the graph represented by the linear equation $x - 2y = 3$, the values of the co-ordinates keep step when marching along. When x increases by 1, y increases by 0.5 from –2 to –1.5 and in the next step, y increases by 0.5 from –1.5 to –1. Thus whenever x steps 1 step forward, y consistently takes ½ step forward, neither more nor less (which means that x increases by 2 when y increases by 1). This is what a linear relationship means: the change in the value of one co-ordinate with a given change in the other will remain the same throughout the line graph.

In the equation $y = x^2 - 2$, when x increases by 1 from –1 to 0, y decreases by 1 from –1 to –2 and in the next step, when x increases by 1 from 0 to 1, y increases by 1 from –2 to –1. The change in y with the given increase of 1 in the x co-ordinate is not the same throughout; sometimes y decreases and at other times y increases when x increases by 1 each time.

It is common knowledge that all along the y–axis, x is zero and that all along the x–axis, y = o. Therefore the equations of the x–axis and the y–axis are respectively $y = 0$ and $x = 0$. We could then see the equation $y = \log x$. Since there are no logarithms for either zero or negative numbers, any graph representing the equation $y = \log_{10} x$ cannot either touch the y-axis or intersect it. It will necessarily be detached from the y –axis. If x is a fraction – let us assume the following values of x: 1/10, 1/100 and 1/1000 – then y= –1, –2 and –3 respectively. When x = 1, y = 0 and when x = 10, 100 or 1000, y = 1, 2 and 3 respectively. If one were to draw a graph of $y = \log_{10} x$, since x = 1/10 would be very close to the origin and x = 1/100 or x = 1/1000 would be perilously close to the y-axis, the co-ordinates (1/10, –1), (1/100, –2) and (1/1000, –3) would mean that the graph would start out as a virtual laminate on the y-axis, slowly distancing itself from the y-axis when it approaches (1, 0) and then again it will rise very gradually to the co-ordinates (10, 1), (100, 2) and (1000, 3). But since there is no direct relationship between y and log x, the graph representing the equation $y = \log_{10} x$ will necessarily be a curve as will all graphs representing equations where there is no direct relationship between x and y.

Every line graph has a fixed gradient that shows the constant rate of change in the y co-ordinate with the corresponding change in the value of the x co-ordinate. This would be easy to understand once we understand what a gradient really is.

When you climb a slope, you pant because the gradient is steep. The gradient of any slope is equal to the distance climbed comparcd to the distance covered on the ground. Visualise yourself on a picnic to three different peaks as in the diagrams below on a bright Sunday morning. While climbing Snow Peak, you can whistle a merry tune as you go along. You might ask your girlfriend to put her arms on your shoulders. This is because the vertical distance climbed as represented by the line AB is small as compared to the horizontal distance covered as shown by line BC. This vertical distance is the numerator and the horizontal distance is the denominator in a fraction called the gradient.

Snow Peak

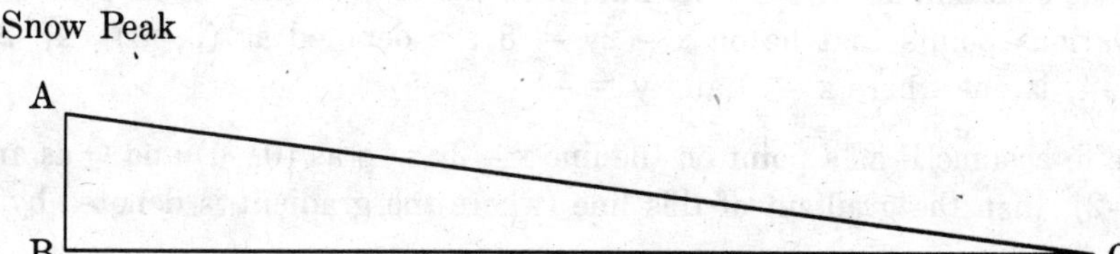

Now let us move on to Old Bailey's Peak.

Old Bailey's Peak

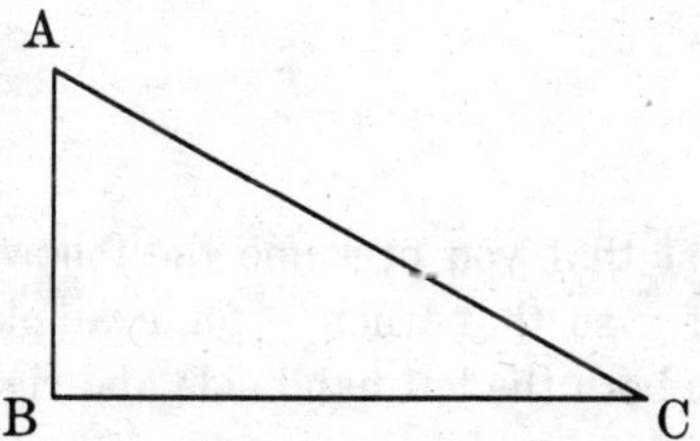

In the case of Old Bailey's Peak, the vertical distance climbed as compared to the horizontal distance covered – meaning AB/BC is a fraction of greater value than in the case of Snow Peak. You have to pause for breath. When your girlfriend puts her arm on your shoulder, you enquire of her with a good deal of irritation whether she thinks you are a ruddy porter and why can't she take her hand off your shoulder?

The Sheer Horn

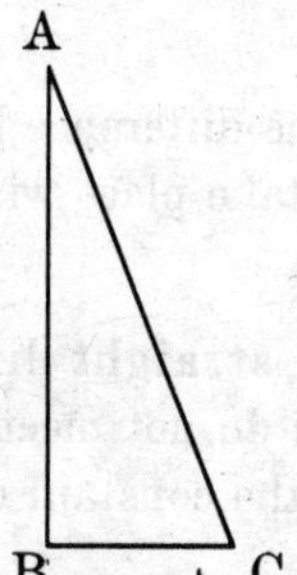

When climbing up Sheer Horn, every step is a pain in the neck. This is because the gradient is too steep. The vertical distance AB that you climb is too large in relation to the horizontal distance BC covered. This is what makes gradients steep.

The gradient of a line graph is always the same anywhere on the line. If the gradient fluctuates you can have a wave or a parabola and so on but not a straight line.

A line graph represented by the equation $y = 4$ is parallel to the x-axis in which case it is not climbing up and therefore has no gradient. A line graph represented by the equation $x = 4$ is parallel to the y-axis in which case it is climbing up like a high-rise building without any slope and its gradient is infinity simply because you climb vertical distance only and no horizontal distance climbed in relation to the vertical distance.

If two points P and Q are on a straight line graph and the co-ordinates of P and Q are respectively as follows: $P = (x_1,y_1)$ and $Q = (x_2,y_2)$, then the gradient is $m = (y_2\text{-}y_1)/(x_2\text{-}x_1)$. It may be noticed that the expression $(y_2 - y_1)$ indicates the change in the values of the y co-ordinates and therefore the vertical distance moved along a line parallel to the y-axis whereas the expression $(x_2 - x_1)$ indicates the change in the values of the x co-ordinates and therefore the corresponding change in the values of x co-ordinates and therefore the corresponding distance covered on the x-axis. This is why the expression $(y_2\text{-}y_1)/(x_2\text{-}x_1)$ indicates the vertical distance climbed in relation to the horizontal distance covered which in turn is what a gradient is.

The various values of x and y that obey the equation $x - 2y = 8$ are known as the co-ordinates of the points on the line graph $x\text{-}2y = 8$. So three of the various points that lie on $x - 2y = 8$ are denoted as (0, -4), (4, -2) and (-4, -6) where, for example the point (0,-4) is one where $x = 0$ and $y = -4$.

Now as per what is given above, we were to assume P as a point on the line $x - 2y = 8$ as (0, -4) and Q as another point on this line with co-ordinates (4, -2), then the gradient of this line (where the gradient is denoted by m) = $(y_2\text{-}y_1)/(x_2\text{-}x_1) = (\text{-}2\text{-} (\text{-}4))/(4\text{-}0) = 0.5$

We would strongly recommend that you plot the three lines with equations as follows on a **SINGLE GRAPH SHEET** and see the result for yourself. This will drive home the point about which line graphs intersect, which run parallel and which will be perpendicular:

Line 1: $x - 2y = 8$

Line 2: $2x + y = 8$

Line 3: $3x - 6y = 12$

In determining the coordinates of points on the three lines, I would suggest that you presume the following five values of x: –2, –1, 0, 1, and 2 and arrive at the corresponding values of y so that when – for example – you substitute the values of both x and y in the equation $x - 2y = 8$, you get 8 on both the left hand side and right hand side of the equation.

You will find that:

- Line 1 will be perpendicular to Line 2
- Line 1 and Line 3 will run parallel to each other.

A line that is not parallel to another will intersect the other. Let us see the line graph $x - 2y = 8$ with slope of 2 and another line graph obeying the equation $x - y = 3$ which has a slope of 1.

You will find these two lines of unequal slopes interesting. It may sometimes so happen that the difference between the slopes of two lines is rather small. In such case the intersection of the two lines may not take place within the constraints of the size of the graph paper.

But fundamentally, every straight line that has a slope different from another straight line will intersect it. It is due to the fact that the railway line is perfectly parallel that its two tracks do not meet even if you go from one end of the rail track to the other even if they are thousands of miles apart. If the constant distance between the tracks were to vary, be sure the train would derail.

When the product of the slopes of two line graphs is –1, then the two lines will intersect each other at right angles and will thus be perpendicular to each other.

The slope of the line x + 2y = 9 can be easily determined. Assume that x = 0 and then x = 2. The corresponding values for y will be 4.5 and 3.5 respectively. As it can be seen, **when the value of the x-co-ordinate increases by 2, there is corresponding reduction of 1 in the value of the y-co-ordinate**. The gradient of this line x + 2y = 9 is equal to (the change in the value of the y co-ordinate) divided by (the corresponding change in the value of the x co-ordinate); the gradient is thus -½. The slope of the line 2x-y = 3 is 2. These two lines are perpendicular to each other. Draw these two lines on graph paper and see for yourself that since the slopes of two lines are such that the product of their slopes is –1, these two lines intersect each other at right angles.

It becomes important to point out the fact that even if one does not remember the formula for the slope of a line graph, it is not a matter to be unduly worried about. If you understand **why** the slope of a line graph is equal to (the difference between the subsequent and prior y co-ordinates) divided by the (the difference between the subsequent and prior x co-ordinates), reconstructing the formula is a matter of a jiffy.

See, for example, the line graph represented by the equation y = 2x – 9. This can be rewritten as y – 2x = –9. One thing is certain as far as this equation is concerned: whatever be the value of y, and the corresponding value of x, y minus twice the corresponding value of x will result in -9; neither more, nor less. So in the line graph representing y – 2x = –9, if the value of y increases by 1, 2x has also got to go up by 1 so that the increase of 1 in y would be cancelled out by the increase of 1 in 2x. This means that if 2x has to go up by 1, x has to go up by ½ and then the ratio of the vertical distance climbed to the corresponding horizontal distance covered is 1/ (1/2) or 2. This means that the gradient of the line representing y – 2x = –9 is 2. Incidentally the gradient is equal to [–1 × coefficient of x] / coefficient of y.

Then see the line 2y + 3x = 4.5. Whatever happens to x and y, 2y + 3x should invariably add up to 4.5; this is what is meant by the constant term in an equation. If you were to climb 1 unit on the y-axis (or on a line parallel to the y-axis), the value of y would go up by 1. This means the value of 2y goes up by 2. This means 3x has to decrease by 2 so as to cancel out the increase of 2 in 2y in order to maintain the constant total of 4.5 when you add 2y and 3x. If 3x has to go down by 2, x has to go down by 2/3. This means that when the value of y increases by 1 unit, the value of x decreases by 2/3 and hence the gradient of the line 2y + 3x = 4.5 is 1/ (-2/3) or –3/2. Incidentally the gradient is equal to [-1 × coefficient of x] / coefficient of y.

We trust that while explaining the rationale behind the formula for the gradient of a line graph, one has been able to drive home the point that the gradient of any line graph is independent of the constant term. **The gradient is determined by the coefficients alone of x and y** in the equation that the line graph represents.

We also trust that it will now be appreciated that the slope of a line representing the equation ax + by + c = 0 will be positive when the coefficients of x and y are different in sign and negative when the coefficients of x and y have the same sign.

Exercise

1. ABCD is a rhombus with the diagonals AC and BD intersecting at the origin on the x – y plane. The equation of the straight line AD is x + y = 1. What is the equation of BC?

   (1) x + y = –1

   (2) x – y = –1

   (3) x + y – 1

   (4) None of the above

2. The area bound by the three curves |x + y| = 1 , |x| = 1 , and |y| = 1, is equal to:

   (1) 4 (2) 3 (3) 2 (4) 1

3. The lines represented by the three equations: $2X + 3Y - 5 = 0$; $3X - 5Y + 2 = 0$; and $-5X + 2Y + 3 = 0$
   a. are parallel
   b. form a triangle
   c. have two perpendicular lines
   d. pass through a common point

4. Which of the following pairs of lines (equations given) are parallel?
   1. $2x - 3y + 4 = 0$ and $10x - 15y - 7 = 0$
   2. $25x + 20y - 8 = 0$ and $5x + 4y + 4 = 0$
   3. $y = -2x + 8$ and $y = -2x + 1$
   4. $y = 3x + 4$ and $y = -3x + 2$

   (1) I and II (2) I and III (3) I,II and III (4) III and IV

5. The distance of point P from the origin is 5. The slope of the segment joining the origin and P is ¾. What are the co-ordinates of P? (1) (-3,-4) (2) (-3,4) (3) (3,4) (4) (4,3)

Detailed answers

Answer 1

It would come in very handy if one were to quickly draw the two axis x and y and mark three roughly equidistant points 1, 2, 3 on both the positive and negative sides of the x and y axis. If one does that and draws line $x + y = 1$, taking values of $x = 0$(the corresponding point would be $y = 1$), $x = 1$(correspondingly $y = 0$) and $x = -1$(correspondingly $y = 2$), one will find that from line AD, the point (1,0) and (0,1) are the only points from where ray will go to the point (0,0) that is the origin on the x,y plane and create a rhombus with(-1,0) and (0,-1) as the other two vertices of the rhombus ABCD. The equation of the other line BC is $x + y = -1$ [Since points (-1,0) and (0,-1) are the two points on BC]. Hence Option 1.

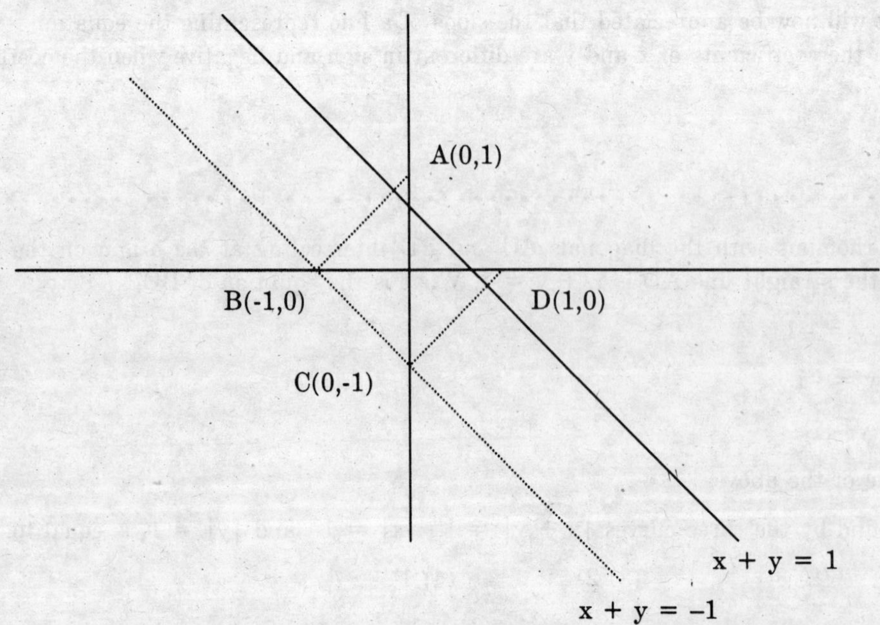

It must be remembered that a rhombus is a plane figure having four equal sides and equal opposite angles (two acute and two obtuse) and the diagonals of which bisect each other at right angles. Therefore in the given question, the crux lies in determining as to which of the lines whose equations have been given is parallel to the line x+y=1 and we find that the only parallel line is x + y = –1 at Option 1.

Answer 2

It would be worth plotting the curves quickly. Taking x as 0, x as 1 and 2 and x as –1 and –2, the image that emerges is set out herein.

Modulus(x + y) = 1; here one first presumes x+y=1 and then x + y = –1

Modulus(x) = 1; here one takes x=1 (which would be a line parallel to the y axis and pass through x=1) and then x = –1 (which would be a line parallel to the y axis and pass through x = –1)

Modulus(y) = 1; here one takes y=1(which would be a line parallel to the x axis and pass through y = 1)and then y = –1(which would be a line parallel to the x axis and pass through y = –1)

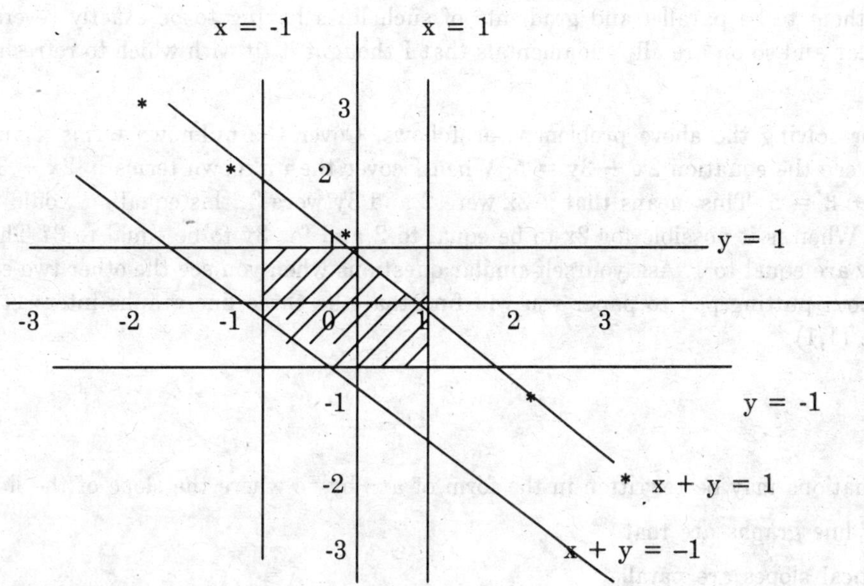

The area of the shaded portion is the area bounded by the three curves is 2 full squares and 2 half-squares and this would add up to 3 sq cms. Hence **Option 2.**

Answer 3

The equations of the three lines and their gradients (- coefficient of x/coefficient of y) are as follows:

	Gradient
Line 1: 2x + 3y – 5 = 0 or 2x + 3y = 5	–2/3
Line 2: 3x – 5y + 2 = 0 or 3x – 5y = –2	3/5
Line 3: –5x + 2y + 3 = 0 or –5x + 2y = –3	5/2

Two lines can be parallel only if they have identical gradients whereas none of these lines have identical gradients.

Two lines can be perpendicular only if the gradient of one is the exact negative of the other.

Thus Option 1: the lines are parallel and Option 3: have two perpendicular lines are eliminated.

Now the choice rests with Option 2: **form a triangle** and 4: **pass through a common point** have to be tested. **If they pass through a common point then the three lines cannot form a triangle** and if one were to test the aspect of passing through a common point, the solution would emerge straight away. It is fundamental to remember that the point of intersection of two lines obeys both equations.

If one were then to take equations of Line 1 and Line 2:

(i) $2x + 3y = 5$ and (ii) $3x - 5y = -2$ then multiplying both sides of equation(i) by 2 and both sides of equation (ii) by 5, one gets equations (iv) $4x + 6y = 10$ and (v) $15x - 25y = -10$. Adding equations (iv) and (v), one gets $19x - 19y = 0$ and hence $x = y$. Substituting the value of $x = y$ in equation (i) $2x + 3y = 5$, one gets equation (vi) $2x + 3x = 5$ and hence $5x = 5$ and hence $x = 1$ and since $y = x$, y is also $=1$, if the three lines were to intersect at the co-ordinates (1,1). If one were to substitute the values of both x and y as=1 in equations (i) $2x + 3y = 5$, (ii) $3x - 5y = -2$ and (iii) $-5x + 2y = -3$, one would find that in all three cases, the left hand side of the equations is equal to the right hand side. This leads to the conclusion that the three lines intersect at the co-ordinates (1,1) and hence **Option 4**.

Here we may add that all the above explanations in regard to gradients of straight line graphs having to be identical in order for them to be parallel and gradients of such lines having to be exactly reverse in sign in order to be perpendicular and so on are all fundamentals that I thought it fit with which to refresh the reader's memory.

The fastest method for solving the above problem is as follows. Cover the unknown terms x and y and ask yourself this when you see the equation $2x + 3y = 5$: When I cover the unknown terms in $2x + 3y = 5$, what do I see? I see that $2 + 3 = 5$. This means that if 2x were 2 and 3y were 3, this equation would not have any unknown terms at all. When is it possible for 2x to be equal to 2 and for 3y to be equal to 3? This is possible only when both x and y are equal to 1. Ask yourself similar questions when you see the other two equations and you will find that without putting pen to paper you will find that the three line graphs intersect at the point whose co-ordinates are (1,1).

Answer 4

The four pairs of equations may be rewritten in the form of $ax+by=c$ where the slope of the line is $-a/b$

The fundamentals of line graphs are that:

(A) lines of identical slopes are parallel

(B) if there are two lines with slopes such that the slope of one is the exact negative of the slope of the other, then the lines are perpendicular to each other and

(C) lines with unequal slopes invariably intersect.

Rewriting the given equations in the form of $ax+by=c$, we get:

1. $2x - 3y = -4$ and $10x - 15y = 7$; the slope of the two lines are respectively equal to 2/3 and 10/15 = 2/3. Hence the lines have identical slopes and they are parallel.

2. $25x + 20y = 8$ and $5x + 4y = -4$; the slope of the two lines are respectively equal to -25/20 = -5/4 and –5/4. Hence the lines have identical slopes and they are parallel.

3. $2x + y = 8$ and $2x + 1y = 1$; the slope of both the lines are –2. Hence the lines have identical slopes and they are parallel.

4. $-3x+y= 4$ and $3x + y = 2$; the slope of the two lines are respectively 3 and -3. Hence the lines have slopes such that the slope of one of the lines is exact negative of the slope of the other line and hence the two lines are not parallel.

   Thus **Option 3**: I,II and III.

Answer 5

The slope of a straight-line graph is defined as the ratio of the vertical and horizontal distances between two points on the line. The slope of the line is 3/4. This means that the vertical distance to the point P is 3 times some unknown quantity and the horizontal distance to the point P is 4 times the same unknown quantity. You would then have a right-angled triangle wherein the ratio of the sides other than the hypotenuse is 3/4 but the hypotenuse itself is 5 units. This is only possible if the two sides were 3 and 4 units respectively. In the present case therefore the horizontal distance as represented by the co-ordinates of P is 4 and the vertical distance to be covered in order to reach P is 3. This means that if you wish to reach the point P, travel 4 units away from the origin along the x axis of the point, thus reaching point say C and then climb 3 units horizontally from C and you would reach point P as in the following diagram.

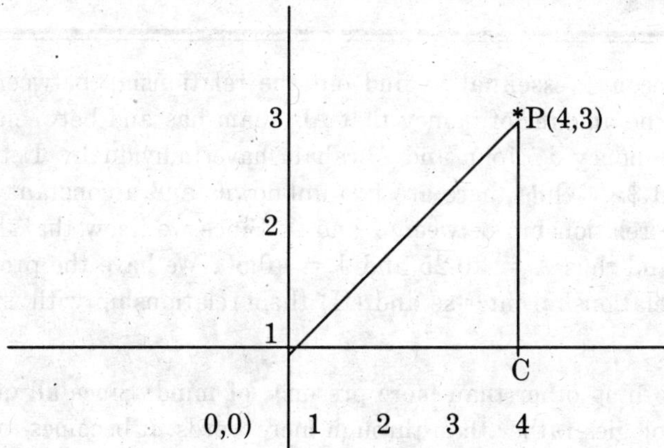

Thus Option 4.

Chapter 22

Linear Equations (and how to form them) and Simultaneous Equations (and how to solve them)

When dealing with unknown quantities, it becomes essential to find out the relationship between such unknown terms. For example, imagine John has twice the amount of money that Abraham has and between them they have $60.75. You are asked to find out how much money do John and Abraham have individually. Let us assume that John and Abraham have, respectively, $J and $A. While there are two unknowns and a constant term, effectively there is only one unknown since we know the relationship between J and A. Since we know that $J = 2A$ and that $J + A = 60.75$, we know that $3A = 60.75$ and thus $A = 20.25$ and $J = 40.50$. We have the precise value of the unknown terms J and A based on (I) their relationship inter-se and (II) their relationship with the constant term (here the constant term is 60.75).

Equation formation is simple and calls for nothing other than mere presence of mind. Since all quantitative skills can be sharpened through illustrative methodologies rather than through mere words, it becomes imperative to skip preambles and leap on to the illustrations bandwagon. So here we go!

Imagine that between A, B and C there are 31 mangoes and A has 3/2 times as many as B and C has $3/5^{th}$ the number of mangoes that B has. You are now asked to find out how many does A have. How do you go about this?

If A has 3/2 times as many as B, and C has $3/5^{th}$ the number of mangoes that B has, the number of mangoes that B has is divisible by both 2 and 5 and therefore if we were to assume that the number of mangoes with A, B and C is a, b and c respectively, we know that b is definitely divisible by 10. The first such number divisible by 10 is 10 itself. Let b be 10. So $a = 15$ and $c = 6$. Do the three unknowns a, b and c add up to 31? Yes, they do. (If they did not we would have to try our luck with 20 which is the next higher multiple of 10). We have solved this harmless looking question through logic alone. At other times we may have to rely on our skills at forming equations. Let us see illustrations of such nature. We shall see problems of a rising level of difficulty. You will see methodologies that will make learning a matter of sheer joy.

Problem 1

Diana is at the banks of a magic stream. She has a basket in which there are some apples. Each time she dips the apples that she has in the stream, the number of apples doubles. She dips the basket for the first time and gives a certain number of apples to Ronald. Then she dips the basket again in the stream. She then gives to Donald the same number of apples that she gave to Ronald. She dips the basket again and gives a like number of apples to Sam and finally she dips the basket and gives the same number of apples to Tim as she gave to the other three boys. She then finds that the basket is empty. What is the minimum number of apples that she could have started with?

Answer 1

Since we do not know how many apples did she have, or how many did she give to each of the four boys (although we know that she gave the same number to each of them), we have no choice but to assume that she started with S number of apples and gave G number of apples to each of the four (Trial and error will get us nowhere).

This means that when she first dipped the apples in the stream, the number doubled to 2S. From this she gave G to the 1st boy. She then had (2S – G) left.

She dipped (2S – G) apples and this doubled to (4S – 2G). From this she gave G number of apples to the 2nd boy. She now had (4S – 3G) apples.

When she dipped the apples for the third time, she had (8S – 6G) apples. From this she gave G to the 3rd boy. She then had (8S – 7G) number of apples left.

When she dipped for the 4th time, the (8S – 7G) apples doubled to (16S – 14G). From this she gave G apples to the 4th lad. Now she reckoned that she had (16S – 15G) number of apples in the basket but in fact there weren't any. This means that (16S – 15G) = 0 and hence 16S= 15G and hence S/G = 15/16. This means that for every 15 apples that she started out with, she gave 16 apples to each of the four boys. The fact that she gave an integral number of apples to each of the lads means that the smallest possible integral value of G is 16. This then also means that the smallest possible integral value of S is 15. So the least number of apples that Diana could have **started with** is **15 apples** and **gave 16 to each** of the boys. To cross check this, if she started with 15 apples, they doubled to 30 on dipping. She gave 16 to the first boy and had 14 left. These doubled to 28 on the second dip and she gave 16 to the second boy and had 12 left which doubled to 24 on the third dip. Out of 24 she gave 16 to the third fellow and had 8 left which doubled to 16 on the fourth dip and she gave all 16 to the fourth boy.

If you have noticed, we have assigned the letter S to the number of apples that the girl **started** with and G to the number of apples that she **gave** to the boys. Someone would ask: why not X and Y? The reason for choosing S and G is obvious. If we find the value of S, we do not have to scratch our head and relate X back to what we had assumed it would stand for: whether X stood for apples that she started with or whether it stands for those that she gave. Time constraints sometime may cost you dear. It may so happen that you have correctly found the value of X but yet mark the wrong answer confusing X with the number of apples that she **gave** to each boy.

Problem 2

In an examination there were 50 questions. Each correct answer carried one mark, each wrong answer carried a negative 1/3rd mark and each question that was not attempted carried negative 1/6th mark. If Michael's net score at the examination was 32, what are his possible numbers of correct answers?

Answer 2

One must assume the number of correct answers as C, wrong answers as W and those unanswered as U. Since the examination had 50 questions in all, anyone writing the examination can afford to do only three things: (I) Answer correctly (II) Answer wrongly (III) Leave the question unanswered. This means that the sum of C, W and U is 50. The first linear equation – which we shall call Equation 1 - is as follows: $C + W + U = 50$.

So far, the net score would be [1 mark for each of C] – [1/3 × W] - [1/6 × U] and hence Equation 2 is: $C - (W/3) - (U/6) = 32$.

If we were to subtract Equation 2 from Equation 1 we would have Equation 3 as follows: $(4W/3) + (7U/6) = 18$. In order that we have integers on both sides of Equation 3 we may multiply both sides with 6 so that we may rewrite Equation 3 as follows: $8W + 7U = 108$.

This is where the methodology of equations will have to stop and logic will have to take over. This is because if you have two unknowns and know what they add up to without knowing their relationship inter-se there can be any number of values to the unknowns. For example, if you are told that two unknown numbers X and Y add up to 14, then there could be millions of values of X and Y if there is no bar to their being both fractional and negative as we shall see from the following table that will attempt to give a few of the possible values of these unknowns X and Y:

If X=	And Y=	Then X+Y=
0.5	13.5	14
-13	27	14
-1000	1014	14
1	13	14
1000	-986	14

But the moment you are told that X= 2.5Y, the equation X+Y = 14 then becomes 2.5Y + Y = 14 or 3.5Y = 14 and hence Y = 4 and X = 10. The moment you know the relationship between X and Y inter-se (meaning, X = 2.5Y) then there can be only **unique** values of X and Y that satisfy the equation X+Y = 14

In the rewritten version of Equation 3 we have arrived at integral values on both sides for two clear reasons:

(1) It is convenient to work with integers than with fractions

(2) The numbers of questions at examinations are in integers and hence working with fractions makes no sense

Equation 3 is 8W + 7U = 108. Knowing that both W and U are necessarily integral values, the very first possible value of W with which we could start off is W = 1. This means that 8 + 7U = 108 and thus 7U = 100 and therefore U will not be integral since 100 is not divisible by 7. We are to try our luck with W = 2 where we will find that 7U = 92 and therefore U will not be integral either. Moving on to W = 3, we find that 7U = 84 and therefore U = 12. This will do.

The question now is whether any higher value for W is feasible. See the equation 8W + 7U = 108. Since W and U are both integral, for every increase of 1 in W, 8W increases by 8 and hence 7U should decrease by 8 in order to maintain the total of 8W and 7U at 108. Thus when W increases by 1, U decreases by 8/7. The message is clear: When W increases by a certain integer U decreases by an amount that is 8/7 times that integer. The decrease in U can be integral (and exactly equal to 8 times the integer) only if W increases by 7 and its multiples. Therefore the next higher value of W that we shall look for is 7 more than 3 (which is the meaning of the words *if W increases by 7*) since at W=3 we found integral value for U. When W = 10, 7U = 28 and hence U = 4. The need for further toiling is eliminated mercifully because of the fact that the next higher value for W would be 17 at which level 8W would cross 108 and one would have negative values for U, which is absurd.

Problem 3

Pizzas are $5 apiece; hamburgers are $12 to the dozen and fries are 20 to the dollar. You are required to spend exactly $100 and you are to buy exactly one hundred items with the condition that you must buy at least one of each kind. How many of each type will you buy?

Answer 3

This is simple once you build the method. What are you asked to find? The number of each of the eatables! But before we proceed, let us remember that there are 100 cents to the dollar.

We shall now proceed to form equations. This is because the other choice is to go by guesswork or trial and error and so on all of which may take so much time and yet there is no guarantee whatsoever that any unscientific method will succeed.

Let us assume that you have purchased P number of pizzas, H number of hamburgers and F number of fries. Since there are 100 items in all, we get Equation 1 as follows: P + H + F = 100.

If one pizza costs $5, then two cost 2 times $5 and P number of pizzas will cost P times $5. Since pizzas cost $5 per piece, hamburgers cost $1 apiece and fries cost 5 cents per piece, then if one were to buy P number of pizzas, H number of hamburgers and F number of fries, the total cost would be $100 and thus we get Equation 2 as follows: 5P + H + 0.05F =100.

You have two equations: (I) P + H + F = 100 and (II) 5P + H + 0.05F = 100. Subtract equation (I) from equation (II) and you have 4P – 0.95F = 0 or 4P= 0.95F or 4P = 95F/100 or 4P = 19F/20 and thus P/F = 19/80. Since the number of items of each type has got to be integral, and all numbers of items are less than 100, this means that the first such instance when P and F can be integral is when P = 19 and F = 80. H then becomes 1.

This means that you can buy 19 pizzas, 1 hamburger and 80 fries.

Problem 4

A young man counts the money in his pocket and tells his father how many dollars and cents he has. His father then gives him a matching amount. The young man now finds that he has (A) twice the number of cents as he had dollars before and (B) as many dollars as he had cents before. How much did his father give him?

Answer 4

When an amount of money comprising some dollars and some cents doubles it is not necessary that the number of dollars doubles and so also the number of cents doubles. Imagine that you have $3 and 55c. If this doubles, you have $7 and 10c. Is $7 the double of $3? Is 10c the double of 55c? The answer in both cases is: no. However there were 355 cents earlier and 710 cents after the money has doubled. 710 cents is the exact double of 355 cents.

That is why if the young fellow had $D and cents C at the beginning, he had effectively (100D+ C) cents. When this doubled he had (200D+ 2C) cents. However, he found that he has twice the number of cents as he had dollars before and as many dollars as he had cents before. This means that now he has $C and 2D cents which if converted to cents comes to (100C + 2D) and this is equal to (200D + 2C) cents.

So (100C + 2D) = (200D + 2C) and thus 98C = 198D and thus D/C = 98/198 or 49/99. The number of $s and cents have got to be integral and that the number of cents cannot exceed 100. This means that the first (and the only) such instance when D and C can be integral is when D = 49 and C = 99. So the young man started out with $49 and cents 99. His father gave him $ 49.99. He now has $99 and 98 cents.

Problem 5

A foreigner studying the weather of Panama City for D number of days observed that:

A. It rained on 7 days, morning or evening.

B. When it rained in the afternoon it was clear in the morning.

C. There were 5 clear afternoons

D. There were 6 clear mornings.

What is the value of D?

Answer 5

A day consists of two principal parts: pre-noon (meaning from 0000 hours midnight to 1200 hours noon) and afternoon (meaning, after 1200 noon till midnight). Anytime after 1200 noon is after noon.

If the foreigner had stayed three days and found that there were two rainy afternoons, it means that there was only one (which is equal to three minus two) clear afternoon.

Similarly if he stayed D number of days and found that there were five clear mornings, it means that there were (D-5)` rainy afternoons. If he found that there were 6 clear mornings there were (D – 6) rainy mornings. If it rains in the morning and is clear in the afternoon even then the day can be called a rainy day. In the converse if it rains in the afternoon and is clear in the morning, even then the day is a rainy day. The total number of rainy days is the total of rainy mornings and rainy afternoons. This means that (D – 5)+ (D – 6) =7 (since we have 7 rainy days in total) and hence 2D – 11 = 7 or 2D = 18 and so D = 9.

Problem 6

At his usual rowing rate, Ricky can travel 12 miles downstream in a certain river in six hours less than it takes him to travel the same distance upstream. But if he could double his usual rowing rate for this 24 mile round trip, the downstream 12 miles would then take only one hour less than the upstream 12 miles. What is the speed of the current in miles per hour?

Answer 6

Let Ricky's rowing speed be R miles/hour and that of the current be C miles/hour. When he goes **with the current** (which means downstream) **his effective speed is the total of his speed and that of the current**. In the converse, when he goes **against the current** (which means upstream) his **effective speed is the difference between his speed and that of the current**. It must be remembered that only if his speed is greater than that of the current, he can hope to travel anywhere in a direction opposite to the current. If his speed equals that of the current then what may happen is that he would be at the same spot so long his arms can keep up a speed equal to that of the current. If his speed is less than that of the current, he will go with the flow of the stream.

The journey downstream is 12 miles and his speed is (R + C) miles per hour. Since speed = distance /time, in the converse, time= distance/ speed. When going downstream, the journey will take 12/(R + C) hours. When going upstream, the time taken is 12/(R-C) hours. Since the downstream journey takes six hours less than the upstream journey this means that :

$$\frac{12}{(R-C)} - \frac{12}{(R+C)} = 6.$$

When you are subtracting one fraction from another you would need to find the LCM of the denominators so that the fractions could be meaningfully expressed - and thereafter added or subtracted as the case may be – with reference to a common denominator. For example, when subtracting 1/21 from 1/7, it would be clear that since 21 is the LCM of the denominators 7 and 21, 1/7 is nothing other than 3/21 and hence 1/7 – 1/21 is nothing other than 3/21 – 1/21 which means 2/21. This is if you are dealing with known quantities. If you are dealing with unknown quantities such as (R - C) and (R + C), how can you find LCM? It is therefore practical to simply multiply the two denominators and proceed as follows:

$$\frac{12}{(R-C)} \quad \frac{-12}{(R+C)} = \frac{12(R+C) - 12(R-C)}{(R-C) \times (R+C)} = \frac{12R+12C - 12R + 12C}{(R^2 - C^2)} = \frac{24C}{(R^2 - C^2)} = 6$$

Therefore we get Equation 1: $(R^2 - C^2) = 4C$.

If R is doubled then 12/(2R – C) – 12/(2R + C) = 1. Therefore we get Equation 2: $(4R^2 - C^2) = 24C$. We have two equations where we have R and C in their squares to the left of the equations and C to the right, This means that if we were to eliminate R in its square, we would be able to strike a relationship with C in its square to the left of the equation and C to the right. This would give us the precise value of C, which is what we want.

About the method of eliminating R in its square from these two simultaneous equations, here it is: Multiply Equation 1 by 4 on both sides and we would get $4(R^2 - C^2) = 16C$ or $4R^2 - 4C^2 = 16C$. If we were to subtract Equation 1 from Equation 2 we would get $3C^2 = 8C$ and thus C = 8/3. So the speed of the current is 8/3 miles per hour.

The equation in this problem looked poised for being a quadratic equation with (R + C) as one of the denominators and (R - C) as the other **but has turned out to be a linear equation because** of the fact that both the equations having (R +C) and (R - C) as denominators had **the same numerator** (the numerator in both cases was the number 12).

Problem 7

A rich businessman's wife asked him how many gold bars did he have. He said that if he were to divide the gold bars into two unequal numbers, then 483 times the difference between the two numbers equals the difference between the squares of the two numbers. How many gold bars did the businessman have?

Answer 7

It must be understood that it is possible for the businessman to divide the number of gold bars into two parts in the following two ways only: (I) Two equal parts (II) Two unequal parts. Had he divided the number of gold bars into two equal parts then the difference between the two parts would have been zero. The total number of gold bars could have been any of the millions of even numbers that Man has devised because only if the number of bars was even then he could hope to divide them into two **equal** parts and yet have an integral number of bar in each of the two equal parts. Since he wanted to divide the gold bars into two unequal halves only then could the difference between the squares of the two unequal parts have been other than zero. Secondly whatever be the number of bars in the two unequal parts, the number of bars in Part 1 + the number of bars in Part 2 = total number of gold bars that he had.

Let us assume that he divided the gold bars into two unequal parts in which one part had X number of bars and the other had Y number of bars. The difference between the squares of these is $(X^2 - Y^2)$. If $(X^2 - Y^2)$ is 483 times the difference between the two unequal parts then $(X^2 - Y^2) = 483\ (X - Y)$. As you know $(X^2 - Y^2)$ is nothing other than $(X - Y) \times (X + Y)$ and therefore $(X - Y) \times (X + Y) = 483\ (X - Y)$ and hence $X + Y = 483$. This means that he had 483 gold bars.

We have seen illustrations in this chapter where some equations involving one unknown and others involving two unknowns are formed and solved. What is presented herein is the methodology of accurately forming equations. The problems are those that might seem insurmountable to someone who is not well versed with equation formation and solving. We are sure that assimilation of the methodology would enable the reader to not only surmount even tougher questions but enjoy solving them.

Chapter 23

Logarithms

Man has all along been looking for ways to make life easier. When he multiplied some numbers with some other numbers, he developed a headache. When he divided some long number with another he had to be woken up from slumber to which he succumbed due to boredom. He then found that adding is always easier by far than multiplying and that subtracting is a good deal easier than dividing. But how can one add when one has to multiply? This question vexed him. He pondered. He twirled his moustache. He fingered his beard. He then hit upon logarithms.

Before we begin this introduction to logarithms, we must dispel all your fears about this topic insofar as the competitive examination is concerned. Listen, no one expects you to work with logarithms, because if they did they would give you logarithm tables or ask you to bring them from home. All you are allowed to carry is a couple of pencils and an eraser. Period!

None can work out the logarithm of any number except 1 and 10 and other powers of 10 in their heads. What the examiner at any competitive examination for admission to management programmes or post-graduate courses wants to find out is whether you have grasped the fundamentals about the topics that you studied while at school of which logarithms is one. All that is required is an awareness of the concepts of logarithms such as the logarithms of fractions are necessarily negative if the base of the logarithm is an integer and that if the logarithms of two numbers are to be added, the resultant logarithm is the logarithm of the product of these two numbers and so on. All very elementary aspects of logarithms!

One must also know that there can be a logarithm for only positive terms and not for negative terms. After all the logarithms are a device for simplifying multiplication and division. The logarithms work only with positive signs. As to what will be the ultimate sign in the multiplication or division, you will have to decide. The square root of a number can be both positive and negative. The square root of 36, for example, is either +6 or –6. Whether you wish to use the positive square root or the negative square root, you will have to decide. If you are calculating the number of persons who will turn up at your party (where you have noticed that the number of persons who actually turn up is very nearly the square root of the number of invitations sent) and are making use of square roots, you may have to rely necessarily on positive square roots. There cannot be negative number of people attending parties. In other cases you may even have to experiment with negative square roots. What you want to do is your business. It is not the business of logarithms. They will simplify things for you. They will not spoon-feed you.

But let us see how logarithms have been evolved. How can addition work in place of multiplication and how can subtraction work in place of division at all? In order to understand the underlying principle in logarithms we must know the following:

- When you multiply 2^3 with 2^5, why do you get 2^8? It is because 2^3 is nothing other than $2 \times 2 \times 2$ and 2^5 is nothing other than $2 \times 2 \times 2 \times 2 \times 2$ and therefore $2^3 \times 2^5$ is $2 \times 2 \times 2 \times 2 \times 2 \times 2 \times 2 \times 2 =$ 2 multiplied by itself eight times which is written as 2^8. Therefore $2^3 \times 2^5 = 2^{(3+5)} = 2^8$. The short point is that when you multiply the different powers of the same number (here that number is 2 and the different powers of 2 are 2^3 and 2^5) then you can short circuit the process of multiplication by merely adding the powers of the number.
- When you divide 2^8 with 2^5, why do you get 2^3? It is because the numerator is $(2 \times 2 \times 2 \times 2 \times 2 \times 2 \times 2 \times 2)$ and the denominator is $(2 \times 2 \times 2 \times 2 \times 2)$ and you are left with $2 \times 2 \times 2$, which is 2^3. Again, the short point is that when you divide the different powers of the same number (here that number is 2

and the different powers of 2 are 2^8 and 2^5) then you can short circuit the process of division by merely subtracting the powers of the number in the denominator from the power of the number in the numerator.

There are some who would take an hour to think about if you were to ask them what the square root of 4 is, in the first place. There are others who would be able to tell you that the square root of 17 to the fifth place of decimal (since 17 is not a perfect square, its square root, if calculated in detail, can a trip around the equator but one has to stop somewhere and that is why the fifth place of decimals might seem fair enough to some).

People of the latter variety found that if you were to raise 10 to the power of 0.3010 (written as $10^{0.3010}$) you would get perilously close to 2. They then found that if you were to divide 10 by 2 you would get 5 but what you would be doing effectively is dividing 10^1 with $10^{0.3010}$ and thus what one would get is $10^{(1-0.3010)} = 10^{0.6990}$. Therefore $10^{0.6990}$ is 5. Now 5^2 is 25 and since 5 is $10^{0.6990}$, 25 is $(10^{0.6990})^2$, which is $10^{(0.6990+0.6990)}$ which is $10^{1.3980}$. These mathematically oriented people then wrote down what power does 10 have to be raised in order to get a whole lot of numbers and then up to decimal points and this tabular representation is what is known as Logarithm Tables in which you will see 0.3010 against 2 and 0.6990 against 5 which means that 10 has to be raised to 0.3010 in order to get 2 and so on. Here the number 10 is known as the base number – meaning the reference number that has to be raised to 0.3010 in order to get 2 and so on.

When you say for example that 10 has to be raised to 0.3010 in order to get 2, what you are saying is that the logarithm of 2 to the base 10 is 0.3010. Thus the logarithm of 10 to the base 10 is 1 and the logarithm of 100 to the base 10 is 2 and so on. Then there is an Antilogarithm Table in which the reverse process takes place. Imagine that you have added the logarithm of 50 (which is 1.6990) and the logarithm of 2 (which is 0.3010) and have come to 2.0000 as the result of this addition. You want to know what will I get when I raise 10 to the power of 2.0000. You see the Antilogarithm Tables and find that the antilogarithm of 2.0000 is 100 meaning that when you raise 10 to the power of 2.0000, you get 100.

To summarise therefore, the logarithm of a number is always stated with respect to a base number of the logarithm. For the purposes of standardisation, the number 10 has been assumed as the base of logarithms while devising the Logarithm Tables. The logarithm of a number (say N) to the base 10 is therefore the power to which 10 has to be raised so as to get N. The antilogarithm of a number (A) is what you would get by raising 10 to the power of A. It is for this reason that the antilogarithm of 1.3980 is 25 since $10^{1.3980} = 25$, as seen in the previous paragraph.

If you wish to multiply for example 1234.8789 with 344.9872, all you have to do is to find the logarithms of 1234.8789 and 344.9872 from logarithm tables and add these two logarithms and whatever total you get, write it down, turn to the Antilogarithm Tables, find the antilogarithm and there you are. You have the product of 1234.8789 and 344.9872 in a flash.

There is, however, no bar in assuming another number as the base of logarithms. Let us see how things would work out with the number 2 as the base number of the logarithm. 4 is 2^2 and 16 is 2^4, and in both cases the base number 2 is raised to certain powers.

The power to which 2 is raised is called the logarithm of the resultant number with reference to the base number 2. Thus the logarithm of 4 to the base 2 is 2 and the logarithm of 16 to the base 2 is 4.

Now just as the logarithm of 64 to the base number 2 is 6 (because you have to raise 2 which is the base number to the power of 6 in order to get 64), so the antilogarithm of 6 (meaning the result of raising the base number 2 to the power of 6) is 64. In order to understand this vital aspect of logarithms, please see the table given hereunder that should drive home the concept once and for all.

The Logarithm of the number	To the Base	Is	Because	And the Logarithm of the number is written as
100	10	2	10^2 is 100	Log_{10} 100
1000	10	3	10^3 is 1000	Log_{10} 1000
4	2	2	2^2 is 4	Log_2 4
32	2	5	2^5 is 32	Log_2 32
27	3	3	3^3 is 27	Log_3 27
49	7	2	7^2 is 49	Log_7 49
0.1	10	-1	10^{-1} is 1/10 or 0.1	Log_{10} 0.1
0.01	10	-2	10^{-2} is 1/100 or 0.01	Log_{10} 0.01
1/4	2	-2	2^{-2} is $1/2^2$ or 1/4	Log_2 1/4
1/49	7	-2	7^{-2} is $1/7^2$ or 1/49	Log_7 1/49

Thus, the logarithm of any number X is the power to which the base number is raised so as to arrive at X.

And thus:

The antilogarithm of the Number	To the Base	Is	Because
2	7	49	7^2 is 49
2	10	100	10^2 is 100
4	3	81	3^4 is 81
5	2	32	2^5 is 32
2	8	64	8^2 is 64
-3	2	1/8	2^{-3} is 1/8
-3	3	1/27	3^{-3} is 1/27

The antilogarithm of any number Y is the result of raising the base number to Y.

It is important to remember that **in the process of carrying out of any one set of calculations through the means of logarithms, the base number is to be kept same.**

Otherwise what may happen is that if one takes the logarithm of 100 to the base 10 as 2 and the logarithm of 16 to the base 2 as 4 and then multiply 100 with 16, the result may be 6 and if the base number is 10 then the antilogarithm of 6 is 1000000 and if the base of the logarithm is 2 then the antilogarithm of 6 is 64. So with assuming two different basis of logarithm in one set of calculations, I may get the product of 100 and 16 as either 1000000 or 64, none of which is correct.

Either you choose the base number as 10 in both cases or you choose 2 as the base number in both cases; but you cannot mix the two.

The base number of logarithms in any calculations made with logarithms has to be kept constant because the powers of only a constant number are respectively added and subtracted in the process of multiplication and division. Only $x^a \times x^b$ will give you $x^{(a+b)}$. But $x^a \times y^b$ will not give you $x^{(a+b)}$.

Logarithms are now used for a variety of purposes in pure and applied mathematics.

If one were to see a logarithm (**log** as it is generally known) table and against the number 2 if the logarithm is 0.3010, then it means that if 10 is raised to the power of 0.3010, the result is 2. This would also mean that if I did not refer further to the log table and wanted to find out as what is the logarithm of 4 is, all I have to do is to multiply 0.3010 with 2 and thus I know that the $\log_{10} 4$ is 0.6020 and $\log_{10} 8$ is 0.9030. This is because:

$\log_{10} 4$ is $\log_{10}(2 \times 2)$ and this means $10^{0.3010} \times 10^{0.3010}$ and this would give me $10^{(0.3010+0.3010)} = 10^{0.6020}$; since I am multiplying two powers of the base number 10, I am able to arrive at the product through only adding the two powers. So it is in the case of $\log_{10} 8$ where I would be effectively multiplying $2 \times 2 \times 2$ and thus effectively $10^{0.3010} \times 10^{0.3010} \times 10^{0.3010}$ and the result would be $10^{0.9030}$.

What if I were to find the log of 20? Now 20 is 10×2. The logarithms of 10 and 2 to the base 10 are 1 and 0.3010 respectively. Thus 10×2 is $10^1 \times 10^{0.3010}$. Since I am multiplying two different powers to which the base number 10 has been raised, I can find the product through adding the two powers. So 20 is $10^{1.3010}$. The logarithm of 20 is thus 1.3010 and similarly the logarithm of 200 would be 2.3010 and the logarithm of 2000 is 3.3010.

The logarithm tables will contain only the logarithm of 2 and not 20. The standard log table – that is based on the number 10 as the base of the logarithms it contains - will give the log of 2 as 0.3010. If I have to find the logarithm of 200 I have to add 2 to 0.3010 and find that the log of 200 is 2.3010. This is because 200 is 100×2 and thus $10^2 \times 2$. Therefore the logarithm of 200 is logarithm of $(10^2 \times 2)$ or $\log 10^2 + \log 2 = 2 + 0.3010 = 2.3010$.

Thus if a log table with 10 as the base of the logarithms that it tabulates contained only the logs of 2 and 5 as respectively 0.3010 and 0.6990, then:

The logarithm of	To base 10 is
20	1.3010
200	2.3010
50	1.6990
500	2.6990

There are two terms associated with logarithms – **characteristic** and **mantissa**. They are nothing much. They are names given to certain aspects of logarithms for the very reason that when you wish to refer to something, you need to have a name that you can use when making the reference. They could as well have been Jack and Jill but for reasons of practicability.

The logarithm of 500 to the base 10, which is given as 2.6990, is the aggregate of two terms: 2 and 0.6990. 2 is known as the **characteristic** or the integral number to which 10 is already raised in the number for which you are searching for a logarithm and 0.6990 is the **mantissa** or the fractional number to which 10 has to be raised so as to get you 5.

The characteristic in logarithm to base 10 is the same as the power to which 10 is raised in the number for which you want to know the logarithm. So far we have seen as to what is the characteristic for the numbers 20 and 200 and 50 and so on.

20 has 1 zero at the end and its characteristic is 1 and 500 has two zeroes at the end and its characteristic is 2. What will be the characteristic for the logarithm to the base 10 of say 2500? Now the log table will give you the logarithm of only 2.5 and this is say 0.3982. But 2500 is nothing other than 1000×2.5 which $10^3 \times 10^{0.3982} = 10^{3.3982}$. So the logarithm of 2500 will have the characteristic of 3 and a mantissa of 0.3982 and will be written as 3.3982. This means that if I am to find out the log to the base 10 of a number with N digits in the integral number, the characteristic will be equal to N-1. **The characteristic is the implied power of 10 in the logarithm to the base 10** and:

In the number	The number of digits N =	Which is effectively	The implied power of 10 is	And the charcteristics in the logarithm of N to the base 10 is	The mantissa will be the logarithm of
253	3	$10^2 \times 2.53$	2	2	2.53
25.3	2	$10^1 \times 2.53$	1	1	2.53
2.53	1	$10^0 \times 2.53$	0	0	2.53
0.253	0	$10^{-1} \times 2.53$	-1	-1	2.53
0.0253	-1	$10^{-2} \times 2.53$	-2	-2	2.53
253.253	3	$10^2 \times 2.53253$	2	2	2.53253

An important thing to remember is that unless the base of the logarithm is specified, it is to be presumed that the base of the logarithm is 10, which is the standard.

Having grasped the fundamentals of logarithms, let us move on to some problems that will ensure assimilation of the concepts that we have been feasting upon.

Problem 1

If the $\log_{10} 2$ is 0.3010 then how do I find out the logarithm of 1.25 without reference to the log table?

The Detailed Solution

1.25 is 125/100 or 5/4 or also 10/8. I know that the log of 10 is 1. I also know that 8 is 2^3 and hence the log of 8 is $3 \times \log_{10} 2$. So the log of 1.25 is effectively $\log_{10} 10/8$ or $\log_{10} 10 - 3 \times \log_{10} 2$. We know that $3 \times \log_{10} 2 = 3 \times 0.3010 = 0.9030$ and thus 1- 0.9030 or 0.0970.

In the alternative, since 1.25 is 5/4, log 1.25 is log (5/4) which is log 5 – log 4 or log(10/2) – log 4 or log 10- log 2 – 2log 2 or log10 – 3log 2= 1 – 0.9030 = 0.0970.

Problem 2

If I know that $\log_4 2$ is 1/2, then how do I find $\log_4 1/4$?

The Detailed Solution

The fraction 1/4 is essentially 4^{-1}. Therefore $\log_4 (1/4)$ is –1 because the base number of the logarithm is 4 and 4 has to be raised to the power of –1 in order to arrive at the number ¼ of which I am trying to find the logarithm to the base 4. The power to which the base of the logarithm has to be raised in order to arrive at the number, of which I am trying to find the logarithm, is the logarithm that I am looking for.

Problem 3

If $\log_Y X$ is 2, then I know that X is Y^2. If I am given that $\log_Y X$ is A and $\log_Y Z$ is 2A, what is the relation between X and Z?

The Detailed Solution

Since $\log_Y X$ is A, $X = Y^A$. Since $\log_Y Z$ is 2A, $Z = Y^{2A}$.

That means Z is $(Y^A)^2$, whereas $X = Y^A$. So Z is X^2. To put this in simpler terms, if $\log_4 16$ is =2 and $\log_4 256$ is = 4, then $256 = 16^2$.

Problem 4

If three terms A, B and C are in Arithmetic Progression, are the terms log A, log B and log C in arithmetic or geometric progression?

The Detailed Solution

Let us assume that the logarithms of A, B and C are respectively 1, 2 and 3 since these are in AP with a constant difference of 1. In which case, since log A =1 and log B = 2 and log C = 3 and presuming that the base of the logarithm is 10, A = 10^1, B = 10^2, and C = 10^3. So A, B and C are respectively, 10, 100 and 1000. These three terms are such that any term multiplied by 10 will give the next term in the series. And hence A, B and C are in geometric progression.

Take any other base of logarithms in the above illustration and you will find the same answer. If we were to take $\log_4 A = 1$, $\log_4 B = 2$ and $\log_4 C = 3$, it would means that A, B and C are respectively 4, 16 and 64. The fact that 4, 16 and 64 are in Geometric Progression is no nuclear secret. The acid test of a geometric progression is like this: in a Geometric Progression, any term divided by its immediately preceding term gives the same result all through the progression.

Problem 5

What is the value of $\log_{10} 0.001$?

The Detailed Solution

We know that 0.001 is 1/1000 or also 10^{-3}. So $\log_{10} 0.001$ is, effectively, $\log_{10} 10^{-3}$. The log of any number N is the power to which the base of the logarithm has to be raised to arrive at N. Here N is 10^{-3}. The base of the logarithm is 10. This means that 10 has to be raised to the power of –3 in order to arrive at 10^{-3} or 0.001. So $\log_{10} 0.001 = -3$.

Problem 6

What is the logarithm of 1728 to the base $2\sqrt{3}$?

The Detailed Solution

$2\sqrt{3}$ is $\sqrt{12}$ or $12^{1/2}$. 1728 is 12^3. We know that 12^3 is, as such, $12^{(6\times 1/2)}$. Therefore if $2\sqrt{3}$ is A, then 1728 is A^6. Therefore effectively $\log_{2\sqrt{3}} 1728$ is the same thing as $\log_A A^6$, which is 6.

Please note that when a number N is raised to a certain power X to give another number M and then M is then raised to another power Y, then M = $(N)^{X\times Y}$. See this in simpler terms. If 2 were raised to the power of 3 we get 8. If 8 were raised to the power of 2 we get 64. Now 64 which we know is 2^6, is 8^2 or $2^{3\times 2}$. Here N = 2, X = 3, Y = 2 and M = 64 and thus M = $(N)^{X\times Y}$.

Problem 7

If $\log_{10} 2 = 0.3010$, then $\log_{10} 0.002 = ?$

The Detailed Solution

We know that 0.002= 2/1000 or 2 × $(10)^{-3}$. Thus $\log_{10} 0.002$ is effectively $\log_{10} [2 \times (10)^{-3}]$. This is therefore $\log_{10} 2 + \log_{10} (10)^{-3}$ and is thus = 0.3010 + (-3)which is – 2.6990.

Thus, $\log_{10} 0.002 = -2.6990$.

It is not normal to represent this logarithm as – 2.6990 but as –3 + 0.3010 where the characteristic of the logarithm is –3, implying that 10 is raised to –3 in the number whose logarithm is being found out and 0.3010 is the mantissa.

In such instances, the characteristic - when it is negative - is represented by a bar sign on it and thus in this case the characteristic is "Bar 3" and the mantissa is 0.3010 but the logarithm (here – 2.6990) is really the sum of the characteristic and the mantissa like in the case of integral numbers that we have seen before.

In the above case, where the characteristic is negative, $\log_{10} 0.002$ is written as $\bar{3}.3010$. The bar-sign on 3 indicates that 3 is negative.

EXERCISE

1. Given that the $\log_{10} 3$ is 0.48, and $\log_{10} 2$ as 0.30, what is the value of $\log_{10} \sqrt{337.50}$?
2. The logarithm of a fraction of value less than 1 is: (A) invariably a fraction (B) invariably a whole number(C) invariably negative (D) Cannot say unless base of logarithm is specified
3. All the following expressions are meaningful except: (A) $\sqrt{\log 0.1}$ (B) $\log \sqrt{0.1}$ (C) $\log \cos 0^0$ (D) $\log_{\sqrt{5}} 5$
4. If $\log[(a + b)/ 5] = ½(\log a + \log b)$, then $a^2 + b^2$ in terms of ab is (A) 16 ab (B) 18 ab

   (C) 20 ab (D) 23 ab (E) 25 ab
5. Given that the logarithm of 5 to the base 10 is 0.6990, what is the logarithm of 0.0005? (A) –3.6990 (B) –4.6990 (C) –4. 3010 (D) –3.3010

ANSWER KEY

1. 1.38
2. Option (D)
3. Option (A)
4. 23ab
5. -3.3010

SOLUTIONS

1. The square root of 337.5 = square root of 675/2 = square root of 5 × 5 × 3 × 3 × 3 ÷ 2. Remember, the digits of 675 add up to 18 and thus it is patently divisible by 9. This should help factorising 675. We have been given the log of 2 but not of 5 but since 5 is nothing other than 10/2, the logarithm of 5 = logarithm of 10 – logarithm of 2 = 1 – 0.30 = 0.70.

   So the log of square root of 675 = 1/2×[log 675] = 1/2×[log (5 × 5 × 3 × 3 × 3 ÷ 2)] =

   1/2×[log5 + log5 + log5 + log3 + log3 – log2] = 1/2 × [0.7 + 0.7 + 0.7 + 0.48 + 0.48 – 0.30]=

   1/2 × [2.10 + 0.96 – 0.30] = 1/2 × [2.76] = **1.38.**
2. Fundamentally, the logarithm of any number N is the power to which the base of the logarithm has to be raised in order to arrive at the number N.

   The logarithm of a fractional number N worth <1, is invariably negative if the base of the logarithm is a number greater than 1.

   The logarithm of a fractional number N can be a whole number or a number greater than 1 if the base of the logarithm has to be raised to a power more than 1 in order to obtain N. Let us see a few examples in the table given below:

If the base of the logarithm is	Then the logarithm of the following fractional number <1	Is
2	1/2	–1, because 1/2 is effectively $(2)^{-1}$
3	1/9	–2, because 1/9 is effectively $(3)^{-2}$
8	1/4	–2/3, because 1/4 is effectively $(8)^{-2/3}$
1/64	1/8	1/2, because 1/8 is effectively $(1/64)^{1/2}$
1/8	1/64	2, because 1/64 is effectively $(1/8)^2$
1/27	1/3	1/3, because 1/3 is effectively $(1/27)^{1/3}$
1/3	1/27	3, because 1/27 is effectively $(1/3)^3$
9	1/3	–1/2, because 1/3 is effectively $(9)^{-1/2}$
1/5	1/25	2, because 1/25 is effectively $(1/5)^2$

Thus whether the logarithm of a fractional number having value less than 1 may be:

(A) a fraction

(B) a whole number

(C) negative

All would depend on the base of the logarithm and thus **Option (D).**

3. The square root of a negative number is not meaningful. The logarithm of 0.1 is effectively log 10^{-1} and is equal to –1. The square root of –1 is not a real number and anything unreal is not meaningful. Thus **Option A.**

4. While on the face of it this may seem to be a question pertaining to logarithms, if one comes to grips with the fact that when log of something is equal to log of another thing, then something is equal to another thing and then logarithms can go for a swim, for all you care.

   If log (a + b)/5 = 1/2 × (log a + log b), then log (a + b)/5 = 1/2 log a + 1/2 log b, and hence (a + b)/5 = $\sqrt{a} \times \sqrt{b} = \sqrt{ab}$.

   So (a+b)= $5\sqrt{ab}$ and squaring (both) sides we get $(a+b)^2$= 25 ab.
   Thus $a^2 + 2ab + b^2$= 25 ab and hence a^2+b^2= **23 ab.**

5. Given that the logarithm of 5 to the base 10 is 0.6990, what is the logarithm of 0.0005? What is 0.0005? It is 5 divided by 10000 or 5 × 10^{-4}. Therefore what is the implied power of 10 in 0.0005? The implied power of 10 is –4.

   The logarithm of 5 × 10^{-4} = log5 + log 10^{-4} = 0.6990 +-4 = -3.3010.

   It may be noted that that the logarithm of 5 to the base 10 is 0.6990 is normally written as hereunder: $\bar{4}$.6990 where the bar-sign above 4 indicates a negative characteristic and thus –4 is the characteristic of the logarithm and .6990 is the mantissa of the logarithm of 0.0005. But the logarithm of 0.0005 is essentially the sum of the characteristic and the mantissa because 0.0005 is 5 ×10^{-4} and hence the logarithm of this is as hereunder:

   log 5 + log 10^{-4} = 0.6690 +(–4) = –3.3010.

Chapter 24

Elementary Aspects of Statistics

The Educational Testing Service -in brief, the ETS (that administers the GRE) – gives a Compact Disc titled POWERPREP to aspirants when they register for the GRE. The Test Taking Tips set out the broad framework of the GRE. Insofar as the Tips relate to statistics, it would be necessary to acquaint the reader with the following topics:

1. Elementary Probability
2. Mean, Median, Mode, Range, Standard Deviation, Frequency Distribution, Percentiles
3. Interpretation of Data in Graphs and Tables: Line Graphs, Bar Graphs and Circle Graphs (also known as Pie Charts).

As regards 1 and 3 above, there are separate chapters in this book that cover not only the elementary aspects of these topics but also have illustrations that will make learning a matter of joy. As regards 2 above, we shall give the relative fundamentals in this chapter. What is elementary and what is advanced is a matter of perception. The concept notes that we give in this chapter (and for that matter all others) are based on a scientific assessment of the skill level needed for answering the **actual** questions administered at the GRE. **One extremely important aspect is ensured in the bargain: Complete Relevance.**

If you will see the actual test papers in this book, it will become clear that problem solving in the Quantitative Skills Section involves breadth of perception and the capacity to think beyond the convention rather than deep knowledge of formulae and so on. The presentation in this book as a whole and in this chapter in particular is designed keeping in view the fact that the matter pertains more to application of what one has learnt rather than to theory.

The Mean

We shall start off with refreshing our memory with the basics of The Mean.

When a family returns from an outing and settles down to a piping hot homemade meal, recalling the wonderful time that they had in the hills, the children ask the father as to how much did they end up spending. The father then tells the family that although this time they stayed in better hotels and ate at better eateries, the average expense per head was much less than the last outing thanks to the bargains that the travel agency struck with hotels and transport suppliers.

The youngest child says (while munching butter-drenched toast dripping with honey) that she has not the faintest idea what the words *average expense* mean. The eldest boy chips in saying that average expense is the same thing as *mean expense*. The little lady is still not able to understand what *mean expense* means. The mother then clarifies that the *average expense* is equal to the total money that they spent on the trip divided by the number of persons who went on the trip. The little lady is somewhat relieved and asks for a spot of marmalade but persists with knowing what is the difference between *mean expense* and *average expense*. The mother says *mean expense* is another way of saying *average expense*.

The father decides to provide a simple illustration. He asks the little daughter to imagine that three people are camping in a forest and the first has three sandwiches, the second has two sandwiches and the third has four sandwiches. If they decide to share the sandwiches equally, how many does each one get? The little girl does a spot of counting and says that there are nine sandwiches in all and since there are three people, each gets three sandwiches. *Precisely,* says the father, *three sandwiches is the **arithmetic average** of the number of sandwiches that the three people have **and three sandwiches is also the mean** of the number of the sandwiches that the three people have between them.*

While explaining to the daughter, the father has even refreshed our concepts about Arithmetic Average and Mean. We shall however have to take leave of the family discussing arithmetic averages and things at the dining table and focus on some important aspects that we must know in order that we can cope with the problems that call for breadth of perception.

The first of these is the fact that if any term in a series of terms (such as 1, 3, 5, 7, 9 and so on or 4, 14, 24, 34, 44 and so on) is the average of A and B [such average will be (A + B)/2)] where A is the term preceding it and B is the term succeeding it, then the series is an Arithmetic Progression. If the term between A and B is the average of A and B –shall we call this middle term as M?- it means that M – A = B – M [which can also be expressed as M = (A + B)/2] [For example, 3 lies between 1 and 5 in the series of odd integers 1,3,5,7,9 and so on and 3 is also the average of 1 and 5]. This means that if in any series of numbers, the difference between any term and its preceding term is the same throughout, then the series has got to be an Arithmetic Progression since this is the very definition of an Arithmetic Progression.

The mean of the series of numbers A, B, C, D, E and F – for example – is equal to (A + B + C + D + E + F)/ 6. This is why if you have to ensure that six children who have respectively 3, 4, 5, 6, 7 and 11 pencils should instead have an equal number of pencils, you can do this by adding the number of pencils (3 + 4 + 5 + 6 + 7 + 11 will give you 36 pencils. Divide 36 by 6 and you get 6 which means that 6 is the mean number of pencils that the children have). If you have noticed, the total number of pencils remains unchanged after the redistribution such that each child has the same (or mean number) of pencils.

The mean of any series of terms in which the difference between any term in the series and its immediately preceding term is the same throughout is the arithmetic average of the first and the last terms. [Or =(first term in the series + the last term in the series)/2].

Therefore if you come across a series of values such as 3, 5, 7, 9, 11, ...57 it is not necessary to add up all the terms in the series and then divide this total by the number of terms. Of course, there is no bar to your doing this. What we have learnt at school is that the average of a series of values is equal to the total of the values divided by the number of values. What calls for a broader perspective at the competitive examination is the fact that you have only half a minute to solve such a question and if you decide to persist with the things that were taught to you at school, you might be able to crack the question before sunset but not within time constraints. The reason why the competitive examination flings questions involving such fundamental aspects is because the examiner wants to know whether you are able to **apply** what you know to situations involving computing things quickly and accurately. That is where the fundamental aspect of the average of a series of values with a constant difference comes in. If you are asked to calculate the average of the series 3, 5, 7, 9, 11...57, all you have to do is to add 3 and 57 when you get 60 and then divide 60 by 2 and you get 30. This means that the average of the series 3,5,7,9..57 is 30.

The Median

If there are 3 terms in any series (arranged either in ascending or descending order) then the term in the middle is the 2nd term. If there are 5 terms in any series then the term in the middle is the 3rd term. If there are 57 terms then the term in the middle term is the 29th term. Let us suppose that the first term is A. Let us also suppose that the common difference between each term in the series and its immediately preceding term is D. Thus the 2nd term is A + D, the 3rd term is A + 2D and so on such that the 57th term is A + 56D and the Nth term is A + D (N – 1). The 29th term will be (A + 28D). Add the first term A and the 57th term (A + 56D) and you get (2A + 56D). Divide (2A + 56D) by 2 and you get (A + 28D) which is the 29th term. Therefore if a series of numbers has N terms, the term in the middle is the [(N + 1)/2]th term. This middle term is known as the **Median** of the series.

Imagine that a class teacher has jotted the weights (in kilograms) of the 17 children in her class whom she called one by one to the weighing machine in the alphabetical order of their names. Imagine that the weights are as follows where the first weight is that of Alfred, the second of Betty and the last is that of Walter: 36, 33, 31, 33, 34, 33, 31, 32, 35, 37, 39, 30, 38, 31, 30, 31 and 36. If the weights are rearranged in ascending order, the arrangement would be as follows: 30, 30, 31, 31, 31, 31, 32, 33, 33, 33, 34, 35, 36, 36, 37, 38, and 39. The middle term in this arrangement in **ascending order** of weights is the 9th term (which is what is meant by the middle term being the [(N+1)/2]th term if there are N terms in a series of numbers). Start counting from the left and you will find that the 9th term or **Median** is 33. On the other hand if the weights were arranged in **descending order** this arrangement would be as follows: 39, 38, 37, 36, 36, 35, 34, 33, 33, 33, 32, 31, 31, 31,31, 30, and 30. **Either way, the Median remains 33. The important thing to remember in finding the Median is that there has got to be an order** (or arrangement) **in the series** (you can take your pick: – the order can be either ascending or descending).

Imagine that the class teacher while jotting the weights of the 17 students in her class missed out the fact that Jonathan was unwell and therefore not present. She then adds Jonathan's weight of 34 kg to the ascending order of weights. The new order would be as follows: 30, 30, 31, 31, 31, 31, 32, 33, 33, 33, 34, 34, 35, 36, 36, 37, 38, and 39. There are 18 weights. The [(N + 1)/2]th term would be the 9.5th term. How does one find the 9.5th term? The teacher then looks up the elements of statistics that she learnt while at school (now that she is teaching botany she has lost touch with the elements of statistics) and finds that if there are an even number of terms in a series, the median term is the average of the two middle terms. This means that if there are 4 terms in a series – let us call then Term 1, Term 2, Term 3 and Term 4 – then Term 2 and Term 3 are in the middle whereas Term 1 and Term 4 are at the extremes of the series and in such a situation the Median is the average of the Term 2 and Term 3. If there are 18 terms in a series then the 9th and 10th terms are in the middle of the series [(there will be 8 terms (Term 1 to Term 8) to the left of Term 9 and 8 terms (Term 11 to Term 18) to the right of Term 10 in a series with 18 terms)]. In the case of the series 30, 30, 31, 31, 31, 31, 32, 33, 33, 33, 34, 34, 35, 36, 36, 37, 38, and 39, both the 9th and 10th terms are 33 and hence the median of this series is the average of 33 and 33 (which too is 33 since the average of two same numbers is equal to either of the numbers).

Determining which terms are in the middle of a series of even number of terms is not difficult at all. If a series has, for example, 56 terms then find (N + 1)/2 and this is 28.5 when N=56. If the 28.5th term is in the middle but yet cannot be located because it is imaginary, the two real terms in the middle are the 28th terms and the 29th term that lie ½ terms to the left and right respectively of the imaginary 28.5th term.

As such the mean is a more precise measure than the median. The mean can, however, be greatly affected by a few numbers very different from the rest. If there are three brothers who have respectively put away $250,000, $510,000, and $ 5,600,000 for their retirement, the mean savings of the three is ($250,000 + $510,000 + $ 5,600,000)/3 =6,360,000/3 = $2,120,000. However if the prudent level of savings is considered to be say $2,000,000, the **mean** savings of the three men would give an impression that all the three men have put away a prudent amount of savings for the days when they shall not be able to earn their living. The reality however is that only one of the three can be considered as having adequate savings. This is because the large savings of only one of the brothers has affected the average significantly and therefore the picture presented is lop-sided. It is for this reason that the median is sometimes used to give a better overall impression of the typical values of the numbers. In the present case the median is $510,000, which is well below the mean. The median shows the central tendency of the series of numbers.

Mode

The Mode is the number in a given set of numbers that appears most frequently. If the ages of children who have recently enrolled for swimming lessons during the last month are 3,4,5,6,6,7,10,13, the mode of this set of numbers is 6. This is because 6 is the number that appears most number of times in the set. If two or more such numbers occur, the set has two or more modes. For example, if the ages of students who enrolled for swimming lessons during the last two months are 3, 4, 5, 5, 5, 5, 6, 6, 6, 6, 6, 7, 10, and 13, there are two modes to this set: these two modes are 5 and 6. The reasons for this set having two modes are obvious.

There are sets of numbers that may not have modes at all. A set of numbers where no number is repeated will not have any mode. For example, imagine that a store clerk writes the daily figures of individual purchases in excess of USD 3,000 in the register of high-value clients. If the entries at the end of a particular day are USD 5,249, USD 4315 and USD 2937 it is clear that no figure is repeated. It is for this reason that there is no mode for the series of numbers as aforesaid.

Range

The range of a given set of data is the difference observed in any sample between the largest and the smallest values of a given variable. It is the difference between the largest and smallest possible values of a random variable.

Consider that K is an unknown quantity. You are given that K = [2 + (7/N)] where N is a natural number. You are asked to find the range between the possible integral values of K.

As we know, natural numbers are those that you can count on your fingers and therefore natural are necessarily positive integers. The very first natural number is 1. There is no upper limit to natural numbers although there is an upper limit to the number of fingers that you have. This is because nothing stops you from counting all over again once you exhaust the number of fingers that you have.

As regards K, we know that it is a sum of two numbers one of which (the number 2) is constant and has nothing to do with the changing values of N and the other is 7/N, which in turn is a fraction (with a constant numerator but variable denominator) the value of which will increase with decrease in the value of N and vice-versa. Therefore what affects the value of K is only the value of 7/N (which is the variable term). As we know, 2 is already an integer. If you want that K [which is 2 + (7/N)] should be an integer, then 7/N has got to be integral as well and this is possible only on two occasions: when N = 1 and when N = 7. This is because 7 is a prime number and has only these two factors: 1 and 7. It is for this reason that 7/N can have integral values only when either N = 1 or N = 7.

Thus when N = 1, K = [2 + (7/N)] = 9 and when N = 7, K = [2 + (7/N)] = 3. Therefore there are two possible integral values of K: 9 and 3. The range in the possible integral values of K is the difference between the highest possible integral value minus the lowest possible integral value of K and this range is 9 – 3 = 6.

Standard Deviation

Standard Deviation is a number representing the **spread** of a set of numbers around their average value. It is calculated from all the individual deviations from the average. It is an important concept in most statistical calculations because it is a precise indicator of the *degree of variability* within the set of numbers.

A simple example is to consider the heights of a group of five children whose names are mentioned in brackets after the respective height in cm. If their heights are 146 (Tim), 148 (Bob), 151 (Anna), 153 (Joe), and 157(Nick), the average of their heights is 151 cm. Therefore young Anna could be said to represent the average height of the group of these 5 children. If you wish to find the difference between Anna's height and those of the others, this difference would be as follows:

(146 – 151) + (148 – 151) + (151 – 151) + (153 – 151) + (157 – 151) = –5 + –3 + 0 + 2 + 6 = 0.

If we wish to find the simple average of the deviations (Meaning, differences from the average), then since such an average is (the sum of the deviations from the average)/ number of persons, it is bound to be zero since – as we have seen above - the sum of the deviations from the average is zero whether in the present case or in any other case.

Try finding the average of the five numbers 3, 5, 19, 15 and 8 and you will see that the average of these five numbers is = (3 + 5 + 19 + 15 + 8) = 50/5 = 10. Find the sum of the deviations from the average and you will see that this sum is (3 – 10) + (5 – 10) + (19 – 10) + (15 – 10) + (8 – 10) = –7 –5 +9 +5 –2 = 0. This illustration is to drive home the point once and for all that the simple average of deviations from the arithmetic mean of a series of numbers is invariably equal to zero and hence cannot be a meaningful indicator of the deviations from the average. This is why a more complicated method of ascertaining the degree of variability is necessary. In practice, the squares of the deviations are averaged (squares are always positive), and then the square root of this is taken.

In the case of the above illustrations involving the heights of five children [146 (Tim), 148 (Bob), 151 (Anna), 153 (Joe), and 157(Nick)], the average of their heights is 151 cm. The deviations are respectively –5, –3, 0, 2 and 6 and the squares of these deviations are respectively 25, 9, 0, 4 and 36. The sum of the squares of the deviations is then 25 + 9 + 0 + 4 + 36 = 74. This sum (74 in the present case) is averaged out over the number of terms (5 terms in this case). Therefore the average of the squares of the deviations is 74/5 = 14.8. All we have to do now is to find the square root of 14.8.

A fairly good approximation of the square root of 14.8 (or for that matter any other number is not too difficult to make if you were to see the following method of determining the square roots of numbers) can be made as follows:

Consider 14.8 as effectively 1480/100. We know that if we can find the square root of 1480, we can divide that figure by 10 (which is the square root of 100) and thus find the square root of 14.8.

We know that 900 is the square of 30 and 1600 is the square of 40 and therefore the square root of 1480 will lie between 30 and 40 but closer to 40 than 30 (meaning, higher than the average of 30 and 40).

Let the square root of 1480 be (40 – X) where X is an unknown term. The square of (40 – X) will be 1600 – 80X + X^2 just as $(A + B)^2 = A^2 + 2AB + B^2$. Let us dump X^2 because what we want is an approximation. Otherwise we would have been allowed to go into competitive examinations with calculators and things and there would have been no options. This means 1600 - 80X = nearly 1480 and therefore 80X = nearly 120 and thus X = 120/80 = nearly 1.5. This means that the square root of 1480 is very nearly (40 – X) or (40 – 1.5) or 38.5 and therefore the square root of 14.8 is 38.5/10 = nearly 3.85. The standard deviation is 3.85 cm.

Imagine that the heights of five children from five different classes are jotted and you see the following data of height in cm: 96, 105, 111, 134, 154. The average height is (96 + 105 + 111 + 134 + 154)/5 = 600/5 = 120 cm. The deviations from the average are –24, –15, –9, 14 and 34 and the squares of the deviations from the average are 576, 225, 81, 196 and 1156 and their sum is 576 + 225 + 81 + 196 + 1156 = 2234. The average of the squares of the deviations (from the average) is 2234/5 = 447 (approximately) and the square root of 447 is a wee bit more than 21 since the square of 21 is exactly 441.

We have seen that the standard deviation in the case of the five children whose heights were 146 (Tim), 148 (Bob), 151 (Anna), 153 (Joe), and 157(Nick) was 3.85 because the shortest among the five was not significantly short as compared to Anna whose height was the average of the five children. The heights of the children moved in a narrow band. The difference between the least height and the greatest height was 11 cm. The range of values was 11 cm. As against this the standard deviation in the case of the five children whose heights in cm were 96, 105, 111, 134, 154 was nearly 21 because the difference in height between the shortest and tallest child was 58 cm and this is significantly higher than in the earlier case.

It is now easy to see that where the values are clustered (meaning where they move in a small range) the standard deviation is bound to be much smaller than when there is large range in the data for which we are to ascertain the standard deviation. Therefore there is a direct correlation between the range in a given series of values and its standard deviation.

Frequency Distribution

Imagine that the following are the marks obtained by 20 boys out of whom there are 8 girls and 12 boys: 70, 74, 74, 74, 76, 76, 76, 76, 76, 76, 78, 78, 80, 82, 82, 82, 84, 84, 88, and 90.

In the above data the frequencies of marks are distributed as under:

The Frequency of	Is
70 marks	1
74 marks	3
76 marks	6
78 marks	2
80 marks	1
82 marks	3
84 marks	2
88 marks	1
90 marks	1
Total	20

Let us see how we can use the given data to answer the following questions.

Problem 1

If 5 boys have scores of 82 or above, how many girls have scores below 82?

(1) 7 (2) 6 (3) 5 (4) 4 (5) 3

Answer 1

There are 8 girls and 12 boys. The number of students having scores of 82 and above is 7 as can be counted as follows: 3 (with scores of 82)+ 2 (with scores of 84) +1 (with score of 88) +1 (with score of 90). There are 5 boys with scores of 82 and above. This means that there are 2 girls in the scores of 82 and above. Since there are 8 girls in all and 2 of them are in the score of 82 and above, there are 6 girls who have score below 82. Hence Option 2.

Problem 2

If 76 were the lowest passing score, what per cent of the class did not get a passing score?

(1) 8% (2) 10% (3) 12% (4) 20% (5) 25%

Answer 2

The number of students getting scores less than 76 is 4 as may be seen by counting the frequencies in the case of 74 (where the frequency is 3) + 70 (where the frequency is 1). There are in all 20 students. If 4 out of 20 do not get passing score, this means 4/20 or (4 × 5)/(20 × 5) or 20/100 did not get passing score. This is 20% and hence Option 4.

In order to express any fraction in percentage terms all you have to do is to multiply both numerator and denominator with such a common number so that you get 100 in the denominator. Then the numerator is the percentage value of the fraction.

Let us remember these few fundamental aspects of the frequency distribution that we have seen in the above illustration, fundamentals that will not vary although the data may vary till it is blue in the face:

- The frequencies that are being distributed are absolute values of marks.
- The relative positions being implied in the absolute values will not undergo changes if the same number of marks are either added to all students' marks or deducted there from. If one were to, for example, deduct five marks for irregular attendance from each of the 20 students in the class, what will change is the

absolute position and not the relative positions: If a boy – let us call him John Sebastian – has scored 90 marks, he will continue to hold first rank even if 5 (or for that matter any number of) marks are uniformly deducted from all students as aforesaid.

- The mean (or arithmetic average) of the marks will change with either increasing a certain number of marks to the marks of all students or decreasing all marks by the same number of marks. So will the median, the mode. **The range will not change** in either of the aforesaid situations **nor** therefore will the **standard deviation** change in any way. It is recommended that you, dear reader, do try working out the average, the mode, the median, the range and then the standard deviation after first adding five marks to each of the marks in the frequency distribution table on which Problems 1 and 2 are based and then after reducing five marks from the frequency distribution as aforesaid. You will see for yourself that the mean, mode, median will all undergo a change each time whereas the range and the standard deviation will not.

Percentiles

People collect data in order to present it to their shareholders, employers, employees, wives (*my expense on alcohol has dwindled from so and so in December last to this September*) and so on. One of the most difficult tasks that people face in presenting data is to keep the audience awake. Sleep sets in rather quickly when people ramble as such. If numbers accompanied the rambling, Man would surrender to sleep in a jiffy. The collective snores of the audience may cause structural problems to the ceiling.

Therefore, collected data must be arranged, tabulated, and presented to permit ready and meaningful analysis and interpretation. To study and interpret the examination-grade distribution in a class of 30 pupils, for instance, the grades are initially arranged in ascending order: 30, 35, 43, 52, 61, 65, 65, 65, 68, 70, 72, 72, 73, 75, 75, 76, 77, 78, 78, 80, 83, 85, 88, 88, 90, 91, 96, 97, 100, 100. This progression shows at a glance that the maximum is 100, the minimum 30, and the **range**, or difference, between the maximum and minimum is 70. As we have seen earlier, there is a direct correlation between range and standard deviation: the smaller the range, the smaller the standard deviation and so on.

Like the standard deviation, the percentile is a measure of variability of distribution. The investigator is frequently concerned with the variability of the distribution, that is, whether the measurements are clustered tightly around the mean or spread over the range. One measure of this variability is the difference between two percentiles, usually the 25th and the 75th percentiles. The Pth percentile is a number such that P per cent of the measurements are less than or equal to it; in particular, the 25th and the 75th percentiles are called the lower and upper quartiles, respectively.

Let us see this at work as follows:

Let us imagine that there are 20 students in a class who have written an examination and the following is the statement of their marks (expressed in percentages rounded off to the nearest half percent).

RollNo.	Marks (%)	RollNo.	Marks (%)
1	84.5	11	62.5
2	43.0	12	65.0
3	71.5	13	88.0
4	88.0	14	47.5
5	93.0	15	55.5
6	57.5	16	90.0
7	57.0	17	82.5
8	81.5	18	74.5
9	88.5	19	45.0
10	57.0	20	52.5

Let us note the following:

- Roll No. 5 stands first with 93%
- Roll no. 2 is at the bottom of the list with 43%
- 20 students make 100% of the students here. Therefore 10% of the students means 2 students and 20% of the students means 4 students and so on.
- There are two students who have scored up to and including 45% (Roll Nos. 2 and 19) and hence 45% marks correspond to 10 Percentile.
- There are five students who have scored up to and including 55.5% (Roll Nos. 2, 19, 14, 20 and 15) and hence 55.5% marks correspond to 25 Percentile.
- There are ten students who have scored up to and including 65% (Roll Nos. 2, 19, 14, 20, 15, 6, 7, 10, 11 and 12) and hence 65% marks correspond to 50 Percentile.
- There are fifteen students who have scored up to and including 84.5% (Roll Nos. 2, 19, 14, 20, 6, 7, 10, 11, 12, 1, 3, 8, 17 and 18) and hence 84.5% marks correspond to 75 Percentile.
- There are eighteen students who have scored up to and including 88.5% (Roll Nos. 2, 19, 14, 20, 6, 7, 10, 11, 12, 1, 3, 8, 17,18, 4, 13 and 9) and hence 88.5% marks correspond to 90 Percentile.
- There are nineteen students who have scored up to and including 90% (Roll Nos. 2, 19, 14, 20, 6, 7, 10, 11, 12, 1, 3, 8, 17,18, 4, 13, 9 and 16) and hence 90% marks correspond to 95 Percentile.
- There are twenty students who have scored up to and including 93% and hence 93% marks correspond to 100 Percentile.

If you have observed, there is a perceptible difference between percentages and percentiles as we learn from this illustration. For example, **roll no. 16 has 90 percent marks but is in 95 percentile**. This means that only 5% of the number of students writing the examination is above him in rank.

Percentiles find numerous applications one of which is as per following. At competitive examinations - for example the Civil Service - it would be difficult to decide beforehand what would be the cut off mark for recruiting persons to the Civil Service. This is because if the written test is easy, there may be throngs of young persons who may score either equal to or more than 90% and then there will be more civil servants in the country than ordinary citizens. On the other hand if the written test is tough, there may be no one who will qualify if you were to set a threshold mark of say 95% for recruitment of commissioned officers in the army. In that case the army will have to make do without directly recruited officers. To obviate such situations, the system of percentiles comes in handy. The cut-off will depend on the number of persons that are planned to be recruited and therefore will depend upon the percentile and not percentages at the written examinations and interviews and so on. If you find that the number of persons taking a competitive test is 150,000 and there are only 1500 vacancies for which you wish to interview 3000 persons, you decide that you shall issue letters for interviews only to those who are in the top 2% (meaning over 98 percentile).

Chapter 25

The Number Line

When you subtract a smaller number from a larger number (such as 2 from 5), you always get a remainder.

When you subtract a number from the same number (such as 3 from 3), you get no remainder.

As long as smaller numbers are being subtracted from larger ones, carrying out the operation of subtraction in arithmetic is not difficult. However if you subtract a larger number from a smaller number (such as subtracting 5 from 3, for instance), the only way to produce a remainder, is to introduce the concept of negative numbers.

Negative numbers have numerous and varied applications in real life situations. For example, when you have an account with a bank, you put money into your bank account. When you draw a cheque for a larger amount than what you have in your bank account and request the bank to honour your cheque, there will be a negative remainder in your bank account. This is what is known as an overdraft. It creates a situation wherein instead of you banking with the bank, the bank banks with you.

Negative numbers may be most easily visualized by considering the familiar numbers of arithmetic, the positive integers, arranged in a line and increasing in a positive direction. Such a line is called the Number Line. Negative numbers are reached by proceeding away from 0 in the opposite direction. The following number line represents both positive and negative numbers:

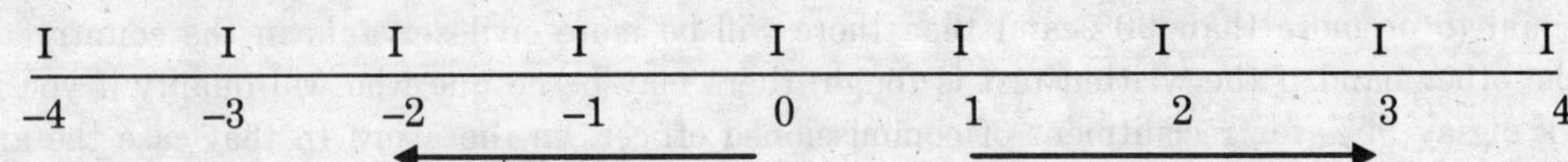

Negative territory of the number line Positive territory of the number line

To the left of zero is the negative territory of the number line. The further you go to the left, the deeper you go into the negative territory. This means that –4 has lower value than –3 and –3 has lower value than –2 and so on. Thus if one is asked as to which is greater in value, –1 or –3 it should not take a moment to visualise the positions of –1 and –3 on the number line and then realising that –3 is further to the left of the number line, it should occur in a flash that –3 is the lower than -1.

To the right of zero is the positive territory of the number line. The further you go to the right, the deeper you go into positive territory. This means that 4 has higher value than 3 and 0 has higher value than –1 and so on.

If you are ever foxed by a question such as which is greater in value –2/3 or –3/4, do visualise a number line and you will find that since 3/4 is closer to 1 than 2/3, –3/4 will occur nearer to –1 than –2/3. Therefore –3/4 is deeper into the negative territory of the number line than –2/3. This means that –2/3 has greater value than –3/4.

Zero is the transition from negative numbers to positive numbers.

If 4 is subtracted from 2, written symbolically as 2 – 4, four units are counted backwards from +2, and –2 is reached. Therefore –2 is the remainder when 4 is subtracted from 2.

Rules for basic arithmetic operations involving negative numbers are set out hereunder:

- The product of a negative number and a negative number is invariably positive (that is why, for example, $-4 \times -3 = 12$)
- The product of a positive number and a negative number is invariably negative (that is why, for example, $4 \times -2 = -8$)
- When you divide a negative number with a negative number, the result is invariably a positive number (that is why, for example, $-14 \div -2 = 7$)
- When you divide a positive number with a negative number or a negative number with a positive number, the result is invariably a negative number (that is why, for example, $15 \div -2 = -7.5$ or $-24 \div 3 = -8$)
- The square of a negative number is invariably positive for no other reason than the fact that the square of a negative number involves multiplying a negative number with a negative number (although it is a different matter that insofar as a square is concerned you are multiplying a negative number with the **same** negative number).
- All even number integral powers of a negative number will invariably yield a positive number. That is why, for example, $(-2)^4$ will give +16 and $(-3)^6$ will give +729 and so on. (It may be mentioned that as such it is not necessary to write the positive sign to precede a positive number yet the positive sign has preceded 16 and 729 in this illustration in order to only **emphasise** the point being made).
- All odd number integral powers of a negative number will invariably yield a negative number. That is why, for example, $(-4)^3$ will give -64 and $(-2)^5$ will give -32 and so on.
- A number is basically presumed to be a positive number if no sign precedes it. That is why if you wish to indicate a negative number, only then is it necessary to write a negative sign preceding the number such as in the case of –3, for example.)

Chapter 26

Mathematical Operators

We are well aware of the broad mathematical operations such as addition, subtraction, multiplication and division. Whenever one sees, for example, X+Y, one knows that one has to add X and Y and find their sum. There is no confusion in these simple operating signs of + for addition, – for subtraction, × for multiplication and / for division.

There are some mathematical operations for which there are no standard signs. For example, there is no sign that will lead you to infer that what you are asked to do is to find out the average of A and B unlike the expression A×B where the whole thing is about finding out the product of A and B.

But one can assign a certain defined function to a sign or a numeral and thereby create temporary mathematical operators. For example, A(X,Y) can be defined as the average of X and Y for the purpose of computing the answer for a particular question or Mo(X,Y) can refer to the most among X and Y. These temporary signs of mathematical operation created in order to serve as a guideline for specific mathematical functions other than the standard mathematical operations such as addition, subtraction and so on are known as mathematical operators. These operators are case specific and do not have standard application.

Let us illustrate:

When I define Mo(X,Y) as the maximum among X and Y and Min(X,Y) as the minimum among X and Y, I have created temporary operators for ascertaining maximum and minimum. So when I ask as to what is the product of Mo(4, 6) and Min(–4, –2), the answer is 6×-4 = –24. This is because Mo(4, 6) is 6 and Min(–4, –2) is –4 and 6 × –4 = –24.

When I define @(X,Y) as the average of X and Y and $(X,Y) as the square of Y divided by the cube of X, I have created temporary mathematical operators for which I have no standard sign. The expression that I have temporarily created are radical in nature. They do not conform to the normal expression of × as multiplication, ÷ as division and so on. So, if asked as to what is @(6, 18) – $(4,8) [given that @(X,Y) = (X + Y)/2 and $(X,Y) = Y^2/X^3], I know that:

(A) @(6, 18) is the average of 6 and 18 and is = (6 + 18)/2 = 12 and

(B) $(4,8) = $8^2/4^3$ = 64/64 = 1

So @(6, 18) – $(4,8) = 12 – 1 = 11

Let us now move on to some problems regarding temporarily created mathematical operators. The problems presented hereunder have a rising level of difficulty and cover the range that you would need for the GRE.

Problem 1

If x(@)y = $x^2 + y^3$, what is the value of z, if 6(@),3(@)z)) = 4949?

Answer

In the expression 6(@),3(@)z)), x = 6 and y = 3(@)z). Now, since x = 6, x^2 = 36, the expression 36,3(@)z)) = 4949 and hence $[3(@)z)]^3$ = 4949-36 = 4913. Thus, 3(@)z) is the cube root of 4913. Now the cube of 10 is 1000 and the cube of 20 is 8000 and hence the cube root of 4913 since 4913 lies between 1000 and 8000, lies between 10 and 20. The last digit in 4913 is 3, this is possible only when a number ending with 7 is multiplied by itself thrice. Thus, the cube root of 4913 is 17. Then 3(@)z = 17.

In the expression 3(@)z), x = 3 and hence x^2 = 9 and since 3(@)z) = 17, 9 + z^3 = 17 and hence z^3 = 8 and therefore z = 2.

Problem 2

If A*B = the remainder when A is divided by B, and A/B = Quotient when A is divided by B, then which of the following is true?

Options: (1): A= A*B + (A/B)

(2): A= A*B + (A/B)A

(3): B= A*B + (B/A)A

(4): A= A*B + (A/B)B

Answer

Let us assume that A = 3 and B = 2. So, A*B = 1 and A/B = 1. With this, now let us go from option to option as follows:

Option (1): will give 3 = 1 + 1; this is incorrect. How can 3 be equal to 2?

Option (2): will give 3 = 1 + (1 × 3); this is incorrect too.

Option (3): will give 2 = 1 + (0 × 3); this is incorrect as well.

Option (4): will give 3 = 1 + (1 × 2); this is correct. Hence **Option 4.**

Problem 3

If A;B = 1 + A + B + AB, and A – B = Remainder of the fraction A/B, then the value of {(7;5) × (5-3)}; (3; 2) is:

Options: (1): 1158

(2): Zero

(3): 1261

(4): None of these

Answer

(7;5) = 1 + 7 + 5 + 35 = 48 and (5 – 3) = 2 (remainder when 5 is divide by 3) and thus, {(7;5) × (5-3)} is = 48 × 2 = 96. Further, (3; 2) = 1 + 3 + 2 + 6 = 12. Thus, {(7;5) × (5 – 3)}; (3; 2) is 96;12 = 1 + 96 + 12 + (96 × 12) = 1 + 96 + 12 + 1152 = 1261. Hence **Option 3.**

The general instructions for Problem 4 and 5 are as follows:

Let x, y and z be three numbers.

Define:

le(x,y) = minimum of x and y;

mo(x,y) = maximum of x and y;

me(x,y) = 1/2{le(x,y) + mo(x,y)}.

Problem 4

Given that x > y > z , which among the following is true?

Option (1): x = mo(me(x,y), mo(y,z)) Option (2): z = le(le(x,y), me(x,y))

Option (3): y = le(me(x,y), me(y,z)) Option (4): y = me(le(x,y),mo(y,z))

Answer

Given that x > y > z , le(x,y) = y and mo(x,y) = x and thus me (x, y) = 1/2(le(x,y) + mo(x,y)) = 1/2(x + y) and therefore **me(x,y) is effectively the average of x and y.**

There are distinct advantages in assuming some **distinct** values for the unknown quantities x, y and z. The first advantage is that the correct answer will get crosschecked with numerical values rather than mere alphabets. If you persist with alphabets, there are chances that you may flounder somewhere. Secondly, even if we assume that the correct answer will emerge with alphabets, there would be need to crosscheck the validity of the answer by assigning numerical values to alphabets. Then why not eliminate unnecessary effort and work right away with numerals alone? Secondly, **it is important to assume distinct values for unknown quantities represented by alphabets.** If indistinct there may be a situation wherein more than one option may turn out to be correct and then one will have to assume certain other numerical values for the alphabets and find out which option among the conflicting options will work. Instead of this it is safer to assume distinct values, for this will throw up only one option as correct.

Let us now assume that x = 3, y = 2 and z = 1 and then go by the options:

Option (1): x = mo(me(x,y), mo(y,z)); me(x,y) = 2.5 and mo(y,z) = 2. but mo(2.5,2) is 2.5 which is not =x which we have assumed to be 3 at the outset. Hence Option 1 is not correct.

Option (2): z = le(le(x,y), me(x,y)) = le(2, 2.5)) = 2 which is not = z which we have assumed to be 1 at the outset. Hence Option 2 is not correct.

Option (3): y = le(me(x,y), me(y,z)) = le(2.5, 1.5) = 1.5 which is not equal to y which we have assumed as 2 at the outset. Hence Option 3 is not correct.

Option (4): y = me(le(x,y),mo(y,z)) = average of (2,2) = 2. This is correct. Thus **Option 4.**

Problem 5

Given that x > y > z, which of the following is not necessarily true?

Option (1): le(x,y) > me(mo(y,z), me(y,z)

Option (2): mo(y,z) < me(me(x,y), me(y,z)

Option (3): me(x,y)e ≥ mo(me(x,y), le(x,y))

Option (4): me(y,z) e ≥ le(me(y,z), mo(y,z)

Answer

Let us go from option to option and see which one is correct:

Option (1): le(x,y) > me(mo(y,z), me(y,z); le (x,y) is y. me(mo(y,z), me(y,z) = me(y, (y + z)/2); average of y and (y + z)/2; me(2y + y + z)/2 = 1/2(3y + z)/2 = 0.75y + 0.25z. If we take y as 2 and z as 1, then 0.75y + 0.25z = 1.5 + 0.25 = 1.75 and is lesser than 2.

So, Option (1) is not correct since it is necessarily true.

Option (2): mo(y,z) < me(me(x,y), me(y,z). mo(y,z) is y. me(me(x,y), me(y,z)

= 1/2 ((x + y)/2, (y + z)/2)) = 1/2 (x + 2y + z)/2) = 1/4 (x + 2y + z).

If one takes x as 3, y as 2 and z as 1, then 1/4 (x + 2y + z) = 1/4*(3 + 4 + 1) = 2. We have taken y as 2 and 2 is equal to 2. So, mo(y,z) < me(me(x,y), me(y,z) is not necessarily true.

Hence **Option 2 is correct**. There is no need to go further.

Chapter 27

Mixtures

The other day, someone asked my brother this question that the fellow saw in a question paper of a competitive test: What percentage of water should I add to milk so as to get a resultant mixture that has 80% milk.

It struck him that 80% is 4 parts out of 5. He solved the problem like this: If I had 4 litres of milk at the outset, then in order to have 5 litres of a mixture of milk and water, I would have to add 1 litre of water to 4 litres of milk. When you add 1 litre to 4 litres, you are adding to the original volume by $1/4^{th}$. When you want to express $1/4^{th}$ in percentage terms, what you want to do is to express ¼ on a standard denominator of 100 because the word *per* means *for every* (which in other words means *divided by*) and the word *cent* means *hundred*. If I want a denominator of 100 in the fraction ¼ without altering the value of the fraction, then I should multiply both numerator and denominator by 25 so that I get 100 in the denominator and 25 in the numerator. ¼ is thus effectively 25/100 or 25%. Thus I should add 25% water to milk so as to get a mixture containing 80% milk. This is regardless of the quantity of milk at the beginning: if there was 2 litres of milk I should add ½ litres of water and if there was 28 litres of milk, I should add 7 litres of water and so on.

It is not as if the above solution defies the conventional manner of calculation: it only quickens the pace while staying within the confines of method. If you were to strike equations after assuming that an unknown quantity of milk mixes with another unknown quantity of water resulting in milk being 80% of the resultant mixture, you would not get any different answer. See this problem from the viewpoint of equations as well as per follows:

Suppose I had M litres of milk to which I should add W litres of water in order to get a mixture that has 80% milk. The volume of the mixture is (M + W) litres and mixture has M litres of milk. The proportion of milk in the mixture is M/(M+W) and this proportion is 80% or $4/5^{th}$. The linear equation that can be struck is as follows:

$M/(M + W) = 4/5$ and hence $5M = 4M + 4W$ and therefore $W = M/4$. This means that if there are M litres of milk, I must add M/4 litres of water and therefore if there are 100 litres of milk, I must add 25 litres of water or 25% water.

In this problem, neither did my brother know what was the volume of milk *before* putting water in it nor what was the volume *after* putting water and yet he was able to arrive at the correct answer in a jiffy only because the question pertained not to mathematics but to one's breadth of perception and to reasoning. The mathematics that you learned at the school level can enable you to express some fraction in percentage terms only if you know what is the numerator and what is the denominator. This is why one has to perceive things very differently if one wants to emerge with flying colours at a competitive examination.

The other day, someone asked me for help with solving this question from the past paper of a major competitive examination: If water constitutes 90% of fresh grapes and 20% of dried grapes, how many kilograms of dried grapes can be made from 20 kilograms of fresh grapes?

I asked him this: Do you know that if 90% is water it means the rest is grape concentrate? He said *yes*. Then I asked him whether he could understand that 90% means 9 parts out of 10 and thus if 9 parts out of 10 were water, 20 kg of fresh grape would have 18 kg of water and 2 kg of grape concentrate? He said *yes*. Then I asked him whether he knew that 20% means 2 parts out of 10 and thus if 2 parts of 10 were water, every kg or 1000 grams of fresh grape would have 200 grams of water and 800 grams of grape concentrate? He said *yes*. Then I asked him if he could appreciate that if 800 grams of grape concentrate could make 1 kg of dried grapes, then 2 kg or 2000 grams of grape concentrate could make 2000/800 or 5/2 or 2.5 kg of dried grapes? He said *yes*. The problem was solved.

The mathematics that we learned at school helped us learn method and methodical presentation; we got marks for method even if the answer was wrong. In the life outside school, what matters is the correct answer. A wrong answer, no matter how well presented, may invite anything between derisive laughter to loss of employment or winding up of one's business. This is why the emphasis is on logic and not on method. However logic cannot work in isolation all the while and this is why we must have conceptual clarity.

There are some fundamental aspects about mixtures that we must know.

(I) The volume or quantity of a mixture resulting from mixing two or more commodities is to be presumed to be the sum of the volumes of the ingredients or the sum of the quantities of the ingredients, unless you are specifically told to the contrary. This is why, for example, when I mix 500 grams of milk with 200 grams of water, I get 700 grams of a mixture of milk and water.

(II) When I mix X kg of a commodity costing \$A per kg with Y kg of the same commodity (or another one if the two of them mix well - not that it makes a difference to the answer) costing \$B per kg, and I get a resultant mixture costing \$C per kg, three things must be noted:

(1) The total cost of X kg of the commodity costing \$A per kg is \$AX and that of Y kg of the other variety at \$B per kg is \$BY and thus the total cost is \$ (AX + BY)

(2) The total quantity that I now have is (X+Y) kg

(3) The average cost of the mixture is \$(AX + BY) ÷ (X + Y) kg and this is equal to C

The equation that emerges is: $(AX + BY) \div (X + Y) = C$ and thus $AX + BY = CX + CY$ or $X(A - C) = Y(C - B)$ and hence this equation: $X/Y = (C - B)/(A - C)$. If I do not know the value of either X or Y, but I know the numerical values of A, B and C (meaning exactly what each component cost per kg and what the resultant mixture costs per kg) then since A, B and C are all numerical values, the fraction $(C - B)/(A - C)$ will yield a numerical. Since the value of X divided by Y will have a clear numerical value, it is possible for me to know the exact proportion in which X and Y are to be mixed although this may not tell me the exact quantities in which they are mixed.

If a fellow wants to remember the equation in the preceding paragraph, no one would stop him. What we would recommend, however, is that he understands the fundamentals rather than the formula. The human mind is built for forgetting. If one grieves over the Alsatian dog (whom one loved very dearly) that died forty years ago, one would be able to do nothing constructive throughout one's life. Anyone grieving lifelong, would do well to know *why* mortal things die rather than *how*. This is why it is important, for example, to remember *why* things obey the Law of Gravitation rather than *how* they obey them. Things can obey this law by falling to the earth. Isaac Newton was lucky that it was only an apple that fell on him. Suppose one were to sit under a balcony and a huge iron hammer were to slip from someone's hands, one may not get a chance to breathe, leave alone sit and analyse why the apple fell down and not soar up in the sky instead. Even if you have forgotten a formula, reconstructing the formula may be a matter of a jiffy once you remember the why aspect rather than the how aspect of things.

The proof of any pudding lies in eating it. If we are to eat puddings, why not start right away?

If I am given the percentages in which two or more things are mixed, it is safe for me to assume each part of the mixture in terms of 100 units of measure (for volume this may be cubic cm or litres and so on and for weight I may opt for grams or kilograms as may be necessary in order to facilitate calculation). This assumption will in no way affect the outcome, as one will see when we actually solve problems in this chapter.

If I am told, for example, that three varieties of items costing respectively \$3, 4 and 6 per kg respectively are mixed so that I get the resultant mixture costing an average price of \$5 per kg, I assume that X kg of item costing \$3 per kg and Y kg of the item costing \$4 per kg and Z kg of the item costing \$6 per kg are mixed so as to get a resultant mixture costing \$5 per kg, then the equation that emerges is as follows:

$3X + 4Y + 6Z = 5(X + Y + Z)$ and hence $3X + 4Y + 6Z = 5X + 5Y + 5Z$ and thus $Z = 2X + Y$. You know only the relationship between three unknowns but that cannot get you any idea of the numerical value of any of the unknowns. An infinite number of combinations are possible. Let us see some of these from the following table:

If X were	If Y were	If Z(which is equal to 2x+y) were	Then 3X=	Then 4Y	Then 6Z=	X+Y+Z=A, where A is the total number of kg of the mixture would be	3X+4Y+6Z=B, the total cost of the mixture in $ would be	B/A=C, cost of the mixture in $ per kg would be
1	2	4	3	8	24	7	35	5
2	3	7	6	12	42	12	60	5
3	4	10	9	16	60	17	85	5

The short point is that if there are three unknowns as regards the ratio of items mixed but the price of each item is known and so also is the price of the resultant mixture, then it is not possible to tell as to what is the exact proportion in which these may be mixed.

Another point to be noted here is that the average cost of the resultant mixture cannot exceed the cost of the costliest among the items mixed nor can it go below the cost of the least costly item. Let us see why.

In what proportion should I mix almonds costing $10 per kg with pistachios costing $12 per kg and cashew nuts costing $15 per kg so that I get a resultant mixture costing $18 per kg?

Let us assume that I mix X kg of almonds with Y kg of pistachios with Z kg of cashew nuts. The equation that emerges is as follows:

10X + 12Y + 15Z = 18(X + Y + Z) and thus 10X + 12Y + 15Z = 18X + 18Y + 18Z and hence 3Z = –8X –6Y or dividing both sides I get Z = –(8X + 6Y)/3. All X, Y and Z have got to be positive since these are quantities. You cannot have negative quantities of almonds or pistachios. So this equation can never be solved. Which means that the average cost of the resultant mixture cannot exceed the cost of the costliest among the items mixed.

In what proportion should I mix almonds costing $10 per kg with pistachios costing $12 per kg and cashew nuts costing $15 per kg so that I get a resultant mixture costing $8 per kg?

Let us assume that I mix X kg of almonds with Y kg of pistachios with Z kg of cashew nuts. The equation that emerges is as follows:

10X + 12Y + 15Z = 8(X + Y + Z) and thus 10X + 12Y + 15Z = 8X + 8Y + 8Z and hence 7Z = –2X –4Y or dividing both sides I get Z= – (2X + 4Y)/7. You cannot have negative quantities of almonds or pistachios. So this equation can never be solved. Which means that the average cost of the resultant mixture cannot go below the cost of the least costly among the items mixed.

We shall now move on to some illustrations involving mixtures. The illustrations are designed in such a way that the level of difficulty rises gradually and by the time one is at the last of these illustrations, all the necessary concepts about mixtures would have gone home.

Illustration 1

Rum contains 32.55% alcohol and Gin contains 45.75% alcohol whereas whiskey contains 51.30% alcohol. What would be the alcohol content in a mixture containing 3 parts of rum, 2 of whiskey and one of gin?

Solution

Since the whole thing is about percentages, why not assume each part to be of 100cc and proceed accordingly?

3 parts of rum, 2 of whiskey and one of gin would make a total of 600 cc of mixture:

300 cc of rum with 32.55 × 3 = 97.65 cc of alcohol

200 cc of whiskey with 51.30 × 2 = 102.60 cc of alcohol

100 cc of gin with 45.75 × 1 = 45.75 cc of alcohol

Total alcohol content

of 600 cc of mixture is = 246.00 cc of alcohol

The alcohol content of the mixture is in percentage terms = 246 × 100 ÷ 600 = 2460045/600 = 41%.

Illustration 2

In what proportion must rice at $6.20 per kg be mixed with rice at $7.20 per kg so that the mixture is worth $6.50 a kg?

Solution:

Let the number of kilograms of rice costing $6.20/kg be X and rice costing $7.20/kg be Y. So the total cost is $(6.20 × X + 7.20 × Y) and the total number of kg is X + Y. The cost of X + Y kg is $6.50/kg and hence the total cost of X + Y kg of rice is $6.50 (X + Y).

Now (6.20 × X + 7.20×Y) =6.50 (X + Y) and hence multiplying both sides with 100 we get 620X + 720Y = 650X + 650Y and hence 70Y = 30X; so X/Y = 7/3. So rice costing $6.20/kg and rice costing $7.20/kg must be mixed in proportion of 7:3 so as to get a resultant mixture worth $6.50/kg.

Illustration 3

How many kg of sugar costing Euro 12.20 per quintal must be mixed with 126 quintals of sugar costing Euro 5.70 per quintal so that 20% may be gained by selling the mixture at Euro 9.60/quintal?

Solution

When do you gain 20% on something costing 100 units of a currency? When you sell it at 120 units of that currency. So if Euro 9.60 here were akin to 120, what would be akin to 100?

9.60 × 100 ÷ 120 = 8.00

Thus while the selling price of the resultant mixture is Euro 9.60/quintal, its cost price is Euro 8.00 per quintal since only then would a gain of 20% be feasible.

The quantity that is unknown here is the number of quintals of sugar costing Euro 12.20/quintal. Let this unknown quantity be X and thus its cost will be 12.20X. The equation that emerges is as follows:
12.20X +126 ×. 5.70 = 8(X + 126).

12.20X + 718.20 = 8X + 1008 and hence 4.2X = 289.80. One would recommend multiplying both sides by 10 so as to obviate working with decimals. If what one recommends is implemented, the equation becomes 42X = 2898 and hence X = 2898 ÷ 42 = 69.

So one must mix 69 quintals of sugar costing Euro 12.20 per quintal with 126 quintals of sugar costing Euro 5.70 per kg so that 20% may be gained by selling the mixture at Euro 9.60/quintal.

Having come to the end of illustrations that have been designed with the objective of driving home the concepts related to this chapter, I present hereunder a small exercise that should ensure complete assimilation of the concepts.

EXERCISE

Question Number	
1	In what proportion must water be mixed with spirit to gain 18.75% by selling it at a cost? (Take the cost of water as nil)
2	An Army officer's batman helped himself from a bottle of sherry that contained 40% of alcohol and he replaced what he had stolen, by sherry containing only 16% alcohol. The resultant strength of alcohol in the bottle of sherry was then of 24% only. What part of the bottle did he steal?
3	The average weekly salary per head of the entire staff of a factory consisting of supervisors and workers is $ 120. The average salary per head of the supervisors is $800 and that of the workers is $ 112. Given that the number of supervisors is 12, find the number of workers in the factory.
4	A lump of two precious metals weighing 18 gm is worth $ 174 but if their weight were interchanged, it would be worth $157.20. If the price of one metal were $ 13.40 per gm, find the weight of the other metal in the mixture.
5	A container contains 80 kg of milk. From this container, 8 kg of milk was taken out and replaced by water. This was repeated for two more times. How much milk now remains in the container.

SOLUTIONS

1. Luckily the cost of water is indicated as nil or else this would be a non-starter. I am asked to state the gain percentage and hence let me assume that there is a litre of sherbet costing $10 and I wish to add water to it so that I pass off the resultant mixture as sherbet itself and make a gain.

   Suppose I were to add 100 cc of water, how much water would I have added to the sherbet as compared to its prior volume? 10%. How much sherbet do I have to sell now? I now have 1.10 litres of sherbet that I can sell @ $10 per litre and charge $ 11 and earn a profit of $1, which is effectively 10% profit.

   Suppose I were to add 200 cc of water, how much water would I have added to the sherbet? 20%. How much sherbet do I have to sell now? I now have 1.20 litres of sherbet that I can sell @ $ 10 per litre and charge $ 12 and earn a profit of $ 2, which is effectively 20% profit.

   The percentage of profit is equal to the percentage of water that I must add. So if I am to gain 18.75% by selling at cost, I may add 18.75% water.

2. Let us assume that the bottle contained 100 cc of sherry at the outset when it contained 40 cc of alcohol (i.e. before the batman started feasting on it). Let us assume that he helped himself to X cc.

   When the fellow takes X cc away, the alcohol content in that X cc is 40% of X cc which is 0.4Xcc. The bottle thus now contained (40 – 0.4X) cc of alcohol.

   When he replaces what he had taken, he puts in X cc of sherry containing 16% alcohol, the content of alcohol now is [(40-0.4X) + 0.16X] cc of alcohol.

   The overall volume of sherry is however only 100 cc whereas what varies is only the alcohol content since if there are 100cc to begin with, and he steals X cc and then he replaces X cc, the total volume of liquid in the bottle remains 100 cc.

   So at the end of it all the 100 cc had 24% alcohol and this is then 24 cc of alcohol. The equation that emerges is as follows:

   [(40 – 0.4X) + 0.16X] =24 and thus 40 – 0.4X + 0.16X = 24 and hence – 0.24X= –16 and thus X = 16/0.24 or 1600/24 = 200/3 cc or **two thirds of the bottle.**

3. Let there be W number of workers. The number of supervisors is given as 12. This makes (W+12) number of staff and since their average salary is \$ 120, the total salary is 120(W+12).

The number of supervisors being 12, $(800 \times 12) + 112 \times W = 120(W + 12)$ and thus $9600 + 112W = 120W + 1440$, hence $8W = 9600 - 1440 = 8160$ and therefore $W = 1020$. So the **number of workers is 1020.**

4. Let us assume that there are X grams of the metal costing \$ 13.40 per gram in the lump. Let us also assume that the price of the other metal is \$ P per gram of which there are (18 – X) grams. This means that: $P(18 - X) + 13.4X = 174$ and thus we get equation A: $18P - PX + 13.4X = 174$

$PX + 13.4(18 - X) = 157.2$ and we get equation B: $PX + (13.4 \times 18) - 13.4X = 157.2$

If we were to add equation B to equation A, we would get $18P + 241.2 = 331.2$ and hence $18P = 90$ and hence $P = 5$.

Now substituting the price of the other metal in equation A we get $90 - 5X + 13.4X = 174$ and hence $8.4X = 84$ and thus $X = 10$. Thus the weight of the other metal in the lump is $18 - 10 =$ **8 grams.**

5. The first time 8 kg of milk was taken out the container had $80 - 8 = 72$ kg of milk. This was replaced by water. The container now has 80 kg of mixture of milk and water of which 72 kg is milk and 8 kg is water. The percentage of milk in the mixture is $72 \times 100 \div 80 = 90\%$.

If another 8 kg of milk were to be taken out then 90% of this 8 kg would be milk and this would be 7.2 kg. So the container now has $72 - 7.2 = 64.8$ kg of milk. The percentage of milk in the container is $64.8 \times 100 \div 80 = 81\%$.

If another 8 kg of milk were to be taken out then 81% of this 8 kg would be milk and this would be $8 \times 81 \div 100$kg. So the container now has $64.8 - (8 \times 81 \div 100\text{kg}) = 64.8 - 6.48 =$ **58.32 kg of milk.** The percentage of milk in the container is now $58.32 \times 100 \div 80 = 5832/80 = 72.9\%$.

The first time the percentage of milk drawn from the container was 10% of its original volume. The percentage of milk in the undiluted mixture was 100%, and then it fell to 90% and then to 81%. Each time the percentage of milk is reduced to 0.9 times its original percentage. So the third time this business of drawing milk and then replacing it with 10% of the volume of the container was carried out, the percentage of milk in the container should have dropped to 0.9 times 81% and this is 72.9% and 72.9% of 80 kg is 58.32 kg.

Chapter 28

Divisibility Rules

A number is divisible by another if there is no remainder as a result of this division. So when you divide 8 by 4, you get a quotient of 2 and no remainder. This means that 8 is divisible by 4. Then if you were to try dividing 163 by 15 and find that you get a quotient of 10 but also a remainder of 13, it means that 163 is not divisible by 15. However, there are some ground rules about divisibility and these are worth remembering – not memorising, but remembering – because these ground rules would enable you to say with a single glance at the number 167 that it is not divisible by 3, nor with 5 nor with 11 and so on. In short, there are some little niceties about divisibility that would be of significant help both in terms of economy of effort when dividing and time saving as well. It will be our objective to learn these rules of divisibility by a method that will make remembering them so easy.

When you have thirty chocolates and give them equally to three boys, you are giving ten to each one of them. When you have thirty chocolates and are to give equally to each of them, you are again dividing them between two young lads who will squeal with joy when they get 15 each in lieu of 10 as in the case of dividing among three boys. But when you give all thirty to just one boy, you are not dividing at all. You are allotting them to a single unit. The chocolates have been united, not divided. Dividing by the number 1 is not division. It is unification.

When you are asked to factorise a number-say, the number 19 - you may have no choice but factorising it as 1 and 19. This is because it is a prime number. Let us see when you would have to factorise 19.

Suppose you are told that the difference between the squares of two integers is 19, and then are asked to find out these integers. If you were to imagine that these two integers are X and Y, then $(X^2 - Y^2) = 19$ and therefore $(X + Y) \times (X - Y) = 19$. Here you have no choice but to factorise 19 as 19 and 1 so that $(X + Y) = 19$ and $(X - Y) = 1$ and therefore $X = 10$ and $Y = 9$.

But if you are told, for example, that $K = (17N^2 + 6N^2 + 19N + 6)/N$ is an expression when N is a natural number – natural numbers incidentally are those that can be counted on your finger tips (up to a point, of course) and therefore start with 1 and then you have 2 and then 3 and so on – then for how many values of N will you get integral values for K, you have to understand that when you are trying to divide $(17N^2 + 6N^2 + 19N + 6)$ with N, up to $(17N^2 + 6N^2 + 19N)$, the expression is divisible by N regardless of the value of N. What is to be seen is for what values of N, will 6 be divisible by N. If $N = 6$, then the entire expression $(17N^2 + 6N^2 + 19N + 6)$ is divisible by N because N itself is 6. But 6 is a composite number and therefore divisible by its factors. This means that when you factorise 6, you can factorise it as 1×6 or 2×3. On the face of it, N could have four values: 1, 2, 3 and 6. But when you factorise 6 as 1×6, since you have seen that when $N = 6$, the entire expression is divisible by N, you might have to put $N = 1$. This means that in the expression $(17N^2 + 6N^2 + 19N + 6)/N$, you are dividing $(17N^2 + 6N^2 + 19N + 6)$ with 1 and this is not on since division with 1 is not division at all; it is unification. Thus you are left with three values for N: 2, 3 and 6. Put N as any one of 2, 3 and 6 and you will get integral values for K.

A number is an even number if it is divisible by 2. The first of such numbers is 2. Incidentally the only even prime number is 2. See the first few even numbers and you will find it so easy to remember that the last digit of an even number is invariably one of these five digits: 0, 2, 4, 6, and 8. A number ending with an odd digit – such as 1, 3, 5, 7 and 9 – can never be an even number.

Suppose you are multiplying some numbers as follows: A × B × C × D × E and so on is a row of numbers that may stretch long enough to take a lap around the Equator, even if all but one number in this long multiplication are odd and just one number is an even number, the result of this multiplication (usually referred to as the *product*) will invariably be even.

An odd number if divided by another odd number would invariably give an odd number if the first odd number (in the numerator) were exactly divisible by the second odd number (in the denominator). This is because any odd number multiplied by another odd number always yields an odd number. So 21 divided by 3 yields 7 and 33 divided by 11 yields 3 which too is an odd number. This is because an odd multiple of 11 for example if denoted by N (10 + 1) – read N times (10 + 1) where N is a real number would give N when divided by 11 which is as such (10 + 1). For example, 33 is 3 (10 + 1) and 11 is (10 + 1) and when you divide 3 (10 + 1) by (10 + 1), the result will be that (10 + 1) in both numerator and denominator will cancel off and you will be left with 3. If there were to be an even number in place of N in N (10 + 1) you cannot get an odd number as a value for N (10 + 1) at all.

A number is an odd number if it is not divisible by 2. Thus the last digit of an odd number is one of these five digits: 1, 3, 5, 7, and 9. When you multiply an odd number with another odd number, the product will invariably be odd. For that matter if you were to raise an odd number to the power of an odd number or an even number, the outcome is invariably an odd number. This is because when you raise an odd number to a power (whether even or odd power) what you are doing is multiplying that odd number with itself a certain number of times. Fundamentally, an odd number multiplied by itself whether once or for a thousand times can yield nothing other than an odd number, the square or cube and so on of an odd number will be invariably odd.

A number is divisible by 3 if its digits add up to 3 or any integral multiple of 3 such as 3, 6, 9, 12 and so on. This is a property of numbers divisible by 3. It is a matter of observation.

There are only 2 single digit numbers divisible by 4 and these are 4 and 8. A two-digit number is divisible by 4 if the last two digits are any of the following 25 combinations: 00, 04, 08, 12, 20, 16, 24, 28, 32, 36, 40, 44, 48, 52, 56, 60, 64, 68, 72, 76, 80, 84, 88, 92, and 96.

If a number ends with either of the digits 0, 4 or 8, then it can be divisible by 4 only if the digit in the tens' place is even. If a number ends with any one of the digits 2 and 6 then it can be divisible by 4 only if the digits in the tens' place is odd.

All hundreds are divisible by 4. This is because 100 = 2 × 2 × 5 × 5. Therefore, all powers of 10, higher than 10^2, are also divisible by 4. Then since 1000 = 2 × 2 × 2 × 5 × 5 × 5, all thousands are divisible by 8. It is also easy to understand that all even thousands will be divisible by 16 for the reason that in an even thousand, there will be one more 2 than in an odd thousand, taking up the number of twos in the factors of even thousands to 4 and since 2 × 2 × 2 × 2 is 16, all even thousands are divisible by 16. Basically if one were to remember that 10 = 2 × 5 and that $10^N = 2^N \times 5^N$, one can quickly see why 40000 is divisible by 64.

A number is divisible by 5 only if the last digit is either 5 or 0. This is a property of numbers divisible by 5. This too is a matter of observation. If the last digit of a number is 5, then this number is an odd multiple of 5 and if the last digit of any number is 0 then this number is an even multiple of 5.

A number is divisible by 6 if it is simultaneously divisible by both 2 and 3. This means that a number divisible by 6 has got to have the following properties:

- It must be an even number and should therefore end with 0, 2, 4, 6 or 8.
- The sum of its digits should be 3 or any integral multiple of 3 such as 3, 6, 9, 12 and so on.

A number is divisible by 9 **only** if its digits add up to 9 or integral multiples of 9 such as 9, 18, 27, 36 and so on. So when you look at the number 188, if you wish to know if it is divisible by 36, you must appreciate that in order for a number to be divisible by 36, it must first be divisible by 9. Add the digits 1, 8 and 8 and you find 17. Since 17 is not divisible by 9, so is 188 not divisible by 9. If you wish to know what number higher than 188 but nearest to 188 is divisible by 9, then add 1 to the total of the digits of 188 and you get 18. Thus 188 + 1 (or 189) is divisible by 9. If you wish to know which number, lower than 188 but nearest to 188, is divisible by 9 then subtract 8 from the total of the digits of 188 and you get 9. This means 188 – 8 (or 180) is the number lower than 188 but nearest to 188 that is divisible by 9.

A number is divisible by 10 only if the last digit is 0. So only 10, 20, 30... 100, 200 and so on will be divisible by 10.

A number is divisible by 11 only if (A – B) is either = 0 or 11 or integral multiples of 11 where:

- A is the sum of its even digits (meaning the second digit which is the digit in the tens' place) + the fourth digit (which is the digit in the thousands' place) and so on, and
- B is the sum of its odd digits, meaning the first digit (which is the digit in the units' place) + the third digit and so on

If I wish to check whether the number 1605857 is divisible by 11 or not let me add the numbers in even digits and I get (A) 6 + 5 + 5 = 16 and the numbers in odd digits and I get (B) 1 + 0 + 8 + 7 = 16 and the difference between A and B is zero. The number 1605857 is divisible by 11. This too is a matter of observation whereby it has come to light that it is the property of numbers divisible by 11 that the difference between the sum of its digits in odd places and the sum of its digits in even places is either zero or integral multiples of 11.

While here onwards, it may be possible to state the rules of divisibility of a number by say 12 where it should be divisible by both 3 and 4 and of 15 which should be divisible by both 3 and 5 and so on, there is really no need for stating such rules. The basic rules stated above should do. Would you need to be told why a number is divisible by 99 only if it is simultaneously divisible by both 9 and 11?

Having acquainted ourselves with the clutch and the brake and the accelerator and so on, let us switch on the ignition and take a go at the steering so as to pick up the nitty-gritty of car driving as we go along. We shall see the concepts that we have presented in the notes here before being reinforced through the medium of illustrations. Here we go!

Illustration 1:

I have a total of $1000. Item A costs $110, item B costs $90, item C costs $70, item D costs $40 and item E costs $45. For every item D that I purchase, I must also buy two of item B. For every item A, I must buy one item C. For every item E, I must also buy two of item D and one of item B. For every item purchased I earn 1000 points and for every dollar not spent I earn a penalty of 1500 points. My objective is to maximise the points I earn. What is the number of items that I must purchase to maximise my points?

The options are as follows: (1) 13 (2) 14 (3) 15 (4) 16

The detailed solution

The information given may be worthwhile mapping.

If I purchase A, I will also have to purchase C; thus one A would mean A+C meaning Rs.180 and 2 items

For every item D, I must also buy 2B;

For every E, I must also buy 2D + 1B.

For every item purchased I earn 1000 points and for every dollar not spent, I earn penalty of 1500 points.

	Item				
	A	B	C	D	E
Cost per item	110	90	70	40	45

A + C = $180; items 2

E + 2D + B + 2(2B on account of having to buy 2B with every D) = E + 2D + 5B = $575; 8 items

D + 2B = $220; 3 items.

Since I am to maximise points, I would be tempted to buy as many items as possible. In this I find myself trying 2 of E that would give me 16 items. But this would mean crossing $1000 since 575 × 2 = 1150.

The first thing to be noted is that there is no compulsion about buying any other item with B and C.

Both buying three of A and two of D would mean my spending $3 × 180 + 2 × 220 = $980 leaving me with $20 and a huge negative 30000 points (20 × 1500); the surplus can buy me nothing thereafter. **The message is clear – I must minimise the surplus.** This can happen only with buying 13 items of C (13 × 70 = 910) and 1 of item C (90); I would spend all of $1000 and have no surplus left. Thus I buy 13 + 1 = 14 items and hence Option 2.

In this illustration there is an important lesson to be learnt as regards divisibility.

We are told that for every item purchased I earn 1000 points and for every dollar not spent, I earn penalty of 1500 points and the cost of the items are as per hereunder:

	Item				
	A	B	C	D	E
Cost per item	110	90	70	40	45

Would it not be sensible to lop off unnecessary zeroes from all the figures in the information that has been provided in regard to this problem as per hereunder?

For every item purchased I earn 1 point and for every dollar not spent, I earn penalty of 1.5 points. Of what use are the three zeroes behind 1000 or the two zeroes behind 1500? Why not divide both by 1000 and keep small numbers to work with comfortably? Whether you get 1000 points or 1 point per dollar spent or lose 1500 points or lose 1.5 points per dollar unspent, will the number of items change because of reducing the number of zeroes in this points system?

What you are asked is to find out the maximum number of items that you can purchase.

Then as regards, the amount of money to be spent of which I have a total of $1000 and the prices of the items, can we not knock off one zero everywhere so that you have $100 to spend and the prices are as per hereunder?

	Item				
	A	B	C	D	E
Cost per item	11	9	7	4	4.5

With this will things not become trim? Will one then not be operating in the tables of small numbers like 11 or 7 or 9? Will it not occur to us that 7 × 13 + 9 = 91 + 9 = 100 and that I can buy 13+1=14 things and yet not have a single rupee unspent and with this I have not to even think of penalty points?

Is this problem anything but a test of your knowledge of tables of small numbers if seen in this fresh light after having noted that there is no compulsion about buying any other item with B and C?

Illustration 2

Let N = 1421 × 1423 × 1425. What is the remainder when 12 divide N?

The detailed solution

The question is: Are you expected to actually calculate the product of 1421, 1423 and 1425 and then divide this product by 12? It will probably run into 11 or 12 digits and might take a few minutes whereas all the time that you can allocate to this question is about a minute.

The answer is: Certainly not!

Then how would you find the answer to such a question?

The first thing to be realised is that 1421, 1423 and 1425 are such that if you add 2 to the previous number, then you have the subsequent number.

Then one has to appreciate that in order to deal with questions like this, one has to reduce the problem to a slightly smaller size and see what would be the remainder if one were to multiply 21, 23 and 25 and divide their product by 12.

If one wanted to find out for sure as to what will be the product of 21, 23, and 25 how would one go about it? How would one multiply 21 and 25 quickly? $4 \times 25 = 100$ and thus $20 \times 25 = 500$ and so $21 \times 25 = 500 + 25 = 525$. $23 \times 525 = 23 \times 500 + 23 \times 25 = 11500 + 575 = 12075$ and if you were to divide 12075 by 12, we know that 12000 would in any case be divisible. Plus 72 is also divisible by 12 and thus $12075 \div 12$ would leave a remainder of 3.

Now how can one build the theme for the larger problem drawing the lesson from its reduced version?

21 is (12 + 9), 23 is (12 + 11) and 25 is ($2 \times 12 + 1$). Let A = 12. So $21 \times 23 \times 25 = (A + 9) \times (A + 11) \times (2A + 1) = (A^2+20A+99) \times (2A+1)$. In this multiplication only the term where you multiply $9 \times 11 \times 1$ will be independent of A. Since we have taken A to be equal to 12, all powers of A will also be divisible by 12 and then the crux of the matter lies in finding out as to what will be the remainder when 99 is divided by 12. If one knows one's tables, $12 \times 8 = 96$ and thus 99 (which is 96 + 3) $\div$ 12 will leave a remainder of 3.

The important thing to see is that the question is limited to finding only the remainder when N, which is equal to $1421 \times 1423 \times 1425$ is divided by 12.

How do we find out as to which is that number that is closest to 1421, 1423 and 1425 and is also divisible by 12? Try dividing 1421 by 12 and you will get a remainder of 5. This means that 1416 (which is 1421 - 5) is the number that you are looking for and that if you were to assume 1416 as equal to A then $1421 \times 1423 \times 1425$ is nothing other than $(A + 5) \times (A + 7) \times (A + 9)$ and that in this multiplication, the only term that will be independent of A will be $5 \times 7 \times 9 = 315$ and thus what you are effectively required to find out is the remainder when you divide 315 by 12 since A and all its higher powers will be invariably divisible by 12. Now 315 divided by 12 will leave a remainder of 3 and hence the answer to the main question is that if $N = 1421 \times 1423 \times 1425$, then 3 is the remainder when 12 divides N.

Illustration 3

The integers 34041 and 32506 when divided by a three digit number *n*, leave the same remainder. What is *n*? The options are: (1) 289 (2) 367 (3) 453 (4) 307

The detailed solution

Now just as we have assumed A to be 1416 which is a multiple of 12 in the previous example, let us assume that:

(A) the number 34041 is X times *n* + the remainder R when 34041 is divided by *n* and

(B) the number 32506 is Y times *n* + the remainder R, where both X and Y are positive integers

Since 34041 > 32506, X > Y and since the remainder is common in both cases of dividing by *n*, we have assumed the remainder to be R in both cases.

Thus when I subtract 32506 from 34041, what I am doing is subtracting (Yn + R) from (Xn + R) and I would get n (X – Y) and since both X and Y are positive integers such that X > Y, (X – Y) will also be a positive integer and thus n (X – Y) is also an integral multiple of *n*. Now let us subtract 32506 from 34041 and we get 1535. So 1535 is an integral multiple of *n*. Which among the options is a clear factor of 1535? 307? Quite obviously for one can spot straightaway that 1535 is 307×5. So Option 4.

Illustration 4

What is the remainder when 48 divides 7^{84}?

The detailed solution

What does one have to know in order to crack this question? We should know these three things:

1. $7^2 = 49$ and therefore $48 = 7^2 - 1$
2. 84 is 42 times 2
3. $(A^N - 1)$ is always divisible by $(A - 1)$ where N is a positive integer

If we know that 84 is 42 times 2, it means that 7^{84} is as such $(7^2)^{42}$. Thus if we were to take 7^2 as A, then 7^{84} is A^{42}. Thus 7^{84} is $7^{84} - 1 + 1$ (or $A^{42} - 1 + 1$); add one to a number and then subtract one and there is no change to the number as such; what you are doing is preparing the ground for dividing 7^{84} by $7^2 - 1$, which you must if you are ever to see what is the result of this division. When you divide $(A^{42} - 1 + 1)$ by $(A - 1)$, there will be no remainder till $(A^{42} - 1)$. The number 1 after $(A^{42} - 1)$ will not be divisible by (A-1).

It must be noted that $(A^N - 1)$ is always divisible by (A-1) where N is a positive integer. Let us see how:

Let N be 2. Then $(A^N - 1) = (A^2 - 1)$ which as such is $(A^2 - A + A - 1)$ or in other words $[(A^2 - A) + (A - 1)]$ or $[A(A - 1) + 1(A - 1)]$ or $[(A + 1) \times (A - 1)]$.

Let N be 3. Then $(A^N - 1) = (A^3 - 1)$ which as such is $(A^3 - A^2 + A^2 - A + A - 1)$ or in other words $[(A^2(A - 1) + A(A - 1) + 1(A - 1)]$ or $[A^2 + A + 1) \times (A - 1)]$.

It can be seen from the above that regardless of the value of N, $(A - 1)$ will always be a factor of $(A^N - 1)$ so long as N is a positive integer. Therefore $(A^N - 1)$ is always be divisible by $(A - 1)$. Thus when you divide 7^{84} by 48, the remainder will be 1.

Illustration 5:

What will be the remainder when 24 divides 5^{84}?

The detailed solution

When you see 24, it must strike a bell that the number 24 is nothing other than $5^2 - 1$. What one is required to do is to divide 5^{84} by $(5^2 - 1)$.

What would you call the level of the syllabus in which you are required to do a sum involving division of another number by 24? Standard V, at best!

How long would it take a calculator to reckon the precise value of 5^{84}? Probably never since it would not have that much space for the number of digits that would be involved. How long would it take for a computer to reckon the precise value of 5^{84}? Again it may not come up with a precise answer since there may not be space for so many digits and then again the computer will not tell you what the remainder will be; it will tell you the result of this division in a large number of decimals but the remainder you will have to work out yourself. Try dividing 15 by 8 in your calculator and you will see 1.875, which is the exact answer to three places of decimals (it stops at three places of decimals because that is all there can be). It will not tell you that the remainder is 7.

Then why is it being given to you to be worked out in a span of a few seconds? Because a seasoned human being can answer this on the basis of sheer reasoning and therefore you can state precisely what the remainder will be.

What if such a sum was given to students appearing for the School Level examination? They would probably start attempting to work out the value of 5^{84} and after realising this is a hopeless task, some of the examinees may faint when realising the enormous dimensions of the problem.

Why is it being administered at the competitive examination? Because by then the person's perception level has become vastly different! He is used to analysing problems differently with the substantially sharpened faculty of logic at his command.

So what would you do in the present circumstances wherein you are required to state what will be the remainder when 24 divides 5^{84}?

First, you see 5^{84} divided by 24 as $(5^{84} - 1 + 1) \div (5^2 - 1)$. Then you take 5^2 as A and thus 5^{84} as $A^{42} - 1 + 1$. Then you would have started wondering whether $(A^{42} - 1)$ will be exactly divisible by $(A - 1)$. But with the methodology that we have seen in the previous illustration, you will have a naughty smile on your face when you tick 1 as the correct answer.

Illustration 6

What will be the remainder when 6 divides 4^{643}?

The detailed solution

The time at your disposal for answering this question may not extend beyond a minute. It might take a supercomputer a miniature eternity to work out the precise value of 4^{643} but having done so it may take only a flash to divide 4^{643} by 6 and yet you shall not be able to see what will be the precise remainder. You will only get a string of decimals. So what do you do? Well, you divide:

- 4^1 by 6 to begin with and you find that the quotient is zero and the remainder is 4
- 4^2 by 6 to carry things forward and you find that the quotient is 2 and the remainder is 4
- 4^3 by 6 to carry things further and you find that the quotient is 10 and the remainder is 4

The writing on the wall is crystal clear:

- There is a clear pattern that emerges and the pattern is that whenever you divide any integral power of 4 by 6, you invariably get a remainder of 4
- The matter pertains not to mathematics but to reasoning

We shall see this from the mathematical point as well so that for those of us who are comfortable with mathematics, the concept is reinforced. What we shall do is to see 4 being raised first to an even power and then to an odd power and see whether the result of dividing this exponential of 4 by 6 is the same all through.

4^2 is $(6\text{-}2)^2$ which is nothing other than $(A\text{-}2)^2$ if you take 6 as A; $(A - 2)^2$ is $(A^2 - 4A + 4)$ and since we have assumed 6 as A, $(A^2 - 4A + 4)/A$ will mean a remainder of 4 since in the expression $(A^2 - 4A + 4)$, up to $(A^2 - 4A)$, division by A will leave no remainder.

4^3 is $(6 - 2)^3$ which is nothing other than $(A - 2)^3$ if you take 6 as A; $(A - 2)^3$ is $(A^3 - 6A^2 + 12A - 8)$ and since we have assumed 6 as A, $(A^3 - 6A^2 + 12A)/A$ will mean no remainder since up to this stage the whole expression is in powers of A. There will be an integral value so far but when it comes to – 8 divided by 6, then you will get – 1 integers and 1/3rd. –1 integers will pull away one integer from the integral value that you will get up to $(A^3 - 6A^2 + 12A)/A$. From this one less integer, – 1/3rd will pull away one more integer and leave you with 2/3rd. Therefore whatever the remainder be, it will be 2/3rd of 6 and this shall be 4 invariably regardless of the power to which 4 is raised.

Another interesting aspect of divisibility that would be interesting is that whenever you divide an integer with 3, 9, 11, 33, 37, 99, 101 and so on, you are likely to see a recurring decimal. In order to appreciate this better, one should have a calculator handy and see for oneself that:

You see recurring decimals when you divide:

1 with 3 you will get 0.33333333....

2 with 3 you get 0.66666666.. (However this rule does not apply to numbers that are divisible by 3, which is why you will not see a recurring decimal when you divide 3, 6 and so on by 3)

7 with 9 you get 0.777777.... or 8 with 9 you get 0.88888888...(However this rule does not apply to numbers that are divisible by 9, which is why you will not see a recurring decimal when you divide 9, 18 and so on by 9)

3 with 11, you get 0.27272727... or 10 with 11 you get 0.90909090...(However this rule does not apply to numbers that are divisible by 11, which is why you will not see a recurring decimal when you divide 22, 33 and so on by 11)

14 with 33, you get 0.42424242... or 29 with 33 you get 0.8787878787...(However this rule does not apply to numbers that are divisible by 33, which is why you will not see a recurring decimal when you divide 66, 99 and so on by 33)

2 with 37, you get 0.054054054054... or 11 with 37 you get 0.297297297297...(However this rule does not apply to numbers that are divisible by 37, which is why you will not see a recurring decimal when you divide 74, 111 and so on by 37)

We find it would suffice if we were to stop here and recommend that you, dear reader, verify whether you would indeed get a recurring decimal if you were to divide numbers less than 99 by 99 and numbers less than 101 by 101 and number less than 111 by 111 and so on.

We would also suggest that you investigate why you get a recurring decimal in each of these cases and write to us the result of your findings to the following e-mail address: jivaishnav@yahoo.com. Do also let us have your feedback about the quality of the presentations in this book and your suggestions if any for improving it further.

Chapter 29

Permutations, Combinations and Probability

Permutations and combinations are two different ways of arranging objects. If a person removes two balls, one at a time, from a billiard pocket containing three balls, then there are six possible permutations. Please see this illustration. If the three balls in a billiards pocket are of three different colours – say, red, blue and white – then you can have the following **permutations** of two balls picked one at a time:

Permutation 1: White and Blue

Permutation 2: White and Red

Permutation 3: Red and Blue

Permutation 4: Red and White

Permutation 5: Blue and Red

Permutation 6: Blue and White

The order of arrangement is important in determining the number of permutations; choosing a red ball then a blue ball is a different permutation from choosing a blue ball then a red ball.

When determining the number of possible **combinations**, however, ordering is not important; choosing a red ball then a blue ball results in the same combination as choosing a blue ball then a red one. The combination is essentially of a red ball and a blue ball regardless of which colour is picked first and which is picked thereafter. As a result, there are effectively only three possible distinct **combinations**. These three combinations are Permutations 1, 2 and 3 as above; Permutation 1 is not distinct from Permutation 6. Similarly Permutation 2 above is not distinct from Permutation 4 above and finally Permutation 3 above is not different form Permutation 5 above. There are three distinct permutations. We shall not argue which of these are distinct: you may consider White and Blue as distinct whereas I may consider Blue and White as distinct. There can be no end to an argument about which is distinct. But we are agreed on the fact that three out of six are distinct. These three distinct permutations are combinations. This is the essential difference between permutations and combinations.

It is important to note that when we permute, we should pursue an absolutely logical sequence. If you are to permute the digits 1, 2, 3, and 4 so as to find out how many **distinct** numbers can be formed with these four digits, it is important to first put down the smallest number that can be formed from these digits, then followed by the next smallest number and rising progressively to the highest number that can be so formed. This sequence would kick off as follows:

000's Place	00's Place	Tens Place	Units Place	000's Place	00's Place	Tens Place	Units Place
1	2	3	4	3	1	2	4
1	2	4	3	3	1	4	2
1	3	2	4	3	2	1	4
1	3	4	2	3	2	4	1
1	4	2	3	3	4	1	2
1	4	3	2	3	4	2	1
2	1	3	4	4	1	2	3
2	1	4	3	4	1	3	2
2	3	1	4	4	2	1	3
2	3	4	1	4	2	3	1
2	4	1	3	4	3	1	2
2	4	3	1	4	3	2	1

The idea is not to miss a single possible permutation. When you sit down to crosscheck, it would be so easy to find out which permutations have you missed or which you have taken more than once. This is because you follow a logical pattern. In the absence of such a logical pattern there would be chaos. Besides, this is the surest way of realising that each digit occurs exactly six times in each of the thousands, hundreds, tens and units place and this is precisely why the number of permutations that are possible from 4 different digits is $4 \times 3 \times 2 \times 1 = 24$. This is four factorial times. Only from a logical arrangement of the digits is it possible to appreciate why the number of distinct arrangements is four-factorial. This is because for the first digit (meaning for the thousands place) if you have four choices, then for the hundreds place you have choice out of the remaining three and then for the hundreds place you may choose from the remaining two and lastly for the units place, you have one choice.

The above sequence should be followed even when arranging letters. If you are to arrange A, B, M and N in different permutations, then it is only proper to arrange A, B, M and N in ascending order as in the alphabet and then permute keeping this order in mind always. A would be least in value and N would be most if one were to mentally assign values to A, B, M and N and proceed according to the above table. This is the only way to ensure that you do not miss a single permutation, which you may if you went about this task in a random sort of way.

Permutations are sequenced arrangements of objects. Consider a small pack of cards consisting of just the Jack, Queen, King, and Ace of Hearts (whom we shall refer to as J, Q, K and A).

The order in which the cards are dealt would be a permutation.

There are 24 such permutations:

JQKA JQAK JKAQ JKQA JAQK JAKQ

QJKA QJAK QKAJ QKJA QAJK QAKJ

KQJA KQAJ KJAQ KJQA KAQJ KAJQ

AQKJ AQJK AKJQ AKQJ AJQK AJKQ

The number of different permutations can be worked out by considering what happens when the cards are being dealt.

The first card dealt and turned over could be 1 of 4 possible cards – it could be either a jack, or a queen or a king or an ace. The second card could be 1 of 3 remaining possibilities, the third card 1 of 2 and there would be only one choice of fourth card.

This gives the total permutations as $4 \times 3 \times 2 \times 1 = 24$, which can also be written as 4! (Read this as *four factorial*).

In general there are n factorial permutations of choosing, or arranging, n objects in sequence, where *n factorial* represents the product of all the positive integers from 1 to n, and 0! is defined as 1.

The above example represents the permutation of four objects taken four at a time; the number of such permutations is denoted by the symbol $4P_4$. If we were to imagine someone holding these cards in one's hands while playing a game of cards, then whether one has arranged the cards according to the order – say – AQKJ or JKAQ, the combination of cards in hand is not going to be only one combination. The order in which J, Q, K and A have been dealt will not make any difference to the cards in hand.

However, when we are to make, say, 4-digit numbers from the digits 1, 2, 3 and 4 there can be 24 combinations [six combinations with 1 as the first digit such as 1234, 1243, 1324, 1342, 1423 and 1432 and six more with each of 2, 3 and 4 as the first digit making 24 numbers each of which has a distinctive value].

We shall now see the elementary but important aspects of probability through the methodology of illustrations.

What is the chance that in two dice thrown together, I will get the number 3 on both surfaces facing me?

Here one must see what is the chance that one will get 3 on a face of a single dice thrown once. There are six faces to a dice. There is one only instance in which the number 3 can turn up on the surface that is facing me. Thus the chance of getting the number 3 on the surface of the dice facing me is 1 out of 6. **(This is true of any number from 1 to 6 on the dice thrown once and not just of 3)**

Now what about two dice thrown together? From what one has learnt at school it should be $(1/6) \times (1/6) = (1/36)$. But how! And why?

When one throws up two dice together the following combinations are possible:

11	21	31	41	51	61
12	22	32	42	52	62
13	23	**33**	43	53	63
14	24	34	44	54	64
15	25	35	45	55	65
16	26	36	46	56	66

There are 6 faces on a dice. When one throws a dice, any one of six different faces can come up. There are 6 faces on the other dice as well. When two dice are thrown, the total number of possible combinations on the face of the two dice is a multiple of the possible number of faces that may come up on each dice. In all therefore there are 36 combinations that are possible. The above table tells you how and why this is so. Out of these 36 possibilities, there is only one instance in which two 3's can come up as highlighted in the above table. The chance of getting the number 3 on two surfaces facing me is 1/36. This explains why one has to multiply the possibility of 1/6 for the number 3 to appear on the surface of the first dice with 1/6 for the number 3 to appear on the surface of the second dice. It makes no difference whether the two dice are thrown together or thrown one by one. The fundamentals would remain the same.

Now if there were to be an examination in which there are two options for answers and you are to mark the correct answer by ticking against the option you think is correct and there are three particulars questions that you know nothing about but you wish to take your chances by ticking an option at random, what is the probability that you will get all three right?

We all learnt at school that the chance of getting one option right out of two is 1/2 and that the chance of getting three such answers right by ticking at random is $1/2 \times 1/2 \times 1/2 = 1/8$. But why do you need to multiply these probabilities? Let us see once for and all why do you need to multiply.

Let us see these three questions and the options and see the whole thing live.

Question 1. The art of flower decoration in Japan is known as (A) Kawasaki (B) Ikebana

Question 2: The language spoken in lower Nigeria is (A_1) Swahili (B_1) Kwacha

Question 3: The art form where the artist paints what his mind perceives and not what his eyes see is known as (A_2) Surrealism (B_2) Realism

Now suppose one did not have the faintest idea and one were to tick the answers at random. What is the chance that all three will be right? Let us assume that the three correct answers are B, B_1, and A_2.

Suppose the space for marking the correct answers looked like this.

A	B
A_1	B_1
A_2	B_2

The following combinations are possible.

$A A_1 A_2$	$A A_1 B_2$	$A B_1 A_2$	$A B_1 B_2$	$B A_1 A_2$	$B A_1 B_2$	$B B_1 A_2$	$B B_1 B_2$

In all therefore, there are eight combinations, which is the number of options in each case multiplied by one another (meaning $2 \times 2 \times 2 = 8$). Out of these eight possible combinations, we can see that the correct sequence that we have assumed as B B_1 A_2 appears only once and is highlighted in the above table.

It is thus that the chance of getting three questions right (with two options against each of them) when one were to tick three options at random is 1/8th. This, we trust, conclusively explains why one has to multiply the three probabilities (or chance if you please) in order to arrive at the overall probability. One has to derive one's concepts from reducing problems to small sizes. This is why we took an illustration that involved three questions and two possible answers against each problem. If we were to devote our attention to, say, 150 questions with 4 possible answers against each question, the task of actually plotting and finding out how many combinations are possible may take months.

Let us see the other aspects of permutations and combinations as we go along with the illustrations hereunder.

Illustration 1

Let n be the number of different five digit numbers, divisible by 4 with the digits 1,2,3,4,5 and 6 no digit being repeated in the numbers. What is the value of n?

The first condition that is to be fulfilled is that the number should be divisible by 4. Remember: all hundreds are divisible by 4 and only the tens digit and the units digit will decide whether a number will be divisible by 4 or not. The second condition is that you are not allowed to repeat a digit. Which means that if for any given place – say the ten thousands place – you have exercised a choice out of 5 numbers, then for the thousands place, you have only four digits to choose from or else you are likely to repeat a digit.

Since one has to first decide as to which of these five digits in the tens and units place will give me a number divisible by 4, I find that there are eight possible combinations of digits in tens and units place that can make the number divisible by 4 and these eight combinations are: 12, 16, 24, 32, 36, 52, 56, and 64. Please note that we have been able to arrive at these eight possible combinations not on basis of any mathematical formula but on the basis of our knowledge of the rule of divisibility by 4.

If the last two digits are say 12, there can be a choice out of the remaining 4 digits in the first place, out of 3 in the second place and out of 2 in the third place. Thus with 12 as the last two digits, there can be $4 \times 3 \times 2 = 24$ combinations. These 24 combinations are possible only with 12 as the last two digits. Since there are 8 combinations in the last digits as per above, the total number of 5 digit numbers out of 1,2,3,4,5 and 6 divisible by 4 is $24 \times 8 = 192$.

Illustration 2

Sam has forgotten his friend's 7-digit telephone number. He remembers the following: the first three digits are either 635 or 674, the number is odd and the number 9 appears once. If Sam were to use a trial and error process to reach his friend, what is the minimum number of trials he has to make before he can be certain to succeed?

Let us presume that he starts out with the initial three digits as 635. This is because he has got to start somewhere. Staring at the telephone will not help him.

In that case he would have to work on the following combinations presented in the table below prepared with the assumption that he places the number 9 first time in the fourth digit and next time in the fifth and then in the sixth and finally in the seventh (which is necessarily an odd digit so as to make the telephone number an odd number):

First 3 Digits	4th Digit	5th Digit	6th Digit	7th Digit (which is necessarily odd)	Number of trials
635	1(No.9)	9 (meaning, any one of the nine numbers from 0 to 8)	9 (0 to 8)	4 (meaning, any one of 1,3,5,7)	9×9×4=324
635	9(0 to 8)	1 (Only No.9)	9 (0 to 8)	4 (1,3,5,7)	9×9×4=324
635	9(0 to 8)	9 (0 to 8)	1 (No.9)	4 (1,3,5,7)	9×9×4=324
635	9(0 to 8)	9 (0 to 8)	9 (0 to 8)	1 (Only No. 9)	9×9×9=729

The total number of combinations with 635 as prefix is 1701 (324 + 324 + 324 + 729). He will have to repeat these 1701 combinations with 674 as prefix. So in all he will have to be prepared to run through 1701 + 1701 = 3402 combinations.

Illustration 3

What is the sum of all the whole numbers that can be formed with the four digits 1, 2, 3 and 4 using each digit once only?

Let us reduce this problem to a slightly smaller level and learn the ropes from that level. Let us therefore deal with only three digits 1, 2 and 3. The strategy of reducing problems and then deriving one's lessons from this reduced level can get amazing results.

The numbers that can be formed from these three digits are 123, 132, 213, 231, 312, and 321; six in all!

Since we have actually seen the number of numbers that can be formed from the digits 1, 2 and 3 without repeating the digits, we may be able to derive the number of numbers that can be formed from three digits without actually writing the numbers so formed. The methodology is simple. If we are to choose a number for the first digit, we have three choices for this. Once we have exercised this choice for the first digit, then we can choose from only out of the remaining two for the second digit and then there is only one number left for the third digit. Hence the total number of combinations of three digit numbers possible from three numbers without repeating any of the digits is thus 3 × 2 × 1 = 6.

From these six numbers, the digit 1 occurs in two places, the digit 2 occurs in two places, and so also the digit 3. This is to be expected since only then can you form 6 numbers.

Thus if one were to add the six numbers formed out of three digits 1, 2 and 3, the hundreds place will have 1 two times and 2 two times and then 3 also two times. So the total of the hundreds place will be 2 times the total of (1+2+3) and would thus be 12. The contribution to the total on account of the hundreds place will be 1200. Similar will be the case of the tens place where since its total will be 12, the contribution to the total on account of the tens place will be 120 and so will it be in the case of the units place which will add 12 to the total.

So the total of all numbers formed with the three digits 1, 2 and 3 without repeating any of the digits is 1200 + 120 + 12 = 1332. If we were to manually add 123, 132, 213, 231, 312, and 321 we should get this total and we indeed do.

Then how many numbers are possible to form with the digits 1,2,3 and 4 without repeating any of the digits? $4 \times 3 \times 2 \times 1 = 24$ where each of the four digits will appear six times in each place. Thus the digits in the thousands place would add up to $6 \times (1 + 2 + 3 + 4) = 60$ and the hundreds place, the tens place and the units place will each add up to 60 and hence the sum of all the 24 possible numbers that can be formed from the digits 1, 2, 3 and 4 without repeating any of the digits is 60000 + 6000 + 600 + 60 = 66660.

Illustration 4:

What is the sum of all the whole numbers that can be formed with the three digits 1, 2, and 4?

Here there is no bar to using each digit more than once and since there are three digits, they can each be used three times so that $3 \times 3 \times 3 = 27$ combinations are possible. Let us see how these 27 combinations emerge in the table that unfolds herein below.

1st Digit	2nd Digit	3rd Digit	1st Digit	2nd Digit	3rd Digit	1st Digit	2nd Digit	3rd Digit
1	1	1	2	1	1	4	1	1
1	1	2	2	1	2	4	1	2
1	1	4	2	1	4	4	1	4
1	2	1	2	2	1	4	2	1
1	2	2	2	2	2	4	2	2
1	2	4	2	2	4	4	2	4
1	4	1	2	4	1	4	4	1
1	4	2	2	4	2	4	4	2
1	4	4	2	4	4	4	4	4

In all, 27 different numbers (meaning 27 different combinations from the three digits) are possible since there are three numbers that may be repeated as well. This means that for each digit we can choose from three numbers and hence the number of combinations when there are 3 digits is $= 3 \times 3 \times 3 = 27$.

Similarly if there were 4 digits with no bar to repeating the digits, then there would be $4 \times 4 \times 4 = 64$ combinations if one were allowed to repeat the digits.

But back to the question of the sum of all the whole numbers that can be formed with the three digits 1, 2, and 4, there are 27 different combinations possible, as we have seen above. It may also be seen that since there are 3 digits and 27 different combinations, each digit occurs in the 100s place 9 times, in the tens place 9 times and in the units place also 9 times. (Please count and ensure that you have understood this). Only then of course could 27 different combinations be possible.

Since each digit occurs in the hundreds place 9 times then the total in the hundreds place on account of say 1 in the above illustration would be 9. Since 2 occurs 9 times in the hundreds place, the total in the hundreds place would be 18 on account of 2 alone in the hundreds place. And since 4 occurs 9 times in the hundreds place 9 times, the total in the hundreds place on account of 4 alone would be 36. Hence the total in the hundreds place on account of the three digits 1, 2 and 4 together would be 9 + 18 + 36 = 63 (meaning $9 \times (1 + 2 + 4) = 9 \times 7 = 63$).

The same would be the case in the other two places (meaning tens and units) and hence the total in the tens place would be 63 and so also would 63 be the total in the units place.

The sum of all the whole numbers that can be formed with the three digits 1, 2, and 4 would then be (63 × 100 = 6300) + (63 × 10 = 630) + (63 × 1 = 63) = **6993.**

Illustration 5

How many distinct arrangements can be made from all six letters of the word BANANA used together?

Before we see the problem as posed above, let us see some fundamentals of how to determine the number of distinct arrangements of some letters that occur more than once.

Please see the table below in which we climb step by step and understand as to why is there a clear relationship between the number of arrangements if all the letters were distinct and the number of distinct arrangements when some letters occur more than once.

We shall then see what is the precise relationship between the two.

Suppose there were	How many distinct arrangements can be made from these?	What is the relation between the number of distinct arrangements and the number of letters that are identical?
Just one letter A from which one had to make distinct arrangements	Only one – the letter A by itself	No letters are identical so far
Two letters A and B from which one had to make distinct arrangements	Two – AB and BA	No letters are identical so far
Three letters, A, B and C from which one had to make distinct arrangements	Six – ABC, ACB, BAC, BCA, CAB and CBA	No letters are identical so far
Three letters, A, B and B from which one had to make distinct arrangements	Three in all - ABB, BAB and BBA	The total number of distinct arrangements is 6 (which is 3! or 3×2×1) and the total number of identical letters is 2 and hence the number of distinct arrangements is 3! / 2! = 3×2×1/2×1= 3
Four letters in all –B, B, C, and C from which one had to make distinct arrangements	Six in all - BBCC, BCBC, BCCB, CBBC, CCBB, CBCB	The total number of distinct arrangements is 24 (which is 4! or 4×3×2×1) and the total number of identical letters is 2 and 2 (meaning two of each kind) and hence the number of distinct arrangements is 4! / (2! × 2!)= 4×3×2×1/(2×1) ×(2×1)= 6

With the concepts as outlined in the above table having become clear, let us see as to how many distinct arrangements can be made from all six letters of the word BANANA used together.

BANANA is a six-letter word that has three A's and two N's. The number of distinct arrangements of six letters (if the six letters were to be different) is 6 Factorial (meaning 6 × 5 × 4 × 3 × 2 × 1) whereas there are two letters that occur more than once - the letter A occurs thrice whereas the letter N occurs twice. Therefore, the number of distinct arrangements that can be made with the six letters of the word BANANA is = 6 × 5 × 4 × 3 × 2 × 1/(3 × 2 × 1) × (2 × 1) = 60. So sixty distinct arrangements can be made from all six letters of the word BANANA used together.

Needless to say, it is important to remember this lesson that we have drawn from the table above for application in larger sums since if we were not to derive this lesson and insist on facing the problem in the case of the BANANA as above on its larger scale, this would be a mammoth task. The number of distinct arrangements of six letters (if the six letters were to be different) is 6 Factorial, which is 720. One cannot hope to draw 720 arrangements and then see which of these are distinct without developing a huge headache.

PROBABILITY

Mathematical probability began in an attempt to answer certain questions arising in games of chance, such as how many times a pair of dice must be thrown if there is to be a 50-50 chance that a 6 will have appeared by then. The probability of an outcome is represented by a number between 0 and 1 both inclusive. If the number of possible outcomes is finite, probability 0 indicates that an outcome will never occur and probability 1 indicates that it will always occur.

The simplest problems are concerned with the probability of a specified favourable result of an event that has a finite number of equally likely outcomes. If an event has n equally likely outcomes and f of them are termed favourable, the probability of a favourable outcome is f/n.

For example, a fair die can be cast in six equally likely ways; therefore, the probability of throwing a 5 or a 6 is 2/6 or 1/3. More involved problems are concerned with events in which the various possible outcomes are not equally likely. For example, in finding the probability of throwing a 5 or 6 with a pair of dice, we are to find out the possibility of a total of 5 (with 1 and 4, 2 and 3) and a total of 6 (with 1 and 5, 4 and 2, 3 and 3) the various outcomes (totals of 2, 3, 4, 7, and so on till 12) are not all equally likely. An event may even have infinitely many possible outcomes, as when a point is chosen at random on a circle. In such cases an outcome may occur and yet have probability 0.

Problems involving repeated trials form one of the connections between probability and statistics. To illustrate, what is the probability that exactly five 3s and at least four 6s will occur in 50 tosses of a fair die?

Let us see this little illustration about probability: A person throws a die and wins 4 cakes if it falls 1, 2, or 3; 3 cakes for 4 or 5; but loses 12 if it falls 6. What is his expected gain on a single throw of the single dice?

We shall see how to determine the probability that any one number out of 1,2 and 3 will come up on the face of the dice and based on this learning we shall on our own determine the probability of the occurrences of the other events. One can readily see that the 1, 2 and 3 means three numbers. A dice has six numbers. Any time a dice is thrown, the possibility that any one of three numbers will come up is 3 out of 6 or ½. The expected value on a single throw is $(3 \times 4/6) + (2 \times 3/6) - (1 \times 12/6) = 1$, or a gain of one cake (on average).

The most common interpretation of probability is used in statistical analysis. For example, the probability of throwing a 7 in one throw of two dice (which can happen when any one of these 6 combinations can come up on the face of the dice: 1 and 6, 2 and 5, 3 and 4, 6 and 1, 5 and 2 and finally 4 and 3) is 1/6 because the total number of combinations that can come up on the face of the dice is 36 as we have seen earlier. If an event has N equally likely outcomes and F of them are termed favourable, the probability of a favourable outcome is F/N. This is why the probability of throwing a 7 in one throw of two dice is 6/36 or $1/6^{th}$.

Thus, if long-range statistics show that out of every 100 people between 20 and 30 years of age, 42 will be alive at age 70, the assumption is that a person between those ages has a 42 per cent probability of surviving to the age of 70.

We shall see some illustrations about probability that rise gradually in the level of difficulty and will ensure that we assimilate completely the relative concepts.

Illustration 1

There are nine boxes in the diagram below. A boy has three coins and he places each coin in one square. What is the possibility that the three coins form a line?

There are nine places in all. The possible number of ways in which the boy will place three coins in the nine spaces is ${}^9C_3 = (9 \times 8 \times 7) / (3 \times 2 \times 1) = 12 \times 7 = 84$.

Let the boxes be numbered A, B, C and so on till I as in the diagram hereunder.

A	B	C
D	E	F
G	H	I

How many ways in which a line can be formed? ABC, DEF, GHI, ADG, BEH, CFI, AEI and CEG: 8 in all. So the probability that the three coins form a line is 8/84 or, in other words, 2/21.

It is important to see how the formula for arranging 3 objects in 9 different spots has been found. This awareness of the fundamentals behind the deriving of this formula would be of great help in cracking problems relating to combinations and probability.

Let us first visualise that there are only three boxes as in the diagram below in which one has to place 3 coins in each box.

A	B	C

There is only one distinct way in which one can put three coins in these three boxes.

Now let us visualise that there are six boxes as in the diagram below in which one has to place 3 coins in each box. ${}^3C_3$ as we know is $(3 \times 2 \times 1) / (3 \times 2 \times 1) = 1$.

A	B	C
D	E	F

One can place the first coin in A. Then if one were to put:

- ✓ The second coin in B, you could have these 4 different combinations: ABC, ABD, ABE, ABF.
- ✓ The second coin in C, you could have these 3 different combinations: ACD, ACE, and ACF. Note that we have not taken the combination ACB into consideration because this combination is already taken care of in the combination ABC (this is because if you were to put a coin each in A, B and C this would be in no way be different from putting coins in A, C and B) in the above instance with A in the first box and B in second box and in further steps we shall ignore those combinations that are taken care of in earlier combinations.
- ✓ The second coin in D, you could have these 2 different combinations: ADE, and ADF.
- ✓ The second coin in E, you could have this 1 combination: AEF.

With the first coin in box A, you have $4 + 3 + 2 + 1 = 10$ different combinations.

Now if one were to put the first coin in B and:

The second coin in C, you could have these 3 different combinations: BCD, BCE, and BCF.

The second coin in D, you could have these 2 different combinations: BDE, and BDF.

The second coin in E, you could have this 1 combination: BEF.

With the first coin in box B, you have $3 + 2 + 1 = 6$ different combinations.

Now if one were to put the first coin in C and:

The second coin in D, you could have these 2 different combinations: CDE, and CDF.

The second coin in E, you could have this 1 combination: CEF.

With the first coin in box C, you have $2 + 1 = 3$ different combinations.

Now if one were to put the first coin in D and the second coin in E, you could have this 1 combination: DEF.

The total number of combinations are $10 + 6 + 3 + 1 = 20$.

${}^6C_3$ as we know is $(6 \times 5 \times 4) / (3 \times 2 \times 1) = 20$.

From the above it should be easy to understand why there are a total of ${}^9C_3$ combinations when there are three coins to be put at random in 9 boxes. The bottom line is: if you know the fundamentals then you can recreate the formula at any time; in situations where an existing formula may not work, one can create one's own formula as one goes along.

Illustration 2

Machine–A produces 40% of the total output and Machine-B produces 60% of the total output. An average of nine units out of a thousand goods manufactured by Machine-A and one unit of 250 units produced by Machine-B prove to be defective. What is the probability that a unit chosen at random from the total daily output of the factory is defective?

Let the total daily output of the factory be 10000 units. So Machine A produces 4000 units, 36 goods will be defective. Out of every 1000 goods produced by Machine-A, 9 units are found to be defective. Machine B manufactures 6000 goods and since one unit out of 250 produced by Machine B is defective, there will be 6000/250 = 24 defective units produced by Machine-B. The total number of defective goods produced by both machines together during the day is 36 + 24 = 60 out of the 10000 units produced together daily. Thus the probability that a unit chosen at random out of the daily production at the factory is defective is 60/10000 = 0.006.

Chapter 30

Prime Numbers

The other day a young student came across a problem from the Quantitative Ability Section of a premier business school entrance test. He wanted to know, first of all, what topic did the thingamajig pertain to and then how to go about it. The question went like this: If X is a natural number such that $12 \le X \le 30$ and N = [(X – 1). (X – 2). (X – 3)...3.2.1)] / X then how many values of N will not be integral?

I asked him if he knew that, for example, (X – 1). (X-2) meant (X – 1) × (X – 2). He answered in the affirmative. But he said what does this (...3.2.1) mean? I told him that it meant that one should multiply (X – 1) with (X – 2) with (X – 3)...and so till one ended the process of multiplication with multiplying 3 with 2 with 1 because at 1 the process will have to stop since 1 is the very least natural number. I then asked him if he understood whether $12 \le X \le 30$ meant that X could be 12 at the very least and 30 at the very most? To this he replied in the affirmative as well. I then asked him to first try with X = 12 and then experiment with steadily rising values of X till he had understood the examiner's game plan.

He first assumed X as 12 and found that N = 11 × 10 × 9 ....3 × 2 × 1/12. He found that 12 in the denominator could be cancelled off against so many factors in the numerator such as 9 × 8 and 6 × 2 and 4 × 3 and so on. There would be an integral value for N with N = 12 since the numerator would be 1 and there would be a string of integers in the numerator after cancelling off some of them against the denominator of 12.

He then assumed N = 13. He then found that N = 12 × 11 × 10 × 9 ....3 × 2 × 1/ 13. There were hordes of factors in the numerator but none for 13. The denominator would not cancel off against any number in the numerator. Thus with X = 13, N would be necessarily fractional.

He then assumed N = 14. He then found that N = 13 × 12 × 11 × 10 × 9 × 8 × 7 ....3 × 2 × 1/ 14. There were hordes of factors in the numerator out of which 8 and 7, 7 and 4, 7 and 2 and so on will come in handy for cancelling off against the denominator of 14. Thus with X = 14, N would be necessarily integral.

He then skipped experimenting with 15 because he said with 15 in the denominator, there would be 10 and 3 – for example – in the numerator that would cancel off against 15 in the denominator. He also skipped experimenting with 16 because he said with 16 in the denominator there would be 8 and 4 (for example) in the numerator that would cancel off against 16 in the denominator. At X = 17, he was stuck again. The numerator had no factors that would cancel off against 17 in the denominator. It dawned on him that the number 17 was also a prime number like 13. The bright young lad realised that the matter pertained to prime numbers and that the whole issue was of finding out the number of prime numbers between 12 and 30 (both inclusive). The rest is not worth the narrative.

It is so important to be able to understand the topic to which questions at competitive examinations pertain since no competitive examination prescribes either a syllabus or a particular textbook. Seldom, if ever, a competitive examination wishes to test any mathematical ability beyond school level. The idea is to test how deeply have you sipped of the concepts that were taught to you while you were at school. The idea is to find out how quick you are on the draw, meaning how quickly you can pull your gun from the holster and meet the need of the hour. It is in this context of the absence of a syllabus and the huge importance of conceptual clarity that we present to you, dear reader, the concepts underlying prime numbers. There will be illustrations to reinforce the concepts and exercises that are designed to ensure complete assimilation.

A prime number is that integer which is:

(A) greater than 1.

(B) divisible by no number other than itself.

A number is divisible by another provided there is no remainder in the process of division.

Every number would leave no remainder if the number 1 divided it. But the most important characteristic of a prime number is that it is not divisible by any number **other than itself**. Thus if 7 is divided by 1 there will be no remainder but here 7 is being divided by a number other than itself and further that division by 1 is not division really since 1 is unity and unity unites but does not divide.

The series of prime numbers starts with 2 and the series of all prime numbers between 1 and 100 would run like this: 2, 3, 5, 7, 11, 13, 17, 19, 23, 29, 31, 37, 41, 43, 47, 53, 59, 61, 67, 71, 73, 79, 83, 89, and 97.

In all, there are 25 prime numbers from 1 to 100. This would not only be worth remembering but also make great common sense remembering lest one may not end up counting the number of prime numbers on one's finger tips and waste valuable if asked a question pertaining to prime numbers between 1 and 100. In order to help memorising there are $100 \div 4 = 25$ prime numbers, from 1 to 100 (where 4 is the first non-prime number other than 1).

We have deliberately avoided giving lessons to the reader of this book on how to find out whether a number is prime or composite. There are several reasons for this. The first is that what is put to test at a competitive test like the GRE is Quantitative Ability and not Mathematics. The second reason is that **we have solved thousands of questions on Quantitative Ability from ACTUAL QUESTION PAPERS (and NOT MOCK PAPERS) during the course of writing the numerous books on how to crack competitive examinations including the toughest of them and have yet to come across a single instance of a problem involving finding out whether any number is prime or composite.** For that matter we have yet to come across a single problem on the topic of Prime Numbers where one is expected to know any prime number other than those 25 prime numbers between the numbers 1 and 100. Since the range of knowledge of prime numbers is so small and involves knowing the tables from $1 \times 1 = 1$ and so on till $10 \times 10 = 100$, we see no need to acquaint the reader with such trifles. The third reason is that we have resolved to be utterly relevant in whatever we present to the reader.

Shall we quickly get on with illustrations in regard to prime numbers and then see our way through the exercise at the end?

Problem 1

How many numbers between 50 and 100 are divisible by no number less than 10?

The Detailed Solution

The pencil and the jotter will never let you down. But before one begins jotting, one has to remember that all even numbers are divisible by 2. This would mean that at least half the numbers between 50 and 100 are not to be reckoned by you at all. Your task gets simpler to that extent. One also has to remember that if you were to add the digits of any number and find that the digits add up to 3 or an integral multiple of 3, the number is divisible by 3. One also has to remember that a number ending with 5 or 0 is definitely divisible by 5. So when one begins jotting, 50, 51 and 52 are not to be jotted at all. 53 is a prime number and will have to be jotted. 54, 55, 56, 57 and 58 are not to be jotted since they are divisible by any of 2, 3 or 5. The next number you will jot is 59, which again is prime. Then you will skip 60 and jot 61, which again is prime. At this stage you must understand that the game is of prime numbers and complete your jottings on that understanding.

Those who are comfortable with numbers may see this from the following slightly different stance. 50 to 100 has, in all, 51 numbers. Every second number after 50 is divisible by 2 since it is an even number. These even numbers are 26 in all starting with 50. Then there are multiples of only 3 but not 2, such as 51, 57,63 and so on till 99, each separated by 6. These are 9 in all. The total so far is $26 + 9 = 35$. Then there are other numbers divisible by 5 but not by 2 or 3 such as 55, 65, 85, 95 each separated by 10 (we have not reckoned 75 because it is included in the list of numbers divisible by 3 but not by 2). This makes 4 more numbers taking the total up to 39. Then there are numbers divisible by only 7 but not by 2, 3, or 5 and these are 77, and 91 each separated by 14. These make two more taking the total to 41. There are in all 51 numbers between 50 and 100 of which 41 are not to be reckoned at all. $51 - 41 = 10$. Thus there are only the prime numbers between 53, 59, 61, 67, 71, 73, 79, 83, 89, 97 – ten in all – that qualify for being divisible by no number less than 10.

Problem 2

What is the sum of all the prime numbers less than 20?

The Detailed Solution

2, 3, 5, 7, 11, 13, 17 and 19 are prime numbers less than 20 and these add up to 77. You will notice that with each problem that we solve together, your awareness of which number is prime and which isn't will rise. Only this awareness can help you solve problems pertaining to prime numbers. No formulae can tell you what number is prime and what isn't. The very topic is such that only hands on experience with problems pertaining to the topic will help you understand its nuances; nothing else.

Problem 3

How many numbers between 1 and 100 (both inclusive) are not divisible by 2, 3 or 5 or by 7?

The Detailed Solution

As such there are 25 numbers that are not divisible by any number other than by themselves and these are known as prime numbers.

Prime numbers between 1 and 100 are: 2, 3, 5, 7, 11, 13, 17, 19, 23, 29, 31, 37, 41, 43, 47, 53, 59, 61, 67, 71, 73, 79, 83, 89, 97. Of these 2, 3, 5 and 7 are divisible by 2, 3, 5 and 7 respectively and have to be excluded from the list of prime numbers between 1 and 100 since we have to find out as to how many numbers between 1 and 100 (both inclusive) are not divisible by 2, 3, 5 and 7. That makes a list of 21 (prime) numbers that are not divisible by 2, 3, 5 and 7.

Problem 4

Let S be the set of prime numbers greater than or equal 2 and less than 63. If one were to multiply all elements of S, how many consecutive zeroes will end the product?

The Detailed Solution

The prime numbers are 2, 3, 5, 7, 11,.........63. Only 2×5 will yield 10 and thus one zero at the end.

$2^x \times 5^x = 10^x$. Here, 10^x will yield x consecutive zeroes at the end. Thus if I were to ascertain the number of zeroes at the end of this multiplication, I should see how many powers of 5 are available from among the multiplicands. I get only 5^1 and 2^1 from both 5 and 2 respectively. The rest of the prime numbers are odd and none other number of the set S is divisible by 5. Since I get only 10^1, the number of consecutive zeroes at the end of the product of all elements of the set S will be 1.

Problem 5

If S is a set of numbers representing the absolute difference between consecutive prime numbers between 2 and 100, then how many members does S have?

The Detailed Solution

All prime numbers between 1 and 100 are as follows: 2, 3, 5, 7, 11, 13, 17, 19, 23, 29, 31, 37, 41, 43, 47, 53, 59, 61, 67, 71, 73, 79, 83, 89 and 97.

The absolute difference – for example – between 2 and 3 is 1, between 3 and 5 is 2, between 7 and 11 is 4, between 23 and 29 is 6 and between 89 and 97 is 8. Thus S has five members: 1, 2, 4, 6, and 8.

EXERCISE

1. If S is a set of values of x such that 100 < x < 200 and x is (A) Odd (B) Divisible by 7 but not by 3 or 5, how many members constitute S? Options: (1) 1 (2) 2 (3) 3 (4) None of these .
2. The difference of the squares of two prime numbers is 648. Which are the two prime numbers?
3. The number of prime numbers among the numbers 201 to 210 both inclusive is: (1) 1 (2) 2 (3) 3 (4) None of these.
4. Consider a number 23571113....and so on made by placing in ascending order, all the prime numbers between 2 and 30. If this number were divided by 16, the remainder will be: (1) 3 (2) 7 (3) 1 (4) 9.
5. The product of all the prime numbers from 11 till 50 will have the last digit as: Options (1) 1 (2) 3 (3) 7 (4) 5.

ANSWER KEY

1. 3 numbers: 119, 133, 161
2. 83 and 79
3. Option 4
4. Option 4
5. Option 1

SOLUTIONS

1. If S is a set of values of x such that 100 < x < 200 and x is (A) Odd (B) Divisible by 7 but not by 3 or 5, this means that:

   (1) You are to bother your little head only about multiples of 7.

   (2) When you divide 100 by 7, you get a remainder of 2, and

   (3) Thus 100+5 would be the first number more than 100 that would be divisible by 7 since 105 is 7×15.

   (4) When you divide 200 with 7, you get a remainder of 4 and this means that the last number divisible by 7 in between 100 and 200 is 196, which is 7×28. This is simple to understand. For example, if you were to divide 33 with 8 you would get a remainder of 1. If you were to subtract 1 from 33, you would get a number that is exactly divisible by 8. The same principle applies when you divide 200 with 7.

   (5) Thus the multiples of 7 that are > 100 but < 200 are 7 × 15, 7 × 16, 7 × 17, ... and so on 7 × 28. 14 in all!

   (6) Since all members of the set S are odd, one will have to ignore all even multiples of 7. If we are to ignore those multiples of 7 that are also multiples of 3 and 5, we are to ignore, the following: 7 × 15, 7 × 16, 7 × 18, 7 × 20, 7 × 21,7 × 22, 7 × 24, 7 × 25, 7 × 26, 7 × 27 and 7 × 28.

   (7) That leaves us with 7 × 17, 7 × 19 and 7 × 23 as the only values of x that qualify to be members of the set S. So S has three members: 119, 133, and 161, all three of them being products of 7 and prime numbers.

   Hence **Option 3: 3.**

2. The difference of the squares of two prime numbers is 648. Let the two prime numbers be A and B. Hence $A^2-B^2 = 648$. Thus $(A + B) \times (A - B) = 648$. If $(A + B) \times (A - B) = C \times D$, then $A = (C + D)/2$ and $B = (C - D)/2$.

If we are to have integral values for A and B, then we are to factorise 648 in such a way that both factors are odd or both factors are even. 648 is an even number and cannot possibly have both factors that are odd. Hence 648 will need to be factorised only in such a way that both factors are even. $648 = 4 \times 162$. So $A = (162 + 4)/2 = 83$ and $B = (162 - 4)/2 = 79$.

The other even factors of 648 are 2 and 324 and these will give $A = (324 + 2)/2 = 163$ and $B = (324 - 2)/2 = 161$. As to whether 163 is prime or otherwise, it is a matter of detailed working that may not be necessary once you are able to establish whether 161 is prime or composite for if 161 is composite, then 161 and 163 will not work for 648 is the difference between two numbers both of which are prime.

As to whether a number is prime or otherwise may call for a whole lot of arithmetic unfortunately because prime numbers do not have distinguishing features such as tails or long moustaches. But generally one starts dividing with 2 (which it is not necessary here since the number 161 is odd) and then with 3 (which too is not necessary since the digits in 161 add up to 8) and then with 5 (by which 161 is obviously not divisible) and then with 7. This is the normal and logical sequence in the process of ascertaining whether a number is prime or otherwise. When we divide 161 with 7 we get 23. Thus 161 is not eligible for being referred to as a prime number (and will therefore not be able to enjoy the advantages – if any, of course – that go to prime numbers).

Thus 83 and 79 are the two prime numbers the difference in squares of which is 648.

3. 201 and 210 are both divisible by 3 since their digits add up to 3. So we are to ignore 201 and 210. Secondly, all even numbers cannot be prime. So we are to ignore, 204, 206, 208. That leaves us with 203, 205, 207 and 209. 205 is patently divisible by 5. 207 adds up to 9 and 207 is thus clearly divisible by 9 and is not prime. The odd digits of 209 add up to 11 and the even digits add up to zero and the difference between sum of odd digits and even digits is 11 and hence 209 is patently divisible by 11. The only number that remains to be seen is 203 which when divided by 7 we find that the quotient is 29 and there is no reminder. So $29 \times 7 = 203$. Even 203 is not prime. Thus there are no numbers between 201 and 210 both inclusive that are prime.

4. A number 23571113....made by placing in ascending order, all the prime numbers between 2 and 30, would have the last six digits as 192329. All ten thousands are divisible by 16. $10000 \div 16 = 625$ and therefore all integral multiples of 10000 will also be divisible by 16. All we have now to see is what will be the remainder when the number represented by the last four digits – meaning 2329 – is divided by 16 and we find that 9 will be the remainder. There is no need to find the quotient simply because one is not asked to find the quotient. There is no need to do anything that the examiner at the competitive examination does not want you to do. There is nothing to be gained by volunteering in this specific case. On the contrary, there will be waste of valuable time if one does things that are not expected of one.

5. The prime numbers between 11 and 50 are 13, 17, 19, 23, 29, 31, 37, 41, 43 and 47. In determining the last digit of the product of all these numbers one will need to quickly multiply the last digits of all these prime numbers that we have enumerated above and we find that the last digit will be 1.

When we multiply $11 \times 13 \times 17 \times 19 \times 23 \times 29 \times 31 \times 37 \times 41 \times 43 \times 47$, what we are really doing is multiplying $(10 + 1) \times (10 + 3) \times (10 + 7) \times (10 + 9) \times (20 + 3)$ and so on till $(40 + 7)$. So if you take $A = 10$, then what you are multiplying is essentially $(A+1) \times (A + 3) \times (A + 7) \times (A + 9) \times (2A+3)$ and so on till $(4A+7)$. In this multiplication only the following product will be independent of the term A: $1 \times 3 \times 7 \times 9 \times 3 \times 9 \times 1 \times 7 \times 1 \times 3 \times 7$. Any term expressed as A or its powers will invariably end with zero since we have assumed A to be 10. So if we are to find the last digit in the multiplication of all these numbers it makes sense to multiply all the last digits alone and see what is the last digit in the product and you will find that the last digit in $1 \times 3 \times 7 \times 9 \times 3 \times 9 \times 1 \times 7 \times 1 \times 3 \times 7$ will be 1.

In the multiplication of $1 \times 3 \times 7 \times 9 \times 3 \times 9 \times 1 \times 7 \times 1 \times 3 \times 7$ also, there is no need to multiply 21 with 9 at the stage of $1 \times 3 \times 7 \times 9$; just multiply 1 in 21 with 9 because the whole objective is to determine the last digit and for the attainment of this extremely limited objective, the principle of ignoring the tens and their multiples, as outlined in the previous paragraph, will work admirably. Stick to the last digit alone, is the name of the game. If the idea is to kill a fly, is there a need to run after it with a sledgehammer? Have we not heard of the fly swatter?

Chapter 31

Profit and Loss

We shall quickly recapitulate a few fundamentals about profit and loss. These have been designed for those who may be students of the humanities, but in the course of preparation for competitive examinations, may need to brush up on what one has learnt at school in regard to profit and loss both of which are generally expressed in percentage terms and hence this chapter on Profit and Loss covers Percentages as well.

When a merchant buys some goods for sale, he normally incurs expenses under different heads of expense, some of them regardless of whether he buys the goods or not, and even if buys goods then regardless of whether he sells the goods or not. These expenses are of course in addition to what he has paid for the goods.

Such expenses that have a direct relationship with the quantity of goods bought by the merchant are called variable costs. These may include transportation, sales tax, municipal taxes levied at the stage of entry of the goods in the town, premium for transit insurance, and so on. The rationale is simple: if you buy nothing, you transport nothing; if you buy less, you insure less, and so on.

Then there are some heads of expenses under which he will have to spend regardless of whether he buys goods or sells them. Some of these heads are salary for his staff, municipal taxes for the commercial establishment, electricity and telephone charges, and so on. Such costs are called fixed costs.

It may therefore be easy to see that since the fixed costs are not dependent on the amount of goods sold and thus their value since the merchant would sell them for value expressed in the currency of the country in which the merchant in our narrative is operating – the more the sales of goods in value terms, the finer is the distribution of the fixed costs over sales. This is because fixed costs are the numerator and with the same numerator, the bigger the denominator (of sales), the smaller the fraction of fixed costs per unit of sales.

While working out a price at which to sell goods, the merchant would endeavour to sell them at such a price at which both variable costs and fixed costs are covered and after this he has surplus to buy bread and possibly butter and jam for his family and to be generally in wealth. So the selling price of each unit that he sells has to comprise of buying price + variable cost + unit fixed cost + surplus for himself. It is this surplus that is known as profit.

If we call the surplus as profit and the amount of sales the merchant has been able to log, his profit = Sales Revenue – (Variable Costs + Fixed Costs). In the converse, loss is an event that happens when the costs exceed revenue.

PERCENTAGES

Per means *for every,* and *cent* means *hundred*.

When I wish to divide 16 chocolates equally between four boys, each one gets 4; or in other words, I would be able to give 4 chocolates per boy. The division is as follows: 16 chocolates/ 4 boys= 4 chocolates/boy. If I were to decide to give 7 chocolates per boy who attends my birthday party, I must know as to how many boys would attend the party so as to be able to buy the required number of chocolates. I may buy, say, 350 chocolates. Yet the denominator is not known because I do not know how many boys will come to the party. In percentages, however, this denominator is certain. The denominator is 100. *Per cent* means that the denominator is 100.

The only difference between fractions and percentages is that in the case of fractions, there are diverse denominators whereas in the case of percentages, the denominator is 100 all through and hence if one is asked to compare some fractions and tell as to which is the highest in value and which the lowest, the sure fire method of telling is to look at the fractions as percentages and then since the denominator is the same in the latter case, one has to compare only numerators and this would enable one to arrange all given fractions in ascending (or for that matter even descending) order of value without any difficulty at all.

Can you tell which of these fractions would be in the middle of the five fractions? The five fractions are: ¾, 13/17, 17/25, 5/7 and 9/13. This can happen in a live situation wherein you may be attempting the Problem Solving Section at a competitive examination and may have been able to calculate the values of, say, year on year growth in turnover as compared to the previous year sales of a firm and may now be required to arrange the fractions as aforesaid in order to arrive at an inference as to which is the year in which the growth was the median of all the five fractions. What do you do then? All the denominators are different. Comparison is feasible only when the denominator is same.

There are two options before you:

1. Find the least common multiple (LCM) of all the fractions and rewrite the numerators with LCM of the five denominators as the standard denominator of all five fractions.

2. Express the fractions as percentages and see for yourself.

The first options would be terribly time consuming; it may involve a whole lot of multiplication since three of the five denominators are prime.

For those aspiring to beat the clock as one might be expected to do in competitive examinations, time management is the key. Converting the fractions into percentage terms is a whole lot easier. Let us see how. See these fractions once again. I would call the first fraction as F_1 and the next as F_2 and so on.

F_1	F_2	F_3	F_4	F_5
3/4	13/17	17/25	5/7	9/13

How would I convert F_1 into percentage terms? The denominator is 4 and if this were to be multiplied by 25, I would get a denominator of 100. Since I am to multiply the denominator by 25, I must also multiply the numerator by 25 so as to retain the same value of the fraction. So F_1 is effectively 75%.

In F_2, I could multiply both numerator and denominator by 6 and I would then have a numerator of 78 and denominator of 102 and this is very nearly 100. F_2 is thus approximately 78%.

In F_3, I could multiply both numerator and denominator by 4 and I would then have a numerator of 68 and denominator of 100 and this makes F_3 exactly 68%.

In F_4, I could multiply both numerator and denominator by 14 and I would then have a numerator of 70 and denominator of 98 and this is very nearly 100. F_4 is thus approximately 70%.

In F_5, I could multiply both numerator and denominator by 8 and I would then have a numerator of 72 and denominator of 104 and this means that the denominator is very nearly 100. F_5 is thus approximately 70%.

Since F_4 and F_5 are both nearly 70%, I do not know which would come in the middle but the choice is between F_4 and F_5. But the fractions F_4 and F_5 are effectively 70/98 and 72/104 respectively. I am at a loss to know as to which is larger. So what do I do?

I should convert F_4 as an exact percentage by multiplying both numerator and denominator by 100/7 and thus the fraction is 500 × 100/7 × 100 % = 500/7% = very nearly 71%.

I also convert F_5 as an exact percentage by multiplying both numerator and denominator by 100/13 and get (900/13) in the numerator and 100 in the denominator. 900/13 is very nearly equal to 69. Thus F_5 is very nearly 69%. Clearly F_4 is bigger than F_5. So the ascending order is: F_3 (68%) F_5 (69%) F_4 (71%) F_1 (75%) and F_2 (78%).

Let us look at another fundamental aspect about percentages.

One may be given a problem in which all terms are expressed in percentages and the answer may also have to be given in percentages. The fundamental thing to remember in such situations is that when all terms are expressed in percentages, and the answer is required to be expressed in percentages, it is convenient to assume 100 as the starting point. It will not make any difference whatsoever to the outcome.

Let us see by way of the following illustration, how assuming 100 as the starting point will not make any difference to an answer required to be expressed in percentages.

Suppose 40% of the employees of a certain company are men, and 75% of the men earn more than $35 per day. If 45% of the company's employees earn more than $35 per day, what percent of the women employed by the company earn $35 per day or less? (1) 18% (2) 25% (3) 33.33% (4) 75%.

If the number of employees is E	100	200	400	1000
The number of men is M where M is 40% of E	40	80	160	400
The number of women is W where W is 60% of E	60	120	240	600
The number of men earning >$35 is 75% of M and M_1=	30	60	120	300
The number of employees earning >$35 is E_1 = 45% of E=	45	90	180	450
The number of women earning>$35 is $W_1 = E_1 - M_1$.	15	30	60	150
The number of women earning <$35 is $W_2 = W - W_1$	45	90	180	450
The percentage of women earning <$35 of total women employees is = $W_2 \times 100/W$	75	75	75	75

Here we have assumed the number of employees as 100 and then taken progressively larger values for this starting point, and yet the answer comes to the same. The short point is that if one is given figures in percentages and asked the answers in percentages, it makes no difference whether you assume 100 or 1000 as the starting point. Secondly, even if one were asked to compute the number of women earning less than $35 as a fraction of the total number of women in the company, the above findings would stand. This is because the value of a fraction when expressed in percentages does not change at all. Percentage is nothing other than what would be the value of the numerator of a given fraction, if the denominator were to be 100.

We shall now move on to some illustrations that will enable us to jog our memory about what we learnt at school in regard to percentages and profit and loss. In addition to this, the illustrations shall demonstrate to us what calls for breadth of perception.

Illustration 1

In a school, there are 15 more girls than boys. If the number of girls is increased by 10% and the number of boys is also increased by 16%, there would be 9 more girls than boys. What is the total number of students in the school?

Solution

Let there be B number of boys and G number of girls in the school. Thus G = B + 15.

If the number of boys is increased by 16%, it increases to 116% of its earlier figure and thus the new number of boys is 116B/100. If the number of girls is increased by 10%, it increases to 110% of its earlier figure and thus the new number of girls is 110G/100 = 110 × (B + 15)/100. After the increase in the number of boys and girls, the number of girls will be 9 more than the number of boys. So 110 × (B + 15)/100 = (116B/100) + 9. If we were to multiply both sides of the equation with 100, we would get 110B + 1650 = 116B+900 and hence 6B = 750 or B = 125. Since G = B + 15, G = 125 + 15 = 140. The number of students in the school was 140 girls + 125 boys = 265 in all.

Illustration 2

When a company decreased the selling price of the tape recorders it manufactured by 20%, the sales in terms of number of units sold increased by 80%. What was the net effect on sale realisations in percentage terms?

Solution

Suppose the company had been selling 10 tape recorders earlier at price of \$10 per piece, its sales realisation was 10 × \$10 = \$100.

After it reduced the price by 20%, the new price was \$8 whereas the new sales were 18 tape recorders. The new sales realisation was \$8 × 18 = \$144. Sales realisation went up from \$100 to \$144 and thus increased by \$44 over its earlier level of \$100 and hence increased by \$44 per \$100 of earlier sales. Hence the sales realisation increased 44%.

It is important to realise that in supposing that the earlier price was \$10 and the earlier sales was 10 pieces (so that the sales revenue is \$100, which would be an extremely convenient figure to work with since we are to find percentages), the result will remain the same. The only difference is that the result will emerge only faster.

May we explain how?

Suppose the company was selling each tape recorder @ \$T per piece and the sales were S pieces. The sales realisation was \$T × S. If the price of a tape recorder went down by 20%, it means that it fell to 80% of its earlier level and the new price of a tape recorder was \$T × 80/100. If the sales went up by 80%, it means that the number of pieces sold went up to 180% of its earlier level and thus the number of units sold increased to 180×S/100. The new sales realisation was (\$T × 80 / 100) × (180 × S / 100) = \$(T × 80 × S × 180) / 10000 = \$14400T × S / 10000 = \$144TS/100. So the sales have increased from TS to 144TS / 100. This means the increase is (144TS /100) – TS = 44TS / 100. Sales realisation has gone up 44%.

Assuming some convenient figures makes no difference to the outcome if you are asked to calculate the answer in percentage terms and not absolute terms. Only, the answer emerges a whole lot faster.

Illustration 3

When Ron gets an increment of \$35 in his salary, his new salary is now just 50% of Sonny's salary. Can you tell as to what is Sonny's present salary?

Solution

If you say that Ron's salary was R and Sonny's salary was S, with an increment of \$ 35, Ron's new salary is R + 35. This R + 35 is 50% of Sonny's present salary. 50% is ½. This means that R + 35 = S/2. If we were to multiply both sides by 2, we would get 2R = S – 70. We get a linear equation with two unknown values R and S and an idea about what is their interrelation but no idea at all of what is the definite value of either R or S. Some possible values of S and R that could fulfil the condition that 2R = S – 70 are as follows:

R =	S =	2R =	S–70 =
10	90	20	20
20	110	40	40
200	470	400	400

The short point is that when an equation gives the relationship between two unknowns, then in order to ascertain the absolute value of any one of the unknown terms, it is imperative to know the absolute value of the other term or else one is back to two unknowns.

Illustration 4

A shopkeeper sells two suits @\$154 each. On one he gains 12% and on the other he loses 12%. What was his net result of these two transactions?

Solution

When he sold one at a loss of 12%, it means that something worth, say, \$100 earlier, he sold at \$88. Thus what \$88 is to \$100, \$154 is to (154 × 100) / 88 = 15400/88 = 175. When I see 154, I know that it is a multiple of 11 since the difference of sum of the odd digits (1 + 4) and the sum of the even digits (here only 5) is either zero or 11 or a multiple of 11.

When he sold another suit at a gain of 12% it means that he sold something worth \$100 at \$112. So what \$112 is to \$100, \$154 is to (154 × 100) / 112 = (15400)/112 = 2200/16 = 137.5.

So the two suits were worth \$175 + \$137.5 = \$312.5. He realised \$154 × 2 = \$308. He thus lost 312.5-308 = \$4.5, overall, in the two transactions.

Illustration 5

If the side of a square is increased by 40%, what is the percentage increase in area of the square?

Solution

If we assume that prior to increase, the side of the square was 10 cm, then its area then was 100 sq cm. If the side increased by 40%, it grew to 14 and the new area was 14 × 14 = 196 sq cm. So the area went up from 100 sq cm to 196 sq cm indicating an increase of 96 sq cm over its earlier area of 100 sq cm. And percent is per 100. Thus the increase in area is 96%. We have assumed the earlier side to be of 10 cm length because that would give the area of the square to be 100 sq cm and since the whole thing is about finding out percentage increase, 100 in the denominator saves a whole lot of time and energy.

Secondly, whatever value one would assume for the length of the side, the answer would be 96% only. So why assume X and Y and so on?

Illustration 6

Two numbers are respectively 20% and 50% of a third number. What percentage is the first number of the second?

Solution

Since there are percentages under mention, let the third number be 100. So the first number is 20 and the second number is 50. Now the first number divided by the second number is 20/50=2/5. In percentage terms 2/5 is equal to 40 parts out of 100 and is thus 40%.

Illustration 7

A trader bears a loss of 25% by selling 40 marbles for a dollar. How many marbles should he sell for a dollar in order to earn a profit of 20%?

Solution

If the trader sells 40 marbles for a dollar, he sells each marble for 100/40=2.5 cents (since there are 100 cents in a dollar).

Selling one marble for 2.5 cents leads him to a loss of 25%. One can incur a loss of 25% when one sells a thing for 75 units of money when the original cost is 100 units. Also, one can make a profit of 20% when one sells something at 120 units of money when one has bought the thing for 100 units of money. So something that the trader earlier sold at 75 units (when he made a loss of 25%), he will have to sell at 120 units, if he wants a profit of 20%. If 75 units is Selling Price-I and 120 units is Selling Price-II then since Selling Price-II means a profit of 20%, he will sell whatever commodity that he has sold at a loss of 25% at 120/75 or 8/5 times Selling Price-I in order to register a profit of 20%. Which means that he will have to sell the marbles instead at 2.5×8/5=4 cents per marble. For a dollar he can sell 100/4 = 25 marbles.

Illustration 8

A man sold a watch for \$119. If the percentage of his profit was the same as the cost price, what was his cost price?

Solution

Let us assume that the cost price of the watch was \$X. In that case a profit of X% means that the $(100 + X) \times (X / 100) = 119$. So $100X + X^2 = 11900$ or $X^2 + 100X - 11900 = 0$. As we know, 119 is 17×7 and hence 11900 is 170×70 and thus $X^2 + 100X - 11900 = (X + 170) \times (X - 70) = 0$ and hence X is either -170 or 70. Since the price of a watch – or for that matter anything at all – cannot be negative, $X = 70$; the man bought the watch for \$70.

Chapter 32

The Pythagoras Theorem

One seldom realises why right angles are so important in everyday life. If a building were not to be at perfect right angles to the plane on which it stands, it would come crashing to the ground with the slightest tremor. The Pythagoras theorem deals with right angles and forms the basis of a branch of mathematics known as trigonometry.

For those who may not have been in touch with this theorem that deals with right-angled triangles, it states that in a right-angled triangle, the square on the hypotenuse is equal to the sum of the squares on the other two sides. See the following figure:

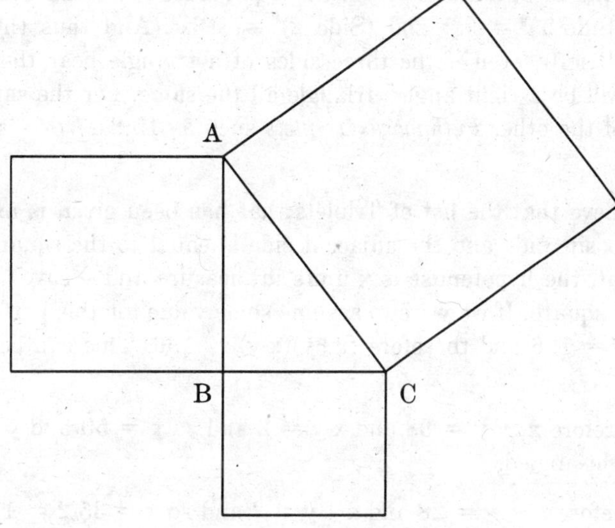

In regard to the right angled triangle ABC that we have drawn above:

- Angle ABC is 90°
- Line AC is the longest of the three sides and is known as the hypotenuse of this right angled triangle; the hypotenuse has got to be the longest side because it lies opposite to the angle of 90° and in any triangle, if one angle is 90°, no other angles can be either greater than or even equal to the angle of 90°
- Line AB is one side and line BC is the other side; insofar as angle C is concerned, AB is the side opposite to it and vis-à-vis angle C, the side AB is known as the *opposite* side whereas BC is adjacent to it and vis-à-vis angle C, the side BC is known as the *adjacent* side.
- If you were to draw a square on the hypotenuse AC, its area would be equal to the sum of the areas of the squares drawn on the sides AB and the side BC. Effectively what the great philosopher Pythagoras said was that in a right angled triangle,
- The $(\text{hypotenuse})^2 = (\text{opposite})^2 + (\text{adjacent})^2$.

Based on this theorem there are some *Pythagoras Triplets* which are the values for hypotenuse and for the other two sides that would satisfy the condition of $(\text{hypotenuse})^2 = (\text{opposite})^2 + (\text{adjacent})^2$.

These are some *Pythagoras Triplets* here, meaning probable sides of right-angled triangles. These would come in handy when dealing with questions relating to the right-angled triangle.

Side 1	Side 2	Hypotenuse	Square on Side 1	Square on Side 2	Square on Hypotenuse
3	4	5	9	16	25
6	8	10	36	64	100
5	12	13	25	144	169
9	40	41	81	1600	1681
8	15	17	64	225	289
20	21	29	400	441	841
7	24	25	49	576	625
60	11	61	3600	121	3721

Integral multiples of 3, 4 and 5 – for example – are also *Pythagoras Triplets*. The reason for this is simple. Let any unknown number x be a multiplicand of 3, 4 and 5. Then the hypotenuse is 5x and the other two sides are 3x and 4x. So, $(\text{Hypotenuse})^2 = 25x^2$; $(\text{Side } 1)^2 = 9x^2$ and $(\text{Side } 2)^2 = 16x^2$. And thus $(\text{hypotenuse})^2 = (\text{Side } 1)^2 + (\text{Side } 2)^2 = 9x^2 + 16x^2 = 25x^2$. Briefly, even if the three sides of a triangle bear the ratio of 3:4:5 and are not actually 3, 4 and 5, the triangle will be a right-angled triangle all the same. For the same reason, even if the ratio of the sides of a triangle is that of the other *Pythagoras Triplets* such as 15:8:17 or – say 9:40:41 - the triangle is sure to be right-angled.

Of course, there is no need to believe that the list of Triplets that has been given is anywhere near exhaustive. If the sum of the squares of the opposite side and the adjacent side is equal to the square of the hypotenuse then it follows that, if we were to say that, the hypotenuse is x units in measure and – say – the adjacent side is y units in measure then $x^2 - y^2$ = a perfect square. If we were to assume some value for this perfect square – say 196 (which is the square of 14) – then $x^2 - y^2 = 196$ and therefore $(x+y)(x-y) = 196$. This can be factorised in several ways, some of them being as follows:

$(x + y)(x - y) = 98 \times 2$ and therefore $x + y = 98$ and $x-y = 2$ and so $x = 50$ and $y = 48$. Thus a triangle with sides of 50, 24 and 14 will be right-angled.

$(x + y)(x - y) = 28 \times 7$ and therefore $x + y = 28$ and $x - y = 7$ and so $x = 35/2 = 17$ and $y = 28 - 7/2 = 10.5$. Thus a triangle with sides of 17.5, 10.5 and 14 will be right-angled as well.

The list of *Pythagoras Triplets* can be endless.

Pythagoras had, I think unknowingly, stumbled onto a finding that it is only the sum of the squares of two numbers that can be equal to the square of a third number. There are no instances that one knows where the sum of the cubes of two numbers is equal to the cube of a third number nor is this seen in any higher powers than cubes. This interesting finding stood me in really good stead when I faced this problem.

Question

If u, v, w, and m are natural numbers such that $u^m + v^m = w^m$, then which one of the following is true.

1. $m \geq \min(u,v,w)$ 2. $m \geq \max(u,v,w)$ 3. $m < \min(u,v,w)$ 4. none of these

Solution

In natural numbers, only the squares of two natural numbers can add up to the square of a third natural number. One has not seen any instance where the cubes of two natural numbers add up to the cube of a third natural number. The smallest possible values of two natural numbers whose squares add up to that of a third natural number is in the case of $3^2 + 4^2 = 5^2$ (After refreshing one's memory on the fundamentals of the Pythagoras Theorem, 3:4:5 is the smallest possible ratio of sides of a right-angled triangle that comes to mind).

In this question, if you were to see $3^2 + 4^2 = 5^2$ in the form of $u^m + v^m = w^m$, you will see that m is the least among m, u, v and w and hence **Option 3**.

We shall now see some illustrations based on the Pythagoras theorem and soak in the fundamentals.

Illustration 1

If the angles in a triangle are in the ratio of 1:2:3, it follows that the sides could be in the ratio of:

(1) 1 : 2 : 3 (2) 1: √3 :2 (3) 3 :2 :1 (4) √2: √3 : 2

Solution

It is a property of the triangle that the three angles in a triangle add up to 180 degrees. If they are in the ratio of 1:2:3, it means that they are 30, 60 and 90°. This means that the triangle is right-angled. This means that the square on the hypotenuse is equal to the sum of the squares on the other two sides as per the theorem of Pythagoras. Only in Option 2, we get the situation where the squares of 1 and √3 are 1 and 3 and they add up to 4 which is the square of the hypotenuse with measure of 2. Thus **Option 2**.

Illustration 2

The measures of a right-angled triangle are in Arithmetic Progression. If the area of the triangle is 96 square cm, what is the perimeter of the triangle?

Solution

If the sides of a right-angled triangle are in arithmetic progression, then the sides are in the ratio of 3:4:5. If you might like to see the illustrations of other Pythagoras combinations that have been furnished hereinabove, no other combination is in Arithmetic Progression.

Let us then assume the three sides to be of measures 3x, 4x and 5x units. If the sides smaller than the hypotenuse are 3x and 4x, the area of the triangle = 1/2 × base × height = 1/2 × 3x × 4x = $6x^2$ = 96. So x^2 = 16 and hence x = 4. The three sides are thus 12, 16 and 20 and the perimeter is = 12 + 16 + 20 = 48.

Illustration 3

In triangle PQR, angle P is 90°. If PM is a median, then PM is:

(1) > 1/2 QR (2) < 1/2 QR (3) = 1/2 QR (4) May be any of these

Solution

A median drawn from any vertex in a triangle is that which divides the opposite side in two equal halves. It is a property of the circle that if the two ends of a diameter of any circle were linked to any point on the circumference of the circle, then the straight lines joining the two ends of the diameter with the point on the circumference would form a right angle at the point on the circumference.

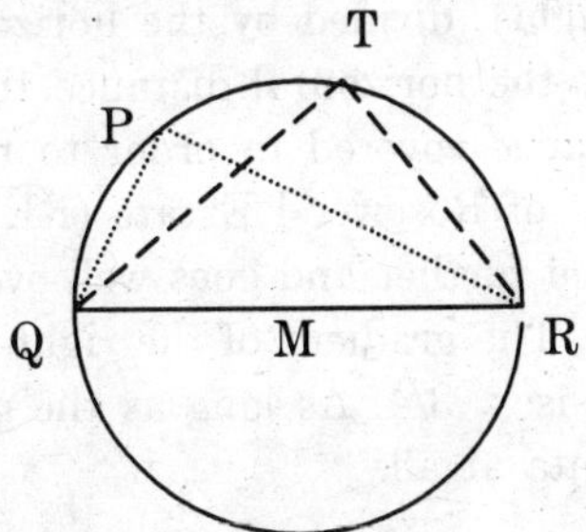

In the above figure, there is a circle with its centre at M. The points Q and R are the two ends of the diameter of the circle. P and T are two distinct points on the circumference of the circle. As per the above property of the

circle, angle QPR in triangle QPR and angle QTR in triangle QTR is bound to be a right angle. QR is the hypotenuse of either triangle. In either of these right-angled triangle, the median from the vertex having the right angle cannot help meeting the hypotenuse QR in point M at its centre. The centre of the circle invariably divides the diameter into two equal halves called the radii of the circle. It is for this reason that PM = 1/2 QR. Hence Option 3.

Directions for Illustrations 4 and 5: Please read the following information and answer the questions 4 and 5 based thereon.

The Atlanta is a high-rise complex of offices and shops. It is under construction. It has come up to 36 meters. Every floor of Atlanta is 5 meters in height.

Rosewood Estate is a high-rise complex of apartments. It is fully occupied. Rosewood Estate is 27 meters tall. Atlanta and Rosewood Estate are 20 meters apart.

Zaheer Khan has a shop 36 meters away from Rosewood Estate and the bases of both Atlanta and Rosewood Estate and the eye-level of Zaheer Khan (when he is standing in his shop) are on a horizontal line with Atlanta first, then Rosewood Estate and thereafter Zaheer Khan's shop.

Illustration 4

How many complete floors of Atlanta can Zaheer Khan see standing in his shop?

Options: (1) 2 (2) 3 (3) 1 (4) None

Solution

Please see the following figure, which is not to scale:

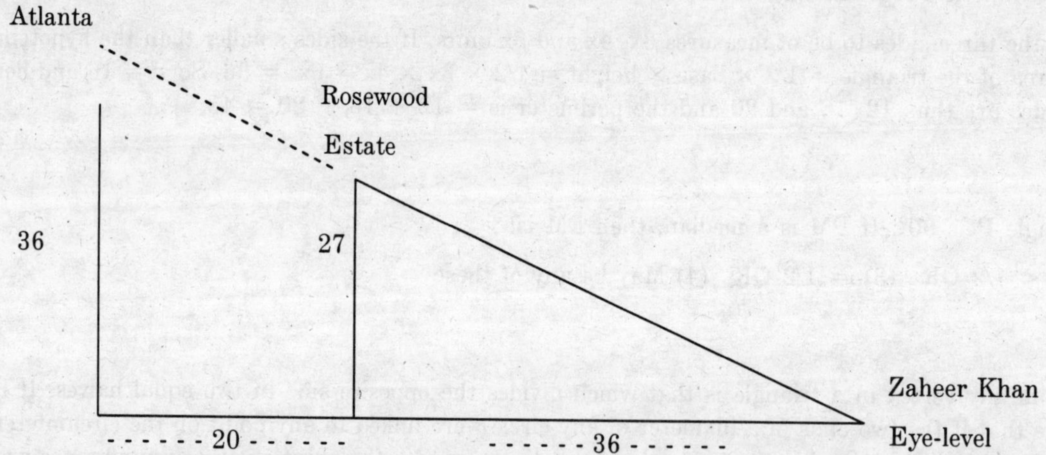

The gradient of a right-angled triangle is the height of the triangle divided by its base. The gradient of a plane is the vertical distance travelled (in order to reach a certain height), divided by the horizontal distance travelled in order to reach that height. A steep gradient would mean that the horizontal distance travelled is less and as the gradient becomes easier, there would be more horizontal distance covered in order to reach a given height. The gradient of the right-angled triangle formed by joining the top of Rosewood Estate (RE) and Zaheer Khan's eye-level (Z) is 27/36 = 3/4. The line linking Z with RE is produced further and goes well over the top of Atlanta. The top of Atlanta does not lie within Zaheer Khan's field of vision. The gradient of the right-angled triangle formed by joining the top of Atlanta (A) with Z is: 36/56 = 9/14, which is < 3/4. As long as the gradient between Z and A is not equal to 3/4, Zaheer Khan will not be able to see Atlanta at all.

Illustration 5

If Atlanta rises by 1 meter and Zaheer Khan's eye-level moves 18 meters away from his shop, which part of Atlanta can he now see?

Options: (1) 2 floors (2) 3 floors (3) 1 floor (4) Only the top

Solution

Please see the following figure:

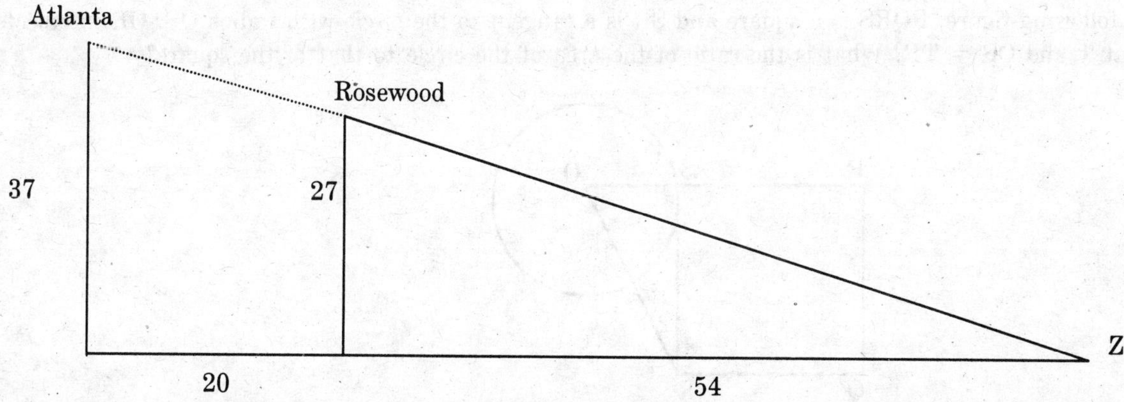

The gradient of the triangle with hypotenuse RZ is 27/54 = 1/2. The gradient of the triangle with hypotenuse AZ is 37/74 = 1/2. Since the two gradients are equal, Zaheer Khan can just about see the top of Atlanta.

EXERCISE

DIRECTIONS: for Question 1 and 2

ABC forms an equilateral triangle in which B is 2 km from A. A person starts walking from B in a direction parallel to AC and stops when he reaches a point D directly east of C. He, then, reverses direction and walks till he reaches a point E directly south of C.

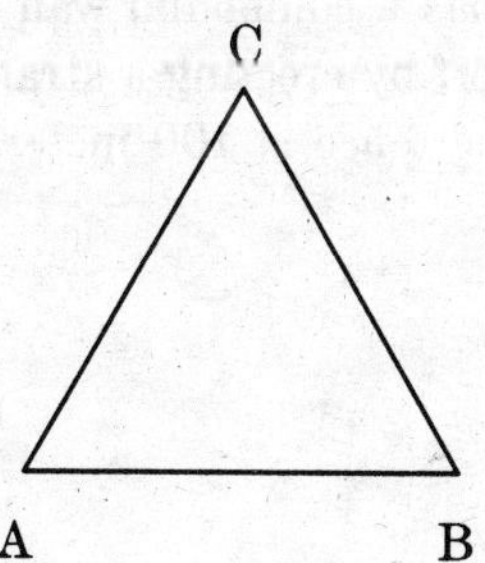

1. Then D is
   1. 3 km east and 1 km north of A.
   2. 3 km east and $\sqrt{3}$ km north of A.
   3. $\sqrt{3}$ km east and 1 km south of A.
   4. $\sqrt{3}$ km west and 3 km north of A.
2. The total distance walked by the person is
   1. 3 km
   2. 4 km

3. $2\sqrt{3}$ km

4. 6 km

3. The three sides of a triangle measure 6 cms, 8 cms and 10 cms. A rectangle equal in area to that of the triangle has a width of 8 cms. The perimeter of the rectangle is

1. 11 cms.

2. 22 cms.

3. 16 cms.

4. None of these

4. In the following figure, PQRS is a square and SR is a tangent to the circle with radius OS. OR intersects the circle at T and OS = TR. What is the ratio of the area of the circle to that of the square?

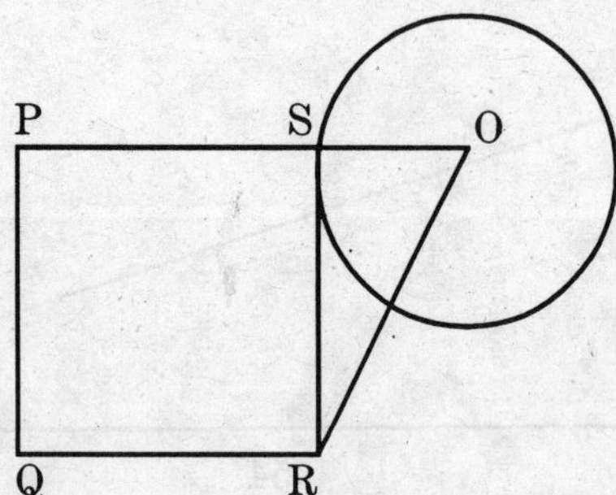

1. 6π

2. $\pi/3$

3. $\pi/9$

4.. None of these

5. The length of a ladder exactly equals the height of a wall. If the ladder is placed on a 2 feet tall stool placed 10 feet away from the wall then its tip can just touch the top of the wall. The height of the wall, in feet is

1. 15

2. 26

3. 28

4. 32

6. There is a square field with each side 500 meters long. It has a compound wall along its perimeter. At one of its corners, a triangular area of the field is to be cordoned off by erecting a straight-line fence. The compound wall and the fence will form its borders. If the length of the fence is 100 meters, what is the maximum area in square meters that can be cordoned off?

1. 2,500

2. 10,000

3. 5,000

4. 20,000

7. A ladder leans against a vertical wall. The top of the ladder is 8m above the ground. When the bottom of the ladder is moved 2m farther away from the wall, the top of the ladder rests against the foot of the wall. What is the length of the ladder?

1. 10m

2. 15m

3. 20m

4. 17m

8. Two sides of a plot measure 32 meters and 24 meters and the angle between them is a perfect right angle. The other two sides measure 25 meters each and the other three angles are not right angles.

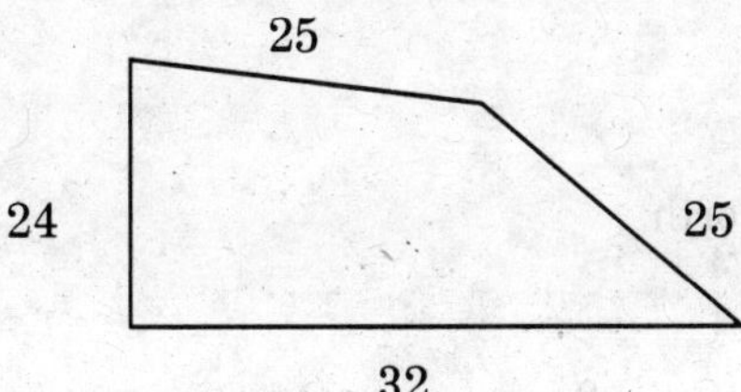

What is the area of the plot?

1. 768

2. 534

3. 696.5

4. 684

9. Euclid has a triangle in mind. Its longest side has length 20 and another of its sides has length 10. Its area is 80. What is the exact length of its third side?

1. $\sqrt{260}$

2. $\sqrt{250}$

3. $\sqrt{240}$

4. $\sqrt{270}$

10. Based on the figure below, what is the value of x, if y=10.

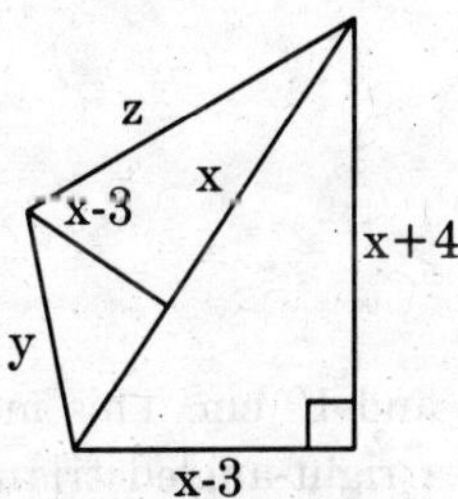

1. 10

2. 11

3. 12

4. None of these

SOLUTIONS

1. It is worth drawing the cardinal points at each of A and C in order to correctly answer this question. Please see the diagram below.

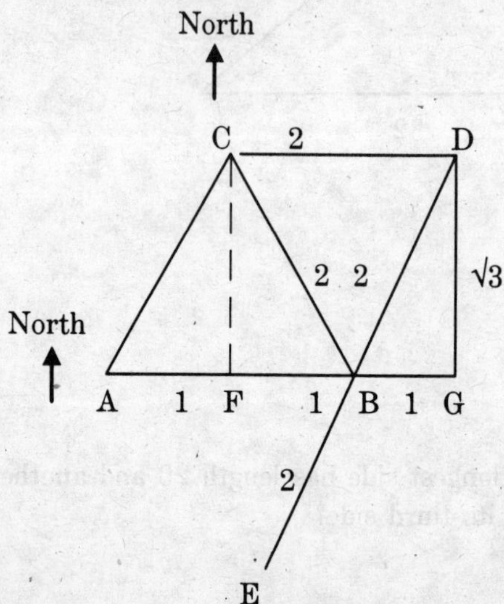

D is to the east of C. Since ABC is equilateral all sides are 2 in length. Drop a perpendicular on AB from C at F. Extend AB and drop another perpendicular from D to meet the extended line AB at G. Triangle CFB is right-angled with 2 as the hypotenuse. So AF = 1 and CF = $\sqrt{3}$. CDFG is a rectangle and thus DG is also $\sqrt{3}$. And hence in order to go to D from A, one has to go 3 km east of A till G and then turn north and go another $\sqrt{3}$ km to reach D. So D is 3 km east of A and $\sqrt{3}$ km north of A. Hence **Option 2**.

2. The person walks from

   B to D = 2 km

   D to B = 2 km and then

   B to E = 2 km.

   In all he walks 6 km. Hence, **Option 4**.

3. The three sides of a triangle measure 6, 8 and 10 cm. This means that they are in the ratio of 3:4:5. This is a clear indication of the triangle being a right-angled triangle. The area of this triangle is $1/2 \times$ base $\times$ height and $= 1/2 \times 6 \times 8 = 24$. The rectangle with side 8 has the same area as the triangle and thus its area is length $\times$ breadth $= 8 \times 3 = 24$ and hence the other side of the rectangle is 3. So its perimeter [the total of the length of all four sides] is $3 + 8 + 3 + 8 = 22$. Hence **Option 2**.

4. OS is the radius which one may assume to be r. OS = TR. So TR = r. Hence OR = r + r = 2r. When a tangent touches a circle, the angle between the tangent and the radius drawn from the point of contact of the tangent to the centre of the circle is always 90°. Thus triangle OSR is a right-angled triangle where the hypotenuse (OR) is 2r and one side (OS) is r. Thus $SR^2 = 4r^2 - r^2 = 3r^2$. Thus SR = $\sqrt{3} \times r$. So the square PQRS has side of $\sqrt{3} \times \pi$ and its area is therefore $3r^2$. The area of the circle is πr^2. So the ratio of the area of the circle to the area of the square is $= (\pi r^2)/3r^2 = \pi/3$.

Hence **Option 2**.

5. Please see the figure below.

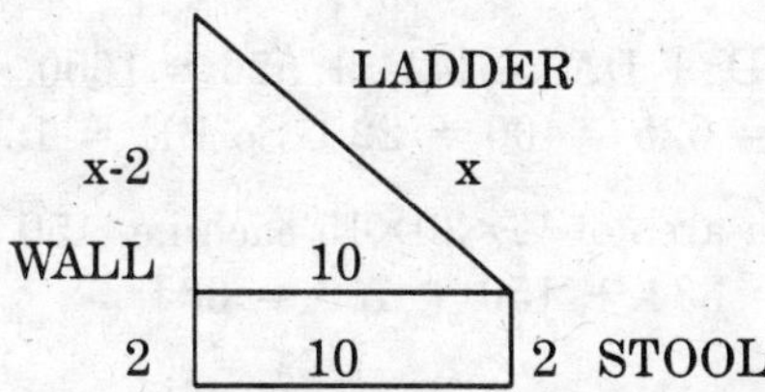

Let the length of the wall be x. Then the length of the ladder will also be x and will not be affected by putting on a stool. The ladder forms the hypotenuse of a right-angled triangle with 10 as the base and x – 2 as the other side. The square on the hypotenuse is the sum of the squares on the other two sides and $x^2 = 10^2 + (x - 2)^2$. Thus $x^2 = 100 + x^2 - 4x + 4$. And hence $4x = 104$ and $x = 26$. So Option 2.

6. The triangular area to be cordoned off will be $1/2 \times b \times h$. The area will be largest when the value of b and h is highest. The triangle at the corner of the square will necessarily be a right-angled triangle. Now the length of the hypotenuse is fixed since the hypotenuse is a wall of 100 meters length. Thus the square of this hypotenuse would be equal to the sum of the squares of the other two sides or $(100)^2 = S^2 + S^2$, i.e. $10000 = 2S^2$ and $S^2 = 5000$ so $S = \sqrt{5000}$. The value of $b \times h$ would be highest when the two sides are equal. This means both the base and the height should be $= \sqrt{5000}$.

   The maximum area that could be cordoned off in the shape of triangle is equal to $(1/2 \times \sqrt{5000} \times \sqrt{5000}) = 1/2 \times 5000 = 2500$ square meters. By way of an illustration, I may take b (the base) to be 25 and h to be 25 in C_1 the first case, 24 and 26 in case C_2, and 23×27 in case C_3, then the value of $b \times h$ is as follows: C_1 – 625, C_2 – 624, C_3 - 621. Clearly, when the two sides are equal, the value of b*h is highest. So **Option 1.**

7. See diagram below.

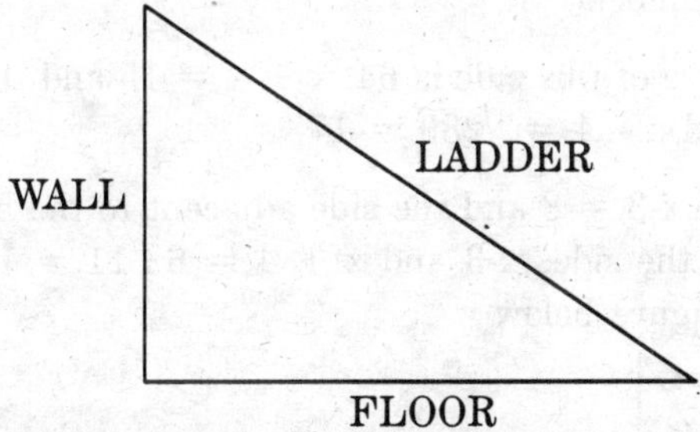

   The ladder forms a right-angled triangle with the wall (walls are always perpendicular to the ground on which they stand and if they are not, than they fall); where the ladder touches the wall at a height of 8 meters from the base of the wall. If one takes the length of the ladder as x, then since the ladder falls to the ground when moved away from the wall by 2 meters, the distance between the base of the wall and the point where the ladder touches the ground is (x – 2) meters. The ladder is the hypotenuse in this right-angled triangle and so $x^2 = (x - 2)^2 + 8^2$ and thus $x^2 = x^2 - 4x + 4 + 64$; from which one gets $4x = 68$ and thus $x = 17$. **Thus Option 4.**

   It is important to remember that 8, 15 and 17 are "Pythagoras Cousins" (since $8^2 + 15^2 = 64 + 225 = 289 = 17^2$).

8. In the figure below, if we draw a line between A and C, we get three triangles.

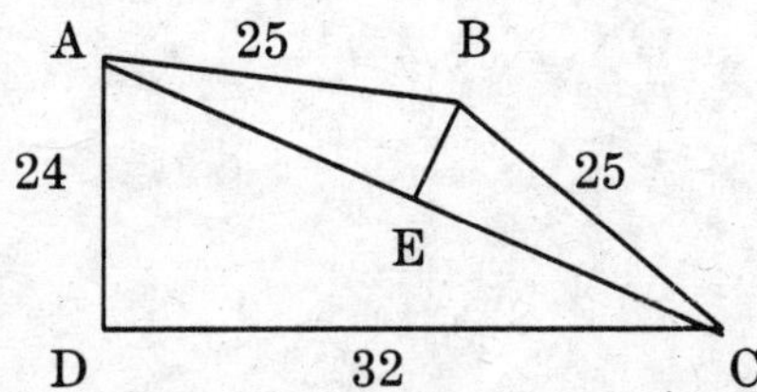

Triangle ADC has an area of ½ × 32 × 24 = 384. Triangle ABC is isosceles and BE, bisects AC.

As per Pythagoras theorem, $AC^2 = CD^2 + DA^2 = 1024 + 576 = 1600$. AC is thus 40. AE and AC are thus 20 each. Further $BE^2 = AB^2 - AE^2 = 625 - 400 = 225$. So BE = 15.

The triangles ABE and BEC have an area of ½×20×15 each i.e. 150 sq units each. The total area of the plot = areas of triangle 1,2 and 3 = 384 + 150 + 150 = 684.

Thus **Option 4**.

9. When one side is 10 and the longest side is 20, the figure would be roughly like this.

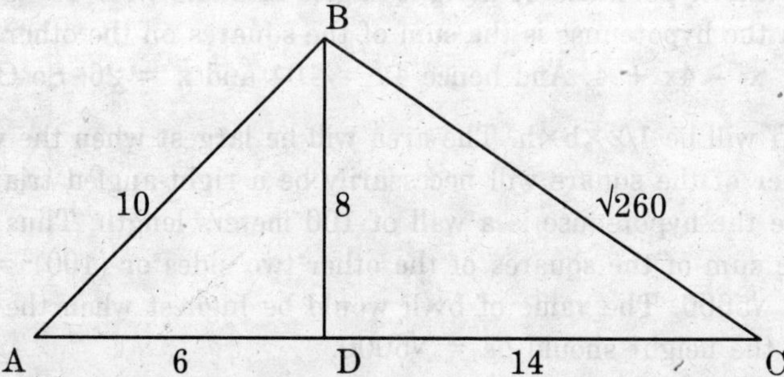

AB = 10; AC = 20, with 20 as base, the height DB of the triangle comes to 8; so AD = 6 (since $AB^2 = BD^2 + AD^2$); thus DC = 14 (since DC = AC – AD = 20 – 6) and (the third side) $BC^2 = (BD^2 + DC^2) = 64 + 196 = 260$; thus the third side is √260. Hence **Option 1**.

10. One will have to be guided by the options since there are two unknowns x and y. If x = 10, x-3 = 7 and the square of this side is 49; x+4 = 14 and the square of this side is 196, then the hypotenuse to the sides x – 3 and x – 4 = √245; this is not a whole number.

Then let us try x = 11; x – 3 = 8 and the square of this side is 64; x + 4 = 15 and the square of this side is 289, then the hypotenuse to the sides x-3 and x – 4 = √289 = 17.

If this is true then the side y = 10 and the side x-3 = 8 and the side adjacent to the hypotenuse y is equal to 6; if this is 6 then the entire hypotenuse to the sides x-3 and x + 4 = 6+11 = 17. This matches. So x = 11 and hence **Option 2**. Please see the figure below.

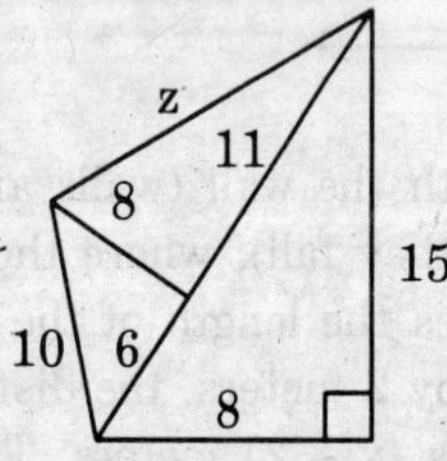

The value of z is irrelevant. Neither does one have to ascertain the value of z nor is it germane to the value of x.

Chapter 33

Quadratic Equations

There are linear equations and quadratic equations and polynomials in algebra that establish a relationship between unknowns. Through solving such equations, one can find the value of unknown(s).

The unknown quantity or number is represented by an alphabet – usually as x and y – to reach an equation. For example, if I do know how old Albert is but if I were to subtract 40 years from his age I would get 2. Here, I write this as A – 40 = 2, where I represent the unknown term (namely Albert's age) as A and strike an equation. The equation A – 40 = 2 is a linear equation where the unknown quantity A does not have an exponent, such as A^2 or A^3 and so on.

While on the issue of representing unknown numerical values by alphabets, it may be mentioned that in the above example, one would assume Albert's unknown age as A. If it had been Bertram in place of Albert, then Bertram's age should be taken as B. This is safer than assuming terms such as X and Y for the ages of Albert and Bertram. This is because once you find the values of X and Y, you have to relate these back to what they stand for. Instead, A or B would not need relating back to Albert or Bertram.

A Quadratic Equation is a mathematical equation in which the second power (the square of an unknown quantity but not any of the higher powers of the unknown quantity such as A^3 or A^4 and so on) appears. A Quadratic Equation therefore has the following form:

$ax^2 + bx + c = 0$

In the above equation $ax^2 + bx + c = 0$, there are three constants: a, b, and c that are respectively (i) the coefficient of x^2 (ii) the coefficient of x and (iii) the numerically constant term in the equation (meaning that term which is not dependent on the value of x).

In a quadratic equation, in the form $ax^2 + bx + c = 0$, the value of a cannot be zero or else the equation effectively becomes $bx + c = 0$, which is a linear equation and not a quadratic equation. If any higher power of x (the unknown quantity) other than x^2 appears in an equation, it ceases to be a quadratic equation. It would than become a polynomial. The difference between a polynomial and a linear equation is that a polynomial has an unknown quantity in a higher power than 1 (such as x^2 and x^3 and so on). The quadratic equation too has the unknown quantity in a higher power than 1. Therefore if you were to group quadratic equations as cows and polynomials as animals, while all cows are animals; but all animals are not cows. Therefore all quadratic equations are polynomials but the converse is not necessarily true.

In the equation $ax^2 + bx + c = 0$, it is possible for either b or c to be 0 (but not both of them simultaneously to be equal to zero) because this will still ensure that the unknown quantity appears in the second power (the square), and that the quadratic equation will have two roots. The meaning of the words *two roots* is that if you were to – for example – see the following quadratic equations, then you will find two values for the unknown quantity in the equation. It will satisfy the following equation if substituted in place of the unknown term:

Equation 1: $x^2 = 4x$. Here two values of x can satisfy the equation: $x = 0$ and $x = 4$. If you were to put 0 as the value of x on both sides – left and right – of the equation, you will get zero. If you put 4 as the value of x then on both sides – left and right – of the equation you will get 16. This means that there are **two real numbers** that would **satisfy** the equation if these real numbers were **substituted** in **place** of the unknown **quantity**.

Equation 2: $x^2 = 2$. Here two values of x can satisfy the equation: $x = \sqrt{2}$ and $x = -\sqrt{2}$. The square root of 2 is a complex number unlike the square roots of numbers such as 4 and 9 and 16 and so on, which are all real numbers. It means that there are two complex numbers that would satisfy an equation such as $x^2 = 2$ if $\sqrt{2}$ and $-\sqrt{2}$ were substituted in place of the unknown quantity in the said equation.

We may put in a word about **quadratic equations without real roots.** If you were to see the equation $x^2 + 1 = 0$, it means that $x^2 = -1$ and therefore x is the square root of a negative number which is impossible to find merely because the square of any number has got to be a positive number.

Equation 3: $x^2 - 4x + 3 = 0$. This equation is really a product of two linear equations as are all quadratic equations that have two real roots. It is simple to understand why quadratic equations with real roots are products of two linear equations. A linear equation has only x but not x^2. If you want x^2 as one of the terms in the equation of the type $x^2 - 4x + 3 = 0$ you have to multiply x with x. Secondly, if you want a constant term such as 3 in the equation that we are presently looking at, 3 can be arrived at by multiplying two real numbers such as the following, which are only illustrative since the list can be endless:

(I) 1 with 3

(II) −1 with −3

(III) 2 with 1.5

(IV) 1/2 with 6

(V) − 1/2 with −6

Therefore, if we are asked to factorise the expression $x^2 - 4x + 3 = 0$, we know that the coefficient of x is = 4 and this is integral even if it is a negative integer. We also know that the two integral factors of 3 that will (A) add up to = 4 and (B) multiply to give 3 are −1 and −3. Therefore $x^2 - 4x + 3$ can be factorised as $(x - 1) \times (x - 3)$. It means that if $x^2 - 4x + 3 = 0$ then any one of $(x - 1)$ or $(x - 3)$ could be equal to zero and therefore x could either be equal to 1 or 3. It means that there are two real roots of the equation $x^2 - 4x + 3 = 0$ and these are $x = 1$ and $x = 3$. If we were to substitute the value of x as 1 in the equation $x^2 - 4x + 3 = 0$, we shall get zero on both sides of the equation and likewise if we were to substitute the value of x as 3 in the equation $x^2 - 4x + 3 = 0$, we shall get zero on both sides of the equation.

We are aware that the square root of a negative number is not a real number but an imaginary number. If we were to assume two imaginary values for X such as $X = \sqrt{-3}$ and $X = \sqrt{-5}$, then we have two equations: $(X - \sqrt{-3}) = 0$ and $(X - \sqrt{-5}) = 0$. If we were to multiply both these equations, we would get the equation $X^2 - X(\sqrt{-3} + \sqrt{-5}) + \sqrt{15} = 0$. If we were to see this in the form of general form of the quadratic equation, we would get the following values for a, b and c: $a = 1$, $b = (\sqrt{-3} + \sqrt{-5})$ and $c = \sqrt{15}$. Then, $b^2 = (\sqrt{-3} + \sqrt{-5})^2 = -3 + 2\sqrt{15} - 5 = 2\sqrt{15} - 8 = \sqrt{60} - 8$ which will be negative since 8 is $\sqrt{64}$ and thus $\sqrt{60} - 8$ is effectively $\sqrt{60} - \sqrt{64}$. As against this, $4ac = 4 \times 1 \times \sqrt{15} = 4\sqrt{15}$ which is positive. This means that if a quadratic equation is to have two real roots, then such as equation seen in the standard form of a quadratic equation must satisfy the condition that b^2 is greater than 4ac or in other words, $b^2 - 4ac$ is greater than 0.

If $b^2 = 4ac$ or $b^2 - 4ac = 0$ as in the case of $x^2 - 4x + 4 = 0$, then the quadratic equation has two **equal** roots (which effectively means one real root). The equation $x^2 - 4x + 4 = 0$ is essentially $(x - 2) \times (x - 2)$ and hence the equation can be satisfied by a unique value for x and this is when $x = 2$. Therefore in such a case, there are two equal roots to this equation and similar equations where $b^2 - 4ac = 0$.

Assuming that both of the linear equations that are factors of a quadratic equation are equal to zero, let us multiply two linear equations and see the outcomes:

If I multiply	$[(x+1)=0]$ with $[(x+2)=0]$	$[(x-2)=0]$ with $[(x+2)=0]$	$[(x-3)=0]$ with $[(x-4)=0]$	$[(x+3)=0]$ with $[(x-4)=0]$
I get the Quadratic Equation	$x^2 + 3x + 2 = 0$	$x^2 - 4 = 0$	$x^2 - 7x + 12 = 0$	$x^2 - x - 12 = 0$
Where the coefficient of x is	+3	0	-7	-1
And this coefficient is the sum of	1 and 2	-2 and 2	-3 and -4	3 and -4
The constant term is	2 which is (1×2)	–4 which is (2×-2)	12 which is (-3×-4)	–12 which is (3×-4)

Now, what one sees is the following:

In the equation	Since both	x can have the values of	The roots of this equation are
$x^2 + 3x + 2 = 0$	$(x+1)$ and $(x+2)=0$	–1 and –2	–1 and –2
$x^2 - 4 = 0$	$(x-2)$ and $(x+2) = 0$	2 and –2	2 and –2
$x^2 - 7x + 12 = 0$	$(x-3)$ and $(x-4) = 0$	3 and 4	3 and 4
$x^2 - x - 12 = 0$	$(x+3)$ and $(x-4) = 0$	–3 and 4	–3 and 4

From the above, the following inferences emerge:

- The coefficient of x is = –1 × (the sum of the roots). [Care: We are talking only about the coefficient of x here and not the coefficient of x^2].
- The constant term is the product of the roots.
- **When both the roots of the equation are negative, the coefficient of x is positive.**
- **When both the roots of the equation are positive, the coefficient of x is negative.**

The skill in solving a quadratic equation would principally involve being able to factorise the constant term c in an equation of the type $ax^2 + bx + c = 0$, so that you get the coefficient of the x term and the x^2 term that appear in the given equation.

So if I were to factorise the equation $x^2 - 2x - 899 = 0$, I should be able to see that 899 is nothing but $(900 - 1)$ and is thus equal to $(30 - 1) \times (30 + 1)$ or 29×31.

And thus the equation $x^2 - 2x - 899 = 0$ can be factorised as $(x - 31) \times (x + 29) = 0$. This would mean that the following two values of x would satisfy the equation $x^2 - 2x - 899 = 0$: $x = 31$ and $x = -29$.

So long as an equation has x^2 (meaning x raised to the power of two but to no higher power than 2) as one of its terms, then it will certainly have two roots (although it is a different matter that in some cases the two roots would be equal as we have seen earlier). Let us see the following equations and what could be the two possible roots of the equation although in one case the coefficient of x is zero and in the other case, the constant term is zero.

In the equation	The coefficient of x is	The constant term is	The possible values of x that satisfy the equation are:
$x^2 - 4 = 0$	0	–4	2 and –2
$x^2 - x = 0$	0	0	0 and 1

We may also observe the following:

If the roots of the equation R_1 and R_2	The Equation is	Coefficient of x in the equation is	$(-R_1)+(-R_2)=$	Constant Term (which is $(-R_1) \times (-R_2)$ =
Equal and each is equal to say 2	$(x-2)(x-2) = x^2-4x+4=0$	–4 or two times the root multiplied by –1	-4	$-2\times-2 = 4$ which is effectively the square of the root.
Equal and each is equal to say 4	$(x-4)(x-4) = x^2 -8x+16=0$	–8 or two times the root multiplied by –1	-8	$-4\times-4 = 16$ which is effectively the square of the root.
Reciprocal and are say 2 and ½	$(x-2) \times (x-½)= x^2-2½\,x+1=0$	-2½	-2½	$-2\times-1/2=1$ which means that the precondition for the roots to be reciprocal is that the constant term should be +1
Reciprocal and are say 5 and 1/5 (which is 0.2)	$(x-5)(x-0.2) = x^2-5.2x+1 = 0$	-5.2	-5.2	$-5\times-0.2 = 1$ which means that the precondition for the roots to be reciprocal should be a constant term +1

To summarise:

- The coefficient of x in a quadratic equation is invariably the sum of the roots of the equation **after each of the roots has changed sign** (meaning from positive to negative and vice versa).
- The coefficient of x in a quadratic equation having equal roots is minus two times the root.
- If a quadratic equation has roots such that one is the negative of the other, (say 2 and -2), then the coefficient of x in such an equation is 0 (meaning there will be no term with x in the equation).
- The constant term in the quadratic equation is equal to the product of the roots after each of the roots has changed sign (meaning from positive to negative and vice versa).
- The constant term in a quadratic equation having equal roots (which effectively means one root) is invariably equal to the square of the root.
- The constant term in a quadratic equation having reciprocal roots is invariably equal to 1.

EXERCISE

1. The quadratic equation, which has 2 and –15 as its roots, is given by (1) $x^2 - 2x + 19 = 4$ (2) $3x^2 + 45x-2 = 4$ (3) $7x^2 + 91x - 206 = 4$ (4) $x^2 - 30 = 0$
2. If R and P are the roots of the quadratic equation $ax^2 + bx + c = 0$, (when c is non-zero), then the roots of the equation $cx^2 + bx + a = 0$ are (1) $R + 1, P + 1$ (2) $R - 1, P - 1$ (3) R^{-1}, P^{-1} (4) $1 - R, 1 - P$
3. If P and Q are the roots of $x^2 - a(x + 1) - 1= 0$, then $(P + 1) \times (Q + 1)$ = ? (1) 0 (2) –1 (3) 1 (4) 2
4. When I worked out a quadratic equation, my younger brother was reading out the equation to me. He first spoke the wrong constant term, and I got 7 and 6 as the roots of the equation and when I worked with the wrong co-efficient of x that he read out to me the second time that he read the equation I got -5 and 6 the roots of the equation. What are the roots of the equation that I was trying to solve if my brother were to read it correctly?

5. Johnny and Tim attempted to solve a quadratic equation. Johnny made a mistake in writing down the constant term and ended up with the roots (4,3). Tim made a mistake in writing down the co-efficient of x. He got the roots as (3,2). What are the exact roots of the original quadratic equation?

6. The roots of the equation $Lx^2 + Mx + N = 0$ are reciprocals of each other provided (A) $L = M$ (B) $L = N$ (C) $M = N$ (D) $M = LN$

7. If P and Q are the roots of the quadratic equation $Lx^2 + Mx + N = 0$, then the value of $[(P/Q) + (Q/P)]$ is given by (A) $(M^2 - 2N)/ 2N$ (B) $(M^2 - 2N)/ N$ (C) $(N - 2M^2)/ M$ (D) $(N - 2M^2)/ 2M$

8. If the roots of the equation $x^2 + 3x + c = 0$ are consecutive integers, then what is the value of c?

9. The equation $x^2 - 2(k - 1)x + 4k = 7$ has equal roots, if k = ? (A) 3 (B) 4 (C) 5 (D) 6

10. The number of real solutions of the equation $x^2 - 5|x| + 6 = 0$ are:

    (1) 0 (2) 2 (3) 4 (4) None of these

SOLUTIONS

1. If the roots of the quadratic equation are 2 and –15, it means that the equation is really a product of $(x-2)$ and $(x + 15)$. Since $(x - 2) \times$ equation $(x + 15) = 0$, the equation is $x^2 + 13x - 30 = 0$. From among the options we may see which of the options yields $x^2 + 13x - 30 = 0$.

   Option (1): $x^2 - 2x + 19 = 4$; this is effectively $x^2 - 2x + 15 = 0$

   Option (2): $3x^2 + 45x - 2 = 4$; this is effectively $3x^2 + 45x + 2 = 0$

   Option (3): $7x^2 + 91x - 206 = 4$; this is effectively $7x^2 + 91x - 210 = 0$, or dividing both sides by 7 we get $x^2 + 13x - 30 = 0$. This is the equation we are looking for and hence **Option 3**.

2. We are given that R and P are the roots of the quadratic equation $ax^2 + bx + c = 0$, (when c is non-zero). We have two choices: (A) Continue with R and P and flounder or (B) Assume some real number and distinct values for R and P and reach the correct inference. Let us assume R = 2 and P= –2 and see what is the quadratic equation that will emerge. The equation will then be $(x - 2) \times (x + 2) = 0$ or $x^2 - 4 = 0$. If one were to see the equation $x^2 - 4 = 0$ in the standard form $ax^2 + bx + c = 0$, then $a = 1$, $b = 0$ and $c = -4$. Then the equation $cx^2 + bx + a = 0$ would be $-4x^2 + 1 = 0$ and this would then be $4x^2 - 1 = 0$ and x^2 would be equal to 1/4 and hence the roots of this equation would be ½ and –1/2 which are reciprocals of the roots in the earlier equation. So **Option 3**: R^{-1}, P^{-1}.

   You can take values such as $x = 5$ and $x = 3$, but taking distinct numerical values for the two roots R and P will help solving the prolem quickly. This means that $x - 5 = 0$ and $x - 3 = 0$ and that multiplying these two equation you would get $x^2 - 8x + 15 = 0$ which has 5 and 3 as its roots. Now see this equation in the standard form of the quadratic equation $ax^2 + bx + c = 0$ and you see that $a = 1$, $b = -8$ and $c = 15$. If you are to find the roots of the equation $cx^2 + bx + a = 0$, this means that we are to find the roots of $15x^2 - 8x + 1 = 0$ and this can be factorised as $(5x - 1) \times (3x - 1) = 0$ and this means that the roots of this latter equation are $x = 1/5$ and $x = 1/3$ which are reciprocals of the roots 5 and 3 of the earlier equation $x^2 - 8x + 15 = 0$.

3. The equation $x^2 - a(x + 1) - 1 = 0$ can be simplified as $x^2 - ax - a - 1 = 0$ and thus further simplified to $x^2 - ax - (a + 1) = 0$. Take $a = 1$. So the equation becomes $x^2 - x - 2 = 0$. Factorise this and you get $(x - 2) \times (x + 1) = 0$. Therefore the roots of the equation $x^2 - x - 2 = 0$ are 2 and –1. Let the value of P be 2 and that of Q be –1. So $(P + 1) \times (Q + 1) = (2 + 1) \times (-1 + 1) = 0$. Whatever value of a that you will assume will get you no other answer for $(P + 1) \times (Q + 1)$ other than zero. Try any other value for a and verify this statement.

We will take another value for a and make sure that this point goes home once and for all. Take $a = 2$ and the equation $x^2 - ax-(a + 1) = 0$ becomes $x^2 - 2x-3 = 0$ and thus $(x + 1) \times (x - 3) = 0$. This means that $P = -1$ and $Q = 3$ and thus $(P + 1) \times (Q + 1) = (3 + 1) \times (-1 + 1) = 0$.

4. When I worked out a quadratic equation, my younger brother was reading out the equation to me. He first spoke the wrong constant term, and I got 7 and 6 as the roots of the equation. It means that the equation I was really working on was $(x - 7) \times (x - 6) = 0$ whereas this is $x^2 - 13x + 42 = 0$. Here, the error is only in regard to the constant term. The coefficient of x in the correct equation is –13. For the equation that I worked with the wrong co-efficient of x that he read out to me, I got -5 and 6 the roots. It means that the equation I was working was $(x + 5) \times (x - 6) = 0$ and thus $x^2 - 1x-30 = 0$. Thus the constant term of the correct equation is –30. Which means that the correct equation was $x^2 - 13x - 30 = 0$ and this correct equation can be factorised as $(x - 15) \times (x + 2) = 0$. The roots of the equation that I was trying to solve, if my brother were to read it correctly, are 15 and –2.

5. With the wrong constant term, Johnny got 4 and 3 as the roots of the equation. This means that the equation Johnny was really working on was $(x - 4) \times (x - 3) = 0$ and this is $x^2 - 7x + 12 = 0$.

   In this the error is only in regard to the constant term. The coefficient of x in the correct equation is –7.

   For the equation that Tim worked (meaning, the equation with the wrong co-efficient of x) he got 3 and 2 as the roots. It means that the equation he was working was $(x - 3) \times (x - 2) = 0$ and thus $x^2 - 5x + 6 = 0$. Thus the constant term of the correct equation is +6.

   It means that the correct equation was $x^2 - 7x + 6 = 0$ and this correct equation can be factorised as $(x - 6) \times (x - 1) = 0$.

   The roots of the original equation are 6 and 1.

6. Let us assume two reciprocal roots for an equation as 2 and 1/2. Thus the equation is $(x - 2) \times [(x-(1/2))] = 0$. This is effectively $x^2 - (5x/2) + 1 = 0$. Consider the equation in the form of $Lx^2 + Mx + N = 0$

   You will see that $L = 1$, $M = 5/2$, and $N = 1$. See which of the Options is feasible:

   (A) L is not equal to M (B) $L = N$ (C) M is not equal to N (D) M is not equal to LN. Thus, only if $L = N$, then the roots can be reciprocal. Hence **Option B**.

7. P and Q are the roots of the quadratic equation $Lx^2 + Mx + N = 0$. Assume the roots of the equation to be 3 and 2. So the quadratic equation is really a multiple of $(x - 3) = 0$ and $(x - 2) = 0$ which is equal to $x^2 - 5x + 6 = 0$. If one were to see this equation $x^2 - 5x + 6 = 0$ in the form of $Lx^2 + Mx + N = 0$, then $L = 1$, $M = -5$ and $N = 6$. So the value of $[(P/Q) + (Q/P)]$ is

   $[(3/2) + (2/3) = 13/6]$ and what we now have to see is which of the options gives us 13/6.

   (A) $(M^2 - 2N)/ 2N = (25 - 12)/12 = 13/12$

   (B) $(M^2 - 2N)/ N = (25 - 12)/6 = 13/6$

   Therefore, **Option (B)**.

8. It must be remembered that:

   (a) The coefficient of x in a quadratic equation is invariably the sum of the roots of the equation after each of the roots has changed sign (meaning from positive to negative and vice versa), and

   (b) The constant term in the quadratic equation is equal to the multiple of the roots after each of the roots has changed sign (meaning from positive to negative and vice versa).

   Since the coefficient of x in the $x^2 + 3x + c = 0$ is 3 and 3 is the sum of the roots of the equation after each of the roots has changed sign, the two roots add up to –3. Further, since the roots are consecutive integers, only –2 and –1 could add up to –3.The equation is effectively $(x + 1) \times (x + 2) = 0$ and this is $x^2 + 3x + 2 = 0$ and thus $c = 2$.

9. Let us see from the given options as to in which case one can have equal roots:

(A) If $k = 3$, then the equation $x^2 - 2(k - 1)x + 4k = 7$ is $x^2 - 2(3 - 1)x + 4 \times 3 = 7$ and thus $x^2 - 4x + 5 = 0$; the factors of this equation are $(x + 1)$ and $(x - 5)$ and the roots are –1 and 5 and these are not equal roots

(B) If $k = 4$, then the equation $x^2 - 2(k - 1)x + 4k = 7$ is $x^2 - 2(4 - 1)x + 4 \times 4 = 7$ and thus $x^2 - 6x + 9 = 0$; the factors of this equation are $(x - 3)$ and $(x - 3)$ and the roots are 3 and 3 and these are equal roots. The easiest way to solve this is by substituting the value of k in only the constant term of the equation and try to obtain a perfect square in the constant term. If there is only one option that would give a perfect square in the constant term, there is no need to go further.

10. An equation deals with unknown quantities. An unknown quantity can be either positive or negative (or zero). Let us call that unknown quantity as x. Therefore:

I. If x is either zero or positive, the modulus sign is unnecessary. In that case the equation $x^2 - 5 \mid x \mid + 6 = 0$ becomes $x^2 - 5x + 6 = 0$.

II. If x is negative, then modulus x is $-x$. If we were to assume that $x = -10$ (for example), then modulus $x = -x = 10$. Thus if x is negative then the equation $x^2 - 5 \mid x \mid + 6 = 0$ effectively becomes $x^2 - 5(-x) + 6 = 0$ or $x^2 + 5x + 6 = 0$.

Thus there can be two distinct quadratic equations on opening up the modulus sign:

- $x^2 - 5x + 6 = 0$
- $x^2 + 5x + 6 = 0$

The factors of the first equation $x^2 - 5x + 6 = 0$ are $(x - 2)$ and $(x - 3)$ and the roots are 2 and 3.

The factors of the second equation $x^2 + 5x + 6 = 0$ are $(x + 2)$ and $(x + 3)$ and the roots are – 2 and – 3.

As may be seen from the above, since both above equations will have two roots each, there will be four roots of the equation $x^2 - 5 \mid x \mid + 6 = 0$.

Chapter 34

Ratio and Proportion

If I am asked to divide 30 chocolates between Sam and Peter in the ratio of 3:2, what am I really supposed to ensure?

I am supposed to ensure that for every 2 chocolates that Peter has, Sam should have 3. But how? I realize that I must have 5 chocolates, at the very least, if I am to give 3 to Sam and 2 to Peter. This means that Sam gets $3/5^{th}$ of the chocolates and Peter gets $2/5^{th}$. I should arrange 30 chocolates in 5 batches such that each batch has an equal number of chocolates and then from these five batches, give three batches to Sam and two batches to Peter.

I can divide 30 into 5 batches with equal number of chocolates in each batch by putting 6 chocolates in each batch. When I give 2 such batches (of six chocolates each) to Peter I give him 12 chocolates and when I give three such batches to Sam then I have given him 18 chocolates. The distribution gets over and it is in line with the proportion of chocolates that I am supposed to maintain between Sam and Peter.

If I am given a pile of 40 blankets and I am told to give out the maximum possible whole number of blankets from the pile to three persons P, Q and R such that the ratio of blankets that they shall get is 2: 3: 7 respectively, I must divide 40 blankets into 12 batches (since I should give 2, 3 and 7 batches of blankets with an equal number of blankets in each such batch to P, Q and R respectively) and this would mean that I shall be able to make 12 batches with 3 blankets in each of them. That would account for 36 blankets and 4 blankets will be surplus. I then give out these 12 batches of 3 blankets each so that P gets 2, Q gets 3 and R gets 7 batches. P, Q and R would thus respectively have 6, 9 and 21 blankets. The 4 surplus blankets are to be put back into the closet.

The lesson to be derived from the above is as follows:

Dividing Z number of items between A and B in the ratio of X:Y means that I divide Z by $(X + Y)$ and give $(Z \times X) / (X + Y)$ to A and $(Z \times Y) / (X + Y)$ to B. Cross check this from the examples given above.

If I am to divide K items between A, B and C in the ratio of X: Y: Z, I divide K by $(X + Y + Z)$ and give $(K \times X) / (X + Y + Z)$ to A, $(K \times Y)/ (X + Y + Z)$ to B and $(K \times Z) / (X + Y + Z)$ to C.

If you wish to crosscheck this, try out with K=36 and X: Y: Z as 2: 3: 7. You will find that A, B and C respectively get 6,9 and 21 items.

If ratios are expressed in fractions, it becomes imperative to convert the fractions into whole numbers by multiplying each of the fractions with the least common multiple of the denominators of the fractions. This makes understanding the ratios rather easy. Multiplying the ratio by the same number does alter the ratio in any way. If I had 1 red shirt and you had 2 red shirts, the ratio of red shirts that you and I have is 1:2. If you and I have 20 red shirts and 40 red shirts respectively, the ratio of red shirts that you and I have would still be 1:2.

See this illustrated as per hereunder:

A grandfather decided to divide $141 among his three grandsons who were attending a summer camp. He gave the money to the three brothers R, S and T in the ratio of 1/2: 1/3: 2/7 respectively. How much more did R get than T?

If the ratio of money divided between three brothers is 1/2: 1/3: 2/7, then one should find the least common multiple of 2, 3 and 7, which are the denominators of the fractions. This LCM is the product of these three integers since all three are prime numbers and have no common factors at all. The LCM of 2, 3 and 7 is 42. Multiplying each of the fractions 1/2, 1/3 and 2/7 by 42, one gets the ratio in whole numbers and this ratio is 21: 14: 12. This means I should divide $141 into 21 + 14 + 12 = 47 parts such that each part is $3. R gets 21 such parts of $3 each and that makes R's share \$63. T gets 12 such parts of \$3 each and he thus gets \$36. Thus R gets \$63 – \$36 = \$27 more than what T gets in the process of distribution.

The topic of Ratio and Proportion has far greater importance insofar as competitive examinations goes. Let us see some important applications of ratio and proportion in some problems as hereunder:

Problem 1

A storekeeper intends to earn a profit of 10% on all his goods. For how much should he sell an item that cost him \$353.50?

Solution

Fundamentally if a man decides to sell his goods at a profit of 10%, all that he has to do is to maintain a ratio of 110: 100 (or 11: 10 or 1.1: 1) between his Selling Price and Cost Price. If he sells any item worth \$100 at \$110, he will earn a profit of 10%. It means that the ratio between his selling price and cost price is 110:100. Thus, if he has to decide the selling price of any item that has cost him \$353.50, all that he has to do in order to arrive at the selling price is to multiply \$353.50 by 1.1. His selling price should thus be \$388.85.

Problem 2

If the marked price of a shirt ensures a profit of 25% on cost, what is the cost price of a shirt which is marked at \$6.75?

Solution

If an item costs \$100, it will fetch a profit of 25% only if sold at \$125. It means that the ratio between Selling Price and Cost Price is 125:100 or 5:4. It also means that if any item is sold at a profit of 25%, the cost price is $4/5^{th}$ of the selling price. Here the selling price is \$6.75 and thus the cost price is $(6.75 \times 4)/5 = 27/5 =$ \$5.40.

Problem 3

If a shopkeeper first increases the price of an item by X% and then offers a discount of X% on the item, will he make a gain or a loss or will he break even?

Solution

If a man were to increase the selling price of the commodity by, say, 50% (so that the marked price is 1.5 times the earlier selling price; let us call the new marked price as M_1) and then mark it down by 50% so that the new selling price is 50% of the marked price (Let us call the new marked price as M_2) and again increase by the new marked price by 1/2 its value (Let us call this marked price as M_3) and then again mark it down by 50% its value (Let us call the new marked price as M_4), then the ratio between M_2 and M_1 will be the same as between M_4 and M_3.

Let us assume that a shopkeeper plans to sell a table that he bought for \$400 and put the marked price building in a profit margin equal to 50% its cost price. His marked price M_1 is thus \$600. Let us assume that he marks it down by 50% this marked price M_1, the new marked price – M_2 will be \$300. He loses \$100 in this transaction.

Let us assume that he marks up M_2 by 50% once again and then the new marked price, M_3, will be \$450. When he marks down this new marked price M_3 by another 50% the latest marked price, M_4, will be \$225. He again loses on the transaction. His loss is \$300 – \$225 = \$75.

Let us see the ratio between M_2 and M_1 and M_4 and M_3.

M_2: M_1 as 300:600 and this is effectively 1:2.

M_4: M_3 as 225:450 and this is also effectively 1:2.

If the shopkeeper were to persist with this marking up and down cycle till he were to fall down with exhaustion, the ratio, each time, between the new marked price and the old marked price at the end of each such cycle would remain unchanged so long as the percentage by which he marks it up and then down remains constant.

But one thing is for certain. If the cost price is \$X and the profit margin is Y% of the cost price (so that the marked price is inclusive of a profit of Y% over the cost price), and then if he were to offer a discount of Y% on the marked price, **he would never cover his cost price (meaning he would certainly make a loss).** Let us see this in tabular form.

If the cost price of an item were to be \$	200	1000	1200
If the margin of profit were to be	25%	10%	20%
Then the marked price would be	250	1100	1440
If he were to offer a discount equal to the profit margin, then the new selling price would be	250–62.50= 187.50	1100–110 = 990	1440 –288= 1152
He would then lose	\$12.50	\$10	\$48
Then the margin of loss would be	12.50×100/200 =6.25%	10×100/1000=1%	48×100/1200=4%
This loss in percentage terms is equal to	25×25/100 = 6.25%	10×10/100= 1%	20×20/100= 4%

The lessons to be learnt from the above are that:

1. If a thing costs a certain amount and the marked price includes a profit margin of Y%, and then if a discount of Y% is offered to the buyer, the transaction would invariably result in a loss.
2. The loss so resulting would increase if the value of Y – meaning the profit margin included in the marked price increases
3. The resultant loss in percentage terms = $Y^2 / 100$.

If the above fundamentals were absorbed, no problem relating to ratio and proportion would be a source of bother, no matter how complex it is.

Problem 4

A train approaches a tunnel AB. Inside the tunnel is a cat located at a point that is 3/8th of the distance AB measured form the entrance A. When the train whistles, the cat runs. If the cat moves to the entrance of the tunnel, A, the train catches the cat exactly at the entrance. If the cat moves to the exit, B, the train catches the cat at exactly the exit. The speed of the train is greater than the speed of the cat by what order? Options are as follows:

1. 3:1 2. 4:1 3. 5:1 4. none of these

Solution

This problem would seem prima facie as one pertaining to Speed and Distance but it isn't really. This seems a fairly difficult nut to crack but it isn't once we see the methodology for cracking it.

Let us make a small sketch of the tunnel where we shall refer to the entrance as A, the exit as B and the cat as C and then proceed as under:

A $3X$ C $5X$ B

Entrance Exit

Let AB be $8X$ meters. So the cat is $3X$ meters from A and hence AC is $3X$. One does not know as to how far is the train from entrance A. Let it be M to the left of A. Let the speed of the train be T meters/second and that of the cat be C meters/second.

When the train whistles, the cat runs. If the cat moves to the entrance of the tunnel, A, the train catches the cat exactly at the entrance. This means that by the time the train covers M meters, the cat covers $3X$ meters. Now, let us go by the options:

Option 1: Train's speed : Cat's speed is 3:1

If we assume that the speed of the train is 3 times that of the cat, then by the time the cat has run $3X$ meters to the entrance, the train has run 3 times the distance that the cat has run since the train runs three times as fast as the cat and thus the train has run $9X$ meters before reaching the entrance of the tunnel.

If the cat moves to the exit, B, the train catches it at exactly the exit. This means that by the time the train covers $9X + 8X$ meters $= 17X$, the cat covers $5X$ meters and thus the train runs $17/5 = 3.4$ times as fast as the cat whereas for Option 1 to be correct, this ratio should be 3:1. Hence Option 1 is not correct.

Option 2: Train's speed : Cat's speed is 4:1

If we assume that the speed of the train is 4 times that of the cat, then by the time, the cat has run $3X$ meters to the entrance, the train has run 4 times the distance that the cat has run. Since the train runs four times as fast as the cat, the train has run $12X$ meters before reaching the entrance of the tunnel.

If the cat moves to the exit, B, the train catches at exactly the exit. This means that by the time the train covers $12X + 8X$ meters $= 20X$ meters, the cat covers $5X$ meters and thus the train runs four times as fast as the cat since the train has covered $20X$ meters in the time the cat has run $5X$ meters. Thus Option 2 is correct.

Problem 5

Sarah got two and a half times as many marks at Arithmetic as at Geography. If the total of her marks in the two subjects is 140, how many marks did she get at Arithmetic?

Solution

For every 2 marks that Sarah got at Geography, she got 5 at Arithmetic. Divide her aggregate marks of 140 in 7 equal parts, and you get each part=20. Allot five such batches of 20 marks to Sarah for Arithmetic and she gets 100 at arithmetic. This means that Sarah's score at Arithmetic is 100. (She therefore gets 40 at Geography).

Problem 6

Two numbers are in the ratio of 1:2. If 7 were added to both, their ratio changes to 3:5. What are the two numbers?

Solution

Let the two numbers be X and Y. We are told that $X/Y = 1/2$. Hence the greater number of the two is Y (which means $Y = 2X$ and hence $X = Y/2$). If 7 is added to both X and Y, we get $(X + 7)$ and $(Y + 7)$. We are given that $(X + 7) / (Y + 7) = 3/5$ or $5 \times (X + 7) = 3 \times (Y + 7)$ or $5X + 35 = 3Y + 21$ and hence $3Y - 5x = 14$.

If one were to substitute the value of X in this we get $[3Y - (5Y/2)] = 14$ and thus $Y/2 = 14$. Thus Y, the bigger of the two numbers is 28 and therefore $X = 14$.

Problem 7

A building contractor employed 25 employees on a job. He was paid $2750 for the work. After retaining 20% thereof, he distributed the remaining amount amongst the employees. If the number of men to women employees was 2:3 and their wages were in the ratio of 5:4, what wages did each woman employee get?

Solution

Since the contractor retains, 20% of $2750, he passes on 80% or 80/100 or 4/5th of $2750, which is $2200 and this $2200 is to be divided among 25 employees.

We are told that the number of men to women employees was 2:3 and their wages were in the ratio of 5:4. This means that the number of women employees was 3/5th of the total number of employees. Suppose there were 2 men and 3 women and each man got $5 and each woman $4, the two men together would get $10 and the three women together would get $12. It means that if there were $22 to be divided among a number of men and women when the ratio of Men: Women is 2:3, then the men would get \$10 and the women would get \$12. If there were \$2200 to be divided, the women would get \$1200. But how many women are there? 3 × 25/5 = 15. Thus 15 women get a total of \$1200 and this means that each woman gets \$1200/15 = \$80 as wages.

Problem 8

There are 200 questions in a 3-hour examination. Among the questions are 50 mathematical problems. It is suggested that twice as much time be allowed for each mathematical problem as for each of the other questions. How many minutes should be allotted for the mathematical problems?

Solution

There are 50 mathematical problems out of 200 overall and, therefore, 150 others. Let us assume that M minutes are allotted for each of the other problems. This makes 150M minutes for others. Thus the time allotted for each mathematical problem is 2M minutes and this makes 50 × 2M= 100M minutes for mathematical problems. This makes 150M + 100M = 250M minutes for the entire 3-hour examination and therefore 250M = 180 minutes (since three hours are exactly 180 minutes). If 250 M = 180 minutes, M= 180 ÷ 250 = 18÷25 minutes. Thus the time allowed for mathematical problems should be 100 × M = 100 × 18/25 = 72 minutes. As for the other problems, the total time allowed should be 180 – 72 = 108 minutes.

Problem 9

There are 200 questions in a 2-hour test. Questions are classified as Easy, Medium and Tough. Easy questions require half the time for medium, and a sixth of the time required for Tough questions. The proportion of Easy, Medium and Tough questions is 2: 2: 1. How much time that should be allocated for solving Medium questions?

Solution

Let us assume that there are 6M minutes allocated for solving each Tough question; 6M because it is possible to divide 6M with 6 to arrive at the time for solving each Easy question (which is then M minutes) and since this is half the time needed for solving Medium questions, the time to be allotted for solving each Medium question is 2M minutes. The proportion of Easy, Medium and Tough questions is 2: 2: 1 and it means that if one were to divide 200 questions in 5 parts (which is necessary to maintain the 2: 2: 1 proportion), each part is 40 and thus there are 80 questions of Easy type, 80 of Medium type and 40 of Tough variety.

Thus the total time required for the different types of questions is as follows: (A) Easy questions: 80 × M = 80 M (B) Medium questions: 80 × 2M = 160 M, and (C) Tough questions: 40 × 6M = 240 M. Thus the total time for all questions put together is (80 × M) + (80 × 2M) + (40 × 6M) = 80M + 160M + 240M = 480M.

Since the total time for the test is 2 hours meaning 120 minutes, 480M = 120 minutes and thus M = 120/480 = ¼ minute. The total time needed for solving Medium questions is 160 × ¼ = 40 minutes. For the others, the time allotted for Easy questions should be 80 × ¼ = 20 minutes. For Tough questions it should be 240 × ¼ = 60 minutes and all these add up to 40 + 20 + 60 = 120 minutes (or two hours) which, indeed, is the duration of the test.

Chapter 35

The Clock

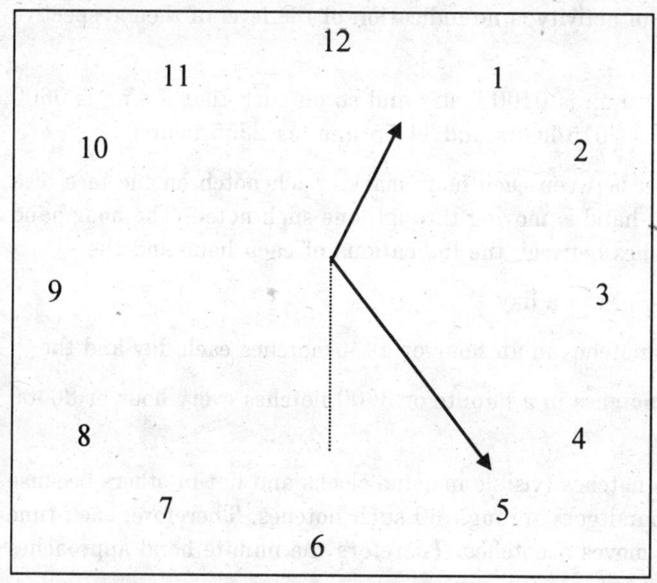

Although the clock is a familiar figure, it is not so familiar at most major competitive examinations. It is reasonable to expect every aspirant to be wearing a watch and since the basic ingredients for solving a poser on the clock are on his corporal self, a problem about clocks may not be too great a challenge for the examinee. However, if you will see some questions about clocks you would find that even if you had worn, for example, the Big Ben around your neck, it would not have helped. What would help are fundamentals of the clock for example, look at the following question:

If we were to refer to that side of the dial plate of a clock which has the numerals 12, 11, 10, …6 as the LEFT side and the part that has the numerals 12,1,2,3…6 as the RIGHT side, at what time between three and four o'clock will the minute hand be nearly as far from twelve on the left side of the dial plate as the hour hand is from twelve on the right side of the dial plate? The options are as follows:

(A) 3:45:09 (B) 3:41:32 (C) 3:40:10 (D) 3:35:30

While you may consider solving this question on your own, it is recommended that you first assimilate the fundamentals about a clock as per follows. (If you wish to crosscheck your answer, you may get in touch with us over e-mail at the following address: jivaishnav@yahoo.com)

Here are some basic and important aspects of clocks:

A clock generally has three hands: the hour hand, the minute hand and the second hand, although some clocks may not be equipped with the second hand.

The three hands move from 12 to 3 to 6 and then to 9 and back to 12. This is a clockwise movement. The reverse of this movement is anticlockwise movement, which does not happen in a clock unless one does it manually.

The day has 24 hours whereas the clock shows intervals only of 12 hours. Thus the hour hand goes twice around the face of the clock each day.

The minute hand indicates minutes, of which there are 60 in every hour. Each movement of the minute hand thus marks the conclusion of a minute. Since there are 24 hours in a day, the minute hand moves exactly 24 × 60 = 1440 times every day. The minute hand goes around the face of the clock once every hour. It thus goes around the face of the clock 24 times every day.

The second hand indicates seconds as its very name suggests. There are 60 seconds in a minute and thus the second hand moves 60 times every minute and in every hour the second hand makes 60 × 60 = 3600 movements. In the span of a day the second hand makes 3600 × 24 = 86400 movements. The second hand goes around the face of the clock once every minute and thus 60 times during the time span of one hour and thus 60 × 24 = 1440 times around the face of the clock every day. The second hand is the busiest of the three of them whereas the minute hand is a little leisurely in movement. The hour hand seems to have the easiest time of them all. Each has, however, its own significance and this comparison of levels of activity is no indication of the level of their respective significance.

These days, time is indicated as 0000 hours at midnight. 1 a.m. is 0100 hours and so on such that 6 a.m. is 0600 hours and noon is 1200 hours and 8:15 p.m. is indicated as 2015 hours and 11.55 p.m. as 2355 hours.

There are sixty notches on the face of a clock, five notches between each hour mark. Each notch on the face of a clock, marks one minute or one second depending on which hand is moving through one such notch. The hour hand moves through 1 notch in 12 minutes. There are five notches between the indications of each hour and the:

- Hour hand moves 5 notches in an hour or 120 notches in a day
- Minute hand moves one notch every minute or 60 notches in an hour or 1440 notches each day and the
- Second hand moves one notch every second or 60 notches in a minute or 3600 notches every hour or 86400 notches every day

When the hour hand goes from 12 to 1, which is as such 5 notches (visible in some clocks and not in others because the notches are not marked in some clocks), the minute hand goes through 60 such notches. Therefore, each time that the minute hand moves sixty notches, the hour hand moves 5 notches. Therefore the minute hand approaches the hour hand at a relative speed of 55 notches.

There are exactly two occasions in a day when the hour hand and the minute hand and the second hand (if the second hand is there, of course) meet, when the number of minutes is a whole number. This is at the indication of 12; first at 0000 hours (or midnight) and then at 1200 hours (or mid-day). The rest of the times when they meet the number of minutes or seconds cannot have an integral value.

Why so? Let us imagine the clock to be a circular track of 60 notches with a common starting point that is the hour of 12 on the face of the clock. The fifth notch away from the starting point corresponds to the 1-hour indication on the clock face so that the tenth notch away from the starting point corresponds to the 2-hour indication on the clock face, and so on.

The hour hand is a runner who runs at the speed of 5 notches per hour (Let us call him H) whereas the minute hand is another runner who runs at the speed of 60 notches per hour (Let us call him M). Both start simultaneously from the aforesaid starting point at the stroke of midnight. For every one notch that H runs, M runs 12 notches. What is the distance that H runs before he reaches the starting point? 60 notches. At what stage does M overtake him?

The relative speed of M and H is 55 notches per hour. H runs at 5 notches per hour whereas M runs at 60 notches per hour and thus when H is 5 notches away from the starting point (meaning it is at 1, the first hour indicator on the clock face), how long has M run? 60 notches. So M is back at the starting point and the distance between him and H is 5 notches. How long would M take to overtake H when the distance separating them is 5 notches and their relative speed is 55 notches per hour? An eleventh part of one hour that is 60/11 minutes. So M and H will meet again at 01 hours and 60/11 minutes. This means that M and H will meet at 0100 hours and 60/11 minutes.

When H has run 10 notches in 2 hours (meaning he is at 2, the second hour indicator on the clock face), M is back again at the starting point. How long would M take to overtake H when the distance separating them is 10 notches and their relative speed is 55 notches per hour?

M and H will meet again at 0200 hours plus $2/11^{th}$ of an hour or 0200 hours and 120/11 minutes (which means very nearly 11 minutes after the hour of 2 but not exactly 11 minutes after 2).

So they will meet at the following times after each hour:

- 0100 hours + 60/11 minutes
- 0200 hours + 120/11 minutes and so on till
- 1100 hours + 660/11 minutes, which incidentally is 1200 hours since 660/11 is 60. Sixty minutes past 1100 hours is 1200 hours. And so on thereafter at:
- 2300 hours and 660/11 minutes, which incidentally is 0000 hours since 660/11 is 60. Sixty minutes past 2300 hours is 0000 hours.

Thus the only time that the minute hand and the hour hand will meet when the number of minutes is a whole number, is at 1200 hours and 0000 hours.

By the time the hour hand goes through 5 notches (that are marked between each hour indication), the minute hand goes through 60 notches.

Thus for each notch that the minute hand moves on the face of the clock, the hour hand moves $1/12^{th}$ of a notch. Thus for example at 1215 hours, when the minute hand is 15 notches away from 12, the hour hand is $15 \div 12 = 5/4^{th}$ notches = 1.25 notches away from 12. The minute hand is thus $15 - (5/4) = 55/4$ notches away from the hour hand at 1215 hours.

At 1230 hours, the minute hand is 30 notches away from 12 whereas the hour hand is 5/2 notches away from 12. Having come so far, it is important to remember that the clock is meant to have a round face and even if it does not, the hands move in a circle and thus there will always be an angle between the hour hand and the minute hand except at 1200 and 0000 hours. A circle subtends an angle of 360° at its centre. Since the three hands of the clock move on a pivot that is at the centre of the circle, the minute hand and the hour hand subtend a twelfth of 360° angle which is equal to 30° – at the centre of the clock at both 0100 hours and 1300 hours.

Therefore the angle between the minute hand and the hour hand is 30° when it is 1300 hours and 60° when it is 1400 hours and so on till it is 0600 hours, when the angle between them is the greatest, that is 180° and then the reverse process starts, with the passage of each hour, the angle between the two reduces. Then the angle between the hour hand and the minute hand reduces by 30° each hour so that it is 150° at 0700 hours, 120° at 0800 hours so that at 1100 hours it is 30° and at 1200 hours it is 0°.

But this is the position of the angles between the hour hand and the minute hand at an integral number of hours. What if we are asked to find the angle between these hands at say 1415 hours?

At 1415 hours, the hour hand has gone through 11.25 notches away (meaning 5 notches between 12 and 1 and 5 more notches between 1 and 2 then again 1.25 notches in the span of 15 minutes after 2). During this time the minute hand has moved through 15 notches. The distance between them is 15 – 11.25=3.75 notches. There are sixty notches on the face of the clock and each notch thus subtends an angle of 6° (meaning $360 \div 60$) at the centre of the clock. Thus 3.75 notches would subtend an angle of 22.5° at the centre and so the angle between the hour hand and the minute hands of the clock at 1415 hours is 22.5°.

Let us see these few illustrations to reinforce the important concepts about clocks that we have learnt in this chapter.

Illustration 1

A clock loses 5 minutes every 12 hours. It is set to correct time at 0900 hours. What would be the angle between the minute hand and the hour hand when the correct time is 1500 hours the same day?

The clock has been working for 6 hours between 0900 hours and 1500 hours when the correct time is 1500 hours. But since it is losing 5 minutes every 12 hours, the time that the clock in our problem shows is 14:57:30. Thus it has lost 2.5 minutes. At 14:57:30, how many notches is the minute hand away from the 12th hour indicator 12-hour mark on the clock face? 2.5 notches.

At 14:57:30, how many notches is the hour hand away from the 12-hour indication on the clock face? If the clock was showing correct time it has been working for 360 minutes but since it has lost 2.5 minutes, it has actually worked for 357.5 minutes and during this time, the hour hand has moved through 357.5/12 notches away from 0900 hours.

This means that if one were to deduct the 15 notches between 0900 hours and 1200 hours, it is (357.5/12) – 15 notches away from the 12-hour mark = (357.5 – 180) ÷ 12 = 177.5 ÷ 12 notches from away from the 12-hour mark. The minute hand is 2.5 notches behind the 12-hour mark and this means that the number of notches between the hour hand and the minute hand is (177.5/12) + 2.5 notches. Since each notch on the clock face is 6° this means that the angle between the hour hand and the minute hand is now = 6 × [(177.5/12) + 2.5]° and this equal to (177.5/2) +15° = 88.75 + 15 = **103.75°**.

Illustration 2

What is the earliest instance between 1700 hours and 1800 hours when the hour hand and the minute hand of a clock are exactly at right angles?

By the time the hour hand goes through 5 notches (that are marked between each hour indication), the minute hand goes through 60 notches. Thus the minute hand approaches the hour hand at a relative speed of 55 notches per hour. When it is 1700 hours, the hour hand is at the 5-hour mark and the minute hand is at 12-hour mark. At this stage the number of notches between them is 25.

A clock is a circle and a circle subtends a total of 360° at its centre. Since there are 60 notches on the face of the clock, each notch subtends an angle of 6° at the centre.

What must be the number of notches between the hour hand and the minute hand so that the angle between them is exactly 90°? 15 notches. Thus there were 25 notches between the hour hand and the minute hand at the stroke of 1700 hours and in order that the two hands are 90° apart, the number of notches between them must be 15. What needs to be done is to find out the time in which the two hands will come closer by 10 notches so that the number of notches between them is reduced from 25 to 15.

If the two hands reduce 55 notches between them in an hour, how long would it take them to reduce this to 10 notches? This would take (10 × 60) / 55 minutes, which is 120/11 minutes (or very nearly 11 minutes) past 1700 hours.

Chapter 36

Setting up Equations to Solve Word Problems

The POWERPREP Compact Disc, that the Educational Testing Service gives students who register for the GRE, contains a list of Test Taking Tips. This list has the various aspects that the student, who plans to write the GRE, is expected to be familiar with. Setting up equations to solve word problems is one of the aspects listed in the Test Taking Tips. Hence this Chapter.

We shall see how to solve seemingly mind-boggling word problems through setting up equations. The methodology has got to be necessarily illustrative and hence we shall proceed with illustrations straight away.

Word Problem 1

I went to visit a home for the aged, where I was told that exactly two-third of the inmates had diabetes, exactly three-fourth had cardiac problems and exactly four-fifth had digestive disorders. "And how many have all three?" I asked. To this the reply was that there were at least 16 such cases. How many inmates did the home have when I went to visit?

The Solution

Let us assume that the home for the aged had H number of inmates. It is to be remembered that:

The number of inmates having each of the three diseases was a positive integer in each case. You cannot have fractional patients.

The number of inmates was divisible by:

- 3 and that is why two-thirds of the inmates had diabetes
- 4 and that is why three-fourth had cardiac problems
- 5 and that is why four-fifth had digestive disorders

This means that the total number of inmates at the very minimum is the least common multiple of 3, 4 and 5. Since 3, 4 and 5 have no common factors, the LCM of these three numbers is their product. Thus the least value for H is 60.

Now two-thirds, three-fourth and four-fifth of 60 are respectively 40, 45 and 48 that adds up to 133. If we assume the number of inmates having only diabetes as D, those having only cardiac ailments as C and those having only stomach disorders as S, we get the following three equations: (I) 40 = D + T, (II) 45 = C + T and (III) 48 = S + T. Adding these three equations we get equation (IV) as follows: D + C + S + 3T = 133.

Since there are only 60 inmates and yet the total number of inmates having the three ailments is 133, we get equation (V) as follows: D + C + S + T = 60. Subtracting equation (IV) from equation (V) we get equation (VI) as follows: 2T = 73 and therefore T = 36.5.

Since you cannot have 36.5 people, it means that we shall have to move on to the next higher common multiple of 3, 4 and 5 and this multiple will have to be at least an even multiple of the LCM of 3, 4 and 5 so that we get a whole number of patients having all three diseases. The least even multiple of 60 is 120.

We will then assume that there were 120 inmates. Since exactly two-third of the inmates had diabetes, exactly three-fourth had cardiac problems and exactly four-fifth had digestive disorders, we would get the following situations:

- The total number of persons having all three is 73.
- The number of persons having only diabetes is 7 that is 73 less than two-third of 120, which is 80.
- The number of persons having only cardiac problems is 17 that is 73 less than three-fourth of 120, which is 90.
- The number of persons having only digestive problems is 23 that is 73 less than four-fifth of 120, which is 96.

To crosscheck, the total number of inmates is 73 + 7 + 17 + 23 = 120. This tallies with the 120 inmates that we have assumed as twice 60. As regards "at least 16 such cases", 16 and more also qualify for "at least 16" and hence 73 is as eligible for "at least 16" as 16 itself.

Word Problem 2

A co-operative housing society decided to hold its annual general meeting on a Sunday. Some houses in the society were occupied by the members of the society whereas others were rented to non-members. Non-members are not allowed to vote at any meeting of the society. However, the notice was not specific on this issue. The result being that when it was decided to seek a mandate on the plan to make a club house in the Society's common plot, all in favour were asked to put up their hands. After counting the number of hands, the Chairman of the meeting declared that the motion was adopted with a majority that was exactly equal to a quarter of those voting against. Then someone pointed out that there were twelve non-members present and all of them had put up their hands. The motion was declared defeated with a majority of one. How many members participated in the annual general meeting?

The Solution

We shall go about this by referring to the number of people voting **for** the resolution as F and those voting **against** as A. We shall bear in mind that we shall have to reckon with only integral values of F and A since you cannot have fractional people either voting or dancing the rumba.

If a resolution is to be passed at all, the first condition is that F must be greater than A. Therefore the difference between F and A has got to be a positive number. After counting the number of hands, the Chairman of the meeting declared that the motion was adopted with a majority that was exactly equal to a quarter of those voting against. Since we have assumed the number of people voting against as A, a quarter of those against, would then be A/4. This should give us the following equation: F – A = A/4 and therefore F = 5A/4.

Now someone pointed out that there were twelve non-members present and all of them had put up their hands. This means that those who were not members, had to put their hands down. This means that the number of people voting for would decrease by 12. This would mean that the number of people now voting for the resolution is F – 12. Since we know that F = 5A/4, the number of people still voting **for** the resolution, after the hands of non-members have come down is [(5A/4) – 12] whereas the number of people voting against remains unchanged at A. Now the situation is that the resolution has been defeated by one vote. This means that the **difference between the number of people voting against** and the number of people **voting for is** 1. The equation that we can now set up is A - [(5A/4) –12] = 1. Solving this equation we get A – (5A/4) + 12 = 1 and therefore – A/4 = –11 and thus A/4 = 11 and then A = 44. The number of people voting against is 44. The number of people voting for, earlier is 5A/4 = (5 × 44)/4 = 55. Thus 55 + 44 = 99 people had voted out of which 12 were non-members. That is why the number of members present in the meeting was 99 – 12 = 87.

Word Problem 3

Mrs. Ronald (whom we shall call Mrs. R hereafter) was a widow and Mr. Stevenson (whom we shall call Mr. S hereafter) a widower. Each had children and it was when both families were on a visit to the zoo that they met. Mrs. R soon thereafter married Mr. S and each of them now has five children. Recently they were out to buy woollens for the children and asked for seven sweaters so that all the children in the family could get one each. How many children were born after the marriage of Mrs. R to Mr. S?

The Solution

Mrs. R had children from her marriage with her husband who died. Mr. S had children from his marriage with Mrs. S who is also no more. Let us refer to the number of children that Mrs. R had prior to her marriage with Mr. S as HERS and to the number of children that Mr. S had prior to his marriage with Mrs. R as HIS. Let us refer to the number of children that Mrs. R and Mr. S had after their marriage as THEIRS. Since each of Mrs. R and Mr. S had five children, we get two equations:

(I) HERS + THEIRS = 5

(II) HIS + THEIRS = 5

If we were to add these two equations we would get equation (III) as follows: HERS + HIS + 2(THEIRS) = 10. Since they bought 7 sweaters, we get equation (IV) as follows: HERS + HIS + THEIRS = 7. If we were to subtract equation (IV) from equation (III) we would get THEIRS = 3. This means that Mrs. R and Mr. S had three children after their marriage and that they had 2 children each from their previous spouses (that would make 5 children to each of Mrs. R and Mr. S) and yet 7 children in all.

Word Problem 4

I was at a friend's furniture shop the other day, trying to buy tea caddies and tables. I had wanted to place a large order and thought it prudent to ask him if he had enough of each variety. Tea caddies are normally three legged while tables are four legged but there was one defective tea caddy that had four legs and one defective table that had six legs. In all there were 45 items and 150 legs. How many items, each of tea caddies and tables, would that make?

The Solution

To err is human. This is why carpenters making six-legged tables and four-legged tea caddies are to be pardoned for their small lapses. We shall move on with the process of setting up equations. We shall refer to the number of tea caddies as C and the number of tables as T so that we do not face any problems while relating to the alphabets assumed for unknown quantities. We could have, for example, if we were to assume X and Y as the number of tea caddies and tables respectively.

Let there be C number of tea caddies and T number of tables. Since the total number of items are 45, it means that $C + T = 45$ and therefore $T = 45 - C$. That would make $(45 - C)$ tables.

C number of tea caddies would normally have 3C legs but there is one defective piece with an extra leg and that makes $3C+1$ legs.

$(45 - C)$ tables would normally have $4 \times (45 - C) = 180 - 4C$ legs but since there is one defective table that has two extra legs, this makes $180 - 4C + 2 = 182 - 4C$ legs.

The number of legs in all are $3C + 1 + 182 - 4C = 183 - C$ legs and this we know is $= 150$.

Thus $183 - C = 150$ and hence $C=33$ and since the number of items are 45 in all, out of which there are 33 tea caddies, there are $45 - 33 = 12$ tables.

Word Problem 5

A class is out on a picnic. A fifth of the students are out swimming. A third of the class is at the merry-go-round and thrice the difference between those on the merry-go-round and those out swimming, are at the seesaw. One student is sitting by himself, not participating in the fun and games. How many students are there in all?

The Solution

The question is about finding out the total number of students and therefore we shall have to first assume this number as T.

Since a fifth of the students are out swimming, the number of students out swimming is T/5.

Since a third of the students are at the merry-go-round, the number of students at the merry-go-round is T/3.

We do not know how many students are at the seesaw. We therefore assume this number as S.

The difference between those on the merry-go-round and those out swimming is [(T/3) – (T/5)] and thrice this difference is 3[(T/3) – (T/5)] or [(3T/3) – (3T/5)]. The number of students at the seesaw is therefore [(3T/3) – (3T/5)]. The total number of students so far is {(T/5) + (T/3) + [(3T/3) – (3T/5)]}. Add the one student to this and we have the total number of students which we have assumed as T. This gives us the following equation: {(T/5) + (T/3) + [(3T/3) – (3T/5)]} + 1 = T. Multiplying both sides of this equation so as to work with integers on both sides, we get 3T + 5T + 15T – 9T + 15 = 15T and hence 14T + 15 = 15T and thus T = 15.

The total number of students out on the picnic is 15.

Word Problem 6

I was to travel on the weekly Kenya Airways flight to Nairobi and reached the airport with three bags weighing in all 60 kgs such that the first and the second bag together weigh 54 kgs and the third bag weighs 30% of the second bag.

Since Kenya Airways allows one to carry, without any extra charge, bags weighing in all 75 kg but with a condition that for every bag weighing in excess of 30 kgs, the extra luggage charge would be $ 3 per kg, how much charge would I have to pay?

The Solution

I have three bags weighing in all 60 kgs whereas Kenya Airways allows one to carry, without any extra charge, bags weighing in all 75 kgs. Therefore there will be a need to pay any extra charge only if any bag exceeds the per bag limit of 30 kgs.

Let us say that the weights (in kgs) of my first bag, second bag, and the third bag are FB, SB and TB respectively.

Since the three bags weigh a total of 60 kgs, we get equation (I) as follows: FB + SB + TB = 60. Since the first bag and the second bag weigh a total of 54 kgs, equation (II) is 54 + TB = 60 and therefore TB = 6.

Since the third bag weighs 30% of SB, TB = 30(SB)/100 and therefore SB = 100TB/30 = 100 × 6/30 = 20.

Since the first bag and the second bag together weigh 54 kg, FB + 20 = 54 and hence FB = 34. The weights of FB, SB and TB are 34, 20 and 6kg respectively.

The first bag is the only bag in excess of 30 kgs. It is 4 kgs above the limit of 30 kg. Since the extra luggage charge would be $ 3 per kg, I would have to pay $ 12 as extra luggage charge.

Word Problem 7

Andy was asked to calculate the Arithmetic Mean of ten positive integers each of which had two digits. By mistake, he interchanged the two digits, say A and B, in one of these ten integers. As a result, his answer for the Arithmetic Mean was 1.8 more than what it should have been. What is the value of (B – A)?

The Solution

Let us assume that the Arithmetic Mean of the ten positive integers is M if Andy were to calculate the mean correctly.

As we know, the Arithmetic Mean of any series of numbers = (Total of the series of numbers)/ (Number of terms in the series). We do not know the total of the series of numbers therefore we assume the total as T. We know that there are ten terms and therefore Number of terms in the series = 10. Thus the first equation that we get is, M = T/10 and hence T = 10M.

By mistake, Andy interchanged the two digits, say A and B, in one of these ten integers. As a result, his answer for the Arithmetic Mean was 1.8 more than what it should have been. This means that the wrong Mean that he got was 10M + 1.8. Let us call this wrong Mean WM. Though he got a wrong mean, the number of terms in the series remains unchanged that is 10, therefore the wrong total = 10(WM) = 10 (M + 1.8) = 10M + 18.

This means that the difference between the wrong total and the correct total = (10M +18) – (10M) = 10M – 10M +18 = 18. This means that as a result of an interchange in its digits that particular number increased by 18 (since all other integers remained unchanged).

Since we are told that the two digits of the number that Andy interchanged in error were A and B, a two digit number of A in the tens place and B in the units place is (10A +B). If you were to see the two-digit number 36 for example, it is [(10 × 3) + 6]. If the two digits of this two digit number AB were mistakenly interchanged, the new number formed was BA, which is (10B + A). If we were to mistakenly interchange the digits in 36, the new number would be 63, which is [(10 × 6) + 3].

We have deduced that the value of the wrong number was more than the value of the correct number because only then it is possible for the wrong total (and therefore the wrong mean) to be more than the correct mean. This means (10B + A) – (10A + B) = or 9B – 9A = 18 and therefore 9(B – A) = 18. This is why (B – A) = 2.

Word Problem 8

Let A and B be two solid spheres such that the surface area of B is 300% higher than the surface area of A. The volume of A is found to be V% lower than the volume of B. What is the value of V?

The Solution

The surface of a solid sphere is $4\pi r^2$ where π is a constant and r is the radius of the sphere. It should be easy to see that the surface area of a sphere is dependent solely on its radius since the radius is the only variable term in the formula for the surface area of the sphere. The greater the radius of the sphere, the greater the area of the sphere. The lesser the radius, the lesser the area of the sphere.

The volume of a solid sphere is $4\pi r^3/3$ where π is a constant and r is the radius of the sphere. It should be easy to see that like the surface area, even the volume of a sphere is also dependent solely on its radius since the radius is the only variable term in the formula for the volume of the sphere.

We are told that the surface area of sphere B was 300% higher than the surface area of A. If one quantity is 300% higher than another quantity then we can assume the lower quantity as L, and the higher quantity as H which is 3L more than L. Hence the relationship between the two is H = 4L. In other words the higher quantity is 4 times the lower quantity.

Let us assume the radius of sphere B as B units and the radius of sphere A, as A units of length. Therefore the surface area of sphere A is $4\pi A^2$ whereas the surface area of sphere B is $4\pi B^2$. We have deduced that the surface area of sphere B was 4 times the surface area of A. This means that $4\pi B^2 = 4(4\pi A^2)$ and thus $4\pi B^2 = 16\pi A^2$ which means that $B^2 = 4A^2$ and therefore B = 2A.

The volume of A is $4\pi A^3/3$ whereas the volume of B is $4\pi B^3/3$ and since B = 2A, the volume of B is $4\pi (8A^3)/3$. Comparing the volume of sphere A with B, we get: $[4\pi A^3/3]/[4\pi (8A^3)/3]$ which is equal to 1/8. This means that the volume of A is an eighth of the volume of B or, in other words, the volume of A = (the volume of B) – (seven-eighth of the volume of B). If we were to work out the value of seven eighths in percentage terms this would be $7 \times 100/8 = 700/8 = 175/2 = 87.5$. The value of V is thus 87.5. Therefore the volume of sphere A is 87.5% less than the volume of sphere B.

Word Problem 9

Anita had to do a multiplication. Instead of taking 35 as one of the multipliers, she took 53. As a result, the product went up by 630. What is the new product?

The Solution

One thing that should stand a mile out is the fact that Anita must have been multiplying at least two numbers because that is the very least number of multipliers that one needs in order to carry out any multiplication. It takes two not only to tango but also to multiply. Although we do not know how many multipliers was Anita multiplying, let us first assume that she was working with two multipliers. Let us call the first multiplier as F and the second as 35. Had she been multiplying correctly, the product would have been 35F. Since she mistakenly took 35 as 53, the wrong product was 630 more than the correct product. Let us call the correct product as C and the wrong product as W. This means that C = 35F and W = 53F and since the wrong product was 630 more than the correct product, W – C = 630 or 53F – 35F = 630 and hence 18F = 630 and thus F = 630/18 = 35. Hence the new product (or wrong product in other words) = 53×35 = 1855.

Now comes the stage for clarifying some concepts. What if Anita had been working with 3 multipliers one of which was 35, which she wrongly took as 53? Let the first two multipliers be F and S respectively. The product of the three multipliers including 35 would have been $F \times S \times 35$ whereas by mistake it was $F \times S \times 53$ and since the wrong product was 630 more than the correct product, $[F \times S \times 53] - [F \times S \times 35] = 630$ and thus 18FS = 630 and therefore FS = 35. The new product (or in other words the wrong product) would have then been 53FS = 53×35 = 1855. Briefly, the number of multipliers she was working with, would not make any impact whatsoever on the ultimate answer, which remains constant at 1855.

The attempt in this chapter is to provide the basic but foolproof methodology of setting up equations to solve word problems. It is very likely that some of you may:

(A) Be able to solve word problems orally and may not need to work with any equations at all to solve any of the word problems, that appear as illustrations in the chapter

(B) Be able to set up equations mentally and solve word problems such as those given in the illustrations in after assimilating the concepts given in this chapter.

There will be many of you who will from now on face any word problem with the confidence that the methodology in this chapter is certain to inspire.

All good things have to come to an end that is why the curtain will now come down on this chapter. We trust, you have enjoyed reading this chapter as well.

Chapter 37

Speed and Distance

Problems involving the fundamentals of speed and distance are frequent features at competitive examinations. However, in a majority of cases, what come into play are the fundamental aspects of speed and distance. Once these aspects are clear, logic can and should take over if the correct answer is to emerge and that too within a short time.

The idea in this chapter will be to build these fundamentals about speed and distance and then put them into application in solving problems.

Speed is the rate at which distance is covered over unit time. The numerator in the expression is therefore distance and time taken is in the denominator.

Thus, speed = Distance/ Time and in the converse, Distance = Speed × Time and also Time = Distance/Speed.

When I travel a distance of say 80 kilometres in two hours although I may have done some distances at 100 kilometres per hour and others at speeds as low as 30 kilometres due to traffic lights, I can say that the rate at which I am travelling is, on average, 40 kilometres to the hour. My average speed for the journey is 40 kilometres per hour.

Suppose you set out at the same time as I do and travel a distance of say 120, kilometres in three hours although you may have done some distance at 100 kilometres per hour and others at speeds as low as 20 kilometres due to traffic lights, your average speed for the journey is 40 kilometres per hour. But if someone were to regularly measure – say at every half hour - the distance that I have travelled from starting point and the distance that you have travelled from starting point, it is not necessary that you and me will both be at the 20th kilometre mark from start after 30 minutes from start, although our average speeds are identical.

If I am driving on a deserted lane and see that for the past 90 minutes the speedometer has indicated 80 kilometres per hour without any variation, then I am travelling at a **uniform** speed – or in other words at a **constant** speed - of 80 kilometres per hour. Suppose you set out after 1 hour after I do and see that for the past 60 minutes the speedometer has indicated 60 kilometres per hour without any variation, then you are said to be travelling at a **uniform** speed of 60 kilometres per hour.

It will be interesting to note that the distance that you and I have travelled at uniform speed would have the same ratio as that of our respective uniform speeds. When my uniform speed is 80 kilometres per hour and your uniform speed is 60 kilometres per hour, the ratio of my uniform speed to your uniform speed is 80:60 or 4:3. Let us see how:

During the first N minutes where N=	15	30	45	60
I have covered X km @ 80km/hour where X =	20	40	60	80
You have covered Y km @ 60 km/hour where Y=	15	30	45	60
The ratio of X:Y is	4:3	4:3	4:3	4:3

Briefly, therefore, when people travel at uniform speeds, the ratio of the distance travelled by them at a given interval of time after start will bear the same ratio as their uniform or constant speeds bear to one another. This is irrespective of the time at which the different persons travelling at different uniform speeds start travelling.

In certain cases such as races, if we assume – or are told – that the participants travel at their respective constant speeds, it is not to be told separately that the participants have started simultaneously. **The simultaneous start is a general presumption regarding races**. Secondly, if people start simultaneously and travel at their respective constant speeds, then the distance covered by them **at any time after start** will bear the same ratio as their respective constant speeds do to one anther.

See this in an illustration that might seem outlandish prima facie where you are not given either speed or time and yet you are required to find out the distance covered. Solving an example like the one that is to follow is possible only if you are aware of the fundamental fact that if people start simultaneously and travel at their respective constant speeds, then the distance covered by them **at any time after start** will bear the same ratio as their respective constant speeds do to one another.

The illustration goes like this: Abraham, Border and Charles ran a race at their respective constant speeds. Abraham finished 12 metres ahead of Border and 16 metres ahead of Charles. Border finished 5 metres ahead of Charles. What was the length of the race?

While apparently the problem might seem to pertain to speed and distance, we all know that in order to find speed, we need to know the distance and time taken to cover the given distance. Do we have any idea of the speeds? No! Do we have any idea of the time taken? No! Even then it is possible to find out the precise distance of the race. What is more, there will be a unique solution and unique methodologies to arrive at the correct answer.

We shall first refer to Abraham, Border and Charles as A, B and C respectively. When can we say that A has won the race? When he just crosses the finishing line. This is true of anyone who wants to finish a race. After crossing the finishing line, one can run till one foams at the mouth and passes out. What matters is the performance up to the finishing line.

Let us see the situation when A finished the race. When A was on the finishing line, B was 12 meters behind the finishing line and C was 16 meters away from the finishing line. B thus had a lead of 4 meters over C.

When B finished, he ran the 12 meters that separated him from the finishing line. Again when B completed the race, C was 5 meters behind B, meaning that when B finished the race, C ran 11 meters (from 16 meters behind the finishing line to 5 meters behind the finishing line).

Thus in the time that B ran 12 meters, C ran 11 meters. Therefore, the ratio of the constant speeds of B and C was 12:11 and so **would be the ratio of the distance covered by B and C respectively at any time during the race.**

If the entire race was of, say, 12X meters, by the time B ran 12X meters, C ran 11X meters and the distance between them was X meters. This X, as one is told, was 5 meters and if X = 5, 12X (the length of the race) is 60 meters.

If you look at this problem from another angle, it would seem even easier. B's lead over C was 4 meters at the stage of the race when A finished. When B finished this lead had climbed to 5 meters. In running 12 meters, B increased the lead by 1 meter (from 4 meters to 5 meters). Since his lead was 5 meters at finish, how much distance did B run to get a lead that was 5 times the lead that he could create in running 12 meters? The distance that B ran was 5 times 12 meters or 60 meters. So the race is of 60 meters. Eventually, the event has turned out to be more about ratio and proportion than of speed and distance.

It is important to remember that when comparing speeds, the same parameters must be employed so as to look sensible and consistent. If I tell you that I have been travelling at 45 kilometres per hour and you say that you have been travelling 30 miles per hour and then I say that I am a whole lot faster than what you are, we are talking through our hats. Comparison is feasible only between equals. You talk in terms of kilometres per hour and this would then mean $(30 \times 1.6) = 48$ kilometres per hour since 1 mile is 1.6 kilometres. I will emerge the slower of the two.

When two bodies approach each other at different – or even the same average speed, then the rate at which they approach each other is known as their relative speed. **Relative speed** in the case of two bodies approaching each other **is the aggregate of their individual average speeds if they are travelling towards each other.** Let us see how:

Imagine that there are two places A and B that are 500 kilometres apart. You set out from Place A towards place B at 1200 noon on a given day at an average speed of 45 kilometres per hour and I set out from place B towards place A simultaneously at 55 kilometres per hour, then:

During the first N hours where N=	0	1	2	3	4	5
When the time is	1200 noon	1 PM	2 PM	3 PM	4 PM	5 PM
I have covered X km where X=	0	55	110	165	220	275
You have covered Y km where Y=	0	45	90	135	180	225
You and I are Z km apart where Z=	500	400	300	200	100	0

The important thing to see is that we were 500 kilometres apart at start and every hour we have been reducing by 100 kilometres the distance separating us. When two people approach each other, the central idea is to reduce the distance separating them from the point at which they start approaching each other. This means that the average speed at which the two of us have been approaching each other is 100 kilometres per hour and this is the total of our average speeds of 55 km/ hour and 45 km/ hour.

This total of 100km/ hour is known as the **relative speed** with which we are approaching each other. Another most important aspect that you may have noticed in the above illustration is that when two bodies approach each other while travelling in opposite directions, the ratio of the distances that each body will have to travel from its respective starting point up to the point which they will meet will be the same as the ratio of their speeds. [In the above illustration you were travelling towards me and I was travelling towards you and this is precisely what is meant when one says that two persons are approaching each other while travelling in opposite directions.] In the above illustration:

I was travelling @ 55km/ hour and you were travelling @45 km/hour. The ratio of our speeds is 55:45 or 11:9. At the spot where we meet, I had covered 275 km from my starting point whereas you covered 225 km from your starting point. The distances that we covered from our respective starting points is in the ratio of 275:225 and this is also 11:9 (if you were to divide both 275 and 225 by 25).

The relative speed in the case of two bodies travelling in the same direction and approaching each other is the difference of their individual average speeds. Let us see how:

Imagine that there are two places A and B that are 500 kilometres apart. You set out from Place A towards place B at 1200 noon on a given day at an average speed of 45 kilometres per hour and I set out also from place A towards place B at the same time as you do at 55 kilometres per hour, then:

During the first N hours where N=	0	1	2	3	4	5
When the time is	1200 noon	1 PM	2 PM	3 PM	4 PM	5 PM
I have covered X km where X=	0	55	110	165	220	275
You have covered Y km where Y=	0	45	90	135	180	225
You and I are Z km apart where Z=	0	10	20	30	40	50

The important thing to see is that we were 0 kilometres apart at start and every hour we have been increasing the distance separating us by 10 kilometres. This means that the average distance between us increases by 10 kilometres every hour and this is the precise difference of my average speed of 55km/ hour and your average speed of 45km/ hour. This difference of 10 kilometres per hour that I am ahead of you each hour is known as our relative speed or the speed at which we are going away from each other.

So far we have been talking about simultaneous starts. We shall now see instances of one starting ahead of the other in a race involving these two persons.

Imagine that there are two places C and D that are 500 kilometres apart. You set out from Place C towards place D at 1200 noon on a given day at an average speed of 45 kilometres per hour and I set out from place C towards place D at 1300 hours on the same day at 55 kilometres per hour, then:

During the first N hours from your start (Where N=)	0	1	2	3	4	5	5.5
I have covered X km where X=	0	0	55	110	165	220	275
You have covered Y km where Y=	0	45	90	135	180	225	247.5
You and I are Z km apart where Z=	0	45	35	25	15	5	0
I have been travelling for how many hours?	0	0	1	2	3	4	4.5
You have been travelling for how many hrs?	0	1	2	3	4	5	5.5

When we meet, you have been travelling for 5.5 hours whereas I have been travelling only 4.5 hours. This means that when I started out we were 45 kilometres apart and every hour I reduced the distance by 10 kilometres since our relative speed is 55 – 45 = 10 kilometres per hour. This means that all through I was catching up on you at the rate of 10 kilometres per hour and I was able to bridge this initial gap (of 45 km between us when I started out) in 45/10 = 4.5 hours.

The way I have learnt to convert kilometres per hour to meters per second is by converting the speed at which the hero of my boyhood days ran the men's 100 meters event and won the Olympic gold in a time of just 10 seconds. I find it a particularly easy yardstick not only to employ but to remember as well. It would also be important to see how one can convert speeds indicated in kilometres per hour into miles per hour and so on. The units of time remain constant – an hour is 60 minutes and each minute is 60 seconds and therefore an hour is 60 times 60 or 3600 seconds irrespective of whether the car in which you are travelling runs on a road that has distance marked by milestones or kilometre stones. What may vary is the units of distance conversion from one to another should not be difficult once we see the following information.

- Every kilometre has 1000 meters. In case you do not know, the prefix KILO means one thousand.
- Every mile has 1760 yards.
- Every yard has 3 feet and this means that every mile has 5280 feet.
- Every kilometre has 3300 feet or 1100 yards.
- Every mile thus has 1600 meters.
- Every mile is 1.6 kilometres.

If the Olympic gold medallist of my boyhood days ran 100 meters in 10 seconds, it means that he ran 10 meters every second on average and that means he could have run 36000 meters in 3600 seconds that make an hour. So his speed in kilometres per hour is 36 kilometres per hour. This is useful to remember.

Thus if a train is running at 90 kilometres per hour, it is running @ 90/36 = 2.5 times my hero's speed of 36 kilometres per hour and since my hero did 10 meters per second, 90km/hour is 25 meters per second.

When during the course of ascertaining as to how many seconds that a train travelling at an average speed of T kilometres per hour will take to run the length of the platform of say P meters, only the train's speed in meters per second will do. In such instances a handy mental ready reckoner such as the one given above will work wonders and save valuable time.

It is also important to remember that average speed is equal to the total distance travelled, divided by the total time taken. Quite frequently, people employ mistaken logic in reckoning average speeds when asked to calculate someone's average speed for the entire journey of four equal stretches but covered at different speeds. The average speed is not the average of the speeds.

See this illustration.

My friend made two return journeys between A to B, which are separated by 200 kilometres. His average speeds for the journeys were as under:

A to B	@60 km/hour
B to A	@40 km/hour
A to B	@80 km/hour
B to A	@20 km/hour

The simple thing that people do is to add the four speeds that add up to 60 + 40 + 80 + 20 = 200 and divide 200 by 4 (which is the number of journeys) and that gives an average speed of 50 kilometres per hour. If this were true, this means that he did 800 kilometres @ 50 km/hour and took 16 hours for the four journeys. Did he? Calculate and see. You will find that he took 20 hours and 50 minutes for the 800-kilometre journey and that his average speed over the entire journey was 38.4 kilometres per hour. Here is the calculation for that average:

Journey	Speed	Distance Travelled	Time taken
A to B	@60 km/hour	200 km	3 hours 20 minutes
B to A	@40 km/hour	200 km	5 hours 00 minutes
A to B	@80 km/hour	200 km	2 hours 30 minutes
B to A	@20 km/hour	200 km	10 hours 00 minutes
	TOTAL	800 km	20 hours 50 minutes

20 hours and 50 minutes is 20 hours + 5/6th of an hour and this is 125/6 hours and when this divides 800 km, what we get is 800 ÷ 125/6 = (800 × 6)/125 = 4800/125 = 192/5 = 38.4 km/hour.

If the speeds of two persons are in the ratio of X:Y, then the time taken by them to travel the same distance at their respective speeds will be in the ratio of Y:X. This means there is an inverse relationship between the time taken for a given length of journey by two persons and the ratio of their speeds.

Consider this.

You and I are to walk 20 kilometres. We vary our average speeds each time we go for the journey. Let us see what is the ratio of time taken by us for the journey of 20 kilometres.

I travel 20 km at	5 km/ hour	4 km/ hour	5 km/ hour
You travel 20 km at	8 km/ hour	5 km/ hour	10 km/ hour
I take	4 hours	5 hours	4 hours
You take	2 hours 30 minutes	4 hours	2 hours
The ratio of our speeds; Yours: Mine	8:5	5: 4	2: 1
The ratio of the time we take; Time you take: Time I take	5/2:4 or 5:8	4:5	1: 2

But this phenomenon of the ratio of time taken being inversely proportional to the ratio of speeds is independent of the distance travelled. Let us change the distance travelled in the above illustration to 40 km and see whether there is any impact on the ratios as aforesaid.

I travel 40 km at	5 km/ hour	4 km/ hour	5 km/ hour
You travel 40 km at	8 km/ hour	5 km/ hour	10 km/ hour
I take	8 hours	10 hours	8 hours
You take	5 hours	8 hours	4 hours
The ratio of our speeds; Yours: Mine	5:8	4: 5	2:1
The ratio of the time we take; Time you take: Time I take	8:5	5:4	1:2

It would be interesting to note that **if someone were to travel any part of a journey – no matter how small – at a speed less than the overall average speed for the journey, then the average speed for the remaining part of the journey would certainly be more than the overall average speed for the journey**. The underlying rationale is not difficult to understand once we appreciate the fact that when we determine the overall average speed for the journey, we know the exact amount of time taken for the entire journey. If we were to take the total time taken for the entire journey as a standard, it would mean that if you wish to cover the entire distance in the fixed amount of time, one would have to maintain - during the entire journey - a speed equal to the overall average speed. This is the only way in which one can cover a given distance within the fixed time allotted for the journey.

Having understood that an overall average speed for a journey of a fixed distance means that the amount of time for the entire journey is also fixed, it is also easy to understand that if one were to travel any part of the journey at a speed less than the average, then the time taken for that part would be more than what it would have taken if that part of the journey had been covered at the overall average speed for the journey.

This means that the time allowed for the remaining part of the journey is less than the time that would be taken for the remaining part of the journey at the overall average speed. This means that one would have to hurry up if one is to reach within the fixed time. This is why the speed during the remaining part of the journey would have to be higher than the overall average.

In the converse, **if someone were to travel any part of a journey – no matter how small – at a speed more than the overall average speed for the journey, then the average speed for the remaining part of the journey would certainly be less than the overall average speed for the journey.**

The other day someone posed this problem and asked how it could be cracked in quick time:

While going upstream from Place A to Place B, a boat travels @ 20 km/hour and while travelling downstream, the boat travels @ 30 km/hour. If the upstream journey takes 3 hours more than the downstream journey, how far is Place A from Place B?

This was easy. Suppose the distance from Place A to Place B was only 1 km, it would take 2 minutes downstream and 3 minutes upstream and hence one would take 1 minute more for the upstream than the time taken for the downstream journey. Since the downstream journey takes 3 more hours (or 180 minutes more) than the upstream journey it means that the distance is 180 times the assumed distance of 1 km and thus Place A is 180 km from Place B.

Assume the distance between Place A and B to be X km. If one were to travel X km @ 30 km/hour one would X/ 30 hours and if one were to travel X km @ 20 km/hour one would X/20 hours. The slower of the two speeds would mean more time for the journey. This means that (X/20) > (X/30).

Now, (X/20) – (X/30) = (30X – 20X)/600 hours = X/60 hours. Thus the upstream journey took X/60 hours more than the downstream journey if the distance between Place A and Place B was X km. Multiplying both X/60 and X by 60, this means that the upstream journey took X hours more than the downstream journey if the distance between Place A and Place B was 60X km. This means that the upstream journey took 1 hour more than the downstream journey if the distance between Place A and Place B was 60 km. If the upstream journey took 3 hours more than the downstream journey, the distance between Place A and Place B is 180 km.

It is important to note that if we assume the distance from Place A to B as X km then it takes X minutes. This itself means that if the distance was 1 km, it would mean 1 more minute and that if the distance was 3 km then it would mean 3 more minutes and so on. Then why assume X at all? Why not assume some simple numerical value, like 1 km, for the distance and simplify the problem so greatly that one can solve it without putting pen to paper?

Suppose the speeds were different and that the downstream journey was @ 12 km/hour and the upstream journey was @ 16 km/hour, even the same methodology can be applied as in the previous case. Imagine that the distance was 1 km. A speed of 12 km/hour means 12 km in 60 minutes or 5 minutes per km. A speed of 16 km/hour means 16 km in 60 minutes or 60/16 or 1 km in 15/4 minutes. Thus for a 1-km journey, the upstream journey would have taken [5 – (15/4)] = 5/4 minutes or 5/4 hours = more than the downstream journey. If the upstream journey actually took 3 hours more, it means it took 180 minutes more. If a journey of 1 km means a time difference of 5/4 minutes between upstream and downstream journeys, a time difference of 180 minutes means that the journey is 180/ (5/4)= 180×4/5= 144 km.

Here too if we were to assume the distance to be X km, then X km @ 12 km/hour would take 5X minutes since a speed of 12 km/hour means 5 minutes for every km and @ 16 km/hour would take 15X/4 minutes a speed of 16 km/hour means 15/4 minutes for every km. Thus the upstream journey would take 5X – (15X/4) minutes = 5X/4 more and this means that if the journey was 1 km, the upstream journey would take 5/4 more. Thus it makes sense to assume 1 km and work accordingly rather than getting into unknowns such as X and Y and so on. This will hold good not just for upstream and downstream journeys but also for any journey of a fixed length covered either:

(A) By the same person at different speeds while going and returning or

(B) Two persons at different speeds and so on.

Now let us see some problems relating to speed and distance and grasp the fundamentals.

DIRECTIONS *for Problems 1 to 3:* Q started to move from point B towards point A exactly an hour after P started from A in the opposite direction but at a speed twice as much as that of P. By the time P covered one-sixth of the distance between A and B, Q also covered the same distance.

Problem 1

The spot where P and Q met is:

(1) Closer to A (2) Exactly half way between A and B (3) Closer to B (4) P and Q did not meet at all

Solution

Let us visualise that P sets out from A towards B and Q sets out from B towards A like this:

Q →   ← P

B————————————————A

Q travels @ twice the speed of P. P and Q are travelling in opposite directions. Let us imagine the distance between A and B as 12 km. Q leaves B one hour later than P. 12 km is ideal for assuming as the distance given that the ratio of the speeds of Q and P is 2: 1 and that Q covers $1/6^{th}$ the distance in the time P covers the same distance; 12 is eminently divisible by 6 and 2.

Let us imagine that Q covers one-sixth the distance in 1 hour. By the time P covers one-sixth the distance Q also covers one sixth. So Q covers 2 km in one hour whereas P covers 2 km in 2 hours since he has started 1 hour earlier than Q. So P's speed is 1 km/hour and Q's speed is 2 km/hour. P is 2 km away from A and Q is 2 km away from B at the same time. The distance separating them is 8 km. When the two move at speeds in the ratio of 2:1, the distance covered by them at any time will always be in that ratio. So Q covers $2/3^{rd}$ of 8 km when P covers $1/3^{rd}$ of km. So Q is now 2+16/3=22/3= 7.33 km away from B and the remaining distance now is 12 – 7.33 = 4.66 km from A. This is nearer to A. Hence **Option 1**.

Problem 2

How many hours would P take to reach B?

(1) 2 (2) 5 (3) 6 (4) 12

Solution

P travels @ 1 km/hour as seen from above and the distance he has to travel is 12 km. So P takes 12 hours. Hence Option 4

Problem 3

How many more hours would P take as compared to Q to complete the journey?

(1) 4 (2) 5 (3) 6 (4) 7

Solution

P would take 12 hours to complete this journey whereas Q would take 6 hours since he is travelling at twice P's speed. So P would take 6 more hours than Q would take to complete the journey. Hence **Option 3**.

Problem 4

Mr. J. Bond can drive (A) X kilometres in Z hours if he drives his Lamborghini at Y kilometres per hour, (B) Y kilometres in 4Z/9 hours if he drives his Aston Martin at X kilometres per hour, then how much time would he take if he were to drive Y kilometres in his Rolls Royce Silver Ghost at Y kilometres per hour if Z = 36?

Solution

The time taken to drive Y kilometres at Y kilometres per hour is one hour regardless of the value of y. If a chap drives 1 kilometre at 1 kilometre per hour he takes 1 hour and if he were to drive 10 kilometres at 10 kilometres per hour he would take 1 hour. The value of X and Z is not of any consequence.

Problem 5

While driving from Amsterdam to Frankfurt, I did a quarter of the journey at an average speed of 160 km per hour, another quarter of the journey at an average speed of 150 km per hour, the third quarter of the journey at an average speed of 120 km per hour and the remaining part of the journey at an average of 100 km per hour. If it took me 3 hours and 45 minutes to reach Frankfurt, how far is Frankfurt from Amsterdam?

Solution

Suppose the distance is D kilometres. So when I do D/4 kilometres (meaning, a quarter of the journey) @ 160 km per hour, I take $D/(4 \times 160) = D/640$ hours.

Thus $D/640 + D/600 + D/480 + D/400 = 15/4$ hours. If the LCM of 64, 60, 48 and 40 is 960, then the LCM of 640, 600, 480 and 400 is 9600.Multiplying both sides of the equation by 9600, we get $15D + 16D + 20D + 24D = 75D = (9600 \times 15)/4 = 36000$ and hence $D = 36000/75 = 480$. The distance between Amsterdam and Frankfurt is 480 kilometres.

It is important to formulate the equation quickly. If the equation is accurately formulated, the answer has got to be correct. If we were to cross check in this case, then we would get: $480/640 + 480/600 + 480/480 + 480/400 = 3/4 + 4/5 + 1 + 6/5 = 3\frac{3}{4}$ hours =3 hours and 45 minutes.

Problem 6

A boy cycles from place A to place B and while returning from place B to place A, he roller-skates. The total time taken by him for this two-way journey is 37 minutes 30 seconds. If he had roller-skated both ways, he would take an hour for the round trip from A to B. How much time would he have taken for the trip from A to B and back had he cycled both ways?

Solution

If he were to take an hour for roller-skating both ways, it would mean that he would take 30 minutes one way. Since he took 37 minutes and 30 seconds when he went cycling one way and roller-skated back, he took 7minutes and 30 seconds for the one-way journey on cycle. Had he done the round trip on cycle, he would have taken twice this time of 7 minutes and 30 seconds and this means he would have been able to complete the round trip in 15 minutes had he cycled both ways.

Problem 7

The Orient Express runs @ 144 kilometres per hour and it reaches the destination 20 minutes ahead of schedule. If it averages 100 km/hour, it reaches 24 minutes behind schedule.. What is the average speed it should maintain in order to reach the destination on schedule?

Solution

If the destination is D kilometres and the speed in order to reach on schedule is S km/hour, the time taken to reach on schedule is D/S hours. Thus we get two equations:

(I) $(D)/144 = (D/S) - 1/3$ and

(II) $(D)/100 = (D/S) + 2/5$.

Subtracting the first equation from the second we get $44D/14400 = 11/15$. Thus $D = (14400 \times 11)/(44 \times 15) = 240$. Substituting the value of D in the second equation we get $240/100 = (12/5) = (D/S) + (2/5)$ and hence D = 2. Thus the scheduled travelling time is 2 hours.

Problem 8

My brother and I started off simultaneously towards the University Library at average speeds of 8 km per hour and 9.6 km per hour respectively. He had to wait at the destination for 10 minutes before I reached. How long would it take for us to walk home if we both were to average 6 km per hour?

Solution

One would be tempted to try and find out what will be my brother's waiting time if the distance were to be a multiple of our speeds and suppose it was 96 kilometres (because $8 \times 12 = 96$ and $9.6 \times 10 = 96$) then I would reach in 12 hours and he would reach in 10 hours. In which case he would have to wait for 2 hours or 120 minutes. Since the waiting time that was actually observed is 10 minutes which is $1/12^{th}$ of the waiting time that would have been necessary if the distance were to be 96 kilometres, the actual distance up to the University Library is $1/12^{th}$ of the 96 kilometres that we had supposed. This means that the distance to the University Library is 8 kilometres. If we were to walk back together, then we would do 8 kilometres in 8/6 hours = 4/3 hours or 1 hour and 20 minutes.

Problem 9

The ratio between the speeds at which A walks on average and so does B is 3:4. If B were to take 49 minutes and 30 seconds to walk a certain distance at his average speed, how long would A take to walk at the same distance at his average speed?

Solution

The time taken to travel a distance by two persons is inversely proportional to the ratio of the speeds – regardless of the distance. Thus the ratio of the time taken by B: time taken by A would be 4: 3 and hence if B takes 49 minutes 30 seconds (which is 49 +1/2 minute or 99/2 minutes) then A takes $(4 \times 99)/(3 \times 2) = 396/6 = 66$ minutes or 1 hour and 6 minutes.

Problem 10

A train covers a distance of K kilometres between two cities in H hours. At what speed should it travel to reach on schedule if it is found that in reaching within H hours it is 2 hours behind schedule?

Solution

Speed = Distance/Time.

If the train reaches in H hours, it is two hours late. This means it will have to reach in (H-2) hours. If the train wants to reach in (H-2) hours its speed should be equal to (Distance) ÷ (Time) allotted for the journey = K/ (H-2) Kilometres per hour. As a concept this must be understood clearly, for in competitive examinations, often the concept is put to severe test.

If the train in the above illustration were to travel the distance in 10 hours and then in order to reach in time it was to reach in 8 hours, what would be a practical distance to presume? 800 kilometres? Could anything be more practical? The speed at which it would have to travel in order to reach in 8 hours is 100 kilometres per hour. Now we have K = 800, H = 10 and see if K/ (H – 2) = 100? It is!

Chapter 38

Squares and Cubes

SQUARES

A number multiplied by itself, gives the square of that number. So $2 \times 2 = 2^2 = 4$ and $N \times N = N^2$.

The number N can be either positive or Negative. If N is positive N^2 will be a positive number since you are multiplying one positive number with itself.

If N is negative, even then N^2 will be a positive number since you are multiplying one negative number with itself and the product of two negative numbers is invariably a positive number.

While the above information is not earth shattering, if you are told, for example that $X^2 = 25$ and then asked to state the precise value of X, one need not rush to the conclusion that $X = 5$ right away; X can also be equal to –5. Insofar as the Graduate Record Examination (GRE) and the Graduate Management Aptitude Test (GMAT) are concerned, however, the convention is that only the positive square root of a number is to be reckoned.

The first few whole number perfect squares are 1, 4, 9, 16 and so on. While it is easy to remember some perfect squares, the list of perfect squares that one could possibly remember cannot be long. One could go bonkers in trying to memorise squares. What is tested at competitive examinations is the breadth of perception and it is for this reason that you could be given some four numbers such that the first of the numbers ends in 2, the second ends in 3, the third ends in 7 and the fourth ends in 9 and you are asked to state as to which of these four is a perfect square, the idea is to judge whether you know that a perfect square cannot end in either of 2, 3, 7 or 8 and hence the number ending with 9 as its units digit is the perfect square.

If you were to see the squares of the first ten natural numbers, they are 1, 4, 9, 16, 25, 36, 49, 64, 81 and 100. None of them ends with 2, 3, 7 or 8. Therefore no prefect square can end with 2, 3, 7 or 8. Why? How can one make such a sweeping statement based on the knowledge that the squares of the first ten natural numbers do not end with 2, 3, 7 or 8? This is not a sweeping statement. It is based on logic and is simple to understand if you look at it like this.

Any natural number more than 10 is either:

(A) (10+ (a natural number less than 10)) [such as 11 or 13 or 19] or

(B) (An integral multiple of 10 + (a natural number less than 10)) [such as 23 (which is 2 times 10 plus 3) or 28 or 119 and so on]

The square of a natural number falling under Category (A) above is $(10 + (\text{a natural number less than } 10))^2$ which is equal to $[10^2 + (2 \times 10 \times (\text{a natural number less than } 10) + (\text{a natural number less than } 10)^2]$. This is because if you were to consider 10 as A and (a natural number less than 10) as B then $(10+(\text{a natural number less than } 10))^2 = (A + B)^2 = [A^2 + 2AB + B^2]$ in which both A^2 and $2AB$ are bound to be multiples of 10 and hence the last digit up to the sum of $A^2 + 2AB$ is bound to be zero. What remains in $[A^2 + 2AB + B^2]$ is B^2 about which we know that it cannot end in 2, 3, 7, or 8 since B is a natural number less than 10. This is why the square of (10 + (a natural number less than 10)) cannot end in 2, 3, 7, or 8.

Having grasped why the square of (10 + (a natural number less than 10)) cannot end in 2, 3, 7, or 8, it is so easy to understand why the square of (An integral multiple of 10 + (a natural number less than 10)) can also not end in 2, 3, 7, or 8. This is because if you were to take (an integral multiple of 10) as A and (a natural number less than 10) as B, in $(A + B)^2$ the total up to $A^2 + 2AB$ is certain to end with zero. As regards B^2, we know that it cannot end with 2,3,7 or 8. The reasoning in the above paragraph would be applicable in this case as well.

Let us see some squares of numbers beginning with either 1 or 2 in the following table:

If N=	1	2	11	21	25	29	199	299
Then N^2=	1	4	121	441	625	841	39601	89401
D [the number of digits in N] =	1	1	2	2	2	2	3	3
Then the number of digits in the perfect square is (2D-1) =	1	1	3	3	3	3	5	5

The following observations about perfect squares are worth noting:

- The last digit in a perfect square cannot be any other than 0, 1, 4, 5, 6 and 9.
- One cannot have any perfect square ending with 2, 3, 7 or 8.
- The last single digit perfect square is 9, which is the square of 3.
- The first perfect square of two digits is 16, which is the square of 4.
- The last perfect square of two digits is 81, which is the square of 9.
- The first perfect square of three digits is 100, which is the square of 10.
- The last perfect square of three digits is 961, which is the square of 31.
- The first perfect square of four digits is 1024, which is the square of 32
- The last perfect square of four digits is the square of 99 since the square of 100 would be 10000, which is the smallest five-digit number.
- ONLY in case of all numbers beginning with either 1 or 2, if the number has D number of digits then its square will definitely have (2D – 1) digits.

At most competitive examinations it would be sufficient if one knew squares of all integral numbers from 1 to 31, since the great majority of sums revolve around three digit perfect squares. For all natural numbers between 32 and 99, the square will have 4 digits.

One should be able to quickly reckon the squares of any number quite easily by using elementary algebra, which tells us that:

$(x + y)^2 = x^2 + 2xy + y^2$ and

$(x - y)^2 = x^2 - 2xy + y^2$

These above expressions would be of immense help in finding the squares of numbers: if you are to find the square of 31 then look at 31 as (30 + 1) and the square of 31 will thus be $[30^2 + (2 \times 30) + 1^2] = (900 + 60 + 1) = 961$. This expression will be most useful till finding the squares with 5 as the last digit. For example, if you are asked to find the square of 35 then look at 35 as (30 + 5) and the square of 35 = $[30^2 + (2 \times 30 \times 5) + 5^2] = [900 + (2 \times 30 \times 5) + 1] = 900 + 300 + 25 = 1225$.

For finding the squares of numbers ending with 6 and more as the last digit, it is better to make use of the expression $(x - y)^2 = x^2-2xy+y^2$.

For example, if you asked to find the square of 46, then look at 46 as (50-4) and the square of 46 will thus be = $[50^2 - (2 \times 50 \times 4) + 4^2] = [2500 - (2 \times 50 \times 4) + 16] = 2500 - 400 + 16 = 2116$.

If you asked to find the square of 58, then look at 58 as (60-2) and the square of 58 will thus be = $[60^2 - (2 \times 60 \times 2) + 2^2] = [3600 - (2 \times 60 \times 2) + 4] = 3600 - 240 + 4 = 3364$.

With a little bit of practice one can master the technique of finding the squares of natural numbers.

Let us suppose that you are asked to see which of the following could be the square root of 12624095449, and these are the options: (1) 1123577 (2) 122357 (3) 112357 (4) 135357. It would help if we were to remember that:

- The number 12624095449 begins with 1 and has 11 digits

- In case of all numbers beginning with either 1 or 2, if the number has D number of digits then its square will certainly have (2D – 1) digits. If (2D – 1) = 11 then D = 6. This will eliminate Option 1 since it begins with 1 and has 7 digits. If a number beginning with 1 has 7 digits, then its perfect square will have [(2×7) – 1] = 13 digits and thus Option 1 will get eliminated on that account alone.
- If a number has the first two digits as 12, then its perfect square will have at least 144 in the first three digits since the square of 12 is 144. That is why if you see the square of (say) 121 [which is not too difficult to find if you look at 121 as (100 + 21)], it is 14641.Similarly, if a number has the first two digits as 13, then its perfect square will have at least 169 in the first three digits since the square of 13 is 169. If you see the square of (sáy) 131, it is 17161.
- The number 12624095449 that has 11 digits and does not have at least 144 or 169 in the first three digits cannot be the square of a number beginning with 12 or 13 as the first two digits from the left. Options 2 and 4 are to be crossed out for this reason alone. Hence the number 112357 is the most likely square root of 12624095449. The number 112357 has 6 digits and its square will have [(2 × 6) –1] = 11 digits and 12624095449 indeed has 11 digits. **Option 3** is to be marked as correct.

One important fundamental aspect of squares is that the difference between the squares of two consecutive numbers X and Y is equal to their sum; in other words $(Y^2 - X^2) = (X + Y)$ provided X and Y are consecutive numbers and therefore Y = X + 1. So if we are asked to find the difference between the squares of 45 and 44 there is no need to go through the trouble of finding first the square of these numbers and then the difference between them. The difference between 45^2 and 44^2 is = 45 + 44 = 89. This is because $(Y^2 - X^2) = (Y + X) \times (Y - X)$ and since X and Y are consecutive numbers, Y is 1 more than X and hence Y – X = 1. Thus $(Y^2 - X^2) = (Y + X)$.

Another thing worth remembering about squares is that the difference between the squares of any two numbers is equal to the product of (A) and (B) where (A) is the sum of the two numbers and (B) is the difference between the two numbers. This is why for example the difference between the squares of 51 and 49 is (51 + 49) × (51 – 49) = 200.

There are some numbers such that if you were to ever look at any one of them it would be easy to discern that the number is a difference between squares of two integers and this might help in factorising them.

- One look at the number 624 and you can see that it is the difference between 625 and 1 and is thus $(25^2 - 1^2)$ and thus 624 = (25 + 1) × (25 – 1) = 26 × 24.
- One look at the number 99 and you can see that it is the difference between 100 and 1 and is thus $(10^2 - 1^2)$ and thus 99 = (10 + 1) × (10 – 1) = 11 × 9.
- One look at the number 2451 and you can see that it is the difference between 2500 and 49 and is thus $(50^2 - 7^2)$ and thus 245 = (50 + 7) × (50 – 7)= 57 × 43.

This kind of understanding of numbers is certain to come in extremely handy. If one were to study this chapter carefully, there is every reason to believe that the necessary level of awareness of numbers would not only build up but would also sharpen considerably as you go along.

For example, if you were told that the difference between the squares of the 8th term and that of the 7th term in an arithmetic progression is 899 and you are asked to find the 9th term in the Arithmetic Progression, how would one proceed from there?

We should assume that the 8th term is Y and the 7th term is X and hence $(Y^2 - X^2) = 899$. Now the moment you look at 899, you see that 899 is the difference between 900 and 1, which is really $(30^2 - 1^2)$ and hence (Y + X) × (Y – X) = 899 = (30 + 1) × (30 – 1) = 31 × 29. So now we have:

Equation 1: Y + X = 31 and

Equation 2: Y – X = 29

Thus adding equations 1 and 2 we get 2Y=60 and hence Y=30. Now substituting the value of Y in Y – X = 29, we get 30 – X = 29 and hence X = 1. Therefore the common difference of the Arithmetic Progression is 29 since the common difference of an AP is = the nth term – $(n-1)^{th}$ term [or, in other words = (any term in the progression) minus (the immediately previous term)] .Since the 8th term is 30, the 9th term is 30 + 29 and the 10th term is 30 + 29 + 29 = 88.

If one is able to factorise the difference between two squares, then finding the two numbers themselves is fairly easy thereafter. If the difference between squares of two numbers X and Y (where Y is the greater number of the two) is a product of two numbers A and B, then Y= (A+B)/2 and X=(A-B)/2. Let us see how:

$(Y^2 - X^2) = A \times B$, then $(Y^2 - X^2) = (Y + X) \times (Y - X) = A \times B$ and hence we get two equations as under:

Equation 1: $Y + X = A$ and

Equation 2: $Y - X = B$.

Adding the two equations we get $2Y = A + B$ and hence $Y = (A + B)/2$. Subtracting equation 2 from equation 1 we get $2X = A - B$ and hence $X = (A - B)/2$.

There is another interesting aspect of squares of consecutive integers starting from 1.

The sum of the squares of the first n integers =n× (n+1) × (2n+1)/6. This formula is worth remembering. For example, the sum of the squares of the first three numbers (1,2 and 3) is equal to 1 + 4 + 9 = 14. If you wish to see the formula as above in operation in the case of adding the squares of 1, 2 and 3 [since we are only looking for the total of the squares of the first 3 numbers] we know that n=3. Hence = $n \times (n + 1) \times (2n + 1)/6$ or = $[3\times (3 + 1) \times [(2 \times 3) + 1]/6 = (3 \times 4 \times 7)/6 = 84/6 = 14$.

Another elementary formula that we have found used widely in most competitive examinations, is about the sum of the various powers of 2 starting with 2^0. The sequence of the steadily rising powers of 2 would run as follows: 2^0, 2^1, 2^2, 2^3, 2^4, 2^5, 2^6 and so on [and this is effectively 1, 2, 4, 8, 16, 32, 64 and so on].

Here a peculiar aspect of the sum of the above series of 1, 2, 4, 8, 16, 32, 64 and so on is observed. The sum of the series up to any term = (next term –1). For example, the sum of the series 1, 2, 4 and so on up to the 3rd term (meaning, 1+2+4) is 7 which is 8 (which is the next term) –1 and the sum up to the 4th term (meaning, 1 + 2 + 4 + 8) is equal to 15 [which is = (fifth term) –1] and so on.

As to how this peculiarity finds mention at competitive examinations we may illustrate with the help of the following question that appeared in the question paper of one of the toughest competitive examinations in the world:

Jones is given $158 in one-dollar bills. He has been asked to allocate these into a number of different bags such that any amount required between $1 and $158 can be given by handing out a certain number of bags without opening them. What is the minimum number of bags required?

Jones has to be ready to give any amount between $1 and $158 without opening any bags. Jones must remember that the **least amount** that he may be asked to give **is $1**. Therefore, he has to be ready to face the prospect of giving $1 without opening any bag. Thus he would need Bag No.1 containing only $1. Then he would have to be ready for the next demand of $2. For this, Bag No.2 will have to contain $2. He can give $ 3 without disturbing any of the bags by giving both Bags Nos. 1 and 2. What about $ 4? He will need a bag containing $4. With this he will be in a position to give $5 (Bag3 + Bag1) or $6 (Bag 3 + Bag 2) and $7 (Bag3 + Bag2 + Bag1) without opening any of these bags. Then he will need Bag No. 4 containing $8 and thus Bag No. 5 containing $16 and Bag No. 6 containing $32 and Bag No. 7 containing $64. The total of the amount packed in bags 1 to 7 with $1, $2, $4, $8, $16, $32 and $64 is (next term –1) or (128 – 1) or $127. He now has $158 -$127= $31 left. The remaining amount of $31 can be packed in Bag No. 8. This precise figure of the remaining amount of $31 is arrived at without going through the grind of actually sitting down to calculate what 1 + 2 + 4 + 8 + 16 + 32 + 64 would add up to. He will need a **minimum** of **8 bags** (that will contain respectively $1,2, 4, 8, 16, 32, 64, and 31).

Sometimes, one may have to assume certain values for unknown squares in order to be able to reach the answer quickly. Look at this sum:

If $x^2 + y^2 = 0.1$ and $|x - y| = 0.2$, then how much is $|x| + |y|$ equal to?

The modulus sign is a clear indication that you should look beyond the convention of assuming only positive square roots. If one is given that $x^2 + y^2 = 0.1$, this means that since 0.1 is 10/100, $x^2 + y^2 = 9/100 + 1/100$ (or even vice versa). Supposing $x^2 = 9/100$, then x = either 3 /10 (or 0.3) or –3/10 and y = 1/10, or (0.1) or –1/10. In this case, $|x-y| = 0.2$ if x = 0.3 and y = 0.1 [or even if x = – 0.3 and y = – 0.1] and thus $|x| + |y| = 0.3 + 0.1 = 0.4$.

If I were posed a sum stating that $x^2 + y^2 = 1$, since 1 is 100/100 or in other words (64+36)/100, I would assume that x = 8/10 = 0.8 and y = 6/10 = 0.6. This, depending on what is to be calculated, would make calculation rather facile.

Imagine that I were to ask you as follows: Based on the information that $x^2+y^2=1$, what would be the likely value of $|x - y|$ among (A) 1.6 (B) 0.4 and (C) 1.4

Given that $x^2 + y^2 = 1$, one must remember Pythagoras Theorem which states that the sum of squares of the measures of two sides of a right triangle is equal to the square of the hypotenuse. If $x^2 + y^2 = 1$, $x^2 + y^2 = 100/100$ and x^2 should be taken as 64/100 and y^2 as 36/100 so that x = either plus or minus 8/10 and y = either plus or minus 6/10. You could straightaway go for Option (C) since if we assume that x = 0.8 and y = – 0.6, $|x - y|$ would be equal to $= |0.8 - (-0.6)| = |0.8 + 0.6| = 1.4$. If you have noticed, the difference between the positive square roots of 64/100 and 36/100 (which is 8/10 – 6/10 = 2/10 = 0.2) is NOT among the options. If you have noticed, here too there is a modulus sign.

CUBES

The cube of a number is equal to the product of the number multiplied by itself three times. So the cube of 4 is $4 \times 4 \times 4 = 4^3 = 64$. The cube of any number N is $N \times N \times N = N^3$.

To my mind, it would be sufficient if one were to remember the cubes of the first 10 numbers that are respectively as follows: 1, 8, 27, 64, 125, 216, 343, 512, 729 and 1000.

The cube of a number formed by adding two numbers *a* and *b* is denoted by $(a + b)^3$ and is $= a^3 + b^3 + 3ab(a + b)$.

If we take a =	2	4	4
And if we take b=	3	1	5
Then $(a+b)^3$ =	$(5)^3 = 125$	$(5)^3 = 125$	$(9)^3 = 729$
And =	8+27+[3×2×3(2+3)] =8+27+90 =125	64+1+[3×4×1(4+1)] =64+1+60 =125	64+125+[3×4×5(4+5)] =64+125+540 =729

The cube of a number formed by subtracting number b from a is denoted by $(a-b)^3$ and is $= a^3 - b^3 - 3ab(a - b)$.

If we take *a* =	2	4	6
And if we take *b*=	3	1	1
Then $(a-b)^3$ =	$(-1)^3 = -1$	$(3)^3 = 27$	$(5)^3 = 125$
And $a^3-b^3-3ab(a-b)$	=8–27–[3×2×3(2–3)] =8–27+18 =–1	64–1–[3×4×1(4–1)] =64–1-36= =27	216–1–[3×6×1(6–1)] 216–1–90=125 125

The sum of the cubes of two numbers denoted by the terms a, and b is $= a^3 + b^3$. This can be factorised as $(a + b) \times (a^2 - ab + b^2)$.

So if we take a =	1	3	2
And if we take b=	2	5	7
Then a^3 =	1	27	8
b^3 =	8	125	343
$a^3 + b^3$=	9	152	351
$(a+b) \times (a^2-ab+b^2)$=	$(1+2)\times[(1^2-1\times2)+2^2]$ $=(3) \times (3)=9$	$(3+5) \times [(3^2-(3\times5)+5^2]$ $=(8) \times (19)=152$	$(2+7) \times [(2^2-(2\times7)+7^2]$ $=(9) \times (39)=351$

The difference of the cubes of two numbers denoted by the terms a, and b is = $a^3 - b^3$. This can be factorised as $(a - b) \times (a^2 + ab + b^2)$.

So if we take a =	3	5	2
And if we take b=	1	3	7
Then a^3 =	27	125	8
So b^3 =	1	27	343
So $a^3 - b^3$=	26	98	-335
$(a-b) \times (a^2+ab+b^2)$ =	$(3-1)\times[(3^2+(3\times1)+1^2]$ $=(2) \times (13) = 26$	$(5-3)\times[(5^2+(5\times3)+3^2]$ $=(2) \times (49) = 98$	$(2-7)\times[(2^2+(2\times7)+7^2]$ $=(-5) \times (67) = -335$

The simultaneous application of these above two formulae has rarely been seen in competitive tests but I have seen the following question at a major competitive examination:

Let N= $55^3+17^3-72^3$. Then N is divisible by (A) Both 7 and 13 (B) both 3 and 13 (C) both 17 and 7 (D) both 3 and 17.

The number 72, as we know, is 55+17. So $72^3 = (55 + 17)^3$. If we take $55 = a$ and $17 = b$, $55^3 + 17^3 - 72^3 = a^3 + b^3 - (a + b)^3 = a^3 + b^3 - (a + b)^3 = a^3 + b^3 - (a^3 + b^3 + 3ab(a + b)) = a^3+b^3 - a^3 - b^3 - 3ab(a + b) = -3ab(a + b)$. Replacing the values of a, and b that we have assumed as 55 and 17, $-3ab(a + b) = -3 \times 55 \times 17 \times (72)$.

So $55^3 + 17^3 - 72^3$ is effectively $= -3 \times 55 \times 17 \times (72)$ and will thus be divisible by both 3 and 17 among the options.

Before we move on to an exercise, we shall see one interesting aspect of the cubes of natural numbers. The first few cubes are 1,8,27,64,125,216 and so on. Interestingly, the sum of the cubes of the first N natural numbers is: (I) 1 when N = 1 (II) 9 when N=2 [because the sum of the cubes of 1 and 2 is 1 + 8 = 9] (III) 36 when N = 3 [because the sum of the cubes of the first three cubes is 1 + 8 + 27 = 36]. This is because the general formula for the sum of the first N natural numbers (meaning, natural numbers starting with 1) is $[N^2 \times (N + 1)^2]/4$, which is bound to be a perfect square since $[N^2 \times (N + 1)^2]/4$ is the square of $[N \times (N + 1)]/2$.

We shall now go on to a small exercise that will ensure that we assimilate all the concepts in regard to squares and cubes that we shall need to meet a major competitive examination head on.

EXERCISE:

1. A class plans to give a gift, worth $49, to the outgoing science master and the contribution collected from each student (in cents) is the same as the number of students. The class teacher puts in $13 to meet the shortfall. How many students does the class have?

2. If $B^2 = C^3 = A$ for some integers A, B and C then the value of smallest positive integer A > 1 must be: (1) 64 (2) 81 (3) 36 (4) 8

3. A garments clearance sale starts on a particular day. There are various items up for sale but the store management realises that the sales of shirts is halving each day from the launch of the sale. If the shirts are sold out on the 10th day of the sale, then what is the minimum number of shirts that were up for sale?

SOLUTIONS

1. If the number of students in the class is S, then the total collection would be S^2 cents. If the class teacher puts in $13 to meet the shortfall, it means the total amount collected is $36 or 3600 cents since a dollar has 100 cents. If $S^2 = 3600$, $S = 60$. There were thus 60 students in the class.

2. If $B^2=C^3=A$ for some integers A, B and C, A which is >1 should meet the following two conditions:

   - A should be a perfect cube and
   - A should be a perfect square.

   Among the options only two numbers qualify for being perfect cubes: 64 and 8. Between these two while 64 is a perfect square as well, 8 is not a perfect square and thus only 64 meets the conditions that it should be a perfect cube and a perfect square. Hence Option 1.

3. The sale of shirts is halving each day from the launch of the sale. If the shirts are sold out on the 10th day of the sale, then the minimum number of shirts sold on the last day could be 1 and then the number of shirts sold on Day 9 could be 2, on Day 8 could be 4 and then if one were to write the number of shirts sold each day starting from sales on Day 1 to sales on Day 10, the figures would be as under: 1, 2, 4, 8, 16, 32, 64...512.

   The total number of shirts sold each day is $2^0, 2^1, 2^2, 2^3....2^9$. The sum of such a series is worth remembering and it is $2^{(n+1)} - 1$ and in this case it will be $2^{10} - 1 = 1024 - 1 = 1023$.

   The minimum number of shirts up for sale could be 1023. [Although we are not concerned with this, the next higher possible number of shirts could be 2×1023 and then 3×1023 and so on.]

Chapter 39

The Triangle

A triangle is a closed, three-sided figure with three straight lines joining at three vertices. A triangle thus has three angles. The measures of the three angles in a triangle add up to 180°. A triangle is called an acute-angled triangle if all three angles in it measure less than 90°. A triangle is called a right-angled triangle if one of the three angles in it is exactly 90° in measure. Not more than one angle in a triangle can measure 90° since it is a characteristic of the triangle that the sum of the measures of its angles is 180°. A triangle is called an obtuse-angled triangle if one of the three angles in it measures more than 90°. Quite clearly, not more than one angle in a triangle can be obtuse.

It is possible to construct a triangle based on the following information that is only illustrative and not exhaustive. There is a clear reason for not giving an exhaustive list of situations wherein you can construct a triangle and another where you cannot. The reason is like this: this book is not a refresher course for the mathematics that you learned at school. This book is about a wider perspective and about reasoning why some things can be and why others cannot. The idea is to develop the sense of reasoning and then let one take off from there on one's own.

(A) The measure of the three sides: If we are given the measures of the three sides of a triangle – say, for example, 5, 7 and 11 inches – it is sufficient for its construction. Draw a straight line of 11 inches as the base. Call it AB as under. You have two vertices of the triangle ABC. What you now want is the exact location of the third vertex C. With A as the centre and a radius of 7 inches, draw an arc. Every point on the arc is exactly 7 inches from A. Likewise, with B as the centre and a radius of 5 inches, draw an arc. Every point on the arc is exactly 5 inches from B. The meeting point of the two arcs will give you the third vertex C that is exactly 7 inches from A as also exactly 5 inches from B. Link C with the vertices A and B with a straight line and you have your triangle.

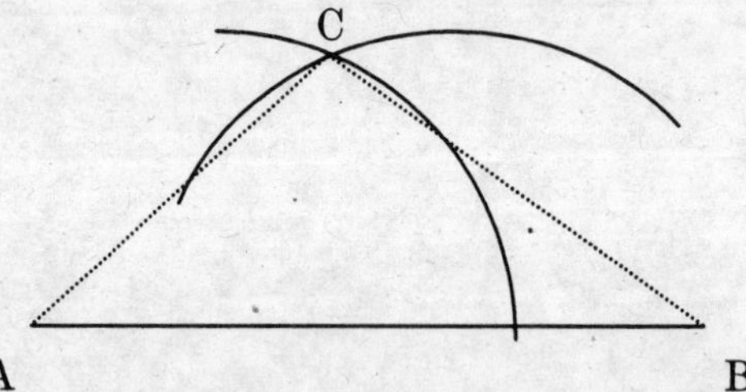

Incidentally, if you were to draw arcs of 6 inches and 5 inches from A and B respectively, when AB is 11 inches, you will find that two arcs will meet on the line AB at a distance of 6 inches from A towards B. The third vertex will elude you. Thus the longest side in any triangle cannot be equal to the sum of the other two sides.

If you were to draw arcs of 6 inches and 4 inches from A and B respectively when AB is 11 inches, you will find that the arc from A will cut AB at a point 6 inches from A towards B, whereas the arc from B will cut AB at a point 4 inches from B towards A, and these two points will lie on the line AB with a difference of one inch from each other. If you want to draw a triangle, you must have a third vertex. It is for this reason that the third vertex cannot lie on the line AB. Thus the longest side in any triangle cannot be greater than the sum of the other two sides.

It is for this reason that if you wish to draw a triangle, the longest side will have to be necessarily less than the sum of the other two sides.

(B) The measure of one side of a triangle is given. The two angles at the end of the straight line is also given. Imagine that we are told that a triangle ABC has AB of 7 inches length and angles CAB and CBA of 30 and 70° respectively. We have two vertices A and B. We know exactly the distance between two vertices. All we have to do is draw a line AB and from A, with a protractor, draw a ray of 30° and from B draw another ray of 70°. When the two rays intersect, the third vertex C is formed at the point of this intersection. Now, you have all three vertices. All you need to do now is to take a rule and link them by straight lines and your triangle is ready.

A triangle that has any two sides of the same measure is known as an isosceles triangle. It is the property of an isosceles triangle that the angles made by the each of two sides of equal measure with the third (and unequal to the other two) side are equal in measure. In the figure below you see an isosceles triangle in which the angles ABC and ACB are the angles made by the two sides of equal measures, AB and AC respectively, with the third side BC (which is unequal to the other two).

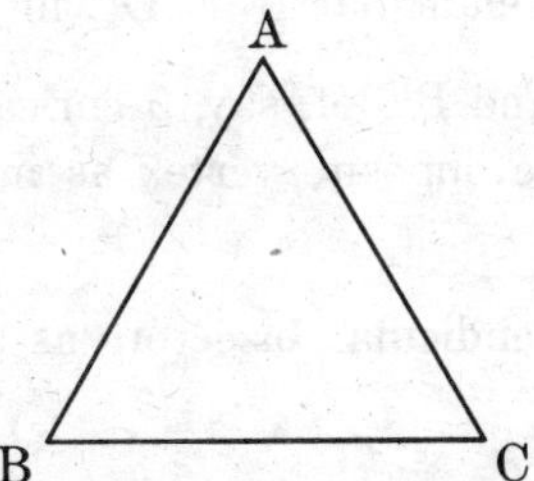

The sides AB and AC are equal in measure and so also are the angles ABC and ACB. Side BC does not measure the same as the two other sides. If it did (i.e., the side BC) then the triangle would become an equilateral triangle. An equilateral triangle is characterized by the following.

1. The measures of the three sides of an equilateral triangle are equal, and
2. Each angle of an equilateral triangle measures exactly 60°.

If one were given the measure of any one of the three angles in an isosceles triangle, it is possible to tell the exact measure of each of the three angles. Suppose in the above isosceles triangle ABC one is given that angle BAC measures 40°, then the sum of the three triangles is 40 + 2(each of the angles ABC and ACB) and since this is equal to 180°, each of the angles ABC and ACB is 70° in measure.

About angles in triangles, the following must be borne in mind: (1) The side opposite the largest angle is necessarily the longest side. (2) The side opposite the smallest angle is necessarily the smallest side.

If you were to see the following situations where the angle between two sides AC and BC of equal measures keeps increasing the length of the side AB, opposite to the angle in the following triangles also increases:

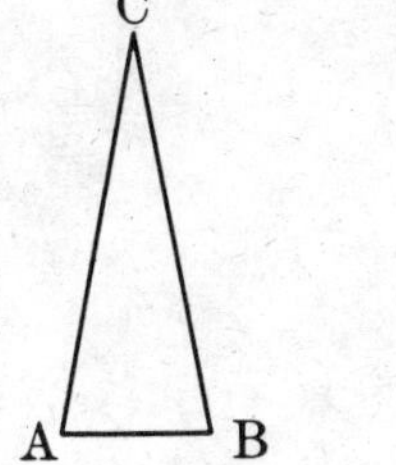

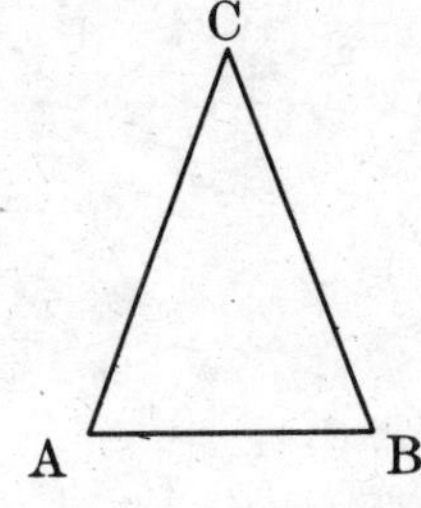

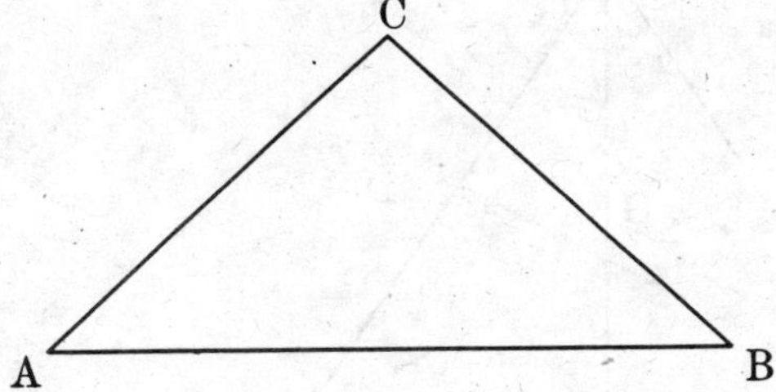

Different types of Triangles are classified in terms of their sides and angles. Scalene triangles have no equal sides. Isosceles triangles have two equal sides. Equilateral triangles have three equal sides. In Acute triangles, all the angles are less than 90°. In Right triangles, one angle is equal to 90°; this is primarily because the three angles in any triangle add up to 180° and therefore if one of the three angles were to be 90°, then since the sum of the other two angles would be 90°, the other two angles would each have to be less than 90°. In Obtuse triangles, one angle is more than 90°.

A line is called an altitude if it is drawn from the vertex perpendicular to the opposite side. In the three triangles drawn on the previous page, the perpendicular from C to AB would be the altitude of the triangle ABC. A line is called a median if it is drawn from the vertex to the midpoint of the opposite side. In the triangles ABC above, the line linking C to the midpoint of AB would be one median and there would be two more such medians: one from B to the midpoint of AC and the other from A to the midpoint of BC. A line is called an angle bisector if it divides an angle into two equal angles.

A line is called a perpendicular bisector if it is drawn perpendicular to a side through its midpoint. Draw a triangle ABC of AB, BC and AC of, say, 4, 6 and 8 cm respectively with D, E and F as the mid points of AB, BC and AC respectively. If you were to place a protractor on points D, E and F in turns and draw lines perpendicular to AB, BC and AC respectively, you will find that these three lines are the perpendicular bisectors of the sides AB, BC and AC respectively. You will also find that the three perpendicular bisectors do not meet at all. What is more, none of the three perpendicular bisectors will connect the midpoint of the line bisected i.e. the perpendicular from F will not go to B, the perpendicular from E will not go to A and the perpendicular from D will not go to C.

Even if you were to draw an isosceles triangle ABC with sides AB and BC of, say, 5 cm each and side AC of, say – 8 cm, the perpendicular bisectors will neither meet nor go to the opposite vertex as in the case of the above triangle with each of the three sides of different measures.

If you were however to draw an equilateral triangle ABC and perpendicular bisectors as aforesaid, you will find that the perpendicular bisectors:

(1) Will pass through a common point.

(2) Will be angle bisectors as well.

(3) Will carry to the opposite vertex.

The three altitudes of a triangle meet in a common point called the orthocentre.

The three medians meet in a point called the centroid. The centroid divides a median through it into two segments, and the segment having a vertex as endpoint is always twice as long as the other segment.

In triangle ABC hereunder, draw the following with a pencil:

(1) The line from A that meets BC at point D, the midpoint of BC.

(2) The line from B that meets AC at point E, the midpoint of AC.

(3) The line from C that meets AB at point F, the midpoint of AB.

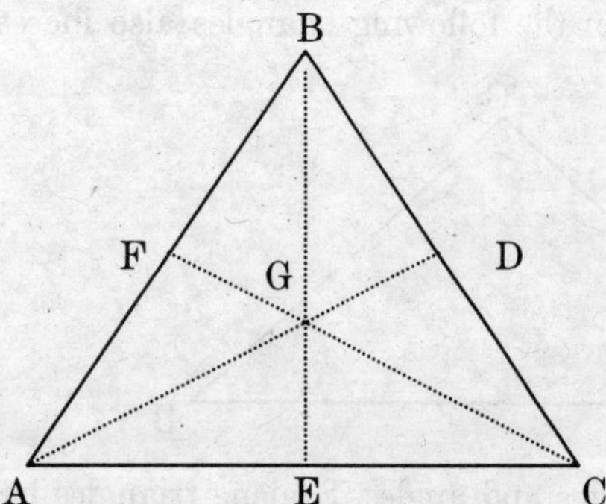

You will find that AD, BE and CF intersect at a point G. You will also find that AG is 2 times GD, BG is 2 times GE, CG is 2 times GF.

In triangle ABC above, erase the lines AD, BE and CF and instead draw the following:

(1) The angle bisector from A (meaning, the ray that divides angle BAC into two equal parts) that meets BC at point D.

(2) The angle bisector from B (meaning, the ray that divides angle ABC into two equal parts) that meets AC at point E.

(3) The angle bisector from C (meaning, the ray that divides angle BCA into two equal parts) that meets AB at point F.

You will find that AD, BE and CF intersect at a point G. You will also find that if you were to take the point G as the centre and the perpendicular distance from G to any of the three sides AB, BC or AC as the radius and draw a circle then each of the three sides AB, BC or AC would be tangents to such a circle that would lie within the triangle ABC and would be the inscribed circle of the triangle ABC.

Please see another noteworthy aspect of the relationship between any two sides of a triangle and their angle bisector. One of the two sides should be smaller than the other.

If you were to draw a triangle ABC such that AB = 6 cm, BC = 8 cm and the angle ABC is – say – an obtuse angle of 120^0, then you will find that the length of BD, the angle bisector of the angle ABC, which meets the opposite side AC at D, is less than the smaller of the two sides AB and BC. You will continue to see this phenomenon each time that you lower the angle ABC from 120 degree to right angle and then to 60^0 although maintaining the same lengths for AB and BC. When angle ABC is at 60^0, the length of BD is almost equal to AB. When angle ABC starts to dip below 60^0, BD becomes equal to AB and then becomes greater than AB.

The three angle bisectors meet at a point called the incentre. If a circle were drawn from the incentre with any of the perpendiculars from the incentre to any of the three sides as radii, then such a circle would touch all three sides of the triangle and is known as the inscribed circle of the triangle. It would be worth noting that the perpendicular distance from the incentre of a triangle to any of the three sides is the same.

The three perpendicular bisectors meet at a point called the circumcentre, H, which is the centre of a circle passing through the three vertices. Such a centre is also known as the circumscribed circle of the triangle.

Please see the following question that would test one's fundamentals in regard to triangles.

What is the minimum information among the following that you must have in order to be able to construct a triangle ABC?

(1) The length of AB and the measures of the angles ABC and ACB.

(2) The length of AB and the measure of the angle ACB.

(3) The measures of the three sides.

(4) The measures of the three angles in the triangle.

Let us see what is the minimum information that one must have in order to be able to construct a triangle and why so.

How many vertices does a triangle have? Three.

Whatever information you have must be able to give you an idea of where exactly the three vertices are. Anything less is not enough. And what can give an idea of the exact location of the three vertices?

(1) The measure of a side and the angles on this side.

How can one construct a triangle on this information alone? Draw the side whose measure is given as the base of the triangle. From its two ends draw the two given angles. Where the rays containing the two angles meet is the third vertex.

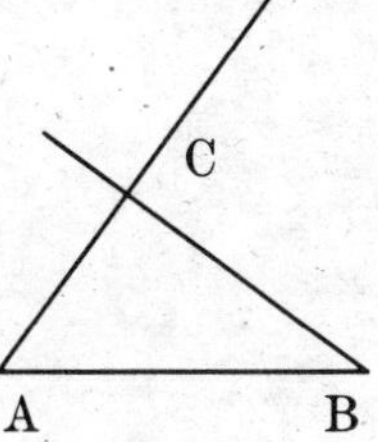

(2) The length of AB and the measure of the angle ABC

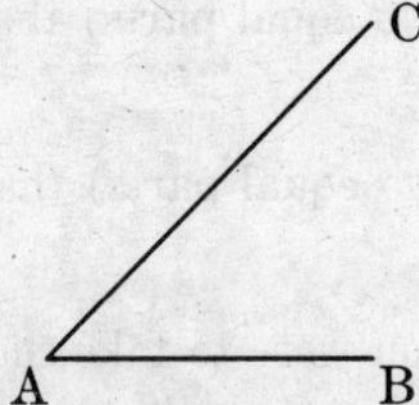

Draw AB as the base of the triangle. Draw the ray containing the angle BAC whose measure is given. One cannot possibly hope to draw a triangle with this much information unless one is told that the triangle is isosceles. If it is indeed isosceles then draw the ray containing an angle equal in measure to the angle BAC from the vertex B. The point where the two rays meet gives you the third vertex. This information would only then suffice to construct a triangle. But in the present case there is no reason to infer that the triangle is isosceles.

(3) The measures of the three sides.

This is sufficient since one can draw a base AB of given measure and then with the help of a compass, draw an arc with A as centre and with radius equal to the measure of one of the given sides and then another arc with B as centre and with radius equal to the measure of one of the third of the given sides and the point where the two arcs meet would give you the third vertex and this information would thus be sufficient for enabling one to construct a triangle.

(4) The measures of the three angles in the triangle.

Here one would not know where to start from and since the first two vertices are unidentifiable, the question of being able to construct a triangle on this basis does not arise.

Although this might seem a trifle elementary to some readers, the idea behind providing this input is that one should not be caught with the wrong foot forward.

Now let us see an exercise about triangles that has an answer key and solutions to each of the questions.

EXERCISE

1. In the adjoining figure, ABCD is a square. BCE is an equilateral triangle. The triangle BAE is isosceles. The angle BAE is

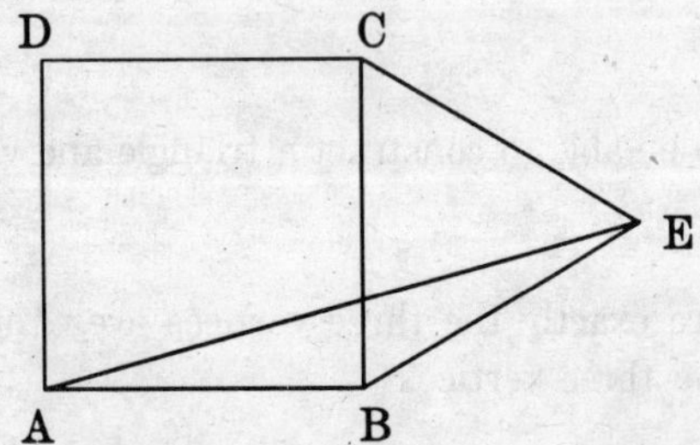

(1) 30^0

(2) 45^0

(3) 15^0

(4) 20^0

2.

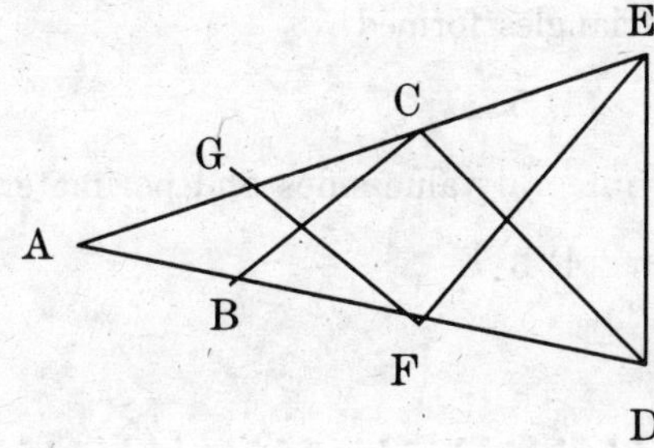

In the figure above, AB = BC = CD = DE = EF = FG = GA. Then angle DAE is approximately:
(1) 15^0 (2) 20^0 (3) 30^0 (4) 25^0

3.

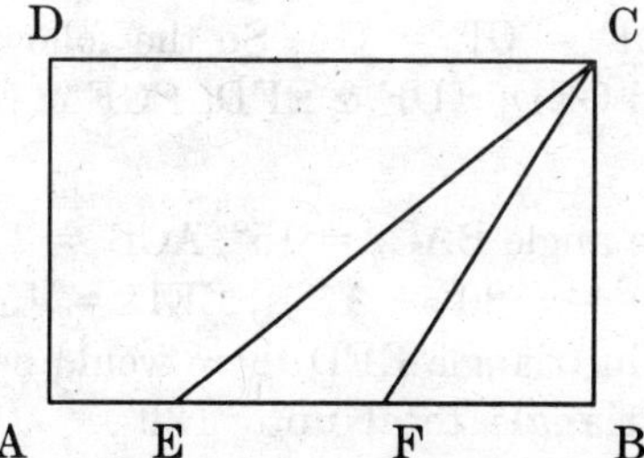

In the above diagram, ABCD is a rectangle with AE = EF = FB. What is the ratio of the area of the triangle CEF and that of the rectangle?

(1) 1/6 (2) 1/8 (3) 1/9 (4) None of these

4.

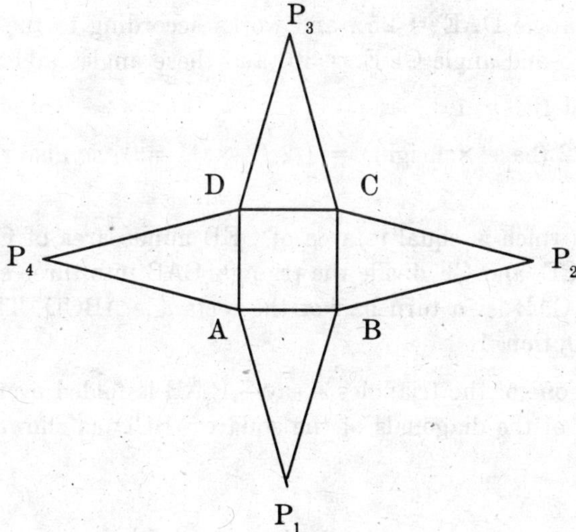

ABCD is a square piece of cardboard. P_1AB, P_2BC, P_3CD and P_4AD are isosceles triangles on the sides. A side of the square is 4 cm and each lateral side of the triangle is 6 cm. Find the vertical height of the pyramid got by bringing together all the four vertices (P's) together.

(1) $2\sqrt{5}$ (2) $2\sqrt{7}$ (3) 6 (4) $4\sqrt{2}$

5. Four straight lines are drawn at random in a plane, no two of which are parallel and no three of which are concurrent. What is the maximum number of triangles formed?

(1) 2 (2) 3 (3) 4 (4) 5

6. What is the number of distinct triangles with integral value sides and perimeter 14?

(1) 6 (2) 5 (3) 4 (4) 3

SOLUTIONS

1. In the figure, angle CBA is 90° since ABCD is a square. Angle CBE is 60° since BCE is an equilateral triangle. Angle ABE is the sum of angles ABC and CBE and is = 90 + 60 = 150°. Thus in triangle ABE, a total of 180 – 150 = 30° is to be divided between angles BAE and AEB. Since triangle BAE is isosceles, angles BAE and AEB are equal and have 15° each. So angle BAE is 15° at **Option 3**.

2. In the figure, AB = BC = CD = DE = EF = GF = GA. So the following angle pairs will be equal: Angle BAC & ACB; CBD and CDB; DCE and CED; EDF & EFD; FGE & GEF; GAF AND GFA. Now let us go by the options.

   Option 1: If angle DAE (which is the same as angle BAC) = 15°, ACB = 15°, ABC = 150°, CBD = 30°, CDB = 30°, BCD = 120°, DCE = 45° (180° – (120° + 15°)), CED = 45°, EDC = 90°, EDF = 120°; now if EDF = 120°, EFD is also =120 and in triangle EFD there would be two angles of 120° each; this is not possible since the all **angles in a triangle total upto 180^0**.

   Option 2: If DAE = 20°, ACB = 20°, ABC = 140°, CBD = 40°, CDB = 40°, BCD = 100° (180° – (40° + 40°)), DCE = 40° (180°–(40° + 100°)), CED = 40°, EDC = 100°, EDF = 140°; so EFD = 140. In triangle EFD, there would be two angles of 140° each and this is not possible.

   Option 3: If DAE (which is the same as angle BAC) = 30°, ACB = 30°, ABC = 120°, CBD = 60°, CDB = 60°, BCD = 60° (180°–(60° + 60°)), DCE = 60°, CED = 60°, CDE = 60°, EDF = 120°. If EDF = 120°, EFD is also = 120°. This is not possible since in triangle DEF, there would be two angles of 120° each.

   Hence Option 4. If one takes angle DAE = 25°, and works according to the above, triangle DEF would have angles DCE = CED = 75 and angle CDE = 30° and these angles add up to 180° in triangle DEF.

3. Let AE = EF = FB = 2, and BC = 1.

   The area of triangle CBF = 1/2 (base × height) = 1/2 (2 × 1) = 1; so also the area of the triangle CEB = 1/2 × 4 × 1 = 2.

   The area of the triangle CEF (which is equal to area of CEB minus area of CFB)= 2 – 1 = 1.Clearly, if one were to join C and A, CA, CE, and CF divide the triangle CAB into three equal portions. Thus triangle CFB is 1/3rd of triangle CAB; CAB is in turn half of the rectangle ABCD. Thus triangle CEF is 1/6th of the rectangle ABCD. Hence **Option 1**.

4. Let us see what happens when one of the triangles – say – P_1AB is folded over AB. P_1 will come vertically above the point of intersection of the diagonals of the square ABCD as shown in the following figure:

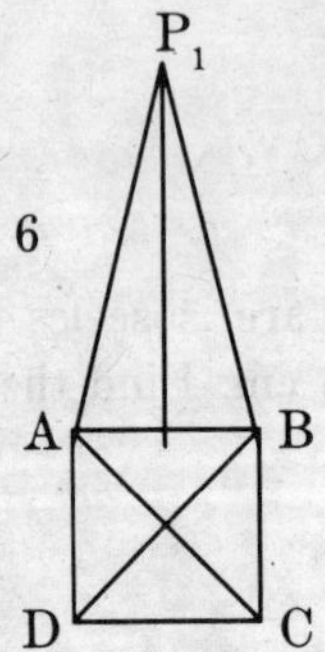

There will be a triangle formed on the point of intersection of the diagonals of the square with three sides as per hereunder:

(I) The height of the triangle P_1AB which will be equal to √(square of P_1A – square of half of the side of the square which has each side equal to 4) = √(36-4) = √32

(II) the line joining the mid point of AB with the intersection of the diagonals which will be 2 cm and

(III) third side that will join P_1 to the intersection of the diagonals and this line will be equal to the height of the pyramid got by folding all four isosceles triangles over the square.

Thus the height of the pyramid = √(square of 32 – 4) = √(28) = 2√7.

5. The idea is to see the maximum number of triangles that can be formed by drawing four straight lines such that no two of them are parallel and no three of which are concurrent. Incidentally if three lines out of four are concurrent, then you have only two lines and then it is impossible to draw a triangle out of just two lines. The statement that no three of them are concurrent is redundant.

Secondly, if two pairs of lines are parallel and they intersect, then all that one can hope to get is a rectangle or parallelogram. The maximum number of triangles can emerge out of four lines only if three of them do not intersect at a common point but these four lines intersect at three different points. If they intersect at a common point then only one line can cut them through them all and thus there can be three triangles at the most as seen from the figure below: ABD, BCD and ADC.

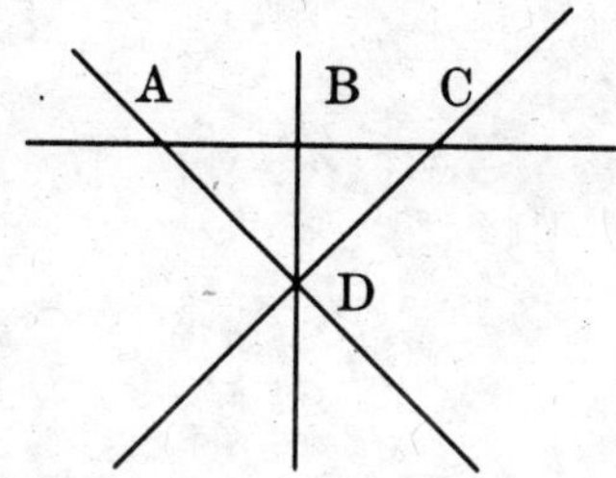

If however, the three lines do not intersect at a common point then four triangles at the most can emerge as seen from the figure below. D is where two lines intersect. B is where the other two intersect.

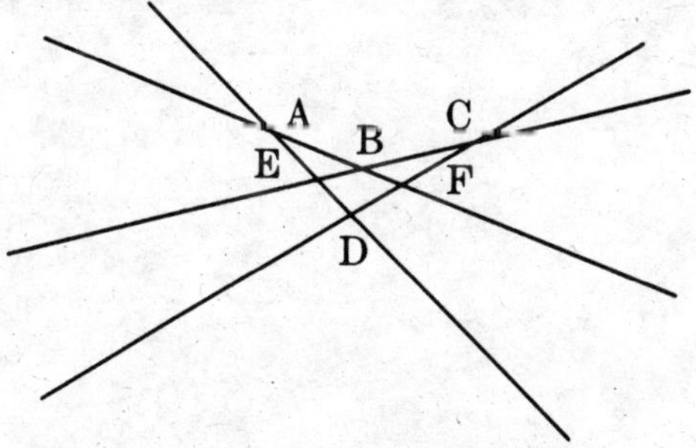

Four distinct triangles emerge: AEB, BCF, ADF, CED.

6. A triangle is feasible only if its longest side is lesser than the sum of its other two sides. In the instant case, the perimeter of all of the triangles is 14. Therefore, the longest side possible is 6 but, if the longest were to be taken at even 7, the sum of the other two sides would be 7, which is equal to **and not more than the longest side**. The combinations of **distinct** triangles with perimeter of 14 are as under:

Longest side	Side 2	Side 3
6	6	2
6	5	3
6	4	4
5	5	4

The longest side cannot be 4 or lesser than 4 because even if it is 4, the sum of the other two sides would have to be 10, which means even if the remaining two sides are equal, each side would be 5, and thus 4 cannot be the longest side.

There can be only four distinct triangles with perimeter 14 and each side of integral value.

It is important to point out that in the above mentioned combinations of triangles with the longest side as 6 or 5, the combination of 6,3 and 5 in the case of 6 as the longest side and 5,4 and 5 in the case of 5 as the longest side have not been reckoned since these would not be distinct from 6,5,3 or 5,5,4. Thus Option 3.

Chapter 40

Work and Time

Work is generally measured in man-days or man-hours or in the number of units of a task. If 1 man can do a job in three days, then the amount of work is said to be of 3 man-days. If 2 men can do a job in $5\frac{1}{2}$ hours, the work is said to be of $2 \times 5\ 1/2 = 11$ man-hours.

If three women can do a particular amount of work in one day that 2 men can do in 1 day, then each woman is said to be capable of doing an amount of work equal to 2/3rd man-day per day. For example, if 2 men together dig six feet in a day, then one man digs three feet in a day. If three women dig six feet in a day, it means that one woman can dig two feet in day and therefore a woman is said to be capable of doing an amount of work equal to 2/3rd man-day per day.

If a job was such that it involves digging a well 36 feet deep and you could do it alone in 6 days and I do it in 12 days, then how much time would we take to complete this work if were asked to do it together? Well, you can do the work alone in 6 days since the work involves digging a 36 feet well, you can dig at the rate of 6 feet per day. Since I can do the job alone in 12 days, I have the capacity to dig 3 feet per day. Together we can dig $(6 + 3) = 9$ feet per day. When we work together, we can dig the 36 feet well in 4 days.

Imagine that a task of laying 9600 bricks involves men, women and children. Every man is capable of independently completing the entire job in 48 days; every woman can do half as much as what a man can do in a day and every child can do only half of what a woman does in a day. How much time would 2 men, 3 women and 10 children take to complete the work if they were to work together?

Since each man can lay 9600 bricks in 48 days, he can lay $9600/48 = 200$ bricks per day. 2 men working together can lay 400 bricks per day. Each woman can do half of what a man does. Each woman can lay 100 bricks per day and so 3 women can lay 300 bricks per day. Each child can do half of what a woman can do. Each child can lay 50 bricks per day so 10 children can lay 500 bricks per day. Therefore 2 men, 3 women and 10 children working together can lay $400 + 300 + 500 = 1200$ bricks per day. There are 9600 bricks to be laid and this will take them $9600/1200 = 8$ days in all.

The time taken by two persons for doing a given amount of work is inversely proportional to the rate at which they can work. Let us see this in the following tabular form:

Suppose a task involved making	30 kg of ice-cream	500 cakes	36 note books
I can make	10 kg/hour	10/day	3/day
You can make	15 kg/hour	25/day	8/day
The ratio of our productivity (I: You) is	2:3	2:5	3:8
For the entire task to be over, I and you take respectively	3 and 2 hours	50 and 20 days	12 and 4 1/2 days;
The ratio of the time we take is (I: You)	3:2	5:2	8:3

If a man can do a piece of work in 20 minutes, it means that he can do 3 pieces of similar work in an hour. If another man can do a piece of work in 30 minutes, it means that he can do 2 such pieces of work in an hour. If a man can do a piece of work in 40 minutes, it means that he can do $60/40 = 1\ 1/2$ pieces of similar work in an hour. If a fellow can do a piece of work in 20 hours, it means that he can do 1/20th of this work in an hour.

Now let us see some problems and the solutions designed in such a way that there is no formula anywhere, nor any mathematics; only common sense. We would like you to solve these problems without setting pen to paper:

Problem 1

A, B and C complete a work in 3 days. A or B alone can do the same work in 8 days. In how many days C alone can finish the same work?

Solution

Let us assume that the work involves binding 24 books (3 x 8 = 24). If A or B alone can do the same work in 8 days, it means that A can bind 3 books per day and B can also bind 3 books per day. Together the two can bind 6 books per day. Since A, B and C can complete binding 24 books in 3 days, the three together bind 8 books every day out of which A and B bind 6 between them. C thus binds 2 books every day. C will take 12 days to bind 24 books on his own. Thus C alone can finish the same work in 12 days.

Problem 2

A cistern is normally filled in 8 hours but takes two hours longer to fill because of a leak in its bottom. If the cistern is full, how much time will it take the cistern to get empty?

Solution

The cistern can fill the tank in 8 hours but because of a leak, it takes two hours more i.e. 10 hours to fill it. Let us assume the capacity of the tank to be 8 × 10 = 80 litres because number 80 is conveniently divisible by both 8 and 10. If the cistern did not leak then the tap filling it in 8 hours would fill 10 litres per hour. But with the leak the cistern can be filled in 10 hours, the cistern retains only 8 litres of water every hour. It means that the leak drains out 2 litres of water every hour. Since we have assumed the capacity of the tank as 80 litres, the leak would empty the full tank in 40 hours.

Problem 3

A can do a piece of work in 20 days, B in 15 days, and C in 12 days. In how many days can A finish the work if he is assisted by B on one day and C on the next, alternately?

Solution

60 is the LCM of 20, 15 and 12. Let us assume that the work involves digging a 60 ft tunnel. Thus A can dig 3 ft, B can dig 4 ft and C can dig 5 ft every day. A is at work everyday. Only his partner changes every day. On day 1, A digs 3 ft and B digs 4 ft. Together they dig 7 ft. On day 2, A digs 3 ft whereas C digs 5 ft and together they dig 8 ft. So in 2 days, A working along with B on one day and C the next day have dug 15 ft in 2 days. Since the task involves digging 60 ft, they will need 4 such time spans of 2 days each and hence 8 days to complete the work.

Problem 4

A garrison having 80 soldiers have food sufficient to last 70 days. How many soldiers should leave after 10 days to ensure that the food lasts another 80 days.

Solution

Assume that each soldier eats 1 loaf of bread every day. The garrison would then need 80 loaves of bread every day since it has 80 soldiers and they have food sufficient for 70 days. In total they would have required 80 × 70 = 5600 loaves of bread. The question of how many soldiers need to leave arises only after 10 days have passed. But in these 10 days, 80 men have eaten 80 × 10 = 800 loaves of bread. The garrison has now 5600 – 800 = 4800 loaves of bread left. With these 4800 loaves, it has to pull on for 80 days. This means that it can afford to give out 4800/80 = 60 loaves of bread per day. Since every soldier is assumed to be eating 1 loaf of bread every day, there is food for only 60 soldiers. So out of 80, 20 will have to leave after 10 days.

Problem 5

If 100 men can do 100 jobs in 100 days; then 1 man can do one job in how many days?

Solution

Suppose each job involves binding 10 books. 100 men can bind 1000 books in 100 days. So every day 100 men can bind 10 books working together. Every day, 1 man can bind $1/10^{th}$ of a book and 1 man can thus bind 10 books in 100 days. So 1 man can do 1 job in 100 days. There is another quick way of looking at this. Since 100 men can do 100 jobs in 100 days, 100 men can do 1 job in 1 day. The job therefore involves work amounting to 100 man-days. One man alone can do a job involving 100 man-days in only 100 days.

Problem 6

3 men or 6 women can do a piece of work in 20 days. In how many days will 12 men and 8 women do the same work? (a) 7/2 days (b) 15/4 days (c) 4 days (d) 5 days

Solution

$3 \times 20 = 60$. Let us assume that the piece of work involves typing 60 pages. So 3 men can type 60 pages in 20 days and hence 3 men can type 3 pages per day, so 1 man can type 1 page per day. 12 men can type 12 pages per day. 6 women can type 60 pages in 20 days and hence 6 women can type 3 pages per day, so 1 woman can type half page per day. 8 women can type 4 pages per day. Together 12 men and 8 women can type $12 + 4 = 16$ pages per day. There are 60 pages to be typed and it should take $60/16 = 15/4$ or 3 3/4 days.

It is time now to move on to a small exercise that will ensure complete assimilation of the concepts that we have learnt so far.

EXERCISE

1. Water enters a tank by tap A, which takes 3 hours to get filled, and can be emptied by two taps B and C, which can empty it in 4 hours and 6 hours respectively. If the tank is full and all three taps are turned on, in how much time will it be empty? (A) 9 hours (B) 10 hours 24 minutes (C) 12 hours 36 minutes (D) 12 hours.
2. If 12 pumps working 7 hours a day can lift 2800 tons of water in 20 days, in how many days can 20 pumps working 9 hours a day lift 3000 tons of water? (A) 11 (B) 8 (C) 9 (D) 10 (E) 12.
3. R, L, and B are employed to do a piece of work for \$1056. The first two together did $7/11^{th}$ of the work and the last two together did the $6/11^{th}$ of the work. What should R be paid? (A) \$480 (B) \$96 (C) \$384 (D) \$672 (E) \$612.
4. Three persons, P, Q, and R can do a piece of work in respectively 30 days, 12 days, and 20 days. In how many days will all the three finish 4 times the original quantum of work? (A) 48 (B) 12 (C) 6 (D) 24 (E) 18.
5. A and B can do a piece of work in 15 days while B and C can do the same work in 12 days, and C and A can do the same work in 10 days. They all work for 5 days, and then B and C leave. How many more days will A take to finish the work? (A) 18 (B) 12 (C) 9 (D) 10 (E) 16.

SOLUTIONS

1. Water enters a tank by tap A, which takes 3 hours to get filled and by two taps B and C, which can empty it in 4 hours and 6 hours respectively. In the context of the figures 3, 4 and 6, let us presume the tank capacity to be 12 litres since 12 is a multiple of 3, 4 and 6.

   If tap A can fill the tank independently in 3 hours, it can fill 4 litres per hour. If taps B and C can empty the tank, whose capacity we have assumed as 12 litres, in 4 and 6 hours respectively, they can individually draw out 3 and 2 litres per hour respectively.

   It means that while tap A fills in 4 litres per hour, tap B and tap C in the aggregate draw out 3 + 2 = 5 litres per hour. It means that when all three taps are turned on together, there is a net outflow of 1 litre of water from the tank. Since we have assumed the tank to be of 12 litres, it would take 12 hours for the three taps operating together to empty the tank, which was full at the outset.

2. If 12 pumps working 7 hours a day can lift 2800 tons of water in 20 days, 12 pumps working 7 hours a day can lift 2800 ÷ 20 = 140 tons of water per day and if 12 pumps worked for 1 hour a day, they would be able to lift 140 ÷ 7 = 20 tons of water per hour.

   If 12 pumps could lift 20 tons of water per hour, 20 pumps could lift 20 × 20 ÷ 12 = 400 ÷ 12 = 100 ÷ 3 tons of water in an hour. 20 pumps working 9 hours a day could lift 9 × 100 ÷ 3 = 300 tons per day and they could lift 3000 tons of water in 3000÷300=10 days.

3. R and L together did 7/11th of the work and L and B together did 6/11th of the work. Let us assume that the work required to make 11 cakes. R and L together, therefore, make 7 cakes. We shall refer to this phenomenon, for example, as Equation 1: R+L=7. Together L and B make 6 cakes and thus we get Equation 2: L+ B = 6.

   We know that R + L + B = 11 and R + L + L + B =13 and thus L = 2.

   If L=2, then from Equation 2, B=4 and if L=2, then from Equation 1, R=5. Since we have assumed the entire work requires making of 11 cakes and R had made 5 cakes, R should be paid for 5/11th of the work and it means that he should get 5× $1056÷11= $480.

4. Three persons, P, Q, and R can do a piece of work in respectively 30 days, 12 days, and 20 days. Since 60 is a multiple of 30, 12, and 20, let us assume that the task involves binding 60 books. P, Q, and R can thus independently bind 2, 5, and 3 books per day respectively and together they can bind 2 + 5 + 3 = 10 books per day. Thus they can finish the entire task (of binding 60 books) in 6 days. If the task were to be 4 times the original quantum of work, it would mean binding 240 books, can be completed in 240 ÷ 10 = 24 days.

5. A and B can do a piece of work in 15 days, while B and C can do the same work in 12 days, and C and A can do the same work in 10 days. 60, will go well with 15, 12, and 10, being a multiple of all three and hence we assume the task of digging a 60 foot well.

   If we were to represent the daily output of A, B, and C with the symbols A, B, and C, then A + B = 4, (since they can dig 60 feet working together for 15 days) and B + C = 5 (since they can dig 60 feet working together for 12 days) and A + C = 6 (since they can dig 60 feet working together for 10 days).

   Thus, if we were to add these three equations, we would get 2A+2B+2C= 15 and hence A+B+C=15/2. If they have been working for 5 days, they dig 5×15/2=75/2 feet. If A+B+C=15/2 and B+C=5, then A=5/2.

   The remaining amount of work is 60 – 75/2 = 45/2 and if A has to work alone thereafter, he can finish the task in 45/2 ÷ 5/2 = 9 days.

   Faster still: 60 will go well with 15, 12, and 10 as 60 is a multiple of all three and hence we assume the task to be digging a 60 foot-well.

- If A and B can do a piece of work in 15 days, it means A and B can together dig 4 feet per day.
- If B and C can do the same work in 12 days, it means B and C can together dig 5 feet per day.
- If A and C can do the same work in 10 days, it means A and C can together dig 6 feet per day.

It means that if A and B work for 1 day, B and C work for 1 day, and A and C work for 1 day, 4 + 5 + 6 = 15 feet will have been dug. This is the result of 2 man-days for each of A, B, and C since each of them has done exactly 2 days' work during the three days. Together A, B, and C can dig 7.5 feet per day. Therefore in 5 days, A, B and C dig 7.5 × 5 = 37.5 feet. Thus 60 – 37.5 = 22.5 feet remains to be dug. B and C alone can dig 5 feet per day. Therefore, A alone can dig 2.5 feet per day. A can dig 2.5 feet per day and 22.5 feet in 9 days.

Chapter 41

Getting into Shape

There is a clear difference between Mathematics and Quantitative Ability. We shall provide some illustrations hereunder to drive home that difference. What the GRE aims to test is Quantitative Ability and not Mathematical skills. This is an inference derived from solutions to hundreds of questions you will see in this book that test the same skills that the GRE aims to test. The basis of the inference is, therefore, scientific and solid.

What you will have seen in previous chapters are concept notes such as on Ages, Quadratic Equations, The Pythagoras Theorem and so on. The exercise in each of these chapters has topic-specific questions. It is now time to move on to an array of topics so as to put to test what we have assimilated so far. This chapter has therefore been designed primarily as a prologue to the Practice Tests and the Question Papers that follow thereafter. This chapter will help you limber up before you take on the Practice Tests and Question Papers.

Illustration 1

If A = [B – (B/10)], where B is a positive integer which increases in value, then does A (I) decrease in value (II) increase in value (III) remain unchanged (IV) first increases and then decreases?

Solution

Since B is a positive integer, B/10 will always be less than B. It means that the difference between B and B/10 will always be positive. Secondly, when B = 1, B/10 = 1/10 and therefore, B – B/10 = 9/10. As we know, (B – B/10) is essentially B (1 – 1/10) or 0.9B, when B increases, 0.9B will increase. Hence A, which is effectively 0.9B, will increase with the increase in value of B.

Illustration 2

If P and R are two different real numbers and P × Q = Q × R, then what is the value of Q?

Solution

If PQ = QR and we were to divide both side by Q, we would get P = R, which is not envisaged since we are told that P and R are different real numbers. So Q has got to be zero only then, P × Q = Q × R, where P and R are not equal.

Illustration 3

If R lies between 0 and 1, which of the following increases as R increases? (A) $1 - R^3$ (B) R – 1 (C) $1/R^3$ (D) $1 - R^2$.

Solution

R remains positive throughout since it remains above zero. Therefore, both R^3 and R^2 will also:

(1) Remain a positive fraction throughout and

(2) Increase in the value with R.

In the case of both $(1 - R^2)$ and $(1 - R^3)$, there is a constant term 1 from which a progressively growing term is subtracted. R is a positive fraction. If for example, R = 1/2, then $(1-R^2)$ = [1 – (1/4)] = 3/4, and $(1-R^3)$ = [1 – (1/8)] = 7/8. If R = 9/10, then $(1-R^2)$ = [1 – (81/100)] = 19/100, and $(1 - R^3)$ = [1 – (729/1000)] = 271/1000 or very nearly 27/100. When R = 1/2, $(1-R^2)$ = 3/4 and when R = 9/10, $(1 - R^2)$ = 19/100. Clearly, as R increases, both $(1 - R^2)$ and $(1 - R^3)$ decrease.

When R = 1/2, (R –1) = –1/2 and when R = 9/10, (R – 1) = –1/10. Clearly, as R increases, (R –1) increases.

When R = 1/2, (1/ R^3) = 1/(1/8) = 8 and when R = 9/10, (1/ R^3) = 1/ (729/1000) = 1000/729 or very nearly 100/73 which is way below 8. Clearly, as R increases, (1/ R^3) decreases. Hence Option B.

Illustration 4

A grocer buys apples @ $J per dozen and sells them at $J/10 per piece. What is his profit per apple in dollars? (A) J/36 (B) J/48 (C) J/60, and (D) 3J/ 80.

Solution

When the grocer buys 12 apples for $J, each apple costs him $J/12. When he sells them @$J/10 per apple, he earns $[(J/10) – (J/12)] per apple, which is $J/60 per apple.

Illustration 5

Which of the following fractions is more than 1/3rd? (A) 23/70 (B) 105/319 (C) 26/75 (D) 117/355

Solution

Let us see three fractions arranged in ascending order as follows: 1/4, 1/3 and 1/2. If you will notice, 1/4 is less than 1/3 because the denominator in 1/4 is a larger multiple of the numerator in 1/4 (since the denominator is four times the numerator) than in the case of 1/3(since the denominator is three times the numerator) and 1/2 is more than 1/3 and even more than 1/4 because in 1/2 the denominator is a smaller multiple of the numerator in 1/3 (since the denominator is twice the numerator).
Therefore, if we were to divide the denominator by the numerator in the four options, we would see as follows:

Option 1: 70/23 = just a wee bit more than 3 since 69/23 is exactly 3.

Option 2: 319/105 = just a wee bit more than 3 since 315/105 is exactly 3.

Option 3: 75/26 = just a wee bit less than 3 since 78/26 is exactly 3.

Option 4: 355/117 = just a wee bit more than 3 since 351/117 is exactly 3.

Only in the case of Option 3 do we see a denominator that is less than three times the numerator and hence Option 3

Illustration 6

If the condition is that $A^B = B^A$, and A and B are distinct positive integers, then how many value pairs of A and B will satisfy this condition.

Solution

An infinite number of value pairs of A and B will satisfy the condition if A and B are not distinct and only two value pairs of A and B will satisfy the condition $A^B = B^A$ if A and B are distinct as may be seen from the following:

If A =	1	2	3
And if B =	1	2	3
Then A^B =	1	4	27
And B^A =	1	4	27

An infinite number of value pairs can satisfy condition if A and B are not to be distinct. If A and B are to be distinct, then only the following value pairs will satisfy the condition that $A^B = B^A$.

If A=	2	4
And if B=	4	2
Then A^B =	16	16
And B^A =	16	16

We shall now move on to a small exercise that should prepare us with thinking beyond the straight and narrow of conventional thought. The detailed solutions follow.

EXERCISE

1. If $x^y + y^x = 1234$, how many positive integer value pairs of x and y satisfy this condition? Options (A) 1 (B) 2 (C) 4 (D) 3

2. Which of the following is the reciprocal of $\frac{a}{b} + \frac{b}{a}$?

   (A) $\frac{a}{b} - \frac{b}{a}$ (B) ab ÷ (a+b) (C) ab ÷ (a^2+b^2) (D) 1÷ (a^2+b^2)

3. How many pairs of natural numbers are such that the difference between whose squares is 39? (A) 1 (B) 2 (C) 3 (D) 4

4. If S is a set of prime numbers where each of its members is >2, and another set S_1 is to be formed by adding a number N to all elements of S so that all members of S_1 are composite numbers, what is the least possible value of N?

5. If $L = \frac{x^{-3} - y^{-3}}{x^{-1} - y^{-1}}$, what is the value of L when x = 3 and y = 2?

   (A) 13/36 (B) 5/6 (C) 7/16 (D) 19/36

6. A red light flashes 3 times per minute and a green light flashes 5 times in two minutes at regular intervals. If both lights start flashing at the same time, how many times do they flash together in each hour? (1) 30 (2) 24 (3) 20 (4) 60

7. Three friends, returning from a movie, stopped to eat at a restaurant. After dinner, they paid their bill and noticed a bowl of mints at the front counter. Sally took 1/3 of the mints, but returned four because she had a momentary pang of guilt. Susan then took 1/4 of what was left but returned three for similar reasons. Enid then took half of the remainder but threw two back into the bowl. The bowl had only 17 mints left when the raid was over. How many mints were originally in the bowl?

   (1) 38 (2) 31 (3) 41 (4) None of these

8. If 09/12/2001 happens to be Sunday, then 09/12/1971 would have been a

   (1) Wednesday (2) Tuesday (3) Saturday (4) Thursday

9. Two full tanks, one shaped like a cylinder and the other like a cone, contain jet fuel. The cylindrical tank holds 500 litres more than the conical tank. After 200 litres of fuel has been pumped out from each tank, the cylindrical tank contains twice the amount of fuel in the conical tank. How many litres of fuel did the cylindrical tank have when it was full?

   (1) 700 (2) 1000 (3) 1100 (4) 1200

10. A farmer has decided to build a wire fence along one straight side of his property. For this, he planned to place several fence-posts at six metre intervals, with posts fixed at both ends of the side. After he bought the posts and wire, he found that the number of posts hc had bought was five less than required. However,

he discovered that the number of posts he had bought would be just sufficient if he spaced them eight metres apart. What is the length of the side of his property and how many posts did he buy?

(1) 100 metres, 15 (2) 100 metres, 16 (3) 120 metres, 15 (4) 120 metres, 16

11. A report consists of 20 sheets each of 55 lines and each such line consists of 65 characters. This report is retyped on to sheets each of 65 lines such that each line consists of 70 characters. The percentage reduction in number of sheets is closest to (1) 15 (2) 20 (3) 25 (4) 30

12. Let $x < 0$, $0 < y < 1$, $z > 1$. Which of the following is false?

a. $(x^2 - z^2)$ has to be positive.

b. yz can be less than one.

c. xy can never be zero.

d. $(y^2 - z^2)$ is always negative.

13. If $\frac{x}{3} = \frac{y}{2} = \frac{z}{5} = \frac{3x+2y-z}{k}$ find the value of k.

(1) 4 (2) 6 (3) 8 (4) –8

14. If $(x + 1)(x + 2)(x + c)$ is identically equal to $x^3 - 7x - 6$, what is c equal to?

(1) 0 (2) 3 (3) -3 (4) 2

15. If $a = \frac{1}{\sqrt{3} + \sqrt{2}}$ and $b = \frac{1}{\sqrt{3} - \sqrt{2}}$, then $\frac{1}{a+1} + \frac{1}{b+1} =$

(1) 0 (2) 1 (3) 2 (4) none of these

16. Find the sum to infinity of $1 + \frac{5}{10} + \frac{9}{10^2} + \ldots$

(1) $\frac{125}{81}$ (2) $\frac{130}{81}$ (3) $\frac{135}{81}$ (4) $\frac{140}{81}$

17. The recurring decimal 1.044 represents the fraction

(1) $\frac{562}{489}$ (2) $\frac{1101}{992}$ (3) $\frac{103}{97}$ (4) $\frac{517}{495}$

18. If 100d = 712.121212 ......, then 17d is

(1) an irrational number (2) a non-recurring infinite decimal

(3) an integer (4) a recurring decimal greater than 100

19. Solve the inequality $\frac{2x - 1}{\log 0.1} < 0$

(1) $x > 1$ (2) $x < 1/2$ (3) $x > 1/2$ (4) Both 1 and 3

20. Find the positive value of x, if the second term in the expansion of $(x + 1)^5$ is 10,00,000.

(1) 200 (2) $100\sqrt{2}$ (3) $10 \times 20^{1/4}$ (4) $(200)^{1/4}$

21. Find the least number that leaves the remainder 6 when divided by 15, 35, or 42.

(1) 216 (2) 232 (3) 426 (4) 78

22. For what values of x is the function $\sqrt{\frac{4 - x}{2x - 5}}$ meaningful?

(1) $\frac{5}{2} < x \le 4$ (2) $x \le \frac{5}{2}$ (3) $x \ge 4$ (4) $0 \le x \le \frac{5}{2}$

23. Which of the following values of x will satisfy $\left|\frac{3x^3 + 1}{2x^2 + 2}\right| = 4$?

(1) – 3 (2) 3 (3) 8 (4) 0

24. Which of the following numbers is closest to the square root of 0.000224?

(1) 0.014 (2) 0.0015 (3) 0.018 (4) 0.015 (5) 0.15

25. A train travels from a Station X to another Station Y, a distance of 192 km, at an average speed of 80 km/hour. It then travels back to X and the total time taken by it for the to and fro journey is 5 hours 36 minutes. What is the average speed on the return trip to X?

(1) 72 km/hour (2) 60 km/hour (3) 64 km/hour (4) 48 km/hour

26. If $x - y = 5$ and $\frac{y}{x} = 6$, what is the value of y?

27. If $3 < p < 4$ and $5 < q < 6$, find which of the following expressions assumes the greatest value?

(A) p^2q (B) $4pq$ (C) p^2/q (D) pq^2 (E) $\frac{4}{5}p^2q$

Here are the detailed solutions.

SOLUTIONS

1. When N, any number, raised to the power of 1 gives N itself and 1 raised to the power of N gives 1. 1234 is effectively 1233 + 1 and hence there are two possible positive integer value pairs of x and y that can satisfy this condition: Hence Option B. (1) x = 1233 and y = 1 and (2) x = 1 and y = 1233.

2. Which of the following is the reciprocal of $\frac{a}{b} + \frac{b}{a}$?

(A) $\frac{a}{b} - \frac{b}{a}$ (B) $ab \div (a+b)$ (C) $ab \div (a^2+b^2)$ (D) $1 \div (a^2+b^2)$

There are two ways at looking at this. One is as follows:

$\frac{a}{b} + \frac{b}{a} = \frac{(a^2+b^2)}{ab}$ and the reciprocal of this is $= \frac{ab}{(a^2+b^2)}$

The other is like this:

Take a = 1 and b = 2. So:

$\frac{a}{b} + \frac{b}{a} = \frac{1}{2} + \frac{2}{1} = \frac{5}{2}$. What is the reciprocal of $\frac{5}{2}$? $\frac{2}{5}$

Which among the options gives $\frac{2}{5}$?

So one has to see only options C and D. D gives 1 in the numerator and 5 in the denominator and hence it is not valid. Thus Option C as it gives 2 in the numerator and 5 in the denominator.

3. 39 can be factorised as (A) 13 × 3 and 39 × 1 or (B) – 13 × –3 and –39× –1

Let A and B be two unknown numbers. If the two numbers whose difference of their squares is 39, this means that $(A^2 - B^2) = 39$ and thus $(A + B) \times (A - B)$ = either 3 × 13 or 1 × 39.

If (A + B) × (A – B) = 13 × 3, then A = 8 and B = 5.

If (A + B) × (A – B) = 39 × 1, then A = 20 and B = 19.

If (A + B) ×(A – B) = –13 × –3, then A = –8 and B = –5.

If (A + B) × (A – B) = –39 × –1, then A = –20 and B = –19.

If (A + B) × (A – B) = –3 × –13, then A = –8 and B = 5.

If (A + B) × (A – B) = –1 × –39, then A = –20 and B = 19.

Since we are to deal only in natural numbers, we are to assume only positive values for A and B and it means that there are only two pairs of natural numbers such that the difference between their squares is 39. Thus Option B.

Incidentally, if the difference between the squares of two natural numbers is a positive number, then the first of the two natural numbers has got to be higher than the second.

4. **A prime number is an integer that can be evenly divided by no other whole number then itself. A composite number is one which that has two clear factors and can be divided by some whole number other than itself.**

Let us see some prime numbers and the next possible composite number.

PRIME NUMBER	THE NEXT COMPOSITE NUMBER AND ITS FACTORS	WHAT LEAST NUMBER SHOULD BE ADDED TO THE PRIME NUMBER SO AS TO MAKE IT A COMPOSITE NUMBER
3	4=2×2	1
7	8=4×2	1
11	12= 6×2 and 3×4	1
13	14= 7×2	1
17	18= 2×9 and 3×6	1
19	20= 2×10 and 4×5	1
23	24= 2×12, 3×8, and 4×6	1
29	30= 3×10 and 5×6	1

Thus the least number that must be added to every member of set S so as to make another set S_1 such that all members of S_1 are composite numbers is 1.

5. $\frac{x^{-3}-y^{-3}}{x^{-1}-y^{-1}} = \frac{3^{-3}-2^{-3}}{3^{-1}-2^{-1}} = \left[\frac{1}{27}-\frac{1}{8}\right] \div \left[\frac{1}{3}-\frac{1}{2}\right] = \frac{-19}{216} \div \frac{-1}{6} = \frac{19\times6}{216} = \frac{19}{36}$

6. **The red light flashes once in 20 seconds and the green light flashes once in 24 seconds. If both start flashing at the same time, they flash simultaneously every 120th second – the LCM of 20 and 24 (or every second minute). They therefore flash simultaneously for $\frac{60}{2}$= 30 times each hour. Thus Option 1.**

7. **Sita took 1/3rd of the mints to begin with. If the number of mints at the very outset was divisible by 3, she could have done without breaking up the number of mints into fractions. None of the first three options are divisible by 3 and so "none of these". Hence Option 4.**

8. 9 December 2001 is a Sunday. 9 December 1971 was precisely 30 years back. Before we start this exercise, we must remember that **7 days make a week** and if 9th December 2001 is a Sunday, so was 2nd December 2001(seven days prior to 9th December) and 25th November 2001(seven days prior to 2nd December 2001). **Each year has 365 days. It means that in a year there are 52 weeks (52 × 7 = 364) plus 1 day.** 9th December 2000 occurred 365 + 1 = 366 days ago (a leap year has 366 days and it is a leap year since 2000 is exactly divisible by 4 and **only an year that is exactly divisible by 4 is a leap year**). These 366 days of the **leap year mean 52 weeks (of seven days each) plus 2 days.** So 366 days

have elapsed between 9th December 2000 and 9th December 2001. Thus 9th December 2000 was a Friday and 9th December 2001 occurs 366 days later, or 364 days (52 weeks) + 2 days later. Between the 9th December 1971 and 9th December 2001, there have been 30 years (i.e. 365 × 30 years) and furthermore there have been 8 leap years in between (1972, 76, 80, ...2000). Since a leap year has 52 weeks plus 2 days, all 30 years that would otherwise have (52 weeks × 30 years) + 30 days, would now have (52 weeks × 30 years + 30 days + 8 days. Thus there will be 30(365)+8 days or 30(364 + 1) + 8 days or (30 × 364) + 30 + 8 days between 9th December 1971 and 2001. Of this number (30 × 364) is per se divisible by 7 since 364 itself is divisible by 7. The remaining number of days is 30+8 or 38. If divided by 7 one gets a remainder of 3. It means that 9th December 1971 was 3 days prior to Sunday; 9th December 1971 was Thursday. Thus **Option 4.**

9. The shapes of the tanks are not important in the context that neither the radius nor, for that matter, any of the dimensions is given. But the fact is that the cylindrical tank has a volume of 500 litres more than the other tank and also that if 200 litres of fuel is pumped out from each tank, then the tank contains 2 times the fuel in the conical tank. Now let us go by the following options:

   Option 1: If the conical tank has a volume of 200 litres of jet fuel and 200 litres were pumped out from both tanks, there would be no fuel left in the conical tank, and the question of comparison with the residual volume in the cylindrical tank does not arise.

   Option 2: If the cylindrical tank were to hold 1000 litres, then the volume of the conical tank would be 500 litres. If 200 litres are taken from both tanks, the residual volume of fuel would be respectively 800 and 300 litres and this is not a case of the residual volume of fuel in the cylindrical tank being twice that in the conical tank.

   Option 3: If the volume of the cylindrical tank were to be 1100 litres, then the volume of the conical tank would be 600 litres and taking away 200 litres from each would mean that the cylindrical tank has 900 litres left whereas the conical tank has 400 litres left and yet again this is not a case of the residual volume in the cylindrical tank being twice the residual volume of fluid in the conical tank.

   Thus **Option 4.**

10. The farmer's earlier plan was to place the poles 6 meters apart and then he had to alter the plan so as to place the poles 8 meters apart. The options where 100 meters is the distance would get eliminated right away since the distance that he has to cover should be an integral multiple of both 6 and 8 and 100 is not an integral multiple of either 6 or 8. Only 120 meters meets this criterion. Now with 120 meters as the distance and each pole 8 meters apart, the farmer would need 16 poles, the first at one end, the second at the 8 meter mark, the third at the 16 meter mark, the 10th at the 88 meter mark and so on till the 16th at the 120 meter mark (which, incidentally, would be the end of the fence). Thus **Option 4.**

11. A report consists of 20 sheets with 55 lines and 65 characters/line. It means that the total number of characters is 20 × 55 × 65. The number of characters will remain the same in the new format. In the new format there will be 65 lines and 70 characters per line. Now, number of characters = number of sheets × number of lines per sheet × number of characters per line.

    The equation that emerges is 20 × 55 × 65 = 65 × 70 × (No. of sheets).

    Therefore, in the new format, number of sheets = number of characters ÷ (number of lines per sheet × number of characters per line) = $\frac{20 \times 55 \times 65}{65 \times 70} = \frac{20 \times 55}{70} = \frac{110}{7} = 15.71$ sheets.

    So the number of sheets is reduced by 20 – 15.71 = 4.29 sheets.

    This reduction of 4.29 sheets as a percentage of the earlier 20 sheets is 4.29 × 100 ÷ 20 = 429 ÷ 20. 20 × 21 = 420. The nearest percentage as per the given options is 20 and hence **Option 2: 20%.**

12. x < 0; 0 < y < 1 and z > 1. x is a negative number. Let us assume the following values of x, y, and z and test the options:

Option1: $(x^2 - z^2)$ has to be positive. If x = –1 and z = 1.5, then $(x^2 - z^2)$ = 1 – 2.25 = –1.25; thus it is not necessary that $(x^2 - z^2)$ has to be positive. Now here, the reason for presuming the respective minimum value for each of x, y, and z is that only then, it can be derived that the expression **$(x^2 - z^2)$ has to be positive**, need not necessarily have a positive value. For example, x can be –11 and z can be even 2 and hence $(x^2 - z^2)$ = 121–4 = 117; this is positive but not necessarily so. Option 1 is false.

If one were to see the other options by taking the values of x = –1, y = 0.1, and z = 1.1, it will be apparent that only Option 1 is necessarily false, since as per the given options, the positions will be as hereunder:

Option 2: yz can be < 1; yz will be 0.1 × 1.1 = 0.11; this will always be positive since, both y and z are positive but if one has presumed the respective minima for y and z; it is not necessarily true since nothing stops one from presuming that z=100 and yz will thus be 0.1 × 100 = 10.

Option 3: xy can never be 0 s; neither x nor y can be zero as per what is given and unless one of the multiplicands of an expression is zero, the value of the expression can never be zero. Option 3 is always true.

Option 4: $(y^2 - z^2)$ is always negative; since y is <1 and z>1; the expression $(y^2 - z^2)$ is always negative.

Hence **Option 1** since it is the only option that is not necessarily true.

13. I would take a logical route to solve this rather than a mathematical one and in doing so I would take x/3 and y/2 and z/5 and (3x+2y-z)/k as all =1. And then since x = 3, y = 2, z = 5, so (3x + 2y-z) = 8. If 8/k = 1 then **k** = 8. Hence Option 3.

14. When you multiply (x + 1) and (x + 2) and (x + c) then all terms will be in powers of x except 1 × 2 × c which will be a constant term and since in the present case 1 × 2 × c = –6, c = –3. Hence Option 3.

15. If $a = \frac{1}{\sqrt{3}+\sqrt{2}}$ and $b = \frac{1}{\sqrt{3}-\sqrt{2}}$, then $ab = \frac{1}{\sqrt{3}+\sqrt{2}} \times \frac{1}{\sqrt{3}-\sqrt{2}} = \frac{1}{(3-2)} = 1.$

Now, $\frac{1}{(a+1)} + \frac{1}{(b+1)} = \frac{b+1+a+1}{(a+1) \times (b+1)} = \frac{a+b+2}{[ab+b+a+1]} = \frac{a+b+2}{[1+b+a+1]}$

since ab=1 and thus = $\frac{[a+b+2]}{[a+b+2]}$ = 1. So **Option 2**: 1.

16. There is something to be taken note of once and for all when you see the row of dots after the progression 1 + 5/10 + 9/10^2 ..... There is a subtle hint that there is no need to go further than 9/10^2, which is the last of the series and means that if you were to add 1 + 5/10 and 9/100 you would get 159/100 = 1.59. Now a/b can be 1.59 provided a = 1.59 times b and among the options, the denominator is constant and is equal to 81. If you were to multiply 81 with 1.59, how much would you get? Look at 1.59 as 1 + 0.5 + 0.09 and then multiplying 1.59 with 81 is easy and the result would be 81 + 40.5 + 7.29 = 128.79. The nearest to this is 130 and thus 130/81 would give you approximately 1.59 and thus **Option 2: 130/81**.

The need to go further would arise only if the result was such that it would be halfway between two options. Then the next term would be (9 + 4)/ 1000 and the sum of 1 + 5/10 + 9/100 + 13/1000 = 1613/ 1000 = 1.61 and if you were to multiply 1.61 with 81 you would get 81 + 48.6 + 0.81 = 130.41, which is still closer to 130 than 128.79. This cross check would put matters beyond all doubt.

17. A recurring fraction can come about by either 3, 11, 9, 37, 99, or 999 and so on in the denominator. Try dividing the following numbers by 9, 99 and so on with your pocket calculator and see for yourself:

When I	By	I get Divide
1	3	0.333333
1	11	0.0909090909
5	11	0.4545454545
1	9	0.11111
2	9	0.222222
1	99	0.0101010101
1	990	0.00101010101
4	99	0.0404040404
1	999	0.001001001001
5	999	0.005005005005
1	37	0.027027027027
1	111	0.009009009009

Please check this on a pocket calculator and let remain permanently in one's memory. The fraction is represented by the decimal 1.0444444 and so on, which means that it is 1 + 44/990 or 1 + 22/495. This is the fraction in Option 4: 517/495.

18. If 100 d = 712.12121212, then d= 7.12121212 and 17 d is 17 × 7.12121212. If we multiply 17 by 7, we get 119 and hence the product of 17 × 7.12121212 is sure to be greater than 100. Now how would one get 7.121212...? By dividing 712 with 99. Because 1 divided by 99 is 0.010101... and thus 712 × (1/99) =7.12121212... So when I multiply 712/99 by 17, the numerator changes but the denominator remains 99 and the genesis of a recurring decimal lies in the denominator being 9, or 99 or 999 and so on. So 17d is (A) sure to be greater than 100 and (B) shall also be a recurring decimal. Hence Option 4.

19. In the expression (2x – 1)/ log 0.1, the numerator is necessarily negative since the log of 0.1 is –1. If (2x – 1)/ log 0.1 < 0, then (2x – 1)/–1 = 1 – 2x is < 0. If we were to subtract 1 from both sides, we get –2x<–1. If:

    (1) x > 1, then –2x will be lesser then –1.

    (2) x < 1/2, then –2x > –1. For example, if we were to assume x as equal to 1/4.

    (3) x > 1/2, then –2x < –1. For example, if we were to assume x = 3/4.

    Hence both 1 and 3.

    It must be mentioned that when we write log 0.1, we mean that the base of the logarithm is 10; the base 10 is a standard base of logarithm and in the absence of a specific base, one presumes 10 to be the logarithm base.

20. The general expansion of $(a + b)^n$ is $a^n + {}^nC_1a^{(n-1)} \times b^1 + {}^nC_2a^{(n-2)} \times b^2 + {}^nC_3a^{(n-3)} \times b^3$..... and so on till b^n. For $(x + 1)^5$, its expansion will be $x^5 + {}^5C_1x^4 \times 1^1 + {}^5C_2x^3 \times 1^2 + \ldots$ The second term in the expansion of $(x + 1)^5$ will thus be ${}^5C_1x^4 \times 1^1 = 5x^4 = 10^6$ as given. So $5x^4 = 10^6 = 100 \times 10^4$. Hence $x^4 = 20 \times 10^4$. And hence $x = 10 \times 20^{1/4}$. Hence **Option 3**.

21. What is that number which when divided by 15, 35 and 42, will leave no remainder? The LCM of 15, 35, and 42 is 210. Add 6 to 210 and try dividing the result with either of 15, 35, or 42 and you will get a remainder of 6. So 216 in **Option 1**.

22. The square root of a negative number is not meaningful. The zero in the denominator of a fraction is not meaningful because it will render the fraction as infinity. So one cannot afford a negative value for $(4 - x)/(2x - 5)$. And one cannot afford a zero in the denominator. If x is lesser than or = 4 then $(4 - x)$ will be negative or zero and since 2x-5 will be positive if $2x - 5 > 0$ for all values of $x > 5/2$, the expression will be meaningful for values of x where **$5/2 < x \leq 4$**. Hence **Option 1**.

23. Let us see the options. Option 1: -3. Substituting $x = -3$, we get $3x^3 + 1 = 3 \times (-27)+1 = -81 + 1 = -80$ and the modulus of -80 is 80. $2x^2 + 2 = 2 \times 3^2 + 2 = 20$ and hence $80/20 = 4$. So **Option 1.**

24. 0.000224 is $224 \div 1000000$ and the square root of this is roughly $15 \div 1000$. So the square root of 0.000224 is nearly **0.015**.

25. A train travels from a Station X to another Station Y, a distance of 192 km, at an average speed of 80 km/hour. This takes $192 \div 80 = 2.4$ hours which is 2 hours and 24 minutes. If the total time taken for the return journey is 5 hours, 36 minutes, the time taken for the return journey is 3 hours and 12 minutes which is 192 minutes. Thus on the return journey of 192 km, it covers 1 km every minute and hence on the return journey, the average speed of the train is 60 km/hour. Hence Option 2.

26. If $x - y = 5$ and $y/x = 6$, then $y = 6x$ and hence $x - 6x = -5x = 5$. Therefore $x = -1$.
Since $y = 6x$ and $x = -1$, **$y = -6$**.

27. Since we are to find the highest value of one expression among five expressions, and each expression has both p and q, we may assume $p = 4$ and $q = 6$ and see which expression gives the highest value. Since both p and q are positive, pq^2 will invariably be $> p^2q$, and p^2/q and $4\ p^2q/5$. The comparison is then only between 4pq and pq^2. But since we have assumed p as 4, then 4pq is also nothing other than p^2q and it means that **pq^2 has the greatest value**. Hence Option D.

Chapter 42

The Axioms

An axiom is a generally accepted principle or rule that requires no proof. A competitive examination – be it the GRE or the GMAT, or what have you – quite frequently, tests a level of awareness with very tight time constraints. To beat the clock, one would do well to be up-to-date on a wide range of mathematical axioms. Those axioms that one has seen to be of great help in solving thousands of questions in our various books are listed herein below for ready reference:

The sum of positive numbers is always positive.	The sum of negative numbers is always negative.
The product of positive numbers is always positive.	The product of two or even number of negative numbers is always positive.
The product of an odd number of negative numbers is always negative	The square of a positive number is always positive because a square of a positive number is nothing other than a positive number multiplied by the same positive number.
The square of a negative number is always positive because a square of a negative number is nothing other than a negative number multiplied by the same negative number. Thus, being the product of an even number of negative numbers, it is always positive.	The whole is always greater than parts; this is why the sum of a series of numbers is always greater than any of the numbers in that series provided all the numbers in the series are positive. If all the numbers in the series are negative then the sum of such a series is always less than any of the numbers in such a series of all negative numbers. If however some of the numbers in a series are positive and others are negative, then the issue whether the whole is greater than the part or the part of such a series is greater than the whole is wide open and the answer can emerge only from the specifics of the situation.
The sum of two odd numbers (or an even number of odd numbers) is always even.	The sum of any number of even numbers (whether odd or even) is always even.
The product of any number of odd numbers is always odd.	The product of any number of even numbers is always even.
If an even number is a multiplicand in any multiplication where there may be any number of odd number multiplicands, the product of such a multiplication is always even.	If a fraction is equal to its inverse, this is only possible under the following two situations: • When the numerator and denominator of the fraction are equal or • When the numerator and denominator of the fraction are opposite in sign. This is why, if you are told, for example, that the circumference of a circle divided by its area is equal to its area divided by

	its circumference, all that has to be done is to equate the numerator and the denominator and thus $2\pi r = \pi r^2$ and hence r = 2. The radius of such a circle can only be two units.
In a fraction, if both numerator and denominator are positive, then the fraction is invariably positive.	In a fraction if both numerator and denominator are negative, then the fraction is invariably positive.
In a fraction if either the numerator or the denominator is negative, then the fraction is invariably negative.	Natural numbers are those that you can count on your fingers. All positive integers starting with one are natural numbers.
The sum of the squares of two distinct natural numbers can be equal to the square of a third natural number. The least of such natural numbers is 3, 4 and 5 where the squares of 3 and 4 add up to the square of 5. Therefore if there are four distinct natural numbers M, N, P and R and if $M^R+N^R=P^R$, there cannot be a higher value than 2 for R.	The sum of any number of consecutive natural numbers is equal to (the first natural number in that series + the last natural number in that series) × the number of natural numbers in that series ÷2. This is why, the sum of all consecutive numbers from – say, 3 to 23 is = (3+23) × 21÷2 = 13×21= 273. Check this out with any series of your choice.
In a series of numbers if the difference between any term and its immediately preceding term is the same throughout the series, then the series is bound to be in arithmetic progression.	The only situation in which an arithmetic progression can also be a geometric progression is when there is no difference (meaning zero difference) between any term in the series and its immediately preceding term throughout the series; the common ratio (meaning the ratio arrived at by dividing any term in a geometric progression with its immediately preceding term in the geometric progression) of such a progression is always 1.
When some persons are A, B and C years old today and the sum of their ages is A+B+C, they shall be respectively aged (A+N), (B+N), and (C+N) years after N years and thus the sum of their ages will be (A+B+C+3N)	When one person is older than the other, the ratio between their ages is always changing, a certain ratio can be only once throughout their lives. This is why if a father is 45 and his son is 15, the ratio of their ages which is 3:1 is only at that stage of their lives when they are 45 and 15 respectively neither before this nor after this can they have this ratio between their ages again.
The ratio between the age of an older person to the younger will always go on diminishing in value from year to year; if a father were to be 25 when his son was born, the ratio of their ages was infinity (the son's age was zero when he was born); five years later it will be 6: 1 and twenty years later it will be 9:4.	If a certain sum A, grows by a certain percentage to another sum B and then diminishes by the same percentage to a sum C, then C is always less than A. When there is an increase and then a decrease by the same percentage from a given starting level, the increase is on a lower number whereas the decrease is on a higher number and thus the absolute decrease will always be higher than the absolute increase. For example, Try increasing, say, 400 by 20% to 480 and then decreasing 480 by 20%; what you will get is 384, which is less than, 400 that you started with.
If a certain sum A grows by a certain percentage P to another sum B and then diminishes by the same percentage to a sum C, then C is always less than A and the difference between A and C expressed as percentage of A is always equal to $P^2/100$.	If all the factors of a product are positive, their sum is least when all the factors are equal in value. This is why, for example, 16 can be factorised in so many ways, some of which are as follows and yet the sum of the factors is least only when each of the factors is 2 as in (D) in the following: (A) 2×1×8×1

	(B) 4×4×1×1 (C) 4×2×2×1 (D) 2×2×2×2
In any triangle, the side facing the larger angle is longer than the side facing the smaller angle.	In any triangle, the side facing the largest angle is the longest side in that triangle; this is why the hypotenuse is the longest side in a right-angled triangle simply because there cannot be another angle either equal to or more than 90° since the three angles of a triangle add up to 180°.
The longest side of any triangle has to be necessarily less than the sum of the measures of the other two sides; this is why – for example – you can have a triangle with two sides as 4 and 5 units in measure and the third side with any measure less than 9 units and more than 5 units; there cannot be a triangle in which the three sides are 4, 5 and 9 units.	If all three sides of a right-angled triangle are diminished by a uniform percentage P, then the area of the resultant right-angled triangle is equal to $[(100 - P)/100]^2$ times the area of the earlier right-angled triangle. For instance a right-angled triangle with three sides of measure being 6, 8 and 10, will have an area of 1/2 × 6× 8= 24 square units. If the three sides were to be diminished uniformly by 50% then the measures of the sides would be 3, 4 and 5 units and the area of the triangle would then be 1/2 × 3× 4= 6 square units. The reduced area is $[(100 - 50)/100]^2$ = 0.25 times the area of the earlier right-angled triangle.
If all three sides of a right-angled triangle are diminished by a uniform percentage P, the hypotenuse of such a triangle will always be parallel to the earlier hypotenuse simply because the ratio of the adjacent and opposite sides to the hypotenuse remains the same whether before or after diminishing. Thus the measure of the angle between the hypotenuse and the other two sides continues to be the same regardless of the change in measures of the three sides (provided the sides changed by the same percentage.)	The square of a number greater than 1 is always greater than the number itself and so are the higher powers of that number; this is why $(1.1)^2$ or $(1.1)^3$ is always greater than 1.1.
The square of a positive number, less than 1, is always less than the number itself and so are the higher powers of that number; this is why $(0.9)^2$ or $(0.9)^3$ is always less than 0.9.	The square of a negative number is always greater than the number itself and so are the higher even powers of that number; this is why $(-2)^2$ or $(-2)^4$ or $(-2)^6$ is always greater than –2.
The cube of a negative number is always less than the number itself and so are the higher odd powers of that number; this is why $(-2)^3$ or $(-2)^6$ or $(-2)^9$ is always less than -2.	There are only two numbers that have the same value even when raised to any powers- whether odd or even; zero whether raised to the power of, say, 2 or 2001 is zero and 1 whether raised to the power of, say, 3 or 3004 is always 1.
Of the two positive fractions, the fraction whose denominator is a higher multiple of its numerator is always less in value than the other fraction; this is why 1/3 is less than 2/5 because in the case of 1/3 the denominator is 3 times the numerator whereas in 2/5 the denominator is 2.5 times the numerator	Two straight lines can be parallel only if they have identical gradients

Two straight lines can be perpendicular only if the product of their gradients is –1.	The product of two numbers A and B that add up to a third number C is highest when A and B are equal. To illustrate, if you were to look at 8 as 4+4, then the product of 4 and 4 is 16. If you were to look at 8 as 5+3, the product of 5 and 3 is 15 which is less than 16. Try any combination of numbers (other than 4 and 4) that add up to 8 and you will see that the product of that combination of numbers is invariably less than 16. This is simple to understand if you could appreciate the following observation: If you take 4 as X, then the product of 4 and 4 is the square of X. If you were to take some numbers other than 4, then these other numbers would essentially be (4+ something) and (4 – the same thing) since (4+ something) and (4 – the same thing) have to add up to 8. The product of (4+ something) and (4 – the same thing) will be (16 – the square of something) that will be invariably less than 16.

Chapter 43

What is Data Interpretation?

Mostly, it is the inadequate knowledge of the event that foxes the person taking a competitive examination.

Suppose you are given the height in cm of a number of boys in a class and are asked to state whose height, if it were converted into inches, would be the greatest among the boys in class, what is required is only a preliminary glance at the figures and – presto! comes the answer. This is because you are asked a relative position. If a fellow is tallest in his class then he is tallest whether you refer to his height in cm or inches or yards and so on. The toil of converting height in cm into inches is to be bypassed even though the examiner wants to know who is the tallest in terms of inches. This is because we need not do anything that is patently unnecessary. We have neither the time nor the need. It is a test of **our** logic and not the logic of the examiner.

Now suppose you are asked what is the average height of the class, then you are asked an absolute position and therefore have no choice but to add the heights and then divide it by the number of boys in the class. There is no other way of finding the average height of the boys in the class.

So many times has one seen questions where one is given, say, the sales of a company over a number of years and is asked to state which among the options would be the year in which one would see the highest percentage growth in sales as compared to the previous year.

It is important to look at the question. Are you asked to state an absolute position or a relative position? The chap setting the question wants you to state in **which year** was the highest percentage growth and **not the** highest **percentage** itself. This means that if you *actually* work out the *percentage* growth from year to year in order to be able to state in which year was the percentage the highest, the writing on the wall is clear: you are inordinately fond of toiling and therefore at least toil you shall get, if not result.

Secondly, even if the examiner had asked you, let us suppose, to state which among the four given options is the highest percentage growth of sales year to year, even then one can safely ignore working out percentages. You have four options. Each of the options has (I) a numerator, which is the increase in sales from sales figure of previous year and (II) a denominator, which is the sales figure of previous year.

What are we to decide really? We have to decide which fraction among the four given fractions has the highest value and then see which option fits the bill. This is because of the reason that the essential difference between (I) a fraction as it is and then (II) the same fraction expressed in percentage terms, is only that the fraction in percentage terms has a standardised denominator of one hundred instead of the existing denominator in (I). In order to ensure that there is no change whatsoever in the value of a fraction during the course of such standardisation, the numerator is aligned according to the standard denominator so that the value of the fraction remains unaltered.

Thus if the fraction were 1 divided by 2 (meaning 1/2), then in order to express this in percentage terms, one would be required to express the value of this fraction with the standard denominator of 100. This means having to multiply the denominator with 50 so as to have 100 in the denominator. Since one is multiplying the denominator with 50 one should also multiply the numerator with 50 so that the value of the fraction remains unchanged. This is why 1/2 is 50/100 or 50%.

So when you are comparing four fractions – say 5/11, 9/13, 5/9 and 7/11 – if you are able to compare these fractions and tell which is the largest, is there any need to work out percentage value of these four fractions before you decide which is the highest? Do you have any idea about how much effort will that take? And how much time? And all this when the central idea is to **interpret data** and not **ruminate** on the **data**.

If the idea was to calculate and state the precise findings, then the examiners would have allowed you to bring in graph paper, rulers, calculators and then they would have not given you any options at all! The examination would not have been objective type at all. If your calculations have been away from a 1% accuracy band, you would get zero and thereafter, possibly, the imposition of holding your earlobes and doing thirty sit-ups.

Again, when you are comparing four fractions – say 5/11, 9/13, 5/9 and 7/11 – you must know that fundamentally the fraction whose denominator is the least multiple of its numerator is the highest in value. If the denominators are expressed as a multiple of the numerators then you are looking at these fractions in a headstand and these fractions would then seem to you as 11/5, 13/9, 9/5 and 11/7. Of these, 11/5 is over 2 and 9/5 is close to 2. 13/9 and 11/7 are far lower than 2 and hence if one were to calculate the value of 13/9 and 11/7 only up to one decimal, one would see that 13/9 is 1.4 and 11/7 is 1.5 till the first decimal. The need to calculate up to the second decimal would arise only if the value up to the first decimal is the same, not otherwise.

Thus among the four fractions 5/11, 9/13, 5/9 and 7/11, 13/9 is the case where the denominator is the smallest multiple of the numerator and thus 9/13 is the highest fraction among these four and will continue to remain the highest fraction among the four fractions even if the four were expressed as percentages. At this stage itself, it is recommended that you try working out the percentage values of these four fractions with your calculator and verify the statement we have made. This is because: (A) seeing is believing and (B) believing will help you assimilate the underlying principle and (C) at the main examination there will be no access to calculators and hence whatever methodologies that we have to learn to be able to bypass the use of calculators, we must learn at this stage itself.

Now if you are asked to state the year of the highest growth in sales compared to the previous year, you need not work out percentages at all. If you are asked to tell the highest percentage sales growth among the given options, all you need is, to convert 9/13 as a percentage. You can do this by multiplying both numerator and denominator by 100/13 so that the denominator becomes 100 and the numerator becomes 900/13. If one remembers one's tables of 13, then 13 sevens are 91 and this means 900/13 would be 69 percent approximately and then one should see which option fits. The need to go to the decimals would arise only if the options are close. This is because the idea is to *interpret* data, not to *ruminate on* it.

We have so far learnt that even if the examiner – at the objective-type competitive examination, of course – tells you to compare and tell what the standing of a fraction is among the other fractions expressed in percentage terms, one can safely avoid calculating the percentage value of the different fractions.

Now let us learn how to safely avoid some more strenuous effort.

Imagine that a company has registered sales as under in the years given there against.

Year	Sales ($s in millions)
1995	11
1996	16
1997	25
1998	40
1999	67

Suppose you are asked to state in which year was the *increase* in sales as percentage of the previous year sales the highest. The question is, is it necessary to find out the incremental sales at all? If the calculation of incremental sales could be avoided, this would save a whole lot of toil since in finding out the incremental sales in four years, one has to subtract sales of the previous year from the sales of the current year four times (if there are four options and five times if there are five options). Is there a safe way to avoid this toil and yet reach a correct conclusion? If yes, what is the logical reason behind a shortcut?

There is a real shortcut. Imagine that you are comparing the sales in the illustration at hand and trying to find out in which year is the incremental sales the highest as a percentage of previous year's sales. You find out the incremental sales just because the examiner has specifically asked you to do so (and if you carry out every instruction of his, he may be motivated to order you to leap out of ten floors; the test is of **your logic, not his**) in the following manner:

Year	Sales ($s in millions)	Current Year Sales C	Previous Year Sales P	Incremental Sales I = C – P
1995	11			
1996	16	16	11	5
1997	25	25	16	9
1998	40	40	25	15
1999	67	67	40	27

You have meticulously calculated the difference between the sales in a year and the sales in its immediately preceding year and have prepared the background for the kill: now you are to find out as to which is the highest growth. The question is: Is all this labour necessary? See whether you could have simply compared a year's sales with the immediately preceding year's sales and reached thé correct answer. We shall see what is the highest growth in sales over previous year (1) when we take into consideration the incremental sales over previous year sales and (2) when we directly compare the current year sales with the previous year sales. If we do get the same answer in each case, we shall also see the logical reason why you are getting the same answer so that the matter goes home once and for all.

Year	Sales $s in millions	Current Year Sales C	Previous Year Sales P	Current Year Sales/Previous Year Sales C/P= (1000/P)%=	Incremental Sales I = C – P	Incremental sales/Previous year sales (C–P)/P= 100 (C–P)/P%
1995	11					
1996	16	16	11	16/11= 145%	5	5/11=45%
1997	25	25	16	25/16=156%	9	9/16=56%
1998	40	40	25	40/25 or 8/5=160%	15	15/25 or 3/5=60%
1999	67	67	40	67/40=167.5%	27	27/40=67.5%

Although it is not necessary to calculate percentages at all, I have done it here, only to drive home the concept that whether you compare an year's sales with the sales of the previous year *directly* or whether you calculate the incremental sale and then do this comparison, you get the same result.

One finds that in the year 1999, the growth of sales over previous year was the highest and this has been thrown up in both the cases:

(I) When we examined the incremental sales as a percentage of previous year sales and then

(II) The current year sales as a percentage of previous year sales. The only difference is that in case of current year sales as a percentage of previous year sales, this percentage is exactly 100% more than the percentage value of incremental sales as a percentage of previous year sales. This 100% is 1, which is what (previous year sales)/(previous year sales) would give you.

Now that we have seen **why** the answers from both routes are the same and that ascertaining percentage growth by placing current year sales in the numerator and previous year sales in the denominator saves a whole lot of labour, it seems that the shorter route should invariably be employed, provided the logic behind the shorter route is explained to your satisfaction.

Here is that logic. Current year sales are as such = (previous year sales) + (increase in sales from previous year). So when you are directly comparing sales, for example, in 1996 over 1995 and sales in 1999 over the sales figure in 1998, what you are effectively comparing is as under:

On the right hand side: [Sales in 1995 + Increase in sales in 1996 over 1995]/(Sales in 1995) with on the left hand side: [Sales in 1998+Increase in sales in 1999 over 1998]/(Sales in 1998). In both cases what you will get is as under:

On the right hand side: (Sales in 1995) /(Sales in 1995) + [Increase in sales in 1996 over 1995]/(Sales in 1995) = 1 +[Increase in sales in 1996 over 1995]/(Sales in 1995)

On the left hand side: (Sales in 1998)/ (Sales in 1998) + [Increase in sales in 1999 over 1998]/(Sales in 1998) = 1 + [Increase in sales in 1999 over 1998]/(Sales in 1998)

So when you are comparing the sales, for example, in 1996 over 1995 and sales in 1999 over the sales figure in 1998, what you are effectively comparing is as under:

1 +[Increase in sales in 1996 over 1995]/(Sales in 1995) with 1 + [Increase in sales in 1999 over 1998]/(Sales in 1998) and since 1 is common to both right and left hand sides, it can be safely crossed out on both sides. Then what you are left with is the comparison between:

[Increase in sales in 1996 over 1995]/(Sales in 1995) with [Increase in sales in 1999 over 1998]/(Sales in 1998) and this is what the examiner has asked you to do in any case, although it is a different matter that you have not worked out the actual percentage increase each time, notwithstanding his instructions. Now having realised that it is just logical to directly compare a year's sales with the immediately previous year sales to be able to tell, in which year was the incremental sales, as a percentage of the previous year sales, the highest (or even lowest for that matter), you can save yourself a whole lot of time and effort.

Please understand that the illustration that we have taken has, for example, $11 million in the year 1995. Real life is not so simple. The examination paper will mention $11.231 million. In other cases it will mention $16.338 million. Imagine what subtracting 11.231 million from 16.338 million and then dividing whatever remainder by 11.231 million would mean in terms of effort and – more important - time! Imagine how much simpler life would be if one were to merely divide 16 by 11 by rounding off 16.338 and 11.231 to the nearest integer. Those who would like to see before believing, may try dividing 16.338 with 11.231 first and then 16 with 11 with their calculators and see whether the earth trembles with the significance of the difference in the results obtained by either method. There will not be any significant difference at all. And let me tell you why this method will do admirably. This is because Data Interpretation is not about hair-splitting.

Let us see some more instances of commonly prevailing false notions about the event that Data Interpretation is and learn how to minimise effort and yet reach the correct answer.

Let us imagine that a company named ABC Ltd, which manufactures a range of products of widely differing prices, has registered total sales of $576 million and the company has identified the principal buyers by value and the top buyers in terms of quantity of goods sold to them.

Let us imagine that the information is represented as per hereunder:

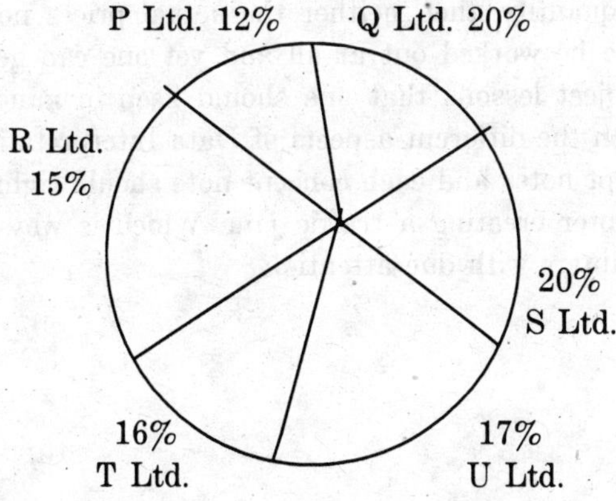

Chart 1

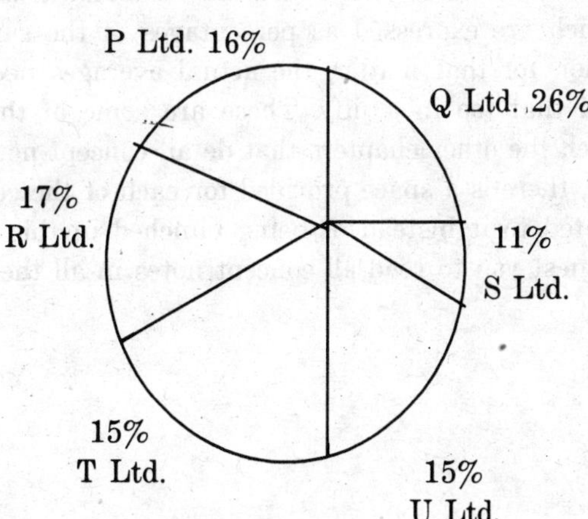

Chart 2

Chart 1 shows the distribution by value of top 6 buyers of the products of ABC Ltd. Chart 2 shows the distribution by quantity of top 6 buyers of ABC Ltd. The total sales are $576 million. The total quantity is 3.321 million tonnes.

Now the question! The buyer who has paid the highest average price, is:

Option (1) U Ltd. Option (2) S Ltd. Option (3) T Ltd. Option (4) Q Ltd.

What would you do? Would you calculate the average prices for all four options to find out which is the highest? What would the finding of the average price in the case of U ltd., for example, involve?

Step 1: Finding out what is 17% of $576 million

Step 2: Finding out what is 15% of 3.321 million tonnes

Step 3: Dividing (1) 17% of $576 million by (2) 15% of 3.321 million tonnes

So if one were to find out the average price in the case of these four options, then it would mean exactly 12 steps and by the time you are through, one may have an awful headache.

So is there a short cut? If yes, what is it? And what is the logic behind the shortcut?

There is a short cut. This short cut is a matter of **sheer logic**. Let us take the case of U Ltd. and S Ltd. only. What are you comparing really?

You are trying to compare (A) (17% of $576 million)/ (15% of 3.321 million tonnes) with (B) (20% of $576 million)/ (11% of 3.321 million tonnes).

So if you were to take 1% of $576 million as X and 1% of 3.321 million tonnes as Y, what you are really comparing is 17X/15Y with 20X/11Y. Is it necessary to calculate any average price? 20X/11Y is clearly higher than 17X/15Y no matter what the value of X and Y since both X and Y are positive.

With this methodology, the following conclusions will emerge:

- In the case of Option (3): T Ltd., the fraction is then 16/15 and since it is less than 17/15 seen in the case of Option (1), Option (3) need not be bothered about at all
- In the case of Option (4): Q Ltd., the fraction is then 20/26 which is less than 1 and since all other options throw up fractions of value greater than 1, Option (4) needs to be caught by its ear and thrown into the waster paper basket
- **Option** (2) is making faces at you from the paper in order to show you that it is the correct option

The fundamental lesson here is that if one has to make a comparative assessment of the average prices of two things, both of which are expressed as percentages of the same quantity, then neither the actual prices nor the actual quantities nor, for that matter, the actual averages need to be worked out at all and yet one can get the correct answer and that too in a jiffy. These are some of the object lessons that one should keep in mind and accordingly approach the other chapters that detail concept notes on the different aspects of Data Interpretation in this book. After all, there is a space provided for each of the concept notes and each concept note should rightly be in the space allocated to it instead of being bunched in this chapter creating a traffic jam. Which is why, dear reader, I would request you to read all concept notes in all the chapters with due attention.

Chapter 44

Reading Bar Charts

What is a chart? Let us see a simple chart and see what it can tell us. Imagine a boy who decides to make and sell sandwiches for a week and donate the earnings to the neighbouring leprosy hospital. He then learns that on six days of the week starting from Monday till Saturday, he earned $25, $25, $35, $50, $35, and $30 respectively. In order to see on what day he got how much, he sets out the information in the following format.

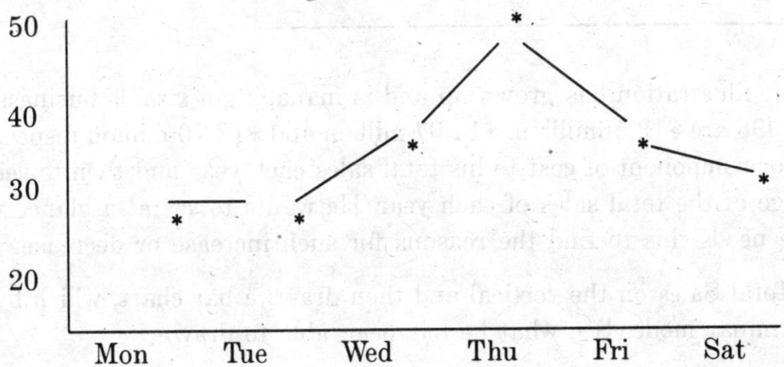

This is a point chart, where each point tells him how much he made on a given day. Linking the points tells him whether his earnings have been climbing or dropping or remaining flat. A situation in which his sales have remained flat is represented in the above graph by a flat horizontal line between points representing equal earnings as may be seen in the case of Monday to Tuesday. A situation in which his earnings have grown is indicated by a rise in the slope of the line linking the points connecting two earnings levels where the end level is higher than the base level as may be seen in the case of Tuesday to Wednesday. A steep rise in earnings is seen in the case of Wednesday to Thursday and then the earnings fall sharply between Thursday and Friday and this fall is a lot less steep from Friday to Saturday.

Thus, if you are asked between which days was the earning unchanged, you do not have to actually calculate anything. You have to only read the chart. You might even be able to hear the chart whispering in your ear that the earnings were flat between Monday and Tuesday. Once you learn how to read the charts, then all you have to do is to wink at the chart in your question paper and the chart will sing the correct answer in your ear.

If the lad in the illustration (remember the lad who decided to donate earnings from sandwiches to the leprosy hospital?) puts a bar rising from each day till the point where the earnings are shown by points, he can have a bar chart.

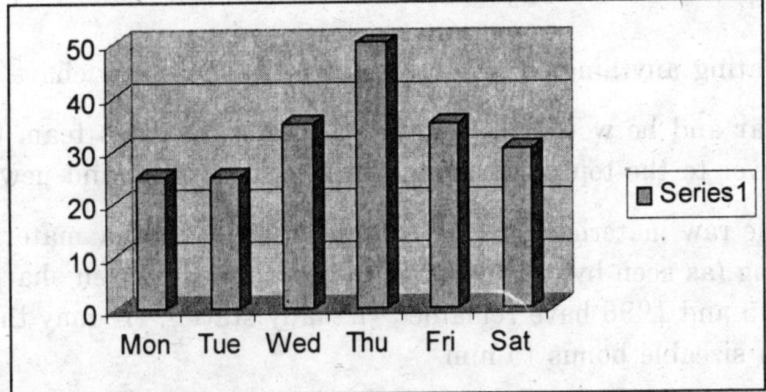

Let us then imagine that the young fellow were to switch to making pies and to learn that the following are the components of cost of making $100 worth of pies: Flour – $20, Butter – $25, Cream – $10, Jam – $15, Sugar – $10, and Fuel – $20. He then wants to represent this information pictorially. He can do so in the form of a pie chart to begin with. This would suit him admirably since he is making pies.

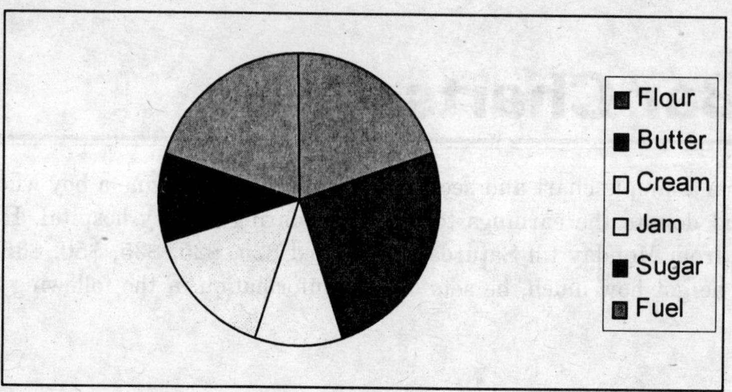

Now let us imagine that the young fellow in our illustration has grown up and is managing a sizable business. His company's sales for the years 1994, 1995 and 1996 are $12.56million, $14.07 million and $16.70 million respectively. He wishes to find the contribution of each major component of cost to his total sales each year and then to see how much is the profit for each year as a percentage of the total sales of each year. He wants to see at a glance which component has risen and which has fallen. He needs this to find the reasons for such increase or decrease.

He puts Years on the horizontal axis and the Total Sales on the vertical and then draws a bar chart, which by now would seem to us as a sort of pie chart in columnar mode. See what he has been able to draw:

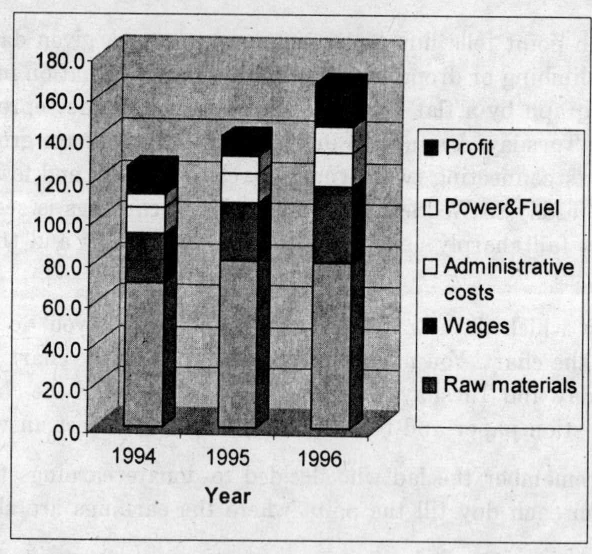

He can now see – without calculating anything, of course – from the above bar chart that:

- Sales have risen each year and he would then consider taking his sales team to Switzerland for a skiing holiday and there hand over to the top performers, the keys to their brand new cars
- He can also see that while raw material costs have been on the rise, raw material as a component of sales value has been diminishing (as seen by the fact that while sales have risen sharply from 1995 to 1996, the raw material costs in 1995 and 1996 have remained virtually static). He may then like to call his Purchase Manager and announce a sizeable bonus to him

When you can see and figure out the information that you want from the graphical representation of data (whether it is in pie chart or bar chart form or whatever other mode of representation), you are **interpreting** data. In some isolated instances you might need to do a small amount of figure work.

We shall now see how to **interpret** data in bar charts from the illustrations hereunder. These illustrations are drawn from the very best questions that have appeared in the past papers of premier business school entrance tests and should serve as the best training grounds for sharpening our data interpretation skills.

Illustration 1

DIRECTIONS *for questions 1 to 4: Answer these questions based on the data presented in the figure below:*

FEI for a country in a year is the ratio (expressed as a percentage) of its foreign equity inflows to its GDP. The following figure displays the FEIs for select Asian countries for the years 1997 and 1998.

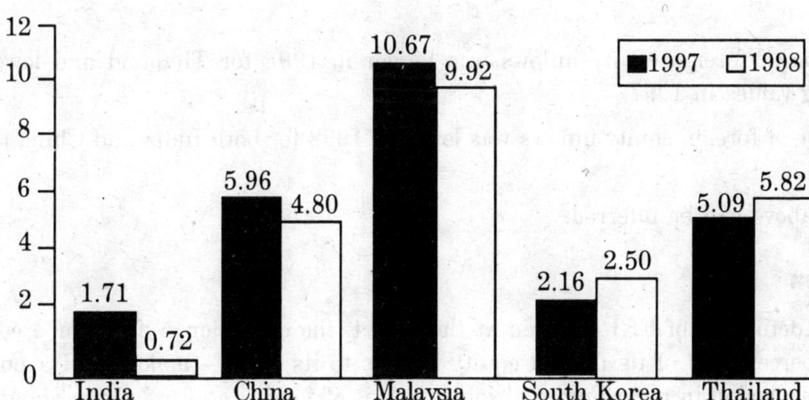

Question 1

The country with the largest change in FEI in 1998 relative to its FEI in 1997, is:

1. India 2. China 3. Malaysia 4. Thailand

Detailed explanation

If you were to link the right hand top corner of the bar representing the FEI of India for 1997 with the right hand top corner of the bar representing the FEI of India for 1998, and do this for all the three other countries namely China, Malaysia, and Thailand – we have done this in the case of India and China in the figures given hereunder to show you what we mean - you will find that the gradient of the line emerging in the case of India is the steepest. Thus Option 1: India.

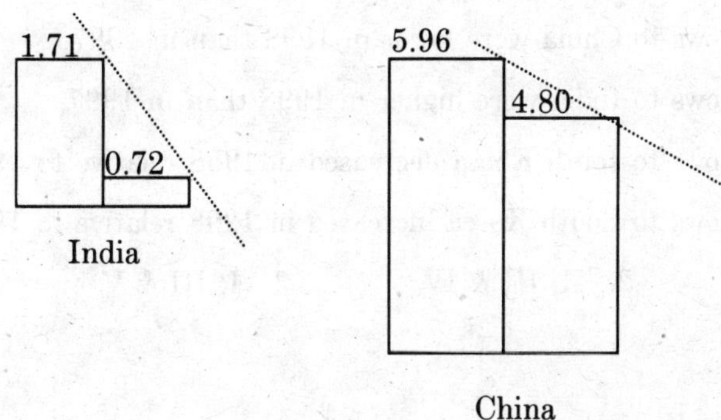

In case it is not easily discernible from the line drawn as suggested as to which is the biggest gradient, it is safer to produce the line on both sides with your pencil. This will leave no room for doubt at all.

As we have seen in an earlier illustration, when asked to state a relative position such as the largest change in FEI in 1998 relative to FEI in 1997, we would do well to compare the ratio (FEI in 1998)/ (FEI in 1997) for the four countries in the options as follows: India 1.71/0.72, China 5.96/4.80, Malaysia 10.67/9.92, Thailand 5.09/5.82. Whereas in the case of Thailand not only there is no increase but there is a drop. In the case of the first three fractions 1.71/0.72, 5.96/4.80 and 10.67/9.92 the fraction in case of India has the highest value since the numerator is more than twice the denominator whereas in the other two cases it is nowhere near twice the denominator. The question of any detailed working does not arise here.

Question 2

Based on the data provided, it can be concluded that:

1. Absolute value of foreign equity inflows in 1998 was higher than that in 1997 for both Thailand and South Korea.
2. Absolute value of foreign equity inflows was higher in 1998 for Thailand and lower for China than the corresponding values in 1997.
3. Absolute value of foreign equity inflows was lower in 1998 for both India and China than the corresponding values in 1997.
4. None of the above can be inferred.

Detailed explanation

If you were to see the definition of FEI as given at the outset, the definition - FEI for a country in a year is the ratio (expressed as a percentage) of its foreign equity inflows to its GDP – makes FEI a purely relative term. We are asked to make a conclusion in regarding to absolute values of foreign equity inflows about various countries but we have no idea about the GDP of any nation. **Till we have the figures of GDP, we can only give comparative figures but not absolute figures of FEI.**

Suppose I were to tell you that I weigh four times as much as my son, can you ever tell my weight unless you know my son's? Can you ever tell my son's weight unless you know mine? Four times someone's weight is an expression of relationship between two unknowns and unless one of the unknowns becomes known, the absolute value of the other can never be found out. So **Option 4.**

Question 3

It is known that China's GDP in 1998 was 7% higher than its value in 1997, while India's GDP grew by 2% during the same period. The GDP of South Korea, on the other hand, fell by 5%. Which of the following statements is/are true?

I. Foreign equity inflows to China were higher in 1998 than in 1997.

II. Foreign equity inflows to China were lower in 1998 than in 1997.

III. Foreign equity inflows to India were higher in 1998 than in 1997.

IV. Foreign equity inflows to south Korea decreased in 1998 relative to 1997.

V. Foreign equity inflows to South Korea increased in 1998 relative to 1997.

1. I, III & IV 2. II, III & IV 3. I, III & V 4. II & V

Detailed explanation

Let us assume that China's GDP was 100 units in 1997. It then grew to 107 units in 1998. Then since FEI of China was 5.96 in 1997, the absolute Foreign Equity Inflows to China would be 5.96 units in 1997 (since we have assumed China's GDP to be 100 units in 1997) and the absolute Foreign Equity Inflows to China in 1998 would be 4.80% of 107, which is around 5 (but yet way below 5.96 in 1997). So Statement II is true. With this our options are down to only 2 and 4. If we check statement III and find it to be true, then Option 2 would be correct and if Statement III is wrong, then Option 4 is correct.

Let us check if foreign equity inflows to India were higher in 1998 than in 1997 as per Statement III. Let us assume that India's GDP was 100 units in 1997. It then grew to 102 units in 1998. Then since FEI of India was 1.71 in 1997, the absolute Foreign Equity Inflows to India would be 1.71 units in 1997 (since we have assumed India's GDP to be 100 units in 1997) and the absolute Foreign Equity Inflows to India in 1998 would be 0.72% of 102, which is jolly nearly 0.72 itself (but yet way below 1.71 in 1997). So Statement III is not true. With this we are left with **Option 4**, which is to be marked correct.

Question 4

China's foreign equity inflows in 1998 were 10 times that into India. It can be concluded that:

1. China's GDP in 1998 was 40% higher than that of India.
2. China's GDP in 1998 was 70% higher than that of India.
3. China's GDP in 1998 was 50% higher than that of India.
4. No inference can be drawn about relative magnitudes of China's and India's GDPs.

Detailed explanation

Suppose India's GDP in 1998 was 100 potatoes and that of China was 100 tomatoes. Thus India's foreign equity inflows in 1998 were 0.72 potatoes and that of China was 4.80 tomatoes. Since China's foreign equity inflows in 1998 were 10 times that into India, it means that 4.80 tomatoes is equal to 7.2 potatoes and thus 48 tomatoes equals 72 potatoes and thus 1 tomato equals 1.5 potatoes. This means that China's GDP was 1.5 times that of India in 1998 and hence Statement III is true. Hence **Option 3**. For those who are not comfortable with 100 potatoes and 100 tomatoes as measures of GDP, they may try 100X and 100Y, although the answer will be no different. The central idea is to interpret data and not knead the data.

Illustration 2

DIRECTIONS *for questions 1 to 6: Answer these questions based on the data given below:*

The figures below present annual growth rate, expressed as the % change relative to the previous year, in four sectors of the economy of the Republic of Reposia during the 9-year period from 1990 to 1998. Assume that the index of production for each of the four sectors, is set at 100 in 1989. Further, the four sectors: manufacturing, mining and quarrying, electricity, and chemicals, constituted 20%, 15%, 10% and 15% respectively of total industrial production in 1989.

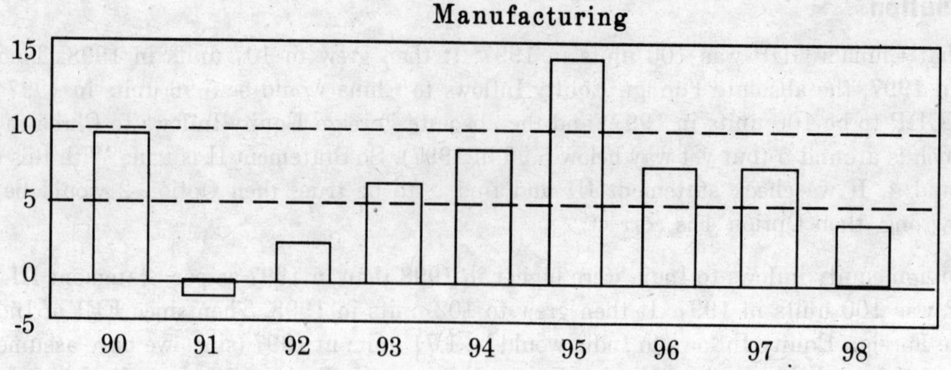
Manufacturing
15
10
5
0
-5
90
91
92
93
94
95
96
97
98

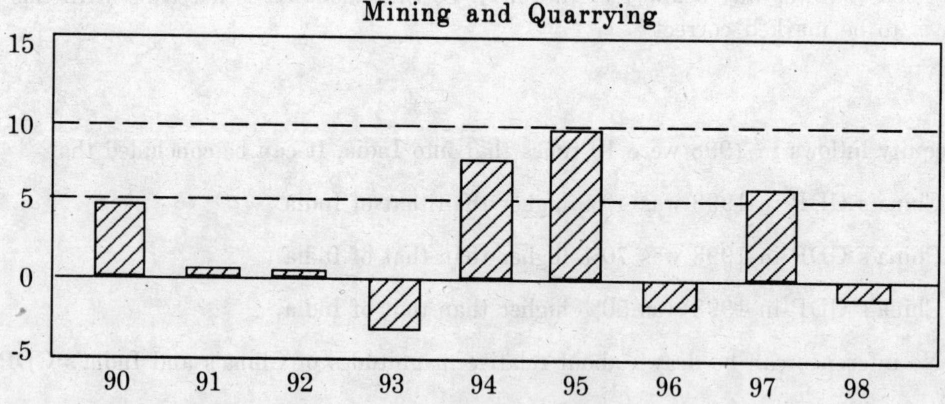
Mining and Quarrying
15
10
5
0
-5
90
91
92
93
94
95
96
97
98

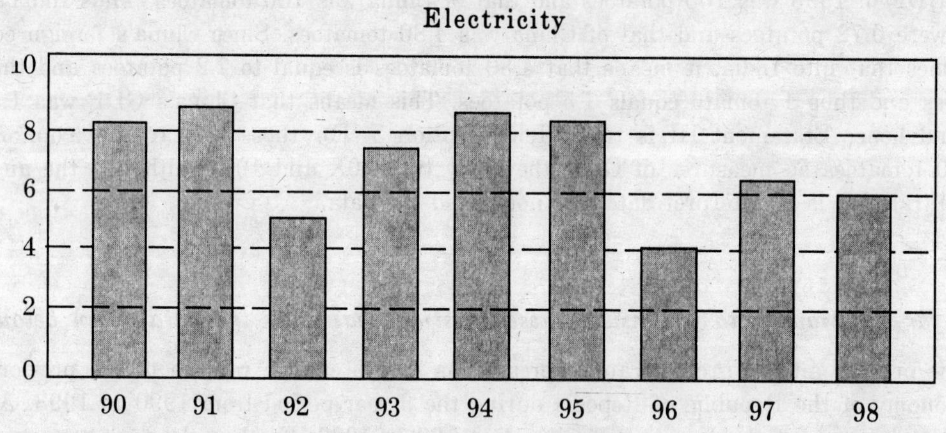
Electricity
10
8
6
4
2
0
90
91
92
93
94
95
96
97
98

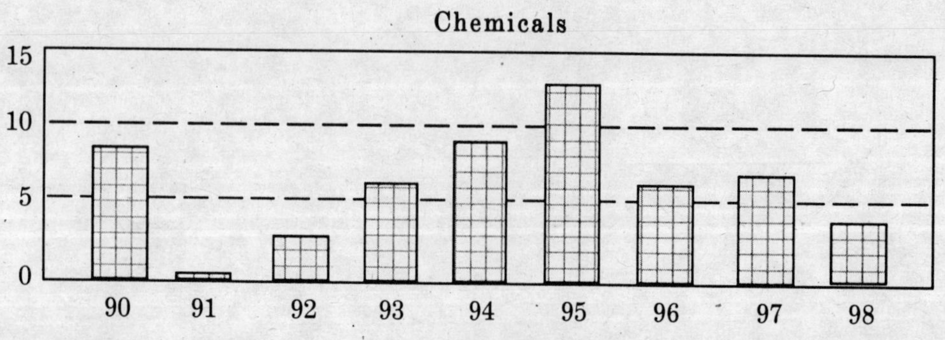
Chemicals
15
10
5
0
90
91
92
93
94
95
96
97
98

Question 1

Which is the sector with the highest growth during the period between 1989 and 1998?

1. Manufacturing
2. Mining and quarrying
3. Electricity
4. Chemicals

Detailed explanation

The different sectors occupy different weights in the economy. But in finding out which sector grew most, it is not necessary to involve their weights in the economy in the calculations.

Let us imagine that you are making vegetable curry, which has the following ingredients: potatoes, onions, cauliflower and cottage cheese. If the prices of cauliflower grew by 10% ,and that of cottage cheese grew by 25%, and the prices of the other ingredients remained unchanged, you can say that the price of cottage cheese grew the most among the four ingredients. This is independent of whether you use 10 gms of cottage cheese or 10 kilograms of cottage cheese for making the curry. If you have to find the impact of the changes in the price of each of the constituents on the cost of the curry, only then do you worry about the curry.

If you were to see the four bar charts, you will see the following:

- The bar charts for manufacturing, quarrying and chemicals have higher percentage growth rates on their y-axis than in the case of the chart of electricity. Thus the previous three have to be compared inter-se first and then the winner of these three is to be compared with the chart of electricity

- The bar charts in case of manufacturing and chemicals are virtually identical, except that in the case of manufacturing there is a small negative growth rate in 1991 whereas in the case of chemicals there is a small positive growth rate in 1991. This means that the overall growth rate for chemicals is, may be higher than in the case of manufacturing. But let us add the year-wise lengths of the bars (starting from 1990 to 1998) in the case of both and see which is higher:

  Manufacturing: 9 –1 + 2 + 6 + 8 + 14 + 7 + 7 + 4 = 56

  Chemicals: 8 + 1 + 3 + 6 + 8 + 13 + 5 + 6 + 4 = 54

  Now it seems manufacturing is higher of the two

- If we are to compare chemicals with electricity to decide as to which is the highest growth rate, imagine that each of the bars is a bar of chocolate. Even if you mentally add the lengths (and, remember, the y-axis tells you how long is the chocolate bar), you will find that the total length of the bars in the case of electricity (9 + 9 + 5 + 7 + 9 + 9 + 4 + 6 + 6 = 64) is greater than that in case of manufacturing. Thus electricity has the highest growth rate and hence Option 3.

Question 2

The overall growth rate in 1991 of the four sectors together is approximately:

1. 10%
2. 1%
3. 2.5%
4. 1.5%

Detailed explanation

What is required, is an approximation of the growth rate in the four sectors together and not in the overall industrial production. So imagine that you are making vegetable curry once again with potatoes, onions, cauliflower and cottage cheese. Now imagine that the prices of these four commodities prior to and after increase were as under:

The commodity and its percentage contribution in the curry if you were to make one	Price per Kg before increase $	Rate of increase	Price per Kg after increase $
Potatoes (10%)	10	20%	12.00
Onions (20%)	20	5%	21.00
Cauliflower (15%)	20	20%	24.00
Cottage Cheese (10%)	100	5%	105.00
Total Price for 4 Kg.	150	8% overall	162.00

What we can see from this example close to everyday life is the fact that the overall increase in the prices of the four commodities has nothing to do with the cost of the curry. The overall impact of the growth in prices of these four commodities on the price of the curry has to be reckoned only when you make the curry. The growth in price of the commodity is independent of how much of the particular commodity you use for making the curry. Remember that it is not the farmer who makes the curry neither does he worry about your curry. Even the greengrocer does not sell you potatoes, for example, with the covenant that they shall be used for nothing other than curry. Once he sells them to you, he does not care even if you feed the potatoes to your pet pigs.

We shall, therefore see how much would each sector grow if we were to assume a base level of 100 units in each sector as at the beginning of 1990.

- Manufacturing: Let us take the base in end-1989 as 100 units: In 1990 it increased by 9% to 109, then decreased by 1% to 108 in 1991. So manufacturing grew from 100 units (assumed base) to 108 units in 1991.
- Mining: Let us take the base in end-1989 as 100 units: In 1990 it increased by 4% to 104, then increased 1% to 105 in 1991. So mining grew from 100 units (assumed base) to 105 units in 1991.
- Electricity: Let us take the base in end-1989 as 100 units: In 1990 it increased 9% to 109, then increased 9% by 10 to 119 in 1991. So electricity grew from 100 units (assumed base) to 119 units in 1991.
- Chemicals: Let us take the base in end-1989 as 100 units: In 1990 it increased 9% to 109, then increased 1% by 1 to 110 in 1991. So chemicals grew from 100 units (assumed base) to 110 units in 1991.

The base level in 1990 was 109+104+109+109 = 431 units and increased to 108+105+119+110=442 units in 1991. This represents an increase of 11 units over a total base level of 431 units and this means an overall increase of less than 2.5% (2.5% is 1/40 and 1/40 of 400 is 10 and thus 1/40 of 431 is nearly 11) and thus nearest to 2.5% at Option 3.

Question 3

When was the highest level of production in the manufacturing sector achieved during the nine-year period 1990–1998?

1. 1998 2. 1995 3. 1990 4. Cannot be determined

Detailed explanation

Logically, the highest level of production, in any sector, can be only after the highest growth rate is recorded and provided there has been no negative growth after the highest growth rate was recorded. We find that in the case of manufacturing, the highest growth rate was in 1995 and thereafter till 1998 (when the field of the data given to us ends) there has only been net growth. Suppose you had a monthly pocket allowance of $100 the year before and when your father raised it by 80% last year, it became $180 per month. This year your brother has further raised it by 5%. You will see that the highest allowance you have ever had is this year although your brother raised the allowance by a much smaller percentage than what your father did. There was a net growth throughout. This is the reason why the current year's allowance is the highest. The matter is as simple as that. Logically therefore the highest production level in manufacturing should be in 1998. Hence **Option 1**.

Question 4

When was the lowest level of production of the mining and quarrying sector hit during the nine-year period 1990–1998?

1. 1996   2. 1993   3. 1990   4. Cannot be determined

Detailed explanation

There are three options to be really considered : 1996, 1993, 1990. If we assume that the level of production was 100 units in end-1989, then in 1990 it is 104 (since the base is 100 units and the growth rate is 4% in 1991 as can be seen from the bar chart) and in 1991 it is up by 1% and so can be taken as 105 and then in 1992, it is up by another 1% and so it can be taken as 106 for end-1992 and then in 1993 it has dropped by 4% so it is down by nearly 4 and so as at end 1993 the level of production can be taken as 102 units if we assume the base level of production as 100 units. Thereafter there is a sizable increase in 1994 (8%) and 1995 (9%) and a nominal decrease in 1996 thus 1996 production level cannot be less than 1993 level.

Thus we have found that the lowest level of production was in 1993 and hence **Option 3**.

We could arrive at the year of the lowest level of production since we were given the relative growth rates of each year till 1998. But we shall not be able to state the absolute value of the lowest production (as we do not have the absolute value of the base figure), however, we can tell when the production was at its lowest level, since that is a matter of relative values and not absolute values. So Option 4 is out of question.

Question 5

The percentage increase of production in the four sectors, namely, manufacturing, mining and quarrying, electricity and chemicals, taken together, in 1994, relative to 1989, is approximately:

1. 25   2. 20   3. 50   4. 40

Detailed explanation

We shall see how much has each sector grown if we were to assume a base level of 100 units in each sector as at the beginning of 1990.

Manufacturing: Let us take the base in end-1989 as 100 units: In 1990 it increased by 9% to 109, then decreased by 1% to 108 in 1991, then increased by 2% to 110 in 1992, then it increased by 6% (i.e. 7 units to 117 in 1993 and then increased by 8% i.e. 10 units to 127 in 1994. So manufacturing grew from 100 units (assumed base) to 127 units in 1994.

Mining: Let us take the base in end-1989 as 100 units: In 1990 it increased by 4% to 104, then increased by 1% to 105 in 1991, then increased by 1% to 106 in 1992, then it decreased by 4% i.e. 4 units to 102 in 1993 and then increased by 7% i.e. 7 units to 109 in 1994. So mining grew from 100 units (assumed base) to 109 units in 1994.

Electricity: Let us take the base in end-1989 as 100 units: In 1990 it increased by 9% to 109, then increased by 9% i.e. 10 units to 119 in 1991, then increased by 5% i.e. by 6 units to 125 in 1992, then it increased by 7% i.e. 9 units to 134 in 1993 and then increased by 9% i.e. 12 units to 146 in 1994. So electricity grew from 100 units (assumed base) to 146 units in 1994.

Chemicals: Let us take the base in end-1989 as 100 units: In 1990 it increased by 9% to 109, then increased by 1% i.e. 1 unit to 110 in 1991, then increased by 2% i.e. 2 units to 112 in 1992, then it increased by 6% i.e. 7 units to 119 in 1993 and then increased by 9% i.e. 11 units to 130 in 1994. So chemicals grew from 100 units (assumed base) to 130 units in 1994.

The overall growth rate was the aggregate of the base level of 100 units in all four cases (which means 400 units) to 127 + 109 + 146 + 130 = 512 units in 1994. This represents an increase of 112 units over a total base level of 400 units and this means an overall increase of 28% and thus nearest to 25% which is Option 1.

Question 6

It is known that the index of total industrial production in 1994 was 50 percent more than that in 1989. Then, the percentage increase in production between 1989 and 1994, in sectors other than the four listed above, is:

1. 57.5
2. 87.5
3. 127.5
4. 47.5

Detailed explanation

In the previous question we have seen that the overall increase in the four sectors was 28% till 1994.

In 1994, the index of industrial production increased by 50% from 100 in 1989. So the index of industrial production in 1994 was 150.

In 1989, the four sectors contributed 60% of the overall sectors in the economy whereas other sectors contributed 40%. If the base level in 1990 was 100 units, then four sectors contributed 60 units and this contribution grew by 28% to 77 units till 1994. If the industrial production index increased to 150 in 1994, it means that the four sectors contributed 77 units and the other sectors contributed 73 units (which is 150 – 77). So the contribution of the other sectors grew by 33 units from 40 units in 1989 to 73 units in 1994. One would do well to remember that 1/40 is 2.5%; 2/40 is 5%. So whenever there is 40 in the denominator, all one has to do to find the percentage, is to multiply the numerator by 2.5. And if one multiplies 33 by 2.5 to find out what would be the value of the fraction 33/40 in percentage terms, the answer would be 82.5. Among the options, 87.5% fits well and hence Option 2.

Chapter 45

Reading Pie Charts

Data can be stored in computers or in tapes, pages and ledgers. Data by itself, can tell us nothing. We have to read the data and derive our lessons and strategies on the basis of the data presented. The importance of visual presentation is significant. Imagine that you are to raise funds for rural housing projects. Imagine that one such project has been implemented. The villagers lived in squalor prior to the housing project. Now they live organised lives: there are decent toilets, waste disposal systems and there is a supply of drinking water through taps. A couple of visuals, which show the situations before and after the project, would have a good deal more impact than merely talking about the improvement in life styles of the rural people to the institutions from whom you expect to raise funds for further housing projects. Nothing works better than visual presentation of data where the message goes home quickly and effectively.

There are several visual ways in which one can present data. There are tables and there are graphs and bar charts and circle charts (or pie charts as they are popularly called) and so on. The pie chart is widely used for presenting data such as changing weight of components of cost, changing age profile of employees in the company, changing market share and so on. The pie chart comes in very handy for depicting comparative positions in particular.

Listing a set of numbers in a table helps a reader to grasp relationships among them. The same numbers can also be represented in a pie chart, with the size of each sector, or slice, corresponding to the size of each number. This gives a good visual impression of the relative size and importance of numbers.

If the idea is to present, for example, the age profile of the company by classifying the employees in diverse age groups, then the total number of employees is the whole pie and the number of employees in the age group of – say - 30 to 35 can be represented as a slice of the whole pie. The fraction of the entire employee strength that is in this age group of 30 to 35 – assuming for a moment that this fraction is an eighth of the entire employee strength - can be diagrammatically represented as a slice of the pie forming an eighth of the pie. A pie is essentially a circle that subtends 360° at its centre. Marking a sector of the circle that subtends forty-five degrees at the centre of the circle, we can draw an eighth part of a circle, since 45 is an eighth of 360.

The pie chart can be used for comparing change in cost composition. For example, a textile mill typically has the following major components of cost in its overall cost of production: raw materials, wages, repairs, transportation charges, power and fuel and so on. Imagine that a textile company has just undergone extensive modernisation. The company wants to tell its shareholders how beneficial the modernisation programme has been. The management is looking for a methodology to present comparative evaluation of the cost composition prior to modernisation and after modernisation. It would do well to use two pies – one representing the composition of total cost prior to modernisation and one depicting the position after modernisation. These two pies may help in understanding, for example, that:

- While interest on borrowings has gone up – which it would since there would be loans to finance the modernisation – the power bill has gone down, since the new equipment is more power efficient
- Rejects have virtually come to zero since the cloth now produced, is of a superior quality. Customers routinely rejected cloth earlier on quality grounds.
- Wages as a percent of the total costs have gone down because the modernisation-cum-rehabilitation scheme involved golden handshake to employees not meeting productivity norms but whom the textile company could not either send home since there was not enough money to pay them terminal dues.

To make a pie, we will start with an illustrative situation close to home. Imagine that there has been a grouse from the children that entertainment is a matter of low priority with their family and the father wants to refute this contention with clear evidence. Whatever evidence must be brought in must be data backed. In the absence of solid evidence only the volume of the person, presenting the contrary view, may decide who wins the argument. This is because, in an argument, people take recourse to shouting their viewpoint when the logic in their argument is exhausted. (Even this is fine as long as people do not take recourse to fisticuffs to close the argument).

Let us imagine that the mother has kept track of exactly where every dollar was spent during the previous two quarters and has the under noted database.

Head of Expense	Quarter 1 Amount Spent $	Quarter 2 Amount Spent $
Grocery and provisions	7800	8500
Telephone & Power	4350	4500
Petrol	4530	4000
Entertainment	3060	1500
Insurance premium	900	900
Travel	660	600
Total expense	**21300**	**20000**

Based on the above database, the father makes the following two pie charts to visually present the data and enable the family to visually compare figures.

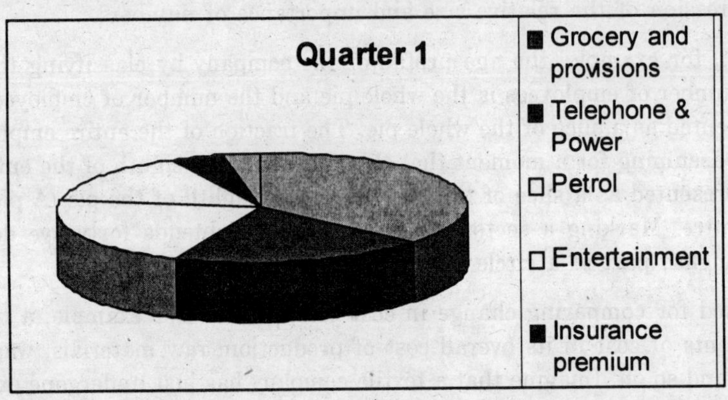

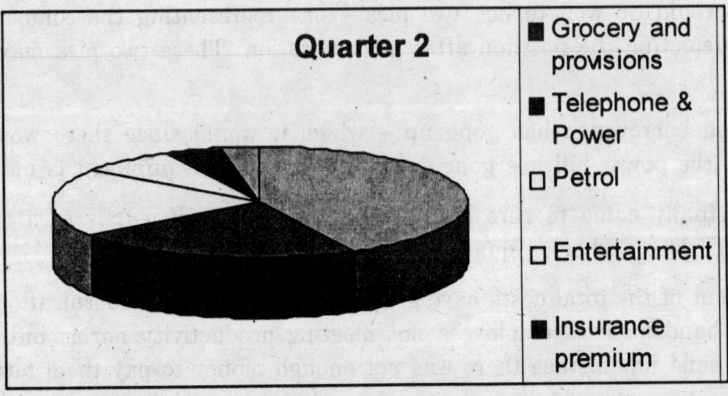

If you see the two pie charts for the two different quarters, each of them will tell a different story. As far as our problem concerned, the sector occupied by Entertainment has shrunk between Quarter 1 and Quarter 2.

What can be seen from pie charts is how much the share of each expense was from among the total expenses. This is provided that the pie represents the total expense. There is no need to presume this since the pie may relate to only the major heads of expense. Secondly, one cannot, for example, tell what the family saved each quarter because you know only what they spent but not what they earned.

You can arrange the various heads of expenses in ascending and descending orders without bothering yourself with the actual figures since the slices in the pie tell you the rank of each head of expense. You can tell which was the highest expense and which the lowest. Briefly, a wide range of relative positions can be seen from the visual representation through the pie chart without actually having to calculate anything at all.

As regards absolute values, the pie tells you what the whole is and each slice tells you the relationship between the slice and the whole pie and thereafter, knowing the absolute values of each of the components of the whole is a matter of mere arithmetic, once you know the absolute value of the whole.

Let us gather further lessons in regard to the pie chart from the illustrations that will follow. The problems that you will see hereunder are crème-de-la-crème and so, we would like to assure you, are the solutions that follow each of the problems.

DIRECTIONS *for Problems 1 to 4: Consider the information provided in the figures below relating to India's foreign trade in 1997–98 and the first eight months of 1998–99. Total trade with a region is defined as the sum of exports to and imports from that region. Trade deficit is defined as the excess of imports over exports. Trade deficit may be negative.*

A	U.S.A	G	Other East Europe
B	Germany	H	OPEC
C	Other E.U.	I	Asia
D	UK	J	Other LDCs
E	Japan	K	Others
F	Russia		

Source of Imports

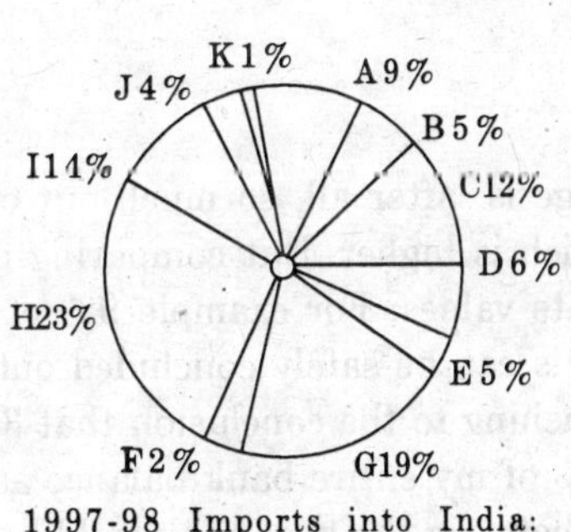

1997-98 Imports into India: $ 40779 million

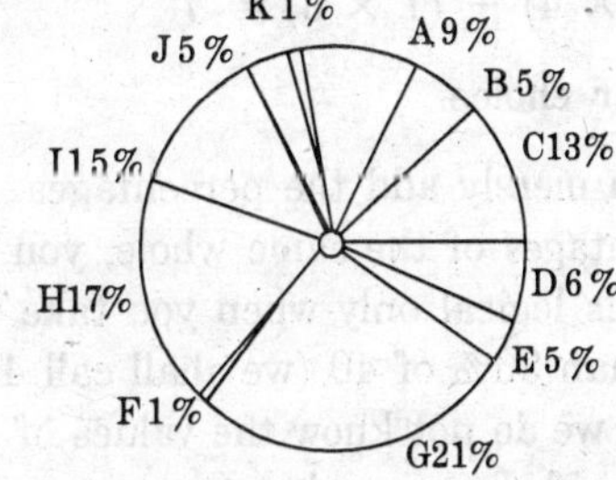

1998-99 Imports into India: (April-November) $ 28125 million

Destination of Exports

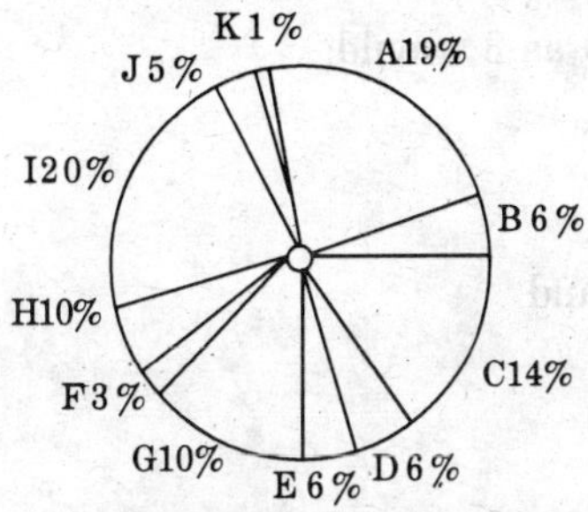

1997-98 Exports from India: $ 33979 million

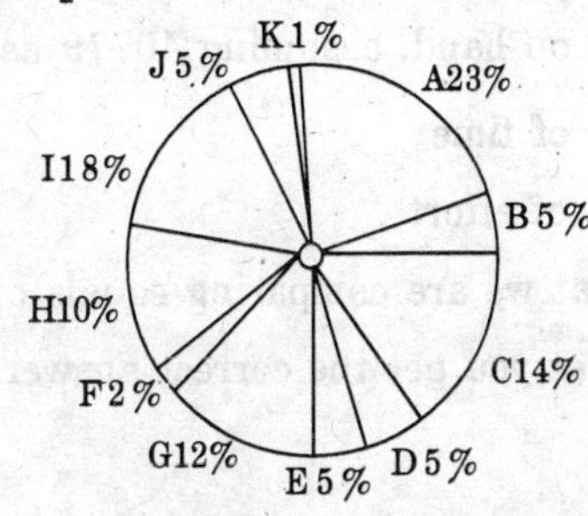

1998-99 Exports from India: (April-Nov.) $ 21436 million

Problem 1

With which region did India have highest total trade in 1997-98?

1. USA 2. Other E.U. 3. OPEC 4. Others

Detailed explanation

Total trade with a region = A + B, where A = imports from that region and B = exports to that region. The question is about a relative position and not an absolute position (since you are not asked what was the highest total trade) and thus, should involve nothing more than glancing at the pie charts and at the very most, some small additions that can be done orally.

Whatever be the figures of total exports and total imports, these will not be necessary since what is asked, is a relative position. If we assume that the total exports is E and total imports is I, then in the case of USA, the imports will be 9I/100 and exports will be 19E/100 and in the case of Other E.U., imports will be 12I/100 and exports will be 14E/100.

When you are comparing [(9I/100) + (19E/100)] with [(12I/100) + (14E/100)], you can safely multiply both sides by 100 so as to get whole numbers on both sides of the comparison. We shall therefore be comparing on the one hand (9I+ 19E) with (12I + 14E) on the other hand. In the present case, Imports into India are USD 40779 million and we may safely take I as 4 (rounding off 40779 to the nearest ten thousand). Exports from India are USD 33979 million here we may again safely take E as 3 (rounding off 33979 to the nearest ten thousand). This is because we are asked only a relative position and not an absolute position.

Comparing (9I + 19E) with (12I + 14E) will mean comparing [(9 × 4) + (19 × 3)] with [(12 × 4) + (14 × 3)] and hence 93 with 90. What we can see is that India's total trade with USA is more than the total trade with Other EUs. In evaluating the options, all that one has to do is to put the percentage of imports and if it is, say 21%, then write 21 and write the imports as 4 and so on. Now see the Options.

Option 1: USA (9 × 4) + (19 × 3) = 93

Option 2: Other EU (12 × 4) + (14 × 3) = 90

Option 3: OPEC (23 × 4) + (10 × 3) = 122

Option 4: Others (1 × 4) + (1 × 3) = 7

Option 3 is the clear choice.

It would be stupid to merely add the percentages. A percentage is, after all, so much out of the whole. If you are comparing the percentages of the same whole, you can tell which is higher. But comparing differing percentages of two different wholes is logical only when you take their absolute values. For example 9% of 200 (we shall call 200 as A) is far higher than 36% of 40 (we shall call 40 as B). This can be safely concluded only because we know the values of A and B. If we do not know the values of A and B, rushing to the conclusion that 36% of B is higher than 9% of A would be stupid. Imagine that I were to offer you 50% of my entire bank balance as a gift and my brother offers you only 2% of his bank balance and you have to choose between the two. You would be prudent to check what is the base of the two percentages. Merely because I offer 50% it does not mean that I am offering a much bigger gift. My bank balance may be $2000 whereas my brother's may be $20 million.

Back to the question on hand, assuming 40779 as 4 and 33979 as 3, would:

(A) Save a lot of time

(B) Save a lot of effort

(C) Ensure that we are comparing equals on both sides and

(D) Ensure that you get the correct answer in a jiffy.

Problem 2

In 1997–98 the amount of Indian exports, in millions US $, to the region with which India had the lowest total trade, is approximately:

1. 750 2. 340 3. 220 4. 440

Detailed explanation

Others occupy 1% of the pie in both imports and exports and *Others* is the area with the lowest total trade. Indian exports aggregate roughly 34000 million and 1% of this is two zeroes off from 34000 and would mean 340. Thus Option 2.

ADDITIONAL DIRECTIONS ***for questions 3 and 4: Solve these questions based on the situation below:***

Assuming that the average monthly exports and imports of India during the remaining four months of 1998–99 would be the same as that for the first eight months of the year.

Problem 3

What is the region to which Indian exports registered the highest percentage growth between 1997–98 and 1998–99?

1. Other East Europe 2. USA 3. Asia 4. Exports have declined, no growth

Detailed explanation

Look at the pie chart for exports in 1997-98, which is for a full year and for 1998-99, which is for eight months only. As per the additional information, we are to assume that the average monthly exports and imports of India during the remaining four months of 1998–99 would be the same as that for the first eight months of the year. If for eight months, the total exports have been 21436 millions, the remaining four months (which is half of eight months) would have brought about additional exports equal to half of 21436 millions, which is 10718 millions and the total exports would then have been 32154 millions.

Since we have to state a comparative position – growth rate in exports in 1997–98 and 1998–99, we can safely ignore the millions. The reason why we should ignore the millions on both sides of the comparison is fairly simple: 11% of 100 is less than 9% of 200 just as 11% of 100 Billion is less than 9% of 200 billion. So what is the need for these millions and billions while stating which is greater?

Secondly, if you are to compare between growth in exports over base year, then you must appreciate that exports in 1998-99= [exports in 1997-98+growth in between] / [exports in 1997-98] = [1+ (growth in between)] / [exports in 1997-98]. By 'growth in between' we mean growth in between the two years; in this case growth in exports between 1997-98 and 1998-99. Thus when you compare the exports of two different regions, you can safely take the exports in the next year as a fraction of the base year instead of finding the difference between the exports in an year and the exports in the base year because when you compare the exports figures of Region 1 with that of Region 2 instead of incremental exports, you will get 1 on both sides of the comparison like this:

1+ [growth in between of exports in Region 1]/[exports in 1997-98] compared with 1+ [growth in between of exports in Region 2]/[exports in 1997-98], and if you strike off the 1 on both sides what you are really comparing is:

[Growth in between of exports in Region 1/exports in 1997-98] with [Growth in between of exports in Region 2/ exports in 1997-98] which is what you want.

Let us see the options.

Option 1: Other East Europe. 10% of 33979 has grown to 12% of 32154. Let 1% of 33979 be A and 1% of 32154 be B. So in the case of Other East Europe, exports in 1998-99/exports in 1997-98 = 12B/10A

Option 2: USA. 19% of 33979 has grown to 23% of 32154. Let 1% of 33979 be A and 1% of 32154 be B. So in the case of USA, exports in 1998-99/exports in 1997-98 = 23B/19A

Option 3: Asia. 20% of 33979 has grown to 18% of 32154. Let 1% of 33979 be A and 1% of 32154 be B. So in the case of Asia, exports in 1998-99/exports in 1997-98 = 18B/20A

Now what we are required to do is to compare among 12B/10A, 23B/19A and 18B/20A and say which is the largest. In that case, neither B nor A in the numerator and denominator respectively are necessary because if you multiply all three fractions by A/B then you get 12/10, 23/19 and 18/20 and yet the relative values of the three fractions will remain unchanged. If you were to multiply three fractions, say, 1/2, 2/3, and 3/4 by one million in the numerator and five million in the denominator, will it alter the fact that 3/4 (as it will seem after all the multiplications) will remain the largest and 1/2 the smallest of these three fractions? See for yourself: The three fractions 1/2, 2/3 and 3/4 will seem like this: 1 million/10 million, 2 million/15 million and 3 million/20 million respectively and yet the last will be the highest and the first will be the lowest.

Thus what you are effectively comparing is 12/10, 23/19 and 18/20 in which 18/20 will have to be booted out since it is less than 1 and then we are left with 12/10 and 23/19. If we divide 12 by 10, we get 1.20. If we divide 23/19 we get 1.2 till the first decimal and when we carry on to the next decimal we get 1.21. We stop here and declare that USA has the highest growth among the three options and thus **Option 2** is correct.

But there is a small googly here. Option 4 says that exports have declined or there has been no growth in any region. This has to be checked. We know that the highest **percentage** growth is in the case of USA. But percentage growth is about relative growth whereas Option 4 talks about absolute growth. Whether there has been no growth or decline in absolute terms can be ascertained only from absolute figures.

Now see the utter logic in this. If this logic goes home, you will be saved a huge lot of calculations. Logic is the name of the game and even if it takes some time for this simple logic to register, it is recommended that you should absorb the fundamentals.

Since we know that in case of USA the percentage growth rate has been the highest, we may just check whether there has been actual growth in this case (we shall choose the highest percentage growth rate to check because if there has not been absolute growth where the percentage growth is highest, then in cases of lower percentage growth, the likelihood of an absolute growth is zero).

In case of USA, export percentage grew from 19% of 33979 million to 23% of 32154 million. For determining whether there was any growth, the millions are unnecessary once again. They would be needed if you were asked how much the growth was. But even then, if the answer is to be given in millions, the millions become redundant once again. Give these millions a well-earned rest. Round off 33979 to 34 (forget the thousands as well) and round off 32154 to 32 (forget the thousands here as well) and see whether 19% of 34 is less than 23% of 32. You will find that exports have indeed grown in the case of USA at least and hence Option 4 (which, if, true would mean that there has not been any growth in exports in any region) does not hold water.

So Option 2 is to be marked as correct.

Problem 4

What is the percentage growth rate in India's total trade deficit between 1997–98 and 1998–99?

1. 43 2. 47 3. 50 4. 40

Detailed explanation

India's trade deficit in 1997-98 in USD (billions) is 40.7 – 33.9 = 6.8. In 1998-99, it is (28.1 × 1.5) – (21.4 × 1.5) = 42.15 – 32.1 = 10.05. The trade deficit has gone up from 6.8 billion USD by 3.25 billion USD to 10.05 billion USD. This increase of 3.25 as a percentage of 6.8 is 3.25 × 100/6.8 = 325/6.8 = 3250/68 = 1625/34. Now 34 × 50 = 1700. 1625 is 75 less than 1700.

Therefore 1625/34 = 50 – (75/34). But 75/34 is more than 2 and thus 1625/34 is likely to be more than 47 and less than 48. From among the options 47% seems the closest answer. So **Option 2: 47%.**

DIRECTIONS *for Problems 5 to 7: The questions are based on the pie charts given below.*

Chart 1 shows the distribution of twelve million tonnes of crude oil transported through different modes over a specific period of time. Chart 2 shows the distribution of the cost of transporting this crude oil. The total cost was $ 30 million.

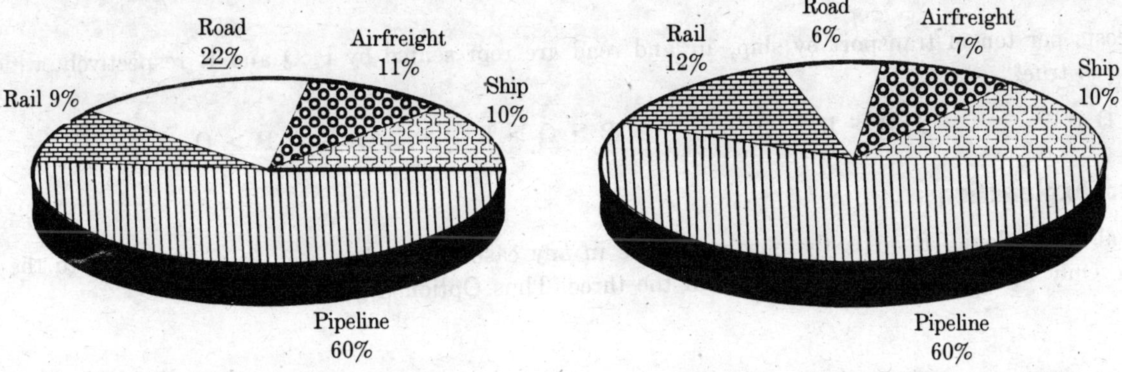

Chart 1: Volume Transported   Chart 2: Cost of Transportation

Problem 5

The cost in $ per ton of oil moved by rail and road happens to be roughly

1. 3   2. 1.5   3. 4.5   4. 8

Detailed explanation

What you are asked is an absolute position and not a relative position or a ratio. You have no choice but to calculate this absolute position.

Total volume of oil transported is 12 million tonnes whereas the total cost of transportation is Rs.30 million. From Chart 1 we find that the volume of oil transported by rail (9%)and road (22%) is 31% of 12 million tones = 3.72 million tonnes. The cost of transportation by rail (12%) and road (6%) comes to 18% of Rs.30 million = Rs.5.4 million. The cost of transportation through road and rail = $ 5.4 million/3.72 million tonnes or Rs.1.5 per tonne approximately. Dividing 5.40 with 3.72 we get 540/372 (multiplying both numerator and denominator with 100 so as to obviate the decimals); this can be further simplified to 45/31 since both 540 and 372 are divisible by 12 (both these quantities are divisible by 4 and 3) which is to all intents and purposes 45/30 which can be further simplified to 3/2 or 1.5. So **Option 2.**

Problem 6

From the charts given, it appears that the cheapest mode of transport is:

1. Road   2. Rail   3. Pipeline   4. Ship

Detailed explanation

Here we are asked a comparative position and it will neither be logical nor necessary to do sit-ups with the absolute figures. The cheapest mode of transportation is that in which you spend the least on transportation per given quantity of goods! The numerator, in this unit cost of transportation, is cost of transportation and the denominator is volume of goods transported. This fraction is likely to be least when the numerator is the least in comparison to the denominator or in other words the denominator is the largest multiple of the numerator.

If one looks at the percentage of the oil sent through the different modes and the cost of transportation of oil as a percentage of the overall cost, it is clear that only in the case of road and airfreight, the percentage of volume transported is more than the corresponding percentage cost of transportation. Between these two, the volume of oil sent by road (22%) is twice that of the volume of oil sent by airfreight (11%), whereas the cost of transportation through road (6%) is lower than the cost of transportation by airfreight (7%). Thus unit cost of transportation by road is the cheapest among all the various modes. So Option 1. Incidentally, we have been able to reach the correct inference by only a glance at the pie chart. No calculation has been necessary.

Problem 7

If the costs per ton of transport by ship, air and road are represented by P, Q and R respectively, which of the following is true?

1. R > Q > P   2. P > R > Q   3. P > Q > R   4. R > P > Q

Detailed explanation

This is all about logic. Road is the cheapest mode in any case as one has seen in the solution to the previous question. Only Option 3 has R as the least of the three. Thus Option 3.

Chapter 46

Reading Tabulated Data

Questions relating to interpretation of tabulated data are frequently asked at competitive examinations in the Data Interpretation Section. Luckily, the Test Taking Tips (that you see in the POWERPREP CD that the Educational Testing Service issues to students registering for the GRE) they expect you to be able to interpret data in graphs and tables and circle graphs. It, therefore, becomes all the more important to acquaint the reader with reading tabulated data.

The logical things to bear in mind are:

(1) When you are asked to state a relative position, you will seldom need to calculate anything

(2) If the comparison is between say X% of a certain quantity A and say Y% of another quantity B then:

If X > Y, and also A > B, you can definitely say that X% of A is > Y% of B. Let us assume that X = 20, Y = 15, A = 100 and B = 80. Then, 0% of 100 is greater than 15% of 80 for the reason that X > Y and A > B.

If you are not given whether A > B, but you are told that X > Y, then merely because X > Y you cannot jump to a conclusion that X% of A is >Y% of B. On the basis of a statement that X > Y, all you can say without actual calculating is X% of A is > Y% of A or X% of B is > Y% of B because in both the last two cases the base is the same and X is higher than Y. That is why you cannot say which is higher: X% of 300 or Y% of 10, unless you know whether X > Y or X = Y or X < Y. For all you know, X may be zero and Y may be 100.

(3) A chart or graph may require only a glance to show you what is the relative position between two variables plotted or represented in the graph or chart and no calculation may become necessary unless one is comparing ratios with different bases.

(4) If you are asked to state an absolute position such as which among the options is the actual number of schoolboys over 35 kilograms weight, you have no choice but to calculate the actual position.

(5) If you are given some base years – such as Year 1, Year 2 and so on - and corresponding performance figures such as sales, and are asked to state as to in which year among the base years does one see the lowest percentage growth, please remember that it is not necessary to calculate.

(A) The actual increase or decrease

(B) The percentage increase or decrease.

(C) This is because if you are asked to compare the increase/decrease between Year 1 and Year 2 and then between Year 2 and Year 3, the Sales figure for Year 2 is actually (the Sales for the Year 1) + (the increase/decrease in Sales from Year 1 to Year 2) and the Sales figure for Year 3 is actually (the Sales for the Year 2) + (the increase/decrease in Sales from Year 2 to Year 3). Instead of working out the increase/decrease in Sales, if you compare the Sales of Year 3 with Sales of Year 2 and the Sales of Year 2 with the Sales of Year 1, the purpose of comparing the incremental sales over year sales will be eminently served. [Please see illustration 3 (Question 2) in this chapter for detailed explanation]

We shall now see some of the best illustrations drawn from the past papers of entrance tests to the very best of management schools and see what concepts are put to test in these illustrations in specific and the competitive examination in general insofar as questions involving reading of tabulated data are concerned. Important lessons can be drawn from these illustrations. We shall then ensure assimilation of whatever we have learnt. We may reinforce concepts that we already know. Then we shall carefully pickle these object lessons and arrange the pickled lessons in our mental larder so that we can quickly retrieve them for use in a feast of logic that the competitive examination essentially is.

Illustration 1

DIRECTIONS *for question 1 to 4: A professor keeps data on students tabulated by performance and sex of the student. The data is kept on a computer disk, but unfortunately some of it is lost because of a virus. Only the following could be recovered:*

	Performance			Total
	Average	Good	Excellent	
Male			10	
Female				32
Total		30		

Panic buttons were pressed but to no avail. An expert committee was formed, which decided that the following facts were self-evident:

(a) Half the students were either excellent or good.

(b) 40% of the students were female.

(c) One third of the male students were average.

Question 1

How many students are both female and excellent?

1. 0 2. 8 3. 16 4. 32

Detailed Explanation

Some data is given; the rest has to be constructed from the statements given.

The statements are as follows: (A) Half the students were either excellent, or good (B) 40% of the students were female, and (C) 1/3rd of the male students were average.

The data can now be filled in as follows on the basis of calculations as stated under:

	Performance			Total
	Average	Good	Excellent	
Male	16	22	10	48
Female	24	8	0	32
Total	40	30	10	80

From statement B since 40% of the students were females and the number of female students is given as 32, this means the total number of students were 80 (since 32 is 40% of 80) and thus the number of males was 48.

Further, from statement C, 1/3rd of the male students were Average and hence 16 males were Average and hence 22 males are Good since 10 males are Excellent as given.

Also since the total number of Good students is 30, the number of female students who fall in the good category is 30-22=8.

From statement A, half the students were either Excellent or Good. Since the number of students in the Good category is already 30 and that 10 males are Excellent, the number of females in the Excellent category is nil. So the table is complete as above.

Now Question no. 1: How many students are both female and Excellent: NIL in Option 1.

Question 2

What proportion of Good students are male?

1. 0 2. 0.73 3. 0.4 4. 1.0

Detailed Explanation

The proportion of Good students to males is 22/30 = 11/15 = 0.73 at Option 2.

Question 3

What proportion of female students are Good?

1. 0 2. 0.25 3. 0.5 4. 1.0

Detailed Explanation

The proportion of female students that is Good is? 8/32 = 1/4 = 0.25 at Option 2.

Question 4

Among Average students, what is the ratio of male to female?

1. 1:2 2. 2:1 3. 3:2 4. 2:3

Detailed Explanation

Among Average students, the ratio of male to female is 16:24 or 2:3 at Option 4.

Illustration 2

DIRECTIONS *for question 1 to 5: Study the following data and answer the questions that follow.*

The number of people planned for a software project requiring 15 months to complete is given below:

Month	1	2	3	4	5	6	7	8	9	10	11	12	13	14	15
People	2	3	3	4	4	5	5	4	4	4	3	3	1	1	1

The project is divided into different phases.

The specific month(s) in which a phase will be executed and the corresponding cost per man-month are shown below:

Phase	Planned months for Execution	Cost per man-month ($ Thousands)
Specifications	1st, 2nd	40
Design	3rd, 4th	20
Code	5th to 8th	10
Test	9th, 10th	15
Maintain	11th to 15th	10

During the actual execution of the project, the design phase was extended by a month i.e., up to the fifth month. The number of people used in the design phase in the 5th month was 4. Because of improved design, the coding time was reduced by a month. So coding was done during the months 6 to 8. The men used during these three months were 4, 5 and 5 respectively.

Question 1

The average number of people planned per month was the least for the phase:

1. Specifications 2. Design 3. Code 4. Maintain

Detailed Explanation

The planned deployment of manpower for the various phases was as under:

	Months	People as Per plan	Average Planned manpower/ number of months
Specifications	1 and 2	2+3=5	5/2=2.5
Design	3 and 4	3+4=7	7/2=3.5
Code	5, 6, 7 and 8	4+5+5+4=18	18/4=4.5
Test	9 and 10	4+4=8	8/2=4
Maintain	11 to 15	3+3+1+1+1=9	9/5=1.8

The average number of people planned was the least for the maintain phase. Hence **Option 4**.

Question 2

The planned cost of design phase as a per cent to the total planned cost of the project was approximately:

1. 14% 2. 19% 3. 15% 4. 25%

Detailed Explanation

	Months	People as per plan	Cost per man-month $ (in 000s)	Total cost per phase
Specifications	1 and 2	2+3=5	40	40×5 = 200
Design	3 and 4	3+4=7	20	20×7 = 140
Code	5, 6, 7 and 8	4+5+5+4=18	10	10×18 = 180
Test	9 and 10	4+4=8	15	15×8 = 120
Maintain	11 to 15	3+3+1+1+1=9	10	10×9 = 90

This will involve actually calculating. Luckily, however, the calculations are small. The total planned cost was 200 + 140 + 180 + 120 + 90 = 730. The planned cost for design phase was 140/730 = 14/73. Now, 14 is 1/5 of 70, and therefore 14/73 is a little less than 1/5 (or 20%). Hence 19% is the nearest among the given options. Hence Option 2.

Question 3

Compared to the plan the actual cost went up by:

1. \$ 40,000 2. \$ 20,000 3. \$ 10,000
4. Did not change

Detailed Explanation

This will involve some very small calculations since what you are asked to find out is an absolute position.

The actual cost per phase was as under:

	Months	People as per actual (\$ in 000s)	Cost per man-month	Total cost per phase
Specifications	1 and 2	2+3=5	40	40×5 = 200
Design	3, 4,5	3+4+4=11	20	20×11 = 220
Code	6,7 and 8	4+5+5=14	10	10×14 = 140
Test	9 and 10	4+4=8	15	15×8 = 120
Maintain	11 to 15	3+3+1+1+1=9	10	10×9 = 90

The total cost thus comes to 200 + 220 + 140 + 120 + 90 = 770. The planned cost is 730 as may be seen in Detailed Explanation to Question 2. The increase in cost is 770 – 730 = 40. So **Option 1: \$40,000.**

Question 4

The actual man-months required for the entire project:

1. Increased by 2 2. Decreased by 1 3. Increased by 1 4. Did not change

Detailed Explanation

If one sees the solutions to questions 2 and 3, the only **changes** in man-months is under design and coding where **what was planned, and what actually transpired was as under:**

	Man-Months as per plan	Man-Months as per actual
Design	7	11
Code	18	14
Sum Total	**25**	**25**

There was no change in the total number of man months actually required for the entire project from what was planned. Hence **Option 4.**

Question 5

The highest actual total cost (\$ '000's) was incurred in the following phase:

1. Specifications 2. Test 3. Design 4. Maintain

Detailed Explanation

If one were to see the solution to question 3 above, the highest actual total cost ($ 000's) was incurred in the design phase. Hence **Option 3**.

Illustration 3

DIRECTIONS *for questions 1 to 5: Answer these questions with reference to the table given below:*

Information Technology Industry in India
(Figures are in million US dollars)

	1994-95	1995-96	1996-97	1997-98	1998-99
Software:					
Domestic	350	490	670	950	1250
Exports 485	734	1083	1750	2650	
Hardware:					
Domestic	590	1037	1050	1205	1026
Exports 177	35	286	201	4	
Peripherals:					
Domestic	148	196	181	229	329
Exports 6	6	14	19	18	
Training	107	143	185	263	302
Maintenance	142	172	182	221	236
Networking & others	36	73	156	193	237
Total	2041	2886	3807	5031	6052

Question 1

The total annual exports lay between 35 and 40 percent of the total annual business of the IT industry, in the years:

1. 1997-98 & 1994-95
2. 1996-97 & 1997-98
3. 1996-97 & 1998-99
4. 1996-97 & 1994-95

Detailed Explanation

It may be seen that the figures relating to software exports/hardware exports and peripherals for 1994-95 are written in the previous column so when reading the data, care will have to be taken to read these correctly. This is not a typing error. It is done on purpose. This is the googly in the question and one has to be careful when dealing with it. This should teach you how to first spot googlies in the future.

For example, the figure of 2650 in relation to software exports written under 1997-98 really pertains to 1998-99 and so on. The total annual exports figures and the total turnover figures are as under (1995-96 is not among the options and therefore not worked out); figures in brackets show how turnover is calculated:

	1994-95	1996-97	1997-98	1998-99
Exports	668 (485+177+6)	1383 (1083+286+14)	1970 (1750+201+19)	2672 (2650+4+18)
Exports/Turnover	0.33	0.35	0.4	0.45

It is important to calculate percentages quickly. 668/2041 is slightly less than 1/3rd (or less than 33%) since 680 is a third of 2040, 1383/3807 is roughly 1400/3800 and this is 7/19 and since 7/20 is 35%, 1383/3807 is a little over 35%; 1970/5031 is nearly 197/500 and since 200/500 is exactly 40%, 1970/5031 is a little below 40%, whereas 2672/6052 is over 40% since 40% of 6000 is 2400 and 2672 is >2400. So Option 2; 1996-97 and 1997-98.

Question 2

The highest percentage growth in the total IT business, relative to the previous year was achieved in:

1. 1995-96 2. 1996-97 3. 1997-98 4. 1998-99

Detailed Explanation

Let us see the figure of total IT business in 1995-96: This is 2886. Which is as such Previous year figure + growth between 1994-95 and 1995-96 (meaning 2886 = 2041 + 845). When I want to compare the figure of total IT business of 1996-97 with 1995-96 and (2) figures of total IT business of 1995-96 with 1994-95, I can directly compare (A) turnover of 1996-97/ turnover of 1995-96 with (B) turnover of 1995-96/ turnover of 1994-95. The resultant ratios are (A) 2886/2041 and (B) 3807/2886. When I compare ratios A with B what I am really doing is comparing (A) (2041+845)/ 2041 with (B) (2886+921)/2886 which is as such (A) 1 + 845/2041 with (B) 1 + 921/2886. I can safely deduct 1 from both sides and then find that what I am effectively comparing is (A) 845/2041 with (B) 921/2886. In comparing turnovers directly, I have actually compared only the incremental growths relative to previous year.

The highest percentage growth relative to previous year is seen from the following figures of turnover:

	1994-95	1995-96	1996-97	1997-98	1998-99
Turnover	2041	2886	3807	5031	6052
Growth (approx.)		845/2041	921/2886	1224/3807	1021/5031
Percentages		>2/5	<1/3	<1/3	Nearly 1/5

Thus the highest growth in turnover in relation to previous year is 1995-96. So **Option 1**. We have deliberately avoided calculating percentages although the examiner has asked you to state in which year is the highest percentage growth in sales as compared to previous year. We were able to find which fraction was the highest among 845/2041, 921/2886, 1224/3807 and 1021/5031. If you can see which fraction is the highest, why convert them into percentage in order to find out which fraction is the highest? The examiner may ask you anything. The test is of your logic, not his.

Question 3

Which one of the following statements is correct?

1. The annual software exports steadily increased but annual hardware exports steadily declined during 1994-1999.
2. The annual peripheral export steadily increased during 1994-1999.
3. The IT business in training during 1994-1999 was higher than the total IT business in maintenance during the same period.
4. None of the above statements is true.

Detailed Explanation

Statement 1 is not true since there has been steady growth in software and hardware exports during 1994-99. Statement 2 is not true since annual peripheral exports have decreased in 1998-99, vis-à-vis previous year. Statement 3: Let us see the totals of IT business in (A) training and (B) maintenance during 1994-99. Training: 107 + 143 + 185 + 263 + 302 = 1000. Maintenance: 142 + 172 + 182 + 221 + 236 = 953. Thus total business in training is greater than the total IT business in maintenance. So Statement 3 is true. Thus Option 3.

ADDITIONAL INSTRUCTIONS *for questions 4 and 5:*

For any activity, A, year X dominates year Y if IT business in activity A, in the year X, is greater than the IT business, in activity A, in the year Y. For any two IT business activities, A & B, year X dominates year Y if

i. the IT business in activity A, in the year X, is greater than or equal to the IT business, in activity A in the year Y,

ii. the IT business in activity B, in the year X, is greater than or equal to the IT business in activity B in the year Y and

iii. there should be strict inequality in the case of at least one activity.

Question 4

For the IT hardware business activity, which one of the following is not true?

1. 1997-98 dominates 1996-97
2. 1997-98 dominates 1995-96
3. 1995-96 dominates 1998-99
4. 1998-99 dominates 1996-97

Detailed Explanation

We are to find out the total hardware business activity (exports + domestic):

	1994-95	1995-96	1996-97	1997-98	1998-99
Hardware exports	177	35	286	201	4
Hardware domestic	590	1037	1050	1205	1026
Total	767	1072	1336	1412	1030

Statement 4 is not true since total hardware in 1998-99 is less than in 1996-97. Thus Option 4.

Question 5

For the two IT business activities, hardware and peripherals, which one of the following is true?

1. 1996-97 dominates 1995-96
2. 1998-99 dominates 1995-96
3. 1997-98 dominates 1998-99
4. None of these

Detailed Explanation

	1994-95	1995-96	1996-97	1997-98	1998-99
Hardware	767	1072	1336	1412	1030
Peripherals	154	202	195	248	347
Total	921	1274	1531	1660	1377

Both hardware and peripherals figures are inclusive of exports figures under each head. **Statement 1**: 1996-97 dominates 1995-96 is not true since peripherals in 1996-97 are lower than in 1995-96. **Statement 2**: 1998-99 dominates 1995-96; hardware business is lower in 1998-99 as compared to 1995-96; so this is not true. Statement 3: 1997-98 dominates 1998-99; this is not true since peripherals at 248 are lower than 347 in 1998-99. So Option 4; "none of these!"

Illustration 4

DIRECTIONS *for questions 1 to 4: Answer the questions based on the table given below: The following is a table describing garments manufactured based upon the colour and size for each lay. There are four sizes: M- Medium, L- Large, XL- Extra Large and XXL- Extra-Extra-Large. There are three colours: Yellow, Red and White.*

Lay	Number of Garments											
	Yellow				Red				White			
Lay No.	M	L	XL	XXL	M	L	XL	XXL	M	L	XL	XXL
1.	14	14	7	0	0	0	0	0	0	0	0	0
2.	0	0	0	0	0	0	0	0	42	42	21	0
3.	20	20	10	0	18	18	9	0	0	0	0	0
4.	20	20	10	0	0	0	0	0	30	30	15	0
5.	0	0	0	0	24	24	12	0	30	30	15	0
6.	22	22	11	0	24	24	12	0	32	32	16	0
7.	0	24	24	12	0	0	0	0	0	0	0	0
8.	0	20	20	10	0	2	2	1	0	0	0	0
9.	0	20	20	10	0	0	0	0	0	22	22	11
10.	0	0	0	0	0	26	26	13	0	20	20	10
11.	0	22	22	11	0	26	26	13	0	22	22	11
12.	0	0	2	2	0	0	0	0	0	0	0	0
13.	0	0	0	0	0	0	0	0	0	0	20	20
14.	0	0	0	0	0	0	0	0	0	0	22	22
15.	0	0	10	10	0	0	2	2	0	0	22	22
16.	0	0	0	0	1	0	0	0	1	0	0	0
17.	0	0	0	0	0	5	0	0	0	0	0	0
18.	0	0	0	0	0	32	0	0	0	0	0	0
19.	0	0	0	0	0	32	0	0	0	0	0	0
20.	0	0	0	0	0	5	0	0	0	0	0	0
21.	0	0	0	18	0	0	0	0	0	0	0	0
22.	0	0	0	0	0	0	0	26	0	0	0	0
23.	0	0	0	0	0	0	0	0	0	0	0	22
24.	0	0	0	8	0	0	0	1	0	0	0	0
25.	0	0	0	8	0	0	0	0	0	0	0	12
26.	0	0	0	0	0	0	0	1	0	0	0	14
27.	0	0	0	8	0	0	0	2	0	0	0	12
Production	76	162	136	97	67	194	89	59	135	198	195	156
Order	75	162	135	97	67	194	89	59	135	197	195	155
Surplus	1	0	1	0	0	0	0	0	0	1	0	1

Question 1

How many lays are used to produce Yellow coloured fabrics?

1. 10   2. 11   3. 12   4. 14

Detailed Explanation

Production of yellow coloured fabrics on different lays on which only yellow coloured fabrics are produced is as under:

Lay No.	No. of garments manufactured			
	M	L	XL	XXL
1	14	14	7	0
3	20	20	10	0
4	20	20	10	0
6	22	22	11	0
7	0	24	24	12
8	0	20	20	10
9	0	20	20	10
11	0	22	22	11
12	0	0	2	2
15	0	0	10	10
21	0	0	0	18
24	0	0	0	8
25	0	0	0	8
27	0	0	0	8

A lay here is the part of a textile loom that closes the weft. **In all 14 lays are** under use for **manufacturing** yellow fabrics. Thus Option 4. Please remember that you need not write anything at all. A lay can be reasonably deemed to produce anything if zero is not marked against it but there is a number against it. Just mark the lays that qualify for this and then count the number of tick marks that you have made with your pencil. Count them in a voice that your neighbour cannot hear. This is a competitive examination and it is on your interest that he does not get the right answer at all and certainly not from you in any case.

Question 2

How many lays are used to produce Extra-Extra Large fabrics?

1. 15   2. 16   3. 17   4. 18

Detailed Explanation

XXL is extra extra-large. To answer the question as to how many lays are used to produce XXD fabrics, we need to see from lay 1 onwards whether these are used to manufacture XXL fabrics. None of the lays from lay 1 to lay 6 is used for manufacturing XXL fabrics of any colour (there is nil production under either yellow, red or white in the XXL category). Only tick mark with your pencil where necessary and then count the ticks. Do no toiling.

The total number of lays used for making XXL garments is 16 as may be seen from the following:

Number of XXL garments manufactured								
Lay no.	Yellow	Red	White		Lay No.	Yellow	Red	White
7	12	0	0					
8	10	1	0		15	10	2	22
9	10	0	11		21	18	0	0
10	0	13	10		22	0	26	0
11	11	13	11		23	0	0	22
12	2	0	0		24	8	1	0
13	0	0	20		25	8	0	12
14	0	0	22		26	0	1	14
27	8	2	12					

Thus 16 lays are used to manufacture XXL fabrics. **Thus Option 2.**

Question 3

How many lays are used to produce Extra-Extra Large Yellow or Extra-Extra Large White fabrics?

1. 8 2. 9 3. 10 4. 15

Detailed Explanation

The number of lays used to produce XXL yellow or XXL white fabrics can be seen from the following:

Number of garments manufactured		
Lay No.	XXL Yellow	XXL White
7	12	0
8	10	0
9	10	11
10	0	10
11	11	11
12	2	0
13	0	20
14	0	22
15	10	22
21	18	0
23	0	22
24	8	0
25	8	12
26	0	14
27	8	12

In all 15 lays are used for manufacturing XXL yellow or XXL white fabrics. Thus **Option 4**.

Question 4

How many varieties of fabrics, which exceed the order, have been produced?

1. 3 2. 4 3. 5 4. 6

Detailed Explanation

When you are given figures of production and the figures of orders and then the figures of surplus, it is very reasonable to infer that the surplus is what production in excess of the order is, really. Fabrics produced in excess of the order are surplus. There is surplus in respect of Medium Yellow, XL Yellow, Large- White and XXL-White. Thus in all 4 varieties of fabrics which exceeded the order have been produced. **Option 2**, therefore.

Illustration 5

DIRECTIONS *for question 1 to 4: Answer these questions based on the table given below concerning the busiest twenty international airports in the world.*

No	Name	International Airport Type	Code	Location	
1.	Hartsfield	A	ATL	Atlanta, Georgia, USA	77939536
2.	Chicago-O'Hare	A	ORD	Chicago, Illionis, USA	72568076
3.	Los Angeles	A	LAX	Los Angeles, California, USA	63876561
4.	Heathrow Airport	E	LHR	London,UnitedKingdom	62263710
5.	DFW	A	DFW	Dallas/Ft. Worth, Texas, USA	60000125
6.	Haneda Airport	F	HND	Tokyo, Japan	54338212
7.	Frankfurt Airport	E	FRA	Frankfurt, Germany	45858315
8.	Roissy-Charles de Gaulle	E	CDG	Paris,France	43596943
9.	San Fransisco	A	SFO	San Fransisco, California, USA	40387422
10.	Denver	A	DIA	Denver, Colorado, USA	38034231
11	Amsterdam Schiphol	E	AMS	Amsterdam, The Netherlands	36781015
12.	Minneapolis-St.Paul	A	MSP	Minneapolis-St. Paul, USA	34216331
13.	Detroit Metropolitan	A	DTW	Detroit, Michigan, USA	34038381
14.	Miami	A	MIA	Miami, Florida, USA	33899246
15.	Newark	A	EWR	Newark, New Jersey, USA	33814000
16.	McCarran	A	LAS	Las Vegas, Nevada, USA	33669185
17.	Phoenix Sky Harbor	A	PHX	Phoenix, Arizona, USA	33533353
18.	Kimpo	FE	SEL	Seoul, Korea	33371074
19.	George Bush	A	IAH	Houston, Texas, USA	33089333
20.	John F. Kennedy	A	JFK	New York, NewYork, USA	32003000

Question 1

How many international airports of type 'A' account for more than 40 million passengers?

1. 4 2. 5 3. 6 4. 7

Detailed Explanation

All the questions in this illustration, you will mark, will involve either ticking them with a pencil or some small calculation. All airports listed at serial no. 1 to 9 carry more than 40 million passengers. Of these 9, the airports listed at serial no. 1,2,3,5 and 9 are A type international airports. Thus the answer is 5 international airports of type A as at Option 2.

Question 2

What percentage of top ten busiest airports is in the United States of America?

1. 60 2. 80 3. 70 4. 90

Detailed Explanation

Of the top ten busiest airports (luckily the airports are arranged according to the number of passengers carried with the airport carrying the highest number being at the head of the list), six airports at serial no. 1,2,3,5,9 and 10 are in the US of A. 6 out of 10 is 60%. So Option 1.

Question 3

Of the five busiest airports, roughly what percentage of passengers is handled by Heathrow airport?

1. 30 2. 40 3. 20 4. 50

Detailed Explanation

The five busiest airports carry roughly 34 (which is 7.8+7.3+6.4+6.2+6.0) million passengers of which Heathrow carries 6.2 million. Among the various options, 20% fits well since among the options 20% is the closest to 6.2/34. Which is as such 62/340 or 31/170 and since 31/155 is exactly 1/5 (or 20%) and 31/186 is exactly 1/6 (or 16.66%), 31/170 would lie between 16.66% and 20%. Thus Option 3.

Question 4

How many international airports not located in the USA handle more than 30 million passengers?

1. 5 2. 6 3. 10 4. 14

Detailed Explanation

All 20 airports listed carry more than 3 million passengers. The six airports at Serial number 4, 6, 7, 8, 11 and 18 are located outside the USA. Thus Option 2.

Chapter 47

Quantitative Comparison

Practice test 1

The section on Quantitative Comparison carries considerable weight. One is given a set of parameters defining a certain quantity on one hand and another quantity on the other hand. What one is required to do is to be able to tell whether:

(I) one of these two quantities is greater than the other and if so which one

(II) both the quantities are equal

(III) based on the given data, one cannot determine whether one is definitely greater than the other or whether they are definitely equal

Looking to its very nature, the concepts underlying the section on quantitative comparison will need to be understood from actual questions alone. This is for more reasons than one. The first reason is that the underlying principles are all a part of our armoury; we have learnt these at school. The second reason is that nothing other than a wide range of actual questions will become workable if the idea is to understand and assimilate a wide range of concepts.

We shall see actual questions as soon as possible. Meantime, we shall begin with the following illustration.

Illustration

The terms v, x and y represent real numbers where $x = 2v$ and $y = v + 2$.

Quantity A is $(x^2 + y^2)$. Quantity B is $(x + y)^2$. You are to tell whether:

(I) Quantity A is bigger than Quantity B or

(II) Quantity B is bigger than Quantity A or

(III) The two quantities are equal or

(IV) One cannot say anything definite from the given information

Let us see what are we comparing. On the one hand we have Quantity A which is $(x^2 + y^2)$ or $[(2v)^2 + (v + 2)^2]$ or $[4v^2 + v^2 + 4v + 4]$ or $[5v^2 + 4v + 4]$. On the other hand we have $(x + y)^2$, which is $[2v + v + 2]^2 = [3v + 2]^2 = 9v^2 + 12v + 4$.

What therefore we are to compare is $5v^2 + 4v + 4$ with $9v^2 + 12v + 4$. Since 4 is common to both sides, it can be safely done away with. If there are two boys and you want to find out who is heavier and find that both of them are carrying schoolbags that each weigh 4 kg, you can safely ask them to leave their school bags to one side. This means that we are now comparing $5v^2 + 4v$ with $9v^2 + 12v$. If v is positive, then 4v will have a positive value and 4v will therefore add equal value to both sides of the comparison. If v is negative, 4v will have a negative value and 4v will therefore subtract equal value to both sides of the comparison. Then why keep 4v? Subtract it from both sides of the comparison and you are now comparing $5v^2$ with $9v^2+8v$. Now we know that $9v^2$ is common to both sides and regardless of whether v is positive or negative, $9v^2$ will invariably be positive and therefore add the same value to both sides of the comparison. Then why allow the two boys whose weights we are trying to compare to hold on to baseball bats of the same weight? Ask them to leave these aside as well and we find that what we are now comparing is $-4v^2$ with 8v. If we were to divide both sides of the comparison with 4, we are then comparing $-v^2$ with

2v. If v is positive, then $-v^2$ will be invariably negative whereas 2v will be invariably positive. Thus when v is positive, the Quantity B is higher than Quantity A. If v is negative, then $-v^2$ will be invariably negative whereas 2v will also be negative.

Having seen that while the Quantity A is invariably negative, Quantity B can be positive as well as negative, the question is: can Quantity A be equal to Quantity B? Let us put this in algebraic form: can $-v^2 = 2v$? Yes it can in two situations: when v = 0 and when v = −2. If there are two quantities that could be equal to each other or one of them could even be greater than the other, one cannot say for certain that one of these quantities is greater than the other or less than the other or equal to the other. This is why one has to choose **Option (IV)**: One cannot say anything definite from the given information.

Now let us move on to practice tests.

GENERAL DIRECTIONS ***to the questions in this practice test:***

The question consists of two quantities, one in Column A and one in Column B. There may be additional information, centres above the two columns, that concerns one or both the quantities. A symbol that appears in both columns represents the same thing in Column A as it does in Column B. You are to compare the quantity in Column A with the quantity in Column B and decide whether:

1. The quantity in Column A is greater
2. The quantity in Column B is greater
3. The two quantities are equal
4. The relation cannot be determined from the information given

Question 1

Column A	Column B
(40% of 50) + 60	(60% of 50) + 40

Question 2

$x + 4 = 10$

Column A	Column B
$x-2$	x/2

Question 3

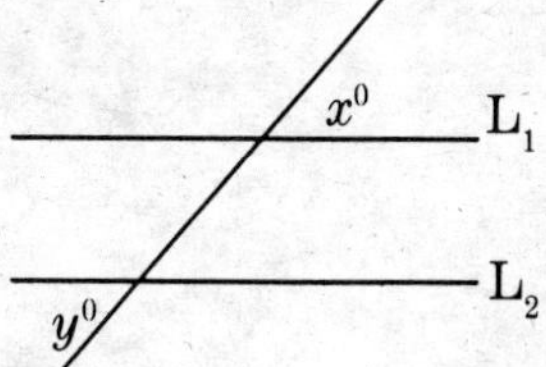

Column A	Column B
X	y

Question 4

Column A	Column B
$\frac{\sqrt{60}}{\sqrt{15}}$	4

Question 5

$0<r<t$

Column A	Column B
$\frac{r}{t}$	$\frac{t}{r}$

Question 6

$7x^2=21$

Column A	Column B
x	2

Question 7

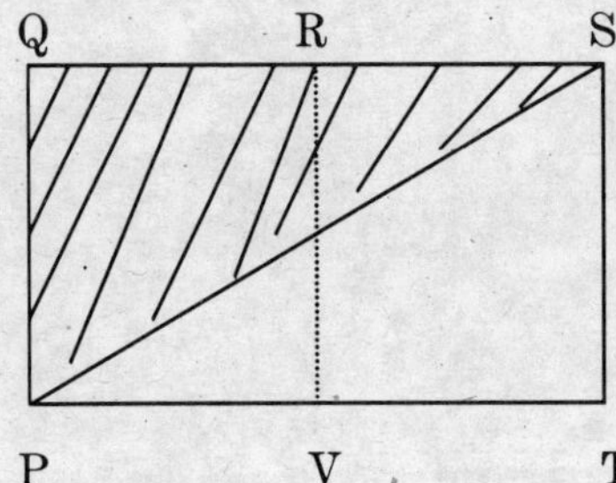

Squares PQRV and VRST have sides of length 6.

Column A	Column B
Area of shaded region PQS	36

Question 8

$x>1$

Column A	Column B
2^x	x^2

Question 9

List X

Value	2	3	4	5
Frequency	7	12	21	22

List Y

Value	6	8	10	14	15
Frequency	8	16	19	10	9

List X and List Y, whose frequency tables are shown, each contain 62 data points. To the nearest tenth, the average (arithmetic mean) of List X is 3.9 and the average of List Y is 10.7. Lists X and Y are to combine into one list.

Column A	Column B
The median of the combined list	The average of the combined list

Question 10

$b=2a+1$

Column A	Column B
$2b$	$4a+1$

Question 11

Column A	Column B
$\frac{1}{2}+\frac{3}{5}$	$\frac{1+3}{2+5}$

Question 12

The price of an article of clothing was reduced from \$25 to \$20. The reduced price of the article was then increased by $x\%$ to return it to \$25.

Column A	Column B
x	20

Question 13

The average (arithmetic mean) of x, y and 6 is 3.

Column A	Column B
$\frac{x+y}{2}$	$\frac{3}{2}$

Question 14

$y^2 = x^2 - 1$ and $x \neq 0$.

Column A	Column B
y^4	x^4+1

Question 15

The circle with centre O has a radius of 5.
Angle ABC is a right angle.

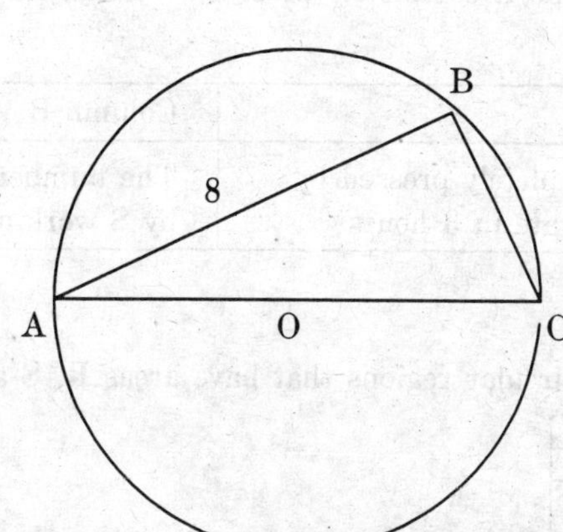

Column A	Column B
The perimeter of triangle ABC	24

Question 16

Kenneth will randomly select one of the 16 candies in a dish. There are 3 red, 5 yellow and 8 blue candies in the dish.

Column A	Column B
The probability that Kenneth will select a blue candy	The probability that Kenneth will select a candy that is either red or yellow

Question 17

m, p and x are positive integers and $mp = x$.

Column A	Column B
m	x

Question 18

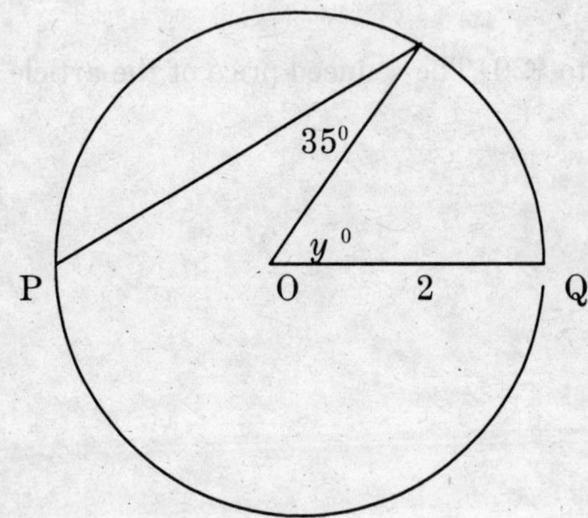

O is the centre of the circle. The distance between P and Q is 4.

Column A	Column B
y	70

Question 19

Working at constant rates, Machine R completely presses x records in 0.5 hour and Machine S completely presses x records in 0.75 hours ($x > 0$).

Column A	Column B
The number of records completely pressed by R working at its constant rate in 3 hours	The number of records completely pressed by S working at its constant rate in 4 hours

Question 20

r, s and t are the radii of three circular regions that have areas R, S and T respectively. R= 2S and S= 2T.

Column A	Column B
r	$2t$

Explanatory Answers

Answer 1

The quantity in Column A =(40% of 50)+60 = 20+60=80

The quantity in Column B =(60% of 50)+40 = 30+40=70

Since the quantity in Column A is greater, mark Option 1 as correct.

Answer 2

Since $x + 4 = 10$, $x = 10 - 4 = 6$.

The quantity in Column A = 6 – 2 = 4

The quantity in Column B = 6/2 = 3

Since the quantity in Column A is greater, mark Option 1 as correct.

Answer 3

Let us first refresh our memory about angles when two straight lines intersect.

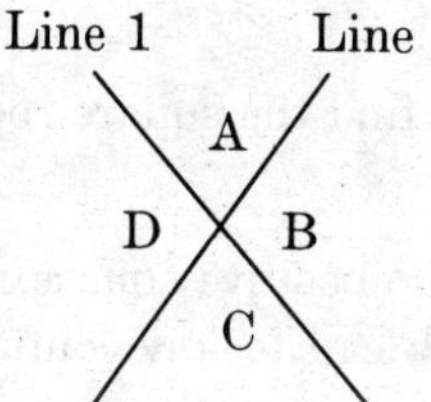

Angles A and C are known as opposite angles. They are equal in measure. Angles B and D are also opposite angles and therefore equal in measure. This is found by observation.

Angles A and B add up to 180^0 since Line 1 is a straight line and a straight line has 180^0.

Angles A and D add up to 180^0 since Line 2 is a straight line and a straight line has 180^0.

Angles D and C add up to 180^0 since Line 1 is a straight line and a straight line has 180^0.

Angles C and B add up to 180^0 since Line 2 is a straight line and a straight line has 180^0.

Let us mark Angles 1 to 8 as shown in the diagram in order to understand some fundamentals of opposite angles and angles in parallel lines.

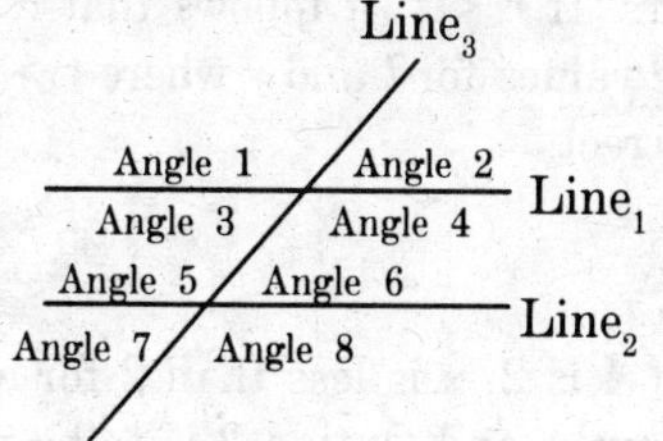

The fundamentals in regard to the angles between parallel lines and a line intersecting both the parallel lines are as under:

Angles 2 and 3 are opposite angles and therefore equal in measure.

Angles 1 and 4 are opposite angles and therefore equal in measure.

Angles 6 and 7 are opposite angles and therefore equal in measure.

Angles 5 and 8 are opposite angles and therefore equal in measure.

Angles 2 and 6 are equal in measure.

Angles 4 and 8 are equal in measure.

Angles 1 and 5 are equal in measure.

Angles 3 and 7 are equal in measure.

Now let us return to the diagram in the question. Let us refer to the line cutting L_1 and L_2 as L_3.

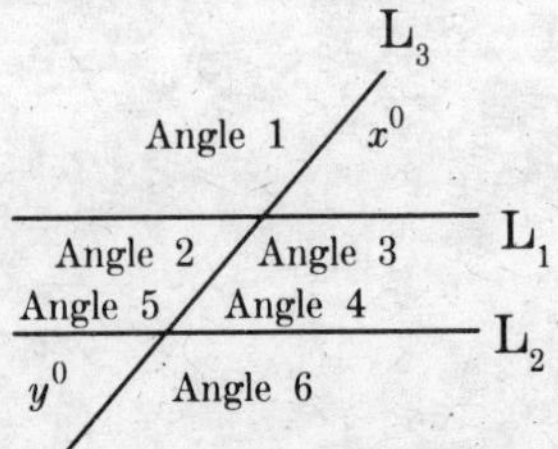

Since Angle of x^0 and Angle 4 are equal in measure and Angle 4 and Angle of y^0 are equal in measure, so $x=y$. Thus Option 3 is correct.

Answer 4

A number can have both positive and negative square roots. If you were to find the square root of 4 – for example- it could be 2 or –2.

However, the convention at the GRE is that unless expressly stated, only the positive square root of a number is to be reckoned in the calculations. This must be borne in mind lest it should lead to any confusion.

The square root of Number A divided by the square root of Number B = Square root of (Number A divided by Number B). Let us see this in operation. We know that the square root of 81 is 9. We also know that the square root of 9 is 3. Is $\sqrt{81}/\sqrt{9} = \sqrt{(81/9)}$? If we were to see $\sqrt{81}/\sqrt{9}$, this would be $9/3 = 3$ and if we were to see $\sqrt{(81/9)}$ this would be $\sqrt{9} = 3$. Since you get the same answer on the left and right sides of the equation, $\sqrt{81}/\sqrt{9} = \sqrt{(81/9)}$ and therefore the general rule is that the square root of Number A divided by the square root of Number B = Square root of (Number A divided by Number B).

$\sqrt{60}$ divided by $\sqrt{15}$ = the square root of (60 divided by 15) = $\sqrt{4} = 2$. The quantity in Column A is 2 and the quantity in Column B is 4, **Option 2** is correct.

Answer 5

We are given that $0 < r < t$. This means that both r and t are positive numbers. If $r < t$, it follows that $t > r$. If $t > r$, then t/r will always be greater quantity than r/t. Try this with any positive values for t and r where $t > r$. The question then pertains to logic more than anything else. Thus **Option 2** is correct.

Answer 6

We are given that $7x^2 = 21$. Thus $x^2 = 3$ and $x = \sqrt{3}$. Since the square root of 4 is 2, x is less than 2 for certain. It is for this reason that the quantity in Column B is greater than that in Column A and **Option 2** is to be marked as correct. Fortunately the convention followed at the GRE in regard to square roots of numbers is that one must always work with positive square roots of numbers unless one is told to the contrary. In the present case, the square root of x could be either positive or negative. When the positive square root is less than 2, the negative square root would be even lesser than 2 because a negative number is always less than a positive number. Thus Option 2 here is correct regardless of the convention at the GRE.

Answer 7

See the figure that has been given. Since Squares PQRV and VRST have sides of length 6, QR = 6 + 6 = 12 and QP = ST = 6. QSTP is thus a rectangle with one side of 12 units and the other side of 6 units. The area of the rectangle QSTP = its length multiplied by its breadth and therefore = 12 × 6 = 72 square units. The shaded portion QSP is essentially the exact half of the area of the rectangle QSTP. The area of the shaded portion is thus equal to 1/2 × 72 = 36 square units.

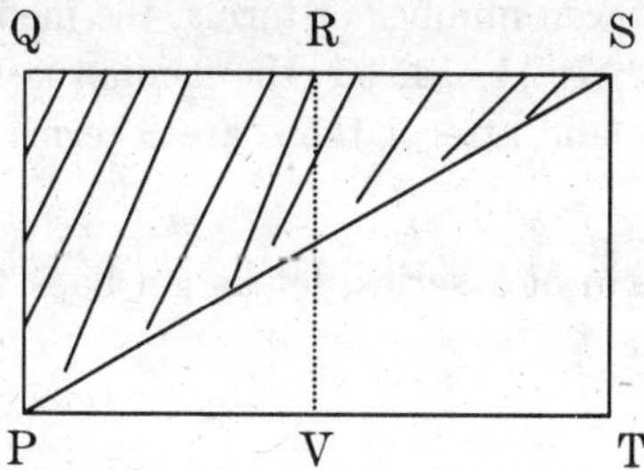

The quantity in Column A = Area of shades region PQS = 36 square units as we have seen above and the quantity in Column B = 36. Clearly, The quantity in Column A = The quantity in Column B and hence **Option 3** is correct.

It does not take a mathematical genius to understand why the area of the shaded region is half the area of the rectangle. If you were to fold the rectangle QSTP along the diagonal SP, you would have Q meeting T such that one face of the folded figure would be right-angled triangle STP and the opposite face will be right-angled triangle PQS. But since Q and T are not distinguishable, you have two right-angled triangles of exactly the same measurements and thus of the same area.

Answer 8

All that you are told that is $x > 1$ and therefore it is certain that x is always a positive number if not n integer. If you are told that $x > 1$, logically the first possible value of x that should come to mind is 2. If $x = 2$, then $2^x = 2^2 = 4$ and then $x^2 = 2^2 = 4$. Thus with the first possible value of x that should logically come to mind, the quantity in Column A is equal to the quantity in Column B.

Now let us see what would the situation be if we were to assume the next higher integral value of x that would be 3. If $x = 3$, then $2^x = 2^3 = 8$ and then $x^2 = 3^2 = 9$. With x = 3, the quantity in Column B is greater than the quantity in Column A. Since the quantity in Column A is equal to the quantity in Column B in the first instance and the quantity in Column B is higher than the quantity in Column A in the second instance you cannot say for sure whether the quantity in column A is greater than quantity in column B. Thus **Option 4** is correct.

Answer 9

The difference between the median of a series of numbers and its average (or, in other words, arithmetic mean) must first be clearly understood.

The median of a series of measurements or other numbers is the value of the middle member of the series of measurements or other numbers when they are arranged in order. In a series having an odd number of terms, the median term has as many terms to its left as it has to its right. Thus in a series having 3 terms, the 2nd term is the median; in a series with 5 terms, the 3rd term is the median and then in a series with – say – 55 terms, the 28th term is the median and so on.

Imagine a series of numbers as follows: 6, 3, 5, 2, 3, 6, 6, 2, 1, 6, 2, 12, 2, 5, 7, 4, 4, 3, 8, 2, 5. There are 21 terms in this series. If the numbers in this series are rearranged in ascending order, this becomes: 1,2, 2, 2, 2, 2, 3, 3, 3, 4, 4, 5, 5, 5, 6, 6, 6, 6, 7, 8, 12. The median of this series is the 11th term, which here is 4.

We have found the median after rearranging the terms in ascending order. Now let us see what the median would be if we were to rearrange the series in descending order. The series would then be as follows: 12, 8, 7, 6, 6, 6, 6, 5, 5, 5, 4, 4, 3, 3, 3, 2, 2, 2, 2, 2, 1. Even then the 11th term is 4. Thus whether you arrange a series in ascending or descending order, the median would remain unaffected.

This gives a series of 21 numbers: the 11th—that is, 4—is the middle one, and is the median of this set of numbers.

About the median term, it must be remembered that if there is an even number of terms, the median is the average of the two middle ones. Therefore in the following series 2, 3, 5, 6, 7, 11, 14, 91, the median is the average of the two middle terms, which are 6 and 7 (prior to 6 there are 3 terms and after 7 there are 3 terms and thus 6 and 7 are the middle terms) which is (6+7)/2 or 13/2 or 6.5.

With this little brushing up of the fundamentals in regard to median of a series, let us get back to the question on hand.

Please see the following two lists.

List X

Value	2	3	4	5
Frequency	7	12	21	22

What is intended when the value 2 has a frequency of 7 is that the number 2 occurs 7 times and 3 occurs 12 times and so on and thus the series would run like this: 2, 2, 2, 2, 2, 2, 2, 3, 3, 3, 3, 3, 3, 3, 3, 3, 3, 3, 3, and so on till the 61st and finally the 62nd term both of which would be 5.

List Y

Value	6	8	10	14	15
Frequency	8	16	19	10	9

The series in List Y would then run as follows: 6, 6, 6, 6, 6, 6, 6, 6, 8, 8, 8, 8, 8,...... and so on till the 61st and 62nd terms both which would be 15.

When the two lists are combined, List Y would join in with List X. The combined list would have 124 terms and since 124 is an even number of terms, the median term would be the average of the average of the 62nd and 63rd terms. Quite naturally, the 62nd and 63rd terms would be in the middle of the new series. The series in List X ends with the 62nd term and the series in List Y starts with the 63rd term and both lists have an equal number of terms. This would be easier to understand if we were to reduce the problem to a small size, derive the fundamentals from the reduced problem and then build the theme for the bigger problem. If a series has four terms and another series also has four terms that would mean that the last term of the first series has 3 terms before it and the first term of the second series has 3 terms after it. Extending this simple logic to a combination of two series having 62 terms each, it follows that the 62nd and 63rd terms would be in the middle of the new series.

In the combined series, the 62nd term would be 5 and the 63rd term would be 6 and the median would be the average of 5 and 6 that would come to 11/2 or 5.5

Now as regards averages, one would do well to reduce the problem and derive one's lessons from the reduced version of the problem. Imagine that a series of 4 terms – let us call it Series $_A$ is as follows: 1, 2, 3, 4 and another Series $_B$ as follows: 5, 6, 7, 8.

The average of Series $_A$ = its total/ the number of terms = (1 + 2 + 3 + 4) /4 = 10/4 = 2.5.

The average of Series $_B$ = its total/ the number of terms = (5+6+7+8) /4 = 26/4 = 6.5.

Now imagine that we are to combine Series $_A$ and Series $_B$. The average of the combined series would then be equal to the total of the combined series, which is = [(the total of Series $_A$)+ (the total of Series $_B$)]/ [(the number of terms in Series $_A$)+(the number of terms in Series $_B$)] = [10 + 26]/[4 + 4] = 36/8 = 9/2 = 4.5. If you were to find the average of the averages of Series $_A$ and Series $_B$, then you will see that it is (2.5 + 6.5)/2 = 9/2 = 4.5. Thus the average of the combined series is also to the average of the averages of the two series or in other words = [(average of Series $_A$) + (average of Series $_B$)]/2. Again, **this is true only of series having the same number of terms.**

Having derived our fundamentals from the smaller version of the problem, let us revert to the larger problem of the average of the combined list resulting out of the merger of List X and List Y. The average (or in other words the arithmetic mean) of the combined list would be = [(average of List X) + (average of List Y)]/2 = [3.9 + 10.7]/2 = 14.6/2 = 7.3

Now the quantity in Column A is 5.5 and the quantity in Column B is 7.3 and hence **Option 2** is correct.

Answer 10

We are given that $b = 2a + 1$. The quantity in Column A is 2b which would then be 2 times $(2a + 1)$ or $4a + 2$. The quantity in Column B is $4a+1$.

Let us remind ourselves that if we are to compare $(4a + 2)$ to the left with $(4a + 1)$ to the right, then the left would invariably be higher in value than the right side regardless of whether the unknown term a has negative values, has no value (meaning that $a=0$), or a has positive values. This is simply because if you are comparing $(4a + 2)$ with $(4a + 1)$, you are essentially comparing 2 and 1 since $4a$ is common to both sides. And then no matter what value does a have, 2 will always be greater than 1.

This is a question of logic more than anything else. If you have say 25 apples and a kilogram of sugar on the left of a scales and say 15 bananas and a kilogram of sugar on the right side of the scales and if you find that the scales is tilting to the left, it means that you would not be making an earthshaking discovery when you announce that 25 apples weigh more than 15 bananas, even if you do not know the precise weight of 25 apples and 15 bananas. Thus **Option 1** is correct.

Answer 11

Let us remember this rather simple method of adding two fractions A/B and C/D. The sum of these two fractions is (AD+BC)/BD.

In the diagram below one cross-multiplies (meaning A with D and C with B) and then adds the products AD and BC to arrive at the numerator and then one multiplies B with D in order to arrive at the denominator of the fraction.

$$\frac{A}{B} + \frac{C}{D} = \frac{AD + BC}{BD}$$

If you were to add 1/4 and 3/4, the result would be [(1 × 4) + (3 × 4)]/(4 × 4) = (4 + 12)/16 = 16/16 = 1. Thus if you were to add the quantity in Column A, you would get (5 + 6)/10 = 11/10 which is more than 1. The quantity in Column B is 4/7, which is less than 1 **as in all cases of positive fractions** where the numerator is less than the denominator. Hence the quantity in Column A is greater than the quantity in Column B and hence **Option 1** is correct.

Answer 12

We are told that the price of an article of clothing was reduced from \$25 to \$20. The reduced price of the article was then increased by $x\%$ to return it to \$25.

Let us see these fundamentals in regard to percentages:

The need for a common denominator arises when you are to compare some fractions that have different denominators. If the denominators are the same, no further effort is necessary to compare them except a mere glance. If you are to compare – for example – two fractions 3/28 and 5/28, you know that if there were 28 candies, then 5 candies out of 28 is a greater share than 3 out of 28.

When you are comparing two or more fractions that have different numerators and different denominators, comparison becomes far easier – and, of course, meaningful - when the different fractions are expressed in terms of the same denominator.

A fraction can be expressed as a percentage terms if the denominator is 100. Thus the fraction 1/4 - for example – can be expressed in percentage terms by multiplying the denominator with 25 so as to get 100 in the denominator. But when you multiply the denominator alone, you are watering down the fraction (meaning reducing its value and then the fraction does not have the same value whereas our intention is to leave the value of the fraction untouched. This is why you multiply the numerator as well so that you can express 1/4 as 25/100 and the fraction ¼ becomes 25%. *Per cent* incidentally is *through 100*, since cent means 100.

When the price is reduced to 20 and then restored to 25, it means that 5 is added to 20. This means that if you were to express this addition of 5 to 20 or 5/20 in percentage terms, you would have to multiply both the numerator and the denominator with 5 so as to get 100 in the denominator as follows: (5 × 5)/(20 × 5) and the fraction 5/20 would then be expressed as 25/100 or 25% in percentage terms. This means that the quantity in Column A is 25 whereas the quantity in Column B is 20 and hence **Option 1** is to be marked as correct.

Answer 13

The arithmetic mean of a series of numbers is = (the total of the terms in the series) ÷ (the number of terms in the series). Thus the total of the terms in a series is = (The arithmetic mean of a series of numbers) × (the number of terms in the series).

If the arithmetic mean of three numbers is 3, it then follows that the total of the three terms is 9. This means that if x, y and 6 add up to 9, x and y would add up to 3.

The quantity in Column A is thus 3/2 and the quantity in Column B is 3/2. Since the quantities in both the columns are equal, **Option 3** is correct.

Answer 14

We are given that $y^2 = x^2 - 1$ and $x \neq 0$. The quantity in column A is y^4 which is the square of y^2 and therefore also the square of $(x^2 - 1)$ since $y^2 = x^2 - 1$.

- When you multiply the sums of some unknown terms, say (A+B) with (C + D), then the product is equal to AC + BC + AD + BD. Thus if you were to multiply, for example, (4 + 3) with (3 + 2) the answer which we all know should be 35 is arrived at in the following manner: (4 × 3) + (3 × 3) + (4 × 2) + (3 × 2) = 12 + 9 + 8 + 6 = 35.
- When you multiply the sums of some unknown terms – say (A – B) with (C – D) then the product is equal to AC – BC – AD + BD. Put some small positive integral values for A, B, C and D and see this for yourself.
- When you multiply the sums of some unknown terms – say (A + B) with (C – D) – then the product is equal to AC + BC – AD – BD. Put some small positive integral values for A, B, C and D and see this for yourself.

Back to the question on hand, the square of $(x^2 - 1) = (x^2 - 1) \times (x^2 - 1) = (x^2 \times x^2) - (1 \times x^2) - (x^2 \times 1)$ $(1 \times 1) = x^4 - x^2 - x^2 + 1 = x^4 - 2x^2 + 1$. The quantity in column A is therefore $(x^4 - 2x^2 + 1)$ and that in column B is $(x^4 + 1)$. You must remember that one substitutes the value of unknown numerical values with alphabets such as x and y. An unknown numerical value can be any one of the following: (A) Negative (B) Zero or (C ositive. When comparing the quantities in the two columns – meaning $(x^4 - 2x^2 + 1)$ with $(x^4 + 1)$, one has to emember that $(x^4 + 1)$ is common to the two sides and therefore what will decide as to which is a greater quantity vill depend on the value of $-2x^2$ that is not common to the two sides. Now if:

A) $x = 0$, then $-2x^2$ will also be zero and hence the two sides shall be equal in value. This is good to remember by vay of a fundamental. In the present case, however, we are given that x is not equal to zero and therefore we need ot consider this scenario for the present case.

B) x has a negative value, then since x^2 will mean $(x \times x)$ and since $(x \times x)$ is a product of two negative values, he product will invariably have a positive value and thus $2x^2$ will have positive value and therefore $-2x^2$ will nvariably have a negative value.

C) x has a positive value, then $-2x^2$ will invariably have a negative value.

his means that the quantity in column A is less than that in column B and thus **Option 2** is correct.

nswer 15

he circle with centre O has a radius of 5. Angle ABC is a right angle.

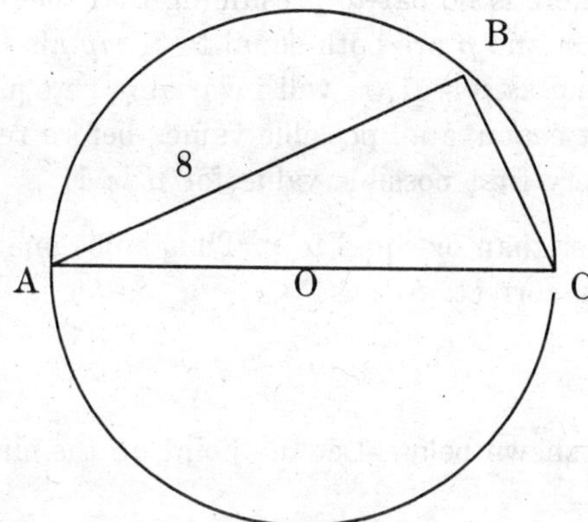

uckily, in the present question, we are given that Angle ABC is a right angle but even if you are not given this formation, it must be borne in mind that it is a property of the circle that when a triangle is formed by joining ny vertex on its circumference to the two ends of its diameter, the angle formed at the vertex shall invariably be right angle.

he diameter of a circle is twice the measure of its radius. Thus AC, which is the hypotenuse of the right triangle BC, is 10. This means that if one were to apply one's knowledge of the Pythagoras Theorem, which says that in right-angled triangle:

Iypotenuse)^2 = (One Side)^2 + (Other side)^2. Thus $(10)^2 = (8)^2 + (BC)^2$ and hence $(BC)^2 = 100 - 64 = 36$ and ence BC = 6.

he perimeter of the triangle ABC is $10 + 8 + 6 = 24$. Hence the quantities in columns A and B are equal in easure and **Option 3** is correct.

nswer 16

hat we are given is: Kenneth will randomly select one of the 16 candies in a dish. There are 3 red, 5 yellow and blue candies in the dish.

et us see what probability means. If an event has N equally likely outcomes and F of them are termed favourable, e probability of a favourable outcome is F/N.

Imagine that Kenneth (shall we call him K for sake of brevity?) who is blindfolded puts his hand into the candy box and pulls one candy out at random. Each time that he dips in, he keeps the candy that he has picked in a separate tray that you and I are jointly holding. We are allowed to sort the candies by their colours. K is blindfolded, but we are not. He can do so 16 times. Out of the 16 times that he dips in, 8 times he has come up with a blue candy since there are 8 blue candies. The number of favourable events – meaning K bringing up blue candies – is 8. The total number of events – meaning K bringing up a candy (blue, red or yellow) is 16. The probability that Kenneth will select a blue candy is 8 out of 16 or 8/16 and hence 1/2.

Now as regards red candies **and** yellow candies (mind the words red **and** yellow which is so different from red **or** yellow), the number of red candies and yellow candies add up to 8. Kenneth can dip in 16 times and if we were to count the number of red and yellow candies, we will find that he has come up with a total of 5 candies that fit the description of being red and 3 that fit the description of being yellow and thus 8 red **and** yellow candies. The probability that Kenneth will select red and yellow candies is 8 out of 16 or 8/16 and hence 1/2.

This means that the quantity in column A is equal to the quantity in column B (since both are equal to 1/2) and hence **Option 3** is correct.

Answer 17

We are given that m, p and x are positive integers and $mp = x$. Positive integers means 1, 2, 3, 4, 5 and so on. We are not told that m and p are unequal. This means that there is no bar to presuming that they are equal. Secondly, the first possible positive integer is 1. This means that if m and p are both equal to 1, mp also $= 1$. Then since all three of m, p and x are equal to 1, $m=x$. Secondly, as long as $p = 1$, m will invariably be equal to x. There is no bar to presuming any value for p and therefore one must examine all possible values before reaching a conclusion and since we are talking about all possible values, the very first possible value for p is 1.

So long as p is more than 1, m can never be either greater than or equal to x. Thus since one cannot say for sure whether m is equal to x or m is less than x, **Option 4** is correct.

Answer 18

In the given diagram, link P and O with a dotted line as shown below. Let the point on the circumference be R as shown in the diagram below.

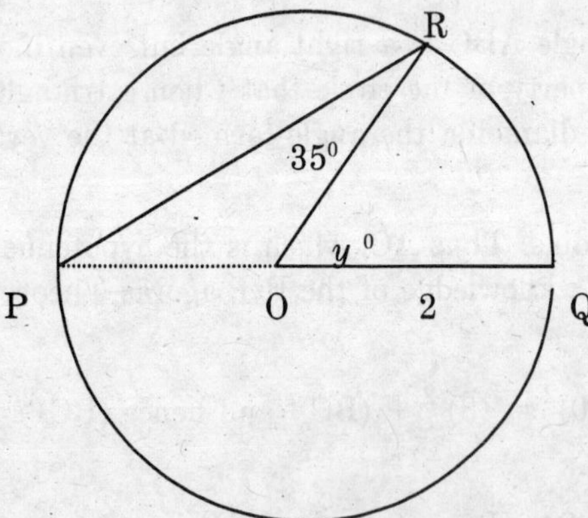

O is the centre of the circle. It is apparent from the diagram that the radius of the circle is 2. PO and OR are the radii of the circle and therefore PO = OR. Since angle PRO is 35^0, then in the triangle PRO, PR + OR, the angles OPR and PRO are equal and thus angle OPR also equals 35^0. This means that in triangle POR, angle POR is $180^0 - (35^0+35^0) = 110$. Since POQ is a straight line, angle ROQ $= 180^0$ – angle POQ$= 180^0 - 110^0 = 70^0$. Since $y^0 = 70^0$, $y = 70$. This means that the quantities in columns A and B are equal and thus **Option 3** is correct.

Answer 19

The comparison of quantities is essentially an exercise in telling which is more and which is less and so on and therefore of being able to decide relative values. This is why you are given an unknown quantity x in the question. For being able to decide which quantity is greater, a little perception becomes necessary. The essential difference between a school level examination in mathematics and a competitive examination involving quantitative ability is that of breadth of perception. The competitive examination tests this breadth.

Now imagine that two of your friends have been telling you of the time they ran at constant speeds while preparing for the school athletics championships. John says that he ran 345 meters in 69 seconds and Ken says that he ran 275 meters in 33 seconds. How can you tell whose speed is greater? Their distances are different and their timings are different. You can do this by finding out how much could they have run in one second if they ran at their constant speeds.

John ran 345 meters in 69 seconds and therefore 345/69 or 5 meters in one second.

Ken ran 275 meters in 33 seconds and therefore 275/33 or 25/3 = more than 8 meters in one second.

Thus Ken's speed is the greater of the two.

Now imagine that Ken and John were to be heard talking of the fish their respective fathers bagged on a fishing vacation. Ken says that his father bagged a huge fish (meaning of unspecified length). John says that his father hooked a fish that was three times as long as the fish that Ken's father bagged. If you are to decide – assuming that both are telling the truth – as to who bagged the longer fish, do you need to persist with the unknown lengths? Divide the lengths of both fish by the same unknown length and even then John's father has bagged a longer fish than Ken's father.

You are told that there are two machines. Working at constant rates, Machine R completely presses x records in 0.5 hour and Machine S completely presses x records in 0.75 hours ($x>0$). Now let us get rid of the unknown term x and let us imagine that both machines could press 1 record in 0.5 and 0.75 hours respectively. Why persist with the unknown quantity x when you are asked to evaluate as to which machine can turn out more presses?

Give x a numerical value – and what could be easier to work with than 1 as a value for x ? If $x = 1$, then since Machine R can press 1 record in 0.5 hour (or ½ hour) R can press 2 records in 1 hour and thus 6 records in 3 hours. Since Machine S can press 1 record in 0.75 hour (or ¾ hour) S can press 4/3 records in 1 hour and thus 16/3 records in 4 hours.

The quantity in Column A is 6 and the quantity in column B is 16/3 (16/3 is more than 5 but less than 6). Thus Option 1.

Answer 20

When one is asked to compare the areas of some circles based on their radii – say r, s and t - one must remember that since the area of a circle is $\pi \times (\text{radius})^2$, the areas of the three circles are $\pi \times r^2$, $\pi \times s^2$ and $\pi \times t^2$. Since π is common to the three areas, it is not necessary to persist with π in comparing the three areas. If A is greater than B, then π times A is greater than π times B. Thus π should be dropped while comparing. This means that when you compare the areas of circles, you are really comparing the squares of their respective radii.

Since the areas of the three circles with radii r, s and t are R, S and T respectively and further that R = 2S and S = 2T, the three areas are 4T, 2T and T respectively which means that the area of the circle with radius r is four times that of the area of circle with radius t. This means that the square of r is 4 times the square of t, or $r^2 = 4t^2$ and hence $r = 2t$. This means that the quantities in columns A and B have the same value and Option 3 is correct.

Chapter 48

Quantitative Comparison

Practice Test 2

GENERAL DIRECTIONS *for the questions in this practice test:*

The question consists of two quantities, one in Column A and one in Column B. There may be additional information, centres above the two columns, that concerns one or both the quantities. A symbol that appears in both columns represents the same thing in Column A as it does in Column B. You are to compare the quantity in Column A with the quantity in Column B and decide whether:

1. *The quantity in Column A is greater*
2. *The quantity in Column B is greater*
3. *The two quantities are equal*
4. *The relation cannot be determined from the information given*

Question 1

$x - 1 < -x$

Column A	Column B
x	0

Question 2

Betty spent $75 for a bicycle and she also spent $27 repairing it. She then sold it for $120.

Column A	Column B
The money Betty received in excess of the total amount she spent	$20

Question 3

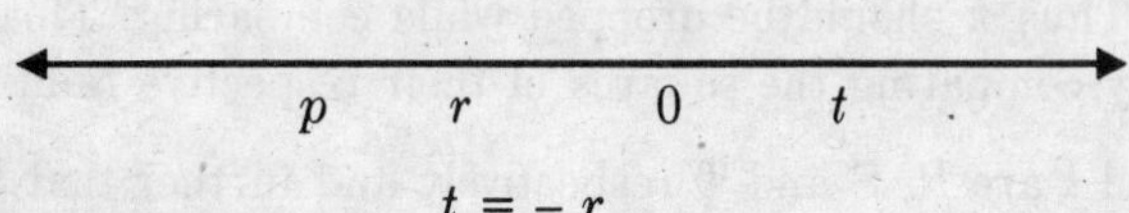

$t = -r$

Column A	Column B
p^2	$-rt$

Question 4

Column A	Column B
23(784)	24(783)

Question 5

Column A	Column B
$(-1)^{10}$	$(-1)^{11}$

Question 6

Column A	Column B
10	$11+x$

Question 7

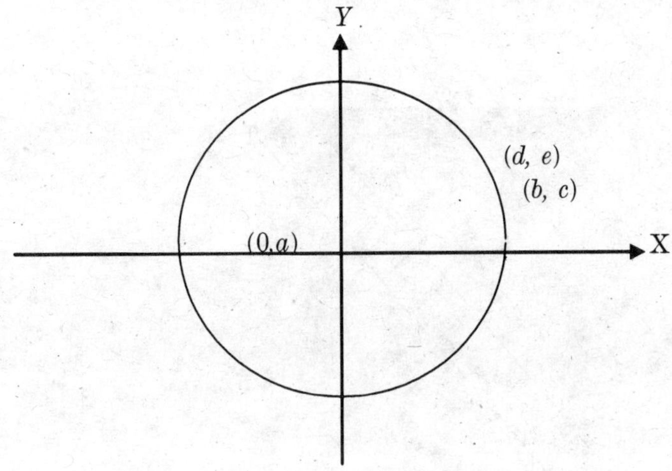

In the xy-plane, the point $(0,a)$ is the centre of the circle and the points (b, c) and (d, e) are on the circle.

Column A	Column B
b^2+c^2	d^2+e^2

Question 8

For each house in Town X, the amount of property tax is p percent of the value of the house. The property tax on a house whose value is \$45,000 is \$ 1,200.

Column A	Column B
The property tax on a house in Town X whose value is \$ 54,000	\$1,300

Question 9

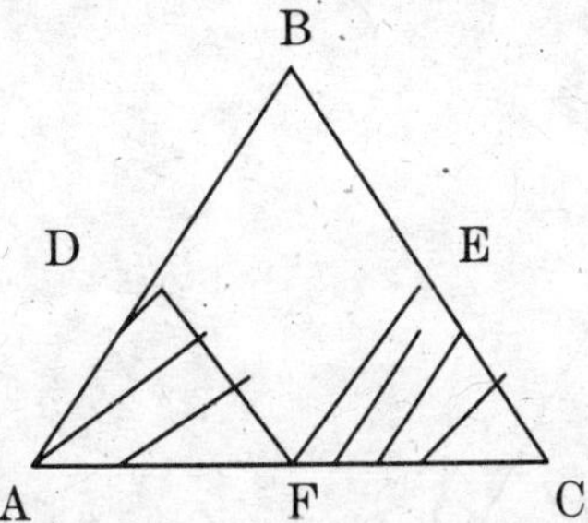

D, E, and F are mid points of the sides of triangle ABC as shown.

Column A	Column B
The sum of the areas of the shaded regions.	The area of the region enclosed by quadrilateral DBEF

Question 10

$x^2+y^2 = 81$

$x^2-y^2 = 0$

Column A	Column B
x^4-y^4	0

Question 11

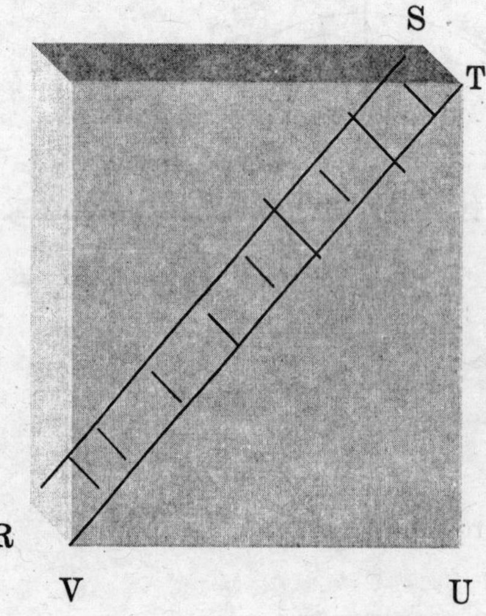

In the rectangular solid shown, TU = 3, UV = 4 and VR = 2.

Column A	Column B
The area of the shaded rectangular region	9

Question 12

A printer numbered consecutively the pages of a book, beginning with 1 on the first page. In numbering the pages, he printed a total of 189 digits.

Column A	Column B
The number of pages in the book	100

Question 13

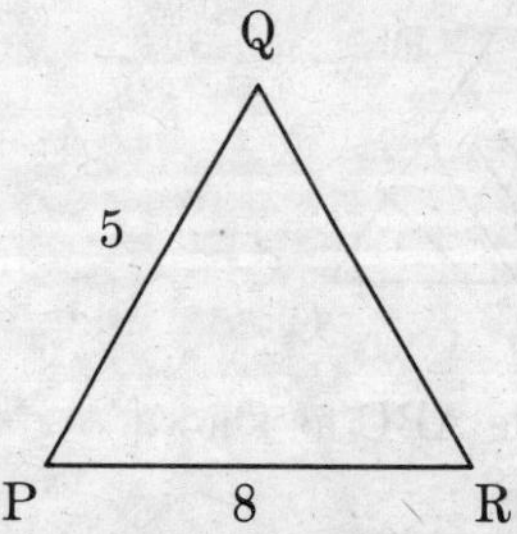

Column A	Column B
QR	6

Question 14

Column A	Column B
The standard deviation of the data 5,5,8,14 and 18	The standard deviation of the data 6,6,8,14 and 16

Question 15

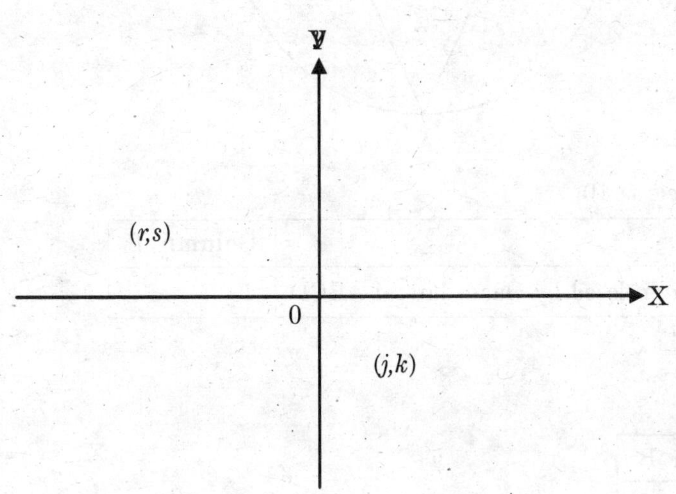

Column A	Column B
$s+j$	$r+k$

Question 16

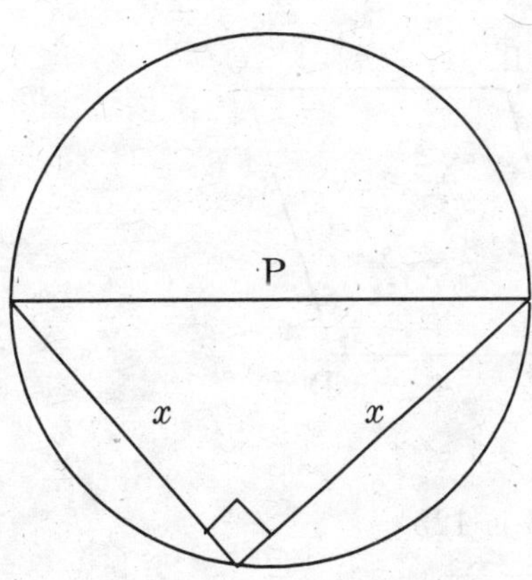

The area of the circular region with centre P is 16π.

Column A	Column B
x	4

Question 17

The length of an edge of cube R is 2 and the length of an edge of cube T is 3.

Column A	Column B
The ratio of the surface area of cube R to that of cube T	The ratio of the volume of cube R to that of cube T

Question 18

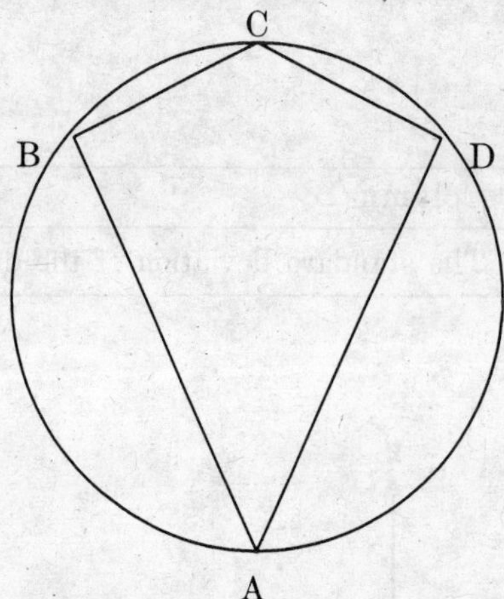

The diameter of the circle is 10.

Column A	Column B
The area of the region enclosed by Quadrilateral ABCD	40

Question 19

$y \neq 5$

Column A	Column B
$(5-y)(y-5)$	0

Question 20

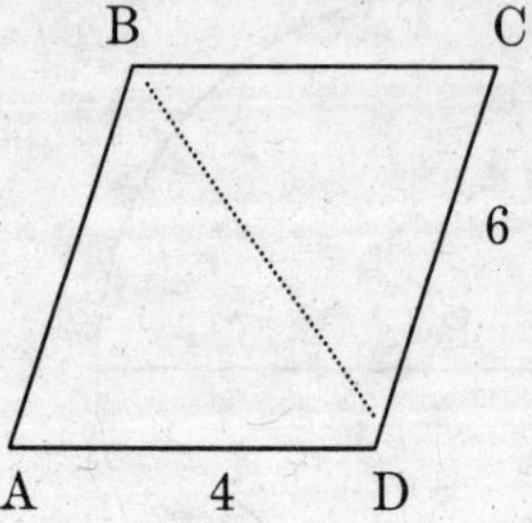

ABCD is a parallelogram and angle B is 125^0.

Column A	Column B
The area of region ABCD	24

Explanatory Answers

Answer 1

When up against such quantitative comparisons, one must remember that in the absence of a specific range of values for the unknown quantity x, there is no bar against assuming negative, zero and positive values for the unknown x. This is why we shall first take a couple of negative integral values for x, then assume x to be zero and then a couple of positive integral values for x.

Secondly one must also remember that one need work with integral values because this will make things simpler.

(i) Let us first assume x to be -1 and then -2. When $x = -1$, $x - 1$ will be $1 - 1 = 0$ whereas $-x$ will be 1. Here the quantity in column A is lower than the quantity in Column B. If you were to assume x to be -2, then $x - 1$ will be $2 - 1 = 1$ whereas $-x$ will be 2. Here the quantity in column A is lower than the quantity in Column B.

(ii) Let us now assume x to be 0. $x - 1$ will be $0 - 1 = -1$ whereas $-x$ will be 0. Here the quantity in column A is equal to the quantity in Column B.

In case (i) the quantity in Column A is lower than that in column B whereas in (ii) the two quantities are equal. The moment you have a situation in which the quantities in the two columns are equal, you have no choice but to mark **Option 4** as correct, since you cannot state whether the quantity in column A is higher or that in column B is higher or whether they are necessarily equal. Now assuming positive values for x is of academic interest only. However we shall take these positive values for x and satisfy ourselves that this is indeed an academic exercise.

(iii) Let us first assume x to be 1 and then 2. When $x = 1$, $x - 1$ will be $1 - 1 = 0$ whereas $-x$ will be -1. Here the basic relationship of $x - 1 < -x$ is not satisfied and hence there is no need to work further with positive values at all.

Answer 2

Since Betty spent \$75 for a bicycle and she also spent \$27 repairing it, she incurred a total of \$102 on the bicycle. She then sold it for \$120. This means that she earned a profit of \$120 – \$102 = \$18. Column A is effectively the profit on the transaction because the profit, in any transaction, is the money received in excess of the total amount spent. Thus the quantity in column B is higher than that in column A. Hence **Option 2**.

Answer 3

We are told that $t = -r$ and thus $-rt = r^2$. Now when you are comparing the quantities in columns A and B what you are effectively comparing is p^2 with r^2. As can be seen in the above diagram, p has further negative value than r. Thus for example, when $r =$ say, -2, $p =$ say, -3 and when $r = -3$ then $p =$ say, -4. Thus irrespective of the values of r and p, p^2will always be higher than the value of r^2. Hence **Option 1** is to be marked as correct.

Answer 4

See how logic will help you surmount this problem that would take a whole lot of time and energy if you were to do actual multiplications. We can see that the two factors in column A are 23 and 784 and those in column B are one more than 23 and one less than 784. This should call for an application of mere logic.

Take 23 as A and 783 as B. This means that the quantity in column A is 23(784) which is A(B + 1) = AB + A and the quantity in column B is (A + 1)(B) = AB + B. Now when you are comparing the quantities in columns A and B, what you are effectively comparing is (AB+A) with (AB + B). AB is common to both and therefore what you are really comparing is A with B. We know A is 23 and B is 783 and therefore 783 is definitely higher than 23. This means that the quantity in column B is definitely higher than the quantity in column A and hence **Option 2** is correct.

Answer 5

When (-1) is raised to an even power the answer will invariably be positive and would be equal to +1. When (–1) is raised to an odd power the answer will invariably be negative and would be equal to –1. This means that the quantity in column A is higher than the quantity in column B and hence **Option 1** is to be marked as correct.

Answer 6

We know that the quantity in column A is 10 whereas the quantity in column B is $11+x$. But the unknown x can have negative values (or for that matter zero and positive values). If x is zero or positive, then the quantity in column B is invariably higher than the quantity in column A but if x is negative, then the following things can happen:

- If $x = -1$, then the quantities in both columns are equal since both would be equal to 10.
- If $x = -2$, then the quantity in column B is 9 whereas the quantity in column A is 10.

Thus we have situations in which the quantity in column A can be higher as well as lower than that in column B and also a situation in which both the quantities are equal. Thus **Option 4** is to be marked as correct.

Answer 7

See the diagram as follows with straight lines linking the centre of the circle with the points on the circle.

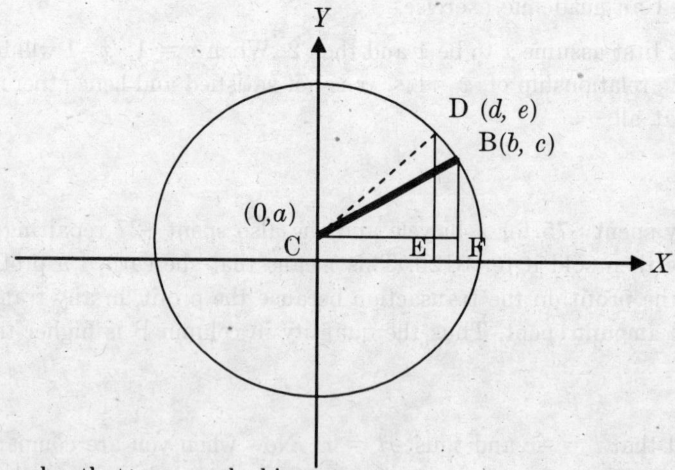

There are two right-angled triangles that you are looking at:

1. Triangle CDE in which CE = d and DE=$e-a$ and
2. Triangle CBF in which CF = b and BF = $c-a$.

Since the two triangles are right angled and both have hypotenuse of the same length (since the hypotenuse in both right angled triangles is the radius of the circle), the sum of the squares of the other two sides in each triangle will be the same as per the theorem of Pythagoras. This means that in triangle CDE, $CE^2 + DE^2 = CD^2$ and in triangle CBF, $CF^2 + BF^2 = CB^2$. Since CD= CB (both being radii of the circle) $CD^2 = CB^2$. This means that $(d)^2 + (e-a)^2 = (b)^2 + (c-a)^2$ or $d^2 + e^2 - 2ea + a^2 = b^2 + c^2 - 2ac + a^2$.

Since a^2 is common to both sides, $d^2 + e^2 - 2ea = b^2 + c^2 - 2ac$ and therefore $b^2 + c^2 = d^2 + e^2 - 2ea + 2ac$ or $b^2 + c^2 = d^2 + e^2 - 2a(e-c)$.

We can see that e has greater value than c and this means that $(e-c)$ will be positive and since a is positive (since a is above the x-axis), $2a(e-c)$ is also positive and thus $b^2 + c^2 = d^2 + e^2$ – *some positive number* (whatever it is).

Since the squares of all numbers except zero are positive, $b^2 + c^2$ is clearly smaller than $d^2 + e^2$ because $b^2 + c^2$ is equal to some positive number **subtracted** from $d^2 + e^2$. Thus **Option 2** is correct.

Answer 8

We are told that the property tax in the town is p percent of the value of the home. Thus if it is p percent in one case, so will it be in another.

If the tax on a house worth $45,000 is $ 1,200, then the tax on a home worth $ 54,000 is 54000/45000 times the tax on the home worth $45,000 or 54/45 times 1200 which is 6/5 times 1200 that comes to $1440. Thus the quantity in column A ($1440) is higher than the quantity in column B ($1300). Hence **Option 1** is correct.

Answer 9.

Join DE with a dotted straight line as shown below:

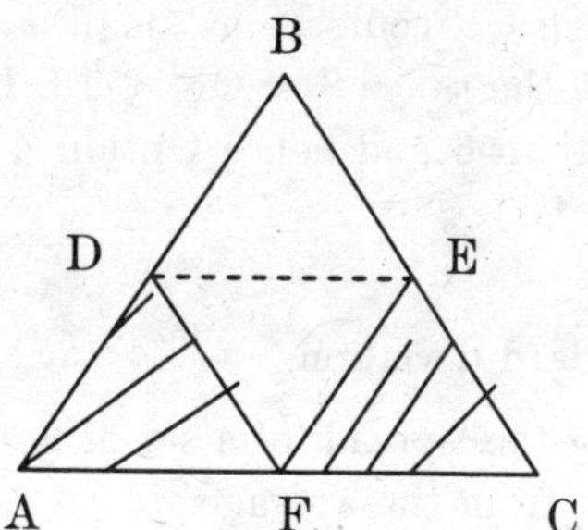

What you now see is four triangles BDE, DEF, ADF and FEC. Triangles BDE and DEF add up to the rectangle DBEF. The area of the triangle ABC is 1/2 its base (AC) multiplied by height (BF). The height of each of the triangles ADF (whose height is the perpendicular from D to AF) and FEC (whose height is the perpendicular from E to FC) is 1/2 BF since DE links the midpoints of the sides AB and BC.

The base of each of the triangles ADF and FEC is 1/2 the base of the triangle ABC. This means that the area of each of the triangles ADF and FEC is 1/2 × 1/2 (the base of the triangle ABC × the height of the triangle ABC)= 1/4th the area of the triangle ABC and this therefore means that the area of the triangles ADF and FEC together adds up to half the area of the triangle ABC. Thus after deducting the areas of the triangles ADF and FEC from the area of the triangle ABC, what you are left with is 1/2 the area of the triangle ABC. Then again, once you deduct the two triangles ADF and FEC from the area of the triangle ABC, what you are left with is the rectangle DBEF. Thus the area of the rectangle DBEF is half the area of the triangle ABC which means that the area of the rectangle DBEF = the sum of the area of the triangles ADF and FEC that makes the area of the shaded region.

Thus the quantity in column A is equal to the quantity in column B and hence **Option 3** is to be marked as correct.

Answer 10

The expression $x^4 - y^4$ is essentially $(x^2 + y^2)$ multiplied with $(x^2 - y^2)$ and if you were to multiply 81 with zero, you would get zero. Thus the quantities in both columns are equal to zero and hence **Option 3**.

Answer 11

Once you realise that all four angles in a rectangle are right angles, it becomes plain that this question pertains to the Pythagoras Theorem that states that the square on the hypotenuse is equal to the sum of the squares on the other two sides.

Since TU = 3 and UV = 4, VT^2, the square on the hypotenuse, in the right-angled triangle TUV $= 3^2 + 4^2 = 9 + 16 = 25$ and therefore VT = 5. The shaded rectangular region STVR is thus a rectangle with one side (meaning VT) of 5 units in measure and the other side (meaning VR) of 2 units in measure and therefore the area of the shaded region is 10 square units in measure. The quantity in column A is greater than that in column B and thus **Option 1**.

Answer 12

The first nine numbers 1 to 9 have one digit each. Thereafter each number has two digits till 99. Since 189 digits have been printed, the number of two digit numbers is (189–9)/2 = 180/2 = 90. Therefore the total number of pages printed is 9 + 90 = 99 and hence the quantity in column B is greater than that in column A. Hence **Option 2** is to be marked as correct.

Answer 13

One of the fundamentals of a triangle is that the longest side is invariably less in measure than the total measure of the other two sides. Here, there may be two situations:

The side PR with 8 units measure may be the longest side in which QR could be as small as, say, 0.1 units but it is definitely less than 3. The measure of side QR could lie in the range $0 < QR < 3$.

The side QR may be the longest side in which QR could be as small as, say, 8.1 units but it is definitely less than 13. The measure of side QR could lie in the range $8 < QR < 13$. Hence you cannot say for sure whether QR is less than 6 or equal to 6 or greater than 6 and hence **Option 4** is to be marked as correct.

Answer 14

Let us first refresh our memory about standard deviation.

Standard Deviation is a number representing the 'spread' of a set of numbers around their average value. It is calculated from all the individual deviations from the average.

A simple example is to consider the heights of a group of five children. If their heights are 146 cm, 148 cm, 151 cm, 153 cm, and 157 cm, the average of their heights is (146 + 148 + 151 + 153 + 157) cm/5 = 755 cm/5 = 151 cm.

A simple average of the deviations (differences from the average) themselves cannot be used. If you are to calculate the deviations in the above example from the average, then the total of the deviations would be equal to $(151 - 146) + (151 - 148) + (151 - 151) + (151 - 153) + (151 - 157) = 5 + 3 + 0 - 2 - 6 = 0$. You will see that the plus and minus values cancel one another out. This is why a more complicated method is necessary. In practice, the squares of the deviations are averaged (squares are always positive), and then its square root is taken. The standard deviation is $(151 - 146)^2 + (151 - 148)^2 + (151 - 151)^2 + (151 - 153)^2 + (151 - 157)^2 = (5)^2 + (3)^2 + (0)^2 + (-2)^2 + (-6)^2 = 25 + 9 + 0 + 4 + 36 = 74$. The square of the deviations is then averaged and this comes to 74/5 or 14.8. The square root of 14.8 is roughly 3.8. Therefore and the standard deviation is approximately 3.8 cm.

In the question, the standard deviation of the quantity in column A is to be calculated as under:

First we must find the average of the data 5, 5, 8, 14 and 18, which would come to 50/5=10. Next, find the difference between the average of the data and each individual data then calculate the square of each and finally add them like this $-(10 - 5)^2 + (10 - 5)^2 + (10 - 8)^2 + (10 - 14)^2 + (10 - 18)^2 = (5)^2 + (5)^2 + (2)^2 + (-4)^2 + (-8)^2 = 25 + 25 + 4 + 16 + 64 = 134$. The sum of the squares of the deviations is then averaged and this comes to 134/5 or nearly 27.

The standard deviation of the quantity in column B is to be calculated in a similar way as under:

First we must find the average of the data 6, 6, 8, 14 and 16, which would come to 50/5=10. The standard deviation of this data is to be found by first adding the difference between the average of the data and each individual data and this would then be $(10 - 6)^2 + (10 - 6)^2 + (10 - 8)^2 + (10 - 14)^2 + (10 - 16)^2 = (4)^2 + (4)^2 + (2)^2 + (-4)^2 + (-6)^2 = 16 + 16 + 4 + 16 + 36 = 88$. The square of the deviations is then averaged and this comes to 88/5 or nearly 18.

Since the square root of 27 is definitely higher than the square root of 18, the quantity in column A is higher than the quantity in column B and thus **Option 1** is correct.

Let us see how we could have short-circuited the process of calculations:

If you have seen from the two sets of data in columns A and B, both have the same arithmetic mean – or average if you please. Secondly both have the same number of data. If you were to add only the absolute deviations – meaning without the sign in front of the deviations or forgetting minuses in other words - in the data in column A you get 5 + 5 + 2 + 4 + 8 = 24 whereas if you were to add only the absolute deviations in the data in column B you get 4 + 4 + 2 + 4 + 6 = 20. The standard deviation in the data in column A is higher because the data in column A is not so clustered around the arithmetic mean – or average – as in the case of the data in column B.

See the following thumb rule. This should be an invaluable tip for those who wish to calculate fast and meet the twin constraints of speed and accuracy. However a tip by itself burdens one's memory unless it is backed by strong illustrations. This is why we have taken pains to explain the fact that a data 'clustered' around the average is sure to have a lower standard deviation than a data that is not so clustered. In order to find out whether a data is clustered or otherwise, it is important to calculate only the absolute deviations.

However, you must remember that **the above thumb rule regarding the standard deviation of the same number of data and the same average being decided by the total of the absolute deviations from the average may or may not apply to cases where the number of observations is different though the average may be the same.**

Answer 15

If you see a above graph, s and j are both positive whereas r and k are both negative. Thus $s+j$ would invariably have a positive value as against $r+k$ which would invariably have a negative value. Hence the quantity in column A is greater than the quantity in column B and hence **Option 1.**

Answer 16

Please see the figure below where we have assigned letters to each of the three vertices of the right-angled triangle in the question.

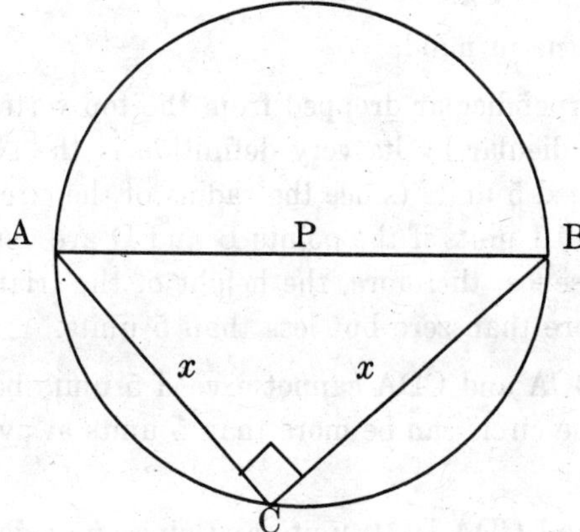

Since the area of the circle with centre P is 16π and since the area of any circle is π times the square of its radius, the square of the radius of the circle is 16 it follows that the radius of the circle is 4 units. This means that AB is 8 units. Since AB is the hypotenuse in the right-angled triangle ABC, and since both AC and BC have the same measure (x units, as is apparent from the diagram in the question) $AB^2 = AC^2 + BC^2$ and thus $64 = 2x^2$. Thus x = square root of 32 which is certainly higher than 4 that is the quantity in column B. Hence Option 1 is to be marked as correct.

Answer 17

A cube has all three sides equal in measure. A cube has six surfaces. The surface area of a cube is equal to six times the product of two of its sides whereas its volume is equal to the product of three of its sides. Thus, when we are comparing the quantities in the two columns, they are as follows:

Column A	Column B
The ratio of the surface area of cube R to that of cube T = (6×2×2)/(6×3×3) = 4/9	The ratio of the volume of cube R to that of cube T = 2×2×2/3×3×3 = 8/27

The question now is: which of the fractions is greater, 4/9 or 8/27. In order to see which fraction has higher value, one must divide the denominator by the numerator and see where one gets the higher value. The fraction in which the denominator is a higher multiple of the numerator, has a lesser value. In case of the fraction 4/9, if we divide the denominator by the numerator we would get 9/4 which is a little over 2 whereas in case of the fraction 8/27, if we divide the denominator by the numerator we would get 27/8 which is a little over 3. This would mean that 4/9 has a higher value than 8/27.

But that is a general rule. In this particular case, the denominator in the fraction 8/27 is 27, which is a multiple of the denominator in the fraction 4/9. This means that if we were to compare the two fractions, one must have the same denominator in order to compare meaningfully. This means that if we were to multiply both the numerator and the denominator with 3 in the fraction 4/9, we would get 12/27 and this is certainly higher than 8/27. Thus Option 1.

Answer 18

Join C and A with a straight line in the figure. It would then be clear that the quadrilateral ABCD is essentially an aggregate of two right-angled triangles BCA and CDA.

We know that the two triangles are right-angled because of the property of a circle according to which if the two ends of the diameter of a circle are linked with any point on the circumference of the circle, then the angle at the vertex on the circumference of the circle is a right angle.

This means that the base of each of the two triangles BCA and CDA is 10 units since the two triangles have a common base. The area of each of the two triangles BCA and CDA is 1/2 × base × height of each of these two triangles. We know only the base of the two triangles but not their height. Thus it is not possible to find, the area of each of the triangles and therefore of the rectangle ABCD since the area of the two triangles BCA and CDA adds up to the area of the rectangle ABCD.

Here some fundamentals must be borne in mind:

- The height of a triangle is the perpendicular dropped from the top vertex to the base. Here the top vertex has to lie on the circle. A perpendicular by its very definition is the shortest distance to the base. This means that the height cannot exceed 5 units (since the radius of the circle is 5 units) but at the same time the height can be as small as say 0.1 units if the points B and D are perilously close to the point C on the circumference of the circle. In essence, therefore, the height of the triangles BCA and CDA is indeterminate but lies within the range more than zero but less than 5 units.
- The height of the two triangles BCA and CDA cannot exceed 5 units because 5 units is the radius of the circle and therefore no point on the circle can be more than 5 units away from the diameter if linked to the it by a perpendicular.
- The base of two triangles BCA and CDA is 10 units and since no side can be longer than 10 units, the base becomes the hypotenuse of the right-angled triangles.
- But merely because the base of a right-angled triangle is 10 units, it does not automatically mean that the other two sides measure 6 and 8 units respectively. If the sides of a triangle are in the ratio of 3:4:5, then it automatically means that the triangle is a right-angled triangle. But merely because the base is 10 units, it does not necessarily mean that the other two sides are in the ratio of 3:4.
- It is also a property of the circle that the area of a triangle drawn in a semi-circle cannot exceed an area equal to the square of its radius. This is because the height of such a triangle can at the most be equal to its radius and the base of such a triangle would be twice the radius. The area of such a triangle with the perpendicular from the vertex being exactly equal to the radius of the circle would then be 1/2 × base × height = 1/2 × 2 times the radius× radius= square of the radius.
- Therefore the area of a rectangle drawn in a full circle cannot exceed twice the square of its radius. Thus the upper limit for the area of the rectangle ABCD is 2 times the square of the radius or in other words 50 square units.

However, since the height of a triangle is indeterminate, so is its area and so is the area of the quadrilateral ABCD. Thus Option 4 is to be marked as correct.

Answer 19

We are told that $y \neq 5$. This means that y can either be less than 5 or more than 5. This means that zero is a candidate for the values of y. We must test this with at least three values of y such that one is negative (say –1), then with zero and thereafter with a positive value more than 5 (say 6).

- If $y = -1$, the quantity in column A which is $(5-y)(y-5)$ becomes $(5 + 1)(-6)$ which will certainly be negative.
- If $y = 0$, the quantity in column A which is $(5 - y)(y - 5)$ becomes $(5)(-5)$ which will certainly be negative.

- If $y = 6$, the quantity in column A which is $(5 - y)(y - 5)$ becomes $(-1)(1)$ which will certainly be negative.

The writing on the wall is clear: $(5 - y)(y - 5)$ **is invariably negative if** $y \neq 5$. This means that Option 2 is to be marked as the correct answer.

Answer 20

Imagine that you are holding a flagpole of 5 feet height. If it rests on the ground and is perpendicular to the ground, then its upper end will be exactly 5 feet from the ground and if you were to make a mark with a pencil where the upper end of the pole touches the wall, you will find that it is 5 feet from the ground.

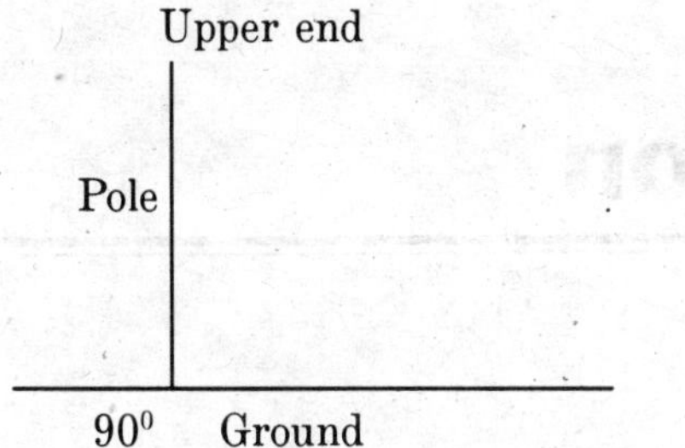

Now imagine that the pole leans on a sofa, such that its one end is on the ground and the upper end touches the wall. Now if you were to make a mark where the upper end touches the wall, you will find that it is less than 5 feet if you measure the perpendicular distance of the mark from the ground shown by the dotted line in the diagram below.

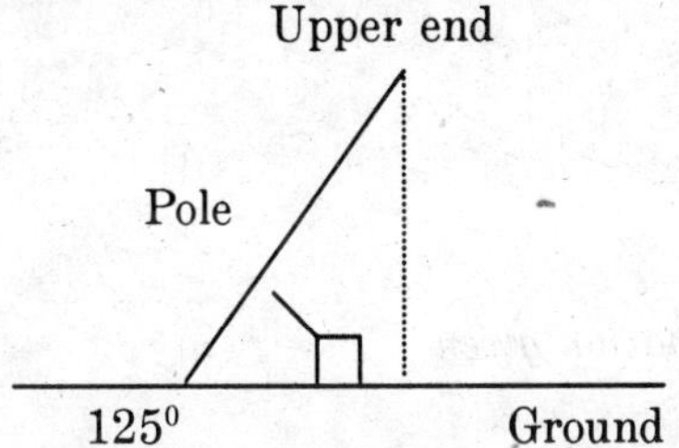

Now coming back to the main question, see the region ABCD as essentially two triangles ABD and BCD of equal area, formed as a result of dividing the region ABCD into two equal halves by the diagonal BD indicated by the dotted line. From the illustration of the pole, it would be clear that the height of the triangles ABD and BCD is definitely less than 6 units if you were to see the side of 6 units as a pole leaning on a sofa and forming an angle CDA of 125°, which is not a right angle.

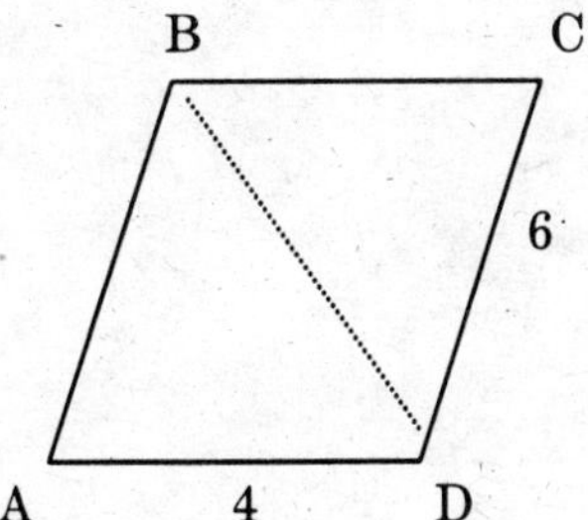

The area of triangle ABD = $1/2 \times$ base $\times$ height = $1/2 \times 4 \times$ (less than 6). The area of the triangle BCD = $1/2 \times$ base $\times$ height= $1/2 \times 4 \times$ (less than 6). The sum of the area of the triangles ABD and BCD = $2 \times 1/2 \times 4 \times$ (less than 6) = $4 \times$ (less than 6)= less than 24. This means that the quantity in column A is less than 24. This also means that the quantity in column B is greater than the quantity in column A and thus Option 2.

Chapter 49

Quantitative Comparison

Practice Test 3

GENERAL DIRECTIONS *for the questions in this practice test:*

The question consists of two quantities, one in Column A and one in Column B. There may be additional information, centres above the two columns, that concerns one or both the quantities. A symbol that appears in both columns represents the same thing in Column A as it does in Column B. You are to compare the quantity in Column A with the quantity in Column B and decide whether:

1. *The quantity in Column A is greater*
2. *The quantity in Column B is greater*
3. *The two quantities are equal*
4. *The relation cannot be determined from the information given*

Question 1

$k + n = 13$

$n + 3 = 8.$

Column A	Column B
k	n

Question 2

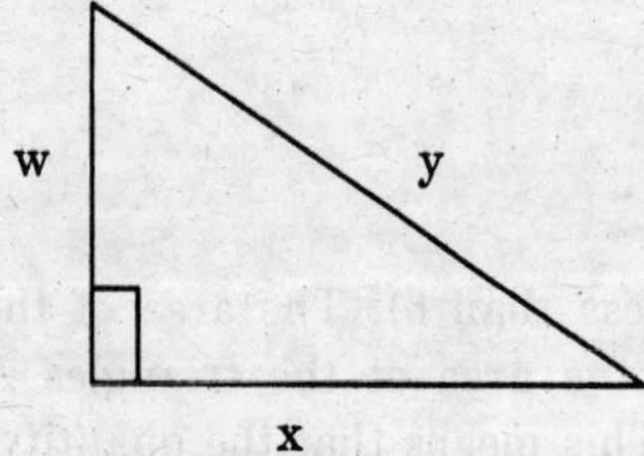

Column A	Column B
x^2	y^2

Question 3

For all positive numbers, x the function of f, is defined by:

$$f(x) = \frac{1}{\frac{1}{x} + \frac{1}{6}}$$

Column A	Column B
$f(12)$	$f(30)$

Question 4

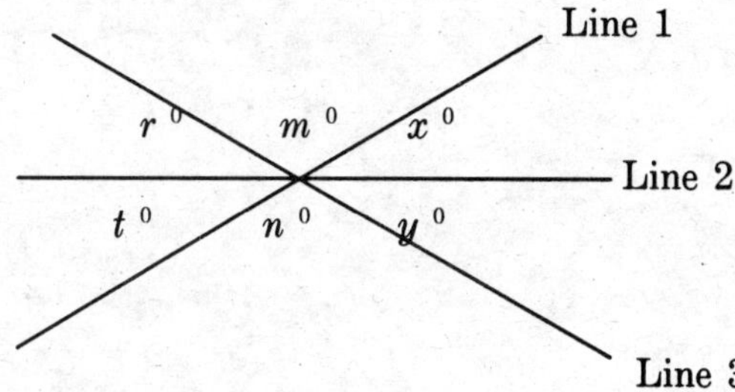

Column A	Column B
$m - (x + y)$	$n - (r + t)$

Question 5

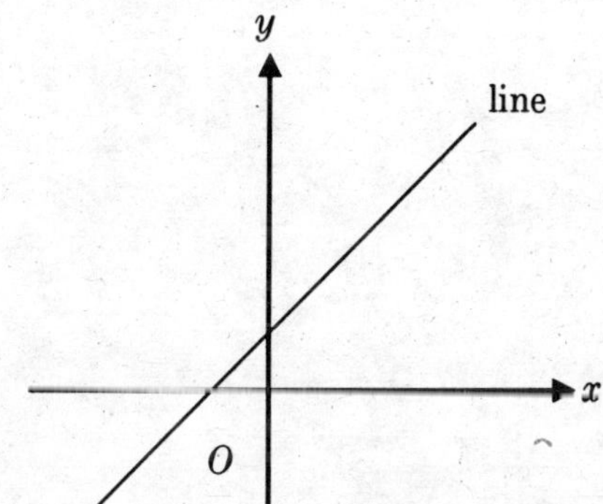

In xy plane, line has slope 1.

Column A	Column B
The value of the x intercept	The value of the y intercept

Question 6

Column A	Column B
The average (arithmetic mean) of 10, 20 and 30	The average (arithmetic mean) of 12, 20 and 28

Question 7

Column A	Column B
1/12th of 17	1/17th of 12

Question 8

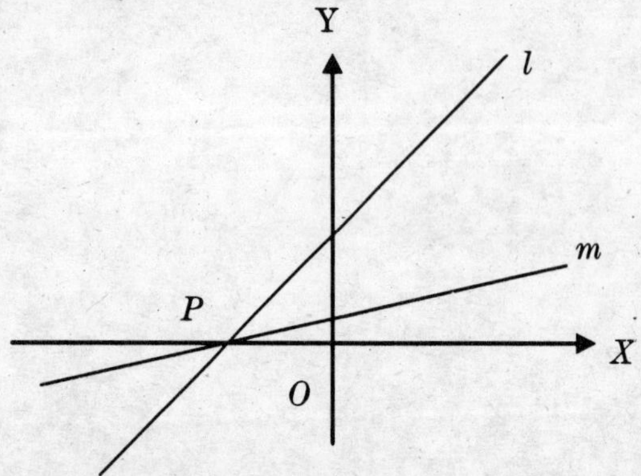

Lines l and m intercept the X-axis at point P.

Column A	Column B
The slope of Line l	The slope of Line m

Question 9

R, S, and T are 3 consecutive odd integers and $R<S<T$.

Column A	Column B
$R+S+1$	$S+T-1$

Question 10

The area of square region S is 36.

Column A	Column B
The perimeter of S	24

Question 11

$n = 7(19^3)$

Column A	Column B
The number of distinct positive factors of n	10

Question 12

$x^2y > 0$

$xy^2 < 0$

Column A	Column B
x	y

Question 13

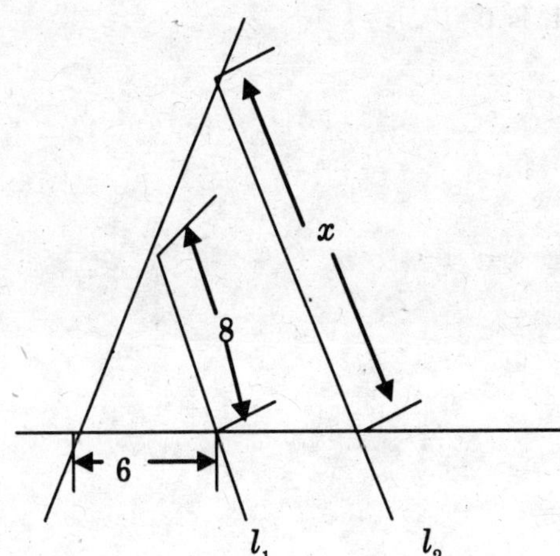

$l_1 \parallel l_2$

Column A	Column B
x	14

Question 14

Triangular regions T_1 and T_2 have equal areas and have heights h_1 and h_2, respectively.

Column A	Column B
$\frac{\text{The area of } T_1}{h_1}$	$\frac{\text{The area of } T_2}{h_2}$

Question 15

Let x = 3, if x is an odd integer;

Let x = 6, if x is an even integer.

r and s are integers, $3r$ is odd, and $5 + s$ is odd.

Column A	Column B
r	s

Question 16

Column A	Column B
4.1 + 1/3	5.1 – 2/3

Question 17

The variable x is normally distributed. The values of x at the 45th, the 15th, and the kth percentiles of the distribution are 550, 350, and 450, respectively.

Column A	Column B
K	30

Question 18

x is an integer, and the remainder, when $2x$ is divided by 4, is 0.

Column A	Column B
The remainder when x is divided by 4	0

Question 19

X, Y, and Z are negative integers.

Column A	Column B
The product of X,Y and Z	The sum of X,Y, and Z

Question 20

$xy = 1$ and $y - x = 0$.

Column A	Column B
y	1

Explanatory Answers

Answer 1

From the equation $n + 3 = 8$, you know that n=5. From the equation $k + n = 13$, you know that since $n = 5$, $k = 8$. The quantity in Column A is greater than the quantity in Column B and hence **Option 1** is correct.

Answer 2

In the right-angled triangle above, y is the hypotenuse. The hypotenuse is opposite to the right angle that measures 90^0. In any triangle, the longest side is opposite to the largest angle. The measures of the three angles of a triangle add up to 180^0. If one angle of the three angles in a triangle measures 90^0, the other two add up to 90^0 so that the measures of the three angles add up to 180^0. This means that the right angle is the largest angle of the three and therefore the hypotenuse is the longest side of the three sides of the triangle.

The quantities under comparison are the squares of two values. The square of a number is invariably positive whereas its square root can be either positive or negative. The measure of the side of a triangle cannot have a negative value and thus both X and Y have got to be positive.

If both x and y are positive and y is greater than x, then y^2 is certainly greater than x^2. Thus **Option 2** is correct.

As far as squares and higher powers of numbers go, see this following illustration that should drive home the underlying concept and should get ingrained on memory:

- If x is a positive fraction, say 1/2, then $x^2 = 1/4$, $x^3 = 1/8$, and so on. The higher powers of x remain positive throughout but diminish in value.
- If x is a negative fraction, say –1/2, then $x^2 = 1/4$, $x^3 = -1/8$, and so on. The even powers of x remain positive throughout but decrease in value whereas the odd powers will remain negative but enhance in value.
- If x is a positive number, say 2, then $x^2 = 4$, $x^3 = 8$, and so on. The even powers of x remain positive throughout but enhance in value.
- If x is a negative number, say -2, then $x^2 = 4$, $x^3 - 8$, and so on. The even powers of x remain positive throughout and enhance in value. The odd powers of x remain negative throughout but decrease in value.

Answer 3

What you are to compare here is between $\dfrac{1}{\frac{1}{12}+\frac{1}{6}}$ and $\dfrac{1}{\frac{1}{30}+\frac{1}{6}}$

The comparison is between two fractions wherein the common numerator is 1 and the denominator is $\frac{1}{12}+\frac{1}{6}$ on the left and $\frac{1}{30}+\frac{1}{6}$ on the right

One need not do any workings at all so long as one knows that when comparing two fractions that have the same numerators, the fraction with a lower denominator has greater value. This is why, for example, 1/3 is greater than 1/6. This is because the denominator in the first fraction is 3 and the denominator in the other fraction is 6 and the fraction with lower denominator has greater value.

This is also why, if we compare 1/(1/2) [which as such is 2] with 1/(1/4) [which as such is 4], we must mark 1/(1/2) has less than 1/(1/4) because the denominator in 1/(1/2) is 1/2, which is greater than 1/4, the denominator in 1/(1/4).

This means that one should know which is higher among the sums of $\frac{1}{12}+\frac{1}{6}$ and $\frac{1}{30}+\frac{1}{6}$

Between the two sides 1/6 is common to both. Therefore what will decide which sum is greater, is the greater of the two fractions 1/12 and 1/30. Since 1/12 is greater than 1/30, the sum of 1/30 and 1/6 will be lower in value than the sum of 1/12 and 1/6. This means the denominator in the quantity in Column B will be lower than the denominator in the quantity in column A and therefore the quantity in column B is greater than the quantity in column A. Thus **Option 2** is to be marked, as the correct choice.

Answer 4

The quantity in Column A is effectively $m - x - y$.

The quantity in Column B is effectively $n - r - t$.

What you are comparing is really $m - x - y$ on the left versus $n - r - t$ on the right.

In the above diagram, $m = n$ because they are opposite angles arising out of Line 1 intersecting with Line 3. Further, $r = y$ because they are opposite angles arising out of Line 2 intersecting with Line 3. And then, $x = t$ because they are opposite angles arising out of Line 1 intersecting with Line 2. Thus effectively, the left hand and right hand sides are $m - x - y$ and $m - x - y$ respectively. This means they are equal and hence Option 3 is correct.

Answer 5

First a word about x and y intercepts: The x intercept is the point where the line graph cuts into the x-axis and the y–intercept is the point where the line graph cuts the y–axis.

The line intercepts the x-axis on its negative side though we do not know precisely where. Thus the x intercept is negative. The line further intercepts the y-axis; we do not know precisely where. What we do know is that it intercepts the y-axis on its positive side. Hence the y-intercept is positive whereas the x-intercept is negative and since a positive value is higher than a negative value, **Option 2** is correct.

Answer 6

As we can see from the above columns, 20 is the median number in both the series that have three terms each. The arithmetic mean of a series is = (The total of the series)/ (the number of terms in the series). Since the number of terms in both the series is 3, when you compare the arithmetic mean, the denominator in the calculation of the arithmetic mean is the same since it is 3 in both cases. This means that if you were to compare only the totals of the two series, you could tell whether the mean is higher in Column A or it is higher in Column B or it is the same in both cases.

In Column A, the three terms are then (20 – 10), 20 and (20 + 10) and if you were to add the three, the total would be 20 – 10 + 20 + 20 + 10 = 60.

In Column B, the three terms are then (20 – 8), 20 and (20 + 8) and if you were to add the three, the total would be 20 – 8 + 20 + 20 + 8 = 60. Since the totals in both columns are equal, **Option 3** is to be marked as correct.

The logical aspect of this question is that the **median of a series is its arithmetic mean if the series is an arithmetic progression** (which means that there is constant difference between any two consecutive terms of the series). Since both the series in the two columns are arithmetic progressions, the median term is the arithmetic mean of each of the series.

Answer 7

When you are comparing fractions, the fraction with the smaller denominator is greater than the fraction with the greater denominator provided the numerator is same in both cases. This is why 1/12 is greater than 1/17.

When you are comparing 1/12th of 17 on the left with 1/17th of 12 on the right, you must remember that the left side is the product of a higher value fraction with a higher positive integer whereas the right side is the product of a lower value fraction with a lower positive integer. Quite naturally, the value of the product to the left will be invariably higher than the value of the product to the right and hence **Option 1** is to be marked as correct.

Answer 8

The slopes of the line are yelling the correct answer. One has only to have the capacity of hearing their roar. Line l has a higher slope or gradient whereas line m has a lower gradient. Thus **Option 1** is to be marked as correct.

Slopes often scream and tell you what is the right inference from the graph. You have to be stone deaf not to hear them. It is also likely that one may not be able to fully appreciate the lingo that the slopes speak while screaming and thus this note.

But first of all, what is a slope at all? A slope is the distance that one would have to rise vertically per unit distance that one would have covered on plain ground. So a hill that is not too high but the climb is many kilometres on foot is likely to have a moderate slope (the other word for slope is *gradient*). A hill that is of middling height but where one can cover the distance to the top in a short climb is likely to have a steep slope. In other words a small vertical climb in relation to a large horizontal distance is an easy slope and a big vertical climb in relation to a small horizontal distance is a steep slope.

Answer 9

One must always remember that when one is told that there are three odd integers, there is no bar to any or all of the numbers being negative. But irrespective of whether any or all of three consecutive odd integers are negative or positive, the one fundamental thing that will be true for every situation is that there will be a difference of 2 between any odd integer in this series of consecutive odd integers and its immediately previous term. Once one remembers this, one will not have to test the above from positive and negative values for the three consecutive odd integers. This should save time. Before we come to the solution, it becomes important to note that if the three consecutive integers were to be even, then the difference of 2 between each term in this series of consecutive even integers would continue to be 2.

If R, S, and T are 3 consecutive odd integers and $R < S < T$, then the three integers R, S, and T are effectively R, $R + 2$, and $R + 4$ respectively. This means that $S = R + 2$ and $T = R + 4$.

The quantity in Column A is then effectively $R + S + 1 = R + R + 2 + 1 = 2R + 3$ and the quantity in Column B is effectively $S + T - 1 = R + 2 + R + 4 - 1 = 2R + 5$. This means that you are comparing $2R + 3$ to the left with $2R + 5$ to the right and thus what you are effectively comparing is 3 with 5 since 2R is common to both sides and will cancel out in the see-saw of the comparison process. Thus the quantity in Column B is higher and **Option 2** is right.

Answer 10

The area of a square is the product of its sides (all of which are equal in length as is the characteristic of a square). This means that the square of its sides is 36 and thus each side is 6. The perimeter of a square (or for that matter of any geometrical figure) is the sum of the measures of all its four sides. Since a square has each side of 6 units, its perimeter is 24. Thus since the quantity in Column A and that in Column B is the same, **Option 3** is right.

Answer 11

$7(19^3)$ is effectively $7 \times 1 \times 19 \times 1 \times 19 \times 1 \times 19 \times 1$ since both 7 and 19 are prime numbers and a prime number has no factors other than 1 and the prime number itself. There would then be eight **distinct** factors of $7(19^3)$ as follows: (1) 1, (2) 7, (3) 19, (4) 7×19, (5) $7 \times 19 \times 19$, (6) 19×19, (7) $19 \times 19 \times 19$, and (8) $7 \times 19 \times 19 \times 19$.

This means that to the left, you have 8 factors whereas to the right you have 10 factors and hence **Option 2** is right.

A word of caution seems necessary here. 7 can be factorised endlessly as $7 \times 1 \times 1 \times 1 \times 1 \times 1 \times 1$ till one turns blue in the face. In such a case, the quantity in column A is indeterminate. But then the word in question that should put you on guard is the word 'distinct'. If one were to factorise 7 as $7 \times 1 \times 1 \times 1 \times 1 \times 1 \times 1$ and so on, the number of 'distinct' factors would be only 7 and 1. This is why **Option 2** is correct.

Answer 12

Since all squares are positive and since $x^2y > 0$, it means that x^2 is positive and x^2y is also positive. This is not possible unless y is also positive.

Since all squares are positive and since $xy^2 < 0$, it means that y^2 is positive and xy^2 is negative. This is not possible unless x is negative.

This means that the quantity in Column A is invariably negative whereas the quantity in Column B is invariably positive. Hence **Option 2** is correct.

Answer 13

Let us mark the given figure as below in order to understand some basics.

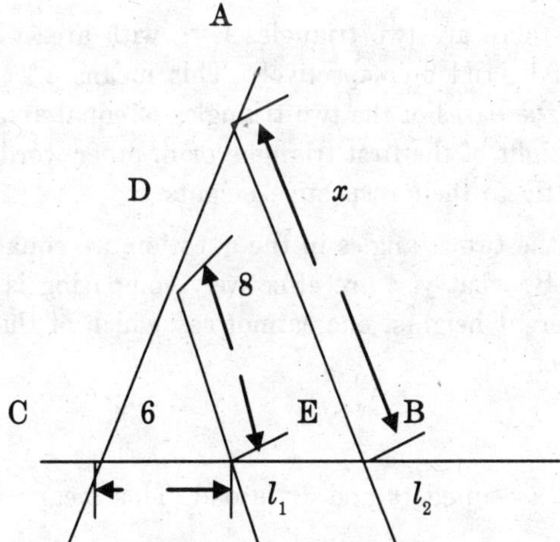

We are given that AB is parallel to DE. We are told that CE = 6 and DE = 8. We are told that AB = x. If AB is parallel to DE, then since angle ACB is common to both triangles ACB and DCE, the ratio of the sides AB and CB should be equal to the ratio of the sides DE and CE. This is because the triangle ACB is effectively a triangle made by extending sides CD and CE till A and B respectively and then AB drawn parallel to DE. Thus the relation between the sides of the original triangle and the extended triangle should remain constant.

This means that:

$\frac{DE}{CE} = \frac{AB}{CB} = \frac{8}{6} = \frac{4}{3} = \frac{x}{CB}$. This means that x= CB× $\frac{4}{3}$. Hence x = $\frac{4CB}{3}$.

This means that the value of x can be determined if one knows the measure of side CB. Since we are not given this measure, we cannot tell what the value of x is. Hence **Option 4**.

There are some fundamental aspects of angles between two straight lines.

The measure of an angle formed by two straight lines emanating from a single point is determined by the ratio of the measures of the two lines emanating from the said point. If you were to verify with a scale you will find that in the diagrams below, the ratio of AC: AB is the same as of AD: AE since BC is parallel to DE. This is because the angle CAB is common to both triangles.

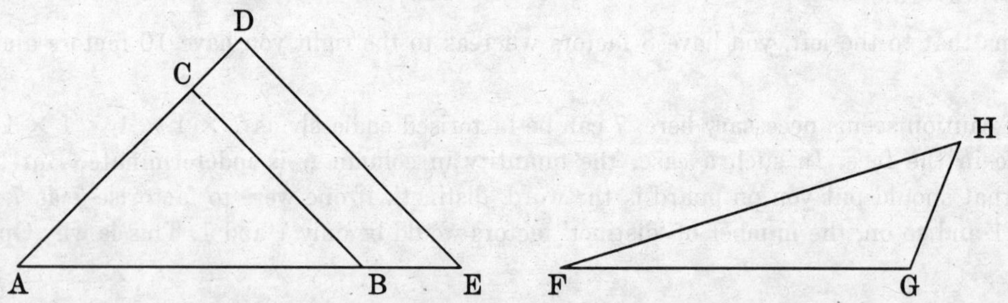

If you were to measure the angle GFH in the other triangle, you will find that the angle has decreased in measure since the ratio between the corresponding sides (FH in the triangle FGH corresponds to AD in the triangle ADE and FG corresponds to AE in triangle ADE) has dropped.

Answer 14

The area of a triangle is equal to 1/2 the product of its base and its height. Let us assume that there are two triangles both with area of, say, 2 units and heights of 2 and 4 units respectively and bases of b_1 and b_2 respectively. This means $1/2 \times b_1 \times 2 = 1/2 \times b_2 \times 4$ and hence $b_1/ b_2 = 2/1$. Thus it is possible for two triangles to have different heights and bases and yet the same area.

Now let us assume that there are two triangles both with area of say 2 units and heights of 4 and 2 units respectively and bases of b_1 and b_2 respectively. This means $1/2 \times b_1 \times 4 = 1/2 \times b_2 \times 2$ and hence $b_1/ b_2 = 1/2$. Thus the ratio of the bases of the two triangles of equal area would be equal to the height of the second triangle divided by the height of the first triangle, or in other words the ratio of the bases of the two triangles would bear an inverse ratio to their respective heights.

Thus, since the areas of the two triangles in the question are equal, when you are comparing the quantities in the two columns A and B, what you are effectively comparing is $1/ h_1$ with $1/ h_2$. Since two triangles with equal area can have different heights, one cannot say which of the two quantities is greater. Hence Option 4 is to be marked as correct.

Answer 15

We are told that r and s are integers and $3r$ is odd. This means that r is also odd and thus the quantity in Column A is 3.

We are told that $5 + s$ is odd. This means that s is even and thus the quantity in Column B is 6. Thus Option 2.

Answer 16

There is no complex calculation at all. Since the denominator in the fractions in both columns is 3, the denominator eventually in both columns is 3 and thus there is no need to simplify more than what follows:

4.1 + 1/3 is really [(4.1 × 3) + 1]/3 or (12.3 + 1)/3 = 13.3/3 and 5.1 – 2/3 is really [(5.1 × 3) –2]/3 or (15.3-2)/3 = 13.3/3. Since both the quantities are equal, **Option 3** is correct. One need not work out the precise value of 13.3/3 since the question pertains to comparative comparison where a common denominator would mean that you are comparing numerators alone. Thus here you are comparing 13.3 with 13.3 and since these are equal, you quickly reach the conclusion that **Option 3** is correct.

Answer 17

The following are the generally mentioned properties of the normal distribution:

1. The normal curve is bell-shaped and symmetrical in appearance.
2. The Mean, the median and the mode coincide.
3. In the normal curve there is only one maximum point.
4. The height of the normal curve is at its maximum at the mean value. This means that the gradient of the bell curve rises continuously till it reaches the maximum height at the mean.
5. The first and third quartiles are equidistant from the median.
6. The curve extends to infinity on both sides of the x-axis **without** touching the x-axis.

As regards percentiles, the Pth percentile is a number such that P per cent of the measurements are less than or equal to it. In the present case, the figure of 550 at 45th percentile is inclusive of the 350 that are in the 15th percentile. The 45th percentile is therefore a cumulative figure that covers those who are in percentiles lower than 45 percentile.

In the present case, the following three possible alternative values for K can exist: Case 1 where K > 30; Case 2 where K = 30 or Case 3 where K < 30. We shall see which of these three can fit in, given that the gradient of the normal distribution curve keeps rising constantly. Before that we must recall that the gradient of a line or the gradient between any two points on a graph is the vertical height gained in going from one point to the next divided by the corresponding distance travelled along a horizontal plane (meaning, either on the x-axis itself or on a plane parallel to the x-axis). We must also remember that in the present case:

- The 15th percentile corresponds to 350
- The Kth percentile corresponds to 450 and
- The 45th percentile corresponds to 550

If K were to be more than 30, let us assume that K = 35. Then in going from 15 to 35 we move 20 units along the vertical whereas we move from 350 to 450, meaning a distance of 100 units along the horizontal. This would make for a gradient of 20/100 or 0.2 between the 15th percentile and 35th percentile. As against this, going from 35 to 45 we move 10 units along the vertical whereas we move from 450 to 550, a distance of 100 units along the horizontal. This would make for a gradient of 10/100 or 0.1 between the 35th percentile and 45th percentile. This would mean that the gradient has actually dropped between the 35th percentile and 45th percentile, which is against the characteristic of a normal distribution since the gradient has to continuously go up till the 50th percentile (or the mean).

If K = 30, then with the background given above, there would be a straight line between the 15th percentile and 45th percentile because the gradient would remain unchanged. This too is against the characteristic of a normal distribution since the gradient has to continuously go up till the 50th percentile (or the mean).

This means that K is definitely less than 30 in order that the gradient between the 35th percentile and 45th percentile is higher than the gradient between the 15th percentile and 35th percentile. Hence **Option 2**.

Answer 18

When you are told that $2x$ leaves no remainder when divided by 4, it means that $2x$ is an integral multiple of 4. Thus $2x$ can have, for example of course, the following range of values and x can have the following corresponding range of values:

$2x=$	4	8	12	16	20	24
$x=$	2	4	6	8	10	12
When x is divided by 4, the remainder is	2	0	2	0	2	0

Since you cannot say what will the remainder be when 4 divides x - it could be either 2 or 0. Thus Option 4 is to marked as correct.

Answer 19

When you are told only that X, Y, and Z are negative integers, there is no bar to presuming that they have equal values to begin with. In that case the first possible negative integer that should come to one's mind is –1.

If X, Y, and Z are all equal to –1, the quantity in Column A is –1 whereas the quantity in Column B is –3 and in this case, the quantity in Column A is greater than that in Column B.

If X, Y, and Z are all equal to –2, the quantity in Column A is –8 whereas the quantity in Column B is –6 and in this case, the quantity in Column B is greater than that in Column A.

Since you cannot say which of the two quantities is definitely greater or whether they are equal, mark Option 4.

Answer 20

Even if you are not proficient at equations, the fact that $y - x = 0$ means that there is no difference between x and y. This means that $x = y$. The fact that $xy = 1$, means that $y \times y = 1$ or $y^2 = 1$. If $y^2 = 1$, it may either mean that $y = 1$ or that $y = -1$. Thus if y = 1, then the two quantities are equal but if y = –1 then the quantity in Column B is greater than that in the other column. Since you cannot tell for sure, Option 4 is correct.

Chapter 50

Problem Solving

Practice Test 1

Questions 1 to 5.

These questions refer to the following data:

SPEED OF WINDS IN THE UNITED STATES (miles per hour)

Station	Up to and including 1967		Up to and including 1979	
	Average	High	Average	High
Atlanta, Ga.	9.2	70	9.1	70
Boston, Mass.	13.0	65	12.6	65
Buffalo, N.Y.	12.6	91	12.3	91
Chicago, Ill.	10.2	60	10.4	60
Cincinnati, Ohio	7.1	49	7.1	49
Denver, Colo.	9.3	56	9.0	56
Helena, Mont.	7.9	73	7.9	73
Miami, Fla.	9.0	132	9.2	132
Montgomery, Ala.	6.9	60	6.7	72
Mt. Washington, N.H.	35.6	231	35.0	231
New York, N.Y.	9.6	70	9.4	70
Omaha, Nebr.	11.1	73	10.8	109
Pittsburgh, Pa.	9.4	58	9.3	58
Salt Lake City, Utah	8.7	71	8.8	71
San Diego, Calif.	6.5	51	6.7	51
Washington, D.C.	9.5	78	9.3	78

SPEED AND OFFICIAL DESIGNATION OF WINDS

Designation	Miles per Hour	Designation	Miles per Hour
Calm	Less than 1	Near Gale	32 to 38
Light Air	1 to 3	Gale	39 to 46
Light Breeze	4 to 7	Strong Gale	47 to 54
Gentle Breeze	8 to 12	Storm	55 to 63
Moderate Breeze	13 to 18	Violent Storm	64 to 73
Fresh Breeze	19 to 24	Hurricane	74 and above
Strong Breeze	25 to 31		

Question 1

Through 1967, what was the ratio of the highest to the average wind speed for Boston, Massachusetts?

(1) 5: 1 (2) 6: 1 (3) 7: 1 (4) 8: 1 (5) 9: 1

Question 2

For the three places whose average wind speeds through 1979 were the three highest, approximately what was the average (arithmetic mean) of those wind speeds in miles per hour?

(1) 157 (2) 151 (3) 60 (4) 20 (5) 12

Question 3

For how many of the places shown did the highest wind speed change from 1967 to 1979?

(1) One (2) Two (3) Three (4) Six (5) Fourteen

Question 4

For which of the places shown was the absolute value of the difference between the average wind speed through 1967 and the average wind speed through 1979 greatest?

(1) Boston (2) Chicago (3) Mt. Washington (4) Omaha (5) San Diego

Question 5

The data imply that, between December 31, 1967, and January 1, 1980, which of the following was (were) true?

(i) There was a hurricane wind recorded in Omaha

(ii) The average wind speed in Montgomery was 6.8 miles per hour

(iii) The wind speed in Chicago was never as high as 60 miles per hour

(1) (i) only (2) (ii) only (3) (i) and (iii) only (4) (ii) and (iii) only (5) (i) (ii) and (iii)

Question 6

From a group of 12 people, a 5-person team is to be formed. After 3 of the team members have been chosen, what is the total number of possible choices of the remaining 2 team members?

(1) 36 (2) 66 (3) 72 (4) 126 (5) 792

Question 7

A secretary typed 6 letters, each of which had either 1 or 2 pages. If the secretary typed 10 pages in all, how many of the letters had 2 pages?

(1) 1 (2) 2 (3) 3 (4) 4 (5) 5

Question 8

What is the remainder when 6^3 is divided by 8?

(1) 5 (2) 3 (3) 2 (4) 1 (5) 0

Question 9

$(3 \times 100) + (4 \times 1) + (5 \times 1000) + (6 \times 10) =$

(1) 3,456 (2) 3,564 (3) 4,635 (4) 5,346 (5) 5,364

Question 10

If $b - c = 3$, and $a + c = 32$, then $a + b =$

(1) 30 (2) 35 (3) 40 (4) 42 (5) 50

Questions 11 to 15

These questions refer to the following graphs.

COLLEGE *R*: ENROLLMENT AND CONTRIBUTIONS: 1976 TO 1980.

In the following charts, School Year 1 corresponds to the year 1976, School Year 2 corresponds to the year 1977 and so on.

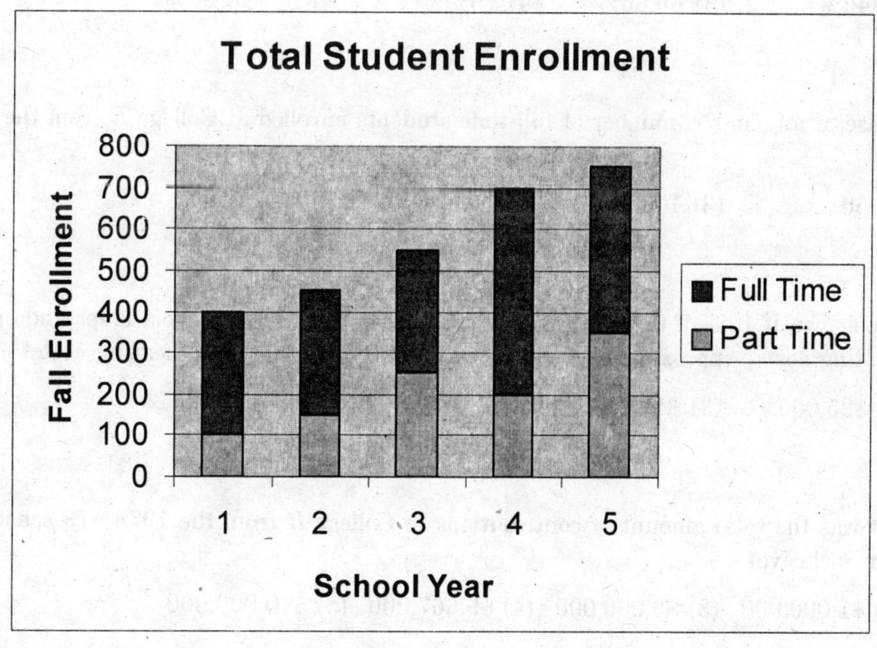

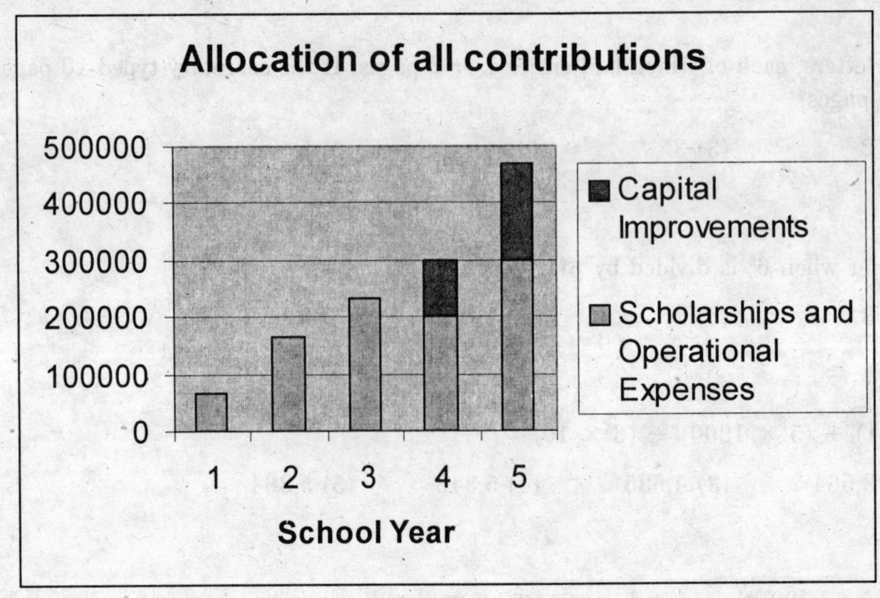

Question 11

What was the total number of students enrolled at College R in the fall of 1979?

(1) 200 (2) 250 (3) 500 (4) 650 (5) 700

Question 12

By what percent did the number of part-time students enrolled increases from the fall of 1979 to the fall of 1980?

(1) 7% (2) 42% (3) 66.66% (4) 75% (5) 80%

Question 13

What was the increase, if any, in the number of full-time students enrolled at College R from the fall of 1976 to the fall of 1977?

(1) 0 (2) 50 (3) 100 (4) 150 (5) 200

Question 14

In the 1978–79 school year, if 12% of the amount of contributions allocated to scholarships and operational expenses was allocated to heating costs, approximately how much was NOT allocated to heating costs?

(1) $2,000 (2) $25,000 (3) $176,000 (4) $205,000 (5) $250,000

Question 15

Approximately what was the total amount of contributions to College R from the 1978 –79 school year through the 1980-81 school year, inclusive?

(1) $967,000 (2) $1,000,000 (3) $9,000,000 (4) $9,667,000 (5) $10,000,000

Question 16

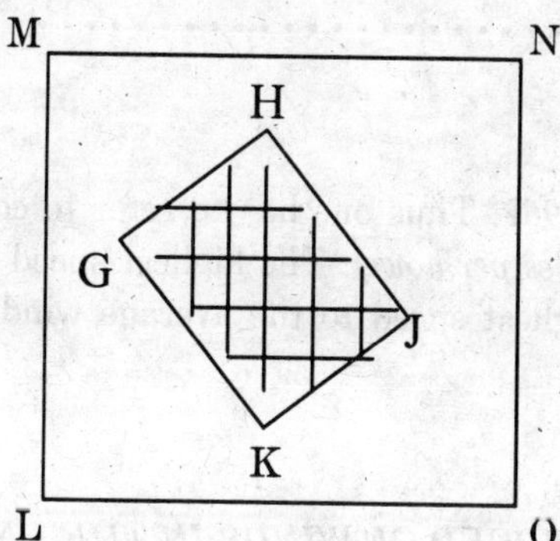

In the figure above, LMNO, and GHJK are rectangles, where GH = 1/2 LM and HJ = 1/2 MN. What fraction of the region bounded by LMNO is NOT shaded?

(1) $\frac{1}{4}$ (2) $\frac{1}{3}$ (3) $\frac{1}{2}$ (4) $\frac{2}{3}$ (5) $\frac{3}{4}$

Question 17

There are 20 rows of seats in an auditorium. If the first row has 20 seats and each successive row has 6 more seats than the previous row, how many seats are in the auditorium?

(1) 1,600 (2) 1,540 (3) 1,440 (4) 1,200 (5) 1,040

Question 18

If a certain object has been moving at the constant rate of x meters per minute, how many meters has the object moved in the last y seconds?

(1) $\frac{xy}{60}$ (2) $\frac{60x}{y}$ (3) $\frac{x}{60y}$ (4) $\frac{60}{xy}$ (5) $60\,xy$

Question 19

Which of the following equals the reciprocal of $x - \frac{1}{y}$ where $x - \frac{1}{y} \neq 0$?

(1) $\frac{1-y}{x}$ (2) $\frac{-y}{x}$ (3) $\frac{y}{x-1}$ (4) $\frac{x}{xy-1}$ (5) $\frac{y}{xy-1}$

Question 20

In a certain survey of a group of people, 87 people indicated they liked raspberries, 91 indicated they liked strawberries, and 91 indicated they liked blueberries. Of the people surveyed, 9 liked only raspberries, 10 liked only strawberries, 12 liked only blueberries, and 40 liked all three berries. How many of the people surveyed liked both strawberries and blueberries, but not raspberries?

(1) 21 (2) 26 (3) 31 (4) 36 (5) 41

Detailed Answers

Answer 1

The words *through 1967* mean *up to and including 1967*. Thus one has to refer to column 2 in the table titled *SPEED OF WINDS IN THE UNITED STATES (miles per hour)*. The highest speed in Boston was 65 and the average was 13 miles per hour. The ratio of the highest speed to the average wind speed in Boston through 1967 was thus 65: 13 or 5:1 and hence **Option 1**.

Answer 2

We now have to refer to column 3 in the table titled *SPEED OF WINDS IN THE UNITED STATES (miles per hour)*. The three highest averages are in Mt. Washington (35), Boston (12.6) and Buffalo (12.3). The average of the three highest averages is (35+12.6+12.3)/3 = 59.9/3 or nearly 20. Hence **Option 4**.

Answer 3

We now have to compare data in column 2 with data in column 3 of the table titled *SPEED OF WINDS IN THE UNITED STATES (miles per hour)* and see how many places shown did the highest wind speed change from 1967 to 1979. The changes were in the case of Montgomery (60 to 72), and Omaha (73 to 109). There are thus 2 cases and hence **Option 2** is to be marked as correct.

Answer 4

We would have to compare data in column 2 with data in column 3 of the table titled *SPEED OF WINDS IN THE UNITED STATES (miles per hour)* and see the absolute value of the difference between the average wind speed through 1967 and the average wind speed through 1979 and see which of these is the greatest. Our search must be limited only to the places mentioned in the five options and nothing beyond. There is no point in looking further than what one is required to see.

See the relevant information reproduced hereunder for ready reference.

Station	Up to and including 1967 Average	Up to and including 1979 Average	Absolute value of the difference between the average wind speed through 1967 and the average wind speed through 1979(When you talk about absolute difference you are to find the difference but ignore the minus signs; thus for example the difference between 13.0 and 12.6 is - 0.4 but the absolute difference is 0.4)
Boston, Mass.	13.0	12.6	0.4
Chicago, Ill.	10.2	10.4	0.2
Mt. Washington, N.H.	35.6	35.0	0.6
Omaha, Nebr.	11.1	10.8	0.3
San Diego, Calif.	6.5	6.7	0.2

The absolute difference is greatest in case of Mt. Washington and hence **Option 3**.

Answer 5

The words *between December 31, 1967 and 1st January 1980* mean *1st January 1968 to 31st December 1979 both days inclusive* and therefore we have to see only column 3 in the table titled *SPEED OF WINDS IN THE UNITED STATES (miles per hour)* along with the table titled SPEED AND OFFICIAL DESIGNATION OF WINDS.

Let us evaluate the three statements one by one:

(i) There was a hurricane wind recorded in Omaha: Wind speed of 74 miles per hour and above it is designated as a hurricane. If you were to see column 3 in the table titled SPEED OF WINDS IN THE UNITED STATES (miles per hour), there was a speed of 109 miles per hour in the case of Omaha. Thus statement (i) is definitely true.

(ii) The average wind speed in Montgomery was 6.8 miles per hour: If you were to see the same table and column as in the case of statement (i) above, it would be seen that the average speed in Montgomery was 6.7 miles per hour. This means that statement (ii) is false. This also means that we have now to verify statement (iii) only.

(iii) The wind speed in Chicago was never as high as 60 miles per hour: The words *never as high as 60 miles per hour* mean *definitely below 60 miles per hour*. If you were to see the same table and column as in the case of statement (i) above, it would be seen that the high speed in Chicago was indeed 60 miles per hour. This means that statement (iii) is also false.

Thus Option 1 is to be marked as correct.

Answer 6

After 3 of the 5 team members have been chosen, you have to select 2 team members from out of the remaining 9 of the original group of 12 people.

Let us see this problem at a slightly smaller level in order to understand how a general formula can be evolved in regard to selecting 2 team members out of a progressively growing number of people:

Let us assume that there are three people A, B and C out of whom you can select 2 team members. You can make these **three** distinct combinations: (1) A and B, (2) A and C and (3) B and C.

Now let us assume that there are four people A, B, C and D out of whom you can select 2 team members. You can make these **six** distinct combinations: (1) A and B, (2) A and C and (3) A and D (4) B and C (5) B and D and (6) C and D. The combinations can be quickly stated as 2 like this: A with B and C, 1 like this: B with C and that makes 3 combinations in all.

If the number of people from whom you can choose from is 3 then you can make 3 distinct combinations and this is equal to the total of all positive integers up to 2 (meaning 1+2) which is the number immediately preceding 3, the number of people from whom you can make 2-member teams.

If the number of people from whom you can choose from is 4 then you can make 6 distinct combinations and this is equal to the total of all positive integers up to 3 (meaning 1+2+3) which is the number immediately preceding 4, the number of people from whom you can make 2-member teams.

If you have to select 2 team members from 9 people, you can make 1 + 2 + 3 + 4 + 5 + 6 + 7 + 8 = 36 distinct combinations. Hence **Option 1**.

The idea in giving the above explanation instead of quoting the formula is that one may forget a formula but if one remembers how a formula is evolved, then one can retrieve the formula at once. One understands the rationale behind formula. Then he is the King of the subject.

If you were to find the total number of distinct combinations that you could make in picking 3 team members out of 5 people, then with logic on your side, it is awfully simple. Name the five people as A, B, C, D and E. See it like this:

- 3 combinations where A is with B and C, then B and D, then B and E
- 3 combinations where A is with C and D, A with C and E and then A with D and E
- 3 combinations where B is with C and D, and then B with C and E and then B with D and E
- 1 combination where C is with D and E

That makes 3+3+3+1=10 combinations. Permutations and combinations is a subject that makes people's knees turn to jelly. Once you assimilate the relative concepts in the chapter about permutations and combinations in this book, you will become the King of the subject.

Answer 7

There can be two different approaches to this question: one based on linear equations and the other based on mere logic.

Approach 1

There were 6 letters typed. Some of these were 2-page letters. Let there be x number of 2-page letters. This means that there were (6 - x) letters of the 1-page variety.

Since the total number of pages was 10, it means that $(6 - x) + 2x = 10$ and thus $6 - x + 2x = 10$ or $6 + x = 10$ and hence $x = 4$. Thus there were 4 letters such that they had 2 pages each.

Approach 2

This approach is for those who harbour the wrong impression that the competitive examination is about mathematics and since they do not know how to form and solve equations, they are at a disadvantage vis-à-vis those who are comfortable with equations. This approach is based on logic alone. Mind you, there is no need to put pen to paper in this approach.

The chart hereunder should not be drawn while working. All that has to be done is an oral exercise. The chart is designed as if you are speaking to yourself.

If according to Option	1	2	3	4
The number of 2-page letters were	1	2	3	4
Then the number of pages on account of the two-page letters would be	2	4	6	8
Since there were in all six letters, this also means that the number of one-page letters was	5	4	3	2
Therefore the number of pages on account of the one-page letters was	5	4	3	2
Therefore the total number of pages would then be	2 + 5 = 7	4 + 4 = 8	6 + 3 = 9	8 + 2 = 10
This means this option is	Wrong	Wrong	Wrong	Right
Since the total number of pages was in all	10	10	10	10

There is no need to go further. Option 4 is correct.

Answer 8

6^3 is essentially $2^3 \times 3^3$. Then again 2^3 is essentially $2 \times 2 \times 2 = 8$. So when you divide 6^3 by 8 what you are dividing is 8×3^3 by 8 and the question of any remainder does not arise. Thus **Option 5**.

Answer 9

This is a matter of logic more than anything else. The moment you see (5×1000), it means that the total of $(3 \times 100) + (4 \times 1) + (5 \times 1000) + (6 \times 10)$ is certainly over 5000. This means that you are to look only at Options 4 and 5 because it is only in these two options that there is a sum over 5000.

Once your range is narrowed down to Options 4 and 5, you must see that what differs in these two options is the digit in the tens place. In the total of $(3 \times 100) + (4 \times 1) + (5 \times 1000) + (6 \times 10)$, there is (6×10) or 60. This means that the tens place is 6 and hence **Option 5** is correct.

Answer 10

There can be two approaches to this simple problem: one based on algebra, the other based on mere logic. The algebraic approach is like this: Equation 1 is $b - c = 3$, and Equation 2 is $a + c = 32$. Add the two equations and you get $b - c + a + c = 3 + 32 = 35$ and thus $a + b = 35$.

The one involving logic is like this: The fact that some unknown term b minus another unknown term c is equal to 3 means that b is 3 more than c. Remember that algebra is after all manmade. Nothing prevents us human beings from assuming some values for the unknown terms.

If b is 3 more than c, then let $c = 0$ and thus $b = 3$. If $a + c = 32$, then $a = 32$ since we have assumed c as 0. This means that $a + b = 32 + 3 = 35$.

If b is 3 more than c, then let $c = 1$ and thus $b = 4$. If $a + c = 32$, then $a = 31$ since we have assumed c as 1. This means that $a + b = 31 + 4 = 35$.

This means that whichever way you look at it, $a + b = 35$ and so **Option 2** is correct.

Answer 11

First, a word about the *fall* season becomes necessary. The fall season is that time of the year when trees shed their leaves. There are two principal seasons in the cold countries: winter and summer. The fall season is the third season when there is transition from summer to winter. In the northern hemisphere the fall season is in the months of September, October and November. The reason behind giving this information is that when appearing for the GRE one must be acquainted with things that one may not have even heard of. For example, a driveway (which is a road leading from the gate of one's bungalow to the porch) is something that someone from the developing world may not be able to understand at all when there may be neither a gate nor a road; one may have to lift one's bicycle and walk into the house.

Back to the question, if you were to see the chart titled *Total Student Enrollment*, 1979 corresponds to Year 4 (since 1976 corresponds to Year 1) and the total number of students enrolled is 700. Thus **Option 5**.

Answer 12

If you were to see the chart titled *Total Student Enrollment*, you would see that the number of part-time students in 1979 was 200 and increased to 350 in 1980. This means there was an increase of 150 students over 200 students. This is a 75% increase. Hence **Option 4**.

Answer 13

If you were to see the chart titled *Total Student Enrollment*, you would see that the number of full-time students in 1976 was 300 and the number of full-time students was 300 in 1977. This means there was no increase of full-time students enrolled at College R from the fall of 1976 to the fall of 1977. Hence **Option 1**.

Answer 14

The fact that 12% (or, in other words, 12 out of 100) of the amount of contributions allocated to scholarships and operational expenses was allocated to heating costs means that the remaining 88% (or, in other words, 88 out of 100) was NOT allocated to heating costs.

In 1978-79 the total amount of contributions allocated to scholarships and operational expenses was somewhere in the region of $230,000 as may be seen from the chart titled *Allocation of All Contributions.* The bar in the bar chart stops a little below halfway between 200,000 and 300,000. The question now is: what is 88% of $230,000? If we were to realise that 88% of $200,000 is $176,000 (since 88 × 2 = 176), Options 1, 2 and 3 are out of the reckoning. Option 5 crosses the upper limit since we are looking for 88% of $230,000 (which means some figure less than $230,000) whereas $ 250,000 at Option 5 is well over $ 230,000. This means that Option 4 is pleading with you to mark it as correct without your having to calculate anything at all. All you have to do is to use your pencil and do the needful.

Answer 15

This is a question of logic more than anything else. From the Bar Chart titled *Allocation of All Contributions*, you can see that the bar representing $230000 in Year 3 is roughly the average allocation of all five years. Thus even if we were to multiply $230000 with 5, we would get **$1,150,000 as the total allocation for all five years**. This means that any Option that talks about over **$1,150,000** has to be ignored. This means Options 3, 4 and 5 are out of the reckoning from the very beginning. This means that we are now to focus on Options 1 and 2 alone.

If we were to add the allocations in Years 3, 4 and 5 (that correspond to years 1978-79, 1979-80 and 1980- 81), the total would come to $230000 + $300000 + $470000 = $1,000,000. Thus **Option 2** is correct.

Answer 16

The area of the rectangle LMNO = LM × MN. The area of the shaded region GHJK = 1/2 LM × 1/2 MN = 1/4 × LM × MN. The area NOT shaded = [LM × MN] – [1/4 × LM × MN] = 3/4 × LM × MN. The fraction of the region bounded by LMNO that is NOT shaded is 3/4 and hence **Option 5**.

Answer 17

The number of seats are 20+ (20 + 6) + (20 + 12) + (20 + 18) + (20 + 24) and so on till (20 + 114) = (20 times 20) + (6 + 12 + 18 + 24 and so on till 114) = 400 +6 (1 + 2 + 3 + 4 and so on till 19) = 400 + 6(the sum of the first 19 natural numbers).

The sum of the first N natural numbers is equal to their average multiplied by the number of natural numbers= (1 + 19)/2 multiplied by 19 = 10 × 19 = 190.

The number of seats in the auditorium are 400+ 6(the sum of the first 19 natural numbers) = 400 + (6 × 190) = 400 + 1140 = 1540. Hence **Option 2**.

Answer 18

There can be two different approaches to this, one based on mathematics and the other based on logic. Let us see both:

Mathematics-based approach: If a body has been moving at a constant rate of x meters per minute, then it has been doing x meters in 60 seconds and thus x /60 meters every second. In y seconds it does y times x / 60 meters and therefore xy /60 meters in the last y seconds.

Logic-based approach: 60 seconds make a minute. The speed of the body and the number of seconds in the last few seconds (the words y seconds may be taken as last few seconds) are both unknown. If the distance covered by a body in a minute is given and you are to find the distance covered in some seconds, the presence of 60 in the denominator in the correct answer is a certainty since you are given the values of neither x nor y. This means that we have to look only at Options 1 and 3.

Now the other thing that must be borne in mind is that Man has fathered algebra. We may thus assume some simple values for x and y. Since the body can cover x meters in 60 seconds, let us assume x to be a small multiple of 60 and thus let x be 120. This means that the body covers 2 meters per second. Let y be 3. This means that the body has covered 6 meters in the last 3 seconds. Let us see all options so that we can see whether the logical approach is infallible and which option gives us 6 as the answer:

Option 1: $xy/60 = 120 \times 3/60 = 360/60 = 6$. This means that **Option 1** is correct.

Option 2: $60x/y = 60 \times 120/3 = 20 \times 120 = 2400$ meters. This means that Option 2 is wrong.

Option 3: $x/60y = 120/60 \times 3 = 120/180 = 2/3$ meters. This means that Option 3 is wrong.

Option 4: $60/xy = 60/120 \times 3 = 60/360 = 1/6$ meters. This means that Option 4 is wrong.

Option 5: $60xy = 60 \times 120 \times 3 = 21600$ meters. This means that Option 5 is wrong

The conclusion is that the logic-based approach is infallible. This is because nothing can be above logic.

Answer 19

Having come to the conclusion that the logic-based approach is infallible and also much simpler, we shall tackle this from the logical standpoint alone. Of course, this is not the only reason why we shall take the logical approach. The examiner has clearly recommended the logical approach in telling us that $x - 1/y \neq 0$. If he wanted the mathematical approach, there is no need for furnishing this information. The inverse of $x - 1/y$ can very well be found through algebra in the absence of this additional information as well. The idea behind telling us that $x - 1/y$ is not equal to zero is that you are to consider assuming some values for the two unknowns such that x and y are not reciprocals of each other (meaning if you assume x to be 1, please do not assume y to be 1 as well and if you assume x to be 2, please do not assume y to be 1/2 and so on). Then again the unseen examiner has imparted an important lesson in assuming values for two unknown terms: Do not assume identical values for two unknown terms.

We must remember that we should assume different values for x and y, and at the same time small natural number values for x and y. After assuming such values for x and y, we must ensure that $x - 1/y$ is not equal to zero as per the question.

Let us assume that x = 1 and y = 2. In that case, $x - 1/y = 1/2$. The reciprocal of 1/2 is 2. Let us see which option gives us 2 as the answer.

Option 1: 1/1 – 2 = –1.

Option 2: 2/1 = –2

Option 3: 2/0 = infinity

Option 4: 1/(2–1) = 1.

Option 5: 2/(2–1) = 2. **Option 5** is correct.

Answer 20

Questions like this should not be tackled without the methodology of the Venn diagram that we shall present hereunder in brief:

The three circles represent raspberries (represented by R), strawberries (suitably represented by S) and blueberries (B).

As to how to read the diagram:

- The area where the legend *Only R* occurs – for example – will have the number of people that like only raspberries.
- Where the circles representing R and S overlap – for example – the area will have the number of people who like exactly two types of berries, R and S.
- Where the three circles overlap, the area will have the number of people who like all three types of berries.

- The number of people who like raspberries – for example- will thus be a sum of the numbers in the four areas (1) Only R (2) R&S (3) R&S&B and (4) R&B.
- The total number of people who like raspberries – for example – will thus be a sum of the numbers in the four areas (1) Only R (2) R&S (3) R&S&B and (4) R&B. Similarly the total number of people who like strawberries – for example – will thus be a sum of the numbers in the four areas (1) Only S (2) R&S (3) R&S&B and (4) S&B.

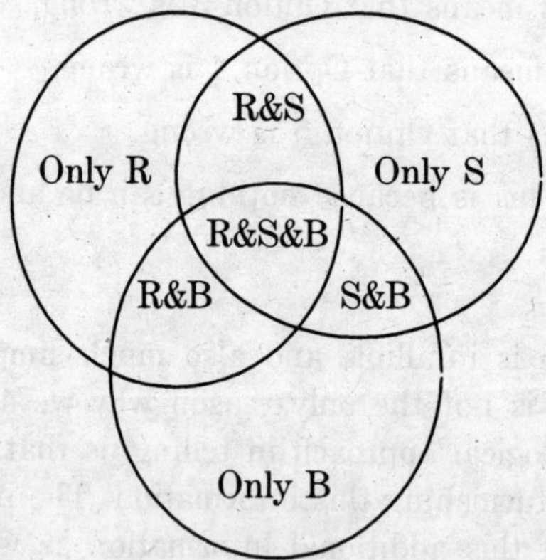

We are given that Only R = 9, Only S = 10 and Only B = 12 and R&S&B = 40. We may fill in the blanks appropriately in the diagram below. We may now go by the options and construct the Venn diagram.

If Option 1 were true, then the number in S&B will be 21, the diagram would be as follows:

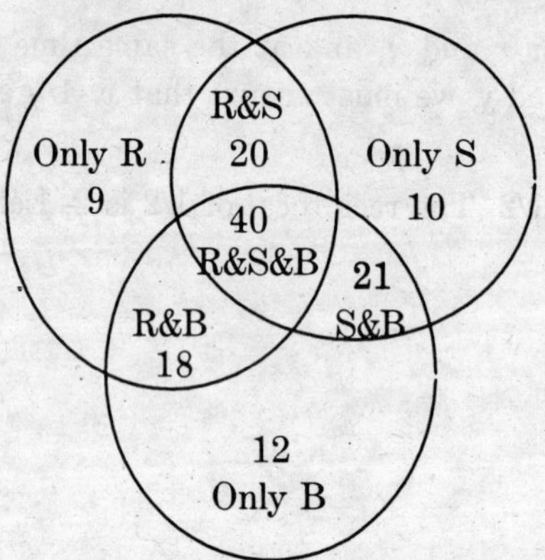

We find that those who like raspberries add up to 9+20+40+18=87, those who like strawberries add up to 10+20+40+21=91 and those who like blueberries add up to 12+18+40+21=91. This is in accordance with the figures given and hence **Option 1** is correct.

If you wish to see whether the other options are workable, you may fill in the figures in the other options and find that they shall not work. For example, you will find that Option 2 is not workable because if you were to construct the Venn diagram with 26 in S&B, you will have the following numbers in S&B, R&S and R&B: 26, 15 and 23 respectively. The numbers in R&S&B, Only R, Only S and Only B are fixed at 40, 9, 10 and 12 respectively. Thus the total number of persons liking blueberries would be 101 instead of 91 as given. This is why Option 2, for example, is not workable.

Chapter 51

Problem Solving

Practice Test 2

Question 1

$\sqrt{(42 - 6)(25 + 11)} =$

(1) 6 (2) 18 (3) 36 (4) 120 (5) 1,296

Question 2

If $2x + 3y = 15$ and $y = 1$, then $2x =$

(1) 18 (2) 12 (3) 10 (4) 9 (5) 3

Question 3

$52.68 \times 1/100 =$

(1) 0.05268 (2) 0.5268 (3) 5.268 (4) 526.8 (5) 52,680

Question 4

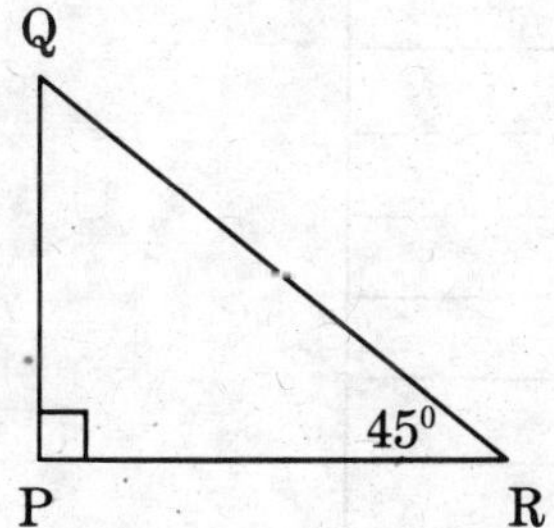

If the area of triangle PQR, with angle QRP measuring 45^0, is 32 what is the length of PR?

(1) 2 (2) 7 (3) 8 (4) 16 (5) 32

Question 5

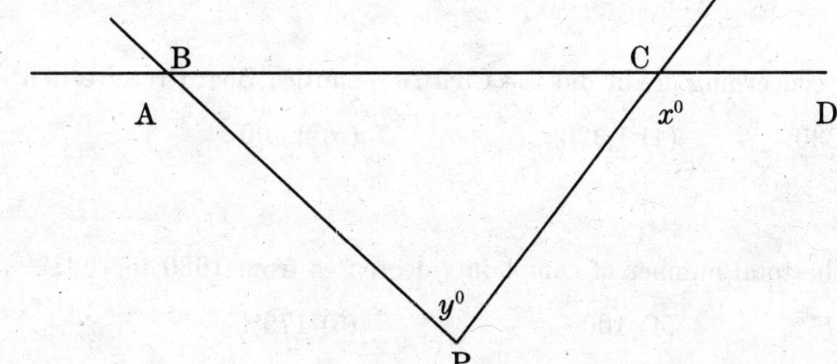

In the figure above, BP = CP. If $x = 120$, then $y =$

(1) 30 (2) 60 (3) 75 (4) 90 (5) 120

Question 6

A membership list of 620 people shows that 31 of them have first and last names that begin with the same letter. If a person is selected at random from the list, what is the probability that the first person's first and last names do not begin with the same letter?

(1) 0.05 (2) 0.25 (3) 0.50 (4) 0.75 (5) 0.95

Question 7

A list of numbers has mean 7 and standard deviation of 2.5. If x is a number in the list that is 2 standard deviations above the mean, then x is equal to

(1) 7 (2) 8 (3) 9 (4) 10 (5) 12

Question 8 to 12

These questions refer to the following table:

CONSUMER COMPLAINTS RECEIVED BY THE CIVIL AERONAUTICS BOARD

Category	1980 (per cent)	1981 (per cent)
Flight problems	20.0%	22.1%
Baggage	18.3	21.8
Customer service	13.1	11.3
Overbooking of seats	10.5	11.8
Refund problems	10.1	8.1
Fares	6.4	6.0
Reservations and ticketing	5.8	5.6
Tours	3.3	2.3
Smoking	3.2	2.9
Advertising	1.2	1.1
Credit	1.0	0.8
Special passengers	0.9	0.9
Other	6.2	5.3
	100.0%	100.0%
Total number of complaints	22,988	13,278

Question 8

Approximately how many complaints concerning credit did the Civil Aeronautics Board receive in 1980?

(1) 133 (2) 220 (3) 230 (4) 1,330 (5) 2,300

Question 9

By approximately what percent did the total number of complaints decreases from 1980 to 1981?

(1) 40% (2) 60% (3) 75% (4) 100% (5) 175%

Question 10

If the categories, except "other", are ranked by per cent of complaints from greatest to least, for how many of the categories would the rank change from 1980 to 1981?

(1) Three (2) Four (3) Six (4) Seven (5) Eight

Question 11

If the circle graphs below (drawn to scale) represent total consumer complaints for 1980, which graph shows a shaded sector that corresponds to flight problems and refund problems combined?

(1)

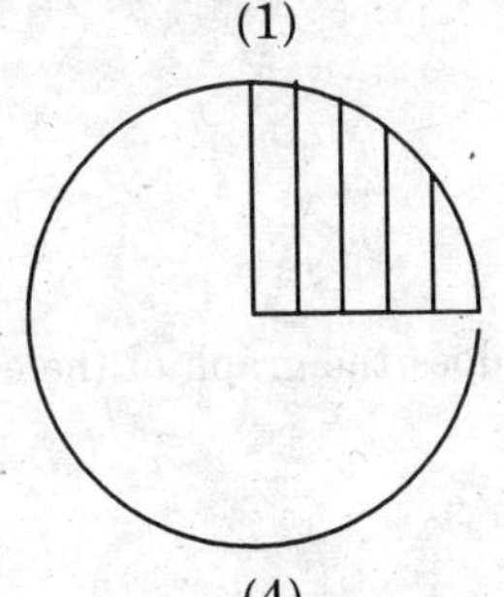

(2)

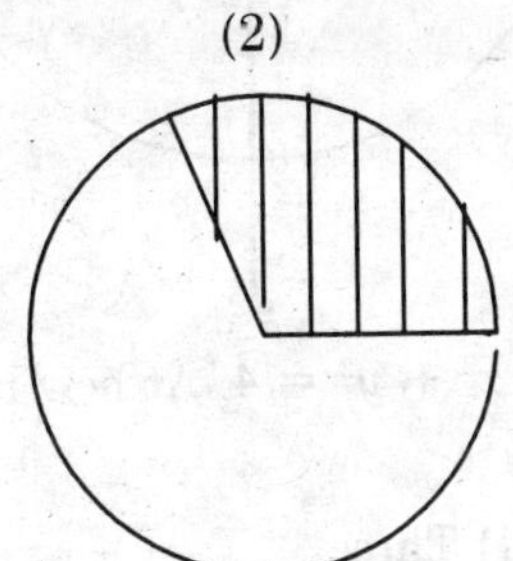

(3)

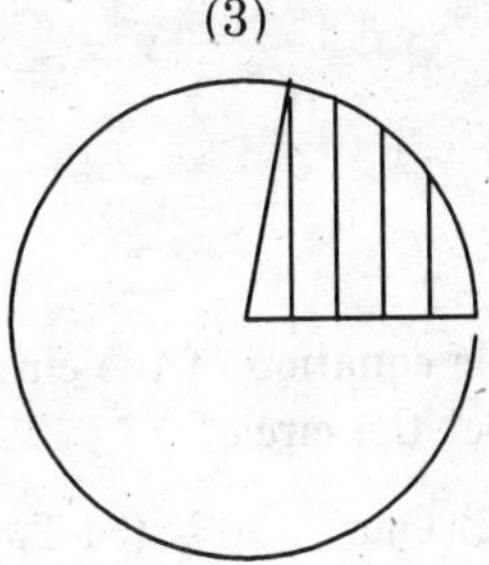

(4)

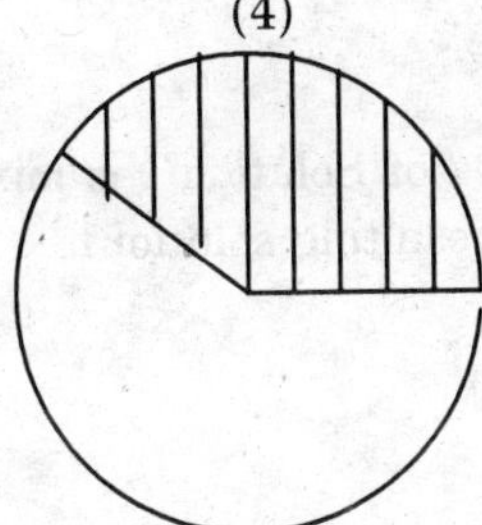

(5)

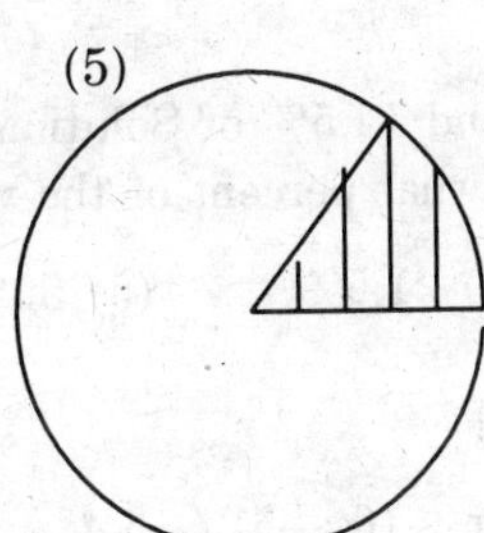

Question 12

Which of the following statements can be inferred from the table?

(i) In 1980 and in 1981, complaints about flight problems, baggage, and customer service together accounted for more than 50% of all consumer complaints received by the Civil Aeronautics Board

(ii) The number of special passenger complaints was unchanged from 1980 to 1981

(iii) From 1980 to 1981, the number of flight problem complaints increased by more than 2%

(1) (i) only (2) (ii) only (3) (i) & (ii) only (4) (i) & (iii) only (5) (i) (ii) & (iii)

Question 13

Ricardo lives 4 kilometres due west of Pat's house. Ann lives 6 kilometres due north of Pat's house and 4 kilometres due west of David's house. What is the straight-line distance, in kilometres, from Ricardo's house to David's house?

(1) 4 (2) 5 (3) 8 (4) 10 (5) 12

Question 14

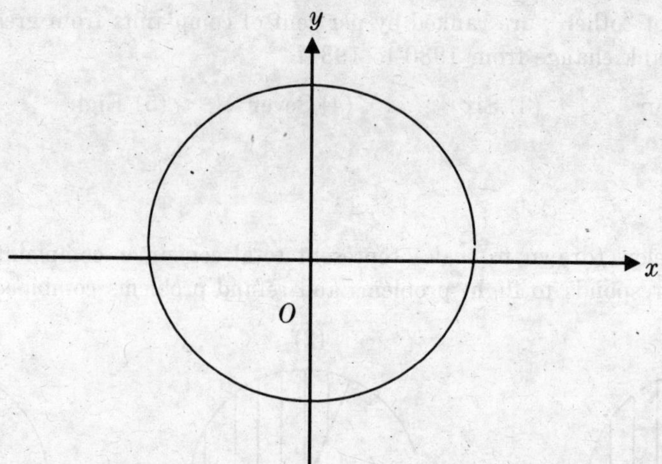

In the xy-plane, the equation of the circle shown is $x^2 + y^2 = 4$. At how many points does the graph of the equation $y = x^2 - 3$ intersect the circle?

(1) None (2) One (3) Two (4) Three (5) Four

Question 15

By weight, liquid A makes up 7.0% of Solution I and 14.5% of Solution II. If 3 grams of Solution I is mixed with 2 grams of Solution II, then liquid A accounts for what percent of the weight of the resulting solution?

(1) 6.09% (2) 10% (3) 10.75% (4) 21.5% (5) 50%

Question 16

Of the following which could be the graph of $2 - 5x \leq (6x - 5) / -3$?

Question 17

If the range of the six measurements 140, 125, 180, 110, 165, and x is 80, which of the following could be the value of x?

(1) 60 (2) 85 (3) 190 (4) 220 (5) 245

Question 18

A certain integer n is a multiple of both 5 and 9 which of the following must be true?

I. n is an odd integer.

II. n is equal to 45.

III. n is a multiple of 15.

(1) III only (2) I and II only (3) I and III only (4) II and III only (5) I, II and III only

Question 19

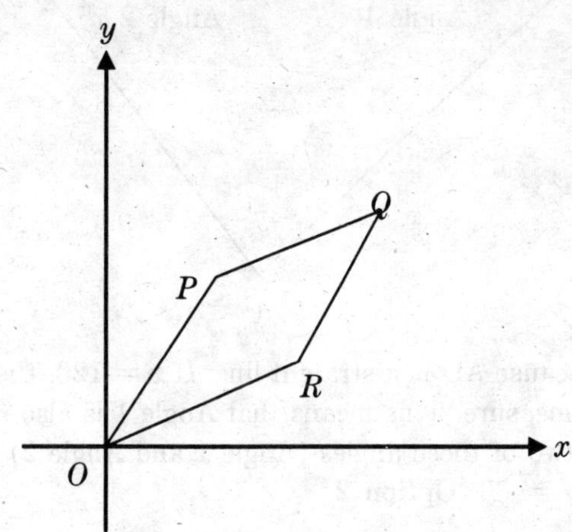

In the xy- plane, point P and Q have the coordinates (1,2) and (3,3) respectively. If $OPQR$ is a parallelogram what are the coordinates of point R?

(1) (1,1) (2) (3/2,1) (3) (2,1) (4) (2,3/2) (5) (5/2,3/2)

Question 20

How many positive whole numbers less than 81 are NOT equal to squares of whole numbers?

(1) 9 (2) 70 (3) 71 (4) 72 (5) 73

Detailed Answers

Answer 1

$\sqrt{(42-6)(25+11)}$ is really the square root of (36 × 36) which is 36. Hence **Option** 3.

Answer 2

If $2x + 3y = 15$ and $y = 1$, then $2x + 3 = 15$ and thus $2x = 12$. Hence **Option** 2.

Answer 3

52.68 × 1/100 = 0.5268. Hence **Option** 2.

Answer 4

A triangle has three angles. The measures of the three angles add up to 180^0. In a right-angled triangle like PQR above, one of the angles is 90^0.and therefore the other two have to add up to 90^0. If one of the two angles is 45^0, the other is also 45^0. This means that the triangle PQR has two sides PQ and PR equal in measure.

The area of a triangle is equal to 1/2 × base × height. In triangle PQR in the question, the base is PR and the height is PQ. Thus the area of the triangle PQR is 1/2 × PR × PQ or in other words 1/2 × PR × PR (since PQ and PR equal in measure).

Thus $1/2 \times PR^2 = 32$ and so $PR^2 = 64$ and thus $PR = 8$. Hence **Option 3**.

Answer 5

In the figure given in the question, mark the following angles:

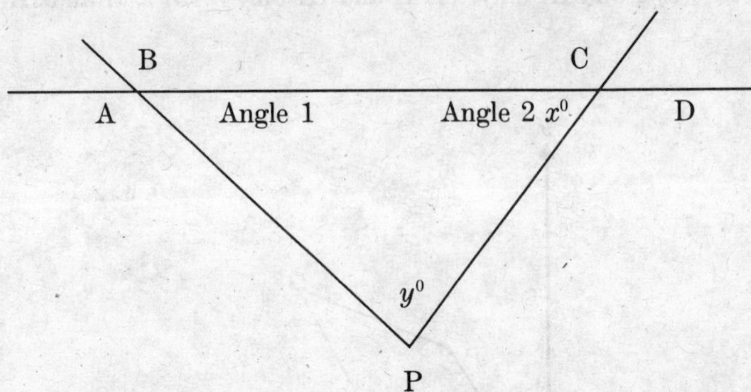

Angle 2 is $180 - x^0$ because AD is a straight line. If $x = 120$, then Angle 2 is 60^0. Since BP = CP, Angle 1 and Angle 2 are equal in measure. This means that Angle 1 is also 60^0. Since the three angles of the triangle BCP add up to 180^0, and two of these angles (Angle 1 and Angle 2) add up to 120^0, the third angle y^0 is $= 180^0 - 120^0 = 60^0$. Hence $y = 60$. **Option 2.**

Answer 6

A membership list of 620 people shows that 31 of them have first and last names that begin with the same letter. This means that 1 out of every 20 in the membership list has first and last names that begin with the same letter (because $31 \times 20 = 620$). This also means that 19 out of every 20 in the membership list has first and last names that do not begin with the same letter. Thus the probability that the first person's first and last names do not begin with the same letter is 19 out of 20 or 19/20 or 0.95 at **Option 5**.

Answer 7

If a monkey has three bananas and a crocodile says that he has two times the number of bananas that the monkey has, the crocodile has six bananas. If a hippopotamus were then to say that he has one banana ***over*** what the crocodile has, then the hippo has seven bananas.

If the standard deviation of a list of numbers has a standard deviation of 2.5, then somebody has a number x that is 2 standard deviations above the mean, this means that the number x is 5 more than 7 and hence x is equal to 12, and thus **Option 5** is correct.

Answer 8

As may be seen from the table, the Civil Aeronautics Board received a total number of 22988 complaints – or approximately 23000 complaints – in 1980. 1% of these pertained to credit and thus $1 \times 23000/100$ or 230 pertained to credit. Hence **Option 3**.

Answer 9

As may be seen from the table, the Civil Aeronautics Board received a total number of 22988 complaints – or approximately 23000 complaints – in 1980 and 13278 or roughly 13300 complaints in 1981. The number of complaints decreased by $23000\text{-}13300 = 9700$ from 23000 and in percentage terms this reduction is $9700 \times 100/23000 = 970/23 = 42$. Option 1 is the nearest to 42 and hence **Option 1**.

A faster approach is like this: The half of 23000 is 11500. 13278 is more than half of 23000. Thus the decrease is not even fifty percent. Option 1 fits in straightaway.

Answer 10

Ranking is not such a difficult thing after all. Let us see the table – without the row pertaining to "others" of course - and how we would allot ranks:

If you were to see the column pertaining to 1980, the percentages are in descending order. If the list of students in a class has the student with the highest percentage marks at the head of the list and the student with the least percentage of marks at the bottom then the position of each student in that list is his rank in class and what is more, the list is in descending order. Since the percentages in the column pertaining to 1980 are in descending order, we can rank them as follows with ease keeping in mind the fact that the highest percentage gets first rank and then the next highest gets second rank and so on:

Category	1980 (%)	Rank	1981 (%)	Rank
Flight problems	20.0%	1	22.1%	1
Baggage	18.3	2	21.8	2
Customer service	13.1	3	11.3	**4**
Overbooking of seats	10.5	4	11.8	**3**
Refund problems	10.1	5	8.1	5
Fares	6.4	6	6.0	6
Reservations and ticketing	5.8	7	5.6	7
Tours	3.3	8	2.3	**9**
Smoking	3.2	9	2.9	**8**
Advertising	1.2	10	1.1	10
Credit	1.0	11	0.8	**12**
Special passengers	0.9	12	0.9	**11**

In all, for **six** categories ranks changed from 1980 to 1981. Where there are changes in rank, the changed rank is highlighted in column 5 of the above table. Hence **Option 3**.

Answer 11

The number of complaints regarding flight problems and refund problems received during 1980 were 20% and 10.1% adding to 30.1% in the aggregate. 30.1% means a little over 25% (and of course 25% is a quarter). A quarter of a circle is 25% of the circle. A half is 50% and so on. The various options represent the following percentages roughly:

Option 1 – 25%; Option 2: 30%; Option 3: Less than 25%; Option 4: More than 30% (say 37%) since it is nearly halfway between 25% and 50%; Option 5: Less than 25%. Thus **Option 2** is to be marked as correct.

Answer 12

Let us see which of the statements can be inferred from the data:

(i) In 1980 and in 1981, complaints about flight problems, baggage, and customer service together accounted for more than 50% of all consumer complaints received by the Civil Aeronautics Board:

Category	1980 (%)	1981 (%)
Flight problems	20.0%	22.1%
Baggage	18.3	21.8
Customer service	13.1	11.3
Sub Total after ignoring the decimal points	>51	>54

A note of caution: Decimals may be taken into reckoning only if the total prior to the decimals comes to less than 50% but not before that; there is no point in toiling unnecessarily, is there? Thus statement (i) is correct.

(ii) The number of special passenger complaints was unchanged from 1980 to 1981: The percentage remained unchanged at 0.9% in the two years but the base – meaning the total number of complaints dropped from 1980 to 1981 and with that the number of complaints is bound to drop if the percentage remains unchanged since 0.9% of 23000 (approximately, of course) is higher than 0.9% of 13300 (approximately, of course). Therefore statement (ii) is false.

(iii) From 1980 to 1981, the number of flight problem complaints increased by more than 2%: The number of flight problems in 1980 was 20% of 23000 whereas in 1981 it was 22.1% of 13300. 20% of 23000 comes to 20 × 23000/100 = 4600 and 22% of 13300 comes to 22 × 13300/100 = 22 × 133. In order to be able to multiply 22 and 133 quickly see 133 as (100+30+3) and then 22×133 becomes 22 × (100 + 30 + 3) =2200 + 660 + 66 which means much less than 4600 (DO NOT CALCULATE MORE THAN NECESSARY) and hence statement (iii) is also false.

Thus since only statement (i) is true, **Option 1** is to be marked as correct.

Answer 13

The question essentially pertains to the Pythagoras Theorem. Let us see how. If we were to refer to Ricardo as R and Ann as A and so on, here is a sketch of the locations of the houses of the four people.

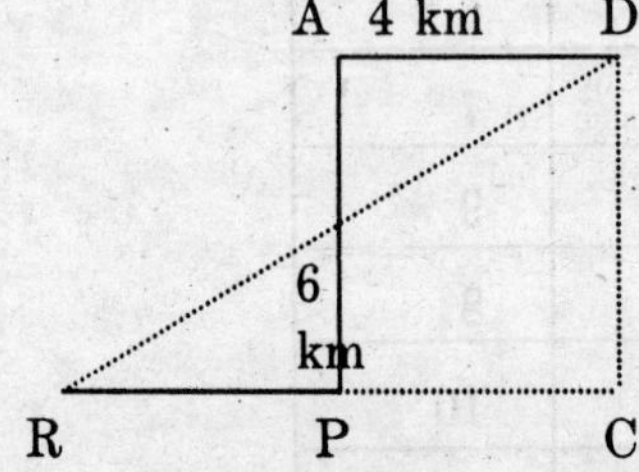

The dotted line RD is the straight-line distance from R to D. The dotted-line perpendicular from D to the line RP extended by a dotted line meets the extended RP at point C. RC is 8 km. DC is 6 km. In the right-angle triangle DRC, RD is the hypotenuse. By Pythagoras Theorem, the square on the hypotenuse = sum of the squares on the other two sides and thus RD = 10. Hence **Option 4**.

Answer 14

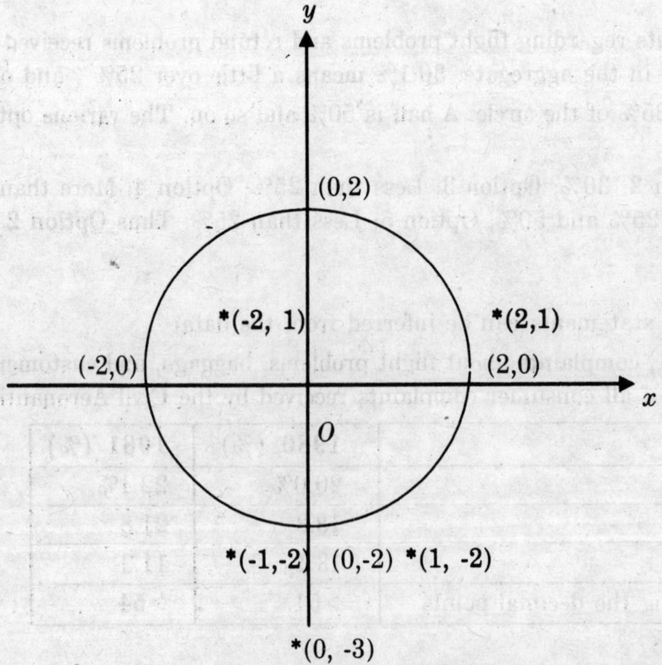

Since the equation of the circle shown is $x^2 + y^2 = 4$, the following four points shall be the co-ordinates for the limits of the circle (0,2), (0,-2), (2, 0) and (-2, 0). This is because when $x = 0$, $y =$ either + 2 or –2 and when $y = 0$, $x =$ either + 2 or –2.

Now let us assume some small values for x such that these values would lie outside the limits of the circle:

When $x = -2$, $y = x^2 - 3$ and therefore $y = 4 - 3 = 1$.

When $x = -1$, $y = x^2 - 3$ and therefore $y = 1 - 3 = -2$.

When x =0, $y = x^2 - 3$ and therefore $y = -3$.

When x =1, $y = x^2 - 3$ and therefore $y = -2$.

When x =2, $y = x^2 - 3$ and therefore $y = 1$.

When $y = -2$, $y = x^2 - 3$, $x^2 = 1$ and therefore $x =$ either +1 or –1.

Plotting these points on the figure above, we learn that the curve represented by the equation $y = x^2 - 3$ would intersect the circle at the following places:

It would intersect the circle twice to the left of the y - axis when traversing from the point (–2, 1) to (–1, –2). It would then dip to (0, -3).

It would intersect the circle twice to the right of the y - axis when traversing from the point (–2, 1) to (–1, –2).

In all, therefore, the curve represented by the equation $y = x^2 - 3$ would intersect the circle at four places. Hence Option 5.

Note that you are not to find out precisely where the curve intersects the circle but only how many times. Assuming some small natural number values for x and y in the equation $y= x^2 - 3$ is enough for the purpose. If you were to notice, the circle itself is bound by + 2 and –2 as maximum and minimum values for both x and y. The whole idea then is to proceed with assuming the following values: +2, 0 and -2 for both x and y in the equation $y= x^2 - 3$.

Answer 15

When 3 grams of Solution I are being mixed with 2 grams of Solution II, then Solution I and Solution II are being mixed in the ratio of 3 : 2.

Let us see how to find what percent of the weight of the resulting solution liquid A accounts in the following steps:

- The weight of liquid A in the resultant solution on account of 7% of liquid A being in 3 grams of Solution I will be 7% of 3 grams.
- The weight of liquid A in the resultant solution on account of 14.5% of liquid A being in 2 grams of Solution I will be 14.5% of 2 grams.
- The weight of the resulting solution will be 2 + 3 = 5 grams.
- The weight of liquid A as a fraction of the resulting solution will be [(7% of 3 grams) + (14.5% of 2 grams)]/ 5 grams = [(7 × 3 grams/100) + (14.5 × 2 grams/100)]/ 5 grams.

When you want to express a fraction in percentage terms, the word *percent* means *per hundred*. Thus both the numerator and the denominator have to be multiplied by such a number so as to get 100 in the denominator. This is why, for example, the fraction 1/4 is (1 × 25)/(4 × 25) = 25/100. The denominator has now become 100. The numerator is the percentage value of the fraction. Thus, for example, 1/4 is 25/100 and this is why 1/4 is 25% because 25 is the numerator when the fraction has a standard denominator of 100.

Similarly when you wish to convert [(7 × 3 grams/100) + (14.5 × 2 grams/100)]/5 grams is percentage terms, you have to multiply both the numerator and denominator by 20 so as to get 20 × [(7 × 3 grams/ 100)+(14.5 × 2 grams/100)]/ (5 × 20) grams. The numerator that you will get over the standard denominator of 100 will be [(7 × 3 grams/5) + (14.5 × 2 grams/5)] = [21 grams) + (29 grams/5)] = (21 + 29)/5 = 50/ 5 =10. Thus the answer is 10% at Option 2 since 10 is the numerator in the fraction [(7 × 3 grams/100) + (14.5 × 2 grams/100)]/5 grams.

Answer 16

This is a question that requires nothing more than logic. There are five line graphs in the five options. All five graphs indicate possible values for x alone. There is no y-axis at all.

If $2 - 5x \le (6x - 5) / -3$, then since $(6x - 5)/ -3$ can be simplified to $5/3 - 2x$, effectively the expression $2 - 5x \le (6x - 5)/ -3$ can be simplified to $2 - 5x \le 5/3 - 2x$. Add $5x$ to both sides of the expression (without fearing that the earth will shake with this addition since if x were to be negative, it would subtract equal amounts from the two sides; if x were to be zero, it will make no difference to both sides; and if x were to be positive, it will add the same quantity to both sides). After adding $5x$ to both sides we shall see the expression $2 - 5x \le (6x - 5)/ -3$ as $2 \le 5/3 + 3x$. In the expression $2 \le 5/3 + 3x$, 5/3 is less than 2 as it is. In order that the left hand side is to be equal to the right hand side (let alone more than the right hand side), we must add some positive quantity to 5/3. This is only possible if x is positive. Therefore x cannot take negative values or zero. Hence **Option 3** is the lone choice for the correct choice.

Answer 17

This too is entirely about logic once we understand what the word *range* indicates.

Let us see an example as follows: When five students have scored 35%, 47%, 73%, 81% and 91% marks, the range of these six scores is the difference between the highest percentage and the lowest percentage. The range of these five scores is 91 – 35 = 56.

In the present question, there are five options in regard to the range.

If Option 1 were true and $x = 60$, then if the range is 80, the difference between the highest and the lowest would be 80. This means that the highest measure could be 60 + 80 = 140, which it is not since among the given measures 180 is the highest measure. On the other hand, since 180 is the highest, 60 cannot be a value for x since that would make 180 – 80 = 100 as the lowest measure which it is not since the lowest among the given measures is 110.

If Option 2 were true and x=85, then since the range is 80, the difference between the highest and the lowest would be 80. This means that the highest measure could be 85 + 80 = 165, which it is not since among the given measures 180 is the highest measure. On the other hand, since 180 is the highest, 85 cannot be a value for x since that would make 180 – 80= 100 as the lowest measure which it is not since the lowest among the given measures is 110.

If Option 3 were true and the value of x were to be 190, then if the range is 80, the difference between the highest and the lowest would be 80. This means that the highest measure is 110 + 80 = 190. 190 can be a value for x since that would make 190 – 80 = 110 as the lowest measure which it is since the lowest among the given measures is 110. Thus **Option 3** is eminently workable.

If Option 4 were true and x=220, then since the range is 80, the difference between the highest and the lowest would be 80. This means that 220 cannot be a value for x since that would make 220 – 80= 140 as the lowest measure which it is not since the lowest among the given measures is 110.

If Option 5 were true and $x = 245$, then since the range is 80, the difference between the highest and the lowest would be 80. This means that 245 cannot be a value for x since that would make 245 – 80 = 165 as the lowest measure which it is not since the lowest among the given measures is 110.

Thus **Option 3** is to be marked as correct.

Answer 18

The integers 5 and 9 have no common factors. Therefore the least common multiple of these two numbers is $5 \times 9 = 45$. The other common multiples of 5 and 9 (higher than the least common multiple) are then the integral multiples of 45 such as 90, 135, 180 and so on which are as such 45×2, 45×3, 45×4 and so on. Since 90 and 180 are possible values for n, and both 90 and 180 are even numbers, statement I is not necessarily true. Furthermore, since 45, 90,135, 180 and so on (meaning integral multiples of 45) are possible values for n, 45 is not the only possible value for n, statement II is not necessarily true.

If we see the first few possible values of n, they are all integral multiples of 45 (which really is 15×3). Since 45 is a multiple of 15, it follows that all integral multiples of 45 are also integral multiples of 15. Thus statement III is necessarily true. Hence **Option 1**.

Answer 19

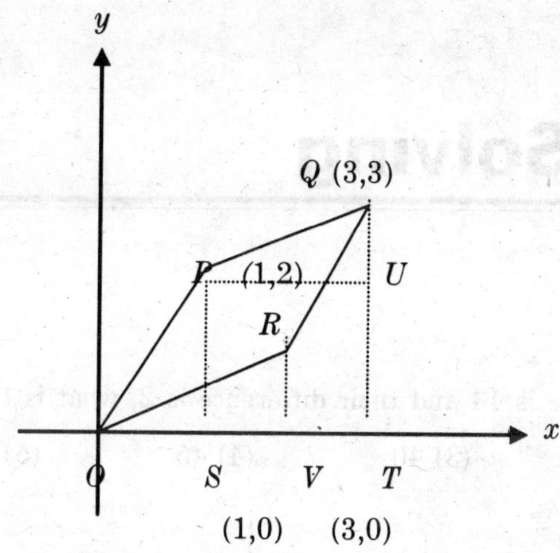

Let us mark the co-ordinates of P and Q in the figure. Let us drop perpendiculars from P and Q to meet the x-axis at S and T respectively. Let us also draw a line parallel to the x-axis from P to meet QT in U. The co-ordinates of S and T are respectively (1.0) and (3,0). Let us remember that the equation of the x-axis is $y = 0$ just as the equation of the y-axis is $x = 0$ and thus the y co-ordinate of any point on the x-axis is invariably zero.

Since $PQRS$ is a parallelogram, PQ can be parallel to OR only if the slopes of these two lines are the same. The slope of the line PQ is $(QU / PU) = 1/2$. Effectively the slope of a straight line is the distance travelled up (or down) the y-axis (or a line parallel to the y-axis if the y co-ordinate lies on a line parallel to the y-axis) divided by the distance travelled along the x-axis (or a line parallel to the x-axis either in positive or negative direction if the x co-ordinate lies on a line parallel to the x-axis) and thus this is effectively = (the difference between the y co-ordinates of the ending and starting points of the line) divided by (the difference between the x co-ordinates of the ending and starting points of the line). Therefore the slope of the line OR is also 1/2. The co-ordinates of the point O are (0,0). Since the slope of the line OR is RV / OV, = 1/2, (the difference between the y co-ordinates of R and O) divided by (the difference between the x co-ordinates of R and O) = 1/2 and this is only feasible with **Option 3** which has (2,1) as possible co-ordinates of R.

Answer 20

One has to read this question carefully as one should read all of them since haste can lead to a wrong answer for such a simple question.

The question should be seen in two parts:

Part (1): How many positive whole numbers are less than 81

Part (2): How many of these positive whole numbers less than 81 are not squares of whole numbers

The answer to the question is Part (1) – Part (2).

Part (1) is simple: There are 80 such whole numbers and these are 1 to 80.

Part (2) is also simple: There are 8 such numbers and these are the squares of positive whole numbers 1 to 8 (1, 4, 9 and so on till 64).

The answer to the question therefore is $80 - 8 = 72$. Hence **Option 4**.

Chapter 52

Problem Solving

Practice Test 3

Question 1

If the sum of two numbers is 14 and their difference is 2, what is the product of the two numbers?

(1) 24 (2) 28 (3) 40 (4) 45 (5) 48

Question 2

The price per pair of Brand X socks is \$2 and the price per pair of Brand Y socks is \$3. If there is no Sales Tax and a customer chooses only from among these two brands, what is the greatest number of pairs of socks that he can buy with exactly \$25?

(1) 9 (2) 10 (3) 11 (4) 12 (5) 20

Question 3

If a small juice can contains 200 ml of juice, how many *litres* of juice is there in 48 small cans contained in a case? (1 litre = 1000 ml)

(1) 0.96 (2) 9.6 (3) 96 (4) 960 (5) 9,600

Question 4

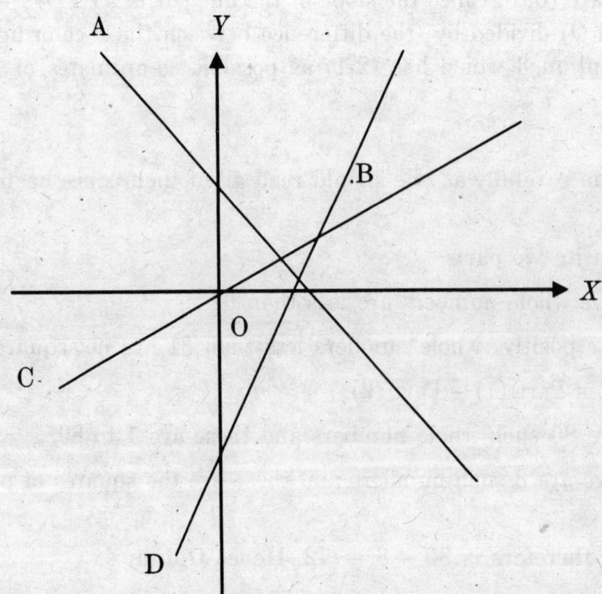

In the *XY*- plane, point B has co-ordinates (E,F), and lines D, C and A have equations y = 3 x –3, y = x/2 and y = –x + 1 respectively. Which of the following inequalities is NOT true?

(1) 2F > E (2) F < 4E (3) E + F > 1 (4) 3E – F < 3 (5) EF > 0

Question 5

$$\frac{\frac{4}{9}+\frac{4}{9}+\frac{4}{9}+\frac{4}{9}+\frac{4}{9}+\frac{4}{9}}{6} =$$

(1) 2/27 (2) 4/9 (3) 2/3 (4) 8/3 (5) 6

Question 6

If y = 3x and z = 2y, then in terms of x, x + y + z =

(1) 10x (2) 9x (3) 8x (4) 6x (5) 5x

Question 7

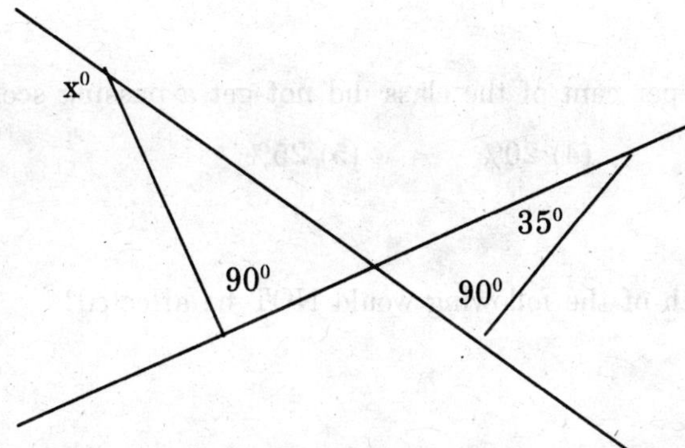

In the figure above x=

(1) 35 (2) 55 (3) 125 (4) 145 (5) 150

Question 8

If $(3/x)+(4/3x) = 1/3$, then x=

(1) 7 (2) 9 (3) 11 (4) 13 (5) 15

Question 9 to 13

These questions refer to the following distribution.

TEST SCORES FOR A CLASS OF 8 JUNIORS AND 12 SENIORS

Frequency

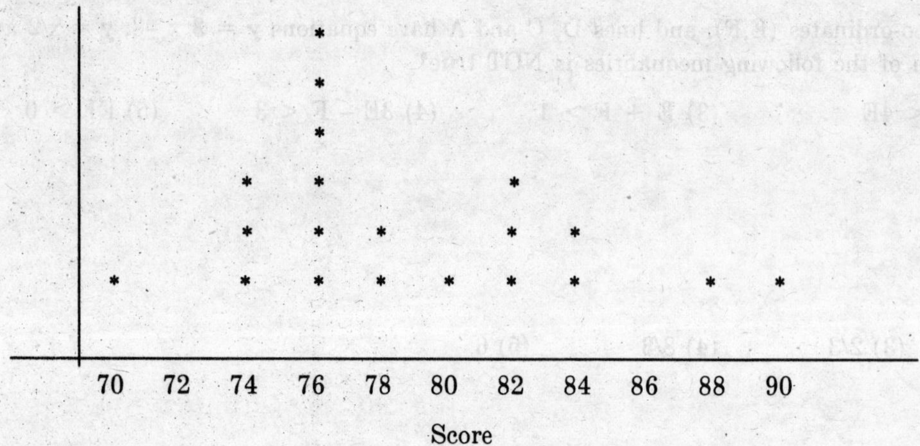

Question 9

If 5 seniors have scores of 82 or above, how many juniors have scores below 82?

(1) 7 (2) 6 (3) 5 (4) 4 (5) 3

Question 10

If 76 were the lowest passing score, what per cent of the class did not get a passing score?

(1) 8% (2) 10% (3) 12% (4) 20% (5) 25%

Question 11

If 5 points were added to each score, which of the following would NOT be affected?

(1) The highest score

(2) The mean for all scores

(3) The median for the seniors' scores

(4) The mode of the juniors' scores

(5) Standard deviation for all scores

Question 12

If the mean score for the juniors were known, which of the following could be calculated from the information given?

(i) The range of the scores for the seniors

(ii) The median score for the juniors

(iii) The mean of the score for the seniors

(1) None (2) (i) only (3) (iii) only (4) (i) and (ii) (5) (ii) and (iii)

Question 13

The median score for the class is:

(1) 76 (2) 77 (3) 78 (4) 79 (5) 80

Question 14

A sequence of numbers a_1, a_2, a_3, … is defined by $a_1 = 5$, $a_2 = 10$ and $a_{(n+1)} = (a_n)^{(a^{n-1})}$ for each positive integer $n > 2$. For example, $a_3 = 10^5$. What is the least value of n for which a_n has at least 5,000,000 digits?

(1) 4 (2) 5 (3) 6 (4) 10 (5) 100

Question 15

If $x \neq 0$, then $x(x^2)^3 / x^2 =$

(1) x^2 (2) x^3 (3) x^4 (4) x^5 (5) x^6

Question 16

At 9 AM, Train T left a train station and 2 hours later Train S left the same station on a parallel track. If Train T averaged 60 km/hour and Train S averaged 75 km/hour until S overtook T, at what time did S overtake T?

(1) 2 PM (2) 5 PM (3) 6 PM (4) 7 PM (5) 9 PM

Question 17

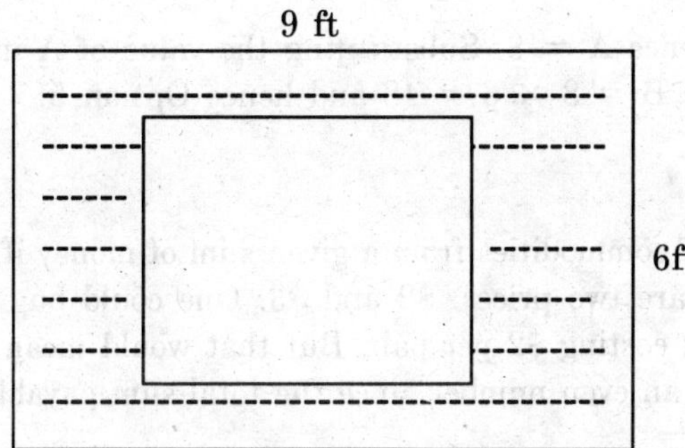

The rectangular rug shown in the figure above has a floral border 1 foot wide on all sides. What is the area, in square feet, of that portion of the rug that excludes the border?

(1) 28 (2) 40 (3) 45 (4) 48 (5) 53

Question 18

One month Susan used one-sixth of her monthly salary for a car payment and one fourth more than the car payment for rent. What fraction of the monthly salary did Susan use that month for the car payment and rent combined?

(1) 5/24 (2) 3/8 (3) 5/12 (4) 1/2 (5) 7/12

Question 19

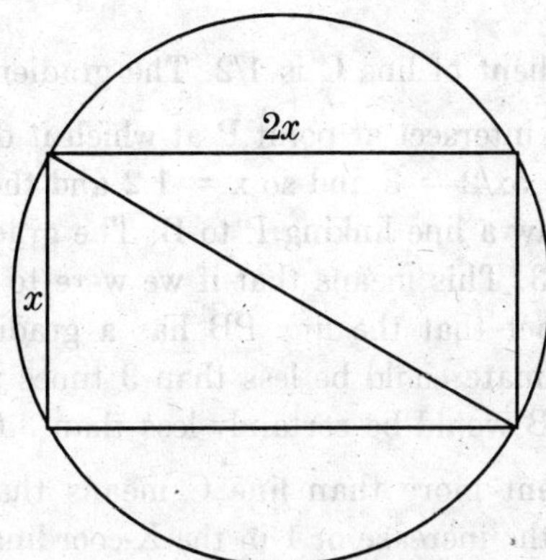

In the figure above, if the area of the inscribed rectangular region is 32, then the circumference of the circle is

(1) 20π (2) $4\pi\sqrt{5}$ (3) $4\pi\sqrt{3}$ (4) $2\pi\sqrt{5}$ (5) $2\pi\sqrt{3}$

Question 20

$A = \pi D^2/X$.

If the formula above gives the area A of a circular region in terms of its diameter D, then X=

(1) 1/4 (2) 1/2 (3) 1 (4) 2 (5) 4

Detailed Answers

Answer 1

Let the two numbers be A and B respectively. The fact that their sum is 14 and their difference is 2 means that we can write the following two equations:

Equation 1: A + B = 14

Equation 2: A – B = 2

Adding Equations 1 and 2 we get 2A = 16 and hence A = 8. Substituting the value of A in either of the Equations 1 or 2, we get B = 6 and therefore A × B = 8 × 6 = 48 and hence **Option 5**.

Answer 2

Fundamentally, one can buy the maximum number of commodities from a given sum of money if one buys only those commodities that have the least price. There are two prices: $2 and $3. One could buy the maximum number of socks if one were to buy only those socks costing $2 per pair. But that would mean that the total sum paid for the socks would necessarily have to be an even number since the total sum payable is a product of the price per pair and the number of pairs bought.

However 25 is an odd number and therefore there will have to be at least one pair priced at $3 per pair. This means that if one were to buy 11 pairs of socks costing $2 per pair and 1 pair of socks costing $3 per pair, one could buy 1+11=12 pairs of socks and spend exactly $25. Hence **Option 4**.

Answer 3

If a small juice can contains 200 ml of juice, 5 such cases would make 1000 ml of juice and since 1000 ml of juice makes 1 litre of juice, 5 small cans make a litre of juice.

Since there are 48 small cans, and every 5 cans make 1 litre, 9×5=45 cans would make 9 litres of juice and the remaining three would make less than one litre. This means that there are more than 9 litres but less than 10 litres of juice. This is only **Option 2**.

Answer 4

The gradient of line A is –1. The gradient of line C is 1/2. The gradient of line D is 3.

Let us imagine that the lines C and D intersect at point P at which it obeys both the equations $y = 3x - 3$ and $y = x/2$. Thus $3x - 3 = x/2$ and hence $5x/2 = 3$ and so $x = 1.2$ and then $y = 0.6$. The co-ordinates of P are (1.2, 0.6). Imagine that we were to draw a line linking P to B. The gradient of such a line would certainly be more than 1/2 but certainly less than 3. This means that if we were to assume that the X-coordinate of B is one more than that of point P, the fact that the line PB has a gradient less than line D means that the corresponding increase in the Y- coordinate could be less than 3 times the increase of 1 in the X-coordinate. This means that the Y- coordinate of B would be certainly less than 3.6.

Then since the line PB has a gradient more than line C means that the corresponding increase in the Y- coordinate would be more than 1/2 the increase of 1 in the X-coordinate. This means that the Y coordinate of B would be certainly more than 1.1.

Thus when E=2.2, F lies within the range $1.1 < F < 3.6$. Now let us go from option to option:

Option 1: $2F > E$. If $E = 2.2$, then since F could be 1.2, 2F could be greater than E.

Option 2: $F < 4E$. If $E = 2.2$, then since F could be 1.2. Then F would certainly be less than 4E which could be as much as 8.

Option 3: $E + F > 1$. If $E = 2.2$, then since F could be 1.2. Thus E+F would certainly be greater than 1.

Option 4: $3E - F < 3$. If $E = 2.2$, $3E = 6.6$. F could be 1.2. 3E-F would then be 5.4 which would mean that $3E - F$ can be greater than 3. This equality is not true. Hence **Option 4**.

Option 5: $EF > 0$. If $E = 2.2$, then since F could be more than 1.1, the product of E and F will certainly be positive and hence this equality is true.

Answer 5

If A + A + A + A + A + A = 6A, and if you were to divide 6A by 6, you would get A. Similarly:

$\frac{4}{9} + \frac{4}{9} + \frac{4}{9} + \frac{4}{9} + \frac{4}{9} + \frac{4}{9} = 6 \times \frac{4}{9}$. If you were to divide $6 \times \frac{4}{9}$ with 6 you would get $\frac{4}{9}$.

Hence Option 2.

Answer 6

Assume x = 1. Then y = 3 and z = 6. Thus x + y + z = 1 + 3 + 6 = 10. Thus x + y + z in terms of x is 10 times 1 and hence 10x. Thus Option 1.

Answer 7

Let us see the following figure and put in values for angles and names for points as we go along.

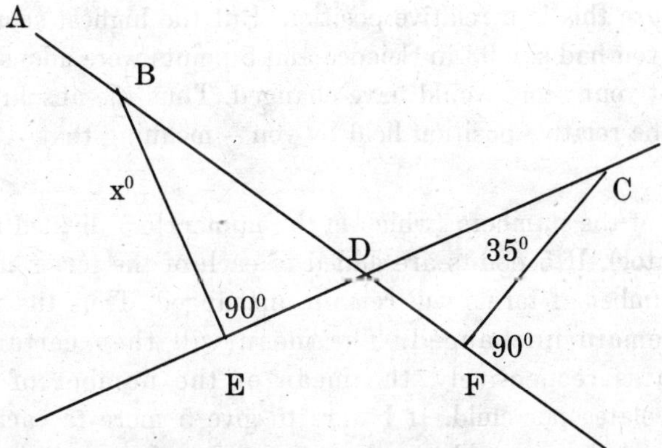

In right-angled triangle CDF, angle CDF = $180^0 - (90^0+35^0) = 55^0$. Angles BDE and CDF being opposite angles, they are equal and so angle BDE is 55^0. In right-angled triangle BDE, angle DBE = $180^0 - (90^0 + 55^0) = 35^0$. Since ABF is a straight line, angle ABE or angle of x^0 is $180^0 - 35^0 = 145^0$. Hence x = 145 in Option 4.

Answer 8

If:

Option 1 is right then $x = 7$ that is, $(3/x) + (4/3x) = (3/7) + (4/21) = 9/21 + 4/21 = 13/21$ but this is not equal to 1/3 because 7/21 is 1/3. Hence Option 1 is not correct.

Option 2 is right then $x = 9$ that is, $(3/x) + (4/3x) = (3/9) + (4/27) = 9/27 + 4/27 = 13/27$ but this is not equal to 1/3 because 9/27 is 1/3. Hence Option 2 is not correct.

Option 3 is right then $x = 11$ that is, $(3/x) + (4/3x) = (3/11) + (4/33) = 9/33 + 4/33 = 13/33$ and this is not equal to 1/3 because 11/33 is 1/3. Hence Option 3 is not correct.

Option 4 is right then $x = 13$ it follows, $(3/x) + (4/3x) = (3/13) + (4/39) = 9/39 + 4/39 = 13/39$ and this is equal to 1/3. Hence **Option 4** is correct.

What is to be learnt from the exercise in the case of Options 1 and 2 is that we shall get 13 in the numerator. Since 13 is a prime number, if you are to get 1/3, the denominator must also be a multiple of 13 and hence if any option should work, it must be Option 4. When you are taking the test, Option 3 need not be examined at all.

Answer 9

There are 8 juniors and 12 seniors. The number of students having a score of 82 and above is 7, as may be seen by counting the number of dots as follows: 3 (with a score of 82)+ 2 (with a score of 84) +1 (with a score of 88) +1 (with a score of 90). There are 5 seniors with a score of 82 and above. This means that there are 2 juniors with the score of 82 and above. Since there are 8 juniors in all and 2 of them have a score of 82 and above, there are 6 juniors who have a score below 82. Hence **Option 2**.

Answer 10

The number of students getting a score less than 76 is 4 as may be seen by counting the dots in the case of 74 (3 dots)+ 70 (1 dot). There are a 20 students in all. If 4 out of 20 do not get passing score, this means 4/20 or $(4 \times 5)/(20 \times 5)$ or 20/100 did not get a passing score. This is 20% and hence **Option 4**.

In order to express any fraction in percentage terms all you have to do is to multiply both numerator and denominator with such a common number so that you get 100 in the denominator. Then the numerator is the percentage value of the fraction.

Answer 11

If you had the highest score in class and if five points were added to the scores of each one, it would not alter the fact that you have the highest score because this is a relative position. But the highest score, which is an absolute value, would increase by 5 points. If you had say 93 in Science and 5 points were added to each score, you would have 98 points and this means that your score would have changed. Thus the absolute position will be changed. What will remain unchanged is the relative position held by you – meaning that your score is the highest in class.

The mean of a series of numbers is the total of the numbers (which is the numerator) divided by the number of terms in the series (which is the denominator). If 5 points are added to each of the terms in a series, this would add to the total as well and yet the number of terms will remain unchanged. Thus the numerator will increase whereas the denominator will remain unchanged. The mean will then certainly increase. If three children had 1, 2 and 3 chocolates respectively, the mean of the number of chocolates is (1 + 2 + 3) chocolates/3 children = 2 chocolates per child. If I were to give 5 more to each of them, the number of chocolates that they would respectively have would then be 6,7 and 8 and the arithmetic average of the number of chocolates that they have would then be (6 + 7 + 8) chocolates/3 children= 7 chocolates per child. The mean is certainly going to change.

As regards the median, the median of a series of terms is that term that lies halfway between the two ends of the series. In the case of 1,2,3 the median term is 2 whereas if 5 were added to each term, you would have a new series of 6,7,8 and this would mean that the median is now up to 7.

What we have seen is that if 5 were to be added to each of the terms, both the mean and median would increase by exactly 5.

The mode, in mathematics, is the number in a given set of numbers that appears most frequently. If a given set of numbers is 1, 2, 3, 3, 3, 4, 5, 6 then 3 is the mode of the series. If another series were to be 1, 2, 2, 2, 3, 4, 5, 5, 5, 6 then 2 and 5 are its modes.

In the set 3, 4, 5, 6, 6, 7, 10, 13 - for example - the mode of the set is 6. To this series if you were to add 5 to each of the terms of the series 3, 4, 5, 6, 6, 7, 10, 13, the series would get changed to 8, 9, 10, 11, 11, 12, 15, 18 and with this, the mode- meaning the number appearing most frequently – would get changed to 11.

Other sets may have no modes. However the set that we have been asked to see has 76 as its mode. So the mode would change as well.

The Standard Deviation is a number representing the **spread** of a set of numbers around their average value. It is calculated from all the individual deviations from the average. It is an important concept in most statistical calculations because it is a precise indicator of the degree of variability within the set of numbers. To illustrate, the standard deviation of a series 2, 5, 8, 9, 10, 12, 17 is calculated as follows:

- First the mean of this series is calculated. The mean of the series is the (total of the series) ÷ (the number of terms) $=63 \div 7=9$.
- Then the absolute difference between each of the terms and the mean is calculated and the average of these absolute differences is arrived at; the absolute difference is the one that is obtained after ignoring the negative signs. The sum of the absolute difference here would be: $(9-2)+(9-5)+(9-8)+(9-9)+(10-9)+(12-9)+(17-9)=7+4+1+0+1+3+8=24$. The average of these absolute differences is 24/7. The square root of this average is the standard deviation and thus in the present case, the standard deviation would be $\sqrt{(24/7)}$. In this series if we were to add 5 points to each of the terms in the series 2, 5, 8, 9, 10, 12, 17, the series would become 7, 10, 13, 14, 15, 17, 22 and would have a mean of $98/7=14$. The absolute differences between the mean and the terms in the series would remain unaltered primarily because if you are subtracting a number B from a number A the answer is $(A-B)$ and then if you were to subtract $(B+5)$ from $(A+5)$ the difference would continue to remain $(A-B)$.

Thus the standard deviation would remain unaffected. Thus **Option 5** is correct.

It is recommended that you find the standard deviation of the new series 7, 10, 13, 14, 15, 17, 22 and satisfy yourself that the standard deviation remains unchanged at $\sqrt{(24/7)}$.

If you have noticed, we have not used the data in the question at all. We have reduced the data to small and manageable integral numbers so that we understand the concepts of the mean, median, mode and standard deviation. Mathematical concepts do not vary with numbers. Thus the understanding of the concepts alone is what is required and not unnecessary toiling.

Answer 12

The information given to us is what is in the diagram as reproduced hereunder:

TEST SCORES FOR A CLASS OF 8 JUNIORS AND 12 SENIORS

Frequency

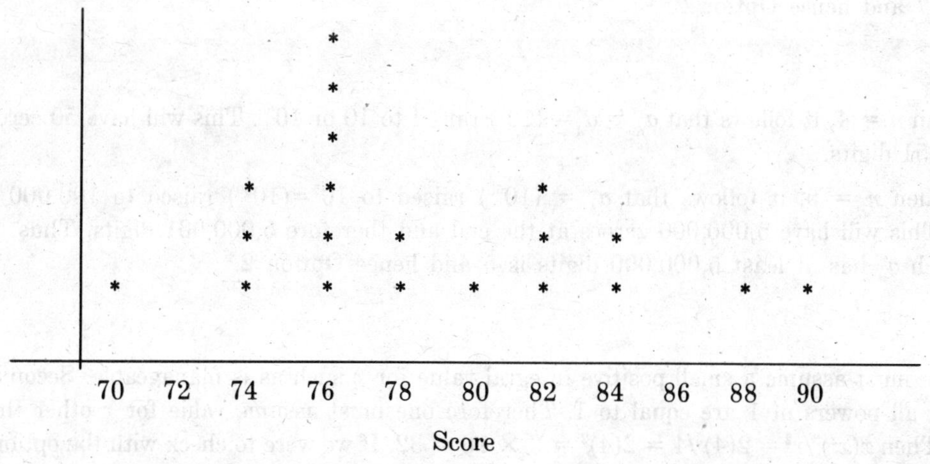

As regards questions 9 to 11 there are IFs and ANDs. What if 5 were added to each score? What if 76 were the lowest passing score? There is nothing concrete. If IFS and ANDS were pots and pans (meaning if what one wishes could be reality) then tinkers and tailors would be soldiers and sailors. You know for sure that there are 8 juniors and 12 seniors. You do not know who got what score. If you were to count the number of asterisks (that represent the scores of the twenty boys in the chart) you will see that there are twenty. If you were to add up the scores represented by each asterisk, you can find the total of the scores of the 20 students. Let us call this total A. If you were given the mean score of the juniors you could then find the total score of the 8 juniors; let us call this total B. If you were to deduct the total score of the juniors from the total score of the twenty students, you would get the total score of the 12 seniors; let us call this total $A - B$. From here finding the average score of the seniors is a matter of a jiffy; all you have to do is to divide $(A - B)$ by 12.

Each asterisk represents a particular student's score. You however do not know whom in particular does the asterisk represents. All you know is that the lowest score is 70 and the highest score is 90 and therefore the range of the scores is 20. But this is the range of the scores of the seniors and juniors combined. You do not know the range of either the seniors or the juniors. The average of the juniors' score can give you the total but not what values comprise the total. If three boys in your class were to tell you that they have an average score of 25 out of 50, can you guess their individual scores? Unless you know the individual scores, how can you tell what is the range of the scores that will involve finding the difference between the lowest and the highest score. The information at Statement (i) cannot be obtained from the given information.

As regards the median scores, the median score cannot be found in the absence of the individual scores. Hence only **Option 3** is correct.

Answer 13

The 20 scores will have to be arranged in ascending order as follows: 70, 74, 74, 74, 76, 76, 76, 76, 76, 76, 78, 78, 80, 82, 82, 82, 84, 84, 88, 90. However when you actually write the examination this must be limited to scribbling like this: 70 (once), 74 (four) 76 (six) and so on. You need not write anything at all if you can get to the 10th and the 11th terms upon which the answer to this question depends. The Lord has given us a fair number of fingers. One could make admirable use of them in counting.

The median of a series of numbers with n terms where n is an odd number is the $[(n + 1)/2]^{th}$ term. Thus if a series has, say, 5 terms, the 3rd term is the median term.

The median of a series of numbers with n terms where n is an even number is the average of $n/2^{th}$ term and the $[(n + 2)/2]^{th}$ term. If a series has 6 terms then the average of the 3rd and the 4th term is the median of the series. This is because the 3rd term has 2 terms preceding it and the 4th term has two terms succeeding it. Thus the 3rd and the 4th terms are exactly in the middle of the series of 6 terms and hence the average of the 3rd and the 4th terms is the median of the series of 6 terms.

Since there is even number of terms, 20 to be precise, the average of the 10th and the 11th term will give the median of the series. The 10th term is 76 and the 11th term is 78 and the average of these is 77. Hence the median of the series is 77 and hence **Option 2**.

Answer 14

If Option 1 were true, then $n = 4$, it follows that $a_n = a_4 = (10^5)$ raised to 10 or 10^{50}. This will have 50 zeroes at the end and therefore 51 digits.

If Option 2 were true, then $n = 5$, it follows that $a_5 = (10^{50})$ raised to $10^5 = (10^{50})$ raised to 100,000 or 10 raised to 5,000,000. This will have 5,000,000 zeroes at the end and therefore 5,000,001 digits. Thus the least value for n for which a_n has at least 5,000,000 digits is 5 and hence **Option 2**.

Answer 15

When told that $x \neq 0$, one must assume a small positive integral value for x such as is manageable. Secondly, when you assume $x = 1$, all powers of 1 are equal to 1. Therefore one must assume value for x other than $x = 1$. Let us take $x=2$. Then $x(x^2)^3/x^2 = 2(4)^3/4 = 2(4)^2 = 2 \times 16 = 32$. If we were to check with the options, we would find that only in the case of **Option 4** would we get 32 with the value of x as 2.

Basically this is a test of one's concepts. Algebra is manmade. Nothing prevents us from assuming some small value for the unknown term x. This is because we are human beings and algebra is our humble servant. As to the question what value to assume, it will involve the knowledge that all powers of 1 whether 1^2 or 1^{20000}

can give exactly 1 and nothing more or less. This is why one should not assume 1 as a value for x. (Incidentally what is true of 1 is also true for zero but the question expressly bars us from assuming zero as a possible value for x).

Answer 16

At 9 AM, Train T left the train station. At 11 AM, Train S left the train station. The fact that S overtook T means that they both were going in the same direction and that S is the faster of the two. This is fundamental.

T moved @ 60 km/hour. By 11 AM, T was already 120 km away from the station when S got into the act. S moved @ 75 km/hour whereas T moved @ 60 km/hour. Every hour, S was reducing the distance between the two trains by 15 km. This means that it would take S 120/15= 8 hours to overtake T. Since S left at 11 AM, if one were to add 8 hours thereto one would find that S overtook T at 7 PM. Hence **Option 4**.

Answer 17

The rug has dimensions of 9 ft by 6 ft and thus has an area of 54 sq ft. The floral border is 1 ft on all sides. Thus the area excluding the border is:

- 1 ft less on either end of the length of the rug that is 9 ft and
- 1 ft less on either end of the breadth of the rug that is 6 ft in measure

This means that the measurements of the area that excludes the border are 7ft by 4ft and thus the area of the portion excluding the border is 28 square feet and hence **Option 1**.

Answer 18

When up against fractions such as one-sixth and one-fourth, one must realise that the denominators in the two fractions are 4 and 6 and hence one may assume Susan's salary as 24 units of currency since 24 is a multiple of both 4 and 6. This means that Susan paid 4 units for the car payment. One-fourth of 4 is 1. So she spent 4 + 1 = 5 units for rent. In all therefore, she spent 4+5=9 units for car payment and rent combined. This means that she spent $9/24^{th}$ of her salary for the aggregate of car payment and rent and this when simplified comes to $3/8^{th}$ and hence **Option 2** is correct.

Answer 19

If the sides of a rectangle are $2x$ and x, then its area is $2x^2$. This means that $2x^2=32$ and thus $x^2=16$ and so $x=4$.

This means that the measures of the rectangle are 8 and 4 units. The diagonal of the rectangle is the hypotenuse of the right-angled triangle with 8 and 4 units as the two sides and is also the diameter of the circle. According to the Pythagoras Theorem the square on the hypotenuse is equal to the sum of the squares on the other two sides and hence the $(\text{diagonal})^2 = 8^2 + 4^2$ or $(\text{diagonal})^2 = 64 + 16 = 80$ and hence the diagonal $= \sqrt{80} = 4\sqrt{5}$ and since the diagonal is also the diameter of the circle, the radius of the circle is $1/2 \times 4\sqrt{5} = 2\sqrt{5}$ and the circumference of the circle is $2 \times \pi \times r$, the circumference of the circle is $2 \times \pi \times 2\sqrt{5} = 4\pi\sqrt{5}$ and hence **Option 2** is correct.

Answer 20

The area of a circular region is given by the following formula:

Area of a circle $= \pi \times r^2$ where r is the radius of the circle. The radius, as we know is half the diameter and hence if we were to refer to the diameter as D, then the area of a circle would be $\pi \times (D/2)^2 = \pi D^2/4$. Since $A = \pi D^2/X = \pi D^2/4$, $X = 4$ and hence **Option 5** is correct.

Chapter 53

Question Paper 1

SECTION I

Time: 45 minutes

Present your perspective on one of the issues below using relevant reasons and/or examples to support your view.

Topic 1

"Wisdom is rightfully attributed not to people who know what to look for in life but to people who know what to overlook"

Topic 2

"The media (books, film, music, television, for example) tend to create rather than reflect the values of a society"

SECTION II

Time: 30 minutes.

Discuss how well reasoned you find this argument.

The following appeared as a letter to the editor of a local newspaper:

"Five years ago, we the residents of Morton, voted to keep the publicly owned piece of land known as Rose Woods, in a natural, undeveloped state. Our thinking was that, if no shopping centres or houses were built there, Rose Woods would continue to benefit our community as a natural parkland. But now that our town planning committee wants to purchase the land and build a school there, we should reconsider this issue. If the land becomes a school site, no shopping centres or houses can be built there, and substantial acreage would probably be devoted to athletic fields. There would be no better use of land in our community than this, since a large majority of our children participate in sports, and Rose Woods would continue to benefit our community as a natural parkland."

SECTION III

VERBAL

Time: 30 minutes.

30 Questions.

This question includes a sentence that has one or two blanks, each blank indicating that a word or a phrase has been omitted. Beneath the sentence are five words or sets of words. Choose the word or set of words for each blank that best fits the meaning of the sentence as a whole.

Question 1

Chinese art has no __________ the powerfully explicit antiwar paintings of the West, but ________ subtlety and indirection to express political thought.

(1) panacea for.. passes by (2) diversion from .. defers to (3) counterpart for .. relies on (4) intimation of .. alludes to (5) derivative of .. refrains from

Choose the word or phrase that is most nearly opposite in meaning to the word in capital letters.

Question 2

SEMINAL

(1) oblique (2) provincial (3) incomplete (4) fluctuating (5) derivative

Question 3

LACONIC

(1) operative (2) acerbic (3) voluble (4) pompous (5) erect

Question 4

SYBARITE

(1) political aspirant (2) habitual malcontent (3) humanitarian (4) veteran (5) ascetic

Question 5

PROSAIC

(1) appropriate (2) propitious (3) ambiguous (4) modern (5) extraordinary

In the following question, a related pair of words or phrases is followed by five-lettered pairs of words or phrases. Select the lettered pair that best expresses a relationship similar to that expressed in the original pair.

Question 6

GRANDSTAND: IMPRESS::

(1) patronise: alienate (2) hedge: reveal (3) equivocate: deceive (4) presume: disprove

(5) upbraid: dislike

Choose the word or phrase that is most nearly opposite in meaning to the word in capital letters.

Question 7

RESTIVENESS

(1) contentment (2) heartiness (3) smugness (4) bashfulness (5) urbanity

In the following questions, a related pair of words or phrases is followed by five lettered pairs of words or phrases. Select the pair that best expresses a relationship similar to that expressed in the original pair.

Question 8

OBSEQUIOUS: SYCOPHANT::

(1) pusillanimous: coward (2) reticent: dupe (3) progressive: entrepreneur

(4) guileless: racketeer (5) acquiescent: rebel

Choose the word or phrase that is most nearly opposite in meaning to the word in capital letters.

Question 9

SUBLIME

(1) weak (2) austere (3) simple (4) base (5) abnormal

This question includes a sentence that has one or two blanks, each blank indicating that some word has been omitted. Beneath the sentence are five words or sets of words. Choose the word or set of words for each blank that best fits the meaning of the sentence as a whole.

Question 10

Just as the authors' book on eels is after a key text for courses in marine vertebrate zoology, their ideas on animal development and phylogeny ________ teaching in this area.

(1) prevent (2) defy (3) replicate (4) inform (5) use

In the following questions, a related pair of words or phrases is followed by five lettered pairs of words or phrases. Select the pair that best expresses a relationship similar to that expressed in the original pair.

Question 11

DOLDRUMS: ENERGY::

(1) joy: euphoria (2) rehabilitation: discipline (3) hunger: thirst

(4) depravity: virtue (5) grief: hope

Question 12

FOOLISH: DISCRETION::

(1) inedible: food (2) gumptious: disrespect (3) isolated: shelter

(4) impecunious: money (5) implacable: determination

Question 13

MISCALCULATION: JUDGEMENT::

(1) breach: fortification (2) fumble: location (3) gaffe: decorum

(4) exaggeration: statement (5) default: loan

Question 14

The ________ of gamblers' unsuccessful decision strategies is one ________ of the illusions built into games of chance in order to misguide players and take their money.

(1) distortion.. outcome (2) restriction .. result (3) maintenance .. function

(4) prediction .. accomplishment (5) demonstration .. prerequisite

Choose the word or phrase that is most nearly opposite in meaning to the word in capital letters.

Question 15

BUCOLIC

(1) cynical (2) cultivated (3) mythical (4) urban (5) gentle

This question includes a sentence that has one or two blanks, each blank indicating that a word has been omitted. Beneath the sentence are five words or sets of words. Choose the word or set of words for each blank that best fits the meaning of the sentence as a whole.

Question 16

Overall, the evidence was inconclusive as to whether the adjustment to the inflated estimates would ________ their accuracy or instead ________ the actual amount.

(1) compromise .. magnify (2) confirm .. validate (3) disprove .. pinpoint

(4) verify .. distort (5) improve .. understate

Question 17 and 18

After reading the passage, choose the best answer to each question. Answer all questions following the passage on the basis of what is stated or implied in the passage.

Since the United States census determines the appointment of federal and state legislative seats, and since it is also used for dividing the annual federal funds for certain social programs, accuracy in taking the census matters is very important. But despite careful standardised procedures undercounts are a persistent problem. Demographic analysis, which uses data on births, deaths, immigration and emigration yields a good estimate of the size of the national undercount. But sheer size is not the main problem. It is the uneven distribution of the undercount across geographic areas and across population groups that makes undercounts so problematic. The current procedure for dealing with that problem is the coverage-measurement survey. The survey, essentially a second, extremely painstaking census, is conducted in a limited number of the blocks into which the census has divided the country. Combining the information from both survey and census, statisticians are able to arrive at improved population estimates, even for areas outside the survey block.

Question 17

According to the passage, which of the following information is useful in gauging the number of people missed by the United States census?

(1) Shifts in federal and state legislative seats

(2) The procedure followed in taking the census

(3) Foreigners who become residents of the United States

(4) Migration patterns within the United States

(5) Persons with two official residences

Question 18

Based on your inference of the passage answer which of the following is true about the coverage measurement survey?

(1) It does away with the need to rely on estimates to arrive at population counts

(2) It is a census-taking method that is appropriate for only certain kinds of geographic areas

(3) It arrives at population counts that are often different from those of the census itself.

(4) It replaces the census proper in a limited number of geographic areas

(5) It analyses data on births, deaths, immigration, and emigration by population group.

In the following questions, a related pair of words or phrases is followed by five lettered pairs of words or phrases. Select the pair that best expresses a relationship similar to that expressed in the original pair.

Question 19

REPROVE: REPRIMAND::

(1) blame: censure (2) control: contain (3) persuade: convince

(4) thwart: confront (5) inconvenience: effect

This question includes a sentence that has one or two blanks, each blank indicating that a word or group of words has been omitted. Beneath the sentence are five words or sets of words. Choose the word or set of words for each blank that best fits the meaning of the sentence as a whole.

Question 20

The meeting seemed __________ , not just because decisions were made with excessive deliberation, but also because the director was so __________ as to provoke extremely lengthy debate.

(1) abbreviated .. distracted (2) interminable .. tendentious (3) methodical .. persuasive

(4) endless .. amenable (5) overwhelming .. withdrawn

Question 21 to 24

After reading the passage, choose the best answer to each question. Answer all questions following the passage on the basis of what is stated or implied in the passage.

In the fields of Delano, California, in 1965, Luis Valdez started the Teatro Campecino (Farmworkers' Theatre), and with it initiated the renaissance of Mexican American theatre. The Teatro Campecino had an avowedly political purpose: to rally campecinos (farmworkers) in support of the farm workers' strike then being organized by Cesar Chavez. Valdez', dramatic presentations, called *actos*, spoke to a campecino audience and addressed topics and themes directly related to the strike. Valdez', early *actos* were composed of a series of scenes about the strike experience acted by campecino volunteers. His later *actos* were presented by a newly constituted professional company, still called the Teatro Campecino, and addressed such themes as the impact of the Vietnam war on Mexican Americans and the dangers of assimilation, themes relevant to urban Mexican Americans as well as to campecinos. All Valdez', *actos* contained elements of song and dance, relied little on stage effects or props, and featured the use of masks. These dramatic elements, along with an intensely social or political purpose and the use of a mixture of Spanish, English, and Mexican American dialects in the dialogues, which realistically capture the flavour of Mexican American conversation, are still characteristic both of the *acto* and of most other forms of Mexican American theatre today.

Innovative as it is, the *acto* owes much to the theatre traditions of other periods and regions. Like early Spanish/American religious dramas, secular folk dramas, and the Mexican *carpas* of a somewhat later period, *actos* are usually performed outdoors by travelling groups of players or by local theatre groups. The improvised comic satire of the *actos* is often attributed to Valdez', study of the Italian *commedia del ' arte* of the sixteenth century although some critics see it as a direct reflection of the comic and improvisational qualities of the more contemporary and local *carpas* of Mexican theatre. The Italian influence is likely, whatever Valdez', immediate source: the Mexican *carpas* themselves are said to have originated from the theatre pieces of a sixteenth-century Spanish writer inspired by encounters with Italian *commedia del ' arte* troupes in towns in Spain. The English language theatre has provided elements as well: Valdez himself has acknowledged his debt to the agitprop socialist theatre that appeared in the United States during the 1920s and 1930s.

In particular, his actos contain the same assortment of semi-allegorical characters and the same blend of music, chorus, and dialogue found in some of the agitprop pieces, as well as the same fierce spirit of social and political critique. Finally, many of Valdez', later theatre pieces freely incorporate characters, plots and symbols drawn from the indigenous myths and rituals of the pre-Hispanic peoples of Latin America. In fact, no other art form illustrates more clearly the depth and complexity of the Mexican American heritage itself than does the *acto* of Luis Valdez and the Teatro Campecino.

Question 21

Which of the following, if true, most strengthen the author's argument concerning the debt of the *acto* to the theatre traditions of other periods and regions?

(1) Many popular forms of theatre rely heavily on improvisation

(2) Plays resembling the *acto* in structure were written in the 1970s by West African playwrights who are interested in dramatizing the richness of their own cultures

(3) The use of masks has, at one time or another, been characteristic of the theatre traditions of almost all cultures, even those most isolated from outside influences.

(4) During a strike, it is common for union members to present musical skits dramatizing the values of solidarity and resistance

(5) Before 1965 Luis Valdez had attended many performances of traditional Mexican theatre groups touring the Western United States.

Question 22

Which of the following best describes the author's evaluation of the views of the critics, cited in lines 5-7 at paragraph two?

(1) Their views if correct, do not preclude the existence of an Italian influence on the acto.

(2) Their views are unlikely to be correct given the difference existing between Mexican and Mexican American theatre.

(3) Their views concerning the Mexican *carpas* are essentially correct, but they lack familiarity with the acto.

(4) Their views are probably more correct than the views of those who have attributed the comic and improvisational elements of the acto to earlier sources.

(5) Their views betray a lack of familiarity with the *commedia del ' arte.*

Question 23

Which of the following does the passage suggest, was true of the later actos of the Teatro Campecino?

(1) They were more politically effective than were earlier actos.

(2) They were presented primarily outdoors, whereas earlier actos were presented inside theatres.

(3) They used a greater mixture of dialects than did the earlier actos.

(4) They addressed a broader audience than did the earlier actos.

(5) They differed from earlier actos in that they contained fewer improvisational elements

Question 24

According to the passage, which of the following elements, characteristic of the acto, are also found in some agitprop theatre pieces?

(1) The use of masks

(2) Comic improvisation

(3) An outdoor setting

(4) Minimal use of complex stage effects or props

(5) An assortment of semi-allegorical characters

Choose the word or phrase that is most nearly <u>opposite</u> in meaning to the word in capital letters.

Question 25

ENERVATE

(1) inculcate

(2) inaugurate

(3) invigorate

(4) fabricate

(5) generate

Question 26 and 27

After reading the passage, choose the best answer to each question. Answer all questions following the passage on the basis of what is stated or implied in the passage.

Months of sub-zero temperatures and blinding snowstorms characterise the polar bear's winter environment. Because the sea ice breaks up frequently, seals, the bear's primary prey, are available only sporadically. To survive, the polar bear must stabilize its body temperature and store energy between meals that may occur at large intervals. Because their fur, hide, and blubber provide excellent insulation, relatively inactive bears can maintain a stable body temperature in extreme cold without consuming excessive energy. But this insulation also makes polar bears overheat quickly. A polar bear walking only about four miles per hour has a body temperature of almost 100^0 F, fever temperature in a human. The polar bear's size and awkward sideways gait cause it to use more than twice as much energy in movement as do most mammals. Bears both stabilize their temperature and conserve energy by still-hunting- lying motionless beside holes in the ice until seals surface for air.

Question 26

The passage is primarily concerned with discussing:

(1) Relationships between predators and prey in a winter environment

(2) Hunting techniques used by predators in winter environments

(3) The effects of the winter environment on the physiology of locomotion in one kind of mammal

(4) Comparative efficiency of energy storage in various mammals living in winter environment

(5) The way that one kind of animal is adapted to its winter environment.

Question 27

According to the passage which of the following would occur in a winter when the sea ice does not break up frequently?

(1) The population of seals would increase.

(2) Seals would spend more time on land and less in the water.

(3) Polar bears would move about much more.

(4) Polar bears would increase the variety of prey in their diet.

(5) Polar bears' chances of regular success in hunting would improve.

Choose the word or phrase that is most nearly opposite in meaning to the word in capital letters.

Question 28

DISGORGE

(1) inter (2) swallow (3) solidify (4) replace (5) include

In the following questions, a related pair of words or phrases is followed by five pairs of words or phrases. Select the word pair that best expresses a relationship similar to that expressed in the original pair.

Question 29

ANNOYING: GADFLY::

(1) brave: underdog (2) conniving: killjoy (3) insipid: bungler

(4) rude: churl (5) vicious: manipulator

This question includes a sentence that has one or two blanks, each blank indicating that a word has been omitted. Beneath the sentence are five words or sets of words. Choose the word or set of words for each blank that best fits the meaning of the sentence as a whole.

Question 30

Often the argument against philanthropy has the effect of ________ the character of philanthropists but not necessarily ________ their work: they may have done good inspite of themselves.

(1) describing .. explaining (2) aggrandizing .. acknowledging (3) emphasizing .. citing

(4) impugning .. discrediting (5) obscuring .. attacking

SECTION IV

QUANTITATIVE

Time: 45 minutes.

28 Questions.

Question 1

$x \neq 0$.

Column A	Column B
$-2x^2$	$x^2/3$

1. The quantity in Column A is greater
2. The quantity in Column B is greater
3. The two quantities are equal
4. The relation cannot be determined from the information given

Question 2

If n is a positive integer, then n^+ denotes a number such that $n<n^+<n+1$.

Column A	Column B
$20^+/4^+$	5^+

1. The quantity in Column A is greater
2. The quantity in Column B is greater
3. The two quantities are equal
4. The relation cannot be determined from the information given

Question 3

S is the set of all integers from 1 to 48, inclusive.

V is the sum of all of the even integers in *S*.

D is the sum of all of the odd integers in *S*.

Column A	Column B
V	$D + 23$

1. The quantity in Column A is greater.
2. The quantity in Column B is greater.
3. The two quantities are equal.
4. The relation cannot be determined from the information given.

Question 4

The "reflection" of a positive integer is obtained by reversing its digits. For example, 321 is the reflection of 123. The difference between a 5-digit integer and its reflection must be divisible by which of the following?

(1) 2 (2) 4 (3) 5 (4) 6 (5) 9

Question 5

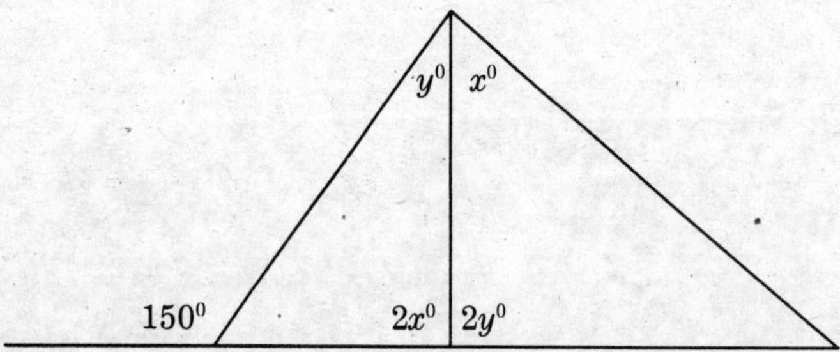

Column A	Column B
$x - y$	30

1. The quantity in Column A is greater.
2. The quantity in Column B is greater.
3. The two quantities are equal.
4. The relation cannot be determined from the information given.

Question 6

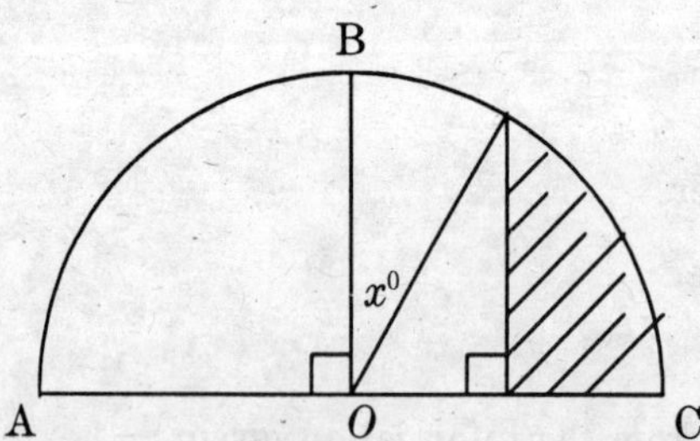

In semicircle ABC shown above, radius $OC = 1$. If $x = 30$, what is the perimeter of the shaded region?

(1) $\pi/3$ (2) $(\pi/3) + 2$ (3) $(\sqrt{3}/2) + (3/2)$ (4) $(\pi/3) - (\sqrt{3}/2) + (1/2)$
(5) $(\pi/3) + (\sqrt{3}/2) + (1/2)$

Question 7

$A > 0$ and $B > 0$

Column A	Column B
$\sqrt{A+B+2\sqrt{AB}}$	$\sqrt{A} + \sqrt{B}$

1. The quantity in Column A is greater
2. The quantity in Column B is greater
3. The two quantities are equal
4. The relation cannot be determined from the information given

Question 8

Let $A_1, A_2, A_3, \ldots, A_N, \ldots$ be a sequence of positive numbers where $A_1 = 1$, and for $n \geq 1$, $A_{N+1} = A_N + 4$. Which of the following represents the Nth term in the sequence?

(1) 4N – 3 (2) 4N – 1 (3) 4N (4) 4N + 1 (5) 4N + 4

Question 9

Column A	Column B
The greatest prime factor of 3^5	The greatest prime factor of 5^3

1. The quantity in Column A is greater.
2. The quantity in Column B is greater.
3. The two quantities are equal.
4. The relation cannot be determined from the information given.

Question 10

The average (arithmetic mean) of W, X, and Y is 9.

Column A	Column B
The average (arithmetic mean) of 2W – Y, 3X + 6, and 3Y – X	20

1. The quantity in Column A is greater
2. The quantity in Column B is greater
3. The two quantities are equal
4. The relation cannot be determined from the information given

Question 11

A circular flowerbed of radius R feet is surrounded by a circular walk of radius R/2 feet.

Column A	Column B
The area of the flower bed	The area of the walk

1. The quantity in Column A is greater.
2. The quantity in Column B is greater.
3. The two quantities are equal.
4. The relation cannot be determined from the information given.

Question 12

If N is an integer, then the units digit of N^2 cannot be

(1) 0 (2) 2 (3) 4 (4) 5 (5) 6

Question 13

Seven 1 dollar bills are to be distributed among Lucy, Gerard, and Dean so that each person gets at least \$1.

Column A	Column B
The number of ways to distribute the bills so that at least one person receives at least \$3	The total number of ways to distribute the bills

1. The quantity in Column A is greater.
2. The quantity in Column B is greater.
3. The two quantities are equal.
4. The relation cannot be determined from the information given.

Question 14 and 15

These questions refer to the following graphs.

INCOME OF ORGANIZATION X IN 1990, BY SOURCE

(total income = \$ 43,000,000)

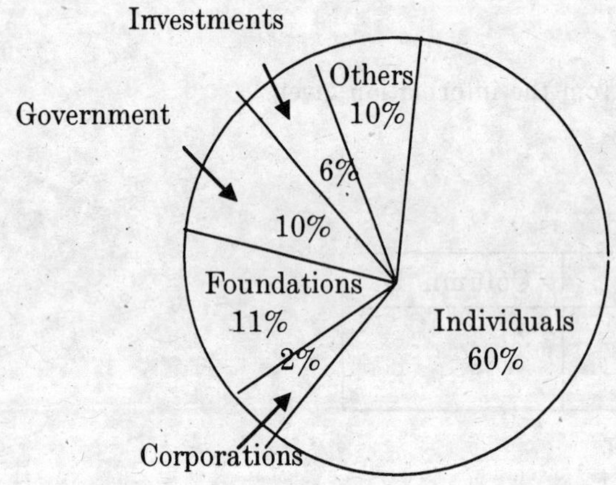

Membership in Organization X 1980-1990

Note: On X axis Year 1 represents year 1980 and 2 represents year 1981 and so on till year 11 that represents 1990.

Question 14

If income from foundations increased 25% from 1989 to 1990, which of the following represents income from foundations in 1989?

(1) (0.75) (0.11) ($43,000,000)

(2) (1.25) (0.11) ($43,000,000)

(3) 0.11/0.25 ($43,000,000)

(4) 0.11/0.75 ($43,000,000)

(5) 0.11/1.25($43,000,000)

Question 15

For the year 1982 through 1985, inclusive, the average (arithmetic mean) membership was approximately

(1) 50,000 (2) 60,000 (3) 75,000 (4) 95,000 (5) 1,20,000

Question 16

$3 < x < 5$

Column A	Column B
$(3 + x) / 3$	$(5 + x) / x$

1. The quantity in Column A is greater.
2. The quantity in Column B is greater.
3. The two quantities are equal.
4. The relation cannot be determined from the information given.

Question 17

Column A	Column B
1 / (1 – 0.03)	1.03

1. The quantity in Column A is greater.
2. The quantity in Column B is greater.
3. The two quantities are equal.
4. The relation cannot be determined from the information given.

Question 18

The jewels in a crown consist of diamonds, rubies and emeralds. If the ratio of diamonds to rubies is 5/6 and the ratio of rubies to emeralds is 8/3, what is the least number of jewels that could be in the tiara?

(1) 16 (2) 22 (3) 40 (4) 53 (5) 67

Question 19

If $ax - by + cx - dy = 0$, $x/y = 2$, and $b + d = -1$, then which of the following statements is true?

(1) $a + c = -1/2$ (2) $c - a = 1/2$ (3) $a + c = 2$ (4) $a + c = -2$ (5) $c - a = -2$

Question 20 and 21

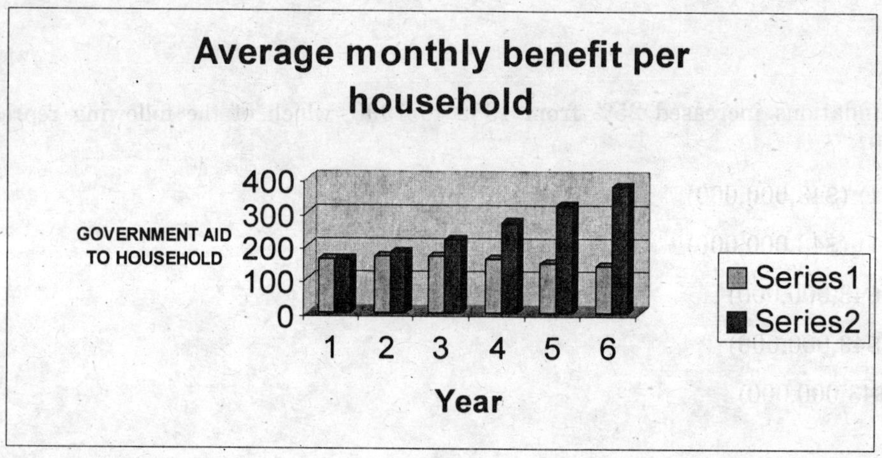

Series 1 = in 1960 dollars

Series 2 = in actual year dollars

Note: In the bar chart above year 1 represents years from 1955 to 1960, year 2 years from 1960 to 1965 and so on till year 6 that represents years from 1980 to 1985.

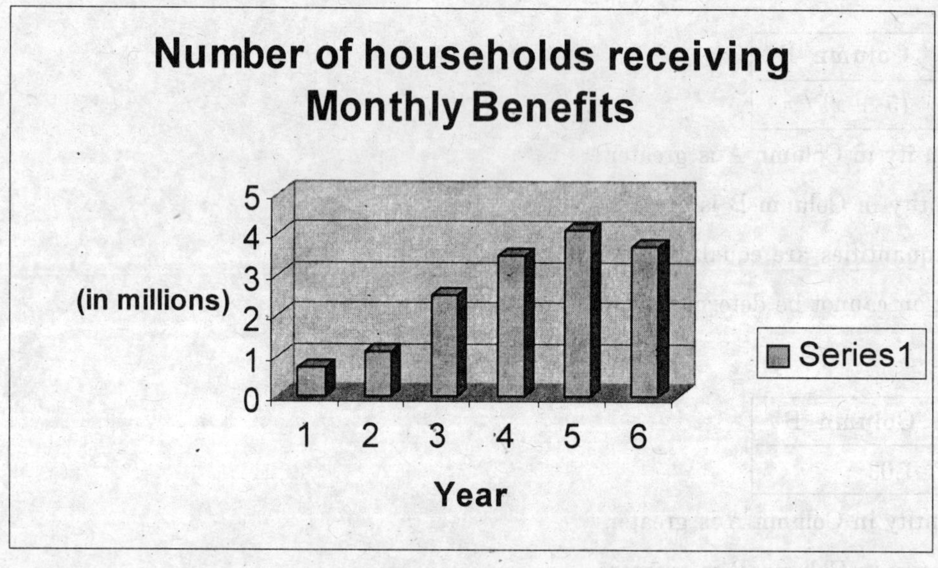

Note: In the bar chart above year 1 represents period from year 1955 to 1960, year 2 period from year 1960 to 1965 and so on till year 6 that represents period from the year 1980 to 1985.

Question 20

If there is an 80% increase from 1970 to 1995 in the number of households receiving monthly benefits, then the increase in the number of households receiving monthly benefits from 1985 to 1995 will be approximately

(1) 1,200,000 (2) 1,100,000 (3) 900,000 (4) 700,000 (5) 500,000

Question 21

Which of the following can be inferred from the data

I. From 1980 to 1985, the average monthly benefit in 1960 dollars decreased by at least 20%.

II. For the five-year periods indicated in the graph, the number of households receiving monthly benefit increased by the greatest percent from 1970 to 1975.

III. In 1975 fewer than 3 million people resided in households that received monthly benefits

(1) none (2) I only (3) II only (4) I & III (5) II & III

Question 22

The total surface area of a cube with edge of length 3 is how many times the total surface area of a cube with edge with length $\sqrt{3}$?

(1) $\sqrt{3}$ (2) 3 (3) 6 (4) $6\sqrt{2}$ (5) 9

Question 23

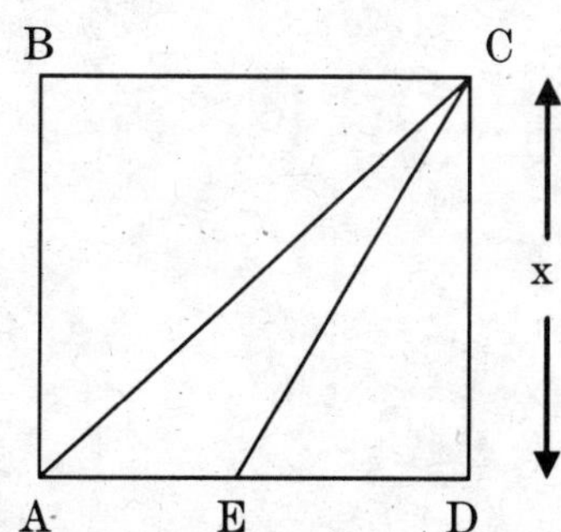

ABCD is a square and AE = ED

Column A	Column B
The perimeter of triangle ACE	5x/2

1. The quantity in Column A is greater.
2. The quantity in Column B is greater.
3. The two quantities are equal.
4. The relation cannot be determined from the information given.

Question 24

Part of a $ 10000 inheritance was invested at 4% and the remainder was invested at 6%. The total simple annual interest earned on the $ 10000 at the end of one year was $ 520.

Column A	Column B
The amount invested @4%	The amount invested @6%

1. The quantity in Column A is greater.
2. The quantity in Column B is greater.
3. The two quantities are equal.
4. The relation cannot be determined from the information given.

Question 25

Column A	Column B
2^{x+x}	4^{x}

1. The quantity in Column A is greater.
2. The quantity in Column B is greater.
3. The two quantities are equal.
4. The relation cannot be determined from the information given.

Question 26

If two trains are 120 miles apart and are travelling towards each other at a constant speed of 30 mph and 40 mph, respectively, how far apart will they be exactly one hour before they meet?

(1) 10 miles (2) 30 miles (3) 40 miles (4) 50 miles (5) 70 miles

Question 27

WEATHER FORECAST FOR JUNE 21

Sunrise: 06:53 Sunset: 16:32 Expected hours of sunshine: 70% of maximum possible sunshine hours

According to the weather forecast above, approximately how many hours of sunshine are expected on June 21?

(1) 5.25 (2) 6.75 (3) 7.5 (4) 8.25 (5) 9.75

Question 28

From the even numbers between 1 and 9, two different even numbers are to be chosen at random. What is the probability that their sum will be 8?

(1) 1/6 (2) 3/16 (3) 1/4 (4) 1/3 (5) 1/2

Answers to SECTION I & II

As you may have noted, while going through the guidelines in the POWERPREP CD regarding essay similarity, the perspectives that you are required to present and the critique of the arguments that you are given have to be in your own words. They are to be entirely original.

The ETS gives those broad parameters that would decide what scores would be allotted to your presentation on the issue and your critique of the argument. You will also find these parameters in the chapter titled Understanding the System in this book. If you wish to have your responses to the questions in the first two sections evaluated by us, you may feel free to forward your responses to us at our e-mail ID as follows:

jivaishnav@yahoo.com

We may just mention that this evaluation shall be at no cost.

Explanatory answers to SECTION III

Answer 1

Let us understand the meanings of some words and then see which option would fit the bill.

The word panacea means a remedy that has an application in a large range of diseases or maladies. Figuratively a panacea is a cure for all sorts of problems. It can be used in the following contexts from which the different shades of its meaning will become clear:

- The tribes in the Lower Congo consider the bark of the cinchona tree a *panacea* for all stomach-related maladies.
- To pull the country out of a deep recession, the party in power tried to apply the *panacea* of governmental spending but this remedy did not work.

Since war paintings are neither diseases nor any other forms of problems, Option 1 will not work.

Let us see what and who can be diverted or who can divert in the following contextual usages of the word *divert*:

- If your train had to *divert* from the coastal railway track because there was a landslide that blocked the rails, your train had to *turn away* from its regular route.
- If the government decides to enhance agricultural subsidies so as to divert the attention of the people from its administrative failures, it *turns* the attention of the people from its lapses.

Anyone or anything capable of turning – such as trains and cars and the attention of human beings and so on - can be diverted. Antiwar paintings cannot either turn away from or be made to turn away from anything. This is why Option 2 will not do either.

A *counterpart* is an equivalent. If the counterpart of an army general in the navy is an admiral, then the two ranks are equivalent. Antiwar paintings of the west can have a counterpart or match in another place that is not in the west. The word *counterpart* can fit into the first blank. **Option 3** can work for this reason alone unless any of the other options throw up a close choice.

If you have booked a flight to New York and the airline rings to give you an *intimation* that the flight will be delayed by three hours, the airline gives *notice* or *information*. Imagine that your country is sending a dozen horses with its team to take part in an international equestrian event and the cargo plane fare is to cost 20% more from the date of journey. To whom will the airline send intimation calling for additional fare? Will they post letters addressed to the horses? Will the horses bother who pays the fare? Intimations can be sent to human beings, not to antiwar paintings. Thus Option 4 will not do either.

As regards Option 5, the word derivative comes from the verb *derive* that comprises of the prefix DE- (that means *down* or *away from*) and the Latin word RIVUS that means stream (or a small river). A *derivative* means something drawn down or away from another source and therefore a derivative is essentially not original. This is why Chinese art form cannot have a derivative of any art form of the West. If it were a derivative of Western art form, Chinese art form would not be original. Then its name would get changed to Western art form. There is a difference between not having and not being able to have. There are couples that do not have children because they have consciously decided not to have children and there are some who cannot have children for reasons of incapability.

Option 3 is to be marked as correct.

Answer 2

The word *seminal* comes from the word *semen*, and means something that has the property of a seed and is therefore highly original. Something seminal thus has a possibility of growth or future development. If the French painter Theodore had *seminal* influence on the 19th century romanticism style of painting, he was the originator of this art form. The opposite of original is something that is imitated or copied or derived from another. It is for this reason that **Option 5** fits like a shot.

Something *oblique* is that which does not go straight. If someone has become rich by *oblique* ways, he has not gathered wealth by straight means; he may have defrauded the bank or sold imitations passing them off as original paintings and so on. The word oblique is the opposite of straight but not of the word original and hence Option 1 will not do. The word *provincial* comes from the word *province* or a particular region. So if you find that you are able to guess someone's hometown from his typical *provincial* dialect, then it means that his dialect (and therefore the dialect of his *origin*) is commonly spoken in a particular region of the country. The word provincial can at best be fai tly synonymous to seminal but not opposite. Thus Option 2 will not do. The words incomplete and fluctuating have nothing to do with the word seminal.

Answer 3

Imagine that you have been trying to talk to the chap in the next seat on a bus journey of some ten hours' duration and all that he has said during these ten hours is *really* and *is that so*. He does not say **yes** or **no** when **hmm** will do. He is *laconic* (or someone who speaks very less). The opposite of laconic is someone who speaks as if today is the last day for all speaking. The word *voluble* fits rather well and hence **Option 3**.

Something *operative* is in working condition. A laconic person may have a tongue in working condition and yet not give it the bother. *Operative* cannot be the antonym for laconic. If someone has been making harsh and bitter criticism of someone, his tone is *acerbic*. It has nothing to do with laconic. Someone may say a few extremely harsh words about someone and shut up for the rest of the ten-hour journey. A pompous person is one who brags or shows off. Typically a *pompous* person feels that most others are below him in rank and status. He brags or shows off. Someone *pompous* may deem it below his dignity to chat with the lesser mortal in the next seat and this may make him seem laconic. An *erect* position means standing or sitting straight. This posture has nothing to do with *laconic*. A sentry has to stand erect and generally does not chatter while on duty although the moment he goes off duty he may give his family members a headache with his babbling. *Erect* has also nothing to do with *laconic*.

Answer 4

The word *sybarite* comes from the ancient Italian city named *Sybaris* that was known for the self-indulgent and luxurious life style of its inhabitants. The opposite of someone self-indulgent is someone who is self-denying.

A political aspirant is keenly aiming to get into political office. He seeks power with fervour. He is not the opposite of sybarite. Option 1 will not do. A habitual malcontent is someone who feels that he is getting a raw deal all the while and keeps grumbling. He is not self-denying. If a person does not want cake at all, he cannot be reasonably expected to crib (or *complain* about the quality of confectionery). Option 2 will not do either. A humanitarian person is one who is concerned about the welfare of his fellow human beings. This does not in any way imply self-denial. He may go about in a swank Mercedes distributing blankets to those who sleep on pavements in freezing winters and thus Option 3 will not work. A veteran is someone who has a long experience. He may have an experience in playing poker. He may be a retired army man. He may live a life of luxury. Option 4 will not do for this reason. An ascetic is someone who lives a life of self-denial for reasons mainly of spirituality and hence an ascetic would qualify for being the opposite of a sybarite. Hence **Option 5**.

Answer 5

Imagine that a young boss and his stunning female secretary are out on a business trip and are sharing a room at the hotel. They are back to the hotel after a day's work. Does this not whip up your imagination? What if he settles down to reading the papers and she knits woollen socks all evening? What if he yawns from time to time and she yawns even louder? They have had a *prosaic* evening, dull, ordinary, and humdrum. The opposite of prosaic, as it would seem so clear from this situational usage of the word prosaic is something that is out of the ordinary and hence **Option 5** fits like a shot.

We shall however not let this chance to strike/ refresh acquaintance with the words in the other options go past.

- When someone comes to play football in *appropriate* clothes, he is dressed in shorts and a T-shirt and football shoes. A tuxedo and a Stetson would be inappropriate when playing football.

- Imagine that someone has borrowed a million dollars from you against the security of blue-chip shares. He does not repay the loan although you have sent him several reminders. You then sell the shares. You realise an amount more than what he owes you. You *appropriate* (or *apply*) the sale proceeds of shares to the loan amount and refund the remaining amount to him.
- Imagine that a passionate painter resides in a poor country. He starves. He migrates to a developed country. Decades later he returns to his homeland and finds that top rung painters are making a killing in art sales; they are minting money, their paintings are fetching whopping prices. He has returned to his homeland at a *propitious* (or *opportune* or *favourable*) time.
- The word *ambiguous* has the prefix AMBI- that means *two*. This is why someone *ambidextrous* is one who can work with his right hand as well as with his left. A statement with double meaning (and therefore *doubtful*, *unclear* and thus *confusing*) is *ambiguous*. So if you are on an archaeological site and find some clay figurines, you need not jump with joy at having been able to establish that toys were in fashion even in prehistoric times. The evidence that you have is *ambiguous* because the figurines may as well be associated with religious beliefs.

Answer 6

A *grandstand* is a place from where spectators can view a race or a sporting event. The word grandstand can also be used as a verb. When someone performs for getting applause from the audience in the grandstand, he is *grandstanding*. If a class is out on a picnic and a particular boy is going great lengths to impress the ladies, he may be asked not to *grandstand*. So one would grandstand to impress someone. The relationship is that of cause and effect.

Now let us see which option will click.

Option (1): patronise: alienate. If you find someone buying regularly from a shop, the person is *patronising* that shop (or *frequenting* that shop as a customer). If the new school in town has been *patronised* by the owners of the industrial valves manufacturing unit nearby, it means that the school has been *funded* or *sponsored* by these industrialists. Imagine that a veteran tennis player plays against a young man and wins. He then tells the young man that it will take him ages to come to his level. He is *patronising* him or *treating him like a child or like an inferior*. So when one would *talk condescendingly* he would *patronise* someone.

If someone is alien to a country, he does not belong there. If someone has procured admission to an engineering college thousands of miles and finds the environment there *alien*, the environment is *unfamiliar* or *strange*. When the boys in a class decide to *alienate* the newly admitted lad who acts high and mighty, they decide to keep him a stranger (or to *turn away* from him)

When someone patronises either a shop or a club, he has to mix with the people there. He cannot alienate either himself or the others. This is why Option 1 will not do.

Option (2): hedge: reveal. A *hedge* is a fence around your garden that bars cattle from strolling in and feasting upon your loveliest roses. When you obtain insurance for your car, you *hedge* against an accident where there may be damage to your car or to you or a third party and therefore a lot of expense in repairs or hospitalisation and so on. The insurance would *protect* you against such unforeseen expense. When you hedge your garden, you do not reveal. You conceal. Thus the relationship between hedge and reveal is certainly not that of cause and effect and this option will not do.

Option (3): equivocate: deceive. The word equivocate has a prefix EQUI- that means *equal* and *vocal* is something that is expressed orally. So when you speak word(s) that has/have more than one meaning, you speak in such a way that would *confuse* or *deceive* the other person or *evade* a point. Therefore when someone exclaims that the great athlete has no pants, people turn towards the athlete expecting him to be nude but the fellow has tried to *deceive* the others by *equivocating* with the use of the word *pants* (which also means *gasps* besides *trousers*). Thus equivocation is the cause of which deception is the effect. Hence Option 3 will do rather well.

Option (4): presume: disprove. Suppose your Private Secretary tells you that one Mrs. Brandon and one Miss Templeton are here to see you. One of the ladies comes in. She is elderly and you say: "Mrs. Brandon, I *presume*? " What you mean is that you *assume* (or *presuppose*) that she is the married lady. When you *presume* something, there is no evidence. When the police officer is trying to *disprove* an allegation that he has been biased towards the ruling party in handling a violent clash between two political groups, he is trying to give evidence that would prove the allegation wrong. There is absence of evidence when you presume and presence of evidence when you disprove. Thus there is no cause and effect relationship in Option 4.

Option (5): upbraid: dislike. When an army officer decides to *upbraid* (or *admonish*, *reprimand*) a junior officer for his sloppy turnout, he does so because he *dislikes* the way he has dressed. If at all there is any relationship between upbraid and dislike, it is of effect and cause, which would go contrary to the relationship that we are looking for.

Answer 7

It is Sunday. Boys in a hostel have been playing football for the past two hours. They are hungry. The mess manager assures them that lunch will be served in 30 minutes. It is past one hour and yet there is no lunch in sight. The boys are now extremely hungry. They start clamouring for lunch. The mess manager feels that the boys may become *restive* or *restless*, or *uncontrollable* or *agitated*. Something that possesses the quality of *restiveness* is *restless*. The opposite of *restiveness* is *satisfaction*, a quality that the boys are quite likely to exhibit once they have been delving into the food for a miniature eternity and have been burping freely. It is the food that has made the boys cease being restive. It is the food that has provided them satisfaction.

Contentment (the prefix CON- means thoroughly and the Latin root TENT- means holding and therefore content means *thoroughly holding* – and can hold no more- or *satisfied*) means a state of satisfaction and would do very well. Thus **Option 1** is to be marked as correct.

As regards the other options, let us see why they will not do.

Just as truthfulness is the quality that makes a person truthful, *heartiness* is the quality that makes a person *hearty* or *jovial* or *warm-hearted* or *sincere*. We need to find out whether someone who possesses *heartiness* (which can also mean that he is *not pretending* or is *thorough* or *whole-hearted*) also has *satisfaction* necessarily. You have a guest who eats with *heartiness*. He has gone through your family's rations for a fortnight and yet shows no signs of letting up. He may laugh all the while. If an elephant had eaten the amount that he has eaten, the poor animal would have keeled over. Thus someone with heartiness is not necessarily satisfied. This is why Option 2 will not do.

While someone smug is satisfied, *smugness* essentially means *self-satisfaction*. Someone has aimed to just pass an examination. He manages to get mere passing mark. He is *smug* (or self-content). His father is rummaging in the cupboard for his pet whip with which to belt the boy. His father is not satisfied at all with the performance. One cannot provide smugness to others. This is why Option 3 will not do either.

Bashfulness can mean *timidity*, *diffidence*, *reserve*, or *sheepishness*. One may want a whole lot of things but in this big bad world, the fittest shall survive and the weak shall go to the wall. One who is bashful does not have the courage to either ask or take what he wants. Someone with bashfulness need not be a satisfied person. This is why Option 4 will not do either.

Urbanity means the qualities associated with the life style of urban areas. It can mean *polished mannerisms* or *sophistication*. The mere fact that one stays in urban areas or is sophisticated does not mean he is satisfied. No urban areas are built overnight. Agriculture has been the principal occupation of people till the early twentieth century with land as the principal means of production. People migrated from rural areas to urban locations with a view to get richer. There is no connection between *urbanity* and *satisfaction* or the lack of it. Thus Option 5 will not do.

Answer 8

Let us first understand a few of the words in the question and then move on to see which option would fit in the light of the appreciation of the meanings and nuances of words highlighted by contextual usage.

The word obsequious has the prefix OB- that means *towards* or *against* + SEQUIOUS that comes from the word *sequence*, which means *something that follows*. Someone who comes towards you and follows what you tell him to do is an *obsequious*, *servile* or *slavish* person.

A *flatterer* or a *yes-man* is known as a *sycophant*. A person can become truly great only if he has the maturity to patiently hear a contradictory viewpoint. People who are truly great always keep sycophants at an arm's length. Sycophants do not have the courage to contradict people in power when the latter are wrong in their judgement. A sycophant possesses the qualities of an obsequious person.

The word PUSILL in Latin means *petty* or *insignificant*. The Latin root ANIM- means *life, mind, soul*, or *spirit*. The word *pusillanimous* means *someone of a petty mind* and therefore *cowardly, chicken-hearted, lily-livered, timid* and so on. A *coward* has got to be *pusillanimous* (which also means *cowardly*) and therefore Option 1 will do very well.

A *reticent* person is one who speaks very little. He is *uncommunicative*, or *silent* or *secretive*. In order to *dupe* (or *cheat*) someone the cheater has to win the confidence of the potential victim. He has to be a glib talker. Once having won someone's confidence, the cheater betrays that confidence or trust. That is how a person dupes another. No man can win another's confidence by remaining silent or uncommunicative. This is why Option 2 will not do.

Someone who is progressive is one who is ahead of the times (or at the very least he is in sync with the times). He keeps rising in life. An entrepreneur is an adventurous person. He employs capital and gets into business. He creates employment. However a progressive person need not be a businessman. Some progressive child in kindergarten can recite *Baba Black Sheep* while all that her classmates are doing is wailing *I want to go to Mummy* all the while. This is why Option 3 will not do either.

Guile means *cunning* or *craftiness*. In a game of cricket, if a batsman is facing a bowler who bowls with (let us say) *guile*, then it means that when the action of the bowler seems to say that the ball would come from the leg side and cut towards the off side, precisely the reverse happens. The batsman then lobs a simple catch to the nearby fielder who cannot stop laughing while holding that lollypop of a catch. A *guileless* person is one who possesses no cunning. So when a grandfather has eaten all the chocolate pie that was in the fridge, he would try to educate his *guileless* grandchild to tell grandma that it was the cat who ate it all. A racketeer is one who runs rackets or illegal businesses through which he cheats or defrauds other people. No one who is guileless, can reasonably aspire to become a racketeer simply because cunning and cheating are the tools of the trade of the racketeer. This is why Option 4 will not work.

Someone who agrees *tacitly* (or *without speaking*) is said to be *acquiescent*. The prefix AC- is another variant of the prefix AD- that means *to*. The word *acquiescent* also has the other element of QUIET, meaning *mum* or *restful* in it. Someone who comes to either to *terms* or to an *agreement* without saying anything, is therefore *acquiescent*. When a powerful businessman takes over many companies, he tries to consolidate his empire by calling for tokens of submission from these companies by asking their directors to resign from their boards. Some directors *rebel* (or *strongly oppose the move*) whereas most others *acquiesce* (or *submit without any protest*). Since someone acquiescent cannot be a rebel, this option will not work either.

Answer 9

If you see a hospital nurse with a *sublime* devotion to her duties, she is *noble* in her devotion. If you have just had a *sublime* meal, you have had a superb dinner. If someone is in *sublime* neglect of his health, he is *utterly* or *completely* careless about his health. The opposite of someone sublime, should therefore be someone who is *ignoble* (or *the opposite of noble*).

A weak person may be very noble. He may be a saint who has been fasting for a month and has become physically weak. This is why Option1 will not do. An *austere* person is one who is severely simple. He does not want luxury. It does not follow that an austere person is the opposite of noble. Sages and saints have got to be austere if they wish to pursue spirituality. You cannot have a saint coming to the dance floor in tuxedos and Ray Ban glasses. This is why Option 2 will not do either; the word simple in Option 3 will not do for similar reasons.

If a chap has a collection of base quality books, his collection is of low value: it can be morally corrupting literature as well. A fellow may have impulses that may either be wise or foolish or noble or base. Clearly base is the opposite of noble. Hence Option 4 is to be marked as correct.

An abnormal child may be born before the normal period of pregnancy; it may even be more than normal in terms of weight or height, it may have less mental growth than other children of the same age. The prefix AB-means *away* or *off from*. Something away from the normal or usual is therefore abnormal. This word has no relation whatsoever with *sublime* which is why Option 5 is not to be looked at.

Answer 10

The word *key* stands for *most important*. The short point made here is just as some authors' book on eels is after a key text on Marine Vertebrate Zoology so are their ideas on animal development and phylogeny teaching. With this, let us see which option will fit:

Option 1: The question is whether important ideas can *prevent* teaching? They can enhance the quality of teaching, if anything. This is why this option will not do.

Option 2: The question is whether important ideas can *defy* teaching (or *protest against teaching* or *deliberately disobey teaching*)? Option 2 will therefore not do.

When someone *replicates* the Statue of Liberty in clay, he makes a clay model of the famous statue. When someone *replicates* the conversation that the two lovers were having in the park, he *repeats* their conversation. Ideas cannot replicate anything. Only living things can replicate something else. The pet parrot may *replicate* (or *imitate*) how the grandma mutters while climbing the stairs. Ideas themselves can replicate nothing at all. Option 3 will not do either. For the same reason that only living beings can *use* something, Option 5 will not do as well.

The word *inform* has the Latin prefix IN- that means the same as it does in English and the word *form* that means *shape* or *body*. When the ideas of someone inform teaching in a subject, they put vital formative inputs in the subject. Thus Option 4 will do.

Answer 11

Let us understand a few words and then move on to the options.

If some tennis professional was in *doldrums* between his winning one major tournament and another, it means he did not have any exceptional achievement in the in between period. He was in *low spirits* or was *sluggish* in the intervening period. Something that does not have *energy* (or *drive*) is bound to be *sluggish*. Therefore the relationship between doldrums and energy is the state that one would be in, if there were no energy.

Euphoria is a *state of cheerfulness* or *optimism*. Without euphoria one can never have joy. The relationship between joy and euphoria is reverse of that seen in the original pair.

RE-, the prefix, means *back*. The word *habilitate* comes from the word *ability*. Therefore if someone has been a drug addict and he is rehabilitated then he is back in a state where he is able to live a normal life. Discipline can mean any of these following things from which it will become clear that there is no relationship between rehabilitation and discipline:

- If a person lives a life of *discipline*, he may be moderate in eating and regular with exercise and so on.
- If a person's *discipline* is mathematics, this is his branch of learning.

One can jolly well have hunger and thirst at the same time but one cannot have doldrums and energy together.

Depravity can mean many things such as *debauchery* (or, in other words, *immorality*), or *corruption*. A person has the *virtue* (or *good quality*) of honesty if he is honest. Clearly, the lack of virtue would lead to depravity and hence Option 4.

Grief is a state when one mourns. *Hope* is expectation. It is possible that one has no hopes and yet no grief. A son of parents who are both doctors with thumping practice may not have any hopes of getting the required marks for securing admission to medical college and yet may not have any grief about not getting them since he is aware of his limitations.

Answer 12

Discretion means so many things such as carefulness or judgement, choice and so on.

- If someone avoids drinking in a region where there is prohibition law in force, he is acting with *discretion* (or *care*) so that the police do not catch him in the wrong.

- If the manager has the *discretion* to grant leave for periods beyond a month to the staff, he has the option to grant (or *reject*, of course) such leave. [This means that he is empowered to grant leave if in his judgement there is adequate merit in the request.]
- If the stock market has been booming and someone feels that *discretion* lies in selling at that juncture rather than waiting further, he feels that there is *prudence* in selling.

From the above, it would be clear that someone who is foolish does not have discretion.

Inedible is that which cannot be eaten. If something does not have food, it is empty. It does not mean it is inedible. Give a paper plate (with no food in it) to a cow and it will be eaten before you can say Mary had a little lamb.

Someone who has an unnecessarily high opinion of his own self is *vain* or *gumptious*. It is very likely that a person who is gumptious is disrespectful. This is because he thinks he is the greatest and in his dealings with others he cares neither for intellectual superiors nor for elders. He is thus *eminently* likely to be rude.

Someone who has been *cut off* from others is *isolated*. It is not necessary that an isolated person does not have shelter. A person may decide to be isolated from others because he has a transmittable disease and yet he may live in a palatial residence.

If someone is passing through pecuniary straits he is short of money. An impecunious person has no money. This relationship is akin (or *similar*) to that in the original pair FOOLISH: DISCRETION; Option 4 is to be marked as correct.

If a lady prisoner has the magnetic personality to charm the most *implacable* of the jailers (meaning, jailers who are *uncompromising*, *relentless*, *adamant* and so on), the chances are that the jailer and this lady would be dancing at a discotheque one evening and then she would escape from there. If a person is implacable, it means he has tremendous determination not to shift from the stand that he has taken. Somebody implacable has got to have determination and hence this option is not workable.

Answer 13

When you try to calculate something you are trying to judge the value or measure or weight and so on of something. If in a boxer's judgement the opponent's jab is directed towards the stomach, he guards the stomach. If, instead, the blow lands on the mouth and the air is thick with blood and broken teeth, then it is *miscalculation*. A *miscalculation* is therefore an *error in judgement*. Now let us see the options.

A breach in a canal is a hole (either made intentionally or because the walls of the canals cannot stand the force of water) in the canal. A breach in the fortification (or fort) is not necessarily due to an error of judgement. Enemies can breach a fortification. The fortification may have been built centuries back and designed to withstand the onslaught of the entire army of the neighbouring country rushing in with battering rams but not the firepower of modern cannons. Therefore a breach is not necessarily an error in fortification.

When someone *fumbles* in his pockets while trying to find the keys to his house, it is not necessary that he makes an error in the location of the keys (or the house for that matter). The location of the keys is clear: they are on his person because if they were not on him, he would not even *try* to find them in his pockets. All that he is not sure about is in which pocket does he have the keys. There is no error of location.

A *gaffe* is a *bloomer* or *howler* or an *act of indiscretion* or a *clumsy remark*. Let us visualise a gaffe. Imagine that a fellow is sitting at his friend's place. It is Sunday. He sees a young lady coming in with the tea service and toast. He tells the host that he is lucky to have housemaids coming in even on Sundays. The young lady rushes away red faced. The host replies icily that the young lady is his sister-in-law. The guest has made a *gaffe*. The error is in *decorum* or *etiquette* or *proper behaviour*. Decorum requires that one should wait for being introduced. What is more, there is no need to assume that everyone bringing in tea and trays is a housemaid. A gaffe being an error in decorum, Option 3 will do very well.

Exaggeration is stating more than what is necessary and is therefore an overstatement. Suppose a mother tells her child: "Have I not told you a thousand times not to go out of our complex on your bicycle?" She is making an exaggeration about the number of times she has deterred the child from going out on the bicycle. There is no error in the statement. The idea may be to emphasise the importance of her advice. This is a case of too much of something as against the original pair where miscalculation is an error in judgement.

If someone makes a *default* in a *loan* he is not paying the loan as per the agreed schedule. A default may be due to the will of the person who is to repay. He has the money but does not want to repay. The default may be due to the person's business not running at all for no fault of his: he may have set up a unit to manufacture pagers whereas mobile telephones may have edged pagers out of the market altogether. A default is not an error in the loan. This is why Option 5 will not do.

Answer 14

The question is: who takes whose money? The people running the gambling dens take the money of the gamblers who come and gamble in these dens. Whose decision strategies should be unsuccessful so that people running gambling dens make money? The decision strategies of the people who gamble in these dens.

The word *distortion* means *misrepresentation* or *twisting*. Suppose I were to go into a gambling den and find that I have lost money. What is the first thing that I would realise? The first thing that I would realises that my decision strategies were unsuccessful. How can this fact that my decision strategies were unsuccessful be misrepresented? The only way to misrepresent this is to say that these decision strategies were indeed successful and that I have actually made money and not lost money. This means that the chap running the gambling den should not only refund my money but also give me some money so that I go out with more in my pocket than what I had when I came in. What would you call the chap who runs such a gambling den where people who lose, get not only refunds but also a bonus? He could at the very least be described as an idiot.

Now about *restricting* my unsuccessful gambling strategies, if someone could restrict me from making wrong decisions at gambling it could be my wife and children who would starve if I went on losing money. Would anyone who took the money that I lose at gambling ever try to *restrict* the unsuccessful decision strategy and thereby restrict his own earnings from my wrong decisions? What would you call him?

About *maintenance* (or *continuation*) of my wrong decision strategies, who will gain from seeing that I *continue* making wrong decisions and thereby lose money? The fellow who runs the gambling den will chuckle all the while that I lose money. It is in his interest to maintain the unsuccessful decision strategies of the gamblers who play in his den. This is why Option 3 will do very well.

About *prediction* – meaning, *telling about an event before it actually occurrs* – when can you say, for example, that the weather bureau predicted heavy rainfall today? The weather bureau has to either write this or tell it to the world. If I were to enter a gambling den and the person running the den meets me at the threshold and tells me that I will lose money today because my decision strategies will be wrong, would I even enter the den? I will run away. He will starve.

About *demonstration* (meaning a *show*) of a gambler's unsuccessful decision strategies, suppose someone were to lose money at a gambling den, who will show others how he has gone wrong – the chap running the gambling den (who has made money) or the loser? The owner of the den would be an utter moron if he were to show how the loser went wrong. Not only the loser but anyone else listening to this demonstration would not make such mistakes again. The number of people winning at the den would increase everyday and the owner of the den would go broke.

Nothing other than Option 3 will do.

Answer 15

The word *bucolic* comes from the Greek BOUKOLOS that means *herdsman* (*or someone minding the cattle* and sheep and things). Anyone herding cattle will be naturally found in the great outdoors and therefore in the rural areas. Someone *bucolic* is *rustic* or *rural*. The opposite of *rural* is *urban* and hence Option 4.

Answer 16

There is mention of *inflated estimates*. How would you know that the estimate that the electrician has given you for repair of the geyser is *inflated* or *blown up*? You can say that the estimate is inflated only when you know (or you can find out from some reliable source):

(A) Whether the parts that he suggests for replacement should indeed be replaced

(B) The correct charge for similar repairs to the geyser and

(C) The prices of the parts that he wants to replace

With this point clear, ask yourself this: how do I adjust the amount of air in the tyre that seems to have been blown up? I should first know how much pressure there is in the tyre. This is something that I can find out only if I have an air pressure gauge. Now assume that I have a gauge and I have measured the tyre pressure. Now imagine that someone has taken the gauge and I have to make do with estimating how much air I must take out. I can afford to take out any air at all only if I know what should be the ideal tyre pressure. Now imagine that there is a list of the ideal tyre pressures for most makes of cars stuck on the wall in front of me from which I can find out that there is more tyre pressure than what is desirable. In the absence of the air pressure gauge, what would happen if I were to remove some air that in my estimate should bring down the pressure to a proper level? Any of the following things can happen:

(I) The tyre pressure comes down to a level closer to the ideal pressure but still remains above the ideal pressure

(II) The tyre pressure comes down to a level equal to the ideal pressure

(III) The tyre pressure comes to a level below the ideal tyre pressure

In Situations (I) and (II) above, there is only improvement since the tyre pressure was more than what was necessary. In Situation (III) above, the tyre pressure is less than ideal.

Drawing a parallel from the above illustration, what happens when you adjust inflated estimates is that either there is an improvement over the inflated estimates or the estimate is now understated. This is why Option 5 will do very well.

As regards Option 1, once one knows that the estimates are inflated, then *adjustment* can only mean *reducing* the estimates. More inflation is not an adjustment. No adjustment to inflated estimates can therefore *magnify* the inflated estimates and hence Option 1 will not do.

As regards Option 2, when can something be confirmed? When it is true! If the estimates were inflated they were not true. Then how can inflated estimates possess accuracy? An estimate by its very nature does not possess accuracy. Then how can one confirm the accuracy of any estimates whether inflated or otherwise when the estimates do not have accuracy in the first place?

As regards Option 3, why it will not work is simple. Something can be disproved if it is wrong. You can disprove that the umbrella that I am holding in my hand is mine provided I am holding any umbrella at all. If an inflated estimate does not have any accuracy, how can you even disprove its accuracy? As regards Option 4 how can you verify the accuracy of something when it does not possess any accuracy at all?

Answer 17

Imagine that you are hosting a dinner in celebration of your brother's twenty-fifth birthday. You have counted the number of guests who have responded to your invitation and confirmed participation. You have come prepared to pay for some 50 guests give or take a few here or there. The dinner is at a restaurant that charges a fat price per plate. The number of plates picked up is equal to the number of people for which you will be billed. You have not cared to ensure that only known people pick up the plates. You get the bill and feel the world spinning around you. You find that many of the people who have wined and dined at your expense are not in your invitation list. You do not even recognise some of them. This means that your painstaking estimate of the number of expected guests has fallen short of the actual number of people who have dined at your cost.

There are some points of difference between a dinner and a census that must be borne in mind. In a census, the people are counted at their respective locations. This could be a rather painstaking exercise. You may decide to count people only on holidays so that you do not count a particular person once at his residence in the morning and again at his office in the afternoon. You meet him only at his residence and if you go to another person's residence, then you count only those who permanently reside there and not those who are merely sitting there and sipping cocktails. At the dinner in the above illustration, the people are counted at a single location. At this location you have counted neither more nor less than those who ate. You have counted only the number of plates picked up and hence those who picked up plates. The realisation that there has been an undercount dawns only when you find that earlier you counted less number of persons than what there actually are.

There are norms for seats in legislative assemblies. If it is decided that a town with a population of between 100,000 and 125,000 will have one seat in the assembly, then if - say- Town A has a population of 110,000 Town A will have a seat in the assembly. If Town B has a population of 85,000 and Town C has a population of 40000, then Town B along with Town C has a seat in the assembly. Now imagine that the recent census finds that the population of Town B is 125,000 whereas that of Town A is 90,000 and that of Town C is 25,000. This may be because Town B has in the meantime developed several thousand job opportunities and there has been migration from Town A to Town B. There could have been a grave natural disaster in Town A leading to thousands of deaths. The findings of this census can mean that the seat will shift from Town A to Town B and Town A will have a seat with another town. You may have missed none at either Town A or Town B because all that is involved is a shift in population with the attendant consequence of a shift in seats.

A shift in seats means that one has counted the number of people who have migrated from one town to another within the country. A census cannot ask those who have died or infants in cradles to raise their hands so that they could be excluded from/added to the population count in the previous census. It has to rely on birth and death records. Immigrants are those who are temporarily in the country. They are like the people who are sipping cocktails at a particular residence when the census people go there. They do not stay there and you do not have to count them. Emigrants are those who are temporarily away from their homes. The number of people temporarily away is available from emigration records just as the number of immigrants is available from immigration records.

With the above facts in mind, let us see which option will work.

Option (1): Shifts in federal and state legislative seats. This could be primarily due to a intra-country migration. When you count the number of persons in Town B, you do not count them in Town A. You do not count someone at two locations: one from where he has migrated and the other to where he has migrated. This information will not be of use in finding out how many were missed in the census.

Option (2): The procedure followed in taking the census.

The passage says that the procedure is painstaking. Even if it were not, a procedure is a system. What one is interested in knowing is how many people were missed, not how they were missed. A procedure is designed with an objective in mind. Its failure is due to factors that were not taken into consideration while devising the procedure. No procedure will outline the factors it has not reckoned when it was devised. It would not fail to achieve its objective otherwise. This too therefore will be of no use.

Option (3): Foreigners who become residents of the United States.

A foreigner who becomes a resident will figure neither in the previous census nor in the intra-country migration nor in births or immigration records (which would have records of people staying temporarily in the country for things such as lecturing or sight-seeing or meeting their relatives and so on). A foreigner becoming a resident of the United States is like a person who came to the dinner that you had hosted but whom you had not expected. This is why Option 3 will work very well.

Option (4): Migration patterns within the United States.

If someone has migrated from Town A to Town B during the period spanning two censuses, he is excluded from the population count at Town A and included in the population count at Town B. No one is omitted. This information will not be of use in estimating the number of people missed because in the present case you miss no one.

Option (5): Persons with two official residences.

If a person has two official residences, he cannot be lolling in the sofas at Residence 1 when the census people call to count those residing at his Residence 2. At any time he can be at only one residence. He can at best be counted at both places. This may lead to an over count. He cannot be missed. This is why Option 5 will not do either.

Answer 18

A word before we begin. If you are asked something that is according to the passage, it will be in the passage and therefore the inference that is required will emerge verbatim. Secondly if you are to find which of the given statements is not true, the one that is not true will certainly not be there in the passage.

In this passage, first the *coverage measurement survey* has been mentioned and then the word *survey* appears in reference to this. Therefore the word *survey* is to be taken as referring to the coverage measurement survey and to nothing else.

Let us see which of the options is true about the coverage measurement survey:

Option 1: It does away with the need to rely on estimates to arrive at population counts. Please see the following words about the coverage measurement survey at the end of the passage: "Combining the information from both survey and census statisticians are able to arrive at improved population estimates..." What the survey does is that it actually adds to what the census does. The survey and census together help in arriving at improved estimates. So if the survey is like bread and the census is like filling, together they help make the sandwich of the estimates; the bread does not do away with the sandwich; on the contrary it helps in making the sandwich. So Option 1 is not true.

Option 2: It is a census-taking method that is appropriate for only certain kinds of geographic areas. Please see the following words in the passage about the coverage measurement survey: "The survey, essentially a second, extremely painstaking census, is conducted in a limited number of the blocks into which the census has divided the country." It is not as if the survey is suitable only for certain kinds of geographic areas. It is conducted in a limited number of blocks into which the country has been divided. There is no reason to assume that the division is in terms of geographical areas. The idea behind a census is to study population and not geography. When you deliberately decide to play a game with only your next-door neighbours, it does not mean that the game itself can be played with only your next-door neighbours. So Option 2 is not true either.

Option 3: It arrives at population counts that are often different from those of the census itself. Please see the following words in the passage: "Combining the information from both survey and census, statisticians are able to arrive at improved population estimates, even for areas outside the survey block". If the information from the survey and the census is the same, what is the need to combine the information from both survey and census? What do you combine? Do you combine two things of the same kind or two things of different kind? Quite clearly, the statement in Option 3 is true and therefore **Option 3** is to be marked as correct.

Option 4: It replaces the census proper in a limited number of geographic areas. Please see the following words: "The survey, essentially a second, extremely painstaking census, is conducted in a limited number of the blocks into which the census has divided the country". The survey is a second census; it is in addition to the census and not in place of the census. Thus Option 4 is not correct.

Option 5: It analyses data on births, deaths, immigration, and emigration by population group. Please see the following words in the passage: "Demographic analysis, which uses data on births, deaths, immigration and emigration yields a good estimate of the size of the national undercount". If anything uses demographic data on births, deaths and so on, it is demographic analysis and not the survey. Thus Option 5 is not workable.

Answer 19

The word *reprove* comes from the Latin verb PROBARE that means *approve*. The prefix RE- means *back* (as in *reject* or *throw back*) or in *opposition* (as in rebel). When someone does something that calls for the opposite of an approval, you *reprove* or *admonish* or *reprimand* or *scold* him. Clearly, therefore, *reprove* and *reprimand* are synonymous. Besides both have negative connotations; one does not get reproved for good work. With this let us see which option bears a similar relationship to that in the original pair.

Option 1: blame: censure. If the court censures the accused, it blames him for the wrong done. If a senior officer censures a junior officer, he blames for breach of propriety or service condition and so on. Blame and censure are synonymous. **Option 1** will do very well.

Option 2: control: contain. If you contain your temper, you control it. But it is not as if contain always means the same thing as control. If a bottle can contain 10 litres of orange juice, it does not mean it can *control* these 10 litres of orange juice. Have you heard of a bottle stopping some human being from drinking what it contains because it wants to control (or *regulate*) the flow of juice? Option 2 will not do.

Option 3: persuade: convince. If a man tries to persuade a girl to marry him, he is trying. The girl may do any of the things out of this illustrative list:

(A) She may tell him to go fly a kite

(B) She may request him to give her some time to think about the proposal

(C) She may agree to marry him

You could say that she has been convinced only in the case of (C) above. Therefore to persuade and to convince are two different things. Option 3 will not do.

Option 4: thwart: confront. Suppose in the above instance, the man comes to propose to the girl. She can *thwart* him by saying that she is married already although she may not be. This way she is able to *frustrate* his plans to marry her. She is able to *avoid* him or *block* his moves. The word confront has the prefix CON- which is also a variant of the prefix COM- that means *together*, or *jointly*. When two persons confront they show each other their fronts and hence take an aggressive stance. One may thwart another by lying or trickery whereas if one confronts another there is a likelihood of aggression. Thus Option 4 will not do as well.

Option 5: inconvenience: effect. The synonym of inconvenience is trouble whereas the synonym of effect is result. The two words are not related at all and therefore the question of striking a relationship between these does not arise.

Answer 20

The word *deliberation* means *discussion*. *Excessive* means more than necessary. If decisions were made with excessive deliberations it means that the meeting lasted rather long.

The word *abbreviated* comes from *abbreviation* (which, in turn, comes from the word *brief* that means *short*). Since the meeting involved more than necessary discussion, it could certainly not have been *abbreviated*. Thus Option 1 is to be ruled out.

The word *interminable* comes from *terminus* that means the end. The prefix IN- means *not*. If a quarrel seems *interminable* or *unending*, it would mean that it seems it would never end. When people discuss more than necessary, the feeling that those getting bored in the bargain get is that this thing is not likely to end at all. Now about the tendentious director, the word tendentious comes from the word *tendency*, which means *propensity* or *leaning*. If the director does not have the inclination to discuss for longer than necessary, he would tell the others - in as polite a manner as possible so as to drive home the point that there is no need to discuss further - to get back to their work places. The meeting would end. If the director has the tendency to discuss for long, then the meeting is very likely to seem *unending*. Option 2 will do very well.

If the meeting were to be methodical, it would have method in it. Then there would be only necessary discussion not excessive debate. Option 3 will not do for this reason.

The word *endless* in Option 4 may fit into the first blank. *Amenable* means open to new ideas and suggestions. Someone who is amenable hears others patiently. He does not *provoke* or *excite* others. This is why Option 4 will not work.

As for Option 5, if the director were to be *withdrawn* (or *not interested* in the meeting and therefore *not participating* in it either physically by going off to the golf club or mentally by drawing cartoons while everyone else is discussing), he would not *provoke* anyone in the meeting to discuss. If at all, he would tell people to discuss this at some other place and time.

Answer 21

In regard to the debt of the acto to the theatre traditions of other periods and regions, this debt is mentioned in the following words at paragraph 2 in the passage reproduced as follows: "Innovative as it is, the *acto* owes much to the theatre traditions of other periods and regions."

The author's argument concerning this debt of the acto is that **Italian influence is likely on the acto** is at paragraph 2 in the passage and is reproduced as follows: "The Italian influence is likely, whatever Valdez' immediate source: the Mexican *carpas* themselves are said to have originated from the theatre pieces of a sixteenth-century Spanish writer inspired by encounters with Italian *commedia del ' arte* troupes in towns in Spain."

What must be noted is that there is no debate regarding the acto having borrowed from other theatres traditions. What needs to be strengthened is the assertion about the Italian influence on the actos whether the influence comes straight from Italy or indirectly through Mexican carpas that have drawn from Italian theatres.

Now let us go from option to option.

Option 1: Many popular forms of theatre rely heavily on improvisation.

When you *improvise* a speech that you are asked to give on your school's Annual Sports Day, you make the speech as you go along. You first thank the ladies and gentlemen for having made the event a grand success. Then you reverse the order by thanking the gentlemen and then the ladies for having made the event a great success. Then you clear your throat a couple of times till something else occurs to you such as how important sport is for physical and mental health and so on. When you *improvise* a quick meal, you throw in the potatoes and the bread and the garlic and so on and make some nondescript dish to fill your tummy. When you *improvise,* there is neither the time nor the need to borrow from other traditions. This is because one *improvises* from one's own resources. This is why Option 1 cannot be true because the main argument is that the actos have been borrowed from Italian theatre traditions.

Option 2: Plays resembling the *acto* in structure were written in the 1970s by West African playwrights who were interested in dramatizing the richness of their own cultures.

The thrust of the argument is about Italian influence. Option 2 says about the reverse of any influence on the actos because it talks about West African people borrowing from the actos. Italy or the Mexican carpas are not even mentioned at Option 2, which is why it will not do.

Option 3: The use of masks has, at one time or another, been characteristic of the theatre traditions of almost all cultures, even those most isolated from outside influences.

Even Option 3 does not mention Italy or the Mexican carpas and is to be shown the door.

Option 4: During a strike, it is common for union members to present musical skits dramatizing the values of solidarity and resistance

Option 4 does not talk about Italy or the Mexican carpas and is to be taken by the ear and chucked out of the window.

Option 5: Before 1965 Luis Valdez had attended many performances of traditional Mexican theatre groups touring the Western United States.

As regards the influences on the actos, there are reportedly direct Italian and indirect influences as may be seen in these words in the passage: "The improvised comic satire of the *actos* is often attributed to Valdez' study of the Italian *commedia del ' arte* of the sixteenth century although some critics see it as a direct reflection of the comic and improvisational qualities of the more contemporary and local *carpas* of Mexican theatre." When can you see your reflection in the mirror? You can see the reflection only when you stand in front of the mirror and secondly, none other than *you* can influence the mirror to reflect *your* image. Therefore one of the arguments is that actos are the image of the Mexican carpas.

About the Mexican theatre, there is mention at paragraph 2 in the passage that the carpas are local dramas and therefore the carpas are traditional Mexican theatre forms. It is also mentioned in the same paragraph that the carpas themselves were inspired by Italian troupes performing in Spain. This Option admits indirect Italian influence on actos. **Option 5** is to be marked as correct.

Answer 22

How helpful can anyone get? You need to see lines 5 to 7 at paragraph 2 in the passage. Let us go there and see the author's evaluation of the views of the critics. We reproduce this evaluation hereunder for ready reference:

"The improvised comic satire of the *actos* is often attributed to Valdez' study of the Italian *commedia del ' arte* of the sixteenth century although some critics see it as a direct reflection of the comic and improvisational qualities of the more contemporary and local *carpas* of Mexican theatre."

The author's evaluation of the views of the critics – or what he feels that the critics are saying - is that the **improvised comic satire of the acto is a direct reflection of comic and improvisational qualities of the more contemporary and local *carpas* of Mexican theatre.**

Now let us go from option to option and see which one is correct and which are wrong and why.

Option 1: Their views if correct, do not preclude the existence of an Italian influence on the acto.

When a club *precludes* those who are not graduates from its membership, it *keeps out* or *excludes* or *debars* non-graduates from enrolling. Option 1 if true therefore would not try to debar any statement admitting Italian influence on the acto. In the same paragraph where you see the author's evaluation of the critics' views, there is mention of Italian influences on Mexican carpas. Thus Italian influence is not precluded. **Option 1** will do very well.

Option 2: Their views are unlikely to be correct given the difference existing between Mexican and Mexican American theatre.

First of all we shall have to see whether there is any difference between Mexican and Mexican American Theatre. If the passage mentions no difference, there is no need to imagine anything.

Please see the following words at the end of the passage: "In fact, no other art form illustrates more clearly a depth and complexity of the Mexican American heritage itself than does the *acto* of Luis Valdez and the Teatro Campecino." At one stage the author holds that the comic satire of the acto is a direct reflection of the more contemporary Mexican *carpas*. Then he also says that the acto best illustrates the depth and complexity of the Mexican American heritage. This means that there is no difference between Mexican theatre and Mexican American theatre. This is why Option 2 will not do.

Option 3: Their views concerning the Mexican *carpas* are essentially correct, but they lack familiarity with the acto.

This is a matter of sheer logic. Imagine that your car has had a breakdown on the highway and someone passes by and says the spark plug for the fourth cylinder needs to be replaced. You then tell him that you have a spare plug but do not know where to put it. You then lift the bonnet and hand him the plug. If he then asks you as to where the engine is, his views about the spark plug are not to be even considered at all leave alone as correct merely because if he wants to have his opinion considered as correct, he must develop complete familiarity with the subject matter of his views. This is why Option 3 needs to be thrown by its ear.

Option 4: Their views are probably more correct than the views of those who have attributed the comic and improvisational elements of the acto to earlier sources.

It is important to see if anyone at all has attributed the comic and improvisational elements of the acto to earlier sources. If yes, then we break our heads on this.

Whatever the critics have attributed about the comic and improvisational elements of the acto is at paragraph 2 and this is as follows: "**the improvised comic satire of the acto is a direct reflection of comic and improvisational qualities of the more contemporary and local *carpas* of Mexican theatre**". No one else has attributed the comic and improvisational elements of the acto to any other source whether earlier or subsequent because there is no mention of these two specific aspects of the acto in the passage except in the highlighted words. There is no need to imagine anything then. Catch Option 4 by its ear and chuck it out.

Option 5: Their views betray a lack of familiarity with the *commedia del ' arte*.

Let us revert to your stalled car on the highway in our analysis of Option 3. If someone passes by and says "What a magnificent rainbow there is in the sky", can you say that his words betray (or *reveal* or *show*) a lack of familiarity with the engine? He has spoken nothing about the engine. When the critics have **said nothing** about the Italian *commedia del ' arte*, how can one say that they do not have familiarity with this Italian thing?

Answer 23

Let us see what the passage says about the later actos of the Teatro Campecino and then try to determine which of the options is true. The words in the passage about the later actos of the Teatro Campecino are as follows and may be seen in the first paragraph in the passage: "Valdez' early *actos* were composed of a series of scenes about the strike experience acted by campecino volunteers. His later *actos* were presented by a newly constituted professional company, still called the Teatro Campecino, and addressed such themes as the impact of the Vietnam war on Mexican Americans and the dangers of assimilation, themes relevant to urban Mexican Americans as well as to campecinos. All Valdez' *actos* contained elements of song and dance, relied little on stage effects or props, and featured the use of masks. These dramatic elements, along with an intensely social or political purpose and the use of a mixture of Spanish, English, and Mexican American dialects in the dialogues, which realistically capture the flavour of Mexican American conversation, are still characteristic both of the *acto* and of most other forms of Mexican American theatre today."

Now let us see which of the options is correct.

Option 1: They were more politically effective than were earlier actos. In order to infer that someone has said that your brother is stronger than you, he must at least mention either you or your brother. Whatever has been said about the actos is said that they had intense political purposes. Having a purpose is one thing and being effective is another. The chap who stopped by your stalled car may have had the purpose of helping you by saying that the spark plug has conked off. He may have said that after having heard somewhere that spark plugs when they go off tend to stall cars. The question is was he effective? Option 1 will not do for this reason.

Option 2: They were presented primarily outdoors, whereas earlier actos were presented inside theatres.

All that the passage says is that actos are performed outdoors. This is in paragraph 1. There is no mention about actos being performed indoors in the passage. Option 2 will not work for this reason.

Option 3: They used a greater mixture of dialects than did the earlier actos.

We can see that Valdez originated the *actos* whether earlier actos or later actos. In the words that we have reproduced at the beginning of Answer 23, there is mention that all Valdez' actos used a mixture of dialects. The word all covers earlier and later actos. Therefore the assertion that later actos used a greater mixture of dialects than did the earlier actos in Option 3 is hogwash.

Option 4: They addressed a broader audience than did the earlier actos.

As regards audiences for the **earlier actos** these are mentioned in the following words at paragraph 1 in the passage: "Valdez' dramatic presentations, called *actos*, **spoke to a campecino audience** and addressed topics and themes directly related to the strike".

The words about the audiences for the later actos are as follows and have been drawn from the quoted text at the beginning of Answer 23: "His **later *actos*** were presented by a newly constituted professional company, still called the Teatro Campecino, and **addressed** such themes as the impact of the Vietnam war on Mexican Americans and the dangers of assimilation, themes relevant to urban Mexican Americans **as well as to campecinos**".

The earlier actos addressed a campecino audience whereas the later actos addressed some other audiences as well as to a campecino audience. **Option 4** is to be marked as correct.

Option 5: They differed from earlier actos in that they contained fewer improvisational elements.

Please see the following words: "All Valdez' *actos* contained elements of song and dance, relied little on stage effects or props, and featured the use of masks". The words *all actos* cover earlier actos and later actos. There is no distinction drawn about the range of elements in the actos performed at two different time frames. Hence Option 5 will not work.

Answer 24

Let us see where we see the agitprop theatre is mentioned in the passage. The reference to the agitprop theatre pieces is in the following words at the last paragraph in the passage: "In particular, **his actos contain the same assortment of semi-allegorical characters and the same blend of music, chorus,** and dialogue found in some of the agitprop pieces, as well as the same fierce spirit of social and political critique". Option 5 emerges verbatim.

Answer 25

Wherever you see the prefix E- at the head of any word, think of the words *eject* (that means *throw out*), *evince* (that means *reveal* and therefore *show in an outwardly* fashion), *evict* (that means *turn out*). This prefix means *out*. If rock-climbing requires *nerve*, it requires *courage* or *spirit*. When something *enervates*, the courage or spirit goes out. The opposite of this means courage or spirit coming in.

When you *inculcate* the habit of reading the newspaper, you *develop* this habit. Reading a newspaper needs no courage, however. When the Governor has consented to *inaugurate* the Mountaineering Institute, he merely cuts a ribbon. He needs no courage to *inaugurate*. If anybody is going to need courage, it is going to be the trainees who shall enrol at the Institute.

If a documentary film of Man's first conquest of Mount Everest will *invigorate* the trainee at the institute, it will put the spirit of adventure in him. Option 3 is to be marked as correct.

If the police have caught a person for driving without a licence and he *fabricates* (or *invents*, *makes up*) a story that the licence has been misplaced, he needs no courage or spirit for adventure for saying this lie simply because courage and spirit are positive attributes and cannot be employed in telling lies. If the power station is designed to *generate* 100 MW of power everyday, it does not require any courage either.

Answer 26

The passage talks about only one predator – the polar and only one prey – the seal. Options 1 and 2 are not to be looked at because they deal with predators in the plural. Option 5 will therefore do very well unless some other option is close.

As regards Option 3, there is mention about the *locomotion* (or *movement*) of two mammals (A) bears, that overheat when they walk and lie still waiting for seals and so on and (B) seals that come up for air which they cannot reasonably do without moving. Had it been a single mammal, this option may have to be looked at a closer range.

The passage talks about how the bear stores energy. The seal is mentioned only as food for the bear. As to how the seal stores energy is not mentioned at all. No seal can store energy and be eaten by the bear at the same time. Option 4 will therefore not do.

Option 5 is to be marked as correct because the polar bear stays in the poles where winters are severe and one cannot hope to go about in half-sleeve sweaters unlike in most Asian countries. Besides, the polar bear has no choice but to adapt to the winter environment.

Answer 27

Let us see where the sea-ice is mentioned in the passage. Please see these words: "Because the sea ice breaks up frequently, seals, the bear's primary prey, are available only sporadically." If there are *sporadic* incidents of violence, it means that violence occurs only *now and then* but not *regularly*.

If the sea ice did not break up frequently, there could be two logical conclusions:

(I) The seals are available not even sporadically, meaning never at all

(II) The seals are available regularly

If we were told that only polar bears eat seals, then Option 1 would have a slight chance in view of the possible conclusion (I) above. But since there is nothing mentioned about other animals (such as – may be - whales) saying *no thank you we'd rather have spinach* when offered seals for dinner by Mother Nature, only Option 5 can be correctly inferred.

Answer 28

When someone who has not had anything to eat for days finds a full meal, he may eat with a sense of urgency that may put a wolf to shame. He stuffs it in. He is said to *gorge* the food.

The prefix DIS- means *away from* (as in *distract* or *away from the path*) or *undo* (as in *disrobe*). When someone *disgorges* – or undoes whatever he has gorged - he *vomits* or *throws up*. Among the options, Option 2 fits like a shot.

We shall see the meaning of the word *inter* in a situational context. If the church has a plot of land where one can *inter* the dead, the plot is meant to *bury* the dead.

Answer 29

A *gadfly* is a parasite that sits on animals and annoys them no end. It hums into a bull's ears and tickles him till a stage comes when the bull goes berserk. A gadfly, figuratively, is *someone who annoys* or *harasses* others. The relationship between ANNOYING and GADFLY is synonymous.

Let us see which option would now fit in.

Option (1): brave: underdog. While the word *brave* needs no introduction, an *underdog* is a weaker party or a person in the process of losing a fight. For years together, the West Indies cricket team was so strong that anyone playing them would start out as underdogs. The relationship between brave and underdog is not synonymous and hence Option 1 will not work.

Option (2): conniving: killjoy. The word *conniving* consists of the prefix CON- (that means *together*) and the word *nictitate* that means *wink*. When some people plot to do harm to another person, they – figuratively – wink at one another symbolising conspiracy. The other connotation of the word *conniving* is overlooking someone's rudeness or *condoning* mistakes by *blinking at* them. A *killjoy* is someone who spoils the fun that people are having. If some youngsters in a family are having a great time swimming in the sea and an elder orders everyone to go back to shore and get dressed for dinner, he is a *party-pooper* or *wet blanket* or *killjoy*. As such there is no relationship between conniving and killjoy hence this option will not do.

Option (3): insipid: bungler. If the vegetable curry that is on one's plate is *tasteless*, it is *insipid*. An *insipid* person (where of course the word *insipid* is being used figuratively) is *lifeless* or *dull*. A *bungle* is a *botch-up* or *blunder*. If the fullback at football inadvertently lobs the ball into his own goal while trying to save a goal, he is said to have made a *bungle*. If he does this more than once, he becomes known as a *bungler*. As such there is no relationship between these two words hence this option will not do either.

Option (4): rude: churl. A *rude* person insults others and has no consideration for the hurt feelings of those to whom he is rude. If you find someone's poetry *rude*, it *lacks finish* or is *roughly made*. A *churl* is a *peasant* or *ill-bred* fellow *lacking refinement*. Thus *rude* and *churl* are synonymous and hence **Option 4** will do very well.

Option (5): vicious: manipulator. The word *vicious* comes from *vice* that means bad habit and thus *vicious* means *depraved* or *immoral* or *corrupt* or *dangerous* as are bad habits. If someone *manipulates* a good posting, he *manages* to get a posting of his choice through sycophancy or political contacts or whatever else goes into getting such a position. A *manipulator* thus manages things but in a negative connotation of the word *manage*. As such there is no relationship between these two words hence this option will not do either.

Answer 30

Let us understand a few words in context so that this could be of help in eliminating the options that are not workable. After all when one races against time in a competitive examination, it would be a great help if one were able to eliminate those of the options that are not workable per se. To that extent, one can focus on those options that seem workable prima facie and beat the clock.

The word philanthropy consists of the prefix PHIL – (that means *love*) and the Greek ANTHROPOS (that means *human beings*). A *philanthrope* is one who does good things (such as donating generously to hospitals or schools) out of his love for human beings. *Philanthropy* is love for mankind. In the converse a *misanthrope* is someone who hates mankind. Anthropology is the science of human evolution.

When someone argues against someone, the idea is to disprove what the other fellow is saying. If someone were saying that Mr. X is a veritable saint, no one who is bent upon arguing against this statement would point out a single virtue of Mr. X. In the converse, if someone were saying that Mr. X is a crook of the first order, no one who is bent upon arguing against this statement would point out a single rotten characteristic of Mr. X. It is likely that Mr. X would have both vices and virtues. But if anyone argues against one aspect of Mr. X, he would deliberately not mention the opposite aspect of Mr. X's personality. It is for this reason that any argument against philanthropy will not describe the character of philanthropists (because it will give only one feature but not both the positive and negative features of philanthropists). This is why Option 1 will not do.

The word *aggrandising* comes from *grand* that means *impressive*, *magnificent*, *vitally important* and so on. Philanthropy as we have seen is a noble quality. Any argument against philanthropy will outline the negative aspects of things done out of love of mankind. For example, some people would feel that giving alms would make the receiver of alms – or *charity* - a beggar forever and therefore may hold a view that no one should give alms. Therefore an argument against philanthropy will try to say a few negative things about it instead of trying to aggrandise philanthropy. This is why Option 2 will not work.

An *emphasis* means further stress on what one wants to say. When you speak with *emphasis*, you speak *forcefully*. If someone is arguing against anything, he will speak forcefully whatever he wants to say. This is because he wants the emphasis to help in proving his point. If he emphasises the other person, he will help the other person and thereby defeat his argument. This is why Option 3 will not do either.

The word *impugning* comes from the French verb PUGNARE that means *to fight*. This is why someone pugnacious is quarrelsome or bad-tempered. The prefix IM- means *in*. If you wish to fight anyone *in* his territory, you cannot avoid *attacking* him. This is why *impugning* means *attacking*. What is more, the central idea of any argument against some point is to attack the point being made and defeat it. This is why Option 4 will do very well not just because *impugning* fits into the first blank but also because discrediting will fit into the second blank. This is because there is a statement at the end of the sentence that they (meaning, *philanthropists*) have done good in spite of themselves. If someone has done admittedly good work, then any argument against such work may attack the character of the person doing the work but not the work itself. This is why the argument may not *discredit* the work.

When something becomes *obscure*, it becomes *unclear* or *hazy* or *confusing*. Imagine that someone donates regularly to charities and pays for the higher education of ten students every year. He is also believed to be a cool and collected person. He is also widely believed to be a virtuous person. When someone cites an instance when this person lost his temper for a very small provocation or another person cites an instance when he saw this so-called virtuous person in the company of a whore, the person's character becomes obscure; you are confused as to what he is. But this argument against a person with noble qualities (which a philanthropist is) cannot be made without *attacking* the person. This is why no word other than something meaning *attacking* will do in the first blank.

Explanatory answers to SECTION IV

Answer 1

This is all about logic once one knows that:

- The square of zero – or for that matter, zero raised to any power - will invariably be zero
- The square of any non-zero number is invariably positive; if the square of a number is either multiplied or divided by any positive number, then the resultant number (or fraction) will invariably be positive
- A minus sign in front of the square of a number will make the resultant number invariably negative: this is why $-2x^2$ will invariably be negative so long as x is non-zero
- A positive number will always be greater in value than a negative number

For the above reasons, the quantity in Column B will invariably be greater than that in Column A. Hence **mark 2**.

Answer 2

In order to crack this, all that one must know is as follows:

There is no regular mathematical usage that will tell you what n^+ denotes; the term n^+ has been temporarily created and as to what n^+ means has been defined and thus this n^+ is a newly created function and may not mean the same thing in other cases unless defined. For example A(X, Y) may be defined as the average of X and Y (or X + Y/2) in a particular question but that does not mean that A(P, Q) is the average of P and Q in another problem; there A(P, Q) may have been defined – for example – as the difference between Q and P.

The expression $n < n^+ < n + 1$ (where n is a positive integer) means that n^+ is certainly more than n and yet certainly less than n+1. This means that – for example if we were to consider only two values up to two places of decimal - 5^+ could be 5.01 at its lowest and 5.99 at its highest.

The values of the expression $20^+/1^+$ could vary between (A) 20.01/ 4.99 in the least (meaning very nearly 20 divided by very nearly 5 or very nearly 4) to (B) 20.99/4.01 at the most (meaning very nearly 21 divided by very nearly 4 or very nearly 5.25). Thus on one hand, the expression $20^+/4^+$ could take any values between very nearly 4 and very nearly 5.25.

On the other hand the expression 5^+ could take any value between very nearly 5 to very nearly 6. So in one instance Quantity A could be higher than Quantity B and in the other instance, the reverse could be true. Since one cannot say for sure which quantity is higher then mark 4.

Answer 3

This is all about logic once one knows that:

If the members of a set are integers, there can be only two varieties of integers: odd and even

In S, the set of all integers from 1 to 48, there shall be exactly 48 members consisting of consecutive positive integers stating from 1 and ending with 48

The even integers in this set S shall start with 2, then followed by 4 and so on till 48: the sub-set of such even integers can be denoted as (2, 4, ...48) or 2(1, 2... 24) and V, the sum of all even integers in S, can be denoted as 2 times the total of the consecutive integers from 1 to 24= 2 times the (average of 1 to 24) multiplied by (the number of terms in 1 to 24) = 2 (25/2) (24) = 600. So V is 600.

The sum of consecutive positive integers starting with 1 and ending with 48 is essentially an arithmetic progression wherein the first term is 1 and the difference between each term and its previous term is the same throughout and this difference is exactly 1 throughout the progression. The sum of the members in set S is = 48 times (1 + 48)/2 = 24 times 49 = 24 times (50 – 1) = 1200 – 24 = 1176.

If we know that the sum of all the members in S is 1176 and the sum of the even integers in S is 600, then since the only other variety of integers in S is odd integers, the sum of all odd integers in S is 1176 – 600 = 576. So D is 576.

Therefore the quantity in Column A is 600 whereas the quantity in Column B is 576 + 23 = 599. This is why the quantity in Column A is bigger than that in column B. Thus **mark 1**.

Answer 4

As to what is the meaning of the reflection is given by way of an example. The example tells it all. The difference between 321 and 123 is 198 and is divisible by 2, 6 and 9. But if we were to assume that the three digits in a number were A, B and C, then the number would be ABC (meaning 100A + 10B + C) and the reflection would be CBA (meaning 100C + 10B + A) and the difference between the number and its reflection would then be (99A – 99C). In ABC there are three digits and the second digit is the middle digit. The middle digit is unaffected by the reflection. It therefore does not have part to play in the difference between the number and its reflection. This is why the difference between 312 and 123 is an integral multiple of 99.

Extending this to a five digit number- say ABCDE, the middle digit C would have no impact on the difference between the number ABCDE and its reflection EDCBA because in both cases it would have a place value of

100C. The difference between ABCDE and EDCBA would then be (10000A + 1000B + 10D + E) –(10000E + 1000D + 10B + A) = 9999A + 990B – 990D – 9999E = 99(101A + 10B + 10D – 101E). The expression (101A + 10B + 10D – 101E) could be either odd or even depending upon the individual values of A, B, D and E. But the difference between ABCDE and EDCBA is sure to be multiple of 99 and hence certainly divisible by 9. Hence **Option 5**.

Answer 5

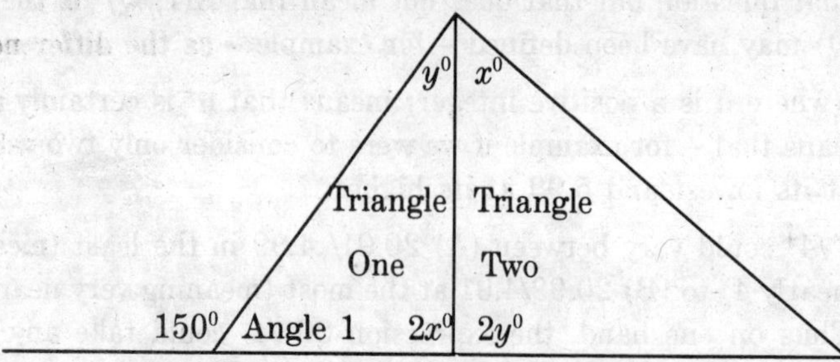

Let us name the two triangles in the figure as Triangle One and Triangle Two. In Triangle One, Angle 1 is 30^0. Angle 1 + $2x^0 + y^0 = 180$ and thus $2x^0 + y^0 = 150$.

The first thing to be seen is that two angles $2x^0$ and $2y^0$ add up to 180^0. One need not presume that $2x$ and $2y$ are each equal to 90^0 and therefore each of x and y is 45^0 merely because the angles $2x$ and $2y$ are apparently right angles. But the first thing that emerges is that $2x + 2y = 180$ and therefore $x + y = 90$.

We now have two equations:

Equation 1: $2x + y = 150$

Equation 2: $x + y = 90$

Subtracting Equation 2 from Equation 1 we get $x = 60$ and hence, since $x + y = 90$, $y = 30$ and thus $x - y = 30$. The quantities in the two columns are equal. Hence **mark 3**.

Answer 6

See the figure.

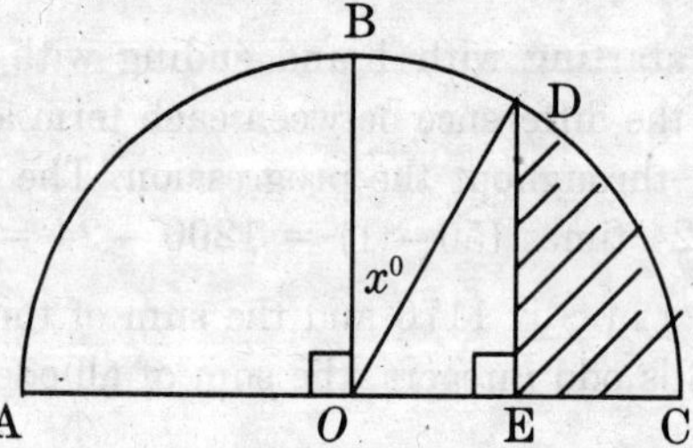

Let us name the point where the ray that forms angle x^0 touches the circle circumference as D. Let us name the point where the perpendicular from D touches the circle as E.

Since angle BOD = $x^0 = 30^0$, $x = 30$ and hence Angle DOC = 60^0, BO is perpendicular to AC. Since Angle DOC is 60^0, and since DC is that arc of the circle that subtends an angle of 60^0 with the centre of the circle, the length of the arc DC bears the same ratio with the circumference of the circle as does the angle DCO with 360^0 that any circle subtends at its centre and so the length of DC is $60^0/360^0$ or 1/6th of the circumference of the circle. Since the radius of the circle is given as 1, the circumference of the circle is 2π and thus the length of DC is $2\pi/6$ or $\pi/3$.

The perimeter of the shaded region comprises of (A) $\pi/3$ that is the length of arc DC + (B) the length of the perpendicular DE which is unknown + (C) length of EC which is half the radius and since the radius is 1 unit, EC = 1/2 unit. Thus the options that we are to look at are those that have all three components of the perimeter of the shaded area: $\pi/3$, the length of DE and 1/2. Only Option 5 will fit the bill.

To cross check, since OED is a right-angled triangle in which OE=1/2, OD=1, we can find by application of the Pythagoras Theorem that DE = $\sqrt{3}/2$. Thus Option 5 gets confirmed as the right choice.

Answer 7

This is all about logic once you understand that if, for example, one is not able to determine which is bigger: √3/7 or 1/4, the problem arises because one does not know the precise value of √3 but the solution to this problem lies in squaring both sides and finding that √3/7 when squared gives 3/49 whereas 1/4 when squared gives 1/16 and then since 3/48 is 1/16, then 3/49 is less than 1/16 and hence, between √3/7 and 1/4, √3/7 is smaller of the two.

Similarly in the present case, it is safer to square both sides and get rid of the large square root sign in the column A. Squaring both sides we get, the square of the quantity in Column A = A + B + 2√AB and the quantity in column B =$(\sqrt{A} + \sqrt{B})^2$ = A + B + 2√AB. Quantities in both columns are equal and hence **mark 3**. One should note that one has taken recourse to squaring both sides ONLY after knowing that (1) both A and B are positive (2) it is the convention at the GRE to assume positive square roots and (3) in view of this convention, the quantities in Columns A and B shall both be positive. Without this knowledge, squaring both sides would be illogical because Column A may, for example, have a negative quantity whereas Column B may have a positive quantity and squaring the quantities in both columns would then mean that you are looking at only positive quantities whereas the comparison may essentially be between one negative and another positive quantity.

Another far better and still eminently logical way of going about this is to assume perfect square values for A and B. This is because the convention at the GRE is that the square root of a number is to be taken as positive unless it is specified to the contrary. If such a convention were not outlined, then while assuming values for A and B we may have to be ready to see what would be the situation when their square roots are negative.

Let us then take A as 16 and B as 9. In column A, the square root of (A + B + 2√AB) is = square root of (16 + 9 + 2√144) = square root of (49) = 7. In column B, √A + √B = √16 + √9 = 4 + 3 = 7. Hence mark 3.

Answer 8

In the sequence of positive numbers A_1, A_2,A_3, ..., A_N, if A_1 = 1, and for n ≥ 1, A_{N+1} = A_N + 4, in simple language it means that:

(I) The first term is 1

(II) Any term is four more than its previous term.

Then the sequence goes like this: 1, 5, 9, 13 and so on where A_2 is 5, A_3 is 9 and so on. Since A_3 is 9, what we have to find is the value of which among the five options would be 9 given that N=3? Option1 will give 9; Option 2 will give 11; Option 3 will give 12; Option 4 will give 13 and Option 5 will give 16. Clearly, Option 1 is to be marked as correct.

Answer 9

Prime numbers are those positive integers that are more than 1 and are divisible only by themselves. Thus the first few prime numbers are 2, 3, 5, 7, 11, 13 and so on.

3 raised to 5 in Column A can be factorised as 3 × 3 × 3 × 3 × 3 and 5 raised to 3 in Column B can be factorised as 5 × 5 × 5. The greatest prime factor of 3 × 3 × 3 × 3 × 3 is 3 itself, because – for example- 3 × 3 is composite and so is 3 × 3 × 3 and so on. The greatest prime factor of 5 × 5 × 5 is 5 itself, because – for example- 5×5 is composite and so is 5 × 5 × 5. Thus the quantity in Column A is 3 whereas the quantity in column B is 5. Hence **mark 2**.

Answer 10

The average (arithmetic mean) of three numbers is equal to their sum divided by 3. If the average (arithmetic mean) of W, X, and Y is 9, it follows that W + X + Y = 27.

As regards the quantity in Column A, the average (arithmetic mean) of 2W – Y, 3X + 6, and 3Y – X = (2W – Y+ 3X + 6 + 3Y – X)/3 = (2W + 2X + 2Y + 6)/3 = [2(W + X + Y) + 6]/3 = (54 + 6)/3 = 20. This is equal to the quantity in Column B. Hence **mark 3.**

Answer 11

This is about logic as such once you know that the area of a circle is π times the square of its radius (where π is a constant and the only factor that can make a difference to the area of the circle is its radius and not π).

The area of the flowerbed is π times the square of R, the area of the walk will be π times the square of (R + R/2) – π times the square of R.

Since we are comparing and not actually calculating any area (specially since we are not given the actual radius without which any effort to calculate the actual area would be wasteful) π can be safely dropped from both sides of the comparison. What we are left with is comparing:

- The square of R in Column A with
- The square of (R + R/2) - the square of R that comes to the square of (3 R/2) - the square of R or 9R square/4 – R square = 5 times R square/4 in Column B.

Since 5 times R square/4 is greater than R square, **mark 2.**

Answer 12

We are given that N is an integer and thus its square is invariably an integer. If we were to see the squares of the positive integers starting from 1 till 10, you will find that these are 1, 4, 9, 16, 25, 36, 49, 64, 81 and 100. The units digit is never 2 in the above squares although 0, 4, 5 and 6 do occur as units digit in some cases of squares. It is not necessary to check integers beyond 10 because – for example – some few integers thereafter are (10 + 1), (20 + 2), (60 + 3), (80 + 4), and (110 + 5) - briefly all subsequent integers are effectively (an integral multiple of 10+ an integral number with possible values of 1 to 9 both inclusive) - and the squares of these numbers – if we were to take them as $(A + B)^2$, would be $A^2 + 2AB + B^2$ wherein A^2 will invariably be a multiple of 100, 2AB will be invariably a multiple of 10 and whatever that could contribute to a units digit would be B^2 that again cannot end with 2 since it is a perfect square. Hence **Option 2.**

Answer 13

This is wholly about logic and has little to do with any permutations and combinations.

If we are to ensure that each person of the three gets at least 1 dollar, then there can be the following ways in which this can be done:

The 1st person gets	The 2nd and 3rd person get collectively	This means that the 2nd and 3rd persons can get \$6 in the following ways:	Remarks
\$1	\$6	\$1 and \$5, \$2 and \$4, \$3 and \$3, \$4 and \$2, \$5 and \$1	Among the different ways of allocating \$6 between two persons in 1 Dollar bills, there is at least one person who gets \$3; when you give \$6 between the 2nd and 3rd persons – say \$1 and \$5 or \$2 and \$4 and so on – exactly one person gets \$3 or more than \$3 and this qualifies for the term "at least one person getting at least \$3"

$2	$5	$1 and $4, $2 and $3, $3 and $2, $4 and $1	Similarly as in the case of the above when you distribute $5 between two persons, exactly one person gets $3 or more than $ 3 and this also qualifies for the term "at least one person getting at least $3"
$3	$4	$1 and $3, $2 and	From here onwards, the first person gets $3 or more and hence the first person qualifies for the term "at least one person getting at least $3"
$4	$3	$1 and $2, $2 and $1	
$5	$2	$1 and $1	

The inference to be drawn is that each possible method of distributing $7 in $1 bills to three people so that each person gets at least $1, is also a possible method of distributing $7 in $1 bills to three persons so that at least one person gets at least $3. Therefore, the number of ways in which to distribute the bills so that at least one person receives at least $3 = the total number of ways to distribute the bills, hence **mark 3**.

Answer 14

The total income in 1990 was $ 43,000,000 of which income from foundations was 11%. This means that income from foundations was 11% of $ 43,000,000 or 0.11 × ($ 43,000,000).

Now let us move on to the second part of the question. Let us assume that the income during 1990 was $100. This means that it increased by 25% from a certain amount in 1989. What was that certain amount? An increase of 25% from 1989 to 1990 means that if something was worth $100 in 1989, it is worth $125 in 1990. So the relationship between its worth in 1989 and 1990 is 100/125. Therefore the income from foundations in 1989 was 100/125 times this income in 1990 or 100/125 × 0.11 × ($ 43,000,000) = 0.11 × ($ 43,000,000)/1.25; 100/125 is 1/1.25 when you divide both numerator and denominator with 100. Hence Option 5.

Answer 15

The logical thing to remember here is that when you are asked what is the average of the membership for some years, you have no choice but to actually calculate. What you are asked is an absolute position and not a comparative one. If two young men are seeking to be commissioned in the army and one of them is asked as to what is the height of the other, he cannot say that he is taller of the two. He has to actually measure the other fellow's height if he does not want to be sent packing. Likewise we have no choice here but to calculate.

When we calculate, we must remember that the figures of memberships are in round thousands and therefore there is no need to add three zeroes to the figure – for example – of 60 that you see for the year 1982.

Year 3 represents 1982 in the chart and Year 6 represents the year 1985 in the chart. Thus the year-wise membership (ignoring the thousands), during 1982 and 1985 was approximately 60 + 70 + 80 + 150 = 360/4 = 90. The nearest to 90000 is **Option 4.**

Answer 16

The logical thing to remember here is to do an extreme analysis without which one is sure to go wrong.

The expression $3 < x < 5$ means that:

- The smallest value of x is definitely more than 3 and if we were to restrict our fancy to two places of decimals, x could be 3.01 in the very least
- The highest value of x is definitely less than 5 and if we were to restrict our fancy to two places of decimals, x could be 4.99 in the very most

This would then mean that if we were to assume the value of x as 3.01, the quantities in Columns A and B would respectively be 6.01/3 and 8.01/3.01 or – say – ever so slightly more than 2 and well over 2.5 respectively. In this case, the quantity in column B is higher.

If we were to assume the value of x as 4.99, the quantities in Columns A and B would respectively be 7.99/3 and 9.99/4.99 or – say – well over 2.5 and ever so slightly more than 2 respectively (this is because 4.99 multiplied by 2 gives 9.98 and 9.99 in the numerator is only slightly more than 9.98). In this case, the quantity in column A is higher.

If we are to say who can eat more sandwiches - Sam or Tim - and find that sometimes Sam eats more than Tim and at other times Tim eats more than Sam, can we say which of the two definitely eats more than the other? We cannot. For similar reasons, **Option 4** is to be marked as correct.

A word of caution: when you read expressions such as $3 < x < 5$, do not leap to any conclusions with middle-of-the-road values such as 4 for x. If you do, you cannot help arriving at a situation wherein the quantity in one column is definitely bigger than that in the other. This is because you have assumed a unique value and for this there can be only a unique answer. This is why the extreme analysis that has been outlined in the solution becomes of paramount importance,

Answer 17

To the left we have 1/0.97 or 100/97. When you divide 100 by 97, you get 1 as quotient and 3 as remainder. This means that when we compare 1/1 – 0.03 and 1.03, the integer 1 is common to both sides and therefore our comparison will have to tell us which is higher: 3/97 or 0.03?

This means that we have now to divide 3 by 97 and find out whether this is more than 0.03. Fundamentally, when you are comparing two fractions both with the same numerator, the fraction with a lower denominator is bound to be higher in value than the other one. That is why 3 divided by 97 is bound to be higher than 0.03 (which is really 3 divided by 100). Hence the quantity in Column A is higher, so **mark 1**.

Answer 18

For every 6 rubies, there are 5 diamonds. There are 8 rubies for every 3 emeralds. We have now to find the least number of rubies that are a multiple of both 6 and 8. The least common multiple of 6 and 8 is 24. Thus the least possible number of rubies is 24. Therefore the least possible number of diamonds is $5/6^{th}$ of 24 or 20. Then the least number of emeralds is $3/8^{th}$ of the least possible number of rubies and thus you have 9 emeralds. The total number of jewels is thus at least 24 + 20 + 9 = 53. Hence **Option 4**.

Let us see why the number of rubies has to be a least common multiple of 6 and 8. If the number of rubies is a multiple of 6 (such as 6, 12, 18, and so on) but not a multiple of 8, then while one would get a whole number of diamonds (since for 6 rubies, there are 5 diamonds) but not a whole number of emeralds (because for every 8 rubies, there are 3 emeralds). In the converse, if the number of rubies is a multiple of 8 but not of 6, then while one would get a whole number of emeralds, one would not get a whole number of diamonds. Since the number of jewels is integral (as seen from the options), the only way one can get the least number of jewels is when the number of rubies is a least common multiple of 6 and 8.

Answer 19

This is not so much a question of logic as it is of simple algebra involving very elementary linear equations,

We are given that x/y = 2. Thus x = 2y.

The equation $ax - by + cx - dy = 0$ can be written as $x(a + c) - y(b + d) = 0$. We are told that $b+d= -1$ and hence $x(a + c) - y(b + d) = x(a + c) - y(-1) = x(a + c) + y = 0$. Substituting the value of x (=2y) in the equation x(a + c) + y = 0, we get 2y(a + c) + y = 0 and thus 2y(a + c) = –y and hence (a + c) = –y/2y = –1/2. Hence **Option 1**.

Answer 20

In the bar chart given in the question, year 1 corresponds to 1960 and year 2 as 1965 and so on till year 6 that represents 1985. Thus Year 3 and 4 would represent the years 1970 and 1975 respectively.

The number of households receiving monthly benefits in 1970 is a little less than about 2.5 million. 80% of anything is its $4/5^{th}$. The $1/5^{th}$ of 2.5 (which is 5/2) is ½ (which in words is a half) and therefore $4/5^{th}$ of 5/2 is 4 such halves that make 2. If there is an 80% increase from 1970 to 1995 in the number of households receiving monthly benefits, then the number of households receiving monthly benefits goes up from 2.5 to a little less than 4.5 million.

If we were to see the relative chart, the number of households receiving monthly benefits in 1985 is about 3.7 million. Therefore the increase in the number of households receiving monthly benefits from 1985 to 1995 will be approximately a little less than 4.5 million minus 3.7 million or less than 0.8 million that comes to a little less than 800,000. **Option 4** seems to be the closest.

Answer 21

Let us go from statement to statement and see which of the three can be inferred:

I. From 1980 to 1985, the average monthly benefit in 1960 dollars decreased by at least 20%: The average monthly benefit in 1960 dollars stood at $120 in 1980 and at $115 in 1985. This shows a decrease of 5/120 or 1/24, which is a little more than 4% but less than 5% since 1/25 is exactly 4% and 1/20 is exactly 5%. This statement can therefore not be inferred.

II. For the five-year periods indicated in the graph, the number of households receiving monthly benefit increased by the greatest percent from 1970 to 1975: Here we are to focus our attention not on absolute terms but on relative terms since we are asked about the percentage growth in the number of households and it is possible that we may be able to derive relative positions from a mere glance at graphs. Fundamentally, when you express relative positions in percent means, you essentially compare growths/declines and so on over a common denominator of 100. Since a percentage is nothing other than a fraction expressed differently (without altering its value in any way) the basics of fraction will hold good. A fraction in which the denominator is a smaller multiple of the numerator is certain to be of higher value than a fraction in which the denominator is a larger multiple of the numerator.

   From 1960 to 1965, the growth (in millions) has been from 0.5 to 1.0 or a 100% growth. From 1965 to 1970, the growth has been from 1.0 to 2.2, which is more than 100%. There are two things that would lead one to believe that the given inference cannot be drawn. The first is that the denominator is lower in a case other than 1970. The second is the quite visibly higher gradient in the rise from the column in 1965 to 1970. Unless expressly told that a graph is drawn to scale, it is quite reasonable to assume that it is to scale. In the latter case the gradient is a reliable indicator of relative rises or falls.

III. In 1975 fewer than 3 million people resided in households that received monthly benefits: This is about absolute positions and not about relative positions. However all that needs to be done is to check whether the column corresponding to 1975 stops short of 3 million, stops at 3 million or goes above 3 million. In this case the column goes above the 3 million mark in year 4 and hence this statement cannot be inferred either.

   Since none of the statements can be inferred **Option 1** is to be marked as correct.

Answer 22

A cube has six faces each of which is square with a surface area of the square of the side. The surface of a cube is thus six times the square of its sides. In comparing the surface areas of two cubes of different dimension – 3 and √3 units -, what we are comparing is six times the area of a square of 9 sq units with six times the area of a square of 3 sq units and hence the area of the cube of side 3 units/ area of cube of √3 units is 9/3= 3. Hence **Option 2**.

Answer 23

Since ABCD is a square and one of its sides is x units, AD is also equal to x. AE = x/2 units. Since AE=ED, both are equal to x/2 units.

The perimeter of triangle ACE is = AE + AC + CE. AC is the hypotenuse of a right triangle with one of its sides x and the other also x. AC = $x\sqrt{2}$ approximately or 1.4x units. CE is the hypotenuse of a right triangle with one of its sides CD of x units and ED - the other – of x/2 units. Therefore CE= square root of $(x^2 + x^2/4) = \sqrt{(5x^2/4)} = \sqrt{1.25\ x^2}$. CE is thus approximately 1.1x units. (When trying to mentally reckon the square root of 1.25 look at 1.25 as 125/100 of which the square root shall be nearly 11/10 or 1.1). The perimeter of ACE is = 0.5x + 1.4x + 1.1x = 3x units.

The quantity in column A is 3x units whereas the quantity in column B is 2.5 x units. Hence **mark 1**.

Answer 24

When you compare the heights of two boys A and B, either A can be taller than B or A can be shorter than B or A and B can be of equal height. There is no fourth possibility. Likewise, there can be only three possible scenarios regarding investment in two parts of a sum at two different rates of interest:

Scenario 1: The part invested at lower interest is more than the part invested at higher interest

Scenario 2: The part invested at higher interest is more than the part invested at lower interest

Scenario 3: Equal amounts have been invested at the two different rates of interest

The total interest in Scenario 1 will be lower than the interest in Scenario 3 and the total interest in Scenario 2 will be greater than the interest in Scenario 3

If we were to assume that half of a $ 10000 inheritance was invested at 4% and the other half was invested at 6%, the interest would then be ½ of 4% of $10000 + ½ of 6% of $10000 = 2% of $10000 + 3% of $10000 = 5% of $10000, which would mean interest of $500. Since the interest received at the year-end was more than $500, it follows that the amount invested at 6% interest was higher than the amount invested at 4% interest. Hence Mark 2.

Answer 25

The whole thing is about logic more than anything else. If you do not know Indices so well, give x one or two small values. First let x be 1. In that case, on the left hand side $2^{x+x} = 2^2 = 4$ and on the right hand side, $4^x = 4$. Both sides are equal.

Now give x another value only to crosscheck. Let x be 2. In that case, on the left hand side $2^{x+x} = 2^4 = 16$ and on the right hand side, $4^2 = 16$. Both sides are equal.
Mark 3 as correct without further ado.

Answer 26

This is a matter of **sheer logic**. One hour before the two trains meet they are at such a place from where one train will take one hour to reach the place where they meet and the other train coming from the opposite direction will also take one hour to reach the place where they meet. Thus the train doing 30 miles per hour is 30 miles away from the place where they meet and the train doing 40 miles per hour is 40 miles away in the opposite direction and thus the two trains are 30+40=70 miles apart one hour before they meet. Hence Option 5 is to be marked as correct.

Answer 27

From 06:53 to 15:53 is 9 hours. From 15:53 to 16: 00 is 7 more minutes. From 16:00 to 16:32 is another 32 minutes.

The total time between sunrise and sunset is 9 hours and 39 minutes. 70% of something is 70/100 or 7/10th part of something. Thus 70% of 9 hours is 7 × 9/10 = 63/10 = 6.3 hours. 70% of 39 (or very nearly 40 minutes) is 7 × 40/10 = 280/10=28 minutes which is very nearly 30 minutes or half an hour or 0.5 hours. The approximate number of hours of sunshine expected on June 21 is nearly 6.3 + 0.5 = 6.8 hours. Hence Mark 2.

Answer 28

There is only one combination of two even numbers between 1 and 9 that will add up to 8. These numbers are 2 and 6 and in this there can be two different ways in which one can choose: the first way of choosing such even numbers is 2 and then 6 and the other way is 6 and then 2. Now let us see what is the possible number of ways in which we can add different even numbers between 1 and 9. There are 4 different even numbers between 1 and 9 and these are 2, 4, 6 and 8. Suppose we pick 2 first, for the second choice one can pick from any of 4, 6 and 8. Now suppose we pick 4 first, for the second choice one can pick from any of 2, 6 and 8.

The different combinations can thus be as follows:

2 + 4, 2 + 6 and 2 + 8

4 + 2, 4 + 6 and 4 + 8

6 + 2, 6 + 4 and 6 + 8

8 + 2, 8 + 4 and 8 + 6

Thus there can be three different ways of choosing the other distinct number with each one of four even numbers between 1 and 9. The total number of ways of choosing even numbers between 1 and 9 is thus 4 times 3, which is equal to 12. The two possible combinations where one can get a total of 8 are highlighted in the above listed possible combinations. If an event has n equally likely outcomes and f of them termed favourable, the probability of a favourable outcome is f/n. In the present case, the probability is 2/12 or $1/6^{th}$. Hence Mark 1.

Chapter 54

Question Paper 2

SECTION I

Time: 45 minutes

Present your perspective on one of the issues below using relevant reasons and/or examples to support your view.

Topic 1

"Our declining environment may bring the people of the world together as no politician, philosopher, or war ever could. Environmental problems are global in scope and respect no nation's boundary. Therefore, people are faced with the choice of unity and co-operation on one hand and disunity or a common tragedy on the other."

Topic 2

"Both the development of technological tools and the uses to which humanity has put them have created modern civilisations in which loneliness is ever increasing."

SECTION II

Time: 30 minutes

Discuss how well reasoned you find this argument.

"Six months ago the region of Dunsinane increased the speed limit for vehicles travelling on the region's highways by 10 miles per hour. Since that change took effect, the number of automobile accidents in that region has increased by 15%. But the speed limit in Inverness, a region neighbouring Dunsinane, remained unchanged, and automobile accidents declined slightly during the same six-month period. Therefore, if the citizens of Dunsinane want to reduce the number of automobile accidents on the region's highways, they should campaign to reduce Dunsinane's speed limit to what it was before the increase."

SECTION III

VERBAL

Time: 30 minutes

30 Questions

The following question includes a sentence with blank spaces, each blank indicating that something has been omitted. Beneath the sentence are five words or sets of words. Choose the word or set of words for each blank that best fits the meaning of the sentence.

Question 1

Because the most recent research has __________ earlier criticism of her work, one has to conclude that scientists who persist in dismissing her contribution are either _____ the latest findings or simply obstinate.

(1) disparaged..satisfied with (2) refined..preoccupied with (3) rejuvenated..unmoved by

(4) confirmed..opposed to (5) invalidated..ignorant of

Choose the word or phrase that is nearly opposite in meaning to the word in capital letters.

Question 2

ABSOLUTE:

(1) inferior (2) tolerant (3) qualified (4) preliminary (5) immeasurable

Question 3

LIMPID:

(1) irrelevant (2) caustic (3) informal (4) unsubstantiated (5) unclear

The following question includes a sentence with blank spaces, each blank indicating that something has been omitted. Beneath the sentence are five words or sets of words. Choose the word or set of words for each blank that best fits the meaning of the sentence.

Question 4

The senator's attempt to convince the public that he is not interested in running for a second term is _______ given the extremely _______ fund-raising activities of his campaign committee.

(1) futile..clandestine (2) sincere..visible (3) specious..apathetic

(4) disingenuous..public (5) straightforward..dubious

In the following questions, a related pair of words or phrases is followed by five pairs of words or phrases. Select the pair that best expresses a relationship similar to that expressed in the original pair.

Question 5

PARSIMONY: MISER::

(1) temerity: despot (2) belligerence: traitor (3) remorse: delinquent

(4) equanimity: guardian (5) rebelliousness: insurgent

Question 6

MOLLIFY: ANGER::

(1) enlighten: seriousness (2) nurture: dependency (3) hearten. dejection

(4) distract: confusion (5) anticipate: outcome

Choose the word or phrase that is most nearly opposite in meaning to the word in capital letters.

Question 7

TRANSITORY:

(1) distinctive (2) gradual (3) persistent (4) distant (5) implicit

The following question includes a sentence with blank spaces, each blank indicating that something has been omitted. Beneath the sentence are five words or sets of words. Choose the word or set of words for each blank that best fits the meaning of the sentence.

Question 8

The critics' evident _______ the new production was somewhat _______ by their high regard for the playwright's earlier work.

(1) admiration for..offset (2) curiosity about..dampen (3) hostility toward..tempered

(4) disappointment in..disguised (5) awareness of..frustrated

Choose the word or phrase that is nearly ***opposite*** *in meaning to the word in capital letters.*

Question 9

LASH:

(1) disembark (2) discharge (3) uncover (4) unburden (5) unbind

In the following question, a related pair of words or phrases is followed by five lettered pairs of words or phrases. Select the lettered pair that best expresses a relationship similar to that expressed in the original pair.

Question 10

ABRADED: FRICTION::

(1) refined: combustion (2) attenuated: coagulation (3) diluted: immersion
(4) strengthen: compression (5) desiccated: dehydration

DIRECTIONS *for Question 11 and 12:*

After reading the passage, choose the best answer to each question. Answer all questions at the end of the passage on the basis of what is stated or implied in the passage.

Neutrinos, perhaps the most abundant sub-atomic particle (particles smaller than an atom), may be useful in foretelling the universe's future. Physicists believe that colliding nuclei of hydrogen atoms in the Sun and other stars release neutrinos that emerge from the stars and stream into space. Although unsure about neutrinos' specific properties, physicists reason that if neutrinos possess mass and are therefore susceptible to gravity, millions of years from now, the countless neutrinos that have been streaming outward through space would over time cause the expanding universe to slow, stop, and begin collapsing inwards.

Neutrinos, however, are extremely difficult to detect and study. Their visible traces– infinitesimal flashes of light appearing when neutrinos collide with atomic nuclei – are virtually indistinguishable from those of other atmospheric phenomena such as the interaction of cosmic rays with atomic nuclei in earth's atmosphere. Physicists are therefore building underground neutrino detectors assuming that the screening capacity of earth will prevent the mistaking of neutrinos for other phenomena.

Question 11

Which of the following, if true, would most tend to strengthen physicists' theories about the release of neutrinos into space referred to in the passage?

(1) Research in space fails to confirm that neutrinos are travelling in a direction outward from the sun.

(2) Underground neutrino detectors confirm the existence of neutrinos in earth's atmosphere in much larger quantities than the theories anticipated.

(3) Neutrinos are invariably detected wherever there is a high concentration of cosmic rays and electromagnetic radiation in earth's atmosphere.

(4) Experiments designed to measure and capture any recurring patterns in the flashes of light created by neutrinos revealed that neutrinos are also produced by colliding nuclei of other elements.

(5) Experiments in which the nuclei of hydrogen atoms are made to collide under conditions presumed to exist at the Sun's centre result in the release and escape of neutrinos.

Question 12

According to the passage, if neutrinos are affected by gravity, it may also be true that neutrinos:

(1) contain information about the origins of the universe .

(2) are the most abundant sub-atomic particles in space.

(3) produce infinitesimal flashes of light when they interact with cosmic rays .

(4) will eventually inhibit the expansion of the universe.

(5) are unaffected by the presence of other sub-atomic particles.

Question 13

Choose the word or phrase that is most nearly ***opposite*** *in meaning to the word in capital letters.*

PENCHANT:

(1) retreat (2) aversion (3) travesty (4) betrayal (5) prodigality

DIRECTIONS *for Question 14 to 17:*

After reading the passage, choose the best answer to each question. Answer all questions following the passage on the basis of what is ***stated*** *or* ***implied*** *in the passage.*

One goal of Puritan missionaries in colonial New England was to teach Native Americans to read and write in English or in native languages transcribed into the English alphabet. These efforts to teach reading and writing using English characters (alphabetic literacy) were an integral part of the larger framework of religious proselytism. How scholars view these attempts to impart alphabetic literacy has therefore been coloured by historians' judgements of the consequences of missionary activity. For instance, prior to the 1960's, colonial New England missions were generally described as benevolent enterprises and were often exempted from criticism even when other aspects of Puritan interactions with Native Americans were not. In the 1960's, however, scholars began to focus on "coercive" cultural change. They saw the Puritan missionaries as "cultural imperialists" who imposed an ethnocentric worldview on Native Americans in colonial New England, and they portrayed Native Americans as not resisting the assaults on their culture.

In contrast, the perspective that emerged among scholars in the 1980's held that Native Americans in colonial New England were not passive in the face of "cultural imperialism"; rather, they acted in a variety of ways to maintain their cultures. The new view suggested that in order to evaluate missionary activity from the viewpoint of Native Americans, scholars must consider whether the adoption of Christianity may have indirectly helped Native Americans to preserve their cultural identity. From this point of view, the Puritan missionaries, in introducing Native Americans to alphabetic literacy, may have provided them with a practical means of adjusting to a new era.

The experience of the Native Americans on Martha's Vineyard, an island off the southeastern coast of Massachusetts, provides an interesting case study. In the 1640's, Thomas Mayhew set out to convert the Wampanoag people, and widespread alphabetic literacy among the Wampanoag was initially the direct consequence of his missionary activity. Members of the Wampanoag nation appeared to have accepted Christianity wholeheartedly and without coercion. Historian William Simmons has called their conversion "the most profound social conversion to occur anywhere in New England".

Shortly after Mayhew's death in 1657, individual members of the Wampanoag nation emerged as leaders of the conversion movement, and the Wampanoag themselves became the chief agents of Christianity. When Christian belief among the Wampanoag began to fade in the early 18th century, alphabetic literacy remained a central feature of Wampanoag life; it came to be regarded by the community as an intrinsically valuable skill that the Wampanoag people themselves taught to their children.

Though initially motivated primarily by the Wampanoag people's to read religious works, alphabetic literacy proved useful in conducting diplomatic correspondence, establishing a legal system, and keeping written records of court decisions. While accepting English rule, the Wampanoag of Martha's Vineyard were able to remain essentially self-governing and culturally independent.

Question 14

The information in the passage suggests that the author believes in which of the following about the 1960's view of interaction between Puritan missionaries and Native Americans in colonial New England?

(1) It is more persuasive than the view held in the 1980's.

(2) It does not accurately describe the experience of one particular group of Native Americans.

(3) It fails to take account of research done on the motivations of Puritan missionaries.

(4) It is credible because it is based on Native American viewpoints about interaction with Puritan missionaries.

(5) It is definitive because it is critical of Puritan missionaries' attempts to impose their culture.

Question 15

The passage is primarily concerned with:

(1) assessing the impact of particular religious beliefs and activities on specific historic events.

(2) developing a theoretical framework within which to determine the effects of interactions between different cultures.

(3) analysing a theory that explains a particular cultural practice and placing the theory in a broad historical context.

(4) depicting particular historical events and determining their causes.

(5) describing successive interpretations of historical events and supporting one interpretation by reporting a specific situation.

Question 16

Which of the following best describes the purpose of the final paragraph of the passage?

(1) It provides a controversial interpretation of interactions between missionaries and the Wampanoag.

(2) It provides an additional example of the effect of missionaries on Native American culture.

(3) It offers evidence in support of the view of missionary activities held by scholars in the 1960's.

(4) It criticizes the view of missionary activities held by historians prior to the 1960's.

(5) It identifies consequences of alphabetic literacy that are consistent with the scholarly view of the 1980's.

Question 17

According to the passage, teaching alphabetic literacy to Native Americans in colonial New England was part of a larger effort to:

(1) facilitate the conversion of Native Americans to Christianity.

(2) encourage Native Americans to develop legal institutions.

(3) enable Native Americans to conduct political correspondence with Europeans.

(4) encourage diplomatic relations between Native Americans and Europeans.

(5) foster cultural understanding between Native Americans and Europeans.

The following questions includes a sentence with blank spaces, each blank indicating that something has been omitted. Beneath the sentence are five words or sets of words. Choose the word or set of words for each blank that best fits the meaning of the sentence.

Question 18

The challenge of interacting fictional works written under politically depressing regimes lies in distinguishing what is ________ to an author's beliefs, as opposed to what is ________ by political coercion.

(1) innate..understood (2) organic..imposed (3) contradictory..conveyed

(4) oblique..captured (5) peripheral..demanded

*Choose the word or phrase that is nearly **opposite** in meaning to the word in capital letters.*

Question 19

DECORUM:

(1) constant austerity (2) false humility (3) impropriety (4) incompetence

(5) petulance

In the following question, a related pair of words or phrases is followed by five lettered pairs of words or phrases. Select the lettered pair that best expresses a relationship similar to that expressed in the original pair.

Question 20

ODIOUS: DISGUST::

(1) awesome: resentment (2) normal: banality (3) scarce: poverty

(4) immobile: stability (5) menacing: fear

The following questions includes a sentence with blank spaces, each blank indicating that something has been omitted. Beneath the sentence are five words or sets of words. Choose the word or set of words for each blank that <u>best</u> fits the meaning of the sentence.

Question 21

Although it seems ________ that there would be a greater risk of serious automobile accidents in densely populated areas, such accidents are more likely to occur in sparsely populated regions.

(1) paradoxical (2) axiomatic (3) anomalous

(4) irrelevant (5) portentous

*Choose the word or phrase that is nearly **opposite** in meaning to the word in capital letters.*

Question 22

ANOMALY:

(1) derivation from estimates (2) conformity to norms (3) return to origins

(4) adaptation to stresses (5) repression of traits

In the following questions, a related pair of words or phrases is followed by five lettered pairs of words or phrases. Select the lettered pair that best expresses a relationship similar to that expressed in the original pair.

Question 23

NARCISSIST: SELF-ABSORBED::

(1) malcontent: resigned (2) braggart: detestable (3) cynic: pensive

(4) sycophant: obsequious (5) perfunctionist: incomplete

Question 24

ABATE: FORCE::

(1) corrode: acid (2) grind: powder (3) congeal: viscosity

(4) intensify: hue (5) decelerate: speed

Choose the word or phrase that is nearly **opposite** in meaning to the word in capital letters.

Question 25

WAX:

(1) disconnect (2) decrease (3) supplement

(4) loosen (5) squander

DIRECTIONS *for Question 26 and 27:*

After reading the passage, choose the best answer to each question. Answer all questions at the end of the passage on the basis of what is stated or implied in the passage.

Certain current short-story writers often use techniques – particularly exposition and description – associated with the essay. As exemplified in the work of Raymond Carver and Ann Beattie, the result is a fiction that is founded on relentless exposition and that bulges with detail - often excessive detail about arcane processes and the external appearance of people and places. This use of detail, which recalls that in certain 19th Century British novels, makes current fiction seem old-fashioned. Moreover, the characters in such stories are often flat – shallow and psychologically uncomplicated. The action consists of a chronicle of everyday life, and thus the work often becomes a report of mundane experiences. This type of story does not, however, herald the death of the short story: it is merely a particular form of fiction currently enjoying critical favour in part because few critics have seen beyond its apparent virtue – the dazzling surface of its prose.

Question 26

The author of the passage is most likely to agree with which of the following statements about the use of essay techniques in the short stories of writers such as Carver and Beattie?

(1) Their use represents a step backward because it heightens the short story's similarity to the 19-century essay.

(2) Their use has emphasised description at the expense of other important elements of fiction.

(3) Their use has produced a style of writing sufficiently dazzling to compensate for the psychological shallowness of such stories.

(4) Their use signals the demise of the short story as a distant form of fiction.

(5) Their use has weakened the traditional emphasis on characters in a short story, pointing instead to a new emphasis on plots.

Question 27

The passage is primarily concerned with:

(1) appraising a particular style of writing present in current short fiction.

(2) asserting that certain short story writers' use of essay technique has made the short story indistinguishable from the essay.

(3) tracing the development of the current short story from its origins in the nineteenth-century British novel.

(4) arguing that certain current short story writers have permanently changed the form of the short story.

(5) contrasting the use of description in the essay with its use in the short story.

The following questions includes a sentence with blank spaces, each blank indicating that something has been omitted. Beneath the sentence are five words or sets of words. Choose the word or set of words for each blank that best fits the meaning of the sentence.

Question 28

Although frequent air travellers remain unconvinced, researchers have found that, paradoxically, the ________ disorientation inherent in jet lag also may yield some mental health ________.

(1) temporal .. benefits (2) acquired .. hazards (3) somatic .. disorders

(4) random .. deficiencies (5) typical .. standards

Choose the word or phrase that is most nearly opposite in meaning to the word in capital letters.

Question 29

DAUNTLESS:

(1) easily discouraged (2) open to persuasion (3) free of prejudice (4) salvageable (5) ethereal

In the following questions, a related pair of words or phrases is followed by five pairs of words or phrases. Select the pair that best expresses a relationship similar to that expressed in the original pair.

Question 30

SYNOPSIS: CONCISENESS::

(1) distillate: purity (2) mutation: viability (3) replication: precedence

(4) illusion: quickness (5) icon: charity

SECTION IV

QUANTITATIVE

Time: 45 minutes

28 Questions

Question 1

On a drawing done to scale, 1/4 inch represents 5 feet.

Column A	Column B
The number of inches on the drawing that represents 150 feet	7.5

1. The quantity in Column A is greater.
2. The quantity in Column B is greater.
3. The two quantities are equal.
4. The relation cannot be determined from the information given.

DIRECTIONS *for Questions 2 and 3: These questions refer to the following graph.*

SELECTED CATEGORIES OF THE UNITED STATES FEDERAL BUDGET, 1993
(in billion of dollars)

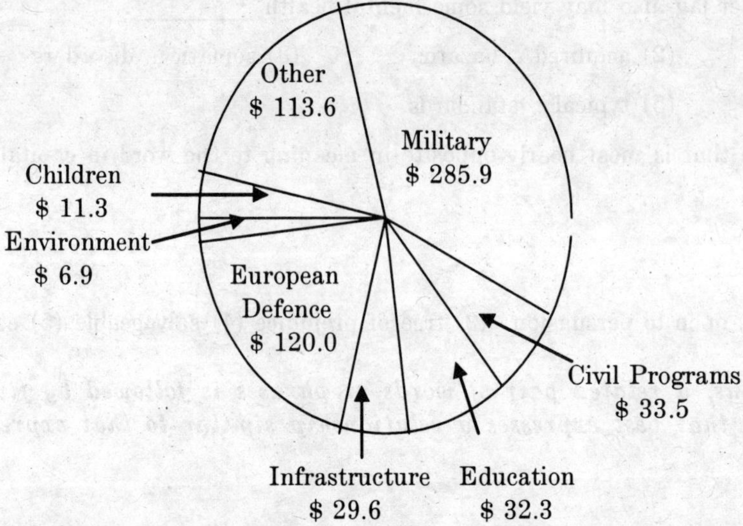

Total: $ 633.1 billion

One billion = 1,000,000,000

Note: Drawn to scale

Question 2

The ratio of the amount budgeted for military and European defence to the amount budgeted for all other categories shown was approximately:

(1) 4:3 (2) 3:1 (3) 2:3 (4) 2:1 (5) 1:2

Question 3

Approximately what percent of the total does the amount budgeted for education represent.

(1) 5% (2) 12.5% (3) 25% (4) 32% (5) 50%

Question 4

Which of the following CANNOT be a factor of $2^n.3^k$, where n and k are positive integer?

(1) 6 (2) 8 (3) 27 (4) 42 (5) 54

Question 5

Bill and Gina both collect coins. The number of coins in Bill's collection is 80 less than twice the number in Gina's collection.

Column A	Column B
The number of coins in Bill's collection	The number of coins in Gina's collection

1. The quantity in Column A is greater.
2. The quantity in Column B is greater.
3. The two quantities are equal.

4. The relation cannot be determined from the information given.

Question 6

A line in the xy-coordinate plane has x-intercept a and y-intercept b, where a and b are nonzero. The slope of this line is:

(1) $1/ab$ (2) $-b/a$ (3) $-a/b$ (4) b/a (5) a/b

Question 7

Column A	Column B
The least positive integer with four different prime factors, each greater than 2	1,155

1. The quantity in Column A is greater.
2. The quantity in Column B is greater.
3. The two quantities are equal.
4. The relation cannot be determined from the information given.

Question 8

The area of rectangular region R is equal to the area of rectangular region T. The ratio of the length to the width of R is 3:1. The length and width of T are 12 and w, respectively.

Column A	Column B
w	4

1. The quantity in Column A is greater.
2. The quantity in Column B is greater.
3. The two quantities are equal.
4. The relation cannot be determined from the information given.

Question 9

T is no more than 20% greater than the integer X, and T is no smaller than a number 20% less than the integer X. If T = 60, which of the following indicates the smallest possible interval for X?

(1) $40 \le X \le 80$

(2) $48 \le X \le 75$

(3) $48 \le X \le 72$

(4) $50 \le X \le 78$

(5) $50 \le X \le 75$

Question 10

A train makes a 50-mile trip at an average speed of 45 miles per hour. The train travels at an average speed of 40 miles per hour for the first 30 miles of the trip.

Column A	Column B
The train's average speed for the last 20 miles of the trip	45 miles per hour

1. The quantity in Column A is greater.
2. The quantity in Column B is greater.
3. The two quantities are equal.
4. The relation cannot be determined from the information given.

Question 11

Which of the following numbers is NOT the sum of three consecutive odd integers?

(1) 15 (2) 75 (3) 123 (4) 237 (5) 313

Question 12

Column A	Column B
$(0.83)^6/(0.83)^7$	1

1. The quantity in Column A is greater.
2. The quantity in Column B is greater.
3. The two quantities are equal.
4. The relation cannot be determined from the information given.

Question 13

If the sum of two positive integers is 43 and the difference of their squares is 43, then the smaller integer is:

(1) 17 (2) 19 (3) 20 (4) 21 (5) 22

Question 14

From the set of 6 letters A, B, C, D, E, and F there are 20 different 3-letter subsets that could be selected

Column A	Column B
The number of 3-letter subsets that include the letter F	10

1. The quantity in Column A is greater.
2. The quantity in Column B is greater.
3. The two quantities are equal.
4. The relation cannot be determined from the information given.

Question 15

P, Q and R are distinct points on a straight line with Q between P and R. S is a point not on the line, and QR = QS.

Column A	Column B
PR	PS

1. The quantity in Column A is greater
2. The quantity in Column B is greater

3. The two quantities are equal
4. The relation cannot be determined from the information given

Question 16

In a group of 80 students, 24 are enrolled in Geometry, 40 in Biology, and 20 in both. If a student were randomly selected from the 80 students, what is the probability that the student selected would not be enrolled in either course?

(1) 0.20 (2) 0.25 (3) 0.45 (4) 0.55 (5) 0.60

Question 17

Column A	Column B
$(2x + 3y)^2$	$4x + 6xy + 9y^2$

1. The quantity in Column A is greater.
2. The quantity in Column B is greater.
3. The two quantities are equal.
4. The relation cannot be determined from the information given.

DIRECTIONS *for Questions 18 and 19: These question refer to the following information:*

Thirty hospital patients who had been treated for the same illness were given a new treatment in a research study. They were then asked to evaluate whether give symptoms, H, L, P, T and V were made better or worse by the new treatment compared to the old treatment. For each symptom, each patient used one of five ratings:

2: Much better

1: Somewhat better

0: Neither better nor worse

-1: Somewhat worse

-2: Much worse

For each symptom, the sum and standard deviation of the ratings are listed below.

Symptom	Sum of 30 ratings	Standard deviation of 30 ratings
H	12	1.40
L	35	0.69
P	-33	0.79
T	-26	0.43
V	2	0.89

Question 18

Based on the sums of the ratings alone, how many of the symptoms must have had at least one rating of –2?

(1) None (2) 1 (3) 2 (4) 3 (5) 4

Question 19

For the symptom whose arithmetic mean rating was closest to 0, approximately what was the arithmetic mean rating?

(1) 0.015 (2) 0.020 (3) 0.067 (4) 0.15 (5) 0.67

Question 20

Column A	Column B
$\frac{1}{\sqrt{5}} \times \left[\left(\frac{1+\sqrt{5}}{2}\right) - \left(\frac{1-\sqrt{5}}{2}\right)\right]$	1

1. The quantity in Column A is greater.
2. The quantity in Column B is greater.
3. The two quantities are equal.
4. The relation cannot be determined from the information given.

Question 21

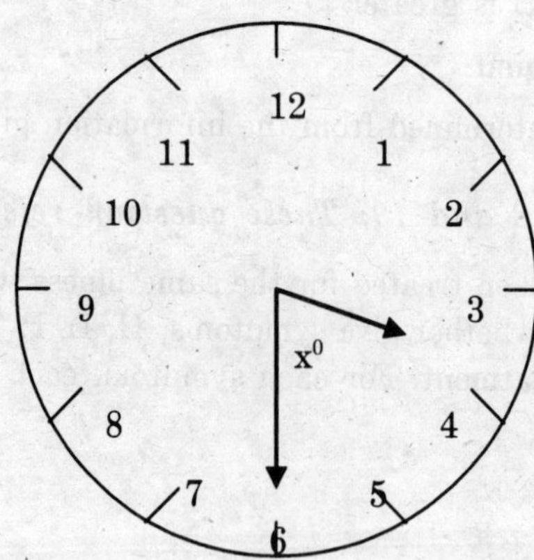

Note: Drawn to scale

The circular clock shows a time of exactly 3:30. What is the value of x?

(1) 60 (2) 75 (3) 85 (4) 90 (5) 105

Question 22

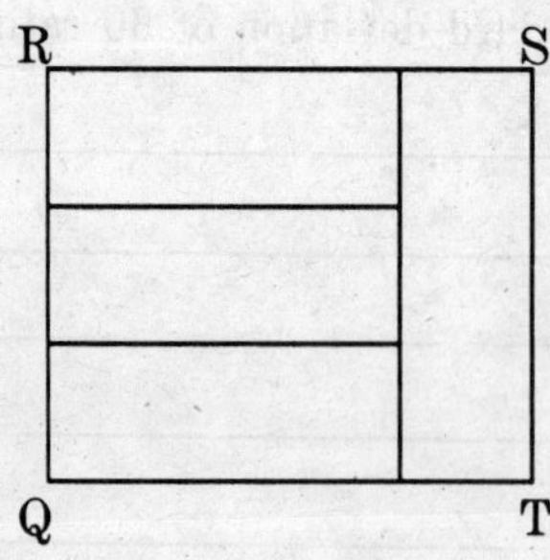

Rectangular region QRST is divided into four smaller rectangular regions with length L and width W.

Column A	Column B
QR/RS	3/4

1. The quantity in Column A is greater.
2. The quantity in Column B is greater.
3. The two quantities are equal.
4. The relation cannot be determined from the information given.

Question 23

Which of the following sums is greater than 1?

(1) 1/2 + 1/3

(2) 7/8 + 3/30

(3) 15/16 + 2/40

(4) 12/25 + 12/30

(5) 35/102 + 2/3

Question 24

If X and Y are negative integers, which of the following must be true?

I. $XY > 0$

II. $X > X + Y$

III. If $X < Y$, then $X^2 > Y^2$

(1) I only (2) I & II only (3) I & III only (4) II & III only (5) I, II & III

Question 25

$B \neq 0$

Column A	Column B
(-B) × (-B)	(-B) / (-B)

1. The quantity in Column A is greater.
2. The quantity in Column B is greater.
3. The two quantities are equal.
4. The relation cannot be determined from the information given.

Question 26

The cost C of an order of N special envelops is given by C = ($0.50)N + $15.00.

Column A	Column B
The cost of an order of 500 special envelops	$260

1. The quantity in Column A is greater.
2. The quantity in Column B is greater.
3. The two quantities are equal.
4. The relation cannot be determined from the information given.

Question 27

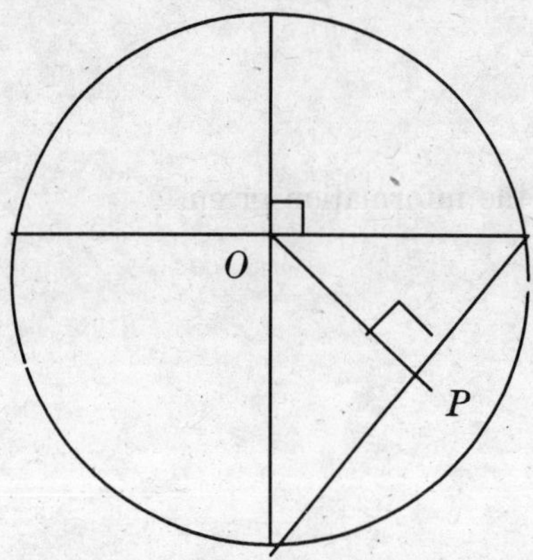

O is the centre of a circle of radius R.

Column A	Column B
OP	$R/\sqrt{2}$

1. The quantity in Column A is greater.
2. The quantity in Column B is greater.
3. The two quantities are equal.
4. The relation cannot be determined from the information given.

Question 28

What is the value of 22/7 – 7/22 to the nearest integer?

(1) 0 (2) 1 (3) 2 (4) 3 (5) 4

Answers to SECTION I & II

As you may have noted while going through the guidelines in the POWERPREP CD in regard to essay similarity, the perspectives that you present and your critique of the arguments are to be provided in your own words. They are to be entirely original.

The ETS gives the broad parameters that would decide what scores would be allotted to your Presentation on the Issue and your Critique of the Argument. You will also find these parameters in the chapter titled Understanding the System in this book. If you wish to have your responses to the questions in the first two sections evaluated by us, you may feel free to forward your responses to us at our e-mail ID as follows:

jivaishnav@yahoo.com

We may just mention that this evaluation shall be at no cost.

Explanatory Answers to Section III

Answer 1

Let us understand a few words from contextual usage before we judge the best option.

A young boy stands on a three-meter diving board in a swimming pool. He is hesitant to leap from that lofty height. His classmates ask him to climb down saying that the high board is not meant for sissies. Not *disparaged* (or *belittled*), he leaps and lands smoothly in the water.

If some one is *preoccupied* preparing for an examination, his thoughts are dominated by the pressure of examination and little does he think of anything else.

The word *rejuvenated* has the prefix RE- that means *back.* It comes from the word *juvenile* that means *young* or *youthful*. (You would have heard of *juvenile* courts that are meant for trials of criminals who are not adults). Anything that *rejuvenates* puts back the vigour or makes someone (figuratively, of course) young once again. Alumni meetings generally have the effect of *rejuvenating* people.

The word invalid has the prefix IN- and means *not.* It comes from the French verb VALERE, which means *to be strong*. (Remember *valour* means *courage* or *strength*) *Invalid* therefore means something that has *no strength* either physical (like an invalid lying on a hospital bed), or in terms of authority (like an act or law becoming invalid by being repealed, or like an argument becoming invalid after being proved wrong).

Now let us go from one option to the other.

Option 1: If a recent research has a *disparaged* criticism of someone's work, it means that the research has pooh-poohed her critics. It means that if the scientists who have been dismissing her work (one can dismiss someone's work by saying that it is useless or irrelevant or foolish and so on) will either:

(A) decide to continue with their dismissal by saying that the findings of the research are bad, biased, incorrect and so on, or

(B) decide to change their earlier stance if they are satisfied with the findings of the research and has proved them wrong.

The scientists who have been dismissing her work cannot continue to dismiss her work and yet be satisfied by the findings of the recent research. This is why Option 1 is not workable.

Option 2: Let us understand what research is meant for, by means of an illustration. Imagine that a beautician says that regular use of shampoo would make one highly vulnerable to pneumonia. What research would do is to see how many people use shampoo and what percentage of them contract pneumonia. Research would try to cover as large a number of persons as possible to find out whether this statement made by the beautician is correct or not. Research does not criticise. Research does not disparage anyone. If at all anyone can disparage the beautician who says such things about the use of shampoo, it can be those who are in favour of shampoo (or those who manufacture shampoo). Research is like an umpire at a cricket test. The umpire tells whether the batsman is out or not out. The umpire does not pooh-pooh the fielder who dropped the catch and tells him that he should first practice cricket with children. This means we are to see only Options 4 and 5 in view of the words *confirmed* and *invalidated* respectively in these options for the first blank in the given sentence.

If Option 4 were correct, since recent research has confirmed earlier criticism, then it would mean that the findings of this research says that the scientists have been right in dismissing her contributions. Why would a person *oppose* someone who says something in his favour? Can such a person ever be a scientist? This is why Option 4 will not do while Option 5 will be a perfect fit.

Answer 2

The word absolute has so many shades of meaning that we shall see in contextual usage as follows:

- If someone has *absolute* mastery over his subject, he has *complete* command over his subject.
- If the nearby factory makes *absolute* alcohol, it is making *pure* or *undiluted* alcohol.
- If the school bus driver tells you that he shall come to pick up your brother at 8 AM sharp tomorrow, his commitment about the time is *absolute (*meaning, *unchanging* or *not dependent on some circumstance).* If the driver then adds that he will reach at 8 AM sharp in case he wakes up in time, his commitment has changed from being *absolute* to being *conditional* or *qualified.*

Option 3 fits like a shot.

Answer 3

The word *limpid* has several shades of meanings that shall emerge in the following contexts:

- If you were to jump into some cool and *limpid* lake in the mountains for a swim, the water is clear and *free of suspended particles or turbid matter.*

- If you find that the film starlet's eyes are *limpid*, they seem to you to be *free from any guile or complication*.

Imagine that you are looking for evidence to validate your theory that Egyptians first designed kites. Someone brings you a newspaper clipping that Egyptians found a way of preserving human corpses. This clipping is not related to what you want and is therefore *irrelevant*.

The word *caustic* comes from *caustic soda* that has the property of corroding and biting into the skin. Thus, if someone is asked about the prospects in the country to which he has migrated and he says that (A) he went there because people told him that the streets here were paved with gold, (B) he soon found that the streets were *not* paved with gold; and (C) the streets were not *paved at all* and (D) in fact, *he has been paving the streets for eking out a living*, he is making *caustic* remarks about the prospects.

If someone gets up to make an *informal* speech, the speech is not structured or pre-arranged.

If someone comes to office in jeans and a t-shirt, he has dressed in an *informal, unconventional*, or *casual* manner.

If the boss has been having a love affair with his secretary and tells her that, in private, she may call him *Jim* instead of *Mr. James* in private, he is asking her to address him in an *informal* manner.

Substance has matter or weight. When you substantiate some statement with evidence, you make your statement solid. Something unsubstantiated is not solid. Therefore, when someone says that railway accidents have become an everyday affair and cannot cite an instance of a railway accident when asked as to when the last accident took place, his statement about railway accidents becoming everyday affairs is *unsubstantiated*.

Since limpid means clear or free from guile, *unclear* is its opposite. Hence Option 5.

Answer 4

Let us understand a few words here before we start analysing as to which option fits.

If someone has been throwing stones at the ripe mangoes hanging from the tree for an hour and then gives up because his arms are aching and yet he has not been able to bring down a single mango, it shows that he gives up because his efforts have been *futile* (meaning, *vain* or *fruitless* – not just because mango is a fruit; the reference to fruit is in the context that could also mean *result*).

If a boy and a girl living next door have been meeting in a clandestine manner, they are probably meeting secretly without the knowledge of their parents. Secret Service organisations generally gather classified information in a *clandestine* (or *cloak and dagger*) manner through informants who should not be detected.

Specious is something that seems true but in reality it is false (and therefore *deceptive* or *misleading*).

Imagine that a ruling monarch asks the prime minister as to why people in the kingdom are so skinny. Imagine that the minister tells him that the people do not have bread to eat. If the monarch then says that why don't they eat cake instead, the monarch is *apathetic* (or *indifferent*) to the condition of the people.

The word disingenuous has the prefix DIS- (that means *away from*) and the Latin root GEN- that means to *give birth*. The word *ingenuous* literally means *in the same way as born* or *simple, artless, sincere, honest, innocent* and so on, depending on the context. *Disingenuous* would mean *away from being honest or artless* and therefore *dishonest* or *deceiving*.

The word *dubious* comes from the word *doubt* and therefore means *doubtful, unsure, questionable* or *unclear* and so on.

With this, let us revert to the question at hand. When would one try to convince another person? You could, for example, try to convince the professor that you have completed the assignment by saying that you have already completed the assignment; the papers are in the cupboard but unfortunately you cannot find the key. If the senator wants to convince the public that he is not running for a second term, he is trying to tell them something that they do not believe. He could then tell the public that he does not want to run for a second term and yet collect money from sources that the public would not come to know. The moment, however, the public comes to know of his fund-raising sources, he cannot convince even an infant that he is not interested in running for the second term.

Now let us see the options:

Option 1: If this option were true and the senator has been collecting funds in a clandestine or secret manner, he could definitely convince the public that he is not interested in a second term. This is because no one knows that he is collecting finds for his campaign. His attempts will on the contrary be successful and not futile. This is why Option 1 will not do.

Option 2: If the senator has been making *sincere* (or *honest*) efforts, there is no need for him to try to *mislead* anyone. An honest person misleading anyone is like a contradiction in terms – something as self- contradictory as boiling ice cream. Option 2 will not do either.

Option 3: If the fund-raising efforts of the committee have been *apathetic*, who will give them a single farthing? If a person comes to you and says: "I have not eaten for a whole day. Give me some money so that I can buy a sandwich. However, if you do not want to give me money, I am not bothered." Will you give him any money? This is why Option 3 will not do either.

Option 4: If the fund-raising activities of the senator's campaign committee have been *public* (meaning, the public knows that he is collecting money for an election campaign) his efforts to convince the people that he is not interested in a second term will certainly be an act of dishonesty. Thus **Option 4** fits.

Option 5: If the fund-raising activities have been *dubious* (or *doubtful*, *questionable*) then again the senator cannot make straightforward or honest efforts; it will again be a huge self-contradiction. This is why Option 5 cannot work.

Answer 5

The word *parsimony* means *miserliness* and it comes from the French verb PARCERE that means to *refrain* or *spare*. Someone who refrains from spending or uses things too sparingly is a miser. Thus parsimony is the attribute that makes a miser.

Let us now see the options in which we shall understand the meanings of different words in their contextual usage.

Option 1: temerity: despot. Imagine that someone has just graduated from a medical school. He is watching a surgery being performed by a renowned surgeon. Suppose this young doctor tries to teach the experienced surgeon to make a proper incision. What the senior surgeon would probably do is that he would ignore the young doctor's *temerity*, or *recklessness*, or *impudence*, or *cheek*. Temerity makes people foolhardy or rash. A *despot* is an autocrat; he is tyrannical. However, the quality that makes a despot is *despotism* and not *temerity*. This is why Option 1 will not do.

Option 2: belligerence: traitor. The word *belligerence* comes from the Latin BELLUM that means *war*. The *inclination to quarrel* or *fight* at the slightest provocation is *belligerence*. A *traitor* is someone who betrays others. If someone wants to run away with someone else's money after betraying him, he needs to win the confidence of the other person before running away. If the other person does not give the traitor the custody of his money, what will the traitor run away with? Winning someone's trust cannot be done with belligerence. No one will trust someone quarrelsome. This is why Option 2 will not do.

Option 3: remorse: delinquent. When a prisoner has been feeling sorry for his crimes, he is stricken with *remorse* or *pangs of conscience*. A delinquent is a *criminal* or a *wrongdoer*. Remorse will, on the contrary, **reform** a delinquent, not make him a delinquent. Option 3 will not do either.

Option 4: equanimity: guardian. *Equanimity* means *balanced mind* or *composure*. A guardian is someone who has someone else's guardianship. Equanimity is the quality that makes people equanimous and composed but it does not make guardians. Option 4 will not do.

Option 5: rebelliousness: insurgent. A *rebel* is someone who rises in revolt against the government, or system, or his superiors. *Rebelliousness* makes someone a rebel. The word *insurgent* comes from the word *surge* that means to *rise* or *rush*. If one wants to revolt against anyone, he can hope to revolt against those who are oppressing him and therefore one can revolt from *within* and not form outside. An army general need not revolt against a major. He can issue legitimate **orders** to the major. Therefore an *insurgent* is an existing part of a system who wants to break away. Thus rebelliousness is what makes insurgents and hence **Option 5**.

Answer 6

If someone has a severe toothache and he takes an aspirin, he does this to *mollify* the pain or *reduce* its *intensity*. If the husband brings home a bouquet to *mollify* his wife's anger at having forgotten their anniversary, he is trying to *appease,* or *pacify* her, or *calm* her *down*. Therefore when someone tries to *mollify*, the idea is to **reduce** anger. With this let us turn to the options, which we shall take one by one.

Option 1: enlighten: seriousness. When you found that the lecture on the art of living could *enlighten* you, it means that the speaker threw light on various aspects about which you were in the dark. You were not very serious about spending quality time with your family. When the lecture did enlighten you, you have become more serious. Seriousness can be increased by enlightenment. This is why Option 1 will not do.

Had it been lighten in place of enlighten, Option 1 would have been correct. If you find that the people in the room that you have just entered are grim and serious and you crack a joke to **lighten** the atmosphere, you can reduce the seriousness in the room.

Option 2: nurture: dependency. When someone *nurtures* the desire to be the inter-collegiate boxing champion; he *fosters* this wish. If the Canadian Hockey Federation has engaged an Indian coach to *nurture* their team; he has been hired to *train* the team. If an eagle preys on a rabbit to feed her young ones; she does this to *nurture* her eaglets. It is possible that dependency may actually **increase** when someone nurtures another. This is why Option 2 will not do.

Option 3: hearten: dejection. If the news of my cousin passing the university examinations managed to *hearten* him considerably, it *made* him *happy*. He had failed at the first trial and this had made him *dejected* or *unhappy*. If something heartens someone, it could certainly reduce dejection and hence **Option 3** will fit.

Option 4: distract: confusion. The word distract has the prefix DIS- (that means *away from*) and the Latin root TRACT- (that means *draw*). Something that *draws away* (attention, for instance) would *distract*. Imagine that a group of students are on a walk in the forest. There is a small trail, which, if missed, would mean that they might even get lost in the forest. Someone points to the rarely seen Tiger Moth butterfly. They chase the butterfly over bush and boulder. When they give up the chase, the trail is nowhere to be seen. They are confused about which path to take. Therefore when you distract someone, there is every possibility of confusion increasing whereas we are looking for the reverse situation. Option 4 will not do.

Option 5: anticipate: outcome. The prefix ANTI- in the word *anticipate* is a variation of the prefix ANTE- that means before and if you *anticipate* that it will rain today, it means that you *take before* or *assume the happening of an event before it takes place*. If you find that the *outcome* of the World Cup Hockey final was decided by penalty strokes, it means that the *result* was decided through a tiebreaker. When you see clouds and anticipate rains, only two things may happen: it may rain or it may not rain. In either event you would be a mere spectator. You cannot influence rainfall unlike when you mollify to reduce anger. Option 5 will not do for that reason.

Answer 7

The prefix TRANS- means *across*. When you *transport* something you *carry it across*. If a dull phase in business is *transitory*, it is *brief, short, not permanent, ephemeral, transient*, and so on.

If someone 5-foot tall seems *distinctive* in a crowd of pigmies, his height is what *sets him apart from others*. You could see him a mile away. However if this person were to be in a group of six-footers, you may not see him at all. He does not stand apart. While his height remained unchanged, his *distinctiveness* was transitory. This is why *distinctive* cannot be the opposite of *transitory*.

When you learn a new language in a *gradual* manner; it means that you go step by step. (This is because the Latin root GRAD- means *step*. If the train moves at a *gradual* pace, it goes slowly. This may be a transitory phase since the track is under repairs. Once the track is repaired, the train may move like greased lightning. The earlier progress of the train was gradual. This was for a short while. it was transient. Something gradual may be transient as well. Thus Option 2 will not do.

When the pain in the jaw is *persistent*, it means that it has been there for long and may continue to be there unless you see a doctor about it. *Persistent* is the opposite of *transitory* and hence **Option 3**.

If the *distant* hill resort is *far away*, it cannot remain distant for long once you start driving towards it. Once you arrive there, it is not distant at all. Therefore merely because something is distant, it does not mean it is permanently distant. Thus *distant* cannot be the opposite of *transitory*.

The word *implicit* comes from the Latin root PLIC- that means *weave* or *fold*. When a boy asks his girlfriend as to what is it that she likes best about him and she points to his head, the boy may take this as an implicit acknowledgement of his intellectual genius. He may then tell her that he has been a brilliant student all along. She then tells him in clear tones that what she meant was his crew-cut hairstyle. He may feel a little peeved when her acknowledgement changes in substance when it transits from implicit to explicit. Something implicit may as well be transitory. Option 5 will not do either.

Answer 8

There could be only one out of three possible things that could have happened:

(A) The new work of the playwright would have added to the high regard that the critics had for the earlier work.

(B) The new work of the playwright would have diluted the high regard that the critics had for the earlier work.

(C) The new work of the playwright would not have made any difference to the level of the regard that the critics had for the earlier work.

If Option 1 were true then the admiration for the new work would mean that any one of (A) or (C) could have happened but not (B). When someone has not been paying the car loan instalments regularly and the bank sells the shares that he pledged as collateral to *offset* the dues, the idea is to *reduce* the dues. Option 1 will thus not do because the word *offset* would make it a case of (B) above, which it is clearly not.

As regards Option 2, high regard does not dampen anything. If you have high regard for your professor and he agrees to visit your home, you would probably go about cleaning up. Your enthusiasm would only increase. Option 2 will not do either.

As regards Option 3, it tallies on two counts: one, since there was *hostility* for the new work, it is a case of (B) and two, the word *tempered* in the second blank means *reduced*. Thus Option 3.

If the critics were disappointed with the new production, then their disappointment would be manifest either in their expressions or in their writing. How can be it disguised by the high regard for the earlier work? On the contrary when someone who is believed to be a veritable saint is found to be freely using foul language and reeling drunkenly in the street, whatever regard that one has for such a person will *evaporate instantly*. After it evaporates, what can it disguise?

Finally, as regards Option 5, if anything can *frustrate* one. Failures or impediments can frustrate someone. High regard can only enthuse someone; high regard cannot *frustrate* anyone.

Answer 9

There are several meanings of the word *lash*, both as a noun and as a verb. If theft is punished with six *lashes* in a certain country, it means that the thief is struck six times or flogged with a *whip*. If the playwright decides to *lash* out at his critics, he would *verbally attack* his critics. If the fishermen *lash* their boats to the pier, they *tie* it to a pole after they are through with the day's fishing. If the senior officer decides to *lash* the junior for his improper behaviour, he would *scold* or *admonish* the junior.

When you *embark* the ship, you *board* it. When you *disembark*, you *leave* or *get off* the ship or train or *alight* from the vehicle. However, one does not get tied with ropes when he boards a train, *disembark* is not the opposite of *lash*.

When the hospital authorities decide to *discharge* a patient finding that he is so fit that he does a thousand sit-ups every day and gorges a dozen eggs for breakfast, they decide that he should be allowed to go home. Since no patients (other than mental cases are tied to beds, *discharge* is not the opposite of *lash*.

When you see the school's elderly vice-principal and the young schoolmistress in each other's arms in a park and tell your classmates all about it in an excited tone, you *uncover* – or *expose* – their secret liaison. You do not *untie* them simply because they were not lashed together in the first place.

If you try to keep the secret about the vice-principal and the schoolmistress to yourself and find it difficult to hold, you may unburden it by telling it to the class. When someone has been having daily squabbles with his wife and decides to tell all about this turbulence in their relationship to a friend, one does not *untie* anything when telling someone about it.

If you unbind a parcel to access the chocolates, you untie the straps that hold the parcel. You *unlash* it. Thus Option 5.

Answer 10

The whetstone that is used for sharpening knife-edges has emery, a substance harder than steel. This emery *abrades* or *scrapes off* the surface of steel making it thinner and the knife sharper. Friction between the emery and the steel makes sparks fly off when the knife touches the whirling whetstone. When people get into a quarrel it is because friction between their viewpoints. They then use *abrasive* or *sharp, cutting* language. Thus friction is necessary if you want something to be abraded. With this we may turn to the options and see which one will fit in.

Option 1: refined: combustion. When cooking oil is passed through several filters it becomes *free of impurities* (and therefore *pure*); it becomes *refined*. When some learned person speaks in a *polished* manner, polite and soft, he is a *refined* person. The automobile that we drive runs on petrol which is burnt inside an internal combustion engine that powers the vehicle. *Combustion* is the process of *burning*. Combustion, however, is not necessary for something to be refined. The refined gentleman does not have to go through combustion in order to become refined, does he? Thus Option 1 will not do.

Option 2: attenuated: coagulation. When someone spends a small fortune on beer and even then does not get a kick, he is probably drinking *attenuated* beer where the alcoholic content in beer is less and hence its kick is *weakened*. I remember having once travelled by ship and was frequently seasick. I reached the destination considerably *attenuated*, or I had *become* quite *thin* when I reached. When you put a dash of curd into milk and let it set overnight, you find that the milk has *changed from a liquid to a solid state*. The milk is said to have *coagulated*. When something coagulates, it may become more solid than before and hence the relationship between attenuate and coagulate is the reverse of that in the original pair.

Option 3: diluted: immersion. When the hostess at a big party is afraid that her husband may topple over after drinking a few glasses of liquor, she may ask the waiter to see that the liquor served to her husband has a lot more water. Whatever her husband drinks is considerably *watered down*, *weakened in force* or *diluted*. Deep-frying involves complete *immersion* (meaning, *plunging in* or *submersion*) of food articles in hot oil. Even learning to swim may mean experiencing immersion in water. If human beings were to get *diluted* or *watered down* when immersed in water, we may dissolve in swimming pools. This is why Option 3 will not work.

Option 4: strengthen: compression. When the army decided to *strengthen* its presence on the border, it decided to send more men or *augment* its *force*. When the text of a speech is so long that the audience is likely to snore away while the speaker is halfway through the speech, the speech needs to be *compressed* or *squeezed* or *abridged*. Compression is the act of pressing together with the object of reducing the volume of the material such as in the case of making cotton bales through *compression* by *squeezing together* huge volumes of cotton to make small, easily manageable bales. It is possible to strengthen things such as the presence of the military on the border without compressing the army men. Option 4 will not do either.

Option 5: desiccated: dehydration. When you find that a container of *desiccated* garlic is being exported, it is the dehydrated garlic that is sent out. The word *desiccate* has the prefix DE- meaning down and comes from the French verb SICCARE that means *to dry*. The idea in drying one's clothes is to remove water from them. When a child suffers from *dehydration* or *loss of water*, the child is administered water with sugar and salt to promote water retention. *Dehydration* is what makes things *desiccated*. Thus Option 5.

Answer 11

Since we are told that the physicists' theories about release of neutrinos into space is given in the passage, we have no choice but to scan the passage and find out where these theories are mentioned. Scanning the passage reveals that these theories are mentioned in the following words in the first paragraph in the passage: "Physicists believe that colliding nuclei of hydrogen atoms in the Sun and other stars release neutrinos that emerge from the stars and stream into space. Although unsure about neutrinos' specific properties, physicists reason that if neutrinos possess mass and are therefore susceptible to gravity, millions of years from now the countless neutrinos that have been streaming outward through space would over time cause the expanding universe to slow, stop, and begin collapsing inwards".

The salient aspects of these theories are summarised as per follows:

- Colliding nuclei of hydrogen atoms in the Sun and the stars release neutrinos into space.
- Neutrinos would cause the expanding universe to slow, stop, and begin collapsing inwards.

Now let us see which of the options will strengthen or support the theories about release of neutrinos into space.

Option 1: Research in space fails to confirm that neutrinos are travelling in a direction outward from the sun.

If the neutrinos, whatever they may be, wish to entertain any hopes of causing the expanding universe to slow, they have to stream through space. For any neutrino moving around the sun, there are only two choices: into the sun or outward from the sun into space. If this option were correct and if neutrinos are not confirmed on the holiday tours leaving the sun, how can they go into space at all? If they cannot go out into space, how can they ever hope to begin slowing down the universe? Option 1 will not do.

Option 2: Underground neutrino detectors confirm the existence of neutrinos in earth's atmosphere in much larger quantities than the theories anticipated.

If the neutrinos wish to slow down the space, they have to go out into the space. The earth's atmosphere is not space. If there is much larger presence of neutrinos in the earth's atmosphere, then the neutrinos are loafing around in the wrong place. The theories want them to stream around in space and not in the earth's atmosphere. If parents theorise that their children will develop great thigh muscles when they cycle several times daily around the track but instead the children develop huge paunches watching television, the theories of the parents would go wrong for sure.

Option 3: Neutrinos are invariably detected wherever there is a high concentration of cosmic rays and electromagnetic radiation in earth's atmosphere.

Neutrinos are expected to stream out from stars and the Sun into space. Once neutrinos realize the fact that the Earth's atmosphere is not space, only then will this theory be strengthened.

Option 4: Experiments designed to measure and capture any recurring patterns in the flashes of light created by neutrinos revealed that neutrinos are also produced by colliding nuclei of other elements.

The passage tells us that neutrinos are produced by colliding nuclei of hydrogen atoms and when they stream out into space, they will – over time of course – stop space from growing. This option talks about neutrinos produced by nuclei of **other elements** whereas the theory is about neutrinos produced by nuclei of **hydrogen atoms**. Option 4 is not even relevant.

Option 5: Experiments in which the nuclei of hydrogen atoms are made to collide under conditions presumed to exist at the Sun's centre result in the release and escape of neutrinos

Here scientific evidence tells that neutrinos will stream into space. If a convict escapes after he has been serving rigorous imprisonment for the last twenty years, where will he escape to? Will he run away to the prison toilet to apply rouge on his cheeks? No way. He is bound to run out from the prison; so will neutrinos run outward from the Sun into space when they escape from the Sun. Thus **Option 5**.

Answer 12

First, let us understand what being affected by gravity means. Imagine that a young man is slim and has supple knees and rosy cheeks. He can bound over fences and hedges. When he leaps up, gravity pulls him down. He is supple and cares two hoots about gravity. He tills a plot of land. He brims with the confidence that he shall toil and grow bountiful crops and from the money that he shall earn, he shall buy the neighbouring plots and his estates shall expand. He toils hard for a few years and indeed buys more land. Then imagine that the boy takes to food in a big way. He eats like a man possessed. A few years later he has a huge paunch, spindly legs and even getting up from the easy chair makes him gasp for breath, so affected is he by gravity that affects him more and more as he grows heavier. Can he now make his estate expand? This is why Option 4 will fit like a shot.

Is it necessary to presume that merely because he has become awfully obese and therefore affected by gravity, the young man in the story also knows where his great grandfather came from (and therefore has information about his origin)? Option 1 will not work.

If a dozen such lads as the fatso in our story have been affected by gravity there is likelihood that they will not even be seen at the local sports contest, let alone being seen in abundance on locations other than their easy chairs. This is why Option 2 will not work either.

If the fatso in our story can produce anything it is snores. In order to produce flashes of light one would need tremendous energy and the capacity to move with great speed. Option 3 will not do.

If the fatso in our story were unaffected by someone telling him to go slow on hogging, will he ever be able to expand his estate. For similar reasons, Option 5 will not work.

Answer 13

If one were to see a toddler strumming a guitar and conclude that the little fellow has a *penchant* for music, it means that he has an *inclination*, or *liking* for music. If a family were to prepare food with so much chilly in the curry that the first morsel makes one's hair stand on end, the family has a *penchant* or *passion* for spicy food. Whatever is opposite of *penchant* must mean *no inclination* or *no liking* for something. Let us now see the options.

Option 1: retreat. When the rain floods the countryside and the flood waters recede when it stops, it *retreats* not because the water has no liking for the land. When a soldier *retreats* in the face of heavy enemy fire, he does so for the love of his life. For this reason, Option 1 will not do.

Option 2: aversion. The word *aversion* has the prefix A- (that means *away from*) and the Latin root VERT- that means *turn*. When you don't like your office job and turn away from it, you have an *aversion* for that job. *Aversion* is the opposite of *penchant* and thus **Option 2**.

Option 3: travesty. Imagine a person from an ethnic minority being tried in a court of law for an alleged crime against someone from the ethnic majority. If the courts invariably rule in favour of the ethnic majority, the trial of the accused will be a *travesty* or *mockery* of justice. The travesty of justice is not because the courts do not like justice. They do not know what justice is. This is why Option 3 will not do.

Option 4: betrayal. Imagine that as part of the election manifesto of a political party, it promises it will not privatise the country's public enterprises. After it assumes power it begins the process of their privatisation. If the opposition now says that this is a *betrayal* of their election promises, they mean that this is *an act of treachery*. The reason for such so-called *betrayal* may not be because of one's dislike either towards election promises or towards public enterprises. The reason may be because the treasury is empty and privatisation may bring in more money to tide over the financial difficulties, or because the public enterprises are making huge losses and draining the government exchequer. This is why Option 4 will not do either.

Option 5: prodigality. Someone who spends money extravagantly and wastefully is a *prodigal*. Someone who has wandered aimlessly and returned home is also referred to as the prodigal. *Prodigality* is the quality that makes people prodigal. A person who spends money recklessly does not do so because he does not have a passion for money. If that were the case he would save money, not spend it. He would then be a miser and not a prodigal. This is why Option 5 will not do.

Answer 14

Since we are asked something about the 1960's view of interaction between Puritan missionaries and Native Americans in colonial New England, we may not waste time and start scanning the passage to find out where this view is mentioned.

We shall find these views in the last sentence of the first paragraph in the passage, summarised as per follows: In the 1960's scholars saw the Puritan missionaries as *cultural imperialists* who imposed an ethnocentric worldview on Native Americans in colonial New England, and they portrayed Native Americans as not resisting the assaults on their culture.

The above are the views of the scholars, the principal aspects of these views being: (A) The Puritan missionaries imposed their culture on Native Americans, and (B) the Native Americans surrendered to this cultural invasion meekly. We have now to see of the following was what the author felt in the matter:

Option 1: It is more persuasive than the view held in the 1980's

The view held in the 1980's is given in the second paragraph of the passage as follows: "In contrast, the perspective that emerged among scholars in the 1980's held that Native Americans in colonial New England were not passive in the face of "cultural imperialism"; rather, they acted in a variety of ways to maintain their cultures". If someone does even a single thing – leave alone a variety of things – to maintain his or her own culture, he/she can never be blamed for surrendering meekly to invasion by another culture. For example, there is a tribe in which all adult males wear a beard. This is a part of the tribe's culture. There is a city nearby where all adult males are clean shaven. If a tribal youth grows up and wears a beard, he cannot be said to have meekly surrendered to the invasion by the culture of the nearby city.

It may be noted that the 1980's views are entirely different from the 1960's views. One can compare between two of the same kind. One view could be more persuasive than the other if the both were in favour of the same thing. When the two views are so different, the question of one being compared with another does not arise.

Option 2: It does not accurately describe the experience of one particular group of Native Americans. From the passage we have inferred that: (A) The Puritan missionaries imposed their culture on Native Americans and (B) the Native Americans surrendered to this cultural invasion meekly. Since, Native Americans, as a whole, surrendered to the cultural invasion of Puritan missionaries, this option seems to be the one to mark as correct provided no other option fits the bill hereafter.

Option 3: It fails to take account of research done on the motivations of Puritan missionaries. Someone invades another with a view to gain dominance over him. A cultural invasion has the motive of bringing another group of persons under one's culture. The motivations – meaning, the factors that motivated an invasion – are clear. Hence Option 3 is not correct.

Option 4: It is credible because it is based on Native American viewpoints about interaction with Puritan missionaries. The whole thing is of scholars' views and not Native Americans' viewpoints. If this was about Native Americans' views, then Native Americans should have referred to themselves as *we* in the passage. Hence Option 4 is not true either.

Option 5: It is definitive because it is critical of Puritan missionaries' attempts to impose their culture. There is no criticism of Puritan missionaries attempts to impose their culture. It may be seen that the 1960's views are those of scholars and not of the author. Option 5 will not work for that reason.

Thus Option 2.

Answer 15

Let us go from option to option in regard to what the passage is primarily concerned with and see which one of them would fit.

Option 1: assessing the impact of particular religious beliefs and activities on specific historic events. For this option to be correct, particular religious beliefs must have an impact on specific historical events and not the reverse. If you see the passage, first of all, whatever impact is being talked about is on the culture of Native Americans and not on specific historical events. Secondly, there is only one specific historical event that is discussed here. It is the event at Martha's Vineyard where one missionary set out to convert a tribe and imparted alphabetic literacy. The tribe accepted Christianity wholeheartedly. If at all, it was this historical event that influenced people of particular religious beliefs and not the reverse.

If you see this option from the point of view of logic alone, historical events can have influence on particular religious beliefs not vice versa. If, for example, some religious sect believes that its members should invariably carry a dagger on their person at all times, it is because frequent attacks on them in the past would have dictated this belief. Option 1 gets ruled out for this reason alone.

Option 2: Developing a theoretical framework within which to determine the effects of interactions between different cultures.

Imagine that a tribe has been living in the heart of a jungle and not wearing anything other than smiles. Some city dwellers arrive in their midst. They teach the tribe how to make clothes and wear them. The tribe learns the art. It is the effect of the interaction between the two cultures. But the tribe still wears nothing. It means that the interactions have had no effect. Back to the passage, there is a clear assertion at the end of the passage that the tribe were able to remain culturally independent even after conversion to Christianity. It means that there was no cultural change in them. One can possibly think of a framework to study some change or complete change. What theoretical framework would you need to study no change?

Option 3: Analysing a theory that explains a particular cultural practice and placing the theory in a broad historical context.

About culture, there is this assertion at the end of the passage that some tribe remained culturally independent. There is no mention of any cultural practice. If a theory analyses any cultural practice it must state what cultural practice it wants to analyse. If a psychoanalyst wants to analyse a patient, there must be a patient in the first place. This is why Option 3 will not do.

Option 4: Depicting particular historical events and determining their causes.

There is only one particular historical event described here and that is about Martha's Vineyard. Secondly whatever is discussed here is about the effect of the event and not its causes. This is why Option 4 will not do either.

Option 5: Describing successive interpretations of historical events and supporting one interpretation by reporting a specific situation.

If one sees the text of the passage, there are different interpretations – or scholars' views – of historical events:

Before 1960s, missionaries were described as benevolent.

In the 1960s, it was felt that missionaries forced cultural change upon Native Americans.

In the 1980s it was felt that the Native Americans took care to preserve their culture in spite of the coercion from missionaries.

The specific event of Martha's Vineyard has been taken as an illustration to support the 1980s view that the Native Americans remained culturally independent. Option 5 fits on all counts.

Answer 16

If we see the final paragraph of the passage we see that alphabetic literacy proved useful in conducting diplomatic correspondence, establishing a legal system, and keeping written records of court decisions. While accepting English rule, the Wampanoag of Martha's Vineyard were able to remain essentially self-governing and culturally independent. The scholarly view of the 1980s is that the Native Americans took care to preserve their culture in spite of the coercion from missionaries. This view is supported in the final paragraph. The phrase "identifying consequences of something that is consistent with the view of someone" means "supporting something". When I say that you should not drink milk when you have a tummy upset and some one says that he too had a tummy upset after he had milk, he is supporting my view since his contention is consistent with mine. This is why Option 5 fits like a shot.

Answer 17

When the question requires that we consult the passage about the larger effort of which alphabetical literacy was a part, we have no choice but to refer to the passage. We see the objective of imparting alphabetical literacy in the following words at paragraph 1 in the passage: *One goal of Puritan missionaries in colonial New England was to teach Native Americans to read and write in English or in native languages transcribed into the English alphabet. These efforts to teach reading and writing using English characters (alphabetic literacy) were an integral part of the larger framework of religious proselytism.* The word *proselytism* means the *practice of conversion* and hence Option 1 fits like a shot.

If, for example, you wish to encourage the people of Zululand to develop legal institutions, teaching the English language to the Zulu people is not necessary at all. The courts may conduct cases in the Zulu language with great ease.

First of all, English is not the only language in Europe. Secondly, for conducting political correspondence or diplomatic relations or fostering cultural relations between Native Americans and Europeans, it is not necessary to teach English to a large number of persons. If some tribe from the deep rain forests of the Amazon basin wishes to correspond with the Europeans, it will suffice if one or two people from the tribe go over to a few different European countries and learn a few European languages such as French, German and English. If, for example, Spain has diplomatic relations with Kenya, is it necessary for each Spaniard to know the Swahili language?

Answer 18

The answer has to be evaluated from the viewpoint of the second blank for which we shall have to appreciate the fact that the word in the second blank has to describe the result of *coercion*.

The word *coercion* means *force* or *duress* or *compulsion*. The confession from an accused is not admitted as evidence in courts if it is in the presence of the police. It is because such a confession may have been under *coercion* (meaning, the confession may have been obtained under *compulsion* by the police after bashing the accused black and blue).

Now let us go form option to option, seeing only the word eligible for the second blank.

Option 1: understood. Suppose an accused is in a police custody for attempted housebreaking. Will the investigating police officer wink at the accused and ask smilingly whether he has *understood* that he has to confess? Will there be the need for any coercion?

Option 2: imposed. When punishment is imposed on a person, he does not have choice; it is *forced upon* him. If a murderer were asked as to what punishment would he like, he might even suggest ten sit-ups. Will he ever opt for hanging? Something can only be *imposed* or *forced upon* through *coercion* or *compulsion*. Option 2 is to be marked as correct.

Option 3: conveyed. When you want to convey something to someone, there need not be any force at all.

- Someone can wink at his girlfriend and show two fingers for two o'clock and convey the time when he will meet her in the park.
- The news of graduating successfully can be conveyed to a girl by e-mail without the slightest need for any force.

This is why Option 3 will not do either.

Option 4: captured. It is possible for a forceful political regime to capture an author. But no matter how coercive is the regime it *cannot capture any of the works of an author*. Works are non-living things. Can you capture carrots, for instance? Option 4 will not do for this reason.

Option 5: demanded. There is no need to assume that whatever is *demanded* is with force. If there is demand for the new flavour of ice cream, people do not twist the arms of the manufacturer when they want it. Option 5 will not do either.

Answer 19

Let us understood what *decorum* means. If *decorum* or *polite behaviour* requires that you greet your teachers, then you say a soft *good morning, teacher* when you meet the drawing teacher in the corridor. If army *decorum* requires that a general visiting your unit must be saluted with a volley of eleven gunshots, then army *protocol* stipulates this manner of greeting. The opposite of *decorum* can be something that is not in keeping with norms of good behaviour. With this let us see the options.

Option 1: constant austerity. The word *austerity* has several shades of meaning that we shall see from appropriate contexts as follows:

- If the professor exuded an air of *austerity* around him so that no one dared to joke with him, he gave an air of *sternness of manner or disposition*.
- If the budget for the school's Annual Day celebrations has been trimmed to half its last-year level for reasons of *austerity*, it is for *economising*.
- If the drawing room at the neighbour's has only a few cane chairs and no carpet and is thus marked by *austerity*, it is marked by *severe simplicity*.

There is no reason to believe that austerity necessarily means something that is not proper. The neighbour's drawing room may be sparsely furnished because they wish to settle overseas and may move as soon as they get the visas.

Option 2: false humility. *Humility* means *humbleness*. When someone displays *false humility*, it becomes apparent that the humbleness is a mere show. But then in order that the show passes off as humility, the fellow would have to be polite, even if he is actually a big braggart. This is why Option 2 will not do.

Option 3: impropriety. The word *impropriety* that means *lack of propriety* has the prefix IM- that means not and comes from the word *proper*, which is something that we all know. This is the precise opposite of decorum and hence **Option 3**.

Option 4: incompetence. *Lack of capability* is *incompetence*. A polite person may have been recruited as a security guard but he may break out in sweat when he reads a ghost story. On night patrol he may shriek and pass out when he sees someone passing by in a white shawl. His *incompetence* for the job on hand would become clear. People who are incompetent may, in order to retain their jobs, become servile sycophants of their bosses so that they do not get the boot. There is no impoliteness whatsoever implied in incompetence.

Option 5: petulance. *Petulance* is that quality that makes people *petulant* or *peevish* or *irritable over trifling matters*. If a child has been asking for chocolates too often, the father may say *no chocolates for the whole week*. Irritated, the child may sulk and not speak for a while and thereby display *petulance*. There would be something indecorous if the child were to use foul language. But when there is no speaking, there need not be any presumed impropriety.

Answer 20

Let us understand some of the words before we start seeing which option would fit the bill.

If compulsory military service after graduation is *odious* to the youth, it is *hateful* or *offensive* to them; it brings up *disgust* in them. Thus something *odious* results in *disgust* for it. With this, let us now see which option will fit the bill.

Option 1: awesome: resentment. Something inspires *awe* or *wonder* in us when either its size or beauty or majesty *impresses* us. When someone makes such a remark that makes you feel like giving him one tight slap, the remark brings *resentment* or *dislike*. One has to be a veritable moron if he were to develop resentment at seeing a girl of awesome elegance. Option 1 will not do.

Option 2: normal: banality. When someone is of *normal* height, he is of the height that is the norm or *average* for people of his age group. When someone has been quarrelling for long with his neighbour and now they are on *normal* terms, their relations are now *adjusted*. If some young lad had a fabulous voice but if he got lost in the *banality* of his office routine, it means that he could not go places in the world of music because he could not step out of the *dullness* of his office job. Something normal may not cause banality at all. It may be normal for a super heavyweight boxer to have biceps that make the trunk of an oak tree seem trifling. If, however, one were to ask him as to what is he doing with these *trifling* or *humdrum* biceps, one punch from him would be disastrous. Option 2 will not do either.

Option 3: scarce: poverty. When something is in *short supply* or *rarely seen*, it could be termed *scarce*. If man-eating tigers have become *scarce*, it does not result in poverty. Option 3 will not do for this simple reason.

Option 4: immobile: stability. Something that is capable of moving or being moved easily is mobile; *immobile* is the precise opposite of mobile. Someone who has had a stroke of paralysis may become bedridden and *immobile*. The word *stability* has several shades of meaning. *Stability* is *steadiness*. When the prices of vegetables move in a small band, there is *price stability* in vegetables. If the flats have withstood the severe earthquake, you are convinced of the *stability* or *solidity* of their structures. If an unknown gentleman with a *salt and pepper* moustache (meaning, *with some grey hair*) in your compartment were to put his tongue out at you every now and then and make faces, it would make you start doubting his *stability* or *sanity*. It is not as if when something becomes immobile, it brings stability. One can have a stroke and become immobile due to paralysis and yet there may be wild fluctuations in blood pressure (meaning, no stability at all). Option 4 will not do either.

Option 5: menacing: fear. If your town has been facing the *menace* of cholera for the past week, it has been facing the *threat* of cholera. If someone has been waving a stick at another with *menacing* looks, this is an *indication of his hostile intent*. Something menacing may cause fear and hence **Option 5**.

Answer 21

Let us understand some words in this question from their following contexts and then see which Option fits in.

- If you were to see vast hutments at a number of places in a developed country, this would be *paradoxical* or *self-contradicting*, *enigmatic* or *absurd*.
- If you find someone sleeping with his eyes open, it is *paradoxical* or *strange* considering that one naturally shuts one's eyes when sleeping.
- It is *axiomatic* (meaning, something so *widely accepted* that there is no need to prove it) that when two integers are multiplied, the product is always an integer. It is axiomatic that the whole is greater than any of its parts.
- Water normally contracts on cooling. Water when cooled below zero degrees shows *anomalous* or *strange* behaviour. Instead of contracting, it actually expands between zero and minus four degrees Celsius.
- If a person were to collect books on a basis that is *irrelevant* to the merit of their literary content, he probably might be guided by issues such as wanting to buy a copy from the first edition, or handmade paper used in the book or the book bearing the signature of a renowned person and so on - things that are not *pertinent* or *germane* to the literary content of the book.
- If the dark skies are *portentous* of a storm, they are *indicative* or *forewarning* of a storm. The word *portentous* comes from the word *portend* that has the prefix PRO- (which is a variation of the prefix PRO- that means *forward* as in the case of *protrude* and *project* or *before* as in the case of *proactive*) and the Latin root TENT- (that means *hold*). When you see the dark clouds and say that they *portend* rain, you say that in the time to come the clouds will rain or pour forward what they *hold*. When the majesty of some sculpture *holds* you *before* (meaning, in front of the sculpture), then the sculpture is *portentous* or *majestic* or *awesome*.

With this, let us see which option will work.

Option 1: As we have seen, paradox occurs when the reverse of what is intended happens. You expect a rich country to be free of hutments and yet paradoxically there are huts in plenty. Generally, there is *greater* perceived risk of automobile accidents in densely populated areas. So it would be *paradoxical* if it were to found that there is a *lower* risk of automobile accidents in densely populated areas. Part one of the sentence talks about densely populated areas whereas part two talks about sparsely populated areas. There is no paradox here.

Option 2: An axiom is something that is generally believed to be true and needs no proof. In densely populated areas, the number of cars and the number of pedestrians would be more whereas the space for driving would be less and hence there seems sufficient reason to believe that there would be a greater risk of accidents in densely populated areas. The word axiomatic can fit here very well.

Option 3: As we have seen in the contextual usages of the word anomaly, it is similar to paradox; if paradox will not do, anomaly will not do either.

Option 4: When both the regions have risk of accidents, then both are relevant in the sentence. There is nothing irrelevant.

Option 5: Serious automobile accidents are neither awesome or majestic nor possible to foretell in any way. This is why Option 5 will not do.

Option 2 is to be marked as correct.

Answer 22

We have seen the instance of anomaly – meaning, *departure from normal* – in the previous answer where we read that water *normally* contracts on cooling but when cooled below zero degrees it actually expands between zero and minus four degrees Celsius thus exhibiting *anomalous* or *strange* behaviour.

If *anomaly* is departure from the norms, the opposite of anomaly could only be *conforming* with norms. Hence Option 2.

As regards Option 1, estimates are not norms. If you estimate that the company whose shares you have bought by the hundreds will post ten-fold increase in profit, then it is not a norm for the company to register such increases in profit. It is in business. It may incur huge losses as well. When you derive something, you derive it from the origin. Thus *derivation* can only be an extraction from *root* or *origin*. When there is *derivation* of joy from the work that you do, you *extract* joy from the work. It is not normal to make lewd remarks at girls passing by. Yet eve-teasers derive joy from doing so.

Answer 23

The word *narcissist* comes from the legendary Greek boy *Narcissus* who fell in love with his own reflection in the mirror (or was it water?). A *narcissist* is someone who *admires himself too much* or who is an *egotist* or *self-conceited* or *vain*. Quite clearly, a narcissist is someone who is self-absorbed. We must thus look for synonymous relationships. Now let us see the options.

Option 1: malcontent: resigned. The word *malcontent* has the prefix MAL- (that means *bad* or *ill*) and comes from the word *content* (that means *satisfied*). Someone *dissatisfied* or *complaining* is *malcontent*. A fellow may get more salary than what he has been getting in his present employment. He resigns not because he is *malcontent*; on the contrary he is happy to move to another job where he is going to earn not just bread but butter and jam as well. Since the two need not be synonymous, Option 1 will not do.

Option 2: braggart: detestable. A braggart is one who boasts about himself. One would not like to be on a long journey in a seat next to a braggart. A braggart is detestable but the reverse need not be true just as it is true that all cows are animals but the reverse of it is not true (all animals are not cows, are they?) One can detest someone who has dressed shabbily. One can detest someone who is a sycophant (who does no bragging at all; he in fact puffs up the other person's ego and not his own). Since braggart and detestable are not synonymous, Option 2 will not do either.

Option 3: cynic: pensive. A *cynic* is someone who is suspicious of everything. He is a merchant of doom. You tell him that our country will return with thirty Olympic gold medals and he says that we will be lucky if we can win a single bronze although he doubts it very much. Someone who has been aspiring to kill a tiger succeeds and then seeing the great animal lying at his feet, he may become *pensive* (meaning, *thoughtful*) at having caused the death of such a majestic animal. A cynic thinks negatively all the time. The pensive person standing near the tiger gasping for his last breath may decide never to do this again nor allow anyone else to kill a tiger. He may have remorse, repentance, or the resolve to protect the earth's heritage. He may think positively. Option 3 will not do since there is no implied synonymy in the relationship between a cynic and someone who is pensive.

Option 4: sycophant: obsequious. A *sycophant* is an *obsequious* or *servile* person forever ready to *dance attendance* on someone, waiting to hear his command. The relationship here is synonymous and hence Option 4.

Option 5: perfunctionist: incomplete. If you have perfunctorily seen the prospectus of the school that you plan to get in through a competitive test, you have seen it superficially; you have not studied it in detail. If you find that what the cook has made is yuck, it may be because he has cooked things *perfunctorily* (or *mechanically*, *without interest* or *enthusiasm*). A perfunctionist may or may not leave things incomplete, like the cook who has cooked five courses (that may mean two more than what you asked him to make).

Answer 24

If a storm *abates*, its force *decreases* till it finally has no force. This is the relationship between *abate* and *force*. Now let us turn to the options.

Option 1: corrode: acid. When the acid from the chemicals factory corrodes the plaster of the homes nearby, it eats into the plaster. The relationship between *corrode* and *acid* is that of effect and cause. When an acid corrodes, it does not decrease the effect of acid. It only does what an acid is supposed to do in the first place.

Option 2: grind: powder. When you grind wheat for example, you actually *increase* the amount of powder content in the wheat that you grind. This is why Option 2 will not do.

Option 3: congeal: viscosity. The word *congeal* has the prefix CON- (that means *thoroughly* or *together*) and comes from the French verb GELARE that means *freeze*. Therefore when something *congeals*, it only *thickens*. If snakebite *congeals* the blood, the blood becomes thicker and thus blockages develop in the heart leading eventually to death unless there is timely medical attention. What happens when the blood congeals is that its viscosity (or its state of semi-fluidity) actually increases and not the reverse as the relationship expresses in the original pair.

Option 4: intensify: hue. Fundamentally, when something *intensifies*, it worsens in condition (if the pain intensifies, it increases). Thus Option 4 will not do either.

Option 5: decelerate: speed. When you press the accelerator in your car (provided of course you are driving and not playing cops and thieves in the car parked in your garage), the speed increases. When you decelerate, the speed decreases. The relationship is similar to that expressed in the original pair and hence Option 5.

Answer 25

The word wax has several shades of meaning that we shall see hereunder in context:

A. You must have seen a wax candle, it is made of beeswax.

B. When you say that the moon has begun to *wane*, you mean it has begun to *decrease* in size but when you see it has begun to *wax*, you mean it has started to *increase* in size.

C. If someone has got into a *wax* at the bill that has some item that he has not ordered, he is in a state of *great annoyance*.

From the options, it would become evident that only the *verb* connotation of the word wax is to be reckoned since all the options are verbs.

When you *disconnect*, you do not necessarily do something opposite of growing. When you disconnect the oxygen supply of a patient who is now fully recovered, you may actually see improvement in the fellow's condition as soon as he gets up from the sickbed. When you *disconnect* the oxygen supply of a patient who has become one of the morning stars; there will be neither growth nor increase.

When you *decrease* the food supply of the boy who has a king-sized paunch while in his teens, you diminish the supply. This is the precise opposite of wax and hence Option 2.

When somebody *supplements* his income by singing to the accompaniment of a harmonica in the street (something that beggars frequently do), he is doing this in order to *increase* his income not decrease it. Hence Option 3 will not do.

When the children ask their father to loosen his purse, their intention is to tell him to *increase* their pocket allowance and not decrease it. Hence Option 4 will not do either. When you squander money, you spend money but do not decrease it. If you spend X units of money, these X units go to the shopkeeper. If you earn Y units of money it merely passes hands. It goes from the employer's hands to your hands. Money in supply remains unaffected whether you squander the money or earn it. Hence Option 5 will not do.

Answer 26

When the question pertains to the use of essay techniques in the short stories of writers such as Carver and Beattie, we would do well to run our eyes up and down the passage and see where the use of these essay techniques are mentioned and we shall see the following highlights about the essay techniques:

- Essay techniques make the work of Carver and Beattie bulge with excessive details about arcane processes and the external appearance of people and places.
- The use of detail that has also been made in certain 19th Century British novels makes current fiction seem old-fashioned.
- The characters in such stories are often flat, shallow and psychologically uncomplicated.
- The work often becomes a report of mundane experiences.
- This type of story is enjoying critical favour in part because few critics have seen beyond its apparent virtue – the dazzling surface of its prose.

Now let us see the options:

Option 1: Their use represents a step backward because it heightens the short story's similarity to the 19-century essay.

Whatever has been mentioned about the 19th century is about 19th century novels and not short stories or essays. This means that this option is not to be considered at all.

Option 2: Their use has emphasised description at the expense of other important elements of fiction.

When the passage says that the essay bulges with the use of excessive detail about arcane (meaning, *mysterious*) processes and the external appearance of people, quite obviously the description is at the expense of other important elements of fiction. When someone returns from a trip to a workshop on Advanced Spirituality and his kith and kin are sitting around him to know what esoteric aspects came to light in the workshop, they would feel like kicking him in the ribs if he persisted with how the cooking suited him and how uncomfortable the beds were and what all vegetables grew in the kitchen garden and so on. Option 2 will do very well and we may keep this option in mind.

Option 3: Their use has produced a style of writing sufficiently dazzling to compensate for the psychological shallowness of such stories.

The passage states that the use of unnecessary details often makes the work a report of mundane (or *insignificant*) experiences. Few (meaning, *not many*) critics have been able to see beyond the dazzling surface of its prose. This means that the fellow who came back from the camp on Advanced Spirituality has mentioned so many complicated names of French cuisine and in such ornate (or *flowery*) language that the poor listeners have not been able to understand that he is talking through his hat. The dazzling prose has actually *hidden* the shallowness of the style of writing and *not compensated* for the shallowness. This is why Option 3 will not do.

Option 4: Their use signals the demise of the short story as a distant form of fiction.

About the short story, the passage says that it is merely a particular form of fiction currently enjoying critical favour. If the demise (or *death*) of something is signalled – like the doctors telling the incurable patient's family to take him home and let him rest there - the fellow who is dying cannot be expected to get up from his death bed and do breathtaking acrobatics on the trapeze so that the spectators give him a standing ovation. Nothing can enjoy critical flavour (meaning, *appreciation from critics*) and yet be dying.

Option 5: Their use has weakened the traditional emphasis on characters in a short story, pointing instead to a new emphasis on plots.

If the fellow who is just back from a camp on Advanced Spirituality talks all the while about vegetables and hard beds and French cuisine, he has nothing of substance to say. This means he has no plot at all. One can put an emphasis on plots, if one can come up with plots in the first place. This is why Option 5 will not do. Mark Option 2.

Answer 27

Let us see which option will fit in and thus let us go from option to option.

Option 1: appraising a particular style of writing present in current short fiction.

The passage is certainly focussed on a particular style of writing involving excessive details so that the essay seems like a huge report about some mundane matter. No other style is even mentioned in the passage. Secondly there are critical observations about the style that lead one to infer that the passage is an evaluation or review of a particular style of writing. Option 1 could fit the bill very well.

Option 2: asserting that certain short story writers' use of essay technique has made the short story indistinguishable from the essay.

All that the passage says is that certain writers use techniques associated with the essay. So if a cook makes fried chicken and also vegetable fried rice, does it mean that you cannot say which is fried rice and which is fried chicken just because both use the process of frying? Hence Option 2 is to be ruled out.

Option 3: tracing the development of the current short story from its origins in the nineteenth-century British novel.

All that the passage says is that when you come across the use of excessive detail in present short stories, you recall that a similar style was employed in some 19th century British novels. When you hear your new neighbour laughing so loud that the windowpanes shudder and you are reminded of your boss who used to laugh in a similar manner, does it mean that the new neighbour is your boss's grandson? Hence, Option 3 is absurd.

Option 4: arguing that certain current short story writers have permanently changed the form of the short story

The passage says that the current short story writers have introduced a style that is merely a particular form of fiction writing that finds critical flavour.

If some tribe in Lower Congo decides to dance the tango wearing a skirt made of leaves whereas the rest of the world wears tuxedos when dancing the tango, does it mean that the tribe has permanently changed the dress code for the tango dance? It is only a variation. Option 4 will not do either.

Option 5: contrasting the use of description in the essay with its use in the short story

Whatever the passage says about the use of description in the essay is that certain current short-story writers often use techniques – particularly exposition and description – associated with the essay. Therefore if the tribe in Lower Congo find that the dress code associated with the tango is tuxedos and then decide to employ that dress code, they will conform to the dress code, not contrast with it. Option 5 is not workable either and hence Option 1 is to be marked as correct.

Answer 28

We shall learn the meanings of a few words before we take on the task of ascertaining which option will fit.

When you go to a new environment you might have some initial problems that may disappear with *orientation* (meaning, *adjustment*) to the new set-up. When someone goes into a military academy and cannot get up early as the rules of the place require nor can he take the strain of extensive physical exercise, he begins to yearn for his mamma's lullabies. He falls ill. He cannot remember whatever he is made to study. He is *disoriented* (or, literally, he is *away from adjustment*).

The word *temporal* comes from the French word TEMP that means *time* and thus something that is *only for a time* (or *temporary*) is *temporal*. If jet lag could lead to permanent disorientation, people would not travel by jet planes.

If there is a paradox, it means that what happens is quite the reverse of what is expected to happen. When you travel with someone who normally vomits when travelling to a hill station you are prepared to see him become sullen after a few hairpin bends. You are also mentally ready to see him refusing food at the cafeteria where the bus stops en route. When you see a paradoxical situation with such a person, it means that you are seeing him whistling merrily at each hairpin bend and stuffing himself at the cafeteria. Similarly when you see something paradoxical with disorientation (which means *adjustment problems*), you should be prepared to see the opposite of adjustment problems. This means that the word in the second blank should indicate a situation where you find the opposite of disorientation. Thus Options 2, 3 and 4 are to be chucked out of the window for this reason alone. *Benefits* in Option 1, is the opposite in effect of disorientation. The question now is whether Option 5 would be workable.

When you want to decide what should be the standard blood pressure for a person, you never set this standard based on the blood pressure of someone who is feeling giddy. When you want to decide what should be the standard time in which a healthy person should digest a 250-gram cake, you do not set this standard on the basis of someone who rushes to the toilet by the time he eats half the cake. Disoriented people cannot yield health standards. This is why **Option 1** is to be marked as correct.

Answer 29

Let us understand the shades of meanings of a few words before we decide which option will work and which will not.

A person who decides to pitch a tent and camp the night in a forest infested with wild animals, is *dauntless*; he is *bold*.

If an army officer is *dauntless* in leading an attack on enemy positions although the enemy have been issuing threats over field loudspeakers that they are hopelessly outnumbered and will get butchered, he is *not intimidated nor cowed down* by the enemy threats.

If someone has failed the graduation examination even after he studies hard and even harder before reappearing at the examination, he is *dauntless* or *not easily disheartened* or *not easily discouraged*.

When someone's wife runs away from him but is ready to talk to him when he rings up and suggests that if she comes back, he will always come straight home from the office instead of going to the pub first, she is open to *persuasion* (or open to *winning over*). If she slams the receiver when he rings, she is not open to persuasion. A person may not be open to persuasion if his decision is firm and will under no circumstances change his decision to open the tiger's cage in the zoo and sock him in the jaw for having scared his children with his roaring.

The word *prejudice* has the prefix PRE- that means *before* and comes from the Latin word JUDICIUM that means *judgement*. Someone who says that she does not like avocado even before she has tasted one has reached a judgement that avocados are yuck before tasting the avocado. She has a *bias* or *preconceived notion*. Someone prejudiced against the use of fenugreek in curry is not necessarily afraid by fenugreek or disheartened by it.

If an industrial unit has been making losses for some time because it does not get continuous power supply that it needs to sustain its continuous process of manufacture and is *salvageable*, it means that it *can be saved* if exempted from power cuts. If a person's prestige is *salvageable* if he gets a loan against mortgage of his huge house to meet his financial commitments, it means that his reputation *can be saved* if he gets some money against the security of his house. Neither an industrial unit nor someone's prestige can be afraid of anything or disheartened by any adverse developments. If at all anyone can be frightened or disheartened it can be a living body.

If an exquisitely beautiful lady enters a room and everyone is awed by her *ethereal* beauty they are amazed to see someone who is so *exquisitely beautiful* that she seems to have descended straight *from paradise*. Exquisite beauty is a quality and not a living body. It can neither be daunted nor dauntless.

The opposite of a dauntless person is someone who is easily frightened or disheartened. **Option 1** fits like a shot.

Answer 30

Imagine that someone has returned from a trip to Tanzania where zebras eat grass and lions eat zebras and so on. He is asked to tell us about his trip. He says: *Great place, Tanzania! Lush green meadows! Majestic lions! Imagine seeing a snow-capped mountain at the equator*! He is giving a *synopsis* or *condensed statement presenting an overall view* of his visit. He is being *concise*. On the other hand, his sister is asked to describe the trip. She says: *First we set an alarm for 5 in the morning because we had to catch the flight. We all woke up but my brother would just not wake up. Actually we could have taken the subsequent flight but then we felt that the early one would be better because then we would not have a stopover. We all hate stopovers. They are sometimes unending, like the other time when we had to stop over at Singapore for eleven hours...* By this time the listener turns and runs away; it might take an hour before she starts talking about the bumpy landing in Dares Salaam and at what other places did they have similar landings. What the sister is indulging in is the opposite of conciseness: she is going on and on. Synopsis has conciseness as its principal quality and hence the relationship between synopsis and conciseness is that of something and its prime quality. With this let us start seeing the options one by one and see which one will fit.

Option 1: distillate: purity.

A *distillate* is a liquid formed by the condensation of liquid vapour; this condensation of liquid vapour is a process known as *distillation*. When an impure liquid is distilled, only the liquid vaporises and the soluble and insoluble impurities are left behind to dance the samba in the container in which the liquid was heated. The distillate formed has purity as its prime quality. Hence Option 1.

Option 2: mutation: viability

The word *mutation* comes from the French verb MUTARE that means *change* and therefore means an *action* or *process of changing*. If one were to see the *mutation* of a tribe of shepherds into office-goers, this means that there is a *change* or *transformation* in this tribe.

The word *viability* comes from the Latin root VITA- that means *life*. *Viability* would then mean the *capability to live*. If an industrial unit is able to generate a surplus after meeting all its expenses, this means that it is profitable and it has economic *viability* or *it can live*. If losses increase, the unit would close and thus, figuratively, die. If the plan to create a reserve for lions in a particular region is not *viable* because it has evergreen forests whereas lions require dry grasslands, then the project is not *workable* or *practicable*.

By now one may have noticed that the prime quality of mutation is change and not viability. Option 2 is not workable.

Option 3: replication: precedence.

The word *replication* comes from the Latin root PLIC- that means to *fold* or *twist* and has the prefix RE- means *back*. To replicate *literally* means to *fold back* and therefore *to repeat*. Mr. A can *replicate* Mr. B's speech (in other words *reproduce it word to word*) provided Mr. A has heard Mr. B before he starts replicating. However he is able to replicate because he remembers the words and diction and not merely because Mr. B has spoken earlier. The prime ingredient of replication is the *capacity to replicate* and not just precedence. If my great grandfather died a hundred years before I was born (and therefore *preceded* me), how can I replicate his voice when I have not heard him speak? This is why Option 3 will not do.

Option 4: illusion: quickness. Synopsis has conciseness as its principal quality and hence the relationship between synopsis and conciseness is that of an object and its prime quality. Quickness need not be the prime quality of illusion.

If somebody suffers from an illusion (or *false impression*) that he is terminally sick, he is not necessarily quick. He may deliberately slow down his level of activity as a consequence of that illusion.

Option 5: icon: charity. A person who has an exceptionally strong physique may be an icon of strength but not charity. He may be a great miser. Thus Option 5 will not do.

Explanatory Answers to Section IV

Answer 1

1/4th of an inch means one part out of the four parts into which you divide one inch. If one part out of four is 5 feet, one whole inch is 4 times 5 feet or in other words 1 inch represents 20 feet. In Column B, 7.5 inches would represent 7.5 times 20 feet or 150 feet. This means that the quantity in Column A is equal to the quantity in Column B. Thus **Mark 3**.

Answer 2

The whole thing is in billions of dollars. There is no need to mention billion dollars just as when students of an all-girls school meet they do not call each other "Miss so and so".

The amount budgeted for Military was 285.9 or 286 when rounded off. The amount budgeted for European defence was 120. These two add up to 406. The total amount budgeted for all categories is 633. Therefore the budget for the categories other than Military and European defence = 633 – 406 = 227.

The ratio of the amount budgeted for military and European defence to the amount budgeted for all other categories shown was 406: 227. Dividing both sides by 100 we get 4.06: 2.27 or approximately 2 : 1 as per Option 4.

When eliminating the options in such calculations, since 406 is way above 227, Option 3 and 5 gets eliminated right away because these would mean that 406 is less than 227 and that would be absurd at the very least. Option 2 too would get eliminated since if it were true than 406 should be thrice 227 which is absurd since 406 is not even twice 227; thrice is out of the question. As regards Option 1, 4: 3 would mean that 227 is 3/4th of 406 which it is not since the 3/4th of 400 is 300 and therefore the 3/4th of 406 should be a wee bit more than 300. If you have seen, we have not actually calculated anything; we have gone straight to the correct answer by logic alone.

Answer 3

The amount budgeted for education is 32.3 whereas the total amount is 633.1. The fraction 32/633 is roughly 32/632 or 4/79 (when you know that 32 is a multiple of 8 and that all even hundreds such as 200 and 400 and 600 and so on are multiples of 8, it makes sense to divide both numerator and denominator in 32/632 by 8) or very nearly 4/80 and thus 1/20. Since we know that 100 is divisible by 20, 1/20 would be exactly 5%. Thus Option 1 will do admirably.

Approximations and rounding off that we have seen in this answer are the only alternatives that you have under time constraints and when you do not have calculators. Try dividing 32.3 by 633.1 with a calculator now and you will find that you will be pretty close to 0.05, which in percentage terms is 5%. The idea is to be able to calculate fast. If the options are far and wide, approximations should be able to help tremendously.

As one's sense of analysis picks up, one should be able to notice that four options are above 10%, which is 10/100 or 1/10th. Since we know that 1/10th of 633 is 63 in the very least and 32.3 is nowhere near 63, Option 1 should be marked as correct without calculating anything at all. This is why it is so important to see the options before rushing off to do calculations.

Answer 4

It must be appreciated that either 2^n or 3^k could be a factor of $2^n.3^k$. With this in our mind, let us see the options.

Option 1: $6 = 2^1.3^1 = 6$ and hence 6 can certainly be a factor of $2^n.3^k$

Option 2: $8 = 2^3$ and hence 8 can certainly be a factor of $2^n.3^k$

Option 3: $27 = 3^3$ and hence 27 can certainly be a factor of $2^n.3^k$

Option 4: $42 = 6 \times 7$ and since neither 2^n nor 3^k can ever be equal to 7 so long as both n and k are positive integers, 42 can never be a factor of $2^n.3^k$. Hence **Mark 4**.

Option 5: $54 = 2^1.3^3$ and hence 54 can certainly be a factor of $2^n.3^k$

Answer 5

Let us represent the number of coins in Bill's collection as B and G as Gina's coins. What we would see is that B=2G-80. There are two unknowns in this linear equation: B and G. Two unknowns can have an infinite number of values some of which we shall see hereunder. But before that, we must know that 2G will definitely be an even number regardless of whether G is even or odd and since 80 is also even, when you subtract an even number from another even number, you shall always get even numbers. This is why any value that one assumes for B should invariably be even and secondly, in order to proceed logically, since there is no upper limit for even positive integers, we must always begin with the lower possible limit for even positive integers that is 2 and then test this bit about infinite possible values for B and G:

If B = 2, then since 2G – 80 = 2, 2G = 82 and hence G = 41

If B = 4, then since 2G – 80 = 4, 2G = 84 and hence G = 42

If B = 6, then since 2G – 80 = 6, 2G = 86 and hence G = 43

To cut a long story short, both B and G can have infinite number of values the least of which are 2 and 41 respectively. It is for this reason that the relation between B and G cannot be determined from the information given. Hence **Mark** 4.

Answer 6

To draw the two axes and the line cutting the x-axis at a, and the y-axis at b is a matter of a jiffy. See hereunder:

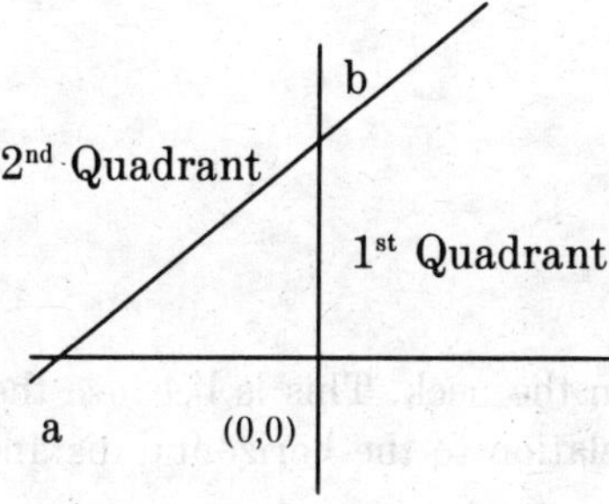

There are four quadrants formed as a result of intersection of the two axes at right angles. While we have named the quadrants in the diagram, the salient aspects of the quadrants are as per hereunder:

1st Quadrant: The region where x is positive and so is y

2nd Quadrant: The region where x is negative and y is positive

3rd Quadrant: The region where x is negative and so is y

4th Quadrant: The region where x is positive and y is negative

Now about gradients, when you climb a slope, you pant because the gradient is steep. The gradient of any slope is equal to the distance climbed compared to the distance covered on the ground. Visualise yourself on a picnic to three different peaks as in the diagrams below on a bright Sunday morning. While climbing 'Snow Peak, you can whistle a merry tune as you go along. You might ask your girlfriend to put her arms on your shoulders. This is because the vertical distance climbed as represented by the line AB is small as compared to the horizontal distance covered as shown by line BC. This vertical distance is the numerator and the horizontal distance is the denominator in a fraction called the gradient.

Snow Peak

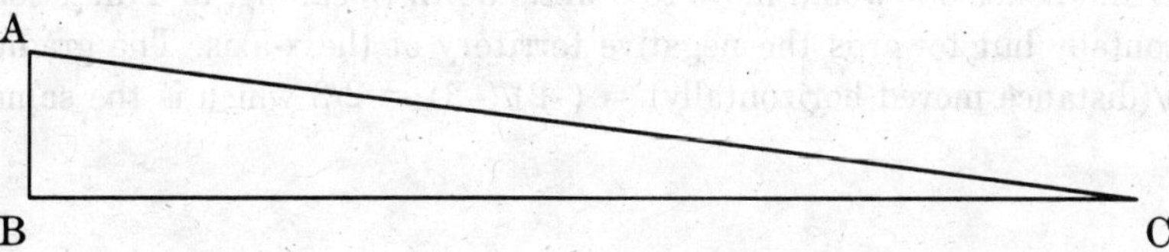

Old Bailey's Peak

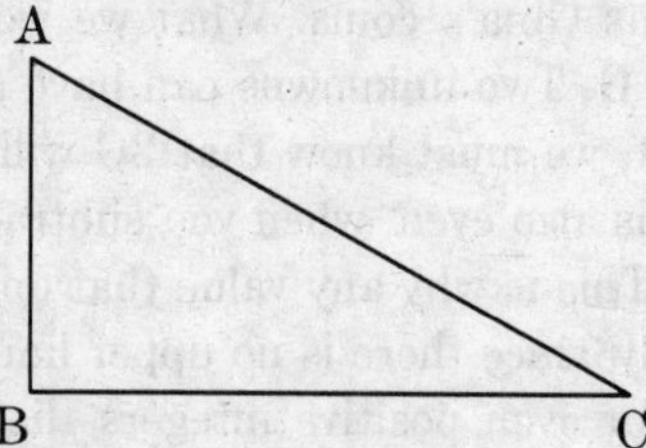

Now let us move on to Old Bailey's Peak. In the case of Old Bailey's Peak, the vertical distance climbed as compared to the horizontal distance covered – meaning AB/BC is a fraction of greater value than in the case of Snow Peak. You have to pause for breath. When your girlfriend puts her arm on your shoulder you enquire of her with a good deal of petulance whether she thinks she is a ruddy osteopath.

The Sheer Horn

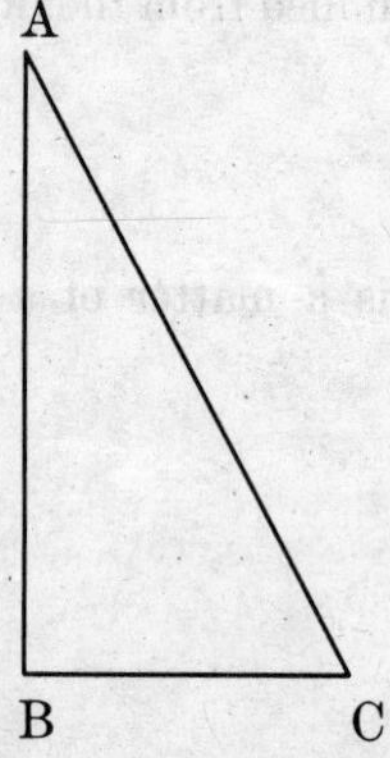

When climbing up the Sheer Horn, every step is a pain in the neck. This is because the gradient is too steep. The vertical distance AB that you climb is too large in relation to the horizontal distance BC covered. This is what makes gradients steep.

Back to the main question, if one were to imagine that a = –2 and b = 3, one would climb 3 units horizontally and in order to do this one would have to move 2 units towards positive territory of the x-axis from x = –2 to x = 0. This means that the gradient of the line is 3/2 which is effectively the (y intercept)/ –(x intercept) or b/ –a which is the same thing as –b/a.

Now let us imagine that the y-intercept was negative (say –2) and the x-intercept was positive (say 3). Then the line graph would look like this:

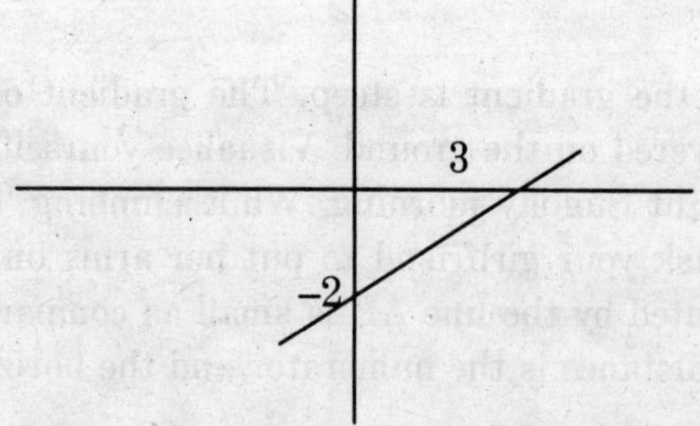

In this case one has to climb down and hence one would move to b units down (meaning, in a direction opposite to the vertical) and a units horizontally but towards the negative territory of the x-axis. The gradient of the line is (distance moved vertically)/(distance moved horizontally) = (–2)/(–3) = 2/3 which is the same thing as –b/a as in the earlier case.

Thus Option 2.

Answer 7

All prime numbers are positive and so would be their product. We shall therefore not persist with the use of the words *positive integer* hereafter insofar as this question is concerned. It is possible to form the least quantity with four different prime factors only with the least possible four prime numbers other than 2. The prime numbers following 2 when arranged in ascending order are 3, 5, 7 and 11. If you are asked to find the least number that has say 2 and 4 as factors, such a number is 4, which is the least common multiple of these two numbers. We are however spared the bother of finding LCMs when finding the least quantity having four different prime factors. By their very definition prime numbers have no common factor with one another the least number that can be formed such that this number will have the four prime factors 3, 5, 7 and 11 is the product of 3, 5, 7 and 11, which in turn is 1155. Hence **Mark 3**.

Answer 8

If the ratio of the length to the width of R is 3:1, let us assume that its width is A and thus its length is 3A. The area of rectangular region R is $3A \times A = 3A^2$. The area of rectangular region T is $12w$. We can say that $3A^2 = 12\ w$ and hence $w = A^2/4$. Since A^2 is a perfect square and so is 4, one can only say that w is definitely a perfect square. Nothing more. The following are among a few of the several possible values of A and w

If A=	Then w=
1	¼
2	1
3	9/4
4	4
6	9
8	16

As can be seen from the above table, so long A is below 4, w is less than 4; as soon as A = 4, w also =4 and then for all values of A above 4, w is more than 4. Thus **Mark 4**.

Answer 9

Mind the words *no more than* and *no smaller than*. We are also told that the value of T is fixed at T=60.

Let us examine the options one by one.

If Option 1 were correct, then X could be no less than 40 but X could be equal to 40. Even if one were to assume that X = 40, since T = 60, T/X is 60/40 or 3/2 and thus T = 3X/2 or in percentage terms 150% of X. This means that T is 50% more than X and this option is not workable since we are given that T is no greater than 20% more than X.

If Option 2 were correct, then X could be no less than 48 but X could be equal to 48. Even if one were to assume that X = 48, since T = 60, T/X= 60/48 or 5/4 and thus T = 5X/4 or in percentage terms 125% of X. This means that T is 25% more than X and this option is not workable since we are given that T is no greater than 20% more than X. Option 3 also gets eliminated on this account alone.

If Option 4 were correct, then X could be no less than 50 but X could be equal to 50. Even if one were to assume that X = 50, since T = 60, T/X= 60/50 or 6/5 and thus T = 6X/5 or in percentage terms 120% of X. This means that T is 20% more than X and this option is workable provided the other condition of T being no smaller than a number 20% less than the integer X (or 80% of the integer X) is also met. In Option 4, X could be equal to 78. In that case, 80% of X is 80 × 78/100 = 4 × 78/5 = 312/5 = >60. Since X is fixed at 60, this option is not workable either.

If Option 5 were correct, this option is workable provided the other condition of T being no smaller than a number 20% less than the integer X (or 80% of the integer X) is also met. In Option 5, X could be equal to

75. In that case, 80% of X is 80×75/100 = 4 × 75/5 = 300/5 = 60. Since X is fixed at 60, Option 5 will do very well.

Answer 10

If the train travels 50 miles at 45 miles per hour, it takes 50/45th or 10/9th of an hour or 10 × 60/9 minutes or 200/3 minutes. When the train travels at 40 miles per hour, it does 40 miles in 60 minutes and therefore it would take 1.5 minutes for every mile. If it is to travel 30 miles, it takes 30 × 1.5 = 45 minutes for the first 30 mile stretch. This means the train will have to cover the remaining 20 miles in (200/3 - 45) minutes. This means that it will run at the rate of 20/(65/3) miles per minute or 20 × 60/(65/3) miles per hour or 1200×3/ 65 or 3600/65 or 720/13 or >55 miles hour. Thus the quantity in Column A is >55 miles per hour. Hence Mark 1.

Fundamentally if the average speed during a journey is say, X miles per hour and even if the smallest part of the journey is performed at a speed that is less than the overall speed, then the average speed during the remaining part of the journey has got to be necessarily higher than the overall average of X miles per hour. From this logic alone, it is possible to mark Option 1 and move on. We shall, however, see the following illustration in regard to the fundamental aspect mentioned here.

Imagine that a train travels 40 miles at an overall average speed of 60 miles per hour. A speed of 60 miles per hour means 1 mile per minute and thus a 40-mile journey would take 40 minutes. If the train were to do say the first mile at an average speed of 50 miles per hour, then since it takes 60 minutes to travel 50 miles, it would take 1.2 minutes to travel a mile. Since it has to do the remaining 39 miles in 40 – 1.2 = 38.8 minutes so as to make the overall journey in 40 minutes, then its speed would be 39/38.8 or more than a mile in a minute. When it travels exactly at one mile per minute, its speed is 60 miles per hour. When it travels more than a mile per minute, its speed is greater than 60 miles per hour. This illustrates the fundamental aspect in the above paragraph.

Answer 11

Fundamentally there is a difference of exactly 2 between:

Each consecutive even integer (such as in the case of 2, 4, 6, 8, 10, 12, 14 and so on), and

Each consecutive odd integer (such as in the case of 1, 3, 5, 7, 9, 11, 13 and so on)

Imagine that the first of three consecutive odd integers is A. This means that the three consecutive odd integers are A, (A + 2) and (A + 4) and their sum is 3A+6 which is as such 3(A+2). As we know A is an odd integer and so will be A+2. Thus 3(A + 2) will be divisible by 3 and will also be an odd integer. The rule of divisibility by 3 is that if you were to add the digits of any number and find that the sum comes to 3 or a number divisible by 3 (such as in the case of say 12 where the digits add up to 3 or say 345 where the digits add up to 12 which in turn is divisible by 3), the number is divisible by 3 and not if the sum of the digits is not divisible by 3 (as in the case of say 232 where the digits add up to 8 which is not divisible by 3).

This is why one should **Mark 5** as correct because the digits in 313 add up to 7 which is not divisible by 3.

Answer 12

As can be seen, 0.83 is as such 83/100, which in turn is a fraction where the numerator is less than the denominator.

The expression $(0.83)^6/(0.83)^7$ is, as such nothing other than the following when expanded:

(0.83 × 0.83 × 0.83 × 0.83 × 0.83 × 0.83) / (0.83 × 0.83 × 0.83 × 0.83 × 0.83 × 0.83 × 0.83) = 1/0.83 = 100/83 which, in turn, is > 1.

The fundamental thing to remember here is that whenever you see a positive number say X raised to a certain power P divided by the same number X raised to Q which is >P (meaning, a higher power than in the numerator), the result is X raised to P – Q which is bound to be negative. This is why say $2^5/2^8 = 2^{(5-8)} = 2^{-3}$. Thus in the case of $(0.83)^6/(0.83)^7$ what we shall get as a result of the division is, $(0.83)^{-1}$ which as such is the inverse of 0.83 or the inverse of 83/100 and therefore equal to 100/83 which is very apparently more than 1.

This is why one should Mark 1 as the correct answer.

Answer 13

Imagine that the two positive integers are X and Y where X > Y. If their sum is 43, it means that X + Y = 43. If the difference between their squares is 43, it means that $(X^2 - Y^2) = 43$.

This means $(X^2 - Y^2) = (X + Y) \times (X - Y) = 43$

Since (X + Y) = 43, (X – Y) = 1.

One has two linear equations as follows:

Equation 1: X + Y = 43

Equation 2: X – Y = 1

Subtracting Equation 2 from Equation 1, we get 21, we get 2Y = 42 and hence Y = 21 and hence X = 22. Hence Mark 4 as the correct answer.

Now let us see a faster method for cracking such questions with accuracy so that one can give more time to the other questions.

Fundamentally, the difference between the squares of two numbers X and Y where X > Y is equal to the product of (I) their Sum and (II) their difference. If X > Y, it could mean any of the following situations:

Situation 1: Their sum is 1, which is possible if Y is 1–X; so long as X is more than 1, Y will invariably be a negative integer in this case.

Situation 2: Their difference is 1, which is possible if the two are consecutive integers.

Situation 3: Their difference and sum are both equal to 1 which is possible if you are looking at X=1 and Y=0

Since we are told that the two integers are positive, Situations 1 and 3 get eliminated and this then means that the integers are consecutive and positive.

All that one has to do after understanding the above fundamental aspect is to see the options. If the smaller number were to be 17 as per Option 1, then the greater number would be 18 and then their sum would be 37 and not 43. Check the options and you will find that only **Option 4** will work.

Answer 14

First let us see some fundamentals by reducing the problem to a smaller scale. When you want to make 3-letter different subsets from 4 letters A, B, C, and D, then the following 24 combinations are possible: (1) ABC and ACB, (2) ABD and ADB, (3) ACD and ADC, (4) BAC and BCA, (5) BAD and BDA, (6) BCD and BDC, (7) CAB and CBA, (8) CAD and CDA, (9) CBD and CDB, (10) DAB and DBA, (11) DAC and DCA, and (12) DBC and DCB. The reason why 24 combinations can be formed without repeating any of the letters is that one can choose from out of 4 letters the letter for the first place and then out of 3 the letter for the second place and finally out of 2 letters the letter for the third place hence making 4 × 3 × 2 = 24 possible combinations.

If one wants to see that the subsets have different letters then (1) ABC and ACB, (4) BAC and BCA, (7) CAB and CBA, have the same three letters A, B, and C. We are not saying which one out of ABC and CAB and BAC is different but all that we are saying is that $1/6^{th}$ of these six are different. Similarly combinations (2), (5), and (10) also have the same letters A, B and D. As can be seen, only$1/6^{th}$ of the combinations out of the 24 combinations are distinct.

When you want to make 3-letter different subsets from the six letters A, B, C, D and F, then one has six choices for the first number and can choose out of any one of the 6 letters. Having done that, one can choose from any of the remaining 5 letters the letter for the second place and then out of the remaining 4 the letter for the third place. One can then have 6 × 5 × 4 = 120 possible combinations. Of these $1/6^{th}$ will be different and hence there can be 20 different combinations: ABC, ABD, ABE, ABF, ACD, ACE, ACF, ADE, ADF and AEF, BCD, BCE, BCF, BDE, BDF, BEF, CDE, CDF, CEF, and DEF. Mark the combinations having the letter F and you will find that there are 10 of them. Hence Mark **3** as the correct statement.

Now let us try to understand this a whole lot faster. If there are 20 different 3-letter subsets, it means that there are in all 60 letters employed. [This is simple to understand; if 20 boys have two candies each it means that there are 40 candies in all]. There are exactly 6 letters. Each letter is employed the same number of times. Only then can one have combinations without repetition of any one letter in any given combination. This means that each letter – whether A, B, C, D, E or F – is employed 10 times in these 20 three-letter subsets. The detailed explanation given in the preceding paragraphs is for conceptual clarity alone. The real method of cracking such questions is the quick method shown in this paragraph.

Answer 15

This is easy once one knows that in any triangle, the side opposite the larger angle is always longer than the side opposite a smaller angle.

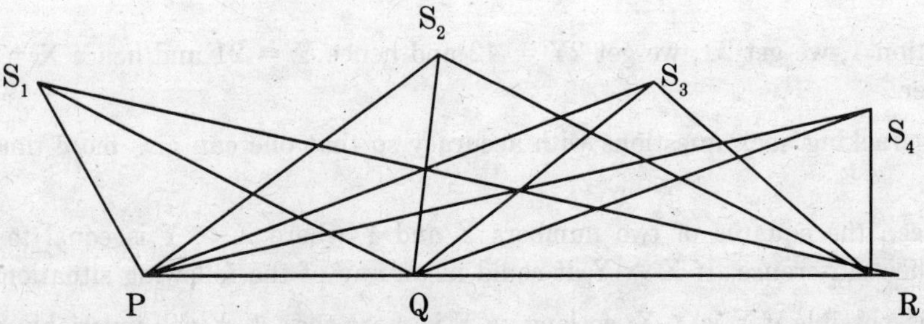

Imagine that the point S first lies at S_1 in such a position that PS_1 (which is nothing other than PS seen with shifting positions of the point S) assumes small values, and then gradually shifts in such a way that PS assumes higher values with PS_4 being almost as large as PR.

Now imagine that in triangle	Then angle	So if we were to assume that the angle	Then angle
PS_1R, $QS_1 = QR$.	$QS_1R = S_1RQ$	$QS_1R = x^0$,then angle $S_1RQ = x^0$.	$PS_1R = QS_1R + QS_1P$. Thus angle PS_1R would be greater than the angle S_1RQ and hence PR, which is the side opposite angle PS_1R, would always be longer than the side PS_1.
PS_3R, $QS_3 = QR$.	$QS_3R = S_3RQ$	$QS_3R = x^0$, then angle $S_3RQ = x^0$.	$PS_3R = QS_3R + QS_3P$. Thus angle PS_3R would be greater than the angle S_3RQ and hence PR, which is the side opposite angle PS_3R, would always be longer than the side PS_3.

As may be seen from the above table, PR is always greater than PS and hence Mark 1 as the correct statement.

Having grasped the fundamentals in this case, one must realise that since any competitive test is about conceptual clarity and primarily about logic, the logical thing to realise here is that PS can be the same length as PR only if the angle S_4PR were zero in which case there would be no QS. This means that PS will invariably have to be less than PR.

Answer 16

There are two approaches to this problem and we would present these one by one so that you, dear reader, may select whichever of the two suits you.

Approach 1: Let us refer to the number of students enrolled in both Geometry and Biology as GB and those exclusively enrolled in Geometry and Biology as G and B respectively and those enrolled in neither, as N. Since, for example, the number of students enrolled in Geometry is an aggregate of those enrolled exclusively in Geometry and those enrolled in both Geometry and Biology, we know that:

(1) G + GB = 24 and since GB = 20, G = 4

(2) B + GB = 40 and since GB = 20, B = 20

(3) G + B + GB + N = 80 and since GB = 20, G = 4 and B = 20, N = 36

If an event has n equally likely outcomes and f of them are termed favourable, the probability of a favourable outcome is f/n. If you were to select at random from the 80 students, the probability that the student selected would NOT be enrolled in either course is 36/80 or 9/20 and hence 0.45 at **Option 3** is to be marked as correct.

Approach 2: Let us refer to the number of students enrolled in both Geometry and Biology as GB and those exclusively enrolled in Geometry and Biology as G and B respectively and those enrolled in neither, as N. Let us represent this diagrammatically as hereunder in order to find out how many students are not enrolled in either of the subjects:

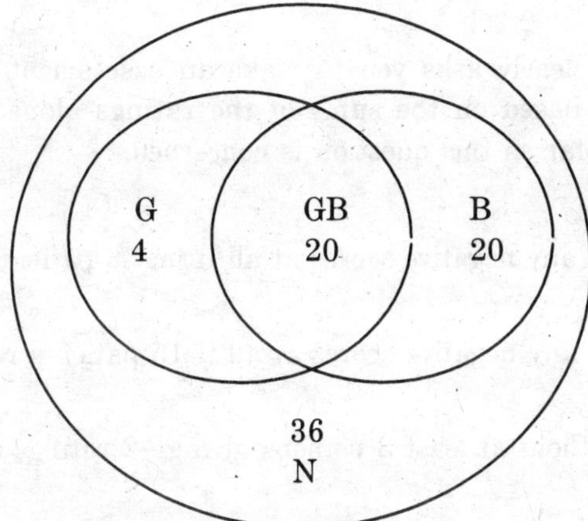

The above diagrammatic method is a fabulous method to drive home the concepts. However, there are some limitations to this method that must be realised so that when the limiting situation arises we ignore this methodology and come quickly to the answer through the method of simple linear equations as above. The most severe limitation of the Venn diagram method is that while it can cope with three intersections it cannot cope beyond. This means that if we were to try this method with a question involving four or more subjects, the method of the Venn diagram would be cumbersome, to say the very least.

Answer 17

The quantity in Column A is effectively $4x^2 + 12xy + 9y^2$ whereas the quantity in column B is $4x + 6xy + 9y^2$. In trying to compare the two, I know for a fact that whatever be the value of y (positive or negative), $9y^2$ will always be positive and hence $9y^2$ adds the same value to each side. I can safely cross out $9y^2$ from both sides and am left with comparing $4x^2 + 12xy$ with $4x + 6xy$. Here too I know that 6xy can be subtracted from both sides since if 6xy is positive, it adds the same value to each side and if it is negative subtracts the same value from each side. Thus I am effectively comparing $4x^2 + 6xy$ with 4x. I can also divide the two sides by 2 and reduce the burden of calculating and hence I am left with comparing $2x^2 + 3xy$ with 2x.

The following fundamentals must be borne in mind while dealing with such questions:

- The square of a number is always greater than the number itself if the number is negative (including negative fractional values for the number, for the simple reason that a positive number – which the square shall always be - is always greater than any negative number).
- The square of a number is always greater than the number itself if the number is >1.
- The square of a number is equal to the number itself if the number is 1.
- The square of a number is always lesser than the number itself if the number is <1 (meaning, the number is a positive fraction).

Thus if x is a fraction, $2x^2$ may be a smaller fraction than 2x (say if x = 1/4, 2x = 1/2 whereas $2x^2$ = 2/16 or 1/8 which is smaller than 1/2). If x = 1/4 and y = 0, $2x^2$ + 3xy will be smaller than 2x. If both x and y are zero, $2x^2$ + 3xy will be equal to 2x since both would mean zero. If x is >1 and y is positive, $2x^2$ + 3xy will be greater than 2x; this is because $2x^2$ will not need the help of 3xy to bash 2x through and through; $2x^2$ will bash 2x black and blue on his own. This is why one would do well to Mark 4 as the correct answer.

The quickest way to deal with this is to read the wording of the question with due care and realise that since we are not told that x and y are non-zero there is no bar to assuming that both of them are simultaneously equal to zero and therefore both sides being zero, the quantity in Column A could be equal to that in Column B. If 2x is fractional and positive and y = 0, then the quantity in Column B could be greater than that in Column A. This much we can derive without putting pen to paper. All the trouble that one need give the pen is to use it for marking **Option 4**.

Answer 18

It is important to remember that the question clearly asks you to make an assessment of the number of symptoms which have at least one rating of –2, **based on the sums of the ratings alone**. Thus there is no need to even look at the standard deviations insofar as this question is concerned.

Now let us go from symptom to symptom.

- Symptom H: A score of 12 is possible without any negative scores at all if just 6 patients rate +2 and the rest rate 0.
- Symptom L: A score of 35 is possible without any negative scores at all if 15 patients rate +2, 5 rate +1 and the rest 10 rate 0.
- Symptom P: A score of –33 is not possible without at least 3 persons giving –2 ratings even if the rest 27 gave –1 each.
- Symptom T: A score of –26 is possible without any –2 scores if 26 patients rate –1 and the rest 4 rate 0.
- Symptom V: A score of 2 is possible without any negative scores if 2 patients rate 1 and the rest 28 rate 0.

Symptom P is the only case where there has to be at least one –2 rating and hence **Option 2**.

Answer 19

The arithmetic mean of a series of numbers is equal to (The sum of the series)/ (The number of terms in the series). Therefore in the present case, if the arithmetic mean of 30 terms is closest to zero, it follows that (The sum of the series)/ 30 = Closest to Zero and therefore (The sum of the series) = 30 × Closest to Zero and thus (The sum of the series) = Closest to Zero. This means that if we have to look for the symptom whose arithmetic mean rating was closest to 0, we have to see which symptom has its sum of ratings closest to Zero. Symptom V fits best. If the sum of 30 terms in a series is 2, the arithmetic mean of the series is 2/30 or 1/15 or 0.067 and hence **Option 3**.

Answer 20

The quantity in Column B is the very first natural number. It is only the quantity in Column A that has to be determined.

[(1 + $\sqrt{5}/2$) – (1 – $\sqrt{5}/2$)] = [(2 + $\sqrt{5}$)/2 – (2 – $\sqrt{5}$)/2] = [(2 + $\sqrt{5}$ – 2 + $\sqrt{5}$)/2] = 2$\sqrt{5}$/2 = $\sqrt{5}$. Therefore 1/$\sqrt{5}$ [(1 + $\sqrt{5}$/2) – (1 – $\sqrt{5}$/2)] = 1/$\sqrt{5}$ × $\sqrt{5}$ = 1. Hence the quantities in columns A and B are equal. Mark 3 as the correct answer.

Answer 21

It is important to remember that the clock is meant to have a round face and even if it does not, the hands move in a circle and thus there will always be an angle between the hour hand and the minute hand except at 1200 and 0000 hours.

A circle subtends an angle of 360° at its centre. Since the hands of the clock move on a pivot that is at the centre of the circle, the minute hand and the hour hand subtend a twelfth of 360° – which is equal to 30° – at the centre of the clock at both 0100 hours and 1300 hours.

So the angle between the minute hand and the hour hand is 30° when it is 1300 hours and 60° when it is 1400 hours and so on until at 0600 hours, when the angle between them is 180° after which the reverse process starts when the angle between the hour hand and the minute hand reduces by 30° with the passing of each hour so that it is 150° at 0700 hours, 120° at 0800 hours so that at 1100 hours it is 30° and at 1200 hours such is 0°.

But this is the position of the angles between the hour hand and the minute hand at an integral number of hours. What if we are asked to find the angle between these hands at say 0330 hours?

At 0300 hours, the hour hand is on the 15th notch (that corresponds to the 3 O' clock mark on the face of the clock) whereas the minute hand is on the 0th notch (that corresponds to the 12 O' clock mark on the face of the clock). At 0330 hours, the minute hand is on the 30th notch, having moved 30 notches between 0300 and 0330 hours. Since the hour hand travels 1 notch for every 12 notches that the minute hand travels, the hour hand has moved 30/12 or 5/2 or 2.5 notches during the time the minute hand has moved through 30 notches. The hour hand is then on the (15 + 2.5)th notch or 17.5th notch. The number of notches separating the minute hand and the hour hand is 30 –17.5 or 12.5.

Since the circular face of the clock having 60 notches subtends an angle of 360° at its centre, the angle between each notch is 360/60 or 6° and hence the angle between the minute hand and the hour hand at 0330 hours is 12.5 times 6° or 75°. Hence Option 2.

Answer 22

Let us name some of the points in the diagram given in the question as follows:

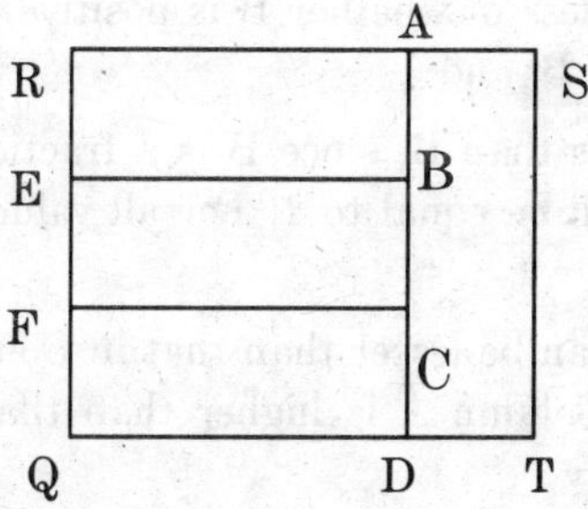

Since rectangular region QRST is divided into four smaller rectangular regions with length L and width W, we know that RA = EB = FC = QD = AD = ST = L and FQ = EF = ER = DT = AS = W.

The area of the rectangular region QRST is RS× QR= (L+W) × 3W. Since the region has been divided into four equal parts (which is simple to infer since each of the sub-rectangles has the same length L and width W), the area of each region is L×W and therefore the area of the four equal parts is 4 L × W.

Since the area of the rectangle QRST is equal to the sum of the areas of the four sub-rectangles, 4 L×W = (L + W) × 3W or 4LW = 3LW + $3W^2$and hence LW = $3W^2$, so L – 3W.

QR = FQ + EF + ER = W + W + W = 3W and RS = RA + AS = L + W = 3W + W = 4W. Hence QR/RS = 3W/4W = 3/4. Since the quantities in the columns A and B are equal, **Mark 3**.

Answer 23

Let us go from Option to Option.

Option 1: If 1/2 + something has to be even equal to 1, then that something has got to be ½ at the very least. The question is: Is 1/3 equal to 1/2? No. So let us move on.

Option 2: If 7/8 + something has to be even equal to 1, then that something has got to be 1/8 at the very least. The question is: Is 3/30 or 1/10 equal to 1/8? No. So let us go to the next option.

Option 3: If 15/16 + something has to be even equal to 1, then that something has got to be 1/16 at the very least. The question is: Is 2/40 or 1/20 equal to 1/16? No. So let us try the next option.

Option 4: If 12/25 + something has to be even equal to 1, then that something has got to be 13/25 at the very least. The question is: Is 12/30 or 2/5 or 10/25 equal to 13/25? No. So let us move on.

Option 5: If 2/3 + something has to be even equal to 1, then that something has got to be 1/3 at the very least. The question is: Is 35/102 equal to 1/3? No. It is greater than 1/3 considering that 35/105 would be 1/3 whereas 35/102 has a lesser denominator than 105. Thus 2/3+ 35/102 would exceed 1. Hence **Option 5**.

Answer 24

If both X and Y are negative integers, XY would mean a product of two negative numbers which would be invariably positive and hence Statement I is true. The sum of two negative numbers would mean an even smaller number [for example (–3) + (–4) which would be –7, would always be less than either –3 or –4]. Hence Statement II is also true.

If X < Y, then if we were to assume that:

(I) $X = -3$ when $Y = -2$, $X^2 = 9$ and $Y^2 = 4$ and hence $X^2 > Y^2$.

(II) $X = -5$ when $Y = -4$, $X^2 = 25$ and $Y^2 = 16$ and hence $X^2 > Y^2$.

Briefly, all three statements are true and hence **Option 5**.

Answer 25

If $B \neq 0$, it would mean that B can be either negative or positive. It is not worth bothering with trying out negative values for B since the two minus signs in the multiplication will make things positive and the quantity in Column B will invariably be 1 regardless of whether B is positive or negative so long as B is non-zero. Then the comparison is essentially between B^2 and 1.

If we assume that B is less than 1, B^2 will be less than B, since B is a fraction; B^2 will be certainly less than 1. If we then assume that B is equal to 1, B^2 will be equal to 1. For all values of B where B is greater than 1, B^2 will be greater than 1.

Since in some cases the quantities in Column A can be lesser than that in Column B, in others the two can be equal and in most other cases the quantity in Column A is higher than that in Column B, **Mark 4** as the correct answer.

Answer 26

If the cost C of an order of N special envelops is given by C = (\$0.50)N + \$15.00, the cost of an order of 500 special envelops = 500(\$0.50) + \$15.00 = \$250 + \$15.00 = \$265.00. Hence Mark 1 as the correct answer.

Answer 27

Let us name a few points in the figure in the question reproduced hereunder to calculate the measure of OP.

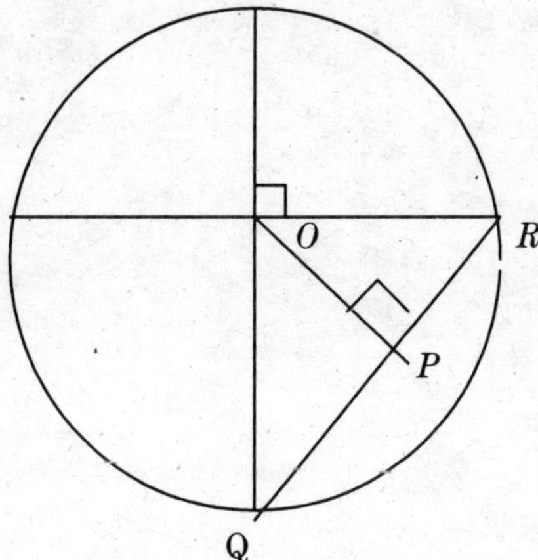

Let Q and R be the two ends of the chord on which the point P lies. In the two triangles OQP and OPR, the two sides OQ and QR are radii of the circle and therefore equal in measure. Both triangles have a common side OP. Both triangles have a right angle. With two sides and an angle of equal measure, the two triangles are congruent. This means that the sides QP and PR are equal in measure and thus OP bisects QR.

Angle QOR is a right angle since the circle subtends an angle of 360° at its centre and since QOR forms one part of four equal parts of the circle, it subtends one fourth of 360°, which implies that angle QOR is a right angle. This means that QR is the hypotenuse of a right-angled triangle with each side of R units and hence QR measures $\sqrt{2}R$ since $QR^2 = OQ^2 + OR^2 = R^2 + R^2 = 2R^2$. This means that OP is $1/2 \times \sqrt{2}R$ or $R/\sqrt{2}$. Thus the quantities in both columns A and B are equal. Hence Mark **3** as the correct statement.

Answer 28

22/7 is a little over 3 since 21/7 is exactly 3. 7/22 is a little less than 1/3 since 7/21 is exactly 1/3. Therefore 22/7 – 7/22 is effectively (A little over 3) – (A little less than 1/3) = A little over 2 and $2/3^{rd}$, the nearest integer to which is 3 in **Option 4**.

As such when you subtract the inverse of a fraction from the fraction itself what you are doing is subtracting B/A from A/B where both A and B are positive integers. $(A/B) - (B/A) = (A^2 - B^2)/AB$. This is worth remembering.

In the present case, A = 22 and B = 7 and hence 22/7 – 7/22 = (484 – 49)/154 = 435/154 that can be rounded off to 430/150 which would make it 43/15 or just a wee bit short of 3.